PENGUIN REFERENCE
The Penguin Pocket English Dictionary

Robert Allen, the editor of this dictionary, is an experienced lexicographer and writer on language. After ten years on the *Oxford English Dictionary* he edited a major new edition of the *Concise Oxford Dictionary*, was an associate editor of the *Oxford Companion to the English Language*, and directed work on the *Chambers 21st Century Dictionary*. He has been a consultant for a number of major publishing houses, has written an updated version of *Fowler's Modern English Usage*, and writes articles in *English Today* and other journals. He is an honorary research fellow of the Department of English Language at the University of Glasgow.

THE PENGUIN POCKET
ENGLISH DICTIONARY

Consultant Editor
Robert Allen

PENGUIN BOOKS

PENGUIN BOOKS

Published by the Penguin Group
Penguin Books Ltd, 80 Strand, London WC2R 0RL, England
Penguin Group (USA) Inc., 375 Hudson Street, New York, New York 10014, USA
Penguin Books Australia Ltd, 250 Camberwell Road, Camberwell, Victoria 3124, Australia
Penguin Books Canada Ltd, 10 Alcorn Avenue, Toronto, Ontario, Canada M4V 3B2
Penguin Books India (P) Ltd, 11 Community Centre, Panchsheel Park, New Delhi – 110 017, India
Penguin Group (NZ), cnr Airborne and Rosedale Roads, Albany, Auckland 1310, New Zealand
Penguin Books (South Africa) (Pty) Ltd, 24 Sturdee Avenue, Rosebank 2196, South Africa

Penguin Books Ltd, Registered Offices: 80 Strand, London WC2R 0RL, England

www.penguin.com

First published as *The Penguin Pocket English Dictionary* 2004
4

Set in Stone Sans and Stone Serif
Typeset by Columns Design Ltd, Reading, Berkshire
Printed in England by Clays Ltd, St Ives plc

Contents

Acknowledgments

Consultant Editor
Robert Allen

Publishing Director
Nigel Wilcockson

Publisher
Martin Toseland

Lexicographers
Stephen Curtis, Rosalind
Fergusson

Database Editor
Rachael Arthur

Proofreaders
David Cumming, Rosalind
Fergusson, Peter Horton

Designer
Richard Marston

Database Systems
Librios Ltd

Typesetting
Columns Design Ltd

Layout of Dictionary Entries

The display below shows the main features of a dictionary entry.

headword	**educate** *v* to teach or instruct in academic, moral, or social matters. ➤ **educator** *n*.
	educated *adj* **1** having had an education, *esp* a good one. **2** based on some knowledge or experience: *an educated guess*.
part of speech	**education** *n* **1** the act of educating or the process of being educated. **2** instruction in some subject. **3** the knowledge resulting from instruction. **4** the field of study that deals mainly with methods of teaching. ➤ **educational** *adj*.
definition	**Edwardian** *adj* of the reign of King Edward VII of England (1901–1910).
	eel *n* a long snakelike fish with a smooth slimy skin.
alternative spelling and inflected forms	**eerie or eery** *adj* (**-ier, -iest**) frighteningly strange or gloomy. ➤ **eerily** *adv*.
	efface *v* **1** to remove from a surface or make indistinct. **2** to make (oneself) inconspicuous.
idioms and phrases	**effect¹** *n* **1** the result produced by a cause or action. **2** the extent to which a cause or action produces results. **3** the state of being operative: *come into effect*. **4** (*in pl*) personal movable property; goods. **5** (*often in pl*) something designed to enhance the drama, realism, or impressiveness of a play or film. ✳ **for effect** in order to impress. **in effect** actually although not officially so. **take effect 1** to become operative. **2** to produce a result.
Usage note on points of grammar and language sensitivity	*Usage note:* Do not confuse this word with **affect**, which is a verb only.
	effect² *v* to bring about, carry out, or accomplish.

effective *adj* **1** producing a decisive or desired effect. **2** impressive or striking. **3** actual or real, though not officially recognized. **4** in force; operative. ➤ **effectiveness** *n*.

effectual *adj* able to produce a desired effect; effective.

effeminate *adj* of a man: having qualities usu thought of as feminine. ➤ **effeminacy** *n*.

derived word with meaning
deducible from headword

effervesce *v* of a liquid: to bubble and hiss as gas escapes.

effervescent *adj* **1** effervescing. **2** lively and exhilarated.

effete *adj* **1** marked by weakness and decadent overrefinement. **2** effeminate.

efficacious *adj formal* effective.

efficacy *n formal* effectiveness.

usage label

efficient *adj* **1** producing desired effects, *esp* with minimum waste. **2** of a person: briskly competent. ➤ **efficiency** *n*, **efficiently** *adv*.

effigy *n* (*pl* -ies) an image or representation of a person, *esp* a hated person.

noun plural form

effluent *n* fluid industrial refuse, sewage, etc discharged into the environment and causing pollution.

effluvium *n* (*pl* **effluvia**, **effluviums**) an offensive gas or smell.

Pronunciation

Guidance on pronunciation is given within slashes // for words that cause particular difficulty. The characters used are those of the English alphabet with their normal values. The following special characters and combinations of characters are used:

dh as in **th**ey
kh as in lo**ch**
aw as in ho**rn**, **aw**ful
ə as in **a**like, gard**e**n
eə as in h**air**, th**ere**
ie as in b**i**te, f**igh**t
iə as in b**eer**, h**ere**
oh as in b**o**ne, l**oa**n
oo as in b**oo**k, p**u**t
ooh as in b**oo**t, l**u**te
ow as in n**ow**, r**ou**t
uh as in b**ir**d, abs**ur**d

The main stress or emphasis in a word of more than one syllable is shown by the symbol ' and any secondary stress by the symbol ₁.

List of Abbreviations

Abbreviations in general use (such as AD and i.e.) are given in the main text. Special abbreviations are as follows:

abbr	abbreviation	*derog*	derogatory	*part.*	participle
adj	adjective	*dimin.*	diminutive	*pers*	person
adv	adverb	*esp*	especially	*pl*	plural
attrib	attributive(ly)	*euphem*	euphemistic	*prep*	preposition
Aus	Australian	*fem*	feminine	*prob*	probably
aux	auxiliary (verb)	*fl*	floruit	*pron*	pronoun
b.	born	*interj*	interjection	*SAfr*	South Africa(n)
Brit	British	*intrans*	intransitive	*Scot*	Scottish
c.	circa	*irreg*	irregular(ly)	*sing.*	singular
Can	Canadian	*masc*	masculine	*specif*	specifically
cent.	century	*n*	noun	*superl*	superlative
cents	centuries	*NAmer*	North American	*trans*	transitive
comb. form	combining form	*N Eng*	Northern English	*usu*	usually
compar	comparative	*NZ*	New Zealand	*v*	verb
conj	conjunction	*orig*	originally	*v aux*	auxiliary verb
d.	died				

A¹ or **a** n (pl **A's** or **As** or **a's**) the first letter of the English alphabet. ✳ **from A to Z** from beginning to end.

A² abbr **1** ampere. **2** answer.

a or **an** *indefinite article* **1** used before a singular noun to denote a person or thing not previously specified. **2** one single. **3** every; per.

AA abbr **1** Alcoholics Anonymous. **2** Automobile Association.

aardvark n an African mammal with a long extendable tongue, large ears, that feeds on ants and termites.

aback ✳ **be taken aback** to be surprised or shocked.

abacus n (pl **abacuses**) an instrument for performing calculations by sliding beads as counters along rods or in grooves.

abaft adv and prep towards or at the stern of a ship.

abandon¹ v (**abandoned, abandoning**) **1** to give up completely. **2** to leave or desert (somebody or something) permanently. **3** to give (oneself) over to a feeling or emotion. ➤ **abandonment** n.

abandon² n freedom from constraint or inhibitions.

abase v to bring down in status or esteem. ➤ **abasement** n.

abashed adj ashamed or embarrassed. ➤ **abashment** n.

abate v to become less intense or widespread. ➤ **abatement** n.

abattoir n a slaughterhouse.

abbess n the superior of an abbey of nuns.

abbey n (pl **abbeys**) the buildings of a monastery or a former monastery.

abbot n the superior of a community of monks.

abbreviate v to make (a word or phrase) shorter.

abbreviation n a shortened form of a written word or phrase.

ABC n (pl **ABC's** or **ABCs**) **1** the alphabet. **2** the rudiments of a subject.

abdicate v to relinquish a power or duty, *esp* to give up the throne. ➤ **abdication** n.

abdomen n **1** the part of the body between the thorax and the pelvis containing the liver, gut, etc. **2** the rear part of the body of an insect or arthropod. ➤ **abdominal** adj.

abduct v to carry off secretly or by force. ➤ **abduction** n, **abductor** n.

aberrant adj deviating from what is right, usual, or natural. ➤ **aberrance** n.

aberration n **1** a departure from a normal state or moral standard. **2** an unsoundness or disorder of the mind.

abet v (**abetted, abetting**) to encourage or approve of somebody in doing wrong.

abeyance ✳ **in abeyance** temporarily suspended or out of use.

abhor v (**abhorred, abhorring**) to detest; to loathe.

abhorrent adj causing horror. ➤ **abhorrence** n.

abide v **1** (*usu* **cannot abide** or **could not abide**) to bear (somebody or something) patiently. **2** to remain stable or fixed. ✳ **abide by** to comply with (a rule or decision).

ability n (pl **-ies**) **1** the power to do something. **2** competence or skill.

abject adj **1** wretched or miserable. **2** humble or servile. ➤ **abjection** n, **abjectly** adv.

abjure v to renounce formally or on oath.

ablaze adj and adv burning strongly.

able adj (**abler, ablest**) **1** having the power, skill, or means to do something. **2** skilful or competent. ➤ **ably** adv.

-able or **-ible** suffix able to act or be acted on in some way: *breakable; reliable*. ➤ **-ably** suffix.

able-bodied adj physically strong and fit.

ablutions n a place with washing and toilet facilities.

abnegate v to relinquish or renounce. ➤ **abnegation** n, **abnegator** n.

abnormal adj deviating from the normal or average. ➤ **abnormality** n, **abnormally** adv.

aboard prep and adv on or onto a ship, aircraft, train, or vehicle.

abode n formal a home or residence.

abolish v to put an end to (a custom or institution). ➤ **abolition** n.

abolitionist n a person who wants to abolish a custom or institution. ➤ **abolitionism** n.

A-bomb n = ATOM BOMB.

abominable adj **1** causing disgust or hatred. **2** *informal* disagreeable or unpleasant. ➤ **abominably** adv.

Abominable Snowman n a large hairy manlike animal reported as existing high in the Himalayas. Also called YETI.

abominate v to hate or loathe.

abomination n **1** a detestable or shameful thing or action. **2** extreme disgust and hatred.

aboriginal[1] adj **1** growing or living in a place from the earliest times. **2** (**Aboriginal**) of Australian Aboriginals. ➤ **aboriginally** adv.

aboriginal[2] n **1** an aboriginal person, animal, or plant. **2** (**Aboriginal**) the indigenous people of Australia.

Aborigine n an Australian Aboriginal.

abort[1] v **1** to induce the abortion of (a foetus). **2** to expel a premature foetus. **3** to end (an activity) because of a fault or failure. **4** to fail to develop completely.

abort[2] n the premature termination of a mission or procedure, esp one involving a military aircraft or spacecraft.

abortion n **1** the induced expulsion of a foetus in order to terminate a pregnancy. **2** the spontaneous expulsion of a foetus before it is able to survive independently.

abortive adj fruitless; unsuccessful. ➤ **abortively** adv.

abound v **1** to exist in large numbers or in great quantity. **2** (+ in/with) to have a large number or amount of.

about[1] adv **1** on or to all sides; round. **2** here and there. **3** in succession or rotation. **4** approximately. **5** almost. **6** in the vicinity. ✳ **about to** on the verge of.

about[2] prep **1** with regard to or concerning. **2** approximately. **3** carried by or associated with. **4** in different parts of. **5** surrounding.

about-turn[1] (NAmer **about-face**) n **1** a turn to face the opposite direction. **2** a reversal of policy or opinion.

about-turn[2] (NAmer **about-face**) v to make an about-turn.

above[1] adv **1** in or to a higher place or position. **2** higher on the same page or on an earlier page. **3** in or to a higher rank or number.

above[2] prep **1** higher than the level of. **2** more than. **3** superior to in rank. ✳ **above all** before every other consideration; especially.

abracadabra interj used to accompany conjuring tricks.

abrade v to roughen or wear away by friction.

abrasion n **1** a process of wearing or rubbing away. **2** an area of scraped skin.

abrasive[1] adj **1** having a rough surface used for grinding or smoothing. **2** rude or unpleasant.

abrasive[2] n an abrasive substance, e.g. emery.

abreast adj and adv **1** side by side and facing in the same direction. **2** (+ of) up-to-date with trends or developments.

abridge v **1** to shorten (a book or other piece of writing). **2** to reduce or curtail (a right or privilege). ➤ **abridgment** n.

abroad adv and adj **1** in or to a foreign country. **2** over a wide area. **3** in wide circulation. **4** dated away from one's home; out of doors.

abrogate v to abolish (a law or agreement) by authoritative action. ➤ **abrogation** n.

abrupt adj **1** occurring without warning; unexpected. **2** unceremoniously curt. **3** rising or dropping sharply; steep. ➤ **abruptly** adv, **abruptness** n.

abscess n an accumulation of pus surrounded by inflamed tissue.

abscond v to leave secretly or hurriedly to avoid discovery or arrest. ➤ **absconder** n.

abseil v to descend a vertical surface by sliding down a rope secured from above and wound round the body.

absence n **1** the state of being absent. **2** a period of being absent. **3** (+ of) a lack of.

absent[1] adj **1** not present or attending. **2** not existing. **3** not paying attention. ➤ **absently** adv.

absent[2] v to take or keep (oneself) away.

absentee n somebody who is absent.

absenteeism n persistent unauthorized absence from work or school.

absentminded adj **1** unaware of one's surroundings or actions. **2** habitually forgetful.

absinthe or **absinth** n **1** = WORMWOOD. **2** a green liqueur flavoured with aniseed.

absolute adj **1** complete; perfect. **2** having no restriction or qualification. **3** independent of external references or comparisons.

absolute zero n the lowest temperature theoretically possible (–273.15°C).

absolution n forgiveness of sins pronounced by a priest.

absolutism n government by an absolute ruler or authority. ➤ **absolutist** n and adj.

absolve v **1** (+ from) to set free from an obligation or guilt. **2** to forgive (a sin or sinner).

absorb v **1** to take in (a liquid or gas). **2** to learn (information). **3** to make part of an existing whole; to incorporate. **4** to engage or occupy wholly. **5** to receive and transform (energy) without reflecting or transmitting it. ➤ **absorption** n.

absorbent adj able to absorb a liquid or gas. ➤ **absorbency** n.

abstain v **1** to refrain from something pleasant. **2** to choose not to vote. ➤ **abstainer** n.

abstemious adj not allowing oneself much food, drink, or enjoyment.

abstention n **1** abstaining. **2** an instance of abstaining from voting.

abstinence n voluntary forbearance, esp from drinking alcohol. ➤ **abstinent** adj.

abstract[1] adj **1** theoretical rather than practical. **2** of art: having little or no element of pictorial representation. **3** of a noun: naming a quality, state, or action rather than a thing.

abstract[2] n a summary of the main points, e.g. of a piece of writing.

abstract[3] v to remove, separate, or extract.

abstracted adj preoccupied or absentminded.

abstraction *n* **1** an abstract idea or term. **2** the act or process of abstracting something. **3** preoccupation or absentmindedness.

abstruse *adj* difficult to understand.

absurd *adj* **1** ridiculously unreasonable or incongruous. **2** lacking order, value, or meaning. ➤ **absurdity** *n*, **absurdly** *adv*.

abundance *n* a large quantity or amount.

abundant *adj* **1** occurring in large quantities. **2** (+ in) having plenty of. ➤ **abundantly** *adv*.

abuse[1] *v* **1** to put to a wrong or improper use. **2** to attack in words; to revile. **3** to harm or injure by wrong or cruel treatment. ➤ **abuser** *n*.

abuse[2] *n* **1** improper use or treatment. **2** strong condemnation or disapproval. **3** physical maltreatment. **4** a corrupt practice or custom.

abusive *adj* **1** involving verbal abuse; insulting. **2** involving physical abuse. **3** improper or corrupt. ➤ **abusively** *adv*.

abut *v* (**abutted**, **abutting**) **1** (+ on/upon) of an area: to touch (another area) along a boundary. **2** (+ on/against) to terminate at a point of contact with. **3** (+ on/upon) to lean on for support. ➤ **abutter** *n*.

abysmal *adj* extremely bad. ➤ **abysmally** *adv*.

abyss *n* **1** a deep chasm or void. **2** a wretched situation.

AC *abbr* **1** air conditioning. **2** alternating current.

Ac *abbr* the chemical symbol for actinium.

acacia *n* a tree or shrub with white or yellow flowers.

academia *or* **academe** *n* the academic environment or an academic community.

academic[1] *adj* **1** relating to formal study or education. **2** theoretical and impractical. ➤ **academically** *adv*.

academic[2] *n* a teacher or research student at a college or university.

academy *n* (*pl* **-ies**) **1** a college in which special subjects or skills are taught. **2** a society of learned people organized to promote the arts or sciences.

acanthus *n* (*pl* **acanthuses** *or* **acanthi**) a prickly plant or shrub with spiny leaves and white or purple flower spikes.

a cappella *or* **a capella** *adj and adv* of music: performed without instrumental accompaniment.

accede *v* (*usu* + to) **1** to give consent to. **2** to take up (an office or position, *esp* the throne). **3** to become a party to (an agreement or treaty).

accelerate *v* **1** to move faster. **2** to increase the speed of. ➤ **acceleration** *n*.

accelerator *n* **1** a pedal in a motor vehicle that controls the speed of the engine. **2** a substance that speeds up a chemical reaction. **3** in physics, an apparatus for giving high velocities to charged particles, e.g. electrons.

accent[1] *n* **1** a distinctive pattern of pronunciation and intonation. **2** prominence given to one syllable over others by stress or a change in pitch. **3** greater stress given to one musical note. **4** rhythmically significant stress on certain syllables of a verse. **5** a mark added to a letter to show how it should be pronounced. **6** special emphasis. ➤ **accentual** *adj*.

accent[2] *v* **1** to stress (a vowel, syllable, or word). **2** to mark (a word or letter) with an accent. **3** to emphasize.

accentuate *v* to accent or emphasize. ➤ **accentuation** *n*.

accept *v* **1** to agree to receive or undertake. **2** to agree to a suggestion. **3** to regard as proper or normal. **4** to recognize as true. ➤ **acceptance** *n*.

acceptable *adj* **1** good enough to be accepted. **2** welcome or pleasing. **3** tolerable. ➤ **acceptability** *n*, **acceptably** *adv*.

access[1] *n* **1** freedom to approach or reach somebody or something. **2** a means of approaching or entering.

access[2] *v* to gain access to.

accessible *adj* **1** of a place: capable of being reached. **2** in a form that can be grasped intellectually. **3** (+ to) able to be influenced by. ➤ **accessibility** *n*, **accessibly** *adv*.

accession *n* **1** the act of entering on a high office. **2** an item added to a library or museum.

accessory *or* **accessary** *n* (*pl* **accessories** *or* **accessaries**) **1** something extra that makes a thing more useful or attractive. **2** a person who helps someone commit a crime without taking part.

accident *n* **1** an unpleasant or harmful event that occurs by chance. **2** lack of intention; chance. **3** an unexpected happening.

accidental *adj* happening unexpectedly or by chance. ➤ **accidentally** *adv*.

acclaim[1] *v* to applaud or praise.

acclaim[2] *n* public praise or approval.

acclamation *n* loud or keen public praise or approval.

acclimatize *or* **-ise** *v* to adapt to a new climate or situation. ➤ **acclimatization** *n*.

accolade *n* a mark of acknowledgment or honour; an award.

accommodate *v* **1** to have adequate room for. **2** to provide with lodgings. **3** (+ to) to make fit or appropriate. **4** to oblige or give help or consideration to.

accommodating *adj* helpful or obliging.

accommodation *n* **1** a building or space in which somebody may live or work. **2** a settlement or agreement.

accompaniment *n* **1** an instrumental or vocal part supporting a principal voice or instrument. **2** an addition or complement.

accompany *v* (**-ies**, **-ied**) **1** to go with as an escort or companion. **2** to perform an accompaniment for a singer or musician. **3** to supplement (one thing) with another.

accomplice *n* somebody who helps another person to commit a crime.

accomplish *v* to manage or achieve (an undertaking).

accomplished *adj* skilled or proficient.

accomplishment *n* **1** successful completion or fulfilment. **2** an achievement or ability.

accord¹ *v* to grant or concede. * **accord with** to be consistent with.

accord² *n* **1** agreement or conformity. **2** a formal treaty of agreement. * **of one's own accord** on one's own initiative; voluntarily.

accordance *n* * **in accordance with** agreeing with or conforming to.

according * **according as** depending on how or whether. **according to** in a way that corresponds to.

accordingly *adv* **1** in an appropriate way. **2** consequently.

accordion *n* a musical instrument played by squeezing hand-operated bellows and pressing keys or buttons. ➤ **accordionist** *n*.

accost *v* to approach and speak to (a person) boldly or challengingly.

account¹ *n* **1** a description of facts or events. **2** a record of money received and spent. **3** a facility for keeping money in a bank or for buying goods on credit. **4** * **on account of** due to; because of. **on no account/not on any account** under no circumstances. **on somebody's account** for somebody's sake. **take into account/take account of** to consider along with other factors.

account² *v* to consider or think of in a certain way. * **account for 1** to give a reason for. **2** to be the explanation for.

accountable *adj* **1** (*often* + to/for) responsible; answerable. **2** able to be explained; explicable. ➤ **accountability** *n*.

accountant *n* a person who keeps financial accounts for a living.

accoutrement (*NAmer* **accouterment**) *n* (*usu in pl*) an additional item of equipment or dress.

accredit *v* (**accredited, accrediting**) **1** to give official authorization to. **2** to give credit or recognition to. **3** to attribute (words) to somebody. ➤ **accreditation** *n*.

accretion *n* **1** increase in size caused by natural growth or addition. **2** something added or formed extraneously.

accrue *v* (**accrues, accrued, accruing**) **1** (*often* + to) to come as an increase or addition. **2** of money: to be received periodically and accumulate. **3** to collect or accumulate. ➤ **accrual** *n*.

accumulate *v* **1** to collect together gradually. **2** to increase in quantity or number. ➤ **accumulation** *n*, **accumulative** *adj*.

accumulator *n* **1** *Brit* a rechargeable electric cell. **2** *Brit* a bet whereby the winnings from one event are staked on the next.

accurate *adj* **1** correct; free from error. **2** reaching the intended target. ➤ **accuracy** *n*, **accurately** *adv*.

accursed or **accurst** *adj* **1** under a curse; ill-fated. **2** *informal* detestable; irritating.

accusation *n* a charge of wrongdoing; an allegation.

accusative *adj* of a grammatical case expressing the direct object of a verb. ➤ **accusative** *n*.

accuse *v* (*often* + of) to charge with a fault or crime. ➤ **accuser** *n*.

accustom *v* to make used to through experience; to habituate.

accustomed *adj* **1** customary or habitual. **2** (+ to) in the habit of or used to.

AC/DC *abbr* alternating current/direct current.

ace¹ *n* **1** a playing card marked with one spot. **2** a service in tennis that an opponent cannot return. **3** *informal* an expert or leading performer. * **within an ace of** on the point of; very near to.

ace² *adj informal* excellent.

acerbic *adj* **1** bitter or sour in taste. **2** sharp or vitriolic in speech. ➤ **acerbically** *adv*, **acerbity** *n*.

acetate *n* **1** a textile fibre made from cellulose acetate. **2** an audio recording disc coated with cellulose acetate.

acetic acid *n* a pungent liquid that gives vinegar its taste.

acetone *n* a volatile liquid used as a solvent.

acetylene *n* a colourless inflammable gas used *esp* as a fuel to produce a bright flame.

ache¹ *v* **1** to suffer a dull persistent pain. **2** (*often* + for) to yearn or long for something. ➤ **achy** *adj*.

ache² *n* a dull persistent pain.

achieve *v* **1** to accomplish successfully. **2** to obtain or win by effort. ➤ **achievable** *adj*, **achiever** *n*.

achievement *n* **1** something achieved; a feat. **2** successful completion or accomplishment.

Achilles' heel *n* a single weak or vulnerable point.

Achilles tendon *n* the tendon joining the muscles in the calf to the heelbone.

acid¹ *adj* **1** sour or sharp to the taste. **2** sharp in speech or manner. ➤ **acidity** *n*.

acid² *n* **1** a compound that turns litmus paper red and is capable of reacting with an alkali or other chemical base to form a salt. **2** *slang* the hallucinogenic drug LSD. ➤ **acidic** *adj*.

acidify *v* (**-ies, -ied**) to make or become acid.

acid rain *n* rain containing high levels of acid caused by pollution from burning fuel into the atmosphere.

acid test *n* a severe or crucial test.

acknowledge *v* **1** to admit to be true or valid. **2** to express gratitude or obligation for. **3** to greet or show recognition of. **4** to confirm receipt of.

acknowledgment or **acknowledgement** n **1** something done or given in recognition of something received. **2** a declaration or avowal of a fact. **3** a mention of people to whom an author is indebted.

acme n the highest point or stage.

acne n a skin disorder characterized by red pustules. ➤ **acned** adj.

acolyte n an assistant or follower.

acorn n the nut of the oak, a smooth oval fruit in a cuplike base.

acoustic adj **1** of sound or the sense of hearing. **2** of a musical instrument having sound produced naturally. **3** deadening or absorbing sound. ➤ **acoustically** adv.

acoustics pl n **1** the science of sound. **2** the sound properties of a room.

acquaint v (+ with) to cause to know something; to make familiar with.

acquaintance n **1** personal knowledge or familiarity. **2** somebody one knows slightly.

acquiesce v (often + in) to submit or comply tacitly. ➤ **acquiescence** n, **acquiescent** adj.

acquire v **1** to gain or come into possession of. **2** to gain as a new characteristic or ability. ➤ **acquirement** n.

acquisition n **1** acquiring or gaining possession. **2** something or somebody acquired.

acquisitive adj fond of acquiring material possessions.

acquit v (**acquitted, acquitting**) **1** (often + of) to declare that somebody is not guilty of an offence. **2** to conduct (oneself) in a specified manner. ➤ **acquittal** n.

acre n a unit of area equal to 4840yd^2 (about 0.405ha). ➤ **acreage** n.

acrid adj **1** unpleasantly pungent. **2** acrimonious.

acrimonious adj characterized by personal hostility or bitterness. ➤ **acrimoniously** adv.

acrimony n caustic sharpness of manner or language. ➤ **acrimonious** adj, **acrimoniously** adv.

acrobat n an entertainer who performs gymnastic feats. ➤ **acrobatic** adj, **acrobatically** adv.

acronym n a word formed from the initial letters of other words, e.g. Aids from acquired immune deficiency syndrome.

across[1] adv **1** from one side to the other. **2** to or on the opposite side.

across[2] prep **1** from one side to the other of. **2** on the opposite side of.

acrylic adj made with acrylic acid, an unsaturated liquid acid, or its derivatives.

act[1] n **1** a thing done, or the process of doing something. **2** a formal record of something done or transacted. **3** a law passed by a legislative body. **4** a division of a play or opera. **5** each part or performance in an entertainment. **6** a display of affected behaviour; a pretence.

act[2] v **1** to take action; to do something. **2** to behave in a specified way. **3** (+ as) to perform a function. **4** to produce an effect. **5** (+ on) to do something in response to advice or instructions. **6** to play a role in a play or film.

action[1] n **1** practical activity directed towards a particular aim. **2** the state of functioning actively. **3** energetic activity. **4** a voluntary act. **5** the events in a story or play. **6** armed combat in war. **7** the operating part of a mechanism or device. **8** the manner in which something operates or moves. **9** a civil legal proceeding. * **out of action** not working or functioning actively. **take action** to begin to act; to do something.

action[2] v to take action on.

actionable adj giving grounds for an action at law.

action stations pl n the positions taken up by forces for military action.

activate v to cause a device or process to start operating. ➤ **activation** n.

active adj **1** moving, working, or operating, not at rest. **2** full of activity; busy. **3** characterized by practical action and involvement. **4** having practical results; effective. **5** of a volcano: liable to erupt. **6** in grammar, of a verb: having as the subject the person or thing doing the action. ➤ **actively** adv.

active service n military service in a war.

activist n a person who advocates vigorous social or political action. ➤ **activism** n.

activity n (pl **-ies**) **1** a state in which things are happening or being done. **2** vigorous or energetic action. **3** a pursuit in which a person takes part.

act of God n a sudden event brought about by uncontrollable natural forces.

actor n **1** a person who takes part in a dramatic production. **2** a participant in an event or situation.

actress n a female actor.

actual adj existing or happening in fact.

actuality n (pl **-ies**) **1** the quality or state of being actual; reality. **2** (often in pl) an existing circumstance; a real fact.

actualize v to make (a plan, etc.) happen.

actually adv really; in fact.

actuary n (pl **-ies**) a person who calculates insurance risks and premiums. ➤ **actuarial** adj.

actuate v **1** to put (a device or machine) into action. **2** to incite to action; to motivate.

acuity n keenness of mental or physical perception.

acumen n keen judgment or ability in practical matters; shrewdness.

acupuncture *n* the puncturing of the body with needles to cure disease or relieve pain. ➤ **acupuncturist** *n*.

acute *adj* **1** intelligent and shrewd. **2** of a sense or feeling: intensely felt or perceived. **3** of something bad: serious or critical. **4** of an angle: measuring less than 90°. ➤ **acutely** *adv*, **acuteness** *n*.

acute accent *n* a mark (´) placed over certain vowels in some languages to show a particular vowel quality or stress.

AD *abbr* anno Domini, used to indicate that a date comes within the Christian era.

Usage Note: AD *and* BC. AD *is traditionally written before a number signifying a year:* AD 1625. *When referring to centuries, however, it is necessary to place* AD *at the end of the phrase:* in the third century AD. BC *always follows a date:* 440 BC; the seventh century BC.

---

adage *n* a maxim or proverb that embodies a general truth.

adagio *adj and adv* of a piece of music: performed in a slow gentle tempo.

adamant *adj* refusing to change one's mind; unyielding. ➤ **adamantly** *adv*.

Adam's apple *n* the projection in the front of the neck, more prominent in men.

adapt *v* (*often* + to) to make or become suited to different circumstances. ➤ **adaptability** *n*, **adaptable** *adj*, **adaptive** *adj*.

adaptation *n* **1** adapting or being adapted. **2** a play or film adapted from a novel or other medium.

adapter *or* **adaptor** *n* **1** a device for connecting two pieces of apparatus not orig intended to be joined. **2** a device for connecting several pieces of electrical apparatus to a single power point.

add *v* **1** to join to something else so as to bring about an increase or improvement. **2** to serve as an addition to something. **3** to say or write further. **4** (*often* + up) to combine into a single number.

addendum *n* (*pl* **addenda**) an extra item at the end of a book.

adder *n* a poisonous viper with a dark zigzag pattern along the back.

addict¹ *v* (*usu in passive*) **1** to cause to become dependent on a habit-forming drug. **2** to cause to indulge habitually or obsessively in (an activity). ➤ **addiction** *n*, **addictive** *adj*.

addict² *n* **1** somebody who is addicted to a drug. **2** an enthusiast or devotee.

addition *n* **1** the process of adding. **2** something or somebody added. ✳ **in addition** also; as well.

additional *adj* added or extra. ➤ **additionally** *adv*.

additive *n* a substance added to another in relatively small amounts.

addled *adj* **1** confused or muddled. **2** of an egg: rotten.

address¹ *v* **1** to mark directions for delivery on (a letter or package). **2** to speak or write directly to. **3** to communicate directly to somebody. **4** to greet by a prescribed form. **5** to deal with or apply oneself to. ➤ **addressee** *n*.

address² *n* **1** a place where a person lives or a building is situated. **2** the details of such a place. **3** a location in the memory of a computer where particular information is stored. **4** a prepared speech delivered to an audience.

adduce *v* *formal* to offer as evidence or proof. ➤ **adducible** *adj*.

add up *v* **1** to come to a total. **2** *informal* to be internally consistent; to make sense.

adenoids *pl n* a mass of tissue at the back of the pharynx that obstructs breathing when enlarged. ➤ **adenoidal** *adj*.

adept¹ *adj* highly skilled or proficient. ➤ **adeptly** *adv*.

adept² *n* a highly skilled person.

adequate *adj* sufficient or acceptable. ➤ **adequacy** *n*, **adequately** *adv*.

adhere *v* **1** to stick or hold fast. **2** to give support or loyalty to. **3** (+ to) to observe or follow exactly. ➤ **adherence** *n*.

adherent¹ *n* a supporter of a leader or cause.

adherent² *adj* sticking or holding fast.

adhesion *n* the action or state of adhering.

adhesive¹ *adj* sticky.

adhesive² *n* an adhesive substance.

ad hoc *adj and adv* for the particular purpose at hand only.

adieu *interj chiefly literary* goodbye.

ad infinitum *adv* without end or limit; indefinitely.

adjacent *adj* **1** (*often* + to) having a common boundary or border. **2** near or next to something or to one another.

adjective *n* a word that modifies a noun or pronoun by describing a particular characteristic of it. ➤ **adjectival** *adj*.

adjoin *v* to be next or joined to.

adjourn *v* **1** to suspend (a meeting) until a later time. **2** to defer for later consideration or resolution. **3** to move to another place. ➤ **adjournment** *n*.

adjudge *v* **1** to declare or judge formally. **2** to award or grant judicially.

adjudicate *v* **1** to decide judicially. **2** to act as judge in a competition. ➤ **adjudication** *n*, **adjudicator** *n*.

adjunct *n* something added as an incidental accompaniment.

adjure *v* *formal* to command or advise solemnly to do something.

adjust *v* **1** to regulate or modify slightly. **2** to adapt oneself to new conditions. **3** to decide the amount to be paid under an insurance policy. ➤ **adjustable** *adj*, **adjustment** *n*.

adjutant n a military officer who assists a commanding officer with administrative matters. ➤ **adjutancy** n.

ad-lib[1] adj spoken or performed without preparation.

ad-lib[2] v (**ad-libbed, ad-libbing**) to speak spontaneously; to improvise.

ad-lib[3] n an improvised speech, line, or performance.

administer v (**administered, administering**) 1 to manage or supervise. 2 to give (a remedy or punishment).

administrate v to manage or supervise the affairs of a business or country. ➤ **administrative** adj.

administration n 1 the business of running the affairs of a business or country. 2 a government in power.

admirable adj deserving the highest respect; excellent. ➤ **admirably** adv.

admiral n 1 the commander-in-chief of a fleet or navy. 2 a senior officer in the Royal Navy or US Navy.

admire v to admire or think highly of. ➤ **admirer** n.

admissible adj 1 acceptable or permissible. 2 entitled to enter a place.

admission n 1 acknowledgment that a fact or allegation is true. 2 being allowed to enter a place or join a group.

admit v (**admitted, admitting**) 1 to concede as true or valid. 2 (+ to) to make an acknowledgment of. 3 to allow to enter a place or join a group. 4 to take into a hospital for treatment.

admittance n 1 permission to enter a place. 2 access or entrance.

admonish v 1 to reprove gently. 2 to urge or warn. ➤ **admonition** n, **admonitory** adj.

ad nauseam adv to a tediously excessive degree.

ado n * **without more/further ado** without further delay.

adolescent[1] adj of the period of life between puberty and maturity. ➤ **adolescence** n.

adolescent[2] n an adolescent person.

Adonis n a strikingly handsome young man.

adopt v 1 to bring up (a child of other parents) as one's own child. 2 to take over or begin to use. 3 to vote to accept. ➤ **adoption** n.

adoptive adj of a parent: adopting a child.

adorable adj lovable or charming. ➤ **adorably** adv.

adore v 1 to admire or love greatly. 2 to worship or honour as a deity. ➤ **adoration** n.

adorn v to decorate with ornaments. ➤ **adornment** n.

adrenal adj 1 of the region of the kidneys. 2 of the adrenal glands.

adrenal glands pl n glands near the front of each kidney, secreting hormones and adrenalin.

adrenalin or **adrenaline** n a hormone produced by the adrenal gland in response to stress or excitement, increasing the heart rate and blood pressure.

adrift adv and adj 1 of a boat: drifting without power or steerage. 2 unfastened or unstuck.

adroit adj clever or skilful. ➤ **adroitly** adv.

adulate v to flatter or admire excessively. ➤ **adulation** n, **adulatory** adj.

adult[1] adj 1 fully developed and mature. 2 appropriate to adults. ➤ **adulthood** n.

adult[2] n an adult person.

adulterate v to corrupt or make impure. ➤ **adulteration** n.

adulterer or **adulteress** n a man or woman who commits adultery.

adultery n (pl -ies) voluntary sexual intercourse between a married person and somebody other than his or her spouse. ➤ **adulterous** adj.

adumbrate v formal 1 to outline broadly without details. 2 to foreshadow vaguely.

advance[1] v 1 to move forward in position or time. 2 to accelerate the growth or progress of. 3 to develop or make progress. 4 to raise in rank. 5 to supply (money or goods) ahead of time or as a loan. 6 to bring (an opinion or argument) forward for notice.

advance[2] n 1 a forward movement. 2 progress in development. 3 (usu in pl) a friendly or amorous approach. 4 money or goods supplied ahead of time. * **in advance** beforehand.

advance[3] adj 1 made, sent, or provided ahead of time. 2 going or situated ahead of others.

advanced adj 1 far on in time or course. 2 more complex or developed.

advancement n 1 promotion to a higher rank or position. 2 furtherance towards perfection or completeness. 3 forward movement or progress.

advantage n 1 a favourable or helpful factor or circumstance. 2 a benefit or gain. 3 the first point won in tennis after deuce. * **take advantage of somebody or something** 1 to use something for one's benefit. 2 to impose on or exploit.

Advent n 1 the period from the fourth Sunday before Christmas to Christmas itself. 2 the coming of Christ to earth as a human being. 3 (**advent**) a coming into being; an arrival.

adventitious adj coming accidentally or unexpectedly.

adventure n 1 an undertaking involving danger and uncertainty. 2 an exciting or remarkable experience. ➤ **adventuresome** adj.

adventurer or **adventuress** n 1 somebody who enjoys adventures. 2 somebody who seeks wealth or position by unscrupulous means.

adventurous adj prepared to take risks or try new experiences. ➤ **adventurously** adv.

adverb *n* a word that modifies a verb, an adjective, another adverb, or a sentence, answering questions such as *how?*, *when?*, or *where?*

adversarial *adj* involving opposition or hostility.

adversary *n* (*pl* **-ies**) an enemy or opponent.

adverse *adj* unfavourable or harmful. ➤ **adversely** *adv.*

adversity *n* (*pl* **-ies**) a condition of suffering or hardship.

advert *n* chiefly Brit, informal an advertisement.

advertise *v* **1** to encourage sales of (a product or service) by emphasizing its qualities. **2** to announce publicly. **3** (+ for) to seek by means of advertising. ➤ **advertiser** *n.*

advertisement *n* something published or broadcast to advertise a product or service.

advice *n* guidance or recommendations about a decision or course of conduct.

advisable *adj* worthy of being recommended; prudent. ➤ **advisability** *n.*

advise *v* **1** to give advice to. **2** to recommend. **3** to give information to.

advised *adj* thought out; considered. ➤ **advisedly** *adv.*

advisory *adj* having the power to advise but not to decide.

advocaat /'advəkah/ *n* a sweet liqueur made with brandy and eggs.

advocate[1] *n* **1** somebody who pleads the cause of another before a tribunal or court. **2** Scot a barrister. **3** somebody who openly supports a cause or proposal.

advocate[2] *v* to recommend or plead in favour of (a cause or proposal). ➤ **advocacy** *n.*

adze (*NAmer* **adz**) *n* a cutting tool with the blade attached at right angles to the handle.

aegis *n* protection or support.

aeon *or* **eon** *n* an extremely long period of time.

aerate *v* **1** to combine or impregnate with a gas. **2** to make (a liquid) effervescent. ➤ **aeration** *n.*

aerial[1] *adj* **1** existing or occurring in the air or atmosphere. **2** operating overhead on elevated cables or rails. **3** of or involving aircraft.

aerial[2] *n* a metal rod or wire designed to transmit or receive radio or television signals.

aerie *n* see EYRIE.

aerobatics *n* the performance of stunts in an aircraft as the entertainment. ➤ **aerobatic** *adj.*

aerobic *adj* **1** to do with aerobics. **2** living or occurring only in the presence of oxygen.

aerobics *n* a system of physical exercises designed to improve respiration and circulation.

aerodrome *n* chiefly Brit a small airport or airfield.

aerodynamics *n* the dynamics of the motion of gases, e.g. air, and solid bodies moving through them. ➤ **aerodynamic** *adj.*

aerofoil *n* chiefly Brit a structure on an aircraft or vehicle for providing lift as the vehicle moves through the air.

aeronautics *n* the science or practice of flight. ➤ **aeronautical** *adj.*

aeroplane *n* a powered aircraft with fixed wings.

aerosol *n* **1** a suspension of fine solid or liquid particles in gas. **2** a substance dispersed from a pressurized container as an aerosol.

aerospace *n* the science or technology of flight in the earth's atmosphere and beyond.

aesthete (*NAmer* **esthete**) *n* somebody who appreciates beauty in art or nature.

aesthetic[1] (*NAmer* **esthetic**) *adj* to do with beauty or the appreciation of the beautiful. ➤ **aesthetically** *adv.*

aesthetic[2] *n* a set of principles on which the work of an artist or artistic movement is based.

aesthetics (*NAmer* **esthetics**) *n* **1** a branch of philosophy dealing with the nature of beauty and aesthetic taste. **2** the principles concerning beauty.

afar *adv* to or at a great distance.

affable *adj* pleasant and friendly. ➤ **affability** *n*, **affably** *adv.*

affair *n* **1** a particular or personal concern. **2** (*in pl*) commercial or public business. **3** a procedure or action. **4** a love affair. **5** a matter causing public controversy or scandal.

affect[1] *v* **1** to have an effect on. **2** to act on (somebody) so as to bring about a response.

Usage Note: Affect is a verb that means 'to influence or change': *How will this affect my pension prospects?* Effect is most commonly used as a noun: *What effect will this have on my pension prospects?* It can also be used, slightly formally, as a verb meaning to 'bring about' or 'carry out': *The police effected an entry into the premises.*

affect[2] *v* **1** to pretend to feel or show (a quality). **2** to assume the character or attitude of. **3** to wear or use ostentatiously.

affectation *n* **1** an insincere or pretended display of a quality or feeling. **2** a deliberately assumed peculiarity of speech or behaviour.

affected *adj* **1** insincere or pretentious. **2** pretended for effect. ➤ **affectedly** *adv.*

affection *n* fondness or liking.

affectionate *adj* showing affection. ➤ **affectionately** *adv.*

affidavit *n* a sworn written statement for use as judicial proof.

affiliate[1] *v* **1** to attach (an organization) as a member or branch. **2** to connect or associate oneself with another. ➤ **affiliation** *n.*

affiliate[2] *n* an affiliated person or organization.

affinity *n* (*pl* **-ies**) **1** a natural liking for or understanding of somebody. **2** an attraction to or taste for something. **3** resemblance based on relationship or causal connection. **4** a chemical attraction or biological relation.

affirm v **1** to validate or confirm. **2** to state positively. **3** to assert (e.g. a judgment of a lower court) as valid.

affirmative¹ adj stating that something is true or correct. ➤ **affirmatively** adv.

affirmative² n a word or statement expressing agreement or assent.

affix¹ v **1** to attach physically. **2** to add in writing.

affix² n a prefix or suffix.

afflict v **1** to distress severely. **2** to cause serious problems or trouble to. ➤ **affliction** n.

affluent adj wealthy. ➤ **affluence** n.

afford v **1** to have enough money or time for. **2** to be able to do without serious harm. **3** to provide or supply. ➤ **affordable** adj.

affray n a brawl in a public place.

affront¹ n an open insult.

affront² v to insult or offend.

aficionado /ə,fishyə'nahdoh/ n (pl **aficionados**) a devotee or fan.

afield adv away or at a distance.

aflame adj and adv on fire.

afloat adj and adv **1** floating on the water. **2** free of debt.

afoot adv and adj happening or imminent.

aforementioned adj mentioned previously.

afraid adj (often + of/to) filled with fear.

afresh adv again or differently.

African n a person from Africa, esp a black person. ➤ **African** adj.

Afrikaans n a language of southern Africa developed from Dutch.

aft adv and adj towards or in the rear of a ship or aircraft.

after¹ prep **1** behind in place or order. **2** later than. **3** in search or pursuit of. **4** in accordance with. **5** in the manner of or in imitation of.

after² adv **1** in the rear; behind. **2** afterwards.

after³ conj later than the time when.

afterbirth n the placenta and foetal membranes expelled from the womb after a birth.

aftereffect n an effect that follows later.

afterlife n an existence after death.

aftermath n the time or result following an unpleasant or disastrous event.

afternoon n the time between noon and lunchtime and evening. ➤ **afternoon** adj.

aftershave n a scented lotion for use on the face after shaving.

afterthought n an idea thought of or added later.

afterwards or **afterward** adv after that; subsequently.

afterword n = EPILOGUE.

Ag abbr the chemical symbol for silver.

again adv **1** once more. **2** so as to be as before. **3** in addition.

against prep **1** in opposition or hostility to. **2** in contact with. **3** opposite to the motion or course of. **4** in preparation or provision for. **5** in exchange for.

agape /ə'gayp/ adj wide open; gaping.

agate n a mineral used as a gem composed of quartz of various colours, often arranged in bands.

age¹ n **1** the length of time a person has lived or a thing existed. **2** a stage of life. **3** a period of past time dominated by a central figure or prominent feature. **4** a division of geological time, shorter than an epoch. **5** informal (usu in pl) a long time. * **come of age** to reach legal adult status.

age² v (**ageing** or **aging**) **1** to become or start to look old. **2** to cause to seem old. **3** to mellow or ripen.

aged /'ayjid/ adj **1** of an advanced age. **2** /ayjd/ of a specified age.

ageism or **agism** n discrimination on grounds of age. ➤ **ageist** adj and n.

ageless adj timeless or eternal.

agency n (pl **-ies**) **1** an establishment that does a particular type of business. **2** an administrative department of a government. **3** intervention or instrumentality.

agenda n **1** a list of items for discussion at a meeting. **2** a plan of procedure.

agent n **1** a person who is authorized to act for another. **2** a representative of a government. **3** a spy. **4** something or somebody that produces an effect or exerts power.

agent provocateur /,ahzhonhprə,vokə'tuh/ n (pl **agents provocateurs**) a person employed to incite suspected people to action that will incriminate them.

age of consent n the age at which a person may legally consent to sexual intercourse.

agglomeration n a collection or mass of things.

aggrandize or **-ise** v to make more powerful or important. ➤ **aggrandizement** n.

aggravate v **1** to make worse or more severe. **2** informal to annoy or irritate. ➤ **aggravation** n.

aggregate¹ adj formed by combining separate elements into a whole.

aggregate² v to combine into a mass or whole.

aggregate³ n **1** a mass of loosely associated parts. **2** the whole amount; the sum total. **3** a rock composed of closely packed mineral crystals or rock fragments. **4** sand, gravel, etc for mixing with cement to make concrete.

aggression n hostile or violent behaviour or attitudes. ➤ **aggressor** n.

aggressive adj **1** hostile or violent in behaviour or attitude. **2** forceful or dynamic. ➤ **aggressively** adv.

aggrieved adj showing or expressing resentment for unfair treatment.

aghast adj shocked or horrified.

agile *adj* **1** able to move easily and gracefully. **2** mentally quick and resourceful. ➤ **agilely** *adv*, **agility** *n*.

agitate *v* **1** to trouble or disturb. **2** to shake or stir. **3** to work to arouse public feeling about an issue. ➤ **agitation** *n*, **agitator** *n*.

AGM *abbr* annual general meeting.

agnostic *n* somebody who believes it is impossible to know whether God exists. ➤ **agnostic** *adj*, **agnosticism** *n*.

ago *adv* before now.

agog *adj* full of excitement or eagerness.

agonize *or* **-ise** *v* **1** to suffer, or cause to suffer, agony or anguish. **2** to make a great effort. **3** to worry excessively over a decision.

agony *n* (*pl* **-ies**) intense physical pain or mental suffering.

agony column *n* a column in a magazine or newspaper offering advice on readers' personal problems.

agoraphobia *n* abnormal fear of open spaces. ➤ **agoraphobic** *n and adj*.

agrarian *adj* to do with farming and agriculture.

agree *v* **1** to have the same opinion or judgment about something. **2** (*often* + to) to approve of something or consent to do something. **3** (*often* + with) to be compatible with; to correspond or be consistent. **4** (+ with) to suit somebody's health or constitution. **5** (*often* + on) to decide together about.

agreeable *adj* **1** to one's liking; pleasing. **2** willing to agree or consent. ➤ **agreeably** *adv*.

agreement *n* **1** a sharing of opinion or feeling. **2** correspondence or consistency. **3** consent. **4** a treaty or contract.

agriculture *n* the theory and practice of farming. ➤ **agricultural** *adj*, **agriculturally** *adv*.

aground *adv and adj* touching the shore or the bottom of a body of water.

ague *n* a malarial fever with attacks of chills and sweating.

ahead *adv and adj* **1** in front or in a forward direction. **2** in the future.

ahoy *interj* used at sea as a greeting or warning.

aid[1] *v* **1** to give help or assistance to. **2** to facilitate.

aid[2] *n* **1** help or assistance. **2** money or supplies given to a country in need. * **in aid of** in order to help or support.

aide *n chiefly NAmer* an assistant to a political leader.

Aids *or* **AIDS** *n* a disease of the immune system, caused by the HIV virus.

aikido *n* a martial art resembling judo.

ail *v archaic* to give pain or trouble to.

ailing *adj* ill or unwell or chronically ill.

ailment *n* a mild illness.

aim[1] *v* **1** to point a weapon, camera, etc at an object or person. **2** to intend or try to do something.

aim[2] *n* **1** a clear intention or purpose. **2** the pointing of a weapon at a target. ➤ **aimless** *adj*, **aimlessly** *adv*.

ain't *contraction non-standard* **1** am not; are not; is not. **2** have not; has not.

air[1] *n* **1** the mixture of invisible gases that surrounds the earth. **2** empty unconfined space. **3** nothingness. **4** the supposed medium of transmission of radio waves. **5** a person's bearing or demeanour. **6** (*in pl*) an artificial or affected manner. **7** a tune or melody. * **in the air** being generally spread round or hinted at. **on the air** being broadcast on radio or television. **up in the air** not yet settled; uncertain.

air[2] *v* **1** to express (an opinion) openly. **2** to broadcast on radio or television. **3** to expose to fresh air or warmth.

air base *n* a base for military aircraft.

airborne *adj* **1** carried in the air. **2** of an aircraft: in the air after taking off.

airbrush[1] *n* an atomizer for spraying paint.

airbrush[2] *v* to paint or spray with an airbrush.

air conditioning *n* an apparatus for controlling the temperature and quality of the air in a building or vehicle. ➤ **air-condition** *v*.

aircraft *n* (*pl* **aircraft**) an aeroplane, helicopter, or other vehicle that can fly.

aircraft carrier *n* a large warship serving as a base for aircraft.

airfield *n* an area of land where aircraft can take off and land.

air force *n* the branch of a country's armed forces that fights with aircraft.

air gun *n* a gun that propels a pellet by compressed air.

air hostess *n* a female member of the cabin crew on a passenger aircraft.

airing *n* exposure to discussion.

airlift *n* the transport of supplies or passengers by air from an otherwise inaccessible area. ➤ **airlift** *v*.

airline *n* a company that provides public air transport.

airliner *n* a large passenger aircraft.

air lock *n* **1** an airtight chamber, e.g. in a spacecraft or submerged vessel, that allows movement between two areas of different air pressure. **2** a stoppage of flow caused by the presence of air in circulating liquid.

airmail *n* mail transported by aircraft, or this system of transporting mail. ➤ **airmail** *v*.

airman *or* **airwoman** *n* (*pl* **airmen** *or* **airwomen**) a military pilot or crew member.

airplane *n chiefly NAmer* = AEROPLANE.

airport *n* an airfield with runways and associated buildings, used as a base for the transport of passengers and cargo by air.

airship *n* a gas-filled lighter-than-air aircraft that has its own means of propulsion and steering.

airspace *n* the area of the atmosphere above a nation and coming under its jurisdiction.

airstrip *n* a strip of ground where aircraft can take off and land.

airtight *adj* **1** not allowing air to pass through. **2** of an argument: unassailable.

airwaves *pl n* the supposed medium of radio and television transmission.

airway *n* **1** a designated route along which aircraft fly. **2** the passage through which air reaches the lungs.

airworthy *adj* of an aircraft: fit for operation in the air. ➤ **airworthiness** *n*.

airy *adj* (**-ier, -iest**) **1** spacious and well-ventilated. **2** showing lack of concern; flippant. **3** light and graceful. ➤ **airily** *adv*.

airy-fairy *adj chiefly Brit* whimsically unrealistic.

aisle *n* **1** a passage between rows of seats in a church or other public building. **2** a passage between rows of shelving in a shop.

ajar *adj and adv* of a door: slightly open.

AKA *or* **aka** *abbr* also known as.

akimbo *adj and adv* with the hands on the hips and the elbow turned outwards.

akin *adj* **1** descended from a common ancestor. **2** essentially similar or compatible.

Al *abbr* the chemical symbol for aluminium.

alabaster *n* a fine-textured white translucent stone often carved into ornaments.

à la carte *adv and adj* according to a menu that prices each item separately: compare TABLE D'HÔTE.

alacrity *n formal* promptness or cheerful readiness.

alarm¹ *n* **1** the fear resulting from the sudden sensing of danger. **2** a signal that warns or alerts, or an automatic device that produces such a signal. **3** = ALARM CLOCK.

alarm² *v* **1** to cause great fear or anxiety in. **2** to warn or alert. **3** to fit with an automatic alarm. ➤ **alarming** *adj*, **alarmingly** *adv*.

alarm clock *n* a clock that can be set to sound an alarm at a required time, used to wake somebody up.

alarmist *n* a person who needlessly alarms other people.

alas *interj* used to express unhappiness, pity, or disappointment.

albatross *n* (*pl* **albatrosses** *or* **albatross**) a very large web-footed seabird with long narrow wings related to the petrels.

albeit *conj formal* even though.

albino *n* (*pl* **-os**) a person or animal with deficient pigmentation resulting in white skin and hair, and eyes with a pink pupil. ➤ **albinism** *n*.

album *n* **1** a blank book for holding or displaying a collection, e.g. of stamps or photographs. **2** a collection of musical recordings issued on a single disc.

albumen *n* the white of an egg.

alchemy *n* (*pl* **-ies**) a medieval form of chemical science that sought to turn base metals into gold. ➤ **alchemic** *adj*, **alchemical** *adj*, **alchemist** *n*.

alcohol *n* **1** a colourless liquid, the intoxicating agent in fermented and distilled drinks and also used as a solvent. **2** drink containing alcohol.

alcoholic¹ *adj* **1** containing or caused by alcohol. **2** affected with alcoholism.

alcoholic² *n* somebody affected with alcoholism.

alcoholism *n* addiction to alcoholic drink.

alcove *n* a recess or arched opening in a wall.

alder *n* a tree or shrub of the birch family with toothed leaves and catkins.

alderman *n* (*pl* **aldermen**) formerly in Britain, a senior member of a county or borough council.

ale *n* **1** beer. **2** an alcoholic drink made with malt and hops.

alert¹ *adj* **1** watchful; aware. **2** active; brisk. ➤ **alertly** *adv*, **alertness** *n*.

alert² *n* a warning of danger. * **on the alert** on the lookout for danger or opportunity.

alert³ *v* to warn about a danger or opportunity.

A level *n* an examination at sixth-form level.

alfalfa *n* a plant of the pea family that is widely grown for fodder.

alfresco *or* **al fresco** *adj and adv* taking place in the open air.

algae *pl noun* aquatic plants that lack differentiated stems, roots, and leaves, e.g. seaweed.

algebra *n* a branch of mathematics in which letters and symbols represent various entities in equations and formulas. ➤ **algebraic** *adj*.

algorithm *n* a systematic mathematical procedure for making a calculation. ➤ **algorithmic** *adj*.

alias¹ *adv* otherwise called or known as.

alias² *n* an assumed name.

alibi *n* (*pl* **alibis**) a plea of having been elsewhere when a crime was committed, or evidence supporting such a claim.

alien¹ *adj* **1** belonging to another person, place, or thing; strange or foreign. **2** from another world; extraterrestrial. **3** differing in nature or character.

alien² *n* **1** a foreign-born resident. **2** a being from another world.

alienate *v* **1** to make hostile or indifferent. **2** to cause (affection or sympathy) to be withdrawn or diverted. **3** to convey or transfer (property or a right) to another.

alight¹ *v* **1** to dismount or disembark from a vehicle. **2** to descend from the air and settle. **3** (+ on) to discover or notice.

alight² *adj* **1** *chiefly Brit* on fire; ignited. **2** animated or alive.

align v **1** to bring into proper relative position, usu in a straight line. **2** to position (oneself) in relation to a party or cause. ➤ **alignment** n.

alike[1] adj showing close resemblance without being identical.

alike[2] adv in the same manner, form, or degree; equally.

alimentary canal n the passage from the mouth to the anus along which food passes.

alimony n chiefly NAmer = MAINTENANCE 2.

alive adj **1** having life; not dead. **2** still in existence or operation; active. **3** (+ to) realizing the existence of; aware of. **4** lively or animated.

alkali n (pl **alkalis**) **1** a soluble chemical base, esp a hydroxide or carbonate of an alkali metal, that combine with acids to form salts. **2** a soluble chemical salt that is present in some soils of dry regions and prevents the growth of crops. ➤ **alkaline** adj.

all[1] adj **1** the whole amount or quantity of. **2** every. **3** any whatever. **4** as much as possible. ✱ **all there** informal alert or shrewd.

all[2] adv **1** wholly or altogether. **2** to a supreme degree. **3** in scores: for each side. ✱ **all but** very nearly; almost. **all together** all at the same time or in the same place. **all too** emphatically so.

all[3] pron (pl **all**) everybody or everything. ✱ **all in all** taking everything into account. **in all** in total.

Allah n the name for the Muslim God.

allay v to reduce the severity of (pain, fear, or suffering).

all clear n a signal that a danger has passed.

allegation n a statement made without proof.

allege v to assert without proof. ➤ **alleged** adj, **allegedly** adv.

allegiance n loyalty to or support of a person, group, or cause.

allegory n (pl **-ies**) a story, poem, or picture that contains a symbolic meaning. ➤ **allegorical** adj.

allegro adj and adv of a piece of music: performed in a brisk lively manner.

alleluia interj and n see HALLELUJAH.

allergic adj **1** having an allergy. **2** inducing an allergy.

allergy n (pl **-ies**) extreme sensitivity to substances that have no such effect on the average individual.

alleviate v to relieve (a problem or anxiety). ➤ **alleviation** n.

alley n (pl **-eys**) **1** a narrow passageway between buildings. **2** a garden walk bordered by trees or a hedge. **3** a long narrow lane for bowling or playing skittles.

alliance n **1** an association or bond for mutual help between nations or groups. **2** a connection or relationship, esp by marriage.

allied adj **1** joined in alliance by agreement or treaty. **2** in close association; united. **3** related genetically.

alligator n a large aquatic reptile related to the crocodile but with a broader head.

all in adj informal tired out; exhausted.

all-in adj **1** chiefly Brit including all costs. **2** Brit said of wrestling: having almost no holds barred.

alliteration n the repetition of initial consonant sounds in neighbouring words or syllables for special effect. ➤ **alliterative** adj.

allocate v to apportion or distribute. ➤ **allocation** n.

allot v (**allotted, allotting**) **1** to apportion or assign. **2** to earmark or designate.

allotment n **1** Brit a small plot of land for growing flowers or vegetables. **2** the act of allotting or a share allotted.

allow v **1** to permit or make it possible for somebody to do something. **2** to assign (time or money) as a share or suitable amount. **3** to grant (a sum of money) as an allowance. **4** (+ for) to take into account. ➤ **allowable** adj.

allowance n **1** a share or portion allowed. **2** a sum paid to a person, usu at regular intervals. **3** an amount of income on which no tax is payable. ✱ **make allowances for** to take (mitigating circumstances) into account.

alloy[1] n **1** a mixture of metals or of a metal with a non-metal. **2** a metal mixed with a more valuable metal.

alloy[2] v **1** to mix (metals) to form an alloy. **2** to spoil by addition.

all right[1] adv well enough.

all right[2] adj **1** satisfactory or acceptable. **2** safe or well. **3** agreeable or pleasing.

all-rounder n somebody who is competent in many fields.

all told adv with everything or everybody taken into account.

allude v (+ to) to refer to indirectly; to mention in passing.

allure[1] v to entice by charm or attraction.

allure[2] n power of attraction or fascination.

allusion n **1** an implied or indirect reference. **2** alluding or hinting. ➤ **allusive** adj.

alluvium n (pl **alluviums** or **alluvia**) clay or silt deposited by running water. ➤ **alluvial** adj.

ally[1] v (**-ies, -ied**) **1** to join or unite with, esp for common benefit. **2** (usu in passive) to combine with. **3** (+ to) to relate by resemblance or common properties.

ally[2] n (pl **-ies**) **1** a state associated with another by treaty. **2** a person or group that helps, supports, or cooperates with another.

alma mater n a school, college, or university that one has attended.

almanac or **almanack** n an annual publication containing statistical information, *esp* a publication containing astronomical and meteorological data.

almighty[1] adj **1** (often **Almighty**) having absolute power over all. **2** having relatively unlimited power. **3** *informal* great in extent, seriousness, force, etc.

almighty[2] adv *informal* to a great degree; very.

almond n an edible oval nut obtained from a small tree of the rose family.

almost adv very nearly but not exactly.

alms pl noun money or food formerly given to help the poor.

almshouse n *Brit* a house for the poor, founded and financed by charity.

aloe n a succulent plant with thick leaves and tall spikes of flowers, and producing a juice used as a laxative.

aloe vera n a jelly-like extract from a species of aloe, used in cosmetic preparations and ointments.

aloft adv at or to a higher place; up in the air.

alone adj and adv **1** separated from others; isolated. **2** considered by itself. **3** free from interference or help.

along[1] prep **1** over the length of or in a line parallel with. **2** in the course of. **3** in accordance with.

along[2] adv forward; onward. * **all along** all the time. **along with** in addition to.

alongside[1] adv along or at the side of something.

alongside[2] prep (also + of) side by side with or along the side of.

aloof adj distant or unsympathetic. ➤ **aloofness** n.

alopecia n abnormal loss of hair.

aloud adv with a normal speaking voice.

alp n **1** a high mountain. **2** in Switzerland, a mountainside pasture.

alpaca n (pl **alpacas** or **alpaca**) a type of mammal related to the llama, found in Peru, producing a fine wool.

alpha n the first letter of the Greek alphabet (A, α).

alphabet n a set of letters used to write a language.

alphabetical or **alphabetic** adj in the order of the letters of the alphabet. ➤ **alphabetically** adv.

alpha particle n a positively charged nuclear particle, identical with the nucleus of a helium atom, ejected from radioactive substances: compare BETA PARTICLE.

alpine adj relating to or growing in mountainous regions.

already adv **1** before a particular time or the expected time. **2** previously.

alright adv, adj, and interj = ALL RIGHT[1].

Usage Note: All right is often preferred.

Alsatian n *chiefly Brit* a large dog of a wolflike breed originating in Germany. Also called GERMAN SHEPHERD.

also adv as well; in additionally.

also-ran n an undistinguished person.

altar n **1** a table on which the communion bread and wine are consecrated in Christian churches. **2** a table-like structure on which offerings are made to a deity.

alter v to make or become different. ➤ **alteration** n.

altercation n an angry discussion or quarrel.

alter ego n (pl **alter egos**) **1** a side of somebody's character that is different from their usual character. **2** a close and trusted friend.

alternate[1] adj **1** of two things: occurring by turns. **2** forming an alternating series. **3** every other; every second. ➤ **alternately** adv.

alternate[2] v **1** of two things or people: to occur or do something by turns. **2** to interchange (one person or thing) with another. **3** to change repeatedly from one state or action to another. ➤ **alternation** n.

alternating current n an electric current that reverses its direction at regularly recurring intervals: compare DIRECT CURRENT.

alternative[1] adj **1** able to be used instead of something else. **2** different from the usual forms or kinds. ➤ **alternatively** adv.

alternative[2] n **1** another person or thing that could act as a replacement. **2** a choice between two or more possibilities.

alternator n an electric generator for producing alternating current.

although conj **1** in spite of the fact or possibility that; though. **2** but.

altimeter n an instrument for measuring altitude.

altitude n the height of an object or place above sea level.

alto n (pl **-os**) **1** a female singer with a range below that of a soprano. **2** an adult male singer with a range above that of a tenor.

altogether adv **1** completely; in every way. **2** with everything taken into account.

altruism n unselfish regard for others. ➤ **altruist** n, **altruistic** adj.

alum n a sulphate of aluminium with potassium.

aluminium (NAmer **aluminum**) n a light silver-white metallic element.

alumnus n (pl **alumni**) a former student of a particular school, college, or university.

always adv **1** at all times; continuously. **2** in all cases. **3** forever. **4** as a last resort.

Alzheimer's disease /'alts·hiemaz/ n a disease leading to premature senile dementia.

AM abbr amplitude modulation.

Am *abbr* the chemical symbol for americium.

am *v* first person sing. present of BE.

a.m. *abbr* ante meridiem, before noon.

amalgam *n* **1** an alloy of mercury with another metal. **2** a mixture of different elements.

amalgamate *v* **1** to combine into a single body. **2** to combine or alloy (a metal) with mercury. ➤ **amalgamation** *n*.

amanuensis *n* (*pl* **amanuenses**) somebody employed to write from dictation or to copy a manuscript.

amass *v* **1** to collect or accumulate. **2** to bring together into a mass.

amateur[1] *n* **1** somebody who undertakes a sport or other activity as a pastime rather than a profession. **2** somebody who does something unskilfully. ➤ **amateurism** *n*.

amateur[2] *adj* **1** of or for amateurs rather than professionals. **2** inexpert.

amateurish *adj* not skilful or competent. ➤ **amateurishly** *adv*.

amatory *adj* expressing sexual love or desire.

amaze *v* to fill with wonder; to astound. ➤ **amazement** *n*.

Amazon *n* a tall strong or athletic woman.

ambassador *n* **1** a diplomat sent to a foreign country as a resident representative of a government or sovereign. **2** somebody who represents or promotes a cause. ➤ **ambassadorial** *adj*.

amber *n* **1** a hard yellowish translucent substance that is the fossilized resin of some extinct trees, used in jewellery. **2** a yellowish colour.

ambergris *n* a waxy substance from the intestines of sperm whales, used in perfumes.

ambidextrous *adj* able to use either hand with equal ease.

ambience *or* **ambiance** *n* a characteristic atmosphere in a place.

ambient *adj* relating to the immediate surroundings of a place.

ambiguity *n* (*pl* **-ies**) **1** an ambiguous or imprecise word or expression. **2** uncertainty of meaning.

ambiguous *adj* **1** capable of more than one interpretation. **2** vague; difficult to classify. ➤ **ambiguously** *adv*.

ambit *n* the scope or range of something; a limit.

ambition *n* a strong drive to achieve something, *esp* status or success.

ambitious *adj* **1** acting from or showing ambition. **2** motivated by a strong ambition and therefore difficult to achieve. ➤ **ambitiously** *adv*.

ambivalence *n* the state of having mixed attitudes or feelings towards a person or thing. ➤ **ambivalent** *adj*.

amble[1] *v* to move at a leisurely pace.

amble[2] *n* a leisurely walk.

ambrosia *n* **1** the food of the Greek and Roman gods. **2** something extremely pleasing to eat or smell.

ambulance *n* a vehicle for transporting injured or sick people to and from hospital.

ambulatory *adj* relating to or adapted for walking.

ambush[1] *v* to attack from a hidden position.

ambush[2] *n* a surprise attack from a hidden position.

ameliorate *v* *formal* to make better or more tolerable. ➤ **amelioration** *n*.

amen *interj* a word used at the end of a prayer with the meaning 'so be it'.

amenable *adj* **1** willing to be persuaded. **2** capable of being judged or tested.

amend *v* to revise or make corrections to.

amendment *n* an alteration to a document or law.

amends ✳ **make amends** to compensate for a wrong.

amenity *n* (*pl* **-ies**) a facility that improves material comfort.

American *n* a native or inhabitant of America, *esp* the USA. ➤ **American** *adj*.

American football *n* a football game played with an oval ball between teams of eleven players, involving kicking and running with the ball and forward passing.

American Indian *n* *dated* a member of any of the indigenous peoples of America.

amethyst *n* a clear purple or violet variety of quartz used as a gemstone.

amiable *adj* friendly and pleasant. ➤ **amiability** *n*, **amiableness** *n*, **amiably** *adv*.

amicable *adj* friendly and peaceable. ➤ **amicably** *adv*.

amid *prep* *formal* in or to the middle of ; among.

amidships *adv and adj* in or towards the middle part of a ship.

amino acid *n* any of the organic acids that are the chief components of proteins.

amir *n* see EMIR.

amiss *adv and adj* wrong; not in order. ✳ **not come/go amiss** to be appropriate or welcome. **take it/something amiss** to be offended or upset by something.

amity *n* friendly relations.

ammeter *n* an instrument for measuring electric current in amperes.

ammo *n* *informal* ammunition.

ammonia *n* a pungent colourless gas used in the manufacture of fertilizers, synthetic fibres, and explosives.

ammonite *n* an extinct sea mollusc that was common during the Mesozoic era.

ammunition *n* **1** a supply of bullets or shells for use in weapons. **2** points used to support an argument.

amnesia *n* loss of memory. ➤ **amnesiac** *adj and n*.

amnesty n (pl **-ies**) **1** a pardon granted to a large group of individuals, esp for political offences. **2** a period during which no legal action is taken against people who admit an offence and comply with conditions.

amniotic fluid n the fluid surrounding a foetus in the uterus.

amoeba (NAmer **ameba**) n (pl **amoebas** or **amoebae**, NAmer **amebas** or **amebae**) a single-celled organism that can change its shape.

amok or **amuck** adv * **run amok** to act wildly or be completely out of control.

among or **amongst** prep **1** in midst of; surrounded by. **2** by or through the whole group of. **3** in the number or class of. **4** shared by.

amoral adj not concerned with or caring about moral principles or ethical judgments: compare IMMORAL. ➤ **amorality** n.

amorous adj showing or feeling sexual love or desire. ➤ **amorously** adv.

amorphous adj having no definite form; shapeless.

amount[1] v **1** (+ to) to add up to. **2** (+ to) to be equivalent to.

amount[2] n **1** a quantity. **2** the total of two or more quantities.

ampere /'ampeə/ n the basic SI unit of electric current.

ampersand n a sign (&) standing for the word and.

amphetamine n a synthetic drug used as a stimulant.

amphibian n **1** a frog, toad, newt, or other member of a class of cold-blooded vertebrates that live in the water when young and on land when fully developed. **2** a vehicle adapted to operate on both land and water. ➤ **amphibious** adj.

amphitheatre (NAmer **amphitheater**) n an open oval or circular building with rising tiers of seats ranged about an arena, used for sports and public spectacles.

ample adj (**ampler**, **amplest**) **1** enough or more than enough. **2** large or extensive. ➤ **amply** adv.

amplifier n an electronic device that increases sounds or electrical signals.

amplify v (**-ies**, **-ied**) **1** to increase the strength or (a sound or electrical signal). **2** to expand (a statement) or make it clearer. ➤ **amplification** n.

amplitude n **1** largeness of size or scope; abundance. **2** the extent of a vibration or oscillation measured from the average position to a maximum.

ampoule (NAmer **ampul** or **ampule**) n a small sealed glass vessel holding a solution for hypodermic injection.

amputate v to remove (a limb) surgically. ➤ **amputation** n.

amputee n somebody who has had all or part of a limb amputated.

amuck adv see AMOK.

amulet n a small stone or piece of jewellery worn as a protection from harm.

amuse v **1** to appeal to the sense of humour of. **2** to entertain or interest.

amusement n **1** the act of amusing or being amused. **2** a pleasant diversion, esp a fairground entertainment.

an indefinite article used in place of a (see A) before words with an initial vowel sound.

anabolic steroid n a synthetic hormone that increases the size and weight of skeletal muscle.

anachronism n **1** the placing of people or things in a period to which they do not belong. **2** a person or thing that belongs or seems to belong to an older time. ➤ **anachronistic** adj.

anaconda n a large snake of the boa family that crushes its prey.

anaemia (NAmer **anemia**) n a condition in which the blood is deficient in red blood cells or haemoglobin, causing a lack of energy.

anaesthetic (NAmer **anesthetic**) n a substance that suppresses pain, so that surgery can be carried out.

anaesthetize or **-ise** (NAmer **anesthetize**) v to administer an anaesthetic to. ➤ **anaesthetist** n.

anagram n a word or phrase made by rearranging the letters of another.

anal adj relating to or in the region of the anus.

analgesic n a drug that relieves pain.

analog adj **1** of a computer: using data supplied in a stream of numbers represented by directly measurable quantities, e.g. voltages or mechanical rotations: compare DIGITAL. **2** of a clock or watch, etc: using a pointer or hands rather than having an electronic display: compare DIGITAL. **3** converting sound waves into a continuous electrical wave form to record sound: compare DIGITAL.

analogous adj **1** (often + to/with) similar in some respects. **2** of plant or animal parts: similar in function but having evolved separately and distinctly.

analogue[1] (NAmer **analog**) n something that is analogous to something else.

analogue[2] adj = ANALOG.

analogy n (pl **-ies**) an explanation or illustration of something that uses a comparison with something similar.

analyse (NAmer **analyze**) v **1** to make a close examination of (something) in order to determine its nature, content, or structure. **2** = PSYCHOANALYSE.

analysis n (pl **analyses**) **1** the examination and identification of the constituents of a complex whole and their relationship to one another. **2** the act or process of breaking something up into its constituent elements. **3** = PSYCHO-ANALYSIS.

analyst *n* **1** a person who analyses or is skilled in analysis. **2** a psychoanalyst.

analytical *or* **analytic** *adj* using analysis. ➤ **analytically** *adv.*

anarchic *or* **anarchical** *adj* **1** advocating anarchy or likely to bring about anarchy. **2** not adhering to conventions or expectations. ➤ **anarchically** *adv.*

anarchist *n* somebody who attacks the established social order or laws; a revolutionary. ➤ **anarchism** *n*, **anarchistic** *adj.*

anarchy *n* **1** a society with no government. **2** a state of lawlessness or disorder.

anathema *n* somebody or something that is hated.

anatomy *n* (*pl* **-ies**) **1** the scientific study of the structure of people, animals, and plants. **2** the structural make-up of an organism. ➤ **anatomical** *adj.* **anatomist** ➤ *noun.*

ancestor *n* **1** somebody from whom a person is descended. **2** an earlier type or model from which a more recent version has developed.

ancestral *adj* of or inherited from an ancestor.

ancestry *n* (*pl* **-ies**) a line of noble descent; a lineage.

anchor[1] *n* a heavy hook or other device dropped from a ship or boat to hold it in a particular place.

anchor[2] *v* **1** to hold in place with an anchor. **2** to secure firmly.

anchorage *n* a place where boats and ships can anchor.

anchorite *n* somebody who lives in seclusion for religious reasons.

anchorman *or* **anchorwoman** *n* (*pl* **anchormen**) in broadcasting, a person who links up with outside reporters from a central studio.

anchovy *n* (*pl* **-ies**) a small fish that resembles a herring, with a strong taste.

ancien régime /,onsi·an ray'zheem/ *n* (*pl* **anciens régimes**) a political or social system that has been superseded.

ancient *adj* **1** belonging to a remote period of history. **2** *informal* very old. ➤ **anciently** *adv.*

ancillary *adj* **1** giving support; auxiliary. **2** subordinate.

and *conj* **1** used to join words, clauses, or sentences. **2** used to express the addition of numbers.

andante *adj and adv* of a piece of music: performed moderately slowly.

androgynous *adj* combining male and female features. ➤ **androgyny** *n.*

android *n* in science fiction, an automaton with a human form.

anecdotal *adj* in the form of an anecdote, without evidence or proof. ➤ **anecdotally** *adv.*

anemometer *n* an instrument for measuring the speed of the wind.

anemone *n* **1** a plant with divided leaves and brightly coloured flowers. **2** = SEA ANEMONE.

aneurysm *or* **aneurism** *n* a swelling of a diseased blood vessel. ➤ **aneurysmal** *adj.*

anew *adv chiefly literary* **1** one more time; again. **2** in a new form or way.

angel *n* **1** a spiritual being, usu depicted in human form with wings, believed to serve as a messenger of God. **2** a good or loving person.

angelica *n* a plant with candied stalks used as a cake decoration.

anger[1] *n* a strong feeling of displeasure.

anger[2] *v* (**angered, angering**) to make or become angry.

angina *n* a disease with severe chest pain, caused by a deficiency of blood to the heart.

angle[1] *n* **1** a space formed by two lines or surfaces extending outwards from the same point or line. **2** a corner. **3** a position from which something is observed. **4** a way of thinking or asking about something. ➤ **angled** *adj.*

angle[2] *v* **1** to place or move in a slanting position. **2** to bend or shape into an angle. **3** to present (information) from a particular point of view.

angle[3] *v* **1** to fish with a hook and line. **2** (*usu* + for) to use indirect or devious means to get something. ➤ **angler** *n.*

Anglican[1] *adj* relating to the Church of England. ➤ **Anglicanism** *n.*

Anglican[2] *n* a member of the Church of England.

anglicize *or* **-ise** *v* to make English in character or form. ➤ **anglicization** *n.*

Anglophile *or* **Anglophil** *n* (*also* **anglophile**) somebody who admires England or Britain.

Anglo-Saxon *n* **1** a member of the Germanic peoples who conquered England in the fifth cent. **2** the Old English language. ➤ **Anglo-Saxon** *adj.*

angora *n* **1** a cat, goat, or rabbit with long soft hair. **2** a fabric made from Angora rabbit or goat hair.

Angostura bitters *n trademark* a bitter aromatic tonic added to alcoholic drinks as a flavouring.

angry *adj* (**-ier, -iest**) **1** feeling or showing anger. **2** caused by or expressing anger. **3** of a wound: painfully inflamed. ➤ **angrily** *adv.*

angst *n* a strong feeling of anxiety about the human condition.

angstrom *n* a unit of length equal to 10^{-10}m, used in measuring electromagnetic radiation wavelength.

anguish *n* extreme mental distress or physical pain.

angular *adj* having or forming angles **1** placed at an angle. **2** of a person: lean and bony. ➤ **angularity** *n.*

animal *n* 1 a living creature that is able to move and respond to stimulation. 2 any living creature apart from a human being. 3 a mammal as distinct from a bird, fish, or insect. 4 a coarse, unfeeling, or cruel person.

animate[1] *v* 1 to make lively and interesting. 2 to create or film using the techniques of animation. 3 to give life to. ➤ **animator** *n*.

animate[2] *adj* possessing life; alive.

animated *adj* 1 lively or vivacious. 2 made using the techniques of animation. ➤ **animatedly** *adv*.

animation *n* 1 being lively or active. 2 the technique of filming a sequence of images or models in different positions so that they appear to be moving.

animism *n* attribution of souls to nature or natural phenomena. ➤ **animist** *n*.

animosity *n* (*pl* **-ies**) a strong feeling of hostility or resentment.

animus *n* ill will or hostility; animosity.

anion *n* a negatively charged ion.

aniseed *n* the seed of anise (a plant of the carrot family) used as a flavouring.

ankle *n* the joint between the foot and the leg.

anklet *n* a band or chain worn round the ankle.

annals *pl noun* a record of events, activities, etc, arranged in yearly sequence.

anneal *v* to toughen (metal or glass) by heating and gradual cooling it.

annex[1] *v* 1 to add as an extra part. 2 to incorporate (another country) within the domain of a state. ➤ **annexation** *n*.

annex[2] *or* **annexe** *n* 1 an extra building providing additional accommodation. 2 an addition to a document.

annihilate *v* to destroy entirely. ➤ **annihilation** *n*.

anniversary *n* (*pl* **-ies**) the date on which a notable event took place in an earlier year.

annotate *v* to provide (a text) with notes. ➤ **annotation** *n*.

announce *v* 1 to make publicly. 2 to indicate in advance; to foretell. ➤ **announcement** *n*.

annoy *v* 1 to make mildly angry. 2 to bother or pester. 3 to be a source of irritation. ➤ **annoyance** *n*.

annual[1] *adj* 1 covering or lasting for the period of a year. 2 occurring once a year. 3 of a plant: completing the life cycle in one growing season. ➤ **annually** *adv*.

annual[2] *n* 1 a publication that appears once a year. 2 an annual plant.

annuity *n* (*pl* **-ies**) an amount payable each year to a person.

annul *v* (**annulled, annulling**) 1 to declare legally invalid. 2 to cancel or abolish. ➤ **annulment** *n*.

annular *adj* in the shape of a ring.

annunciation *n* (**the Annunciation**) the announcement by Gabriel to the Virgin Mary that she would be the mother of Jesus Christ celebrated by Christians on 25 March.

anode *n* the electrode by which electrons leave a device and enter an external circuit.

anodize *or* **-ise** *v* to coat (metal) with a protective film by means of electrolytic action.

anodyne[1] *adj* dully mild or inoffensive.

anodyne[2] *n* a painkilling drug.

anoint *v* to put oil on (somebody) as part of a religious ceremony.

anomalous *adj* deviating from what is usual or expected.

anomaly *n* (*pl* **-ies**) something that deviates from what is usual or expected.

anon *adv* *archaic or informal* in a short while; soon.

anonymous *adj* 1 having or giving no name. 2 nondescript. ➤ **anonymity** *n*, **anonymously** *adv*, **anonymousness** *n*.

anorak *n* *chiefly Brit* a short weatherproof coat with a hood.

anorexia *or* **anorexia nervosa** *n* a disorder with prolonged loss of appetite.

another[1] *adj* 1 being a different or additional one. 2 some other.

another[2] *pron* a different or additional one.

answer[1] *n* 1 a spoken or written reply to a question or statement. 2 the solution to a problem.

answer[2] *v* 1 to give an answer to. 2 to provide a solution to (a problem). 3 to act in response to. 4 (+ for) to be responsible or accountable for something. 5 (+ to) to have to explain oneself to (somebody). 6 to be adequate or usable.

answerable *adj* (+ to/for) responsible to somebody for something.

answering machine *n* a telephone device that responds to calls with a recorded reply and records messages spoken by callers.

ant *n* a small insect that lives in large organized groups.

antacid *n* a medicine that combats excessive acidity, *esp* in the stomach.

antagonism *n* open hostility or antipathy.

antagonist *n* an opponent or adversary. ➤ **antagonistic** *adj*.

antagonize *or* **-ise** *v* to cause to become antagonistic.

Antarctic *adj* of the South Pole or the surrounding region.

anteater *n* a mammal with a long snout and bushy tail that feeds chiefly on ants and termites.

antecedent[1] *n* 1 a preceding thing, event, or circumstance. 2 (*in pl*) family origins; ancestry.

antecedent[2] *adj* earlier in time or order.

antedate *v* to precede in time.

antediluvian adj **1** belonging to the period before the flood described in the Bible. **2** ridiculously out-of-date or antiquated.

antelope n (pl **antelopes** or **antelope**) a fast-running hoofed mammal native to Africa and Asia.

antenatal adj relating to pregnancy. ➤ **antenatally** adv.

antenna n **1** (pl **antennae** /-nee/) a long thin sense organ on the head of insects, crustaceans, and centipedes. **2** (pl **antennas** or **antennae**) an aerial.

anterior adj **1** before in time. **2** situated towards the front.

anteroom n an outer room that leads to a larger one.

anthem n **1** a solemn song sung as an expression of national identity. **2** a musical setting of a religious text.

anther n an organ at the tip of a flower's stamen that contains and releases pollen.

anthill n a mound of soil and leaves thrown up by ants or termites making a nest.

anthology n (pl **-ies**) a selection of literary or musical pieces or passages. ➤ **anthologist** n.

anthracite n a hard variety of coal that burns slowly and with a non-luminous flame.

anthrax n a disease of cattle and sheep caused by a spore-forming bacterium and capable of being transmitted to humans.

anthropoid adj resembling human beings in form or behaviour.

anthropology n the scientific study of human societies and behaviour. ➤ **anthropological** adj, **anthropologist** n.

anthropomorphic adj **1** having human form. **2** ascribing human characteristics to non-human things. ➤ **anthropomorphically** adv, **anthropomorphism** n.

anti- or **ant-** prefix against or opposing.

antibiotic n a substance that kills bacteria. ➤ **antibiotic** adj.

antibody n (pl **-ies**) a protein, e.g. a blood protein, that is produced by the body in response to a specific ANTIGEN (toxin, virus, etc).

Antichrist n (often **the Antichrist**) an enemy of Christ predicted to appear shortly before the end of the world.

anticipate v **1** to foresee and deal with in advance; to forestall. **2** to discuss or think about in advance or too early. **3** to use or spend before the right or natural time. **4** to look forward to. ➤ **anticipation** n, **anticipatory** adj.

anticlimax n an event that is strikingly less important or exciting than expected. ➤ **anticlimactic** adj.

anticlockwise adj and adv in a direction opposite to that in which the hands of a clock rotate.

antics pl n foolish or entertaining behaviour.

anticyclone n a system of winds that rotates about a centre of high atmospheric pressure,

usually bringing calm, fine weather. ➤ **anticyclonic** adj.

antidote n a remedy that counteracts the effects of poison.

antifreeze n a substance added to a liquid to lower its freezing point.

antigen n a harmful substance that stimulates the body to produce an antibody.

anti-hero n (pl **anti-heroes**) a main character in a story, film, play, etc, who lacks traditional heroic qualities.

antihistamine n a drug that opposes the actions of histamine and is used esp for treating allergies.

antimacassar n a cover put over the backs or arms of furniture to protect it from grease and dirt.

antimatter n hypothetical matter composed of antiparticles.

antimony n a silver-white metallic chemical element used as a strengthening constituent of alloys.

antipathy n (pl **-ies**) (often + to) a deep-seated aversion or dislike.

antiperspirant n a substance used to reduce perspiration.

antiphon n a verse said or sung as part of a church service. ➤ **antiphonal** adj.

Antipodes pl n (**the Antipodes**) Australia and New Zealand. ➤ **Antipodean** adj and n.

antiquarian adj **1** relating to ancient relics. **2** said of books other works of art: old and rare.

antiquated adj outmoded or out-of-date.

antique[1] adj **1** valuable because of its age. **2** suggesting the style of an earlier period.

antique[2] n an object or work of art made in an earlier period and sought by collectors.

antiquity n (pl **-ies**) **1** ancient times. **2** the quality of being ancient. **3** (in pl) relics or monuments of ancient times.

anti-Semitism n hostility towards or discrimination against Jewish people. ➤ **anti-Semite** n, **anti-Semitic** adj.

antiseptic adj preventing the growth of microorganisms that cause disease. ➤ **antiseptic** n, **antiseptically** adv.

antisocial adj **1** of a person or behaviour: causing annoyance to others. **2** tending to avoid the company of others; unsociable. ➤ **antisocially** adv.

antithesis n (pl **antitheses**) **1** somebody or something that is a direct opposite. **2** a contrast of ideas.

antithetical or **antithetic** adj directly opposed or contrary. ➤ **antithetically** adv.

antler n one of a pair of branched horns of a male deer.

antonym n a word that means the opposite of another. ➤ **antonymy** n.

anus n the opening through which solid waste matter leaves the body.

anvil n a heavy iron block on which metal is shaped by hammering.

anxiety n (pl -ies) 1 uneasiness of mind because of possible trouble or danger. 2 a cause of anxiety.

anxious adj 1 uneasy in the mind because of possible trouble or danger. 2 causing anxiety; worrying. 3 ardently or earnestly wishing to do something. ➤ **anxiously** adv.

any[1] adj one or some, no matter which.

any[2] pron (pl **any**) any person or thing.

any[3] adv to any extent or degree.

anybody pron any person.

anyhow adv 1 in a haphazard manner. 2 anyway.

anyone pron any person.

anything pron any thing whatever.

anyway adv 1 in any case; inevitably. 2 used when resuming a narrative. 3 nevertheless.

anywhere[1] adv in or to any place. ✶ **get anywhere**

anywhere[2] n any place.

aorta n the main artery carrying blood from the heart to be distributed by branch arteries throughout the body. ➤ **aortic** adj.

apace adv at a quick pace; swiftly.

apart adv 1 at a distance from something or somebody in space, time, or quality. 2 in or into two or more parts. ✶ **apart from** except for.

apartheid /ə'paht·(h)ayt, -(h)iet/ n a policy of racial segregation formerly operated in South Africa.

apartment n 1 chiefly NAmer a flat. 2 a suite of rooms used for living in. ➤ **apartmental** adj.

apathetic adj lacking interest; indifferent. ➤ **apathetically** adv.

apathy n lack of interest or enthusiasm.

apatosaurus n a large dinosaur with a long neck and tail and short forelegs, formerly called brontosaurus.

ape[1] n a large tailless primate belonging to the group which includes gorillas, chimpanzees, orang-utans, and gibbons.

ape[2] v to imitate closely but clumsily.

aperitif n an alcoholic drink taken before a meal to stimulate the appetite.

aperture n 1 an opening or gap. 2 the adjustable opening in a camera through which the light passes.

apex n (pl **apexes** or **apices**) the top or uppermost point; a tip.

aphid n a small insect that sucks the juices of plants, e.g. a greenfly.

aphorism n a pithy phrase expressing a truth.

aphrodisiac n a food, drink, or drug that stimulates sexual desire.

apiary n (pl -ies) a place where bees are kept.

apiece adv for each one; individually.

aplenty adj archaic or literary in abundance.

aplomb n calm self-assurance.

apocalypse n 1 a cataclysmic event. 2 (**the Apocalypse**) the ultimate destruction of the world, as depicted in the Book of Revelation in the Bible.

apocalyptic or **apocalyptical** adj momentous or catastrophic.

apocryphal adj of an account or story: probably untrue.

apogee n 1 the point farthest from the earth reached by the moon or a satellite in its orbit. 2 the farthest or highest point; the culmination.

apolitical adj having no interest in politics.

apologetic adj regretfully acknowledging a fault or failure; contrite. ➤ **apologetically** adv.

apologia n a reasoned defence of a faith, cause, or institution.

apologist n a person who speaks or writes in defence of something.

apologize or **-ise** v (often + for) to make an apology.

apology n (pl -ies) 1 a regretful admission of error or discourtesy. 2 (+ for) a poor substitute; a specimen.

apoplectic adj 1 relating to or causing apoplexy. 2 informal extremely angry.

apoplexy n (pl -ies) a stroke.

apostasy n (pl -ies) renunciation of a belief.

apostate n a person who renounces a belief. ➤ **apostate** adj.

apostle n 1 (often **Apostle**) an early Christian teacher sent out to preach the gospel. 2 an advocate, or supporter of a system, movement, etc.

apostrophe n a punctuation mark (') used to indicate the omission of letters or figures, the possessive case, or the plural of letters or figures.

apothecary n (pl -ies) archaic a pharmacist or pharmacy.

apotheosis n (pl **apotheoses**) a supreme example of something at its most developed.

appal (NAmer **appall**) v (appalled, appalling) to overcome with horror or dismay. ➤ **appalling** adj, **appallingly** adv.

apparatus n (pl **apparatuses** or **apparatus**) equipment designed for a particular use.

apparel n literary clothing.

apparent adj 1 easily seen or understood; evident. 2 seemingly real but not necessarily so. ➤ **apparently** adv.

apparition n an unusual or unexpected sight; esp the appearance of a ghost.

appeal[1] n 1 the power of arousing a sympathetic response; attraction. 2 an earnest plea or request. 3 a legal proceeding by which a case is brought to a higher court for review.

appeal[2] v (often + to) 1 to arouse a sympathetic response. 2 to make an earnest plea or request. 3 to take a case to a higher court for review.

appealing *adj* having appeal; attractive. ➤ **appealingly** *adv*.

appear *v* **1** to become visible or present. **2** to arrive. **3** to give the impression of being; to seem.

appearance *n* **1** an act of appearing or being present. **2** the way someone or something looks or seems.

appease *v* **1** to pacify or calm (somebody) by agreeing to what they want. **2** to assuage or allay (hunger, thirst, etc). ➤ **appeasement** *n*.

appellation *n literary* a name or title.

append *v* to attach or add as a supplement.

appendage *n* something added to something larger or more important.

appendicitis *n* inflammation of the appendix.

appendix *n* (*pl* **appendixes**) a short tube that extends from the lower end of the large intestine. **2** (*pl* **appendices** /-seez/) a supplement at the end of a book or other piece of writing.

appertain *v* **1** (*usu* + to) to relate to. **2** to be relevant.

appetite *n* **1** a desire to eat. **2** a strong desire or inclination.

appetizer *or* **appetiser** *n* a food or drink that stimulates the appetite.

appetizing *or* **appetising** *adj* appealing to the appetite.

applaud *v* to express approval by clapping or cheering.

applause *n* approval or admiration expressed by clapping.

apple *n* a round fruit with red or green skin and crisp white flesh. ✳ **the apple of one's eye** somebody or something greatly cherished.

appliance *n* an instrument or device designed for a particular use.

applicable *adj* able to be applied; appropriate or related. ➤ **applicability** *n*.

applicant *n* a person who applies for something.

application *n* **1** a formal request or petition. **2** an act of applying. **3** a use to which something is put. **4** close attention; diligence. **5** a computer program that performs a particular function.

applicator *n* a device for applying a substance.

applied *adj* of a subject of study: put to practical use.

appliqué /a'pleekay, aplee'kay/ *n* decorative work in which a cutout decoration is attached to a larger piece of material.

apply *v* (-ies, -ied) **1** to bring to bear or put to use. **2** to lay or spread on a surface. **3** to devote (oneself) to something. **4** (*usu* + to) to be relevant. **5** (*usu* + for/to) to make a formal request for something.

appoint *v* **1** to select for an office or position. **2** *formal* to decide on (a time) officially.

appointment *n* **1** an act of appointing. **2** an office or position to which somebody is appointed. **3** an arrangement for a meeting or other engagement.

apportion *v* **1** to divide or distribute. **2** to assign (blame). ➤ **apportionment** *n*.

apposite *adj* appropriate or apt.

appraisal *n* an act of appraising, e.g. a valuation of property or an assessment of an employee's performance.

appraise *v* **1** to evaluate the worth or status of. **2** to make a valuation of (property).

Usage Note: Do not confuse this word with *apprise*.

appreciable *adj* large enough to notice; substantial. ➤ **appreciably** *adv*.

appreciate *v* **1** to recognize the value or importance of. **2** to esteem. **3** to realize or be aware of. **4** to increase in value.

appreciation *n* **1** recognition of the value of something. **2** admiration, approval, or gratitude. **3** an increase in value. **4** a favourable critical assessment.

appreciative *adj* showing appreciation; pleased or grateful. ➤ **appreciatively** *adv*.

apprehend *v* **1** to arrest or seize (a suspect). **2** to understand or perceive.

apprehension *n* **1** nervous anxiety or fear. **2** understanding; comprehension. **3** the arrest of a suspect.

apprehensive *adj* nervously fearful or uneasy. ➤ **apprehensively** *adv*.

apprentice[1] *n* a person who is learning a skill or trade from an employer. ➤ **apprenticeship** *n*.

apprentice[2] *v* (*usu in passive*) to employ as an apprentice.

apprise *or* **apprize** *v formal* to inform of something.

Usage Note: Do not confuse this word with *appraise*.

approach[1] *v* **1** to draw close to. **2** to come near to in quality or character. **3** to make an offer or request to. **4** to begin to consider or deal with.

approach[2] *n* **1** a means of access. **2** a manner or method of doing something. **3** (*usu in pl*) an offer or request.

approachable *adj* friendly and easy to talk to.

approbation *n* **1** approval. **2** praise or commendation.

appropriate[1] *v* **1** to take possession of without approval. **2** (*often* + to) to set (money) apart for a purpose. ➤ **appropriation** *n*.

appropriate[2] *adj* suitable or apt. ➤ **appropriately** *adv*.

approval *n* **1** a favourable opinion or judgment. **2** formal or official permission. ✳ **on approval** of goods: able to be returned if unsatisfactory.

approve v **1** (often + of) to take a favourable view. **2** to sanction or ratify. **3** to accept as satisfactory.

approximate[1] adj **1** nearly correct or exact. **2** of a term, etc: loose; inexact. ➤ **approximately** adv.

approximate[2] v **1** (often + to) to come close in quality or character. **2** (often + to) to average out. ➤ **approximation** n.

appurtenances pl noun things needed for an activity or purpose.

après-ski /ˌapray'skee/ n social activity after a day's skiing.

apricot n an oval orange-coloured fruit with soft juicy flesh.

April n the fourth month of the year.

a priori adj and adv using reasoning from self-evident propositions.

apron n **1** a garment tied round the waist and used to protect clothing. **2** the part of a theatre stage extending in front of the curtain. **3** a paved area at an airport, used for loading and moving aircraft.

apropos /aprə'poh/ prep (also + of) concerning; with regard to.

apse n a projecting and rounded part of a church or other building.

apt adj **1** likely to do something. **2** suited to a purpose. **3** keenly intelligent. ➤ **aptly** adv, **aptness** n.

aptitude n **1** a natural ability or talent. **2** (usu + for) fitness or suitability.

aqualung n an underwater breathing apparatus.

aquamarine n **1** a bluish green gemstone. **2** a pale bluish green colour.

aquaplane v of a vehicle: to slide out of control on the surface of a wet road.

aquarium n (pl **aquariums** or **aquaria**) a glass tank filled with water for keeping fish and other sea animals.

Aquarius n the eleventh sign of the zodiac (the Water Carrier).

aquatic adj **1** growing or living in water. **2** taking place in or on water.

aqueduct n a bridge-like structure built to carry a canal across a valley.

aqueous adj resembling or containing water.

aquiline adj **1** relating to or like an eagle. **2** of the human nose: hooked.

Ar abbr the chemical symbol for argon.

Arab n a member of a Semitic people of the Middle East and North Africa. ➤ **Arab** adj, **Arabian** adj.

arabesque n **1** a ballet posture in which the dancer is supported on one leg with one arm extended forwards and the other arm and leg backwards. **2** an intricate decorative design or style with intertwining motifs. **3** an ornamental musical passage.

Arabic n the Semitic language of the Arab peoples. ➤ **Arabic** adj.

Arabic numeral n any of the number symbols 0, 1, 2, 3, 4, 5, 6, 7, 8, 9.

arable adj of land: used or suitable for crop farming.

arachnid n an arthropod having a body in two segments, e.g. a spider or scorpion. ➤ **arachnid** adj.

arachnophobia n irrational fear of spiders.

arbiter n **1** a person or agency who settles disputes. **2** a person respected for authority in a subject.

arbitrary adj **1** based on whim or random choice rather than reason. **2** of power or of rule: despotic or tyrannical. ➤ **arbitrarily** adv.

arbitrate v **1** to act as an arbitrator. **2** to submit for decision to an arbitrator.

arbitrator n a person or group chosen to settle a dispute.

arboreal adj inhabiting or relating to trees.

arboretum n (pl **arboretums** or **arboreta**) a place where trees and shrubs are cultivated for study and display.

arbour (NAmer **arbor**) n a garden alcove formed by climbing plants or branches. ➤ **arboured** adj.

arc[1] n **1** a continuous portion of a curve. **2** the apparent path followed by a planet or other celestial body. **3** a luminous discharge of electricity across a gap in a circuit.

arc[2] v (**arced**, **arcing**) to form or move in an arc.

arcade n **1** a passageway or covered walk with shops on both sides. **2** a series of arches with their columns or piers.

Arcadian adj ideally quiet and rural; idyllic.

arcane adj secret and esoteric.

arch[1] n **1** a curved structure spanning an opening or supporting a structure. **2** the inner bony structure of the foot.

arch[2] v to form or bend into an arch.

arch[3] adj consciously or playfully sly or teasing. ➤ **archly** adv, **archness** n.

archaeology (NAmer **archeology**) n the study of the material remains of past human life and activities. ➤ **archaeological** adj, **archaeologist** n.

archaeopteryx n the oldest fossil bird, with the wings and feathers of a bird and the teeth and tail of a dinosaur.

archaic adj **1** old or antiquated. **2** belonging to an earlier time. ➤ **archaism** n.

archangel n a chief or principal angel.

archbishop n a bishop of the highest rank.

archdeacon n a senior member of the clergy with administrative functions.

archer n a person who shoots with a bow and arrows. ➤ **archery** n.

archetype n **1** an original pattern or model. **2** a perfect example. ➤ **archetypal** adj.

archipelago n (pl **-os** or **-oes**) a group of scattered islands.

architect n **1** a person who designs buildings. **2** a person who originates an idea or plan.

architecture n **1** the designing and erecting of buildings. **2** the design and structure of anything. ➤ **architectural** adj.

architrave n **1** in classical architecture, a beam resting on the capitals of the columns. **2** the frame round a a door or window.

archive[1] n a collection of historical documents and records. ➤ **archival** adj.

archive[2] v to collect in an archive.

archivist n a person who organizes archives.

archway n an arch with a passage or entrance beneath it.

Arctic adj relating to the North Pole or the surrounding region.

ardent adj eager or zealous. ➤ **ardently** adv.

ardour (NAmer **ardor**) n **1** intense or passionate feelings, **2** great enthusiasm.

arduous adj difficult or strenuous. ➤ **arduously** adv.

are[1] v second person sing. present or pl present of BE.

are[2] n a metric unit of area equal to 100m^2.

area n **1** the extent of a surface measured in square units. **2** a piece of ground. **3** a particular space or surface. **4** a range of activity.

arena n **1** an enclosed area used for public entertainment. **2** a sphere of interest or activity.

aren't contraction **1** are not. **2** used in questions: am not.

areola n (pl **areolae**) a coloured ring round a nipple.

argon n a gaseous chemical element used in vacuum tubes and electric light bulbs.

argot n the jargon or slang of a particular group.

arguable adj able to be argued or disputed. ➤ **arguably** adv.

argue v (**argues**, **argued**, **arguing**) **1** to disagree in words; to bicker or quarrel. **2** to give reasons for or against something. ✳ **argue the toss** to dispute a settled decision. ➤ **arguer** n.

argument n **1** a quarrel or disagreement. **2** the act or process of arguing; debate. **3** a coherent reason or series of reasons offered as proof.

argumentative adj tending or liking to argue.

aria n (pl **arias**) an accompanied melody sung by one voice.

arid adj **1** of land: excessively dry from lack of rainfall. **2** dull or unproductive. ➤ **aridity** n.

Aries n the first sign of the zodiac (the Ram).

arise v (**arose**, **arisen**) **1** to originate from a source. **2** (often + from) to come into being or to the attention.

aristocracy n (pl **-ies**) hereditary nobility ranking socially above the ordinary or common people and below royalty.

arithmetic n a branch of mathematics dealing with real numbers and calculations. ➤ **arithmetical** adj.

ark n **1** in the Bible, the ship built by Noah to escape the Flood. **2** (**Ark/Ark of the Covenant**) the sacred chest containing the Ten Commandments. **3** (also **Holy Ark**) a repository for the scrolls of the Torah. ✳ **out of the ark** informal very antiquated.

arm[1] n **1** either of the human upper limbs extending from the shoulder to the hand. **2** a support for the forearm on a chair. **3** an inlet of water from the sea. **4** a division of a group or activity. ✳ **with open arms** with welcoming enthusiasm.

arm[2] v **1** to supply with weapons. **2** to provide with something that strengthens or protects. **3** to activate the fuse of (a bomb).

armada n (pl **armadas**) a fleet of warships.

armadillo n (pl **-os**) a burrowing South American mammal with a body and head encased in bony plates.

Armageddon n **1** the final battle between good and evil in the New Testament. **2** a vast decisive conflict.

armament n **1** (often in pl) the arms and equipment of a nation or military force. **2** preparation for war.

armature n **1** the central rotating part of an electric motor or generator. **2** a bar of iron placed across the poles of a magnet to close the circuit.

armchair n an upholstered chair with armrests.

armed adj having or using a gun.

armed forces pl n the army, navy and air force of a country.

armistice n a suspension of hostilities.

armorial adj relating to or bearing heraldic arms.

armour (NAmer **armor**) n **1** a covering of metal or chain mail worn by medieval soldiers in combat. **2** a protective covering for a military ship or aircraft. **3** armoured forces and vehicles.

armourer (NAmer **armorer**) n a person who repairs, assembles, and tests weapons or armour.

armoury (NAmer **armory**) n (pl **-ies**) a store of arms and military equipment.

armpit n the hollow between the arm and shoulder.

arms pl noun **1** weapons, esp guns. **2** a set of heraldic insignia. ✳ **up in arms** protesting strongly.

army n (pl **-ies**) **1** a large organized force for fighting on land. **2** a large crowd or group.

aroma n a pleasant smell. ➤ **aromatic** adj.

aromatherapy n the use of natural oils to relieve symptoms, promote healing, and reduce tension. ➤ **aromatherapist** n.

arose v past tense of ARISE.

around¹ *adv* **1** in the vicinity. **2** in various directions; to and fro. **3** approximately. **4** so as to face the opposite way. **5** so as to move in a circle.

around² *prep* **1** here and there in (a place). **2** so as to encircle.

arouse *v* **1** to stimulate (a feeling or response). **2** to rouse to action. **3** to excite sexually. **4** to awaken from sleep. ➤ **arousal** *n*.

arpeggio *n* (*pl* **-os**) a chord with notes that are played in quick succession.

arraign *v* to charge formally with an offence in a court of law. ➤ **arraignment** *n*.

arrange *v* **1** to put in order or into sequence. **2** to make preparations for. **3** to adapt (music) for different voices or instruments. ➤ **arranger** *n*.

arrangement *n* **1** a preparation or plan. **2** an informal agreement or settlement. **3** something made by arranging parts together. **4** a musical adaptation.

arrant *adj* complete; utter.

array¹ *v* **1** to set or place in order. **2** to dress or decorate impressively.

array² *n* **1** an imposing collection or large number. **2** an orderly arrangement.

arrears *pl n* an unpaid or overdue debt. ✳ **in arrears 1** behind in the payment of a debt. **2** of rent or wages: paid at the end of each period.

arrest¹ *v* **1** to seize and keep in custody by legal authority. **2** to bring to a stop or make inactive.

arrest² *n* **1** the act of arresting somebody. **2** a sudden stopping.

arresting *adj* catching the attention; striking. ➤ **arrestingly** *adv*.

arrival *n* **1** the act or time of arriving. **2** somebody or something that has arrived.

arrive *v* **1** to reach a destination. **2** to come. **3** to achieve success. ✳ **arrive at** to reach by effort or thought.

arrogant *adj* having or showing a feeling of superiority over others. ➤ **arrogance** *n*, **arrogantly** *adv*.

arrogate *v* to claim or take without justification. ➤ **arrogation** *n*.

arrow *n* **1** a slender pointed shaft with feathers at the end, shot from a bow. **2** a symbol shaped like an arrow, showing direction.

arrowroot *n* a starch obtained from a tropical plant, used as a thickening agent in cooking.

arse *n Brit, coarse slang* the buttocks or anus.

arsenal *n* a store of weapons and ammunition.

arsenic *n* a grey element that forms many poisonous compounds.

arson *n* the criminal act of intentionally setting fire to property. ➤ **arsonist** *n*.

art¹ *n* **1** the use of skill and creative imagination in producing visual representations. **2** paintings, sculptures, and other works produced by creative imagination. **3** an activity which requires imagination as well as practical knowledge. **4** (**the Arts**) the humanities as contrasted with science.

art² *v* archaic second person sing. present of BE.

artefact *or* **artifact** *n* a tool or other useful object made by human effort.

artery *n* (*pl* **-ies**) **1** any of the vessels that carry blood from the heart to the lungs and through the body. **2** a road or other important channel of communication.

artesian well *n* a well in which the water reaches the surface under its own pressure.

artful *adj* cunningly or deceitfully clever. ➤ **artfully** *adv*.

arthritis *n* inflammation and stiffness of the joints.

arthropod *n* an animal with a jointed body and limbs, such as an insect, spider, or crab.

artichoke *n* (*also* **globe artichoke**) the flower head of a tall thistle-like plant, used as a vegetable.

article¹ *n* **1** a particular or separate object. **2** a distinct piece of non-fictional writing in a magazine or newspaper. **3** a separate item in a document. **4** (*in pl*) a period of professional work with a firm undertaken by a trainee. **5** *a*, *an*, and *the*, used with nouns. ✳ **article of faith** a strongly held belief.

article² *v* to employ as an apprentice.

articulate¹ *adj* **1** expressing oneself clearly. **2** clearly expressed. **3** having joints. ➤ **articulacy** *n*, **articulately** *adv*.

articulate² *v* **1** to say (words) or express (an idea) clearly. **2** to join (a body part) with a joint. **3** of bones: to fit together to form a joint. ➤ **articulation** *n*.

artifact *n* see ARTEFACT.

artifice *n* **1** an artful device or scheme. **2** clever or artful skill.

artificer *n* a skilled or artistic worker or designer.

artificial *adj* **1** made by human skill and labour imitating what is natural. **2** affected or insincere. ➤ **artificiality** *n*, **artificially** *adv*.

artificial intelligence *n* a capacity of computers or programs to emulate human behaviour or understanding.

artificial respiration *n* the forcing of air into and out of the lungs of somebody whose breathing has stopped.

artillery *n* (*pl* **-ies**) **1** heavy weapons used in land warfare. **2** a branch of an army using artillery.

artisan *n* a skilled manual worker.

artist *n* **1** a person who practises an imaginative art such as painting or sculpture. **2** a skilled performer.

artiste /ah'teest/ *n* a professional public entertainer.

artistic *adj* **1** showing creative skill. **2** characteristic of art or artists. ➤ **artistically** *adv*.

artistry *n* artistic quality or ability.

artless adj **1** sincere or natural. **2** free from deceit or artifice. ➤ **artlessly** adv.

artwork n the pictures and illustrations in a publication.

arty adj (**-ier, -iest**) showily or pretentiously artistic. ➤ **artily** n.

Aryan n **1** a member of an ancient people who appeared as invaders in North India in the second millennium BC. **2** in Nazi ideology, a white non-Jewish person of European origin. ➤ **Aryan** adj.

As abbr the chemical symbol for arsenic.

as[1] adv to the same degree or amount; equally; so.

as[2] conj **1** used in comparisons, often in pairs. **2** used to give a reason. **3** in accordance with. **4** while.

as[3] prep **1** in the capacity of. **2** used with certain verbs of regarding and describing.

a.s.a.p. abbr as soon as possible.

asbestos n a mineral of thin fibres, used to make non-combustible or chemically resistant materials.

ascend v **1** to move or slope upwards. **2** to rise from a lower level or degree.

ascendant or **ascendent** adj **1** rising. **2** superior or dominant. ➤ **ascendancy** n.

ascension n **1** the act of rising in position or degree. **2** (**Ascension**) in Christianity, Christ's ascent to heaven after the Resurrection.

ascent n **1** the act of going up. **2** a way up. **3** an advance in status.

ascertain v to find out or learn. ➤ **ascertainable** adj.

ascetic or **ascetical** adj **1** practising strict self-denial. **2** austere in appearance or manner. ➤ **asceticism** n.

ascorbic acid n a compound occurring in citrus fruits and green vegetables and essential for healthy connective tissue.

ascribe v to refer or attribute to a cause or source. ➤ **ascription** n.

aseptic adj **1** preventing infection. **2** free from micro-organisms.

asexual adj **1** having no sex or sex organs. **2** lacking sexual interest. ➤ **asexually** adv.

ash[1] n a tall tree of the olive family with tough elastic wood.

ash[2] n **1** the solid residue left when material has been burned. **2** (in pl) the remains of a dead body after cremation.

ashamed adj feeling shame or guilt.

ashen adj deadly pale from fear or shock.

ashore adv on or to the shore.

ashram n a Hindu religious retreat or sanctuary.

Asian adj relating to Asia or its people. ➤ **Asian** n.

Asiatic adj relating to Asia.

aside[1] adv and adj **1** to or towards the side. **2** out of the way. **3** in reserve for future use.

aside[2] n **1** an actor's speech supposedly not heard by other characters on stage. **2** a digression or incidental remark.

asinine adj extremely foolish or stupid.

ask v **1** to say something that calls for an answer. **2** to make a request of. **3** to provoke an unpleasant consequence). **4** to invite. **5** (often + for) to make a request about or seek information from. **6** (+ after) to enquire about somebody's welfare.

askance ✳ **look askance at** to regard with disapproval or distrust.

askew adv and adj out of line; awry.

aslant prep, adv, and adj in a slanting direction.

asleep adj **1** in a state of sleep. **2** of a limb: numb.

asp n a small viper with an upturned snout.

asparagus n a spike-shaped shoot of a tall plant, used as a vegetable.

aspect n **1** a particular feature of a situation or plan. **2** appearance to the eye or mind. **3** the side of a building facing a particular direction.

aspen n a poplar with fluttering leaves.

asperity n (pl **-ies**) **1** roughness of manner. **2** unevenness.

aspersion n ✳ **cast aspersions on** to attack the reputation of.

asphalt n **1** a black substance like tar, **2** a composition from asphalt used for surfacing roads.

Usage Note: Note the spelling with as- not ash-.

asphyxia n a lack of oxygen in the body resulting in unconsciousness or death.

asphyxiate v to make unconscious or kill by depriving of oxygen. ➤ **asphyxiation** n.

aspic n a savoury jelly of fish or meat stock.

aspidistra n a plant of the lily family with large leaves.

aspirant n somebody seeking to achieve an objective.

aspirate[1] /'aspirayt/ v **1** to pronounce (a vowel, consonant, or word) with a forceful exhalation of breath. **2** to draw or remove (e.g. blood) by suction. **3** technical to inhale.

aspirate[2] /'aspirat/ n **1** an independent /h/ sound, or the character representing this sound. **2** an aspirated consonant, e.g. the p of pit.

aspiration n a strong desire or ambition. ➤ **aspirational** adj.

aspire v (usu + to) to seek to achieve a particular objective.

aspirin n (pl **aspirin** or **aspirins**) a compound (acetylsalicylic acid) used in the form of a tablet to relieve pain and reduce fever.

ass[1] n **1** a long-eared hardy mammal related to and smaller than the horse. **2** a stupid or obstinate person.

ass[2] n chiefly NAmer = ARSE.

assail v **1** to attack violently with blows or words. **2** of a feeling: to prey on.

assailant n an attacker.

assassin n a murderer of a political or religious leader.

assassinate v to murder (a political or religious leader). ➤ **assassination** n.

assault[1] n **1** a violent attack. **2** an attempt to attack a fortified position.

assault[2] v to make an assault on.

assault course n an obstacle course for training soldiers.

assay[1] n analysis of an ore or drug, etc to determine its purity.

assay[2] v to analyse (an ore) for its purity.

assemblage n **1** a collection or gathering. **2** a three-dimensional collage.

assemble v **1** to come or bring together. **2** to fit together the parts of (a kit or model).

assembly n (pl **-ies**) **1** a group of people gathered together. **2** a legislative or deliberative body. **3** the fitting together of parts.

assembly line n a sequence of machines for assembling a product.

assent[1] v to agree to something.

assent[2] n formal agreement or approval.

assert v **1** to state or declare formally. **2** to demonstrate (a quality or attribute). **3** to insist on (a right or claim). * **assert oneself** to compel recognition of one's rights.

assertion n a declaration or positive statement.

assertive adj self-confident and firm in dealing with others. ➤ **assertively** adv, **assertiveness** n.

assess v **1** to determine the rate or amount of. **2** to estimate the quality or worth of. ➤ **assessment** n, **assessor** n.

asset n **1** (in pl) the total property of a person or company. **2** a single item of property. **3** an advantage or resource.

assiduity n persistent application or diligence.

assiduous adj showing careful attention or application. ➤ **assiduously** adv.

assign v **1** to allot (something) to somebody. **2** to appoint to a particular role or task. **3** to transfer (property) to another person. **4** to ascribe as a motive or reason.

assignation n a secret meeting with a lover.

assignment n a specified task or amount of work assigned to somebody.

assimilate v **1** to take in or absorb (a substance). **2** to absorb and understand (information). **3** to make (one thing) similar to another. **4** to absorb (people or pinciples) into a different culture. ➤ **assimilation** n.

assist v to help (somebody).

assistance n help or support.

assistant n a person whose job is to help somebody.

assize n (usu in pl) a civil and criminal court formerly held in each English and Welsh county.

associate[1] v **1** to involve (a person or group) with another more powerful one. **2** to connect (somebody or something) mentally with a particular thing, quality, or feeling. **3** (often + with) to mix socially.

associate[2] adj **1** sharing a function or office with another. **2** having subordinate status.

associate[3] n **1** a fellow worker or colleague. **2** a person admitted to a subordinate degree of membership.

association n **1** an organization of people having a common interest. **2** a mental connection between sensations or ideas.

Association Football n football played with a round ball by teams of eleven players.

assonance n repetition of the vowel sounds in two or more words as an alternative to rhyme.

assorted adj consisting of various kinds.

assortment n a mixed collection of various kinds.

assuage v **1** to ease or lessen the intensity of (suffering or discomfort). **2** to relieve or satisfy (thirst or desire).

assume v **1** to take (something) as granted or true without proof. **2** to take on (a role or duty). **3** to pretend to have (a feeling or attitude). **4** to adopt (a new name or identity).

assumption n **1** a supposition that something is true. **2** a fact or statement taken for granted. **3** the act of laying claim to or taking possession of something. **4** (**Assumption**) the taking up of the Virgin Mary into heaven, celebrated by Christians on 15 August.

assurance n **1** a declaration that something is true. **2** freedom from doubt. **3** confidence of mind or manner. **4** chiefly Brit life insurance.

assure v **1** to inform positively that something is true. **2** to give confidence to. **3** to ensure. **4** to protect with life insurance.

assured adj **1** self-confident and sure of one's competence. **2** certain; guaranteed. ➤ **assuredly** adv.

asterisk n the sign (*) used as a reference mark.

astern adv behind or towards the rear of a ship or aircraft.

asteroid n a small rocky planet between Mars and Jupiter.

asthma n an allergic condition with laboured breathing and chest constriction. ➤ **asthmatic** adj and n.

astigmatism n a defect of the eye resulting in blurring of the image. ➤ **astigmatic** adj.

astir adj **1** in a state of bustle or excitement. **2** out of bed.

astonish v to affect with sudden wonder or surprise. ➤ **astonishment** n.

astound v to affect with bewilderment and wonder.

astrakhan /astrəˈkan/ *n* **1** a woollen fabric with curled and looped pile. **2** wool of Russian origin.

astral *adj* relating to or consisting of stars.

astray *adv* **1** off the right path or route. **2** in error.

astride¹ *adv* with the legs wide apart.

astride² *prep* **1** with one leg on each side of. **2** extending over or across.

astringent *adj* **1** causing the soft tissues of the body to contract. **2** dry or caustic. ➤ **astringency** *n*.

astrolabe *n* an instrument formerly used to show the positions of the planets and stars.

astrology *n* the study of the supposed influences of the planets and their motions on human affairs. ➤ **astrologer** *n*, **astrological** *adj*.

astronaut *n* a person trained to travel in space.

astronomical *or* **astronomic** *adj* **1** relating to astronomy. **2** *informal* extremely large. ➤ **astronomically** *adv*.

astronomy *n* the scientific study of the stars, planets, and universe. ➤ **astronomer** *n*.

astrophysics *pl n* the scientific study of the physical nature of astronomical bodies and phenomena. ➤ **astrophysicist** *n*.

astute *adj* shrewd and perceptive. ➤ **astutely** *adv*, **astuteness** *n*.

asunder *adv literary* into parts or pieces.

asylum *n* **1** protection from arrest or danger. **2** a place of retreat and security. **3** *dated* an institution for the care of the mentally ill.

asymmetric *or* **asymmetrical** *adj* not symmetrical. ➤ **asymmetric** *adj*, **asymmetry** *n*.

At *abbr* the chemical symbol for astatine.

at *prep used to indicate:* **1** position in or movement towards a place. **2** time. **3** a rate or value. **4** the object of an action. **5** a state.

atavistic *adj* relating to or typical of ancestors.

ate *v* past tense of EAT.

atheism *n* the belief or doctrine that there is no God. ➤ **atheist** *n*, **atheistic** *adj adv*.

athlete *n* a person who is trained or skilled in exercises and sports, *esp* in athletics.

athlete's foot *n* a form of fungal infection of the feet affecting the skin between the toes.

athletic *adj* **1** relating to athletes or athletics. **2** vigorous or active. **3** muscular and well-proportioned. ➤ **athletically** *adv*, **athleticism** *n*.

athletics *pl n* the sport of running and other track and field events.

athwart *prep* across.

-ation *suffix* denoting an action or process.

Atlantic *adj* of or near the Atlantic Ocean.

atlas *n* a book of maps or charts.

atmosphere *n* **1** the gas enveloping the earth or other celestial body. **2** the air or climate of a locality. **3** a surrounding feeling or mood encountered in some environment. **4** a unit of pressure equal to the typical pressure of the air at sea level.

atmospheric *adj* **1** relating to the atmosphere of the earth. **2** having a strong aesthetic or emotional atmosphere. ➤ **atmospherically** *adv*.

atmospherics *pl n* lightning and other atmospheric phenomena that cause radio interference.

atoll *n* a coral reef surrounding a lagoon.

atom *n* **1** the smallest particle of an element that can exist. **2** a tiny particle; a bit.

atom bomb *or* **atomic bomb** *n* a bomb whose violent explosive power is due to the sudden release of atomic energy derived from the splitting of the nuclei of plutonium, uranium, etc by neutrons in a very rapid chain reaction.

atomic *adj* **1** relating to atoms, atom bombs, or atomic energy. **2** existing as separate atoms.

atomize *or* **-ise** *v* to reduce to minute particles or a fine spray.

atonal *adj* of music: not written in a particular key and using the notes of the chromatic scale impartially. ➤ **atonality** *n*.

atone *v* to make amends for a crime or wrong.

atrium *n* (*pl* **atria** *or* **atriums**) **1** an inner courtyard open to the sky or with a glazed roof. **2** either of the two upper chambers of the heart.

atrocious *adj* **1** extremely wicked or cruel. **2** *informal* very horrible or bad. ➤ **atrociously** *adv*.

atrocity *n* (*pl* **-ies**) **1** a wicked or cruel act. **2** *informal* something ugly; an eyesore.

atrophy¹ *n* (*pl* **-ies**) a wasting away or progressive decline of something. ➤ **atrophic** *adj*.

atrophy² *v* (**-ies**, **-ied**) to waste away or degenerate.

attach *v* **1** to join or fasten. **2** to ascribe or attribute. **3** to appoint (a person) to serve with an organization.

Usage Note: Note the spelling with -*ach* not -*atch*.

attaché /əˈtashay/ *n* a technical expert on a diplomatic staff.

attaché case *n* a slim case used for carrying papers.

attachment *n* **1** the process of attaching. **2** a device for attaching to a machine or implement. **3** fondness or fidelity. **4** computer data sent with an email message.

attack¹ *v* **1** to try to hurt or injure. **2** to take the initiative against (an opponent or opposing team). **3** to criticize in a hostile way. **4** to have a harmful effect on. **5** to begin (a task) vigorously. ➤ **attacker** *n*.

attack² *n* **1** the act of attacking; an assault. **2** an act of attacking. **3** an onset of sickness or disease.

attain *v* **1** to achieve (an objective). **2** *formal* to reach (a certain age). ➤ **attainable** *adj*.

attainment *n* something achieved.

attar *n* a fragrant perfume obtained from rose petals.

attempt[1] *v* to make an effort to accomplish (something).

attempt[2] *n* an instance of attempting something.

attend *v* 1 to go to or be present at. 2 to look after or tend to. 3 to accompany in a formal role. 4 (+ to) to deal with a task or problem. 5 (*often* + to) to pay attention to what is being said or done. 6 (+ on) to result from something.

attendance *n* 1 the number of people present. 2 the number of times a person attends something.

attendant[1] *adj formal* (*often* I on/upon) accompanying or following.

attendant[2] *n* a person who performs a service for another.

attention *n* 1 application of the mind to an object of sense or thought. 2 (*usu in pl*) an act of civility or courtesy. 3 sympathetic consideration of the needs of others. 4 a formal position of readiness assumed by a soldier.

attentive *adj* 1 paying close attention. 2 concerned for the welfare of another. ➤ **attentively** *adv*.

attenuate *v* 1 to weaken or lessen the force of. 2 to make thinner. ➤ **attenuation** *n*.

attest *v* 1 to be proof of or bear witness to. 2 to affirm the truth or existence of. ➤ **attestation** *n*.

attic *n* a room or space in the roof of a building.

attire[1] *n formal* dress or clothing of a particular kind.

attire[2] *v formal* (*usu in passive*) to dress in a particular way.

attitude *n* 1 a way of regarding or thinking about a topic, person, etc. 2 a posture. 3 *informal* a confrontational or deliberately challenging manner.

attitudinize or **-ise** *v* to assume an affected mental attitude.

attorney *n* (*pl* **-eys**) 1 a person who has legal authority to act for another. 2 *NAmer* a lawyer.

attract *v* 1 to fascinate or arouse the affection or interest of. 2 to have the power to draw (things) towards itself. 3 to become the focus of (attention). 4 to be liable for (an obligation).

attraction *n* 1 an attractive quality or aspect. 2 the ability to draw a response. 3 something that draws visitors or spectators. 4 the power of attracting. 5 personal charm.

attractive *adj* 1 good-looking or sexually interesting. 2 arousing interest or pleasure. ➤ **attractively** *adv*, **attractiveness** *n*.

attribute[1] *n* a characteristic or quality.

attribute[2] *v* 1 to credit a person or group with (something). 2 (+ to) to put (a happening, etc) down to a particular cause. ➤ **attributable** *adj*, **attribution** *n*.

attrition *n* the process of weakening or exhausting an opponent by constant harassment. ➤ **attritional** *adj*.

attune *v* 1 to cause or allow (people or their bodies) to become accustomed to new circumstances. 2 (*often* + to) to train (the ear) to respond to certain sounds.

atypical *adj* not typical.

Au *abbr* the chemical symbol for gold.

aubergine *n* a large purple fruit used as a vegetable.

auburn *n* a reddish brown colour.

auction[1] *n* a public sale in which each item is sold to the buyer offering the highest bid.

auction[2] *v* to sell (property) at an auction.

auctioneer *n* an official who conducts an auction.

audacious *adj* 1 boldly daring. 2 insolent or presumptuous. ➤ **audaciously** *adv*, **audacity** *n*.

audible *adj* loud enough to be heard. ➤ **audibility** *n*, **audibly** *adv*.

audience *n* 1 a group of listeners or spectators at a theatre or concert or at a lecture. 2 a formal hearing or interview.

audit[1] *n* an official examination of company accounts.

audit[2] *v* (**audited, auditing**) to perform an audit on (accounts, etc).

audition[1] *n* a trial performance to assess the ability of a candidate for joining an orchestra, choir, etc.

audition[2] *v* to test (a performer) for a part.

auditorium *n* (*pl* **auditoria** or **auditoriums**) the part of a theatre or concert hall where the audience sits.

auditory *adj* relating to hearing or the ear.

au fait /oh 'fay/ *adj* fully informed about or familiar with.

auger *n* a tool for boring holes.

aught *pron archaic* anything at all.

augment *v* to make or become greater or more numerous. ➤ **augmentation** *n*.

augur *v* to be a sign of (a future state or event).

augury *n* (*pl* **-ies**) an omen or portent.

August *n* the eighth month of the year.

august *adj* marked by dignity or grandeur.

auk *n* a diving seabird with a short neck and black-and-white plumage.

aunt *n* the sister of one's father or mother, or the wife of one's uncle.

au pair /oh 'pea/ *n* a young foreign woman who does domestic work for a family in return for accommodation.

aura *n* a distinctive atmosphere surrounding a person or place.

aural *adj* relating to the ear or hearing. ➤ **aurally** *adv*.

aureole *n* a circle of light surrounding the sun or moon when seen through thin cloud.

au revoir /oh rə'vwah/ *interj* goodbye.

aurora borealis n streamers of light sometimes seen in the sky over the North Pole.

auspice n archaic a favourable sign. ✳ **under the auspices of** under the patronage or guidance of.

auspicious adj being a sign of likely success. ➤ **auspiciously** adv.

Aussie n informal an Australian.

austere adj 1 stern and forbidding in appearance and manner. 2 plain or simple. ➤ **austerely** adv, **austerity** n.

Australian n a native or inhabitant of Australia. ➤ **Australian** adj.

authentic adj know to be genuine or trustworthy. ➤ **authentically** adv, **authenticity** n.

authenticate v 1 to prove or declare to be genuine. 2 to corroborate (a story) independently. ➤ **authentication** n.

author n 1 the writer of a book or article. 2 the source or inventor of something. ➤ **authorship** n.

authoritarian[1] adj 1 enforcing strict obedience; 2 dictatorial.

authoritarian[2] n an authoritarian person.

authoritative adj 1 depending on good authority; definitive or reliable. 2 commanding respect and obedience. ➤ **authoritatively** adv.

authority n (pl **-ies**) 1 the power to issue orders and expect obedience. 2 (**the authorities**) people in command; the government or law-enforcers. 3 a government body that administers a public service or enterprise. 4 an individual or book regarded as an expert.

authorize or **-ise** v 1 to give (a person or body) powers to act in a certain way. 2 to allow (a proceeding or activity). ➤ **authorization** n.

autism n a mental disorder marked by acute difficulty in forming relations with other people. ➤ **autistic** adj and n.

autobiography n (pl **-ies**) an account of one's life written by oneself. ➤ **autobiographical** adj.

autocracy n (pl **-ies**) government by a single ruler with total power.

autocrat n 1 a person who rules with total power. 2 a dictatorial person. ➤ **autocratic** adj, **autocratically** adv.

autograph[1] n 1 a celebrity's handwritten signature as a memento. 2 an original manuscript or work of art.

autograph[2] v to write an autograph on.

automate v to convert (a machine or system) to automatic operation.

automatic adj 1 acting or done spontaneously or unconsciously. 2 resembling an automaton; mechanical. 3 able to operate without human intervention. 4 of a gun: able to fire repeatedly from a round of ammunition. 5 happening or implemented as a matter of course. ➤ **automatically** adv.

automatic pilot n a device for steering a ship or aircraft without human control.

automaton n (pl **automatons** or **automata**) 1 a robot. 2 a mechanism designed to respond to encoded instructions.

automobile n chiefly NAmer a motor car.

automotive adj relating to motor vehicles.

autonomous adj self-governing; independent. ➤ **autonomously** adv.

autonomy n (pl **-ies**) 1 self-government. 2 freedom to act independently.

autopsy n (pl **-ies**) a postmortem examination.

autumn n chiefly Brit the season between summer and winter. ➤ **autumnal** adj.

auxiliary[1] adj 1 subsidiary. 2 kept in reserve; extra.

auxiliary[2] n (pl **-ies**) a person, group, or device that is extra or kept in reserve.

avail[1] v 1 to help or benefit. 2 to be of use or advantage. ✳ **avail oneself of** to make use of or take advantage of.

avail[2] n benefit; use. ✳ **of little/no avail** in vain useless.

available adj 1 present or ready for use. 2 obtainable. ➤ **availability** n.

avalanche n 1 a mass of snow or ice falling rapidly down a mountain. 2 a sudden overwhelming rush.

avant-garde adj daringly modern or innovative.

avarice n extreme desire for wealth or gain. ➤ **avaricious** adj.

avenge v 1 to take vengeance on behalf of. 2 to exact satisfaction for (a wrong). ➤ **avenger** n.

avenue n 1 a broad street or road, esp one bordered by trees. 2 a way of doing something or making progress.

aver v (**averred**, **averring**) formal to declare positively.

average[1] n 1 a value obtained by adding several values together and dividing by the number of them. 2 a level typical of a group.

average[2] adj 1 in arithmetic and geometry, equalling a mean. 2 midway between extremes. 3 common or typical.

average[3] v to have (an amount) as an average.

averse adj (usu + to) strongly opposed to or disliking.

Usage Note: Do not confuse this word with adverse.

aversion n a strong dislike or antipathy.

avert v 1 to turn away (the eyes). 2 to avoid or prevent (something unwelcome).

avian adj relating to birds.

aviary n (pl **-ies**) an enclosure for keeping birds.

aviation n the manufacture and operation of aircraft.

aviator n dated a pilot.

avid *adj* very eager or keen. ➤ **avidly** *adv*, **avidness** *n*.

avionics *pl noun* the use of electronic equipment in aircraft. ➤ **avionic** *adj*.

avocado *n* (*pl* **-os** *or* **-oes**) a pear-shaped fruit with a green flesh.

avoid *v* **1** to keep away from or shun. **2** to prevent the occurrence of. **3** to refrain from (doing something). ➤ **avoidable** *adj*, **avoidance** *n*.

avoirdupois /ˌavwahdooh'pwah, ˌavədə'poyz/ *n* the series of units of weight based on a pound of 16 ounces.

avow *v* **1** to declare with assurance. **2** to acknowledge openly. ➤ **avowal** *n*, **avowed** *adj*.

avuncular *adj* kindly or genial towards somebody younger.

await *v* **1** to wait for. **2** to be in store for.

awake[1] *v* (**awoke, awoken**) **1** to come out of sleep. **2** (*usu* + to) to become aware of. **3** to arouse from sleep.

awake[2] *adj* **1** not asleep. **2** (*usu* + to) aware of.

awaken *v* **1** to wake. **2** to wake up. **3** to stir up (a feeling).

award[1] *v* to confer or bestow (something deserved or complimentary).

award[2] *n* **1** something that is conferred as an honour or reward. **2** the act of awarding something.

aware *adj* knowing about or conscious of something. ➤ **awareness** *n*.

awash *adj* covered or flooded with water.

away[1] *adv* **1** at a distance. **2** into a secure place. **3** out of existence. **4** constantly or without interruption.

away[2] *adj* of a sports fixture: played at the opponent's ground.

awe[1] *n* a feeling of dread and wonder.

awe[2] *v* to fill with awe.

awesome *adj* **1** inspiring awe. **2** *informal* impressive. ➤ **awesomely** *adv*.

awful *adj* **1** extremely unpleasant. **2** *informal* used as an intensive: *an awful headache.* **3** *archaic* inspiring awe. ➤ **awfully** *adv*.

awhile *adv* for a short time.

awkward *adj* **1** difficult to use or handle. **2** lacking dexterity; clumsy. **3** lacking social grace and assurance. **4** causing or feeling embarrassment. ➤ **awkwardly** *adv*.

awl *n* a pointed tool for making small holes.

awning *n* a canvas cover used to protect something from the weather.

awoke *v* past tense of AWAKE[1].

awoken *v* past part. of AWAKE[1].

AWOL *adj* absent without leave.

awry *adv and adj* out of the right position or course; amiss.

axe[1] (*NAmer* **ax**) *n* **1** a tool with a large heavy blade, used for chopping. **2** (**the axe**) a drastic reduction or removal. ✳ **have an axe to grind** to have a private purpose to pursue.

axe[2] (*NAmer* **ax**) *v* to cancel or dismiss abruptly.

axiom *n* a principle or rule generally recognized as true.

axis *n* (*pl* **axes**) **1** a straight line about which a body or figure can rotate. **2** a reference line in a system of coordinates. **3** (**Axis**) the alliance between Germany and Italy in World War II.

axle *n* a shaft on which a wheel rotates.

ayatollah /ie-ə'tolə/ *n* a leader of Shiite Muslims in Iran.

aye *or* **ay** *interj archaic or dialect* yes.

azalea *n* a rhododendron with bright flowers.

azimuth *n* the direction of a star in relation to the observer, measured as the angle from a point on the horizon due north or south.

azure *n* **1** sky blue. **2** in heraldry, blue.

B¹ or **b** n (pl **B's** or **Bs** or **b's**) the second letter of the English alphabet.

B² abbr the chemical symbol for boron.

BA abbr Bachelor of Arts.

Ba abbr the chemical symbol for barium.

baa¹ v (**baas**, **baaed** or **baa'd**, **baaing**) to make the bleat of a sheep.

baa² n (pl **baas**) the bleating sound of a sheep.

babble¹ v 1 to utter meaningless or unintelligible sounds. 2 to talk foolishly; to chatter.

babble² n meaningless or unintelligible sounds.

babe n 1 chiefly literary an infant or baby. 2 informal a girl or woman.

babel n a scene of noise or confusion.

baboon n a large monkey with a long doglike muzzle and a medium-length tail.

baby¹ n (pl **-ies**) 1 a very young child or animal, esp one that has recently been born. 2 (used before a noun) comparatively small of its type. 3 a childish or immature person. ➤ **babyhood** n, **babyish** adj.

baby² v (**-ies**, **-ied**) to treat with excessive or inappropriate care.

babysit v (**babysitting**, past tense and past part. **babysat**) to look after a child while the parents are out. ➤ **babysitter** n.

baccalaureate n a qualification in some countries to allow students to enter higher education.

baccarat /'bakərah/ n a card game in which players bet against the dealer.

bacchanalia pl n a drunken feast; an orgy. ➤ **bacchanalian** adj.

bachelor n 1 an unmarried man. 2 a recipient of a first degree from a university. ➤ **bachelorhood** n.

bacillus n (pl **bacilli**) a rod-shaped bacterium that causes disease.

back¹ n 1 the rear part of the human body from the neck to the end of the spine. 2 the upper part of an animal's body. 3 the side or surface behind the front or face. 4 a defensive player in a team game. ✳ **back to front** in such a way that the back and the front are reversed in position. **behind somebody's back** without a person's knowledge or permission. **get/put somebody's back up** to annoy or irritate somebody. **the back of beyond** informal a remote place. **turn one's back on** to reject or deny (somebody or something).

back² adv 1 to or at the rear. 2 in or into a reclining position. 3 in or into the past. 4 nearer the beginning. 5 to or in a place from which somebody or something came. 6 to or towards a former state. 7 in return or reply. ✳ **back and forth** backwards and forwards repeatedly.

back³ adj 1 at or in the back. 2 distant from a central or main area; remote.

back⁴ v 1 to give support to. 2 to provide a musical accompaniment for. 3 to drive (a vehicle) backwards. 4 to be at or form the back of. 5 to place a bet on (a competitor in a race). 6 of the wind: to shift anticlockwise. 7 (+ on/onto) of a building: to have its back adjacent to or closely facing. ➤ **backer** n.

back-bencher n an MP who does not hold a post in the government or opposition.

backbiting n mean and spiteful talk.

backbone n 1 the spine. 2 the most substantial part of something. 3 firmness of character.

backchat n chiefly Brit rude or impertinent remarks.

backdate v 1 to apply retrospectively. 2 to date (a document) with an earlier date than the actual date.

backdoor adj using unfair or underhand methods.

back down v to concede defeat.

backdrop n 1 a painted cloth hung at the back of a theatre stage. 2 a setting for an event.

backfire v 1 of an engine: to make a loud bang when fuel ignites prematurely. 2 to cause difficulty by having the reverse of the expected effect.

backgammon n a board game for two players played with dice and counters.

background n 1 the scenery or ground behind something. 2 the part of a painting or photograph that depicts what lies behind objects in the foreground. 3 the conditions forming a setting for an experience. 4 information that helps to explain a problem or situation. 5 a person's experience and upbringing.

backhand n a stroke in tennis, squash, etc made with the back of the hand turned in the direction of the stroke.

backhanded *adj* of a compliment: apparently complimentary but with an uncomplimentary edge to it.

backhander *n* 1 a backhanded blow or stroke. 2 *informal* a bribe.

backing *n* 1 financial support or aid. 2 endorsement. 3 something forming a back or reverse side. 4 the musical or vocal accompaniment to a song or singer.

backlash *n* a strong adverse reaction to a political or social development.

backlog *n* an accumulation of things still needing to be done.

back off *v* to withdraw from a confrontation.

back out *v* to withdraw from a commitment.

backpack *n* a rucksack. ➤ **backpacker** *n*.

backpedal *v* (**backpedalled, backpedalling,** *NAmer* **backpedaled, backpedaling**) to withdraw from a previous opinion or stand.

backroom *adj* done or working behind the scenes.

backside *n informal* the buttocks.

backslapping *n* excessive cordiality or praising.

backsliding *n* lapsing after a period of improvement.

backstage *adj and adv* behind the stage out of view of the audience.

backstreet *n* a quiet or minor street in a town.

backstroke *n* a swimming stroke performed on the back using reverse overarm strokes and kicking movements of the feet.

backtrack *v* 1 to retrace a path or course. 2 to reverse one's position or stand.

back-up *n* 1 support. 2 a copy of computer data made for security.

back up *v* 1 to give support to. 2 in computing, to make a security copy of (data). 3 of traffic: to form a queue behind a hazard or congestion.

backward *adj* 1 directed or turned towards the back. 2 not developed as far as normal.

backwards (*NAmer* **backward**) *adv* 1 towards the back. 2 with the back foremost. 3 in a reverse direction or towards the beginning. 4 perfectly; thoroughly. 5 towards the past. 6 towards or into a worse state. ✳ **bend/fall/lean over backwards** to make extreme efforts.

backwash *n* the backward movement of a receding wave.

backwater *n* 1 an area of stagnant water. 2 an isolated or backward place or condition.

backwoods *n* a remote or culturally backward area.

bacon *n* cured and salted or smoked meat cut from the side of a pig.

bacteria *n* pl of BACTERIUM.

bacterium *n* a microscopic organism living in organic matter and often carrying disease.

bad *adj* (**worse, worst**) 1 poor or inadequate in quality; below an acceptable standard. 2 morally objectionable. 3 mischievous or disobedient. 4 (*often* + at) unskilful or incompetent. 5 disagreeable or unpleasant. 6 (+ for) injurious or harmful. 7 worse than usual; severe. 8 unwell. 9 unhealthy or diseased. 10 (*often* + about) regretful or remorseful. 11 of a debt: not going to be paid. 12 *chiefly NAmer, informal* excellent. ✳ **not bad** *informal* quite good.

bade *v* past tense of BID[1].

badge *n* 1 a token of membership in a society or group. 2 an emblem awarded for a particular accomplishment.

badger[1] *n* a black or dark grey mammal with white striped facial markings, active at night and living underground.

badger[2] *v* to harass or annoy persistently.

badinage *n* playful repartee or banter.

badlands *pl n* a barren region marked by extensive rock erosion.

badly *adv* 1 in an unsatisfactory or unpleasant way. 2 unkindly; cruelly. 3 unsuccessfully. 4 severely. 5 very much. ✳ **badly off** poor.

badminton *n* a game played with light rackets and a shuttlecock that is volleyed over a net.

baffle *v* to puzzle or perplex. ➤ **bafflement** *n*.

bag[1] *n* 1 a flexible container for storing or carrying things. 2 a handbag or shoulder bag. 3 a sagging of the skin under the eyes. 4 *chiefly Brit, informal* (*in pl*) a great deal; lots. 5 *informal, derog* an old woman. 6 *informal* a person; special interest. ✳ **in the bag** *informal* as good as achieved. ➤ **bagful** (*pl* **bagfuls**) *n*.

bag[2] *v* (**bagged, bagging**) 1 to swell out or bulge. 2 to hang loosely. 3 to put into a bag. 4 to get possession of. 5 *informal* to steal. 6 to take (animals) as game.

bagatelle *n* 1 a game in which balls are struck up a board past obstacles into holes. 2 something unimportant or of little value.

bagel /'baygl/ *n* a hard ring-shaped bread roll.

baggage *n* luggage for travel.

baggy *adj* (**-ier, -iest**) loose or puffed out.

bagpipe or **bagpipes** *n* a wind instrument with pipes, played by squeezing air through from a bag.

baguette /ba'get/ *n* a long thin French loaf.

bail[1] *n* 1 money paid as security that a person released from custody will return to stand trial. 2 temporary release by payment of bail.

bail[2] *v* to release on payment of bail.

bail[3] *n* in cricket, each of the two crosspieces that rest on the stumps to form the wicket.

bail[4] or **bale** *v* 1 (*usu* + out) to clear (water) from a ship or boat. 2 (*usu* + out) to jump from an aircraft, using a parachute. 3 (*usu* + out) to rescue somebody in danger or difficulty.

bailey *n* (*pl* **-eys**) the outer wall of a castle.

bailiff *n* 1 *chiefly Brit* an official who serves writs and seizes property on which rent is owed. 2 *chiefly Brit* somebody who manages an estate or farm.

bailiwick *n* the area of jurisdiction of a bailiff.

bait[1] n something put on a hook or trap to lure an animal.

bait[2] v 1 to provoke or tease. 2 to harass (a chained animal) with dogs. 3 to provide with bait.

baize n a green woollen cloth used as a covering for billiard tables.

bake v 1 to cook (food) in an oven. 2 to dry or harden by heat. 3 to become extremely hot.

baker n a person who bakes and sells bread and cakes. ✳ **a baker's dozen** thirteen.

bakery n (pl **-ies**) a place where bread is made and sold.

baking soda n sodium bicarbonate.

balaclava n a close-fitting woollen hood that covers the head leaving the face free.

balance[1] n 1 stability produced by even distribution of weight on each side of a vertical axis. 2 the ability to retain a physical equilibrium. 3 mental and emotional steadiness. 4 equilibrium between contrasting elements. 5 equality between the totals of the two sides of an account. 6 the difference between credits and debits in an account. 7 something left over. 8 a weighing instrument consisting of a beam pivoted at the centre with pans suspended from the ends. ✳ **in the balance** with the fate or outcome still to be determined. **on balance** all things considered. ➤ **balanced** adj.

balance[2] v 1 to make or become in a position or state of balance. 2 to compare the relative value or importance of the factors in (a situation). 3 of accounts: to have the debit and credit totals equal. 4 to counterbalance or offset.

balance of payments n the difference between a country's payments for imports and receipts for exports.

balance sheet n a statement of the financial state of an organization.

balcony n (pl **-ies**) 1 a platform with a railing built out from the wall of a building. 2 a gallery inside a theatre or other building.

bald adj 1 having no hair on the head. 2 of a tyre: having little or no tread. 3 plainly or bluntly expressed. ➤ **baldly** adv, **baldness** n.

balderdash n nonsense.

balding adj becoming bald.

bale[1] n a large bundle of cloth, paper, or hay.

bale[2] v to tie into bales or bundles.

bale[3] n and verb Brit see BAIL[4].

baleen n whalebone.

baleful adj pernicious or menacing. ➤ **balefully** adv.

balk (Brit **baulk**) v 1 (usu + at) to stop short and refuse to go on. 2 (often + at) to refuse abruptly. 3 to check or thwart.

ball[1] n 1 a solid or hollow spherical object used in a game or sport. 2 a delivery or play of the ball in a game. 3 coarse slang (in pl) the testicles. ✳ **on the ball** knowledgeable and competent; alert.

ball[2] v to form or gather into a ball.

ball[3] n a large formal gathering for social dancing. ✳ **have a ball** informal to enjoy oneself.

ballad n 1 a rhythmic poem or song that tells a story. 2 a slow, romantic or sentimental popular song.

ballast n 1 heavy material carried in a ship or airship to improve stability. 2 broken stone laid in a bed for railway lines or the lower layer of roads.

ball bearing n a bearing of steel balls that roll with minimal friction in a groove between a shaft and a support.

ballcock n an automatic valve in a cistern controlled by the rise and fall of a float.

ballerina n a female ballet dancer.

ballet n a form of artistic dancing based on conventional positions and steps, usu performed to music. ➤ **balletic** adj.

ballistic adj 1 relating to the movement of projectiles under their own momentum and the force of gravity. 2 informal violently angry.

ballistic missile n a missile guided in ascent and falling freely on its target.

ballistics pl n the science of the movement of projectiles.

balloon[1] n 1 a baglike container filled with hot air or a gas lighter than air so as to rise and float in the atmosphere. 2 an inflatable coloured rubber bag used as a toy or decoration. 3 an outline enclosing words spoken or thought by a character in a cartoon.

balloon[2] v 1 to ascend or travel in a balloon. 2 (often + out) to swell or puff out. 3 to increase rapidly.

ballot[1] n 1 an election in which votes are cast in secret. 2 the number of votes cast.

ballot[2] v (**balloted**, **balloting**) 1 (often + for) to vote by ballot. 2 to ask (people) to vote.

ballpoint or **ballpoint pen** n a pen having a tiny rotating ball as the writing point.

ballroom n a large room for formal dancing.

ballroom dancing n formal dancing by couples.

ballyhoo n noisy talk or fuss.

balm n 1 an aromatic and medicinal resin. 2 something that soothes or heals.

balmy adj (**-ier, -iest**) of weather: pleasantly mild.

baloney or **boloney** n (pl **-eys**) nonsense.

balsa n (also **balsa wood**) the strong light wood of a tropical American tree, used in making models.

balsam n an oily resin obtained from certain plants, or a medicinal preparation containing it.

baluster n each of the upright supports for a rail.

balustrade n a row of balusters topped by a rail.

baptize

bamboo n a tropical giant grass with strong hollow stems.

bamboozle v 1 to deceive or cheat. 2 to confuse or mystify.

ban[1] v (**banned, banning**) to prohibit or forbid officially.

ban[2] n a legal or social prohibition.

banal adj lacking originality or novelty; dull. ➤ **banality** n, **banally** adv.

banana n a long curved fruit growing in bunches, with a thick yellow skin and soft pulpy flesh.

band[1] n 1 a narrow strip of material used as trimming on an article of dress. 2 a strip distinguishable by colour, texture, or composition. 3 a strip or belt serving to join or hold things together or to transmit motion. 4 a range of radio wavelengths.

band[2] v 1 (often + together) to unite for a common purpose. 2 to fasten with a band. 3 to mark with a band.

band[3] n 1 a group of musicians playing jazz, pop, rock, or marching music. 2 a group of people sharing an interest or purpose.

bandage[1] n a strip of fabric used to dress and bind up wounds.

bandage[2] v to bind or dress with a bandage.

bandanna n a large patterned piece of cloth worn round the head.

b and b abbr (often **B and B**) Brit bed and breakfast.

bandit n a member of a band of armed robbers. ➤ **banditry** n.

bandolier or **bandoleer** n a belt worn across the chest with pockets or loops for cartridges.

bandstand n a roofed outdoor stand for a brass band.

bandwagon n a fashionable cause or activity.

bandwidth n a range of frequencies used in radio transmission and telecommunications.

bandy[1] v (**-ies, -ied**) (often + about) to use or make reference to in a glib or offhand manner. ✳ **bandy words** to argue angrily.

bandy[2] adj (**-ier, -iest**) of a person's legs: bowed.

bane n a cause of ruin or trouble.

bang[1] v 1 to strike sharply. 2 to cause to make a loud sharp or metallic noise.

bang[2] n 1 a sudden loud noise. 2 a resounding blow. 3 a burst of energy or activity.

bang[3] adv informal 1 right or directly. 2 exactly.

banger n Brit 1 a firework that explodes with a loud bang. 2 informal a sausage. 3 informal an old usu dilapidated car.

bangle n a rigid ornamental bracelet.

banish v 1 to send (somebody) permanently away from a place as a punishment. 2 to dispel (an unpleasant thought) from one's mind. ➤ **banishment** n.

banister or **bannister** n 1 (also in pl) a handrail with its upright supports at the edge of a staircase. 2 an upright support of such a handrail.

banjo n (pl **-os** or **-oes**) a stringed musical instrument with a round flat body and long neck. ➤ **banjoist** n.

bank[1] n 1 a mound of earth or snow. 2 a mass of cloud or fog. 3 the rising ground bordering a lake or river or forming the embankment along a road or railway. 4 a slope.

bank[2] v 1 (often + up) to rise in or form a bank. 2 of an aircraft: to incline laterally.

bank[3] n 1 an establishment for keeping, lending, and issuing money and for the transmission of funds. 2 a collection of something kept available for use. 3 a container for collecting materials for recycling.

bank[4] v to deposit (money) in a bank. ✳ **bank on** to rely on.

bank[5] n 1 a group or series of objects arranged together. 2 a row of keys on a typewriter or computer keyboard.

bankable adj popular and therefore likely to be a source of profit.

bank holiday n a public holiday when banks and some businesses are closed.

banknote n money in paper form.

bankroll[1] n 1 a roll of banknotes. 2 NAmer a supply of money; funds.

bankroll[2] v to finance.

bankrupt[1] adj legally declared to be incapable of paying outstanding debts.

bankrupt[2] n a bankrupt person.

bankrupt[3] v to make bankrupt.

banner[1] n a usu square or oblong flag bearing heraldic arms or a symbolic design, held up high.

banner[2] adj NAmer distinguished from all others, esp in excellence: a banner year for business.

bannister n see BANISTER.

banns pl n the public announcement in church of a proposed marriage.

banquet[1] n a large and elaborate ceremonial meal.

banquet[2] v (**banqueted, banqueting**) to provide or entertain with a banquet.

banshee n a female spirit in Gaelic folklore whose wailing warns of death.

bantam n a small domestic fowl.

banter[1] n light-hearted teasing or badgering.

banter[2] v to speak or act playfully or wittily.

bap n Brit a soft round bread roll.

baptism n the Christian sacrament of admission to the church by sprinkling with or immersion in water. ➤ **baptismal** adj.

baptism of fire n a severe initial experience.

Baptist adj belonging to a Protestant denomination which baptizes full adult believers rather than babies. ➤ **Baptist** n.

baptize or **-ise** v 1 to administer baptism to. 2 to give a name to at baptism.

bar[1] *n* **1** a long firm piece of hard material. **2** something that obstructs or prevents progress or action. **3** a counter at which alcoholic drinks are served, or a room or premises containing this. **4** in a court of law, the dock or the railing that encloses the dock. **5** (*usu* **the Bar**) *Brit* the profession or body of barristers. **6** a straight stripe or band. **7** a group of notes and rests in music, marked on each side by a line. * **behind bars** in prison.

bar[2] *v* (**barred, barring**) **1** to fasten with a bar. **2** to shut in or out. **3** to prevent or forbid. ➤ **barred** *adj*.

bar[3] *prep* except for.

barb *n* **1** a sharp projection extending backwards from the point of an arrow, fishhook, etc. **2** a pointedly critical remark.

barbarian *n* **1** a person belonging to a land, culture, or people regarded as uncivilized or inferior. **2** a cruel or uncivilized person.

barbaric *adj* **1** unsophisticated or uncivilized. ➤ **barbarically** *adv*.

barbarism *n* **1** primitive or unsophisticated social or intellectual condition. **2** merciless cruelty.

barbarous *adj* **1** mercilessly cruel. **2** lacking culture or refinement.

barbecue[1] *n* **1** an outdoor meal at which food is cooked over a charcoal fire. **2** a piece of equipment for use at a barbecue.

barbecue[2] *v* (**barbecues, barbecued, barbecuing**) to cook on a barbecue.

barbed *adj* **1** having barbs. **2** of a remark: sarcastic or spiteful.

barbed wire *n* twisted wires with sharp points set along them.

barbel *n* **1** a thin projecting organ on the lips of some fishes. **2** a freshwater fish with four barbels on its upper jaw.

barbell *n* a bar with adjustable weighted discs attached to each end, used for weight-lifting.

barber *n* a person who cuts and styles men's hair and shaves or trims beards.

barbiturate *n* a sedative drug used in the treatment of epilepsy and formerly in sleeping pills.

bar code *n* an identifying code printed on a product for sale, consisting of parallel lines of varying thickness that can be read by an electronic scanner.

bard *n* *archaic or literary* a poet who sang or recited verses about heroes. **2** a poet. **3** (**the Bard**) Shakespeare. ➤ **bardic** *adj*.

bare[1] *adj* **1** not wearing any clothes. **2** lacking a natural or usual covering. **3** open to view; exposed. **4** unfurnished or empty. **5** having nothing left over or added; mere. **6** not disguised or embellished in any way. ➤ **bareness** *n*.

bare[2] *v* to reveal or uncover.

bareback *or* **barebacked** *adv and adj* on the back of a horse without a saddle.

barefaced *adj* lacking scruples; shameless.

bargain[1] *n* **1** something bought at a very favourable price. **2** an agreement between people to help or support each other. * **into the bargain** in addition.

bargain[2] *v* (*often* + with) to negotiate over the terms of a purchase or agreement. * **bargain for** to be prepared for. **bargain on** to expect.

barge[1] *n* a long flat-bottomed boat used for transporting goods on inland waterways.

barge[2] *v* **1** to move clumsily or forcefully. **2** (+ in/into) to intrude noisily or clumsily.

baritone *n* a male singer having a voice between base and tenor.

barium *n* a silver-white soft metallic chemical element.

bark[1] *v* **1** to make the short loud cry of a dog. **2** to speak loudly or angrily. * **bark up the wrong tree** to proceed under a misapprehension.

bark[2] *n* the sound made by a barking dog.

bark[3] *n* the tough exterior covering of a tree.

bark[4] *v* to scrape the skin off (the knee or shin) by accident.

barley *n* (*pl* **-eys**) a cereal grass used in foods and for cattle feed.

barley sugar *n* a brittle sweet made of boiled sugar .

barman *n* (*pl* **barmen**) somebody who serves drinks in a bar.

bar mitzvah /bah 'mitsvə/ *n* the religious ceremony marking the time when a Jewish boy takes on adult duties and responsibilities at the age of 13.

barmy *adj* (**-ier, -iest**) *informal* foolish or slightly mad.

barn *n* a large farm building for storage.

barnacle *n* a marine crustacean that is fixed to rocks or floating objects.

barn dance *n* a social gathering with country dancing.

barnstorm *v* *chiefly NAmer* to travel staging theatrical performances or conducting a political campaign.

barnyard *n* *NAmer* a farmyard.

barometer *n* **1** an instrument for measuring atmospheric pressure in order to predict the weather. **2** a gauge of fluctuations in public opinion. ➤ **barometric** *adj*.

baron *n* **1** a member of the lowest rank of the peerage in Britain. **2** formerly, a feudal tenant who received his rights and title directly from the sovereign in return for his allegiance.

baroness *n* **1** the wife or widow of a baron. **2** a woman having the rank of a baron.

baronet *n* a man holding a title below a baron and above a knight. ➤ **baronetcy** *n*.

baroque *adj* of a 17th-cent. ornamental style of European art, architecture, and music.

barrack *v* *chiefly Brit* to jeer or scoff at (a player or performer).

barracks *pl n* a group of buildings providing accommodation for soldiers.

barracuda *n* (*pl* **barracudas** *or* **barracuda**) a predatory fish of warm seas.

barrage[1] *n* **1** a continuous bombardment of intensive artillery fire. **2** an overwhelming series of questions or complaints. **3** *Brit* an artificial dam placed in a watercourse or estuary.

barrage[2] *v* to overwhelm with questions or complaints.

barrel *n* **1** a cylindrical container for liquids, with bulging sides and flat ends. **2** the tube of a gun, from which the bullet is fired. ✳ **over a barrel** *informal* in a weak position.

barrel organ *n* a street organ with a revolving cylinder played by turning a handle.

barren *adj* **1** incapable of producing offspring. **2** of a tree: habitually failing to fruit. **3** of land: not productive. **4** lacking interest or information.

barricade[1] *n* an obstruction thrown up to block a road or entrance.

barricade[2] *v* to block or defend with a barricade.

barrier *n* something that prevents entry or progress.

barring *prep* except for.

barrister *n Brit* a lawyer who has the right to plead as an advocate in a lawcourt.

barrow[1] *n* a cart with two wheels and shafts for pushing it.

barrow[2] *n* a large mound of earth or stones over an ancient grave.

bartender *n chiefly NAmer* a barman.

barter[1] *v* to trade by exchanging goods without the use of money.

barter[2] *n* trade by bartering.

basalt *n* a dark igneous rock.

base[1] *n* **1** the bottom or lowest part of something; a support or foundation. **2** a side or face of a geometrical figure on which it is regarded as standing. **3** the fundamental part of something; a basis on which other activities or institutions depend. **4** a centre from which a start is made in an activity or from which operations proceed. **5** the locality or installations on which a military force relies for supplies or from which it starts operations. **6** the number with reference to which a number system is constructed. **7** any of the stations at each of the four corners of the inner part of a baseball field to which a batter must run in turn in order to score a run. **8** a chemical compound capable of taking up a hydrogen ion from or donating an unshared pair of electrons to an acid to form a salt.

base[2] *v* **1** to make or serve as a base for. **2** (*usu* + on/upon) to use as a base or basis for; to found. **3** (*usu* + in/at) to have (a place) as an operational base.

base[3] *adj* **1** lacking higher values; degrading. **2** lacking or showing a lack of moral values such as honour, chivalry, or loyalty. **3** of a metal: of comparatively low value and having relatively inferior properties.

baseball *n* a game played with a bat and ball between two teams on a field with four bases arranged in a diamond marking the course a batsman must run to score.

baseball cap *n* a close-fitting round cap with a large peak.

baseless *adj* not supported by fact; unfounded.

baseline *n* **1** a basis or starting point for measurements or comparisons. **2** the back line at each end of a court in tennis, badminton, or volleyball.

basement *n* the part of a building wholly or partly below ground level.

bases[1] *n* pl of BASE[1].

bases[2] *n* pl of BASIS.

bash[1] *v informal* **1** to strike violently. **2** (*often* + up) to make a violent physical attack on.

bash[2] *n informal* **1** a heavy blow. **2** *chiefly Brit* (*often* + at) an attempt. **3** a party.

bashful *adj* self-consciously shy or timid. ➤ **bashfully** *adv.*

basic[1] *adj* **1** forming the base or essence; fundamental. **2** simple; elementary. **3** having the character of a chemical base. ➤ **basically** *adv.*

basic[2] *n* (*usu in pl*) a fundamental fact or principle.

basil *n* an aromatic plant of the mint family with leaves used as a herb in cooking.

basilica *n* an oblong building used in ancient Rome as a place of assembly or as a lawcourt, or an early Christian church similar to this.

basilisk *n* **1** a mythical reptile with a fatal breath and glance. **2** a crested tropical American lizard related to the iguanas.

basin *n* **1** a rounded open container used for holding liquid. **2** a bowl used for mixing food. **3** a depression in the surface of the land or ocean floor. **4** the region drained by a river and its tributaries.

basis *n* (*pl* **bases**) the principal component of something.

bask *v* **1** to lie enjoying warmth or sunshine. **2** (*usu* + in) to enjoy favour or approval.

basket *n* **1** a rigid receptacle made of interwoven strips of wicker or wood. **2** a net, open at the bottom and suspended from a metal ring, that constitutes the goal in basketball.

basketball *n* a team game in which players score goals by throwing a ball through a raised basket.

bass[1] *n* (*pl* **basses** *or* **bass**) an edible spiny-finned sea and freshwater fish.

bass[2] *n* **1** a male singer with a voice of the lowest range. **2** a double bass or bass guitar. **3** the lower portion of the audio frequency range. ➤ **bassist** *n.*

bass³ adj **1** of low pitch. **2** deep or grave in tone.

bass clef n a musical clef placing the F below middle C on the fourth line of the staff.

basset hound n a hunting dog of a short-legged breed with a long body and drooping ears.

bassoon n a large woodwind musical instrument of the oboe family. ➤ **bassoonist** n.

bastard n **1** offensive or archaic a child of unmarried parents. **2** informal an offensive or disagreeable person.

bastardize or **-ise** v to debase.

baste¹ v to sew with loose stitches.

baste² v to pour fat and juices over (meat) during cooking.

baste³ v to beat soundly; to thrash.

bastion n **1** a projecting part of a fortification. **2** something considered as providing defence or protection.

bat¹ n **1** a wooden implement used for hitting the ball in sports and games. **2** an implement like a rounded bat for guiding aircraft on the ground. ✷ **off one's own bat** through one's own efforts.

bat² v (**batted, batting**) **1** to strike or hit with a bat. **2** to take one's turn at batting.

bat³ n **1** a nocturnal flying mammal. **2** (**old bat**) derog a disagreeable old woman.

bat⁴ v (**batted, batting**) to blink (an eye) in surprise or emotion. ✷ **not bat an eyelid** not to be at all surprised.

batch¹ n a quantity of goods produced at one time.

batch² v to gather (things) together or process as a batch.

bated ✷ **with bated breath** in a state of nervous suspense.

bath¹ n **1** a large open container for filling with water and lying in for washing. **2** an act of washing in a bath. **3** (usu in pl) a building containing a swimming pool or rooms for bathing.

bath² v Brit to wash in a bath.

bathe¹ v **1** to wash in a bath. **2** chiefly Brit to swim for pleasure. **3** to wash or clean with water or other liquid. **4** to suffuse with light. ➤ **bather** n.

bathe² n Brit an act of swimming.

bathos n a sudden change from something serious to something trivial. ➤ **bathetic** adj.

bathroom n **1** a room containing a bath or shower and usu a washbasin and toilet. **2** NAmer a toilet.

batik n a method of hand-printing by coating with wax the parts to be left undyed.

baton n **1** a small stick with which a conductor directs a band or orchestra. **2** a stick passed by the runners in a relay team. **3** a short stick carried as a symbol of military rank. **4** a long metal rod twirled by a drum major.

batsman n (pl **batsmen**) a player who bats or is batting in cricket.

battalion n **1** a military unit composed of a headquarters and two or more companies. **2** a large number of troops, people, or things.

batten¹ n a thin narrow strip of squared timber, plastic, or metal.

batten² v (often + down) to fasten (esp a ship's hatches) with battens.

batten³ v (+ on/upon) to thrive at the expense of somebody else.

batter¹ v to strike heavily and repeatedly; to break or damage with heavy persistent blows. ➤ **battered** adj.

batter² n a mixture of flour, egg, and milk or water, used for making pancakes or coating food for frying. ➤ **battered** adj.

batter³ n in baseball, etc, the player who is batting.

battery n (pl **-ies**) **1** a source of power consisting of two or more cells connected together to provide an electric current. **2** a number of similar things connected or used together. **3** chiefly Brit a series of cages or compartments for raising poultry. **4** the unlawful use of force or violence on a person without their consent. **5** a fortified gun emplacement.

battle¹ n **1** an extensive fight between opposing armed forces. **2** an extended struggle or controversy.

battle² v **1** to fight vigorously. **2** to struggle to do something. ➤ **battler** n.

battle-axe n **1** a large axe used formerly in warfare. **2** a domineering older woman.

battledress n uniform worn by soldiers in battle.

battlefield or **battleground** n a piece of ground where a battle is fought.

battlement n a parapet on a wall, with gaps originally used for firing through.

battleship n a heavily armed warship.

batty adj (**-ier, -iest**) informal eccentric or crazy.

bauble n a trinket or trifle.

baulk v Brit see BALK.

bauxite n a mineral that is the principal ore of aluminium.

bawdy adj (**-ier, -iest**) boisterously or humorously indecent. ➤ **bawdiness** n.

bawl v to cry or shout out. ➤ **bawl** n.

bawl out v chiefly NAmer, informal to reprimand loudly or severely.

bay¹ n a wide curving inlet of a sea or lake.

bay² n a small evergreen tree of the laurel family with leaves used for flavouring.

bay³ n **1** a special area or compartment within a larger structure. **2** a structure projecting from the wall of a building. **3** a section of wall between two columns or buttresses.

bay⁴ adj of a horse: reddish brown.

bay⁵ *v* **1** of a dog: to bark fiercely. **2** (+ for) to demand insistently. * **hold/keep at bay** to prevent from coming close to or affecting one.

bayonet¹ *n* a blade attached to the muzzle of a firearm and used in hand-to-hand combat.

bayonet² *v* (**bayoneted, bayoneting**) to stab with a bayonet.

bay window *n* a window projecting outwards from the wall.

bazaar *n* **1** a market in the Middle East. **2** a sale to raise money for charity.

bazooka *n* a short-range antitank rocket launcher.

BBC *abbr* British Broadcasting Corporation.

BC *abbr* **1** used after a date, before Christ. **2** British Columbia.

Usage Note: BC comes after the date, e.g. 133BC.

Be *abbr* the chemical symbol for beryllium.

be *v* (*sing. present* **am, are, is,** *pl present* **are,** *first and third person sing. past* **was,** *second person sing. past and pl past* **were,** *past part.* **been**) **1** to exist or be present. **2** to occur in time. **3** to have a specified state, function, or value. **4** used instead of *go* or *come* in the perfect tense: *I've been to New York.* ➤ *verb aux.* **1** used with a present participle to form continuous or progressive tenses. **2** used with a past participle to form the passive voice. **3** used with *to* and an infinitive to express a wish or future action: *You are not to worry.* * **be oneself** to behave normally or naturally. **the be-all and end-all** the most important factor or part.

beach¹ *n* the shore of a sea or lake, covered by sand or pebbles.

beach² *v* to bring ashore from the water.

beachcomber *n* a person who searches a beach for useful or saleable objects.

beacon *n* **1** a signal fire lit at the top of a hill. **2** a light or signal used to guide shipping or aircraft.

bead *n* **1** a small piece of wood or glass, threaded on a string or wire to make a necklace. **2** a drop of liquid. ➤ **beaded** *adj*.

beadle *n* a minor parish official.

beady *adj* (-**ier, -iest**) of the eyes: small and round, and vigilant.

beagle *n* a hound of a breed with short legs and a smooth coat.

beak *n* a bird's hard projecting mouth structure. ➤ **beaked** *adj*.

beaker *n* **1** a tall drinking vessel without a handle. **2** a cylindrical flat-bottomed vessel used by chemists and pharmacists.

beam¹ *n* **1** a long piece of heavy timber used in building. **2** a bar for balancing on in gymnastics. **3** the width of a ship at its widest part. **4** a ray or shaft of light or other radiation. **5** a radio signal transmitted continuously in one direction as an aircraft navigation aid. * **off beam** wrong; irrelevant.

beam² *v* **1** to smile broadly. **2** to transmit (a broadcast signal). **3** to emit a bright light.

bean *n* **1** a seed of a climbing plant, growing in a pod and used as a vegetable. **2** *informal* the smallest possible amount. * **full of beans** lively or energetic.

beanbag *n* **1** a small bag filled with beans, used in games or as a toy. **2** a large loosely stuffed cushion used as an informal low chair.

bear¹ *n* **1** a large heavy mammal with long shaggy hair and a short tail. **2** a surly, uncouth, or shambling person.

bear² *v* (**bore, borne**) **1** to carry or transport. **2** to behave in a particular way. **3** to have or show as a feature. **4** to give birth to. **5** of a plant or tree: to produce (fruit or flowers). **6** to support the weight of. **7** to tolerate. **8** to sustain or incur (e.g. a cost). **9** to go in a specified direction. **10** (+ on) to be relevant to something. **11** (+ with) to show patience or indulgence towards somebody. * **bear fruit** to have good results. **bear in mind** to remember or consider. ➤ **bearable** *adj*, **bearably** *adv*, **bearer** *n*.

beard¹ *n* a growth of hair on the lower part of a man's face. ➤ **bearded** *adj*.

beard² *v* to confront boldly or defiantly.

bear down *v* * **bear down on 1** to approach purposefully or threateningly. **2** to weigh heavily on.

bearing *n* **1** a person's manner of standing, moving, or behaving. **2** (*often in pl*) a machine part in which another part turns or slides. **3** the compass direction of a course or of one point with respect to another. **4** (*in pl*) comprehension of one's position or situation. **5** (*usu* + on) connection or relevance to something. **6** an emblem or figure on a heraldic shield.

bear out *v* to confirm or substantiate.

bear up *v* to remain cheerful or resolute in a difficult situation.

beast *n* **1** an animal, *esp* a large or wild animal. **2** a cruel or contemptible person.

beast of burden *n* an animal used to carry loads.

beat¹ *v* (**beat, beaten**) **1** (*often* + up) to hit repeatedly, *esp* so as to inflict pain. **2** to strike repeatedly in order to produce a noise or signal. **3** to mix (food) by stirring. **4** to shape or flatten thin by repeated blows. **5** to overcome or defeat (an opponent). **6** to surpass. **7** of a heart or pulse: to pulsate. **8** *informal* to bewilder or baffle. * **beat about the bush** to fail to come to the point. **beat it** *informal* to hurry away. **beat somebody to it** to act ahead of somebody. **off the beaten track** remote or isolated.

beat² *n* **1** a pulsation or throb. **2** a sound produced by beating. **3** metrical or rhythmic stress in poetry or music. **4** an area patrolled by a police officer.

beat³ *adj informal* exhausted.

beatific

beatific *adj* blissfully happy. ➤ **beatifically** *adv*.

beatify *v* (**-ies, -ied**) to authorize the veneration of (a dead person) by the Roman Catholic Church by giving the title 'Blessed'. ➤ **beatification** *n*.

beatnik *n* in the 1950s and 1960s, a young person who rejected established society.

beat up *v* to assault and harm by repeated punching or kicking.

beat-up *adj informal* dilapidated or worn out.

beau *n* (*pl* **beaux** *or* **beaus**) *chiefly NAmer* a boyfriend.

beautician *n* somebody who gives beauty treatments.

beautiful *adj* **1** producing aesthetic or sensual pleasure. **2** generally enjoyable and good; excellent. ➤ **beautifully** *adv*.

beautify *v* (**-ies, -ied**) to make beautiful.

beauty *n* (*pl* **-ies**) **1** a quality that gives pleasure to the senses. **2** a beautiful woman. **3** a brilliant or extreme example of something. **4** a particularly advantageous or excellent quality.

beaver[1] *n* a large semiaquatic rodent with webbed hind feet and a broad flat tail.

beaver[2] *v* (*also* + away) to work energetically.

becalm *v* (*usu in passive*) to keep (a sailing vessel) motionless by lack of wind.

because *conj* for the reason that; since.

beck[1] *n N Eng* a brook; *esp* a pebbly mountain stream.

beck[2] * **at somebody's beck and call** constantly ready to obey somebody.

beckon *v* **1** to summon or signal somebody to come. **2** to look appealing.

become *v* (**became, become**) **1** to begin to be. **2** to suit or be suitable for. * **become of** to happen to.

becquerel *n* the SI unit of radiation.

bed[1] *n* **1** a piece of furniture for sleeping on. **2** sleep, or a time for sleeping. **3** a plot of ground prepared for plants. **4** the bottom of a body of water. **5** a supporting surface or structure. * **go to bed with** to have sexual intercourse with.

bed[2] *v* (**bedded, bedding**) **1** (*often* + down) to provide with a bed. **2** (*often* + down) to go to bed. **3** (*often* + out) to plant (seedlings, etc) in beds.

bedclothes *pl n* the covers used on a bed.

bedding *n* **1** bedclothes. **2** straw used as a bed for livestock.

bedevil *v* (**bedevilled, bedevilling**, *NAmer* **bedeviled, bedeviling**) to be a continual problem or nuisance to.

bedlam *n* a place or state of uproar and confusion.

bedpan *n* a shallow vessel used as a toilet by a person in bed.

bedraggled *adj* looking limp and untidy.

bedridden *adj* confined to bed by illness or old age.

bedrock *n* **1** a layer of solid rock under the soil. **2** the basis of something.

bedroom *n* a room for sleeping in.

bed-sit *n or* **bed-sitter** *Brit, informal* a rented room used as both a sitting room and bedroom, often also with cooking facilities.

bedsore *n* a sore caused by prolonged pressure on part of the body of a bedridden invalid.

bedspread *n* an ornamental cloth cover for a bed.

bedstead *n* the framework of a bed.

bee *n* a winged insect kept in a hive for the honey that it produces. * **a bee in one's bonnet** an obsessive idea. **the bee's knees** *informal* somebody or something that is outstandingly good.

beech *n* a hardwood deciduous tree with smooth grey bark.

beef[1] *n* **1** meat from a bullock, cow, or bull. **2** (*pl* **beeves**, *NAmer* **beefs**) a full-grown ox, cow, or bull, *esp* when fattened for food. **3** *informal* a complaint.

beef[2] *v* **1** *informal* (*usu* + up) to add weight or strength to. **2** *informal* to complain.

beefburger *n* a hamburger.

beefy *adj* (**-ier, -iest**) brawny or powerful.

beehive *n* a structure for keeping bees.

beeline * **make a beeline for** to hurry directly towards.

Beelzebub *n* the Devil.

been *v* past part. of BE.

beep[1] *n* a sound from a horn or electronic device, that serves as a signal or warning.

beep[2] *v* to make a beep. ➤ **beeper** *n*.

beer *n* an alcoholic drink brewed from fermented malt flavoured with hops.

beeswax *n* a yellowish substance secreted by bees for constructing honeycombs, used as a wood polish.

beet *n* a plant with a swollen root used as a vegetable or a source of sugar.

beetle[1] *n* an insect with hard coverings over its wings.

beetle[2] *v Brit, informal* (*often* + off) to move swiftly.

beetroot *n* (*pl* **beetroots** *or* **beetroot**) *chiefly Brit* a beet with a red edible root used as a vegetable.

befall *v* (**befell, befallen**) of something unwelcome: to affect or happen to.

befit *v* (**befitted, befitting**) to be appropriate or suitable for. ➤ **befitting** *adj*.

before[1] *adv* **1** earlier in time. **2** so as to be in advance of others; ahead.

before[2] *prep* **1** in front of. **2** earlier than. **3** in a higher or more important position than. **4** in preference to.

before[3] *conj* **1** earlier than the time when. **2** rather than.

beforehand *adv and adj* ahead of time.

befriend *v* to seek to be a friend of.

befuddled *adj* muddled or confused.

beg *v* (**begged, begging**) **1** to ask for alms or charity. **2** to ask for earnestly. **3** of a dog: to sit up and hold out its forepaws. ✱ **beg the question** to assume something as established or proved without justification. **go begging** to be available but unwanted.

beget *v* (**begetting, begot,** *archaic* **begat, begotten**) *archaic* **1** to produce (offspring) as the father. **2** to cause (an effect). ➤ **begetter** *n*.

beggar[1] *n* **1** a person who lives by asking for money or food. **2** a very poor person. **3** *informal* a person of a specified kind: *a lucky beggar*
➤ **boggary** *n*

beggar[2] *v* to make very poor.

begin *v* (**beginning, began, begun**) **1** to do the first part of an action; to start. **2** to bring or come into existence. **3** (+ with) to have as a starting point. **4** to come first in. ➤ **beginner** *n*.

begonia *n* a plant with bright flowers, cultivated as an ornamental garden and house plant.

begrudge *v* **1** to give reluctantly. **2** to envy (somebody) the pleasure or enjoyment of something.

beguile *v* to please or charm, often deceptively.

behalf ✱ **on behalf of 1** in the interest of. **2** as a representative of.

behave *v* **1** to act in a specified way. **2** to conduct oneself properly.

behaviour (*NAmer* **behavior**) *n* **1** the way in which a person behaves. **2** the way in which something functions. ➤ **behavioural** *adj*.

behead *v* to execute (somebody) by cutting off their head.

behemoth *n* a huge and monstrous creature.

behest *n* a command or urgent request.

behind[1] *adv* **1** in or towards the back. **2** in a place now departed from. **3** in a secondary or inferior position. **4** (*usu* + in/with) in arrears. **5** (*usu* + with) late.

behind[2] *prep* **1** at or to the rear of. **2** remaining after. **3** obscured by. **4** less advanced than. **5** not keeping up with (a plan or schedule). **6** responsible for (something unwelcome). **7** supporting and helping.

behind[3] *n informal* the buttocks.

behold *v* (*past tense and past part.* **beheld**) to see or admire. ➤ **beholder** *n*.

beholden *adj* (*usu* + to) under an obligation for a favour or gift.

behove *v* to be necessary or advantageous for.

beige *adj* of a yellowish grey colour.

being *n* **1** life or existence. **2** the essential qualities of somebody or something. **3** a living thing; *esp* a person.

bejewelled (*NAmer* **bejeweled**) *adj* decorated with jewels.

belated *adj* delayed beyond the usual time. ➤ **belatedly** *adv*.

belay *n* in mountain climbing, a rope securing a climber.

belch[1] *v* **1** to expel gas from the stomach through the mouth. **2** to emit (smoke, steam, etc) violently.

belch[2] *n* an act of belching.

beleaguer *v* **1** to harass. **2** to besiege. **beleaguered** *adj*.

belfry *n* (*pl* **-ies**) a room in which a bell is hung in the bell tower of a church.

belie *v* (**belies, belied, belying**) **1** to give a false impression of. **2** to show to be false.

belief *n* **1** something widely believed. **2** conviction of the truth or reality of something. **3** trust in somebody or something.

believe *v* **1** to consider (something) to be true or (somebody) to be telling the truth. **2** to have as an opinion. **3** to have a firm religious faith. **4** (*often* + in) to have a firm conviction as to the reality or goodness of something. ➤ **believable** *adj*, **believer** *n*.

Usage Note: Note the spelling *-ie-*.

belittle *v* to undermine the value or importance of.

bell *n* **1** a hollow metallic device that makes a ringing sound when struck. **2** the sound of a bell as a signal. **3** something with the shape of a bell.

belladonna *n* **1** deadly nightshade. **2** an extract of deadly nightshade containing atropine.

belle *n* a beautiful young woman.

bellicose *adj* aggressive and fond of fighting. ➤ **bellicosity** *n*.

belligerence *n* **1** an aggressive attitude or disposition. **2** the state of being at war.

belligerent[1] *adj* **1** engaged in war. **2** aggressive or combative.

belligerent[2] *n* a country or person engaged in war.

bellow[1] *v* **1** to make a loud deep roar. **2** to shout in a deep voice.

bellow[2] *n* **1** a bellowing sound. **2** a loud deep shout.

bellows *pl n* (*treated as sing.*) a device with handles and pleated expandable sides used to create a current of air to fan a fire.

belly[1] *n* (*pl* **-ies**) **1** the abdomen. **2** the undersurface of an animal's body. **3** the stomach and associated organs. **4** an internal cavity; the interior.

belly[2] *v* (**-ies, -ied**) (*often* + out) to swell or fill.

bellyache[1] *n* colic.

bellyache[2] *v informal* to complain peevishly. ➤ **bellyacher** *n*.

belly flop *n* a dive into water in which the front of the body strikes flat against the surface.

belong *v* **1** (+ to) to be somebody's property. **2** to be in a proper situation or position. **3** (+ to) to be attached by birth, allegiance, or membership. **4** (+ to) to be an attribute or function of a person or thing.

belongings *pl n* possessions.

beloved[1] *adj* dearly loved.

beloved[2] *n* a dearly loved person.

below[1] *adv* **1** in or to a lower place or position. **2** lower on the same page or on a following page.

below[2] *prep* **1** lower than the level of. **2** less than. **3** inferior to in rank.

belt[1] *n* **1** a strip of leather or material worn round the waist to hold clothing or a weapon. **2** an endless band of material for transmitting motion and power or conveying objects. **3** an area characterized by some distinctive feature. **4** *informal* a heavy blow. ✳ **below the belt** unfairly. **tighten one's belt** to reduce expenditure. **under one's belt** successfully attained or accomplished. ➤ **belted** *adj*.

belt[2] *v* **1** to fasten with a belt. **2** *informal* to strike or hit hard. **3** *informal* (*usu* + out) to sing in a forceful manner or style. **4** *informal* to move or act vigorously or violently.

belt up *v Brit, informal* to stop talking.

bemoan *v* to express regret or displeasure over.

bemused *adj* confused or bewildered.

bench[1] *n* **1** a long seat for two or more people. **2** (*often* **the Bench**) a judge's seat in court. **3** a long worktable. **4** (**the bench**) seating for substitute players at a sports match.

bench[2] *v* **1** to exhibit (a dog) at a show. **2** *NAmer* to remove (a player) from or keep them out of a game.

benchmark *n* a standard or point of reference.

bend[1] *v* (*past tense and past part.* **bent**) **1** to move into or out of a curve or angle. **2** to make submissive; to subdue. **3** to incline the body, *esp* in submission; to bow. **4** (*often* + to) to yield or compromise. **5** to alter or modify (a rule) to make it more acceptable.

bend[2] *n* **1** a curved part of a road or stream. **2** (**the bends**) (*treated as sing. or pl*) = DECOMPRESSION SICKNESS. ✳ **round the bend** *informal* mad or crazy.

bender *n informal* a drinking spree.

beneath[1] *prep* **1** in or to a lower position than. **2** directly under. **3** not suitable to; unworthy of. **4** under the control or influence of.

beneath[2] *adv* in or to a lower position.

benediction *n* a blessing in public worship.

benefactor *n* a person who gives financial or other aid.

benefice *n* an ecclesiastical office to which an income is attached. ➤ **beneficed** *adj*.

beneficiary[1] *n* (*pl* **-ies**) a person who benefits from the terms of a trust or will.

beneficiary[2] *adj* of a benefice.

benefit[1] *n* **1** an advantage or helpful thing. **2** good or welfare. **3** (*also in pl*) financial help provided by the state to those in need. **4** a

payment provided by a pension scheme or insurance policy. **5** a game or social event to raise funds for a person or cause.

benefit[2] *v* (**benefited, benefiting**) **1** to be useful or profitable to. **2** to receive a benefit.

Usage Note: Note the spellings *benefited* and *benefiting* with one *t*.

benevolent *adj* **1** disposed to do good; charitable. **2** characterized by goodwill. ➤ **benevolence** *n*.

benighted *adj* intellectually, morally, or socially unenlightened.

benign *adj* **1** gentle or gracious. **2** favourable or mild. **3** of a tumour: not malignant.

bent[1] *v* past tense and past part. of BEND[1].

bent[2] *adj* **1** not straight or even; curved. **2** (+ on) determined to. **3** *Brit, informal* corrupt; dishonest.

bent[3] *n* a special talent or interest.

benzene *n* a liquid found in petroleum and used as a solvent.

bequeath *v* **1** to leave (personal property) in a will. **2** to transmit or hand down. ➤ **bequeathal** *n*.

bequest *n* **1** a legacy. **2** the act of bequeathing.

berate *v* to scold or condemn angrily.

bereave *v* (*past part.* **bereaved** *or* **bereft**) (**be bereaved**) to suffer loss by the death of a loved person. ➤ **bereavement** *n*.

bereft *adj* deprived or robbed of; completely without.

beret *n* a round flat cloth cap.

bergamot *n* an essential oil found in some oranges and used as a flavouring.

beriberi *n* a disease caused by a lack of vitamin B1.

berk *n Brit, slang* a stupid person.

berry *n* (*pl* **-ies**) a small, pulpy, edible fruit without a stone.

berserk ✳ **go berserk** to become wildly frenzied.

berth[1] *n* **1** a place for sleeping on a ship or train. **2** a place in a harbour for a ship. ✳ **give a wide berth to** to remain at a safe distance from.

berth[2] *v* **1** of a ship: to dock. **2** to allot a berth to.

beryllium *n* a steel-grey light metallic chemical element.

beseech *v* (**beseeched** *or* **besought**) to ask earnestly or pleadingly.

beset *v* (**besetting**, *past tense and past part.* **beset**) **1** to trouble constantly. **2** to surround and attack.

beside *prep* **1** by the side of. **2** in comparison with. **3** unconnected with. ✳ **beside oneself** extremely agitated or worried.

besides[1] *adv* **1** in addition. **2** moreover.

besides[2] *prep* **1** other than. **2** as an addition to.

besiege *v* **1** to surround with armed forces. **2** to crowd round. **3** to importune with questions or complaints.

besmirch *v* to sully or soil.

besotted *adj* **1** infatuated. **2** drunk or intoxicated.

bespoke *adj* *Brit* made to individual requirements.

best[1] *adj* **1** of the highest quality or most excellent type. **2** most appropriate or advisable. * **the best part of** most of something.

best[2] *adv* **1** in the best manner; to the best extent or degree. **2** as a preference or ideal. * **had best** would be well advised to do something.

best[3] *n* (**the best**) what is most excellent or desirable. * **get the best of** to defeat or get an advantage over. **make the best of** to get some benefit from (an unfavourable situation).

best[4] *v* to outdo or outwit (somebody).

bestial *adj* brutally cruel.

bestiality *n* brutally cruel behaviour.

bestir *v* (**bestirred, bestirring**) to rouse (oneself) to action.

best man *n* a male friend or relative who attends the bridegroom at a wedding.

bestow *v* (*usu* + on/upon) to present as a gift or honour. ➤ **bestowal** *n*.

bestrew *v* (**bestrewed, bestrewed** or **bestrewn**) *literary* **1** to strew (something) somewhere. **2** (+ with) to lie scattered over (a place): *The ground was bestrewn with leaves.*

bestride *v* (**bestrode, bestridden**) **1** to ride or stand astride. **2** to tower over; to dominate.

bestseller *n* a book or other product that achieves a high level of sales. ➤ **bestselling** *adj*.

bet[1] *n* **1** the act of risking a sum of money or other stake on the forecast outcome of a future event, e.g. a race or contest. **2** a stake. **3** an opinion or belief. **4** a person or thing likely to be successful.

bet[2] *v* (**betting, bet** or **betted**) **1** (*usu* + on) to stake (an amount of money) as a bet. **2** to make a bet with. **3** *informal* to be convinced that a guess or prediction) is true.

beta *n* the second letter of the Greek alphabet (B, β).

beta-blocker *n* a drug used to treat high blood pressure.

beta particle *n* an electron or positron emitted from the nucleus of an atom during beta decay: compare ALPHA PARTICLE.

bête noire *n* (*pl* **bêtes noires**) a person or thing strongly detested.

betide *v* * **woe betide** used as a warning of retribution or punishment.

betoken *v* **1** to show. **2** to presage or portend.

betray *v* **1** to give up or reveal (somebody or something) to an enemy by treachery. **2** to be disloyal to. **3** to show (a feeling) inadvertently. **4** to disclose (a secret). ➤ **betrayal** *n*.

betrothed *adj* engaged to be married.

better[1] *adj* **1** of a higher quality. **2** more appropriate or advisable. **3** improved in health; partly or wholly recovered from an illness or injury. * **better off** enjoying better circumstances, *esp* financially. **get the better of** to overcome or defeat.

better[2] *adv* **1** in a way that is more excellent or desirable. **2** to a greater degree; more. * **had better** would be well advised (to do something).

better[3] *v* to surpass or improve on. * **better oneself** to improve one's living conditions or social status.

betterment *n* improvement.

between[1] *prep* **1** in or into the time or space that separates. **2** in intermediate relation to. **3** from one to the other of (two places). **4** through the common action of. **5** in shares to each of. * **between you and me** in confidence.

between[2] *adv* in or into an intermediate space or interval.

betwixt *adv and prep archaic* between. * **betwixt and between** in a midway position; neither one thing nor the other.

bevel[1] *n* a sloping or slanting edge or surface, usu between two other surfaces meeting at right angles.

bevel[2] *v* (**bevelled, bevelling,** NAmer **beveled, beveling**) to cut or shape to a bevel.

beverage *n* a drink.

bevy *n* (*pl* **-ies**) a group of people.

bewail *v* to express deep sorrow for.

beware *v* to be wary of (a threat or danger).

bewilder *v* to perplex or confuse.

bewitch *v* **1** to attract or charm. **2** to cast a spell over.

beyond[1] *prep* **1** on or to the farther side of. **2** out of the reach of. **3** in a degree or amount surpassing. **4** out of the comprehension of.

beyond[2] *adv* on or to the farther side.

beyond[3] *n* (**the beyond**) something that lies outside the scope of ordinary experience; *specif* life after death, the hereafter.

Bi *abbr* the chemical symbol for bismuth.

biannual *adj* occurring twice a year. ➤ **biannually** *adv*.

bias *n* **1** an inclination to favour or disfavour certain people or things. **2** a line diagonal to the grain of a fabric. **3** the tendency of a bowl to take a curved path when rolled.

bias binding *n* a narrow folded strip of fabric cut on the bias used for hemming, to cover raw edges, or for decoration.

biased *adj* or **biassed** having a bias; prejudiced.

biathlon *n* an athletic contest consisting of cross-country skiing and rifle shooting.

bib *n* **1** a cloth or plastic covering placed over a child's front to protect the clothes while it is eating. **2** a small rectangular section of a garment above the waist.

bible n 1 (**the Bible**) the sacred book of Christians, comprising the Old Testament and the New Testament. 2 an authoritative book.

biblical adj of or in accordance with the Bible. ➤ **biblically** adv.

bibliography n (pl -ies) a list of books and articles relating to a particular topic. ➤ **bibliographer** n, **bibliographical** adj.

bibliophile n a collector of books.

bibulous adj prone to over-indulgence in alcoholic drinks.

bicameral adj having two legislative chambers.

bicarbonate n an acid carbonate; esp SODIUM BICARBONATE.

bicentenary n (pl -ies) the celebration of a 200th anniversary.

biceps n a large muscle at the front of the upper arm that bends the arm at the elbow.

bicker v to engage in petty bad-tempered argument.

bicycle[1] n a two-wheeled pedal-driven vehicle with handlebars and a saddle. ➤ **bicyclist** n.

bicycle[2] v to ride a bicycle.

bid[1] v (**bidding, bid** or **bade, bid** or **bidden**) 1 to offer (a price) for payment or acceptance, e.g. at an auction. 2 to make a bid of or in (a suit at cards). 3 to make an attempt to do something. ➤ **bidder** n.

bid[2] n 1 an act of bidding. 2 an offer of a price.

biddable adj easily led or controlled; docile.

biddy n (pl -ies) informal an old woman.

bide v archaic or dialect to remain for a while. * **bide one's time** to wait patiently for an opportunity to act.

bidet n a low basin used for washing the genitals and anus.

biennial adj 1 occurring every two years. 2 of a plant: growing for two years and then dying.

bier n a stand for a corpse or coffin before burial.

biff[1] n informal a whack or blow.

biff[2] v informal to hit sharply or roughly.

bifocal adj of a lens: having one part that corrects for near vision and one for distant vision.

big adj (**bigger, biggest**) 1 large in size, amount, number, or scale. 2 important in influence, standing, or wealth. 3 of a sibling: older or grown-up. 4 of great force or intensity. 5 magnanimous or generous.

bigamy n the crime of marrying while legally married to another person. ➤ **bigamist** n, **bigamous** adj.

big bang n 1 the theoretical explosion of material from which the universe originated. 2 a sudden reorganization or change.

big end n Brit the end of an engine's connecting rod nearest the crankshaft.

big game n large animals hunted or fished for sport.

bighead n informal a conceited person. ➤ **bigheaded** adj.

bigot n an unpleasantly prejudiced and intolerant person. ➤ **bigoted** adj, **bigotry** n.

big top n the main tent of a circus.

bigwig n informal an important person.

bijou adj small and attractively elegant.

bike[1] n informal a bicycle or motorcycle.

bike[2] v to ride a bicycle or motorcycle.

biker n a member of a gang of motorcyclists.

bikini n a woman's two-piece swimsuit.

bilateral adj having two sides or parts.

bilberry n (pl -ies) a bluish edible soft fruit.

bile n 1 a fluid secreted by the liver to aid the digestion of fats. 2 a tendency to become angry.

bilge n 1 the lowest part of a ship's hull. 2 informal nonsense.

bilingual adj 1 able to use two languages fluently. 2 expressed in two languages.

bilious adj 1 suffering from a feeling of nausea. 2 relating to bile.

bilk v to cheat by swindling.

bill[1] n 1 an itemized statement of charges. 2 a draft of a law presented to a law-making body. 3 a programme of entertainment in a theatre or cinema. 4 chiefly NAmer a banknote. * **fill/fit the bill** to be suitable.

bill[2] v 1 to submit a bill of charges to. 2 (+ as) to announce or proclaim to be something.

bill[3] n 1 the beak of a bird. 2 a narrow piece of land projecting into the sea.

bill[4] v * **bill and coo** to caress and talk lovingly.

billboard n chiefly NAmer a large board for advertisements.

billet[1] n a private home where soldiers are given board and lodging.

billet[2] v (**billeted, billeting**) (often + on) to provide (soldiers) with a billet.

billet-doux /ˌbili'dooh, ˌbeeyay/ n (pl **billets-doux**) a love letter.

billhook n a pruning tool having a blade with a hooked point.

billiards n a game played with three balls, in which scores are made by causing the cue ball to hit the other two balls in succession.

billing n the relative prominence given to each performer in advertising programmes.

billion n a thousand millions or 1,000,000,000 (10^9). ➤ **billionth** adj and n.

billionaire n somebody whose wealth is estimated at a billion or more pounds or dollars.

billow[1] n 1 a large wave in the open sea. 2 a swirling mass of flame or smoke.

billow[2] v to rise or swell out in billows.

billy n (pl -ies) a metal can with a handle and lid, used for outdoor cooking.

billy goat n informal a male goat.

bimbo n (pl -os) informal, derog an attractive but unintelligent young woman.

bin[1] n 1 Brit a container for rubbish. 2 a large container used for storage.

bin² v (**binned, binning**) to discard or throw away.

binary adj 1 relating to a system of numbers that has two as its base and uses only the digits 0 and 1. 2 involving a choice of two alternatives (e.g. on or off). 3 consisting of two things or parts.

bind¹ v (past tense and past part. **bound**) 1 (also + up) to tie together, or make secure by tying. 2 to put under an obligation or legal requirement. 3 (often + up) to enclose by wrapping something round. 4 to stick together. 5 to strengthen or decorate with a band or binding. 6 to apply a binding to (a book). 7 to form a cohesive mass. 8 to become unable to move or operate freely.

bind² n informal a nuisance or annoyance.

binder n 1 a cover for holding sheets of paper. 2 a person who binds books. 3 a harvesting machine that binds straw into bundles.

bindi n (pl **bindis**) a decorative mark in the middle of the forehead, worn by Indian women.

binding¹ n 1 a covering that fastens the leaves of a book together. 2 a narrow strip of fabric used to finish raw edges.

binding² adj (often + on) imposing an obligation.

bind over v to impose a specific legal obligation on.

bindweed n a twining plant such as convolvulus.

binge¹ n informal a period of excessive eating or drinking.

binge² v (**binged, bingeing**) informal to eat or drink excessively.

bingo¹ interj used to express sudden success or welcome surprise.

bingo² n a game in which players mark off numbers on a card as they are randomly called out, the winner being the first to complete a card.

binocular adj relating to or using both eyes.

biobank n a collection of genetic material established to facilitate research, esp into genetic links to disease.

biochemistry n the study of the chemical processes in living organisms. ➤ **biochemical** adj, **biochemist** n.

biodegradable adj capable of being broken down into simpler harmless products by the action of bacteria and other living organisms.

biodiversity n the variety of living species in the world or a particular environment.

biofeedback n the technique of making involuntary bodily processes perceptible to the senses so that they can be affected by conscious mental control.

biography n (pl **-ies**) 1 an account of a person's life. 2 biographical writing as a literary genre. ➤ **biographer** n, **biographical** adj.

biological adj 1 relating to biology or living organisms. 2 acting on or produced by living organisms. 3 of a detergent: containing an enzyme. ➤ **biologically** adv.

biology n the study of the life processes of living organisms. ➤ **biologist** n.

biometric adj 1 relating to records of a person's fingerprints, iris image, voice pattern, etc. 2 relating to the use of such data as a means of identification, as in an identify card.

bionic adj 1 of an artificial body part: designed to replace or simulate a living part. 2 informal having exceptional powers.

biopsy n (pl **-ies**) the removal and examination of tissue from the living body.

biorhythm n (usu in pl) a periodic cycle of biological activity affecting mood and behaviour. ➤ **biorhythmic** adj.

bipartite adj 1 consisting of two parts. 2 affecting both parties to a treaty.

biped n a two-footed animal. ➤ **bipedal** adj.

biplane n an aeroplane with two pairs of wings, one above the other.

bipolar adj 1 having positive and negative electrical poles. 2 characterized by two opposed statements or views. ➤ **bipolarity** n.

birch¹ n 1 a deciduous tree with a thin bark that peels readily. 2 (**the birch**) punishment by flogging with a bundle of birch twigs.

birch² v to flog with a birch.

bird n 1 an animal with feathers, a beak, and wings, laying eggs and usually able to fly. 2 chiefly Brit, informal a girlfriend or young woman. * **the birds and the bees** informal the facts of sex and sexual reproduction.

birdie n 1 a small bird. 2 a golf score of one stroke less than par on a hole.

bird of prey n a bird that feeds on carrion or on meat taken by hunting.

bird's-eye view n a view from above.

Biro n (pl **-os**) trademark a kind of ballpoint pen.

birth n 1 the emergence of a new individual from the body of its parent. 2 family origin and social status. 3 a beginning or start. * **give birth** to produce a baby as a mother.

birth control n use of contraception and other means to control the number of children born.

birthday n an anniversary of the day a person was born.

birthmark n a blemish existing on the skin at birth.

birthrate n the number of live births per unit of population.

birthright n something to which a person is entitled by being born into a particular family, nation, etc.

biscuit n 1 Brit a small flat crisp sweet or savoury cake. 2 a light yellowish brown colour.

bisect v to divide into two parts. ➤ **bisection** n.

bisexual¹ *adj* **1** sexually attracted to both sexes. **2** possessing characteristics of both sexes. ➤ **bisexuality** *n*.

bisexual² *n* a bisexual person.

bishop *n* **1** a senior member of the Christian clergy, typically governing a diocese. **2** a chess piece that moves diagonally across the board.

bismuth *n* a heavy brittle reddish white metallic element used in alloys.

bison *n* (*pl* **bison**) a large ox with a shaggy mane and a humped back.

bistro *n* (*pl* **-os**) a small bar or restaurant.

bit¹ *n* **1** a small piece or quantity of something. **2** (**a bit**) a short period or distance. **3** a small coin. * **a bit** *informal* somewhat; rather. **bit by bit** by small amounts. **bits and pieces/bobs** miscellaneous things of little value. **do one's bit** *Brit* to make one's personal contribution to a task or cause.

bit² *n* a unit of computer information corresponding to a choice between two alternatives (e.g. *on* or *off*).

bit³ *n* **1** a bar of metal attached to a horse's bridle and inserted in its mouth. **2** a piece of a tool for drilling or boring. **have the bit between one's teeth** to act with determination.

bit⁴ *v* past tense and past part. of BITE¹.

bitch¹ *n* **1** a female dog. **2** *slang* a spiteful and domineering woman. **3** *informal* something difficult or unpleasant.

bitch² *v informal* **1** to make malicious or spiteful comments. **2** to complain.

bitchy *adj* (**-ier, -iest**) *informal* malicious or spiteful. ➤ **bitchiness** *n*.

bite¹ *v* (**bit, bitten**) **1** to seize or cut into with the teeth or jaws. **2** to sting with a fang or other specialized part of the body. **3** to take a strong hold of; to grip. **4** to have an effect. * **be bitten by/with something** to have great enthusiasm for. **bite somebody's head off** to speak to or scold somebody angrily. **bite the bullet** to endure stoically something unpleasant that cannot be avoided. **bite the dust 1** to fall dead, *esp* in a fight. **2** to collapse or be destroyed.

bite² *n* **1** an act of biting. **2** a wound made by biting. **3** the amount of food taken with one bite. **4** a strong grip. **5** sharpness or pungency of taste.

biting *adj* **1** of a wind: strong and intensely cold. **2** of a remark: unkind or sarcastic.

bit part *n* a minor acting role.

bitter¹ *adj* **1** having a sharp or sour taste. **2** intense or severe. **3** showing or stemming from great dislike or resentment. **4** of a wind: intensely cold. **5** characterized by or causing severe grief or regret. ➤ **bitterly** *adv*, **bitterness** *n*.

bitter² *n Brit* a bitter beer heavily flavoured with hops.

bittersweet *adj* **1** bitter and sweet at the same time. **2** pleasant but with elements of sadness.

bitty *adj* (**-ier, -iest**) scrappy or disjointed. ➤ **bittily** *adv*.

bitumen *n* tar or other black sticky substance obtained from petroleum and used in surfacing roads. ➤ **bituminous** *adj*.

bivalve *n* an aquatic mollusc having a shell composed of two valves.

bivouac¹ *n* a temporary encampment under little or no shelter.

bivouac² *v* (**bivouacked, bivouacking**) to camp in a bivouac.

bizarre *adj* odd or eccentric. ➤ **bizarrely** *adv*.

Bk *abbr* the chemical symbol for berkelium.

blab¹ *v* (**blabbed, blabbing**) **1** to reveal (a secret). **2** to talk indiscreetly or thoughtlessly. ➤ **blabber** *n*.

blab² *n* somebody who blabs.

blabber *v* (**blabbered, blabbering**) **1** to babble. **2** to talk indiscreetly.

black¹ *adj* **1** of the darkest colour. **2** relating to people having dark skin pigmentation. **3** of coffee or tea: served without milk or cream. **4** sinister or evil. **5** indicative of hostility or disapproval. **6** showing a financial profit: compare RED¹. **7** characterized by grim or grotesque humour. ➤ **blackness** *n*.

black² *n* **1** a black colour. **2** a black person. * **in the black** financially in credit.

black³ *v* **1** to make black. **2** *chiefly Brit* to declare (e.g. a business or industry) subject to boycott by trade-union members.

black-and-blue *adj* darkly discoloured from bruising.

black-and-white *adj* **1** reproducing visual images in black, white, and tones of grey. **2** evaluating things in extremes.

blackball *v* **1** to vote against (a candidate for membership). **2** to ostracize.

black belt *n* a black belt worn by an expert in a martial art.

blackberry *n* (*pl* **-ies**) a black edible fruit that grows on a prickly shrub.

blackbird *n* a bird with black feathers and an orange beak.

blackboard *n* a hard smooth board used for writing on with chalk.

black box *n* an aircraft's flight recorder.

blackcurrant *n* a small black edible soft fruit.

black economy *n* illegal or unofficial business activity.

blacken *v* **1** to make or become black. **2** to injure or destroy (somebody's reputation).

black eye *n* an area of bruising round the eye.

blackfly *n* a small dark-coloured insect that feeds on plants.

blackguard *n* a coarse or unscrupulous person; a scoundrel.

blackhead *n* a small dark-coloured oily plug blocking a pore on the face.

black hole *n* an area in space with an intense gravitational field, from which no radiation can escape.

black ice *n Brit* transparent slippery ice on a road.

blackleg *n chiefly Brit* a worker who continues working during an official strike.

blacklist[1] *n* a list of people or organizations who are disapproved of or are to be boycotted.

blacklist[2] *v* to put on a blacklist.

black magic *n* magic performed by invoking evil spirits.

blackmail[1] *n* **1** extortion with the threat of exposing secret or compromising information. **2** political or moral pressure to do something undesirable.

blackmail[2] *v* to subject to blackmail. ➤ **blackmailer** *n*.

black mark *n* a mark of censure or disapproval.

black market *n* illicit trade in violation of official regulations. ➤ **black marketeer** *n*.

blackout *n* **1** a period of darkness enforced as a precaution against air raids. **2** a sudden loss of electrical power. **3** a temporary loss of consciousness. **4** a holding back or suppression of something. **5** a brief loss of radio signal.

black out *v* to become unconscious.

black pudding *n chiefly Brit* a dark sausage made from suet and pigs' blood.

black sheep *n* a disreputable member of a family or organization.

blacksmith *n* somebody who works iron at a forge. ➤ **blacksmithing** *n*.

black spot *n Brit* a stretch of road on which accidents occur frequently.

blackthorn *n* a spiny shrub with hard wood and small white flowers.

black widow *n* a venomous spider of which the female is black with a red mark on the underside.

bladder *n* **1** a sac in animals in which urine collects before being discharged. **2** an air-filled rubber bag inside a ball.

blade *n* **1** the cutting part of a knife, razor, or other tool. **2** a long narrow leaf of a grass or cereal. **3** the runner of an ice skate. **4** the broad flattened part of an oar, paddle, bat, propeller, etc.

blag *v* (**blagged, blagging**) **1** *Brit, informal* to rob with violence. **2** to steal. **3** to bluff. ➤ **blagger** *n*.

blame[1] *v* **1** to hold responsible for wrongdoing or misfortune. **2** to find fault with.

blame[2] *n* **1** responsibility for wrongdoing or misfortune. **2** disapproval or reproach. ➤ **blameless** *adj*, **blameworthy** *adj*.

blanch *v* **1** to make or become pale. **2** to scald (almonds) to remove the skin. **3** to prepare (vegetables) by plunging them briefly in boiling water.

blancmange *n* a sweetened and flavoured dessert made from cornflour and milk.

bland *adj* **1** without character or excitement; dull or insipid. **2** of food: with little flavour or texture. **3** showing no emotion or anxiety.

blandishments *pl n* pleasing things said to coax or flatter somebody.

blank[1] *adj* **1** with nothing marked, written, or recorded on it. **2** not filled in. **3** dazed or nonplussed. **4** showing no expression. **5** temporarily without memory or understanding. **6** absolute or unqualified. ➤ **blankly** *adv*, **blankness** *n*.

blank[2] *n* **1** an empty space to be filled in on a form. **2** a void, without thought, memory, or understanding. **3** a vacant or uneventful period. **4** a piece of material prepared to be made into something, e.g. a key or coin. **5** a gun cartridge containing powder but no bullet. ✱ **draw a blank** to obtain no positive results.

blanket[1] *n* **1** a large thick piece of fabric used as a warm covering. **2** a thick covering or layer.

blanket[2] *v* (**blanketed, blanketing**) to cover with a thick layer.

blanket[3] *adj* applying generally.

blank out *v* to hide or erase.

blank verse *n* verse with no rhyme.

blare[1] *v* **1** to emit a loud harsh sound. **2** to proclaim loudly or sensationally.

blare[2] *n* a loud harsh sound.

blarney *n* **1** pleasing but insincere talk or flattery. **2** nonsense.

blasé /'blahzay/ *adj* indifferent to pleasure or excitement because of over-familiarity.

blaspheme *v* to use a holy or sacred name with impiety. ➤ **blasphemer** *n*.

blasphemy *n* (*pl* **-ies**) disrespect for a holy or sacred name. ➤ **blasphemous** *adj*.

blast[1] *n* **1** an explosion or violent detonation. **2** a violent wave of increased atmospheric pressure produced by this. **3** a strong gust of wind. **4** a violent outburst. **5** the sound made by a wind instrument or whistle. ✱ **at full blast** at top speed or full capacity.

blast[2] *v* **1** to shatter, remove, or open with an explosive. **2** to destroy (hopes, etc). **3** to curse or denounce.

blast[3] *interj Brit, informal* used to express annoyance.

blast furnace *n* a furnace for converting iron ore into iron, using currents of air under pressure.

blast off *v* of a spacecraft or missile: to leave the launching pad.

blatant *adj* obvious and unashamed. ➤ **blatancy** *n*, **blatantly** *adv*.

blather[1] *n* foolish voluble talk.

blather[2] *v* (**blathered, blathering**) to talk foolishly or volubly. ➤ **blatherer** *n*.

blaze[1] *n* **1** an intensely burning flame or fire. **2** intense direct light. **3** a dazzling display. **4** a sudden outburst. * **like blazes** *informal* intensely.

blaze² *v* **1** to burn or shine strongly. **2** to be conspicuously brilliant. **3** (+ away) to shoot rapidly and repeatedly.

blaze³ *n* a broad white mark on a horse's face.

blaze⁴ *v* * **blaze a trail 1** to mark out a path or way. **2** to lead or be a pioneer in some activity.

blazer *n* a jacket with patch pockets, worn for casual wear or as part of a school uniform.

blazon *v* to proclaim widely and ostentatiously.

bleach¹ *v* to make whiter or remove the colour from (e.g. fabric) by chemical or physical means.

bleach² *n* a strong chemical substance used in bleaching.

bleak *adj* **1** barren and exposed. **2** cold or raw. **3** lacking in warmth or kindness. **4** of circumstances: not hopeful or encouraging. **5** severely simple or austere. ➤ **bleakly** *adv*, **bleakness** *n*.

bleary *adj* (-ier, -iest) **1** of the eyes or vision: dull and indistinct from fatigue or sleep. **2** poorly outlined or defined. ➤ **blearily** *adv*.

bleat¹ *v* **1** to make the cry of a sheep or goat. **2** to talk complainingly or feebly.

bleat² *n* the cry of a sheep or goat.

bleed¹ *v* (*past tense and past part.* **bled**) **1** to emit or lose blood. **2** formerly in medicine, to remove or draw blood from. **3** (+ for) to feel anguish, pain, or sympathy. **4** of colour or dye: to flow over into an adjoining area. **5** to extort money from. **6** to drain the vitality or lifeblood from. **7** to let out liquid or gas from (a container).

bleed² *n* an act or instance of bleeding.

bleep¹ *n* a short high-pitched sound made by an electronic device.

bleep² *v* **1** to emit a bleep. **2** to summon by means of a bleeping device. ➤ **bleeper** *n*.

blemish¹ *n* **1** a flaw or disfiguring mark. **2** a defect of character.

blemish² *v* to spoil the appearance of.

blench *v* to draw back or flinch from fear or pain.

blend¹ *v* **1** to mix or combine separate constituents. **2** (*often* + in) to produce a harmonious effect.

blend² *n* a mixture.

blender *n* an electrical device for grinding or mixing food.

bless *v* **1** to consecrate by a prayer or religious rite. **2** to invoke divine care for. **3** to confer prosperity or happiness on.

blessed *adj* **1** holy and venerated. **2** bringing pleasure or contentment. ➤ **blessedly** *adv*.

blessing *n* **1** the invocation of God's favour upon a person. **2** the words used in this. **3** approval or moral support. **4** something conducive to happiness or welfare.

blew *v* past tense of BLOW¹.

blight¹ *n* **1** a disease of plants resulting in withering. **2** something that impairs or destroys. **3** a condition of disorder or decay.

blight² *v* **1** to affect (e.g. a plant) with blight. **2** to impair or destroy.

blighter *n* *chiefly Brit, informal* a troublesome or unfortunate person or thing.

blind¹ *adj* **1** unable to see. **2** (*often* + to) unable to perceive clearly or judge rationally. **3** acting or done without adequate knowledge or judgment. **4** having only one opening or outlet. * **turn a blind eye** to overlook mistakes or wrongdoing. ➤ **blindly** *adv*, **blindness** *n*.

blind² *v* **1** to make blind. **2** (*often* + to) to rob of judgment or discernment.

blind³ *n* **1** a flexible screen for covering a window. **2** a cover or subterfuge.

blind date *n* a date between people who have not previously met.

blindfold¹ *v* to cover the eyes of (somebody) with a piece of material.

blindfold² *n* a piece of cloth tied around a person's head to prevent them from seeing.

blindfold³ *adj and adv* wearing a blindfold.

blinding *adj* **1** of light: overpoweringly bright. **2** extremely obvious. ➤ **blindingly** *adv*.

blindman's buff *n* a game in which a blind-folded player tries to catch other players.

blind spot *n* **1** a point in the retina of the eye that is not sensitive to light. **2** a part of a visual field that cannot be seen. **3** an area in which one lacks knowledge or discrimination.

blink¹ *v* **1** to close and open the eyes rapidly or involuntarily. **2** to shine intermittently.

blink² *n* an act of blinking. * **on the blink** *informal* not working properly.

blinker¹ *n* **1** a warning or signalling light that flashes on and off. **2** (*in pl*) something that restricts understanding or awareness. **3** *chiefly Brit* each of two flaps over a horse's eyes to prevent it from seeing to the sides.

blinker² *v* **1** to put blinkers on (a horse). **2** to restrict or lessen the understanding or awareness of. ➤ **blinkered** *adj*.

blip¹ *n* **1** a bleep. **2** an image on a radar screen. **3** a brief deviation from the norm; an aberration.

blip² *v* (**blipped, blipping**) to deviate briefly from the norm.

bliss *n* complete happiness. ➤ **blissful** *adj*, **blissfully** *adv*.

blister¹ *n* **1** a raised part of the outer skin containing watery liquid. **2** a bubble or raised spot on a surface.

blister² *v* to be affected with blisters.

blistering *adj* **1** of heat: extremely intense or severe. **2** of speed: extremely fast.

blithe *adj* **1** cheerful and light-hearted. **2** casual or heedless. ➤ **blithely** *adv*.

blithering *adj informal* **1** stupid. **2** talking nonsense.

blitz[1] n **1** an intensive aerial bombardment. **2** a period of intensive action.

blitz[2] v **1** to attack in a blitz. **2** to deal with by intensive action.

blizzard n a severe snowstorm with a strong wind.

bloat v to swell with gas or liquid. ➤ **bloated** adj.

bloater n a salted smoked herring or mackerel.

blob n **1** a small drop of a sticky substance. **2** an amorphous shape. ➤ **blobby** adj.

bloc n an alliance of nations for a common purpose.

block[1] n **1** a large building divided into separate functional units. **2** a rectangular area of buildings enclosed by streets. **3** a compact solid piece of material. **4** an obstacle or blockage.

block[2] v **1** to be a barrier that obstructs (a passage, road, pipe, etc.). **2** to hinder the movement or progress of.

blockade[1] n the surrounding of an enemy area to prevent people and supplies from passing in and out.

blockade[2] v to subject to a blockade.

blockage n something that causes something to be blocked.

blockbuster n informal something particularly outstanding or effective.

block capitals pl n plain capital letters.

bloke n chiefly Brit, informal a man.

blonde[1] or **blond** adj **1** esp of hair: golden or pale yellow. **2** having blonde hair.

blonde[2] or **blond** n a woman with blonde hair.

blood[1] n **1** the red fluid that circulates in the arteries and veins of a vertebrate animal. **2** family background; ancestors. * **in one's blood** part of a person's character or life. **one's blood is up** one is ready for a fight.

blood[2] v to give an initiating experience to.

bloodbath n a slaughter or massacre.

blood-curdling adj horrifying.

blood group n any of the classes by which human blood is classified.

bloodhound n a large hound used for tracking and following a scent.

bloodless adj **1** without the shedding of blood. **2** lacking in spirit or vitality. **3** of the complexion: pale from lack of blood.

bloodletting n **1** the draining of blood as a former medical treatment. **2** conflict with bloodshed.

blood pressure n the pressure exerted by the blood as it passes through blood vessels.

bloodshed n the killing or injuring of people.

bloodshot adj of an eye: having the white part tinged with red.

blood sport n a sport in which animals are hunted or killed.

bloodstream n the blood circulating in the body.

bloodthirsty adj eager for bloodshed.

blood vessel n any of the veins, arteries, or capillaries through which the blood circulates.

bloody[1] adj (-ier, -iest) **1** covered with blood. **2** involving bloodshed. **3** murderous or bloodthirsty. **4** informal used to express annoyance.

bloody[2] v (-ies, -ied) to cover or mark with blood.

bloody-minded adj obstructive and unhelpful.

bloom[1] n **1** a flower. **2** the state of having flowers. **3** a time of freshness and vigour. **4** a rosy or healthy complexion. **5** a light coating on some fruits and leaves.

bloom[2] v **1** to produce flowers. **2** to support abundant plant life. **3** to flourish.

bloom[3] n a thick bar of hammered or rolled iron or steel.

bloomer n **1** informal a foolish blunder. **2** chiefly Brit a long loaf marked with diagonal cuts.

bloomers pl n **1** a former women's costume consisting of a short skirt and loose trousers gathered at the ankles. **2** women's full loose knickers.

blossom[1] n **1** the flower of a plant. **2** the mass of flowers on a tree or shrub.

blossom[2] v (blossomed, blossoming) **1** to bloom. **2** to develop or flourish.

blot[1] n **1** a spot of ink or other liquid. **2** a fault or bad act.

blot[2] v (blotted, blotting) **1** to spot or stain. **2** to dry with an absorbent material. **3** to spoil (one's reputation) by committing an error or wrongdoing. * **blot one's copybook** to spoil a good record or reputation.

blotch[1] n an irregular spot or mark. ➤ **blotchy** adj.

blotch[2] v to mark with blotches.

blot out v **1** to obscure or eclipse. **2** to exclude from one's mind.

blotter n a piece of blotting paper.

blotting paper n absorbent paper for drying or soaking up ink.

blouse[1] n a loose-fitting woman's upper garment like a shirt.

blouse[2] v **1** to fall in folds. **2** to make (e.g. a piece of clothing) fall in folds.

blouson n a short loose jacket gathered at the waist.

blow[1] v (blew, blown) **1** of air or wind: to move perceptibly. **2** to send a current of air through the mouth or nose. **3** to force air through (a musical instrument) to produce a sound. **4** of a tyre: to burst and lose the air inside it. **5** of a fuse: to break when overloaded. **6** informal to explode or detonate. **7** to burst or destroy with explosives. **8** to shape (e.g. glass or bubbles) by the action of blown air. **9** informal to waste (a chance of success). **10** informal to spend (money) extravagantly. **11** informal to reveal (a secret or disguise). **12** *informal* to leave hurriedly. ✳ **blow hot and cold** to vary unpredictably in one's support for something; to vacillate. **blow one's own trumpet** to boast. **blow one's top** *informal* to lose one's temper.

blow² *n* **1** an act of blowing. **2** a strong wind or windy storm.

blow³ *n* **1** a hard hit delivered with the hand or a weapon. **2** a shock or misfortune. ✳ **come to blows** to start fighting; to end up as a fight.

blowfly *n* (*pl* **-ies**) a fly that deposits eggs in meat.

blowhole *n* a nostril in the top of the head of a whale or dolphin.

blowout *n* **1** *informal* a large meal or other lavish entertainment. **2** the bursting of a tyre or fuse. **3** an uncontrolled eruption of an oil or gas well.

blow over *v* of a difficulty: to pass without harm.

blowsy *or* **blowzy** *adj* (**-ier**, **-iest**) *esp* of a woman: slovenly and overweight.

blowtorch *or* **blowlamp** *n* a portable burner that produces an intense flame.

blow up *v* **1** to shatter or destroy by an explosion. **2** to exaggerate. **3** to inflate with air or gas. **4** to enlarge (a photograph). ➤ **blowup** *n*.

blowy *adj* (**-ier**, **-iest**) windy.

blub *v* (**blubbed**, **blubbing**) *informal* to sob uncontrollably.

blubber¹ *n* **1** the fat of whales and seals. **2** *informal* body fat. ➤ **blubbery** *adj*.

blubber² *v informal* to sob uncontrollably.

bludgeon¹ *n* a heavy club used as a weapon.

bludgeon² *v* **1** to hit or beat with a bludgeon. **2** (*also* + into) to force (somebody) to do something.

blue¹ *adj* **1** of the colour of a clear sky. **2** low in spirits. **3** depressing or dismal. **4** indecent or pornographic. **5** *Brit* politically conservative. ✳ **once in a blue moon** very rarely.

blue² *v* (**blues**, **blued**, **blueing** *or* **bluing**) *Brit, informal* to spend (money) wastefully.

bluebell *n* a plant with blue bell-shaped flowers.

blueberry *n* (*pl* **-ies**) a dark blue fruit produced by a shrub of the heath family.

blue blood *n* high or noble birth. ➤ **blue-blooded** *adj*.

bluebottle *n* a large fly with an iridescent blue body.

blue cheese *n* cheese marked with veins of mould.

blue chip *n* a high-quality stock that is a sound investment. ➤ **blue-chip** *adj*.

blue-collar *adj* relating to manual work and workers.

blueprint¹ *n* **1** a plan or drawing done in white on a blue background. **2** a programme of action.

blueprint² *v* **1** to make a blueprint of (a plan, etc). **2** to plan out (a programme of action).

blues *n* (*pl* **blues**) **1** (**the blues**) low spirits; melancholy. **2** (*often* **the blues**) a melancholy style of music which originated among American blacks. ➤ **bluesy** *adj*.

bluestocking *n derog* a woman with intellectual or literary interests.

blue tit *n* a bird with a bright blue crown and yellow underside.

blue whale *n* a large bluish whale found *esp* in northern European waters.

bluff¹ *v* to deceive by a pretence of strength or confidence.

bluff² *n* an act or instance of bluffing. ✳ **call somebody's bluff** to challenge (somebody) to prove a claim one believes to be untrue.

bluff³ *adj* good-naturedly frank and outspoken.

bluff⁴ *n* a high steep bank or cliff.

blunder¹ *v* **1** to move unsteadily or confusedly. **2** to make a blunder.

blunder² *n* a careless or clumsy mistake.

blunderbuss *n* an obsolete short gun with a a flared muzzle.

blunt¹ *adj* **1** without a sharp edge or point. **2** direct and straightforward in manner. ➤ **bluntly** *adv*.

blunt² *v* to make or become blunt.

blur¹ *n* **1** something vague or indistinct. **2** a smear or stain. ➤ **blurry** *adj*.

blur² *v* (**blurred**, **blurring**) to make or become indistinct or confused.

blurt out *v* to say abruptly and impulsively.

blush¹ *v* to become red in the face from modesty or embarrassment.

blush² *n* **1** an instance of blushing. **2** a red or rosy tint.

blusher *n* a cream or powder for adding colour to the cheeks.

bluster¹ *v* **1** to talk or act in a showy manner. **2** of wind or rain: to blow in stormy gusts. ➤ **blustery** *adj*.

bluster² *n* loud boastful or threatening talk.

boa *n* **1** a large snake that crushes its prey. **2** a long fluffy stole of fur or feathers.

boa constrictor *n* a large American boa.

boar *n* **1** a male pig. **2** a wild pig with large tusks.

board¹ *n* **1** a long thin narrow piece of sawn timber. **2** a flat piece of material with a surface designed for a special purpose. **3** a group of people managing an organization or enterprise. **4** provision of daily meals. ✳ **go by the board** to be rejected or overlooked. **on board** aboard.

board² *v* **1** to go aboard a ship, train, aircraft, or vehicle. **2** to come alongside and attack (a ship). **3** (+ over/up) to cover with boards. **4** to live in school as a boarder.

boarder *n* a resident pupil at a boarding school.

board game *n* a game that is played by moving pieces on a special board.

boarding house *n* a lodging house that supplies meals.

boarding school *n* a school at which meals and lodging are provided.

boardroom *n* a room in which a board of directors meets.

boast[1] *n* an act of self-praise. ➤ **boastful** *adj*, **boastfully** *adv*, **boastfulness** *n*.

boast[2] *v* 1 to praise oneself or one's achievements openly. 2 to have or display as a source of pride.

boat *n* 1 a small open vessel for travelling across water. 2 a boat-shaped dish. ✻ **in the same boat** in the same situation.

boater *n* a straw hat with a flat crown and a brim.

boatswain or **bosun** or **bo's'n** *n* an officer responsible for maintenance and equipment on a ship.

bob[1] *v* (**bobbed, bobbing**) 1 to move repeatedly up and down. 2 to curtsy briefly.

bob[2] *n* a short quick bobbing movement.

bob[3] *n* 1 a short straight hanging hairstyle for women. 2 a hanging ball or weight on a plumb line or kite's tail.

bob[4] *v* (**bobbed, bobbing**) to cut (hair) in a bob.

bob[5] *n* (*pl* **bob**) *Brit, informal* a shilling.

bobbin *n* a cylinder or spindle for holding yarn or thread.

bobble *n* a small fluffy ball made from pieces of wool.

bobby *n* (*pl* **-ies**) *Brit, informal, dated* a police officer.

bobsleigh *n chiefly Brit* a sledge used for racing down an ice-covered slope.

bode *v* ✻ **bode ill/well** to be a bad or good sign for the future.

bodge *v Brit, informal* to make or repair clumsily.

bodice *n* 1 the upper part of a woman's dress. 2 formerly, a woman's corset-like undergarment.

bodily[1] *adj* 1 relating to the body. 2 physical or actual, as distinct from spiritual.

bodily[2] *adv* 1 involving the whole body. 2 in bodily form; in the flesh.

bodkin *n* a blunt thick needle with a large eye.

body *n* (*pl* **-ies**) 1 the physical structure of a person or animal. 2 a corpse. 3 the main part of a human or animal body. 4 the main part of a building. 5 an expanse of water. 6 a star or planet. 7 a material object. 8 a group of people or things working or acting together. 9 firmness or fullness of texture or substance.

body bag *n* a bag in which a dead body is placed for transportation.

body blow *n* 1 a hard punch on the body. 2 a serious setback.

body-building *n* strengthening the body and developing a muscular physique. ➤ **body-builder** *n*.

bodyguard *n* an escort who protects a person from bodily harm.

body language *n* the unconscious expressing of feelings by looks and movements.

body shop *n* a workshop where bodywork of vehicles is repaired.

body stocking *n* a light one-piece garment covering the trunk.

bodywork *n* the outer structure of a vehicle.

Boer /'bawə, 'boh-ə/ *n* a South African of Dutch descent.

boffin *n chiefly Brit, informal* a scientist or technical expert.

bog *n* an area of wet spongy ground. ➤ **boggy** *adj*.

bog down *v* 1 to cause (a vehicle) to sink into soft ground. 2 to hinder with complications or obstructions.

bogey or **bogy** *n* (*pl* **-eys** or **-ies**) 1 a golf score of one stroke over par on a hole. 2 a spectre or ghost. 3 a source of recurring fear. 4 *Brit, informal* a piece of dried nasal mucus.

bogeyman or **bogyman** *n* (*pl* **bogeymen** or **bogymen**) a frightening evil spirit.

boggle *v informal* (+ at) to hesitate from fear or scruples. ✻ **the mind boggles** used in mock bewilderment or ironic speculation: goodness knows.

bogie or **bogy** *n* (*pl* **-ies**) *chiefly Brit* a swivelling framework with one or more pairs of wheels and springs to carry and guide one end of a railway vehicle.

bogus *adj* spurious or sham.

Bohemian *n* a writer or artist living an unconventional life. ➤ **Bohemian** *adj*.

boil[1] *v* 1 of a fluid: to reach a temperature at which it bubbles and changes into vapour. 2 to cook (food) in boiling water. 3 to heat (a vessel) until its contents boil. ✻ **boil down to** to amount in essence to.

boil[2] *n* (**the boil**) the act or state of boiling; boiling point.

boil[3] *n* a pus-filled swelling of the skin.

boiler *n* a tank in which water is heated and stored.

boiler suit *n chiefly Brit* a pair of overalls used for messy or oily work.

boisterous *adj* noisily and cheerfully rough. ➤ **boisterously** *adv*.

bold *adj* 1 showing a fearless adventurous spirit. 2 impudent or presumptuous. 3 conspicuous. 4 of type: darker and thicker than normal. ➤ **boldly** *adv*, **boldness** *n*.

bole *n* the trunk of a tree.

bolero /bə'leəroh/ *n* (*pl* **-os**) a Spanish dance in triple time.

boll *n* the seed pod of cotton or similar plants.

bollard *n* **1** *Brit* a short post used to guide vehicles or prevent their access. **2** a post on a wharf for fastening mooring lines.

Bolshevik *n* a member of the party that seized power in Russia in 1917. ➤ **Bolshevism** *n*.

bolshie or **bolshy** *adj* (**-ier, -iest**) *Brit, informal* stubborn and uncooperative. ➤ **bolshiness** *n*.

bolster¹ *n* a long pillow or cushion.

bolster² *v* to strengthen or support.

bolster³ *n* a heavy chisel used for cutting bricks or stone slabs.

bolt¹ *n* **1** a sliding bar or rod used to fasten a door. **2** a metal rod or pin for fastening objects together. **3** a rod or bar that closes the breech of a gun. **4** a short blunt arrow shot from a crossbow. **5** a lightning stroke. * **bolt from the blue** something totally unexpected and unwelcome. **bolt upright** with a straight back.

bolt² *v* **1** to move rapidly; to flee. **2** of plants: to produce seed prematurely. **3** to secure or fasten with a bolt. **4** to swallow (food) hastily.

bolt³ *n* an attempt to escape or flee. * **make a bolt for** to dash towards (a door, etc).

bolt-hole *n chiefly Brit* a place to escape to and find refuge in.

bomb¹ *n* **1** a device that explodes and causes widespread damage. **2** (**the bomb**) nuclear weapons. * **cost a bomb** *Brit, informal* to be very expensive. **go like a bomb** *informal* to move very fast.

bomb² *v* **1** to attack with bombs. **2** *informal* to be a failure. **3** *Brit, informal* to move very fast.

bombard *v* **1** to attack with heavy artillery or with bombs. **2** (*usu* + with) to direct an unremitting flow of questions or facts at. **3** to subject (a substance) to the impact of electrons or other particles. ➤ **bombardment** *n*.

bombardier *n* **1** a non-commissioned officer in the British artillery. **2** a US bomber-crew member who releases the bombs.

bombast *n* pretentious inflated speech or writing. ➤ **bombastic** *adj*.

bomber *n* **1** an aircraft designed for dropping bombs. **2** somebody who throws or plants bombs.

bombshell *n* **1** an astounding occurrence or piece of news. **2** *informal* a stunningly attractive woman.

bona fide /ˌbohnə ˈfiedi/ *adj* genuine or real.

bonanza *n* an unexpected supply of wealth or prosperity.

bonbon *n* a sweet.

bond¹ *n* **1** something that binds or restrains. **2** an adhesive or cementing material. **3** the adhesion achieved between surfaces cemented together. **4** something that unites or binds. **5** a feeling or purpose that unites people. **6** a binding agreement or contract. **7** a certificate of intention to pay the holder a specified sum, with or without other interest, on a specified date.

bond² *v* **1** to fasten or secure together. **2** to form a strong close emotional bond.

bondage *n* **1** slavery or serfdom. **2** sexual gratification involving the physical restraint of one partner.

bone¹ *n* **1** the hard material of which the skeleton of vertebrates is chiefly composed, or a piece of this. **2** a hard substance resembling bone. **3** a hard strip used to stiffen a corset or dress. * **bone of contention** a cause of argument. **feel in one's bones** to know instinctively or intuitively. **have a bone to pick with** *informal* to have a cause of complaint against. **make no bones about** to have no hesitation in. **near/close to the bone** of a remark: risqué, indecent, or too close to the truth. ➤ **boneless** *adj*.

bone² *v* to remove the bones from (fish or meat).

bone china *n* a translucent white hard-paste porcelain.

bone-dry *adj* completely dry.

bone-idle *adj* thoroughly lazy.

bone meal *n* fertilizer or feed made of ground bones.

bonfire *n* a large open-air fire.

bongo *n* (*pl* **-os** or **-oes**) each of a pair of small drums played with the hands.

bonhomie /ˈbonəmee, bonəˈmee/ *n* good-natured friendliness.

bonk¹ *v informal* **1** to hit or knock. **2** *Brit* to have sexual intercourse with.

bonk² *n informal* **1** a light blow or hit. **2** *Brit* an act of sexual intercourse.

bonkers *adj Brit, informal* mad or crazy.

bonnet *n* **1** a woman's or child's hat, tied under the chin. **2** *Brit* the hinged metal covering over the engine of a motor vehicle.

bonny *adj* (**-ier, -iest**) *chiefly Scot, N Eng* fresh-looking and attractive.

bonsai /ˈbonsie/ *n* (*pl* **bonsai**) the art of growing miniature trees.

bonus *n* (*pl* **bonuses**) **1** something extra or unexpected. **2** an extra sum of money paid to employees or shareholders.

bon voyage /ˌbon vwahˈyahj, -ˈyahzh/ *interj* good wishes to somebody starting on a journey.

bony *adj* (**-ier, -iest**) **1** consisting of or resembling bone. **2** full of bones. **3** skinny or scrawny.

boo¹ *interj* used to express disapproval or to startle or frighten.

boo² *v* (**boos, booed, booing**) to show disapproval by shouting 'boo!'

boob¹ *n Brit, informal* a stupid mistake or blunder.

boob² *v Brit, informal* to make a stupid mistake.

boob³ *n informal* a woman's breast.

booby¹ *n* (*pl* **-ies**) *informal* an awkward foolish person.

booby² *n* (*pl* **-ies,**) *informal* a woman's breast.

boogie¹ *n informal* a dance to rock music.

boogie² *v* (**boogies, boogied, boogieing**) *Informal* to dance to rock music.

book¹ *n* **1** a set of written, printed or blank sheets bound together down one edge. **2** a printed work in this form. **3** a major division of a literary work. **4** (*in pl*) financial records or accounts. ✳ **by the book** following rules or guidelines exactly. **throw the book at** to reprimand or punish severely.

book² *v* **1** to reserve or hire in advance. **2** to take the name of (an offender) with a view to prosecution or other action.

bookcase *n* a piece of furniture with shelves for holding books.

book club *n* an association that offers books to its members at a discount.

booked up *adj* fully booked.

bookend *n* a support placed at the end of a row of books.

bookie *n informal* a bookmaker.

book in *v* to register on arrival at a hotel.

bookish *adj* fond of reading and studying.

bookkeeper *n* a person who records the accounts or transactions of a business. ➤ **bookkeeping** *n*.

booklet *n* a small slim book with a paper cover.

bookmaker *n* a person who receives and pays bets. ➤ **bookmaking** *n*.

bookmark *n* **1** a strip of card or leather used to mark a place in a book. **2** a computing facility for recording the address of a file or web page for future access.

bookworm *n informal* a person who enjoys reading and study.

boom¹ *n* **1** a booming deep low sound or cry. **2** a rapid and widespread expansion of economic activity.

boom² *v* **1** to make a deep low sound or cry. **2** to experience rapid economic growth.

boom³ *n* **1** a spar at the foot of a mainsail. **2** a long movable arm carrying a microphone. **3** a cable or line of spars forming a barrier across a river or harbour mouth.

boomerang *n* a bent piece of wood shaped so that it curves round and returns when thrown.

boon *n* a benefit or blessing.

boor *n* a coarse or insensitive person. ➤ **boorish** *adj*.

boost¹ *v* **1** to increase or raise the level of. **2** to encourage or give a fillip to.

boost² *n* **1** an increase in amount. **2** a support or encouragement.

booster *n* **1** a supplementary dose of vaccine renewing the effectiveness of an earlier dose. **2** an auxiliary engine which provides extra thrust to a rocket or spacecraft. **3** a device that increases voltage or amplifies an electrical signal.

boot¹ *n* **1** a piece of footwear that extends above the ankle. **2** *informal* a kick. **3** *Brit* the luggage compartment of a motor car. **4** (**the sack**) *informal* dismissal from employment.

boot² *v* **1** to kick roughly. **2** *informal* (+ out) to eject or discharge (a person) summarily. **3** to start (a computer).

boot³ ✳ **to boot** besides; as well.

bootee *n* **1** a baby's boot-shaped sock. **2** a woman's short boot.

booth *n* **1** a stall or stand for the sale or exhibition of goods. **2** a small enclosure affording privacy for telephoning, voting, etc.

bootleg *adj* **1** of alcoholic drink or recordings: smuggled or illegally produced. **2** of trousers: having legs that flare slightly at the bottom.

booty *n* (*pl* **-ies**) **1** plunder taken in war. **2** a rich gain or prize.

booze¹ *n informal* alcoholic drink, *esp* spirits.

booze² *v informal* to drink alcohol heavily.

bop¹ *n chiefly Brit, informal* **1** a dance to popular music. **2** a disco or dance.

bop² *v* (**bopped, bopping**) *informal* to dance to popular music. ➤ **bopper** *n*.

bop³ *v* (**bopped, bopping**) *informal* to punch smartly.

bop⁴ *n informal* a punch.

boracic *adj* containing boron.

borage *n* a coarse hairy herb with blue flowers.

borax *n* natural or synthetic hydrated sodium borate used *esp* as a flux and cleansing agent.

border¹ *n* **1** an outer part or edge. **2** a boundary or frontier. **3** a narrow flower bed along the edge of grass. **4** an ornamental design at the edge of something.

border² *v* **1** to form a border along the edge of. **2** of a country or region: to adjoin (another country or region). **3** (+ on) to be close to a feeling or state.

borderline *adj* verging on one or other place or state.

bore¹ *v* **1** to make (a hole) in something using a drill. **2** to hollow out (a gun barrel). ➤ **borer** *n*.

bore² *n* **1** the hollow interior of a gun's barrel. **2** the interior diameter of a tube.

bore³ *n* a dull or tedious person or situation.

bore⁴ *v* to make (somebody) weary by being dull or monotonous. ➤ **bored** *adj*, **boring** *adj*.

bore⁵ *v* a tidal flood that moves rapidly up an estuary.

bore⁶ *v* past tense of BEAR².

boredom *n* the state of being bored.

borehole *n* a hole drilled in the earth to find water or oil.

boric acid *n* a white crystalline solid acid used *esp* as an antiseptic.

born *adj* **1** brought into existence by birth. **2** having a natural ability or aptitude: *a born teacher*. **3** (+ of) resulting from (e.g. a feeling or cause).

born-again *adj* recently converted to Christianity or some other belief.

borne *v* past part. of BEAR².

boron n a metalloid chemical element found in nature only in combination.

borough n 1 an urban area in Britain with powers of local self-government granted by royal charter. 2 a local-government area of London. 3 a political division of New York City.

borrow v 1 to take or receive (something) with the intention or requirement of returning it. 2 to get (a sum of money) from a bank under an arrangement to pay it back, usu with interest. ➤ **borrower** n.

Borstal n Brit formerly, a penal institution providing training for young offenders.

bosom n 1 the front of the human chest; esp the female breasts. 2 the deep heart or centre of something, e.g. the family.

boss¹ n informal a person who exercises control or authority.

boss² v informal to give orders to in a domineering manner.

boss³ n 1 a stud or knob at the centre of a shield. 2 the enlarged part of a shaft, on which a wheel is mounted. 3 the middle part of a propeller.

bossa nova n a Brazilian dance similar to the samba.

boss-eyed adj Brit, informal having a squint; cross-eyed.

bossy adj (-ier, -iest) informal domineering or dictatorial. ➤ **bossiness** n.

bosun n see BOATSWAIN.

botany n the study of plant life. ➤ **botanical** adj, **botanist** n.

botch v informal 1 to repair in a makeshift or inept way. 2 to bungle.

both¹ adj affecting or involving the one as well as the other of two people or things.

both² pron the one as well as the other of two people or things.

bother¹ v 1 to disturb or distract. 2 to cause to be troubled or perplexed. 3 to cause discomfort or pain to. 4 to take the trouble to do something. 5 to concern oneself about something.

bother² n 1 unnecessary fuss or effort. 2 a cause of difficulty or fuss.

bothersome adj causing bother; annoying.

bottle¹ n 1 a glass or plastic container with a narrow neck, used for liquids. 2 Brit, informal courage.

bottle² v 1 to store (liquid) in a bottle. 2 Brit to preserve (fruit) in glass jars.

bottleneck n a narrow stretch of road where the flow of traffic is impeded.

bottle out v informal to lose one's nerve.

bottle up v to restrain (an emotion).

bottom¹ n 1 the underside of something, or the surface on which it rests. 2 the buttocks or rump. 3 the lowest or deepest part or place. 4 the lowest position or last place in order of precedence. 5 (also in pl) the lower part of a two-piece garment. ＊ **get to the bottom of** to find out the truth or basis of.

bottom² v of a submarine: to reach the sea bed.

bottom³ adj relating to or situated at the bottom or lower part of something. ➤ **bottommost** adj.

bottom line n (the bottom line) informal the crucial factor.

bottom out v of a bad situation: to reach its worst point and level out.

botulism n an acute form of food poisoning caused by a toxin in food.

boudoir /'boohdwah/ n a woman's bedroom or private room.

bouffant /'boohfong/ adj of hair: puffed out in a rounded shape.

bougainvillea or **bougainvillaea** n a tropical climbing plant with bright floral bracts.

bough n a main branch of a tree.

bought v past tense and past part. of BUY¹.

boulder n a large stone or rock.

boulevard n a broad avenue.

bounce¹ v 1 to cause (a ball, etc) to rebound. 2 to rebound after striking a surface. 3 to move with a springing step. 4 informal of a cheque: to be returned by a bank because there are not enough funds in the payer's account. 5 Brit, informal to coerce into doing something.

bounce² n 1 a sudden leap or bound. 2 a rebound. 3 verve or liveliness.

bouncer n a person employed in a nightclub to remove disorderly people.

bouncy adj (-ier, -iest) 1 bouncing readily. 2 buoyant; exuberant.

bound¹ adj 1 going somewhere specified: bound for home. 2 confined to a place: housebound. 3 certain or sure to do something. 4 placed under legal or moral obligation: duty-bound.

bound² n (usu in pl) 1 a limiting line or boundary. 2 something that limits or restrains. ＊ **out of bounds** 1 outside the permitted limits. 2 of the ball in team sport: outside the area of play.

bound³ v 1 to set limits to. 2 to form the boundary of (a country, region, etc).

bound⁴ n 1 a leap or jump. 2 a bounce.

bound⁵ v 1 to move by leaping. 2 to rebound or bounce.

bound⁶ v past tense and past part. of BIND¹.

boundary n (pl -ies) 1 a dividing line that indicates or fixes a limit or extent. 2 a border or frontier.

boundless adj limitless.

bounteous adj giving or given freely. ➤ **bounteously** adv.

bountiful adj 1 generous; liberal. 2 abundant; plentiful. ➤ **bountifully** adv.

bounty n 1 a financial reward paid for the capture of a criminal or outlaw. 2 literary something given generously. 3 literary generosity.

bouquet n 1 a bunch of flowers. 2 a distinctive fragrance.

bourbon *n* an American whisky distilled from maize with malt and rye.

bourgeois *adj* belonging to or characteristic of the middle class.

bourgeoisie /booəzhwah'zee/ *n* the middle class.

bout *n* **1** a spell of activity. **2** a boxing or wrestling match. **3** an attack of an illness.

boutique *n* a small fashionable shop selling clothes or other specialized goods.

bouzouki /boo'zoohki/ *n* (*pl* **bouzoukis**) a Greek stringed instrument resembling a mandolin.

bovine¹ *adj* **1** relating to cattle. **2** slow, stolid, or dull.

bovine² *n* an ox or related animal.

bow¹ *v* **1** to bend the head or upper body in respect or greeting. **2** to submit or yield to something or somebody. ✳ **bow and scrape** to act in an obsequious manner.

bow² *n* a bending of the head or body in respect or greeting. ✳ **take a bow** to acknowledge applause or praise.

bow³ *n* **1** a knot tied with two loops and two free ends. **2** a weapon for shooting arrows, consisting of a strip of wood or other flexible material held bent by a taut cord at the two ends. **3** a rod with horsehairs stretched from end to end, used for playing a stringed instrument.

bow⁴ *n* (*also in pl*) the front end of a ship.

bowdlerize or **-ise** *v* to remove parts from (a book) because they are considered indecent or offensive.

bowel *n* **1** (*in pl*) the intestines. **2** the large intestine or the small intestine. **3** (*in pl*) the innermost parts of something.

bower *n* **1** a shelter in a garden. **2** an attractive dwelling or retreat.

bowl¹ *n* **1** a round deep dish for holding or mixing food. **2** the hollow rounded part of something. **3** a bowl-shaped geographical region or formation.

bowl² *n* **1** a weighted shaped ball used in the game of bowls. **2** a ball used in skittles or tenpin bowling. **3** (*in pl*) a game played outdoors on a green, in which players roll bowls as close as possible to a target bowl.

bowl³ *v* **1** to roll (a ball) in a game of bowls. **2** to deliver (a ball) to a batsman in cricket. **3** of a bowler: to dismiss (a batsman in cricket) by hitting the wicket. **4** (*often* + along) to travel quickly.

bowlegged *adj* having legs that curve outwards at the knees.

bowler¹ *n* the person who bowls in a team sport.

bowler² *n* a man's stiff felt hat with a rounded crown and narrow brim.

bowling *n* a game in which balls are rolled at one or more objects.

bowl over *v informal* to impress or astonish.

bow tie *n* a short tie fastened in a bow.

bow window *n* a curved bay window.

box¹ *n* **1** a flat-sided container with a lid. **2** a small compartment for a group of people, e.g. in a theatre or sports ground. **3** (**the box**) *chiefly Brit, informal* television. **4** a space or area marked out with straight lines or as a grid.

box² *v* **1** to enclose in a box. **2** to confine or restrict.

box³ *v* **1** to engage in boxing. **2** to slap (somebody's ears) with the hand.

box⁴ *n* a punch or slap on the ear.

box⁵ *n* an evergreen shrub or small tree used for hedges.

boxer¹ *n* a person who engages in boxing.

boxer² *n* a dog of a breed having short brown hair and a flat pug-like face.

boxer shorts *pl n* men's loose-fitting underpants.

boxing *n* the sport of attack and defence with the fists enclosed in thickly padded gloves.

Boxing Day *n* 26 December, observed as a public holiday.

box number *n* the number of a box at a post office, for delivering and collecting mail.

box office *n* the place in a cinema or theatre where tickets are sold.

boxroom *n Brit* a small storage room in a house.

boxy *adj* (**-ier, -iest**) **1** resembling a box; boxlike. **2** of a room: cramped or poky.

boy *n* a male child or young person. ➤ **boyhood** *n*, **boyish** *adj*.

boycott¹ *v* to refuse to have dealings with or trade with, as a protest or penalty.

boycott² *n* an act of boycotting.

boyfriend *n* a regular male companion or lover.

Br *abbr* the chemical symbol for bromine.

bra *n* a woman's undergarment for supporting the breasts.

brace¹ *n* **1** a diagonal piece of structural material that serves to strengthen. **2** an appliance for supporting a weak leg or other body part. **3** a dental fitting for correcting irregular teeth. **4** a rope attached to a yard on a ship that swings the yard horizontally to trim the sail. **5** a mark ({ or }) used to connect words or items to be considered together. **6** a pair. **7** (*also* **brace and bit**) a crank-shaped drilling instrument that holds a bit.

brace² *v* **1** to prepare (oneself, or a part of one's body) for receiving an impact. **2** to prepare (oneself) for something unpleasant. **3** to support with a brace.

bracelet *n* an ornamental band or chain worn round the wrist.

braces *pl n Brit* a pair of elasticated straps worn over the shoulders and attached to the trousers to keep them up.

bracing *adj* refreshing or invigorating.

bracken *n* a large coarse fern of moorland areas.

bracket[1] *n* **1** each of a pair of marks ( ), [ ], < >, or { }, used to enclose matter in writing or printing. **2** a social group. **3** a projecting fixture that supports a load or strengthens an angle.

bracket[2] *v* (**bracketed, bracketing**) **1** to place (written or printed matter) within brackets. **2** (+ **together**) to put (people or things) in the same category.

brackish *adj* of water: slightly salty.

bract *n* a small leaf near a flower or floral axis.

brag[1] *v* (**bragged, bragging**) to talk boastfully.

brag[2] *n* a card game resembling poker.

braggart *n* a loud arrogant boaster.

braid[1] *v* **1** to plait (hair). **2** to decorate with ribbon or braid.

braid[2] *n* **1** a plaited strip of cord or ribbon. **2** a length of plaited hair. **3** a narrow plait of hair.

Braille *n* a system of writing or printing for the blind, with characters made up of raised dots.

brain[1] *n* **1** the organ of thought and neural coordination enclosed within the skull. **2** (*in pl*) intelligence. **3** *informal* an intelligent or intellectual person. **4** (**the brain/the brains**) *informal* the chief planner of an organization or enterprise. ✳ **on the brain** *informal* constantly recurring in one's head.

brain[2] *v informal* to hit hard on the head.

brainchild *n* something that results from a particular person's creative imagination.

brain drain *n informal* the loss of highly qualified people through emigration.

brainless *adj* stupid or foolish.

brainstorm *n informal* a mental abberation or lapse in concentration.

brainwash *v* to attempt to instil beliefs into (somebody), or change existing beliefs, by systematic repetition.

brain wave *n* **1** a rhythmic fluctuation of voltage between parts of the brain. **2** *informal* a sudden bright idea.

brainy *adj* (**-ier, -iest**) *informal* intelligent.

braise *v* to cook (meat) slowly by frying it briefly and then stewing it at a low heat.

brake[1] *n* (*also in pl*) a device for slowing down or stopping a vehicle.

brake[2] *v* to apply a brake on a vehicle.

brake[3] *n* an open carriage drawn by horses.

brake[4] *n* **1** a toothed instrument used for crushing flax and hemp. **2** (*also* **brake harrow**) a machine formerly used for breaking up large clumps of earth.

bramble *n* a prickly rambling shrub, *esp* a blackberry. ➤ **brambly** *adj*.

bran *n* the broken husk of cereal grain separated from the flour or meal by sifting.

branch[1] *n* **1** a thick shoot growing from the trunk of a tree. **2** a road, railway line, or river that deviates from a main one. **3** a division of a family, organization, or group. **4** a section of a subject of study.

branch[2] *v* **1** to put out branches. **2** to spring from a main stem.

branch out *v* to try new activities or experiences.

brand[1] *n* **1** a product identified by name as made by a single firm or manufacturer. **2** a mark made on farm animals by burning with a hot iron, e.g. to designate ownership. **3** a charred or smouldering piece of wood.

brand[2] *v* **1** to mark with a hot iron. **2** to identify (goods) with a brand name. **3** to stigmatize (somebody, or their conduct).

brandish *v* to shake or wave (a weapon, etc) menacingly or ostentatiously.

brand name *n* a maker's name for a product.

brand new *adj* completely new.

brandy *n* (*pl* **-ies**) a spirit made by distilling wine or fermented fruit juice.

brash *adj* **1** aggressively self-assertive. **2** tastelessly showy. ➤ **brashly** *adv*, **brashness** *n*.

brass *n* **1** an alloy of copper and zinc. **2** the brass instruments of an orchestra. **3** *Brit* a brass memorial tablet set into the wall or floor of a church. **4** a round flat brass ornament for a horse's harness. **5** (*also* **the top brass**) *informal* the people in authority.

brass band *n* a band consisting of brass instruments.

brasserie *n* a small informal French-style restaurant.

brassy *adj* (**-ier, -iest**) **1** shamelessly bold or showy. **2** resembling brass in colour.

brat *n informal* an ill-disciplined child. ➤ **brattish** *adj*.

bravado *n* bold conduct intended to impress or deceive people.

brave[1] *adj* showing courage. ➤ **bravely** *adv*.

brave[2] *v* to face or endure (unpleasant or dangerous conditions) with courage.

brave[3] *n dated* a Native American warrior.

bravery *n* courage or valour.

bravo[1] *interj* used by an audience to applaud a performer.

bravo[2] *n* (*pl* **-os** *or* **-oes**) a villain or desperado; *esp* a hired assassin.

bravura /brəˈv(y)ooərə/ *n* **1** a flamboyant brilliant style of performance. **2** a display of daring.

brawl[1] *v* to quarrel or fight noisily.

brawl[2] *n* a noisy quarrel or fight.

brawn *n* **1** muscular strength. **2** *Brit* pork trimmings pressed into a mould.

bray *v* to utter the loud harsh cry of a donkey. ➤ **bray** *n*.

brazen[1] *adj* **1** shamelessly bold. **2** *literary* resembling or made of brass. ➤ **brazenly** *adv*.

brazen[2] ✳ **brazen it out** to face danger, trouble, or criticism with defiance or impudence.

brazier[1] /'brayzi-ə, 'brayzhə/ *n* **1** a receptacle or stand for holding burning coals. **2** *NAmer* a barbecue.

brazier[2] *n* a person who works in brass.

brazil nut *n* a large three-sided nut.

breach[1] *n* **1** a violation of a law or obligation. **2** a gap made in a wall or barrier. **3** a temporary quarrel or disagreement. ✲ **step into the breach** to replace somebody who has been suddenly prevented from doing a job.

breach[2] *v* **1** to make a breach in (a wall or barrier). **2** to break or violate (a law or agreement).

bread *n* **1** a food made from flour or meal which is baked and leavened with yeast. **2** *informal* money.

bread and butter *n* one's means of sustenance or livelihood.

breadcrumb *n* a small fragment of bread.

breadline *n* ✲ **on the breadline** *Brit* earning barely enough for survival.

breadth *n* **1** the distance from side to side of something. **2** wide range or scope.

breadwinner *n* the member of a family whose income provides the chief means of support.

break[1] *v* (**broke, broken**) **1** to separate into pieces from a blow, mishap, etc. **2** to stop working. **3** to fracture (a limb), or to become fractured. **4** to fail to keep (an agreement or rule). **5** to defeat or crush. **6** to reduce the impact of (a fall). **7** to interrupt (a journey) for a rest or diversion. **8** to exceed or surpass. **9** to solve (a code). **10** to make (news) known to people. **11** of news: to become known. **12** of the day: to begin at dawn. **13** of weather: to change after a settled period. **14** of a storm: to develop suddenly. **15** of a person: to give way under pressure. **16** in tennis, to win a game against (an opponent's service). **17** of a boy's voice: to deepen at puberty. ✲ **break even** to recoup an initial investment or outlay. **break into** to start an activity. **break loose** to escape. **break the back of** to complete the most difficult part of. **break the bank** to cause financial ruin. **break wind** to release gas from the anus. **break with** to end a relationship with after a quarrel. ➤ **breakable** *adj*.

break[2] *n* **1** an act or action of breaking. **2** a place where something is broken. **3** a gap. **4** a brief rest or respite. **5** a dash or rush. **6** *informal* an opportunity or a stroke of good luck. **7** in tennis, an instance of breaking an opponent's service. **8** in snooker, a sequence of successful shots or strokes. **9** in jazz, a short ornamental passage between phrases.

breakage *n* **1** something that has been broken. **2** the action of breaking something.

breakaway *n* **1** somebody or something that breaks away. **2** a breaking away from a group or tradition.

break away *v* **1** to escape. **2** to separate from a main group.

breakdown *n* **1** a failure to function. **2** a physical or nervous collapse. **3** the process of decomposing. **4** a classification or detailed analysis.

break down *v* **1** to fail or stop working. **2** of an agreement, talks, etc: to fail or become unworkable. **3** to give way to feelings. **4** to cause to collapse. **5** to separate into components or elements.

breaker *n* a wave breaking into foam.

breakfast[1] *n* the first meal of the day.

breakfast[2] *v* to eat breakfast.

break in *v* **1** to enter a building by force. **2** to intrude or interrupt. **3** to train (a horse) to carry a rider. **4** to use (new shoes) until they become comfortable.

break-in *n* an act of forcing an entry into a building.

breakneck *adj* dangerously fast.

break off *v* **1** to stop abruptly. **2** to discontinue (a connection or relationship).

break out *v* **1** of something unwelcome: to start suddenly. **2** to escape from confinement.

breakthrough *n* a sudden advance or discovery.

break up *v* **1** to bring or come to an end. **2** to break into pieces. **3** to finish an activity and disperse.

breakwater *n* a barrier protecting a harbour or beach from the sea.

bream *n* (*pl* **breams** *or* **bream**) a silvery freshwater fish with a deep narrow body.

breast[1] *n* **1** either of the two milk-producing organs on a woman's chest. **2** the front part of the body between the neck and the abdomen.

breast[2] *v* **1** to confront resolutely. **2** to meet or lean against with the breast or front.

breastbone *n* a narrow flat bone extending down the chest, to which some of the ribs are attached.

breast-feed *v* (*past tense and past part.* **breast-fed**) to feed (a baby) with milk from the breast.

breaststroke *n* a swimming stroke performed by pushing the arms forward then sweeping them out and back, while kicking the legs out and back.

breath *n* **1** air inhaled and exhaled in breathing. **2** an act of breathing. **3** a slight movement of air. **4** a slight indication. ✲ **out of breath** breathing very rapidly from strenuous exercise. **under one's breath** in a whisper.

breathalyse *or* **breathalyze** *v* to test (a driver's breath) with a breathalyser.

breathalyser *or* **breathalyzer** *n* a device used to test the alcohol level in a driver's blood.

breathe *v* **1** to draw air into the lungs and expel it. **2** to let air or moisture out. **3** to say or express.

breather *n informal* a short break in an activity.

breathless *adj* **1** gasping for breath after strenuous exercise. **2** gripping or intense. ➤ **breathlessly** *adv*.

breathtaking *adj* extremely exciting or thrilling. ➤ **breathtakingly** *adv*.

breathy *adj* (-**ier**, -**iest**) accompanied by audible breathing.

breech *n* the part of a firearm at the rear of the barrel.

breech birth *n* a birth in which the baby's feet or buttocks emerge first.

breeches *pl n* knee-length trousers fastened at the knees.

breed[1] *v* (*past tense and past part.* **bred**) **1** to produce offspring by sexual union. **2** to propagate (plants or animals). **3** to produce or engender.

breed[2] *n* **1** a particular group of animals or plants having similar characteristics. **2** a class or kind.

breeder reactor *n* a nuclear reactor in which more radioactive fuel is produced than is consumed.

breeding *n* good behaviour regarded as resulting from family background.

breeze[1] *n* **1** a light wind. **2** *informal* something easily done.

breeze[2] *v* to come or go casually or nonchalantly.

breeze-block *n* a building block made from ashy residue mixed with sand and cement.

breezy *adj* (-**ier**, -**iest**) **1** fresh and windy. **2** brisk and cheerful. ➤ **breezily** *adv*.

brethren *n* pl of BROTHER, used in religious contexts.

breve *n* a musical note with the time value of two semibreves.

brevity *n* **1** conciseness of expression. **2** shortness of duration.

brew[1] *v* **1** to make (beer) by fermentation. **2** to make (tea) by infusion in hot water. **3** (*often* + up) to contrive or plot. ➤ **brewer** *n*.

brew[2] *n* a brewed drink.

brewery *n* (*pl* -**ies**) a place in which beer is brewed.

briar *n* see BRIER.

bribe[1] *v* to offer money or other inducement to persuade (somebody) to do something illegal or wrong.

bribe[2] *n* something offered to bribe somebody.

bribery *n* the practice of giving a bribe.

bric-a-brac *n* miscellaneous small articles or curios.

brick[1] *n* **1** a rectangular block of baked clay used in building. **2** a small block used as a children's toy. ✳ **bricks and mortar** buildings and housing.

brick[2] *v* (+ up) to enclose or pave with bricks.

brickbat *n* a critical or hostile remark.

bricklayer *n* a person who is employed to lay bricks.

bridal *adj* of or for a bride or wedding.

bride *n* a woman at the time of her wedding.

bridegroom *n* a man at the time of his wedding.

bridesmaid *n* a woman or girl who attends a bride.

bridge[1] *n* **1** a structure spanning a river or road or other obstacle. **2** the upper bony part of the nose. **3** an arch supporting the strings of a musical instrument. **4** an enclosed platform on a ship for the captain and officers. **5** a denture filling a gap.

bridge[2] *v* to make a bridge over or across (a river or road).

bridge[3] *n* a card game for four players, with bidding.

bridgehead *n* an advanced position in enemy territory, taken as a foothold for further advance.

bridle[1] *n* a framework of leather straps attached to a horse's head and used to control it.

bridle[2] *v* **1** to put a bridle on (an animal). **2** to restrain or control. **3** to show hostility or resentment.

bridleway *n* a path with right of way for horse riding.

Brie /bree/ *n* a cream-coloured soft French cheese.

brief[1] *adj* **1** short in length or time. **2** using few words. **3** of clothing: covering only a small area. ➤ **briefly** *adv*.

brief[2] *n* **1** a set of instructions describing a task and setting its limits. **2** a statement of a client's case drawn up for legal counsel. **3** *Brit, informal* a barrister or solicitor assigned to a case.

brief[3] *v* to provide with instructions or information for a task.

briefcase *n* a flat rectangular case for carrying papers.

briefing *n* a meeting for giving instructions or information.

briefs *pl n* short underpants.

brier *or* **briar** *n* a plant with woody and thorny or prickly stems.

brig *n* a two-masted square-rigged sailing ship.

brigade *n* **1** a large section of an army including a headquarters and several fighting units. **2** *informal* a group of people who have a particular point of view.

brigadier *n* an officer in the British Army ranking below a major general.

brigand *n* a member of a gang of bandits.

bright *adj* **1** radiating a lot of light; shining. **2** lively and cheerful. **3** of a colour: bold and brilliant. **4** quick to learn or understand. **5** promising success or good fortune. ➤ **brightly** *adv*, **brightness** *n*.

brighten *v* (*often* + up) to make or become brighter or happier.

brill *n* (*pl* **brill**) a flatfish related to the turbot.

brilliant adj **1** very bright or bold. **2** having great intellectual ability. **3** strikingly impressive or distinctive. **4** Brit, informal of high quality; good. ➤ **brilliance** n, **brilliantly** adv.

brim[1] n **1** the edge or rim of a container. **2** the projecting edge of a hat.

brim[2] v (**brimmed, brimming**) to be full to the brim.

brimful adj full to the brim.

brimstone n archaic = SULPHUR.

brindled or **brindle** adj of an animal: having dark streaks on a grey or tawny background.

brine n **1** a solution of salty water. **2** sea water.

bring v (past tense and past part. **brought**) **1** to carry or convey to a place. **2** to cause to reach a particular condition. **3** to force (oneself) to do something. **4** to cause to occur; to lead to. **5** to present or initiate.

bring about v to cause to happen.

bring down v **1** to reduce. **2** to cause the collapse of (a government).

bring in v **1** to earn (an amount of income). **2** to introduce (a measure).

bring off v to achieve successfully.

bring on v **1** to cause (a feeling or symptom) to occur. **2** to help to make progress.

bring out v **1** to publish or produce. **2** to emphasize or make more obvious.

bring round (NAmer **bring around**) v **1** to persuade (somebody) to adopt a particular opinion. **2** to revive (an unconscious person).

bring up v **1** to educate and look after (a child). **2** to raise for consideration.

brink n **1** the edge of land at the top of a steep place or by water. **2** the point at which something is about to happen.

brinkmanship n the art of going to the very brink of conflict, danger, etc before drawing back.

briny[1] n (**the briny**) Brit, informal the sea.

briny[2] adj (**-ier, -iest**) salty.

brio n enthusiasm and liveliness.

brioche n a light, slightly sweet French bread roll.

brisk adj **1** energetic and fast. **2** fresh and invigorating. **3** sharp in tone or manner. ➤ **briskly** adv.

brisket n a joint of beef cut from the breast.

brisling n (pl **brislings** or **brisling**) a small herring.

bristle[1] n a short stiff hair.

bristle[2] v **1** of hair or fur: to rise and stand stiffly erect. **2** to react peevishly or resentfully.

bristly adj (**-ier, -iest**) **1** resembling bristles. **2** covered with bristles.

British[1] n (**the British**) (treated as pl) the people of Britain.

British[2] adj of Britain or its people.

Briton n a native or inhabitant of Britain.

brittle adj **1** hard and easily broken. **2** of the voice: light and thin in tone.

broach v **1** to raise (a subject) for discussion. **2** to pierce (a container).

broad adj **1** large in size or extent from side to side. **2** of a specified size in width. **3** widely applicable or applied. **4** relating to the main features and not details. **5** clear or easily noticed. **6** extending far; vast. **7** of an accent: marked. **8** of humour: coarse. ➤ **broadly** adv.

broad bean n a large flat green bean.

broadcast[1] v (past tense **broadcast**, past part. **broadcast** or **broadcasted**) **1** to transmit (a television or radio programme). **2** to make widely known. ➤ **broadcaster** n.

broadcast[2] n a radio or television programme.

broaden v to make or become broad or broader.

broad-minded adj tolerant of other views or forms of behaviour.

broadsheet n a newspaper printed on large folded sheets.

broadside n **1** a forceful verbal or written attack. **2** formerly, the firing together of all the guns on one side of a ship.

brocade n a rich fabric woven with raised patterns. ➤ **brocaded** adj.

broccoli n a vegetable with a green or purplish flower head.

brochure n a small pamphlet containing promotional material.

brogue[1] n a stout shoe with decorative perforations in the leather.

brogue[2] n a dialect or regional accent.

broil v **1** NAmer to grill (food). **2** to become extremely hot.

broke[1] v past tense of BREAK[1].

broke[2] adj informal having no money.

broken[1] v past part. of BREAK[1].

broken[2] adj of language: hesitant and containing errors.

broken-down adj in a state of disrepair; dilapidated.

brokenhearted adj overcome by sorrow or grief.

broken home n a family that has been affected by separation of the parents.

broker[1] n **1** an agent who negotiates contracts of purchase and sale. **2** an intermediary in business or politics.

broker[2] v to negotiate (a deal).

bromide n a compound of bromine.

bromine n a non-metallic chemical element with a pungent vapour.

bronchial adj relating to the tubes leading from the windpipe to the lungs.

bronchitis n inflammation of the bronchial tubes.

bronco n (pl **-os**) a wild or partially broken horse of the American West.

brontosaurus n a former name for apatosaurus.

bronze[1] *n* **1** a yellowish brown alloy of copper and tin. **2** a sculpture made of bronze. **3** a yellowish brown colour.

bronze[2] *v* **1** to give the appearance of bronze to. **2** to make brown or suntanned.

Bronze Age *n* (**the Bronze Age**) the period of human history in which bronze and copper tools and weapons were common, coming between the Stone Age and the Iron Age.

bronze medal *n* a medal of bronze awarded for third place in a competition.

brooch *n* an ornament fastened to clothing with an attached pin.

brood[1] *n* **1** a group of young birds or animals born or hatched at one time. **2** *humorous* the children of a family.

brood[2] *v* **1** of a bird: to sit on eggs to hatch them. **2** to worry at length about something unpleasant. **3** to hover menacingly.

broody *adj* (**-ier, -iest**) **1** of a hen: ready to hatch eggs. **2** *informal* of a woman: feeling a strong desire to have a baby. **3** constantly occupied with melancholy thoughts. ➤ **broodily** *adv.*

brook[1] *n* a small stream.

brook[2] *v formal* to tolerate.

broom *n* **1** a long-handled brush for sweeping. **2** a shrub with small leaves and showy yellow flowers.

broomstick *n* a brush of twigs on a long thin handle, ridden by a witch in children's stories.

bros. *or* **Bros.** *abbr* brothers.

broth *n* a soup or stock in which meat, fish, cereal grains, or vegetables have been cooked.

brothel *n* a premises in which prostitutes can be visited.

brother *n* **1** a man or boy having the same parents as another person. **2** a male colleague. **3** a male member of a religious order. ➤ **brotherly** *adj.*

brotherhood *n* **1** the state of being brothers. **2** a religious body founded for a particular purpose. **3** fellowship or friendship between human beings.

brother-in-law *n* (*pl* **brothers-in-law**) **1** the brother of one's husband or wife. **2** the husband of one's sister.

brought *v* past tense and past part. of BRING.

brow *n* **1** the forehead. **2** an eyebrow. **3** the top point of a hill.

browbeat *v* (**browbeat, browbeaten**) to intimidate with persistent threats.

brown[1] *adj* **1** of the colour of wood or soil, between red and yellow. **2** of dark or tanned complexion.

brown[2] *v* to make brown by cooking.

browned-off *adj informal* annoyed or disheartened.

brownfield *adj* of a site: located in an urban area where buildings previously stood.

brownie *n* **1** (**Brownie**) a member of the junior section of the Guides Assoiaction, for girls aged from seven to ten. **2** a small square of rich chocolate cake. **3** in stories, a goblin believed to perform household chores secretly at night.

browse[1] *v* **1** to look idly through a book or mass of things. **2** of animals: to nibble at leaves or other vegetation. **3** to look at (the contents of computer data).

browse[2] *n* a period of browsing.

browser *n* **1** a person or animal that is browsing. **2** a computer program for viewing information on the World Wide Web.

bruise[1] *n* **1** an area of discoloration on the skin, caused by a blow or injury. **2** an area of discoloration caused by damage to plant tissue.

bruise[2] *v* **1** to inflict a bruise on. **2** to be damaged by a bruise.

bruiser *n informal* a large burly person.

brunch *n* a meal eaten in the late morning, combining breakfast and lunch.

brunette (*NAmer* **brunet**) *n* a girl or woman with dark brown hair.

brunt *n* the principal force of an attack or a blow.

brush[1] *n* **1** an implement of hair, bristle, or wire set into a handle and used for grooming hair, painting, or cleaning. **2** an act of brushing. **3** a momentary touch or contact. **4** a conductor that makes electrical contact between a stationary part and a moving part. **5** the bushy tail of a fox.

brush[2] *v* **1** to clean or groom with a brush. **2** to apply (paint) with a brush. **3** to remove with sweeping strokes. **4** to touch lightly.

brush[3] *n* scrub vegetation, or land covered with it.

brush[4] *n* a brief antagonistic encounter or skirmish.

brush off *v* to dismiss in an offhand way.

brush up *v* to renew one's skill in.

brushwood *n* undergrowth of broken twigs and small branches.

brusque *adj* blunt or abrupt in manner or speech. ➤ **brusquely** *adv.*

Brussels sprout *n* a bud of a plant of the cabbage family, used as a vegetable.

brutal *adj* **1** cruel and violent. **2** harsh or severe. **3** unpleasantly direct or uncompromising. ➤ **brutalism** *n,* **brutality** *n,* **brutally** *adv.*

brutalize *or* **-ise** *v* **1** to make brutal or unfeeling. **2** to treat brutally.

brute[1] *n* **1** a cruel and violent person. **2** a large aggressive animal. ➤ **brutish** *adj.*

brute[2] *adj* **1** purely physical. **2** cruel or savage.

bryony *n* (*pl* **-ies**) a climbing plant with large leaves and red or black fruit.

BSE *abbr* bovine spongiform encephalopathy, a fatal disease of cattle affecting the central nervous system.

BSI *abbr* British Standards Institution.

BST *abbr* British Summer Time.

Btu *or* **BTU** *abbr* British thermal unit.

bubble¹ *n* **1** a small body of gas within a liquid or solid. **2** a thin transparent film of liquid inflated with air or vapour. **3** a transparent dome.

bubble² *v* **1** to form or produce bubbles. **2** to be highly excited.

bubble gum *n* chewing gum that can be blown into bubbles.

bubbly¹ *adj* (-ier, -iest) **1** full of bubbles. **2** lively and in good spirits.

bubbly² *n informal* champagne.

bubonic plague *n* a highly infectious and fatal form of plague.

buccaneer *n* **1** a pirate. **2** an unscrupulous adventurer. ➤ **buccaneering** *adj*.

buck¹ *n* **1** a male animal, *esp* a male deer or rabbit. **2** *archaic* a fashionable young man.

buck² *v* **1** of a horse: to spring into the air with the back curved. **2** to fight against or refuse to comply with; to oppose.

buck³ *n* a plunging leap by a horse.

buck⁴ *n NAmer, Aus, NZ, informal* a dollar.

bucket¹ *n* **1** an open container with a handle, used for holding or carrying liquids. **2** a tool or part of a machine shaped like a bucket. **3** *informal* (*in pl*) large quantities. ➤ **bucketful** (*pl* **bucketfuls**) *n*.

bucket² *v* (**bucketed, bucketing**) to move about jerkily or recklessly.

buckle¹ *n* a fastening consisting of a rigid rim with a hinged pin.

buckle² *v* **1** to fasten with a buckle. **2** to bend or warp under stress.

buckle down *v* to apply oneself vigorously.

buckshot *n* a coarse lead shot used for shooting large animals.

buck up *v* **1** to become encouraged or more cheerful. **2** to hurry up.

buckwheat *n* a plant with pinkish white flowers and seeds used to make flour.

bucolic *adj* relating to pastoral or country life.

bud¹ *n* a small growth on the stem of a plant that develops into a flower, leaf, or shoot.

bud² *v* (**budded, budding**) of a plant: to produce buds.

Buddhism *n* a religion or philosophy based on the teaching of Gautama Buddha. ➤ **Buddhist** *n and adj*.

budding *adj* in an early and usu promising stage of development.

buddleia *n* a shrub or tree with showy clusters of yellow or violet flowers.

buddy *n* (*pl* **-ies**) *chiefly NAmer, informal* a friend or colleague.

budge *v* (*usu in negative contexts*) **1** to move a little. **2** to change an opinion.

budgerigar *n* a small Australian bird often kept in captivity.

budget¹ *n* **1** a statement of income and expenditure over a period. **2** the amount of money available for or required for a particular purpose. **3** (**the Budget**) a statement of the government's financial position presented annually by a country's finance minister. **4** (*used before a noun*) simple and inexpensive. ➤ **budgetary** *adj*.

budget² *v* (**budgeted, budgeting**) to plan or provide for the use of available resources.

budgie *n informal* a budgerigar.

buff¹ *n* **1** a pale yellowish brown colour. **2** *informal* somebody who has a keen interest in a subject. ✳ **in the buff** *informal* naked.

buff² *v* to polish or shine with a soft cloth.

buffalo *n* (*pl* **buffaloes** *or* **buffalo**) **1** an American bison. **2** a large African ox with a short mane and large curving horns.

buffer¹ *n* **1** a spring-loaded metal disc on a railway vehicle or at the end of a railway track, for absorbing shocks. **2** a device that serves to protect or cushion against shock. **3** a temporary storage area in a computer.

buffer² *n Brit, informal* a silly or ineffectual man.

buffet¹ *n* **1** a self-service meal set out on tables or a sideboard. **2** a counter where refreshments are sold.

buffet² *v* (**buffeted, buffeting**) to batter or strike repeatedly.

buffoon *n* an absurd but amusing person. ➤ **buffoonery** *n*.

bug¹ *n* **1** a tiny insect. **2** *informal* a microorganism, or a disease caused by one. **3** a fault in a computer program. **4** a hidden listening device.

bug² *v* (**bugged, bugging**) **1** *informal* to bother or annoy. **2** to plant a listening device in.

bugbear *n* a cause of concern or difficulty.

bug-eyed *adj* with protruding eyes.

bugger¹ *n coarse slang* **1** a disagreeable or contemptible person. **2** *chiefly Brit* a cause of annoyance or difficulty. **3** a man who has anal intercourse.

bugger² *v coarse slang* **1** (*often + up*) to damage or ruin. **2** *Brit* (+ around/about) to behave foolishly or annoyingly. **3** to have anal intercourse with.

buggery *n* anal intercourse.

buggy *n* (*pl* **-ies**) **1** a lightweight foldable pushchair. **2** a small open motor vehicle. **3** a light one-horse carriage.

bugle *n* a valveless brass instrument like a small trumpet. ➤ **bugler** *n*.

build¹ *v* (*past tense and past part.* **built**) **1** to construct by putting materials together. **2** (+on) to develop (a plan or idea). **3** to increase gradually. ➤ **builder** *n*.

build² *n* the physical proportions of a person or animal.

build in v to construct or develop as an integral part.

building n 1 a permanent structure with walls and a roof. 2 the business or act of building structures.

building society n an organization providing financial services for members and making mortgage loans.

buildup n 1 a gradual increase. 2 advance praise or publicity.

build up v 1 to accumulate or develop. 2 to develop gradually by increments.

built v 1 past tense and past part. of BUILD[1]. 2 proportioned or formed in a specified way.

built-in adj forming part of a larger structure.

built-up adj occupied by many houses and other buildings.

bulb n 1 a short stem base of a plant, with one or more buds enclosed in overlapping leaves, from which the roots develop. 2 (also **light bulb**) a glass bulb with a filament and gas, giving light when an electric current is passed through it. 3 a part shaped like a bulb.

bulbous adj 1 round like a bulb. 2 of a plant: growing from bulbs.

bulge[1] n 1 a swelling or convex curve on a flat surface. 2 informal a temporary increase or expansion.

bulge[2] v to swell or curve outwards.

bulimia n an emotional disorder with periods of compulsive overeating alternating with fasting or self-induced vomiting. ➤ **bulimic** adj and n.

bulk[1] n 1 the volume or size of something. 2 a large or heavy mass. 3 (+ of) the main or greater part. 4 dietary fibre; roughage. ✳ **in bulk** in large amounts or quantities.

bulk[2] v 1 (often + out) to swell or thicken. 2 to appear as an unwelcome factor.

bulkhead n an internal partition or wall in an aircraft or ship.

bulky adj (-ier, -iest) large and cumbersome.

bull[1] n 1 an adult male bovine animal. 2 an adult male elephant, whale, or other large animal. ✳ **take the bull by the horns** to face up to a problem.

bull[2] n a papal edict.

bull[3] n informal nonsense.

bulldog n a sturdy breed of dog with a short neck and wide head.

bulldoze v to clear or demolish.

bulldozer n a vehicle with caterpillar tracks and a broad horizontal blade at the front, for clearing ground.

bullet n 1 a small projectile fired from a gun. 2 a large dot in in printing.

bulletin n 1 a brief news item or broadcast. 2 a journal published at regular intervals.

bullfight n a public spectacle in which a bull is taunted and killed. ➤ **bullfighter** n, **bullfighting** n.

bullfinch n a finch with a rosy red breast and throat.

bullfrog n a large frog with a deep croak.

bullion n gold or silver in bars.

bullish adj energetically optimistic or enterprising.

bullock n a young castrated bull.

bullring n an arena for bullfights.

bull's-eye n the centre of a target, or a shot that hits it.

bull terrier n a short-haired breed of terrier.

bully[1] n (pl -ies) a person who habitually intimidates weaker people.

bully[2] v (-ies, -ied) to intimidate.

bulrush n a grasslike plant growing in wet areas.

bulwark n 1 a defensive wall or barrier. 2 (usu in pl) the side of a ship above the upper deck.

bum[1] n Brit, informal the buttocks.

bum[2] adj informal bad or worthless.

bum[3] n NAmer, informal 1 an idler or loafer. 2 a homeless vagrant.

bum[4] v (bummed, bumming) chiefly NAmer, informal (+ around) to spend time idly.

bumble v to speak or act in a faltering or confused manner. ➤ **bumbler** n.

bumblebee n a large bee with a loud hum.

bumf or **bumph** n chiefly Brit, informal unwanted documents and printed information.

bump[1] v 1 to strike or knock with force. 2 to collide with. 3 to move in a series of bumps or jolts. ✳ **bump into** to meet unexpectedly.

bump[2] n 1 a sudden blow or jolt. 2 a swelling or protuberance.

bumper[1] n a bar fitted at either end of a motor vehicle for absorbing shock.

bumper[2] adj unusually large or fine.

bumpkin n an awkward and unsophisticated country person.

bump off v informal to murder.

bumptious adj unpleasantly self-assertive.

bump up v informal to increase.

bumpy adj (-ier, -iest) 1 covered with bumps. 2 marked by jolts.

bun n 1 a small bread roll or cake. 2 a tight knot of hair at the back of the head.

bunch[1] n 1 a compact group of things loosely held together. 2 informal a group of people. ➤ **bunchy** adj.

bunch[2] v (often + up) to form into a bunch.

bundle[1] n 1 a collection of things held loosely together. 2 informal a large sum of money.

bundle[2] v 1 to form into a bundle or package. 2 informal to hustle or hurry unceremoniously. 3 (+ into) to force hastily into a container or vehicle.

bung[1] n a stopper in the hole of a cask.

bung[2] v 1 (often + up) to block or close. 2 chiefly Brit, informal to throw or put clumsily.

bungalow n a house with one storey.

bungee jumping *n* the sport of diving from a high place to which the feet are attached by an elastic cord.

bungle *v* to do clumsily; to botch. ➤ **bungler** *n*.

bungle² *n* something done clumsily.

bunion *n* an inflamed swelling on the big toe.

bunk¹ *n* a narrow built-in bed.

bunk² *v* (*often* + down) to sleep in a makeshift bed.

bunk³ *n* informal, dated nonsense.

bunk⁴ ✽ **do a bunk** chiefly Brit, informal to escape hurriedly.

bunker *n* **1** a bin or compartment for storing fuel. **2** a fortified underground shelter. **3** a sand-filled hazard on a golf course.

bunk off *v* chiefly Brit, informal to play truant from school.

bunny *n* (*pl* **-ies**) informal a rabbit.

Bunsen burner *n* a gas burner used in laboratories.

bunting¹ *n* a small bird with a short strong beak.

bunting² *n* flags and streamers used as outdoor decorations.

buoy¹ *n* a moored float serving as a navigational aid.

buoy² *v* (+ up) to raise the spirits of.

Usage Note: Note the spelling *buoy* not *bouy*.

buoyant *adj* **1** capable of floating. **2** cheerful and resilient. ➤ **buoyancy** *n*.

burble¹ *v* **1** to make a bubbling sound. **2** to speak rapidly or ramblingly.

burble² *n* **1** a burbling sound. **2** rapid or rambling speech.

burden¹ *n* **1** a heavy load or thing to be carried. **2** an oppressive or troubling duty or responsibility.

burden² *v* to load or oppress with a burden.

burdensome *adj* oppressive or troublesome.

bureau /'byoooaroh/ *n* (*pl* **bureaus** or **bureaux**) **1** a government department. **2** a public office or agency. **3** Brit a writing desk with a sloping top. **4** NAmer a low chest of drawers.

bureaucracy *n* (*pl* **-ies**) **1** government based on fixed rules and a hierarchy of authority. **2** excessive official procedure. ➤ **bureaucratic** *adj*.

bureaucrat *n* a government official who follows procedures rigidly.

burgeon *v* **1** to send forth new growth. **2** to grow and expand rapidly.

burger *n* a hamburger.

burgher *n* archaic an inhabitant of a borough or town.

burglar *n* somebody who commits burglary.

burglary *n* (*pl* **-ies**) the offence of burgling a building.

burgle *v* to steal from (a building).

Burgundy *n* (*pl* **-ies**) a red or white wine from Burgundy in France.

burial *n* the burying of a dead body.

burlesque *n* **1** a literary or dramatic work that imitates or ridicules. **2** NAmer a variety show.

burly *adj* (**-ier**, **-iest**) strongly and heavily built.

burn¹ *v* (*past and past part.* **burned** or **burnt**) **1** to undergo or cause to undergo combustion by fire. **2** to damage or become damaged by exposure to fire or heat. **3** of a fire: to consume fuel and give off heat. **4** (+ with) to experience a strong emotion or desire. ✽ **burn one's bridges/boats** to commit oneself to a course of action. **burn one's fingers** see FINGER¹. **burn the candle at both ends** to be active at night as well as by day.

burn² *n* an injury resulting from burning.

burn³ *n* chiefly Scot a small stream.

burner *n* the part of a fuel-burning device that produces the flame.

burning *adj* **1** on fire or very hot. **2** ardent or intense. **3** urgent.

burnish *v* to make shiny or lustrous by rubbing.

burnout *n* extreme exhaustion caused by overwork and stress.

burnt *v* chiefly Brit past tense and past part. of BURN¹.

burp¹ *n* informal a belch.

burp² *v* informal to belch.

burr¹ *n* **1** a rough or prickly covering of a fruit or seed. **2** a rough edge. **3** the rolled pronunciation of /r/ made at the back of the throat or the front of the mouth.

burr² *v* to make a whirring sound.

burrow¹ *n* a hole or passage in the ground made by a small animal.

burrow² *v* **1** to make (a hole or passage) by tunnelling. **2** to conceal oneself under something. **3** to search as if by digging.

bursar *n* chiefly Brit an official in charge of the financial affairs of an institution.

bursary *n* (*pl* **-ies**) a grant of money awarded to a student.

burst¹ *v* (*past tense and past part.* **burst**) **1** to break suddenly and violently apart or into pieces. **2** (+ into/out) to give vent suddenly to laughter or tears. **3** (+ into) to begin suddenly and forcefully. **4** to emerge or appear suddenly. **5** (+ with) to be filled to the point of breaking or overflowing.

burst² *n* **1** a sudden outbreak or eruption. **2** a brief period of effort or exertion. **3** an act of bursting.

bury *v* (**-ies**, **-ied**) **1** to place or hide in the earth or underground. **2** to conceal. **3** (+ in) to engross (oneself). ✽ **bury the hatchet** to settle a disagreement.

bus¹ *n* (*pl* **buses**, NAmer **busses**) **1** a large motor vehicle that carries passengers along a fixed route. **2** a conductor carrying data from one part of a computer to another.

bus² v (**bused** or **bussed, busing** or **bussing**) to travel or transport by bus.

busby n (pl **-ies**) a tall ceremonial fur hat worn by members of some regiments.

bush¹ n **1** a shrub with a woody stem and thickly growing branches. **2** (usu **the bush**) a large wild area in Africa or Australia.

bush² or **bushing** n an insulated lining through which an electrical wire passes.

bush baby n a small African primate with large eyes and ears.

bushel n **1** a unit of volume for dry goods and for liquids, equal to 8 imperial gallons (about 36.4l). **2** a US unit of volume, equal to 64 US pints (about 30.3l).

bushy adj (**-ier, -iest**) **1** growing thickly. **2** overgrown with bushes.

business n **1** commercial activity. **2** a commercial or industrial enterprise. **3** one's regular employment. **4** an immediate task or objective. **5** a matter that concerns one. * **mean business** to speak or act with serious intent.

businesslike adj efficient and systematic.

businessman or **businesswoman** n (pl **businessmen** or **businesswomen**) a person who is engaged in business.

busk v to play music in the street to collect money from passers-by. ➤ **busker** n.

bust¹ n **1** a woman's breasts. **2** a sculpture of the head, neck, and shoulders.

bust² v (past tense and past part. **busted** or **bust**) informal **1** to break or smash. **2** chiefly NAmer to arrest or raid.

bust³ adj informal **1** broken. **2** bankrupt.

bust⁴ n informal **1** a police raid or arrest. **2** a period of economic collapse.

bustle¹ v **1** to move briskly and ostentatiously. **2** to be full of people and activity.

bustle² n noisy and energetic activity.

bustle³ n a pad or framework formerly worn by women to give extra fullness at the back of a skirt.

bust-up n informal a quarrel or brawl.

busty adj (**-ier, -iest**) informal of a woman: having large breasts.

busy¹ adj (**-ier, -iest**) **1** fully engaged in an activity. **2** full of activity; bustling. ➤ **busily** adv.

busy² v (**-ies, -ied**) to occupy (oneself).

busybody n (pl **-ies**) a meddlesome person.

but¹ conj used to join words, clauses, or sentences to express reservation: poor but proud. * **but for** were it not for: He might have died but for your help.

but² prep with the exception of; other than: all but one.

butane n an inflammable gas obtained from petroleum or natural gas and used as a fuel.

butch adj informal aggressively masculine.

butcher¹ n **1** a person who slaughters animals for their meat. **2** a person who sells or deals in meat. **3** a ruthless or brutal killer of people.

butcher² v **1** to slaughter and prepare (an animal) for sale. **2** to kill (people) indiscriminately. **3** to spoil or ruin. ➤ **butchery** n.

butler n the chief male servant of a household.

butt¹ v to strike or push with the head or horns.

butt² n a blow or thrust with the head or horns.

butt³ n **1** the thicker end of a tool or weapon. **2** the unsmoked remnant of a cigar or cigarette. **3** NAmer, informal the buttocks.

butt⁴ n **1** an object of abuse or ridicule. **2** a target in archery or shooting.

butt⁵ v **1** to place end to end. **2** (+ against/on to) to adjoin.

butt⁶ n a large barrel.

butter¹ n a pale yellow fatty substance made by churning milk or cream.

butter² v to spread or coat with butter.

butter bean n a large dried bean of a tropical plant.

buttercream n a creamy cake filling made with butter and icing sugar.

buttercup n a wild plant with bright yellow cup-shaped flowers.

butterfingers n (pl **butterfingers**) informal somebody who tends to drop things.

butterfly n (pl **-ies**) **1** an insect with large, broad, brightly coloured wings. **2** a frivolous person. **3** a swimming stroke performed by moving both arms together forwards out of the water and then sweeping them back. **4** informal (in pl) a queasy feeling caused by nervous tension.

buttermilk n **1** the liquid left after butter has been churned. **2** slightly sour milk made by adding bacteria to milk.

butterscotch n a brittle toffee made from brown sugar, and butter.

butter up v informal to charm or persuade with flattery.

buttery¹ n (pl **-ies**) Brit a room in a college, in which food and drink are sold.

buttery² adj similar to or containing butter.

butt in v to intrude or interrupt.

buttock n the back of a hip that forms one of the two fleshy parts on which a person sits.

button¹ n **1** a small disc secured to a piece of clothing and fastened by passing it through a buttonhole or loop. **2** a knob on a piece of equipment that is pressed to activate a function.

button² v (often + up) to fasten with buttons.

buttonhole¹ n **1** a slit or loop on a piece of clothing, through which a button is passed. **2** Brit a flower worn in the buttonhole of a lapel.

buttonhole² v informal to seek out and detain in conversation.

buttress¹ n **1** a supporting structure built

against a wall or building. **2** a projecting part of a mountain or rock cliff.

buttress[2] v **1** to support with a buttress. **2** to give support or strength to.

buxom adj of a woman: with an attractively rounded figure and large breasts.

buy[1] v (past tense and past part. **bought**) **1** to pay for (something) in order to own it. **2** to obtain by making a sacrifice. **3** informal to believe or accept (something said or proposed). ➤ **buyer** n.

buy[2] n informal a purchase.

buyout n the purchase of all the shares in a business.

buzz[1] v **1** to make a continuous low humming sound. **2** to be filled with activity or conversation. **3** to move in a hurried or busy manner. **4** to summon or signal with a buzzer.

buzz[2] n **1** a continuous low humming sound. **2** a flurry of activity or excitement. **3** informal rumour or gossip. **4** a signal conveyed by a buzzer or bell. **5** informal a telephone call. **6** informal a thrill.

buzzard n **1** chiefly Brit a large hawk with broad wings and a soaring flight. **2** chiefly NAmer a large bird of prey.

buzzer n an electrical device that makes a buzzing sound.

buzz off v informal to go away.

buzzword n informal a technical word or phrase that has become fashionable.

by[1] prep **1** through the action or creation of. **2** near to. **3** up to and beyond. **4** during: by night. **5** not later than. **6** by means of. **7** in conformity with.

by[2] adv past.

bye[1] n **1** the right of a competitor to proceed to the next round when there is no opponent or the opponent has withdrawn. **2** in cricket, a run scored off a ball that passes the batsman without contact.

bye[2] interj informal used as an expression of farewell.

by-election n Brit a mid-term election to fill a vacancy in a constituency.

bygone[1] adj belonging to an earlier time. ✳ **let bygones be bygones** to forgive past quarrels.

bygone[2] n a domestic or industrial implement of an early and now disused type.

bylaw or **byelaw** n a law made by a local authority and valid only within its area.

by-line n **1** a line in a newspaper or magazine article naming the author. **2** a goal line on a football pitch.

bypass[1] n **1** a road built to take traffic round a town centre. **2** a passage created surgically between two blood vessels to divert blood.

bypass[2] v **1** to go round by means of a bypass. **2** to neglect or ignore.

byplay n action apart from the main action of a film or play.

by-product n **1** something produced in the manufacture of something else. **2** a secondary result.

byre n Brit a cow shed.

bystander n somebody present but not involved in a situation or event.

byte n in computing, a unit equal to a string of eight adjacent bits (binary digits).

byway n a quiet or minor road.

byword n **1** a saying or proverb. **2** a noteworthy or typical example of a quality.

Byzantine adj **1** of the ancient city of Byzantium or its empire. **2** excessively complex. **3** characterized by trickery and deception.

C¹ or **c** n (pl **C's** or **Cs** or **c's**) the third letter of the English alphabet.

C² abbr **1** Celsius. **2** centigrade. **3** century.

C³ abbr the chemical symbol for carbon.

Ca abbr the chemical symbol for calcium.

cab n **1** a taxi. **2** a compartment for the driver of a train, bus, or large vehicle. **3** formerly, a horse-drawn carriage used for hire.

cabal n a clandestine political faction.

cabaret /'kabəray/ n a stage show at a night-club.

cabbage n **1** the leaves of a plant with a a dense round head, used as a vegetable. **2** informal an inactive or apathetic person.

caber n a tree trunk thrown in the Scottish sport of tossing the caber.

cabin n **1** a private room or compartment on a ship. **2** the passenger compartment in an aircraft. **3** a small simple wooden house.

cabinet n **1** a cupboard usu with doors and shelves for storing or displaying articles. **2** an upright case housing a radio, television, etc. **3** (often **Cabinet**) a body consisting of the prime minister and senior ministers.

cabinetmaker n a craftsman who makes furniture in wood.

cable n **1** a strong thick rope of fibre or metal. **2** a set of electrical wires surrounded by a sheath.

cable car n a small cabin hanging from a cable, carrying passengers up and down a mountainside.

cable television n a television service to subscribers via a cable.

caboodle * **the whole caboodle** informal the whole lot.

caboose n NAmer a wagon for the crew, attached to a goods train.

cabriolet /ˌkabrioh'lay/ n a car with a folding or removable roof.

cacao n (pl **-os**) the seeds of a South American tree used in making cocoa and chocolate.

cache n a hiding place, esp for provisions or weapons.

cachet¹ n prestige or esteem.

cackle¹ v **1** to make the squawking cry of a hen. **2** to talk or laugh noisily.

cackle² n **1** a cackling noise made by a hen. **2** a cackling laugh.

cacophony n (pl **-ies**) a discordant combination of sounds. ➤ **cacophonous** adj.

cactus n (pl **cacti** or **cactuses**) a plant with a fleshy stem and scales or spines instead of leaves.

cad n dated a dishonourable man. ➤ **caddish** adj.

cadaver n a corpse, esp one intended for dissection.

cadaverous adj unhealthily pale or thin.

caddie¹ or **caddy** n (pl **-ies**) somebody who carries a golfer's clubs and gives advice.

caddie² or **caddy** v (**-ies, -ied**) to work as a caddie.

caddy¹ n (pl **-ies**) a small container for tea.

caddy² n see CADDIE¹.

caddy³ v see CADDIE².

cadence n **1** the rhythmic flow and intonations of speech. **2** in music, a sequence of chords moving to a harmonic close.

cadenza n an elaborate solo passage in a concerto.

cadet n **1** a trainee officer in the armed forces or the police force. **2** a young person receiving basic military training.

cadge v informal to ask for and get (something) one does not deserve.

cadmium n a bluish white metallic chemical element used in batteries.

cadre n a group of trained people forming the nucleus of a military force or political organization.

Caesar n a title for a Roman emperor.

Caesarean section (NAmer **Cesarean section**) n an operation for delivering a baby by cutting through the mother's abdominal wall.

café n chiefly Brit a small restaurant serving light meals and drinks.

cafeteria n a self-service restaurant.

cafetière /kaf'tyeə/ n a coffee pot with a plunger used to force the grounds to the bottom.

caffeine n a stimulant occurring naturally in tea and coffee.

caftan n see KAFTAN.

cage¹ n an enclosure with bars for confining or carrying animals.

cage² v **1** to put or keep in a cage. **2** to confine as if in a cage.

cagey or **cagy** adj (**-ier, -iest**) informal hesitant about speaking or committing oneself. ➤ **cagily** adv, **caginess** n.

cagoule or **kagoul** n a lightweight waterproof jacket with a hood.

cahoots ✳ **in cahoots** informal working together secretly.

caiman n see CAYMAN.

cairn n 1 a pile of stones built as a memorial or landmark. 2 a breed of small terrier with coarse hair.

cajole v to persuade with flattery or deception. ➤ **cajolery** n.

cake¹ n 1 a sweet baked food made from a mixture of flour, sugar, fat, and eggs. 2 a flat round mass of savoury food.

cake² v 1 to cover and encrust. 2 to form or harden into a mass.

calabrese n a type of sprouting broccoli.

calamine n a pink powder used in soothing or cooling lotions.

calamity n (pl -ies) an extremely grave event; a disaster. ➤ **calamitous** adj.

calcify v (-ies, -ied) 1 to harden with calcium carbonate or other calcium compounds. 2 to convert into a solid compound of calcium.

calcium n a silver-white metallic chemical element.

calcium carbonate n a chemical compound occurring naturally as chalk, marble, and limestone, etc.

calculate v 1 to determine by mathematical processes. 2 to reckon or estimate. 3 (+ on) to count or rely on. ➤ **calculable** adj.

calculated adj planned to accomplish a purpose; intentional.

calculating adj devious or scheming.

calculation n 1 the process or result of calculating. 2 studied care in planning.

calculator n an electronic device for making mathematical calculations.

calculus n a branch of mathematics dealing with rates of change of functions.

caldron n see CAULDRON.

calendar n 1 a system for fixing the length and divisions of the year. 2 a chart or table showing the days of the year. 3 a chronological list of events or activities.

calf¹ n (pl **calves** or **calfs**) 1 a young cow or bull. 2 the young of some other large animals, e.g. the elephant or whale.

calf² n (pl **calves**) the fleshy back part of the leg below the knee.

calibrate v 1 to mark the graduations of (a gauge or thermometer). 2 to determine the correct reading of (a scale or instrument) by comparison with a standard. ➤ **calibration** n.

calibre (NAmer **caliber**) n 1 the internal diameter of a gun barrel or bullet. 2 degree of quality or ability.

calico n (pl -**oes** or -**os**) 1 white or unbleached cotton cloth. 2 NAmer brightly printed cotton fabric.

caliper n NAmer see CALLIPER.

caliph or **calif** n formerly, a secular and spiritual Islamic leader.

calk n see CAULK.

call¹ v 1 to cry out loudly. 2 to cry out to (somebody) to attract attention. 3 of a bird or animal: to utter a characteristic note or cry. 4 to telephone. 5 to summon to a meeting. 6 to use a name or description for. 7 (often + in/by/round) to make a short visit. 8 to stop at a particular place. ✳ **call for** to need or demand. **call on/upon** to require (somebody) to do something. **call the shots/tune** to be in control. **call to account** to demand an explanation from. ➤ **caller** n.

call² n 1 an act of calling with the voice. 2 the cry of a bird or animal. 3 a request or command to come. 4 need or justification. 5 a strong inner prompting. 6 a short visit. 7 an act of telephoning. ✳ **on call** ready to be used or summoned when needed.

call centre n an office dealing with large numbers of telephone enquiries for an organization.

call girl n a prostitute making appointments by telephone.

calligraphy n the art of producing decorative handwriting. ➤ **calligrapher** n, **calligraphic** adj.

calling n 1 a profession or occupation. 2 a strong inner impulse.

calliper (NAmer **caliper**) n 1 (usu in pl) a measuring instrument with two hinged arms. 2 a support for the human leg.

callisthenics (NAmer **calisthenics**) pl n rhythmic bodily exercises. ➤ **callisthenic** adj.

call off v to cancel (an arrangement).

callous adj cruelly insensitive. ➤ **callously** adv.

callow adj immature and lacking experience.

call up v to summon for military service.

callus n (pl **calluses**) a hard thickened area on skin or bark.

calm¹ adj 1 free from anger, nervousness, or excitement. 2 quiet or still. ➤ **calmly** adv, **calmness** n.

calm² n a calm state.

calm³ v (often + down) to make or become calm.

calorie or **calory** n (pl -**ies**) a unit for measuring energy.

calorific adj relating to the energy-producing content of food or fuel.

calumniate v formal to make false statements about.

calumny n (pl -**ies**) a maliciously false statement about somebody.

calve v to give birth to (a calf).

calves¹ n pl of CALF¹.

calves² n pl of CALF².

calypso n (pl -**os**) a style of West Indian music with improvised lyrics on topical themes.

calyx n (pl **calyxes** or **calyces**) the outer leafy part of a flower surrounding the bud.

cam *n* a wheel or shaft with a projecting part that transforms circular motion into back-and-forth motion.

camaraderie *n* a spirit of good humour and trust among friends.

camber *n* a slight arching or curved shape given to a flat surface such as a road.

cambric *n* a fine white linen or cotton fabric.

camcorder *n* a video camera with a built-in video recorder.

came *v* past tense of COME.

camel *n* a mammal with a long neck and either one or two humps on its back, used for riding in desert regions.

camellia *n* a shrub with glossy leaves and bright flowers.

cameo *n* (*pl* **-os**) **1** a piece of jewellery carved with a contrasting raised design of a head in profile. **2** a short piece of writing highlighting a plot or character. **3** a small dramatic role played by a well-known actor.

camera *n* a device for taking photographs or moving images. ✳ **in camera** in private, often in a judge's private rooms.

camisole *n* a short bodice worn as an undergarment by women.

camomile *or* **chamomile** *n* a strong-scented plant with leaves and flowers that are used in herbal remedies.

camouflage[1] *n* **1** the disguising of military personnel and equipment so that they blend in with their surroundings. **2** clothing and other covering used for this purpose. **3** animal markings and colouring that match the natural surroundings.

camouflage[2] *v* to conceal or disguise with camouflage.

camp[1] *n* **1** an area of ground where tents or other temporary shelters are erected. **2** a place with accommodation and other facilities for troops, holidaymakers, prisoners, etc. **3** the members of a political party or supporters of a particular cause.

camp[2] *v* **1** to pitch or occupy a camp. **2** to live temporarily in a tent or other outdoor accommodation. ➤ **camper** *n*.

camp[3] *adj informal* **1** exaggeratedly effeminate. **2** deliberately and outrageously affected or inappropriate.

camp[4] *v* ✳ **camp it up** *informal* to act or behave in a camp manner.

campaign *n* **1** a series of military operations forming a distinct phase of a war. **2** a series of coordinated actions for achieving a particular result.

campanology *n* the art of bell ringing. ➤ **campanologist** *n*.

camp bed *n* a small collapsible bed.

camphor *n* a chemical compound obtained from the camphor tree and used as a liniment and insect repellent.

campus *n* (*pl* **campuses**) **1** the grounds and buildings of a university. **2** *NAmer* the grounds of a school or college.

camshaft *n* a shaft to which cams are attached.

can[1] *v aux* (*third person sing. present tense* **can**, *past tense* **could**) **1** to be able to. **2** to have permission to. **3** to have a certain tendency.

can[2] *n* a cylindrical metal container for food or drink.

can[3] *v* (**canned, canning**) to preserve food or drink) in a can.

Canadian *n* a native or inhabitant of Canada. ➤ **Canadian** *adj*.

canal *n* **1** an artificial waterway for ships or boats. **2** any channel or watercourse used for drainage or irrigation. **3** a tubular passage in an animal or plant.

canapé *n* a small piece of bread or pastry with a savoury topping.

canard *n* a false report or story.

canasta *n* a card game for four players using two full packs plus jokers.

cancan *n* an energetic stage dance with high kicks.

cancel *v* (**cancelled, cancelling,** *NAmer* **canceled, canceling**) **1** to decide that (something arranged) will not take place. **2** to annul or revoke. **3** to mark (a ticket or postage stamp) to show that it has been used. **4** (*often* + out) to match in force or effect; to counterbalance or offset. ➤ **cancellation** *n*.

cancer *n* **1** a malignant tumour that develops when cells multiply in an unlimited way. **2** the medical condition that is characterized by this. **3** a spreading evil in a person, society, etc. **4** (**Cancer**) the fourth sign of the zodiac. ➤ **cancerous** *adj*.

candela *n* the basic SI unit of luminous intensity.

candelabrum *n* (*pl* **candelabra**) a branched candlestick or lamp with several lights.

candid *adj* frank or sincere. ➤ **candidly** *adv*.

candidate *n* **1** somebody who applies for a job or award. **2** somebody who is taking an examination. **3** somebody or something regarded as deserving or suitable for something. ➤ **candidacy** *n*.

candied *adj* of fruit: preserved in a heavy syrup.

candle *n* a cylindrical length of wax with a wick that is burned to give light. **not worth the candle** not justified by the result.

candlestick *n* a holder for a candle.

candlewick *n* a fabric made with thick soft cotton yarn cut in a raised tufted pattern.

candour (*NAmer* **candor**) *n* sincerity or frankness.

candy *n* **1** crystallized sugar formed by boiling down sugar syrup. **2** *chiefly NAmer* sweets.

candy floss *n Brit* a light fluffy mass of spun sugar, wound round a stick.

cane¹ *n* **1** a hollow stem of some reeds and grasses. **2** a length of cane used as a walking stick or for beating somebody.

cane² *v* to beat with a cane. ➤ **caning** *n*.

canine¹ *adj* resembling or being a member of the dog family.

canine² *n* a pointed tooth next to each incisor.

canister *n* a small round container for storage.

canker *n* **1** an ulcer or spreading sore. **2** an area of dead tissue in a plant. **3** an inflammatory disease of animals. **4** a source of spreading corruption or evil. ➤ **cankerous** *adj*.

cannabis *n* the dried leaves of hemp plants, used as a drug.

canned *adj* **1** sold or preserved in a can. **2** *informal* drunk.

cannelloni *pl n* rolls of pasta served with a filling of meat, vegetables, or cheese.

cannery *n* (*pl* **-ies**) a factory for canning foods.

cannibal *n* a human being who eats human flesh. ➤ **cannibalism** *n*, **cannibalistic** *adj*.

cannibalize *or* **-ise** *v* to dismantle (e.g. a machine) for spare parts.

cannon *n* (*pl* **cannons** *or* **cannon**) **1** a large gun on a carriage, used formerly in warfare. **2** an automatic shell-firing gun mounted in an aircraft or tank.

cannonball *n* a metal or stone ball for firing from a cannon.

cannon fodder *n* soldiers seen as expendable in war.

cannot *contraction* can not.

canny *adj* (**-ier, -iest**) cautious and shrewd; astute. ➤ **cannily** *adv*.

canoe¹ *n* a long light narrow boat with pointed ends, propelled with a paddle.

canoe² *v* (**canoes, canoed, canoeing**) to travel in a canoe. ➤ **canoeist** *n*.

canon¹ *n* **1** a regulation or dogma decreed by a church council. **2** an accepted rule or criterion. **3** a body of principles or standards. **4** an authoritative list of books accepted as Holy Scripture. **5** the authentic works of a writer. **6** a musical composition in which a melody is repeated by parts entering in succession and overlapping.

canon² *n* a clergyman attached to a cathedral.

canonical *adj* **1** conforming to a general rule; orthodox. **2** conforming to canon law. **3** accepted as authentic.

canonize *or* **-ise** *v* to recognize (a dead person) officially as a saint. ➤ **canonization** *n*.

canon law *n* the law governing a church.

canoodle *v* *informal* to kiss and cuddle amorously.

canopy *n* (*pl* **-ies**) **1** a cloth covering hung over a bed or throne. **2** an ornamental rooflike structure. **3** the lifting or supporting surface of a parachute. **4** the spreading leafy branches at the top of a forest.

cant¹ *n* **1** insincere or hypocritical talk suggesting piety. **2** the jargon of a specific group.

cant² *n* slope or slanting surface.

cant³ *v* to tilt or slope.

can't *contraction* can not.

cantaloupe *or* **cantaloup** *n* a type of melon with a hard rind and orange flesh.

cantankerous *adj* ill-natured or quarrelsome.

cantata *n* a musical setting of a religious text, comprising choruses, solos, recitatives, and interludes.

canteen *n* **1** a restaurant in a school or factory. **2** *Brit* a box for holding cutlery. **3** a small water flask used by soldiers or campers.

canter¹ *n* a gait of a horse that is smoother and slower than a gallop.

canter² *v* (**cantered, cantering**) to move or ride at a canter.

canticle *n* a hymn based on a text from the Bible and used in services of worship.

cantilever *n* a projecting beam or member supported at only one end. ➤ **cantilevered** *adj*,.

canto *n* (*pl* **-os**) a major division of a long poem.

canton *n* a territorial division of a country.

canvas *n* (*pl* **canvases** *or* **canvasses**) **1** a strong closely woven cloth used for making sails, tents, etc. **2** a cloth surface for painting in oils. **3** the floor of a boxing or wrestling ring.

canvass *v* to visit (voters) to seek political support or to find out their opinions. ➤ **canvasser** *n*.

canyon *n* a deep valley or gorge.

cap¹ *n* **1** a soft close-fitting hat with a peak and no brim. **2** *chiefly Brit* a head covering awarded to a member of a sports team. **3** a cover or lid for a container. **4** an upper financial limit. **5** a small container holding an explosive charge that bangs when struck. **6** *Brit* a contraceptive diaphragm fitting over the cervix of the womb. **7** a protective covering for the external part of a tooth. ✳ **cap in hand** in a deferential manner.

cap² *v* (**capped, capping**) **1** to provide or protect with a cap. **2** to form a cap over. **3** *chiefly Brit* to select (a player) for a sports team. **4** to follow (something) with a better example. **5** to impose an upper financial limit on (e.g. a tax or charge).

capability *n* (*pl* **-ies**) the ability to do something.

capable *adj* **1** able or competent. **2** (+ of) having the ability or propensity to do something. ➤ **capably** *adv*.

capacious *adj* able to hold a great deal; roomy.

capacitance *n* the ability to store an electric charge.

capacitor *n* a component in an electrical circuit that can store an electric charge.

capacity *n* (*pl* **-ies**) **1** the maximum amount that can be contained or produced. **2** the power or ability to do something. **3** a position or role that somebody has.

cape¹ *n* a short cloak.

cape² *n* an area of land jutting out into the sea.

caper¹ *v* to leap about playfully.

caper² *n* **1** a playful or carefree leap. **2** a high-spirited escapade or prank.

caper³ *n* (*usu in pl*) the flower bud or berry of a shrub, pickled and used as a seasoning.

capillarity *n* the pressure on the surface of a liquid in contact with a solid, e.g. in a fine-bore tube, raising or lowering it.

capillary¹ *n* (*pl* **-ies**) a blood vessel connecting small arteries with veins.

capillary² *adj* **1** slender and elongated, like a hair. **2** of a tube, passage, etc: having a very fine bore.

capillary action *n* the force on a liquid in a tube, making it rise or fall.

capital¹ *n* **1** a city serving as a seat of government. **2** wealth or goods used to produce further wealth or goods. **3** the excess of the assets of a business over its liabilities. **4** a capital letter. * **make capital out of** to turn (a situation) to one's advantage.

capital² *adj* **1** punishable by death. **2** of a letter: of the series used to begin sentences or proper names, e.g. *A, B, C* rather than *a, b, c*. **3** *dated* excellent.

capital³ *n* the top part of a pillar or column.

capitalism *n* an economic system based on private ownership and control of the means of production. ➤ **capitalist** *n and adj*.

capitalize *or* **-ise** *v* **1** (+ on) to gain by turning (something) to advantage. **2** to supply capital for. **3** to convert into capital. **4** to write or print (in capitals or with an initial capital). ➤ **capitalization** *n*.

capital punishment *n* the punishment of a crime by death.

capitulate *v* to surrender or cease resisting. ➤ **capitulation** *n*.

capon *n* a castrated male chicken fattened for eating.

cappuccino /kapoo'cheenoh/ *n* (*pl* **-os**) frothy coffee made with steamed milk.

caprice *n* a sudden unexpected change of mind.

capricious *adj* changing mood suddenly or unpredictably. ➤ **capriciously** *adv*.

Capricorn *n* the tenth sign of the zodiac (the Goat).

capsicum *n* a fleshy fruit of a tropical plant, used as a vegetable.

capsize *v* of a boat: to overturn in the water.

capstan *n* a rotating cylinder or shaft on which rope or cable is wound.

capsule *n* **1** a gelatin shell enclosing a dose of a medicine. **2** a small compartment or container.

captain¹ *n* **1** a person in command of a ship or civil aircraft. **2** a naval officer ranking below a

commodore. **3** an army officer ranking below a major. **4** a leader of a team. ➤ **captaincy** *n*.

captain² *v* to be captain of.

caption *n* **1** a comment or description accompanying a pictorial illustration. **2** a piece of text appearing on a film or television screen.

captivate *v* to fascinate or charm irresistibly. ➤ **captivating** *adj*.

captive¹ *adj* **1** taken and held prisoner. **2** confined and unable to escape. ➤ **captivity** *n*.

captive² *n* somebody who has been taken prisoner.

captor *n* somebody who takes another as captive.

capture¹ *n* **1** the act of gaining control or possession. **2** somebody or something that has been captured. **3** the storing of data on a computer.

capture² *v* **1** to take captive. **2** to represent or preserve in words, pictures, etc. **3** to remove (a piece) from the playing board by the rules of a game. **4** to store (data) in a computer.

capybara *n* (*pl* **capybaras**) a large South American rodent.

car *n* **1** a motor vehicle designed for carrying a small number of people. **2** a railway carriage.

carafe *n* a glass bottle with a flaring lip and open top, used for serving wine.

caramel *n* **1** sugar or syrup heated to a brown colour and used as a colouring and flavouring. **2** a chewy soft toffee.

carapace *n* a hard case on the back of a turtle, crab, etc.

carat *n* **1** a unit of weight used for precious stones. **2** (*NAmer chiefly* **karat**) a unit of fineness for gold.

caravan *n* **1** *Brit* a vehicle designed to be towed and for living in when parked. **2** a group of travellers on a journey through a desert.

caraway *n* the seeds of an aromatic plant, used in cookery.

carbide *n* a chemical compound of carbon with a metallic element.

carbine *n* a light automatic rifle.

carbohydrate *n* a compound of carbon, hydrogen, and oxygen, forming a major class of energy providing animal foods.

carbolic *or* **carbolic acid** *n* a chemical compound used as a disinfectant.

carbon *n* a chemical element occurring naturally as diamond and graphite or forming a constituent of organic compounds. ➤ **carbonaceous** *adj*.

carbonate¹ *n* a salt or ester of carbonic acid.

carbonate² *v* **1** to convert (something) into a carbonate. **2** to impregnate (a drink) with carbon dioxide.

carbon copy *n* **1** a copy made with carbon paper. **2** a duplicate or exact replica.

carbon dating n a method of dating organic material by recording the deterioration of carbon 14 in it.

carbon dioxide n a gas formed by the burning and decomposition of organic substances and absorbed by plants in photosynthesis.

carbonic acid n a weak acid that is a solution of carbon dioxide in water.

carbon monoxide n a toxic gas formed by the incomplete combustion of carbon.

carbon paper n thin paper coated with dark pigment, used to make a copy of a document.

Carborundum n trademark an abrasive material.

carbuncle n 1 a painful inflammation of the skin. 2 a red gemstone.

carburettor or **carburetter** (NAmer **carburetor**) n a device for mixing the fuel with air in an internal-combustion engine.

carcass or **carcase** n the body of a slaughtered animal.

carcinogen n a susbtance that causes cancer. ➤ **carcinogenic** adj.

carcinoma n (pl **carcinomas** or **carcinomata**) a cancerous tumour originating in the skin or tissue lining a body cavity. ➤ **carcinomatous** adj.

card[1] n 1 thin cardboard or stiff paper. 2 a postcard, greetings card, visiting card. 3 a playing card. 4 a game played with playing cards. 5 a rectangular piece of plastic with machine-readable information, used to withdraw cash, make payment, etc. 6 informal an amusing or eccentric person. ✳ **get one's cards** Brit, informal to be dismissed/resign from employment. **on the cards** possible or likely.

card[2] v to disentangle (fibres) with a toothed implement before spinning.

cardamom n the fruit and seeds of a plant of the ginger family, used as a spice or condiment.

cardboard n a stiff material made from paper pulp.

cardiac adj relating to the heart.

cardigan n a knitted garment with buttons down the front.

cardinal[1] n 1 a high official of the Roman Catholic Church who takes part in the election of a new pope. 2 a deep scarlet colour.

cardinal[2] adj of primary importance; fundamental.

cardinal number n a number used in counting, e.g. one, two, three, etc.

cardiograph n an instrument for recording movements of the heart. ➤ **cardiography** n.

cardiology n the branch of medical science concerned with the heart and its diseases. ➤ **cardiologist** n.

cardiovascular adj relating to the heart and blood vessels.

cardsharp n a cheat at cards.

care[1] n 1 a cause for anxiety. 2 close attention or effort. 3 attention to or provision for the welfare of somebody or something. 4 charge or supervision. 5 Brit legal responsibility for children by a local authority. 6 a sense of loving protection. ✳ **care of** at the address of (somebody other than the addressee). **take care of** to deal with or look after.

care[2] v 1 to be concerned about something or somebody. 2 to feel an interest or involvement. 3 (+ for) to have a liking or taste for. 4 to wish (to do something).

careen v of a ship: to lean over to one side.

career[1] n a field of employment to which a person devotes much of their working life, hoping to make progress in it.

career[2] v to move swiftly in an uncontrolled way.

careerist n somebody who is primarily intent on advancing their career. ➤ **careerism** n.

carefree adj free from anxiety or responsibility.

careful adj 1 exercising or taking care. 2 marked by attentive concern. 3 cautious or prudent. ➤ **carefully** adv.

careless adj 1 not taking enough care. 2 indifferent or unconcerned. ➤ **carelessly** adv, **carelessness** n.

carer n Brit a person who looks after somebody who is ill, elderly, or disabled.

caress[1] n 1 a gentle or loving touch or stroke. 2 a kiss.

caress[2] v to touch or stroke lightly and lovingly.

caretaker n a person who looks after a school or other public building.

careworn adj showing the effects of anxiety.

cargo n (pl **-oes** or **-os**) goods carried by a ship, aircraft, or vehicle.

Caribbean adj of the Caribbean Sea and its islands.

caribou n (pl **caribou**) a large North American deer with broad branching antlers.

caricature[1] n a picture or description that comically or grotesquely exaggerates the appearance or main features of a person or thing.

caricature[2] v to make a caricature of.

caries n (pl **caries**) decay of a tooth or bone.

carmine n a rich crimson or scarlet colour.

carnage n great slaughter.

carnal adj relating to sexual pleasures and appetites.

carnation n a plant with fragrant red, pink, or white flowers.

carnelian n see CORNELIAN.

carnival n a festival with music, dancing, and processions.

carnivore n a flesh-eating mammal.

carnivorous adj eating meat.

carob n the edible pod of a Mediterranean tree, used as the source of a chocolate substitute.

carol[1] n a Christmas song or hymn.

carol[2] v (**carolled, carolling**, *NAmer* **caroled, caroling**) **1** to sing carols. **2** to sing joyfully. ➤ **caroller** n.

carotene n an orange or red pigment found in carrots and a source of vitamin A.

carotid artery n either of the arteries that supply the head with blood.

carouse v to take part in a drinking spree or drunken revel.

carousel or **carrousel** n **1** a merry-go-round. **2** a rotating delivery system for baggage at an airport.

carp[1] n (pl **carp**) a large edible freshwater fish.

carp[2] v informal (+ at) to complain or find fault peevishly.

carpal adj of or forming part of the wrist.

carpel n the female reproductive organ of a flowering plant.

carpenter n a person who builds with wood. ➤ **carpentry** n.

carpet[1] n **1** a floor covering made of a heavy woven material. **2** a thick layer. * **on the carpet** being reprimanded.

carpet[2] v (**carpeted, carpeting**) to cover with a carpet.

carpetbag n a travelling bag made of carpet-like fabric.

carpet bomb v to bomb (an area) thoroughly.

carport n an open-sided shelter for a car.

carriage n **1** Brit a railway passenger vehicle. **2** a horse-drawn passenger vehicle. **3** a movable part of a machine that supports another part. **4** the carrying or conveying of goods. **5** the manner of bearing the body.

carriage clock n a small clock in a glass-sided frame.

carriageway n Brit the part of a road used by vehicles.

carrier n **1** an organization that transports goods or people. **2** a bag with handles for carrying shopping. **3** a device or mechanism that carries something. **4** a messenger. **5** a person or animal that can transmit a disease while being immune to it themselves.

carrion n dead and putrefying flesh.

carrot n **1** a long orange root vegetable. **2** a promised reward or advantage.

carry v (-ies, -ied) **1** to move or transport from one place to another. **2** to wear or have on one's person. **3** to support the weight of. **4** to bear or transmit (a disease). **5** to accept (blame or responsibility). **6** to have as a consequence or attribute. **7** to win acceptance of. **8** to broadcast or publish (a feature or story). **9** of sounds: to be audible at a distance. * **be/get carried away** to lose self-control. **carry the can** informal to accept blame or responsibility. **carry the day** to win or prevail.

carrycot n Brit a transportable bed with handles, for carrying a baby.

carry forward v to transfer a total to a new column or account.

carry off v **1** to take away by force. **2** to perform successfully.

carry on v **1** to conduct or manage. **2** to continue. **3** informal to behave in a rowdy or improper manner. **4** Brit, informal to have a love affair.

carry-on n Brit, informal a fuss.

carry out v to perform (a task).

carry over v **1** to postpone. **2** = CARRY FORWARD.

carry through v to complete (a task).

cart[1] n **1** an open vehicle used for transporting loads. **2** a small wheeled container for pushing by hand.

cart[2] v **1** to carry or convey in a cart. **2** informal (+ off) to take or drag away by force. **3** informal to carry (something heavy) with difficulty.

carte blanche /ˌkaht ˈblonhsh/ n full discretionary power.

cartel n an association of commercial enterprises aimed at limiting competition by agreeing to keep prices high.

carthorse n a strong horse used for pulling heavy loads.

cartilage n a firm tissue that becomes mostly converted into bone in adults and forms structures such as the external ear and the larynx. ➤ **cartilaginous** adj.

cartography n the science of drawing maps and charts. ➤ **cartographer** n, **cartographic** adj.

carton n a container of cardboard or plastic.

cartoon n **1** a satirical drawing in a newspaper or magazine. **2** a series of drawings telling a story or narrative. **3** an animated film made from a sequence of drawings. **4** a preparatory design or drawing. **cartoonist** n.

cartridge n **1** a tube containing a bullet and explosive, for firing from a gun. **2** a case holding ink, magnetic tape, or photographic film for inserting into a device.

cartridge paper n thick paper for drawing on.

cartwheel n **1** a sideways handspring with arms and legs extended. **2** a wheel of a cart.

carve v **1** to cut and shape (wood or stone). **2** to cut (meat) into pieces or slices.

carvery n (pl -ies) chiefly Brit a buffet or restaurant where roast meat is carved for customers.

carving n an object carved from wood or stone.

Casanova n a promiscuous and unscrupulous male lover.

casbah n see KASBAH.

cascade[1] n **1** a small waterfall, esp one of a series. **2** a series or succession of stages, processes, etc in which each item derives from, is triggered by, or acts on the product of the one before. **3** an arrangement of fabric that falls in a wavy line. **4** something that comes suddenly in large amounts.

cascade² v to fall or pour in a cascade, or in large amounts.

case¹ n **1** a situation or set of circumstances. **2** a situation requiring investigation or action. **3** an instance. **4** a suit or action in a court of law. **5** the evidence or arguments supporting a conclusion. **6** in grammar, a form of a noun, pronoun, or adjective indicating its grammatical relation to other words. * **in case** for use or as a precaution if something happens.

case² n **1** a box or receptacle for holding something. **2** an outer covering. **3** chiefly Brit a suitcase. **4** a box together with its contents. **5** a shallow divided tray for holding printing type.

case³ v **1** to enclose in a case; to encase. **2** informal to inspect or study (a place) before robbing it.

casement n a window that opens on hinges at the side.

cash¹ n **1** money in notes and coins. **2** money paid at the time of purchase.

cash² v to pay or obtain cash for (a cheque, money order, etc).

cash crop n a crop produced for sale.

cashew n the edible kidney-shaped nut of a tropical American tree.

cash flow n the flow of money into and out of a business.

cashier¹ n a person who handles payments and receipts in a shop, bank, etc.

cashier² v to dismiss from service in the armed forces.

cash in v **1** to convert into cash. **2** (+ on) to exploit financially.

cashmere n fine wool from the undercoat of the Kashmir goat.

cash register n a machine used in a shop to record the amount of a sale and hold the money received.

casing n **1** an outer cover or shell. **2** a frame round a door or window.

casino n (pl **-os**) a building or room used for gambling.

cask n a large barrel for holding liquids.

casket n **1** a small chest or box for jewels. **2** chiefly NAmer a coffin.

cassava n the fleshy edible rootstock of a tropical plant, used as food.

casserole¹ n **1** a heatproof covered dish for cooking food in an oven. **2** a stew cooked in a casserole.

casserole² v to cook in a casserole.

cassette n a sealed case containing magnetic tape or film for inserting into a player or camera.

cassock n an ankle-length garment worn by Christian clergy and choristers.

cassowary n (pl **-ies**) a large flightless bird found in New Guinea and Australia.

cast¹ v (past and past part. **cast**) **1** to throw with force. **2** to direct (one's eyes or mind). **3** to send forth or emit. **4** to cause (doubt) to occur. **5** to cause (a spell) to have an effect. **6** to record (a vote). **7** to discard or shed. **8** to assign the parts for (a play or film) or select (an actor) for a role. **9** to shape (metal, plastic, etc) in a mould. **10** to throw out a line and bait with a fishing rod. **11** (+ about/around) to look or search.

cast² n **1** the performers in a dramatic production. **2** a reproduction, e.g. of a statue, formed by casting. **3** an impression taken from an object with a molten or plastic substance. **4** = PLASTER¹ 3. **5** the act or an instance of casting something. **6** a slight squint in the eye. **7** the excrement of an earthworm or a pellet regurgitated by a bird. **8** a shape or appearance.

castanets pl n a pair of small wooden or plastic shells clicked together in the hand by flamenco dancers.

castaway n a person who is cast adrift or ashore after a shipwreck.

caste n any of the hereditary social groups in Hinduism.

castellated adj having battlements like a castle.

castigate v formal to punish or reprimand severely. ➤ **castigation** n.

casting vote n a deciding vote cast by a presiding officer in the event of a tie.

cast iron n a hard alloy of iron and carbon cast in a mould.

castle n **1** a large fortified building or set of buildings. **2** = ROOK³. * **castles in the air** unrealistic schemes.

cast off v to unfasten or untie a boat or a line.

cast-off adj given up or discarded.

castor or **caster** n **1** a small wheel set in a swivel mounting on the base of a piece of furniture. **2** a container with a perforated top for sprinkling sugar, flour, or salt.

castor oil n a laxative oil made from the seeds of a tropical plant.

castor sugar n fine white sugar.

castrate v **1** to remove the testes of (a male animal). **2** to deprive of vitality or effect. ➤ **castration** n.

casual adj **1** existing or occurring by chance. **2** occurring without regularity; occasional. **3** of workers: employed for irregular periods. **4** nonchalant or offhand. **5** of clothes: designed for informal wear. ➤ **casually** adv.

casualty n (pl **-ies**) **1** a person killed or injured in action or in an accident. **2** a person or thing that has been injured or lost. **3** the accident and emergency department of a hospital.

casuistry n the false application of general principles to particular instances.

cat n **1** a small furry mammal kept as a pet. **2** a wild animal of the same family as this. **3** informal a malicious woman. * **let the cat out of**

the bag to divulge a secret inadvertently. **the cat's whiskers** *informal* an excellent person or thing. **put/set the cat among the pigeons** to cause trouble.

cataclysm *n* an event marked by violent upheaval or destruction. ➤ **cataclysmic** *adj*.

catacomb *n* an underground cemetery of galleries with recesses for tombs.

catalepsy *n* a trancelike state in which the body remains rigid and immobile for prolonged periods. ➤ **cataleptic** *adj and n*.

catalogue[1] (*NAmer* **catalog**) *n* **1** a list of items arranged systematically. **2** a series of unwelcome feelings.

catalogue[2] (*NAmer* **catalog**) *v* (**catalogue, catalogued, cataloguing**, *NAmer* **catalogs, cataloged, cataloging**) to list in a catalogue.

catalyse (*NAmer* **catalyze**) *v* to cause the catalysis of (a chemical reaction).

catalysis *n* a change in the rate of a chemical reaction induced by a catalyst.

catalyst *n* **1** a substance that increases the rate of a chemical reaction but itself remains unchanged. **2** somebody or something that causes an important event. ➤ **catalytic** *adj*.

catalytic converter *n* a device in a motor vehicle that reduces the polluting substances in exhaust fumes.

catamaran *n* a boat with twin hulls side by side.

catapult[1] *n* **1** *chiefly Brit* a Y-shaped stick with a piece of elastic material fixed between the two prongs, used for shooting small stones. **2** formerly, a military device used for hurling missiles. **3** a device for launching an aircraft at flying speed.

catapult[2] *v* **1** to throw or launch by means of a catapult. **2** to move suddenly or abruptly.

cataract *n* **1** a large steep waterfall. **2** a clouding of the lens of the eye, causing blurred vision.

catarrh *n* inflammation of a mucous membrane in the nose and throat, causing an excess of mucus.

catastrophe *n* a sudden momentous or tragic event. ➤ **catastrophic** *adj*, **catastrophically** *adv*.

catatonia *n* **1** a form of schizophrenia marked by catalepsy. **2** = CATALEPSY. ➤ **catatonic** *adj and n*.

cat burglar *n* a burglar who enters buildings by climbing up them.

catcall[1] *n* a loud or shrill cry expressing disapproval.

catcall[2] *v* to make a catcall.

catch[1] *v* (*past tense and past part.* **caught**) **1** to capture or seize (a person or animal), *esp* after pursuing them. **2** to take or entangle in a snare. **3** to discover (somebody) unexpectedly. **4** to become or cause to become entangled, fas-

tened, or stuck. **5** to intercept and keep hold of (a moving object). **6** of a container: to take in and retain. **7** to become infected with (a disease). **8** to hit or strike. **9** to be struck or affected by. **10** to attract or arrest (somebody's attention). **11** to get or get momentarily or quickly. **12** to be in time for. **13** to grasp with the senses or the mind. **14** to capture a likeness of. **15** of a fire: to start to burn. * **catch sight of** to see (something or somebody) suddenly or momentarily.

catch[2] *n* **1** the total quantity caught at one time. **2** the act of catching. **3** a game in which a ball is thrown and caught. **4** a device for fastening a door or window. **5** a concealed difficulty or snag. **6** *informal* an eligible marriage partner. **7** a break in the voice, *esp* one caused by emotion.

catch-22 *n* a predicament from which there is no escape because this depends on mutually exclusive prior conditions.

catchment area *n* **1** the area from which a river, lake, reservoir, etc gets its water. **2** the area from which the pupils of a school or patients of a hospital are drawn.

catch on *v informal* **1** to become popular. **2** to understand or become aware.

catch out *v* to expose or detect in wrongdoing or error.

catchphrase *n* a well-known phrase associated with a particular person or group.

catch up *v* **1** to succeed in reaching (somebody ahead). **2** to complete (remaining or overdue work).

catchword *n* a word or expression associated with an idea or principle.

catchy *adj* (**-ier, -iest**) of a tune: easy to remember.

catechism *n* a summary of religious doctrine in the form of questions and answers.

categorical *adj* absolute and unqualified. ➤ **categorically** *adv*.

categorize *or* **-ise** *v* to put into a category; to classify. ➤ **categorization** *n*.

category *n* (*pl* **-ies**) a division or group of people or things within a system of classification.

cater *v* **1** (*often* + for) to provide and serve a supply of prepared food. **2** (+ for/to) to supply what is required or desired by. ➤ **caterer** *n*.

caterpillar *n* the wormlike larva of a butterfly or moth.

caterwaul *v* to make a loud wailing cry.

catgut *n* a tough cord made from the intestines of sheep and used for the strings of musical instruments.

catharsis *n* (*pl* **catharses**) **1** releasing of the emotions through drama. **2** the process of bringing repressed ideas and feelings to consciousness during psychoanalysis. ➤ **cathartic** *adj*.

cathedral *n* the principal church of a diocese.

Catherine wheel *n* a firework in the form of a flat spinning coil.

catheter *n* a flexible tube inserted into a hollow body part to draw off fluid.

cathode *n* **1** the electrode by which electrons leave an external circuit and enter a device. **2** the electrode in a thermionic valve that emits the electrons.

cathode-ray tube *n* a vacuum tube in which a beam of electrons is projected onto a screen e.g. to produce a television picture.

catholic *adj* **1** comprehensive or universal. **2** broad in tastes or interests. **3** (**Catholic**). **4** Roman Catholic. ➤ **Catholicism** *n*.

cation *n* a positively charged ion.

catkin *n* a spike of flowers hanging from a tree, e.g. a willow or hazel.

catnap *n* a brief period of sleep during the day.

Catseye *n* *trademark* each of a series of small reflecting studs set in the road to mark the middle or edge of the carriageway.

cat's-paw *n* somebody used by another as a tool or dupe.

catsuit *n* a tightly fitting one-piece garment combining top and trousers.

cattery *n* (*pl* **-ies**) a place for the breeding or care of cats.

cattle *pl n* cows and oxen.

catty *adj* (**-ier, -iest**) spiteful or malicious. ➤ **cattily** *adv*.

catwalk *n* **1** a narrow stage extending into the audience at a fashion show. **2** a narrow walkway.

Caucasian *adj* of the white race of humankind as classified according to physical features. ➤ **Caucasian** *n*.

caucus *n* (*pl* **caucuses**) **1** a closed political meeting to decide on policy. **2** a group of people forming a faction within a larger organization.

caught *v* past tense of CATCH[1].

caul *n* a membrane covering the head of a foetus at birth.

cauldron or **caldron** *n* a large metal cooking pot.

cauliflower *n* a vegetable of the cabbage family with a white flower head.

caulk or **calk** *n* waterproof material used as a filler and sealant.

causal *adj* being or expressing a cause. ➤ **causally** *adv*.

causation *n* **1** the process of causing. **2** the relationship between cause and effect.

cause[1] *n* **1** somebody or something that brings about an effect. **2** a reason or motive. **3** a principle or movement worth defending or supporting.

cause[2] *v* to be the cause of; to make happen.

causeway *n* a raised road or path across wet ground.

caustic *adj* **1** capable of destroying or eating away by chemical action. **2** sarcastic or cutting.

caustic soda *n* = SODIUM HYDROXIDE.

cauterize or **-ise** *v* to sear or burn (a wound) with a hot iron to stop bleeding or destroy infection.

caution[1] *n* **1** prudent forethought to minimize risk. **2** an official warning given to somebody who has committed a minor offence.

caution[2] *v* **1** to warn or advise caution to. **2** to give a legal caution to. **3** to admonish or reprove.

cautionary *adj* serving as a warning.

cautious *adj* careful or prudent. ➤ **cautiously** *adv*.

cavalcade *n* a procession of people on horseback or in vehicles.

cavalier[1] *n* **1** formerly, a gallant gentleman. **2** (**Cavalier**) a supporter of Charles I of England in the Civil War.

cavalier[2] *adj* offhand or dismissive in attitude.

cavalry *n* (*pl* **-ies**) the mounted troops of an army. ➤ **cavalryman** *n*.

cave[1] *n* a natural hollow chamber underground or in the side of a hill or cliff.

cave[2] *v* to explore underground caves. ➤ **caver** *n*.

caveat *n* *formal* a warning or reservation.

cave in *v* **1** to collapse. **2** to submit.

cavern *n* a large underground chamber or cave.

cavernous *adj* oppressively large and spacious.

caviar or **caviare** *n* the salted roe of a sturgeon or other large fish.

cavil[1] *v* (**cavilled, cavilling**, *NAmer* **caviled, caviling**) (*often* + at) to raise trivial objections.

cavil[2] *n* a trivial objection.

cavity *n* (*pl* **-ies**) **1** a hollowed-out space within a mass. **2** an area of decay in a tooth.

cavort *v* to prance or leap about.

caw *v* to utter the harsh cry of the crow. ➤ **caw** *n*.

cayenne *n* a pungent red pepper made from dried chillies.

cayman or **caiman** *n* (*pl* **caymans** or **cayman**) an American reptile closely related to the alligators.

CBE *abbr Brit* Commander of the (Order of the) British Empire.

cc *abbr* **1** carbon copy. **2** cubic centimetre.

CCTV *abbr* closed-circuit television.

CD *abbr* **1** compact disc. **2** diplomatic corps.

Cd *abbr* the chemical symbol for cadmium.

CD-ROM *n* a compact disc on which large amounts of data can be stored for use by a computer.

Ce *abbr* the chemical symbol for cerium.

cease *v* to come or bring to an end.

cease-fire *n* a suspension of hostilities.

ceaseless *adj* continuing without stopping. ➤ **ceaselessly** *adv*.

cedar *n* a tall evergreen tree of the pine family.

cede v to yield or surrender (territory or power).

cedilla n a mark (¸) placed under a c in French to change its sound from /k/ to /s/.

ceilidh /'kayli/ n a Scottish or Irish party with traditional country dancing and music.

ceiling n 1 the overhead inside surface of a room. 2 an upper limit on prices, expenditure, etc.

Usage Note: Note the spelling *-ei-*.

celebrate v 1 to mark an occasion with special activities. 2 to mark (a holy day or feast day) ceremonially. ➤ **celebration** n, **celebratory** adj.

celebrity n (pl **-ies**) 1 a famous person. 2 the state of being famous.

celeriac n a type of celery with a large edible root.

celestial adj 1 of or relating to heaven. 2 of or in the sky.

celibate adj abstaining from sexual relations. ➤ **celibacy** n.

cell n 1 a small room in a prison, convent, or monastery. 2 the smallest unit of living matter. 3 a compartment of a honeycomb or a receptacle for seeds in a plant. 4 a subversive political group within a larger organization. 5 a vessel for generating electricity by chemical action.

cellar n 1 an underground room used for storage. 2 a stock of wine.

cello n (pl **-os**) a large stringed musical instrument of the violin family that is held upright between the player's knees. ➤ **cellist** n.

Cellophane n trademark thin transparent material for wrapping.

cellular adj 1 relating to or consisting of cells. 2 of a phone or radio system: based on 'cells' or areas each having its own transmitter.

cellulite n a type of body fat that produces a dimpled effect on the skin.

celluloid n a transparent plastic photographic film.

cellulose n a carbohydrate derived from plant cell walls and used to make paper, rayon, paint, and cellophane.

cellulose acetate n a chemical compound formed by the action of acetic acid on cellulose and used for making textile fibres, packaging sheets, photographic films, and varnishes.

Celsius adj of a scale of temperature on which water freezes at 0° and boils at 100°.

Celt or **Kelt** n a member of a pre-Roman people living in Britain and parts of Europe.

Celtic¹ or **Keltic** adj of the Celts or their languages.

Celtic² or **Keltic** n a group of languages including Welsh, Cornish, Breton, Irish and Scottish Gaelic, and Manx.

cement¹ n 1 a powder containing lime and clay, used as the binding agent in mortar and concrete. 2 concrete or mortar. 3 a substance used for sticking objects together.

cement² v 1 to join or fix with cement. 2 to make firm and strong.

cemetery n (pl **-ies**) a burial ground.

cenotaph n a monument in honour of members of the armed forces killed in war.

censer n a covered incense burner used in religious rituals.

censor¹ n an official who examines publications and films and removes parts that are unacceptable or offensive.

censor² v to remove unacceptable parts of (a publication or film). ➤ **censorship** n.

Usage Note: Do not confuse this word with *censure*.

censorious adj severely critical.

censure¹ n strong disapproval or condemnation.

censure² v to criticize or disapprove of.

census n (pl **censuses**) an official counting of the population.

cent n a unit of currency worth 100th of the dollar or other monetary unit.

centaur n a mythological creature with the head, arms, and upper body of a man, and the lower body and back legs of a horse.

centenarian n somebody who has reached the age of 100 years.

centenary n (pl **-ies**) a 100th anniversary.

centennial¹ adj 1 marking a 100th anniversary. 2 occurring every 100 years.

centennial² n a 100th anniversary.

center n and v NAmer see CENTRE¹, CENTRE².

centigrade adj of a scale of 100 degrees, esp the Celsius scale of temperature.

centilitre (NAmer **centiliter**) n a metric unit of capacity equal to 100th of a litre (about 0.35fl oz).

centime n a unit of currency worth 100th of a franc.

centimetre (NAmer **centimeter**) n a metric unit of length equal to 100th of a metre (about 0.4in.).

centipede n a long animal with a flattened segmented body and many legs.

central adj 1 at or near the centre. 2 of primary importance; principal. 3 having overall power or control. ➤ **centrally** adv.

centralize or **-ise** v to bring (power or authority) under central control. ➤ **centralization** n.

centre¹ (NAmer **center**) n 1 the middle point or part of something. 2 a building in which a particular activity is concentrated. 3 the part of a town or city where most of the shops, banks, offices, etc are situated. 4 a focus of attention or activity. 5 (often **Centre**) a political group holding moderate views.

centre² v 1 (+ on/round/around) to have as a centre; to focus on. 2 to place or fix in a centre.

centre back n a player or position in football in the middle of the defence.

centrefold n an illustration or feature occupying the two centre pages of a magazine.

centre forward n a player or position in football in the middle of the forward line.

centre of gravity n the point from which the mass of a body may be considered to act.

centrepiece n the most important or outstanding item.

centrifugal force n a force that appears to act outwardly on an object moving on a circular path.

centurion n an officer commanding a century in the ancient Roman army.

century n (pl **-ies**) **1** a period of 100 years. **2** a score of 100 runs made by a cricketer in one innings. **3** a unit of 100 men in the ancient Roman army.

cephalic adj relating to the head.

ceramic adj made from clay by firing at high temperatures.

ceramics pl n the process of making ceramic articles.

cereal n **1** a plant yielding grain suitable for food. **2** the edible grain of such a plant. **3** a breakfast food made from grain.

cerebellum n (pl **cerebellums** or **cerebella**) a part of the brain that projects at the back of the skull.

cerebral adj **1** of the brain or cerebrum. **2** intellectual, or appealing to the intellect.

cerebral palsy n a disability involving speech disturbance and lack of muscular coordination.

cerebrum n (pl **cerebrums** or **cerebra**) the expanded front portion of the brain.

ceremonial¹ adj marked by or used in ceremony. ➤ **ceremonially** adv.

ceremonial² n a prescribed system of formalities or rituals.

ceremonious adj devoted to form and ceremony; punctilious. ➤ **ceremoniously** adv.

ceremony n (pl **-ies**) **1** a formal act or series of acts prescribed by ritual or convention. **2** established procedures of civility or politeness. ✻ **stand on ceremony** to act in a formally correct manner.

cerise adj of a light purplish red colour.

cerium n a grey soft metallic chemical element.

certain¹ adj **1** assured in one's mind. **2** established beyond doubt or question. **3** able to be relied on; inevitable. **4** of a known but unspecified character. **5** named but not known. ✻ **for certain** without doubt.

certain² pron some; unspecified ones.

certainly adv **1** undoubtedly; definitely. **2** yes; of course.

certainty n (pl **-ies**) **1** something indisputable or inevitable. **2** somebody or something that cannot fail. **3** the quality or state of being certain.

certifiable adj **1** able to be certified. **2** informal insane.

certificate n a document officially stating a particular qualification or achievement of the holder. ➤ **certification** n.

certify v (**-ies, -ied**) **1** to confirm officially in writing. **2** to declare officially to be insane.

certitude n the state of being or feeling certain.

cervical adj relating to the cervix.

cervical smear n a test for signs of cancer in cells from the cervix.

cervix n (pl **cervices**) the narrow outer end of the uterus.

cessation n a stop or ending.

cession n yielding of rights or territory.

cesspool n an underground basin for sewage.

cetacean n a mammal such as a whale, dolphin, or porpoise.

Cf abbr the chemical symbol for californium.

cf. abbr compare.

CFC abbr chlorofluorocarbon, a gas formerly used in aerosols and refrigerators and thought to harm the ozone layer.

CFE abbr College of Further Education.

chador n a cloth worn round the head and top part of the body by some Muslim women.

chafe v **1** to make or become sore by rubbing. **2** to rub (something) so as to wear it away. **3** to warm (part of the body) by rubbing. **4** to feel irritation or discontent.

chaff¹ n husks and other debris separated from the seed in threshing grain.

chaff² v to tease good-naturedly.

chaffinch n a finch with a reddish breast and white wing bars.

chagrin¹ n a feeling of humiliating disappointment.

chagrin² v (usu in passive) to disappoint or annoy.

chain¹ n **1** a series of connected links used for support or restraint, or to form a boundary or barrier. **2** a unit of length equal to 66ft (about 20.12m). **3** a series of linked or connected things.

chain² v (often + up/down) to fasten or restrict with a chain.

chain mail n flexible armour made of interlinked metal rings.

chain reaction n **1** a series of related events, each one initiating the next. **2** a chemical or nuclear reaction yielding energy or products that cause further reactions.

chain saw n a power saw with teeth linked in a continuous revolving chain.

chain-smoke v to smoke continuously by lighting one cigarette from the butt of the previous one.

chain store n each of a series of shops under the same ownership.

chair¹ n **1** a seat for one person, with legs, a

back, and sometimes arms. **2** a professorship. **3** the chairperson at a meeting.

chair² v to preside as chairperson at (a meeting).

chair lift n a ski lift with seats for passengers.

chairman or **chairwoman** n (pl **chairmen** or **chairwomen**) somebody who presides over a meeting or board of directors. ➤ **chairmanship** n.

chairperson n (pl **chairpersons**) a person who presides at a meeting.

chaise longue n (pl **chaises longues**) a low sofa with a partial backrest and only one armrest, for reclining on.

chalet n **1** a wooden house with a steep roof and overhanging eaves, common in rural Switzerland. **2** a cabin at a holiday camp.

chalice n a large drinking cup or goblet.

chalk¹ n **1** a soft white limestone. **2** a piece of chalklike material used for writing and drawing. * **not by a long chalk** by no means. ➤ **chalky** adj.

chalk² v **1** to write or mark with chalk. **2** (+ up) to achieve as a success.

challenge¹ v **1** to invite or call to fight or compete. **2** to dispute the validity or truth of. **3** to order to provide proof of identity. **4** to test the ability of. ➤ **challenger** n.

challenge² n **1** an invitation to fight or compete. **2** a calling to account or into question. **3** a command to halt and prove identity. **4** a formal objection. **5** something demanding or stimulating.

challenging adj testing one's ability in a stimulating way.

chamber n **1** an enclosed space or cavity. **2** a legislative or judicial body. **3** a reception room in an official building. **4** archaic a bedroom. **5** (in pl) a set of rooms used by barristers. **6** (usu in pl) a room where a judge hears private cases. **7** the part of a gun that holds the charge or cartridge.

chamberlain n **1** a chief officer of a royal or noble household. **2** a treasurer of a corporation.

chambermaid n a woman who cleans and tidies bedrooms in a hotel.

chamber music n classical music written for a small group of instruments.

chamber pot n a bowl for urine and faeces, kept in a bedroom.

chameleon n a small lizard that can change the colour of its skin to match its surroundings.

chamfer v to cut a narrow angled surface on the edge of (a piece of wood). ➤ **chamfer** n.

chamois n (pl **chamois**) **1** a small antelope of Europe and the Caucasus. **2** a soft leather made from the skin of the chamois or sheep.

chamomile n see CAMOMILE.

champ¹ v to munch noisily. * **champ at the bit** to be impatient.

champ² n informal a champion in a sport or game.

champagne n **1** a white sparkling wine from the Champagne region of France. **2** a pale golden cream colour.

champion¹ n **1** the winner of a competitive event. **2** an active supporter of a person or cause. **3** formerly, a person who did battle on behalf of another.

champion² v to protect or fight for as a champion.

champion³ adj chiefly N Eng, informal excellent or splendid.

championship n **1** a contest to find a champion. **2** the position or title of champion.

chance¹ n **1** an element in existence that makes events unpredictable. **2** an event without an observable cause. **3** an opportunity. * **by chance** without planning or intention. **take a chance/chances** to do something risky.

chance² adj happening by chance.

chance³ v **1** to take place or come about by chance. **2** (+ on/upon) to find by chance. **3** to take a risk with.

chancel n the part of a church near the altar.

chancellor n **1** the chief minister of state in some European countries. **2** the titular head of a British university.

Chancellor of the Exchequer n the British government minister in charge of public finances.

chancer n Brit, informal an unprincipled opportunist.

chancy adj (-ier, -iest) uncertain or risky.

chandelier n a branched ornamental lighting fixture suspended from a ceiling.

chandler n a dealer in supplies for ships and boats.

change¹ v **1** to make or become different. **2** (often + over) to replace (one thing) with another. **3** to convert into something else. **4** to give (money of one currency) in exchange for an equivalent amount in another currency. **5** to put on fresh clothes. * **change hands** to become the property of somebody else.

change² n **1** a process of becoming different. **2** an alternative set of clothes. **3** money returned when a payment exceeds the amount due. **4** coins of low denominations.

changeable adj **1** likely to vary. **2** capable of being altered or exchanged. **3** unpredictable or fickle.

changeling n a child believed to have been left in place of a human child by fairies.

change-over n a conversion to a different system or function.

channel¹ n **1** a narrow region of sea between two land masses. **2** the bed of a stream of water. **3** the navigable part of a river or harbour. **4** a path for communication or information. **5** a band of frequencies for radio or television transmission, e.g. from a radio or television station. **6** a television station. **7** a gutter, groove, or furrow.

channel² v (**channelled, channelling,** NAmer **channeled, channeling**) **1** to direct towards a particular purpose. **2** to convey through a channel.

chant¹ v to sing or recite in a rhythmic monotonous tone.

chant² n **1** a repetitive melody used for liturgical singing. **2** a psalm or canticle sung in this way. **3** a rhythmic monotonous utterance, recitation, or song.

Chanukah n see HANUKKAH.

chaos n **1** a state of utter confusion. **2** a confused mass. ➤ **chaotic** adj, **chaotically** adv.

chap n informal a man or fellow.

chapati or **chapatti** n (pl **chapatis** or **chapattis**) in Indian cookery, a flat round piece of unleavened bread.

chapel n **1** a room or small church used for prayer or worship. **2** a part of a church set aside with its own altar. **3** the members of a printing trade union.

chaperon¹ or **chaperone** n an older woman who accompanies an unmarried younger woman on social occasions.

chaperon² or **chaperone** v to act as chaperon to.

chaplain n a clergyman attached to a branch of the armed forces, an institution, or a private family. ➤ **chaplaincy** n.

chapped adj of the skin: cracked and sore from exposure to the wind or cold.

chapter n **1** a major division of a book. **2** a significant period or sequence of events. **3** the canons of a cathedral or collegiate church, or the members of a religious house. **4** a local branch of a society or fraternity.

char¹ v (**charred, charring**) to burn slightly.

char² n Brit, informal a woman employed to clean in a private house.

character n **1** the qualities that distinguish a particular person or thing from others. **2** a person portrayed in a novel, film or play. **3** informal an interesting or eccentric person. **4** a person's good reputation. **5** moral strength or integrity. **6** a letter or other symbol used in writing or printing. ➤ **characterful** adj, **characterless** adj.

characteristic¹ adj typical of a particular person or thing. ➤ **characteristically** adv.

characteristic² n a distinguishing trait or quality.

characterize or **-ise** v **1** to describe the character or quality of. **2** to distinguish. ➤ **characterization** n.

charade n **1** a game in which a word or phrase is acted out for other players to guess. **2** a ridiculous pretence.

charcoal n **1** a black porous carbon prepared by

partly burning wood. **2** fine charcoal used in pencil form for drawing. **3** a dark grey colour.

chard n a vegetable with large dark green leaves and succulent stalks.

charge¹ v **1** to ask (a price) or ask for payment from (somebody). **2** to accuse (somebody) of having committed an offence. **3** (often + with) to entrust with a task or responsibility. **4** to command or exhort with right or authority. **5** to rush forward in attack. **6** to load or fill. **7** (often + up) to store electrical energy in (a battery). **8** to fill (somebody or something) with passionate emotion, feeling, etc. ➤ **chargeable** adj.

charge² n **1** a price asked or paid for something. **2** a formal accusation. **3** an instruction or command. **4** an obligation or requirement. **5** supervision or custody. **6** somebody or something committed to another's care. **7** a rush forwards in attack. **8** the quantity that something is intended to receive and hold, esp the quantity of explosive for a gun or cannon. **9** a basic property of matter responsible for electrical activity and characterized as negative or positive. **10** a definite quantity of electricity held by a battery. ✳ **in charge** in control or command.

charge card n a card issued by a large shop for buying goods on credit.

chargé d'affaires /ˌshahzhay daˈfeə/ n (pl **chargés d'affaires**) **1** a diplomat who deputizes for an ambassador or minister. **2** a diplomatic representative inferior in rank to an ambassador.

charger n **1** a device used to charge a battery. **2** a horse for battle or parade.

chargrill v to grill (food) quickly over charcoal.

chariot n a two-wheeled horse-drawn vehicle used in ancient warfare and racing. ➤ **charioteer** n.

charisma n the special appeal or charm of an individual that inspires loyalty and enthusiasm.

charitable adj **1** liberal in giving to the poor; generous. **2** merciful or kind in judging others. ➤ **charitably** adv.

charity n (pl **-ies**) **1** kindly generosity and helpfulness shown to those in need. **2** an institution set up to help those in need. **3** money or other help given to those in need.

charlatan n somebody who pretends to have special knowledge or ability.

charm¹ n **1** the quality of alluring or delighting others. **2** a particularly pleasing or attractive quality or feature. **3** an act or phrase believed to have magic power. **4** something worn to ward off evil or attract good fortune. **5** a small ornament worn on a bracelet or chain. ➤ **charmless** adj.

charm² v **1** to delight with attractive qualities or manner. **2** to gain (something) or influence (somebody) by the use of personal charm. **3** to affect as if by magic. **4** to control (an animal) by the use of rituals. ➤ **charmer** n.

charming adj extremely pleasing or delightful. ➤ **charmingly** adv.

charnel house n a place formerly used for depositing dead bodies or bones.

chart¹ n **1** a sheet giving information in the form of a table or graph. **2** a map used for sea or air navigation. **3** (**the charts**) a weekly list of best-selling pop records.

chart² v **1** to make a chart of. **2** to mark or record on a chart. **3** to outline the course or progress of.

charter¹ n **1** a document that defines the rights of a city, educational or professional institution, or company. **2** a special privilege or exemption. **3** a lease of a ship or aircraft for a particular use or group. **4** (used before a noun) relating to such a lease: charter flights.

charter² v (**chartered, chartering**) **1** to grant a charter to. **2** to hire a ship or aircraft.

chartered adj officially qualified for membership of a professional institution.

chary adj (**-ier, -iest**) cautious and wary. ➤ **charily** adv.

chase¹ v **1** to follow rapidly in order to catch. **2** to rush or hurry. **3** chiefly Brit (+ up) to try to find or contact.

chase² n **1** an act of chasing. **2** (**the chase**) hunting. **3** unenclosed land set aside for breeding animals.

chase³ v to engrave with raised or incised work.

chaser n a strong alcoholic drink taken after a milder one.

chasm n **1** a deep cleft in the earth. **2** a big difference or disagreement.

chassis n (pl **chassis**) **1** the framework supporting the body of a vehicle. **2** a frame supporting a piece of equipment.

chaste adj **1** not having sexual intercourse, or sexual intercourse outside marriage. **2** pure in thought and behaviour.

chasten v **1** to correct by punishment or rebuke. **2** to subdue or restrain.

chastise v **1** to punish, esp by beating. **2** to criticize severely. ➤ **chastisement** n.

chastity n the state of being chaste.

chasuble n a sleeveless outer vestment worn by a priest.

chat¹ v (**chatted, chatting**) to talk informally.

chat² n informal conversation.

château /'shatoh/ n (pl **châteaux** or **châteaux**) a large country house in France.

chattel n an item of personal property.

chatter¹ v **1** to talk idly or incessantly. **2** of teeth: to click together repeatedly from cold.

chatter² n **1** idle talk or conversation. **2** the sound or action of chattering.

chatterbox n informal somebody who likes to chatter.

chat up v Brit, informal to talk to in a flirtatious or scheming way.

chauffeur¹ or **chauffeuse** n a person employed to drive somebody in a private car.

chauffeur² v to act as driver for (somebody).

chauvinism n **1** undue belief in the superiority of one's own group, cause, etc. **2** excessive or blind patriotism. ➤ **chauvinist** n and adj, **chauvinistic** adj.

cheap adj **1** low in price. **2** charging a low price. **3** of inferior quality or worth. **4** gained with little effort or by dubious means. ➤ **cheaply** adv.

cheapen v to reduce the value or quality of.

cheapskate n informal a miserly or stingy person.

cheat¹ v **1** to violate the rules of a game or competition dishonestly. **2** to deceive or swindle. **3** to deprive (somebody) of something by deceit or fraud. **4** (+ on) to be sexually unfaithful to.

cheat² n **1** somebody who cheats. **2** a trick or fraud.

check¹ n **1** a test of the accuracy, state, or quality of something. **2** a pause or stoppage. **3** somebody or something that restrains. **4** in chess, exposure of a king to direct attack. **5** a pattern of squares of alternating colours. **6** NAmer a bill in a restaurant. **7** under restraint or control.

check² v **1** to test or inspect for satisfactory condition, accuracy, or quality. **2** to slow or bring to a stop. **3** to restrain or block the progress of. **4** in chess, to put (the opposing king) in check. **5** chiefly NAmer (often + out) to tally. ✳ **check up on** to make inquiries about. ➤ **checkable** adj.

checker¹ v see CHEQUER².

checker² n informal see CHEQUER¹.

check in v to arrive and register at a hotel or airport. ➤ **check-in** n.

checklist n a list of checks to be made or tasks to be done.

checkmate n in chess, the act of putting an opponent's king in check from which escape is impossible. ➤ **checkmate** v.

checkout n **1** a cash desk at a supermarket or large shop. **2** the act of checking out of a hotel etc.

check out v **1** to complete the formalities for leaving a hotel. **2** to get information about.

checkpoint n a place where travellers are checked for security.

checkup n a routine medical or dental examination.

Cheddar n a hard smooth-textured cheese.

cheek¹ n **1** the side of the face below the eye. **2** insolent boldness or impudence. **3** informal a buttock. ✳ **cheek by jowl** close together.

cheek² v informal to speak rudely to.

cheekbone *n* the bone forming the rounded part of the face below the eye.

cheeky *adj* (**-ier, -iest**) impudent or insolent. ➤ **cheekily** *adv*.

cheep *n* a faint shrill sound made by a young bird. ➤ **cheep** *v*.

cheer¹ *n* **1** a shout of joy, congratulation, or encouragement. **2** happiness or gaiety.

cheer² *v* **1** to shout with pleasure or, in applause. **2** to acclaim or encourage by shouting. **3** (*often* + up) to make or become happier or more hopeful.

cheerful *adj* **1** full of good spirits; happy. **2** ungrudging. **3** conducive to good spirits. ➤ **cheerfully** *adv*, **cheerfulness** *n*.

cheerleader *n* in North America, somebody who leads organized cheering at sports events.

cheerless *adj* gloomy or miserable.

cheers *interj* used as a drinking toast or an informal farewell or expression of thanks.

cheery *adj* (**-ier, -iest**) cheerful and optimistic. ➤ **cheerily** *adv*.

cheese *n* a food made from processed milk curds.

cheesecake *n* a dessert with a filling of cream cheese on a biscuit or pastry base.

cheesecloth *n* a lightweight loosely woven cotton fabric.

cheesy *adj* (**-ier, -iest**) **1** resembling cheese. **2** *informal* poor in quality and taste.

cheetah *n* a long-legged spotted African cat that can run very fast.

chef *n* a cook in a restaurant or hotel.

chemical¹ *adj* **1** used in or produced by chemistry. **2** involving or made from chemicals. ➤ **chemically** *adv*.

chemical² *n* a substance produced by a chemical process.

chemise *n* a woman's loose-fitting dress or undergarment.

chemist *n* **1** *Brit* a pharmacist. **2** *Brit* a retail shop where medicines and other articles, e.g. cosmetics and films, are sold. **3** somebody who studies chemistry.

chemistry *n* **1** a science that deals with the composition and properties of substances and the transformations they undergo. **2** the composition and chemical properties of a substance. **3** a natural attraction between people.

chemotherapy *n* the use of chemical agents in the treatment of cancer.

chenille *n* a soft velvety fibre or the fabric made from it.

cheque (*NAmer* **check**) *n* chiefly *Brit* a written order for a bank to pay money to a named person or account.

cheque card *n* a card guaranteeing payment on a cheque.

chequer¹ (*NAmer* **checker**) *n* (*also in pl*) a pattern of squares of alternating colours.

chequer² (*NAmer* **checker**) *v* (**chequered, chequering**, *NAmer* **checkered, checkering**) to mark with squares of alternating colours.

cherish *v* **1** to feel or show affection for. **2** to keep or nurture with care and affection. **3** to keep in the mind.

cheroot *n* a cigar cut square at both ends.

cherry *n* (*pl* **-ies**) **1** a smooth red or blackish fruit with sweet flesh and a hard stone. **2** a bright red colour.

cherub *n* **1** (*pl* **cherubim**) a biblical attendant of God often represented with large wings, a human head, and an animal body. **2** (*pl* **cherubs**) a winged chubby child in painting and sculpture. **3** an innocent-looking chubby and pretty young person. ➤ **cherubic** *adj*.

chervil *n* an aromatic plant with leaves used as a herb and vegetable.

chess *n* a board game for two players with the object of putting the opponent's king into checkmate.

chest *n* **1** a storage box with a lid. **2** the part of the body enclosed by the ribs and breastbone. **3** the front of the body from the neck to the waist. * **get something off one's chest** to admit or confess something.

chesterfield *n* a padded leather sofa with arms and back of the same height.

chestnut *n* **1** an edible nut with shiny brown skin. **2** a reddish brown colour. **3** a horse chestnut. **4** *informal* an often repeated joke or story.

chest of drawers *n* a piece of furniture with a set of drawers.

chesty *adj* (**-ier, -iest**) inclined to or suffering from catarrh.

chevron *n* **1** a V-shaped sleeve badge indicating the wearer's rank. **2** a V-shaped heraldic design with the point uppermost. **3** (*in pl*) a row of V-shaped stripes marked on a road.

chew¹ *v* **1** to grind or gnaw with the teeth. **2** (+ over) to consider at length. * **chew the fat** *informal* to chat informally.

chew² *n* **1** the act of chewing. **2** a sweet for chewing.

chewing gum *n* a flavoured gum for chewing.

chewy *adj* tough and difficult to chew.

chi *n* the 22nd letter of the Greek alphabet (X, χ).

chic *adj* (**chicer, chicest**) elegant and fashionable.

chicane *n* a series of tight turns in a motor-racing track.

chicanery *n* clever trickery or deception.

chick *n* **1** a newly hatched chicken or bird. **2** *informal* a young woman.

chicken¹ *n* **1** the common domestic fowl. **2** *informal* a coward.

chicken² *adj informal* scared or cowardly.

chicken feed *n informal* an insignificant amount of money.

chicken out v informal (often + of) to lose one's nerve.

chickenpox n an infectious disease marked by a rash of small blisters.

chickweed n a plant with small leaves that occurs as a weed.

chicory n (pl -ies) 1 a plant with edible thick roots and leaves used in salads. 2 the root of this plant, used as a coffee additive.

chide v (past tense **chided** or **chid**, past part. **chided** or **chidden**) to rebuke or scold.

chief[1] n the head of an organization or group of people.

chief[2] adj 1 of the highest rank. 2 of greatest importance; main.

chiefly adv 1 principally or especially. 2 mostly or mainly.

chieftain n the leader of a tribe or clan.

chiffon n a sheer silky fabric.

chignon n a smooth knot of hair worn at the nape of the neck.

Chihuahua n a dog of a very small breed with a round head and large ears.

chilblain n an inflammatory sore on the feet or hands, caused by exposure to cold.

child n (pl **children**) 1 a young person between infancy and youth. 2 a son or daughter. ▶ **childhood** n.

childbirth n the process of giving birth to a child.

childish adj 1 of a child or childhood. 2 silly or immature.

childlike adj marked by the innocence and trust associated with children.

childminder n chiefly Brit a person who looks after other people's children.

chill[1] v 1 to make or become cold. 2 to frighten or horrify. 3 to dispirit. 4 informal (also + out) to relax. ▶ **chillingly** adv.

chill[2] n 1 an unpleasant sensation of coldness. 2 a feverish cold. 3 a moderate degree of cold.

chill[3] adj unpleasantly cold.

chilli (NAmer **chili**) n (pl **chillies**, NAmer **chilies**) the pod of a hot pepper used as a flavouring or spice.

chilly adj (-ier, -iest) 1 unpleasantly cold. 2 aloof or unfriendly.

chime[1] n 1 a musically tuned set of bells. 2 a set of hanging metal bars or tubes sounding like bells when struck. 3 (usu in pl) a musical ringing sound.

chime[2] v 1 to make a musical ringing sound. 2 (usu + together/with) to be or act in accord.

chimera or **chimaera** n (pl **chimeras** or **chimaeras**) 1 (**Chimera**, **Chimaera**) in Greek mythology, a fire-breathing female monster with a lion's head, a goat's body, and a serpent's tail. 2 an unrealizable hope or dream. ▶ **chimerical** adj.

chimney n (pl -eys) a vertical structure for carrying off smoke and extending above a roof.

chimney breast n a projecting part of an inside wall enclosing a chimney.

chimpanzee n an African ape with black coloration.

chin n the lower portion of the face below the mouth. ✳ **keep one's chin up** to remain cheerful.

china n fine porcelain or crockery.

china clay n a soft white clay for making porcelain.

chinchilla n a small South American rodent with soft pearly-grey fur.

Chinese n (pl **Chinese**) 1 a native or inhabitant of China. 2 a group of languages spoken in China, including Mandarin. ▶ **Chinese** adj.

chink[1] n 1 a narrow slit or fissure. 2 a means of evasion or escape.

chink[2] n a short sharp metallic sound.

chink[3] v to make a sharp ringing sound.

chino n (pl -os) 1 a cotton twill fabric. 2 (in pl) trousers made of chino.

chintz n a printed plain-weave fabric of glazed cotton.

chintzy adj 1 made or decorated with chintz. 2 gaudy and cheap.

chip[1] n 1 a small thin flat piece cut or flaked off a hard substance. 2 a flaw left after a chip is removed. 3 chiefly Brit a strip of potato fried in deep fat. 4 NAmer a potato crisp. 5 a counter used as a token in gambling games. 6 an integrated circuit or microchip. 7 a short high shot with a ball.

chip[2] v (**chipped, chipping**) 1 (often + off/away) to cut or break (a small piece) from something. 2 to break off in small pieces. 3 to kick or hit (a ball, pass, etc) in a short high arc. 4 Brit to cut (potatoes) into chips.

chipboard n a board made from compressed wood chips.

chip in v informal to contribute to or interrupt in a conversation.

chipmunk n a small striped American squirrel.

chipolata n a small sausage.

chipper adj informal cheerful and bright.

chiropody n the care and treatment of the feet. ▶ **chiropodist** n.

chiropractic n a system of healing using manipulation of the spinal column and other body structures. ▶ **chiropractor** n.

chirp[1] v of a small bird or insect: to make a short shrill sound.

chirp[2] n a chirping sound.

chirpy adj (-ier, -iest) informal lively and cheerful. ▶ **chirpily** adv.

chisel[1] n a metal tool with a cutting edge, used in shaping wood, stone, or metal.

chisel[2] v (**chiselled, chiselling**, NAmer **chiseled, chiseling**) to cut or work with a chisel.

chit[1] n a small young woman.

chit[2] n a small slip of paper with a note of money owed.

chivalrous adj **1** courteous and considerate to women. **2** honourable or generous. ► **chivalrously** adv.

chivalry n **1** the spirit or customs of medieval knighthood. **2** courteous behaviour towards women. **3** chivalrous conduct.

chive n (usu in pl) a plant with long thin leaves used to flavour and garnish food.

chivvy or **chivy** v (**-ies, -ied**) informal to harass or pester.

chloride n a compound of chlorine with another element or radical.

chlorinate v to treat (water) with chlorine. ► **chlorination** n.

chlorine n a chemical element that is a pungent greenish yellow gas.

chloroform[1] n a liquid used as a solvent and formerly as an anaesthetic.

chloroform[2] v to administer chloroform to make unconscious.

chlorophyll (NAmer also **chlorophyl**) n the green colouring matter of plants that enables them to absorb sunlight.

chloroplast n a part of a green plant that contains chlorophyll and is the site of photosynthesis.

chock n a wedge or block placed under a wheel or door to prevent it from moving.

chock-a-block adj and adv crowded or tightly packed.

chocolate n **1** a sweet food prepared from ground roasted cacao seeds. **2** a sweet made or coated with chocolate. **3** a drink made by mixing chocolate with hot water or milk. **4** dark brown.

choice[1] n **1** the act of choosing. **2** the power of choosing. **3** somebody or something chosen. **4** a sufficient number and variety to choose from.

choice[2] adj **1** of high quality. **2** selected with care.

choir n **1** an organized group of singers. **2** the part of a church between the sanctuary and the nave.

choirboy or **choirgirl** n a boy or girl singer in a church choir.

choke[1] v **1** to stop (somebody) breathing by compressing or obstructing the windpipe, or by poisoning the air. **2** to become unable to breathe. **3** (often + back/down) to suppress (tears) or prevent the expression of (emotion). **4** (also + up) to make or become speechless with emotion.

choke[2] n **1** the act or sound of choking. **2** a valve in a petrol engine for controlling the mixture of fuel and air.

choker n a short necklace or decorative band fitting closely round the throat.

cholera n an epidemic disease marked by severe disorders of the stomach and intestines.

choleric adj formal angry or irate.

cholesterol n a steroid present in animal and plant cells and thought to be a factor in hardening of the arteries.

chomp v to chew noisily.

choose v (**chose, chosen**) **1** to decide on and take (somebody or something) from several alternatives. **2** to decide (to do something).

choosy or **choosey** adj (**-ier, -iest**) fastidious in making choices.

chop[1] v (**chopped, chopping**) **1** (usu + off/down) to cut into or sever by a blow or repeated blows of a sharp instrument. **2** (often + up) to cut into pieces. **3** to strike with a short sharp blow.

chop[2] n **1** a forceful blow or cutting stroke. **2** a small cut of meat often including part of a rib. **3** (**the chop**) informal an abrupt dismissal or cancellation.

chop[3] v (**chopped, chopping**) esp of the wind: to change direction. ✳ **chop and change** Brit to keep changing one's mind, plans, etc.

chopper n **1** Brit a short-handled axe or cleaver. **2** informal a helicopter. **3** informal (in pl) teeth.

choppy adj (**-ier, -iest**) of the sea: rough with small waves.

chopstick n each of two slender sticks used in oriental countries for eating food.

choral adj accompanied with or designed for singing by a choir.

chorale n a traditional hymn or psalm for singing in church.

chord n a combination of notes sounded together. ✳ **strike/touch a chord** produce a sympathetic response.

chore n a routine or tedious task.

choreograph v to compose or arrange the steps and dances for (a ballet or piece of music). ► **choreographer** n, **choreography** n.

chorister n a choirboy or choirgirl.

chortle v to laugh or chuckle.

chorus[1] n **1** an organized group of singers who sing the choral parts of music, opera, or musicals. **2** a composition sung by a chorus. **3** a section of a song or hymn repeated at intervals.

chorus[2] v (**choruses, chorused, chorusing**) to sing or utter (something) together.

chose v past tense of CHOOSE.

chosen v past part. of CHOOSE.

choux pastry n a light pastry used for profiteroles, eclairs, etc.

Christ n a title given by Christians to Jesus.

christen v **1** to give a name to (a baby) at baptism. **2** informal to use for the first time.

Christian[1] n a follower of Christianity.

Christian[2] adj relating to Christianity or Christians.

Christianity n the religion based on the life and teachings of Jesus Christ and the New Testament.

Christian name n a forename.

Christmas n a festival of the Christian Church commemorating the birth of Christ, held on 25 December.

Christmas tree n an evergreen tree decorated with lights and trinkets at Christmas.

chromatic adj 1 relating to colour. 2 of a musical scale: based entirely on semitones. 3 of music: using intervals or notes outside the diatonic scale.

chrome n a plating of chromium.

chromium n a blue-white metallic element used in alloys.

chromosome n a gene-carrying body that contains DNA and protein and is found in the cell nucleus.

chronic adj 1 of an illness or difficulty: lasting for a long time. 2 suffering from a long-lasting disease. 3 habitual or persistent. 4 Brit, informal very bad. ➤ **chronically** adv.

chronicle[1] n 1 an account of events arranged chronologically. 2 a narrative.

chronicle[2] v to record (events) in chronological order. ➤ **chronicler** n.

chronological adj arranged in or according to the order in which things happen. ➤ **chronologically** adv.

chronology n (pl **-ies**) 1 the study of the dating of past events and the evidence for this. 2 a system of dates for past events.

chronometer n an instrument for measuring time.

chrysalis n (pl **chrysalises**) a pupa of a butterfly or moth.

chrysanthemum n a garden plant with brightly coloured flowers.

chub n a freshwater fish of the carp family.

chubby adj (**-ier, -iest**) round and plump. ➤ **chubbiness** n.

chuck[1] v 1 informal to toss or throw casually. 2 (often + out/away) to discard. 3 to pat or tap gently.

chuck[2] n a pat or nudge under the chin.

chuck[3] n a device for holding a drill or other working piece in a tool or lathe.

chuckle[1] v to laugh inwardly or quietly.

chuckle[2] n a quiet laugh.

chuff v to move with the sound of a steam engine.

chuffed adj Brit, informal very pleased.

chug v (**chugged, chugging**) to move with a repeated heavy sound like a labouring engine. ➤ **chug** n.

chum n informal, dated a friend or mate.

chump n 1 a cut of meat taken from between the loin and hindleg. 2 informal a foolish person.

chunk n a thick or solid lump.

church n 1 a building for public Christian worship. 2 (**the Church**) the whole body of Christians. 3 a Christian denomination.

churchyard n an enclosed piece of ground surrounding a church.

churlish adj uncooperative and unfriendly. ➤ **churlishly** adv.

churn[1] n 1 a vessel for agitating milk or cream to make butter. 2 Brit a large metal container for transporting milk.

churn[2] v 1 to agitate (milk or cream) to make butter. 2 to stir or agitate (liquid) violently. 3 to be in violent motion.

churn out v chiefly informal to produce routinely and in large quantities.

chute n 1 an inclined channel down which things pass to a lower level. 2 a slide into a swimming pool.

chutney n a spicy relish containing fruits, vegetables, sugar, vinegar, and spices.

chutzpah n informal brazen audacity.

CIA abbr NAmer Central Intelligence Agency.

ciabatta /chə'bahtə/ n (pl **ciabattas**) a flat Italian bread made with olive oil.

cicada /si'kahdə/ n (pl **cicadas**) an insect that produces a shrill singing noise.

CID abbr Brit Criminal Investigation Department.

cider n an alcoholic drink of fermented apple juice.

cigar n a roll of tobacco leaf for smoking.

cigarette (NAmer also **cigaret**) n a cylinder of cut tobacco rolled in paper for smoking.

cilium n (pl **cilia**) an eyelash or other minute hairlike part.

cinch n informal something very easy or certain.

cinder n a piece of partly burned coal or wood.

cinema n 1 chiefly Brit a theatre where films are shown. 2 the film industry.

cinematic adj to do with films or the cinema.

cinematography n the art or science of cinema photography. ➤ **cinematographer** n.

cinnamon n a spice obtained from the dried bark of an Asian tree.

cipher[1] or **cypher** n 1 a code. 2 a key to a code. 3 a nonentity.

cipher[2] or **cypher** v (**ciphered** or **cyphered, ciphering** or **cyphering**) to put into code.

circa prep approximately.

circadian adj of a biological activity: occurring in day-long periods or cycles.

circle[1] n 1 a shape in the form of a closed curved line every point of which is the same distance from the centre. 2 a balcony or tier of seats in a theatre. 3 a group of people sharing a common interest or activity.

circle[2] v 1 to move in a circle. 2 to enclose in a circle.

circuit n 1 a closed loop enclosing an area, or the area enclosed. 2 a racetrack. 3 a regular tour of an official round an assigned area. 4 a complete path of an electric current. 5 a system of electrical components connected so as to allow the passage of current. **6** a regular series of sports events or competitions.

circuitous *adj* indirect in route or method.

circuitry *n* (*pl* **-ies**) a system of electrical circuits.

circular¹ *adj* **1** having the form of a circle. **2** of a letter or advertising material: intended for circulation to a number of people. ➤ **circularity** *n*.

circular² *n* a letter or leaflet intended for wide distribution.

circulate *v* **1** to follow a course round an area. **2** to flow freely. **3** to become well known or widely available. **4** to go from group to group at a social gathering.

circulation *n* **1** movement through a system or circuit. **2** the movement of blood through the vessels of the body induced by the pumping action of the heart. **3** the passing of things from one person to another. **4** the number of copies of a publication sold over a given period.

circumcise *v* to cut off the foreskin of (a male) or the clitoris of (a female). ➤ **circumcision** *n*.

circumference *n* **1** the perimeter of a circle. **2** the external boundary or distance round something.

circumflex *n* a mark (ˆ) over a vowel in some languages to show a particular vowel sound.

circumlocution *n* the use of an unnecessarily large number of words to express an idea.

circumnavigate *v* to travel by sea or air round the earth. ➤ **circumnavigation** *n*.

circumscribe *v* to restrict the range or activity of.

circumspect *adj* careful to consider all circumstances. ➤ **circumspection** *n*.

circumstance *n* **1** a fact or detail relating to an event, story, etc. **2** (*usu in pl*) the situation one finds oneself in and for which one is not responsible. **3** (*in pl*) one's financial or material situation. ✳ **in/under the circumstances** considering the situation.

circumstantial *adj* of evidence: tending to prove a fact indirectly by proving related events or circumstances. ➤ **circumstantially** *adv*.

circumvent *v* to find a way round (a difficulty). ➤ **circumvention** *n*.

circus *n* (*pl* **circuses**) **1** a group of performers, including acrobats and clowns, who entertain with trained animals. **2** (**Circus**) *Brit* a large open road junction in a town enclosed by a circle of buildings.

cirrhosis *n* hardening of the liver.

cirrus *n* (*pl* **cirri**) a wispy white cloud formation occurring at high altitudes.

CIS *abbr* Commonwealth of Independent States (formed in succession to the USSR).

cistern *n* **1** a water reservoir for a toilet. **2** a tank at the top of a house or building. **3** *chiefly NAmer* a tank, usu underground, for storing rainwater.

citadel *n* a fortress that commands a city.

citation *n* **1** an act of quoting. **2** a quotation. **3** an official mention of something praiseworthy.

cite *v* **1** to quote for authority. **2** to refer to or name officially.

citizen *n* **1** a member of a state, *esp* a native or naturalized one. **2** an inhabitant of a city or town. ➤ **citizenship** *n*.

citric acid *n* an acid occurring in lemons, limes, and other sharp-tasting fruits.

citrus *n* (*pl* **citruses**) any of a group of juicy fruits, including the orange, lemon, lime, and grapefruit.

city *n* (*pl* **-ies**) **1** a large town, *esp* (in Britain) one that has been created by charter and has a cathedral. **2** (**the City**) *Brit* the financial and commercial area of London.

city-state *n* an autonomous state consisting of a city and surrounding territory.

civet *n* **1** an African and Asian cat with a long body and short legs. **2** a musky-smelling perfumed obtained from the civet.

civic *adj* of a city or citizenship.

civil *adj* **1** courteous and polite. **2** involving the general public as opposed to the military or clergy. **3** relating to private rights as distinct from criminal proceedings. ➤ **civilly** *adv*.

civil engineer *n* an engineer who designs large-scale public works, e.g. roads and bridges. ➤ **civil engineering** *n*.

civilian *n* somebody who is not a member of the armed forces or the police. ➤ **civilian** *adj*.

civility *n* (*pl* **-ies**) **1** courtesy or politeness. **2** (*usu in pl*) a polite act or remark.

civilization *or* **-isation** *n* **1** a high level of cultural and technological development. **2** the culture characteristic of a particular time or place. **3** the process of becoming civilized.

civilize *or* **-ise** *v* **1** to bring to a technically and socially advanced stage of development. **2** to educate or refine. ➤ **civilized** *adj*.

civil liberty *n* an individual's right or freedom in relation to the state.

civil rights *pl n* the rights of citizens, *esp* to equality between races or groups.

civil servant *n* a member of a civil service.

civil service *n* (*treated as sing. or pl*) the administrative service of a government or international agency.

civil war *n* war between citizens of the same country.

CJD *abbr* Creutzfeldt-Jakob disease, a progressive disease characterized by dementia and muscular wasting, of which one variant is thought to be linked to BSE.

Cl *abbr* the chemical symbol for chlorine.

cl *abbr* centilitre.

clack¹ *v* **1** to make an abrupt striking sound. **2** *informal* to chatter.

clack² *n* a sound of clacking.

clad v past tense and past part. OF CLOTHE.

cladding n a thin protective covering or overlay.

claim[1] v **1** to ask for as a right. **2** to require or demand. **3** to take as the rightful owner. **4** to assert; to maintain without proof. **5** to end (somebody's life). **6** (+ for) to make a claim under the terms of an insurance policy. ➤ **claimant** n.

claim[2] n **1** an assertion open to challenge. **2** a demand for something due. **3** an act of claiming under an insurance policy. **4** (+ to/on) a right or title to something.

clairvoyance n the ability to perceive matters beyond the range of ordinary perception. ➤ **clairvoyant** adj and n.

clam n a large mollusc with a tightly closed hinged shell.

clamber v (**clambered, clambering**) to climb awkwardly or with difficulty. ➤ **clamberer** n.

clammy adj (**-ier, -iest**) **1** unpleasantly damp and clinging. **2** of the weather: humid.

clamour[1] (NAmer **clamor**) n **1** noisy shouting. **2** a loud continuous noise. **3** (often + against/for) insistent public support or protest. ➤ **clamorous** adj.

clamour[2] (NAmer **clamor**) v **1** to make a din. **2** (usu + for) to make one's wishes or views known loudly and insistently.

clamp[1] n **1** a device that holds two or more things firmly together. **2** a device placed round the wheel of an illegally parked vehicle to immobilize it.

clamp[2] v to hold or fasten with a clamp.

clamp down v to impose restrictions.

clam up v informal to become silent.

clan n **1** a group of related families of Scottish descent. **2** a group of people united by a common interest. ➤ **clansman** n, **clanswoman** n.

clandestine adj held or done in secret. ➤ **clandestinely** adv.

clang v to make a loud metallic sound. ➤ **clang** n.

clank v to make a sharp metallic sound. ➤ **clank** n.

clannish adj associating only with a select group of similar background or interests.

clap[1] v (**clapped, clapping**) **1** to strike (the hands) together repeatedly in applause. **2** to applaud (a person or an act). **3** to strike (somebody) with the flat of the hand in a friendly way. **4** to put (something or somebody) forcefully or suddenly in a certain place or condition. **5** to impose (e.g. a restriction). * **clap hold of** informal to seize forcefully.

clap[2] n **1** the act or sound of clapping hands. **2** a loud sound of thunder. **3** a friendly slap.

clapped out adj Brit, informal old and worn out.

clapper n the tongue of a bell.

clapperboard n in filming, a hinged board banged together to synchronize the beginning and end of each take.

claret n a dry red Bordeaux wine.

clarify v (**-ies, -ied**) **1** to make or become easier to understand. **2** to make (liquid) clear by freeing it from suspended matter. **3** to melt (butter) to make it clear. ➤ **clarification** n.

clarinet n a woodwind instrument with a single reed, a flared end, and holes stopped by keys. ➤ **clarinettist** n.

clarion[1] n a medieval trumpet, or the sound of one.

clarion[2] adj loud and clear.

clarity n the quality or state of being clear.

clash[1] n **1** a noisy metallic sound of collision. **2** a conflict or hostile encounter.

clash[2] v **1** to make a clash. **2** to come into conflict. **3** to form a displeasing combination. **4** to be incompatible or irreconcilable.

clasp[1] n **1** a device for holding objects or parts together. **2** an embrace.

clasp[2] v **1** to fasten with a clasp. **2** to enclose and hold with the arms. **3** to seize with the hand.

clasp knife n a knife with a single folding blade.

class[1] n **1** a group in society sharing the same economic or social status. **2** the system of differentiating society by classes. **3** informal high quality; elegance. **4** a regular group of students being taught. **5** a lesson at a school or college. **6** a distinct group of things sharing common characteristics.

class[2] v to classify or grade.

classic[1] adj **1** serving as a standard of excellence. **2** traditional and enduring. **3** being an archetypal example of some particular thing or occurrence.

classic[2] n **1** a work of lasting excellence. **2** (**Classics**) the study of Greek and Latin literature, history, and philosophy.

classical adj **1** relating to the ancient Greek and Roman world. **2** relating to music of the traditional European forms including orchestral music, chamber music, and opera. **3** constituting an early influential approach to a subject that becomes standard. ➤ **classically** adj.

classicism n **1** adherence to traditional standards having universal and lasting worth. **2** the principles or style embodied in classical literature, art, or architecture.

classicist n a scholar or student of Classics.

classification n **1** systematic arrangement of things in defined groups. **2** a class or category.

classified adj **1** of information, documents, etc: withheld from general circulation for reasons of security. **2** of newspaper or magazine advertisements: organized according to their subjects.

classify v (**-ies, -ied**) **1** to arrange in classes. **2** (often + as) to assign to a category. **3** to designate (a document, information, etc) as secret. ➤ **classifiable** adj.

classroom n a room in a school where classes are held.

classy adj (**-ier, -iest**) informal elegant and stylish.

clatter v **1** to make a loud rattling or banging noise. **2** to move or go noisily. ➤ **clatter** n.

clause n **1** a group of words containing a subject and verb and forming part of a sentence. **2** a distinct article or condition in a formal document.

claustrophobia n abnormal fear of being in confined spaces. ➤ **claustrophobic** adj.

clavicle n a shoulder bone linking the shoulder blade and breastbone; the collarbone.

claw[1] n **1** a sharp curved nail on an animal's toe. **2** a pincer on the end of some limbs of a shellfish, scorpion, etc. **3** a tool or device resembling a claw.

claw[2] v to scratch or dig with the claws or fingernails.

clay n **1** an earthy material, soft when moist but hard when fired, used for making bricks and pottery. **2** thick and clinging earth or mud. ➤ **clayey** adj.

clean[1] adj **1** free or relatively free from dirt. **2** habitually keeping oneself clean. **3** free from contamination or disease. **4** producing little or no radioactive fallout. **5** not obscene. **6** unused or unmarked. **7** having no record of wrongdoing or offences. **8** of an action: smooth and effective. ➤ **cleaner** n, **cleanly** adv.

clean[2] adv all the way; completely.

clean[3] v **1** to make clean. **2** (often + out) to strip or empty (something).

clean[4] n an act of cleaning.

clean-cut adj clean and neat in appearance.

cleanliness n care in keeping things or one's person clean. ➤ **cleanly** adj.

cleanse v to clean or purify thoroughly. ➤ **cleanser** n.

clean-shaven adj with the beard and moustache shaved off.

clear[1] adj **1** easy to understand. **2** easy to see or hear. **3** transparent. **4** of the air or sky: free from cloud, mist, or dust. **5** free from obstructions or interruptions. **6** (+ of) not touching. **7** free from doubt. ✲ **in the clear** free of suspicion or danger. ➤ **clearly** adv.

clear[2] adv **1** clearly. **2** chiefly NAmer all the way.

clear[3] v **1** to free from obstructions or unwanted things. **2** to evacuate (an area or building). **3** (often + off/up/away) to remove or dispose of (something). **4** to go over (an obstacle) without touching it. **5** in football, to kick (the ball) away from the goal as a defensive measure. **6** to free from accusation or blame. **7** (often + off) to settle or discharge (a debt). **8** to

deal with (work) until it is finished or settled. **9** to put (a cheque) through a clearing house. **10** to authorize or cause to be authorized. **11** (often + up) of the weather: to become fine again. ✲ **clear the air** to remove tension or hostility by open discussion. **clear the decks** to prepare for action.

clearance n **1** the removal of obstructions or unwanted things. **2** clear space allowing one thing to pass another. **3** official authorization. **4** in football, a kick to clear the ball.

clear-cut adj easily seen or understood.

clearing n an area of land cleared of wood and brush.

clear off v informal to go away.

clear up v **1** to remove (dirt or mess). **2** to tidy by removing unwanted things. **3** to provide a solution for (a problem or mystery). **4** of an illness, etc: to be cured or alleviated.

clearway n Brit a road on which vehicles may stop only in an emergency.

cleat n **1** a projecting piece on a shoe, for providing a grip. **2** a wedge-shaped piece serving as a support or check. **3** a fitting with projecting horns, for securing a rope.

cleavage n **1** the hollow space between a woman's breasts. **2** a split or division.

cleave[1] v (past tense **clove** or **cleft** or **cleaved**, past part. **cloven** or **cleft** or **cleaved**) **1** to split along the grain. **2** to create (a path) as if by cutting.

cleave[2] v (past tense **cleaved** or archaic **clave**) **1** (+ to) to stick firmly and loyally. **2** (+ to) to be devoted.

cleaver n a butcher's chopping implement with a large heavy blade.

clef n a sign placed on a musical stave to indicate the pitch of the notes following it.

cleft[1] n **1** a space or opening made by splitting. **2** a hollow between ridges or protuberances.

cleft[2] v past tense and past part. of CLEAVE[1].

cleft lip n a harelip.

cleft palate n a congenital split in the roof of the mouth.

clematis n a climbing plant with white, pink, or purple flowers.

clement adj **1** of the weather: pleasantly mild. **2** merciful or lenient. ➤ **clemency** n.

clementine n a small citrus fruit with bright orange skin.

clench v **1** to close or hold together (the fists or teeth) tightly. **2** to grip or clutch firmly. **3** of a set of muscles: to contract suddenly.

clerestory n (pl **-ies**) the part of an outside wall of a church that rises above an adjoining roof.

clergy n the priests or ministers of a Christian Church.

clergyman or **clergywoman** n (pl **clergymen** or **clergywomen**) an ordained priest or minister.

cleric *n* a Christian minister or religious leader.

clerical *adj* **1** relating to routine office work such as typing and filing. **2** relating to the clergy.

clerk *n* **1** a person who keeps records or accounts or does general office work. **2** an official who keeps records for a council or court.

clever *adj* (**cleverer, cleverest**) **1** mentally quick and intelligent. **2** skilful or adroit with the hands or body. ➤ **cleverly** *adv*, **cleverness** *n*.

cliché *n* a hackneyed idea or expression. ➤ **clichéd** *adj*.

click[1] *n* **1** a light sharp sound made by hard parts locking into one another. **2** in computing, an action of pressing and releasing a mouse button.

click[2] *v* **1** to produce or make (something) produce a click. **2** in computing, to press and release (a button on a mouse). **3** *informal* to become friendly or successful. **4** *Brit* to be suddenly recognized.

client *n* somebody who uses the services of a professional person or organization.

clientele *n* the clients of a business, shop, etc.

cliff *n* a steep high face of rock on the coast.

cliffhanger *n* an episode in a story ending in extreme suspense.

climacteric *n* **1** the menopause, or a corresponding period in men. **2** a major turning point or critical stage.

climate *n* **1** the average weather conditions in a particular area over a long period. **2** the prevailing state of affairs or feelings of a group or period. ➤ **climatic** *adj*.

climax[1] *n* **1** the highest point or point of maximum intensity. **2** a sexual orgasm. ➤ **climactic** *adj*.

climax[2] *v* to come or bring to a climax.

climb[1] *v* **1** to go up to or down from a higher position. **2** of a plant: to ascend while growing. **3** to go gradually upwards; to rise. **4** to slope upwards. **5** to get into or out of a confined space with effort.

climb[2] *n* **1** an act of climbing. **2** a route up a mountain. **3** a steep slope or ascent.

climb down *v* to withdraw from a position in an argument. ➤ **climbdown** *n*.

climbing frame *n Brit* a framework of bars for children to climb on.

clime *n chiefly literary* (*usu in pl*) a region of the earth having a particular climate.

clinch[1] *v* **1** to make final; to settle. **2** to fasten (a nail) by turning it over and flattening it. **3** *informal* to embrace or hug.

clinch[2] *n* **1** a tight hold or embrace. **2** a fastening with a clinched nail.

cling *v* (*past tense and past part.* **clung**) **1** (+ to/onto) to hold on tightly. **2** (+ to/onto) to stick to. **3** to have a strong emotional dependence. **4** (+ to) to remain convinced of something. ➤ **clingy** *adj*.

clingfilm *n* a thin clear plastic film used for wrapping food.

clinic *n* a place where medical treatment or advice is given.

clinical *adj* **1** relating to the medical observation and treatment of patients. **2** analytic or detached in attitude. **3** of a place: severely plain and functional. ➤ **clinically** *adv*.

clink *v* to make or cause to make a slight sharp sound. ➤ **clink** *n*.

clinker *n* stony matter left by a fire.

clip[1] *v* (**clipped, clipping**) to clasp or fasten with a clip.

clip[2] *n* **1** a device that grips or holds things. **2** a piece of jewellery held in position by a spring clip.

clip[3] *v* (**clipped, clipping**) **1** to cut (hair or wool) with shears or scissors. **2** to cut off the end or outer part of. **3** to hit with a sharp blow.

clip[4] *n* **1** a sharp blow. **2** a short excerpt from a film or broadcast. **3** *informal* a rapid pace or speed.

clipboard *n* a small writing board with a spring clip for holding papers.

clipped *adj* of speech: tersely quick and distinct.

clipper *n* **1** (*usu in pl*) an implement for trimming hair or nails. **2** a fast sailing ship.

clipping *n* **1** a piece cut or trimmed from something. **2** an extract cut from a newspaper or magazine.

clique *n* an exclusive group of people. ➤ **cliquey** *adj*.

clitoris *n* an organ at the front of the vulva that is a centre of sexual sensation in females.

cloak[1] *n* **1** a long sleeveless outer garment that hangs loosely. **2** something that conceals.

cloak[2] *v* to cover or hide.

cloak-and-dagger *adj* involving melodramatic intrigue and secrecy.

cloakroom *n* **1** a room in which clothing or bags may be left. **2** *chiefly Brit* a room with a toilet.

clobber[1] *n Brit, informal* clothing or paraphernalia.

clobber[2] *v informal* to hit with force.

cloche *n* **1** a cover used for outdoor plants. **2** a woman's soft close-fitting rounded hat.

clock[1] *n* **1** a device for indicating or measuring time. **2** *informal* a speedometer or other metering device. ✳ **round the clock** all day and night.

clock[2] *v* **1** *esp* in sports, to time with a stopwatch or electric timing device. **2** to register (a time, distance, or speed) on a recording device. **3** *Brit, informal* (*often* + up) to achieve (a time, speed, etc). **4** *Brit, informal* to see or observe.

clock in *or* **clock on** *v* to record the time of arriving at work.

clock out or **clock off** v to record the time of leaving work.

clockwise adv and adj in a direction in which the hands of a clock rotate.

clockwork n a mechanism with toothed gearwheels and powered by a coiled spring. * **like clockwork** smoothly and with no hitches.

clod n 1 a lump of earth or clay. 2 informal a clumsy or stupid person.

clodhopper n informal 1 a large heavy shoe. 2 an awkward or clumsy person.

clog[1] n a shoe with a thick wooden sole.

clog[2] v (**clogged, clogging**) (often + up) to block or become blocked.

cloister n a covered passage along the wall of a courtyard in a church, monastery, college, etc.

cloistered adj 1 surrounded with a cloister. 2 sheltered from everyday life.

clomp v to walk heavily or clumsily.

clone[1] n 1 an asexually produced individual identical to its parent. 2 informal an exact or very close copy.

clone[2] v 1 to cause (a cell or organism) to grow as a clone. 2 to make a copy of.

close[1] adj 1 near in space or time. 2 of relatives: near in relationship. 3 intimate or affectionate. 4 of a connection: strong. 5 of a resemblance: showing only small variations. 6 having little space in between; dense. 7 of a game or contest: evenly contested. 8 very careful and concentrated. 9 of the weather: hot and stuffy. 10 secretive or reticent. 11 mean with money. * **at close quarters** in a position close to somebody or something. ➤ **closely** adv.

close[2] adv (**closer, closest**) in or into a close position or manner. * **close on** almost.

close[3] n 1 Brit a road closed at one end. 2 Brit the precinct of a cathedral.

close[4] v 1 to move in a position to cover an opening. 2 to cover or shut. 3 to prevent access to (a road or entrance). 4 to bring or come to an end. 5 (often + down) of a business, etc: to suspend or stop operations. 6 of a shop: to stop trading for the day. 7 (often + on/in on) to come closer to (somebody), in order to challenge them. ➤ **closable** adj.

close[5] n the end or conclusion of something.

close call n a narrow escape.

closed adj 1 not open. 2 not allowing entry; blocked. 3 of a system or society: forming a self-contained unit; self-sufficient. 4 limited or restricted.

closed-circuit television n a television system or installation used for surveillance in a building or area.

closed shop n an establishment which employs only union members.

close in v (often + on) to approach and surround a place.

close-knit adj bound together by strong ties of familiarity and affection.

close season n Brit a period during which fishing or hunting is not allowed, or a sport is not played.

close shave n informal a narrow escape.

closet[1] n 1 a small or private room. 2 chiefly NAmer a cupboard.

closet[2] v (**closeted, closeting**) to shut away in a private place.

close up v to become closer together.

close-up n a photograph or film sequence taken at close range.

closure n 1 the act of closing. 2 the closing by voting of a debate in a legislative body. 3 a device that closes or seals a container.

clot[1] n 1 a coagulated mass produced by clotting of blood. 2 a viscous lump formed by coagulation of cream or other liquid. 3 Brit, informal a foolish person.

clot[2] v (**clotted, clotting**) to form clots.

cloth n (pl **cloths**) 1 a fabric made by weaving or knitting fibres. 2 a piece of cloth used for a particular purpose. 3 (**the cloth**) the clergy.

clothe v (past tense and past part. **clothed** or **clad**) 1 to cover with clothing. 2 to provide with clothes.

clothes pl n articles of cloth or other material worn to cover the body.

clothing n clothes.

clotted cream n a thick cream made by heating and cooling whole milk and then skimming the top.

cloud[1] n 1 a mass of water particles at a great height in the air. 2 a light billowy mass of smoke or dust in the air. 3 a feeling of gloom. * **under a cloud** disliked or under suspicion. **with one's head in the clouds** out of touch with reality.

cloud[2] v 1 (+ over/up) to become cloudy. 2 of facial features: to become troubled or anxious. 3 to make or become blurred or unclear.

cloudburst n a sudden heavy fall of rain.

cloud-cuckoo-land n a fantasy world.

cloudy adj (-ier, -iest) 1 overcast with clouds. 2 not clear or transparent.

clout[1] n 1 informal a heavy blow. 2 informal power or influence.

clout[2] v informal to hit forcefully.

clove[1] n a small bulb that makes up a larger bulb of garlic.

clove[2] n the dried unopened flower bud of a tropical tree, used as a spice.

clove[3] v past tense of CLEAVE[1].

clove hitch n a knot used to secure a rope to a spar or another rope.

cloven v past part. of CLEAVE[1].

cloven hoof n the divided hoof of a sheep, cow, or other animals.

clover n a plant with leaves that have three leaflets and flowers in dense heads. * **in clover** in luxury.

clown[1] *n* **1** a comic entertainer in a circus. **2** a person who jokes and fools about. ➤ **clownish** *adj*.

clown[2] *v* (*usu* + about/around) to behave in a comic or silly way.

cloy *v* of something normally pleasing: to satiate with an excess. ➤ **cloying** *adj*.

club[1] *n* **1** an association of people who enjoy a common interest or activity. **2** premises available for members to stay, eat, or socialize. **3** a nightclub. **4** a thick heavy stick used as a hand weapon. **5** a stick used to hit the ball in golf. **6** (*in pl*) the suit in a pack of playing cards that is marked with black figures in the shape of a clover leaf.

club[2] *v* (**clubbed, clubbing**) **1** to beat or strike with a club or other heavy weapon. **2** (+ together) to share a cost or expense. **3** *informal* to visit nightclubs.

club foot *n* a misshapen foot twisted out of position from birth.

clubhouse *n* a building used for a club's activities.

cluck *v* to make the guttural sound of a hen. ➤ **cluck** *n*.

clue *n* **1** something that provides evidence to solve a problem or mystery. **2** a phrase or anagram that has to be solved as part of a crossword puzzle. ✳ **not have a clue 1** to know nothing. **2** to be incompetent.

clued-up *adj informal* well informed.

clueless *adj informal* completely ignorant or incompetent.

clump[1] *n* **1** a group of trees or bushes growing close together. **2** a compact mass or cluster. **3** a heavy tramping sound.

clump[2] *v* **1** to form clumps. **2** to tread clumsily and noisily.

clumsy *adj* (**-ier, -iest**) **1** awkward and ungraceful in movement. **2** lacking tact or subtlety. ➤ **clumsily** *adv*, **clumsiness** *n*.

clung *v* past tense and past part. of CLING.

clunk *v* to make the dull sound of one heavy object striking another. ➤ **clunk** *n*.

cluster[1] *n* a compact group of similar things or people.

cluster[2] *v* (**clustered, clustering**) to form a cluster or into a cluster.

clutch[1] *v* **1** to grasp or hold tightly. **2** (*often* + at) to try to grasp and hold.

clutch[2] *n* **1** the act of grasping or seizing firmly. **2** (*in pl*) control or possession. **3** a device that connects and disconnects the engine and the wheels in a vehicle.

clutch[3] *n* a nest of eggs laid at one time, or a brood of chicks hatched from them.

clutter[1] *v* to fill or cover untidily with scattered things.

clutter[2] *n* an untidy scattering of things.

Cm *abbr* the chemical symbol for curium.

cm *abbr* centimetre.

Co *abbr* the chemical symbol for cobalt.

co. *or* **Co.** *abbr* **1** company. **2** county.

co- *prefix* with or together: *coexist; co-pilot*.

coach[1] *n* **1** *chiefly Brit* a comfortable single-deck bus used for long-distance travel. **2** a railway carriage. **3** somebody who gives training in a sport. **4** a person who gives private lessons in a subject.

coach[2] *v* **1** to train in a sport. **2** to give private lessons to.

coagulate *v* of a liquid: to thicken or curdle. ➤ **coagulant** *n*, **coagulation** *n*.

coal *n* a black solid mineral consisting of carbonized vegetable matter and used as a fuel.

coalesce *v* to fuse into a whole. ➤ **coalescence** *n*.

coalface *n* the exposed seam in a coalmine.

coalfield *n* a region in which deposits of coal occur.

coalition *n* a temporary alliance of political parties to form a government.

coalmine *n* a mine from which coal is extracted. ➤ **coalminer** *n*.

coal tar *n* tar obtained from coal.

coarse *adj* **1** rough in texture or tone. **2** composed of large particles. **3** crude or unrefined in manners or language. ➤ **coarsely** *adv*.

coarse fish *n* *chiefly Brit* any freshwater fish not belonging to the salmon family.

coarsen *v* to make or become coarse.

coast[1] *n* **1** the edge of land where it reaches the sea. **2** the land near a shore. ✳ **the coast is clear** there is no danger. ➤ **coastal** *adj*.

coast[2] *v* **1** to move downhill by the force of gravity. **2** to move along without, or as if without, further application of propulsive power. **3** to proceed easily without making any special effort or becoming greatly involved. **4** to sail along the shore.

coaster *n* **1** a small mat for resting drinks on. **2** a ship that sails from port to port along a coast.

coastguard *n* an official or organization that keeps guard over coastal waters.

coastline *n* the outline of the land at a coast.

coat[1] *n* **1** a full-length outer garment with sleeves. **2** the external covering of hair or fur on an animal. **3** a layer of paint or other liquid covering.

coat[2] *v* to cover or spread with a protective or enclosing layer. ➤ **coater** *n*.

coat of arms *n* (*pl* **coats of arms**) a heraldic design belonging to a particular family or institution.

coax *v* **1** to urge or influence gently. **2** to manipulate into a desired condition.

coaxial *adj* **1** of a cable: having a central wire insulated from another wire wrapped round it. **2** using or connected to a coaxial cable. ➤ **coaxially** *adv*.

cob n 1 a male swan. 2 the core on which sweet corn grows. 3 a cobnut. 4 a horse of a short-legged stocky breed. 5 Brit a small rounded loaf.

cobalt n a silver-white metallic chemical element used in alloys.

cobber n Aus, informal a friend.

cobble¹ v 1 to repair or make shoes. 2 (+ together) to make or assemble roughly or hastily.

cobble² n a small rounded stone used for paving a street. ➤ **cobbled** adj.

cobbler n 1 a person who makes and mends shoes. 2 NAmer a deep fruit pie with a thick crust. 3 Brit stewed meat with rounds of pastry.

cobnut n the nut of a hazel tree.

cobra n a poisonous Asiatic and African snake with grooved fangs.

cobweb n a spider's web.

cocaine n an addictive alkaloid drug obtained from coca leaves.

coccyx n (pl **coccyges** or **coccyxes**) a small triangular bone at the base of the spinal column.

cochineal n a red dye used as a colouring agent for food.

cochlea n (pl **cochleae**) a coiled part of the inner ear filled with liquid through which sound waves are transmitted.

cock¹ n 1 the male of the domestic fowl or other birds. 2 coarse slang the penis.

cock² v 1 to turn or tip to one side. 2 to draw back and set the hammer of (a gun) for firing. 3 to turn up (the brim of a hat). * **cock a snook** to react with disdain or defiance.

cockade n a rosette or knot of ribbon worn on the hat as a badge.

cock-a-hoop adj informal delighted.

cock-and-bull story n an improbable story.

cockatoo n (pl **cockatoos**) a large parrot with a crest and brightly coloured plumage.

cockcrow n literary dawn.

cockerel n a young male domestic fowl.

cocker spaniel n a small spaniel with long ears and a silky coat.

cock-eyed adj informal 1 askew. 2 foolish or crazy.

cockle n an edible mollusc with a ribbed shell.

cockney n (pl **-eys**) 1 a native of the East End of London. 2 the dialect or accent of East London.

cockpit n 1 a space in the fuselage of an aircraft or spacecraft for the pilot and crew. 2 the driver's compartment in a racing car.

cockroach n an insect like a beetle with a flattened body and long antennae.

cocksure adj informal arrogantly self-confident.

cocktail n 1 an alcoholic drink of mixed spirits or of spirits mixed with flavourings. 2 a mixture of different things.

cocky adj (**-ier**, **-iest**) informal self-confident in an arrogant or cheeky way.

cocoa n a drink made from roasted and powdered cacao seeds.

coconut n the large oval fruit of a tropical palm, with a hard hairy outer husk, thick edible white flesh, and sweet milk.

Usage Note: Note the spelling coco not cocoa.

coconut shy n a funfair stall at which people throw balls to knock down coconuts on stands.

cocoon¹ n 1 a silk envelope which an insect larva forms about itself when passing the pupa stage. 2 a protective covering like a cocoon.

cocoon² v to wrap in a cocoon.

cod n (pl **cod**) a large grey sea fish used for food.

coda n a distinct concluding section to a piece of music.

coddle v 1 to cook (eggs) slowly in liquid. 2 to treat (a person or animal) with excessive care.

code¹ n 1 a system of letters, numbers, or symbols used to represent and replace the normal ones for secrecy. 2 a system of numbers and symbols for conveying instructions to a computer. 3 a body of laws. 4 a set of rules or principles governing behaviour. ➤ **coded** adj.

code² v to put into the form of a code.

codeine n a derivative of morphine used to relieve pain.

codger n informal an elderly man.

codicil n a clause added to a will to modify an existing part.

codify v (**-ies**, **-ied**) to organize (laws or rules) in a systematic form. ➤ **codification** n.

cod-liver oil n an oil obtained from the liver of the cod and used as a source of vitamins A and D.

codpiece n formerly, a pouch covering an opening in the front of men's breeches.

codswallop n chiefly Brit, informal nonsense.

co-education n the education of students of both sexes at the same school. ➤ **co-educational** adj.

coefficient n 1 a number placed before the variable factor or factors in an algebraic expression and multiplying them. 2 a number that serves as a measure of some property.

coerce v 1 (often + into) to compel (somebody) to do something. 2 to restrain by authority or force. ➤ **coercion** n.

coexist v 1 to exist together or at the same time. 2 to live together harmoniously. ➤ **coexistence** n.

C of E abbr Church of England.

coffee n a drink made from the roasted seeds of a tropical shrub.

coffee table n a low table placed in a living room.

coffer n 1 a chest or box for valuables. 2 (usu in pl) a treasury or exchequer.

coffin *n* a box or chest for the burial or cremation of a corpse.

cog *n* 1 a tooth on the rim of a wheel or gear. 2 a toothed wheel that engages with others to transmit motion.

cogent *adj* of an argument: clear and convincing. ➤ **cogency** *n*, **cogently** *adv*.

cogitate *v formal* to think carefully about something. ➤ **cogitation** *n*.

cognac /'konyak/ *n* a French brandy from the Cognac region of France.

cognition *n* the process of acquiring knowledge through perception, awareness, and judgment. ➤ **cognitive** *adj*.

cognizance or **cognisance** *n* 1 *formal* the ability to perceive or understand. 2 notice or heed.

cognoscenti /konyoh'shenti/ *pl n* people having expert knowledge in a subject.

cohabit *v* (**cohabited, cohabiting**) to live together as unmarried sexual partners. ➤ **cohabitation** *n*.

cohere *v* 1 to hold together firmly. 2 to be logically consistent.

coherent *adj* 1 able to speak clearly and understandably. 2 of an argument: logically consistent. ➤ **coherence** *n*, **coherently** *adv*.

cohesion *n* 1 the process of acting or working together effectively. 2 the act of cohering. ➤ **cohesive** *adj*.

cohort *n* 1 a division of a Roman legion. 2 a group of individuals sharing certain characteristics.

coif[1] *n* a close-fitting cap worn by nuns under a veil.

coif[2] *v* (**coiffed, coiffing,** *NAmer* **coifed, coifing**) to arrange (hair) by brushing or combing.

coiffure *n* a hairstyle. ➤ **coiffured** *adj*.

coil[1] *v* 1 to wind (something long) into rings or spirals. 2 to move in a circular or winding course. 3 to form a coil.

coil[2] *n* 1 a length of rope, cable, etc gathered into loops. 2 a spiral of wire used for providing electrical resistance or supplying a high voltage. 3 a contraceptive device in the form of a small coil fitted into the womb.

coin[1] *n* a small disc of metal used as money.

coin[2] *v* 1 to make (coins) by stamping metal. 2 to invent (a new word or phrase). 3 to make or earn (a lot of money).

coinage *n* 1 coins collectively. 2 the coins in use in a particular country. 3 a new word or phrase.

coincide *v* 1 to occur at the same time or place. 2 to have the same form or nature; to correspond.

coincidence *n* 1 the chance occurrence of two or more events at the same time or place. 2 a state of correspondence. ➤ **coincidental** *adj*, **coincidentally** *adv*.

coitus *n technical* sexual intercourse. ➤ **coital** *adj*.

coke[1] *n* a solid porous fuel that remains after gases have been driven from coal by heating.

coke[2] *n informal* cocaine.

colander or **cullender** *n* a perforated bowl for washing or draining food.

cold[1] *adj* 1 having a low temperature. 2 of a person or manner: aloof and unemotional. 3 depressing or cheerless. 4 dead or unconscious. 5 retaining only faint scents or traces. 6 far from a goal or solution being sought. 7 unprepared. ✴ **give somebody the cold shoulder** to be unfriendly. **in cold blood** with premeditation; deliberately. **leave somebody cold** to fail to impress somebody. ➤ **coldly** *n*.

cold[2] *n* 1 a condition of low temperature. 2 cold weather. 3 an infection characterized by a runny nose and sneezing. ✴ **out in the cold** ignored or neglected.

cold-blooded *adj* 1 done or acting without-feeling; ruthless. 2 having a body temperature approximating to that of the environment.

cold feet *pl n informal* a loss of nerve.

cold sore *n* a blister round or inside the mouth, caused by a viral infection.

cold turkey *n informal* unpleasant symptoms suffered by somebody who has stopped taking a narcotic drug.

cold war *n* (**the Cold War**) the period of hostility between the Western and Soviet blocs between 1945 and 1989.

coleslaw *n* a salad of chopped raw cabbage and carrots mixed with mayonnaise.

colic *n* abdominal pain in the intestines caused by obstruction or wind. ➤ **colicky** *adj*.

collaborate *v* 1 to work together on a common project. 2 to cooperate with an enemy. ➤ **collaboration** *n*, **collaborative** *adj*, **collaboratively** *adv*, **collaborator** *n*.

collage *n* a composition made of pieces of different materials fixed to a surface.

collapse[1] *v* 1 to fall down or break completely. 2 to fail suddenly and completely. 3 to suffer a breakdown through exhaustion or disease. 4 to fold down into a more compact shape. ➤ **collapsible** *adj*.

collapse[2] *n* 1 an instance of collapsing. 2 a sudden failure or breakdown.

collar[1] *n* 1 a band of fabric round the neckline of a garment. 2 a band fitted round the neck of a pet animal. 3 a ring or round flange to restrain motion or hold something in place. 4 a cut of bacon from the neck of a pig.

collar[2] *v informal* to seize or apprehend.

collarbone *n* the clavicle.

collate *v* to collect and compare (information).

collateral[1] *adj* 1 secondary or less important. 2 sharing the same ancestry but not in a direct line of descent.

collateral² *n* property pledged by a borrower to secure a loan.

colleague *n* a fellow worker.

collect *v* **1** to bring together. **2** to exact (payments) from a number of sources. **3** to come together in a group. **4** to fetch (something or somebody) from a place. **5** to regain control of (one's thoughts).

collected *adj* **1** calm and composed. **2** assembled from a number of sources.

collection *n* **1** the act or process of collecting. **2** an accumulation of objects gathered for study or exhibition. **3** a range of similar clothing products presented to the public.

collective¹ *adj* **1** of individuals considered as one group. **2** made or held in common by a group of individuals. ➤ **collectively** *adv*.

collective² *n* **1** a collective body or group. **2** an organization or business owned by those who work in it.

college *n* **1** a building used for an educational or religious purpose. **2** *Brit* an independent institution forming part of a university. **3** an institution offering vocational or technical instruction.

collegiate *adj* **1** relating to or comprising a college. **2** of a university: made up of separate colleges.

collide *v* **1** to come together forcibly. **2** to come into conflict.

collier *n* **1** a coalminer. **2** a ship for transporting coal.

colliery *n* (*pl* **-ies**) a coalmine and its associated buildings.

collision *n* an act or instance of colliding; a clash.

colloquial *adj* in the style of familiar and informal speech; conversational. ➤ **colloquially** *adv*.

colloquy *n* (*pl* **-ies**) **1** a formal conversation or dialogue. **2** a religious conference.

collude *v* to cooperate with somebody secretly. ➤ **collusion** *n*.

collywobbles *pl n informal* **1** discomfort in the stomach. **2** a nervous or anxious feeling.

cologne *n* scented toilet water.

colon¹ *n* the part of the large intestine that extends to the rectum. ➤ **colonic** *adj*.

colon² *n* a punctuation mark (:) used to introduce a quotation, a list of items, or an expansion or explanation of the words it follows.

colonel *n* an officer in the army or US air force ranking below brigadier or brigadier general.

colonial¹ *adj* **1** relating to or characteristic of a colony. **2** possessing or composed of colonies.

colonial² *n* an inhabitant of a colony.

colonialism *n* the policy or practice by a state of acquiring control over other countries or peoples. ➤ **colonialist** *n and adj*.

colonist *n* an inhabitant of a colony.

colonize *or* **-ise** *v* **1** to establish a colony in (a place). **2** of plants and animals: to begin to live and breed in (a new area or environment). ➤ **colonization** *n*.

colonnade *n* a row of columns placed at regular intervals and supporting a roof.

colony *n* (*pl* **-ies**) **1** a body of settlers living in a new territory that is subject to control by the settlers' parent state. **2** the territory settled or controlled in this way. **3** a group of individuals with common interests or origins living close together. **4** a distinguishable localized population within a species.

coloration (*Brit also* **colouration**) *n* **1** colouring or complexion. **2** an arrangement or range of colours.

colossal *adj* very large or great. ➤ **colossally** *adv*.

colossus *n* (*pl* **colossuses** *or* **colossi**) **1** a statue of gigantic size. **2** a person or thing of great size or importance.

colostomy *n* (*pl* **-ies**) the surgical formation of an artificial anus in the wall of the abdomen after a shortening of the colon.

colour¹ (*NAmer* **color**) *n* **1** a visual sensation, e.g. of things being red, blue, etc, caused by the wavelength of perceived light. **2** a hue, e.g. red or blue, or such hues in general, as opposed to black, white, and grey. **3** a pigment or other substance that gives colour when applied to an object. **4** the use of colours by a painter. **5** the skin pigmentation characteristic of a particular race. **6** the tint characteristic of good health. **7** (*usu in pl*) an identifying badge or uniform. **8** vitality or interest.

colour² (*NAmer* **color**) *v* **1** to give colour to. **2** to misrepresent or distort. **3** to influence or affect. **4** to blush.

colour-blind *adj* unable to distinguish certain colours. ➤ **colour blindness** *n*.

coloured¹ (*NAmer* **colored**) *adj* **1** having colour. **2** marked by exaggeration or bias. **3** *offensive* of a race other than white.

coloured² (*NAmer* **colored**) *n* (*often* **Coloured**) *offensive* a person of mixed descent.

colourfast *adj* having colour that will not fade or run.

colourful (*NAmer* **colorful**) *adj* **1** having striking colours. **2** full of variety or interest. ➤ **colourfully** *adv*.

colouring (*NAmer* **coloring**) *n* **1** the application or combination of colours. **2** the effect produced by colours. **3** something that produces colour.

colourist (*NAmer* **colorist**) *n* a painter who uses colour in special ways.

colourless (*NAmer* **colorless**) *adj* **1** lacking colour. **2** dull or uninteresting.

colt *n* a young male horse.

coltish *adj* frisky or playful.

column *n* **1** a round pillar with a capital and a base. **2** a long narrow formation of soldiers, vehicles, etc in rows. **3** a vertical section of printing on a page. **4** a regular feature in a newspaper or magazine.

columnist *n* a writer of a newspaper or magazine column.

coma *n* (*pl* **comas**) a state of prolonged deep unconsciousness.

comatose *adj* in a state of coma.

comb[1] *n* **1** a toothed instrument used for arranging or holding the hair. **2** a toothed device used in separating or ordering textile fibres. **3** a fleshy crest on the head of a domestic fowl or a related bird. **4** a honeycomb.

comb[2] *v* **1** to draw a comb through (the hair) to arrange it. **2** to prepare (wool or cotton) for use in manufacturing by cleaning and arranging its fibres with a comb. **3** to search systematically.

combat[1] *n* **1** a fight or contest. **2** active fighting in a war.

combat[2] *v* (**combated** or **combatted, combating** or **combatting**) to act to prevent (something bad or unwelcome).

combatant[1] *n* a person or state engaged in or prepared for combat.

combatant[2] *adj* actively participating in combat.

combative *adj* eager to fight or contend.

combe *n Brit* see COOMB.

combination *n* **1** an act or the process of combining things. **2** a collection of people or things that have been combined or brought together. **3** the sequence of letters or numbers that will open a combination lock.

combination lock *n* a lock operated by entering a specific combination of letters or numbers.

combine[1] *v* **1** to bring together; to unite or mix. **2** to act together.

combine[2] *n* a combination of people or organizations for commercial activities.

combine harvester *n* a harvesting machine that cuts, threshes, and cleans grain while moving over a field.

combust *v* to burn or be burned.

combustible *adj* able to catch fire easily.

come *v* (**came, come**) **1** to move in a direction towards the speaker. **2** to arrive or occur. **3** to happen. **4** to move into a certain state: *to come loose*. **5** to reach a certain position or limit. **6** to be available in a specified form. **7** *informal* to have an orgasm. ✳ **come across 1** to produce a specified impression. **2** to meet or find by chance. **come by** to manage to get. **come clean** *informal* to admit everything. **come into** to inherit (money or property). **come of** to result from. **come over** to affect (somebody) suddenly and strangely. **come to 1** to recover consciousness. **2** to reach a total. **come upon** to meet (somebody) by chance.

come about *v* **1** to occur or take place. **2** of a ship: to change course.

comeback *n* **1** a return to former success or popularity. **2** *informal* a sharp or witty reply.

comedian *n* an entertainer who aims at making people laugh.

comedown *n informal* **1** a loss of rank or dignity. **2** a disappointment.

come down *v* **1** to decrease in amount or value. **2** of an aircraft: to land or crash.

comedy *n* (*pl* **-ies**) **1** a play, film, etc of light and amusing character. **2** a ludicrous or farcical event or series of events.

come-hither *adj* of a look: flirtatious.

come in *v* to be useful.

comely *adj* (**-ier, -iest**) pleasing in appearance.

come off *v* to succeed, or to finish as specified.

come on *v* **1** to advance or begin by degrees. **2** to make an entrance.

come out *v* **1** to be published or made public. **2** to declare oneself in favour of or opposed to something. **3** to end up as specified. **4** to declare one's homosexuality. **5** *Brit, dated* to make one's first appearance in society as a debutante. ✳ **come out with** to say (something) unexpected.

come over *v* **1** to make a casual visit. **2** to change sides. **3** to be affected by a feeling.

come round *v* **1** to recover consciousness. **2** to be persuaded to adopt an opinion.

comestibles *pl n formal* food.

comet *n* a moving celestial body consisting of an icy nucleus surrounded by a trailing cloud of gas and dust.

come up *v* to arise or occur.

comeuppance *n informal* a deserved rebuke or punishment.

comfort[1] *n* **1** contented well-being; physical ease. **2** consolation or encouragement in time of trouble or worry.

comfort[2] *v* to cheer or console. ➤ **comforter** *n*.

comfortable *adj* **1** providing or enjoying physical comfort. **2** of a win or success: achieved with ease. **3** free from stress or tension. ➤ **comfortably** *adv*.

comfy *adj* (**-ier, -iest**) *informal* comfortable.

comic[1] *adj* **1** of or marked by comedy. **2** causing laughter or amusement.

comic[2] *n* **1** a comedian. **2** a children's magazine containing strip cartoons.

comical *adj* causing laughter from being ridiculous or funny. ➤ **comically** *adv*.

comma *n* a punctuation mark (,) used to separate parts of a sentence or list.

command[1] *v* **1** to give an order to. **2** to be able to ask for and receive. **3** to overlook or dominate. **4** to have military charge of.

command[2] *n* **1** an authoritative order. **2** the ability or power to control; mastery. **3** the authority or right to command. **4** a computer instruction that actuates the performance of a function. **5** the unit or personnel under a commander.

commandant *n* a commanding officer.

commandeer *v* to seize for military purposes.

commander *n* **1** a person having command. **2** a naval officer ranking below a captain.

commander-in-chief *n* (*pl* **commanders-in-chief**) an officer in supreme command of an armed force.

commanding *adj* **1** having command or authority. **2** deserving respect and obedience. **3** dominating or having priority.

commandment *n* a rule or law, *esp* one of the Ten Commandments.

commando *n* (*pl* **-os**) a soldier trained to carry out raids.

commemorate *v* to mark or formally remember (an event or a person). ➤ **commemoration** *n*, **commemorative** *adj*.

Usage Note: Note the spelling with *-mm-* and then *-m-*.

commence *v* to start or begin.

commencement *n* a beginning.

commend *v* **1** to praise or approve of. **2** to recommend as worthy of confidence or notice. **3** to entrust for care or preservation. ➤ **commendable** *adj*, **commendation** *n*.

commendable *adj* deserving praise; admirable. ➤ **commendably** *adv*.

commensurable *adj* having a common measure. ➤ **commensurably** *adv*.

commensurate *adj* **1** (*usu* + with) approximately equal in measure or extent. **2** (*often* + to/with) corresponding in size or amount.

comment[1] *n* **1** a remark expressing an opinion or attitude. **2** discussion of a topical issue.

comment[2] *v* **1** to make a comment. **2** (+ on) to explain or interpret.

commentary *n* (*pl* **-ies**) **1** a systematic series of explanations or interpretations. **2** a series of spoken comments describing an event as it happens.

commentate *v* to give a commentary of an event.

commerce *n* the buying and selling of goods.

commercial[1] *adj* **1** involving or relating to commerce. **2** having a good financial prospect. **3** supported by advertising. ➤ **commercially** *adv*.

commercial[2] *n* a television or radio advertisement.

commercialism *n* **1** commercial institutions or methods. **2** excessive emphasis on profit.

commercialize *or* **-ise** *v* **1** to make commercial. **2** to exploit for profit. ➤ **commercialization** *n*.

commiserate *v* to feel or express sympathy. ➤ **commiseration** *n*.

commissar *n* a Communist party official responsible for teaching party principles and ideals.

commission[1] *n* **1** an authorization or command to perform a task. **2** a group of people directed to perform some duty. **3** a percentage fee paid to an agent or employee. **4** a formal warrant granting various powers. **5** military rank above a certain level. **6** authority to act as agent for another. * **out of commission** out of use or working order.

commission[2] *v* **1** to order or appoint (somebody) to perform a task or function. **2** to order (a task) to be done. **3** to put into working order.

commissionaire *n* *chiefly Brit* a uniformed attendant at a hotel, theatre, etc.

commissioner *n* **1** a member or the head of a commission. **2** the government representative in an area.

commit *v* (**committed, committing**) **1** to carry out (a wrong act). **2** to obligate or bind (oneself) to a course of action or a set of beliefs. **3** to assign to a particular course or use. **4** to entrust (something or somebody) to somebody's care. **5** to place in a prison or psychiatric hospital.

commitment *n* **1** an agreement or pledge to do something. **2** an engagement or obligation. **3** loyalty to a system of thought or action. **4** an act of committing to a charge or trust.

Usage Note: Note the spelling with *-mm-* and then one *-t-*.

committal *n* **1** the sending of somebody to prison or a psychiatric hospital, or for trial. **2** the burial of a body.

committee *n* **1** a body of people appointed for a purpose by a larger organization. **2** a body of people delegated to report on some matter.

Usage Note: Note the spelling with *-mm-* and *-tt-*.

commode *n* an upright chair with a removable seat covering a chamber pot.

commodious *adj* *formal* comfortably or spacious.

commodity *n* (*pl* **-ies**) **1** something that can be bought and sold. **2** something useful or valuable.

commodore *n* **1** the senior captain of a merchant shipping line. **2** the chief officer of a yacht club.

common[1] *adj* **1** occurring or appearing frequently. **2** of the most familiar kind. **3** widespread or general. **4** characterized by a lack of privilege or special status. **5** simply satisfying accustomed criteria and no more. **6** lacking refinement. **7** belonging to or shared by two or more individuals. **8** of the community at large; public. **9** in grammar, belonging to a gender that includes masculine and feminine. ✷ **common or garden** ordinary or everyday. ➤ **commonly** adv.

common² n an area of land available for public recreation. ✷ **in common 1** shared together. **2** used jointly.

common denominator n **1** in mathematics, a number into which the denominators of several fractions can be divided with no remainder. **2** a common feature or theme.

commoner n a member of the common people and not of noble rank.

common ground n shared opinions.

common market n (**the Common Market**) the economic association that became the European Union.

common noun n a noun that designates any one of a class of beings or things.

commonplace¹ adj ordinary or unremarkable.

commonplace² n an obvious or trite observation.

common room n chiefly Brit a room in a school or college for the recreational use of staff or students.

commons pl n **1** (**the Commons**) the House of Commons. **2** the common people as a political group.

common sense n sound and prudent judgment. ➤ **commonsensical** adj.

commonwealth n **1** an independent state; a republic. **2** (**the Commonwealth**) an association consisting of the UK and states that were formerly British colonies.

commotion n **1** a disturbance or tumult. **2** noisy confusion and bustle.

communal adj shared or used in common by members of a group or community. ➤ **communally** adv.

commune¹ n a community of individuals or families sharing possessions.

commune² v (usu + with) to communicate intimately.

communicable adj of a disease: able to be transmitted to others.

communicant n a church member who receives Communion.

communicate v **1** to convey or share information about something. **2** to cause (something) to pass from one person to another. **3** of rooms: to give access to each other. **4** to receive Communion. ➤ **communicator** n.

communication n **1** the exchange of knowledge or information. **2** a verbal or written message. **3** (in pl) a system of travelling or communicating information.

communicative adj tending to communicate; talkative.

communion n **1** intimate fellowship or rapport. **2** a body of Christians having a common faith. **3** (often **Communion**) the religious service consecrating and receiving the Eucharist in Christian churches.

communiqué n an official announcement.

communism n **1** a political theory or system advocating elimination of private property. **2** (**Communism**) a system based on revolutionary Marxist socialism, followed in China and formerly in the Soviet Union. ➤ **communist** n and adj.

community n (pl **-ies**) **1** a group of people living in a particular area or sharing the same religion, ethnic group, etc. **2** a group of individuals sharing a profession or activity. **3** a body of people or nations having a common history or common interests.

community care n the provision of care to enable people to stay in their own community rather than in a hospital or institution.

community service n work undertaken by offenders for the benefit of the community, as an alternative to a prison term.

commute v **1** to travel regularly between home and work. **2** to exchange (a penalty) for a less severe one. ➤ **commuter** n.

compact¹ adj **1** having parts or units closely packed or joined. **2** efficiently occupying a small space.

compact² v to press into a small space.

compact³ n a small slim case for face powder.

compact⁴ n an agreement or contract.

compact disc n a small disc on which sound or information is stored in digital form.

companion n **1** a person who accompanies or spends time with somebody else. **2** something belonging to a pair or set of matching things. ➤ **companionship** n.

companionable adj friendly and sociable.

company n (pl **-ies**) **1** a business or commercial organization. **2** friendly association with other people. **3** companions or associates. **4** visitors or guests. **5** a group of people or things. **6** a unit of soldiers. **7** an organization of musical or dramatic performers.

comparable adj **1** capable of or suitable for comparison. **2** approximately equivalent; similar. ➤ **comparably** adv.

comparative adj **1** considered in comparison to something else. **2** involving comparison between different branches of a subject. **3** in grammar, denoting a degree of comparison expressing a higher degree or quantity, e.g. smaller. ➤ **comparatively** adv.

compare v **1** (usu + to) to represent as similar to another thing or person. **2** (often + to/with) to examine the character or qualities of (something or somebody) in order to discover resemblances or differences. **3** (+ with) to be similar.

comparison n **1** the comparing of one thing or person to or with another. **2** identity or similarity of features.

compartment *n* **1** a part into which an enclosed space is divided. **2** a separate division or section.

compartmentalize *or* **-ise** *v* to separate into compartments or categories.

compass[1] *n* **1** an instrument that indicates directions, typically by having a needle that points to magnetic north. **2** (*usu in pl*) an instrument for drawing circles, consisting of two arms joined at one end by a pivot. **3** range or scope.

compass[2] *v archaic* **1** to encompass. **2** to travel round (a place).

compassion *n* sympathetic concern for the hardships of others.

compassionate *adj* **1** having or showing compassion. **2** of leave: granted because of special distressing circumstances. ➤ **compassionately** *adv*.

compatible *adj* **1** (*often* + with) capable of existing or living together in harmony. **2** of equipment: able to be used in combination. ➤ **compatibility** *n*.

compatriot *n* a person from the same country.

compel *v* (**compelled, compelling**) **1** to drive or force (somebody) to do something. **2** to cause (something) to occur.

compelling *adj* having an irresistible power of attraction. ➤ **compellingly** *adv*.

compendium *n* (*pl* **compendiums** *or* **compendia**) **1** a set of information on a subject. **2** a collection of indoor games and puzzles.

compensate *v* **1** (*often* + for) to make a payment or give a benefit to (somebody) to make amends for something disadvantageous or unpleasant. **2** to have an equal and opposite effect to. **3** (+ for) to supply an equivalent. ➤ **compensatory** *adj*.

compensation *n* **1** a payment for damage or loss. **2** something that counterbalances a disadvantage.

compere[1] *n Brit* the presenter of a radio or television programme or a variety show.

compere[2] *v Brit* to be a compere for.

compete *v* (*often* + with) to strive against others for an objective.

competent *adj* **1** having or done with adequate ability. **2** legally qualified to deal with a particular matter. ➤ **competence** *n*, **competently** *adv*.

competition *n* **1** the process of competing; rivalry. **2** an organized test of skill, performance, etc. **3** people who are competing with an individual or organization.

competitive *adj* **1** relating to or based on competition. **2** inclined or desiring to compete. **3** at least as good as those offered by rivals. ➤ **competitively** *adv*.

competitor *n* a person or thing that competes; a contestant or rival.

compilation *n* **1** the act or process of compiling. **2** something compiled from different sources.

compile *v* to collect or compose from various materials.

complacent *adj* smugly uncritical of oneself or one's concerns. ➤ **complacency** *n*, **complacently** *adv*.

complain *v* **1** to express feelings of discontent. **2** to say that one has a pain or symptom.

complainant *n* in law, a plaintiff.

complaint *n* **1** an expression of discontent. **2** something that is the cause of protest. **3** a minor illness or disease.

complaisant *adj* inclined to please or comply. ➤ **complaisance** *n*.

complement[1] *n* **1** something that completes a whole or adds extra features. **2** the quantity required to make something complete.

Usage Note: Do not confuse this word with *compliment*.

complement[2] *v* to add to or enhance (something).

complementary *adj* **1** serving to complete or enhance something. **2** of medicine: not forming part of conventional scientific practice.

complete[1] *adj* **1** having all necessary parts; whole or entire. **2** fully carried out; thorough. **3** total or absolute. **4** totally competent or skilled in an activity. ➤ **completely** *adv*.

complete[2] *v* **1** to bring to an end; to finish doing. **2** to make whole or perfect. **3** to mark the end of. **4** to execute or fulfil. **5** to enter information on (a form). ➤ **completion** *n*.

complex[1] *adj* **1** composed of two or more parts. **2** hard to separate, analyse, or solve. ➤ **complexity** *n*.

complex[2] *n* **1** a whole made up of interrelated parts. **2** a set of buildings forming a unit. **3** a group of repressed feelings that adversely affects personality and behaviour.

complexion *n* **1** the appearance of the skin of a person's face. **2** the overall aspect or character of something.

compliance *n* the act of complying with the wishes of others. ➤ **compliant** *adj*.

complicate *v* to make complex or difficult.

complicated *adj* **1** difficult to analyse, understand, or explain. **2** consisting of parts intricately combined.

complication *n* **1** intricacy or complexity. **2** the act of making something difficult or intricate. **3** a complex or intricate feature or element. **4** a factor or issue that occurs unexpectedly and affects a situation. **5** a secondary disease or condition developing in the course of a primary disease or condition.

complicit *adj* participating in a wrongful act.

complicity *n* association or participation in a wrongful act.

compliment[1] n **1** an expression of esteem or admiration. **2** (in pl) best wishes; regards.

Usage Note: Do not confuse this word with *complement*.

compliment[2] v (often + on) to pay a compliment to.

complimentary adj **1** expressing or containing a compliment. **2** given free of charge.

comply v (-ies, -ied) **1** (usu + with) to do as somebody asks. **2** (usu + with) to meet a certain standard.

component[1] n a constituent part, *esp* of a machine.

component[2] adj of parts: helping to constitute a whole.

comportment n *formal* bearing or demeanour.

compose v **1** to create (a work of art, *esp* music or poetry). **2** to form (something) by putting it together. **3** (usu in passive) to form the substance of (something). **4** to calm or settle (oneself).

composite[1] adj made up of distinct parts or constituents.

composite[2] n a composite material.

composition n **1** a piece of writing or music. **2** the act or process of composing works of art. **3** a mixture of various elements or ingredients. **4** the way in which the parts of something make up the whole.

compositor n a printer who sets type.

compos mentis adj of sound mind.

compost n decayed organic matter used as a fertilizer.

composure n calmness of mind or bearing.

compound[1] n **1** something formed by a union of elements or parts. **2** in chemistry, a distinct substance formed by combination of chemical elements in fixed proportion.

compound[2] adj **1** made from a union of separate elements or parts. **2** of a bone fracture: causing the bone to pierce the skin.

compound[3] v **1** to put together (parts) to form a whole; to combine. **2** to augment or add to (something bad).

compound[4] n an enclosed area containing a group of buildings.

comprehend v to grasp the nature or meaning of.

comprehensible adj able to be comprehended; intelligible.

comprehension n **1** the process of or capacity for understanding. **2** *Brit* an exercise testing understanding of a passage.

comprehensive[1] adj **1** including everything involved or all aspects of something. **2** wideranging in scope. **3** *Brit* relating to the education of children of all abilities in one type of secondary school. ➤ **comprehensively** adv.

comprehensive[2] n *Brit* a comprehensive school.

compress[1] v **1** to press or squeeze together. **2** to force into a smaller space. ➤ **compression** n.

compress[2] n a pad pressed on to a part of the body to ease the pain and swelling of a bruise.

compressor n a machine for compressing gases.

comprise v **1** to be made up of. **2** to make up or constitute.

compromise[1] n **1** a settlement reached by each side conceding points. **2** a state of opinion or action intermediate between extremes.

compromise[2] v **1** to come to agreement by mutual concession. **2** to expose to discredit or danger. **3** to go against (one's principles) for expediency.

comptroller n a public finance officer.

compulsion n **1** being compelled to do something. **2** a strong impulse to perform an irrational act.

compulsive adj caused by or suffering from a psychological compulsion. ➤ **compulsively** adv.

compulsory adj required to be done by a law or rule.

compunction n anxiety arising from a feeling of guilt; remorse.

computation n **1** a process or system of calculating. **2** the use or operation of a computer. ➤ **computational** adj.

compute v to calculate (a quantity or number).

computer n an electronic device that can store, retrieve, and process data according to programmed instructions.

computerize or **-ise** v **1** to equip with computers. **2** to carry out by means of a computer.

comrade n **1** a friend or associate; a member of the same organization. **2** a fellow soldier. ➤ **comradeship** n.

con n *informal* a confidence trick.

concatenate v to link together in a series or chain. ➤ **concatenation** n.

concave adj hollowed or rounded inwards like the inside of a bowl.

conceal v **1** to place out of sight. **2** (often + from) to prevent disclosure or recognition of. ➤ **concealment** n.

concede v **1** to accept as true, valid, or accurate. **2** to acknowledge grudgingly or hesitantly. **3** to grant or yield (a right or privilege). **4** to allow (a goal or point by an opponent) through error.

conceit n **1** excessively high opinion of oneself. **2** *literary* a fanciful idea.

conceited adj having an excessively high opinion of oneself. ➤ **conceitedly** adv.

conceivable adj able to be conceived in the mind; imaginable. ➤ **conceivably** adv.

conceive v **1** to become pregnant with (a baby). **2** to visualize or imagine.

Usage Note: Note the spelling *-ei-*.

concentrate[1] v **1** (often + on) to focus or direct (the mind or attention) on something. **2** to gather into one body or mass. **3** to make (a solution) stronger.

concentrate[2] n something in concentrated form, esp food.

concentration n **1** the process of concentrating on something. **2** a concentrated mass or thing. **3** the relative amount of a substance in a mixture or a solution.

concentration camp n a camp where political prisoners are confined.

concentric adj of shapes: having a common centre. ➤ **concentrically** adv, **concentricity** n.

concept n a thought or notion conceived in the mind. ➤ **conceptual** adj, **conceptually** adv.

conception n **1** the process of conceiving a baby; the beginning of pregnancy. **2** a general idea or concept. **3** the originating of something in the mind.

conceptualize or **-ise** v to form an idea of in the mind.

concern[1] v **1** to be about; to relate to. **2** to involve or have an influence on. **3** to be a cause of trouble or distress to. **4** to engage or occupy (oneself).

concern[2] n **1** something that relates to or involves one. **2** anxiety or a cause of anxiety. **3** a matter for consideration. **4** a business or organization.

concerned adj anxious or troubled.

concerning prep relating to.

concert n **1** a public performance of music. **2** agreement. ✳ **in concert** working together.

concerted adj **1** planned or done together; combined. **2** performed in unison.

concertina[1] n a small hexagonal musical instrument of the accordion family.

concertina[2] v (**concertinas, concertinaed, concertinaing**) to collapse or fold up like the bellows of a concertina.

concerto n (pl **concertos** or **concerti**) a piece of music for an orchestra and one or more soloists.

concession n **1** the act of conceding something. **2** a reduction in price for people in certain categories. **3** a grant or right made in return for services. **4** a small shop or business operating on the premises of a larger business. ➤ **concessionary** adj.

conch n (pl **conchs** or **conches**) a large mollusc with a spiral shell.

concierge n a doorkeeper or caretaker in a large building.

conciliate v **1** to appease or pacify. **2** formal to reconcile (people). ➤ **conciliation** n, **conciliatory** adj.

concise adj brief and clear, with a minimum of detail. ➤ **concisely** adv, **conciseness** n.

conclave n a private meeting or assembly.

conclude v **1** to bring or come to an end. **2** to arrive at (an opinion) by reasoning. **3** to reach an agreement on.

conclusion n **1** the act of concluding. **2** a final summing up of an argument or essay. **3** a reasoned judgment. **4** a result or outcome.

conclusive adj putting an end to debate or a question; decisive. ➤ **conclusively** adv.

concoct v **1** to prepare (food) from various ingredients. **2** to devise or invent (a story or excuse). ➤ **concoction** n.

concomitant adj formal accompanying in a subordinate or incidental way.

concord n **1** a state of agreement or harmony. **2** a treaty or covenant.

concordance n an alphabetical index of the principal words in a book or text.

concordat n a compact or agreement.

concourse n a large open space in a building or where roads or paths meet.

concrete[1] adj **1** real or tangible. **2** specific or particular.

concrete[2] n a building material made by mixing cement, sand and gravel with water.

concrete[3] v to cover or set with concrete.

concubine n in a polygamous society, a woman who lives with a man in addition to his lawful wife or wives.

concur v (**concurred, concurring**) **1** (often + with) to express agreement. **2** of events: to coincide.

concurrent adj operating or occurring at the same time. ➤ **concurrence** n, **concurrently** adv.

concussion n temporary unconsciousness caused by a blow to the head. ➤ **concussed** adj.

condemn v **1** to declare (a person or an action) to be utterly wrong or bad. **2** to sentence to death. **3** (usu + to) to cause to suffer something unpleasant. **4** to declare unfit for use. ➤ **condemnation** n.

condensation n **1** droplets of water formed on a cold surface when water vapour in the air cools and becomes liquid. **2** the process of changing from a vapour or gas to a liquid.

condense v **1** to make denser or more compact; to compress. **2** to change from a vapour or gas to a liquid.

condensed milk n milk thickened by evaporation and sweetened.

condescend v **1** to adopt a patronizing attitude of superiority. **2** to descend to less formal or dignified action or speech. **3** to agree to do something thought to be unworthy. ➤ **condescending** adj, **condescendingly** adv, **condescension** n.

condiment n a flavouring for food, such as pepper or mustard.

condition[1] *n* **1** the state of something with regard to appearance or fitness for use. **2** a defective state of health. **3** a state of physical fitness. **4** (*in pl*) attendant circumstances. **5** something that is necessary for something else to exist or occur. * **on condition that** providing that.

condition[2] *v* **1** to train (a person or animal) to act or respond in a particular way. **2** to put into a proper state for work or use. **3** to give a certain condition to. **4** to make subject to or dependent on a condition.

conditional *adj* **1** subject to a condition or conditions. **2** in grammar, expressing a condition, often with the word 'if'. > **conditionally** *adv*.

conditioner *n* a substance applied to hair or fabric to improve its condition.

condole *v* (+ with) to express sympathy.

condolence *n* **1** sympathy with somebody in sorrow. **2** (*also in pl*) an expression of sympathy.

condom *n* a rubber sheath worn over the penis during sexual intercourse to prevent conception.

condominium *n* (*pl* **condominiums**) *NAmer* a block of individually owned apartments.

condone *v* to pardon or overlook (an offence).

condor *n* a large South American vulture.

conducive *adj* (+ to) likely to bring about a desirable result.

conduct[1] *n* **1** a mode or standard of personal behaviour. **2** the act or manner of directing an operation.

conduct[2] *v* **1** to guide or escort (somebody) somewhere. **2** to carry on or direct (an operation). **3** to convey (water or other fluid material) in a channel, pipe, etc. **4** to act as a medium for transmitting (heat or light). **5** to behave (oneself) in a specified manner. **6** to direct the performance or execution of (a musical or artistic work).

conductance *n* the ability of a material to conduct electricity.

conductor *n* **1** a person who directs the performance of a group of musicians. **2** a substance or body capable of transmitting electricity or heat. **3** a collector of fares on a bus. **4** *chiefly NAmer* a guard in charge of a train.

conduit *n* **1** a channel for conveying fluid. **2** a tube protecting electric wires or cables.

cone *n* **1** the tapering fruit of a coniferous tree. **2** a solid figure tapering evenly to a point from a circular base. **3** a cone-shaped wafer for holding a portion of ice cream.

coney *n* = CONY.

confect *v* to prepare (something elaborate) from assorted materials.

confection *n* **1** an elaborately prepared item of sweet food. **2** an elaborately contrived article of dress.

confectionery *n* (*pl* **-ies**) sweets and chocolate.

confederacy *n* (*pl* **-ies**) **1** an alliance of independent states. **2** (**the Confederacy**) the eleven southern states that withdrew from the USA in 1860–61.

confederate[1] *adj* **1** united in a league; allied. **2** (**Confederate**) belonging or relating to the Confederacy.

confederate[2] *n* an ally or accomplice.

confederate[3] *v* to unite in a confederacy.

confederation *n* a league or alliance of states.

confer *v* (**conferred, conferring**) **1** to bestow (an honour or award) on somebody. **2** (*often* + with) to consult or discuss. > **conferral** *n*.

conference *n* a formal meeting of people, e.g. members of a certain profession, for discussions.

confess *v* **1** to admit (a wrongdoing). **2** to acknowledge reluctantly. **3** to acknowledge one's sins to a priest.

confession *n* **1** an acknowledgement of a wrongdoing. **2** a disclosure of one's sins in confidence to a priest.

confessional *n* an enclosed cubicle in a church where a priest hears confessions.

confessor *n* a priest who hears confessions and gives absolution.

confetti *n* small pieces of coloured paper for throwing over the bride and groom at a wedding.

confidant *or* **confidante** *n* a friend that one can confide in.

confide *v* (+ in) to tell secrets and other private matters to somebody.

confidence *n* **1** faith or trust in something or somebody. **2** a feeling that one's powers or abilities are sufficient. **3** certainty or strong expectation. **4** a secret. * **in confidence** as private or secret information.

confidence trick *n* a swindle performed by gaining the victim's confidence.

confident *adj* **1** characterized by confidence or assurance. **2** (*also* + of) full of conviction; certain. > **confidently** *adv*.

confidential *adj* intended to be kept secret. > **confidentiality** *n*, **confidentially** *adv*.

configuration *n* an arrangement of parts relative one to another.

configure *v* to arrange (things) in a certain way relative to one another.

confine *v* **1** (*often* + to) to restrict within certain limits. **2** to shut (somebody) up. **3** of an illness or injury: to keep (somebody) in bed or a wheelchair.

confined *adj* of a space: cramped or enclosed.

confinement *n* **1** a state of being confined. **2** the time when a woman is about to give birth.

confirm *v* **1** to establish the correctness of (a report, fear, etc). **2** (+ in) to vindicate or strengthen (somebody) in a belief, etc. **3** to be evidence of or prove. **4** to commit oneself definitely to (an arrangement). **5** to administer the rite of confirmation to.

confirmation *n* **1** confirming proof; corroboration. **2** the confirming of an arrangement. **3** a religious ceremony admitting a person to full membership of a Christian church.

confirmed *adj* fixed in habit or attitude.

confiscate *v* to seize (property) by authority. ➤ **confiscation** *n*.

conflagration *n* a large and disastrous fire.

conflate *v* to combine (two or more things) into one. ➤ **conflation** *n*.

conflict[1] *n* **1** a sharp disagreement or clash. **2** mental struggle resulting from incompatible impulses. **3** a prolonged hostile encounter.

conflict[2] *v* to be incompatible or in opposition; to clash.

confluence *n* the meeting of two rivers or streams.

conform *v* **1** to be obedient or compliant. **2** (+ to/with) to accord with a certain standard or pattern.

conformist *n* a person who conforms to an accepted view or practice.

conformity *n* **1** correspondence with a certain model or standard. **2** (+ to) behaviour that is in compliance with a convention or specified requirements. **3** similarity in form.

confound *v* **1** to surprise or disconcert. **2** to prove (an argument or prediction) wrong. **3** to defeat or overthrow (a person or plan).

confront *v* **1** of a problem, etc: to require attention from (somebody). **2** to face up to and tackle (a problem or an opponent). **3** to present (somebody) with unwelcome facts.

confrontation *n* a state of hostile opposition or argument. ➤ **confrontational** *adj*.

confuse *v* **1** to bewilder or perplex. **2** to make more incomprehensible. **3** (*often* + with) to mistake (one person or thing) for another. ➤ **confusable** *adj*.

confused *adj* **1** bewildered. **2** disorganized or muddled.

confusion *n* **1** a state of being confused. **2** disorder or panic.

confute *v* **1** to defeat in argument. **2** to refute (an argument). ➤ **confutation** *n*.

conga *n* a dance performed by a group in single file.

congeal *v* to become solid during cooking or freezing; to coagulate.

congenial *adj* agreeably suited to one's nature or tastes.

congenital *adj* **1** of a disease or abnormality: existing from birth. **2** *informal* having an ingrained tendency to be a certain thing.

conger eel *n* a large edible sea eel.

congested *adj* **1** heavily crowded with people or traffic. **2** of the lungs or respiratory system:

blocked by mucus. **3** of other parts of the body: over-full of blood. ➤ **congestion** *n*.

conglomerate[1] *v* to gather into a mass, to accumulate. ➤ **conglomeration** *n*.

conglomerate[2] *n* **1** a composite mixture. **2** a large business company formed from acquisitions of other firms.

congratulate *v* (+ on) to express pleasure to (somebody) at their success or good fortune. ➤ **congratulation** *n*, **congratulatory** *adj*.

congratulations *pl n* good wishes expressed at somebody's success or good fortune.

congregate *v* to gather together.

congregation *n* **1** an assembly of people for religious worship. **2** a collection of people or things.

congress *n* **1** a formal meeting or programme of meetings between delegates. **2** (**Congress**) the supreme legislative body of the USA and some other countries. **3** *formal* the act or action of coming together and meeting. ➤ **congressional** *adj*.

congruent *adj* **1** in agreement or harmony. **2** geometrically identical size and shape. ➤ **congruence** *n*.

conical *adj* having the shape of a cone.

conifer *n* a tree that bears cones. ➤ **coniferous** *adj*.

conjecture[1] *n* a conclusion or opinion based on incomplete evidence. ➤ **conjectural** *adj*.

conjecture[2] *v* **1** to guess. **2** to form a conjecture.

conjoin *v formal* to unite or join.

conjugal *adj* relating to marriage or married people.

conjugate *v* to give the inflections of (a verb). ➤ **conjugation** *n*.

conjunction *n* **1** in grammar, a word such as *and*, *or*, *but*, *if*, or *when*, that joins words or clauses. **2** in astrology, the apparent meeting or passing of two or more planets in the same part of the sky. **3** occurrence together in time or space.

conjunctivitis *n* inflammation of the membrane lining the eyelid.

conjure *v* **1** (+ up) to produce from one's imagination or by using one's creative powers. **2** (+ up) of a word, sensation, etc: to evoke (ideas, images, etc). **3** to perform conjuring tricks.

conk *n informal Brit* the nose.

conker *n* the hard shiny brown nut of the horse chestnut tree.

conk out *v informal* **1** of a machine: to break down. **2** of a person: to faint or fall asleep.

conman *n* (*pl* **conmen**) *informal* a person who swindles with confidence tricks.

connect *v* **1** to link together. **2** (*often* + with) to associate (two things) mentally. **3** to constitute a link or relationship between. **4** to link (two callers) by telephone. ➤ **connective** *adj*, **connectively** *adv*, **connectivity** *n*.

connection (*Brit* **connexion**) *n* **1** something that connects; a link. **2** a relationship or association. **3** a train, bus, plane, etc, that one transfers to to continue a journey. **4** (*also in pl*) somebody connected to one by friendship, professional interests, etc.

connive *v* **1** (*often* + in/at) to ignore or secretly support a wrong. **2** (*often* + with) to cooperate secretly to do wrong. ➤ **connivance** *n*.

connoisseur /konə'suh/ *n* an expert judge in matters of taste or appreciation.

connotation *n* something suggested by a word as distinct from its direct meaning.

connote *v* of a word: to convey (ideas or feelings) in addition to its explicit meaning.

connubial *adj* concerning marriage or the relationship between husband and wife.

conquer *v* **1** to defeat and gain control over (a country or its people) by force. **2** to overcome or master (a challenge or weakness). ➤ **conqueror** *n*.

conquest *n* **1** the act or process of conquering. **2** a conquered territory. **3** a person who has been won over by love or sexual attraction.

conscience *n* the consciousness of the moral quality of one's conduct or intentions.

conscientious *adj* meticulous or careful in one's work; hard-working. ➤ **conscientiously** *adv*.

conscious *adj* **1** aware of one's surroundings and responding to them. **2** (+ of) aware of something. **3** of an action: intentional, deliberate. ➤ **consciously** *adv*, **consciousness** *n*.

conscript[1] *n* a person who has been called for military service.

conscript[2] *v* to enlist compulsorily for military service. ➤ **conscription** *n*.

consecrate *v* **1** to make or declare sacred by a solemn ceremony. **2** to ordain to a religious office. ➤ **consecration** *n*.

consecutive *adj* following in order without gaps. ➤ **consecutively** *adv*.

consensual *adj* relating to consent or consensus. ➤ **consensually** *adv*.

consensus *n* general agreement; unanimity.

Usage Note: Note the spelling with -*sus* not -*cus*.

---

consent[1] *v* **1** to give assent or approval to something. **2** to agree (to do something).

consent[2] *n* approval or acquiescence.

consequence *n* **1** a result or effect. **2** importance or relevance.

consequent *adj* **1** *formal* (+ to) following as a result or effect. **2** observing logical sequence; rational. ➤ **consequently** *adv*, **consequential** *adj*.

conservation *n* **1** preservation and protection of the environment and its natural resources. **2** the preservation of historic or archaeological artefacts or sites. **3** in physics, the conserving of a quantity. ➤ **conservationist** *n*.

conservative[1] *adj* **1** holding established views and tending to resist change. **2** (**Conservative**) relating to a political party associated with support of established institutions. **3** moderate or cautious. ➤ **conservatism** *n*, **conservatively** *adv*.

conservative[2] *n* **1** (**Conservative**) a supporter of a Conservative party. **2** a person who holds traditional views.

conservatory *n* (*pl* -**ies**) a room with a glass roof and large windows, built on to a house.

conserve[1] *v* **1** to keep in a state of safety or wholeness. **2** to maintain (a resource) and avoid wasteful use of it.

conserve[2] *n* a jam made from boiled fruit.

consider *v* **1** to think about carefully. **2** to deem or judge. **3** to have sympathetic regard for. **4** to have in mind.

considerable *adj* **1** worth consideration; significant. **2** large in extent or degree. ➤ **considerably** *adv*.

considerate *adj* showing concern for the welfare of others. ➤ **considerately** *adv*.

consideration *n* **1** careful thought. **2** a factor taken into account in making a decision. **3** the bearing of something in mind. **4** concern for others. **5** a payment for a service.

considering[1] *prep and adv* taking into account.

considering[2] *conj* in view of the fact that.

consign *v* **1** to entrust (something) to somebody's care. **2** to commit (something) to a place where it will be got rid of.

consignment *n* a batch of goods for delivery.

consist *v* **1** (+ of) to be made up or composed of. **2** (+ in) to be essentially.

consistency *n* (*pl* -**ies**) **1** the degree of thickness or firmness of a substance. **2** the quality of not varying or of being consistent.

consistent *adj* **1** not varying over a period of time. **2** (*often* + with) in agreement; not contradictory. **3** logically coherent. ➤ **consistently** *adv*.

consolation *n* **1** comfort received by somebody who has suffered loss or disappointment. **2** something that affords comfort.

consolation prize *n* a prize given to a competitor who just fails to win a main prize.

console[1] *v* to comfort (somebody) in grief or disappointment. ➤ **consolable** *adj*.

console[2] *n* **1** a panel, or switchboard housing a set of controls. **2** an electronic device for playing computerized video games.

consolidate *v* **1** to strengthen or make more stable. **2** to combine (several elements) into a unit. ➤ **consolidation** *n*.

consommé *n* a thin clear soup made from meat broth.

consonance *n* *formal* harmony or agreement.

consonant[1] *n* a letter representing one of the speech sounds, e.g. /p/, /g/, /n/, /l/, /s/, /t/, characterized by constriction or closure at one or more points in the breath channel.

consonant[2] *adj formal* (+ with) in agreement or harmony with.

consort[1] *n* **1** a husband or wife, *esp* of a reigning monarch. **2** a companion.

consort[2] *n* a group of musicians performing together.

consort[3] *v formal* (+ with) to keep regular company with.

consortium *n* (*pl* **consortia** or **consortiums**) a temporary combination of businesses.

conspicuous *adj* **1** obvious to the eye or mind. **2** attracting attention. ➤ **conspicuously** *adv.*

conspiracy *n* (*pl* **-ies**) a secret plot to do wrong.

conspire *v* **1** to plot secretly with others to do wrong. **2** of circumstances: to seem to be acting together to produce undesirable results.

constable *n Brit* a police officer of the lowest rank.

constabulary *n* (*pl* **-ies**) a local police force.

constant[1] *adj* **1** faithful and resolute. **2** invariable or uniform. **3** continually occurring or recurring; regular. ➤ **constancy** *n*, **constantly** *adv.*

constant[2] *n* **1** a number that has a fixed value. **2** something that stays the same in a given situation.

constellation *n* a group of stars forming patterns identified with mythical figures.

consternation *n* a state of confused dismay.

constipated *adj* affected by constipation.

constipation *n* difficulty in emptying the bowels because of compacted faeces.

constituency *n* (*pl* **-ies**) an electoral district or the body of voters resident in it.

constituent[1] *n* **1** an essential part; a component. **2** a member of an MP's constituency.

constituent[2] *adj* serving to form a unit or whole.

constitute *v* **1** of a group of people or things: to compose (something) together. **2** to be or amount to. **3** to establish or set up.

constitution *n* **1** the body of principles and laws of a nation, state, or social group. **2** the act of establishing or setting up. **3** the physical and mental make-up of a person. ➤**constitutionless** *adj.*

constitutional *adj* **1** relating to or in accordance with the constitution of a state or society. **2** relating to the constitution of body or mind. ➤ **constitutionally** *adv.*

constrain *v* of circumstances: to force (somebody) to do something. **2** to restrict or inhibit.

constraint *n* a constraining force or check.

constrict *v* **1** to make (a passage or opening) narrow. **2** to compress or squeeze. **3** to limit or inhibit. ➤ **constriction** *n.*

constrictor *n* a snake that kills its prey by crushing it.

construct[1] *v* **1** to build or erect. **2** to form (a theory or hypothesis).

construct[2] *n* a developed idea or concept.

construction *n* **1** the process of constructing. **2** a building or other structure. **3** a particular interpretation.

constructive *adj* **1** of a criticism, suggestion, etc: positive and helpful. **2** inferred rather than explicit. ➤ **constructively** *adv.*

construe *v* (**construes, construed, construing**) to interpret (something) in a certain way. ➤ **construal** *n.*

consul *n* **1** an official appointed by a government to reside in a foreign country and look after the interests of citizens of the appointing country. **2** either of two elected chief magistrates of the Roman republic. ➤ **consular** *adj.*

consulate *n* the office of a consul.

consult *v* **1** to seek the advice or opinion of (a professional person). **2** to look up (a reference book, etc). **3** to deliberate together; to confer. ➤ **consultation** *n*, **consultative** *adj.*

consultancy *n* (*pl* **-ies**) **1** an agency that provides consulting services. **2** the post of a consultant.

consultant *n* **1** an expert who gives professional advice or services. **2** a senior British hospital doctor.

consume *v* **1** to eat or drink (food or drink). **2** to use or use up (a fuel or other resource). **3** of fire: to destroy completely. **4** (*usu in passive*) of an emotion: to obsess (somebody).

consumer *n* somebody who uses goods or services.

consumerism *n* the promotion and protection of the consumer's interests. ➤ **consumerist** *n* and *adj.*

consummate[1] *adj* **1** extremely skilled and accomplished. **2** of the highest degree. ➤ **consummately** *adv.*

consummate[2] *v* **1** to make (a marriage) complete by sexual intercourse. **2** to complete (a business deal). ➤ **consummation** *n.*

consumption *n* **1** the process of consuming. **2** an amount consumed. **3** *dated* a wasting disease, *esp* tuberculosis of the lungs.

contact[1] *n* **1** the action of physically touching. **2** meeting or communication. **3** a useful business acquaintance or relationship. **4** an individual who has been in association with an infected person. **5** an electrical connection or junction.

contact[2] *v* to communicate with. ➤ **contactable** *adj.*

contact lens *n* a thin lens placed over the cornea of the eye to correct a sight defect.

contagion *n* the transmission of a disease from one person to another by contact.

contagious *adj* **1** of a disease: communicable by contact. **2** of a person: suffering from a contagious disease. **3** of a mood or attitude: tending to communicate itself to others.

contain v **1** to have or hold (something) within itself. **2** to comprise or include. **3** to keep (something) within limits. **4** to check or restrain.

container n **1** a box, tin, etc that contains things. **2** a large metal case for transporting.

containment n the action of keeping something harmful or unwelcome under control.

contaminate v **1** to render impure or unfit for use. **2** to make radioactive. ➤ **contamination** n.

contemplate v **1** to consider or meditate on. **2** to look at attentively. **3** to consider as a course of action.

contemporaneous adj existing or happening in the same period of time. ➤ **contemporaneously** adv.

contemporary¹ adj **1** happening or existing in the same period of time. **2** modern or fashionable.

contemporary² n (pl **-ies**) a person living or active in the same period of time as another.

contempt n **1** a feeling one has that somebody or something is bad or worthless. **2** (**contempt of court**) the offence of wilful disrespect for a court. ✻ **beneath contempt** utterly despicable.

contemptible adj deserving contempt. ➤ **contemptibly** adv.

contemptuous adj showing or expressing contempt. ➤ **contemptuously** adv.

contend v **1** to struggle or compete. **2** (+ with) to try to overcome difficulties. **3** to debate or argue. **4** to maintain or assert. ➤ **contender** n.

content¹ adj happy or satisfied. ➤ **contentment** n.

content² v to satisfy or appease.

content³ n a state of happy satisfaction. ✻ **to one's heart's content** as much as one wants.

content⁴ n **1** (in pl) the things that are contained in something. **2** (in pl) the topics treated in a book. **3** the matter dealt with in a literary work, lecture, etc, as distinct from its form or style. **4** the amount or proportion of a specified material contained in something.

contented adj **1** satisfied or happy. **2** willing to accept a situation. ➤ **contentedly** adv.

contention n **1** strong disagreement or rivalry. **2** a point advanced in a debate. ✻ **in contention** contending for a prize or success.

contentious adj likely to cause disagreement or controversy. ➤ **contentiously** adv.

contest¹ n **1** a struggle for superiority or victory. **2** a competition or competitive event.

contest² v **1** to stand as a candidate in (an election). **2** to dispute (a claim or decision). **3** (+ with/against) to strive or vie.

contestant n a participant in a contest.

context n **1** the parts surrounding a written or spoken word or passage that clarify its meaning. **2** the conditions in which something exists or occurs. ➤ **contextual** adj.

contiguous adj **1** in contact. **2** touching along a line or at a point; adjacent. **3** next or near in time or sequence.

continent¹ n **1** a large division of land on the globe (Europe, Asia, Africa, N and S America, Australia, and Antarctica). **2** (**the Continent**) Europe regarded from the British Isles.

continent² adj **1** able to control the bladder and bowels. **2** exercising self-restraint. ➤ **continence** n.

continental¹ adj relating to or characteristic of a continent, esp Europe.

continental² n an inhabitant of a continent, esp Europe.

continental breakfast n a light breakfast of bread rolls and coffee.

contingency n (pl **-ies**) **1** an event that may occur but cannot be definitely predicted; an eventuality. **2** the absence of certainty in the occurrence of events.

contingent¹ adj **1** subject to chance or unforeseen causes. **2** (+ on/upon) dependent on or conditioned by.

contingent² n a group of people forming part of a larger body.

continual adj happening constantly: continual interruptions. ➤ **continually** adv.

Usage Note: Do not confuse this word with continuous.

continuation n **1** the process of continuing. **2** resumption after an interruption. **3** something that continues or adds to something.

continue v **1** to maintain without interruption; to carry on (doing something). **2** to resume (an activity) after interruption. **3** to remain or endure. **4** to say something further.

continuity n (pl **-ies**) **1** uninterrupted connection or succession. **2** persistence without essential change. **3** uninterrupted duration in time. **4** a film script or scenario giving the details of the sequence of individual shots. **5** speech or music used to link parts of a radio or television programme.

continuous adj continuing uninterrupted; unbroken: a continuous humming. ➤ **continuously** adv.

Usage Note: Do not confuse this word with continual.

continuum n (pl **continua**) **1** a continuous succession of parts that are not distinguishable. **2** a sequence of minute gradations between extremes.

contort v to twist (something) out of shape. ➤ **contortion** n.

contortionist n a performer who contorts the body into strange postures.

contour[1] n **1** an outline of a curving or irregular figure. **2** a line on a map connecting points of equal elevation or height.

contour[2] v **1** to shape the contour or outline of. **2** to construct in conformity to a contour.

contraband n goods that have been brought out of or into a country illegally.

contraception n the use of contraceptives to prevent pregnancy.

contraceptive n a device or drug that aims at preventing a woman becoming pregnant. ➤ **contraceptive** adj.

contract[1] n **1** a legally binding agreement. **2** informal an arrangement for the murder of somebody by a hired killer. ➤ **contractual** adj.

contract[2] v **1** to reduce to a smaller size. **2** to draw together or tighten. **3** to shorten (a word) by omitting letters. **4** to establish or undertake by legal contract. **5** to catch (a disease). **6** to incur (a debt).

contraction n **1** the process of contracting. **2** the periodic contracting of the muscles of the womb during childbirth. **3** a shortening of a word.

contractor n a person who contracts to do work, esp a builder.

contradict v **1** to state the opposite of (a statement or speaker). **2** to deny the truthfulness of (a statement or speaker).

contradiction n **1** the act of contradicting. **2** a statement or series of statements containing contradictory parts. **3** opposition of factors inherent in a system or situation.

contradictory adj **1** incompatible or inconsistent with one another. **2** of propositions: logically such that only one can be true.

contradistinction n a distinction made by contrasting qualities.

contraflow n a temporary two-way traffic-flow system introduced on one carriageway of a motorway while the other is closed off.

contralto n (pl **-os**) a female singer with the lowest singing voice.

contraption n a strange or complicated device or gadget.

contrapuntal adj relating to musical counterpoint.

contrariwise adv in an opposite direction or way.

contrary[1] adj **1** completely different or opposed in nature or meaning. **2** /kən'treəri/ stubbornly inclined to oppose the wishes of others. **3** of the wind or weather: unfavourable. **4** /kən'treəri/ opposite in position or direction.

contrary[2] n ＊ **on the contrary** just the opposite.

contrast[1] n **1** comparison of similar objects to set off their dissimilar qualities. **2** a person or thing against which another may be contrasted. **3** juxtaposition of dissimilar elements in a work of art. **4** the degree of difference between the lightest and darkest parts of a photograph, television picture, etc.

contrast[2] v **1** (+ with) to be different or opposite. **2** to compare (two things) in respect to differences.

contravene v of a person or act: to break (a law or principle). ➤ **contravention** n.

contretemps /'kɒntrətɒnh, 'kon-/ n (pl **contretemps**) a minor disagreement or quarrel.

contribute v **1** to give something towards a common cause or objective. **2** (+ to) to help bring about an end or result. ➤ **contribution** n, **contributor** n.

contributory adj **1** helping to cause something. **2** contributing to a common fund or enterprise. **3** of a pension scheme or insurance plan: contributed to by both employers and employees.

contrite adj sorry for a wrongdoing. ➤ **contritely** n.

contrivance n **1** the process of contriving something. **2** an ingenious device or a plan.

contrive v **1** to devise or plan (something) with ingenuity. **2** to manage (to do something foolish).

contrived adj of art, language, etc: unnatural or forced.

control[1] v (**controlled**, **controlling**) **1** to supervise and direct (something). **2** to operate (a machine). **3** to restrain (oneself or one's emotions). **4** to regulate (the finances of an organization, etc). ➤ **controllable** adj, **controllability** n, **controller** n.

control[2] n **1** power or authority to control. **2** the activity or situation of controlling. **3** the direction and coordination of business activities. **4** mastery in the use of a tool or technique. **5** restraint or reserve. **6** a thing or person used as a gauge for checking something else. **7** (in pl) the devices and mechanisms used to regulate the operation of a machine or system. **8** an organization that directs a space flight. ＊ **in control** having control or command. **out of control** dangerously out of control.

control tower n a tall airport building from which movements of aircraft are controlled.

controversial adj likely to cause controversy. ➤ **controversially** adv.

controversy n (pl **-ies**) **1** debate or disagreement on an important matter. **2** a dispute over a specific issue.

contumely n formal contemptuous language or treatment.

contusion n a bruise.

conundrum n (pl **conundrums**) **1** a riddle, esp one involving a pun. **2** an intricate and difficult problem.

conurbation n a large urban area, formed when the suburbs of two or more towns merge.

convalesce v to recover gradually after illness or injury. ➤ **convalescence** n, **convalescent** adj and n.

convection n the transfer of heat by the movement of a heated gas or liquid in relation to a colder part.

convector n a heater in which heated air circulates by convection.

convene v to assemble for a meeting. ➤ **convener** n, **convenor** n.

convenience n 1 ease of use or access. 2 personal comfort or advantage. 3 a useful appliance or service. 4 Brit a public toilet.

convenient adj 1 suited to personal comfort or easy use. 2 suited to a particular situation. 3 near at hand; easily accessible. ➤ **conveniently** adv.

convent n a community of nuns.

convention n 1 accepted social custom or practice. 2 a generally agreed principle. 3 an agreement between states. 4 an assembly or conference.

conventional adj 1 conforming to or sanctioned by convention. 2 lacking originality or individuality. 3 of warfare: not using nuclear weapons. ➤ **conventionally** adv.

converge v 1 to come together towards a common point. 2 (+ on/upon) to come together in a common interest or focus. ➤ **convergence** n, **convergent** adj.

conversant adj (+ with) fully acquainted or familiar with facts, principles, etc.

conversation n an informal verbal exchange. ➤ **conversational** adj.

converse[1] v to have a conversation.

converse[2] adj opposite in order or relation. ➤ **conversely** adv.

converse[3] n a situation, fact, etc that is the opposite of something else.

conversion n 1 the process of converting, or something converted. 2 a building that has been altered to a different purpose. 3 the adoption of a new or different religious faith. 4 in rugby, successful kick at goal awarded after a try.

convert[1] v 1 to change (something) from one form or function to another. 2 to alter (a building) to a new purpose. 3 to persuade (somebody) to follow a principle, religious belief, etc. 4 in rugby, to complete (a try) by successfully kicking a conversion.

convert[2] n a person who has undergone a religious conversion.

convertible[1] adj 1 capable of being converted. 2 of a car: having a top that can be lowered.

convertible[2] n a convertible car.

convex adj curved or rounded outwards like the outside of a bowl.

convey v 1 to take or carry from one place to another. 2 to communicate (a feeling or idea).

3 in law, to transfer (property or rights) to another person.

conveyance n 1 the conveying of something. 2 a means of transport. 3 the legal transfer of rights to property. ➤ **conveyancing** n.

conveyor belt n a moving belt or set of linked plates for moving objects from one part of a building to another.

convict[1] v to prove and declare (somebody) to be guilty of a crime.

convict[2] n a person who has been convicted of a crime and imprisoned.

conviction n 1 a strongly held persuasion or belief. 2 the state of being convinced. 3 the process of convicting someone of a crime, or an instance of this.

convince v 1 to cause (somebody) to believe or accept something. 2 to persuade (somebody) to follow a course of action.

convincing adj 1 serving to convince. 2 of a victory, etc: secured by a large margin. ➤ **convincingly** adv.

convivial adj 1 sociable or friendly. 2 enjoying good company. ➤ **conviviality** n.

convoluted adj 1 complex and difficult to understand. 2 technical having twists or coils.

convolution n 1 a twist or coil. 2 something intricate or complicated.

convoy n (treated as sing. or pl) a group of ships or vehicles travelling together.

convulse v 1 to cause (a person) to be shaken violently by spasms of rage, laughter, etc. 2 to be convulsed. ➤ **convulsive** adj.

convulsion n 1 an involuntary contraction or series of contractions of the muscles. 2 a violent disturbance. 3 (in pl) an uncontrolled fit of laughter.

cony or **coney** n (pl **conies** or **coneys**) a rabbit.

coo v (**coos, cooed, cooing**) 1 to make the low soft cry of a dove or pigeon. 2 to talk lovingly or appreciatively. ➤ **coo** n.

cook[1] v 1 to prepare food for eating by heating it. 2 of food: to be cooked by heating. 3 informal to falsify (financial accounts) in order to deceive. ➤ **cooking** n.

cook[2] n a person who cooks food.

cooker n Brit 1 an appliance for cooking food, with an oven, hot plates, and a grill. 2 informal an apple or other fruit suitable only for cooking.

cookery n (pl **-ies**) the art or practice of cooking.

cookie n 1 NAmer a sweet biscuit. 2 informal a person of a specified type: a tough cookie. 3 in computing, data downloaded from an Internet website to identify a user on future visits.

cool[1] adj 1 moderately cold. 2 bringing relief from heat. 3 unfriendly or lacking enthusiasm. 4 calm and self-controlled. 5 informal used as an intensive: a cool million. 6 informal fashionable or attractive. **7** *informal* very good. ➤ **coolly** *adv*, **coolness** *n*.

cool² *v* to make or become cool.

cool³ *n informal* poise or composure.

coolant *n* a liquid or gas used in cooling an engine or machine.

coomb *n* a valley or hollow on a hillside running up from a coast.

coon *n NAmer* a raccoon.

coop¹ *n* a small enclosure for poultry.

coop² *v* (*usu* + up) to confine in a small space.

cooper *n* a person who makes or repairs barrels and casks.

cooperate or **co-operate** *v* **1** to act or work together for a common purpose. **2** to do or agree to what is asked. ➤ **cooperation** *n*.

cooperative¹ or **co-operative** *adj* **1** showing a willingness to work with others. **2** of an organization: owned by and operated for the benefit of its members. ➤ **cooperatively** *adv*.

cooperative² or **co-operative** *n* a cooperative organization or business.

co-opt *v* **1** of a committee or other body: to choose or elect (somebody) as a member. **2** to appropriate (an idea). ➤ **co-option** *n*.

coordinate¹ or **co-ordinate** *v* **1** to combine (diverse elements) into a common condition or action. **2** to combine or act together harmoniously. ➤ **coordinator** *n*.

coordinate² or **co-ordinate** *n* in mathematics, a set of numbers used to specify the location of a point on a line or surface, or in space.

coordinate³ or **co-ordinate** *adj* equal in rank or importance.

coordinated or **co-ordinated** *adj* able to move one's body efficiently and effectively.

coordination or **co-ordination** *n* **1** the process of coordinating. **2** the ability to move one's body efficiently and effectively.

coot *n* a water bird with dark plumage and a white bill.

cop¹ *n informal* a police officer. ✳ **not much cop** *Brit, informal* fairly bad.

cop² *v* (**copped, copping**) *Informal* **1** to capture or arrest. **2** to suffer (something bad or unwelcome). ✳ **cop it 1** *Brit, informal* to be in serious trouble. **2** *Brit, informal* to be killed.

cope¹ *v* to deal effectively with something difficult or awkward.

cope² *n* a long vestment worn by a priest on special occasions.

copier *n* a machine for making copies of documents.

co-pilot *n* a second pilot in an aircraft.

coping *n* a sloping, course of brick or stone on the top of a wall.

copious *adj* abundant or plentiful. ➤ **copiously** *adv*.

cop-out *n informal* avoidance of a responsibility.

cop out *v informal* to avoid a responsibility.

copper¹ *n* **1** a reddish metallic chemical element. **2** a reddish brown colour. **3** *Brit* a coin or token made of copper or bronze.

copper² *n Brit, informal* a police officer.

copper-bottomed *adj Brit* completely reliable.

copperplate *n* a style of fine handwriting marked by lines of contrasting thickness.

coppice *n* a woodland area in which the trees are regularly cut back to promote growth.

copse *n* a small area of trees.

copulate *v* to have sexual intercourse. ➤ **copulation** *n*.

copy¹ *n* (*pl* **-ies**) **1** something made to imitate or be identical to something else. **2** a single specimen of a book, CD, etc. **3** material ready to be printed and published.

copy² *v* (**-ies, -ied**) **1** to make a copy of. **2** to imitate. **3** to model oneself on.

copycat *n informal* somebody who slavishly copies another.

copy-edit *v* (**copy-edited, copy-editing**) to prepare (manuscript copy) for printing by correcting errors and making the style consistent. ➤ **copy editor** *n*.

copyright¹ *n* the exclusive right to publish or perform a literary, musical, or artistic work for a fixed period.

copyright² *v* to secure a copyright on (a literary, musical, or artistic work).

copywriter *n* a writer of copy for advertising or publicity. ➤ **copywriting** *n*.

coquette *n* a woman who flirts with men. ➤ **coquetry** *n*, **coquettish** *adj*.

coracle *n* a small round boat made of waterproof material over a wicker frame.

coral *n* a hard substance produced by certain marine invertebrate animals.

cor anglais /ˌkawrˈongglay, kawrongˈglay/ *n* (*pl* **cors anglais**) a woodwind musical instrument of the oboe family, with a rounded end.

corbel *n* a projection from a wall which supports a weight. ➤ **corbelled** *adj*.

cord *n* **1** a length of several strands of thread or yarn woven or twisted together. **2** an electric flex. **3** corduroy. **4** (*in pl*) trousers made of corduroy. ➤ **cordless** *adj*.

cordial¹ *adj* **1** warm and affable. **2** sincerely or deeply felt. ➤ **cordiality** *n*, **cordially** *adv*.

cordial² *n* **1** *Brit* a non-alcoholic sweetened fruit drink. **2** *NAmer* a liqueur.

cordite *n* a smokeless explosive.

cordon¹ *n* a line of troops, police, preventing access to an area.

cordon² *v* (+ off) to form a cordon round.

cordon bleu /ˌkawdonh ˈbluh/ *adj* of cookery: of the highest standard.

corduroy *n* a cotton pile fabric with lengthways ribs.

core¹ *n* **1** the central part of some fruits. **2** the essential or central part of something.

core² v to remove a core from (fruit).

co-respondent n a person alleged to have committed adultery with the respondent in a divorce case.

corgi n (pl **corgis**) a dog of a breed with short legs and a fox-like head.

coriander n a plant of the carrot family with leaves and seeds used in cooking.

cork¹ n **1** the tough outer tissue of a type of oak tree. **2** a cork stopper for a bottle.

cork² v to fit or close (a bottle) with a cork.

corker n informal a very good example of a person or thing.

corkscrew¹ n an implement for removing corks from bottles.

corkscrew² v to move or twist in a spiral.

corm n a rounded thick underground base of some plants.

cormorant n a dark-coloured seabird with a long neck and hooked bill.

corn¹ n **1** chiefly Brit the most important cereal crop of a region. **2** NAmer, Aus, NZ maize. **3** informal something trite or sentimental.

corn² n a painful hardening of the skin on the top of a toe.

cornea n the transparent membrane covering the iris and pupil of the eye.

corned beef n beef preserved in brine.

cornelian or **carnelian** n a hard reddish mineral used in jewellery.

corner¹ n **1** the point or angle where converging lines, edges, or sides meet. **2** the place where two streets or roads meet. **3** in football, a free kick from a corner of the pitch, awarded to the attacking team. **4** the part of a boxing or wrestling ring in which a fighter rests between rounds. **5** a private or remote place. **6** an awkward or difficult situation.

corner² v **1** to drive (a person or animal) into a place of no escape. **2** to detain and talk to (somebody). **3** to gain control of (an economic market) by acquiring a substantial supply of a commodity. **4** to go round a corner in a road.

cornerstone n **1** a block of stone forming the base of a corner of a building. **2** the most basic part of something.

cornet n **1** a brass musical instrument resembling a trumpet but shorter. **2** Brit an ice cream cone.

cornflour n Brit ground flour made from maize.

cornflower n a plant with narrow leaves and blue, purple, or white flowers.

cornice n an ornamental plaster moulding between the wall and ceiling of a room.

cornucopia n a plentiful supply or store.

corny adj (**-ier, -iest**) **1** informal sentimental and trite. **2** overused and hackneyed.

corolla n the petals of a flower.

corollary n (pl **-ies**) **1** a conclusion drawn from a proved proposition. **2** a natural consequence or association.

corona n (pl **coronas** or **coronae**) **1** a coloured circle of light seen round the sun, the moon, or a star. **2** the outermost part of the atmosphere of the sun and other stars.

coronary¹ adj relating to the arteries and veins that supply the heart with blood.

coronary² or **coronary thrombosis** n (pl **coronaries** or **coronary thromboses**) a blockage in an artery of the heart.

coronation n the ceremony of crowning a sovereign.

coroner n a public officer who enquires into the cause of a sudden or suspicious death.

coronet n **1** a small crown. **2** an ornamental wreath or band for the head.

corpora n pl of CORPUS.

corporal¹ n a non-commissioned army officer ranking below sergeant.

corporal² adj of or affecting the body.

corporal punishment n physical punishment, e.g. caning.

corporate adj **1** relating to companies or businesses. **2** of or belonging to a body of individuals.

corporation n **1** a body of people authorized to act as a single person with its own legal identity. **2** (treated as sing. or pl) the municipal authorities of a British town or city.

corporeal adj **1** relating to a physical material body; not spiritual. **2** not immaterial or intangible; substantial.

corps n (pl **corps**) **1** an army unit consisting of two or more divisions organized for a particular purpose. **2** a body of people engaged in a specific activity.

corpse¹ n a dead body, esp a dead human body.

corpse² v informal to stifle laughter with difficulty, e.g. on a solemn occasion or while acting in a play.

corpulent adj excessively fat; obese. ➤ **corpulence** n.

corpus n (pl **corpora** or **corpuses**) a collection of writings or texts.

corpuscle n a blood cell.

corral¹ n NAmer an enclosure for livestock.

corral² v (**corralled, corralling**) chiefly NAmer to enclose (livestock) in a corral.

correct¹ adj **1** true or right. **2** conforming to an accepted standard or to an ideology. ➤ **correctly** adv, **correctness** n.

correct² v **1** to make or set right. **2** to alter so as to remove an error or imperfection. **3** to point out the faults in.

correction n **1** the process of correcting. **2** a change made in order to correct something. **3** punishment.

corrective adj intended to correct.

cottage cheese

correlate v **1** to relate to and affect one another. **2** to bring together for comparison.

correlation n **1** a relationship between things having a mutual effect. **2** the act or an instance of correlating two things.

correspond v **1** to conform or be compatible. **2** to be equivalent or similar. **3** to communicate by exchanging letters.

correspondence n **1** letters, or communication by letter. **2** agreement or similarity.

correspondence course n a course of study in which students send and receive material by post.

correspondent n **1** a person who communicates by letter. **2** a newspaper or broadcasting journalist who reports on a particular subject.

corridor n **1** a passage with doors leading into rooms. **2** a strip of land through foreign-held territory. **3** a restricted path for air traffic.

corroborate v to support (a claim or an opinion) with evidence or authority. ➤ **corroboration** n, **corroborative** adj.

corrode v **1** to eat or wear away (metal) by chemical action. **2** to weaken or destroy gradually. ➤ **corrosion** n.

corrosive[1] adj **1** causing corrosion. **2** harmful or destructive.

corrosive[2] n a substance that causes corrosion.

corrugate v to fold into ridges and grooves. ➤ **corrugated** adj, **corrugation** n.

corrupt[1] adj **1** open to or characterized by bribery or other improper conduct. **2** morally degenerate. **3** of computer data: damaged and unusable. **4** of a text: containing errors. ➤ **corruptly** adv.

corrupt[2] v to make corrupt. ➤ **corruptible** adj.

corruption n **1** the process of corrupting. **2** improper or immoral conduct.

corsage n a small posy of flowers pinned to a woman's dress.

corset n a supporting undergarment for the middle part of a woman's body.

cortège or **cortege** n a funeral procession.

cortex n (pl **cortices**) the outer part of an organ of the body, esp of the brain.

coruscate v literary to flash or sparkle. ➤ **coruscating** adj.

corvette n a small armed escort ship.

cos abbr cosine.

cosh[1] n Brit a short heavy stick used as a weapon.

cosh[2] v Brit to hit with a cosh.

cosine n in mathematics, the ratio in a right-angled triangle between the side adjacent to a particular angle and the hypotenuse.

cos lettuce n a crisp variety of lettuce with long leaves.

cosmetic[1] n a preparation designed to be applied to the skin or hair to improve its appearance or texture.

cosmetic[2] adj **1** intended to improve beauty, e.g. of the hair or complexion. **2** affecting or improving something superficially without substantial change. ➤ **cosmetically** adv.

cosmic adj relating to the universe.

cosmonaut n a Russian astronaut.

cosmopolitan adj **1** composed of people or elements from many parts of the world. **2** having worldwide rather than provincial scope or bearing.

cosmos n the universe as an orderly system.

Cossack n a member of a people of South Russia and the Ukraine famous for skilful horseriding.

cosset v (**cosseted, cosseting**) to treat (a person or animal) in an excessively protective way.

cost[1] n **1** the price paid or charged for something. **2** the expenditure of effort or sacrifice made to achieve something. **3** the loss or penalty incurred in gaining something. **4** (in pl) legal expenses. * **at all costs** regardless of the price or difficulties.

cost[2] v (past tense and past part. cost) **1** to have a price of (a specified amount). **2** to cause (somebody) to suffer or lose something. **3** (past tense and past part. costed) to estimate or set the cost of.

co-star[1] n a performer who has equal billing with another performer in a film or play.

co-star[2] v (**co-starred, co-starring**) **1** to appear as a co-star in a film or play. **2** to feature (an actor) as a co-star.

cost-effective adj economically worthwhile.

costermonger n Brit, dated a person who sells fruit or vegetables from a street barrow or stall.

costly adj (**-ier, -iest**) **1** expensive or valuable. **2** achieved with considerable sacrifice.

costume[1] n a set of clothing belonging to a specific time, place, or character.

costume[2] v to provide with a costume.

costume jewellery n inexpensive imitation jewellery.

costumier (NAmer **costumer**) n a person who deals in or makes costumes, e.g. for theatrical productions.

cosy[1] (NAmer **cozy**) adj (**-ier, -iest**) **1** affording warmth and comfort; snug. **2** informal suggesting close association or connivance. ➤ **cosily** adv, **cosiness** n.

cosy[2] (NAmer **cozy**) n (pl **-ies**) a cover for a teapot or boiled egg, to keep it hot.

cosy up (NAmer **cozy up**) v (**-ies, -ied**) informal (usu + to) to seek friendship or intimacy in a self-serving way.

cot n Brit a small bed for a baby or young child, with high sides of vertical bars.

cot death n Brit the unexplained death of a baby while asleep.

coterie n a small exclusive group of people.

cottage n a small house in the country.

cottage cheese n a soft white cheese made from the curds of skimmed milk.

cotter pin *n* a pin for fastening parts of a mechanism together.

cotton *n* **1** a soft white fibrous substance surrounding the seeds of a tropical plant. **2** yarn or fabric made of cotton.

cotton wool *n* **1** *Brit* fluffy soft material in balls or pads, used for cleaning the skin. **2** *NAmer* raw cotton.

cotyledon *n* the first leaf developed by the embryo of a seed plant.

couch[1] *n* a long upholstered piece of furniture for sitting or lying on.

couch[2] *v* to phrase in a specified manner.

couch potato *n* *informal* somebody who watches a lot of television.

cougar *n* *NAmer* a puma.

cough[1] *v* **1** to expel air from the lungs with an explosive noise. **2** *Brit, informal* to reveal information.

cough[2] *n* **1** an act or sound of coughing. **2** a condition marked by repeated or frequent coughing. ➤ **cougher** *n*.

cough mixture *n* *Brit* a medicated liquid used to relieve coughing.

cough up *v* **1** to expel (mucus) by coughing. **2** *informal* to produce or hand over (money or information) unwillingly.

could *v aux* the past tense of CAN[1].

couldn't *contraction* could not.

coulomb *n* the SI unit of electric charge.

council *n* **1** an elected or appointed body with administrative or legislative powers. **2** a locally elected body administering a city, county, or district.

council house *n* a house rented to tenants by a local council.

councillor (*NAmer* **councilor**) *n* a member of a council. ➤ **councillorship** *n*.

Usage Note: Do not confuse this word with *counsellor*.

counsel[1] *n* **1** formal or personal advice. **2** a barrister or other lawyer engaged in a court case.

counsel[2] *v* (**counselled, counselling,** *NAmer* **counseled, counseling**) **1** to advise. **2** to give (somebody) help with psychological or personal problems. ➤ **counselling** *n*.

counsellor (*NAmer* **counselor**) *n* **1** a person who gives professional advice or guidance. **2** *NAmer* a barrister.

Usage Note: Do not confuse this word with *councillor*.

count[1] *v* **1** to find the total number of. **2** to name the numbers in order. **3** to include in a reckoning. **4** to think of (somebody or something) as having a particular quality or function. **5** (+ in/out) to include or exclude. **6** to have value or importance. ✳ **count on 1** to look forward to (something) as certain. **2** to rely on (somebody).

count[2] *n* **1** the act of counting. **2** a total obtained by counting. **3** in law, a charge in an indictment. **4** a specific point under consideration; an issue. ✳ **out for the count 1** in boxing, knocked down and unable to rise again during a count of ten. **2** *informal* unconscious or deeply asleep.

count[3] *n* a European nobleman.

countdown *n* a continuous count down to zero of the time remaining before an event.

countenance[1] *n* a person's face as an indication of mood or character.

countenance[2] *v* to allow or tolerate.

counter[1] *n* **1** a level surface over which goods are sold or food is served. **2** a small disc used in counting or in board games. **3** a person or machine that counts. ✳ **under the counter** obtained by illegal or surreptitious means.

counter[2] *v* **1** to act in opposition to; to oppose. **2** to challenge attacks or arguments.

counter[3] *adv* (+ to) in an opposite direction.

counteract *v* to lessen or neutralize the ill effects of. ➤ **counteractive** *adj*.

counterattack[1] *or* **counter-attack** *n* an attack made in reply to an attack.

counterattack[2] *or* **counter-attack** *v* to make a counterattack.

counterbalance[1] *n* **1** a weight that balances another. **2** a force or influence that offsets or checks an opposing force.

counterbalance[2] *v* to oppose or balance with an equal weight or force.

counterespionage *or* **counter-espionage** *n* activities directed towards detecting and thwarting enemy espionage.

counterfeit[1] *adj* made in imitation of something with intent to deceive or defraud.

counterfeit[2] *n* a forgery.

counterfeit[3] *v* to imitate or copy fraudulently.

counterfoil *n* *chiefly Brit* the part of a cheque, ticket, etc that is kept as a record or receipt.

counterintelligence *or* **counter-intelligence** *n* activity designed to block an enemy's sources of information; counterespionage.

countermand *v* to revoke (a command) by a contrary order.

countermeasure *n* a measure designed to counter a danger or difficulty.

counterpane *n* a bedspread.

counterpart *n* a person or thing with the same function or characteristics as another.

counterpoint *n* **1** the combination of two or more independent melodies into a single harmonic texture. **2** one or more independent melodies added above or below a given melody.

counterproductive *adj* having effects opposite to those intended.

countersign *v* to add a signature to (a document) as a witness to another signature. ➤ **countersignature** n.

countersink v (past tense and past part. **countersunk**) **1** to enlarge the exposed surface of (a hole) so that the head of a bolt or screw will fit into it. **2** to set the head of (a bolt or screw) into the surface.

countertenor n a male singer having a voice higher than tenor.

countervail v to counterbalance the effect of; to offset.

countess n **1** the wife or widow of an earl or count. **2** a woman who has the rank of earl or count in her own right.

countless adj too numerous to be counted; innumerable.

countrified or **countryfied** adj rural in style or manner.

country n (pl **-ies**) **1** a political state or nation or its territory. **2** rural as opposed to urban areas. **3** an expanse of land. ✳ **go to the country** Brit to hold a general election.

country music n folk music of the southern USA.

countryside n a rural area.

county n (pl **-ies**) each of the principal territorial divisions of Britain and some other countries or states for administrative purposes.

county town n Brit the administrative centre of a county.

coup /kooh/ n (pl **coups**) **1** (also **coup d'état** /koohday'tah/) the violent overthrow of a government from within a country. **2** a sudden brilliant stroke or act.

coupe n a dessert of fruit and ice cream served in a shallow dish.

coupé n a two-door car with a fixed roof and a sloping rear.

couple[1] n **1** two things considered together; a pair. **2** two people who are married or living together. **3** informal an indefinite small number; a few. **4** in mechanics, two forces that together cause rotation.

couple[2] v **1** to link or fasten. **2** to copulate.

couplet n a unit of two successive rhyming lines of verse.

coupling n a device that connects adjacent parts or objects, e.g. electrical circuits or railway carriages.

coupon n **1** a voucher that entitles the holder to a discount or other benefit. **2** a part of a printed advertisement that can be cut out and filled in to make an enquiry or enter a competition.

courage n mental or moral strength to confront danger, suffering, or difficulty.

courageous adj having or showing courage; brave. ➤ **courageously** adv.

courgette n Brit a variety of small vegetable marrow used as a vegetable.

courier n **1** a person who collects and delivers parcels and documents. **2** a person employed to assist tourists abroad.

course[1] n **1** the path over which something moves. **2** a movement or progression in space or time. **3** the direction of travel of an aircraft. **4** the usual procedure or normal action of something. **5** a chosen manner of conducting oneself; a plan of action. **6** a series of lessons or lectures relating to a subject. **7** a part of a meal served at one time. **8** a medical treatment administered over a period. **9** an area of land marked out for a sport, e.g. golf or racing. **10** a layer of brick or masonry in a wall.

course[2] v **1** of a liquid: to run or flow. **2** to hunt or pursue (hares) with dogs.

court[1] n **1** an official assembly of people authorized to hear judicial cases. **2** a place in which such a court is held. **3** a space marked off for playing tennis or other ball games. **4** a space enclosed by buildings. **5** the residence or the family and retinue of a sovereign.

court[2] v **1** dated to seek the affections of; to woo. **2** to seek to win the favour or support of. **3** to act in a way that provokes (a bad outcome).

court card n Brit a king, queen, or jack in a pack of cards.

courteous adj showing respect and consideration; polite. ➤ **courteously** adv.

courtesan n a prostitute with wealthy or upper-class clients.

courtesy n (pl **-ies**) **1** polite and courteous behaviour. **2** a courteous act or expression. ✳ **by courtesy of** through the generosity or permission of.

courtier n an attendant or companion to a king or queen.

courtly adj (**-ier**, **-iest**) elegant and refined.

court-martial[1] n (pl **courts-martial** or **court-martials**) **1** a court that tries members of the armed forces. **2** a trial by such a court.

court-martial[2] v (**court-martialled**, **court-martialling**, NAmer **court-martialed**, **court-martialing**) to try by court-martial.

courtship n **1** a period of courting. **2** the courting rituals of animals. **3** the process of courting favour.

court shoe n Brit a plain woman's shoe with high heels and no fastenings.

couscous n a North African dish of steamed ground wheat.

cousin n a child of one's uncle or aunt.

couture n the business of designing and making fashionable custom-made women's clothing.

couturier or **couturière** n a person who makes and sells couture clothes.

cove n a small sheltered inlet or bay.

coven n a group or gathering of witches.

covenant n 1 a formal agreement or contract. 2 an agreement to make regular payments to a charity.

cover[1] v 1 to place or set something over (a thing) to conceal or protect it. 2 to lie or spread over. 3 to extend thickly or conspicuously over the surface of. 4 to hide from sight or knowledge. 5 to travel (a specified distance). 6 of an amount of money: to be enough to pay for. 7 to include or take into account. 8 to report news about. 9 to have as one's field of activity. 10 to insure or provide protection against (a risk or contingency). 11 to protect (somebody) by being in a position to fire at an attacker. 12 of a male animal: to copulate with (a female animal). 13 to record a cover version of (a song). 14 (+ for) to act as a substitute for. ✳ **cover one's tracks** to conceal evidence of one's past actions. ➤ **covering** n.

cover[2] n 1 something put over to conceal or give protection. 2 a jacket for a book. 3 natural shelter for an animal. 4 shelter or protection from attack. 5 a pretext or disguise. 6 Brit protection under an insurance policy. 7 a place setting in a restaurant. 8 (also **cover version**) a new version of a pop song previously recorded by another performer. ✳ **break cover** to leave shelter and face pursuit.

coverage n 1 an area or amount covered. 2 inclusion within the scope of something.

cover charge n a charge for service in a restaurant.

covering letter n a letter explaining an enclosed item.

coverlet n a bedspread.

covert[1] adj not openly shown or acknowledged; secret. ➤ **covertly** adv.

covert[2] n a thicket providing cover for game.

cover-up n an attempt to conceal an error or a crime.

covet v (**coveted**, **coveting**) to long to have (something that belongs to somebody else). ➤ **covetous** adj.

covey n (pl -**eys**) a small flock of game birds.

cow[1] n 1 the mature female animal of domestic cattle. 2 a mature female of other large animals. 3 informal an unpleasant woman. ✳ **till the cows come home** for ever.

cow[2] v to intimidate with threats or a show of strength.

coward n somebody who lacks courage or resolve. ➤ **cowardice** n, **cowardly** adj.

cowboy n 1 a man on horseback who herds cattle in North America. 2 informal an incompetent or dishonest trader.

cower v to crouch down or shrink away in fear.

cowl n 1 a monk's hood or long hooded cloak. 2 a chimney covering designed to improve ventilation. 3 a cowling.

cowling n a removable metal covering over an engine.

cowrie or **cowry** n (pl -**ies**) a sea mollusc with a glossy shell.

cowslip n a plant of the primrose family with fragrant yellow flowers.

cox[1] n a person who steers a racing boat and directs the rowers.

cox[2] v to be cox of (a boat).

coxcomb n archaic a conceited foolish person.

coxswain n 1 a cox of a racing rowing boat. 2 a sailor who commands a ship's boat.

coy adj 1 self-consciously shy or unassuming. 2 provocatively playful or coquettish. 3 showing reluctance to reveal details of a sensitive issue. ➤ **coyly** adv.

coyote n (pl **coyotes** or **coyote**) a wolflike wild dog of North America.

coypu n (pl **coypus** or **coypu**) a South American rodent like a beaver.

cozy[1] adj NAmer see COSY[1].

cozy[2] n NAmer see COSY[2].

Cr abbr the chemical symbol for chromium.

crab n a sea crustacean with a broad flat shell and pincers at the front.

crab apple n a small wild sour apple.

crabbed adj 1 of writing: difficult to read or understand. 2 morose or peevish.

crabby adj (-**ier**, -**iest**) bad-tempered.

crack[1] v 1 to make or cause (something) to make a sudden sharp noise. 2 to break or split without coming apart. 3 to break (something) with a crack. 4 to tell (a joke). 5 to work out (a code or mystery). 6 to break into (a safe). 7 of the voice: to change pitch suddenly. 8 to collapse emotionally under stress.

crack[2] n 1 a sudden sharp loud noise. 2 a narrow opening where something has split or broken. 3 a sharp resounding blow. 4 informal a witty remark. 5 informal an attempt at something. 6 (also **crack cocaine**) informal a strong and addictive variety of cocaine.

crack[3] adj informal very able or skilled: a crack shot.

crackdown n informal a period of harsh treatment of bad behaviour or wrongdoing.

crack down v informal (+ on) to deal harshly with.

cracker n 1 a paper tube that makes a cracking noise when pulled sharply apart and contains a toy and a paper hat. 2 a firecracker. 3 a thin savoury biscuit. 4 Brit, informal something or somebody exceptional.

crackers adj chiefly Brit, informal mad or eccentric.

cracking adv informal, dated exceptionally good or fast.

crackle[1] v to make a series of small cracking noises.

crackle[2] n a crackling noise. ➤ **crackly** adj.

crackling n the crisp skin of roast pork.

crackpot n informal a crazy or eccentric person.

crack up *v informal* **1** to suffer an emotional breakdown. **2** to laugh uncontrollably.

cradle[1] *n* **1** a baby's bed or cot on rockers. **2** a supporting framework of wood or metal. **3** a place where something important originates.

cradle[2] *v* to shelter or hold protectively.

craft[1] *n* **1** an activity or trade requiring manual dexterity or artistic skill. **2** skill in making or executing something; dexterity. **3** (*pl* **craft** or **crafts**) a boat, ship, aircraft, or spacecraft. **4** skill in deception.

craft[2] *v* to make using skill and dexterity.

craftsman *or* **craftswoman** *n* (*pl* **craftsmen** *or* **craftswomen**) a man or woman who practises a skilled craft. ➤ **craftsmanship** *n*.

crafty *adj* (**-ier, -iest**) showing subtlety and guile. ➤ **craftily** *adv*.

crag *n* a steep rugged rock or cliff.

cram *v* (**crammed, cramming**) **1** to pack or jam (a container) tight. **2** (+ in/into) to thrust forcefully into something. **3** *informal* to eat voraciously. **4** to study intensively for an examination.

crammer *n Brit, informal* a school that prepares students intensively for an examination.

cramp[1] *n* **1** a painful spasmodic contraction of a muscle. **2** (*in pl*) severe abdominal pain.

cramp[2] *n* a device used to hold timbers or blocks of stone together.

cramp[3] *v* **1** to affect with cramp. **2** to confine or restrain.

cramped *adj* **1** too small or crowded for comfort. **2** of handwriting: small and hard to read.

crampon *n* a spiked metal frame fitted to a boot for climbing on ice or hard snow.

cranberry *n* (*pl* **-ies**) a sour red berry used in sauces and jellies.

crane[1] *n* **1** a machine with a swinging arm or a hoisting apparatus, used for moving heavy weights. **2** a tall wading bird.

crane[2] *v* to stretch (the neck) in order to see better.

crane fly *n* a fly with wide wings and long legs.

cranium *n* (*pl* **craniums** or **crania**) the part of the skull that encloses the brain. ➤ **cranial** *adj*.

crank[1] *n* **1** a part of an axle or shaft bent at right angles to convert back-and-forth motion into circular motion. **2** an eccentric person.

crank[2] *v* **1** (*often* + up) to turn a crank, or to start (an engine) using a crank. **2** (+ up) to increase in intensity.

crankshaft *n* a shaft driven by a crank.

cranky *adj* (**-ier, -iest**) **1** *informal* odd or eccentric. **2** *NAmer* bad-tempered.

cranny *n* (*pl* **-ies**) a small crack or slit.

crap[1] *n* *coarse slang* **1** excrement. **2** nonsense; rubbish.

crap[2] *v* (**crapped, crapping**) *coarse slang* to defecate.

crap[3] *adj* *coarse slang* of poor quality.

crape *n* black artificial silk, formerly used for mourning clothes.

craps *pl n* (*treated as sing. or pl*) a gambling game played with two dice.

crash[1] *v* **1** to break or smash violently and noisily. **2** to make or cause to make a crashing sound. **3** to damage (a vehicle or aircraft) in a collision. **4** of a vehicle or aircraft: to collide with another vehicle or the ground and be damaged. **5** to move or force (one's way) somewhere noisily. **6** of a computer system: to fail and become inoperative. **7** of shares: to fall suddenly in value. **8** *informal* to enter (a party, etc) without being invited. **9** *informal* (*also* + out) to go to sleep.

crash[2] *n* **1** a loud noise. **2** the noise of things smashing. **3** the act of crashing; a violent collision. **4** a sudden decline or failure.

crash[3] *adj* designed to achieve a rapid result: *a crash diet*.

crash helmet *n* a padded helmet worn to protect the head.

crash-land *v* of an aircraft: to land clumsily in an emergency.

crass *adj* insensitive and coarse. ➤ **crassly** *adv*.

crate[1] *n* **1** a wooden framework or box for holding or transporting goods. **2** *informal* an old dilapidated vehicle.

crate[2] *v* to pack in a crate.

crater *n* a bowl-shaped depression in the ground caused by an impact or explosion or forming the mouth of a volcano.

cravat *n* a decorative band worn round the neck by men.

crave *v* **1** to have a strong desire for. **2** *formal* to ask for.

craven *adj* cowardly. ➤ **cravenly** *adv*.

craving *n* a strong desire or longing.

craw *n* the crop of a bird or insect.

crawl[1] *v* **1** to move slowly on hands and knees. **2** to move or progress slowly or laboriously. **3** to be swarming with creeping or unwelcome things. **4** of the skin: to have an unpleasant sensation as of insects crawling over it. **5** *informal* (*often* + to) to behave obsequiously.

crawl[2] *n* **1** the act or an instance of crawling. **2** slow or laborious motion. **3** a swimming stroke performed with alternating overarm strokes while kicking the legs.

crayfish *n* (*pl* **crayfish** or **crayfishes**) a freshwater crustacean like a small lobster.

crayon[1] *n* a stick of coloured chalk or wax used for drawing.

crayon[2] *v* to draw with a crayon.

craze *n* a short-lived popular enthusiasm; a fad.

crazed *adj* **1** mad or crazy. **2** having a mesh of fine cracks.

crazy *adj* (**-ier, -iest**) *informal* **1** insane or eccentric. **2** foolish or impractical. **3** (+ about) very fond of or enthusiastic about. ➤ **crazily** *adv*, **craziness** *n*.

crazy paving *n* a paved surface of irregular flat stones.

creak[1] *v* to make a grating or squeaking noise.

creak[2] *n* a creaking sound. ➤ **creaky** *adj*.

cream[1] *n* **1** the thick yellowish part of milk which forms a surface layer when milk is allowed to stand. **2** a food prepared with or resembling cream. **3** a biscuit, chocolate, etc filled with whipped cream or a soft preparation resembling it. **4** a thick liquid cosmetic applied to the skin. **5** (**the cream**) (+ of) the best part or members of a group. **6** a pale yellowish white colour. ➤ **creamy** *adj*.

cream[2] *v* **1** to prepare (food) with a cream sauce. **2** to mash (vegetables) with added milk or cream. **3** to work or blend (butter and sugar) to the consistency of cream. **4** (*also* + off) to take (the best part of something).

cream cheese *n* a mild soft cheese.

creamery *n* (*pl* **-ies**) an establishment where butter and cheese are made.

crease[1] *n* **1** a ridge or line made in fabric, paper, etc by crushing or folding. **2** a line marked on a cricket pitch.

crease[2] *v* **1** to make creases in (cloth or paper). **2** to become creased. **3** *chiefly Brit, informal* (*often* + up) to double up with laughter.

create *v* **1** to bring into existence. **2** to produce or cause. **3** to invest (somebody) with a new form or rank. **4** *Brit, informal* to make a loud fuss.

creation *n* **1** something created. **2** an original work of art. **3** the world. **4** (**the Creation**) the act of making the universe.

creative *adj* **1** showing the ability or power to create. **2** having the quality of something imaginatively created. ➤ **creatively** *adv*, **creativeness** *n*, **creativity** *n*.

creator *n* **1** a person who creates something. **2** (**the Creator**) God.

creature *n* an animate being, *esp* a non-human one.

creature comforts *pl n* material things that provide comfort.

crèche *n Brit* a centre where young children are looked after while their parents are at work.

credence *n* acceptance of something as true or real.

credential *n* (*usu in pl*) a letter or other document that gives proof of identity or status.

credible *adj* able to be believed; likely or reasonable. ➤ **credibly** *adv*.

Usage Note: Do not confuse this word with *creditable*.

credit[1] *n* **1** a source of honour or repute. **2** acknowledgment or approval. **3** influence derived from enjoying the confidence of others; standing. **4** the balance in a person's favour in an account. **5** an amount or sum placed at a person's disposal by a bank and usu to be repaid with interest. **6** time given for payment for goods or services. **7** an entry in an account recording money received. **8** (*usu in pl*) an acknowledgment of a contributor at the beginning or end of a film or television programme. **9** recognition that a student has fulfilled a course requirement. ✽ **in credit** having money avaiable for use. **on credit** with the cost charged to an account and paid later.

credit[2] *v* (**credited, crediting**) **1** to believe (something). **2** to place an amount to the credit of (an account). **3** (+ with) to ascribe favourable characteristics to. **4** (+ to) to attribute (e.g. an invention, a saying, etc) to.

creditable *adj* deserving acknowledgment even if not successful. ➤ **creditably** *adv*.

Usage Note: Do not confuse this word with *credible*.

credit card *n* a card allowing the holder to obtain goods and services on credit.

creditor *n* a person to whom a debt is owed.

credo *n* (*pl* **-os**) a statement of beliefs.

credulous *adj* too ready to believe. ➤ **credulity** *n*, **credulously** *adv*.

creed *n* **1** a set of religious beliefs. **2** a tenet or set of tenets. **3** a statement of beliefs.

creek *n* **1** a small narrow inlet of a lake or sea. **2** *NAmer* a stream or brook. ✽ **up the creek** *informal* in bad trouble.

creel *n* a basket for newly caught fish.

creep[1] *v* (*past tense and past part.* **crept**) **1** to move along with the body close to the ground. **2** to go very slowly. **3** to move cautiously or quietly. **4** *informal* to behave in a servile manner.

creep[2] *n* **1** a creeping movement. **2** *Brit, informal* an ingratiatingly servile or unlikeable person. ✽ **give one the creeps** *informal* to unnerve or disgust one.

creeper *n* a plant growing along a surface.

creepy *adj* (**-ier, -iest**) **1** producing a sensation of fear or apprehension. **2** *informal* slightly sinister or unpleasant.

cremate *v* to reduce (a dead body) to ashes by burning. ➤ **cremation** *n*.

crematorium *n* (*pl* **crematoriums** *or* **crematoria**) a place where dead bodies are cremated.

crème de la crème /ˌkrem də lah ˈkrem/ *n* (the crème de la crème) the very best or most exclusive.

crenellation *n* an indentation in a battlement.

Creole *n* **1** a person of European descent in the West Indies or Spanish America. **2** a descendant of French or Spanish settlers in the USA. **3** a person of mixed French or Spanish and black descent. **4** (**creole**) a language based on a combination of an African and a European language.

creosote *n* a brownish oily liquid obtained from coal tar and used as a wood preservative.

crepe or **crêpe** n 1 (*also* crape) a light crinkled fabric. 2 a thin pancake.

crept v past tense and past part. of CREEP[1].

crepuscular adj *formal* relating to or resembling twilight.

crescendo n (pl **crescendos** or **crescendi**) a gradual increase in volume in a musical passage.

crescent n 1 a narrow rounded shape coming to a point at each end. 2 *Brit* a curved street.

cress n a plant with mildly pungent leaves, used in salads.

crest[1] n 1 a showy tuft or projection on the head of a bird or other animal. 2 a plume on a helmet. 3 a symbol of a family or organization above the shield in a coat of arms. 4 the ridge or top of a wave, roof, or mountain. ➤ **crested** adj.

crest[2] v to reach the crest of (a hill, ridge, wave, etc).

crestfallen adj disheartened or dejected.

cretin n a foolish person. ➤ **cretinous** adj.

crevasse n a deep wide crack in a glacier.

crevice n a narrow opening resulting from a split or crack.

crew[1] n 1 the personnel of a ship or boat, excluding the captain and officers. 2 the people who work on an aircraft or train. 3 a number of people working together.

crew[2] v chiefly *Brit* past tense of CROW[2].

crew[3] v 1 to serve as a member of a crew on (a ship, aircraft, etc). 2 to provide with a crew.

crew cut n a short bristly haircut.

crew neck n a round neckline on a knitted pullover.

crib[1] n 1 chiefly *NAmer* a child's cot. 2 a cattle stall. 3 a manger or rack for animal fodder. 4 a literal translation of a text used by students. 5 the card game cribbage.

crib[2] v (**cribbed, cribbing**) to copy (somebody else's work) dishonestly.

cribbage n a card game for two to four players.

crick[1] n a painful stiff feeling in the muscles of the neck or back.

crick[2] v to cause a crick in (the neck or back).

cricket[1] n a team game played with a bat and ball on a large field with two wickets near its centre. ➤ **cricketer** n.

cricket[2] n a leaping insect noted for the chirping sounds produced by the male.

cried v past tense and past part. of CRY[1].

crime n 1 a violation of a law. 2 a grave offence against morality. 3 criminal activity. 4 *informal* something deplorable or disgraceful.

criminal[1] adj 1 relating to or guilty of a crime. 2 *informal* disgraceful. ➤ **criminality** n, **criminally** adv.

criminal[2] n a person who has committed or been convicted of a crime.

crimp v 1 to make (the hair) wavy or curly. 2 to pinch or press (material) together to seal or join it.

crimson n a deep purplish red colour.

cringe v 1 to shrink or cower in fear. 2 to feel acute embarrassment.

crinkle[1] v 1 to wrinkle. 2 to cause (something) to crinkle.

crinkle[2] n a small wrinkle. ➤ **crinkly** adj.

crinoline n a full skirt or hooped petticoat formerly worn by women.

cripple[1] n *offensive* a lame or partly disabled person.

cripple[2] v 1 to make (somebody) a cripple. 2 to impair mentally or emotionally. 3 to hamper or severely limit (a person, operation, etc).

crisis n (pl **crises**) 1 a time of acute difficulty or danger. 2 the turning point in an acute disease.

crisp[1] adj 1 brittle or easily crumbled. 2 desirably firm and fresh. 3 decisive or sharp in manner. 4 of the weather: cold and fresh. ➤ **crisply** adv.

crisp[2] n *Brit* a thin slice of fried potato.

crispbread n a plain dry biscuit made from rye or other grain.

crisscross[1] adj marked with a pattern or network of intersecting lines.

crisscross[2] v 1 to pass back and forth across. 2 to mark with intersecting lines.

criterion n (pl **criteria** or **criterions**) a standard on which a judgment may be based.

Usage Note: Note that *criteria* is the plural form: *these criteria not this criteria.*

critic n 1 a person who evaluates works of art, literature, or music. 2 a person who tends to judge harshly.

critical adj 1 inclined to criticize severely. 2 consisting of or involving criticism. 3 involving careful evaluation. 4 crucial or decisive. 5 in a state of crisis or danger. ➤ **critically** adv.

criticism n 1 an instance of criticizing or disapproving. 2 a critical observation or remark. 3 a detailed or reasoned assessment; a critique.

criticize or **-ise** v 1 to find fault with. 2 to evaluate (a literary or artistic work).

critique n a critical estimate or discussion.

croak v 1 to give the cry of a frog or crow. 2 to speak in a hoarse voice. 3 *informal* to die. ➤ **croak** n, **croaky** adj.

crochet[1] n the art of making designs by drawing a yarn or thread into a pattern of interlocked loops using a hooked needle.

crochet[2] v (**crocheted, crocheting**) to make (a garment or design) by crochet.

crock[1] n *Brit, informal* 1 an elderly infirm person. 2 an old broken-down vehicle.

crock[2] n a thick earthenware pot or jar.

crock[3] v *informal* 1 (*also* + up) to injure, weaken, or disable (somebody or something): *I've cracked my back.* 2 *NAmer* to make (somebody)

drunk: *The man was crocked*. **3** *informal* (*also* +
up) to break down; to collapse.

crockery *n* earthenware or china tableware.

crocodile *n* **1** a large reptile with a thick skin,
long jaws, and a long body with a tail. **2** *Brit* a
line of people or schoolchildren walking in
pairs.

crocodile tears *pl n* insincere or affected sorrow.

crocus *n* (*pl* **crocuses** *or* **croci**) a spring plant
with a single brightly-coloured flower.

croft *n* a small farm, *esp* in Scotland, worked by
a tenant. ➤ **crofter** *n*.

croissant *n* a flaky crescent-shaped roll.

crone *n* a withered old woman.

crook[1] *n* **1** an implement having a bent or
hooked shape. **2** a shepherd's staff or bishop's
crozier. **3** a bend or curve. **4** *informal* a criminal.

crook[2] *v* to bend or curve.

crooked *adj* **1** having a crook or curve; bent. **2**
informal not morally straightforward; dishonest.

croon *v* to sing in a low or soft voice.
➤ **crooner** *n*.

crop[1] *n* **1** a plant grown and harvested for food.
2 a group or quantity appearing at any one
time. **3** a short riding whip. **4** a short haircut. **5**
a pouch in a bird's gullet in which food is stored
and prepared for digestion.

crop[2] *v* (**cropped, cropping**) **1** to trim or cut
short. **2** of an animal: to graze on (grass, etc) **3**
to cut and harvest (mature plant produce).

cropper ✳ **come a cropper** *informal* to fall or
fail dramatically.

crop up *v informal* to happen or appear unexpectedly.

croquet *n* a game in which wooden balls are
driven by mallets through a series of hoops.

croquette *n* a small roll of minced meat or
vegetable fried in breadcrumbs.

crosier *or* **crozier** *n* a bishop's staff like a shepherd's crook.

cross[1] *n* **1** a figure formed by two intersecting
lines (+ or x). **2** a cross-shaped upright stake
used in antiquity for executions. **3** (**the Cross**)
the cross on which Christ was crucified. **4** a
monument or badge in the form of a cross. **5** a
cross-bred animal or plant. **6** a person or thing
that combines characteristics of two different
types. **7** the act of crossing the ball in football.
✳ **at cross purposes** misunderstanding each
other or having different objectives. **make the
sign of the cross** to indicate the shape of the
Cross on one's front.

cross[2] *v* **1** to go across or from one side to the
other of. **2** to lie or be situated across. **3** of a line,
road, etc: to intersect (another). **4** to pass simultaneously in opposite directions. **5** (+ off/out/
through) to cancel (an item) by drawing a line
across it. **6** to draw two parallel lines across (a
cheque) to restrict payment to a named

account. **7** to finish off (a letter *t* or *f*) with the
horizontal bar. **8** in sitting, to put (the arms or
legs) so that one is resting on the other. **9** to
make the sign of the cross in front of (oneself).
10 to oppose or frustrate (somebody). **11** to
produce (an animal or plant) by mixing two
breeds. **12** to kick or pass (the ball) across the
field in football. ✳ **cross swords** (*often* + with)
to come into conflict.

cross[3] *adj* angry or annoyed. ➤ **crossly** *adv*.

crossbar *n* **1** a transverse bar between the
uprights of a football goal. **2** a bar extending
from the handlebars of a bicycle to the saddle.

crossbow *n* a mechanical bow formerly used to
fire bolts in warfare.

crossbreed[1] *v* (*past tense and past part.* **cross-
bred**) to produce (an animal or plant) by mixing two breeds.

crossbreed[2] *n* an animal or plant produced by
crossbreeding.

cross-check *v* to check (information) by referring to more than one source.

cross-country *adj and adv* **1** over countryside
rather than by roads. **2** across the whole of a
country.

cross-dressing *n* the wearing of clothing of
the opposite sex. ➤ **cross-dresser** *n*.

cross-examine *v* to question (a witness) testi-
fying for the other side in a law case. ➤ **cross-
examination** *n*.

cross-eyed *adj* having one or both eyes squint-
ing inwards.

cross-fertilize *or* -**ise** *v* to fertilize (a plant) by
joining the ova with pollen or sperm from a
different individual of the same species.
➤ **cross-fertilization** *n*.

crossfire *n* **1** firing from two or more points in
crossing directions. **2** rapid or heated interchange.

crossing *n* **1** part of a road marked for pedestrians to cross. **2** a place where roads or railway
lines cross. **3** a journey across a stretch of water.

cross-legged *adv and adj* sitting on the floor
with ankles crossed and knees bent outwards.

crossover *n* **1** a crossing. **2** the changing of
style from one type of music to another.

cross-question *v* to question or cross-
examine intensively.

cross-reference *n* a reference from one part of
a book to another, for additional information.

crossroads *pl n* a place where two or more
roads cross.

cross-section *n* **1** a surface made by cutting
across something at right angles to its length. **2**
a representative sample of a group.

crosswise *or* **crossways** *adv* so as to cross
something; across.

crossword *n* a puzzle in which words are
entered horizontally and vertically in a pattern
of numbered squares according to clues.

crotch n 1 the angle of the body between the inner thighs. 2 a fork in a tree. ➢ **crotched** adj.

crotchet n Brit a musical note with the time value of half a minim.

crotchety adj informal bad-tempered.

crouch[1] v to lower the body by bending one's knees and bending the upper body forward.

crouch[2] n a crouching position.

croup[1] n a children's disease of the larynx, causing rasping breathing.

croup[2] n the rump of a horse.

croupier n a person who runs the gaming tables in a casino.

crouton n a small cube of crisp bread served with soup or used as a garnish.

crow[1] n a large black bird with a loud cry. ✷ **as the crow flies** in a direct line across country.

crow[2] v (past tense **crowed** or **crew**, past part. **crowed**) 1 to make the shrill cry of a cock. 2 (+ over) to boast about a success or gloat over another's discomfort.

crowbar n an iron or steel bar with a flattened end, used as a lever.

crowd[1] n 1 a large number of people gathered together. 2 a particular social group.

crowd[2] v 1 to collect in large numbers. 2 to fill (a place). 3 to force or thrust into a small space. 4 (+ off/out of) to push (others) out of the way. 5 to press close to (somebody).

crown[1] n 1 a round metal headdress worn by a sovereign. 2 (**the Crown**) the sovereign as head of state. 3 a wreath or band worn on the head as a symbol of victory. 4 a mark of honour or victory. 5 the topmost part of something. 6 the part of a tooth visible outside the gum, or an artificial substitute for it. 7 the high point or culmination. 8 a former British coin worth five shillings (25 pence).

crown[2] v 1 to place a crown on the head of (somebody), esp as a symbol of investiture. 2 to recognize as the leader in a particular field, esp a sport. 3 literary to form the top of. 4 to bring to a successful conclusion. 5 to put an artificial crown on (a tooth). 6 informal to hit on the head.

crow's-foot n (pl **crow's-feet**) a wrinkle round the outer corners of the eyes.

crow's nest n a high lookout platform on a ship's mast.

crozier n see CROSIER.

crucial adj 1 essential to resolve a crisis. 2 very important or significant. ➢ **crucially** adv.

crucible n a vessel for melting a substance at a high temperature.

crucifix n a representation of Christ on the cross.

crucifixion n 1 execution by crucifying. 2 (**Crucifixion**) the crucifying of Christ.

cruciform adj forming a cross.

crucify v (**-ies, -ied**) 1 to execute (somebody) by fastening them to a cross. 2 informal to criticize ruthlessly.

crud n informal 1 dirt or mess. 2 nonsense. ➢ **cruddy** adj.

crude adj 1 in a natural unprocessed state. 2 coarse or vulgar. 3 rough or inexpert. ➢ **crudely** n.

cruel adj (**crueller, cruellest**, NAmer **crueler, cruelest**) 1 liking to inflict pain or suffering; pitiless. 2 painful. ➢ **cruelly** adv.

cruelty n (pl **-ies**) 1 being cruel. 2 cruel behaviour.

cruet n 1 Brit a small container for salt, pepper, mustard, etc at table. 2 Brit a set of cruets on a stand.

cruise[1] v 1 to travel by sea for pleasure. 2 to go about without any definite destination. 3 of a vehicle: to travel at a steady speed.

cruise[2] n a sea voyage for pleasure.

cruiser n 1 a yacht or motor boat with passenger accommodation. 2 a large fast warship.

crumb n 1 a small fragment of bread, cake, biscuit, or cheese. 2 a small amount.

crumble[1] v 1 to break into small pieces. 2 to disintegrate. ➢ **crumbly** adj.

crumble[2] n a dessert of stewed fruit with a crumbly topping.

crummy or **crumby** adj (**-ier, -iest**) informal disagreeable or inferior; squalid.

crumpet n 1 a small round unsweetened cake that is eaten toasted. 2 Brit, informal women collectively as sexual objects.

crumple v 1 to crush out of shape. 2 to become creased or wrinkled. 3 to collapse.

crunch[1] v 1 to chew or bite with a noisy crunching sound. 2 to make or move with a crushing sound.

crunch[2] n 1 a crunching sound or action. 2 (**the crunch**) informal the decisive situation or moment.

crusade[1] n 1 (usu **the Crusades**) a series of medieval Christian military expeditions to win the Holy Land from the Muslims. 2 a reforming enterprise enthusiastically undertaken.

crusade[2] v to take part in a crusade. ➢ **crusader** n.

crush[1] v 1 to deform or flatten by pressing. 2 to reduce to particles by pounding or grinding. 3 to subdue or overwhelm.

crush[2] n 1 a crowd of people in a small space. 2 a soft fruit drink. 3 informal a strong infatuation.

crust[1] n 1 the hardened surface of a loaf of bread. 2 the pastry cover of a pie. 3 a hard or brittle surface layer. 4 the outer rocky layer of the earth. 5 a deposit built up on the inside of a wine bottle.

crust[2] v to form a crust on.

crustacean n a sea creature with a hard shell, e.g. a lobster or crab.

crusty adj (-ier, -iest) 1 having a hard well-baked crust. 2 morose or surly.

crutch n 1 a long stick of wood or metal used to support an injured person in walking. 2 a prop or support. 3 a person's crotch.

crux n (pl **cruxes**) an essential or decisive point.

cry¹ v (-ies, -ied) 1 to shed tears; to weep or sob. 2 to call loudly. 3 of a bird or animal: to utter its call. 4 informal (+ out for) to require or suggest strongly a certain response or treatment. ✻ **a crying shame** something very regrettable.

cry² n (pl **-ies**) 1 a spell of shedding tears. 2 a loud call or shout. 3 a general public demand or complaint. 4 the call of an animal or bird. ✻ **in full cry** in pursuit.

cry off v to call off an arrangement.

cryogenics pl n the branch of physics dealing with very low temperatures. ➤ **cryogenic** adj.

crypt n an underground chamber beneath a church.

cryptic adj 1 mysterious or secret. 2 obscure in meaning. ➤ **cryptically** adv.

crystal n 1 a piece of a natural solid material with plane faces symmetrically arranged. 2 a clear transparent mineral, esp colourless quartz. 3 a fine clear glass.

crystalline adj like or made of crystal.

crystallize or **-ise** v 1 to form crystals. 2 to give (a thought) a definite form. 3 to coat or preserve(fruit) with sugar. 4 to become crystallized.

Cs abbr the chemical symbol for caesium.

Cu abbr the chemical symbol for copper.

cu. abbr cubic.

cub n 1 the young of a fox, bear, lion, or other flesh-eating mammal. 2 (**Cub** or **Cub Scout**) a member of the junior branch of the Scout Association.

cubbyhole n a small room or enclosed space.

cube¹ n 1 a three-dimensional shape with six equal square faces. 2 the result of multiplying a number by itself twice.

cube² v 1 to multiply (a number) by itself twice. 2 to cut (food) into small cubes.

cube root n the number that produces a given number when cubed.

cubic adj 1 having the shape of a cube. 2 three-dimensional. 3 used before a unit of length: denoting a volume equal to that of a cube whose edges are of the specified length.

cubicle n a small partitioned space or compartment.

cubism n an art movement that used geometric patterns to show perspectives from several aspects at the same time. ➤ **cubist** n and adj.

cubit n an ancient unit of length based on the length of the forearm.

cuckoo¹ n (pl **cuckoos**) 1 a greyish brown bird that lays its eggs in the nests of other birds. 2 the two-note call of the cuckoo.

cuckoo² adj informal crazy or eccentric.

cucumber n a long green fruit eaten raw in salads.

cud n partly digested food brought up into the mouth by a ruminating animal to be chewed again.

cuddle¹ v 1 to hold close in the arms and hug for warmth or comfort or in affection. 2 (often + up to) to nestle or lie close.

cuddle² n an act of cuddling.

cuddly adj (-ier, -iest) attractively soft and plump.

cudgel¹ n a short heavy club. ✻ **take up the cudgels** to engage vigorously in a defence.

cudgel² v (**cudgelled, cudgelling**, NAmer **cudgeled, cudgeling**) to beat with a cudgel.

cue¹ n 1 a signal to a performer to begin a speech or action. 2 a signal or hint prompting action. ✻ **on cue** at exactly the right time.

cue² v (**cuing, cueing**) 1 to give a cue to; to prompt. 2 to set audio or video equipment to play (a preselected section of a recording).

cue³ n a long tapering rod for striking the ball in billiards, snooker, or pool.

cue⁴ v (**cuing, cueing**) to strike (a ball) with a cue.

cuff¹ n 1 a fold or band at the end of a sleeve which encircles the wrist. 2 NAmer a turned-up hem of a trouser leg. ✻ **off the cuff** without preparation. ➤ **cuffed** adj.

cuff² v to strike with the palm of the hand.

cuff³ n a blow with the hand.

cuff link n a device of two linked parts used to fasten a shirt cuff.

cuisine /kwi'zeen/ n a partiuclar manner of preparing or cooking food.

cul-de-sac n (pl **culs-de-sac** or **cul-de-sacs**) a street or path that is closed at one end.

culinary adj relating to cookery.

cull v 1 to reduce the population of (animals) by selective killing. 2 to select (a body of people or things) from a source or a range of sources. ➤ **cull** n.

culminate v (often + in) to reach the highest or decisive point. ➤ **culmination** n.

culottes /kyoo'lots/ pl n women's full knee-length shorts.

culpable adj deserving blame. ➤ **culpability** n, **culpably** adv.

culprit n a person who is guilty of an offence or wrong.

cult n 1 a system of religious beliefs and ritual, or its followers. 2 a religion regarded as unorthodox or spurious. 3 great devotion among a group to a particular person, idea, or thing.

cultivate v 1 to prepare or use (land) for the growing of crops. 2 to grow (a plant or crop) on a large scale. 3 to grow (bacteria, tissue, etc) in a culture. 4 to improve or refine (one's mind). 5 to seek or affect (a manner or quality). 6 to encourage or foster the friendship of. ➤ **cultivation** n.

cultural adj **1** relating to the arts and education. **2** relating to a society's culture and traditions. ➤ **culturally** adv.

culture n **1** the development of the mind, esp by education. **2** intellectual and artistic enlightenment. **3** the customary beliefs, social forms, etc of a people or group. **4** the cultivation of living cells, viruses, etc in prepared nutrient media.

cultured adj **1** well educated; cultivated. **2** of a pearl: grown under controlled conditions by inserting a foreign body in the oyster.

culvert n a small passage taking water under a road or railway.

cum prep combined with; along with.

cumbersome adj heavy and unwieldy.

cumin or **cummin** /'kumin/ n the seeds of a plant, used as a flavouring.

cummerbund n a broad sash worn round the waist as part of a man's formal evening wear.

cumulative adj increasing by successive additions. ➤ **cumulatively** adv.

cuneiform /'kyoohnifawm/ adj of ancient writing: using wedge-shaped characters.

cunning[1] adj **1** clever in a deceitful way; crafty. **2** ingenious. ➤ **cunningly** adv, **cunningness** n.

cunning[2] n craftiness.

cup[1] n **1** a small bowl-shaped drinking vessel with a handle on one side. **2** an ornamental metal cup with two handles awarded as a prize in a sports competition. **3** a sports competition with a cup as prize. **4** something resembling a cup in shape. **5** either of two parts of a bra that are shaped to fit over the breasts. * **one's cup of tea** informal exactly what one likes. ➤ **cupful** n (pl **cupfuls**).

cup[2] v (**cupped, cupping**) **1** to curve (one's hands) into the shape of a cup. **2** to curve one's hands round (something).

cupboard /'kubəd/ n a piece of furniture with a door, used for storage.

cupid n **1** (**Cupid**) the Roman god of sexual love, depicted as a winged naked boy holding a bow and arrow. **2** a representation of Cupid in art.

cupidity n excessive desire for wealth or possessions.

cupola /'kyoohpələ/ n a small domed structure built on top of a roof.

cur n **1** a mongrel or inferior dog. **2** informal a surly or cowardly man.

curate n an assistant to a rector or priest in a parish.

curate's egg n Brit something with both good and bad parts.

curative adj used to cure disease.

curator n a person in charge of a museum or gallery.

curb[1] n **1** a check or restraint. **2** a chain or strap used to restrain a horse, attached to the sides of the bit and passing below the lower jaw. **3** chiefly NAmer = KERB.

curb[2] v to check or control.

curd n (also in pl) the thick part of coagulated milk used as a food or made into cheese.

curdle v to separate into solid curds or lumps and liquid.

cure[1] n **1** a drug or treatment that gives relief or recovery from an illness. **2** relief or recovery from an illness. **3** something that puts right a wrong or difficulty.

cure[2] v **1** to restore to health. **2** to bring about recovery from (an illness or other disorder). **3** to rectify (a harmful or troublesome situation). **4** to free from something objectionable or harmful. **5** to preserve (meat or fish) by salting, drying, or smoking. ➤ **curable** adj.

curfew n **1** a regulation requiring people to be indoors by a stated time. **2** the time at which a curfew begins, or the period during which it is in effect.

curie n a unit of radioactivity.

curio n (pl **-os**) an object that is considered unusual or rare.

curiosity n (pl **-ies**) **1** desire to know something. **2** inquisitiveness. **3** a strange, interesting, or rare object, fact, etc.

curious adj **1** eager to learn and find things out. **2** inquisitive. **3** strange or unusual. ➤ **curiously** adv.

curl[1] v **1** to form into waves or coils. **2** to adopt or grow in a twisted or spiral shape. **3** to move in curves or spirals.

curl[2] n **1** a curled lock of hair. **2** something with a spiral or coiled form. **3** a curling movement.

curler n a small roller on which hair is wound for curling.

curlew n (pl **curlews** or **curlew**) a wading bird with long legs and a long curved bill.

curling n a team game in which players slide heavy flat stones over ice towards a marked circle.

curmudgeon n a bad-tempered old man. ➤ **curmudgeonly** adj.

currant n a small seedless dried grape.

Usage Note: Do not confuse this word with *current*.

currency n (pl **-ies**) **1** a system of money used as a medium of exchange. **2** the state of being in general use.

current[1] adj **1** occurring now or belonging to the present time. **2** generally accepted or used. ➤ **currently** adv.

Usage Note: Do not confuse this word with *currant*.

current[2] n **1** a body of water, air, etc that moves in a certain direction. **2** a flow of electricity.

current account n Brit a bank account allowing immediate payments and withdrawals.

curriculum n (pl **curricula** or **curriculums**) the courses offered by an educational institution. ➤ **curricular** adj.

curriculum vitae /veetie/ n (pl **curricula vitae**) a summary of a person's career and qualifications.

curry[1] v (-ies, -ied) **1** to groom the coat of (a horse). **2** to dress (tanned leather). ∗ **curry favour** to seek approval by flattery or attention.

curry[2] n (pl -ies) a dish of Indian origin, seasoned with hot spices and sauces.

curry[3] v (-ies, -ied) to flavour or cook (food) with hot spices and sauces.

curse[1] n **1** an appeal to a deity invoking harm or injury on somebody. **2** a swearword or other offensive expression. **3** a cause of misfortune.

curse[2] v **1** to doom or damn with a curse. **2** to swear or use offensive language. **3** to bring evil upon.

cursor n **1** a movable pointer on a computer or radar screen, indicating the position where input will take effect. **2** a transparent slide locating marks on a slide rule.

cursory adj rapid and superficial. ➤ **cursorily** adv.

curt adj rude or brusque. ➤ **curtly** adv.

curtail v to limit or cut short. ➤ **curtailment** n.

curtain[1] n **1** a piece of fabric hung at a window or at the front of a theatre stage, forming a screen when pulled across. **2** informal (in pl) death or catastrophe.

curtain[2] v to cover or screen with a curtain.

curtsy[1] or **curtsey** n (pl -ies) a woman's or girl's gesture of respect made by flexing the knees with one leg behind the other.

curtsy[2] or **curtsey** v (-ies, -ied) to make a curtsy.

curvaceous adj having an attractively curved figure.

curvature n **1** the fact or extent of being curved. **2** an abnormal curving of the spine.

curve[1] v to deviate gradually from a straight line or course.

curve[2] n a curving line or surface. ➤ **curvy** adj.

cushion[1] n **1** a soft pillow or padded bag used for sitting or leaning on. **2** a pad along the inside of a billiard table. **3** something that mitigates the effects of disturbances or disorders. ➤ **cushiony** adj.

cushion[2] v **1** to furnish with a cushion or cushions. **2** to protect against force or shock. **3** to mitigate the effects of (something unpleasant).

cushy adj (-ier, -iest) informal easy or effortless.

cusp n **1** either horn of a crescent moon. **2** a pointed projection formed by or arising from the intersection of two arcs. **3** a point on the grinding surface of a tooth. ∗ **on the cusp** between one state and another.

custard n a thick sweetened sauce made with milk and eggs or a preparation of cornflour.

custodial adj **1** involving imprisonment. **2** relating to guardianship or custody.

custodian n a person who guards and protects.

custody n **1** care or guardianship. **2** imprisonment or detention.

custom n **1** an established or socially accepted practice. **2** (in pl) duties imposed on imports or exports, or the officials that collect them. **3** chiefly Brit the use of a business by its customers.

customary adj established by or according to custom; usual. ➤ **customarily** adv.

custom-built adj built to individual specifications.

customer n **1** a person who buys a commodity or service. **2** an individual with a specified unfavourable quality: an awkward customer.

customize or **-ise** v to build or adjust (something) to individual requirements.

cut[1] v (**cutting**, past tense and past part. **cut**) **1** to penetrate or make an opening in (something) with a sharp object. **2** to shorten, divide, or detach by cutting. **3** to make or shape by cutting. **4** to reduce the amount of. **5** to shorten or edit. **6** to break or interrupt (a flow, supply, etc.) **7** to cross or intersect. **8** to divide (a pack of cards) into two parts. **9** to ignore deliberately or spitefully. **10** to switch off (an engine or machine). **11** to stop filming or recording. **12** to change from one sound or image to another. **13** to go by a shorter route. ∗ **cut both ways 1** to be equally valid for and against an argument. **2** of a procedure: to have advantages and disadvantages. **cut corners** to do something cheaply or quickly by making risky economies. **cut no ice** to fail to impress or make a difference. **cut one's teeth** to get early experience of an activity. **cut short** to interrupt (a speaker).

cut[2] n **1** an opening or wound made with an edged instrument. **2** a reduction or economy. **3** the style in which the hair or a piece of clothing is cut. **4** something cut or cut off. **5** a piece of meat cut from a carcass. **6** informal a share. **7** a sharp blow or stroke. **8** a version of an edited film. ∗ **a cut above** superior to. **cut and thrust** a competitive and stimulating environment.

cut-and-dried adj completely decided and unalterable.

cutaneous adj relating to or affecting the skin.

cutback n a reduction or decrease.

cut back v to reduce expenditure.

cut down v **1** to make (something growing) fall by cutting through it. **2** to reduce or restrict an activity, expenditure, etc.

cute adj **1** informal appealingly attractive or pretty. **2** shrewd; knowing. ➤ **cutely** adv.

cut glass *n* glass with patterns cut into its surface.

cuticle *n* **1** dead skin round the base and sides of a fingernail or toenail. **2** the outer layer of a hair.

cut in *v* **1** to interrupt. **2** to pull in too closely after overtaking a vehicle. **3** of a device: to start functioning automatically.

cutlass *n* a short curved sword used formerly by sailors.

cutlery *n* knives, forks, and spoons for cutting and eating food.

cutlet *n* **1** a small slice of meat from the neck. **2** a fried cake of minced meat or vegetables.

cutoff *n* a stopping-point or limit.

cut off *v* **1** to remove by cutting. **2** to stop the supply of. **3** to block access to. **4** to disconnect during a telephone call. **5** to disinherit.

cutout *n* **1** something cut out from a larger piece. **2** a device that stops the flow of an electric current or the operation of a machine.

cut out *v* **1** to make by cutting from a larger piece. **2** to eliminate or exclude. **3** to stop doing (something). **4** of an engine: to stop operating. * **be cut out for** be suited to. **cut it out** *informal* to stop doing something.

cutter *n* **1** a person or implement that cuts. **2** a ship's boat for carrying stores or passengers. **3** a light fast boat.

cutthroat¹ *n dated* a murderous thug.

cutthroat² *adj* ruthless or unprincipled.

cutting¹ *n* **1** a piece cut from a newspaper or magazine. **2** a piece cut from a plant for growing into a new plant. **3** an excavation through high ground, for a railway, road, etc.

cutting² *adj* **1** of a remark: likely to hurt or offend. **2** of wind: piercingly cold. * **the cutting edge** the most advanced or ambitious stage of an activity.

cuttlefish *n* a sea mollusc like a squid, having ten arms.

CV *abbr* curriculum vitae.

cwt *abbr* hundredweight.

cyan *n* a greenish blue colour.

cyanide *n* an extremely poisonous salt.

cybernetics *pl n* the comparative study of the automatic control systems in the nervous system of humans and in machines such as computers. ➤ **cybernetic** *adj*.

cyberspace *n* the notional environment in which electronic network communication takes place.

cyclamen /'sikləmən/ *n* a plant with drooping pink, red, or white flowers.

cycle¹ *n* **1** a series of related events happening in a set order. **2** one complete performance of a periodic process, e.g. a vibration or electrical oscillation. **3** a group of poems, plays, novels, operas, or songs on a particular theme. **4** a bicycle.

cycle² *v* to ride a bicycle.

cyclic *adj* occurring in cycles.

cyclone *n* **1** a system of winds rotating about a centre of low atmospheric pressure and often bringing rain. **2** a violent storm. ➤ **cyclonic** *adj*.

cygnet *n* a young swan.

cylinder *n* **1** a three-dimensional shape with circular cross section and parallel sides. **2** the piston chamber in a steam or internal-combustion engine.

cymbal *n* a percussion instrument consisting of a concave brass plate that produces a clashing tone when struck with a stick or against another cymbal.

cynic /'sinik/ *n* **1** a person who doubts the existence of human sincerity or of any motive other than self-interest. **2** a person who is habitually pessimistic or sardonic. ➤ **cynicism** *n*.

cynical *adj* **1** doubting the existence of human sincerity. **2** motivated by selfish interests. ➤ **cynically** *adv*.

cypher¹ *n* see CIPHER¹.

cypher² *v* see CIPHER².

cypress *n* an evergreen tree with overlapping leaves resembling scales.

Cypriot /'sipri·ət/ *or* **Cypriote**/-oht/ *n* **1** a native or inhabitant of Cyprus. **2** the form of Greek spoken on Cyprus. ➤ **Cypriot** *adj*.

Cyrillic *n* the alphabet used for writing Russian and other Slavic languages.

cyst *n* a sac of watery liquid or gas developing abnormally in a plant or animal.

cystic *adj* **1** containing a cyst or cysts. **2** of the bladder or gall bladder. **3** enclosed in a cyst.

cystic fibrosis *n* a hereditary disease marked *esp* by faulty digestion and difficulty in breathing.

cystitis *n* inflammation of the bladder.

cytoplasm *n* the substance of a plant or animal cell outside the nucleus.

czar *n* see TSAR.

Czech /chek/ *n* **1** a native or inhabitant of the Czech Republic or formerly of Czechoslovakia. **2** the Slavonic language of the Czechs. ➤ **Czech** *adj*.

D^1 or **d** *n* (*pl* **D's** or **Ds** or **d's**) **1** the fourth letter of the English alphabet. **2** the Roman numeral for 500.

D^2 *abbr* the chemical symbol for deuterium.

'd *contraction* **1** had. **2** would.

DA *abbr NAmer* district attorney.

dab^1 *v* (**dabbed, dabbing**) **1** to touch lightly and repeatedly. **2** to apply (a liquid or powder) with light strokes.

dab^2 *n* **1** a small amount of something soft or moist. **2** a gentle touch or stroke.

dabble *v* **1** to dip (the fingers or toes) in water and move them about. **2** (*often* + in) to have a casual or superficial involvement or interest. ➤ **dabbler** *n*.

dab hand *n Brit, informal* a person who is skilful at something; an expert.

dace *n* (*pl* **dace**) a small European freshwater fish.

dachshund /'daksənd/ *n* a dog of a breed having a long body, short legs, and long drooping ears.

dad *n informal* one's father.

daddy *n* (*pl* **-ies**) *informal* one's father.

daddy longlegs *n* (*pl* **daddy longlegs**) *Brit* a crane fly.

daffodil *n* a plant having yellow flowers with elongated trumpet-shaped centres.

daffy *adj* (**-ier, -iest**) *informal* crazy or foolish. ➤ **daffiness** *n*.

daft *adj chiefly Brit, informal* silly or foolish.

dagger *n* a short knife used as a stabbing weapon.

daguerreotype *or* **daguerrotype** /də'gerətiep/ *n* an early photograph produced on a silver-covered plate.

dahlia /'dayli-ə, 'daylyə/ *n* an ornamental garden plant with showy flowers.

daily^1 *adj* of or occurring every day or every weekday.

daily^2 *adv* every day.

daily^3 *n* (*pl* **-ies**) *informal* a newspaper published daily from Monday to Saturday.

dainty^1 *adj* (**-ier, -iest**) **1** delicately beautiful or graceful. **2** fastidious, *esp* about food. ➤ **daintily** *adv*.

dainty^2 *n* (*pl* **-ies**) something pleasant to eat; a delicacy.

dairy *n* (*pl* **-ies**) **1** a place where milk is processed and butter or cheese is made. **2** (*used before a noun*) involving milk or other dairy products.

dais /'day-is/ *n* a raised platform in a large room, e.g. for a speaker.

daisy *n* (*pl* **-ies**) a common small European plant whose flowers have yellow centres and slim white petals.

dale *n* a valley.

dally *v* (**-ies, -ied**) **1** to waste time; to dawdle. **2** (+ with) to behave flirtatiously with. ➤ **dalliance** *n*.

Dalmatian *n* a large dog of a short-haired breed with a white coat with black or brown spots.

dam^1 *n* a barrier built across a watercourse to hold back and store the water.

dam^2 *v* (**dammed, damming**) **1** to build a dam across (a river). **2** to block (a flow of something).

dam^3 *n* a female parent of a domestic animal.

damage^1 *n* **1** loss or harm resulting from injury. **2** (*in pl*) compensation in money imposed by law for loss or injury.

damage^2 *v* **1** to cause damage to. **2** to become damaged. ➤ **damaging** *adj*.

damask *n* a lustrous fabric with patterns woven into a plain background.

dame *n* **1** (**Dame**) in the UK, the title of, and form of address for, a woman who has been given an honour equivalent to a knighthood. **2** *Brit* the part of a comic old woman in a pantomime, usu played by a male actor. **3** *NAmer, informal* a woman.

damn *v* **1** to condemn to eternal punishment in hell. **2** to condemn as worthless. **3** to curse. ✳ **damn all** *Brit, informal* nothing at all.

damnable /'damnəbl/ *adj* **1** very bad. **2** deserving damnation.

damnation /dam'naysh(ə)n/ *n* condemnation to hell.

damned *adj* (**damnedest**) *informal* used as an intensive.

damp^1 *adj* slightly or moderately wet.

damp^2 *n* moisture or humidity.

damp^3 *v* **1** to make damp. **2** (*often* + down) to restrain, decrease or make less intense.

damp course *n* a horizontal damp-resistant layer near the ground in a masonry wall.

dampen *v* **1** to make damp. **2** to reduce in strength or intensity.

date

damper *n* **1** a small felted block that stops the vibration of a piano string. **2** a valve or plate in the flue of a furnace for regulating the draught. ✳ **put a damper on** to have a dulling or restraining influence on.

damp squib *n Brit* something that proves to be less effective or impressive than expected.

damsel *n archaic or literary* a young unmarried woman.

damson *n* a small purple fruit similar to a plum.

dance¹ *v* **1** to move the body in a rhythmic way, *esp* in a set sequence of steps and in time to music. **2** to move quickly and lightly. ➤ **dancer** *n*.

dance² *n* **1** a series of steps and bodily movements, usu in time to music. **2** a social event with dancing. **3** a piece of music for dancing to.

dandelion *n* a common plant with yellow flowers and downy seed heads.

dander ✳ **get/have one's dander up** *informal* to lose one's temper.

dandle *v* to move (a baby or small child) up and down in one's arms or on one's knee.

dandruff *n* dead skin that comes off the scalp in small white or greyish scales.

dandy¹ *n* (*pl* **-ies**) a man obsessively concerned with looking fashionable. ➤ **dandified** *adj*.

dandy² *adj* (**-ier, -iest**) *chiefly NAmer, informal* very good.

Dane *n* a native or inhabitant of Denmark.

danger *n* **1** exposure to the possibility of injury, pain, or loss. **2** a cause of danger. **3** the possibility of something unwelcome.

dangerous *adj* able or likely to do harm or inflict injury. ➤ **dangerously** *adv*.

dangle *v* **1** to hang or swing loosely. **2** to offer enticingly. ➤ **dangly** *adj*.

dank *adj* unpleasantly moist or wet.

dapper *adj* of a man: neat and spruce in dress.

dapple¹ *v* to mark (a surface) with patches of varying shade.

dapple² *n* a spot or patch of a colour different from its background.

dare¹ *v* **1** to have sufficient courage or boldness to do something. **2** to challenge (somebody) to do something. ✳ **I dare say/daresay** it is likely or probable that.

dare² *n* a challenge to do something bold or rash.

daredevil *n* somebody who is recklessly bold.

daring¹ *adj* adventurously bold in action or thought. ➤ **daringly** *adv*.

daring² *n* adventurous boldness.

dark¹ *adj* **1** with little or no light. **2** of a colour: not light or pale. **3** of the hair or complexion: not fair. **4** secret or mysterious. **5** sinister or evil. **6** dismal or sad. ➤ **darkly** *adv*, **darkness** *n*.

dark² *n* **1** the absence of light; darkness. **2** night or nightfall. ✳ **in the dark** in a state of ignorance.

Dark Ages *pl n* the period of European history from the fall of the Roman Empire (AD 476) to about 1000, perceived as devoid of culture or learning.

darken *v* **1** to make or become dark or darker. **2** of something unwelcome: to spoil or blight. **3** to make or become unhappy or angry.

dark horse *n* **1** somebody or something that is little known about. **2** a secretive person.

darkroom *n* a room with subdued light for handling and processing photographic materials.

darling¹ *n* **1** used as an affectionate form of address. **2** a dearly loved person.

darling² *adj* **1** dearly loved. **2** charming.

darn¹ *v* to mend (knitted material) by stitching up holes.

darn² *n* a darned area of a garment.

darn³ *or* **darned** *adj informal, euphem* damned.

dart¹ *n* **1** a small pointed projectile with flights of feather or plastic, used as a weapon or in the game of darts. **2** a tapering fold put in a garment to shape it. **3** a quick movement or dash.

dart² *v* to move suddenly or rapidly.

darts *pl n* (*usu treated as sing.*) an indoor game in which darts are thrown at a round board marked in numbered sections.

dash¹ *v* **1** to move with speed or haste. **2** to hurl with great force. **3** to destroy (a hope or plan).

dash² *n* **1** a punctuation mark (–) used to indicate a break or an omission. **2** a hasty movement or journey. **3** *chiefly NAmer* a sprint. **4** a small amount of a substance. **5** panache or stylishness. **6** = DASHBOARD.

dashboard *n* an instrument panel in a car or other vehicle.

dashing *adj* **1** vigorous and spirited. **2** smart and stylish in dress.

dash off *v* to write (something) hurriedly.

dastardly *adj dated* despicably malicious or cowardly.

data *pl n* **1** factual information used as a basis for reasoning, discussion, or calculation. **2** the numbers, characters, etc stored and processed by a computer.

Usage Note: Data is, strictly speaking, a plural noun with the singular form *datum*, but it is increasingly used as a singular mass noun like *information* or *news*: *The data is currently being processed.*

database *n* a large structured set of data held in a computer.

date¹ *n* **1** a particular day of the month or year, identified by a number. **2** the time at which an event occurred or will occur. **3** *informal* an appointment, *esp* a romantic or social engagement, or the person one goes to meet. **4** a show or concert, *esp* one of a series performed in different venues. ✳ **to date** up to now.

date² *v* **1** to determine the date of. **2** to mark with a date. **3** *informal* to go on a date or dates with. **4** to have been in existence for a specified time. **5** to become old-fashioned. ➤ **datable** or **dateable** adj.

date³ n a small brown oval fruit with a sweet taste, eaten fresh or dried.

dated adj out of date or old-fashioned.

dative adj of a grammatical case expressing an indirect object. ➤ **dative** n.

datum n (pl **data**) a piece of information used as a basis for reasoning, measuring or calculating.

daub¹ v to apply, or cover (a surface) with, a soft thick substance crudely. ➤ **dauber** n.

daub² n **1** a mixture of plaster or clay and straw, used with wattle to build a wall. **2** a smear. **3** a crude painting.

daughter n **1** a girl or woman having the relation of child to parent. **2** a female descendant.

daughter-in-law n (pl **daughters-in-law**) the wife of one's son.

daunt v to discourage or dishearten. ➤ **daunting** adj.

dauntless adj courageous and fearless.

dawdle v to move slowly or lackadaisically.

dawn¹ n **1** the first appearance of light in the morning. **2** a first appearance or beginning.

dawn² v **1** of the day, to begin to grow light. **2** to begin to appear or develop. **3** (usu + on) to be realized or begin to be understood.

dawn chorus n birdsong in the early morning.

day n **1** a period of 24 hours beginning at midnight. **2** the period of daylight between sunrise and sunset. **3** the hours spent daily at work, school, etc. **4** (also in pl) a particular time or period in the past. * **call it a day** to stop work or activity for the time being. **day in, day out** continually for a long time. **these days** in the present times.

daybreak n dawn.

daydream¹ n a pleasant fantasy or reverie indulged in while awake.

daydream² v to have a daydream.

daylight n **1** the light of the sun during the day. **2** dawn.

daylight robbery n Brit, informal exorbitant pricing or charging.

daze¹ v to stupefy or stun.

daze² n a state of confusion or shock.

dazzle¹ v **1** to blind temporarily with a sudden bright light. **2** to impress or overwhelm. ➤ **dazzling** adj.

dazzle² n sudden blinding brightness.

dB abbr decibel(s).

DC abbr **1** direct current. **2** District of Columbia (US postal abbreviation).

de- prefix denoting removal, or the reversal of an action: decapitate, deactivate.

deacon n **1** in some Christian Churches, an ordained minister ranking below a priest. **2** a lay minister in various Protestant Churches.

deactivate v to make (e.g. a bomb) inactive or ineffective.

dead¹ adj **1** no longer alive. **2** of a body part: numb. **3** unresponsive. **4** of equipment: no longer working. **5** no longer used, active, or relevant. **6** informal lacking in activity or interest. **7** informal complete or absolute.

dead² n the time when something is at its most intense.

dead³ adv **1** absolutely or exactly. **2** Brit, informal very.

deadbeat n informal an idle person.

dead duck n informal somebody or something that is unlikely to succeed.

deaden v **1** to reduce the resonance of (a sound). **2** to make (pain, etc) less intense. **3** to numb (a part of the body).

dead end n **1** a street or passage without an exit. **2** a situation in which no progress can be made.

deadhead v chiefly Brit to remove dead flower heads from (a plant).

dead heat n a race or contest where two or more competitors finish level.

deadline n a date or time before which something must be completed.

deadlock n **1** a situation in which no progress can be made. **2** Brit a lock that can be opened and shut only by a key.

deadlocked adj brought to a standstill by irreconcilable disagreements.

dead loss n a useless person or thing.

deadly¹ adj (-ier, -iest) **1** likely or able to cause death. **2** vicious, malicious, or irreconcilable. **3** unerring. **4** informal dull or tedious.

deadly² adv extremely.

deadpan adj and adv without feeling or expression.

dead reckoning n the calculation of the position of a ship or aircraft from the record of the course and distance travelled.

dead ringer n a person or thing strongly resembling another.

deadweight n **1** the weight of an inert person or object. **2** the total weight of a ship's contents, including cargo, fuel, passengers, etc.

deadwood n unproductive people or things.

deaf adj **1** unable to hear, or having deficient hearing. **2** (+ to) unwilling to listen to. * **fall on deaf ears** to be ignored. ➤ **deafness** n.

deafen v to overpower with noise.

deal¹ v (past tense and past part. **dealt** /delt/) **1** to distribute (cards) in a game. **2** (+ out) to distribute or apportion. **3** to administer or inflict (e.g. a blow). **4** (often + in) to sell or trade in commercially. **5** informal to buy and sell drugs illegally. * **deal with 1** to take action with regard to. **2** to cope with. **3** to have business relations with. **4** to be concerned with (a theme or subject).

deal² n **1** an agreement. **2** a particular kind of treatment. **3** the process of distributing cards in a game. ✻ **a good/great deal 1** a lot. **2** considerably.

deal[3] *n* fir or pine timber.

dealer *n* **1** a person who deals in goods or services. **2** a person who deals in shares, securities, etc, through an agent. **3** a drugs pusher. **4** the player who deals the cards in a game. ➤ **dealership** *n*.

dealings *pl n* business or personal relationships.

dean *n* **1** the head of the chapter of a collegiate or cathedral church. **2** the head of a university division, faculty, or school. ➤ **deanery** *n*.

dear[1] *adj* **1** much loved; precious or cherished. **2** used as a polite form of address in letters. **3** sweet; appealing. **4** expensive.

dear[2] *n* **1** used as an affectionate form of address. **2** a lovable person.

dearly *adv* **1** very much. **2** at a great cost.

dearth *n* a scarcity.

death *n* **1** the end of life. **2** an instance of dying. **3** the state of being dead. **4** extinction or disappearance. ✻ **at death's door** seriously ill. **like death warmed up** *informal* looking very ill.

death knell *n* the ringing of a bell to mark a death. **2** a sign of the ending of something.

deathly *adj* (**-ier**, **-iest**) suggestive of death.

death penalty *n* punishment by execution.

death row *n* a part of a prison containing the cells of those condemned to death.

deathwatch beetle *n* a small beetle that bores into woodwork making an ominous ticking sound.

debacle /di'bahkal/ *n* a complete failure.

debar *v* (**debarred, debarring**) (+ from) to prevent from doing something.

debase *v* to lower in status, quality or value. ➤ **debasement** *n*.

debatable *adj* open to debate; questionable.

debate[1] *n* **1** a formal discussion of a motion. **2** an argument or controversy.

debate[2] *v* **1** to discuss a question by considering opposed arguments. **2** to consider from different viewpoints.

debauch *v* to corrupt or pervert.

debauchery *n* unrestrained indulgence in sensual pleasures. ➤ **debauched** *adj*, **debauchee** *n*.

debilitate *v* to make weak and lifeless.

debility *n* weakness or infirmity.

debit[1] *n* **1** an entry in an account recording money owed. **2** a charge against a bank account.

debit[2] *v* (**debited, debiting**) **1** to record (an amount) as a debit. **2** of a bank: to take (a sum of money) from an account as payment.

debit card *n* a bank card enabling purchases to be charged electronically to the holder's account.

debonair *adj* **1** suave or urbane. **2** lighthearted or nonchalant. ➤ **debonairly** *adv*.

debrief *v* to interrogate (a soldier, diplomat, etc) about a mission. ➤ **debriefing** *n*.

debris /'debri/ *n* **1** scattered remains or rubbish left after something has been broken down. **2** an accumulation of fragments of rock.

debt *n* **1** money owed or due. **2** the state of owing money or gratitude.

debtor *n* somebody who owes a debt.

debug *v* (**debugged, debugging**) **1** to eliminate malfunctions in (computer software or equipment). **2** to remove concealed listening devices from (a place).

debunk *v* to expose as false or exaggerated.

debut[1] /'dayb(y)ooh/ *n* a first public appearance.

debut[2] *v* (**debuted, debuting**) to make a debut.

debutant *n* somebody making a debut.

debutante *n* an aristocratic young woman making her formal entrance into society.

decade *n* a period of ten years.

decadent *adj* **1** marked by moral or cultural decline. **2** self-indulgent in an immoral way. ➤ **decadence** *n*.

decaffeinated *adj* of coffee: having had most of the caffeine removed.

decagon *n* a polygon with ten angles and ten sides.

decahedron *n* (*pl* **decahedra** or **decahedrons**) a polyhedron with ten faces.

decamp *v* to depart secretly or suddenly.

decant *v* to pour (liquid) from one vessel into another.

decanter *n* an ornamental glass bottle into which an alcoholic drink is decanted.

decapitate *v* to cut off the head of. ➤ **decapitation** *n*.

decathlon *n* an athletic contest in which each competitor takes part in ten events. ➤ **decathlete** *n*.

decay[1] *v* **1** to rot or decompose. **2** to decrease gradually in soundness or vigour.

decay[2] *n* **1** the state or process of decaying. **2** decayed material or tissue.

decease *n* *formal* death.

deceased[1] *n* (*pl* **deceased**) (**the deceased**) *formal* a person who has recently died.

deceased[2] *adj* *formal* recently dead.

deceit *n* **1** the act or practice of deceiving. **2** an attempt to deceive.

deceitful *adj* having a tendency to deceive. ➤ **deceitfully** *adv*.

deceive *v* to cause to accept as true something that is false. ➤ **deceiver** *n*.

Usage Note: Note the spelling with *-ei-*.

decelerate *v* to slow down. ➤ **deceleration** *n*.

December *n* the twelfth month of the year.

decency *n* (*pl* **-ies**) **1** behaviour that conforms to normal standards of propriety. **2** (*usu in pl*) a standard of propriety.

decennial *adj* **1** lasting for ten years. **2** occurring every ten years.

decent *adj* **1** conforming to normal standards of propriety. **2** adequate or satisfactory. **3** *chiefly Brit, informal* kind or helpful. **4** *informal* sufficiently clothed to be seen without impropriety. ➤ **decently** *adv*.

decentralize *or* **-ise** *v* to redistribute functions and powers from a central authority to regional authorities. ➤ **decentralization** *n*.

deception *n* **1** the act of deceiving or the state of being deceived. **2** something that deceives.

deceptive *adj* having the power to deceive.

deceptively *adv* **1** so as to disguise the reality; misleadingly: *Her voice was deceptively calm.* **2** despite appearances to the contrary: *a deceptively spacious room.*

decibel *n* a unit for expressing the intensity of sounds or the power of an electric signal.

decide *v* **1** to make a definite choice or come to a firm conclusion. **2** to influence (somebody) to make a choice. **3** to settle the outcome of.

decided *adj* **1** definite. **2** unhesitating; firm. ➤ **decidedly** *adv*.

decider *n* a final point or additional contest that decides who wins a competition.

deciduous *adj* of a tree: having leaves that are shed seasonally.

decimal¹ *adj* **1** based on the number ten. **2** divided into units that are tenths, hundredths, etc of one another.

decimal² *n* a fraction that is expressed by a dot followed by digits for the number of tenths, hundredths, etc.

decimal place *n* the position of a digit to the right of a decimal point.

decimal point *n* the dot placed between a decimal fraction and a whole number.

decimate *v* **1** to kill a large number from among (a group or population). **2** to destroy a large part of. ➤ **decimation** *n*.

decipher *v* **1** to convert (something coded) into intelligible form. **2** to make out the meaning of (something obscure).

decision *n* **1** a choice or conclusion reached after considering various alternatives. **2** promptness and firmness in deciding.

decisive *adj* **1** of crucial importance in determining the outcome of something. **2** unambiguously settling an issue. **3** having the ability to make firm decisions. ➤ **decisively** *adv*, **decisiveness** *n*.

deck¹ *n* **1** a platform dividing a ship's hull horizontally, *esp* the top platform, open to the air. **2** a floor in e.g. a bus, or a wooden platform, e.g. in a garden. **3** the upper operating surface of a record player. **4** *NAmer* a pack of playing cards. **5** (**the deck**) *informal* the ground or floor.

deck² *v* **1** (*often* + out) to decorate or adorn. **2** *informal* to knock down.

deck chair *n* a folding chair made of canvas stretched over a wooden frame.

decking *n* material used to make a deck.

declaim *v* to speak loudly and dramatically or pompously.

declamation *n* the art or act of declaiming. ➤ **declamatory** *adj*.

declaration *n* **1** an emphatic announcement or formal statement. **2** the act of declaring.

declare *v* **1** to make known formally or explicitly. **2** to make evident. **3** to make a full statement of (something taxable or dutiable). **4** of a cricket captain or team: to end the team's innings before all the batsmen are out. * **declare oneself** admit one's intentions.

declassify *v* (**-ies, -ied**) to declare (e.g. documents, information) no longer secret.

declension *n* **1** a schematic arrangement of noun, adjective, or pronoun inflections. **2** a class of nouns or adjectives with the same inflectional forms.

decline¹ *v* **1** to become gradually smaller, less strong, or less good. **2** to refuse, *esp* courteously. **3** to slope downwards or descend. **4** in grammar, to list the inflectional forms of (a noun, pronoun, or adjective).

decline² *n* **1** a gradual reduction or change for the worse. **2** the period when something is approaching its end.

declivity *n* (*pl* **-ies**) *formal* a descending slope.

decode *v* to convert (a coded message) into intelligible language. ➤ **decoder** *n*.

décolletage /daykol'tahzh/ *n* the low-cut neckline of a dress.

décolleté /daykol'tay, day'koltay/ *adj* of a dress: low-necked.

decommission *v* to take (a ship, weapon, nuclear reactor etc) out of service.

decompose *v* to decay or rot. ➤ **decomposition** *n*.

decompress *v* **1** to release from pressure or compression. **2** to return (computer data) to its normal size after compression. ➤ **decompression** *n*.

decompression sickness *n* a condition suffered by deep-sea divers who surface too quickly, caused by the expansion of nitrogen bubbles in the blood and tissue.

decongestant *n* a drug that relieves *esp* nasal congestion. ➤ **decongestant** *adj*.

deconstruct *v* **1** to analyse (e.g. a film or text) by treating its elements as having meanings independent of the work as a whole. **2** to dismantle. ➤ **deconstruction** *n*.

decontaminate *v* to rid of contamination, e.g. radioactivity. ➤ **decontamination** *n*.

decor *or* **décor** *n* the style and layout of interior decoration and furnishings.

decorate *v* **1** to give a more attractive appearance by adding colour or ornament. **2** to apply paint, wallpaper, etc to (a room or building). **3** to award a medal or honour to.

decoration *n* **1** the act or process of decorating. **2** an ornament. **3** a badge of honour, *esp* a medal.

decorative *adj* serving to decorate; ornamental. ➤ **decoratively** *adv*.

decorator *n* somebody whose job is painting and wallpapering rooms or buildings.

decorous *adj* marked by propriety and good taste. ➤ **decorously** *adv*.

decorum *n* behaviour that is in accordance with propriety and good taste.

decoy[1] *n* **1** something used to lure a person or animal into a trap. **2** somebody or something used to divert the attention, e.g. of an enemy.

decoy[2] *v* to lure by a decoy.

decrease[1] *v* to make or become progressively less in size, number, or intensity.

decrease[2] *n* **1** the process of decreasing. **2** the amount by which something decreases.

decree[1] *n* **1** an order, *esp* one having legal force. **2** a judicial decision, *esp* in an equity, probate, or divorce court.

decree[2] *v* (**decrees, decreed, decreeing**) to command or impose by decree.

decrepit *adj* **1** weakened, *esp* by the infirmities of old age. **2** worn-out, ruined, or in disrepair. ➤ **decrepitude** *n*.

decriminalize or **-ise** *v* to stop treating as a criminal offence.

decry *v* (**-ies, -ied**) to express strong disapproval of.

decrypt *v* to decode.

dedicate *v* **1** to make a long-term commitment of (e.g. oneself, one's time) to a particular goal. **2** to set apart for a specific use. **3** to address (a book, song, etc) to somebody as a mark of esteem or affection. ➤ **dedicatee** *n*, **dedicatory** *adj*.

dedicated *adj* **1** devoted to a cause, ideal, or purpose. **2** given over to a particular purpose.

dedication *n* **1** commitment to achieving a particular purpose, ideal, etc. **2** the act of dedicating. **3** words used to dedicate a book, song, etc to somebody.

deduce *v* to establish (a fact, the truth, etc) by reasoning and making use of the information available.

deduct *v* to subtract (an amount) from a total. ➤ **deductible** *adj*.

deduction *n* **1** the act of deducting. **2** an amount that is deducted. **3** the act of deducing. ➤ **deductive** *adj*.

deed *n* **1** something that is done. **2** an illustrious act. **3** in law, a document containing a transfer, bargain, or contract.

deem *v formal* to judge or consider to be.

deep[1] *adj* **1** extending far downwards, inwards, or back from a surface or area. **2** having a specified extension in this direction. **3** of a

colour: rich and dark; dark. **4** of a sound: having a low pitch. **5** intellectually demanding or difficult to understand. **6** capable of serious and significant thought. **7** intense or extreme. **8** in sport, near or towards the outer limits of the playing area. ✳ **go off the deep end** to become very excited or angry. ➤ **deeply** *adv*.

deep[2] *n* (**the deep**) the sea.

deepen *v* to make or become deeper.

deep freeze *n* a freezer.

deep-fry *v* (**-ies, -ied**) to fry (food) by complete immersion in hot fat or oil.

deer *n* (*pl* **deer**) a ruminant mammal with antlers, *esp* in the male.

deerstalker *n* a close-fitting hat with peaks at the front and the back and ear-flaps.

deface *v* to spoil the external appearance of.

de facto[1] /day 'faktoh/ *adv* in reality; actually.

de facto[2] *adj* existing in fact; effective.

defame *v* to injure the reputation of (somebody) by libel or slander. ➤ **defamation** *n*, **defamatory** *adj*.

default[1] *n* **1** failure to do something required by law, e.g. to pay debts or appear in court. **2** a pre-selected option or setting, e.g. in computing, that remains in effect until cancelled. ✳ **by default** in the absence of an alternative.

default[2] *v* **1** (*often* + on) to fail to meet an obligation, *esp* a financial one. **2** to revert to a pre-selected option or setting.

defeat[1] *v* **1** to win a victory over. **2** to frustrate (e.g. a hope). **3** to prevent (a motion, bill) from being passed.

defeat[2] *n* **1** failure to win. **2** a contest, battle, etc in which one is the loser. **3** the act of defeating.

defeatism *n* resignation to defeat. ➤ **defeatist** *n and adj*.

defecate *v* to discharge faeces from the bowels. ➤ **defecation** *n*.

defect[1] *n* a fault or shortcoming.

defect[2] *v* to desert a cause or party, often in favour of another. ➤ **defection** *n*, **defector** *n*.

defective *adj* unable to function properly; faulty.

defence (*NAmer* **defense**) *n* **1** the act of defending. **2** a means or method of defending, or a defensive structure. **3** an argument in support or justification. **4** a defendant's case. **5** the lawyers representing a defendant in a court. **6** in sport, defending players or moves. ➤ **defenceless** *adj*.

defend *v* **1** to protect from attack. **2** to attempt to retain (a military position, sporting title, or parliamentary seat) that others wish to gain. **3** to maintain (something) by argument against opposition or criticism. **4** in sport, to attempt to prevent an opponent from scoring, e.g. by protecting a goal. **5** to act as legal representative in court for (an accused or defendant). ➤ **defender** *n*.

defendant *n* a party against whom a criminal charge or civil claim is made.

defensible *adj* capable of being defended by argument or in a war.

defensive *adj* **1** serving to defend or protect. **2** sensitive to criticism and eager to justify one's own actions or views. ✳ **on the defensive** having to defend oneself against attack or criticism. ➤ **defensively** *adv*, **defensiveness** *n*.

defer[1] *v* (**deferred, deferring**) to postpone (an action, decision, etc). ➤ **deferment** *n*, **deferral** *n*.

defer[2] *v* (**deferred, deferring**) (*usu* + to) to acknowledge somebody's superiority or allow their opinion to prevail.

deference *n* the respect due to a superior or an elder.

deferential *adj* **1** respectful. **2** obsequious. ➤ **deferentially** *adv*.

defiance *n* bold resistance or disobedience.

defiant *adj* boldly resisting or disobeying. ➤ **defiantly** *adv*.

deficiency *n* (*pl* -**ies**) **1** inadequacy. **2** a lack or shortage.

deficient *adj* **1** (*usu* + in) lacking in some necessary quality or element. **2** inadequate.

deficit *n* **1** a deficiency in amount or quality. **2** an excess of expenditure over revenue or of liabilities over assets.

defile[1] *v* to make unclean or impure.

defile[2] *n* a narrow passage or gorge.

define *v* **1** to describe the essential nature or scope of. **2** to set forth the meaning of (e.g. a word). **3** to fix or mark the limits of. **4** to make clear or precise in outline. ➤ **definable** *adj*.

definite *adj* **1** free of ambiguity or uncertainty. **2** clearly apparent. **3** having distinct or certain limits. ➤ **definitely** *adv*.

definite article *n* the word *the*.

definition *n* **1** a statement of what a word or phrase means. **2** the act of defining. **3** distinctness of outline or detail, e.g. in a photograph.

definitive *adj* **1** serving to provide a final solution. **2** authoritative and apparently exhaustive. ➤ **definitively** *adv*.

deflate *v* **1** to release air or gas from (e.g. a balloon or a tyre). **2** to reduce in self-confidence or self-importance. **3** to cause deflation in (an economy or price levels).

deflation *n* **1** the act of deflating. **2** a reduction in the amount of money and credit available in an economy, and a resulting decline in economic activity and price levels. ➤ **deflationary** *adj*.

deflect *v* to turn from a straight course or fixed purpose. ➤ **deflection** *n*.

deflower *v* *dated or literary* to deprive (a woman) of her virginity.

defoliate *v* to deprive (a tree or an area) of leaves. ➤ **defoliant** *n*, **defoliation** *n*.

deforest *v* to clear (an area) of forests. ➤ **deforestation** *n*.

deform *v* to spoil the form or appearance of. ➤ **deformed** *adj*, **deformation** *n*.

deformity *n* (*pl* -**ies**) **1** the state of being deformed. **2** a physical blemish or distortion; a disfigurement.

defraud *v* to cheat (somebody) of something, *esp* money.

defray *v* to provide for the payment of (an expense).

defrock *v* to unfrock (e.g. a priest).

defrost *v* **1** to thaw out (frozen food). **2** to free (a refrigerator or freezer) from ice.

deft *adj* marked by facility and skill. ➤ **deftly** *adv*, **deftness** *n*.

defunct *adj* **1** no longer existing or in use. **2** dead.

defuse *v* **1** to remove the fuse from (a mine, bomb, etc). **2** to make (a situation) less dangerous or tense.

defy *v* (-**ies**, -**ied**) **1** to resist by refusing to obey. **2** to challenge. **3** to do something considered impossible.

degenerate[1] *adj* having sunk to a lower and usu morally or physically corrupt state. ➤ **degeneracy** *n*.

degenerate[2] *n* a degenerate person.

degenerate[3] *v* to pass from a better to a worse state. ➤ **degeneration** *n*, **degenerative** *adj*.

degrade *v* **1** to cause to lose self-respect or the respect of others. **2** to reduce the quality of. **3** in chemistry, to cause to decompose or disintegrate. ➤ **degradable** *adj*, **degrader** *n*.

degree *n* **1** the extent or level of an action, condition, or relation. **2** an amount or measure. **3** a division of a scale of measurement, *esp* a unit for measuring temperature. **4** a 360th part of the circumference of a circle. **5** an academic title conferred on university students who successfully complete a course.

dehumanize or -**ise** *v* to deprive of human qualities or personality.

dehumidify *v* (-**ies**, -**ied**) to remove moisture from (e.g. air). ➤ **dehumidifier** *n*.

dehydrate *v* **1** to remove water from (a chemical compound, foodstuff, etc). **2** to cause to lose water or body fluids. ➤ **dehydrated** *adj*, **dehydration** *n*.

de-ice *v* to keep free from ice or rid of ice.

deify /'deeifie, 'day-/ *v* (-**ies**, -**ied**) to worship or treat as a god. ➤ **deification** *n*.

deign *v* to see fit to do something that one is usually too proud to do.

deity /'deeiti, 'day-/ *n* (*pl* -**ies**) **1** a god or goddess. **2** (**the Deity**) God.

déjà vu /,dayzhah 'vooh/ *n* the illusion of remembering scenes and events when they are experienced for the first time.

dejected *adj* cast down; depressed. ➤ **dejection** *n*.

delay[1] *n* the time during which something is delayed.

delay[2] *v* **1** to put off to a later time. **2** to detain or hinder for a time. **3** to fail to act or move immediately.

delectable *adj* highly pleasing; delightful or delicious. ➤ **delectably** *adv*.

delectation *n formal* delight or enjoyment.

delegate[1] *n* a person delegated to represent or act for somebody else, e.g. at a conference.

delegate[2] *v* **1** to entrust (e.g. a duty or responsibility) to somebody else. **2** to appoint as one's representative. **3** to assign responsibility or authority to other people.

delegation *n* **1** a group of people chosen to represent others. **2** the act of delegating.

delete *v* to eliminate by erasing. ➤ **deletion** *n*.

deleterious /deli'tiari·əs/ *adj formal* harmful or detrimental.

deli *n* (*pl* **delis**) *informal* a delicatessen.

deliberate[1] *adj* **1** characterized by awareness of the nature of an action and its consequences; intentional. **2** slow or unhurried. ➤ **deliberately** *adv*.

deliberate[2] *v* to ponder or discuss carefully and thoroughly before reaching a decision.

deliberation *n* **1** careful and serious thought or consideration. **2** slow and careful movement or action. ➤ **deliberative** *adj*.

delicacy *n* (*pl* -**ies**) **1** daintiness. **2** fragility. **3** refined sensibility in feeling, perception, or conduct. **4** something pleasing to eat that is considered rare or luxurious.

delicate *adj* **1** very finely made. **2** easily damaged. **3** pleasing to the senses in a mild or subtle way. **4** marked by extreme precision. **5** having or showing extreme sensitivity. **6** requiring tact or careful treatment. **7** weak or sickly. ➤ **delicately** *adv*.

delicatessen *n* a shop where delicacies and foreign foods, e.g. cooked meats, are sold.

delicious *adj* **1** highly pleasing to the sense of taste. **2** delightful. ➤ **deliciously** *adv*.

delight[1] *v* **1** to take great pleasure in. **2** to give enjoyment to.

delight[2] *n* **1** great pleasure or satisfaction. **2** something that gives great pleasure.

delighted *adj* highly pleased. ➤ **delightedly** *adv*.

delightful *adj* highly pleasing; charming. ➤ **delightfully** *adv*.

delineate *v* to describe or depict in sharp or vivid detail. ➤ **delineation** *n*.

delinquency *n* (*pl* -**ies**) antisocial or illegal conduct.

delinquent[1] *n* somebody who has behaved in an antisocial or criminal way.

delinquent[2] *adj* guilty of wrongdoing.

deliquesce *v* to dissolve gradually in water attracted and absorbed from the air. ➤ **deliquescence** *n*, **deliquescent** *adj*.

delirious *adj* **1** suffering from delirium. **2** wildly joyful; ecstatic. ➤ **deliriously** *adv*.

delirium *n* **1** confusion, disordered speech, hallucinations, etc, occurring as a mental disturbance. **2** frenzied excitement or emotion.

deliver *v* **1** to bring or take to a specified place or person. **2** (*often* + up) to surrender. **3** to guide (e.g. a blow) to an intended target. **4** to utter or pronounce (a speech, verdict, etc). **5** to set free. **6** to assist in the birth of (a baby). **7** (*often* **be delivered of**) to give birth to (a baby). **8** *informal* to produce the promised, desired, or expected results.

deliverance *n* liberation or rescue.

delivery *n* (*pl* -**ies**) **1** the act of delivering something. **2** an item or items delivered at one time. **3** the act of giving birth. **4** an instance of throwing or bowling, *esp* in cricket.

dell *n* a small secluded hollow or valley.

delphinium *n* (*pl* **delphiniums**) a garden plant with blue or purple flowers in showy spikes.

delta *n* **1** a triangular area at the mouth of a river formed by deposited silt. **2** the fourth letter of the Greek alphabet (Δ, δ).

delude *v* to mislead the mind or judgment of; to deceive.

deluge[1] *n* **1** a great flood. **2** an overwhelming amount or number.

deluge[2] *v* **1** to overwhelm or swamp. **2** to flood.

delusion *n* a false belief or impression. ➤ **delusional** *adj*.

de luxe *adj* of superior quality.

delve *v* **1** to make a careful search for information. **2** to reach inside something and search about in it. **3** *archaic* to dig.

demagnetize or -**ise** *v* to remove magnetic properties from.

demagogue (*NAmer* **demagog**) *n* **1** an agitator who makes use of popular prejudices in order to gain power. **2** a leader of the common people in ancient times.

demand[1] *n* **1** a claim or forceful request. **2** (*in pl*) requirements. **3** desire or need, *esp* of consumers for a product. ✲ **in demand** sought after; popular. **on demand** whenever asked for.

demand[2] *v* **1** to ask for in an authoritative or peremptory way. **2** to call for urgently or insistently. **3** to require.

demanding *adj* **1** needing much effort or skill. **2** difficult to please.

demarcate *v* to mark the limits of.

dematerialize or -**ise** *v* to lose material form; to vanish.

demean *v* to degrade or debase.

demeanour (*NAmer* **demeanor**) *n* behaviour towards others, or outward manner.

demented *adj* insane; crazy.

dementia n a state of chronic mental impairment, characterized by memory failure and personality changes.

demerara sugar n brown cane sugar from the West Indies.

demerit n a fault or defect.

demigod or **demigoddess** n a mythological superhuman being with less power than a god.

demilitarize or **-ise** v to strip (an area) of military forces, weapons, etc. ➤ **demilitarization** n.

demimonde n a class of people, *esp* courtesans and kept women, on the fringes of respectable society.

demise n **1** *technical or euphem* death. **2** the end of something, e.g. an industry.

demist v *Brit* to remove mist from (e.g. a car windscreen). ➤ **demister** n.

demo n (pl **demos**) *informal* **1** a political demonstration. **2** a version of a computer game or piece of recorded music used for demonstration purposes.

demob v (**demobbed**, **demobbing**) *chiefly Brit, informal* to demobilize (troops).

demobilize or **-ise** v to release at the end of a period of military service. ➤ **demobilization** n.

democracy n (pl **-ies**) **1** a form of government in which the supreme power is exercised by the people. **2** a state governed in this way. **3** control of a group by its own members or a majority of them.

democrat n **1** an adherent of democracy. **2** (**Democrat**) a member of the Democratic party of the USA.

democratic adj **1** practising or favouring democracy. **2** (*often* **Democratic**) denoting a political party of the USA associated with policies of social reform and internationalism. ➤ **democratically** adv.

democratize or **-ise** v to make (a state or organization) democratic. ➤ **democratization** n.

demography n the statistical study of human populations. ➤ **demographic** adj.

demolish v **1** to destroy, smash, or tear down. **2** to defeat or refute (an argument). **3** *informal* to devour (food). ➤ **demolition** n.

demon n **1** an evil supernatural being; a devil. **2** (*used before a noun*) very forceful or enthusiastic.

demoniac or **demoniacal** adj = DEMONIC.

demonic adj **1** of or resembling a demon or evil spirit. **2** intense or frenzied.

demonize or **-ise** v to make seem evil or wicked.

demonstrable adj capable of being demonstrated. ➤ **demonstrably** adv.

demonstrate v **1** to show clearly. **2** to prove or make clear by reasoning, evidence, or example. **3** to show how something is done by doing it. **4** to take part in a political demonstration. ➤ **demonstrator** n.

demonstration n **1** the act of demonstrating. **2** a mass meeting, procession, etc to display group feelings about grievances or political issues.

demonstrative adj **1** inclined to display feelings openly. **2** (+ of) demonstrating something to be real or true. ➤ **demonstratively** adv.

demoralize or **-ise** v to weaken the morale or self-respect of. ➤ **demoralizing** adj.

demote v to reduce to a lower grade or rank. ➤ **demotion** n.

demotivate v to make less motivated to do something.

demur[1] v (**demurred**, **demurring**) to show hesitation about accepting something.

demur[2] n hesitation or objection.

demure adj (**demurer**, **demurest**) reserved or modest. ➤ **demurely** adv.

demystify v (**-ies**, **-ied**) to make less mysterious; to clarify.

den n **1** the lair of a wild animal. **2** a centre of secret or unlawful activity. **3** a comfortable usu secluded room.

denationalize or **-ise** v to remove from the ownership or control of the state.

denial n **1** an assertion that an allegation or statement is false. **2** a refusal to satisfy a request or desire. **3** in psychology, an unconscious refusal to acknowledge feelings or thoughts that may be painful.

denier n a unit of fineness for silk, rayon, or nylon yarn.

denigrate v to make negative or critical statements about, usu unjustly. ➤ **denigration** n.

denim n **1** a durable usu blue cotton fabric used for jeans and work clothes. **2** (*in pl*) denim clothes; *esp* jeans.

denizen n *literary or humorous* an inhabitant or resident.

denominate v *formal* to give a name to.

denomination n **1** a distinctive group within a religious faith. **2** a value shown on a coin or stamp. **3** *formal* a name or designation.

denominator n the part of a vulgar fraction below the line, indicating how many parts the numerator is divided into.

denote v **1** to indicate or mean. **2** to be a sign or symbol of.

denouement /day'noohmonh/ n the final part of a literary work in which all the complications of the plot are resolved.

denounce v **1** to condemn, *esp* publicly. **2** to inform against or accuse.

dense adj **1** marked by compactness or a crowding together of its parts. **2** *informal* stupid. ➤ **densely** adv.

density n (pl **-ies**) **1** the state of being dense. **2** the mass of a substance per unit of volume. **3**

the average number of individuals per unit of space.

dent[1] *n* a depression made by a blow or pressure.

dent[2] *v* **1** to make a dent in. **2** to affect adversely.

dental *adj* relating to the teeth or dentistry.

dentine (*NAmer* **dentin**) *n* a calcium-containing material, similar to bone, of which a tooth is composed.

dentist *n* somebody who treats diseases of, and injuries to, the teeth, mouth, and gums. ➤ **dentistry** *n*.

denture *n* **1** an artificial replacement for one or more teeth. **2** (*in pl*) a set of false teeth.

denude *v* to strip of all covering.

denunciation *n* the act of denouncing, or a public condemnation.

deny *v* (**-ies, -ied**) **1** to declare to be untrue or invalid. **2** to refuse to give or permit something to (somebody). **3** to refuse to grant (e.g. a request or access). ✳ **deny oneself** to refrain from self-indulgence or pleasure.

deodorant *n* a substance that masks unpleasant smells, *esp* body odour.

deodorize *or* **-ise** *v* to remove an unpleasant smell from.

depart *v* **1** to go away; to leave. **2** (*usu* + from) to do something different from what is usual or was prearranged.

departed *adj euphem* having died.

department *n* **1** a major division of a government, institution, or business. **2** a major administrative subdivision, e.g. in France. **3** *informal* a distinct sphere, e.g. of activity or thought; an area of responsibility. ➤ **departmental** *adj*.

department store *n* a large shop with several different sections selling different types of goods.

departure *n* the act of departing; a going-away.

depend *v* **1** (*usu* + on/upon) to be determined by a particular condition or action. **2** (+ on/upon) to rely.

dependable *adj* reliable or trustworthy. ➤ **dependability** *n*, **dependably** *adv*.

dependant (*NAmer* **dependent**) *n* a person who relies on another person, *esp* for financial support.

Usage Note: Dependent is an adjective and dependant is a noun meaning 'a dependent person'.

dependency *n* (*pl* **-ies**) **1** a territorial unit under the jurisdiction of a nation but not formally annexed to it. **2** dependence.

dependent *adj* **1** relying on somebody or something else for support or help. **2** (*often* + on/upon) determined or conditioned by. **3** having a need for something, e.g. a drug.

Usage Note: See note at DEPENDANT.

depict *v* **1** to represent by a picture. **2** to describe. ➤ **depiction** *n*.

depilate *v* to remove hair from (a part of the body). ➤ **depilation** *n*, **depilatory** *adj*.

deplete *v* to lessen markedly in quantity or content. ➤ **depletion** *n*.

deplorable *adj* extremely bad. ➤ **deplorably** *adv*.

deplore *v* to regret or disapprove of strongly.

deploy *v* **1** to spread out (e.g. troops or ships), *esp* in battle formation. **2** to bring into action. ➤ **deployment** *n*.

depopulate *v* to reduce greatly the population of (an area). ➤ **depopulation** *n*.

deport *v* to expel (e.g. an alien) legally from a country. ➤ **deportation** *n*.

deportment *n Brit* the manner in which one stands, sits, or walks; posture.

depose *v* to remove from a position of authority, e.g. the throne.

deposit[1] *v* (**deposited, depositing**) **1** to place for safekeeping or as a pledge. **2** to put (money) in a bank. **3** to put down in a particular place. **4** to let (e.g. sediment) fall and form a layer.

deposit[2] *n* **1** money given as a pledge or down payment. **2** money or valuables deposited in a bank. **3** matter deposited by a natural process.

deposition *n* **1** removal from a position of authority. **2** a sworn statement presented as evidence. **3** an act or process of depositing.

depository *n* (*pl* **-ies**) a storehouse where things are put for safekeeping.

depot *n* **1** *Brit* a place where buses or trains are kept, or taken for maintenance. **2** *NAmer* a railway or bus station. **3** a place for storing goods.

deprave *v* to corrupt morally. ➤ **depraved** *adj*.

depravity *n* moral corruption.

deprecate *v* **1** to express disapproval of, *esp* mildly or regretfully. **2** to disparage.

depreciate *v* **1** to lessen in value. **2** to belittle or disparage. ➤ **depreciation** *n*.

depredation *n* (*usu in pl*) an act of plundering or robbery.

depress *v* **1** to sadden or dispirit. **2** to lessen the activity or strength of. **3** to push or press down.

depressant *n* a drug that slows down natural functions. ➤ **depressant** *adj*.

depressed *adj* **1** very sad or dispirited, *esp* suffering from depression. **2** suffering from economic depression.

depression *n* **1** a mental disorder marked by inactivity, difficulty in thinking and concentration, and *esp* by sadness. **2** an unhappy state or mood. **3** a period of low economic activity and rising levels of unemployment. **4** a lowered or sunken place. **5** an area of low atmospheric pressure that usually brings bad weather. **6** the act of depressing.

depressive adj **1** tending to depress. **2** characterized by psychological depression.

deprivation n **1** hardship caused by lack of basic necessities such as food or shelter. **2** the act of depriving somebody of something.

deprive v (usu + of) to prevent from making use of or benefiting from something.

deprived adj lacking the necessities of life.

dept abbr department.

depth n **1** the measurement downwards from a surface. **2** the distance from front to back. **3** a part that is far from the outside or surface. **4** a profound or intense state, e.g. of thought or feeling: *the depths of despair*. **5** the degree of intensity of a feeling. **6** the quality of having or containing far-reaching insights and great wisdom. ✳ **out of one's depth 1** in water that is deeper than one's height. **2** faced with a situation beyond one's ability to deal with.

depth charge n an explosive device for use underwater against submarines.

deputation n a small group of people chosen to represent the members of a larger group.

depute v to appoint (somebody) to do something on one's behalf.

deputize or **-ise** v (usu + for) to act as a deputy.

deputy n (pl **-ies**) a person appointed as a substitute for another.

derail v **1** to cause (a train) to leave the rails. **2** to throw off course. ➤ **derailment** n.

derange v **1** to disarrange. **2** to make insane. ➤ **derangement** n.

deranged adj mad or insane.

derby n (pl **-ies**) **1** (**the Derby**) a flat race for three-year-old horses held annually at Epsom. **2** a sporting match against a major local rival.

deregulate v to remove from government control or management. ➤ **deregulation** n.

derelict¹ adj **1** left to decay; abandoned or ruined. **2** chiefly NAmer lacking a sense of duty; negligent.

derelict² n a down-and-out.

dereliction n **1** conscious neglect, esp of duty. **2** a decaying or ruined state.

deride v to mock or scorn (something).

de rigueur /dɜɹɪ'guh/ adj required by fashion or etiquette.

derision n scorn or ridicule.

derisive adj mocking or scornful. ➤ **derisively** adv.

derisory adj **1** ridiculously small and inadequate. **2** derisive.

derivation n **1** the fact of being obtained or originating from a particular source. **2** the formation of a word from another word or root.

derivative¹ adj made up of derived elements; not original.

derivative² n something derived, e.g. a word formed by derivation.

derive v **1** to obtain or receive, esp from a specified source. **2** (+ from) to come, result, or originate from.

dermatitis n a disease or inflammation of the skin.

dermatology n the branch of medicine dealing with the skin and skin diseases. ➤ **dermatological** adj, **dermatologically** adv, **dermatologist** n.

derogatory adj expressing a low opinion; insulting or disparaging.

derrick n **1** a hoisting apparatus with a swivelling beam, similar to a crane. **2** a framework over an oil well for supporting drilling tackle.

derring-do n archaic or literary daring action.

dervish n a member of a Muslim religious order noted for its energetic whirling dances that lead to a trance.

descant n an additional melody sung or played above the main tune.

descend v **1** to pass from a higher to a lower level. **2** to incline, lead, or extend downwards. **3** (usu **be descended from**) to have as an ancestor. **4** (+ on/upon) to make a sudden attack on, or a sudden disconcerting visit to. **5** (+ to) to lower or degrade oneself.

descendant n somebody descended from a particular ancestor.

descent n **1** the act or process of descending. **2** a downward slope. **3** family origins or lineage.

describe v **1** to give an account of in words. **2** to trace the outline of.

description n **1** an account in words. **2** the act of describing. **3** a kind or sort.

descriptive adj serving to describe, esp vividly. ➤ **descriptively** adv.

descry v (**-ies, -ied**) formal to notice or see, esp at a distance.

desecrate v to treat (something sacred) irreverently or contemptuously. ➤ **desecration** n.

desegregate v to eliminate racial segregation in (e.g. a school). ➤ **desegregation** n.

deselect v of a constituency political party: to refuse to readopt (somebody) as a parliamentary candidate. ➤ **deselection** n.

desensitize or **-ise** v to make less sensitive.

desert¹ n **1** a barren region incapable of supporting much life. **2** a place that is deprived of something important: *a cultural desert*.

Usage Note: The noun *desert* has the stress on the first syllable; the verb *desert* has the stress on the second. Do not confuse these with *dessert* (sweet course), which has the stress on the second syllable.

desert² n (usu in pl) deserved reward or punishment: *just deserts*.

desert³ v **1** to abandon (somebody), esp somebody to whom one owes a duty. **2** to quit one's post, military service, etc without leave or justification. ➤ **deserter** n, **desertion** n.

deserted adj left empty of people.

deserve v to be worthy of (a reward, punishment, or particular type of treatment). ➤ **deservedly** adv.

deserving adj worthy of something, esp financial aid.

déshabillé /dayza'beeay/ or **deshabille** /-'beel, disa'beel/ n the state of being partially or carelessly dressed.

desiccate v to remove moisture from, esp as a means of preservation.

design[1] v **1** to draw the plans for (e.g. a building). **2** to devise for a specific purpose.

design[2] n **1** a drawing showing how something is to be constructed. **2** the act of producing such a plan. **3** a decorative pattern. **4** a particular purpose held in view. **5** deliberate purposeful planning. * **have designs on** to wish to obtain, often dishonestly.

designate[1] v **1** to nominate for a particular office or duty. **2** to call by a distinctive name or title.

designate[2] adj chosen for an office but not yet installed: ambassador designate.

designation n **1** a distinguishing name or title. **2** the act of indicating or identifying.

designer n **1** somebody who designs esp manufactured objects. **2** (used before a noun) made by a well-known fashion designer: designer jeans.

desirable adj **1** worth having as advantageous or beneficial. **2** attractive, esp sexually. ➤ **desirability** n.

desire[1] v **1** to long or hope for. **2** to wish to have sexual relations with.

desire[2] n **1** a longing or craving, esp a sexual longing. **2** something desired.

desirous adj formal (usu + of/to) eagerly wanting; desiring.

desist v formal (often + from) to cease to proceed or act.

desk n **1** a table with a sloping or horizontal surface, designed for writing and reading. **2** a counter at which cashiers, receptionists, etc work.

desktop n **1** the working surface of a desk. **2** a compact computer suitable for use on a desk. **3** the visible screen on a VDU, on which icons, the cursor, etc are displayed.

desolate[1] adj **1** barren, lifeless, or uninhabited. **2** extremely unhappy.

desolate[2] v **1** to make barren or lifeless. **2** (be **desolated**) to be extremely unhappy. ➤ **desolation** n.

despair[1] v (often + of) to lose all hope or confidence. ➤ **despairing** adj.

despair[2] n utter loss of hope.

despatch[1] v see DISPATCH[1].

despatch[2] n see DISPATCH[2].

desperado n (pl **-oes** or **-os**) dated a reckless or violent criminal.

desperate adj **1** in despair because beyond hope. **2** reckless because of despair. **3** (often + for) suffering extreme need. **4** fraught with extreme danger. **5** violent or dangerous. ➤ **desperately** adj, **desperation** n.

Usage Note: Note the spelling with -er-.

despicable adj morally contemptible. ➤ **despicably** adv.

despise v to regard with contempt or distaste.

despite prep notwithstanding; in spite of. * **despite oneself** in spite of one's intentions, wishes, character, etc.

despoil v to plunder or pillage.

despondent adj extremely discouraged or dejected. ➤ **despondency** n, **despondently** adv.

despot n a ruler with absolute power. ➤ **despotic** adj, **despotism** n.

dessert n a sweet course or dish served at the end of a meal.

Usage Note: See note at DESERT[1].

dessertspoon n a spoon intermediate in size between a teaspoon and a tablespoon.

destabilize or **-ise** v to make (a government, an economy, etc) unstable.

destination n a place where a journey is set to end, or to which something is sent.

destine v **1** (usu be **destined for/to do**) to designate or set apart for a particular purpose or fate: She was destined for great things. **2** (be **destined for**) to be going to a place: freight was destined for various English ports.

destiny n (pl **-ies**) **1** the power held to determine the course of events. **2** a person's fate or future course of life.

destitute adj lacking the basic necessities of life; extremely poor. ➤ **destitution** n.

destroy v **1** to demolish or ruin. **2** to put an end to. **3** to kill (an animal) humanely.

destroyer n **1** somebody or something that destroys. **2** a small fast multi-purpose warship.

destruction n the act of destroying.

destructive adj **1** causing destruction. **2** of criticism, etc: pointing out faults without offering ideas for improvement. ➤ **destructively** adv.

desultory adj **1** passing aimlessly from one subject or activity to another. **2** happening on and off.

detach v **1** to separate (something), esp from a larger object, organization, or group. **2** to keep (oneself) emotionally detached. ➤ **detachable** adj.

Usage Note: Note the spelling with -ach not -atch.

detached *adj* **1** separate; not connected to e.g. another house. **2** of a person: free from prejudice or emotional involvement.

detachment *n* **1** freedom from bias or emotional involvement. **2** a section of a body of troops, ships, etc, designated for a special mission.

detail¹ *n* **1** (*usu in pl*) an individual relevant part or fact. **2** such small parts or facts collectively. **3** a small part of a work of art considered in isolation. **4** a small military detachment selected for a particular task. ✶ **in detail** item by item; thoroughly.

detail² *v* **1** to describe in detail. **2** to assign to a particular task.

detailed *adj* marked by abundant detail or thorough treatment.

detain *v* **1** to delay. **2** to hold in custody.

detainee *n* a person held in custody, *esp* for political reasons.

detect *v* **1** to discover the existence or discern the presence of. **2** to discover (a crime or criminal). ➤ **detectable** *adj*, **detection** *n*.

detective *n* a police officer or other person engaged in investigating crimes.

detector *n* a device used to detect the presence of e.g. radiation, smoke, or metal.

détente *or* **detente** *n* a relaxation of strained relations, e.g. between hostile nations.

detention *n* **1** the act of detaining, *esp* in custody. **2** *chiefly Brit* a period during which a pupil is kept in school after normal hours as a punishment.

deter *v* (**deterred, deterring**) **1** (*often* + from) to discourage or prevent (somebody) from doing something. **2** to prevent (something) happening. ➤ **deterrence** *n*, **deterrent** *adj*.

detergent *n* a cleansing agent; *esp* a chemical one.

deteriorate *v* to grow worse. ➤ **deterioration** *n*.

determination *n* **1** firmness and persistence in carrying out one's intentions. **2** the act of determining something.

determine *v* **1** to regulate or condition the nature or scope of. **2** to ascertain or work out. **3** to settle or decide conclusively or authoritatively.

determined *adj* firm; resolute. ➤ **determinedly** *adv*.

determiner *n* **1** something or somebody that determines. **2** a basic type of word, such as *this, that, my, his,* etc, that comes before a noun and any descriptive adjective applied to that noun.

deterrent *n* something that deters, e.g. nuclear weapons held by one nation to deter another from attacking it.

detest *v* to feel intense dislike for.

detestable *adj* arousing or deserving intense dislike.

detestation *n* extreme dislike.

dethrone *v* to remove (*esp* a monarch) from a position of power or authority.

detonate *v* **1** to cause (a bomb, etc) to explode. **2** of a bomb, etc: to explode. ➤ **detonation** *n*.

detonator *n* a device used for detonating a high explosive.

detour¹ *n* a roundabout route that is an alternative to a shorter or planned route.

detour² *v* to make a detour.

detoxify *v* (**-ies, -ied**) **1** to remove a poison or toxin from. **2** to treat for dependency on alcohol or drugs.

detract *v* (+ from) to make less valuable, interesting, etc.

detractor *n* a person who denigrates somebody or their ideas or beliefs.

detriment *n* injury or damage.

detritus *n* debris or waste material.

deuce *n* **1** a score of 40 all in tennis, after which two consecutive points are needed to win a game. **2** (**the deuce**) *informal* the devil.

Deutschmark /'doychmahk/ *or* **Deutsche Mark** /'doychə mahk/ *n* the basic monetary unit of Germany before the Euro.

devalue *v* **1** to reduce the exchange value of (money). **2** to lessen the value or reputation of. ➤ **devaluation** *n*.

devastate *v* **1** to reduce (a place) to ruin. **2** to overwhelm (somebody), e.g. with grief or horror. ➤ **devastation** *n*.

devastating *adj* **1** causing great destruction. **2** shocking; horrifying. **3** *informal* extremely attractive or impressive. ➤ **devastatingly** *adv*.

develop *v* (**developed, developing**) **1** to go through a process of natural growth or evolution. **2** to cause to grow, mature, or increase. **3** to become gradually visible or apparent. **4** to unfold (an idea) gradually or in detail. **5** to show signs of (an illness). **6** to use chemicals to produce a visible image on (a photograph). **7** to acquire gradually: *He developed a taste for good wine*. **8** to build on or change the use of (land).

development *n* **1** the act of developing. **2** an innovation or new product. **3** something which changes a situation. **4** an area of new building. ➤ **developmental** *adj*.

deviant¹ *adj* deviating from a norm. ➤ **deviance** *n*.

deviant² *n* a person whose sexual or social behaviour differs markedly from the norm.

deviate *v* to stray, *esp* from a principle, norm, or straight course.

device *n* **1** a piece of equipment designed for a special purpose. **2** a scheme to trick or deceive. **3** a heraldic symbol. ✶ **leave somebody to their own devices** to leave somebody to do as they please.

devil *n* **1** (*usu* **the Devil**) the supreme spirit of evil in Jewish and Christian belief. **2** a malignant spirit; a demon. **3** an extremely cruel or wicked person. **4** *informal* a person of the specified type: *You're a lucky devil.* **5** (**the devil**) *informal* something provoking, difficult, or trying. ✳ **the devil to pay** a lot of trouble.

devilish *adj* **1** characteristic of a devil; wicked. **2** mischievous. ➤ **devilishly** *adv.*

devil-may-care *adj* heedless of authority or convention.

devilment *n* wild mischief.

devilry *n* **1** mischief. **2** action performed with the help of the devil.

devil's advocate *n* a person who champions the less accepted cause, *esp* for the sake of argument.

devious *adj* **1** of a person: not straightforward or wholly sincere. **2** roundabout or circuitous. ➤ **deviously** *adv*, **deviousness** *n.*

devise *v* to formulate (a plan) in the mind; to invent.

devoid *adj* (+ of) totally without.

devolution *n* the surrender of powers to regional or local authorities by a central government.

devolve *v* **1** (*usu* + on/upon/to) to surrender (power) by devolution. **2** (*usu* + on/upon/to) to be passed, usu as an obligation or responsibility.

devote *v* (+ to) to set apart for, or give over entirely to.

devoted *adj* **1** very loving. **2** loyally attached. **3** dedicated. ➤ **devotedly** *adv.*

devotee *n* **1** an enthusiast. **2** a person devoted to a particular religious cult or practice.

devotion *n* **1** great love, affection, or dedication. **2** the act of devoting. **3** religious zeal; piety. **4** (*usu in pl*) a special act of prayer or supplication. ➤ **devotional** *adj.*

devour *v* **1** to eat (food) up greedily or ravenously. **2** *literary* to swallow up. **3** (**be devoured**) to be preoccupied or absorbed. **4** to take in eagerly through the mind or senses.

devout *adj* **1** devoted to religion; pious. **2** sincere; genuine. ➤ **devoutly** *adv.*

dew *n* moisture that condenses on cool surfaces, *esp* at night.

dewlap *n* a hanging fold of skin under the neck of an animal, e.g. a cow.

dewy *adj* (**-ier, -iest**) moist with dew, or as if with dew.

dexterity *n* skill, *esp* in using the hands.

dexterous or **dextrous** *adj* skilful, *esp* with the hands. ➤ **dexterously** *adv.*

diabetes *n* an illness characterized by the secretion of excessive amounts of urine, *esp* diabetes mellitus in which the body is unable to process sugar as a result of not producing enough insulin.

diabetic[1] *adj* affected with diabetes.

diabetic[2] *n* a person affected with diabetes.

diabolical *adj* **1** of the devil. **2** *chiefly Brit, informal* dreadful; appalling. ➤ **diabolically** *adv.*

diadem *n* a crown.

diagnose *v* to recognize (a disease, etc) by signs and symptoms. ➤ **diagnostic** *adj.*

diagnosis *n* (*pl* **diagnoses**) **1** the act of identifying a disease from its signs and symptoms. **2** the investigation of the cause or nature of a problem.

diagonal[1] *adj* **1** of a line: straight and slanting. **2** joining two opposite or nonadjacent angles of a rectangle or other figure. ➤ **diagonally** *adv.*

diagonal[2] *n* a diagonal line.

diagram *n* a line drawing, made for mathematical or scientific purposes or to show the arrangement of parts. ➤ **diagrammatic** *adj.*

dial[1] *n* **1** a face with marks or numbers on which something is measured by a pointer, *esp* the face of a clock. **2** a disc-shaped control mechanism, *esp* for selecting numbers on a telephone.

dial[2] *v* (**dialled, dialling,** *NAmer* **dialed, dialing**) to operate a dial, or press buttons, to select (a telephone number).

dialect *n* a variety of a language, usu differing in grammar and vocabulary from the standard, used by a particular regional or social group. ➤ **dialectal** *adj.*

dialectic *n* (*usu in pl*) systematic reasoning or argument that juxtaposes opposed ideas and seeks to resolve their conflict. ➤ **dialectical** *adj.*

dialogue (*NAmer* **dialog**) *n* **1** a conversation between two or more people. **2** the conversational element in a literary work. **3** discussion between two groups with conflicting interests.

dialysis *n* (*pl* **dialyses**) the use of a membrane to separate out substances in solution, *esp* the purification of blood by such means in a kidney machine.

diamanté *n* **1** sparkling particles, or fabric decorated with these. **2** (*used before a noun*) decorated with diamanté.

diameter *n* a straight line passing through the centre of a circle or sphere, or the length of this line.

diametric or **diametrical** *adj* completely opposed or opposite. ➤ **diametrically** *adv.*

diamond[1] *n* **1** a precious stone formed of very hard crystalline carbon. **2** a square or rhombus turned so that it rests on one of its angles. **3** a playing card marked with red diamond-shaped figures.

diamond[2] *adj* marking a 60th anniversary: *diamond wedding.*

diaper *n NAmer* a nappy.

diaphanous *adj* of fabrics: so fine as to be almost transparent.

diaphragm *n* **1** the layer of muscle separating the chest and abdominal cavities in mammals.

2 a contraceptive cap that fits over the cervix. **3** a device that controls the amount of light entering a camera lens. **4** a thin vibrating disc in a sound-reproduction system, e.g. in an earphone.

diarist n somebody who keeps a diary.

diarrhoea (NAmer **diarrhea**) n abnormally frequent bowel movements with fluid faeces.

diary n (pl **-ies**) a book containing a daily record of personal experiences or observations, or for noting appointments, etc.

diatonic adj relating to a standard major or minor musical scale of eight notes to the octave.

diatribe n a lengthy piece of bitter and abusive criticism.

dice[1] n (pl **dice**) a small cube marked on each face with from one to six spots, used in various games.

dice[2] v to cut (food) into small cubes. * **dice with death** to take a big risk.

dicey adj (**dicier, diciest**) informal risky; unpredictable.

dichotomy n (pl **-ies**) a sharp division or contrast, between two things.

dicky adj (**-ier, -iest**) Brit, informal weak or unsound.

dictate[1] v **1** to read out the text of (a letter, etc) for someone else to write down. **2** (often + to) to give orders authoritatively or overbearingly. **3** to impose or control the nature, scope, etc of with authority. ➤ **dictation** n.

dictate[2] n an authoritative rule, principle, or command.

dictator n an absolute ruler, esp an oppressive and unconstitutional one. ➤ **dictatorial** adj.

dictatorship n a state or form of government where absolute power is wielded by one person.

diction n **1** choice of words in speech or writing. **2** pronunciation of words in speaking.

dictionary n (pl **-ies**) a reference book that lists words alphabetically and gives their meanings or their equivalents in a foreign language.

dictum n (pl **dicta** or **dictums**) an authoritative statement on some topic.

did v past tense of DO[1].

didactic adj intended to teach something, esp a moral lesson.

diddle v informal to cheat or swindle.

didgeridoo n (pl **didgeridoos**) an Australian wind instrument consisting of a long wooden tube.

didn't contraction did not.

die[1] v (**dies, died, dying**) **1** to stop living. **2** (also + out) to cease to exist; to become extinct. **3** (often + away) to become weaker or fainter, or to cease. **4** (also + for) to long keenly or desperately. **5** (+ of) to be almost overwhelmed with (e.g. boredom). * **never say die** informal never give up. **to die for** informal excellent or desirable.

die[2] n **1** (pl **dice**) a dice. **2** (pl **dies**) a tool for pressing or moulding materials or impressing a design on e.g. coins. * **the die is cast** the irrevocable decision or step has been taken.

die away v to become weaker or fainter, then disappear.

die-cast v (past tense and past part. **die-cast**) to make (an object) by forcing molten plastic, metal, etc into a die.

die down v to diminish or subside.

die-hard n **1** a person who strongly resists change. **2** (used before a noun) strongly resisting change.

die off v to die one by one.

die out v **1** to become extinct. **2** to cease to exist, be done, etc.

diesel n **1** an internal-combustion engine in which the fuel is ignited by the heat generated by compressing the air in the cylinders. **2** a diesel-engined vehicle. **3** a heavy mineral oil used as fuel in diesel engines.

diet[1] n **1** the food habitually eaten by a person or animal. **2** the kind and amount of food prescribed for a special purpose, esp losing weight. **3** (used before a noun) of food or drinks: low in calories or fat content.

diet[2] v (**dieted, dieting**) to eat and drink sparingly, esp to lose weight.

dietary adj **1** of a diet. **2** present in the food a person eats.

dietitian or **dietician** n a specialist in diet and nutrition.

differ v **1** (+ from) to be unlike. **2** of people: to disagree.

difference n **1** unlikeness between two or more people or things. **2** a disagreement or dispute. **3** a remainder left after subtracting one number from another. **4** a significant effect on a situation.

different adj **1** partly or totally unlike. **2** distinct. **3** other. **4** informal unusual; special. ➤ **differently** adv.

Usage Note: **different from/to/than.** The preferred combination is *different from.* British English also accepts *different to. Different than* is acceptable only in American English.

differential[1] adj of or involving a difference.

differential[2] n **1** the amount by which the rate of pay differs for workers doing comparable types of work. **2** in mathematics, a very small change in the value of a variable. **3** an arrangement of gears that allows one of a pair of driving wheels to turn faster than the other when cornering.

differentiate v **1** to show the difference in (things). **2** to distinguish between (different things). ➤ **differentiation** n.

difficult adj **1** hard to do, make, carry out, or understand. **2** hard to deal with, manage, or please.

difficulty n (pl -ies) **1** the state of being difficult. **2** (often in pl) a cause of trouble or embarrassment; a problem.

diffident adj lacking in self-confidence; shy. ➤ **diffidence** n, **diffidently** adv.

diffract v to cause (a beam of light) to split into bands as it passes the edge of an opaque body, through narrow slits, etc. ➤ **diffraction** n.

diffuse¹ adj **1** not concentrated; scattered. **2** lacking conciseness; verbose.

diffuse² v **1** to spread out. **2** of atomic particles: to become intermingled in a substance as a result of their spontaneous movements. ➤ **diffusion** n.

dig¹ v (**digging**, past tense and past part. **dug**) **1** to turn up, loosen, or remove earth. **2** to hollow out (a hole or tunnel) by removing earth. **3** (often + into) to search for information. **4** to poke or prod. **5** slang, dated to appreciate. ➤ **digger** n.

dig² n **1** a thrust or poke. **2** informal a cutting or snide remark. **3** an archaeological excavation site. **4** chiefly Brit, informal (in pl) lodgings.

digest¹ v **1** to convert (food) into a form the body can use. **2** to assimilate mentally. ➤ **digestible** adj.

digest² n a summary, abridgment, or compilation of essential information.

digestion n the process or capability of digesting something, esp food.

digestive adj relating to digestion.

digestive biscuit or **digestive** n Brit a slightly sweet biscuit made from wholemeal flour.

dig in v **1** of a soldier: to dig defensive positions. **2** informal to hold stubbornly to a position. **3** informal to begin eating. ✻ **dig one's heels in** informal to refuse to move or change one's mind.

digit n **1** an element that can be used in forming a number, esp an Arabic numeral from 0 to 9. **2** a finger or toe.

digital adj **1** presented, stored, or manipulated in the form of numerical digits. **2** of a computer: operating with numbers expressed as discrete pulses representing digits in binary notation. **3** of a clock or watch: presenting information in the form of numerical digits rather than by a pointer and a dial. **4** of sound recording: involving the conversion of sounds into digital form to reduce background noise and distortion. **5** relating to fingers or toes. ➤ **digitally** adv.

digital pen n a pen that makes a digital record of what is written for later downloading onto a computer or transmission by mobile phone.

digitize or **-ise** v to put (data, etc) into digital form.

dignified adj showing or having dignity.

dignify v (-ies, -ied) to confer dignity or distinction on.

dignitary n (pl -ies) a person of high rank.

dignity n **1** composure and self-control. **2** the quality of being worthy or esteemed. **3** a high opinion of oneself.

dig out v **1** to remove by digging. **2** to search for and find.

digress v to turn aside from the main subject in writing or speaking. ➤ **digression** n.

dig up v **1** to remove by digging. **2** to discover by searching.

dike¹ n see DYKE¹.

dike² n informal, derog see DYKE².

diktat n a dictatorial order or ruling.

dilapidated adj decayed or fallen into partial ruin. ➤ **dilapidation** n.

dilate v to become wider or wider open. ➤ **dilation** n.

dilatory adj **1** intended to cause delay. **2** slow, tardy.

dilemma n **1** a situation involving choice between two equally unsatisfactory alternatives. **2** informal a seemingly insoluble problem.

dilettante /dili'tanti/ n (pl **dilettantes** or **dilettanti**) a person with a superficial interest in an art or a branch of knowledge.

diligent adj hard-working and conscientious. ➤ **diligence** n, **diligently** adv.

dill n a herb used in flavouring foods, e.g. pickles.

dillydally v (-ies, -ied) informal to waste time by loitering; to dawdle.

dilute¹ v **1** to make (a liquid) thinner or weaker by adding more liquid. **2** to make less powerful or effective by adding other elements. ➤ **dilution** n.

dilute² adj weak; diluted.

dim¹ adj (**dimmer, dimmest**) **1** giving out a weak or insufficient light. **2** seen or remembered indistinctly. **3** not seeing clearly. **4** informal unintelligent. ✻ **take a dim view of** to have an unfavourable attitude to. ➤ **dimly** adv.

dim² v (**dimmed, dimming**) to make or become dim.

dime n a coin worth ten US cents.

dimension n **1** a measurement giving the length, breadth or height of an object. **2** (in pl) size or scope. **3** an aspect. ➤ **dimensional** adj.

diminish v to reduce or become gradually less.

diminution n a diminishing or decrease.

diminutive¹ adj exceptionally small; tiny.

diminutive² n a word or affix, e.g -ette, indicating a smaller-sized version of something.

dimmer n a device for regulating the brightness of electric lighting.

dimple n a slight indentation, esp in the cheek or chin. ➤ **dimpled** adj.

dimwit n informal a stupid person. ➤ **dimwitted** adj.

din¹ n a loud continued discordant noise.

din² v (**dinned, dinning**) ✳ **din something into** to instil something into (somebody) by perpetual repetition.

dine v to eat dinner.

diner n **1** somebody who is dining. **2** NAmer a small restaurant, often beside the road. **3** chiefly NAmer a dining car.

dinghy n (pl -**ies**) **1** a small open sailing boat. **2** a small inflatable rubber boat.

dingo n (pl -**oes** or -**os**) a wild dog of Australia.

dingy adj (-**ier, -iest**) **1** dirty; discoloured. **2** gloomy; dim.

dinky adj (-**ier, -iest**) chiefly Brit, informal neat and dainty.

dinner n **1** the principal meal of the day taken either in the evening or at midday. **2** a formal evening meal.

dinner jacket n a jacket, usu black, for men's semi-formal evening wear.

dinosaur n **1** an extinct, typically very large reptile of a type that existed from 245 to 65 million years ago. **2** a person or organization that is outdated and reluctant to change.

dint ✳ **by dint of** by means or application of.

diocese n the area under the jurisdiction of a bishop. ➤ **diocesan** adj.

diode n a semiconductor device having only two terminals.

dioxide n an oxide containing two atoms of oxygen.

dip¹ v (**dipped, dipping**) **1** to plunge or immerse in a liquid. **2** to drop or decrease, often temporarily and by a small amount. **3** to lower (something) and then raise it again. **4** to lower (the beam of headlights) so as to reduce glare. **5** (+ in/into) to reach (a hand, etc) into a container to take something out. **6** to slope down. ✳ **dip into 1** to make inroads into for funds or supplies. **2** to read superficially.

dip² n **1** the act of dipping. **2** a brief bathe. **3** a soft mixture into which food is dipped before being eaten. **4** a brief drop or downward slope followed by a rise.

diphtheria n an acute infectious disease marked by the formation of a false membrane in the throat, causing difficulty in breathing.

diphthong n a sound that combines two vowels in one syllable, e.g. /oy/ in toy.

diploma n a certificate awarded for a qualification, usu in a specialized subject.

diplomacy n **1** the art of conducting international relations. **2** skill and tact in dealing with people.

diplomat n **1** a person, e.g. an ambassador, employed in diplomacy. **2** a tactful person.

diplomatic adj **1** of diplomats or international relations. **2** employing tact and conciliation. ➤ **diplomatically** adv.

dipper n **1** a small bird that swims underwater to feed. **2** something, e.g. a long-handled cup, used for dipping.

dippy adj (-**ier, -iest**) informal crazy; eccentric.

dipsomania n alcoholism. ➤ **dipsomaniac** n.

dipstick n **1** a graduated rod for measuring the depth of a liquid, esp the oil in a car. **2** informal a stupid person.

dire adj **1** desperately urgent. **2** informal dreadful; awful.

direct¹ v **1** to control the activities or course of. **2** to control the way (a film, play, or broadcast) is performed. **3** to order or instruct. **4** to show or point out the way for. **5** to cause to turn, move, or point in a particular direction. **6** to address or aim (a remark).

direct² adj **1** going from one point to another in space without deviation or interruption; straight. **2** going by the shortest way. **3** stemming immediately from a source. **4** operating without an intervening agency. **5** frank; straightforward.

direct³ adv **1** by the shortest way. **2** without an intervening agency.

direct current n an electric current flowing in one direction only.

direct debit n an order to a bank to pay sums not specified in advance from one's account to another account at specified times.

direction n **1** the line or course along which somebody or something moves or is aimed. **2** the point towards which somebody or something faces. **3** the act of directing. **4** guidance or supervision. **5** (in pl) explicit instructions on how to do something or get to a place. ➤ **directional** adj.

directive n an authoritative instruction from an official body.

directly¹ adv **1** in a direct manner. **2** immediately; soon.

directly² conj chiefly Brit, informal immediately after; as soon as.

director n **1** the head of an organized group or administrative unit. **2** a member of a management board of a company. **3** somebody who supervises the artistic and technical aspects of a film or play. ➤ **directorial** adj, **directorship** n.

director-general n (pl **directors-general** or **director-generals**) the senior director of a large organization.

directory n (pl -**ies**) **1** an alphabetical or classified list, e.g. of names, addresses, telephone numbers, etc. **2** a list of the files contained in a computer disk.

dirge n **1** a song of grief or lamentation, esp to accompany a funeral. **2** an unduly slow or mournful piece of music.

dirigible n an airship.

dirk n a dagger, formerly used by Scottish Highlanders.

dirt n **1** a filthy or soiling substance. **2** earth; soil. **3** informal excrement. **4** informal obscene or pornographic material. **5** *informal* scandalous gossip. ✳ **treat like dirt** *informal* to treat very badly.

dirty¹ *adj* (**-ier, -iest**) **1** not clean or pure. **2** base, dishonest, or unsporting. **3** low; despicable: *a dirty trick*. **4** indecent; obscene. **5** of the weather: rough or stormy. **6** conveying resentment or disgust: *a dirty look*.

dirty² *v* (**-ies, -ied**) to make or become dirty.

dis- *prefix* denoting removal, exclusion, or the opposite of (a specified action): *disarm; disbar; disappear*.

disability *n* (*pl* **-ies**) **1** an inability to do something because of physical or mental impairment. **2** a handicap.

disable *v* **1** to impair physically; to cripple. **2** to make incapable of operating.

disabled *adj* **1** having physical disabilities. **2** incapable of operating.

disabuse *v* (*usu* + of) to free from a mistaken impression.

disadvantage¹ *n* something which causes one to be in an unfavourable position. ➤ **disadvantageous** *adj*.

disadvantage² *v* to place at a disadvantage.

disadvantaged *adj* underprivileged, *esp* socially.

disaffected *adj* discontented and resentful, *esp* towards authority. ➤ **disaffection** *n*.

disagree *v* **1** (*often* + with) to differ in opinion. **2** to be unlike or at variance with. **3** (+ with) to have a bad effect on. ➤ **disagreement** *n*.

disagreeable *adj* **1** unpleasant; objectionable. **2** ill-tempered.

disallow *v* **1** to prohibit. **2** to refuse to recognize the validity of.

disappear *v* **1** to cease to be visible. **2** to cease to exist. **3** *informal* to leave or depart, *esp* secretly. ➤ **disappearance** *n*.

disappoint *v* to fail to meet the expectations or hopes of, and to sadden by so doing. ➤ **disappointed** *adj*, **disappointing** *adj*.

Usage Note: Note the spelling with *-s-* and *-pp-*.

disappointment *n* **1** a sad feeling caused by being disappointed. **2** somebody or something that disappoints.

disapprobation *n formal* disapproval.

disapprove *v* to have or express an unfavourable opinion of. ➤ **disapproval** *n*, **disapproving** *adj*.

disarm *v* **1** to deprive of weapons. **2** to reduce or abolish weapons and armed forces. **3** to make (a bomb, etc) harmless, *esp* by removing a fuse or warhead. **4** to dispel the hostility or suspicion of, *esp* through personal charm. ➤ **disarming** *adj*.

disarmament *n* the relinquishment or reduction of weapons and armed forces.

disarrange *v* to disturb the arrangement or order of. ➤ **disarrangement** *n*.

disarray¹ *n* a lack of order or sequence; disorder.

disarray² *v* to throw into disorder.

disassociate *v* = DISSOCIATE.

disaster *n* **1** a sudden event bringing great damage, loss, or destruction. **2** a great misfortune. **3** *informal* a failure. ➤ **disastrous** *adj*.

disavow *v formal* to deny knowledge of or responsibility for. ➤ **disavowal** *n*.

disband *v* **1** of a group: to break up and separate. **2** to break up (a group).

disbar *v* (**disbarred, disbarring**) to deprive (a barrister) of the right to practise.

disbelief *n* mental rejection of something as untrue.

disbelieve *v* not to believe or believe in.

disburse *v* to pay out (money), *esp* from a fund. ➤ **disbursement** *n*.

disc (*NAmer* **disk**) *n* **1** a thin flat circular object. **2** a computer disk. **3** a cartilaginous disc between the spinal vertebrae. **4** a gramophone record.

Usage Note: Disc is the correct spelling in British English, except in the context of computers where *disk* is preferred.

discard¹ *v* to get rid of as useless or superfluous.

discard² *n* something discarded, e.g. a playing card.

discern *v* **1** to detect with one of the senses, *esp* to see, often with difficulty. **2** to perceive mentally. ➤ **discernible** *adj*.

discerning *adj* showing insight and understanding. ➤ **discernment** *n*.

discharge¹ *v* **1** to dismiss from employment or service. **2** to release from custody or care. **3** to fulfil (a debt or obligation). **4** to send or pour out (a liquid or gas). **5** to shoot (a firearm).

discharge² *n* **1** the act of discharging. **2** something discharged or emitted.

disciple *n* **1** a person who learns from a teacher or instructor. **2** a follower of Christ during his life on earth, *esp* any of Christ's twelve apostles.

disciplinarian *n* a person who enforces strict discipline.

disciplinary *adj* undertaken to enforce order or correct conduct.

discipline¹ *n* **1** order obtained by enforcing obedience, e.g. in a school or army. **2** self-control. **3** training designed to produce obedience and self-control. **4** a field of study.

discipline² *v* **1** to punish (a person or animal) for the sake of discipline. **2** to train (a person or animal) in obedience and self-control.

disciplined *adj* showing obedience, order, or self-control.

disc jockey *n* a person who plays recorded music on a radio programme or at a nightclub or party.

disclaim *v* to deny or disavow.

disclaimer *n* **1** a denial or repudiation. **2** a denial of legal responsibility.

disclose *v* **1** to make (information) known. **2** to expose to view.

disclosure *n* **1** something disclosed; a revelation. **2** the act of disclosing.

disco *n* (*pl* **-os**) **1** a discotheque. **2** a party with dancing to recorded music. **3** a type of soul-based dance music popular in the 1970s.

discolour (*NAmer* **discolor**) *v* to change, or cause to change, colour for the worse; to stain. ➤ **discoloration** *n*, **discolouration** *n*.

discomfit *v* (**discomfited, discomfiting**) to cause perplexity and embarrassment to. ➤ **discomfiture** *n*.

discomfort[1] *n* mental or physical unease.

discomfort[2] *v* to make uncomfortable or uneasy.

discompose *v formal* to disturb the composure of. ➤ **discomposure** *n*.

disconcert *v* to startle and unsettle; to fluster.

disconnect *v* **1** to break the connection between two things or of something to e.g. a power supply. **2** to cut off the supply of e.g. electricity or the telephone to (a person, etc). **3** to cut (somebody) off during a telephone call. ➤ **disconnection** *n*.

disconsolate *adj* dejected; downcast.

discontent *n* dissatisfaction.

discontented *adj* unhappy; dissatisfied. ➤ **discontentment** *n*.

discontinue *v* (**discontinues, discontinued, discontinuing**) **1** to cease or stop. **2** to cease production of. ➤ **discontinuation** *n*.

discontinuous *adj* lacking continuity; interrupted. ➤ **discontinuity** *n*.

discord *n* **1** lack of agreement or harmony; conflict. **2** a combination of musical sounds that strikes the ear as harsh or unpleasant.

discordant *adj* **1** musically dissonant or unpleasant. **2** disagreeing; at variance.

discotheque *n* a nightclub for dancing to recorded music.

discount[1] *n* **1** a reduction in the price of goods or in the amount payable on a debt, etc. **2** (*used before a noun*) selling or sold at reduced prices.

discount[2] *v* **1** to make a deduction from (a price). **2** to leave out of account as unreliable, unimportant, or irrelevant.

discourage *v* **1** to make less confident or less willing to undertake something. **2** to hinder or deter, *esp* by showing disapproval. ➤ **discouragement** *n*, **discouraging** *adj*.

discourse[1] *n* **1** talk, conversation, or continuous text. **2** a formal speech or piece of writing.

discourse[2] *v literary* (+ on/upon) to express one's ideas in speech or writing.

discourteous *adj* rude or impolite.

discourtesy *n* (*pl* **-ies**) rudeness, incivility, or a rude action.

discover *v* **1** to find by searching or by chance. **2** to be the first to see, find, or know about. **3** to realize or find out.

discovery *n* (*pl* **-ies**) **1** the act of discovering something. **2** somebody or something discovered.

discredit[1] *v* (**discredited, discrediting**) **1** to reject as untrue. **2** to cast doubt on the trustworthiness or reputation of (a person or their ideas, work, etc).

discredit[2] *n* loss of reputation, or a discredited state.

discreditable *adj* bringing discredit or disgrace; shameful.

discreet *adj* **1** careful and reliable, *esp* unlikely to betray secrets. **2** subtle; trying not to attract attention. ➤ **discreetly** *adv*.

discrepancy *n* (*pl* **-ies**) an inconsistency between two accounts, etc.

discrete *adj* individually distinct. ➤ **discretely** *adv*.

discretion *n* **1** the quality of being discreet. **2** the freedom to act as one sees fit.

discretionary *adj* left to or exercised at one's own discretion.

discriminate *v* **1** (+ between) to make a distinction between (two things). **2** (+ against) to treat differently and *esp* unfavourably on the grounds of race, sex, religion, etc.

discriminating *adj* discerning in matters of taste, etc.

discrimination *n* **1** prejudicial treatment, e.g. on the grounds of race or sex. **2** the recognition of the difference between one thing and another. **3** good judgment, *esp* in matters of taste.

discriminatory *adj* showing discrimination, *esp* of an unfavourable kind.

discursive *adj* **1** of a person's writing style, etc: ranging over a variety of topics, often unsystematically. **2** relating to discourse of various kinds.

discus *n* a solid disc, thrown in athletic contests.

discuss *v* **1** to consider (a topic) in speech or writing. **2** to talk about (an issue, problem, etc) so as to make decisions.

discussion *n* **1** a conversation or debate about something. **2** a consideration of a topic in writing.

disdain[1] *n* the feeling one has for something one despises; scorn.

disdain[2] *v* **1** to regard with disdain. **2** to refuse (to do something) because of disdain.

disease *n* a condition that impairs a vital function in a living animal or plant. ➤ **diseased** *adj*.

disembark *v* to alight from a ship, plane, etc. ➤ **disembarkation** *n*.

disembodied *adj* **1** existing apart from the body. **2** coming from an invisible source: *a disembodied voice*.

disembowel *v* (**disembowelled, disembowelling**, *NAmer* **disemboweled, disemboweling**) to remove the entrails of.

disempower *v* (**disempowered, disempowering**) to deprive (a person or group) of initiative or confidence.

disenchant *v* to disillusion. ➤ **disenchanted** *adj*, **disenchantment** *n*.

disenfranchise *v* to deprive of the right to vote.

disengage *v* **1** to release or detach from something that holds or entangles. **2** to remove (troops) from combat areas. ➤ **disengagement** *n*.

disentangle *v* **1** to free from an entanglement. **2** to unravel (tangled wool, string, etc).

disestablish *v* to deprive (*esp* a national Church) of established status.

disfavour (*NAmer* **disfavor**) *n* disapproval or dislike.

disfigure *v* to spoil the appearance of. ➤ **disfigurement** *n*.

disgorge *v* **1** to allow to stream out. **2** to vomit (food) from the stomach. **3** to give up (dishonestly acquired funds).

disgrace[1] *v* to bring reproach or shame to.

disgrace[2] *n* **1** loss of favour, honour, or respect. **2** somebody or something shameful.

disgraceful *adj* shameful or shocking. ➤ **disgracefully** *adv*.

disgruntled *adj* aggrieved and dissatisfied.

disguise[1] *v* **1** to change the appearance of (a person or thing) to conceal their identity. **2** to hide the true state or character of.

disguise[2] *n* **1** a costume or other means of concealing one's identity. **2** the state of being disguised.

disgust[1] *n* a feeling of loathing, revulsion, or moral outrage.

disgust[2] *v* to arouse repugnance or indignation in (somebody). ➤ **disgusted** *adj*, **disgusting** *adj*.

dish *n* **1** a shallow open vessel for holding or serving food. **2** (**the dishes**) the utensils used in preparing and serving a meal. **3** a type of food prepared in a particular way. **4** something resembling a dish in shape. **5** *informal* an attractive person.

disharmony *n* lack of harmony.

dishearten *v* to cause to lose enthusiasm or morale. ➤ **disheartening** *adj*.

dishevelled (*NAmer* **disheveled**) *adj* unkempt or untidy in appearance.

dishonest *adj* not honest, truthful, or sincere. ➤ **dishonesty** *n*.

dishonour[1] (*NAmer* **dishonor**) *n* a state of shame or disgrace.

dishonour[2] (*NAmer* **dishonor**) *v* **1** to treat in a disrespectful manner. **2** to bring shame on. **3** of a bank, etc: to refuse to pay (a cheque, etc).

dishonourable (*NAmer* **dishonorable**) *adj* base or shameful.

dish out *v* **1** to serve out (food) from a dish, pan, etc. **2** *informal* to give (advice, criticism, etc) freely.

dish up *v* **1** to serve (food) onto dishes. **2** to present (facts or information).

dishwasher *n* an electrical machine that washes dishes.

dishwater *n* water used to wash dishes.

dishy *adj* (**-ier, -iest**) *chiefly Brit, informal* very attractive.

disillusion[1] *v* to disappoint (somebody) by revealing the unpleasant truth about somebody or something they admire. ➤ **disillusioned** *adj*.

disillusion[2] *n* the state of being disillusioned.

disincentive *n* something that discourages action or effort.

disinclination *n* unwillingness to do something.

disinclined *adj* unwilling to do something.

disinfect *v* to cleanse (a place, etc) by destroying harmful micro-organisms. ➤ **disinfection** *n*.

disinfectant *n* a chemical that destroys harmful micro-organisms.

disinformation *n* deliberately false or misleading information.

disingenuous *adj* insincere, especially in pretending ignorance of something one knows about.

disinherit *v* (**disinherited, disinheriting**) to deprive (an heir) of the right to inherit.

disintegrate *v* **1** to break into fragments or constituent elements. **2** to lose unity or cohesion.

disinter *v* (**disinterred, disinterring**) to dig up (something buried).

disinterest *n* **1** lack of self-interest; impartiality. **2** *non-standard* lack of interest.

disinterested *adj* **1** free from selfish motives; impartial. **2** *non-standard* uninterested.

Usage Note: Do not use this word to mean 'not interested'; use *uninterested* for this.

disjointed *adj* lacking an orderly sequence; incoherent.

disjunction *n* **1** a lack of coordination; a mismatch. **2** a cleavage or separation.

disk *n* **1** (*Brit also* **disc**) a round plate coated with a magnetic substance for storing computer data. **2** *chiefly NAmer* = DISC.

Usage Note: See note at DISC.

disk drive *n* a device that enables a computer to transfer data to, and retrieve it from, magnetic disks.

diskette *n* a floppy disk.

dislike [1] *n* **1** a feeling of aversion or disapproval. **2** something one dislikes. ✲ **take a dislike to**

dislike [2] *v* to regard with dislike.

dislocate *v* **1** to displace (a bone) from its normal position in a joint. **2** to disrupt the normal order or working of. ➤ **dislocation** *n*.

dislodge *v* to force out of a fixed position.

disloyal *adj* not loyal; unfaithful. ➤ **disloyalty** *n*.

dismal *adj* **1** causing or expressing gloom or sadness. **2** *informal* incompetent. ➤ **dismally** *adv*.

dismantle *v* to take to pieces.

dismay [1] *v* to fill with consternation or sadness.

dismay [2] *n* consternation or sadness.

dismember *v* **1** to cut or tear off the limbs of (a person or animal). **2** to divide up (a territory, etc) into parts. ➤ **dismemberment** *n*.

dismiss *v* **1** to order or allow to leave. **2** to discharge from employment or service. **3** to reject (a suggestion, etc) as unworthy of serious consideration. **4** of a judge: to refuse a further hearing to (a court case). **5** in cricket, to bowl out (a batsman or side). ➤ **dismissal** *n*.

dismissive *adj* of somebody's attitude: disparaging or disdainful. ➤ **dismissively** *adv*.

dismount *v* to get off a horse, bicycle, etc.

disobedient *adj* refusing or failing to obey. ➤ **disobedience** *n*.

disobey *v* to fail to obey (somebody, an order, etc).

disorder *n* **1** lack of order; confusion. **2** breach of the peace or public order. **3** an abnormal physical or mental condition. ➤ **disordered** *adj*.

disorderly *adj* **1** untidy or disarranged. **2** unruly, violent, or disruptive.

disorganized *adj* **1** lacking coherence or system. **2** of a person: unmethodical.

disorientate *v* (*often* **be disorientated**) to confuse by depriving of the normal sense of position and relationship to one's surroundings. ➤ **disorientation** *n*.

disown *v* to repudiate any connection with (a relative, *esp* one's own child, a belief, etc).

disparage *v* to speak slightingly of. ➤ **disparaging** *adj*.

disparate *adj* quite separate and distinct.

disparity *n* (*pl* **-ies**) difference or inequality.

dispassionate *adj* not influenced by strong feeling; impartial. ➤ **dispassionately** *adv*.

dispatch [1] *or* **despatch** *v* **1** to send (a letter, etc) somewhere. **2** to send (personnel) to carry out a particular task. **3** to carry out (a task) rapidly or efficiently. **4** *euphem* to kill.

dispatch [2] *or* **despatch** *n* **1** a message; *esp* a diplomatic or military message. **2** promptness and efficiency. **3** the act of dispatching.

dispel *v* (**dispelled**, **dispelling**) to drive away or disperse (fears, doubts, depression, etc).

dispensable *adj* that can be dispensed with; inessential.

dispensary *n* (*pl* **-ies**) a part of a hospital or chemist's shop where drugs, medical supplies, etc are dispensed.

dispensation *n* **1** an exemption from a law, vow, etc, *esp* one granted by the Roman Catholic Church. **2** the act of dispensing. **3** the religious system prevailing during a particular period.

dispense *v* **1** to distribute in portions. **2** to prepare and give out (drugs, medicine, etc on prescription). **3** to administer (law or justice). **4** (+ with) to get rid of or do without.

disperse *v* **1** to spread or distribute widely. **2** of a crowd, etc: to break up and leave in different directions. **3** to cause (fog, etc) to vanish. ➤ **dispersal** *n*, **dispersion** *n*.

dispirit *v* (**dispirited**, **dispiriting**) to dishearten. ➤ **dispirited** *adj*, **dispiriting** *adj*.

displace *v* **1** to take the place of. **2** to remove or force from its usual or proper place.

displacement *n* **1** the act of displacing. **2** the volume or weight of water displaced by a ship floating in it, used as a measure of the ship's size. **3** the difference between the initial position of a body and any later position.

display [1] *v* **1** to set out or expose to view. **2** of a computer, etc: to show (information) on screen. **3** to demonstrate (a quality).

display [2] *n* **1** a public presentation, e.g. a performance or exhibition. **2** the displaying of something, e.g. the demonstration of a type of behaviour or feeling. **3** ostentation; showing off. **4** an electronic device for presenting data on screen.

displease *v* to annoy or upset.

displeasure *n* disapproval or annoyance.

disport *v archaic* to amuse (oneself) actively; to frolic.

disposable *adj* **1** designed to be used once and then thrown away. **2** of financial resources: available for use.

disposal *n* the act of getting rid of something. ✲ **at one's disposal** available for one's use.

dispose *v* **1** to put (things or personnel) in position. **2** (+ of) to transfer or sell to somebody else. **3** (+ of) to get rid of (rubbish or waste).

disposed *adj* **1** willing to do something. **2** having a particular attitude to somebody or something.

disposition *n* **1** a person's temperament. **2** a tendency or inclination. **3** a particular arrangement of people or things.

dispossess *v* **1** to deprive of possession or occupancy. **2** in football, etc, to deprive (an opponent) of the ball. ➤ **dispossession** *n*.

disproportionate *adj* out of proportion. ➤ **disproportionately** *adv*.

disprove *v* to prove (a statement, etc) to be false.

disputation n debate or argument.

disputatious adj argumentative.

dispute[1] v 1 (often + about) to argue. 2 to call a statement, claim etc) into question. 3 to contest (e.g. a leading position) with somebody. ➤ **disputable** adj.

dispute[2] n a quarrel or disagreement, esp between workers and management.

disqualify v (-ies, -ied) to make or declare unfit or ineligible to do something. ➤ **disqualification** n.

disquiet n anxiety or worry. ➤ **disquieting** adj.

disquisition n a long or elaborate discussion or essay on a subject.

disregard[1] v to pay no attention to.

disregard[2] n lack of attention; neglect.

disrepair n the state of being in need of repair.

disrepute n lack of good reputation or respectability.

disrespect n lack of respect or politeness. ➤ **disrespectful** adj.

disrobe v to undress.

disrupt v 1 to throw into disorder. 2 to interrupt the continuity of (a schedule, etc). ➤ **disruption** n, **disruptive** adj.

dissatisfy v (-ies, -ied) to disappoint or fail to satisfy. ➤ **dissatisfied** adj.

dissect v 1 to cut (an animal or plant) into pieces, esp for scientific examination. 2 to analyse (a literary work, etc) in detail. ➤ **dissection** n.

Usage Note: Note the spelling with -ss-.

dissemble v to conceal facts, intentions, or feelings under some pretence.

disseminate v to spread (ideas, information, etc) about freely or widely. ➤ **dissemination** n.

dissension n disagreement in opinion that makes for discord.

dissent[1] v 1 to differ in opinion. 2 to reject the doctrines of an established Church. 3 in sport: to show disagreement with a referee's verdict. ➤ **dissenter** n.

dissent[2] n disagreement esp with religious doctrine or political policy.

dissertation n a long detailed essay, esp one submitted for a degree, diploma, etc.

disservice n an action which works to somebody's disadvantage.

dissident[1] n a person who rebels against government policy or established opinion. ➤ **dissidence** n.

dissident[2] adj opposed to official policy.

dissimilar adj not similar; unlike. ➤ **dissimilarity** n.

dissimulate v to conceal or disguise one's real feelings or motives. ➤ **dissimulation** n.

dissipate v 1 to dispel or scatter. 2 to use up (money, energy, etc) aimlessly or foolishly.

dissipated adj dissolute; debauched.

dissociate v 1 to declare (oneself) to have no connection with or responsibility for somebody or something. 2 to separate (two ideas) in the mind.

dissolute adj morally unrestrained; debauched.

dissolution n 1 the act of dissolving. 2 the termination of an association or union, esp a marriage. 3 the breaking up of an assembly, etc.

dissolve v 1 to terminate (a partnership, esp a marriage) officially. 2 to break up (an assembly, etc). 3 to cause (a substance) to pass into solution. 4 (usu + into) to be emotionally overcome.

dissonant adj not harmonious; discordant.

dissuade v (+ from) to deter or discourage by persuasion. ➤ **dissuasion** n.

distaff n in spinning, a staff for holding the flax, wool, etc that is to be spun.

distaff side n the female side of a family.

distance[1] n 1 the space between two points or places, or the length of this. 2 a far-off point. 3 wide separation or remoteness. * **go the distance** to keep going until the end of a contest, etc. **keep one's distance** to avoid getting involved.

distance[2] v to keep (oneself) aloof from a situation, etc.

distant adj 1 a certain distance away. 2 remote in space or time. 3 not closely related. 4 reserved or aloof in personal relationships. ➤ **distantly** adv.

distaste n aversion to something.

distasteful adj causing distaste; offensive.

distemper[1] n a viral disease of dogs, with fever and coughing.

distemper[2] n a type of paint used mainly for walls.

distend v to cause (a part of the body, e.g. the belly) to swell from internal pressure. ➤ **distension** n.

distil (NAmer **distill**) v (**distilled, distilling**) 1 to produce (a liquid) in purified form by heating it till it evaporates and then cooling it again. 2 to make (whisky or other spirits) by this method. 3 to extract the essential matter from (previously amassed material). ➤ **distillation** n, **distiller** n.

distillery n (pl -ies) a factory where whisky, etc is distilled.

distinct adj 1 different or separate. 2 readily perceptible to the senses or mind; clear. ➤ **distinctly** adv.

distinction n 1 a difference between things that are similar but not the same. 2 outstanding merit or special talent. 3 the highest level of excellence in passing an exam.

distinguish v 1 (+ between/from) to recognize the difference between (two or more things). 2 to perceive; to make out. 3 of a feature, etc: to serve to identify (a person or thing). 4 to do something to make (oneself) notable. ➤ **distinguishable** adj.

distinguished adj **1** characterized by eminence or excellence. **2** dignified in manner or appearance.

distort v **1** to cause to take on an abnormal shape. **2** to alter the true meaning of (words, a statement, etc). ➤ **distortion** n.

distract v to draw (somebody or their attention) away from the task in hand, etc. ➤ **distracting** adj.

distracted adj **1** not able to concentrate on the matter in hand, etc. **2** crazy; out of one's mind.

distraction n **1** something that distracts one's attention. **2** an amusement or activity.

distraught adj mentally agitated; frantic.

distress[1] n **1** mental or physical anguish. **2** a state of danger or desperate need.

distress[2] v to cause distress to (somebody). ➤ **distressing** adj.

distribute v **1** to divide among a number of recipients. **2** (usu **be distributed**) to scatter over an area. **3** to supply (goods) to retail outlets.

distribution n **1** the act of distributing. **2** the position, arrangement, or frequency of occurrence of things dispersed in space or time.

distributor n **1** a person or company that manages the distribution of goods. **2** an apparatus for directing current to the sparking plugs of an internal-combustion engine.

district n an area or region with a particular character.

distrust[1] n suspicion or lack of trust. ➤ **distrustful** adj.

distrust[2] v to regard as untrustworthy or unreliable.

disturb v **1** to break in upon or interrupt. **2** to alter the position or arrangement of. **3** to destroy the peace of mind or composure of. ➤ **disturbing** adj.

disturbance n **1** the act of disturbing. **2** an interruption. **3** a riot or outbreak of public disorder.

disturbed adj suffering from emotional or mental instability.

disunite v to divide or cause to differ in opinion. ➤ **disunited** adj.

disuse n the state of no longer being used.

ditch[1] n a long narrow excavation for defence, drainage, irrigation, etc.

ditch[2] v **1** of a pilot or aircraft: to make a forced landing on water. **2** informal to get rid of or abandon (a plan, project, etc).

dither v to act nervously or indecisively.

ditto n **1** used to avoid repeating a word: the same. **2** a mark (,, or ") used to indicate repetition usu of the word directly above.

ditty n (pl **-ies**) a short simple song.

diuretic adj of a drug: acting to increase the flow of urine.

diurnal adj occurring during the day or daily.

diva /'deevə/ n (pl **divas**) a principal female opera singer.

divan n **1** a long low couch, usu without arms or back. **2** a bed without a head or foot board.

dive[1] v (past tense and past part. **dived** or NAmer **dove**) **1** to plunge into water headfirst. **2** to swim underwater using breathing equipment. **3** of a submarine: to submerge. **4** of a bird or an aircraft: to descend steeply through the air. **5** to move quickly, esp downwards or under cover.

dive[2] n **1** a headlong plunge into water. **2** a steep descent by an aircraft. **3** informal a disreputable bar or meeting place. **4** a ploy in football in which a player falls over deliberately and pretends to have been fouled.

dive-bomb v to bomb (a place) while making a steep dive towards the target.

diver n **1** a person who dives as a competitive sport or who works or explores underwater. **2** a large fish-eating diving bird.

diverge v **1** to move in different directions from a common point. **2** (often + from) to differ in character or opinion. ➤ **divergence** n, **divergent** adj.

diverse adj **1** different or unlike. **2** varied or assorted.

diversify v (**-ies, -ied**) **1** to make (things) diverse. **2** of a company: to engage in varied types of business or production to reduce risk. ➤ **diversification** n.

diversion n **1** a turning aside from a course or activity. **2** a detour for traffic when the usual route is closed. **3** an amusement or pastime. **4** something that draws the attention away from the main scene of activity. ➤ **diversionary** adj.

diversity n (pl **-ies**) **1** the condition of having differences. **2** a variety or assortment.

divert v **1** to redirect from one course or use to another. **2** to distract. **3** to entertain or amuse (somebody).

divest v **1** (+ of) to dispossess of property, authority, title, etc. **2** (+ of) to rid or free (oneself) of something oppressive.

divide[1] v **1** to separate into parts, branches, groups, etc. **2** to share (something) between recipients. **3** to be what separates (one thing and another). **4** to provoke disagreement between (people, groups, etc). **5** in mathematics, to find out how many times a larger number will contain a smaller one.

divide[2] n a line of division; a split.

dividend n **1** a sum of money to be divided and distributed, esp the part of a company's profits payable to shareholders. **2** an individual shareholder's portion of this. **3** (usu in pl) a reward or benefit.

divider n **1** (in pl) a compasslike instrument used for measuring. **2** a partition used to separate parts of a room.

divination *n* the art of trying to foresee the future, e.g. by using supernatural powers.

divine[1] *adj* **1** of or from God or a god. **2** *informal* delightful or superb. ► **divinely** *adv*.

divine[2] *v* **1** to discover, perceive, or foresee intuitively or by supernatural means. **2** to locate (water or minerals) using a rod. ► **diviner** *n*.

divinity *n* (*pl* **-ies**) **1** the quality or state of being divine. **2** a male or female deity. **3** theology.

divisible *adj* **1** capable of being divided. **2** of a number: that can be divided by another without remainder.

division *n* **1** the act of dividing. **2** a part into which a whole is divided. **3** a major army formation. **4** an administrative or operating unit of an organization. **5** a competitive class or category, e.g. of a football league. **6** a dividing line or partition. **7** disagreement or disunity. ► **divisional** *adj*.

division sign *n* the mathematical symbol (÷) used to indicate division.

divisive *adj* tending to cause disunity or dissension.

divorce[1] *n* the legal dissolution of a marriage.

divorce[2] *v* **1** to end marriage with (one's spouse) by divorce. **2** to dissociate (one thing) from another.

divorcee /divaw'see/ *n* a divorced person.

divot *n* a piece of turf, *esp* one struck out by a golfer making a shot.

divulge *v* to make known or reveal (a confidence or secret).

Diwali /di'wahli/ *or* **Divali** /di'vahli/ *n* the Hindu or Sikh Festival of Lights, celebrating the end of the monsoon.

DIY *n chiefly Brit* amateur repair and building work around the home.

dizzy[1] *adj* (**-ier**, **-iest**) **1** experiencing a whirling sensation in the head and a tendency to lose balance. **2** *informal* foolish or silly. ► **dizzily** *adv*, **dizziness** *n*.

dizzy[2] *v* (**-ies**, **-ied**) to make dizzy; to bewilder.

DJ *n* (*pl* **DJs**) **1** = DISC JOCKEY. **2** = DINNER JACKET.

DNA *n* the material, deoxyribonucleic acid, in the nuclei of cells that makes up genes.

do[1] *v* (**did**, **done**) **1** to effect or perform (an action or activity). **2** to make or provide. **3** to have a particular effect: *A rest will do you good.* **4** to work at for a living or as a course of study. **5** to be adequate or acceptable. **6** to achieve (a particular speed). **7** to serve (a number of years) in prison. ► *v aux* **1** used to form questions and negative statements. **2** used for emphasis: *I do hope you can come.* **3** used as a substitute for a verb already mentioned: *I am earning more than I did last year.* ✳ **do away with** *informal* abolish or kill. **do out of** to deprive of unjustly. **do without** to manage in spite of not having.

have done with to have no further concern with. **to do with** concerned with.

do[2] *n* (*pl* **dos** *or* **do's**) **1** (*usu in pl*) something one ought to do: *dos and don'ts.* **2** *chiefly Brit, informal* a party or festive occasion.

docile *adj* easily led or managed. ► **docility** *n*.

dock[1] *n* an enclosed body of water in a port, where a ship can moor for unloading, repair work, etc.

dock[2] *v* **1** of a ship: to go into a dock. **2** of spacecraft: to join together while in space.

dock[3] *n* the prisoner's enclosure in a criminal court.

dock[4] *v* **1** to cut (an animal's tail) short. **2** to take away (a specified amount) from wages, a score etc.

dock[5] *n* a coarse weed with leaves used to alleviate nettle stings.

docker *n* a person employed in loading and unloading ships.

docket *n* a document recording the contents of a shipment or the payment of customs duties.

dockyard *n* a place where ships are built or repaired.

doctor[1] *n* **1** a person qualified to practise medicine. **2** a holder of the highest academic degree conferred by a university.

doctor[2] *v* (**doctored**, **doctoring**) **1** to give medical treatment to. **2** to adapt, modify, or add to (something), often for a dishonest purpose. **3** *euphem* to castrate or spay (a dog or cat).

doctoral *adj* relating to a doctorate.

doctorate *n* the highest academic degree, awarded by a university for original postgraduate research.

doctrinaire *adj* concerned with abstract theory and ignoring practical considerations.

doctrine *n* a principle, or the set of principles, underlying a branch of knowledge or system of belief. ► **doctrinal** *adj*.

document[1] *n* a written or printed paper, or electronic record, giving information about or proof of something.

document[2] *v* to record (e.g. an event) in detail.

documentary[1] *adj* **1** consisting of documents. **2** presenting or based on factual material.

documentary[2] *n* (*pl* **-ies**) a broadcast or film that presents a factual account of a subject.

documentation *n* documents providing evidence, instructions, support for a claim, etc.

dodder *v* to walk feebly and unsteadily. ► **doddery** *adj*.

doddle *n chiefly Brit, informal* a very easy task.

dodecagon *n* a polygon with twelve angles and twelve sides.

dodecahedron *n* (*pl* **dodecahedrons** *or* **dodecahedra**) a polyhedron with twelve faces.

dodge *v* **1** to shift position suddenly, e.g. to avoid a blow. **2** to evade (a duty, etc) usu in an underhand way.

dodgem n a small electric car designed to be bumped into others as a funfair amusement.

dodgy adj (-ier, -iest) chiefly Brit, informal **1** shady or dishonest. **2** risky or dangerous. **3** liable to collapse or break down.

dodo n (pl -oes or -os) a large extinct flightless bird that formerly lived on Mauritius.

doe n **1** the adult female fallow deer. **2** the adult female of various mammals, e.g. the rabbit.

does v third person sing. present tense of DO[1].

doesn't contraction does not.

doff v to take off (one's hat) as a greeting or sign of respect.

dog[1] n **1** a four-legged flesh-eating domesticated mammal, kept as a pet, for hunting, or to work. **2** a member of the dog family, e.g. a wolf, jackal, or fox. **3** (often used before a noun) a male dog, wolf, fox, etc. * **go to the dogs** informal to decline or deteriorate.

dog[2] v (**dogged, dogging**) **1** to pursue (somebody) closely. **2** of something unwanted: to haunt (somebody).

dog collar n informal a clerical collar.

dog-eared adj **1** of a book: having pages with turned-down corners. **2** worn or shabby.

dog-end n informal a cigarette end.

dogfight n a fight between aircraft, usu at close quarters.

dogfish n (pl **dogfishes** or **dogfish**) a small long-tailed shark.

dogged /'dogid/ adj stubbornly determined. ➤ **doggedly** adv.

doggerel n verse that lacks any poetic quality.

doggo * **lie doggo** to stay quiet and motionless, to avoid detection.

doggy paddle n a simple form of swimming in which the arms paddle and the legs kick.

doghouse n chiefly NAmer a dog kennel. * **in the doghouse** informal in disgrace.

dog in the manger n a person who selfishly deprives others of something he or she does not need.

dogleg n a sharp bend, e.g. in a road.

dogma n a doctrine, or body of doctrines, authoritatively stated by a Church.

dogmatic adj **1** of statements or opinions: insisted on as if authoritative. **2** of a person: inclined to make dogmatic statements. ➤ **dogmatically** adv.

dogsbody n (pl -ies) chiefly Brit, informal a person who carries out routine or menial work for others.

dogtooth n an architectural moulding resembling dog's teeth.

doily n (pl -ies) a small decorative lacy mat, placed under cakes, biscuits, etc on a plate.

do in v informal **1** to kill. **2** to exhaust (somebody).

doings n chiefly Brit, informal a word used to refer to an unspecified fitting, tool, etc.

doldrums pl n * **in the doldrums 1** in a state of depression. **2** of the economy: stagnating.

dole n Brit, informal the government unemployment benefit.

doleful adj sad or mournful. ➤ **dolefully** adv.

dole out v to hand out or distribute.

doll n **1** a child's toy in the form of a human being. **2** informal an attractive person, esp a woman.

dollar n the basic monetary unit of the USA, Canada, Australia, and various other countries.

dollop[1] n a soft shapeless blob, esp of food.

dollop[2] v (**dolloped, dolloping**) (+ out) to serve out (food) carelessly or clumsily.

dolour (NAmer **dolor**) n mental suffering or anguish.

dolphin n a small whale with its snout elongated into a beak.

dolphinarium n (pl **dolphinariums** or **dolphinaria**) an establishment where dolphins perform in public in a large pool.

dolt n an extremely stupid person.

domain n **1** a territory over which control is exercised. **2** a sphere of influence or activity. **3** a group of Internet addresses with the same suffix.

dome n **1** a hemispherical roof or vault. **2** a dome-shaped structure or building with a dome-shaped roof.

domestic adj **1** of, for, or devoted to the home or the family. **2** of one's own country; not foreign. **3** of an animal: tame, or bred by human beings for a specific purpose, e.g. food or hunting. ➤ **domestically** adv.

domesticate v to bring (an animal) under human control, e.g. for carrying loads, hunting, or food. ➤ **domestication** n.

domesticity n home or family life.

domicile[1] n a home; esp a person's permanent home for legal purposes.

domicile[2] v (be **domiciled**) to live in a particular country or place.

dominant adj **1** controlling or prevailing over all others. **2** of a position: commanding a view from a superior height. ➤ **dominance** n.

dominate v **1** to exert controlling influence or power over. **2** to overlook from a superior height. ➤ **domination** n.

domineer v to exercise arbitrary or overbearing control. ➤ **domineering** adj.

dominion n **1** the power or right to rule. **2** the territory of a ruler. **3** (often **Dominion**) a self-governing nation of the British Commonwealth.

domino n (pl -oes or -os) **1** a flat rectangular block with a face divided into two equal parts that are either blank or bear from one to six dots. **2** (in pl) a game played with a set of 28 dominoes.

don[1] n a university teacher, esp at Oxford or Cambridge.

don² v (**donned, donning**) to put on (an item of clothing).

donate v 1 to make a gift of (money, etc), esp to a charitable cause. 2 to give (blood, semen, organs, etc) for use in the medical treatment of others.

donation n something donated, esp money.

done¹ v past part. of DO¹.

done² adj 1 completed. 2 of food: cooked sufficiently. 3 physically exhausted. 4 socially acceptable or expected.

done³ interj used when accepting a deal or bet.

doner kebab /'dohnə, 'donə/ n slices of spiced lamb cut from a large block grilled on a spit.

donkey n (pl -**eys**) a domesticated animal of the horse family with long ears.

donkey jacket n a thick hip-length jacket and with a strip of leather or plastic across the shoulders.

donkey's years pl n chiefly Brit, informal a very long time.

donor n a person who donates something.

don't contraction do not.

donut n NAmer a doughnut.

doodle¹ v to draw in a bored or aimless manner.

doodle² n an aimless scribble or sketch.

doom¹ n an unhappy, terrible, or unavoidable fate.

doom² v to cause to fail or be ruined.

doomsday n the end of the world, or some remote point in the future.

door n a hinged or sliding panel closing the entrance to a building, room, or vehicle. * **out of doors** in or into the open air.

doorman n (pl **doormen**) an employee who stands at the entrance to a hotel, theatre, etc to assist people going in or out.

doormat n 1 a mat placed at a doorway for wiping dirt from shoes. 2 informal a very submissive person.

doorstep n a step in front of an outer door.

doorstop n a device for holding a door open.

dope¹ n 1 a drug given illegally to a racehorse, greyhound, etc to make it run faster or slower. 2 slang marijuana, opium, or another illegal drug. 3 informal a stupid person.

dope² v to administer an illegal or narcotic drug to.

dopey or **dopy** adj (-**ier**, -**iest**) 1 sleepy or drugged. 2 informal stupid.

doppelgänger /'doplgengə, -gangə/ n a ghostly counterpart of a living person.

Doppler effect n a change in the apparent frequency of sound or light waves when the source and the observer move closer together or farther apart.

dorm n informal = DORMITORY 1.

dormant adj 1 asleep or inactive, e.g. during hibernation. 2 temporarily showing no signs of activity or growth.

dormer or **dormer window** n a window set vertically in a sloping roof.

dormitory n (pl -**ies**) 1 a large room containing a number of beds. 2 (often used before a noun) a residential community whose inhabitants commute to their places of work.

dormouse n (pl **dormice**) a small rodent that resembles a mouse with a long bushy tail.

dorsal adj relating to the back or top surface: compare VENTRAL.

dose¹ n 1 a measured quantity of medicine to be taken at one time. 2 a quantity of radiation administered or absorbed.

dose² v to give a dose of medicine to.

dosh n Brit, informal money.

doss v chiefly Brit, informal 1 (often + down) to sleep rough or in a makeshift bed. 2 to be lazy or a shirker.

dossier /'dosi-ə, 'dosiay/ n a file of papers containing a detailed report or information.

dot¹ n a small round spot or mark. * **on the dot** exactly; precisely. **the year dot** Brit, informal a very long time ago.

dot² v (**dotted, dotting**) 1 to mark with a dot or dots. 2 to scatter marks, objects, etc at random over (an area).

dotage n a period of mental decline in old age.

dotcom n a company that operates exclusively or mainly on the Internet.

dote v (+ on/upon) to show great or excessive fondness for. ▶ **doting** adj.

dotty adj (-**ier**, -**iest**) informal eccentric, crazy, or absurd, often in an endearing way.

double¹ adj 1 consisting of two similar parts. 2 of twice the usual size, quantity, etc. 3 designed for two people. 4 having two interpretations; ambiguous. ▶ **doubly** adv.

double² n 1 something twice the usual amount, number, size, etc. 2 somebody who closely resembles another person. 3 somebody who replaces an actor in scenes calling for special skills. * **at the double** very quickly.

double³ adv to twice the extent or amount.

double⁴ v 1 to make or become twice as much or as many. 2 to fold into two thicknesses. 3 (+ up/over) to bend over, e.g. in pain or laughter. 4 (+ back) to turn back on one's course. 5 (+ as) to serve the additional purpose of. 6 (+ for) to be a stand-in or substitute for.

double agent n a spy pretending to serve one government while actually serving another.

double-barrelled adj 1 of a firearm: having two barrels. 2 of a surname: having two parts.

double bass n the largest and lowest-pitched instrument of the violin family.

double bed n a bed for two people.

double-breasted adj of a coat, jacket, etc: having a large overlapping front, usu with two sets of buttons and buttonholes.

double chin n a chin with a fleshy fold under it.

double cream *n* thick heavy cream containing a high proportion of fat.

double-cross *v* to betray or cheat while pretending to help.

double-dealing *n* underhand or deceitful action. ➤ **double-dealer** *n*.

double-decker *n* something with two levels or layers, *esp* a bus with two floors.

double Dutch *n informal* unintelligible or nonsensical language.

double entendre /,doohbl on'ton(h)dr/ *n* (pl **double entendres** /,doohbl on'ton(h)dr/) an ambiguous expression, one of whose meanings is usu risqué.

double figures *pl n* the numbers from 10 to 99.

double glazing *n* windows having two panes of glass separated by an air space. ➤ **double-glaze** *v.*

double jeopardy *n* the act of prosecuting a person for the same offence twice.

double-jointed *adj* of a person: having exceptionally flexible joints.

doubles *pl n* a game between two pairs of players, e.g. in tennis.

double standard *n* an *esp* moral principle applied more rigorously to one group than another.

doublet *n* a man's close-fitting jacket of the 15th to 17th cents.

double take *n* a delayed reaction to a surprising situation.

doubloon *n* a former Spanish gold coin.

doubt[1] *v* **1** to be uncertain about; to feel inclined to disbelieve. **2** to consider unlikely.

doubt[2] *n* **1** uncertainty. **2** an inclination not to believe something. ✳ **no doubt** certainly; probably.

doubtful *adj* **1** causing doubt; open to question. **2** uncertain; unconvinced. **3** unlikely. **4** of questionable worth or honesty. ➤ **doubtfully** *adv.*

doubtless *adv* **1** without doubt; certainly. **2** probably.

douche /doohsh/ *n* a jet of fluid, directed on or into part of the body, *esp* the vagina.

dough *n* **1** a stiff mixture of flour and liquid used to make bread, pastry, etc. **2** *informal* money.

doughnut (*NAmer also* **donut**) *n* a small round or ring-shaped cake of deep-fried yeast dough.

doughty /'dowti/ *adj* (**-ier, -iest**) *chiefly literary or humorous* bold and resolute.

do up *v* **1** to wrap or fasten. **2** *informal* to repair or refurbish.

dour /dooə, 'dowə/ *adj* **1** stern or harsh. **2** gloomy; sullen.

douse *or* **dowse** *v* **1** to drench with liquid. **2** to extinguish (a flame, light, etc).

dove[1] /duv/ *n* **1** a bird similar to but smaller than the domestic pigeon. **2** an advocate of peace, negotiation, or compromise.

dove[2] /dohv/ *v NAmer* past tense of DIVE[1].

dovecot *or* **dovecote** *n* a structure with nesting compartments for domestic pigeons.

dovetail[1] *n* a joint formed by fitting a wedge-shaped projection into a similarly shaped cavity.

dovetail[2] *v* **1** to join (wood) by means of dovetails. **2** to fit together neatly or conveniently.

dowager *n* **1** a widow holding property or a title from her deceased husband. **2** a dignified elderly woman.

dowdy *adj* (**-ier, -iest**) old-fashioned or dull in appearance, clothing etc.

dowel *n* a wooden or metal pin used to hold components together.

down[1] *adv* **1** at or towards a relatively low level. **2** in or into a lying or sitting position. **3** *chiefly Brit* away from the capital of a country or a university city. **4** southwards. **5** in or into a relatively worse condition. **6** into a state of relatively low intensity, heat, volume, etc. **7** to a lower amount, price, figure, or rank. **8** in writing. **9** from an earlier time.

down[2] *adj* **1** directed or going downwards. **2** depressed; dejected. **3** of a computer system: temporarily out of action. ✳ **down to 1** attributed to. **2** the responsibility of.

down[3] *prep* **1** in a downward direction along, through, etc. **2** at or to a position further along. **3** *Brit, informal* to; at: *I'm going down the shops.*

down[4] *v informal* to drink or swallow quickly.

down[5] *n* fine soft feathers or hairs.

down[6] *n* (*usu in pl*) a rounded ridge or hill, *esp* in southern England.

down-and-out *adj* destitute and homeless.

downbeat *adj* **1** pessimistic; gloomy. **2** relaxed; informal.

downcast *adj* **1** dejected or depressed. **2** directed downwards.

downer *n* **1** *informal* a depressing experience or situation. **2** *slang* a depressant drug.

downfall *n* a sudden loss of power or status.

downgrade *v* to lower in rank or importance.

downhearted *adj* discouraged or dejected.

downhill[1] *adv* towards the bottom of a hill or slope. ✳ **go downhill** to decline or deteriorate.

downhill[2] *adj* going or sloping downhill.

download *v* to transfer (programs or data) from one computer to another.

down-market *adj* designed to appeal to less wealthy or sophisticated consumers.

down payment *n* an initial payment for something bought on credit.

downplay *v* to treat as being less significant than it is.

downpour *n* a heavy fall of rain.

downright[1] *adv* thoroughly; altogether.

downright[2] *adj* **1** absolute; thorough. **2** plain or blunt.

downriver *adv and adj* towards the mouth of a river.

downside *n* a drawback or undesirable feature.

Down's syndrome *n* a chromosomal disorder causing intellectual impairment and distinctive physical characteristics.

downstairs *adv and adj* on or to a lower floor.

downstream *adv and adj* in the direction of the flow of a stream.

down-to-earth *adj* practical or realistic.

downtown *adv and adj chiefly NAmer* of, to, or in the central part of a town or city.

downtrodden *adj* oppressed by those in power.

down under *adv informal* in or to Australia or New Zealand.

downward *adj* moving or extending downwards.

downwards *adv* from a higher to a lower place or level.

downwind *adv and adj* in the direction towards which the wind is blowing.

downy *adj* (-ier, -iest) covered in soft fluffy feathers or fine hairs.

dowry *n* (pl -ies) the money or property that a woman brings to her husband in marriage.

dowse[1] *v* to search for hidden water or minerals with a divining rod.

dowse[2] *v* see DOUSE.

doyen *or* **doyenne** *n* the most experienced or highly respected member of a group.

doze[1] *v* to sleep lightly.

doze[2] *n* a short light sleep.

dozen *n* (pl **dozens** *or* **dozen**) 1 a group of twelve. 2 (in pl) an indefinitely large number. * **talk nineteen to the dozen** *Brit* to talk non-stop and very quickly.

DPhil *abbr* Doctor of Philosophy.

Dr *abbr* doctor.

drab *adj* (**drabber, drabbest**) 1 dull or cheerless. 2 of a dull brown or grey colour.

draconian *adj* of laws, measures, etc: extremely severe.

draft[1] *n* 1 a preliminary sketch or version. 2 (used before a noun) constituting a preliminary version or sketch. 3 an order for the payment of money drawn by one person or bank on another. 4 chiefly NAmer conscription for military service.

draft[2] *v* 1 to produce a draft of (a letter, design, etc). 2 to select for a particular job or purpose. 3 NAmer to conscript for military service.

drag[1] *v* (**dragged, dragging**) 1 to pull along slowly or with difficulty. 2 to cause to trail along a surface. 3 to move (e.g. an icon) across a computer screen. 4 to search (a body of water) with a large net or hook. 5 to pass or proceed laboriously or tediously. 6 informal (+ on) to draw smoke from (a cigarette, pipe, etc) into the mouth. * **drag one's feet/heels** to act in a deliberately slow manner.

drag[2] *n* 1 the retarding force acting on a body moving through air, water, etc. 2 informal an inhalation of cigarette, pipe, or cigar smoke. 3 informal women's clothing worn by a man. 4 informal a dull or boring person or experience.

dragnet *n* a net drawn along the bottom of a body of water or the ground to catch fish or small game.

dragon *n* a mythical monster usu represented as a winged, fire-breathing reptile.

dragonfly *n* (pl -ies) a long slender-bodied insect with two pairs of delicate wings.

dragoon[1] *n* a soldier belonging to a cavalry unit.

dragoon[2] *v* to force to do something.

drag out *v* to prolong unduly.

drag race *n* an acceleration contest between cars over a short course. ➤ **drag racing** *n*.

drain[1] *v* 1 to draw off (liquid) gradually. 2 of liquid: to flow off gradually. 3 to empty by allowing liquid to drain away. 4 to empty (e.g. a glass) by drinking the contents. 5 to exhaust physically or emotionally.

drain[2] *n* 1 a pipe or other means by which liquid is drained away. 2 something that uses up energy or resources. * **go down the drain** to be wasted.

drainage *n* 1 the process of draining. 2 a system of drains.

draining board *n Brit* a slightly sloping surface beside a sink, on which washed dishes are placed to drain.

drainpipe *n* a pipe that carries rainwater from a roof.

drake *n* a male duck.

dram *n chiefly Scot* a tot of spirits, usu whisky.

drama *n* 1 a play. 2 plays collectively or as a genre. 3 an exciting or emotionally charged situation.

dramatic *adj* 1 characteristic of drama or acting. 2 vivid or exciting. 3 striking in appearance or effect. ➤ **dramatically** *adv*.

dramatics *pl n* the study or practice of acting and stage management.

dramatist *n* a writer of plays.

dramatize *or* **-ise** *v* 1 to adapt (e.g. a novel) for performance by actors. 2 to exaggerate the seriousness, excitement, etc of. ➤ **dramatization** *n*.

drank *v* past tense of DRINK[1].

drape[1] *v* 1 to cover with cloth or clothing hanging in loose folds. 2 to place (oneself, one's arm, etc) casually on, over, or around something.

drape[2] *n* 1 a piece of drapery. 2 chiefly NAmer (usu in pl) a curtain.

draper *n chiefly Brit, dated* a person who sells fabrics and haberdashery.

drapery *n* (pl -ies) cloth, clothing, etc arranged in loose folds.

drastic adj radical in effect; severe. ➤ **drastically** adv.

draught[1] (NAmer **draft**) n **1** a current of air in an enclosed space. **2** an act of drinking or inhaling, or a portion drunk or inhaled. **3** the act of drawing liquid, e.g. from a cask. **4** the depth of water a vessel requires to float in.

draught[2] (NAmer **draft**) adj **1** of an animal: used for drawing loads. **2** of beer or cider: served from the barrel.

draughts pl n Brit a board game for two players each of whom moves twelve disc-shaped pieces across a chessboard.

draughtsman or **draughtswoman** (NAmer **draftsman** or **draftswoman**) n (pl **draughtsmen** or **draughtswomen**) **1** a person who draws technical plans and sketches. **2** an artist skilled in drawing.

draughty (NAmer **drafty**) adj (-ier, -iest) of a room, house, etc: having cold draughts blowing through it.

draw[1] v (**drew, drawn**) **1** to produce (a picture, diagram, portrait, etc) by making lines on a surface. **2** to pull or haul (a vehicle, etc). **3** to move (somebody) in a particular direction. **4** to pull (curtains) to an open or closed position. **5** (often + out) to bring out of a container, sheath, etc. **6** to take in (a breath). **7** to attract: to draw the crowds. **8** to bring about (a response): drew gasps from the crowd. **9** to reach (a conclusion). **10** to receive (a salary). **11** (often + out) to take (money) from a bank account. **12** to select, often at random, from among things offered. **13** to have equal scores at the end of (a game). **14** to come or go steadily. ✳ **draw on/upon** to use as a source of supply. **draw the line** to fix a limit for an activity.

draw[2] n **1** a random process of choosing, e.g. in a lottery or raffle, or in organizing a sports competition. **2** a contest that ends with the scores even. **3** something that attracts public attention or a large audience. **4** a sucking action on something held between the lips, e.g. a pipe.

drawback n an undesirable feature; a disadvantage.

drawbridge n a bridge that can be raised or let down, e.g. over a castle moat.

drawer n **1** /draw/ an open-topped storage box that slides out of a piece of furniture. **2** /'draw-ə/ somebody who draws something. **3** /draw-ə/ the person who writes a cheque. **4** /drawz/ dated or humorous (in pl) knickers or underpants.

draw in v of successive days: to grow shorter.

drawing n a representation of something in lines made with pencil, crayon, etc.

drawing pin n Brit a pin with a broad flat head used esp to fasten sheets of paper to boards.

drawing room n a formal reception room.

drawl[1] v to speak slowly or lazily with prolonged vowels.

drawl[2] n a drawling manner of speaking.

drawn[1] v past part. of DRAW[1].

drawn[2] adj **1** looking strained, tired, or ill. **2** of a game, competition, etc: ended in a draw.

draw on v to approach.

draw out v **1** to extend (a process) beyond its normal duration. **2** to encourage (somebody) to speak freely. **3** of successive days: to grow longer.

drawstring n a string or tape that can be pulled to close a bag, tighten clothes, etc.

draw up v **1** to prepare (a document or proposal). **2** to come to a halt.

dray n a strong low cart, used esp by brewers.

dread[1] v **1** to be extremely apprehensive about. **2** to fear greatly.

dread[2] n great fear or apprehension.

dreadful adj **1** extremely unpleasant or shocking. **2** very disagreeable. **3** extreme. ➤ **dreadfully** adv.

dreadlocks pl n long plaited or tightly curled locks of hair worn esp by male Rastafarians.

dream[1] n **1** a series of images or emotions occurring during sleep. **2** a state of absentmindedness. **3** a strongly desired goal; an ambition. **4** something especially beautiful, excellent, etc. **5** (used before a noun) perfect.

dream[2] v (past tense and past part. **dreamed** or **dreamt** /dremt/) **1** to have a dream. **2** to indulge in daydreams or fantasies. **3** to consider as a possibility; to imagine. ➤ **dreamer** n.

dream up v informal to devise or invent.

dreamy adj (-ier, -iest) **1** given to daydreaming or fantasy. **2** suggestive of a dream. **3** informal very pleasing or attractive. ➤ **dreamily** adv.

dreary adj (-ier, -iest) causing feelings of cheerlessness or gloom; dull. ➤ **drearily** adv, **dreariness** n.

dredge[1] n a machine for removing earth, mud, etc, esp from the bottom of a waterway.

dredge[2] v **1** (often + up/out). **2** to deepen (e.g. a waterway) with a dredge. **3** informal (+ up) to bring to light by thorough searching. ➤ **dredger** n.

dregs pl n **1** sediment contained in or deposited by a liquid. **2** the most undesirable part.

drench v to make thoroughly wet.

dress[1] v **1** to put clothes on (oneself or somebody else). **2** to put on clothing. **3** to choose or wear one's clothes in a particular way or for a particular purpose. **4** to make more attractive by decorating, arranging, grooming, etc. **5** to apply dressings or medicaments to (e.g. a wound). **6** to prepare (food) for cooking or eating.

dress[2] n **1** a woman's one-piece outer garment including both top and skirt. **2** clothing, esp garments suitable for a particular occasion or time.

dressage /'dresahzh/ *n* the performance by a trained horse of precise movements in response to its rider.

dress circle *n* the first or lowest curved tier of seats in a theatre.

dress down *v* **1** to reprove severely. **2** to wear informal clothes. ➤ **dressing down** *n*.

dresser *n* a sideboard with a high back with open shelves for holding dishes.

dressing *n* **1** a usu cold sauce for adding to food, *esp* salads. **2** material applied to cover a wound, sore, etc.

dressing gown *n* a loose robe worn *esp* over nightclothes.

dressing room *n* a room used chiefly for dressing, *esp* for changing costumes in a theatre.

dressing table *n* a table with drawers and a mirror for use while applying make-up, combing one's hair, etc.

dressmaker *n* a person who makes clothes for female clients. ➤ **dressmaking** *n*.

dress rehearsal *n* a full rehearsal in costume and under performance conditions shortly before the first performance of a play, etc.

dress up *v* to dress in formal or smart clothes or in a particular costume.

dressy *adj* (**-ier**, **-iest**) of clothes: stylish, smart, or formal.

drew *v* past tense of DRAW[1].

dribble[1] *v* **1** to fall or flow in drops or in a thin stream. **2** to let saliva trickle from the mouth. **3** in football, hockey, basketball, etc, to propel (a ball) by successive slight taps or bounces.

dribble[2] *n* **1** a small trickling flow. **2** an act of dribbling in sport.

dribs and drabs *pl n informal* small usu scattered amounts.

dried *v* past tense and past part. of DRY[2].

drier[1] or **dryer** *n* a machine for drying something.

drier[2] *adj* compar of DRY[1].

drift[1] *v* **1** to be carried along by a current of water or air. **2** to move in an aimless or casual way. **3** of snow, leaves, etc: to pile up under the force of wind.

drift[2] *n* **1** the motion of drifting. **2** a gradual shift in attitude. **3** a mass of snow, leaves, etc deposited by wind. **4** a general underlying meaning.

drifter *n* somebody who travels about aimlessly.

driftwood *n* wood floating on water or cast up on a beach.

drill[1] *v* **1** to make (a hole) with a drill. **2** to drill a hole in. **3** to fix in somebody's mind by repetitive instruction. **4** to train in military drill.

drill[2] *n* **1** a boring tool for making a hole in a solid substance. **2** military training in marching, the handling of arms, etc. **3** an exercise to improve skill by regular practice. **4** *chiefly Brit, informal* the approved or correct procedure.

drily or **dryly** *adv* in a subtly ironic way.

drink[1] *v* (**drank, drunk**) **1** to swallow (a liquid), usu for refreshment or nourishment. **2** to drink alcohol, *esp* habitually or to excess. **3** (+ in) to take in avidly. ✳ **drink to** to drink a toast to. ➤ **drinkable** *adj*, **drinker** *n*.

drink[2] *n* **1** liquid suitable for drinking. **2** alcoholic drink. **3** a portion of liquid for drinking.

drink-driving *n Brit* the crime of driving a vehicle while under the influence of alcohol. ➤ **drink-driver** *n*.

drip[1] *v* (**dripped, dripping**) to let (liquid) fall in drops.

drip[2] *n* **1** a drop of liquid. **2** the act of falling in drops. **3** a device used to administer drugs or nutrients in solution slowly into a vein. **4** *informal* a weak or insipid person.

drip-feed *v* to put liquid into gradually.

dripping[1] *n* the fat that runs out from meat during roasting.

dripping[2] *adj* extremely wet.

drive[1] *v* (**drove, driven**) **1** to direct the course of (a vehicle). **2** to transport in a vehicle. **3** to propel by physical force. **4** to apply pressure on (somebody) to act in a certain way. **5** to provide the motive power for (a machine or engine). ✳ **be driving at** to be implying or suggesting. ➤ **driver** *n*.

drive[2] *n* **1** a journey or trip in a car. **2** a private road giving access to a building, *esp* a private house. **3** a motivating instinctual need. **4** great zeal in pursuing one's ends. **5** a campaign. **6** a powerful shot in golf, cricket, etc.

drivel *n* foolish or childish nonsense.

drizzle[1] *v* **1** to rain in small drops or very lightly. **2** to let (liquid) fall in minute drops.

drizzle[2] *n* a fine misty rain.

droll *adj* amusing, *esp* in an odd way.

dromedary *n* (*pl* **-ies**) a one-humped camel.

drone[1] *n* **1** a male bee whose sole function is to mate with the queen. **2** a remote-controlled aircraft, missile, or ship. **3** a droning sound.

drone[2] *v* **1** to make a deep murmuring or buzzing sound. **2** (*often* + on) to talk persistently and tediously.

drool *v* **1** to let saliva dribble from the mouth. **2** (*often* + over) to make an effusive show of pleasure.

droop[1] *v* **1** to hang or bend downwards. **2** to become tired or depressed.

droop[2] *n* the condition or appearance of drooping. ➤ **droopy** *adj*.

drop[1] *n* **1** a round or pear-shaped mass of falling liquid. **2** a minute quantity, *esp* of liquid. **3** a small globular sweet. **4** a fall, decrease, or decline. **5** a parachute descent, or the things dropped by parachute. ✳ **at the drop of a hat** without hesitation; promptly.

drop² v (**dropped, dropping**) **1** to fall or cause to fall vertically. **2** to fall in a state of collapse. **3** to become weaker or less. **4** to give up or abandon (an idea, accusation, friendship, etc). **5** to leave out of a team, etc. **6** to set down (passengers or cargo) from a vehicle, ship, etc. **7** to lose (a point or game) in a series.

drop kick n a kick made, e.g. in rugby, by dropping a ball and kicking it as it rebounds.

droplet n a small drop of liquid.

drop off v **1** to fall asleep, esp unintentionally. **2** to become less.

dropout n **1** somebody who withdraws from conventional society. **2** a student who fails to complete a course.

drop out v **1** to withdraw from an activity. **2** to adopt an alternative lifestyle.

droppings pl n animal excrement.

dross n waste or rubbish. ➤ **drossy** adj.

drought /drowt/ n a prolonged period with little or no rainfall.

drove¹ n **1** a group of animals moving together. **2** (also in pl) a crowd of people moving together.

drove² v past tense of DRIVE¹.

drown v **1** to die or cause to die through suffocation by submersion in water. **2** to submerge, esp by a rise in the water level. **3** (often + out) to cause (a sound) not to be heard by making a loud noise.

drowsy adj (**-ier, -iest**) sleepy. ➤ **drowsily** adv, **drowsiness** n.

drub v (**drubbed, drubbing**) **1** to beat severely. **2** to defeat decisively. ➤ **drubbing** n.

drudge n a person who does hard, menial, or monotonous work.

drudgery n hard, menial, or monotonous work.

drug¹ n **1** a substance intended for the treatment or prevention of disease. **2** a substance that has a particular effect on the body, e.g. a stimulant. **3** something that causes addiction.

drug² v (**drugged, drugging**) to administer a drug to.

drugstore n chiefly NAmer a pharmacy, esp one that also sells refreshments and other goods.

druid n (often **Druid**) a member of an ancient Celtic order of priests.

drum¹ n **1** a hollow cylindrical percussion instrument that is played by beating with sticks or the hands. **2** the sound made by striking a drum, or any similar sound. **3** a cylindrical container or mechanical part.

drum² v (**drummed, drumming**) **1** to beat a drum. **2** to throb or sound rhythmically. **3** (usu + into) to instil (an idea or lesson) by constant repetition.

drum and bass n a type of modern dance music characterized by insistent drum beats and low bass lines.

drumstick n **1** a stick for beating a drum. **2** a fowl's leg between the thigh and foot when cooked.

drunk¹ v past part. of DRINK¹.

drunk² adj under the influence of alcohol.

drunk³ n a person who is drunk, esp habitually.

drupe n a fruit, e.g. a cherry or plum, with a stone enclosed by a fleshy layer.

dry¹ adj (**drier** or **dryer, driest** or **dryest**) **1** not or no longer wet. **2** of wine, etc: not sweet. **3** uninteresting. **4** marked by a matter-of-fact, ironic, or terse manner of expression. ➤ **dryness** n.

dry² v (**-ies, -ied**) **1** to make or become dry. **2** to preserve by removing moisture.

dry-clean v to clean (a fabric, garment, etc) with organic solvents rather than water. ➤ **dry cleaner** n, **dry cleaning** n.

dryer n see DRIER¹.

dry ice n solidified carbon dioxide used esp to produce the theatrical effect of white mist.

dryly adv see DRILY.

dry rot n a decay of seasoned timber caused by fungi.

dry run n a rehearsal or trial.

drystone adj of a wall: constructed of stone without the use of mortar.

dry up v of a supply: to dwindle and stop.

dual adj **1** consisting of two parts or elements. **2** having a double nature. ➤ **duality** n.

dual carriageway n chiefly Brit a road that has traffic travelling in two or more, usu separated lanes in each direction.

dualism n **1** the state of being dual. **2** a theory that considers reality to consist of two independent and contrasting principles, e.g. mind and matter. ➤ **dualist** n, **dualistic** adj.

dub¹ v (**dubbed, dubbing**) **1** to call by an unofficial name or nickname. **2** to confer knighthood on, esp by ceremonial touching on the shoulder with a sword.

dub² v **1** to provide (a film, television broadcast, etc) with a new soundtrack, esp in a different language. **2** (often + in) to add (sound effects, music, etc) to a film or broadcast. ➤ **dubbing** n.

dubbin n a grease used for softening and waterproofing leather.

dubious adj **1** doubtful; uncertain. **2** of questionable quality or origin. ➤ **dubiously** adv.

ducal adj of a duke or duchy.

ducat n a gold coin formerly used in many European countries.

duchess n **1** the wife or widow of a duke. **2** a woman having the rank of a duke.

duchy n (pl **-ies**) the territory of a duke or duchess.

duck¹ n (pl **ducks** or **duck**) **1** a swimming bird with a short neck, short legs, webbed feet, and a broad flat beak. **2** a female duck: compare DRAKE.

duck² v **1** to lower one's head or body suddenly, e.g. to avoid being seen or hit. **2** to thrust momentarily under water. **3** to evade (a duty, question, responsibility, etc).

duck³ n a score of nought, esp in cricket.

duck-billed platypus = PLATYPUS.

duckboard n (usu in pl) a wooden board used to make a path over muddy ground.

duckling n a young duck.

duct n **1** a pipe or channel that carries air, power lines, telephone cables, etc. **2** a bodily tube that carries a glandular secretion.

ductile adj of metals: capable of being drawn out or hammered thin.

dud¹ n informal **1** something that fails to perform as it should. **2** (in pl) clothes.

dud² adj informal ineffectual.

dude n chiefly NAmer, informal a man.

dudgeon n ✱ **in high dudgeon** in a state of great indignation.

due¹ adj **1** owed or owing as a debt. **2** owed or owing as a natural or moral right. **3** proper or appropriate. **4** expected in the prearranged or normal course of events. ✱ **due to 1** ascribable to. **2** because of. **in due course** after a normal passage of time.

due² n **1** something that rightfully belongs to somebody. **2** (in pl) fees; charges. ✱ **give somebody their due** to give somebody the credit they deserve.

due³ adv directly or exactly.

duel¹ n **1** a formal combat with weapons fought between two people to settle a quarrel or point of honour. **2** a conflict between usu evenly matched people, ideas, or forces.

duel² v (**duelled, duelling,** NAmer **dueled, dueling**) to fight a duel.

duet n **1** a composition for two performers. **2** a performance by two musicians, singers, dancers, etc.

duff adj Brit, informal not working; useless.

duffel bag n a cylindrical canvas bag closed by a drawstring.

duffel coat n a hooded coat made of heavy woollen material, usu fastened with toggles.

duffer n informal an incompetent or clumsy person.

dug¹ v past tense and past part. of DIG¹.

dug² n an udder, teat or nipple.

dugout n **1** a boat made by hollowing out a log. **2** a shelter dug in the ground, esp for troops. **3** a shelter at the side of a sports ground where trainers, substitutes, etc sit.

duke n **1** a member of the highest rank of the British peerage. **2** a sovereign ruler of a European duchy. ➤ **dukedom** n.

dulcet adj of sounds: sweetly pleasant or soothing.

dulcimer /'dulsimə/ n a musical instrument played by striking its strings with light hammers.

dull¹ adj **1** boring or uninteresting. **2** cloudy or overcast. **3** lacking brightness or intensity. **4** slow in perception or understanding. ➤ **dullness** n, **dully** adv.

dull² v to make or become dull.

dullard n a stupid or insensitive person.

duly adv in a due manner, time, or degree; properly.

dumb adj **1** lacking the power of speech; mute. **2** unwilling or temporarily unable to speak. **3** chiefly NAmer, informal stupid. ➤ **dumbly** adv.

dumbbell n a short bar with adjustable weights at each end used for weight training.

dumb down v informal to make less intellectually challenging.

dumbfound v to amaze.

dumbstruck adj too astonished to speak.

dumb waiter n a small lift for conveying food and dishes from the kitchen to the dining area of a restaurant.

dumdum n a bullet that expands on impact and inflicts a severe wound.

dummy n (pl **-ies**) **1** an imitation or copy of something used as a substitute, for demonstration purposes, etc. **2** a model of the human body used e.g. for fitting or displaying clothes. **3** chiefly Brit a rubber or plastic teat given to babies to suck. **4** informal a dull or stupid person. **5** the act of deceiving an opponent in sports by pretending to pass or release the ball.

dummy run n a rehearsal or trial run.

dump¹ v **1** to unload or deposit (something unwanted, e.g. refuse). **2** to deposit carelessly or heavily. **3** to get rid of unceremoniously or irresponsibly.

dump² n **1** a place where discarded materials are dumped. **2** an accumulation of military materials or the place where they are stored. **3** informal an unpleasant or dilapidated place.

dumpling n a small round mass of dough cooked by boiling or steaming, often in a stew.

dumps pl n ✱ **down in the dumps** informal gloomy; despondent.

dumpy adj (**-ier, -iest**) of a person: short and thick in build.

dun n a brownish grey colour.

dunce n a stupid person or slow learner.

dune n a ridge of sand piled up by the wind.

dung n the excrement of an animal.

dungarees pl n a one-piece outer garment consisting of trousers and a bib with shoulder straps.

dungeon n a dark underground prison.

dunk v **1** to dip (a biscuit, a piece of bread, etc) into liquid, e.g. a drink or soup, before eating it. **2** to submerge temporarily in water.

dunnock n a small dull-coloured European bird.

duo n (pl **-os**) **1** a pair of people or things, esp a pair of performers. **2** a duet.

duodenum n (pl **duodena** or **duodenums**) the first part of the small intestine, extending from the stomach to the jejunum.

dupe[1] n somebody who is easily deceived or cheated.

dupe[2] v to cheat or deceive.

duple adj of musical rhythm: having two beats per bar.

duplex n **1** NAmer a house divided into two flats. **2** NAmer, Aus a semi-detached house.

duplicate[1] adj **1** consisting of two corresponding or identical parts. **2** being the same as another.

duplicate[2] n **1** either of two things that exactly resemble each other. **2** a copy.

duplicate[3] v **1** to make an exact copy of. **2** to repeat or equal. ➤ **duplication** n.

duplicity n malicious deception in thought, speech, or action. ➤ **duplicitous** adj.

durable adj able to be used for a long time without deteriorating. ➤ **durability** n.

duration n the time during which something exists or lasts.

duress n **1** compulsion by threat, violence, or imprisonment. **2** forcible restraint or restriction.

during prep **1** throughout the whole duration of. **2** at some point in the course of.

dusk n the darker part of twilight.

dusky adj (-ier, -iest) **1** somewhat dark in colour. **2** shadowy; gloomy.

dust[1] n **1** fine dry particles of any solid matter. **2** the fine particles of waste that settle on household surfaces.

dust[2] v **1** to make free of dust, e.g. by wiping or brushing. **2** (+ down/off) to prepare to use again, esp after a long period of disuse. **3** to sprinkle with fine particles.

dustbin n Brit a large container for holding household refuse.

dustcart n Brit a vehicle for collecting household refuse.

duster n a cloth for removing dust from household surfaces.

dustman n (pl **dustmen**) Brit somebody employed to remove household refuse.

dustpan n a shovel-like utensil into which household dust and litter is swept.

dust-up n informal a quarrel or fight.

Dutch n **1** (**the Dutch**) (treated as pl) the people of the Netherlands. **2** the language of the people of the Netherlands. * **go Dutch** to divide expenses equally. ➤ **Dutch** adj.

Dutch courage n courage induced by drinking alcohol.

dutiable adj subject to a duty.

dutiful adj motivated by or expressive of a sense of duty. ➤ **dutifully** adv.

duty n (pl **-ies**) **1** a task or function arising from one's position or job. **2** official service or busi-

ness. **3** a moral or legal obligation. **4** a tax, e.g. on imports or the transfer of property. * **on/off duty** engaged or not engaged in one's usual work.

duty-bound adj morally or legally obliged.

duty-free adj exempt from duty.

duvet /'doohvay/ n a large quilt, used in place of an upper sheet and blankets.

DVD abbr digital videodisc (or digital versatile disc), a disc with a large capacity for storing audio, video, or other information.

dwarf[1] n (pl **dwarfs** or **dwarves**) **1** a person of abnormally small stature. **2** an animal or plant that is much smaller than normal size. **3** in mythology, a small human-like creature often depicted as having magical powers.

dwarf[2] v to cause to appear smaller or less significant by comparison.

dwell v (past tense and past part. **dwelt** or **dwelled**) formal to live; to reside. * **dwell on/upon** to think, write, or speak about at length.

dwelling n formal a place, e.g. a house or flat, in which people live.

dwindle v to become steadily less in quantity or size.

Dy abbr the chemical symbol for dysprosium.

dye[1] n a substance used to colour something.

dye[2] v (**dyes, dyed, dyeing**) to impart a new and permanent colour to (e.g. fabric or hair) with a dye.

dyed-in-the-wool adj uncompromising or unchanging.

dying v present part. of DIE[1].

dyke[1] or **dike** n **1** a watercourse or ditch. **2** a bank, usu of earth, constructed to control or confine water.

dyke[2] or **dike** n informal, derog a lesbian.

dynamic adj **1** of physical force or energy in motion. **2** marked by continuous activity or change. **3** energetic and forceful. **4** relating to variation in sound intensity or volume. ➤ **dynamically** adv.

dynamics pl n **1** the branch of mechanics that deals with forces and their relation to motion. **2** a pattern of change or growth, or the forces that produce it. **3** variation in the intensity of sound, esp in music.

dynamism n the quality of being energetic and forceful.

dynamite[1] n **1** a blasting explosive made of nitroglycerine. **2** informal somebody or something that has a potentially dangerous or spectacular effect.

dynamite[2] v to blow up or destroy with dynamite.

dynamo n (pl **-os**) a machine for converting mechanical into electrical energy.

dynasty n (pl **-ies**) **1** a succession of hereditary rulers. **2** a powerful group or family that main-

tains its position for a considerable time.
➤ **dynastic** *adj.*

dysentery /'dis(ə)ntri/ *n* an infection of the intestines characterized by severe diarrhoea.

dysfunctional *adj* **1** not functioning properly. **2** characterized by the breakdown of social behaviour and relationships.

dyslexia *n* difficulties with reading, writing, and spelling, caused by a neurological disorder.
➤ **dyslexic** *adj and n.*

dyspepsia *n* indigestion.

dyspeptic *adj* **1** relating to or having dyspepsia. **2** ill-tempered.

E e

E¹ or **e** n (pl **Es** or **E's** or **e's**) the fifth letter of the English alphabet.

E² abbr **1** East. **2** Eastern.

E³ n (pl **Es** or **E's**) **1** the drug Ecstasy. **2** an Ecstasy tablet.

e- prefix electronic; using the Internet: email; e-commerce.

each¹ adj and pron every one of the individuals within a group, considered separately.

each² adv to or for each.

eager adj showing keen desire or interest. ➤ **eagerly** adv.

eagle n **1** a large bird of prey noted for its strength, size, and keenness of vision. **2** a golf score of two strokes less than par on a hole.

eagle-eyed adj having very good eyesight.

ear¹ n **1** the organ of hearing in humans and other vertebrates. **2** sensitivity to musical tone and pitch. **3** sympathetic attention. * **be all ears** to listen very attentively. **play it by ear** to act according to circumstances.

ear² n the seed-bearing spike of a cereal plant.

earache n pain in the ear.

eardrum n a vibrating membrane in the ear that responds to sound waves.

earl n a member of the British peerage ranking below a marquess and above a viscount. ➤ **earldom** n.

early adj and adv (-ier, -iest) **1** before the usual or expected time. **2** near the beginning of a period of time or series.

earmark v to designate (e.g. funds) for a specific use or recipient.

earmuffs pl n a pair of ear coverings worn as protection against cold or noise.

earn v **1** to receive (money) as return for work done or services rendered. **2** to deserve (a title, reward, etc) because of one's behaviour or efforts.

earnest adj determined and serious. * **in earnest** serious or sincere; wholeheartedly. ➤ **earnestly** adv.

earnings pl n money or other income earned.

earphone n a device worn directly over or in the ear that reproduces sound from a radio, personal stereo, etc.

earpiece n the part of an instrument, e.g. a telephone, held to the ear.

earplug n a device inserted into the the ear for protection against water, loud noise, etc.

earring n an ornament attached to the lobe or edge of the ear.

earshot n the range within which something, esp the unaided voice, may be heard: out of earshot.

earth¹ n **1** (often **Earth**) the planet on which we live. **2** land or solid ground. **3** soil. **4** chiefly Brit an electrical connection to the ground, used to carry current safely from a circuit in the event of a fault. **5** the lair of a fox, badger, etc. * **go to earth** to go into hiding.

earth² v chiefly Brit to connect (an electrical device) to earth.

earthen adj made of earth or baked clay.

earthenware n ceramic ware made of clay fired at a low temperature.

earthling n an inhabitant of the earth, esp in science fiction.

earthly adj **1** characteristic of the earth or human life on earth. **2** possible: no earthly reason.

earthquake n a sudden violent earth tremor caused by pressures within the earth's crust.

earthwork n an embankment, fortification, etc made of earth.

earthworm n a common hermaphroditic worm that lives in the soil.

earthy adj (-ier, -iest) **1** resembling earth or soil. **2** dealing frankly or cheerfully with sex and bodily functions.

earwig¹ n a small insect with a slender body and a pair of appendages like forceps at its rear end.

earwig² v (**earwigged, earwigging**) informal to eavesdrop.

ease¹ n **1** lack of difficulty in doing something; effortlessness. **2** freedom from pain, anxiety, embarrassment, or constraint. **3** rest or relaxation.

ease² v **1** to make (pain, suffering, etc) less severe or intense. **2** to manoeuvre gently or carefully. **3** (often + off/up) to decrease in activity, intensity, severity, etc.

easel n a frame for supporting something, esp an artist's canvas.

east¹ n **1** the direction of sunrise, 90° clockwise from north. **2** regions or countries lying to the east. ➤ **eastbound** adj and adv.

east² adj and adv **1** at or towards the east. **2** of the wind: blowing from the east.

Easter n a Christian feast commemorating Christ's resurrection, observed on a Sunday between 21 March and 25 April.

Easter egg n a chocolate egg given as a present at Easter.

easterly adj and adv **1** in an eastern position or direction. **2** of a wind: blowing from the east.

eastern adj **1** in or towards the east. **2** (often **Eastern**) relating to countries or continents east of Europe, or their traditions.

Easterner n a person from the eastern part of a country.

eastward adj and adv towards the east; in a direction going east. ➤ **eastwards** adv.

easy adj (-**ier**, -**iest**) **1** causing or involving little difficulty. **2** marked by peace, comfort, or freedom from constraint. **3** free from pain, annoyance, or anxiety. **4** chiefly Brit, informal not having strong preferences on a particular issue. * **go easy on 1** to be lenient with. **2** to be sparing with. **take it easy** to relax or rest. ➤ **easily** adv, **easiness** n.

easygoing adj relaxed and tolerant.

easy listening n music that is undemanding and pleasant to listen to.

eat v (**ate, eaten**) **1** to put (food) in the mouth and swallow it. **2** (+ away/into/through) to destroy, erode, or corrode gradually. **3** (+ into) to use a great deal of (a limited resource). **4** informal to worry or annoy (somebody). * **eat one's words** to retract what one has said. ➤ **eatable** adj.

eatery n (pl -**ies**) informal a restaurant.

eau de cologne /,oh də kə'lohn/ n (pl **eaux de cologne** /,oh/) a variety of toilet water with a characteristic perfume.

eaves pl n the lower border of a roof that overhangs the wall.

eavesdrop v (**eavesdropped, eavesdropping**) to listen secretly to what is said in private.

ebb[1] n the flowing out of the tide towards the sea. * **at a low ebb** in a poor state.

ebb[2] v **1** of tidal water: to recede from the highest level. **2** (often + away) to decline or disappear gradually.

ebony n **1** a hard heavy black wood from a tropical tree. **2** a dark brown or black colour. ➤ **ebony** adj.

ebullient adj full of liveliness and enthusiasm. ➤ **ebullience** n.

EC abbr **1** European Commission. **2** European Community.

eccentric[1] /ik'sentrik/ adj unusual, unconventional, and, usu amusingly, odd. ➤ **eccentrically** adv, **eccentricity** n.

eccentric[2] n an eccentric person.

ecclesiastical adj relating to the Church.

echelon /'eshəlon/ n a level or grade, e.g. of authority or responsibility, in some organized field of activity.

echo[1] /'ekoh/ n (pl -**oes**) **1** the repetition of a sound caused by the reflection of sound waves. **2** the reflection by an object of transmitted radar signals. ➤ **echoey** adj.

echo[2] v (**echoes, echoed, echoing**) **1** to produce an echo. **2** to produce a continuing effect. **3** to repeat or imitate (somebody or somebody's words).

echo chamber n a room with sound-reflecting walls used for making acoustic measurements and for producing echoing sound effects, esp in radio broadcasting.

éclair or **eclair** /i'kleə, ay'kleə/ n a small cylindrical cake of choux pastry filled with cream and topped with chocolate icing.

éclat /ay'klah/ n brilliant or conspicuous success.

eclectic adj selecting elements from a variety of sources, methods, or styles.

eclipse[1] n **1** the total or partial obscuring of one celestial body by another. **2** a falling into obscurity or decay.

eclipse[2] v **1** to cause an eclipse of (a celestial body). **2** to surpass (a person, achievement, etc).

eco-friendly adj not harmful to the environment.

E. coli /'kohlie/ n a bacterium that can sometimes cause severe food poisoning.

ecology n the interrelationship of living organisms and their environments, or the scientific study of this. ➤ **ecological** adj, **ecologist** n.

economic adj **1** relating to economics or an economy. **2** profitable. ➤ **economically** adv.

economical adj **1** thrifty. **2** efficient; not wasting money, fuel, etc. ➤ **economically** adv.

economics pl n a social science concerned with the production, distribution, and consumption of goods and services. ➤ **economist** n.

economize or -**ise** v (often + on) to be frugal or not wasteful.

economy n (pl -**ies**) **1** the system whereby a country produces and sells goods and services and creates wealth. **2** thrifty and efficient use of money or resources. **3** an instance of economizing; a saving. **4** (often used before a noun) a cheaper standard of travel.

ecosystem n a community of plants and animals and its environment, functioning as an ecological unit in nature.

Ecstasy n an illegal drug taken recreationally for its stimulant and euphoric effects.

ecstasy n (pl -**ies**) **1** a feeling of great joy or happiness. **2** a state of frenzied emotion.

Usage Note: Note the spelling -asy not -acy.

---

ecstatic adj extremely happy or enthusiastic. ➤ **ecstatically** adv.

ectoplasm n a substance supposed to emanate from a spiritualist medium in a state of trance and in which a spirit manifests itself.

ecumenical *adj* **1** representing several different Churches. **2** promoting worldwide Christian unity.

eczema /'eksimə/ *n* an inflammatory condition of the skin characterized by itching and oozing blisters.

eddy[1] *n* (*pl* **-ies**) a current of water, air, etc running counter to the main current and causing a small whirlpool.

eddy[2] *v* (**-ies, -ied**) to move in an eddy or with circular motion.

edelweiss /'aydlvies/ *n* a small perennial Alpine plant covered in dense white hairs.

edema *n NAmer* see OEDEMA.

Eden *n* **1** the garden where, according to Genesis, Adam and Eve lived before the Fall. **2** a paradise.

edge[1] *n* **1** the line where an object or area begins or ends; a border. **2** a line where two surfaces of a solid meet. **3** the cutting side of a blade. ✻ **have the edge on/over somebody** to have an advantage over somebody. **on edge** anxious or nervous.

edge[2] *v* **1** to provide with an edge. **2** to move gradually or cautiously.

edgeways *or* **edgewise** *adv* with the edge foremost; sideways. ✻ **get a word in edgeways** to be allowed to contribute to a conversation.

edgy *adj* (**-ier, -iest**) tense, anxious, or irritable.

edible *adj* fit to be eaten as food.

edict *n* an official public decree or command.

edifice *n* a building, *esp* a large or massive structure.

edify *v* (**-ies, -ied**) to instruct and improve, *esp* in moral knowledge. ➤ **edification** *n*, **edifying** *adj*.

edit[1] *v* (**edited, editing**) **1** to alter (e.g. written material), *esp* to condense or improve it. **2** to assemble (e.g. a film or recording) by deleting, inserting, and rearranging material. **3** to be the editor of (a newspaper or periodical).

edit[2] *n* an editorial change or correction.

edition *n* **1** the form in which a text is published. **2** a number of copies published at one time or place. **3** a particular broadcast or instalment of a radio or television programme.

editor *n* **1** a person in overall charge of the content of a newspaper, magazine, book by various writers, or radio or television programme. **2** a person who edits text, films, recordings, etc.

editorial[1] *adj* of or written by an editor. ➤ **editorially** *adv*.

editorial[2] *n* a newspaper or magazine article giving the opinions of the editor.

educate *v* to teach or instruct in academic, moral, or social matters. ➤ **educator** *n*.

educated *adj* **1** having had an education, *esp* a good one. **2** based on some knowledge or experience: *an educated guess*.

education *n* **1** the act of educating or the process of being educated. **2** instruction in some subject. **3** the knowledge resulting from instruction. **4** the field of study that deals mainly with methods of teaching. ➤ **educational** *adj*.

Edwardian *adj* of the reign of King Edward VII of England (1901–1910).

eel *n* a long snakelike fish with a smooth slimy skin.

eerie *or* **eery** *adj* (**-ier, -iest**) frighteningly strange or gloomy. ➤ **eerily** *adv*.

efface *v* **1** to remove from a surface or make indistinct. **2** to make (oneself) inconspicuous.

effect[1] *n* **1** the result produced by a cause or action. **2** the extent to which a cause or action produces results. **3** the state of being operative: *come into effect*. **4** (*in pl*) personal movable property; goods. **5** (*often in pl*) something designed to enhance the drama, realism, or impressiveness of a play or film. ✻ **for effect** in order to impress. **in effect** actually although not officially so. **take effect 1** to become operative. **2** to produce a result.

Usage Note: Do not confuse this word with *affect*, which is a verb only.

effect[2] *v* to bring about, carry out, or accomplish.

effective *adj* **1** producing a decisive or desired effect. **2** impressive or striking. **3** actual or real, though not officially recognized. **4** in force; operative. ➤ **effectiveness** *n*.

effectual *adj* able to produce a desired effect; effective.

effeminate *adj* of a man: having qualities usu thought of as feminine. ➤ **effeminacy** *n*.

effervesce *v* of a liquid: to bubble and hiss as gas escapes.

effervescent *adj* **1** effervescing. **2** lively and exhilarated.

effete *adj* **1** marked by weakness and decadent overrefinement. **2** effeminate.

efficacious *adj formal* effective.

efficacy *n formal* effectiveness.

efficient *adj* **1** producing desired effects, *esp* with minimum waste. **2** of a person: briskly competent. ➤ **efficiency** *n*, **efficiently** *adv*.

effigy *n* (*pl* **-ies**) an image or representation of a person, *esp* a hated person.

effluent *n* liquid industrial refuse, sewage, etc discharged into the environment and causing pollution.

effluvium *n* (*pl* **effluvia, effluviums**) an offensive gas or smell.

effort *n* **1** conscious exertion of physical or

mental power. **2** a serious attempt; a try. **3** something produced by exertion or trying.

effortless *adj* involving no effort; done easily and without strain. ➤ **effortlessly** *adv*.

effrontery *n* the quality of being shamelessly bold; insolence.

effusion *n* **1** an act of emitting or pouring out. **2** an unrestrained expression of feelings in words.

effusive *adj* unduly emotionally demonstrative, *esp* in speech; gushing. ➤ **effusively** *adv*.

e.g. *abbr* for example.

egalitarian *adj* believing in social, political, and economic equality among human beings. ➤ **egalitarian** *n*, **egalitarianism** *n*.

egg[1] *n* **1** a reproductive cell enclosed in a hard or soft casing, produced by a female bird, fish, or reptile. **2** = OVUM. **3** the egg of domestic poultry, etc, used as food. **4** *dated, informal* a person. * **have egg on one's face** to be made to look foolish.

egghead *n derog or humorous* an intellectual or highbrow.

egg on *v* to incite to action.

eggplant *n chiefly NAmer* an aubergine.

ego *n* (*pl* **egos**) **1** self-esteem. **2** excessive self-esteem. **3** in psychoanalytic theory, a part of the mind that mainly controls a person's sense of identity, behaviour and relations with reality.

egocentric *adj* self-centred or selfish.

egoism *n* self-seeking or self-centredness. ➤ **egoist** *n*, **egoistic** *adj*.

egomania *n* extreme self-centredness.

egotism *n* **1** the practice of talking about oneself too much. **2** extreme self-importance. ➤ **egotist** *n*, **egotistic** *adj*.

egregious *adj* conspicuously or shockingly bad.

egress *n formal* **1** going or coming out. **2** an exit.

egret *n* a species of heron that has long plumes during the breeding season.

Eid /eed/ *n* a Muslim festival marking the end of the fast of Ramadan.

eider *n* (*pl* **eiders** *or* **eider**) a large northern sea duck with fine soft down.

eiderdown *n chiefly Brit* a thick warm quilt filled with feathers or other insulating material.

eight *n* **1** the number 8. **2** an eight-person racing boat or its crew. ➤ **eight** *adj*.

eighteen *adj and n* the number 18. ➤ **eighteenth** *adj and n*.

eighth *adj and n* **1** having the position in a sequence corresponding to the number eight. **2** one of eight equal parts of something.

Usage Note: Note the spelling with -*h*- before -*th*.

eighty *adj and n* (*pl* -**ies**) **1** the number 80. **2** (*in pl*) the numbers 80 to 89. ➤ **eightieth** *adj and n*.

eisteddfod *n* (*pl* **eisteddfods** *or* **eisteddfodau**) a Welsh-language competitive festival of music and poetry.

either[1] *adj* **1** both of the two: *on either side of the path.* **2** being the one or the other of two: *Take either road.*

either[2] *pron* the one or the other.

either[3] *conj* used to indicate that what immediately follows is the first of two or more alternatives.

either[4] *adv* for that matter; likewise: *I can't drive and I can't ride a bike either.*

ejaculate *v* **1** to eject (semen) from the body in orgasm. **2** *formal* to utter suddenly and vehemently. ➤ **ejaculation** *n*.

eject *v* **1** to drive or throw out, *esp* by physical force. **2** to escape from an aircraft by using the ejector seat. ➤ **ejection** *n*.

ejector seat *n* an emergency escape seat that propels its occupant out of an aircraft.

eke out *v* **1** to make (a supply) last longer by using it frugally. **2** to make (e.g. a living) laboriously or precariously.

elaborate *adj* **1** planned with great care and attention to detail. **2** marked by complexity and wealth of detail. ➤ **elaborately** *adv*.

élan /ay'lonh, ay'lan/ *n* vigorous spirit or enthusiasm; verve.

elapse *v* of a period of time: to pass by.

elastic[1] *adj* **1** of a material: capable of resuming its former shape after being stretched, squashed, etc. **2** flexible or adaptable. ➤ **elasticity** *n*.

elastic[2] *n* an easily stretched material made of yarns containing rubber.

elasticated *adj* of fabric: made stretchy by the insertion of elastic.

elastic band *n Brit* = RUBBER BAND.

elated *adj* filled with joy or pride.

elation *n* a feeling of great joy or pride.

elbow[1] *n* **1** the joint between the human forearm and upper arm. **2** (**the elbow**) *informal* an abrupt rejection or dismissal.

elbow[2] *v* **1** to shove aside with one's elbow. **2** to strike with one's elbow.

elbow grease *n informal* hard work to clean something.

elder[1] *adj* older.

elder[2] *n* **1** somebody who is older. **2** somebody having authority by virtue of age and experience. **3** an official of a Presbyterian, Quaker, etc congregation.

elder[3] *n* a common shrub or small tree with white flowers and black or red berries.

elderly *adj* rather old.

eldest *adj* oldest.

elect[1] *v* **1** to select by vote for an office, position, etc. **2** *formal* to choose to do something. ➤ **electable** *adj*.

elect[2] *adj* **1** picked out in preference to others. **2** chosen for office but not yet installed.

election n **1** a procedure for electing somebody, e.g. to public office. **2** the act of electing or fact of being elected.

electioneering n **1** activities aimed at getting a person or party elected to political office. **2** insincere or unscrupulous election campaigning.

elective adj **1** chosen or filled by election. **2** that can be freely selected; optional.

elector n somebody qualified to vote in an election.

electoral adj relating to elections or electors.

electoral roll n the official list of those who are entitled to vote in an election.

electorate n a body of electors.

electric[1] adj **1** of, producing, or operated by electricity. **2** thrilling. **3** (often + with) tense.

electric[2] n (in pl) electrical parts or electric circuitry.

electrical adj of, using, or producing electricity. ➤ **electrically** adv.

electric blue n a bright slightly greenish blue.

electric chair n a chair used to electrocute criminals condemned to death.

electrician n somebody who installs or repairs electrical equipment.

electricity n **1** a form of energy derived from charged particles. **2** electric current or electric charge. **3** contagious excitement.

electric shock n the violent effect on the nerves and muscles caused by electricity passing through the body.

electric storm n a thunderstorm.

electrify v (-ies, -ied) **1** to charge with electricity. **2** to equip for the use of electric power. **3** to excite or thrill. ➤ **electrification** n.

electroconvulsive therapy n a treatment for serious mental disorder, esp severe depression, in which an electric current is passed through the brain.

electrocute v to execute or kill by electric shock. ➤ **electrocution** n.

electrode n a conductor that makes electrical contact with a non-metallic part of a circuit, e.g. the acid in a car battery.

electrolysis n **1** the process of passing an electric current through a solution to separate out the solution's constituents. **2** the destruction of hair roots, warts, moles, etc by an electric current. ➤ **electrolytic** adj.

electrolyte n a non-metallic electric conductor, e.g. battery acid.

electromagnet n a metal core, surrounded by a coil of wire, which is magnetized when an electric current is passed through the wire.

electromagnetic adj relating to electromagnets and the interaction of electricity and magnetism. ➤ **electromagnetism** n.

electromotive adj producing an electric current.

electron n an elementary particle carrying a negative electrical charge, which occurs in atoms outside the nucleus.

electronic adj **1** relating to electrons or electronics. **2** involving devices, e.g. transistors or microchips, in which a flow of electrons is controlled by a voltage. **3** involving computers or other electronic systems. ➤ **electronically** adv.

electronic mail n email.

electronics pl n **1** the branch of physics dealing with the behaviour and effects of electrons in transistors, microchips, etc. **2** the circuits, devices, etc of a piece of electronic equipment.

electron microscope n a microscope in which a highly magnified image is produced by a beam of electrons.

electroplate v to plate (an object) with a metallic coating by electrolysis.

elegant adj **1** gracefully refined, dignified, or stylish. **2** of ideas: simple and ingenious. ➤ **elegance** n, **elegantly** adv.

elegiac adj **1** characteristic of an elegy. **2** expressing sorrow, often for something past.

elegy n (pl -ies) a song, poem, or other work expressing sorrow, esp for a dead person.

element n **1** in chemistry, a fundamental substance consisting of atoms of only one kind. **2** a constituent part that makes up a whole. **3** a specified group within a human community. **4** a small quantity; a hint. **5** the part of an electric device, e.g. a kettle, that contains the heating wire. **6** a substance, air, water, fire, or earth, formerly believed to compose the physical universe. **7** the state or sphere natural to someone or something. **8** (in pl) the weather esp bad weather.

elemental adj **1** fundamental. **2** of or resembling a powerful force of nature.

elementary adj of or dealing with the basic elements of something; simple.

elephant n a very large mammal having a muscular trunk instead of a snout and two long ivory tusks, found in Africa and South Asia.

elephantine adj **1** huge or massive. **2** clumsy or ponderous.

elevate v **1** to lift up. **2** to raise in rank or status.

elevated adj **1** raised above a surface. **2** on a high moral or intellectual plane; lofty.

elevation n **1** the height to which something is elevated, esp above sea level. **2** the act of elevating. **3** a scale drawing of the front, back, or side of a building.

elevator n **1** chiefly NAmer = LIFT[2] 1. **2** an endless belt with scoops or buckets for raising grain, liquids, etc. **3** NAmer a building for storing grain. **4** a movable horizontal part of the tailplane of an aircraft for controlling climb and descent.

eleven *n* **1** the number 11. **2** a cricket, football, or hockey team. ➤ **eleven** *adj,* **eleventh** *adj* and *n.*

eleven-plus *or* **11-plus** *n* an examination taken, *esp* formerly, at the age of 10–11 to determine which type of British state secondary school a child should attend.

elevenses *pl n Brit* light refreshment taken in the middle of the morning.

eleventh hour *n* (**the eleventh hour**) the latest possible time.

elf *n* (*pl* **elves**) a fairy, *esp* a small mischievous one.

elfin *adj* small and delicate.

elicit *v* (**elicited, eliciting**) (*often* + from) to call forth or draw out (e.g. a response or reaction).

elide *v* to omit (e.g. a vowel or syllable) in speaking or writing.

eligible *adj* **1** qualified to do or receive something. **2** desirable, *esp* as a marriage partner. ➤ **eligibility** *n.*

eliminate *v* **1** to get rid of completely. **2** to remove (a competitor, team, etc) from a competition by defeating them. ➤ **elimination** *n.*

elision *n* omission of a vowel or syllable, e.g. reducing *I am* to *I'm.*

elite *or* **élite** *n* a group considered to be intellectually, professionally, or socially superior.

elitism *or* **élitism** *n* **1** the belief in leadership by an elite. **2** the belief that some people are superior and deserve special treatment. ➤ **elitist** *n* and *adj.*

elixir *n* a substance believed to have magical properties, *esp* that of prolonging life indefinitely.

Elizabethan *adj* of the reign of Queen Elizabeth I of England (1558–1603).

elk *n* (*pl* **elks** *or* **elk**) the largest deer of Europe and Asia.

ellipse *n* a flattened circle.

ellipsis *n* (*pl* **ellipses**) **1** the omission of words needed to make a construction grammatically complete. **2** a mark (e.g. ... or *** or —), indicating the omission of letters or words.

elliptical *adj* **1** of or shaped like an ellipse. **2** of or marked by ellipsis. **3** of speech or writing: extremely or excessively concise, usu through omitting words.

elm *n* a large tree with serrated leaves.

elocution *n* the art of effective public speaking, *esp* of good diction.

elongate *v* to make or become longer. ➤ **elongated** *adj.*

elope *v* to run away secretly with a lover, usu with the intention of getting married.

eloquence *n* fluent, forceful, and persuasive speech.

eloquent *adj* **1** fluent, forceful, and persuasive in the use of language. **2** vividly expressive or revealing. ➤ **eloquently** *adv.*

else *adv* **1** different from the person, place, etc previously mentioned: *somewhere else.* **2** also; besides. * **or else** if not; otherwise.

elsewhere *adv* in or to another place.

elucidate *v* to make clear, *esp* by explanation. ➤ **elucidation** *n.*

elude *v* **1** to avoid cunningly or adroitly. **2** to escape the memory or notice of.

elusive *adj* difficult to find, catch, obtain, or remember.

elver *n* a young eel.

elves *n* pl of ELF.

emaciated *adj* excessively thin or feeble. ➤ **emaciation** *n.*

email[1] *or* **e-mail** *n* **1** a system for transmitting messages from one computer to another, usu through a modem and telephone line. **2** a message sent in this way.

email[2] *or* **e-mail** *v* to send (a message, document, etc) by email.

emanate *v* **1** to come out from a source. **2** to send out or give off.

emancipate *v* to free from slavery or restrictions imposed by society or law. ➤ **emancipation** *n.*

emasculate *v* **1** to deprive of effectiveness or strength. **2** to castrate. **3** to rob (a man) of his male identity or role. ➤ **emasculation** *n.*

embalm *v* to treat (a dead body) in order to protect it against decay.

embankment *n* a raised structure to hold back water or to carry a road or railway.

embargo[1] *n* (*pl* **-oes**) a legal prohibition, *esp* on commerce.

embargo[2] *v* (**embargoes, embargoed, embargoing**) to place an embargo on.

embark *v* **1** to go on board a ship or aircraft. **2** (+ on) to make a start on. ➤ **embarkation** *n.*

embarrass *v* **1** to cause to experience awkward self-consciousness or shame. **2** to involve in financial difficulties. ➤ **embarrassed** *adj,* **embarrassing** *adj,* **embarrassment** *n.*

Usage Note: Note the spelling with *-rr-* and *-ss-.*

---

embassy *n* (*pl* **-ies**) the official residence or offices of an ambassador.

embattled *adj* **1** hemmed in by adversaries, difficulties, etc. **2** involved in battle.

embed *or* **imbed** *v* (**embedded** *or* **imbedded, embedding** *or* **imbedding**) to fix firmly or deeply in surrounding matter.

embellish *v* **1** to make beautiful by adding ornaments; to decorate. **2** to make (speech or writing) more interesting by adding fictitious detail.

ember *n* a glowing fragment of coal or wood in a dying fire.

embezzle *v* to take (money or property entrusted to one's care) fraudulently for one's own use. ➤ **embezzler** *n.*

embittered *adj* feeling bitter or resentful.

emblazon v **1** to display conspicuously on. **2** to decorate with a heraldic or other emblem.

emblem n a design or symbol used as an identifying mark.

emblematic adj acting as an emblem or symbol.

embody v (-ies, -ied) **1** to represent (an idea or belief) in a concrete and perceptible form. **2** (+ in) to make (e.g. ideas or principles) part of a body or system. ➤ **embodiment** n.

embolden v to make bold or courageous.

embolism n the sudden obstruction of a blood vessel by a clot or air bubble.

emboss v to carve a raised design on (a surface).

embrace[1] v **1** to take and hold in one's arms as a sign of affection. **2** to take up (a cause or opportunity) eagerly. **3** to include as an integral part.

embrace[2] n the act of embracing.

embrocation n a liquid rubbed into the skin, esp to relieve pain.

embroider v **1** to ornament (e.g. cloth or a garment) with decorative stitches. **2** to embellish with exaggerated or fictitious details.

embroidery n (pl -ies) **1** the art of embroidering. **2** embroidered work.

embroil v to involve in conflict or difficulties. ➤ **embroilment** n.

embryo n (pl -os) an animal in the early stages of growth before birth or hatching, esp an unborn baby less than eight weeks old.

embryonic adj **1** relating to an embryo. **2** in an early stage of development.

emend v to remove errors from (a text).

emerald n **1** a bright green gemstone. **2** a bright green colour. ➤ **emerald** adj.

emerge v **1** to come out into view. **2** to become known. **3** to survive a difficult or unpleasant experience.

emergency n (pl -ies) an unforeseen and potentially dangerous occurrence that calls for immediate action.

emergent adj in the early stages of development.

emeritus adj retaining a title on an honorary basis after retirement.

emery board n a strip of cardboard or wood coated with abrasive powder and used as a nail file.

emetic adj causing vomiting.

emigrant n a person who emigrates.

emigrate v to leave one's country for permanent residence abroad. ➤ **emigration** n.

émigré or **emigré** /'emigray/ n a person who emigrates, esp for political reasons.

eminence n **1** a position of prominence or superiority. **2** a person of high rank or attainments.

eminent adj **1** conspicuous or notable. **2** highly regarded; distinguished. ➤ **eminently** adv.

emir or **amir** n a ruler of a Muslim state.

emissary n (pl -ies) a person sent on a mission to represent a government or head of state.

emission n **1** the act of emitting. **2** something emitted, e.g. fumes or radiation.

emit v (**emitted, emitting**) **1** to send out or give off (e.g. light, smoke, or radiation). **2** to make (a sound).

emollient adj **1** softening or soothing, esp to the skin. **2** making a situation calmer.

emolument n formal a salary or fee.

emotion n **1** a strong feeling, e.g. anger, fear, or joy. **2** such feelings collectively. **3** instinctive feelings as opposed to reason.

emotional adj **1** relating to the emotions. **2** feeling or expressing emotion. **3** inclined to show excessive emotion. ➤ **emotionally** adv.

emotive adj arousing or appealing to emotion.

empathize or **-ise** v (usu + with) to understand and share the feelings of another person.

empathy n the capacity for understanding and sharing another's feelings.

emperor n the ruler of an empire.

emphasis n (pl **emphases**) **1** special importance given to something, esp in speaking or writing. **2** special stress given to a word or sound.

emphasize or **-ise** v to give emphasis to.

emphatic adj **1** spoken with or marked by emphasis. **2** clear or definite. ➤ **emphatically** adv.

emphysema n a disorder of the lungs, causing breathlessness.

empire n **1** a large group of countries under the authority of a single ruler or state. **2** an extensive territory or enterprise controlled by a single person or entity.

empirical adj based on experience or experiment rather than theory. ➤ **empirically** adv, **empiricism** n, **empiricist** n.

emplacement n a prepared position for large guns to fire from.

employ v **1** to pay (somebody) in return for their work. **2** to give (somebody) a task or occupation. **3** to use (something) for a specific purpose.

employee n somebody employed by another for wages or a salary.

employer n a person or company that employs people.

employment n **1** the act of employing. **2** paid work. **3** a job or occupation.

emporium n (pl **emporiums** or **emporia**) a large shop or commercial centre.

empower v **1** to give authority or power to. **2** to give (somebody) the confidence to act on their own initiative. ➤ **empowerment** n.

empress *n* **1** the wife or widow of an emperor. **2** a woman having the rank of emperor.

empty[1] *adj* (-**ier**, -**iest**) **1** containing nothing, *esp* lacking typical contents. **2** not inhabited. **3** lacking substance, meaning, or sincerity; hollow. ➤ **emptiness** *n*.

empty[2] *v* (-**ies**, -**ied**) **1** to remove the contents of. **2** to become empty. **3** of a river: to flow into a sea or lake.

empty[3] *n* (*pl* -**ies**) a bottle or other container that has been emptied.

emu *n* a flightless Australian bird, related to but smaller than the ostrich.

emulate *v* to imitate closely, *esp* in order to equal. ➤ **emulation** *n*.

emulsify *v* (-**ies**, -**ied**) to convert (e.g. an oil) into an emulsion.

emulsion *n* **1** a substance consisting of one liquid dispersed in droplets throughout another. **2** a light-sensitive coating for photographic film. **3** a type of water-based paint used *esp* on walls and ceilings.

enable *v* **1** to provide with the means or opportunity to do something. **2** to make possible.

enact *v* **1** to make (e.g. a bill) into law. **2** to perform (a role, scene, etc). ➤ **enactment** *n*.

enamel[1] *n* **1** a usu opaque glassy coating applied to the surface of metal, glass, or pottery. **2** a white substance forming a hard layer on teeth. **3** a paint that dries with a glossy appearance.

enamel[2] *v* (**enamelled, enamelling,** *NAmer* **enameled, enameling**) to cover or decorate with enamel.

enamoured (*NAmer* **enamored**) *adj* (*usu* + of/with) fond of or in love with a person or thing.

en bloc /onh 'blok/ *adv and adj* all together; in a mass.

encamp *v* to set up a camp, or place (people) in a camp.

encampment *n* a camp, *esp* a large one for troops.

encapsulate *v* **1** to express in a concise form. **2** to enclose in a capsule.

encase *v* to enclose in a case.

encephalitis *n* inflammation of the brain.

enchant *v* **1** to cast a spell on. **2** to attract and delight. ➤ **enchanter** *n*, **enchantment** *n*, **enchantress** *n*.

enchanting *adj* charming; delightful.

encircle *v* to form a circle round.

enclave *n* a unit of one country's territory enclosed within another country.

enclose *v* **1** to include in a package or envelope, *esp* along with something else. **2** to shut in or surround completely.

enclosure *n* **1** a fenced-off area of ground. **2** an area reserved for certain spectators in a sports ground. **3** something included with a letter in the same envelope.

encode *v* to convert (a message) into code.

encompass *v* **1** to encircle or enclose. **2** to include, *esp* in a comprehensive manner.

encore *n* an additional or repeated performance at the request of the audience.

encounter[1] *v* **1** to meet, *esp* unexpectedly. **2** to be faced with.

encounter[2] *n* **1** a chance meeting. **2** a clash between hostile factions or people.

encourage *v* **1** to inspire with confidence or hope. **2** to give support or approval to (e.g. a process or action). ➤ **encouragement** *n*, **encouraging** *adj*.

encroach *v* **1** (+ on/upon) to intrude gradually on somebody's possessions or rights. **2** (*often* + on/upon) to advance beyond the proper limits. ➤ **encroachment** *n*.

encrust *v* to cover with a hard or decorative layer.

encrypt *v* to convert into code. ➤ **encryption** *n*.

encumber *v* to impede or weigh down.

encumbrance *n* an impediment or burden.

encyclopedia *or* **encyclopaedia** *n* a work containing general information on all branches of knowledge.

encyclopedic *or* **encyclopaedic** *adj* comprehensive.

end[1] *n* **1** the point at which something stops, is completed, or ceases to exist. **2** the last part of something. **3** either of the parts farthest from the middle of something. **4** death or destruction. **5** a goal or purpose. **6** either half of a sports field, court, etc. **7** (**the end**) *informal* something or somebody particularly unpleasant. ✳ **in the end** eventually. **make ends meet** to cope financially. **no end 1** exceedingly. **2** a huge quantity. **on end** in an upright position.

end[2] *v* **1** to bring or come to an end. **2** (*often* + up) to reach a particular situation, condition, place, etc eventually.

endanger *v* to put in danger.

endangered *adj* at risk, *esp* threatened with extinction.

endear *v* (*often* + to) to cause to become beloved or admired. ➤ **endearing** *adj*.

endearment *n* a word or phrase expressing affection.

endeavour[1] (*NAmer* **endeavor**) *v* to attempt (to do something).

endeavour[2] (*NAmer* **endeavor**) *n* **1** serious determined effort. **2** an attempt or undertaking.

endemic *adj* **1** of a disease: prevalent within a particular area or group of people. **2** of a species: native to a particular region.

ending *n* the final part of something, e.g. a book, film, etc.

endive *n* a plant resembling a lettuce, whose bitter leaves are used in salads.

endless *adj* **1** being or seeming without end. **2** extremely numerous. ➤ **endlessly** *adv*.

endocrine *adj* of a gland: producing secretions that are discharged directly into the bloodstream.

endorphin *n* a natural painkiller secreted by the brain.

endorse *or* **indorse** *v* **1** to express approval of or support for publicly. **2** to sign the back of (a cheque, bill, etc) as an instruction regarding payment. **3** *Brit* to record details of a motoring offence on (a driver's licence). ➤ **endorsement** *n*.

endow *v* **1** to provide with a continuing source of income, often by bequest. **2** to provide with an ability or attribute.

endowment *n* **1** money or property given to an institution or person to provide them with an income. **2** a natural ability or characteristic.

endowment mortgage *n* a mortgage that is paid back by the money received when a life insurance policy matures.

endpaper *n* a folded sheet of paper pasted to the front or back inside cover of a book.

endurance *n* the ability to withstand hardship, adversity, or stress.

endure *v* **1** to undergo (e.g. a hardship), *esp* without giving in. **2** to tolerate. **3** to last.

enema *n* an injection of liquid into the intestine through the anus, e.g. to ease constipation.

enemy *n* (*pl* **-ies**) **1** a person who is opposed to or seeking to harm somebody or something. **2** a nation or military force with whom one is at war.

energetic *adj* marked by energy or vigour. ➤ **energetically** *adv*.

energize *or* **-ise** *v* to give energy or enthusiasm to.

energy *n* (*pl* **-ies**) **1** the natural strength and vitality required for action. **2** (*in pl*) physical and mental powers. **3** fuel and other sources of power, *esp* electricity.

enervate *v* to lessen the mental or physical vitality of. ➤ **enervated** *adj*, **enervating** *adj*.

enfant terrible /ˌɒnfonh teˈreeblə/ *n* (*pl* **enfants terribles**) a person whose outspoken remarks or unconventional actions cause controversy.

enfeeble *v* to make weak.

enfold *v* **1** (*usu* + in) to envelop. **2** to embrace.

enforce *v* **1** to cause (a rule or law) to be obeyed. **2** to impose or compel (e.g. obedience). ➤ **enforceable** *adj*, **enforced** *adj*, **enforcement** *n*, **enforcer** *n*.

enfranchise *v* **1** to give the right of voting to. **2** to set free, *esp* from slavery.

engage *v* **1** to attract and hold (somebody's thoughts, attention, etc). **2** to participate or become involved. **3** to arrange to employ. **4** of a mechanical part: to interlock with (another part).

engaged *adj* **1** involved in activity; occupied. **2** pledged to be married. **3** *chiefly Brit* of a telephone line: already in use.

engagement *n* **1** an agreement to marry. **2** an appointment. **3** a hostile encounter between military forces. **4** the state of being involved in something.

engaging *adj* attractive or pleasing.

engender *v* to cause to exist or develop.

engine *n* **1** a machine for converting energy into mechanical force and motion. **2** a railway locomotive.

engineer[1] *n* **1** a person who is trained in engineering. **2** a person who maintains or operates an engine. **3** *NAmer* a driver of a railway locomotive.

engineer[2] *v* **1** to design or construct as an engineer. **2** to contrive or plan, usu with subtlety.

engineering *n* the study of the design and construction of machines, structures, etc.

English *n* **1** the Germanic language spoken in Britain, the USA, and most Commonwealth countries. **2** (**the English**) (*used as pl*) the people of England. ➤ **English** *adj*.

engorge *v* to make swollen with blood, water, etc.

engrained *adj* see INGRAINED.

engrave *v* **1** to cut (a design or lettering) on metal or stone. **2** to impress deeply on somebody's mind. ➤ **engraver** *n*.

engraving *n* **1** a print made from an engraved surface. **2** the art of cutting designs on hard surfaces.

engross *v* to occupy all the time and attention of.

engulf *v* **1** to flow over and completely cover. **2** to overwhelm.

enhance *v* to improve the value, desirability, or attractiveness of. ➤ **enhancement** *n*.

enigma *n* somebody or something hard to understand or explain. ➤ **enigmatic** *adj*, **enigmatically** *adv*.

enjoin *v formal* to order (somebody) to do something.

enjoy *v* **1** to take pleasure in. **2** to have the use or benefit of. ✴ **enjoy oneself** to take pleasure in what one is doing. ➤ **enjoyment** *n*.

enjoyable *adj* giving pleasure.

enlarge *v* **1** to make or become larger. **2** (+ on/upon) to speak or write at greater length.

enlargement *n* **1** a photographic print that is larger than the negative or an earlier print. **2** the act of enlarging.

enlighten *v* to give knowledge or spiritual insight to. ➤ **enlightenment** *n*.

enlightened *adj* rational, well-informed, and free from prejudice.

enlist *v* **1** to enrol for duty in the armed forces. **2** to secure and employ (somebody, resources, etc) in advancing a cause, etc. ➤ **enlistment** *n*.

enliven v 1 to make more lively or interesting. 2 to make more cheerful.

en masse /onh 'mas/ adv in a body; as a whole.

enmesh v to entangle as in a net.

enmity n (pl -ies) a feeling or state of hostility or hatred.

ennoble v 1 to make finer or more dignified. 2 to raise to the nobility.

ennui n weariness and dissatisfaction resulting from boredom.

enormity n (pl -ies) 1 the state of being enormous. 2 great wickedness. 3 a terribly wicked act.

enormous adj extraordinarily large. ➤ **enormously** adv.

enough[1] adj fully adequate in quantity, number, or degree.

enough[2] adv 1 to a fully adequate degree. 2 to a moderate degree.

enough[3] pron a sufficient quantity or number.

enquire or **inquire** v 1 to seek information by questioning; to ask. 2 (often + into) to make an investigation. * **enquire after** to ask about the health, etc of.

Usage Note: Enquire is the commoner British English spelling; inquire is generally used in American English.

enquiry or **inquiry** n (pl -ies) 1 a request for information. 2 a systematic investigation.

enrage v to make very angry.

enrapture v to fill with delight.

enrich v 1 to make wealthy or wealthier. 2 to improve or enhance, esp by adding additional ingredients. ➤ **enrichment** n.

enrol (NAmer **enroll**) v (**enrolled, enrolling**) to register as a member or student. ➤ **enrolment** n.

en route /on 'rooht/ adv and adj on or along the way.

ensconce v to settle (e.g. oneself) comfortably or snugly.

ensemble n 1 a group that works together as a whole. 2 a complete outfit of matching garments. 3 a group of actors, musicians, etc who perform together.

enshrine v to preserve as sacred and protect from change.

enshroud v to cover and conceal completely.

ensign n a flag flown esp by a ship.

enslave v 1 to reduce to slavery. 2 to make dependent on. ➤ **enslavement** n.

ensnare v 1 to catch in a snare. 2 to lure into a situation from which there is no escape.

ensue v (**ensues, ensued, ensuing**) to take place afterwards or as a result.

en suite /on 'sweet/ adv and adj of a room: opening off another room.

ensure v to make sure or certain.

Usage Note: Do not confuse this word with insure, which means 'to take out insurance on'.

entail v to involve as a necessary accompaniment or result.

entangle v 1 to cause to become tangled. 2 to involve in a difficult situation. ➤ **entanglement** n.

entente n a friendly relationship between two or more countries.

enter v 1 to go or come into (a place). 2 to record (a piece of information) in a diary, account, computer file etc. 3 to become a member of. 4 to register as contestant in a competition. 5 (+ into/on/upon) to embark on something. * **enter into 1** to make oneself a party to or in (e.g. an agreement). 2 to be a factor in.

enterprise n 1 a project or undertaking. 2 a business organization. 3 boldness and initiative.

enterprising adj marked by boldness and initiative; resourceful.

entertain v 1 to give enjoyment or amusement to. 2 to show hospitality to. 3 to have in one's mind (a doubt, suggestion, etc).

entertainment n 1 something that is enjoyable to watch or take part in. 2 the act of entertaining.

enthral (NAmer **enthrall**) v (**enthralled, enthralling**) to hold the complete interest and attention of; to captivate.

Usage Note: Note the spelling with -al and not -all.

enthrone v to place on a throne, esp to mark the beginning of a period in office. ➤ **enthronement** n.

enthuse v 1 to make enthusiastic. 2 to show enthusiasm.

enthusiasm n keen interest and excited admiration.

enthusiast n somebody who is extremely interested in and attached to a cause or pursuit.

entice v to tempt or lure by arousing hope or desire. ➤ **enticement** n, **enticing** adj.

entire adj having no element or part left out; whole.

entirely adv 1 wholly or completely. 2 solely.

entirety n the whole or total. * **in its entirety** with nothing omitted.

entitle v 1 to give a title to. 2 to give the right to do or have something. ➤ **entitlement** n.

entity n (pl -ies) something that has separate and distinct existence.

entomb v 1 to place (e.g. a body) in a tomb. 2 to shut away.

entomology n the study of insects. ➤ **entomological** adj, **entomologist** n.

entourage n a group of attendants or associates of an important person.

entrails pl n internal organs, esp the intestines.

entrance[1] /'entrəns/ n 1 the act of entering. 2 a means or place of entry. 3 right or permission to enter.

entrance² /in'trahns/ v to fill with delight or wonder. ➤ **entrancing** adj.

entrant n somebody who enters a contest, profession, etc.

entrap v (**entrapped, entrapping**) **1** to catch in a trap. **2** to trick into making a compromising statement or committing a crime. ➤ **entrapment** n.

entreat v to beg or plead with or for.

entreaty n (pl **-ies**) a humble or heartfelt plea.

entrée or **entree** n **1** chiefly Brit a dish served before the main course of a formal dinner. **2** the principal dish of a meal. **3** right of entry or access.

entrench or **intrench** v **1** to establish (something) so solidly that it is difficult to change. **2** to dig and occupy trenches for defence. ➤ **entrenchment** n.

entrepreneur n somebody who sets up a business and assumes the risks of running it. ➤ **entrepreneurial** adj.

entropy n a measure of the amount of energy that is unavailable for doing work in a thermodynamic system.

entrust v **1** (+ with) to give (somebody) the responsibility of looking after or dealing with something. **2** (+ to) to put (something) into somebody's care.

entry n (pl **-ies**) **1** the act of entering. **2** the right or privilege of entering. **3** a door, gate, hall, or other way in. **4** a record made in a diary, account book, index, etc.

entwine v to twine together or round.

E number n a number with the letter E in front of it, used to denote a particular additive to food.

enumerate v to list or name one by one. ➤ **enumeration** n.

enunciate v **1** to articulate distinctly. **2** to state or formulate precisely. ➤ **enunciation** n.

envelop v (**enveloped, enveloping**) to wrap, cover, or surround completely. ➤ **envelopment** n.

envelope n **1** a flat container, usu of folded and gummed paper, e.g. for a letter. **2** a wrapper, cover, or casing, e.g. the gasbag of an airship.

enviable adj worthy of envy; highly desirable. ➤ **enviably** adv.

envious adj feeling or showing envy. ➤ **enviously** adv.

environment n **1** the objects or conditions by which somebody or something is surrounded. **2** (**the environment**) the natural surroundings and plant and animal life, among which people live. ➤ **environmental** adj, **environmentally** adv.

environmentalism n concern for the protection or quality of the natural environment. ➤ **environmentalist** n.

environs pl n the area surrounding something.

envisage v **1** to have a mental picture of. **2** to consider as a possibility in the future.

envoy n **1** a diplomatic agent, esp one ranking immediately below an ambassador. **2** a messenger or representative.

envy¹ n (pl **-ies**) **1** a wish to possess an advantage enjoyed by somebody else. **2** somebody or something that is envied.

envy² v (**-ies, -ied**) to feel envy for.

enzyme n a protein produced by living cells that promotes biochemical reactions without undergoing change itself.

eon n see AEON.

epaulette (NAmer **epaulet**) n an ornamental strip attached to the shoulder of a garment, esp a military uniform.

ephemera pl n items of short-lived duration, use, or interest.

ephemeral adj lasting a very short time.

epic¹ n **1** a long narrative poem recounting the deeds of a legendary or historical figure or the events in a nation's history. **2** a novel, film, etc that resembles an epic.

epic² adj **1** of an epic. **2** extending beyond the usual in size or scope. **3** heroic.

epicentre (NAmer **epicenter**) n the part of the earth's surface directly above the origin of an earthquake.

epicure n a connoisseur of food or wine. ➤ **epicurean** n and adj.

epidemic n **1** an outbreak of a disease affecting many individuals within a population or region. **2** a sudden rapid spread of something undesirable.

epidermis n **1** the outer layer of the skin of an animal that covers the dermis. **2** a protective surface layer of cells in plants. ➤ **epidermal** adj.

epidural n an injection of local anaesthetic into the canal housing the spinal cord, esp during childbirth.

epiglottis n a thin plate of cartilage behind the tongue that folds back to cover the entrance to the larynx during swallowing.

epigram n **1** a short witty or satirical poem. **2** a concise, witty remark or saying. ➤ **epigrammatic** adj.

epigraph n **1** an engraved inscription. **2** a quotation at the beginning of a book, chapter, etc.

epilepsy n a disorder affecting the electrical rhythms of the brain and resulting in convulsive attacks and loss of consciousness. ➤ **epileptic** n and adj.

epilogue n a concluding section of a literary work commenting on the main theme or revealing the later fate of the characters.

epiphany n (pl **epiphanies**) **1** (**Epiphany**) the coming of the Magi to see the infant Christ, commemorated on 6 January. **2** a revelation of the nature or meaning of something.

episcopacy n (pl -ies) **1** government of the Church by bishops. **2** the bishops of a Church or country.

episcopal adj **1** of a bishop. **2** governed by bishops. **3** (**Episcopal**) of the Anglican Church in the USA or Scotland.

episcopalian adj **1** of or supporting the episcopal form of Church government. **2** (**Episcopalian**) of the Episcopal Church.

episode n **1** a distinct event that is part of a larger series, e.g. in history or somebody's life. **2** an instalment of a serialized literary work, radio or television programme, etc.

episodic adj **1** made up of separate episodes. **2** occasional or sporadic.

epistemology n the philosophical study of knowledge.

epistle n **1** a letter. **2** (**Epistle**) any of the letters from the apostles adopted as books of the New Testament.

epistolary adj **1** of letters or letter-writing. **2** written in the form of a series of letters.

epitaph n a commemorative inscription on a tombstone or monument.

epithet n a descriptive word or phrase accompanying or replacing the name of a person or thing.

epitome n a typical or ideal example.

epitomize or **-ise** v to serve as a typical or ideal example of.

epoch n an extended period of historical time with its own distinctive character.

eponym n **1** a word, e.g. cardigan, derived from a person's name. **2** a person after whom something is named.

eponymous adj denoting a character in a film, book, etc, whose name is in its title.

epsilon n the fifth letter of the Greek alphabet (E, ε).

equable adj **1** even-tempered or placid. **2** free from extremes or sudden changes. ➤ **equably** adv.

equal[1] adj **1** of the same quantity, size, value, or status as another. **2** identical for each member of a group. **3** evenly balanced or matched. **4** (+ to) capable of meeting the requirements of (e.g. a task). ➤ **equally** adv.

equal[2] v (**equalled, equalling,** NAmer **equaled, equaling**) **1** to be equal to. **2** to achieve the same standard as.

equality n the state of being equal, esp of having the same rights and status as others.

equalize or **-ise** v **1** to make equal. **2** to bring the scores level, e.g. in a football match. ➤ **equalization** n, **equalizer** n.

equanimity n evenness of temper; composure.

equate v to treat or regard as equal.

equation n **1** a statement of the equality of two mathematical expressions. **2** an expression representing a chemical reaction by means of chemical symbols. **3** the act of equating.

equator n the imaginary circle around the earth, equidistant from the two poles, that divides the northern and southern hemispheres.

equatorial adj **1** of, at, or near the equator. **2** of climate: consistently hot and rainy.

equerry n (pl -ies) an officer of the British royal household in personal attendance on a member of the royal family.

equestrian[1] adj of horses or horse riding. ➤ **equestrianism** n.

equestrian[2] n a person who rides on horseback.

equidistant adj equally distant.

equilateral adj of e.g. a triangle: with all its sides of equal length.

equilibrium n (pl **equilibria**) **1** a state of balance between opposing forces. **2** a state of physical balance. **3** a calm intellectual or emotional state.

equine adj of or resembling a horse.

equinoctial adj **1** relating to or occurring at an equinox. **2** relating to the equator.

equinox n either of the two times each year, around 21 March and 23 September, when day and night are of equal length.

equip v (**equipped, equipping**) **1** to provide with appropriate tools, supplies, etc. **2** to provide with the necessary abilities and intellectual or emotional resources for something.

equipment n the tools and resources needed for a particular purpose.

equitable adj fair and just. ➤ **equitably** adv.

equity n (pl -ies) **1** fairness. **2** a system of natural justice developed to supplement common law. **3** the value of a property when monetary claims against it, e.g. mortgages, have been subtracted. **4** the value of shares issued by a company.

equivalent[1] adj **1** equal in force, amount, or value. **2** corresponding or virtually identical in effect, function, or meaning. ➤ **equivalence** n, **equivalently** adv.

equivalent[2] n something or somebody that is equivalent.

equivocal adj subject to two or more interpretations; ambiguous. ➤ **equivocally** adv.

equivocate v to use equivocal language, esp in order to deceive or avoid committing oneself. ➤ **equivocation** n.

Er abbr the chemical symbol for erbium.

-er[1] suffix forming the comparative of adjectives and adverbs: hotter; sooner.

-er[2] suffix denoting somebody or something that performs an action: recorder; baker.

era n a historical period typified by some characteristic feature.

eradicate v to destroy or do away with completely. ➤ **eradication** n.

erase v **1** to rub out (something written). **2** to

remove (recorded matter) from a tape. **3** to remove from existence or memory completely.

eraser *n* something, e.g. a piece of rubber or a felt pad, used to erase pencil, chalk, etc.

ere *prep and conj literary* before.

erect¹ *adj* **1** upright and rigidly straight. **2** in a state of physiological erection. ➤ **erectly** *adv*, **erectness** *n*.

erect² *v* **1** to build. **2** to establish; to set up.

erectile *adj* capable of physiological erection. ➤ **erectility** *n*.

erection *n* **1** a process in which a limp body part, *esp* the penis, becomes firm through being dilated with blood. **2** something erected, *esp* a building. **3** the act of erecting.

ergo *adv* therefore.

ergonomics *pl n* a science concerned with the relationship between human beings and their working environment.

ERM *abbr* exchange-rate mechanism.

ermine *n* (*pl* **ermines** *or* **ermine**) **1** a stoat that has a white winter coat. **2** the winter fur of this animal.

erode *v* **1** to wear away by the action of water, wind, etc. **2** to diminish or destroy by degrees.

erogenous *adj* of part of the body: sensitive to sexual stimulation.

erosion *n* the process of eroding.

erotic *adj* concerned with or arousing sexual desire. ➤ **erotically** *adv*.

erotica *pl n* literature or art with an erotic theme.

eroticism *n* **1** an erotic quality or character. **2** sexual arousal or excitement.

err *v* **1** to make a mistake. **2** to do wrong.

errand *n* a short trip to attend to some business, often for somebody else.

errant *adj* **1** *formal* doing wrong. **2** *archaic* travelling in search of adventure.

erratic *adj* lacking consistency or regularity; unpredictable. ➤ **erratically** *adv*.

erratum *n* (*pl* **errata**) **1** an error in a printed work, shown with its correction. **2** (*in pl*) a list of such errors and corrections inserted into a publication.

erroneous *adj* incorrect. ➤ **erroneously** *adv*.

error *n* **1** a mistake or inaccuracy. **2** the state of being wrong.

ersatz *adj* denoting an artificial and inferior substitute or imitation.

erstwhile *adj* former; previous.

erudite *adj* possessing or displaying extensive knowledge; learned. ➤ **erudition** *n*.

erupt *v* **1** of a volcano: to release lava, steam, etc suddenly and violently. **2** to become suddenly active or violent. **3** to become violently angry. **4** of a rash, spot, etc: to appear on the skin.

Es *abbr* the chemical symbol for einsteinium.

escalate *v* to increase in amount, intensity, or seriousness, usu rapidly. ➤ **escalation** *n*.

escalator *n* a power-driven set of stairs on an endless belt.

escalope *or* **escallop** /'eskəlɒp/ *n* a thin slice of meat coated with egg and breadcrumbs, and fried.

escapade *n* a reckless and often mischievous adventure.

escape¹ *v* **1** to get away, *esp* from confinement or restraint. **2** of gases, liquids, etc: to leak out gradually. **3** to avoid a threatening evil, danger, etc. **4** to fail to be noticed or recalled by. ➤ **escapee** *n*, **escaper** *n*.

escape² *n* **1** the act of escaping. **2** a means of escape.

escapism *n* activity or entertainment intended to take one's mind off unpleasant realities. ➤ **escapist** *adj and n*.

escapology *n* the theatrical art of escaping from restraints such as chains, handcuffs, or locked boxes. ➤ **escapologist** *n*.

escarpment *n* a long steep slope separating two comparatively level surfaces.

eschew *v* *formal* to avoid habitually.

escort¹ *n* **1** one or more people, cars, ships, etc accompanying somebody or something to give protection or show courtesy. **2** a person who accompanies another person socially.

escort² *v* to accompany as an escort.

escutcheon *n* a shield on which a coat of arms is displayed.

Eskimo *n* (*pl* **Eskimos** *or* **Eskimo**) a member of an indigenous people of northern Canada, Greenland, Alaska, and eastern Siberia.

esoteric *adj* understood by or restricted to a small group, *esp* of the specially initiated.

ESP *abbr* extrasensory perception.

espadrille *n* a flat sandal with a canvas upper and rope sole.

especial *adj* **1** particularly special. **2** distinctly personal.

especially *adv* **1** in particular. **2** very much.

espionage *n* the use of spies to obtain information.

esplanade *n* a level open stretch of paved or grassy ground, *esp* along a shore.

espouse *v* to take up and support (a cause, belief, etc). ➤ **espousal** *n*.

espresso *n* coffee brewed by forcing steam through finely ground coffee beans.

Usage Note: Note the spelling with *esp-* and not *exp-*.

esprit de corps /də 'kaw/ *n* a spirit of loyalty and common purpose uniting the members of a group.

espy *v* (**-ies**, **-ied**) *literary* to catch sight of.

Esq. *abbr* Esquire.

esquire *n* *Brit* used instead of Mr as a man's courtesy title and usu placed after the surname.

-ess *suffix* denoting a female person or animal: *actress*; *lioness*.

essay[1] *n* **1** a short piece of prose writing on a specific topic. **2** *formal* an attempt. ➤ **essayist** *n*.

essay[2] *v formal* to attempt.

essence *n* **1** the most important qualities of an individual being or thing, those that make it what it is. **2** the special qualities of a plant, drug, etc, extracted in concentrated form, and used to make e.g. a perfume or flavouring. * **of the essence** of the utmost importance.

essential[1] *adj* **1** of the utmost importance; necessary. **2** fundamental or inherent. ➤ **essentially** *adv*.

essential[2] *n* something indispensable or fundamental.

essential oil *n* an oil with a characteristic odour extracted from a plant for use in perfumes and flavourings.

-est *suffix* forming the superlative of adjectives and adverbs: *nearest; dirtiest*.

establish *v* **1** to make stable, secure, or permanent. **2** to bring into existence. **3** to place (somebody, e.g. oneself) in a permanent or secure position. **4** to put beyond doubt; to prove.

establishment *n* **1** the act of establishing. **2** a place of business or residence with its furnishings and staff. **3** (**the Establishment**) the group of institutions and people who control public life and support the existing order of society.

estate *n* **1** a large landed property, usu with a house on it. **2** *Brit* an area devoted to buildings of a particular type, e.g. housing, or commercial or retail premises. **3** the assets and liabilities left by somebody at death.

estate agent *n chiefly Brit* a person who sells land, houses, and flats for clients.

estate car *n Brit* a car with a rear door opening onto a large luggage compartment.

esteem[1] *v* to admire and respect.

esteem[2] *n* admiration and respect.

ester *n* a chemical compound formed by the reaction between an acid and an alcohol.

esthetic *adj NAmer* see AESTHETIC[1].

estimable *adj* worthy of esteem.

estimate[1] *n* **1** a rough calculation. **2** a statement of the expected cost of a job. **3** an opinion or judgment.

estimate[2] *v* **1** to make an estimate of. **2** to judge or conclude. ➤ **estimation** *n*.

estranged *adj* of a husband or wife: no longer living with his or her spouse.

estrogen *n NAmer* see OESTROGEN.

estuary *n* (*pl* **-ies**) a sea inlet at the mouth of a river.

eta *n* the seventh letter of the Greek alphabet (H, η).

et al *adv* and others.

etc *abbr* et cetera.

et cetera *adv* and other things; and so forth.

etch *v* **1** to produce (a picture or letters) on metal or glass by the corrosive action of an acid. **2** to delineate or imprint clearly.

etching *n* **1** the art of printing from an etched metal plate. **2** a picture produced by etching.

eternal *adj* **1** lasting or existing for ever. **2** *informal* incessant or interminable. ➤ **eternally** *adv*.

eternity *n* (*pl* **-ies**) **1** infinite time. **2** *informal* a seemingly endless time.

ethane *n* a gas obtained from petroleum or natural gas and used as a fuel.

ether *n* **1** an inflammable liquid used *esp* as a solvent and formerly as a general anaesthetic. **2** *literary* the sky or upper regions of the atmosphere.

ethereal *adj* **1** intangible. **2** unusually delicate and light. **3** *literary* celestial; heavenly.

ethic *n* **1** (*also in pl*) a set of moral principles or values governing the conduct of an individual or group. **2** (*in pl*) the study of the nature of moral principles and judgments.

ethical *adj* **1** conforming to accepted standards of conduct or morality. **2** relating to ethics. ➤ **ethically** *adv*.

ethnic *adj* **1** relating to the basic factors, e.g. race, culture, or language, that a group of people have in common. **2** belonging to a particular group by birth or descent. **3** of a traditional, *esp* peasant or non-Western, culture. ➤ **ethnically** *adv*, **ethnicity** *n*.

ethnic cleansing *n* the systematic removal of all members of a particular ethnic group from a region.

ethnic minority *n* an ethnic group that constitutes a minority of the population of a country.

ethos *n* the guiding beliefs of a person, institution, etc.

ethyl *n* a chemical group (CH_3CH_2) derived from ethane and present in alcohol.

etiquette *n* the conventionally accepted standards of proper social or professional behaviour.

etymology *n* (*pl* **-ies**) the history of the origin and development of a word. ➤ **etymological** *adj*.

EU *abbr* European Union.

Eu *abbr* the chemical symbol for europium.

eucalyptus *n* (*pl* **eucalyptuses** or **eucalypti**) an Australasian evergreen tree.

Eucharist *n* **1** the Christian sacrament in which consecrated bread and wine are consumed in accordance with Christ's injunctions at the Last Supper. **2** the consecrated bread and wine consumed in the Eucharist. ➤ **Eucharistic** *adj*.

eugenics *pl n* a science dealing with the improvement of the hereditary qualities of a race, e.g. by careful selection of parents.

eulogize or **eulogise** v to praise highly in speech or writing.

eulogy n (pl -ies) a speech or piece of writing in praise of somebody or something.

eunuch n a castrated man.

euphemism n a mild or indirect expression substituted for an offensive or unpleasant one. ➤ **euphemistic** adj, **euphemistically** adv.

euphonious adj pleasing to the ear. ➤ **euphoniously** adv.

euphonium n a brass musical instrument resembling a tuba but smaller.

euphony n (pl -ies) a pleasing or sweet sound.

euphoria n an intense feeling of well-being or elation. ➤ **euphoric** adj.

Eurasian adj 1 of mixed European and Asian origin. 2 relating to or from Europe and Asia considered as a single landmass.

eureka interj used to express triumph at a discovery.

euro n (pl -os) the single European currency used by many member countries of the European Union.

European[1] adj 1 of, from, or relating to Europe. 2 relating to the European Union. ➤ **Europeanism** n.

European[2] n 1 a native or inhabitant of Europe. 2 a person of European origin; a white person.

European Union n an economic and political association of European states.

euthanasia n the mercy killing of incurably sick or injured individuals.

evacuate v 1 to remove (people) from a dangerous place. 2 to vacate (a dangerous place). 3 to discharge urine, faeces, etc from the body. ➤ **evacuation** n.

evacuee n a person evacuated from a dangerous place.

evade v 1 to avoid, esp by skill or deception. 2 to avoid facing up to or answering. 3 to fail to pay (taxes, etc).

evaluate v to determine the amount, value, or significance of. ➤ **evaluation** n.

evanescent adj chiefly literary tending to dissipate or vanish like vapour. ➤ **evanescence** n.

evangelical[1] adj 1 of or in accordance with the Christian message in the four Gospels. 2 (often **Evangelical**) denoting a Protestant denomination emphasizing salvation by faith, personal conversion, and the authority of Scripture. 3 fervent; zealous. ➤ **evangelicalism** n.

evangelical[2] n (often **Evangelical**) a member of an evangelical denomination.

evangelist n 1 (often **Evangelist**) a writer of any of the four Gospels. 2 a person who preaches the Christian gospel and seeks converts. 3 a person with crusading zeal. ➤ **evangelistic** adj.

evangelize or **-ise** v to preach the Christian gospel to and seek to convert.

evaporate v 1 to change from liquid to vapour. 2 to disappear or fade. ➤ **evaporation** n.

evaporated milk n unsweetened milk concentrated by partial evaporation.

evasion n the act or a means of evading something or somebody.

evasive adj 1 intended to avoid something. 2 tending to avoid committing oneself; equivocal. ➤ **evasively** adv.

eve n 1 the evening or day before a special day, esp a religious holiday. 2 the period immediately preceding an event. 3 chiefly literary the evening.

even[1] adj 1 flat or level. 2 smooth. 3 without variation; uniform. 4 of a person's temper: calm; equable. 5 equal. 6 fair. 7 in equilibrium; balanced. 8 of a number: exactly divisible by two. * **get even with somebody** take revenge on somebody. ➤ **evenly** adv, **evenness** n.

even[2] v (often + up/out) to make or become even.

even[3] adv used to emphasize something: even better than last time. * **even if/though** in spite of the possibility or fact that. **even so** in spite of that.

even[4] n archaic or literary the evening.

evenhanded adj fair; impartial.

evening n the latter part of the day and early part of the night.

evening star n the planet Venus, seen in the western sky at sunset.

evensong n (often **Evensong**) the daily evening service of the Anglican Church.

event n 1 a happening or occurrence, esp an important one. 2 a public or social occasion. 3 any of the contests in a sporting programme. * **in the event of/that** if the specified thing should happen.

eventful adj marked by noteworthy or exciting occurrences.

eventual adj taking place at an unspecified later time; ultimately resulting. ➤ **eventually** adv.

eventuality n (pl -ies) a possible, esp unwelcome, event or outcome.

ever adv 1 at any time. 2 always: an ever-growing need. 3 used as an intensive: why ever not?

evergreen adj 1 having leaves that remain green throughout the year. 2 always retaining popularity.

everlasting adj 1 lasting for all time. 2 continuing for a very long time. 3 tediously persistent. ➤ **everlastingly** adv.

evermore adv archaic or literary always; forever.

every adj 1 all, without exception, of a group larger than two. 2 each or all possible: She was given every chance. 3 once in each: every 5000 miles. * **every now and then/so often/once in a while** at intervals; occasionally. **every other** each alternate.

everybody pron every person.

everyday *adj* **1** daily. **2** encountered routinely; ordinary.

everyone *pron* every person.

everything *pron* **1** all that exists. **2** all that is necessary or that relates to the subject. **3** something of the greatest importance.

everywhere *adv* **1** in, at, or to every place. **2** in many places.

evict *v* to remove (a tenant) from rented accommodation or land by a legal process. ➤ **eviction** *n*.

evidence[1] *n* **1** outward sign or indication. **2** something that gives reason for believing or agreeing with something; *esp* information used by a court to arrive at the truth. * **in evidence** to be seen; conspicuous.

evidence[2] *v* to show.

evident *adj* clear; obvious. ➤ **evidently** *adv*.

evil[1] *adj* **1** not morally good; sinful or wicked. **2** disagreeable or offensive: *an evil smell*. ➤ **evilly** *adv*.

evil[2] *n* **1** wickedness; sin. **2** something that is socially harmful or morally wrong.

evince *v formal* to show clearly; to reveal.

eviscerate *v* to disembowel.

evocative *adj* evoking something, e.g. a memory or image, strongly.

evoke *v* **1** to call forth. **2** to bring to mind. ➤ **evocation** *n*.

evolution *n* **1** a theory that existing types of animals and plants are derived from preexisting types by natural selection. **2** a process of change and development, *esp* a gradual and peaceful one. ➤ **evolutionary** *adj*.

evolve *v* **1** to work out or develop gradually. **2** of a species: to develop by natural evolution.

ewe *n* a female sheep.

ewer *n* a wide-mouthed pitcher or jug.

ex *n informal* a former spouse, boyfriend, or girlfriend.

ex- *prefix* **1** out of; outside. **2** denoting deprivation or removal. **3** former: *the ex-president*.

exacerbate *v* to make worse; to aggravate. ➤ **exacerbation** *n*.

exact[1] *adj* **1** precise or accurate. **2** marked by thorough consideration of all details. ➤ **exactitude** *n*, **exactness** *n*.

exact[2] *v* to demand and obtain by force, threats, etc. ➤ **exaction** *n*.

exacting *adj* making rigorous demands, *esp* requiring careful attention and accuracy.

exactly *adv* **1** accurately; precisely. **2** altogether; entirely. **3** used to express complete agreement.

exaggerate *v* **1** to say or believe that (something) is greater, better, etc than it is. **2** to make more pronounced than normal. ➤ **exaggeration** *n*.

exalt *v* **1** to raise to a high rank or status. **2** to praise highly.

exaltation *n* **1** intense happiness. **2** the act of exalting.

exam *n* an examination, *esp* associated with a course of study.

examination *n* **1** a close inspection. **2** an exercise designed to test knowledge or proficiency. **3** the act of examining.

examine *v* **1** to inspect closely. **2** to investigate the health of (a patient). **3** to test the knowledge, proficiency, etc of. ➤ **examinee** *n*, **examiner** *n*.

example *n* **1** something representative of the group or type to which it belongs. **2** somebody or something that may be copied by others people. **3** something that illustrates a general rule.

exasperate *v* to anger or irritate intensely. ➤ **exasperating** *adj*, **exasperation** *n*.

excavate *v* **1** to form (e.g. a hole or tunnel) by digging. **2** to dig out and remove (e.g. soil or earth). **3** to expose (e.g. archaeological remains) to view by digging away a covering. ➤ **excavation** *n*.

exceed *v* **1** to be greater than or superior to. **2** to go beyond the limits of.

exceedingly *adv* very; extremely.

excel *v* (**excelled**, **excelling**) **1** (*often* + at/in) to be extremely good at. **2** *formal* to be better than. * **excel oneself** to do something better than ever before.

excellency *n* (*pl* -**ies**) (**Excellency**) used as a title for certain high dignitaries of State and Church.

excellent *adj* outstandingly good. ➤ **excellence** *n*, **excellently** *adv*.

except[1] *prep* excluding. * **except for 1** with the exception of. **2** but for.

except[2] *conj* only; but.

except[3] *v* to exclude.

excepting *prep* = EXCEPT[1].

exception *n* **1** the act of excepting. **2** somebody or something that is left out, *esp* a case to which a rule does not apply. * **take exception to** to object to.

exceptionable *adj formal* likely to cause disapproval; objectionable.

exceptional *adj* **1** unusual. **2** not average; superior. ➤ **exceptionally** *adv*.

Usage Note: Do not confuse *exceptional* meaning 'unusual' or 'outstanding' and *exceptionable* meaning 'objectionable'.

excerpt *n* a passage taken from a book, musical composition, film, etc, e.g. for quoting.

excess *n* **1** an amount that is more than necessary, prescribed, or desirable. **2** (*also in pl*) unrestrained behaviour or immoderate indulgence. **3** an amount an insured person agrees to pay towards a claim. **4** (*used before a noun*) denoting an amount that is more than normal or allowed: *excess baggage*. ✳ **in excess of** more than.

excessive *adj* exceeding normal or desirable limits. ➤ **excessively** *adv*.

exchange[1] *n* **1** the act of giving one thing for another. **2** a brief interchange of words or blows. **3** the conversion of one currency into another. **4** an organized market for trading in securities or commodities. **5** equipment controlling the connection of telephone calls between many different lines.

exchange[2] *v* to give (something) in return for something received as an equivalent.

exchange rate *n* the value of a unit of one currency in units of another.

exchequer *n* **1** (*often* **Exchequer**) *Brit* the department of state in charge of the national revenue. **2** a national or royal treasury.

excise[1] *n* a tax levied on the manufacture, sale, or consumption of a commodity within a country.

excise[2] *v* **1** to remove (something) by cutting it out, *esp* surgically. **2** to delete (e.g. a passage of text). ➤ **excision** *n*.

excitable *adj* easily excited. ➤ **excitability** *n*.

excite *v* **1** to cause to feel pleasurably stimulated, enthusiastic, or expectant. **2** to arouse sexually. **3** to provoke (an action or response). **4** to increase the activity of (an organ, tissue, etc); to stimulate. ➤ **excitation** *n*, **excited** *adj*, **exciting** *adj*, **excitingly** *adv*.

excitement *n* **1** a feeling of lively, pleasurable eagerness or anticipation. **2** something that produces this feeling. **3** the act of exciting or arousing.

exclaim *v* to cry out.

exclamation *n* a word or remark uttered suddenly. ➤ **exclamatory** *adj*.

exclude *v* **1** to decide not to include or consider. **2** to bar from participation. **3** to shut out.

exclusion *n* **1** the act of excluding; the fact of being left out. **2** something not covered by a contract, insurance policy, etc.

exclusive[1] *adj* **1** limited to a single individual, a particular group, etc. **2** excluding others from participation, membership, or entry. **3** stylish and expensive. **4** whole or undivided: *gave her his exclusive attention*. **5** (+ of) not including. ➤ **exclusively** *adv*, **exclusiveness** *n*.

exclusive[2] *n* an interview, article, etc published by only one newspaper or broadcast by only one television channel or radio station.

excommunicate *v* to deprive officially of the rights of church membership. ➤ **excommunication** *n*.

excoriate *v* **1** to wear away the skin of. **2** *formal* to censure scathingly. ➤ **excoriation** *n*.

excrement *n* faeces.

excrescence *n* an abnormal outgrowth or enlargement.

excreta *pl n* excrement.

excrete *v* to discharge (waste) from the body. ➤ **excretion** *n*, **excretory** *adj*.

excruciating *adj* **1** causing great pain; agonizing. **2** intensely embarrassing. **3** very bad or tedious. ➤ **excruciatingly** *adv*.

exculpate *v* to clear from blame or guilt.

excursion *n* a short pleasure trip, e.g. for sightseeing.

excuse[1] *v* **1** to try to remove blame from (somebody, oneself). **2** to be an acceptable reason for; to justify. **3** to forgive entirely. **4** to overlook as unimportant. **5** to allow to leave. **6** *Brit* to free from a duty. ✳ **excuse oneself** to announce politely that one is leaving. ➤ **excusable** *adj*.

excuse[2] *n* **1** a reason given to explain or justify a fault, mistake, etc. **2** a pretext. **3** (*in pl*) an expression of regret for failure to do something or for one's absence. **4** *informal* (+ for) a very poor example of.

ex-directory *adj Brit* not listed in a telephone directory at the subscriber's request.

execrable *adj* detestable or appalling.

execrate *v* to detest utterly; to abhor. ➤ **execration** *n*.

execute *v* **1** to put into effect (a plan, order, etc). **2** to put to death as a punishment. **3** to carry out or perform (e.g. a movement). **4** in computing, to run (a file, program, etc).

execution *n* **1** the act of carrying something out. **2** the act of putting somebody to death as a punishment.

executioner *n* a person legally appointed to carry out capital punishment.

executive[1] *adj* concerned with carrying out laws, decisions, plans, etc, rather than formulating them.

executive[2] *n* **1** a person with administrative or managerial responsibility. **2** a person or group that controls an organization. **3** the executive branch of a government.

executor *n* a person appointed to carry out the provisions of another person's will.

exegesis *n* (*pl* **exegeses**) an explanation or critical interpretation of a text.

exemplar *n* somebody or something that serves as a typical example or ideal model.

exemplary *adj* **1** worthy of imitation; outstanding. **2** of a punishment: serving as a warning.

exemplify *v* (**-ies**, **-ied**) **1** to serve as an example of. **2** to illustrate with an example. ➤ **exemplification** *n*.

exempt[1] *adj* free from some liability or requirement to which others are subject.

exempt[2] *v* to make exempt; to excuse. ➤ **exemption** *n*.

exercise[1] *n* **1** physical exertion for the sake of maintaining bodily fitness. **2** an activity or test intended to develop or display a physical or mental skill. **3** something done for a particular purpose. **4** the use of a power or right.

exercise² v **1** to engage in physical exertion for the sake of fitness. **2** to use or exert (e.g. a right). **3** to cause anxiety, alarm, or indignation in.

exercise book n a booklet of blank pages used for written work in schools.

exert v to bring (strength or authority) to bear on a situation. ❋ **exert oneself** to make an effort. ➤ **exertion** n.

exeunt v used as a stage direction instructing more than one character to leave the stage.

exfoliate v **1** to cast (skin or bark) off in scales, layers, etc. **2** to remove surface cells, layers, etc from (the skin). ➤ **exfoliation** n.

exhale v **1** to breathe out. **2** to emit (gas or vapour). ➤ **exhalation** n.

exhaust¹ v **1** to tire out. **2** to consume entirely; to use up. **3** to deal with (a subject) so fully that there is no more to say about it. ➤ **exhaustible** adj.

exhaust² n **1** used gases or vapour expelled from an engine. **2** the pipe or system through which these gases escape.

exhaustion n **1** extreme tiredness. **2** the act of exhausting.

exhaustive adj dealing with every aspect of a subject; comprehensive. ➤ **exhaustively** adv.

exhibit¹ v (**exhibited, exhibiting**) **1** to show (a work of art, etc) publicly. **2** to show (a feeling, symptom, etc) outwardly.

exhibit² n **1** something exhibited, e.g. in a museum. **2** something produced as evidence in a court of law.

exhibition n **1** a public showing, e.g. of works of art. **2** the act of exhibiting. ❋ **make an exhibition of oneself** to behave foolishly in public.

exhibitionism n behaviour intended to attract attention to oneself. ➤ **exhibitionist** n.

exhilarate v **1** to make very happy or cheerful. **2** to enliven or invigorate. ➤ **exhilarating** adj, **exhilaration** n.

exhort v to urge or advise strongly.

exhortation n a strongly worded appeal to somebody to do something.

exhume v to dig (something buried, esp a dead body) up again.

exigency n (pl **-ies**) formal **1** an emergency. **2** desperate or urgent nature.

exigent adj formal requiring immediate aid or action.

exiguous adj formal excessively scanty; meagre.

exile¹ n **1** a state of banishment from one's country or home. **2** somebody who is sent into exile.

exile² v to send into exile.

exist v **1** to have being or life, or to be real. **2** to live at an inferior level.

existence n **1** the state of existing or being. **2** a manner of living.

existential adj **1** of or grounded in existence. **2** relating to existentialism. ➤ **existentially** adv.

existentialism n a philosophical movement characterized by enquiry into human beings' experience of themselves in relation to the world, esp insofar as they are free individuals, responsible for their own moral choices in a universe where there are no absolute concepts of right and wrong. ➤ **existentialist** n and adj.

exit¹ v (**exited, exiting**) **1** used as a stage direction to tell a particular character to leave the stage. **2** to leave or depart.

exit² n **1** a way out of a room or building. **2** the act of going out, away, or off stage. **3** a point at which vehicles can leave a major road, roundabout, etc.

exit poll n a survey of voting trends conducted by questioning people as they leave a polling station.

exodus n a mass departure; an emigration.

exonerate v **1** to free from blame. **2** (often + from) to relieve of a responsibility. ➤ **exoneration** n.

exorbitant adj of prices, demands, etc: much greater than is reasonable. ➤ **exorbitantly** adv.

exorcize or **-ise** v to expel (an evil spirit) from a person or place. ➤ **exorcism** n, **exorcist** n.

exotic adj **1** introduced from another country. **2** strikingly or excitingly different or unusual. ➤ **exotically** adv, **exoticism** n.

expand v **1** to make or become larger, greater, etc. **2** (often + on) to speak or write at greater length. **3** to grow genial; to become more sociable. ➤ **expandable** adj, **expander** n.

expanse n a wide area of something.

expansive adj **1** covering a large area. **2** genial and freely communicative. ➤ **expansively** adv.

expat n informal = EXPATRIATE.

expatiate v (usu + on/upon) to speak or write at length on.

expatriate n a person who lives outside their native country.

expect v **1** to consider (an event) probable or certain. **2** to consider (e.g. respect, obedience) to be reasonable or due. **3** to consider (somebody) to be duty-bound or obligated to do something. **4** to look forward to or to be waiting for. **5** to be waiting for the arrival of. ❋ **be expecting** informal to be pregnant.

expectancy n (pl **-ies**) **1** expectation, esp eager or joyful expectation. **2** the expected amount or length of something.

expectant adj **1** having, showing, or characterized by expectation. **2** of a woman: pregnant. ➤ **expectantly** adv.

expectation n **1** the state of expecting something; anticipation. **2** (also in pl) something expected.

expectorant n a medicine that promotes the bringing up of phlegm from the throat or lungs.

expectorate v to eject (phlegm or similar matter) from the throat or lungs by coughing or spitting.

expedient[1] adj **1** suitable for achieving a particular end. **2** characterized by concern with what is advantageous rather than what is right or ethical. ➤ **expediency** n.

expedient[2] n a means to an end, esp a makeshift or improvised one.

expedite v formal to hasten the progress of.

expedition n a journey undertaken for a specific purpose, e.g. for exploration. ➤ **expeditionary** adj.

expeditious adj formal prompt and efficient. ➤ **expeditiously** adv.

expel v (**expelled, expelling**) **1** to drive or force out. **2** to force to leave a school, society, etc.

expend v to spend or use up (e.g. time, care, or attention) on dealing with somebody or something.

expendable adj **1** not intended to be kept or re-used. **2** regarded as available for sacrifice in order to accomplish an objective.

expenditure n **1** the act of spending money. **2** the amount of money spent.

expense n **1** financial outlay; cost. **2** (in pl) the charges incurred by an employee in performing their duties. **3** a cause of expenditure. * **at somebody's expense** with somebody paying the bill or suffering the consequences. **at the expense of** disregarding or damaging.

expensive adj costing a great deal of money. ➤ **expensively** adv.

experience[1] n **1** direct participation or observation. **2** the knowledge or skill derived from direct involvement with something over a period of time. **3** something personally encountered or undergone. **4** the sum total of events encountered during an individual life.

experience[2] v to have experience of.

experienced adj skilful or wise as a result of experience.

experiment[1] n **1** a controlled scientific operation carried out to make a discovery, test a hypothesis, or illustrate a known law. **2** a procedure or policy that has not been tried before.

experiment[2] v to carry out an experiment or experiments. ➤ **experimentation** n.

experimental adj **1** used as a means of trying something out. **2** based on or relating to scientific experiments. **3** innovative and unconventional. ➤ **experimentally** adv.

expert[1] adj showing special skill or knowledge derived from training or experience. ➤ **expertly** adv.

expert[2] n a person who has special skill or knowledge in a particular field.

expertise n skill in or knowledge of a particular field.

expiate v to make amends for (a sin, crime, etc). ➤ **expiation** n.

expire v **1** of e.g. a permit: to cease to be valid. **2** of a period: to come to an end. **3** formal to die. **4** to breathe (air) out from the lungs.

expiry n a termination, esp of a period of validity.

explain v **1** to make plain or understandable, esp by giving details. **2** to give the reason for. * **explain oneself** to clarify the reasons for one's conduct. ➤ **explanation** n.

explanatory adj serving to explain.

expletive n an obscenity or profanity.

explicable adj capable of being explained.

explicit adj **1** clear and unambiguous. **2** graphically explicit or detailed. ➤ **explicitly** adv.

explode v **1** to burst violently as a result of pressure or a chemical or nuclear reaction. **2** to expand suddenly. **3** to give expression violently and usu noisily to emotion. **4** to demonstrate the falsity of (a belief or theory).

exploit[1] n a notable or heroic action.

exploit[2] v **1** to use or develop (resources, materials, etc) fully. **2** to take unfair advantage of. ➤ **exploitation** n, **exploitative** adj.

explore v **1** to travel through (an unfamiliar place), esp for purposes of discovery. **2** to examine or enquire into thoroughly. ➤ **exploration** n, **exploratory** adj, **explorer** n.

explosion n **1** the act of exploding. **2** a rapid large-scale expansion or increase.

explosive[1] adj **1** capable of exploding. **2** threatening to cause trouble or controversy. **3** sudden, rapid, and powerful. ➤ **explosively** adv.

explosive[2] n an explosive substance.

exponent n **1** somebody that expounds, advocates, or exemplifies something. **2** a skilled practitioner of an art, etc. **3** a symbol written above and to the right of a number to indicate that it is to be multiplied by itself that many times, e.g. $2^3 = 2 \times 2 \times 2$.

exponential adj **1** involving a a mathematical exponent. **2** increasing with accelerating rapidity. ➤ **exponentially** adv.

export[1] v **1** to send (a commodity) to another country for purposes of trade. **2** to take (an idea, custom, etc) to another country. ➤ **exportation** n, **exporter** n.

export[2] n **1** something exported. **2** the act of exporting.

expose v **1** to lay open to view; to uncover or display. **2** to lay open to attack, danger, etc. **3** to subject (a photographic film) to the action of light. **4** to bring (something shameful) to public notice. * **expose oneself** to engage in indecent exposure.

exposé n **1** a formal exposition of facts. **2** an exposure of something discreditable.

exposition n **1** the art of expounding or explaining. **2** a large public exhibition. **3** the first part of a musical composition in which the themes are presented.

expostulate v formal to remonstrate with somebody, esp in order to dissuade them. ➤ **expostulation** n.

exposure n **1** the fact of being exposed, esp to something harmful or unpleasant. **2** lack of protection from cold weather. **3** the act of exposing a sensitized photographic film to light. **4** a section of a film with one picture on it. **5** the disclosure esp of something shameful or criminal. **6** publicization, esp by means of the mass media.

expound v to state and explain (an idea, theory, etc) carefully.

express[1] v **1** to show or make known in words or by other means. **2** to force out (air or liquid) by pressure.

express[2] adj **1** firmly and explicitly stated. **2** specific. **3** travelling at high speed, usu with few stops along the way. **4** Brit designated to be delivered without delay.

express[3] adv by express.

express[4] n **1** an express train. **2** Brit an express delivery service.

expression n **1** the act or a means of expressing. **2** a significant word or phrase. **3** a look on somebody's face that indicates their feelings. **4** a mathematical or logical symbol or combination of symbols. ➤ **expressionless** adj.

expressionism n a style in art, literature, or music that attempts to depict subjective emotions and responses to objects and events. ➤ **expressionist** n and adj.

expressive adj vividly expressing something. ➤ **expressively** adv, **expressiveness** n, **expressivity** n.

expropriate v to deprive of owner's rights to a piece of property, esp with official sanction. ➤ **expropriation** n.

expulsion n the act of expelling.

expunge v formal to erase or obliterate completely.

expurgate v to remove objectionable parts from (a text) before publication. ➤ **expurgation** n.

exquisite adj **1** extremely beautiful, and usu delicate. **2** keenly sensitive, esp in feeling. **3** acute or intense. ➤ **exquisitely** adv.

extant adj still or currently existing.

extemporary adj spoken, done, etc on the spur of the moment without preparation.

extempore /ik'stempəri/ adj and adv spoken or done without preparation.

extemporize or **-ise** v to improvise or make something up on the spur of the moment.

extend v **1** to lengthen or enlarge. **2** to prolong in time. **3** to continue over a particular distance, area, or length of time. **4** to hold out or stretch out (e.g. one's hand or arm). **5** to give or offer. ➤ **extendable** adj, **extendible** adj, **extensible** adj.

extended family n a family unit that includes three or more generations of near relatives living close together.

extension n **1** the act of extending. **2** a part added to make something longer or larger, e.g. an extra room or rooms added to a building. **3** an extra telephone connected to the principal line.

extensive adj **1** extending over a large area. **2** large-scale. ➤ **extensively** adv.

extent n **1** the distance or area over which something extends. **2** the scale or scope of something. **3** the degree to which something is applicable.

extenuate v to lessen the seriousness of (a crime, etc) by providing a reason or excuse for it. ➤ **extenuating** adj, **extenuation** n.

exterior[1] adj on the outside or an outside surface.

exterior[2] n **1** an exterior part or surface; outside. **2** an outward appearance.

exterminate v to destroy or kill off completely. ➤ **extermination** n, **exterminator** n.

external[1] adj **1** on or intended for the outside. **2** arising or acting from outside. **3** relating to dealings with foreign countries or other organizations. ➤ **externally** adv.

external[2] n (usu in pl) an external feature or aspect.

externalize or **-ise** v to express (e.g. a feeling) in externally visible form.

extinct adj **1** no longer existing as a species. **2** of a volcano: no longer active.

extinguish v **1** to cause (a flame, fire, etc) to cease burning. **2** to put out (a light). **3** to destroy completely. ➤ **extinguisher** n.

extirpate v to remove or destroy completely. ➤ **extirpation** n.

extol (NAmer **extoll**) v (**extolled**, **extolling**) to praise highly.

extort v to obtain (e.g. money or a confession) by force or threats. ➤ **extortion** n.

extortionate adj of a price: excessive or exorbitant. ➤ **extortionately** adv.

extra[1] adj more than is due, usual, or necessary.

extra[2] n **1** something extra, e.g. an additional charge. **2** somebody hired to act in a group scene in a film or stage production.

extra³ *adv* beyond the usual size or amount.

extra- *prefix* outside; beyond: *extramural*.

extract¹ *v* **1** to pull out from within something. **2** to obtain, *esp* against resistance or with effort. **3** to separate out (e.g. a mineral) by a physical or chemical process.

extract² *n* **1** a short passage taken from a book, film, etc. **2** a substance containing the essential constituents of e.g. an aromatic plant in concentrated form.

extraction *n* **1** the act of extracting. **2** ancestry or origin.

extractor fan *n* a type of ventilator designed to expel fumes, stale air, etc.

extradite *v* to hand (somebody) over to a foreign country to stand trial for an offence committed there. ➤ **extradition** *n*.

extramarital *adj* of sexual relations: occurring outside marriage.

extramural *adj chiefly Brit* for students of a university, college, etc who do not attend on a full-time basis.

extraneous *adj* **1** not forming an essential or vital part; irrelevant. **2** coming from the outside.

extraordinaire *adj* (*used after a noun*) outstanding: *a decorator extraordinaire*.

extraordinary *adj* **1** highly exceptional; remarkable. **2** held for a special reason: *an extraordinary general meeting*. ➤ **extraordinarily** *adv*.

extrapolate *v* to use (known data or experience) as a basis for working out something unknown. ➤ **extrapolation** *n*.

extrasensory perception *n* perception by means other than the known senses, e.g. by telepathy and clairvoyance.

extraterrestrial¹ *adj* from outside the earth or its atmosphere.

extraterrestrial² *n* an extraterrestrial being.

extravagant *adj* **1** wasteful, *esp* of money. **2** unreasonably high in price. **3** lacking in moderation and restraint. **4** excessively elaborate or showy. ➤ **extravagance** *n*, **extravagantly** *adv*.

extravaganza *n* a lavish or spectacular show.

extreme¹ *adj* **1** existing in a very high degree. **2** not moderate; doctrinaire. **3** exceedingly severe or drastic. **4** situated at the farthest possible point from a centre. ➤ **extremely** *adv*.

extreme² *n* **1** something situated at one end or the other of a range. **2** (*also in pl*) a very pronounced or extreme degree. **3** (*also in pl*) an extreme measure.

extremist *n* somebody who holds extreme views.

extremity *n* (*pl* **-ies**) **1** the furthest part or point. **2** (*also in pl*) a human hand or foot. **3** extreme misfortune or danger or death.

extricate *v* to disentangle with considerable effort.

extrinsic *adj* not forming part of or belonging to a thing; extraneous.

extrovert *n* a gregarious or outgoing person: compare INTROVERT. ➤ **extrovert** *adj*.

extrude *v* **1** to force or push out. **2** to shape (metal, plastic, etc) by forcing it through a die. ➤ **extrusion** *n*.

exuberant *adj* **1** joyously unrestrained and enthusiastic. **2** abundant or luxuriant. ➤ **exuberance** *n*, **exuberantly** *adv*.

exude *v* **1** to ooze out or allow (a liquid or smell) to ooze out. **2** to display (a quality, feeling, etc) in abundance.

exult *v* to rejoice openly and triumphantly. ➤ **exultant** *adj*, **exultantly** *adv*, **exultation** *n*.

eye¹ *n* **1** an organ of sight. **2** the faculty of sight, perception, or appreciation: *an eye for beauty*. **3** the hole through the head of a needle. **4** a loop, *esp* one of metal into which a hook is inserted. **5** an undeveloped bud, e.g. on a potato. **6** a calm area in the centre of a storm, hurricane, etc. ✻ **be all eyes** to watch intently. **have/keep one's eye on** to watch *esp* constantly and attentively. **in the eye/eyes of** in the judgment or opinion of. **make eyes at** to ogle. **more than meets the eye** more than is at first apparent. **see eye to eye** to have a common viewpoint; to agree. **with an eye to** having as an aim or purpose.

eye² *v* (**eyes, eyed, eyeing** or **eying**) to look at *esp* carefully.

eyeball *n* the more or less spherical capsule of the eye of a vertebrate animal. ✻ **eyeball to eyeball** *informal* face to face, *esp* with hostility.

eyebrow *n* the ridge over the eye or the line of hair that grows on it.

eyeful *n informal* **1** an attractive person. **2** a look or gaze.

eyeglass *n* a lens worn to aid vision.

eyelash *n* the fringe of hair edging the eyelid or a single hair of this fringe.

eyelet *n* **1** a small reinforced hole that a cord, lace, etc may be passed through. **2** a small metal ring to reinforce an eyelet.

eyelid *n* a movable lid of skin and muscle that can be closed over the eyeball.

eyeliner *n* a cosmetic for emphasizing the outline of the eyes.

eye-opener *n informal* something surprising and revelatory.

eyepiece *n* the lens looked through at the eye end of an optical instrument.

eyeshade *n* a small shield, fastened to the head, that shades the eyes from strong light.

eye shadow *n* a coloured cream applied to the eyelids to accentuate the eyes.

eyesight *n* the ability to see.

eyesore *n* something offensive to the sight, *esp* an ugly building.

eyetooth *n* (*pl* **eyeteeth**) a canine tooth of the upper jaw.

eye up *v informal* to look at (somebody) in order to assess their sexual attractiveness.

eyewash *n* **1** *informal* nonsense. **2** lotion for the eyes.

eyewitness *n* a person who sees an event take place.

eyrie *or* **aerie** *n* the nest of a bird of prey.

F¹ or **f** n (pl **F's** or **Fs** or **f's**) the sixth letter of the English alphabet.

F² abbr Fahrenheit.

F³ abbr the chemical symbol for fluorine.

FA abbr Football Association.

fable n 1 a short story intended to convey a moral. 2 a legendary story of supernatural happenings.

fabled adj 1 famous or legendary. 2 fictitious.

fabric n 1 a pliable material made by weaving or knitting; cloth. 2 the floor, walls, and roof of a building. 3 the underlying structure of an organization or society.

fabricate v 1 to invent or create (facts), esp to deceive. 2 to manufacture (a product) from various parts. ➤ **fabrication** n.

fabulous adj 1 incredible or extraordinary. 2 informal excellent. 3 told of in or based on fable. ➤ **fabulously** adv.

facade or **façade** n 1 the front of a building. 2 a false or superficial appearance.

face¹ n 1 the front part of the human head from the chin to the forehead. 2 a facial expression, esp a grimace. 3 a front, upper, or outer surface. 4 in geometry, each of the plane surfaces of a solid. 5 the side of a mountain or cliff. 6 one aspect of something. * **on the face of it** at first glance; apparently.

face² v 1 to have the face or front turned in a specific direction. 2 to meet or deal with (a situation or problem) firmly. 3 to have the prospect of (something unpleasant). 4 to cover the front or surface of. * **face the music** to confront unpleasant consequences. **face up to** to confront (a difficulty or problem).

facecloth n a small cloth for washing the face.

face down v to prevail against (somebody) by defiant confrontation.

faceless adj lacking identity; anonymous.

face-lift n 1 an operation to remove wrinkles or sagging skin. 2 a renovation or overhaul.

face-pack n a cream or paste applied to the face to improve the complexion and remove impurities.

face-saving adj serving to preserve one's dignity or reputation.

facet n 1 a plane surface of a cut gem. 2 an aspect of something.

facetious adj inappropriately humorous or flippant. ➤ **facetiously** adv.

face value n 1 the value indicated on a coin or postage stamp. 2 the apparent value or significance of something.

facia n chiefly Brit see FASCIA.

facial¹ adj relating to the face. ➤ **facially** adv.

facial² n a beauty treatment for the face.

facile adj 1 indicating a lack of thought; superficial and glib. 2 easily or readily accomplished or performed.

facilitate v to make (a task or procedure) easier. ➤ **facilitation** n.

facility n (pl -ies) 1 a building, piece of equipment, or resource designed to provide a particular service. 2 a natural ability or aptitude.

facing n 1 a lining at the edge of a garment, for stiffening or ornament. 2 an ornamental or protective layer applied to a wall.

facsimile n 1 an exact copy of printed material. 2 a fax.

fact n 1 an actual event or occurrence. 2 a piece of information. 3 reality or truth. * **the facts of life** information about sexual reproduction. **in fact** in reality; actually.

faction n a minority group within a party. ➤ **factional** adj.

factious adj caused by or inclined to dissension.

Usage Note: Do not confuse this word with *fractious*.

factitious adj produced artificially; sham or unreal.

factor¹ n 1 a condition, force, or fact that contributes to a result. 2 in mathematics, one of two or more numbers that can be multiplied together to produce a given number. 3 formerly, in biology, a gene. 4 a substance in the blood that causes it to clot. 5 a person who acts for another; an agent.

factor² v to express (a number) as the product of factors. * **factor in/out** to include or exclude as a matter to be considered.

factory n (pl -ies) a building containing machinery used for manufacturing.

factory farming n a system of dairy or meat farming that uses intensive production methods.

factotum n (pl **factotums**) a person employed to carry out many types of work.

factual adj restricted to or based on fact. ➤ **factually** adv.

faculty *n* (*pl* **-ies**) **1** an inherent capability or function. **2** a natural aptitude or talent. **3** *chiefly Brit* a group of related departments in a university.

fad *n* **1** a short-lived interest or craze. **2** an idiosyncratic taste or habit. ➤ **faddish** *adj*, **faddy** *adj*.

fade[1] *v* **1** to disappear gradually; to vanish. **2** to lose freshness or colour. **3** of an image or sound: to come gradually into or out of view or hearing.

fade[2] *n* an instance of fading.

faeces (*NAmer* **feces**) *pl n* bodily waste discharged from the bowels. ➤ **faecal** *adj*.

fag[1] *n Brit, informal* a cigarette.

fag[2] *n chiefly Brit, informal* **1** a tiring or tedious task. **2** a pupil at a public school who does tasks for an older pupil.

fag[3] *v* (**fagged, fagging**) *chiefly Brit, informal* to work hard.

faggot *n* **1** *Brit* a fried mass of minced meat and herbs. **2** a bundle of sticks used as fuel. **3** *chiefly NAmer, informal, derog* a male homosexual.

Fahrenheit *adj* of a scale of temperature on which water freezes at 32° and boils at 212°.

fail[1] *v* **1** to be unsuccessful at something. **2** to neglect to do something. **3** to stop functioning. **4** to be insufficient or inadequate. **5** to weaken or die away. **6** to become bankrupt or insolvent. **7** to be unable to reach the required standard in an examination. **8** to judge (somebody or something) as having failed a test or examination. **9** to disappoint or prove inadequate for.

fail[2] *n* a mark indicating the failing of an examination. ✳ **without fail** whatever the circumstances.

failing[1] *n* a defect in character.

failing[2] *prep* in the absence or default of.

failsafe *adj* **1** of a machine: designed to return to a safe condition in the event of failure or breakdown. **2** foolproof.

failure *n* **1** lack of success. **2** an unsuccessful person or thing. **3** an instance of failing to perform something expected. **4** an instance of failing to function normally.

faint[1] *adj* **1** not easy to see or hear. **2** slight. **3** on the point of losing consciousness. ➤ **faintly** *adv*.

faint[2] *v* to lose consciousness briefly.

faint[3] *n* a brief loss of consciousness.

faint-hearted *adj* lacking courage or resolve; timid.

fair[1] *adj* **1** honest and just. **2** conforming with the rules; allowed. **3** of hair or complexion: light in colour. **4** moderately good or large. **5** of weather: fine and dry. **6** of wind: favourable. ➤ **fairness** *n*.

fair[2] *n* **1** an outdoor event with sideshows and amusements. **2** an exhibition for promoting products of a particular type. **3** a gathering of buyers and sellers.

fair copy *n* the final corrected version of a document.

fair game *n* a person or thing open to legitimate attack or ridicule.

fairground *n* an area where an outdoor fair is held.

fairing *n* a smooth structure intended to reduce air resistance on a vehicle or aircraft.

fairly *adv* **1** impartially or honestly. **2** in a proper or legal manner. **3** to a moderate degree. **4** positively.

fair trade *n* trade that supports producers in developing countries.

fairway *n* the mown part of a golf course between a tee and a green.

fair-weather friend *n* a friend who is loyal only in untroubled times.

fairy *n* (*pl* **-ies**) a small mythical being in human form with magical powers.

fairy godmother *n* in fairy stories, a woman who comes to the aid of the heroine or hero.

fairy lights *pl n* small coloured electric lights hung up for decoration.

fairy story *n* **1** a children's story about magical or imaginary people and places. **2** a made-up account or excuse.

fait accompli /ˌfayt əˈkompli/ *n* something accomplished that cannot be changed.

faith *n* **1** complete confidence or belief. **2** a system of religious beliefs. **3** belief in the traditional doctrines of a religion.

faithful[1] *adj* **1** loyal or steadfast. **2** true to the facts; accurate. ➤ **faithfully** *adv*.

faithful[2] *n* (*treated as pl*) (**the faithful**) the people who belong to a religion.

faithless *adj* disloyal or untrustworthy.

fake[1] *adj* not genuine; counterfeit.

fake[2] *n* a person or thing that is not genuine.

fake[3] *v* **1** to forge or counterfeit. **2** to pretend to have (an illness or emotion).

fakir *n* a Muslim or Hindu holy man.

falcon *n* a hawk with long pointed wings.

falconry *n* the art of training falcons to pursue game. ➤ **falconer** *n*.

fall[1] *v* (**fell, fallen**) **1** to descend freely by the force of gravity. **2** to collapse to the ground. **3** to hang down. **4** of a place: to be defeated or captured. **5** of a government: to lose office. **6** to become less or weaker. **7** to pass into a new state or condition: *to fall in love.* **8** to occur at a specified time. **9** to come within the scope or limits of something. ✳ **fall for** *1 informal* to fall in love with. **2** *informal* to be deceived by (a trick, etc). **fall into place** to begin to make sense or progress. **fall on** to attack suddenly or fiercely. **fall over oneself** *informal* to make great efforts. **fall short** to fail to achieve a goal or target. **fall to** to be the responsibility of.

fall² n 1 an instance of falling. 2 something that falls or has fallen. 3 NAmer autumn. 4 a drop in height. 5 (in pl) a steep waterfall. 6 a downward slope. 7 a decrease in quantity or value. 8 a collapse or defeat.

fallacy n (pl -ies) 1 a mistaken idea. 2 a false argument. ➤ **fallacious** adj.

fallback n an alternative or reserve option if the main one fails.

fall back v to retreat. ✻ **fall back on** to have recourse to in difficulty.

fall behind v to fail to keep up.

fall down v 1 to collapse or drop to the ground. 2 to fail to meet expectations.

fall guy n informal a scapegoat.

fallible adj capable of being wrong. ➤ **fallibility** n.

fall in v 1 to sink or collapse inwards. 2 of a soldier: to take a place in a formation. ✻ **fall in with** 1 to concur with (an arrangement). 2 to encounter and join (a group).

fall off v 1 to become detached and drop to the ground. 2 to become less or weaker.

Fallopian tube n either of the pair of tubes conducting the egg from the ovary to the uterus in female mammals.

fallout n 1 radioactive particles resulting from a nuclear explosion. 2 unfavourable secondary results or effects.

fall out v 1 to have a disagreement. 2 to happen in a certain way.

fallow adj 1 of land: left unsown after ploughing. 2 of a sow: not pregnant.

fall through v to fail to be carried out.

false adj 1 untrue or incorrect. 2 not according to law or rules; invalid. 3 intended to deceive; artificial. 4 illusory. 5 disloyal or treacherous. ➤ **falsely** adv, **falseness** n, **falsity** n.

false alarm n a warning that proves to be groundless.

falsehood n 1 an untrue statement; a lie. 2 absence of truth or accuracy.

false pretences pl n acts or claims intended to deceive.

falsetto n (pl -os) a high-pitched male voice.

falsify v (-ies, -ied) to make (information, etc) false. ➤ **falsification** n.

falter v 1 to hesitate in purpose or action. 2 to lose strength or effectiveness. 3 to move or speak unsteadily.

fame n the state of being famous.

famed adj famous.

familial adj relating to a family.

familiar¹ adj 1 frequently seen or experienced; common or well-known. 2 (+ with) having knowledge of. 3 close or intimate. ➤ **familiarity** n.

familiar² n 1 an intimate associate; a companion. 2 a spirit that waits on a witch.

familiarize or **-ise** v to make (somebody) familiar with something. ➤ **familiarization** n.

family n (pl -ies) 1 a group of parents and their children. 2 the children of a parent or parents. 3 a group of people related by descent or marriage. 4 a group of related things. 5 in biology, a category above genus and below order.

family planning n control of the number of children born in a family by means of contraception.

family tree n a diagram showing a family's history and relationships.

famine n an extreme scarcity of food.

famished adj informal very hungry.

famous adj 1 well-known. 2 informal, dated excellent or first-rate. ➤ **famously** adv.

fan¹ n 1 a device of rotating vanes, for producing a current of air. 2 a folding semicircular device that is waved to and fro to cool the face.

fan² v (**fanned**, **fanning**) 1 to cause a current of air to blow on. 2 to drive (something) away by waving. 3 to spread out in the shape of an open fan. 4 to increase the intensity of (a fire) by agitating the air around it. 5 to stir up or stimulate (an emotion).

fan³ n a supporter or admirer of a sport or celebrity.

fanatic n a person who is excessively enthusiastic about a religion, cause, or activity. ➤ **fanatical** adj, **fanatically** adv, **fanaticism** n.

fan belt n a belt driving the cooling fan of a motor vehicle.

fancier n a person who breeds a specified kind of animal: a pigeon fancier.

fanciful adj 1 existing in fancy only; imaginary. 2 marked by fancy or whim; elaborate or contrived. ➤ **fancifully** adv.

fancy¹ v (-ies, -ied) 1 to feel a liking or desire for. 2 to consider (somebody or something) likely to do well. 3 to believe or imagine. ✻ **fancy oneself** informal to have a high opinion of one's own worth, ability, etc. ➤ **fanciable** adj.

fancy² adj (-ier, -iest) 1 of a fine quality. 2 highly decorated or decorative.

fancy³ n (pl -ies) 1 a liking based on whim rather than reason. 2 a notion or whim. 3 a mental image. 4 capricious use of imagination. 5 the power of mental conception in art.

fancy dress n unusual or amusing dress worn at some parties.

fancy-free adj free because not involved in an amorous relationship.

fandango n (pl -os) a lively Spanish dance for two people.

fanfare n 1 a flourish of brass instruments on a ceremonial occasion. 2 a showy display.

fang n 1 a tooth by which an animal seizes and holds its prey. 2 a tooth of a venomous snake.

fanlight n a semicircular window over a door or window.

fanny n (pl -ies) **1** Brit, coarse slang the female genitals. **2** NAmer, informal the buttocks.

fantasize or **-ise** v to form imaginative ideas about something desirable.

fantastic adj **1** unreal or imaginary. **2** so extreme as to be incredible. **3** strange or unrealistic. **4** informal wonderful; excellent. ➤ **fantastical** adj, **fantastically** adv.

fantasy n (pl -ies) **1** the process of creating extravagant mental images or daydreams. **2** a fantastic design or idea. **3** imaginative fiction or drama characterized by strange or unrealistic elements.

fanzine n a magazine for fans of a sports team or performer.

far[1] adv (**farther** or **further, farthest** or **furthest**) **1** to or at a large distance in space or time. **2** by a broad interval. **3** (+ from) in total contrast to. **4** to or at a considerable distance or degree. **5** very much. ✳ **a far cry from** totally different to. **as far as** to the extent that. **by far** by a considerable margin. **go far** to be successful in life. **go too far** to behave in an unacceptable way. **so far** up to the present.

far[2] adj (**farther** or **further, farthest** or **furthest**) **1** remote in space, time, or degree. **2** extreme.

farad n the SI unit of electrical capacitance.

faraway adj **1** situated at a great distance; remote. **2** dreamy or abstracted.

farce n **1** a comedy based on an improbable plot. **2** a ridiculous or nonsensical situation. **3** a travesty or mockery.

farcical adj ludicrous or absurd. ➤ **farcically** adv.

fare[1] n **1** the price charged to travel on public transport. **2** a paying passenger. **3** food provided for a meal.

fare[2] v **1** formal to get along; to succeed or do. **2** to happen.

Far East n China, Japan, Indochina, and other countries of east Asia.

farewell[1] interj archaic goodbye.

farewell[2] n an act of leave-taking.

farfetched adj exaggerated and improbable.

far-flung adj remote or widely spread.

farm[1] n **1** an area of land and associated buildings for growing crops or raising animals. **2** a farmhouse. **3** an area of water used to breed fish.

farm[2] v **1** to engage in the production of crops or livestock. **2** to cultivate or rear (crops or livestock) on a farm. **3** to manage and cultivate (land) as farmland or as a farm. **4** (+ out) to allocate (work) to several people. ➤ **farmed** adj, **farming** n.

farmer n somebody who owns or runs a farm.

farmhouse n a house on a farm.

farrago n (pl -oes or -os) a confused collection.

farrier n a blacksmith who shoes horses.

farrow[1] n a litter of pigs.

farrow[2] v of a sow: to give birth to (piglets).

fart[1] v informal to expel wind from the anus.

fart[2] n informal **1** an expulsion of wind from the anus. **2** a tiresome or unpleasant person.

farther[1] adv at or to a greater distance; further.

farther[2] adj more distant or remote; further.

farthest[1] adj most distant in space or time; furthest.

farthest[2] adv to or at the greatest distance in space or time; furthest.

farthing n a former British coin, worth a quarter of an old penny.

fascia (chiefly Brit **facia**) n **1** a flat horizontal piece of stone or board, under projecting eaves. **2** a nameplate over the front of a shop. **3** chiefly Brit the dashboard of a motor vehicle.

fascinate v to arouse the interest or curiosity of. ➤ **fascination** n.

fascism n **1** a political system that is aggressively nationalistic and supports a centralized autocratic government. **2** informal brutal or intolerant dictatorial control. ➤ **fascist** n and adj.

fashion[1] n **1** a prevailing custom or style. **2** the prevailing style of dress, or the business of producing it. **3** a manner or way. ✳ **after a fashion** in an approximate or rough way. **in/out of fashion** fashionable or unfashionable.

fashion[2] v to give shape or form to.

fashionable adj conforming to the latest custom or fashion. ➤ **fashionably** adv.

fast[1] adj **1** moving or able to move at a high speed. **2** needing only a short time; accomplished quickly. **3** of a clock or watch: showing a time later than the actual time. **4** of a colour: not liable to fade. **5** firmly fixed or attached.

fast[2] adv **1** quickly. **2** in a firm or fixed manner. **3** sound or deeply: fast asleep.

fast[3] v to go without foods or drink for a time.

fast[4] n an act or time of fasting.

fasten v **1** to attach or secure. **2** to fix or direct (something) steadily. **3** (+ on) to choose and concentrate on.

fastener or **fastening** n a device used to fasten a piece of clothing.

fastidious adj **1** difficult to satisfy or please. **2** showing or demanding great delicacy or care. ➤ **fastidiously** adv.

fastness n **1** the quality of being fixed. **2** the durability of a dyed colour. **3** a fortified or secure place.

fat[1] n **1** animal tissue consisting of greasy or oily matter. **2** a solid or semisolid substance derived from animal tissue, as distinct from an oil.

fat[2] adj (**fatter, fattest**) **1** having an unusually large amount of fat. **2** large or thick. **3** profitable or substantial. ✳ **a fat chance** informal no chance at all. ➤ **fatness** n.

fatal adj **1** causing death. **2** bringing ruin. ➤ **fatally** adv.

fatalism *n* the belief that events are predetermined and outside the control of human beings. ➤ **fatalist** *n*, **fatalistic** *adj*.

fatality *n* (*pl* -**ies**) a death resulting from a war or disaster.

fat cat *n informal, derog* a wealthy businessman.

fate[1] *n* **1** a power beyond human control that is believed to determine events. **2** an outcome, *esp* one that is unpleasant and inevitable.

fate[2] *v* ✶ **be fated** to be certain to turn out in a particular way.

fateful *adj* having momentous unpleasant or deadly consequences.

father[1] *n* **1** a male parent. **2** a male ancestor. **3** a priest. **4** somebody who originates or institutes something. ➤ **fatherhood** *n*.

father[2] *n* one's native land.

father-in-law *n* (*pl* **fathers-in-law**) the father of one's husband or wife.

fatherland *n* one's native land.

fatherly *adj* affectionate and caring.

fathom[1] *n* a unit of length for measuring the depth of water, equal to 6ft (about 1.83m).

fathom[2] *v* (*often* + out) to consider and begin to understand.

fatigue[1] *n* **1** physical or nervous tiredness. **2** the tendency of a material to break under repeated stress. **3** manual or menial military work. **4** (*in pl*) the uniform or work clothing worn on fatigue.

fatigue[2] *v* (**fatigues, fatigued, fatiguing**) to weary or exhaust.

fatten *v* (*often* + up) to make or become fatter.

fatty[1] *adj* (-**ier**, -**iest**) **1** containing large amounts of fat. **2** oily; greasy. ➤ **fattiness** *n*.

fatty[2] *n* (*pl* -**ies**) *informal* a fat person.

fatuous *adj* foolish and useless. ➤ **fatuity** *n*, **fatuously** *adv*.

fatwa *n* a legal opinion given by an Islamic religious authority.

faucet *n chiefly NAmer* a tap.

fault[1] *n* **1** a failing or defect. **2** responsibility for wrongdoing or failure. **3** a misdemeanour or mistake. **4** in tennis, a service that does not land in the prescribed area. **5** a fracture in the earth's crust. **6** a break in rock structures caused by strain. ✶ **at fault** liable for blame. **to a fault** excessively. ➤ **faultless** *adj*.

fault[2] *v* to find a fault in.

faulty *adj* (-**ier**, -**iest**) having a fault or defect.

faun *n* in Roman mythology a figure with a human body and a goat's horns and legs.

fauna *n* the animal life of a region or period.

faux pas /ˌfoh ˈpah/ *n* (*pl* **faux pas** /ˌfoh ˈpahz/) a social blunder.

favour[1] (*NAmer* **favor**) *n* **1** positive approval or liking. **2** partiality or favouritism. **3** an act of kindness. ✶ **in favour of 1** in agreement or sympathy with. **2** to the advantage of. **3** out of preference for.

favour[2] (*NAmer* **favor**) *v* **1** to regard or treat with favour. **2** (+ by/with) to do a favour or kindness for. **3** to show partiality towards; to prefer.

favourable (*NAmer* **favorable**) *adj* **1** expressing or winning approval. **2** disposed to favour; partial. **3** successful. ➤ **favourably** *adv*.

favourite[1] (*NAmer* **favorite**) *n* **1** a preferred person or thing. **2** the competitor thought most likely to win.

favourite[2] (*NAmer* **favorite**) *adj* preferred to all the others.

favouritism (*NAmer* **favoritism**) *n* the showing of unfair favour.

fawn[1] *n* **1** a young deer. **2** a light brown colour.

fawn[2] *v* (+ on/upon) to court favour with somebody by flattery.

fax[1] *n* **1** a copy of a document that is scanned and transmitted electronically over a telephone line. **2** a machine for sending and receiving faxes.

fax[2] *v* to send a fax to.

faze *v informal* to disturb or disconcert.

FBI *abbr NAmer* Federal Bureau of Investigation.

FC *abbr* Football Club.

Fe *abbr* the chemical symbol for iron.

fear[1] *n* **1** an unpleasant emotion caused by awareness of danger. **2** a reason for alarm; a danger. ➤ **fearless** *adj*.

fear[2] *v* **1** to be afraid of. **2** to be anxious or regretful about. **3** (+ for) to be apprehensive.

fearful *adj* **1** full of fear; afraid. **2** showing or arising from fear. **3** causing fear. **4** *informal* extremely bad or great. ➤ **fearfully** *adv*.

fearsome *adj* **1** causing fear. **2** awesome or frightening. ➤ **fearsomely** *adv*.

feasible *adj* **1** capable of being done or carried out. **2** *informal* reasonable or likely. ➤ **feasibility** *n*, **feasibly** *adv*.

feast[1] *n* **1** a grand or elaborate meal. **2** a periodic religious observance.

feast[2] *v* to have or take part in a feast. ✶ **feast one's eyes on** to look appreciatively at.

feat *n* a notable or courageous act or achievement. **2** an act of skill or ingenuity.

feather[1] *n* a light horny growth that forms part of the external covering of a bird's body, consisting of a shaft with two sets of interlocking barbs. ✶ **a feather in one's cap** an achievement or distinction in which one can take pride. ➤ **feathery** *adj*.

feather[2] *v* to turn (an oar) so that the blade is horizontal when lifting it from the water. ✶ **feather one's nest** to provide for oneself, *esp* dishonestly.

feature[1] *n* **1** a prominent or distinctive part or characteristic. **2** a part of the face. **3** (*in pl*) the face. **4** the main film on a cinema programme. **5** an important article or story in a newspaper or magazine. ➤ **featureless** *adj*.

feature[2] v **1** to give special prominence to. **2** to have as a characteristic or feature. **3** (+ in) to play an important part.

febrile adj symptomatic of a fever; feverish.

February n (pl **-ies**) the second month of the year.

Usage Note: Note the spelling with -br-.

---

feces pl n NAmer see FAECES.

feckless adj **1** ineffectual or weak. **2** worthless or irresponsible.

fecund adj fruitful or prolific. ➤ **fecundity** n.

fed v past tense and past part. of FEED[1].

federal adj **1** of a system of government in which constituent states subscribe to a central government while retaining self-government in local matters. **2** of the central government of a federation. **3** loyal to the federal government of the USA in the American Civil War. ➤ **federalism** n, **federalist** n and adj, **federally** adv.

federate v to join in a federation. ➤ **federate** adj.

federation n **1** a group of states forming a federal union. **2** a union of organizations. **3** the act of forming a federal union.

fee n a sum of money paid esp for entrance or for a professional service.

feeble adj **1** lacking in strength; weak. **2** deficient in authority or force. ➤ **feebly** adv.

feed[1] v (past tense and past part. **fed**) **1** to give food to. **2** to provide regular food for. **3** to provide something essential to the growth, sustenance, or operation of. **4** to satisfy or gratify (a feeling). **5** to supply continuously for use or processing. **6** (usu + off/on/upon) to eat or be satisfied by.

feed[2] n **1** an instance of feeding or eating. **2** food for livestock.

feedback n **1** information given to the originator about the results of an action or process. **2** the return to the input of a part of the output of a machine or system, e.g. noise fed back to a microphone.

feeder n **1** a person or animal that feeds in a specified way. **2** a device or apparatus for supplying food. **3** a device feeding material into or through a machine. **4** a road, railway, airline, or aircraft that links remote areas with the main transport system.

feel[1] v (past tense and past part. **felt**) **1** to handle or touch (something) to examine or explore it. **2** to perceive by a physical sensation. **3** to give a particular sensation when touched. **4** to experience (an emotion or physical sensation). **5** to be affected by. **6** to be aware of (something) without direct experience. **7** to believe or think. **8** (+ for) to have sympathy or pity for. ✻ **feel like** to have a passing fancy for. **feel up to** to be well or fit enough to.

feel[2] n **1** the sense of feeling or touch. **2** sensation or feeling. **3** the quality of a thing as imparted through touch. **4** a particular quality or atmosphere. **5** intuitive skill or knowledge.

feeler n **1** an animal's feeling organ. **2** (usu in pl) a cautious attempt to ascertain the views of others.

feeling[1] n **1** an emotional state or reaction. **2** (in pl) susceptibility to impression; sensibility. **3** a conscious recognition; a sense. **4** an opinion or belief. **5** bodily consciousness or awareness. **6** capacity to respond emotionally. **7** the sensation of touching or being touched.

feeling[2] adj **1** expressing emotion or sensitivity. **2** able to feel or respond emotionally; sensitive. **3** easily moved emotionally; sympathetic.

feet n pl of FOOT[1].

feign v **1** to give a false appearance or impression of. **2** to pretend (something).

feint[1] n a mock blow or attack made as a diversion.

feint[2] v to make a feint.

feint[3] adj of rulings on paper: faint or pale.

feisty adj (**-ier, -iest**) informal spirited and determined.

felicitations pl n congratulations.

felicitous adj formal very well suited or expressed.

felicity n (pl **-ies**) formal **1** great happiness. **2** in the ability to use art or language effectively. **3** an apt expression.

feline[1] adj **1** of cats or the cat family. **2** resembling a cat.

feline[2] n a member of the cat family.

fell[1] v past tense of FALL[1].

fell[2] v to cut or knock down.

fell[3] n a rugged stretch of high moorland, esp in northern England.

fell[4] adj ✻ **at one fell swoop** all at once.

fellow n **1** informal a man or a boy. **2** an equal in rank, power, or character. **3** either of a pair; a mate. **4** (usu in pl) a comrade or associate. **5** (used before a noun) belonging to the same group: fellow travellers. **6** Brit a member of a learned society. **7** an incorporated member of a college.

fellowship n **1** friendly relations between people. **2** community of interest or experience. **3** the state of being a fellow or associate. **4** a group of people with similar interests; an association. **5** the position of a college fellow.

felon n somebody who has committed a felony.

felony n (pl **-ies**) a serious crime. ➤ **felonious** adj.

felt[1] n a cloth made by compressing wool or fur.

felt[2] v past tense and past part. of FEEL[1].

felt-tip pen n a pen with a soft felt writing tip.

female[1] adj **1** relating to the sex that bears offspring or produces eggs. **2** of a plant or flower: having an ovary but no stamens. **3** designed with a hollow part for receiving a corresponding male part.

female[2] n a female animal, person, or plant.

feminine adj **1** female. **2** characteristic of women. **3** of the gender that includes most words or grammatical forms referring to females. ➤ **femininity** n.

feminism n the advocacy or furtherance of women's rights and interests. ➤ **feminist** n and adj.

feminize or **-ise** v **1** to give a feminine quality to. **2** to cause to take on feminine characteristics. ➤ **feminization** n.

femme fatale /ˌfam fə'tahl/ n (pl **femmes fatales**) a seductive and dangerous woman.

femur n (pl **femurs** or **femora**) the thighbone. ➤ **femoral** adj.

fen n an area of low marshy or flooded land.

fence[1] n **1** a barrier of wire or boards enclosing an area. **2** an upright obstacle to be jumped by a horse. **3** informal a receiver of stolen goods. ✳ **sit on the fence** to remain undecided or uncommitted.

fence[2] v **1** (usu + in) to enclose (an area) with a fence. **2** (usu + off) to separate (an area) with a fence. **3** informal to receive or sell (stolen goods). **4** to practise fencing. ➤ **fencer** n.

fencing n **1** the sport of attack and defence with a sword or foil. **2** fences, or material used for building them.

fend v (+ for) to provide a livelihood for somebody, esp oneself.

fender n **1** a cushion of rope or wood hung over the side of a ship to absorb impact. **2** a low metal guard to prevent coal spilling from a fire. **3** NAmer a wing or mudguard of a vehicle.

feng shui /ˌfung 'shway, ˌfeng 'shooh-i/ n a Chinese system of rules for the position and arrangement of a building, room, etc, according to the flow of energy in the environment.

fennel n a plant cultivated for its aromatic seeds and foliage.

feral adj **1** of an animal: not or no longer domesticated, wild. **2** fierce or savage.

ferment[1] v **1** of a substance: to undergo a chemical breakdown, e.g. by the action of bacteria. **2** to cause (a state of agitation). ➤ **fermentation** n.

ferment[2] n a state of unrest or upheaval.

fern n (pl **ferns** or **fern**) a flowerless plant with leaflike fronds. ➤ **ferny** adj.

ferocious adj extremely fierce or violent. ➤ **ferociously** adv, **ferociousness** n, **ferocity** n.

ferret[1] n a small fierce animal used for hunting small rodents or rabbits. ➤ **ferrety** adj.

ferret[2] v (**ferreted, ferreting**) **1** informal (+ about/around) to search about or around. **2** to hunt with ferrets.

ferret out v informal to find (information) by searching.

Ferris wheel n a fairground amusement consisting of a large upright revolving wheel with seats round the rim.

ferrous adj containing iron.

ferrule n a metal ring or cap on the end of a stick, umbrella, etc.

ferry[1] v (**-ies, -ied**) **1** to carry by boat or ship over a body of water. **2** to convey by car from one place to another.

ferry[2] n (pl **-ies**) a boat or ship that carries passengers and vehicles across a body of water.

fertile adj **1** of land or soil: capable of producing or bearing fruit; productive. **2** of the mind: imaginative or inventive. **3** of a person or animal: capable of breeding or reproducing. **4** of an egg: capable of growing or developing. ➤ **fertility** n.

fertilize or **-ise** v **1** to make (an ovule, egg, etc) capable of developing into a new individual by uniting with a male germ cell. **2** to apply a fertilizer to. ➤ **fertilization** n.

fertilizer or **-iser** n a substance used to make soil more fertile.

fervent adj showing deep emotion. ➤ **fervently** adv.

fervid adj passionately intense. ➤ **fervidly** adv.

fervour (NAmer **fervor**) n passionate intensity of feeling.

festal adj relating to a festival.

fester v **1** of a wound: to generate pus. **2** of food: to putrefy or rot. **3** to become worse; to intensify.

festival n **1** a time marked by special celebration. **2** a programme of cultural events or entertainment. **3** a religious feast.

festive adj **1** of or suitable for a feast or festival. **2** joyous or merry.

festivity n (pl **-ies**) **1** festive activity; a party or celebration. **2** a festival.

festoon[1] n a decorative hanging chain or strip.

festoon[2] v to decorate with festoons.

fetal adj = foetal (see FOETUS).

fetch[1] v **1** to go or come after (something or somebody) and bring them back. **2** to be sold for (a particular price).

fetch[2] n **1 a** the distance along open water or land over which the wind blows. **b** the distance traversed by waves without obstruction. **2** the act or an instance of fetching. **3** archaic a trick or stratagem.

fetching adj attractive or becoming.

fetch up v informal to arrive or come to rest.

fete[1] or **fête** n Brit an outdoor bazaar or other event held to raise money.

fete[2] or **fête** v to honour or celebrate extravagantly.

fetid or **foetid** adj having an unpleasant smell; stinking.

fetish n **1** an object believed to have magical power. **2** a form of sexual desire related to an object or bodily part.

fetlock n **1** a projection bearing a tuft of hair on

the back of a horse's leg above the hoof. **2** the joint of the limb or tuft of hair at the fetlock.

fetter[1] *n* **1** a shackle for the feet. **2** (*usu in pl*) something that confines; a restraint.

fetter[2] *v* to carry on a feud.

fettle *n* a state of physical or mental fitness.

fettuccine /fetə'cheeni/ *pl n* pasta in narrow ribbons.

fetus *n* see FOETUS.

feud[1] *n* a lasting state of hostilities.

feud[2] *v* to carry on a feud.

feudal *adj* of feudalism. ➤ **feudally** *adv*.

feudalism *n* the medieval social system in which vassals held land from a lord in return for allegiance and service.

fever *n* **1** a rise of body temperature above the normal. **2** a state of intense emotion or activity. ➤ **feverish** *adj*.

fevered *adj* **1** hot or flushed with fever. **2** agitated or excited.

few[1] *adj* **1** amounting to only a small number. **2** (**a few**) some but not many. ✻ **few and far between** scarce.

few[2] *n* **1** (*pl*) not many. **2** (**the few**) an exclusive group of people.

fey *adj* **1** unworldly and irresponsible. **2** able to see into the future.

fez *n* (*pl* **fezzes**) a red brimless hat with a flat top, worn by men in some Muslim countries.

ff *abbr* following pages.

fiancé *or* **fiancée** *n* a man or woman to whom a person is engaged to be married.

fiasco *n* (*pl* **-os**) a complete and ignominious failure.

fiat *n* an authoritative order or decree.

fib[1] *n* informal a trivial or childish lie.

fib[2] *v* (**fibbed, fibbing**) informal to tell a fib. ➤ **fibber** *n*.

fibre (*NAmer* **fiber**) *n* **1** an elongated tapering plant cell with thick walls. **2** a filament composing part of the intercellular matrix of connective tissue. **3** an elongated contractile cell of muscle tissue. **4** a slender natural or manufactured thread or filament, e.g. of wool or cotton. **5** material made of fibres. **6** the part of food that helps digestion. **7** strength or fortitude. ➤ **fibrous** *adj*.

fibreboard *n* a building material made by compressing wood fibres.

fibreglass *n* **1** a tough material made from glass fibres. **2** a combination of this with synthetic resins.

fibre optics *pl n* the use of glass or plastic fibres to transmit information as optical signals. ➤ **fibre-optic** *adj*.

fibrillation *n* **1** the forming of fibres or fibrils. **2** rapid irregular contractions of muscle fibres of the heart resulting in a lack of synchronization between heartbeat and pulse.

fibula *n* (*pl* **fibulae** *or* **fibulas**) the outer of the two bones between the knee and ankle.

fickle *adj* inconsistent in one's loyalties.

fiction *n* **1** literature describing imaginary people and events. **2** something untrue or invented. ➤ **fictional** *adj*.

fictionalize *or* **-ise** *v* to make into fiction.

fictitious *adj* invented or unreal.

fiddle[1] *n* **1** informal a violin. **2** Brit, informal a dishonest practice or swindle.

fiddle[2] *v* **1** to move one's hands or fingers restlessly. **2** Brit to falsify (accounts, etc). **3** Brit to get or contrive by cheating or deception. ✻ **fiddle with** informal to tamper or meddle with. ➤ **fiddler** *n*.

fiddly *adj* (**-ier, -iest**) Brit, informal intricate or awkward to use.

fidelity *n* **1** the quality of being faithful; loyalty. **2** accuracy in detail or reproduction.

fidget[1] *v* (**fidgeted, fidgeting**) to move or act restlessly or nervously. ➤ **fidgety** *adj*.

fidget[2] *n* **1** somebody who fidgets. **2** (*usu in pl*) restlessness.

fief *n* formerly, a feudal estate. ➤ **fiefdom** *n*.

field[1] *n* **1** an enclosed area of land used for cultivation or pasture. **2** a large expanse of ice. **3** an outdoor area marked for a game or sport. **4** an area of activity or knowledge. **5** (**the field**) the participants in a sports activity. **6** a region or space in which a given effect, e.g. magnetism, exists. **7** the area visible through an optical instrument.

field[2] *v* **1** to try to intercept (a ball struck in cricket or baseball). **2** to deal with (a question) by giving an impromptu answer. **3** to put (a team) into the field of play. ➤ **fielder** *n*.

field day *n* a time of freedom to enjoy oneself.

field event *n* an athletic event that is not a race, e.g. discus.

field marshal *n* an officer of the highest rank in the British army.

field sport *n* an open-air sport such as hunting or shooting.

fiend *n* **1** a demon. **2** a person of great wickedness or cruelty. **3** informal an enthusiast or devotee of an activity.

fiendish *adj* **1** extremely cruel or wicked. **2** extremely wicked or unpleasant. **3** informal difficult or complex. ➤ **fiendishly** *adv*.

fierce *adj* **1** violently hostile or aggressive. **2** extremely intense or severe. ➤ **fiercely** *adv*, **fierceness** *n*.

fiery *adj* (**-ier, -iest**) **1** consisting of or looking like fire. **2** showing strong emotion or spirit; passionate. **3** irascible.

fiesta *n* **1** a religious festival in Spain or Latin America. **2** a festive occasion.

fife *n* a small flute used in military bands.

fifteen *adj and n* the number 15. ➤ **fifteenth** *adj and n*.

fifth *adj and n* **1** having the position in a sequence corresponding to the number five. **2** one of five equal parts of something. ➤ **fifthly** *adv*.

fifty *adj and n* (*pl* **-ies**) **1** the number 50. **2** (*in pl*) the numbers 50 to 59. ➤ **fiftieth** *adj and n*.

fig *n* a fleshy fruit with many seeds.

fight[1] *v* (*past tense and past part.* **fought**) **1** to contend in battle or physical combat. **2** to disagree verbally; to argue. **3** (*often + for/against*) to strive or struggle. **4** to contend against or try to prevent. * **fight shy of** to avoid facing or getting.

fight[2] *n* **1** an act or spell of fighting. **2** a heated argument. **3** a protracted struggle for an objective.

fighter *n* **1** somebody or something that fights. **2** a fast manoeuvrable military aircraft.

fighting chance *n* a small chance that may be realized with an effort.

fighting fit *adj* in excellent health.

fight off *v* to ward off or repel by fighting or resisting.

figment *n* something fabricated or imagined.

figurative *adj* **1** characterized by or using figures of speech, *esp* metaphor. **2** representing or by a figure or likeness. ➤ **figuratively** *adv*.

figure[1] *n* **1** a number symbol, *esp* an Arabic one. **2** bodily shape or form, *esp* of a woman. **3** an important or well-known person. **4** a diagram or pictorial illustration. **5** a geometrical diagram or shape.

figure[2] *v* **1** (*often + in*) to take an important or conspicuous part. **2** to calculate. **3** *informal* to seem reasonable or expected. **4** *chiefly NAmer, informal* to regard or consider (something). **5** to represent or portray by a figure or outline. * **figure on** *informal* to take into consideration.

figurehead *n* **1** an ornamental carved figure on a ship's bow. **2** a head or chief in name only.

figure of speech *n* a form of expression used to convey a special meaning or effect, e.g. metaphor.

figure out *v informal* **1** to discover or determine. **2** to solve or fathom.

figure skating *n* skating in distinctive circular patterns.

figurine *n* a small statue of a human figure.

filament *n* **1** a single threadlike object or part. **2** a slender conductor in an electric light bulb, made to glow by the passage of an electric current. **3** the stalk of a stamen that bears the anther.

filbert *n* a sweet hazelnut with a thick shell.

filch *v* informal to steal or pilfer.

file[1] *n* **1** a box or folder for keeping papers in order. **2** a collection of letters and documents on a subject. **3** a collection of data stored under one name in a computer.

file[2] *v* **1** to store or organize (papers) in files. **2** to submit or record (a lawsuit) officially.

file[3] *n* a row of people, animals, or things arranged one behind the other.

file[4] *v* to walk or move one behind the other.

file[5] *n* a steel tool with a rough surface for shaping or smoothing.

file[6] *v* to shape or smooth with a file.

filial *adj* relating to a son or daughter's relationship to a parent.

filibuster *n* the use of delaying tactics in a legislative assembly.

filigree *or* **filagree** *n* delicate ornamental work in fabric or metal.

filing *n* (*usu in pl*) a metal fragment rubbed off in filing.

fill[1] *v* **1** to make or become full. **2** to stop up or plug (a hole or gap). **3** to satisfy or fulfil (a need or requirement). **4** to spread through or occupy the whole of. **5** to exercise or appoint somebody to (an office or post).

fill[2] *n* as much as one needs or can tolerate.

filler *n* a substance used to fill holes or increase the bulk of something.

fillet[1] (*NAmer* **filet**) *n* **1** a fleshy boneless piece of meat. **2** a long slice of fish with the bones removed. **3** a narrow strip of material used as a headband. **4** a narrow flat architectural moulding.

fillet[2] *v* (**filleted, filleting**) **1** to remove the bones from (a fish). **2** to cut (meat or fish) into fillets.

fill in *v* **1** *Brit* to complete (a form). **2** (*often + on*) to give (somebody) information. **3** (*often + for*) to act as a temporary substitute.

filling[1] *n* something used to fill a hole or container.

filling[2] *adj* of food: pleasantly satisfying.

fillip *n* a boost or stimulus.

fill out *v* **1** to become fatter. **2** *chiefly NAmer* to complete (a form).

filly *n* (*pl* **-ies**) **1** a young female horse. **2** *informal* a lively young woman.

film[1] *n* **1** a roll or strip of plastic coated with a light-sensitive emulsion for taking photographs or moving pictures. **2** a thin transparent sheet of plastic used as a wrapping. **3** a story, documentary, etc, recorded on film for showing in cinemas or on television. **4** a thin layer or covering.

film[2] *v* **1** to make a film of. **2** (*often + over*) to become covered with a thin layer.

filmy *adj* (**-ier, -iest**) **1** resembling or made of film. **2** covered with a mist or film.

filter[1] *n* **1** a substance or device that allows liquid or gas to pass through and separates out solid matter. **2** a device or material for suppressing light or sound waves of certain frequencies. **3** *Brit* a signal that allows traffic to turn left or right while the main flow is stopped.

filter² v **1** to pass or move through a filter. **2** of information: to become known gradually. **3** Brit of traffic: to turn left or right from the main flow.

filth n **1** dirt or refuse. **2** obscene or pornographic material.

filthy adj (-ier, -iest) **1** extremely or offensively dirty. **2** vile or lewd. **3** informal of the weather: stormy. **4** informal of books or magazines: obscene or pornographic. * **filthy rich** extremely wealthy.

filtrate n material that has passed through a filter.

filtration n the process of passing liquid through a filter.

fin n **1** a flattened appendage on a fish or whale, used in propelling or guiding the body. **2** a flattened projecting part attached to a vessel or aircraft to guide or stabilize it. **3** a flipper used in underwater swimming.

final¹ adj **1** being the last; occurring at the end. **2** conclusive or unchangeable.

final² n **1** the last game in a sport or competition, which determines the overall winner. **2** (in pl) a set of examinations at the end of an academic or professional course.

finale n the last part or item in a piece of music or other entertainment.

finalist n a contestant or team taking part in the final round of a competition.

finality n **1** the condition of being final. **2** a determined air or tone.

finalize or **-ise** v **1** to put into a final or finished form. **2** to give final approval to.

finance¹ n **1** the circulation and use of money in business and banking. **2** the management of large amounts of money. **3** (in pl) resources of money.

finance² v to raise or provide money for.

financial adj relating to money or finance. ➤ **financially** adv.

financial year n a fixed period of twelve months reckoned for tax and accounting purposes.

financier n a person who manages large-scale finance or investment.

finch n a songbird with a short conical beak.

find¹ v (past tense and past part. **found**) **1** to come upon or encounter accidentally or by searching. **2** to experience or be aware of. **3** to recognize (something) to be present in something or native to an area. **4** to seek or provide (money or time) for a purpose. **5** to discover or obtain by effort or experiment. **6** to seek or experience (a feeling). **7** to attain or reach (a level, etc). **8** to perceive (oneself) to be in a specified place or condition. **9** to discover (a person or thing) to have a specified quality, attribute, etc. **10** of a jury: to pronounce (a defendant) guilty or innocent after deliberation. * **find fault** (often + with) to criticize

unfavourably. **find one's feet** to gain confidence with experience.

find² n a valuable object or talented person discovered.

finding n the result of an investigation or enquiry.

find out v **1** to learn or discover by study or inquiry. **2** to detect (a person) in a wrongdoing.

fine¹ adj **1** superior in quality. **2** satisfactory or acceptable. **3** of weather: dry and sunny. **4** in good health or spirits. **5** characterized by elegance or refinement. **6** performed with extreme care and accuracy. **7** narrow in gauge or width. **8** consisting of relatively small particles. **9** of a distinction: subtle or precise. * **cut it fine** to act at the last available moment. **go over with a fine-tooth comb** to search or examine in great detail. ➤ **finely** adv.

fine² v (often + down) to make finer in quality or size.

fine³ n a sum payable as punishment for an offence.

fine⁴ v to punish with a fine.

fine art n an aesthetic art such as painting or sculpture.

fine print n small print in which parts of some legal documents are printed.

finery n elaborate or special clothes or jewellery.

finesse n **1** refinement or delicacy of workmanship. **2** skilful and subtle handling of a situation.

fine-tune v to make small adjustments to.

finger¹ n **1** each of the five parts at the end of the hand, esp one other than the thumb. **2** something that resembles a finger in being long and narrow. **3** the breadth of a finger used as a measure of alcoholic drink. * **keep one's fingers crossed** to hope for the best. **not lift a finger** to make no effort to help. **put one's finger on** to identify a problem or cause.

finger² v to touch or handle.

fingerboard n the part of a stringed instrument against which the fingers press the strings to vary the pitch.

fingering n the use or position of the fingers in sounding notes on an instrument.

fingernail n the thin horny plate on the upper surface at the tip of a finger.

fingerprint¹ n an ink impression of the lines upon the fingertip taken for purposes of identification.

fingerprint² v to make an impression of the fingerprints of (somebody) for identification purposes.

finial n an ornament at the top of a spire, gable, etc, or on a piece of furniture.

finicky adj **1** having exacting taste or standards; fussy. **2** requiring delicate attention to detail.

finish[1] v **1** to reach or bring to an end. **2** to stop (doing something). **3** to eat, drink, use, or dispose of entirely. **4** to end a competition, etc in a specified place or order. **5** to complete or perfect (something). **6** to complete (something) by giving it an attractive surface or edge. **7** *informal* (*also* + off) to bring about the death or ruin of. **8** to exhaust utterly. **9** (*often* + up) to reach a specified place or state. ✳ **finish with 1** to have no further need of. **2** to break off relations with. ➤ **finisher** *n*.

finish[2] *n* **1** the end or final stage. **2** the place where a race ends. **3** the final treatment or coating of a surface. **4** the final appearance of a manufactured article.

finishing school *n* a private school that trains girls in social refinement.

finite *adj* **1** having limits of size or extent. **2** subject to natural limitations.

Finn *n* a native or inhabitant of Finland.

fiord *n* see FJORD.

fir *n* an evergreen tree with flat needle-shaped leaves.

fire[1] *n* **1** the flames, heat, and light, produced when something burns. **2** a mass of burning fuel. **3** a destructive process of burning e.g. of a building or forest. **4** *Brit* a small domestic heater using gas or electricity. **5** intense energy or emotion. **6** the discharge of guns. **7** criticism or verbal attack. ✳ **catch fire** to begin to burn. **hang fire** to hesitate or delay. **on fire** burning. **open/cease fire** to begin/stop shooting a weapon. **play with fire** to take foolhardy risks. **set fire to/set on fire** to start (something) burning, *esp* accidentally or maliciously. **under fire 1** being shot at. **2** being harshly criticized.

fire[2] *v* **1** to discharge a bullet or other projectile from (a gun or other weapon). **2** to direct (questions, commands, etc) in quick succession at somebody. **3** to dismiss (an employee). **4** to supply (a heating system) with fuel. **5** to set fire to (something). **6** to bake (pottery, ceramics, or bricks) in a kiln. **7** to kindle or stimulate (a person's imagination). **8** (*also* + up) to inspire or fill with enthusiasm. **9** of an internal-combustion engine: to become active on ignition of its fuel. ✳ **in the firing line** most likely to be attacked or criticized.

fire alarm *n* a device that sounds to give warning of a fire.

firearm *n* a portable gun, *esp* a pistol or rifle.

fireball *n* **1** a ball of fire or flame. **2** *informal* a highly energetic person.

firebomb[1] *n* an incendiary bomb.

firebomb[2] *v* to attack or damage with a firebomb.

firebrand *n* **1** a piece of burning wood. **2** a person who creates unrest or strife.

firebreak *n* a strip of cleared land intended to check the spread of a fire.

fire brigade *n* an organization for controlling and putting out fires.

firecracker *n* a small firework that explodes with a series of bangs and jumps.

fire door *n* a fire-resistant door in a building.

fire drill *n* a practice of the emergency drill to be followed in the event of a fire.

fire engine *n* a vehicle that carries firefighting equipment and firefighters.

fire escape *n* a staircase or other means of escape from a burning building.

fire-extinguisher *n* an apparatus for putting out fires with chemicals.

firefighter *n* a person trained to fight and put out fires. ➤ **firefighting** *n*.

firefly *n* (*pl* -**ies**) a night-flying beetle that produces a bright intermittent light.

fireguard *n* a protective framework placed in front of an open fire.

fire irons *pl n* a set of tongs, poker, and shovel for tending a household fire.

fireman *n* (*pl* **firemen**) a male firefighter.

fireplace *n* an opening at the base of a chimney to hold a domestic fire.

firepower *n* the capacity to deliver effective fire on a target.

fireproof *adj* able to withstand fire or high temperatures.

fire-raising *n Brit* the act of deliberately setting fire to property. ➤ **fire-raiser** *n*.

fire station *n* a building where firefighting apparatus is kept and firefighters are on duty.

firestorm *n* a large fierce fire sustained by strong currents of air.

firetrap *n* a building that is difficult to escape from in case of fire.

firewood *n* wood used for fuel.

firework *n* **1** a device containing explosive material that goes off with dramatic light and sound effects when ignited. **2** (*in pl*) a display of temper or disagreement. **3** a sparkling display of brilliance.

firing line *n* **1** the troops stationed in the front line of battle. **2** the battle line from which fire is discharged against the enemy. ✳ **in the firing line** in the forefront of an activity, *esp* one involving risk, difficulty, or criticism.

firing squad *n* a detachment of soldiers detailed to execute a condemned person.

firm[1] *adj* **1** solidly or securely fixed. **2** not yielding to pressure; solid and compact. **3** having a sustained strength. **4** of an opinion or principle: unchanging and steadfast. **5** having a strong relationship. **6** of a decision or arrangement: settled or definite. **7** resolute in dealing with people or situations. ✳ **a firm hand** strong control or guidance. **hold/stand firm** to remain steadfast and unyielding. ➤ **firmly** *adv*, **firmness** *n*.

firm[2] *v* **1** to make firm. **2** (*also* + up) to settle or complete (an arrangement).

firm³ *n* a business organization.

firmament *n* the heavens.

first¹ *adj* **1** having the position in a sequence corresponding to the number one. **2** preceding all the rest; earliest. **3** in the top or winning place. **4** most important. ∗ **first thing** early in the morning.

first² *adv* **1** before anybody or anything else. **2** to start with. **3** for the first time.

first³ *n and pron* **1** a person, thing, or group, that is first. **2** a thing that has never happened before. **3** the lowest forward gear of a motor vehicle. **4** in Britain, a first-class honours degree. ∗ **at first** to start with; initially.

first aid *n* emergency treatment given to an ill or injured person. ➤ **first-aider** *n*.

firstborn *n* an eldest child.

first class *n* **1** the first or highest group in a system of classification. **2** the highest class of travel accommodation.

first-degree *adj* of a burn: mild and causing only a reddening of the skin.

first-foot *n esp* in Scotland, the first person to cross one's threshold in the New Year.

first-footing *n* the practice of visiting friends at New Year to be the first across the threshold in that year.

first-hand *adj* coming directly from the original source or personal experience. ∗ **at first hand** directly; without an intermediary.

first lady *n* the wife of a US president.

first name *n* a personal or given name.

first person *n* in grammar, the term used to refer to the speaker or speakers, represented by the pronouns *I* or *we*.

first-rate *adj* of the best class or quality; excellent.

firth *n* a sea inlet or estuary.

fiscal *adj* relating to income from taxation. ➤ **fiscally** *adv*.

fish¹ *n* (*pl* **fishes** or **fish**) **1** a cold-blooded animal that lives in water, with a long scaly body, fins, and gills. **2** the flesh of a fish used as food. **3** a person of a specified kind: *a strange fish*. ∗ **have other fish to fry** to have more important things to do.

fish² *v* **1** to try to catch fish. **2** to feel about looking for something. **3** (*often* + for) to try to obtain something by cunning or devious means.

fisherman *n* (*pl* **fishermen**) a person who catches fish as a living or for sport.

fishery *n* (*pl* **-ies**) a place or establishment for catching fish and other sea animals.

fish-eye lens *n* a wide-angle lens with a protruding front, covering an angle up to 180°.

fishing rod *n* a rod with a reel, used with a line and hook for catching fish.

fishmonger *n chiefly Brit* a person who sells fish for food.

fishnet *n* a coarse open-mesh fabric.

fishwife *n* (*pl* **fishwives**) a vulgar or loud-mouthed woman.

fishy *adj* (**-ier**, **-iest**) **1** resembling fish, *esp* in taste or smell. **2** *informal* causing doubt or suspicion.

fissile *adj* **1** of an atom or element: capable of undergoing nuclear fission. **2** of rock: easily split.

fission *n* **1** a splitting or breaking up into parts. **2** the splitting of an atomic nucleus with the release of large amounts of energy. **3** reproduction by division of cells into two or more parts which grow into new organisms.

fissure *n* a long narrow opening in rock.

fist *n* the hand clenched with the fingers doubled into the palm. ➤ **fistful** *n*.

fisticuffs *pl n* fighting with the fists.

fit¹ *adj* (**fitter**, **fittest**) **1** adapted or suited to a purpose. **2** in a suitable state. **3** strong and healthy. **4** acceptable or worthy. ∗ **see/think fit** to consider it proper or advisable. ➤ **fitness** *n*.

fit² *v* (**fitting**, *past tense and past part.* **fitted** or *NAmer* **fit**) **1** to be the right size or shape for. **2** to insert or adjust (something) so that it is correctly in position. **3** to install (a device or component). **4** to supply with equipment. **5** to match or correspond to. **6** to make (somebody) suitable for something. ➤ **fitter** *n*.

fit³ *n* the manner in which something fits.

fit⁴ *n* **1** a sudden violent attack of a disease accompanied by convulsions or unconsciousness. **2** an outburst of coughing, sneezing, etc. **3** a rapid burst of an activity. ∗ **by/in fits and starts** in an impulsive or irregular manner.

fitful *adj* spasmodic or intermittent. ➤ **fitfully** *adv*.

fitment *n* a fixed piece of equipment or furniture.

fitted *adj* **1** made to fit a space or shape closely. **2** (+ for/to) suitable or qualified for something.

fitting¹ *adj* appropriate to a situation. ➤ **fittingly** *adv*.

fitting² *n* **1** the trying on of clothes which are being made or altered. **2** a small standardized part. **3** (*in pl*) items in a property, e.g. carpets, curtains, etc, that the owner is entitled to remove if the property is sold. **4** the act of installing or securing something.

five *n* the number 5. ➤ **five** *adj*.

fiver *n informal Brit* a five-pound note.

fix¹ *v* **1** to position and attach firmly. **2** to make firm or stable or permanent. **3** to decide on (a date, price, etc). **4** to arrange (something) or make it possible. **5** to repair or mend (something). **6** to put right. **7** *chiefly NAmer* to prepare (food or drink). **8** to influence by illicit means. ➤ **fixer** *n*.

fix² *n informal* **1** a difficult or embarrassing situation. **2** a dose of a narcotic drug.

fixate v to focus one's eyes or attention on. ✳ **be fixated on** to be obsessed with.

fixation n an excessive attachment to or preoccupation with somebody or something.

fixative n a substance used to protect or hold something.

fixity n the state of being fixed or stable.

fixture n **1** a piece of equipment or furniture that is fixed in position. **2** (in pl) items in a property, e.g. plumbing, cupboards, worktops, etc, that the owner leaves if the property is sold. **3** chiefly Brit a sporting event scheduled for a particular date.

fix up v **1** to organize or arrange. **2** informal to provide with something.

fizz[1] v **1** to make a hissing or sputtering sound. **2** of a liquid: to produce bubbles of gas.

fizz[2] n **1** the act or sound of fizzing. **2** spirit or liveliness.

fizzle v to make a weak fizzing sound.

fizzle out v informal to fail or end feebly or disappointingly.

fizzy adj (-ier, -iest) **1** of a drink: effervescent. **2** lively and exuberant.

fjord or **fiord** n a narrow inlet of the sea, esp in Norway.

fl. abbr fluid.

flab n informal soft loose body tissue.

flabbergast v informal to shock or astonish greatly.

flabby adj (-ier, -iest) of flesh: lacking resilience or firmness. ➤ **flabbiness** n.

flaccid /'flaksid, 'flasid/ adj **1** soft or limp. **2** lacking vigour or force. ➤ **flaccidity** n.

flack n see FLAK.

flag[1] n a piece of fabric of distinctive design used as an identifying symbol of a nation, or as a signalling device.

flag[2] v (flagged, flagging) **1** to mark for attention. **2** to direct by signalling with a flag.

flag[3] v (flagged, flagging) to become tired and lose energy.

flag[4] or **flagstone** n a slab of stone used for paving.

flag[5] n a plant with long bladelike leaves.

flag down v to signal to (a driver or vehicle) to stop.

flagellate v to whip (somebody) as a religious punishment or for sexual gratification. ➤ **flagellation** n.

flagon n a large squat jug or bottle for holding cider, wine, etc.

flagpole or **flagstaff** n a tall pole on which to hoist a flag.

flagrant adj conspicuous and outrageous. ➤ **flagrantly** adv.

flagship n **1** the ship that carries the commander of a fleet. **2** something considered the best thing produced by an organization.

flail[1] n a threshing implement consisting of a short swinging stick attached to a handle.

flail[2] v (often + about/around) to wave the arms and legs violently.

flair n **1** (+ for) a natural ability or talent. **2** style and originality.

flak or **flack** n **1** the fire from anti-aircraft guns. **2** informal heavy criticism.

flake[1] n **1** a small loose particle. **2** a thin flattened piece or layer.

flake[2] v **1** (+ off) to come away in flakes. **2** to separate into flakes. ➤ **flaky** adj.

flambé[1] adj of food: sprinkled with brandy, rum, etc and set alight.

flambé[2] v (flambés, flambéed, flambéing) to sprinkle (food) with brandy, rum, etc and set it alight.

flamboyant adj **1** lively and ostentatious. **2** colourful or exotic. ➤ **flamboyance** n, **flamboyantly** adv.

flame[1] n **1** a bright mass of burning gas coming from something that is on fire. **2** a brilliant reddish orange colour. **3** informal a former lover.

flame[2] v **1** to burn strongly. **2** to set alight. **3** of an emotion: to be felt or displayed with intensity. **4** to send an abusive email message to.

flamenco n (pl -os) a lively style of Spanish guitar music accompanied by singing and dancing.

flamethrower n a weapon that sends out a burning stream of liquid.

flamingo n (pl -os or -oes) a wading bird with long legs, curved beak, and rosy-white and pink plumage.

flammable adj easily set on fire.

flan n a dish of a pastry case baked with a sweet or savoury filling.

flange n a projecting rib or rim for strengthening or guiding something.

flank[1] n **1** the side of a person or animal between the ribs and the hip. **2** the side of something large, such as a mountain. **3** the right or left of a formation of troops or ships.

flank[2] v to be at the side of.

flannel[1] n **1** a loosely woven wool or worsted fabric with a slightly napped surface. **2** (in pl) trousers made of flannel. **3** Brit a small square of towelling used for washing. **4** chiefly Brit, informal vague or meaningless talk.

flannel[2] v (flannelled, flannelling, NAmer flanneled, flanneling) chiefly Brit, informal to speak or write in a vague or meaningless way.

flannelette n a cotton fabric resembling flannel.

flap[1] n **1** a flexible or hinged piece that hangs loose or covers an opening. **2** a movable surface on an aircraft wing for controlling its upward or downward movement. **3** a flapping movement. **4** informal a state of excitement or panic.

flap[2] v (flapped, flapping) **1** to move up and down or from side to side, creating a noise. **2** of a bird or bat: to move its wings in flight. **3** *informal* to be agitated or panic.

flapjack *n* **1** a soft biscuit made with oats and syrup. **2** *NAmer* a pancake.

flapper *n informal* a fashionable young woman of the 1920s.

flare¹ *v* **1** to shine or blaze with a sudden flame. **2** (*usu* + up) to become suddenly angry. **3** (*usu* + up) of violence, etc: to break out. **4** (*usu* + out) to get wider at one end. ➤ **flareup** *n*.

flare² *n* **1** a sudden glaring light or flame. **2** a device producing a very bright light used as a signal. **3** a sudden outburst of anger. **4** a gradual widening at one end. **5** (*in pl*) flared trousers.

flash¹ *v* **1** to shine with a bright light briefly or intermittently. **2** to move past at high speed. **3** to direct (a smile, look, etc) briefly. **4** to show quickly or briefly. **5** to display ostentatiously. **6** *informal* of a man: to show his genitals in public. ➤ **flasher** *n*.

flash² *n* **1** a sudden burst of light. **2** a sudden burst of perception or feeling. **3** a camera attachment that produces a flash of light for photography in poor light. **4** a fleeting glimpse. **5** an armband or patch worn on a uniform as a distinguishing symbol. ✳ **flash in the pan** a sudden brief success. **in a flash** very quickly.

flash³ *adj informal* vulgarly ostentatious.

flashback *n* **1** a scene in a book, play, or film that shows events earlier than the time of the main action. **2** a sudden recollection of a past event.

flash flood *n* a sudden local flood caused by heavy rainfall.

flashgun *n* a device that produces a flash of bright artificial light, used for taking photographs in poor light.

flashing *n* a sheet of metal used in waterproofing a roof or the angle between a vertical surface and a roof.

flashlight *n* **1** a flashgun. **2** a powerful electric torch.

flash point *n* **1** the temperature at which vapour from a volatile substance ignites. **2** a point at which violence or anger erupts.

flashy *adj* (**-ier, -iest**) **1** tastelessly ostentatious or flamboyant. **2** superficially brilliant.

flask *n* **1** a glass container with a narrow neck. **2** a vacuum flask.

flat¹ *adj* (**flatter, flattest**) **1** of a surface: horizontal, not sloping. **2** smooth, without raised or hollow areas. **3** having a broad surface and little thickness. **4** clearly unmistakable; downright: *a flat refusal.* **5** of a charge: fixed. **6** dull or monotonous. **7** having lost effervescence or sparkle. **8** of a tyre: lacking air, deflated. **9** of a battery: completely or partially discharged. **10** of a musical note: lowered a semitone in pitch. **11** lower than the proper musical pitch. ✳ **that's flat** *informal* that's final. ➤ **flatly** *adv*.

flat² *n* **1** a flat part or surface. **2** (*in pl*) an area of level ground near water. **3** a musical note one semitone lower than a specified or particular note, or the character (♭) indicating this. **4** *informal* a flat tyre. **5** (*often* **the Flat**) the flat-racing season. ✳ **on the flat** on level ground.

flat³ *adv* **1** on or against a flat surface. **2** so as to be spread out; at full length. **3** *informal* completely, utterly. ✳ **fall flat** to fail to achieve the intended effect. **flat out** as hard or fast as possible.

flat⁴ *n* a self-contained set of rooms within a larger building used as a dwelling.

flat feet *pl n* a condition with the arches of the insteps flattened so that the soles rest entirely on the ground.

flatfish *n* (*pl* **flatfishes** *or* **flatfish**) a sea fish with both eyes on the upper surface of its flattened body.

flat-footed *adj* **1** affected with flat feet. **2** *informal* inept or clumsy.

flatmate *n Brit* someone who shares a flat with another person.

flat race *n* a race for horses on a course without jumps. ➤ **flat racing** *n*.

flatten *v* **1** (*also* + out) to make or become flat or flatter. **2** to press (oneself) flush against a surface. **3** to knock or raze to the ground.

flatter *v* **1** to praise insincerely out of self-interest. **2** (*usu in passive*) to make (somebody) feel valued or needed. **3** to display (a person or thing) to advantage. ➤ **flatterer** *n*.

flattery *n* insincere or excessive praise.

flatulent *adj* suffering from an accumulation of gas in the alimentary canal. ➤ **flatulence** *n*.

flatworm *n* a worm with a flattened body.

flaunt *v* to display ostentatiously or impudently.

Usage Note: Do not confuse this word with *flout,* which means 'to treat with contemptuous disregard': *to flout the rules.*

flautist *n* a person who plays the flute.

flavour¹ (*NAmer* **flavor**) *n* **1** the particular taste of a substance in the mouth. **2** a characteristic quality. **3** a representative sample. ✳ **flavour of the month** a person or thing that is currently fashionable. ➤ **flavouring** *n,* **flavourless** *adj*.

flavour² (*NAmer* **flavor**) *v* to give or add flavour to. ➤ **flavoured** *adj*.

flaw *n* **1** a blemish or imperfection. **2** a hidden defect that can cause failure under stress. **3** a weakness or error. ➤ **flawless** *adj*.

flawed *adj* blemished or imperfect.

flax *n* **1** a slender blue-flowered plant cultivated for its strong woody fibre and seeds. **2** the fibre of the flax plant.

flaxen *adj* of hair: pale soft yellow.

flay *v* **1** to strip off the skin. **2** to whip savagely.

flea *n* a wingless jumping insect that feeds on the blood of animals. ✳ **a flea in one's ear** a sharp reprimand.

flea market *n* an open-air market selling secondhand articles.

fleapit *n Brit, informal* a shabby cinema or theatre.

fleck[1] *n* **1** a small spot of colour or light. **2** a grain or particle.

fleck[2] *v* to cover with small spots or marks.

fledged *adj* of a young bird: having wing feathers developed enough for it to fly.

fledgling *or* **fledgeling** *n* a young bird that has just begun to fly.

flee *v* (**flees, fleeing,** *past tense and past part.* **fled**) to run away from danger or harm.

fleece[1] *n* **1** a sheep's coat of wool. **2** a soft warm fabric with a thick pile. **3** a jacket made of a synthetic fabric with a thick pile. ➤ **fleecy** *adj.*

fleece[2] *v informal* to overcharge or swindle.

fleet[1] *n* **1** a number of warships under a single command. **2** a group of vehicles operating together or owned by one management.

fleet[2] *adj* quick and nimble.

fleeting *adj* brief or transitory. ➤ **fleetingly** *adv.*

flesh *n* **1** the soft parts of the body. **2** an edible pulpy part of a plant or fruit. **3** the physical being of humans. **4** the physical or sensual aspect of human nature. ✳ **in the flesh** in person.

fleshly *adj* (**-ier, -iest**) belonging to or relating to the body; carnal or sensual.

flesh out *v* to add detail to (an idea or proposal).

fleshpots *pl n* places that offer exciting or sensual forms of entertainment.

fleshy *adj* (**-ier, -iest**) **1** plump. **2** succulent or pulpy.

fleur-de-lis *or* **fleur-de-lys** *n* (*pl* **fleurs-de-lis** *or* **fleurs-de-lys**) a stylized representation of three lily petals bound together at the base.

flew *v* past tense of FLY[1].

flex[1] *v* **1** to bend (a limb or joint). **2** to contract or tense (a muscle). **3** to bend and revert to an original position or shape.

flex[2] *n chiefly Brit* an electrical cable used to connect an appliance to a socket.

flexible *adj* **1** capable of being bent. **2** adaptable or versatile. ➤ **flexibility** *n*, **flexibly** *adv.*

flexitime (*NAmer* **flextime**) *n* a system by which employees can vary their working hours.

flick[1] *n* **1** a quick sharp movement with a hand. **2** *informal* a cinema film.

flick[2] *v* **1** to make a quick sharp movement of a hand. **2** to move with a flick. **3** to move lightly or jerkily. ✳ **flick through** to look at or read cursorily.

flicker[1] *v* **1** to burn or shine unsteadily. **2** to move irregularly or unsteadily. **3** to appear irregularly or indistinctly.

flicker[2] *n* **1** an instance of flickering. **2** a momentary feeling or sensation.

flick knife *n* a knife with a blade that springs out from the handle when a button is pressed.

flier *n* see FLYER.

flight *n* **1** the act of flying. **2** a journey made in an aircraft or spacecraft. **3** the path of a struck ball or other object moving through the air. **4** escape from danger or captivity. **5** a group of birds or aircraft flying together. **6** a series of stairs leading from one floor to the next. ✳ **flight of fancy** an imaginative idea. ➤ **flightless** *adj.*

flight deck *n* **1** the cockpit of a passenger aircraft. **2** the deck of an aircraft carrier.

flight path *n* the course taken by an aircraft or spacecraft.

flighty *adj* (**-ier, -iest**) irresponsible or flirtatious.

flimsy *adj* (**-ier, -iest**) **1** weak and insubstantial. **2** thin and light. **3** implausible or unconvincing. ➤ **flimsily** *adv.*

flinch *v* **1** to make a nervous shrinking movement in response to fear or pain. **2** (+ from) to avoid something from fear or nervousness.

fling[1] *v* (*past tense and past part.* **flung**) **1** to throw or hurl with force. **2** to send or put somewhere unceremoniously. **3** (+ into) to involve (oneself) energetically in an activity. **4** to move in a hasty or violent manner.

fling[2] *n* **1** a brief period of enjoyment. **2** *informal* a brief sexual relationship. **3** a vigorous Scottish reel or dance.

flint *n* **1** a hard quartz found in chalk or limestone. **2** a flaked piece of this used in antiquity to form a tool or weapon. **3** a metal alloy used for producing a spark in a cigarette lighter.

flintlock *n* an old type of gun with the charge ignited by sparks struck from a flint.

flip[1] *v* (**flipped, flipping**) **1** to turn over with a quick neat movement. **2** to propel with a flick of the fingers. **3** *informal* to lose self-control. ✳ **flip one's lid** *informal* to become angry or lose self-control ✳ **flip through** to read through quickly or casually.

flip[2] *n* **1** a flipping movement or action. **2** a somersault.

flip[3] *adj informal* flippant or impertinent.

flip-flop *n* a light sandal with two diagonal straps anchored between the big and second toes.

flippant *adj* not showing proper respect or seriousness. ➤ **flippancy** *n*, **flippantly** *adv.*

flipper *n* **1** a broad flat limb of seals and turtles, used for swimming. **2** a flat rubber paddle worn on each foot for underwater swimming.

flip side *n informal* **1** the less important side of a pop record. **2** the less familiar or more unwelcome side of a person or situation.

flirt[1] *v* to show playful sexual interest. ✳ **flirt with 1** to show superficial or casual interest in. **2** to risk (danger or death) deliberately for excitement. ➤ **flirtation** *n*, **flirty** *adj*.

flirt[2] *n* a person who likes to flirt.

flirtatious *adj* liking to flirt. ➤ **flirtatiously** *adv*.

flit[1] *v* (**flitted, flitting**) to move or fly lightly and quickly.

flit[2] *n Brit* a hurried departure or escape.

flitter *v* to move about in a random or agitated way.

float[1] *n* **1** something that rests on the surface of a fluid without sinking. **2** a platform of a lorry supporting an exhibit in a parade. **3** an electrically powered delivery vehicle. **4** a sum of money available for giving change at a stall, in a shop, etc.

float[2] *v* **1** to rest on the surface of a fluid without sinking. **2** to drift on or through a liquid, or move gently in the air. **3** to wander aimlessly. **4** in sport, to send (a ball) on a high smooth flight. **5** to present (an idea) for consideration. **6** of a currency: to find its own level in the international exchange market. **7** to offer the shares of (a company) for the first time for sale on the stock market.

floatation *n* see FLOTATION.

flock[1] *n* **1** a group of birds or mammals in one place. **2** (*also in pl*) a large group. **3** a Christian congregation.

flock[2] *v* to gather or move in a crowd.

flock[3] *n* **1** a tuft of wool or cotton fibre. **2** woollen or cotton material used as stuffing. **3** short or pulverized fibre used to form a velvety pattern on cloth or paper. ➤ **flocky** *adj*.

floe *n* a sheet of floating ice.

flog *v* (**flogged, flogging**) **1** to beat with a stick or whip. **2** *Brit, informal* to sell. ✳ **flog a dead horse** to waste time pursuing already settled issues.

flood[1] *n* **1** an overflowing of water onto dry land. **2** (**the Flood**) the biblical flooding of the earth caused by God as a punishment for human wickedness. **3** the inflow of water associated with a rising tide. **4** *literary* a body of water such as a river or the sea. **5** an overwhelming quantity or volume.

flood[2] *v* **1** to cover with or become submerged under water that has overflowed. **2** of a river: to rise and overflow its banks. **3** to arrive in a continuous stream or overwhelming quantities. **4** of sound, light, etc: to fill (a place).

floodgate *n* **1** a gate for shutting out or admitting water. **2** (*also in pl*) something that keeps back a potentially overwhelming flow.

floodlight[1] *n* a powerful lamp used for artificially illuminating a theatre stage or a sports ground.

floodlight[2] *v* (*past tense and past part.* **floodlit**) to illuminate with floodlights.

floodplain *n* a low-lying area beside a river that is subject to flooding.

flood tide *n* a tide while flowing in.

floor[1] *n* **1** the lower surface of a room or passage. **2** the bottom inside surface of a cave, the sea, etc. **3** a storey of a building. **4** (**the floor**) the part of a legislative or other assembly in which members sit and speak. **5** an area in a stock exchange where trading is done. **6** a lower limit. ✳ **take the floor 1** to make a formal speech. **2** to begin dancing.

floor[2] *v* **1** to fit with a floor. **2** to knock to the floor or ground. **3** to confuse or disconcert.

floorboard *n* a long board or plank forming part of a wooden floor.

floor show *n* a cabaret or other entertainment at a nightclub.

floozy or **floozie** or **floosie** *n* (*pl* -**ies**) *informal* a disreputable or promiscuous woman or girl.

flop[1] *v* (**flopped, flopping**) **1** to swing or hang loosely and heavily. **2** to move or drop in a heavy or clumsy manner. **3** *informal* to fail completely.

flop[2] *n* **1** a flopping movement. **2** *informal* a complete failure.

floppy *adj* (-**ier**, -**iest**) limp and hanging loosely. ➤ **floppily** *adv*.

floppy disk *n* in computing, a flexible disc used for storing data.

flora *n* the plant life of a region or period.

floral *adj* relating to or composed of flowers.

floret *n* **1** each of the small flowers forming the head of a composite plant. **2** each of the flowering stems making up a cauliflower or broccoli head.

florid *adj* **1** tinged with red; ruddy. **2** excessively ornate in style.

florin *n* a former British coin worth two shillings.

florist *n* a person or shop that sells cut flowers.

floss[1] *n* **1** soft silk or cotton thread used in embroidery. **2** soft thread for cleaning between the teeth. **3** silky plant fibres on maize cobs or cotton bolls.

floss[2] *v* to clean the teeth with dental floss.

flotation or **floatation** *n* **1** the act or process of floating. **2** the launching of a company on the stock market by offering shares for the first time.

flotilla *n* a small fleet of ships or boats.

flotsam *n* floating wreckage of a ship or its cargo. ✳ **flotsam and jetsam** odds and ends.

flounce[1] *v* (*often* + out/off/about/away) to move in an exaggerated or petulant manner.

flounce[2] *n* an instance of flouncing.

flounce[3] *n* a wide strip of fabric attached to the hem of a skirt or dress.

flounder[1] *n* (*pl* **flounders** or **flounder**) a small sea flatfish.

flounder[2] v **1** to stagger about in soft mud or water. **2** to behave or speak in a blundering or incompetent way.

flour n **1** finely ground meal, *esp* of wheat. **2** a fine soft powder. ➤ **floury** *adj*.

flourish[1] v **1** to grow or thrive. **2** to achieve success; to prosper. **3** to be in good health. **4** to wave or brandish with dramatic gestures.

flourish[2] n **1** a decorative embellishment in handwriting. **2** an ostentatious or dramatic gesture. **3** a fanfare on brass instruments.

flout v to disregard or ignore (a rule or custom).

Usage Note: See note at FLAUNT.

flow[1] v **1** to move or pour steadily and continuously. **2** to hang or stream gracefully.

flow[2] n a continuous flowing or stream.

flow chart n a diagram showing the successive stages of a procedure or system.

flower[1] n **1** the part of a plant having bright petals, from which the seeds or fruit develop. **2** the finest part or example of something.

flower[2] v **1** to produce flowers. **2** to develop and flourish.

flowerpot n a container for growing plants.

flowery *adj* **1** patterned with flowers. **2** of language: highly ornate.

flown v past part. of FLY[1].

flu n influenza.

fluctuate v to rise and fall or change unpredictably. ➤ **fluctuation** n.

flue n a channel in a chimney for flame and smoke to escape.

fluent *adj* **1** able to speak, write, or read without difficulty. **2** effortlessly smooth and rapid. ➤ **fluency** n, **fluently** *adv*.

fluff[1] n **1** small loose bits of waste material gathered in sticking clumps. **2** soft light fur, down, etc. **3** *informal* a blunder in speaking or performing.

fluff[2] v **1** (+ out/up) to make fuller, plumper, or fluffier. **2** *informal* to do or say badly.

fluffy *adj* (**-ier, -iest**) **1** like or covered with fluff. **2** light and soft or airy. ➤ **fluffily** *adv*.

flugelhorn n a brass musical instrument resembling a cornet.

fluid[1] n **1** a liquid or gas. **2** a liquid in the body of an animal or plant.

fluid[2] *adj* **1** capable of flowing. **2** not fixed or firm. **3** of plans not yet definite. **4** effortlessly graceful. ➤ **fluidity** n, **fluidly** *adv*.

fluid ounce n a British unit of liquid capacity equal to one twentieth of a pint (about 28.4ml).

fluke[1] n a parasitic flatworm.

fluke[2] n a lucky success that happens by chance. ➤ **fluky** *adj*.

flume n **1** a sloping water channel. **2** a water chute at an amusement park or swimming pool.

flummery n (pl **-ies**) *informal* empty or pretentious talk.

flummox v to bewilder or confuse completely.

flung v past tense and past part. of FLING[1].

flunk v *chiefly NAmer, informal* to fail an examination or course.

flunky or **flunkey** n (pl **-ies** or **-eys**) **1** a person performing menial duties. **2** a liveried servant.

fluoresce v to glow brightly.

fluorescent *adj* **1** producing a bright light by emitting electromagnetic radiation. **2** brightly colourful. ➤ **fluorescence** n.

fluoridate v to add fluoride to (a water supply). ➤ **fluoridation** n.

fluoride n a compound of fluorine added to toothpaste or drinking water to reduce tooth decay.

fluorine n a pale yellowish toxic gas.

fluorite n = FLUORSPAR.

fluorspar n a mineral used in glass-making and as a flux in the manufacture of metals.

flurry[1] n (pl **-ies**) **1** a gust of wind. **2** a small mass of snow, rain, or leaves blown about by a light wind. **3** a state of nervous excitement. **4** a short burst of activity.

flurry[2] v (**-ies, -ied**) to make or become agitated and confused.

flush[1] n **1** a tinge of red in the cheeks. **2** an instance of flushing. **3** a fresh and vigorous state. **4** a transitory sensation of extreme heat. **5** a surge of emotion. **6** a sudden flow of water.

flush[2] v **1** to glow brightly with a rosy colour. **2** to blush. **3** to cleanse by causing liquid to flow over or through. **4** to dispose of (waste) by carrying it away on a stream of liquid. ✱ **be flushed with** to feel proud of and excited by.

flush[3] *adj* **1** level with a surface. **2** arranged edge to edge so as to fit snugly. **3** *informal* having plenty of money.

flush[4] v **1** to cause (a game bird) to take flight suddenly. **2** (*often* + out) to force (somebody) to leave a place of concealment.

flush[5] n in poker, a hand of playing cards of the same suit.

fluster[1] v to make or become agitated or confused. ➤ **flustered** *adj*.

fluster[2] n a state of agitated confusion.

flute n **1** a high-pitched woodwind instrument that consists of a cylindrical tube with finger holes stopped at one end, held horizontally and played by blowing air across a side hole. **2** a grooved pleat or frill. **3** a tall narrow wineglass.

flutter[1] v **1** to flap the wings rapidly. **2** to move or fall with quick wavering or flapping motions. **3** to beat or vibrate in irregular spasms. **4** to move about or behave in an agitated aimless manner. ➤ **flutterer** n.

flutter[2] n **1** a state of nervous confusion or excitement. **2** abnormal spasmodic fluttering of the heart. **3** *chiefly Brit* a small gamble or bet. ➤ **fluttery** *adj*.

fluvial *adj* relating to a stream or river.

flux n 1 a continuous flow. 2 continual change. 3 a substance used in soldering or brazing.

fly[1] v (**flies, flying, flew, flown**) 1 to move through the air by means of wings. 2 to float or wave in the air. 3 to operate (an aircraft or spacecraft) in flight. 4 to travel or transport in an aircraft. 5 to move or pass swiftly. 6 to pass suddenly and violently into a rage or other specified state. 7 informal to leave hurriedly. ✴ **fly at** to attack suddenly. **fly in the face of** 1 to disobey. 2 to be contrary to. **fly off the handle** informal to become suddenly angry. **with flying colours** with great success or distinction.

fly[2] n (pl **flies**) 1 (usu in pl) an opening in the front of a pair of trousers, closed with buttons or a zip and covered by a fold of cloth. 2 (in pl) the space over a stage where scenery and equipment can be hung.

fly[3] n (pl **flies**) 1 a flying insect with two thin wings. 2 an artificial fly attached to a fishhook as bait. ✴ **fly in the ointment** a minor irritant or difficulty in a generally satisfactory situation. **fly on the wall** a hidden observer.

fly[4] adj (**flyer, flyest**) chiefly Brit, informal clever and knowing.

flyaway adj esp of the hair: tending not to stay in place.

flyblown adj contaminated by the eggs or young larvae of flies.

fly-by-night adj disreputable or untrustworthy.

flycatcher n a small bird that feeds on insects caught while flying.

flyer or **flier** n 1 a person or thing that flies or moves very fast. 2 a passenger on an aircraft. 3 a small leaflet or handbill. 4 informal a flying start in athletics.

flying picket n a person who travels to picket a place of work other than their own.

flying saucer n a round flying object supposed to come from outer space.

flying squad n a police unit ready to act swiftly in an emergency.

flying start n a successful beginning giving an advantage over competitors.

flyleaf n (pl **flyleaves**) a blank page at the beginning or end of a book and fastened to the cover.

flyover n Brit a crossing of two roads, railways, etc at different levels.

flypaper n a strip of sticky paper hung up to attract and kill flies.

flypast n Brit a ceremonial flight by aircraft over a gathering of people.

flyposting n the unauthorized posting of advertisements in public places.

fly sheet n 1 a protective sheet covering a tent or its entrance. 2 a small pamphlet or circular.

flywheel n a heavy wheel that revolves to make a machine or engine run smoothly.

FM adj frequency modulation (a broadcasting and receiving system).

foal[1] n a young animal of the horse family.

foal[2] v to give birth to a foal.

foam[1] n 1 a light frothy mass of fine bubbles formed on the surface of a liquid. 2 a substance in the form of a light frothy mass of bubbles. 3 a rubber or plastic material filled with small holes by the introduction of gas bubbles during manufacture. ➤ **foamy** adj.

foam[2] v to produce or form foam.

fob n 1 a tab on a key ring. 2 a short chain attached to a watch for carrying in a pocket.

fob off v (**fobbed, fobbing**) 1 (+ with) to put (somebody) off with a trick or excuse. 2 (+ on) to pass or offer (something spurious or inferior) as genuine or perfect.

focal adj of or located at a focus.

focal length n the distance between the optical centre of a lens or mirror and the focal point.

focal point n 1 the point or source at which rays of light converge or appear to converge. 2 a centre of activity or attention.

fo'c'sle n see FORECASTLE.

focus[1] n (pl **focuses** or **foci**) 1 a point at which rays of light or sound converge. 2 the point at which an object must be placed for an image formed by a lens or mirror to be sharp. 3 = FOCAL LENGTH. 4 adjustment of the eye to produce clear vision. 5 a centre of activity or attention. ✴ **in/out of focus** of an image: having or lacking sharpness of outline.

focus[2] v (**focused** or **focussed, focusing** or **focussing**) 1 to adjust (a camera or telescope) to obtain a sharp image. 2 to become able to see clearly. 3 to concentrate one's thoughts or attention on. 4 of rays: to converge on a point.

focus group n a group of people gathered together to discuss a new product or policy.

fodder n 1 food for cattle or other domestic animals. 2 something used to supply a constant demand.

foe n literary an enemy or adversary.

foetid adj see FETID.

foetus or **fetus** n (pl **foetuses** or **fetuses**) an unborn human baby or young of a mammal. ➤ **foetal** adj.

fog[1] n 1 fine particles of water suspended in the lower atmosphere causing a loss of visibility. 2 a state of confusion or bewilderment.

fog[2] v (**fogged, fogging**) 1 to cover or obscure with fog or condensation. 2 to make confused or confusing.

fogey or **fogy** n (pl **fogeys** or **fogies**) a person with old-fashioned ideas.

foggy adj (**-ier, -iest**) 1 thick with fog. 2 vague or confused.

foghorn n a deep horn sounded in a fog to give warning to ships.

foible n a minor weakness or shortcoming.

foil[1] *n* **1** metal in thin sheets. **2** a person or thing that serves as a contrast to another.

foil[2] *v* **1** to prevent (somebody) from doing something. **2** to frustrate or defeat (an attempt).

foil[3] *n* a light fencing sword with a blunted tip.

foist *v* (*usu* + on) to force acceptance of (something or somebody unwanted) on somebody.

fold[1] *v* **1** (*often* + over) to lay one part of (something) over another part. **2** (*often* + up) to reduce the length or bulk of (something) by doubling it over. **3** (*often* + up) to become folded or be capable of being folded. **4** to clasp (the arms) together. **5** to clasp closely. **6** to wrap or envelop. **7** (+ in/into) to gently incorporate (a food ingredient) into a mixture. **8** *informal* of a business: to stop operating. ➤ **foldable** *adj*.

fold[2] *n* **1** a part folded over. **2** a line or crease made by folding.

fold[3] *n* **1** an enclosure for sheep. **2** (**the fold**) a group of people adhering to a faith.

folder *n* a folded cover or envelope for holding loose papers.

foliage *n* the leaves of a plant or clump of plants.

folic acid *n* a vitamin found in green leafy vegetables and liver.

folio *n* (*pl* **-os**) **1** a sheet of paper folded once into four sides. **2** a book printed on pages of this size.

folk *n* **1** *informal* (*also* **folks**) people in general. **2** *informal* (**one's folks**) the members of one's own family or community. **3** = FOLK MUSIC.

folk dance *n* a traditional dance of a people or region.

folklore *n* the traditional customs and stories of a people.

folk music *n* the traditional music and songs of a people or region.

folk song *n* a traditional song of a people or region. ➤ **folksinger** *n*.

folksy *adj* (**-ier, -iest**) *informal* informal or familiar in manner or style.

folk tale *n* an anonymous traditional story that is transmitted orally.

follicle *n* a small cavity surrounding the root of a hair.

follow *v* **1** to go or come after. **2** to go after (somebody or something) to observe them or watch their movements. **3** to accept as a guide or leader. **4** to obey or act in accordance with (rules or instructions). **5** to copy or imitate. **6** to walk or proceed along (a path or route). **7** to engage in (an activity) as a calling or way of life. **8** to undertake (a course of action). **9** to come or take place after in time or order. **10** (+ with) to cause (something) to be followed by something else. **11** (*often* + from) to come into existence or take place as a result of. **12** to support or watch the progress of. **13** to understand the meaning

or logic of. * **follow suit** to do as somebody else has done.

follower *n* **1** somebody who follows the opinions or teachings of another. **2** a fan or supporter.

following[1] *adj* **1** next after. **2** now to be mentioned.

following[2] *n* a group of followers or adherents.

following[3] *prep* subsequent to.

follow on *v* **1** to continue. **2** to come as a consequence.

follow through *v* to pursue or complete (an activity or process).

follow up *v* to continue or enquire into (something) further.

folly *n* (*pl* **-ies**) **1** a lack of good sense or prudence. **2** a foolish act or idea. **3** a fanciful building built for scenic effect.

foment *v* to incite (trouble, rebellion, etc).

fond *adj* **1** (+ of) having an affection or liking for. **2** affectionate; loving. **3** foolishly tender; indulgent. **4** foolish; naive. ➤ **fondly** *adv*, **fondness** *n*.

fondant *n* a soft creamy mixture of flavoured sugar and water, or a sweet made from this.

fondle *v* to handle or caress tenderly and lovingly or erotically.

fondue *n* a dish in which small pieces of food are dipped in a hot oil or a sauce.

font[1] *n* a receptacle in a church for the water used in baptism.

font[2] *n* = FOUNT[2].

food *n* material taken into the body of a living organism to provide energy and sustain life. * **food for thought** something that needs thinking about.

food chain *n* a sequence of organisms each of which uses the next as a food source.

food poisoning *n* a disorder caused by the toxic products of bacteria or by chemical residues in food.

foodstuff *n* a substance with food value.

fool[1] *n* **1** a person lacking in sense or understanding. **2** a jester employed by a royal or noble household. * **act/play the fool** to misbehave. **make a fool of oneself** to behave in an embarrassing way. ➤ **foolery** *n*.

fool[2] *v* **1** to trick or deceive. **2** to say or do something as a joke. **3** to behave in a silly or irresponsible way.

fool[3] *n* chiefly *Brit* a cold dessert made from fruit and whipped cream.

fool about *v* to behave in a silly or irresponsible way.

foolhardy *adj* (**-ier, -iest**) foolishly bold or rash.

foolish *adj* **1** unwise; silly. **2** absurd; ridiculous. ➤ **foolishly** *adv*, **foolishness** *n*.

foolproof *adj* extremely simple or reliable.

foolscap *n* chiefly *Brit* a size of paper usu 17 × 13½ in. (432 × 343mm).

fool's gold *n* a yellowish mineral that looks like gold.

fool's paradise *n* a state of illusory happiness.

foot[1] *n* (*pl* **feet**) **1** the end part of the leg on which an animal or person stands. **2** (*pl also* **foot**) a unit of length equal to 0.305m (12in.). **3** the lower edge or lowest part; the bottom. **4** the end of something that is opposite the head or top. **5** the basic unit of verse metre consisting of a group of syllables. ✷ **feet of clay** a weakness in a generally admired person. **have/keep one's feet on the ground** to remain sensible and practical. **not put a foot wrong** to make no mistakes at all. **on/by foot** walking or running, as opposed to using transport. **put one's foot down** to take a firm stand. **put one's foot in it** to make an embarrassing blunder.

foot[2] *v* to pay (a bill).

footage *n* a length of cinema or television film.

foot-and-mouth disease *n* a disease of cattle, sheep, pigs, and goats, with ulcers in the mouth, round the hoofs, and on the udders.

football *n* **1** a team game that involves kicking a ball, *esp* Association Football in the UK or American football in the US. **2** the inflated round or oval ball used in a game of football. ➤ **footballer** *n*.

footbridge *n* a bridge for pedestrians.

footfall *n* the sound of a footstep.

foothill *n* a hill at the foot of a mountain.

foothold *n* **1** a place where the foot can be placed securely while climbing. **2** an established position or basis from which to progress.

footing *n* **1** a stable placing of the feet. **2** an established position from which progress can be made. **3** a position or rank in relation to others. **4** an enlargement at the lower end of a foundation, wall, or column.

footlights *pl n* a row of lights set across the front of a stage floor.

footling *adj* unimportant or trivial.

footloose *adj* free to go or do as one pleases.

footman *n* (*pl* **footmen**) a servant in livery who receives and attends to visitors.

footnote *n* an extra note or comment placed at the bottom of a printed page.

footpad *n archaic* a person who robbed passers-by on foot.

footpath *n* a path or pavement for people on foot.

footprint *n* an impression made by a foot or shoe.

footsore *adj* having sore feet from much walking.

footstep *n* a step or tread taken in walking.

footstool *n* a low stool used to support the feet when sitting.

fop *n* a man who is too concerned about his clothes and appearance. ➤ **foppish** *adj*.

for[1] *prep* **1** used to indicate purpose or reason. **2** used to indicate direction or intention. **3** because of. **4** in place of. **5** on behalf of. **6** in favour of. **7** considering: *tall for her age.* **8** with respect to: *a stickler for detail.* **9** used to indicate cost or payment: *work for nothing.*

for[2] *conj* because.

forage[1] *n* **1** food for animals, e.g. hay or straw. **2** a search.

forage[2] *v* **1** to search for food. **2** (*usu* + for) to rummage.

foray[1] *v* to make a raid or incursion.

foray[2] *n* **1** a sudden attack or raid into an enemy's territory. **2** a brief attempt in a new sphere.

forbear[1] *v* (**forbore**, **forborne**) to hold oneself back from (doing something), *esp* with difficulty.

forbear[2] *n* see FOREBEAR.

forbearance *n* patience or self-restraint.

forbid *v* (**forbidding**, *past tense* **forbade** or **forbad**, *past part.* **forbidden**) **1** to refuse to allow. **2** to refuse access to or use of. **3** to hinder or prevent.

forbidding *adj* looking threatening or unfriendly.

force[1] *n* **1** strength or energy exerted or brought to bear. **2** moral or mental strength. **3** capacity to persuade or convince. **4** violence or compulsion used to achieve something. **5** legal validity. **6** an organized body of soldiers or workers. **7** (*in pl*) the armed services of a nation or commander. ✷ **in force 1** in great numbers. **2** valid or operative.

force[2] *v* **1** to compel (somebody) to do something. **2** to bring about by compulsion, violence, or great effort. **3** to press or drive (something) with a violent effort. **4** to break open (a door, lock, etc).

force-feed *v* (*past tense and past part.* **force-fed**) to feed (e.g. a person) against their will.

forceful *adj* powerful or effective. ➤ **forcefully** *adv.*

forcemeat *n* a savoury seasoned stuffing of breadcrumbs and meat.

forceps *n* (*pl* **forceps**) a pair of large pincers used in surgery.

forcible *adj* **1** effected by force. **2** powerful; forceful. ➤ **forcibly** *adv.*

ford[1] *n* a shallow part of a river or stream that can be crossed in a vehicle or on foot.

ford[2] *v* to cross (a river or stream, etc) at a ford. ➤ **fordable** *adj.*

fore[1] *adj and adv* situated in or towards the front.

fore[2] *n* a front part. ✷ **to the fore** in a prominent position.

forearm[1] /'fawrahm/ *n* the human arm between the elbow and the wrist.

forearm[2] /faw'rahm/ *v* to prepare against attack or danger.

forebear *or* **forbear** *n* an ancestor or forefather.

foreboding[1] *n* a feeling of something bad about to happen.

foreboding[2] *adj* presaging something bad.

forecast[1] *v* (*past tense and past part.* **forecast** *or* **forecasted**) to estimate or predict (a future event or condition). ➤ **forecaster** *n*.

forecast[2] *n* a prediction of a future happening or condition.

forecastle *or* **fo'c'sle** *n* **1** a short raised deck at the bow of a ship. **2** a forward part of a merchant ship where the living quarters are situated.

foreclose *v* to cancel a mortgage and repossess a property because of nonpayment. ➤ **foreclosure** *n*.

forecourt *n* **1** an open or paved area in front of a building. **2** the part of a tennis court between the net and the service line.

forefather *n* an ancestor.

forefinger *n* the finger next to the thumb.

forefoot *n* (*pl* **forefeet**) each of the front feet of a four-footed animal.

forefront *n* the foremost part or place.

forego *v* see FORGO.

foregoing *adj* going before; immediately preceding.

foreground *n* **1** the part of a picture or view nearest to the viewer. **2** a prominent position.

forehand *n* a stroke in tennis, squash, etc made with the palm of the hand turned in the direction of movement.

forehead *n* the part of the face above the eyes.

foreign *adj* **1** born in or belonging to a country other than one's own. **2** relating to other nations. **3** occurring in an abnormal situation in the living body. **4** (*usu* + to) not characteristic of or relevant to.

foreign body *n* a piece of unwanted material that has entered something.

foreigner *n* **1** a person from a foreign country. **2** a stranger or outsider.

foreign exchange *n* currency of foreign countries.

foreknowledge *n* knowledge of an event before it happens.

forelock *n* a lock of hair growing just above the forehead.

foreman *n* (*pl* **foremen**) **1** a worker who supervises other workers. **2** the chairman and spokesman of a jury.

foremast *n* the mast nearest the bow of a ship.

foremost[1] *adj* **1** first in a series or progression. **2** of first rank or position; preeminent.

foremost[2] *adv* most importantly.

forename *n* a name that comes before a surname.

forensic *adj* **1** relating to the scientific investigation of crime. **2** belonging to courts of law.

foreplay *n* erotic stimulation preceding sexual intercourse.

forerunner *n* a person or thing that comes before a better known one exists.

foresee *v* (**foresaw**, **foreseen**) to be aware of (a development or event) beforehand. ➤ **foreseeable** *adj*.

foreshadow *v* to indicate or suggest beforehand.

foreshore *n* the part of a seashore between high-tide and low-tide marks.

foreshorten *v* (**foreshortened**, **foreshortening**) **1** to shorten (a detail in a drawing or painting) so as to create an illusion of depth. **2** to make more compact in scale or time.

foresight *n* the ability to foresee events, or the prudence arising from this.

foreskin *n* the fold of skin that covers the tip of the penis.

forest[1] *n* **1** a dense growth of trees covering a large area of land. **2** a large number of standing things.

forest[2] *v* to cover with trees or forest. ➤ **forestation** *n*.

forestall *v* to hinder or prevent by taking action in advance.

forestry *n* the scientific study or practice of managing forests.

foretaste *n* an advance indication or sampling.

foretell *v* (*past tense and past part.* **foretold**) to predict.

forethought *n* careful consideration of what is likely to happen or be needed.

forever *adv* **1** (*also* **for ever**) for all future time; indefinitely. **2** persistently; incessantly.

forewarn *v* to warn in advance. ➤ **forewarner** *n*.

forewent *v* past tense of FOREGO.

foreword *n* a preface to a book written by somebody other than the author of the text.

forfeit[1] *n* something lost, taken away, or imposed as a penalty.

forfeit[2] *v* (**forfeited**, **forfeiting**) to lose the right to (a privilege, etc) as a penalty. ➤ **forfeiture** *n*.

forfeit[3] *adj* lost as a forfeit.

forge[1] *n* an open furnace or workshop where metal is heated and worked.

forge[2] *v* **1** to shape (metal) by heating and hammering it. **2** to bring into being by an expenditure of effort. **3** to make a counterfeit copy of (a signature, document, or banknote). ➤ **forger** *n*, **forgery** *n*.

forge[3] *v* to move forwards slowly and steadily.

forge ahead *v* to make rapid progress.

forget *v* (**forgetting**, *past tense* **forgot**, *past part.* **forgotten**, *archaic or NAmer* **forgot**) **1** to be unable to remember. **2** to disregard or give no attention to. **3** to reject the possibility of. * **forget oneself** to act unsuitably or unworthily. ➤ **forgettable** *adj*.

forgetful adj likely or apt to forget. ➤ **forget-fully** adv, **forgetfulness** n.

forget-me-not n a small low-growing plant with blue flowers.

forgive v (**forgave, forgiven**) **1** to stop feeling angry about (something) or resentful towards (somebody). **2** to pardon (somebody, an offence, etc). ➤ **forgivable** adj.

forgiveness n forgiving or being forgiven; pardon.

forgo or **forego** v (**forgoes** or **foregoes, forgoing** or **foregoing**, past tense **forwent** or **forewent**, past part. **forgone** or **foregone**) to abstain or refrain from (something desirable).

fork¹ n **1** an implement with two or more prongs for eating or serving food. **2** a similar larger tool for digging, carrying, etc. **3** either of two divided supports for a bicycle or motorcycle wheel. **4** a place where a road or river divides into two, or each of these divisions.

fork² v **1** to divide into two or more branches. **2** to make a turn into one of the branches of a fork. **3** to dig or work with a fork. **4** informal (+ out) to make a payment or contribution.

forked adj having one end divided into branches or points.

forklift truck n a vehicle for lifting heavy loads by means of two horizontal prongs at the front.

forlorn adj **1** miserably sad and lonely. **2** nearly hopeless. ➤ **forlornly** adv.

form¹ n **1** the shape and structure of something. **2** a kind or variety of something. **3** an established or correct method of proceeding or behaving. **4** a prescribed and set order of words. **5** a document with blank spaces for inserting information. **6** a long seat without a back. **7** chiefly Brit a school class organized for the work of a particular year. **8** the past performances of a competitor. **9** condition suitable for performing well. **10** Brit, informal a criminal record. ➤ **formless** adj.

form² v **1** to give shape or existence to. **2** to mould into a particular shape. **3** to come into existence; to take shape. **4** to serve to make up or constitute. **5** to arrange or be arranged in (a shape).

formal adj **1** characterized by dignity and the observance of correct procedure. **2** suitable for an important or ceremonial occasion. **3** done in accordance with established procedure. **4** arranged in a symmetrical or orderly pattern. ➤ **formally** adv.

formaldehyde n a pungent gas used chiefly as a disinfectant and preservative.

formalin n a clear solution of formaldehyde in water.

formality n (pl -ies) **1** the state of being formal. **2** observance of formal or conventional rules. **3** an established form or procedure. **4** something of little real significance that is required by rule or custom.

formalize or **-ise** v **1** to give formal status or approval to. **2** to give a definite shape to.

format¹ n **1** the general plan of organization or arrangement. **2** the shape, size, and general make-up of a book. **3** in computing, the structure by which data is held.

format² v (**formatted, formatting**) **1** to arrange in a particular format. **2** in computing, to prepare (a disk, etc) to receive data.

formation n **1** the giving or taking of form or shape. **2** the manner in which a thing is formed or arranged. **3** a group of people or things arranged in a special way.

formative adj having a significant influence on growth or development.

former adj **1** occurring in the past or having been previously. **2** (**the former**) denoting the first of two things mentioned or understood.

formerly adv at an earlier time; previously.

Formica n trademark a laminated plastic used to make heat-resistant surfaces for worktops, etc.

formic acid n a pungent corrosive liquid acid naturally produced by ants.

formidable adj **1** of a task, etc: difficult or challenging. **2** of a person: causing fear or respect. ➤ **formidably** adv.

formula n (pl **formulas** or **formulae**) **1** a mathematical rule or principle expressed in symbols. **2** a symbolic expression of the chemical composition of a substance. **3** a set form of words for use in a ceremony or ritual. **4** a set form or method of speaking or writing, often followed uncritically. **5** a recipe or the list of ingredients in it. **6** liquid baby food made from milk or soya. **7** a method or procedure for bringing something about. ➤ **formulaic** adj.

formulate v **1** to state as a formula or reduce to a formula. **2** to devise or develop (a plan, product, etc). ➤ **formulation** n.

form up v to arrange or be arranged in a particular formation.

fornicate v formal to have sexual relations with a person one is not married to. ➤ **fornication** n.

forsake v (**forsook, forsaken**) **1** to renounce. **2** to desert or abandon.

forsooth adv archaic indeed; actually.

forswear v (**forswore, forsworn**) **1** to renounce solemnly. **2** to perjure (oneself).

forsythia n a shrub with bright yellow flowers.

fort n a strongly fortified building maintained to resist attack. ✳ **hold the fort** to take charge temporarily.

forte /'fawtay/ n something at which a person excels.

forth adv archaic **1** onwards in time, place, or order. **2** into notice or view. ✳ **and so forth** and so on.

forthcoming adj 1 about to occur or appear. 2 made available. 3 willing to give information.

forthright adj unhesitatingly outspoken.

forthwith adv immediately.

fortify v (-ies, -ied) 1 to strengthen (a place) against attack. 2 to give strength or endurance to. 3 to add (alcohol to wine or vitamins to food) to strengthen or enrich it. ➤ **fortification** n.

fortissimo adj and adv of a piece of music: to be performed in a very loud manner.

fortitude n courage or endurance in the face of difficulty.

fortnight n chiefly Brit two weeks.

fortnightly adj and adv occurring or appearing once a fortnight.

fortress n a large fortified building or town.

fortuitous adj occurring by chance. ➤ **fortuitously** adv.

fortunate adj 1 unexpectedly bringing good luck; favourable. 2 lucky. ➤ **fortunately** adv.

fortune n 1 a large quantity of money or possessions. 2 luck or chance seen as a force affecting human affairs. 3 one's future destiny. 4 (in pl) a person's experiences.

forty adj and n (pl -ies) 1 the number 40. 2 (in pl) the numbers 40 to 49. ➤ **fortieth** adj and n.

forty winks pl n informal **a short sleep during the day**.

forum n (pl **forums** or **fora**) 1 a meeting place or gathering for exchanging opinions. 2 the marketplace or central public place of an ancient Roman city, used for public business.

forward[1] adj 1 directed or turned towards the front. 2 brash or assertive.

forward[2] adv 1 (also **forwards**) towards what is ahead or in front. 2 into the future. 3 to an earlier time. 4 into prominence or open view.

forward[3] n an attacking player in football, hockey, etc.

forward[4] v to send onwards to a further destination.

forwent v past tense of FORGO.

fossil n 1 the petrified remains of an animal or plant of a past geological age. 2 an outdated person or thing. ➤ **fossilize** v.

fossil fuel n a fuel, e.g. coal, that is derived from the remains of living things.

foster[1] v 1 to promote the growth or development of. 2 to give parental care to (a child not one's own by birth).

foster[2] adj providing or receiving care by fostering.

fought v past tense and past part. of FIGHT[1].

foul[1] adj 1 offensive to the smell or taste. 2 morally or spiritually evil. 3 particularly unpleasant or disagreeable. 4 obscene or abusive. 5 infringing the rules of a game or sport. 6 polluted. ✳ **fall/run foul of** to come into conflict with. ➤ **foully** adv.

foul[2] n an infringement of the rules in a game or sport.

foul[3] v 1 to make dirty; to pollute. 2 in sport, to commit a foul. 3 to obstruct or block. 4 to entangle or collide with.

foulmouthed adj using coarse or abusive language.

foul play n 1 murder or violence. 2 play that infringes the rules in a game or sport.

foul up v 1 to do badly. 2 to spoil or confuse by making mistakes. 3 to entangle or block. ➤ **foul-up** n.

found[1] v past tense and past part. of FIND[1].

found[2] v 1 to establish (an institution or organization). 2 (often + on/upon) to set or ground (e.g. a plan or system of thought) on something sure or solid.

found[3] v to melt (metal) and pour it into a mould to make an object.

foundation n 1 (also in pl) an underlying base or support, esp the part of the structure on which a building rests. 2 the basis or principle underlying something. 3 a reason or justification. 4 the act of establishing something. 5 an organization or institution established with provision for future maintenance. 6 a cream or lotion applied to the face as a base for other make-up.

founder[1] n a person who establishes an institution or organization.

founder[2] v 1 of a ship: to sink. 2 of a plan or project: to fail.

foundling n an infant abandoned by unknown parents and discovered and looked after by others.

foundry n (pl -ies) a place for casting metals.

fount[1] n 1 literary a fountain or spring. 2 a source of something pleasant or useful.

fount[2] or **font** n in printing: a complete set of characters for printing in one style.

fountain n 1 an ornamental structure that sends a jet of water into the air. 2 a spring of water issuing from the ground.

fountainhead n the main source of something.

fountain pen n a pen with a reservoir or cartridge of ink.

four n 1 the number 4. 2 a shot in cricket that crosses the boundary after having hit the ground and scores four runs. ➤ **four** adj.

four-letter word n a short vulgar or offensive word.

four-poster n a bed with corner posts supporting curtains or a canopy.

foursome n a group of four people or things.

foursquare adj and adv 1 solid; squarely based. 2 bold and resolute.

fourteen adj and n the number 14. ➤ **fourteenth** adj and n.

fourth adj and n 1 having the position in a sequence corresponding to the number four. 2

one of four equal parts of something. ➤ **fourthly** adv.

fowl n (pl **fowls** or **fowl**) **1** a domestic bird such as a chicken, turkey, or duck. **2** = WILDFOWL.

fox¹ n **1** an animal of the dog family with a pointed muzzle, large erect ears, and a long bushy tail. **2** a clever or crafty person.

fox² v to outwit or baffle.

foxglove n a tall plant with white or purple tubular flowers.

foxhole n a pit dug as improvised cover against enemy fire.

foxhound n a hound of a breed developed to hunt foxes.

foxtrot¹ n a ballroom dance that includes slow walking and quick running steps.

foxtrot² v (**foxtrotted, foxtrotting**) to dance the foxtrot.

foxy adj (**-ier, -iest**) **1** clever or crafty. **2** like a fox.

foyer n an entrance hall or lobby in a theatre or large building.

Fr abbr the chemical symbol for francium.

fracas n (pl **fracas**) a noisy quarrel or brawl.

fraction n **1** a number that is not a whole number, and usu less than one, e.g., 0.75. **2** a small portion or amount. **3** in chemistry, a portion, e.g. of a distillate, separable by fractionation.

fractional adj **1** relating to or being a fraction. **2** relatively small. ➤ **fractionally** adv.

fractious adj irritable and hard to control.

Usage Note: Do not confuse this word with *factious*.

fracture¹ n **1** a break in or the breaking of something, *esp* hard tissue such as bone. **2** a split or breach.

fracture² v **1** to cause a fracture in. **2** to undergo fracture. **3** to break into separate parts.

fragile adj **1** easily broken or shattered. **2** not secure. **3** of a person: weak or vulnerable. ➤ **fragility** n.

fragment¹ n a part that is incomplete or broken off something larger. ➤ **fragmentary** adj.

fragment² v to break or fall to pieces. ➤ **fragmentation** n.

fragrance n **1** a sweet or pleasant smell. **2** a perfume or aftershave.

fragrant adj smelling sweet or pleasant.

frail adj **1** weak and delicate. **2** easily broken.

frailty n (pl **-ies**) **1** being frail. **2** a moral or physical weakness.

frame¹ n **1** a structure that gives shape or strength to a building, opening, vehicle, etc. **2** a rigid surrounding structure for displaying a painting or photograph. **3** the physical structure of the human body. **4** (in pl) the outer structure holding the lenses of a pair of glasses. **5** a single picture of the series on a length of film. **6** one round of play in snooker or bowling.

frame² v **1** to put a frame round. **2** to plan or formulate. **3** to shape or construct. **4** to fit or adjust for a purpose. **5** informal to make up evidence against (an innocent person).

frame of mind n a particular mental or emotional state.

framework n **1** a supporting frame or structure. **2** a basic structure of ideas.

franc n the basic monetary unit of Switzerland, and formerly of France, Belgium, and Luxembourg (replaced by the euro in 2002).

franchise¹ n **1** (usu **the franchise**) the right to vote. **2** the right granted to an individual or group to market goods or services. **3** a business or service holding a franchise.

franchise² v to grant a franchise to.

frank¹ adj **1** honest and straightforward. **2** undisguised. ➤ **frankly** adv, **frankness** n.

frank² v to mark (a piece of mail) with an official stamp showing that postal charges have been paid.

frankfurter n a cured cooked sausage made from beef and pork.

frankincense n a fragrant gum resin which is burned as incense.

frantic adj **1** emotionally out of control. **2** marked by fast and nervous activity. ➤ **frantically** adv.

fraternal adj **1** relating to brothers; brotherly. **2** relating to a fraternity or society.

fraternity n (pl **-ies**) **1** a group of people organized for a common purpose or interest. **2** a club for male students in some US universities. **3** mutual friendly support.

fraternize or **-ise** v to be on friendly terms. ➤ **fraternization** n.

fratricide n **1** the act of killing one's brother or sister. **2** somebody who does this. ➤ **fratricidal** adj.

fraud n **1** deception for unlawful gain. **2** an act of deception; a trick. **3** a person who is not what they pretend to be; an impostor.

fraudster n somebody who commits a fraud.

fraudulent adj involving fraud. ➤ **fraudulently** adv.

fraught adj **1** (+ with) filled with (something unwelcome). **2** characterized by anxiety and tension.

fray¹ v **1** of fabric or rope: to become worn at the edges. **2** of a person's temper or nerves: to show strain.

fray² n **1** (**the fray**) a dispute or competition. **2** a brawl or fight.

frazzle n informal **1** a burnt state. **2** a state of exhaustion. ➤ **frazzled** adj.

freak n **1** a person, animal, or plant with a physical abnormality. **2** a highly unconventional person. **3** a highly unusual and unforeseeable event. **4** informal an obsessive enthusiast: *a sci-fi freak.* ➤ **freakish** adj.

freak out *v informal* to behave irrationally or wildly.

freckle *n* a small brown spot on the skin. ➤ **freckled** *adj*, **freckly** *adj*.

free[1] *adj* (**freer**, **freest**) **1** not subject to the control of another person. **2** not bound or detained by force. **3** (+ of/from) not subject to or affected by (something unwelcome). **4** having no obligations or commitments. **5** not obstructed or impeded; clear. **6** not being used or occupied. **7** not hampered or restricted. **8** not costing or charging anything. **9** (*usu* + with) lavish or unrestrained. **10** outspoken or familiar. **11** not determined by external influences. **12** voluntary or spontaneous. **13** of a translation: not literal or exact. ✻ **free and easy** unrestrained or casual. **a free hand** freedom of action. ➤ **freely** *adv*.

free[2] *adv* **1** in a free manner. **2** without charge or cost.

free[3] *v* (**frees**, **freed**, **freeing**) **1** to cause to be free. **2** (*often* + up) to make available.

freebie *n informal* a gift or service offered free.

freedom *n* **1** the state of being free. **2** the right to speak or act as one wishes. **3** liberation from slavery or imprisonment. **4** (+ from) being exempt or released from something onerous. **5** (+ of) unrestricted use of something. **6** the rights and privileges of a citizen of a city, granted as an honour to a distinguished person.

free enterprise *n* an economic system that relies on private business operating competitively for profit.

free fall *n* unrestrained motion under gravity.

free-for-all *n* a disorganized contest or situation in which anyone may take part.

free-form *adj* not having a fixed structure; spontaneous.

freehand *adj and adv* drawn or written by hand without the aid of instruments.

freehold *n* ownership of land or property with an unconditional right to sell it. ➤ **freeholder** *n*.

free house *n* a public house that is entitled to sell products of more than one brewery.

free kick *n* in football or rugby, an unhindered kick awarded after a breach of the rules by the other side.

freelance[1] *n* a self-employed person who works for several companies. ➤ **freelance** *adj and adv*.

freelance[2] *v* to work as a freelance.

freeload *v informal* to take advantage of somebody else's generosity or hospitality. ➤ **freeloader** *n*.

freeman *n* (*pl* **freemen**) **1** somebody who has been granted the freedom of a city. **2** formerly, somebody who is no longer a slave.

free market *n* an economic market operating by free competition.

Freemason *n* a member of a secret fraternity who offer each other support and friendship. ➤ **Freemasonry** *n*.

free-range *adj* of farm animals: reared in the open air and allowed to move about.

freesia *n* a sweet-scented plant with red, white, yellow, or purple flowers.

freestanding *adj* standing alone; not supported by something else.

freestyle *n* a competition in which contestants use a style of their choice.

freethinker *n* a person who rejects or questions accepted opinions.

free trade *n* trade based on the unrestricted international exchange of goods.

freeway *n NAmer* a motorway or highway without tolls.

freewheel *v* to coast on a bicycle without using the pedals.

free will *n* the power of making one's own moral choices.

freeze[1] *v* (**froze**, **frozen**) **1** of a liquid: to turn solid from cold. **2** to convert (liquid) to a solid by cold. **3** to stick solidly by freezing. **4** to become or cause to become clogged with ice. **5** to become or make chilled with cold. **6** to preserve (food) by maintaining it at a temperature below 0°C. **7** to become fixed or motionless from fear or surprise. **8** of a computer screen: to stop responding to commands because of a fault. **9** to anaesthetize (a part of the body). **10** to cause to become fixed or unalterable.

freeze[2] *n* **1** freezing cold weather. **2** an act or period of freezing something.

freeze-dry *v* (**-ies**, **-ied**) to preserve (food) by dehydrating it while in a frozen state in a vacuum.

freeze-frame *n* the facility of a video camera or recorder to produce a static picture.

freezer *n* an insulated cabinet or room for freezing and storing food.

freezing *adj* **1** *informal* very cold. **2** below 0°C.

freight[1] *n* **1** goods transported commercially. **2** the commercial transport of goods.

freight[2] *v* to transport (goods) commercially.

freighter *n* a ship or aircraft used chiefly to carry freight.

French[1] *adj* relating to France, its people, or their language.

French[2] *n* **1** the language of France and parts of Belgium, Switzerland, Canada, and Africa. **2** (**the French**) the people of France.

French cricket *n* a game of cricket in which the legs of the player who is batting serve as a wicket.

French dressing *n* a salad dressing of oil, vinegar, and seasonings.

french fries *pl n chiefly NAmer* chips.

French horn *n* a brass instrument with a coiled tube that flares out at the end.

French kiss *n* a kiss with contact between tongues.

French polish *n* a solution of shellac used as a wood polish.

French windows *pl n Brit* a pair of glazed doors opening onto the exterior of a house.

frenetic *adj* frenzied or frantic. ➤ **frenetically** *adv.*

frenzy *n* (*pl* **-ies**) a state of extreme agitation or excitement. ➤ **frenzied** *adj.*

frequency *n* (*pl* **-ies**) **1** the rate at which something occurs over a period of time. **2** the state of occurring frequently. **3** the number of complete alternations per second of an alternating current of electricity. **4** the number of complete oscillations per second of an electromagnetic wave. **5** the number of sound waves per second produced by a sounding body.

frequent[1] *adj* **1** often repeated or occurring. **2** habitual or persistent. ➤ **frequently** *adv.*

frequent[2] *v* to visit (a place) often or habitually.

fresco *n* (*pl* **-oes** *or* **os**) a painting done by applying watercolours to plaster before it is dry.

fresh *adj* **1** new or different. **2** newly come or arrived; inexperienced. **3** of food: newly made, not stale or preserved. **4** of water: not salty. **5** not worn or rumpled; clean. **6** of wind: cool and invigorating. **7** refreshed and alert. **8** of colours: clear and bright. **9** *informal* disrespectful or presumptuous. ➤ **freshly** *adv*, **freshness** *n.*

freshen *v* **1** to make or become fresh or fresher. **2** of wind: to increase in strength. **3** (**freshen up**) to wash and tidy oneself.

fresher *n chiefly Brit, informal* a first-year student at college or university.

freshman *n* (*pl* **freshmen**) a first-year student at university or (in the US) at high school.

fret[1] *v* (**fretted, fretting**) to be anxious or agitated.

fret[2] *n* each of a series of ridges fixed across the fingerboard of a guitar or other stringed instrument.

fretful *adj* anxious and nervous. ➤ **fretfully** *adv.*

fretwork *n* ornamental designs cut in thin wood.

friable *adj* easily crumbled.

friar *n* a member of a male religious order.

friary *n* (*pl* **-ies**) a building housing a community of friars.

fricassee *n* a dish of small pieces of stewed meat served in a white sauce.

friction *n* **1** the rubbing of one body against another. **2** resistance to relative motion between two bodies in contact. **3** disagreement between people or parties.

Friday *n* the day of the week following Thursday.

fridge *n chiefly Brit* a refrigerator.

fried *v* past tense and past part. of FRY[1].

friend *n* **1** a person one knows and likes. **2** somebody who supports a cause or institution. **3** (**Friend**) a Quaker. **make friends** to become friendly. ➤ **friendless** *adj*, **friendship** *n.*

Usage Note: Note the spelling with *-ie-*.

friendly[1] *adj* (**-ier, -iest**) **1** like a friend; kind. **2** not hostile. **3** inclined to be favourable. **4** adapted to the needs of: *user-friendly.* ➤ **friendliness** *n.*

friendly[2] *n* (*pl* **-ies**) *chiefly Brit* an informal match not played as part of a competition.

frieze *n* a sculptured or painted band on a building.

frigate *n Brit* a small warship.

fright *n* **1** fear excited by sudden danger or shock. **2** *informal* something unsightly or shocking.

frighten *v* **1** to make (somebody) afraid. **2** to force (somebody) by frightening them. ➤ **frightened** *adj*, **frightening** *adj.*

frightful *adj* **1** causing intense fear or shock. **2** *informal* unpleasant or difficult. ➤ **frightfully** *adv.*

frigid *adj* **1** intensely cold. **2** *formal* unenthusiastic or unfriendly. **3** *esp* of a woman: resistant to sexual contact. ➤ **frigidity** *n.*

frill *n* **1** a gathered or pleated fabric edging used on clothing or as ornament. **2** something decorative but not essential; a luxury. ➤ **frilly** *adj.*

fringe[1] *n* **1** an ornamental border of threads or tassels on a curtain or clothing. **2** a border. **3** *chiefly Brit* the hair that falls over the forehead. **4** something marginal or secondary. **5** (*treated as sing. or pl*) an unconventional or extreme group.

fringe[2] *v* **1** to provide or decorate with a fringe. **2** to serve as a fringe for.

fringe benefit *n* an extra benefit received by an employee in addition to wages.

frippery *n* (*pl* **-ies**) **1** showy ornamentation. **2** affected elegance or ostentation.

Frisbee *n trademark* a plastic disc thrown through the air with a flip of the wrist.

frisk[1] *v* **1** *informal* to search (a person) by running the hands over their clothing. **2** to leap or dance playfully.

frisk[2] *n* **1** *informal* an act of frisking somebody. **2** a playful leap or dance.

frisky *adj* (**-ier, -iest**) lively and energetic.

frisson *n* a shudder or thrill.

fritillary *n* (*pl* **-ies**) **1** a plant with bell-shaped flowers. **2** a butterfly with orange and black wings.

fritter[1] *n* a piece of food fried in batter.

fritter[2] *v* (*usu* + away) to waste (money or time) gradually.

frivolous *adj* **1** lacking value or purpose. **2** of a person: unconcerned and carefree. ➤ **frivolity** *n*, **frivolously** *adv.*

frizz[1] *v* of hair: to form a mass of tight curls.

frizz² n hair in a mass of tight curls.

frock n 1 Brit a woman's or girl's dress. 2 a loose garment, esp a monk's or friar's habit.

frock coat n a long jacket with knee-length skirts, formerly worn by men.

frog n a tailless leaping amphibian with a smooth skin and webbed feet. ✷ **have a frog in one's throat** to be hoarse.

frogman n (pl **frogmen**) a diver equipped with a rubber suit, flippers, and an air supply for extended periods underwater.

frogmarch v to force (a person) to move forwards by holding their arms firmly from behind.

frogspawn n a gelatinous mass of frogs' eggs.

frolic¹ v (**frolicked, frolicking**) to play and run about happily.

frolic² n 1 a playful expression of high spirits. 2 a light-hearted game. ➤ **frolicsome** adj.

from prep 1 used to indicate a starting point of a journey or process. 2 used to indicate a starting point in measuring or reckoning. 3 used to indicate separation or removal. take one from the shelf. 4 used to indicate a source or cause: suffering from the cold.

fromage frais /ˌfromahzh 'fray/ n a soft smooth cheese.

frond n a leaf of a palm or fern.

front¹ n 1 the part or surface of something that usually faces forward. 2 the part of the human body opposite to the back. 3 a line of battle. 4 a political coalition. 5 a particular situation or sphere of activity. 6 in meteorology, the boundary between two dissimilar air masses. 7 something that masks true identity or purpose. 8 demeanour or bearing in the face of a challenge or danger. ✷ **in front of 1** directly ahead of. 2 in the presence of. **up front** as payment in advance.

front² v 1 to face towards. 2 to be in front of.

front³ adj of or situated at the front.

frontage n 1 the front of a building. 2 the land between the front of a building and the street.

frontal adj situated at or showing the front. ➤ **frontally** adv.

front bench n Brit the benches in the House of Commons on which party leaders sit. ➤ **front-bencher** n.

frontier n 1 a border between two countries. 2 a region that forms the limit of settled territory. 3 (also in pl) the boundary between the known and the unknown.

frontispiece n an illustration facing the title page of a book or magazine.

front line n an army's position nearest the enemy.

front man n a person serving as a representative or figurehead.

front-runner n the leading contestant in a competition.

frost¹ n 1 a covering of ice crystals formed on a cold surface when the temperature falls below freezing. 2 a period of freezing weather.

frost² v to cover or be covered with frost.

frostbite n damage to the body caused by partial freezing.

frosted adj 1 covered with frost. 2 of glass: having a roughened translucent surface.

frosting n 1 a dull or roughened finish on metal or glass. 2 chiefly NAmer icing.

frosty adj (-ier, -iest) 1 marked by frost; freezing. 2 covered with frost; hoary. 3 cool and reserved in manner. ➤ **frostily** adv.

froth¹ n 1 a mass of bubbles formed on or in a liquid. 2 something insubstantial or of little value.

froth² v 1 (often + up) to cause (a liquid) to foam. 2 (often + up) to produce or emit froth. ➤ **frothy** adj.

frown¹ v 1 to contract the brow in anger, worry, or concentration. 2 (often + on) to show disapproval of.

frown² n a frowning expression.

frowsty adj (-ier, -iest) chiefly Brit lacking fresh air; stuffy.

frowzy or **frowsy** adj (-ier, -iest) having a slovenly or uncared-for appearance.

froze v past tense of FREEZE¹.

frozen v past part. of FREEZE¹.

fructose n a sweet sugar found in fruit and honey.

frugal adj economical in the use of resources. ➤ **frugality** n, **frugally** adv.

fruit¹ n 1 the usu edible reproductive body of a seed plant; esp one having a sweet pulp associated with the seed. 2 in botany, the ripened ovary of a flowering plant together with its contents. 3 the beneficial effect or consequence of an action. 4 chiefly NAmer, informal, offensive a male homosexual.

fruit² v to bear fruit.

fruiterer n chiefly Brit a person who sells fruit.

fruitful adj 1 yielding or producing fruit; fertile. 2 having beneficial results. ➤ **fruitfully** adv.

fruition n the realization or fulfilment of a project.

fruitless adj useless or unsuccessful. ➤ **fruitlessly** adv.

fruit machine n Brit a coin-operated gambling machine.

fruity adj (-ier, -iest) 1 resembling or having the flavour of fruit. 2 of a voice: deep and mellow. 3 chiefly Brit, informal sexually suggestive. ➤ **fruitiness** n.

frump n a dowdy unattractive girl or woman. ➤ **frumpy** adj.

frustrate v 1 to prevent (somebody) from carrying out a plan or intention. 2 to prevent (a plan) from being carried out or (a hope) from

function

being realized. **3** to make (somebody) feel frustrated or vexed. ➤ **frustrating** *adj*, **frustration** *n*.

fry[1] *v* (**-ies, -ied**) **1** to cook in hot oil or fat over direct heat. **2** *informal* to feel very hot in the sun.

fry[2] *n* (*pl* **-ies**) **1** a dish of fried food. **2** (*in pl*) *chiefly NAmer* chips.

fry[3] *pl n* recently hatched fish.

frying pan *n* a shallow pan with a long handle, used for frying food. * **out of the frying pan into the fire** free of one difficulty only to encounter a worse one.

ft *abbr* foot or feet.

fuchsia *n* a shrub with hanging deep red or purple flowers.

fuddled *adj* confused and dazed.

fuddy-duddy *n* (*pl* **-ies**) *informal* a person who is old-fashioned and pompous.

fudge[1] *n* **1** a soft creamy sweet made of sugar, milk, and butter. **2** a statement or decision that is intentionally vague and evades the central issues.

fudge[2] *v* to present (facts or figures) in a vague or misleading way.

fuel[1] *n* **1** a material used to produce heat or power when it is burned. **2** a material from which atomic energy can be produced in a nuclear reactor. **3** a source of strength or encouragement.

fuel[2] *v* (**fuelled, fuelling**, *NAmer* **fueled, fueling**) **1** to provide (a machine or vehicle) with fuel. **2** to stimulate (an emotion or activity).

fuel cell *n* a cell that continuously changes chemical energy to electrical energy.

fuel injection *n* the introduction of liquid fuel directly into the cylinders of an engine.

fug *n Brit, informal* a stuffy airless atmosphere. ➤ **fuggy** *adj*.

fugitive[1] *n* a person who flees or tries to escape.

fugitive[2] *adj* running away or trying to escape.

fugue *n* a musical composition in which a theme is repeated by successively entering voices, instruments, or parts.

führer *or* **fuehrer** *n* a tyrannnical leader, *esp* Hitler, leader of the Nazis in Germany.

fulcrum *n* (*pl* **fulcrums** *or* **fulcra**) the support about which a lever turns.

fulfil (*NAmer* **fulfill**) *v* (**fulfilled, fulfilling**) **1** to cause to happen as required or expected. **2** to put into effect; to carry out. **3** to satisfy (a requirement or condition). **4** to develop the full potential of. ➤ **fulfilment** *n*.

full[1] *adj* **1** containing as much or as many as possible or normal. **2** complete in detail, number, or duration: *the full story*. **3** (+ of) possessing or containing a great number or amount of. **4** at the highest or greatest degree; maximum. **5** of the face or figure: rounded in outline; plump. **6** of a garment: having much

material. **7** rich and strong. * **full of oneself** conceited. **full up** completely full. **in full swing** at a high level of activity. ➤ **fullness** *n*, **fulness** *n*.

full[2] *adv* **1** very. **2** exactly or squarely.

full[3] *n* (**the full**) the highest or fullest state, extent, or degree. * **in full** completely or entirely.

fullback *n* in football, rugby, etc, a defensive player stationed close to the defended goal.

full-blooded *adj* forceful or vigorous; hearty.

full-blown *adj* fully developed or mature.

full board *n Brit* accommodation with all meals included.

full-bodied *adj* rich and full in flavour.

fuller *n* a person who cleanses and finishes woollen cloth.

full-frontal *adj* exposing the whole front of the body.

full house *n* **1** a full theatre or other venue. **2** in poker, a hand containing three of a kind and a pair. **3** a winning set of numbers at bingo.

full moon *n* the moon when its whole disc is illuminated.

full-scale *adj* **1** of a reproduction: identical in proportion and size to the original. **2** involving full use of resources.

full time *n* the end of a match or game.

full-time *adj and adv* working for all the available time.

fully *adv* **1** completely. **2** at least.

fully-fledged *adj* **1** of a bird: having all its feathers and able to fly. **2** completely developed.

fulminate *v* to protest or complain angrily. ➤ **fulmination** *n*.

fulsome *adj* **1** unnecessarily effusive or obsequious. **2** overabundant or copious. ➤ **fulsomely** *adv*.

fumble[1] *v* **1** to handle something clumsily or awkwardly. **2** to feel or handle (a ball) clumsily. **3** to deal with (something) awkwardly or clumsily.

fumble[2] *n* an act of fumbling.

fume[1] *n* a dirty and smelly effusion of smoke, vapour, or gas. ➤ **fumy** *adj*.

fume[2] *v* **1** to emit fumes. **2** to be very angry. ➤ **fuming** *adj*.

fumigate *v* to disinfect (a place) with chemical fumes. ➤ **fumigation** *n*.

fun *n* **1** amusement or enjoyment. **2** good humour. * **in fun** not intended to be taken seriously. **make fun of** to make (somebody or something) an object of amusement or ridicule.

function[1] *n* **1** the purpose or primary use of a person or thing. **2** a large social gathering. **3** a mathematical relationship between each element of one set and at least one element of the same or another set.

function[2] v **1** to have a function; to serve. **2** to operate.

functional adj **1** designed for practical use. **2** relating to or performing a function. ➤ **functionality** n, **functionally** adv.

functionary n (pl -ies) an official.

fund[1] n **1** a sum of money set apart for a specific purpose. **2** (in pl) an available supply of money. **3** an available quantity of materials or resources.

fund[2] v to provide funds for.

fundamental[1] adj of central importance; principal. ➤ **fundamentally** adv.

fundamental[2] n a minimum constituent that characterizes something.

fundamentalism n a belief in the literal truth of a religious scripture or teaching. ➤ **fundamentalist** n and adj.

funeral n a formal ceremony at which a dead person is buried or cremated. ＊ **be somebody's funeral** informal to be somebody's own problem or fault.

funeral director n an undertaker.

funerary adj used for or associated with burial.

funereal adj gloomy or solemn.

fun fair n chiefly Brit an outdoor fair with amusements, sideshows, and rides.

fungicide n a substance used for destroying fungus. ➤ **fungicidal** adj.

fungus n (pl **fungi** or **funguses**) an organism, such as a mushroom or toadstool, that reproduces by means of spores. ➤ **fungal** adj.

funicular railway n a cable railway on a steep slope.

funk[1] n informal a state of paralysing fear or panic.

funk[2] v informal to lose the courage to do (something daunting).

funk[3] n dance music with a strong rhythm.

funky adj (-ier, -iest) informal **1** of dance music: having a strong rhythm. **2** informal original and stylish.

funnel[1] n **1** a utensil consisting of a hollow tapering cone with a tube at the smaller end, for pouring liquid or powder into a small opening. **2** a stack or flue for smoke or steam to escape.

funnel[2] v (**funnelled, funnelling,** NAmer **funneled, funneling**) to pass through a funnel or a narrow space.

funny adj (-ier, -iest) **1** causing amusement and laughter. **2** strange or odd. **3** involving deception or dishonesty. **4** unwilling to be helpful. **5** informal slightly unwell. ➤ **funnily** adv.

funny bone n the place at the elbow where a sensitive nerve rests against the bone.

fur[1] n **1** the soft thick hair of a mammal. **2** the dressed skin of an animal used for clothing. **3** an article of clothing made of or with fur. **4** a coating formed in kettles or pipes by the scale from hard water. ➤ **furred** adj.

fur[2] v (**furred, furring**) to become coated or clogged with scaly fur.

furbelow n **1** a flounce on women's clothing. **2** something showy or superfluous.

furious adj **1** extremely or violently angry. **2** having a stormy appearance. **3** intense or excited. ➤ **furiously** adv.

furl v to fold or roll tightly.

furlong n a unit of length equal to 220 yards (about 0.2km).

furlough n a leave of absence.

furnace n an enclosed apparatus in which intense heat is produced.

furnish v **1** to provide or supply. **2** to equip (a room or building) with furniture and fittings.

furnishings pl n articles of furniture and fittings used to make a room comfortable.

furniture n the movable articles that make an area suitable for living in or use.

furore (NAmer **furor**) n an outburst of general excitement or anger.

furrier n a fur dealer.

furrow[1] n **1** a trench in the earth made by a plough. **2** a deep wrinkle on the face.

furrow[2] v to make a furrow or line in.

furry adj (-ier, -iest) like or covered with fur.

further[1] adv **1** to a greater degree or extent. **2** moreover. **3** = FARTHER[1].

further[2] adj **1** extending beyond what exists or has happened; additional. **2** coming after the one referred to. **3** = FARTHER[2].

further[3] v to bring closer to completion. ➤ **furtherance** n.

further education n Brit education for people after leaving school.

furthermore adv in addition; moreover.

furthest[1] adj most distant in space or time.

furthest[2] adv **1** to or at the greatest distance in space, time, or degree. **2** by the greatest degree; most.

furtive adj using stealth; surreptitious or sly. ➤ **furtively** adv.

fury n (pl -ies) **1** intense or violent rage. **2** wild force or activity. **3** (**Fury**) each of three avenging deities who in Greek mythology punished crimes.

furze n = GORSE.

fuse[1] n **1** a length of combustible material for detonating an explosive charge. **2** the detonating device for setting off the charge in a bomb. **3** a wire or strip of metal that melts and interrupts an electrical circuit when the current exceeds a safe level.

fuse[2] v **1** to blend (two things) by melting them together. **2** to join to form a whole. **3** to become blended or combined. **4** to cause (an electrical appliance) to fail by fusing. **5** of an electrical appliance: to fail when a fuse melts. **6** to equip (a device) with an electrical fuse. **7** to fit a fuse to (a bomb or explosive).

fuselage n the central body of an aircraft.

fuzzy

fusible *adj* able to be fused or melted easily.

fusilier *n* a member of a British regiment formerly armed with fusils (light muskets).

fusillade *n* a number of shots fired simultaneously or in rapid succession.

fusion *n* **1** the process of joining things to form a whole. **2** the union of light atomic nuclei to form heavier nuclei, resulting in the release of large quantities of energy.

fuss[1] *n* **1** needless or useless bustle or excitement. **2** an objection or protest.

fuss[2] *v* **1** to pay undue attention to small details. **2** to become unnecessarily agitated or upset.

fusspot *n* *informal* a person who fusses a lot.

fussy *adj* (**-ier, -iest**) **1** showing too much concern over details. **2** fastidious. ➤ **fussily** *adv*, **fussiness** *n*.

fusty *adj* (**-ier, -iest**) **1** stale or musty. **2** old-fashioned.

futile *adj* ineffective or pointless. ➤ **futilely** *adv*, **futility** *n*.

futon *n* a padded quilt laid down to serve as a bed.

future[1] *n* **1** (**the future**) time that is to come. **2** a likelihood of success. **3** in grammar, the verb tense that expresses action or state in the future. ✳ **in future** from now on.

future[2] *adj* **1** that is to be. **2** of or constituting the future tense.

futuristic *adj* **1** revolutionary or technologically advanced. **2** of a story: set in future time. ➤ **futuristically** *adv*.

futurity *n* time in the future.

fuzz *n* **1** fine light particles or fibres. **2** a distortion in vision or sound. **3** (**the fuzz**) *informal* the police.

fuzzy *adj* (**-ier, -iest**) **1** having the appearance or feel of fuzz. **2** blurred or indistinct. ➤ **fuzziness** *n*.

G or **g** n (pl **G's** or **Gs** or **g's**) the seventh letter of the English alphabet.

g abbr **1** gram(s). **2** gravity, or acceleration due to gravity.

Ga abbr the chemical symbol for gallium.

gab v (**gabbed, gabbing**) informal to chatter or blab.

gabble[1] v to talk rapidly or unintelligibly.

gabble[2] n rapid or unintelligible talk.

gaberdine or **gabardine** n a firm durable fabric used esp for making waterproof coats.

gable n the vertical triangular section of wall between two slopes of a pitched roof.

gad v (**gadded, gadding**) (+ about/around) to go about aimlessly, restlessly, or in search of pleasure.

gadfly n (pl **-ies**) **1** a fly that bites livestock. **2** a persistently annoying, provoking, or critical person.

gadget n a usu small and often novel mechanical or electronic device. ➤ **gadgetry** n.

Gaelic n the Celtic language of Ireland, the Isle of Man, and Scotland.

gaff[1] n a pole with a hook for landing heavy fish.

gaff[2] n Brit, informal a house or other dwelling place.

gaffe n a social or tactical blunder.

gaffer n Brit, informal **1** a boss or foreman. **2** an old man.

gag[1] n **1** something put over a person's mouth to stop them speaking. **2** a joke.

gag[2] v (**gagged, gagging**) **1** to put a gag over the mouth of. **2** to prevent (somebody) from having free speech. **3** to retch.

gaga adj informal **1** senile. **2** slightly mad.

gage[1] n NAmer see GAUGE[1].

gage[2] v NAmer see GAUGE[2].

gaggle n **1** a flock of geese. **2** informal a noisy or disorderly group of people.

gaiety n cheerfulness or merriment.

gaily adv **1** cheerfully or merrily. **2** with bright colours. **3** blithely; unthinkingly.

gain[1] v **1** to get possession of, win, or acquire. **2** (often + on) to start catching up with (somebody one is pursuing). **3** to arrive at (a place). **4** to increase in (e.g. speed, weight). **5** to get advantage; to profit. **6** of a watch or clock: to run fast.

gain[2] n **1** something acquired. **2** profit or a profit. **3** an increase in amount or degree.

gainful adj income-producing; profitable. ➤ **gainfully** adv.

gainsay v (**gainsays, gainsaid**) formal to deny or dispute (e.g. an allegation).

gait n a manner of walking.

gaiter n usu in pl a cloth or leather legging worn by men.

gala n **1** a festive gathering or entertainment. **2** Brit a special sports meeting.

galactic adj relating to a galaxy.

galaxy n (pl **-ies**) **1** a large star system. **2** (**the Galaxy**) the Milky Way.

gale n **1** a strong wind. **2** a noisy outburst of laughter.

gall[1] n **1** brazen and insolent audacity. **2** rancour or bitterness.

gall[2] n **1** exasperation. **2** a skin sore caused by rubbing.

gall[3] v to mortify and irritate. ➤ **galling** adj.

gallant[1] adj **1** nobly chivalrous and brave. **2** courteously attentive, esp to women. ➤ **gallantly** adv.

gallant[2] n a man who is particularly attentive to women.

gallantry n (pl **-ies**) **1** conspicuous bravery. **2** courteous attention to a lady.

galleon n a large sailing ship with several decks used for war or commerce.

galley n (pl **-eys**) **1** a large low single-decked ship propelled by oars and sails. **2** a narrow kitchen esp on a ship or aircraft.

Gallic adj of Gaul or France.

gallivant v to roam about looking for pleasure.

gallon n **1** a unit of liquid capacity equal to eight pints. **2** informal (in pl) large quantities.

gallop[1] n **1** the fastest natural gait of the horse. **2** a ride or run at a gallop.

gallop[2] v (**galloped, galloping**) **1** to go or ride at a gallop. **2** to read, talk, or proceed at great speed.

gallows n (pl **gallows** or **gallowses**) **1** a frame for hanging criminals. **2** (**the gallows**) hanging.

gallows humour n grim humour that makes fun of a very serious or terrifying situation.

gallstone n a rounded solid mass formed in the gall bladder or bile ducts.

galore *adj* (*used after a noun*) abundant or plentiful: *bargains galore*.

galosh *n* a rubber overshoe.

galumph *v informal* to bound along or around clumsily and exuberantly.

galvanic *adj* producing a direct current of electricity from chemical action.

galvanize *or* **-ise** *v* **1** to stimulate or shock into action. **2** to coat (iron or steel) with zinc as a protection from rust. ➤ **galvanized** *adj*.

galvanometer *n* an instrument for measuring a small electric current.

gambit *n* **1** a calculated move or remark. **2** a set of opening moves in chess.

gamble[1] *v* **1** to play a game of chance for money. **2** to take a risk with in the hope of gaining an advantage. **3** to risk (e.g. money) by gambling. ➤ **gambler** *n*.

gamble[2] *n* something involving an element of risk.

gambol *v* (**gambolled**, **gambolling**, *NAmer* **gamboled**, **gamboling**) to skip or leap about in play.

game[1] *n* **1** an activity engaged in for amusement. **2** a physical or mental competition conducted according to rules. **3** a sports match or similar contest. **4** a division of a larger contest, *esp* a tennis match. **5** (*in pl*) an organized event with contests in various types of sport. **6** a type of activity seen as competitive or governed by rules. **7** animals that are hunted; *esp* wild mammals, birds, and fish.

game[2] *v* to play for money; to gamble. ➤ **gaming** *adj*.

game[3] *adj* ready to take risks or try something new. ➤ **gamely** *adv*.

game[4] *adj* of somebody's leg: crippled or lame.

gamekeeper *n* somebody who breeds and protects game animals or birds on a private estate.

gamesmanship *n* the art of winning games by means other than superior skill without actually cheating.

gamete *n* a germ cell capable of fusing with another gamete of the other sex to form a zygote from which a new organism develops.

gamine *adj* of a girl or woman: having an impish, boyish appeal.

gamma *n* the third letter of the Greek alphabet (Γ, γ).

gamma radiation *n* radiation composed of gamma rays.

gamma rays *pl n* streams of high-energy electromagnetic radiation that have a shorter wavelength than X-rays.

gammon *n* **1** ham that has been smoked or cured. **2** the lower end of a side of bacon, including the hind leg.

gammy *adj* (**-ier**, **-iest**) *Brit, informal* of somebody's leg: injured or lame.

gamut *n* an entire range or series. **✻ run the gamut** to go through the whole range of something.

gander[1] *n* an adult male goose.

gander[2] *n informal* a look or glance.

gang[1] *n* **1** a group of people associating for criminal or disreputable ends. **2** a group of people working together, e.g. as labourers. **3** a group of people who regularly spend time together.

gang[2] *v* (+ together) to move or act as a gang.

gangling *adj* tall, thin, and awkward.

ganglion *n* (*pl* **ganglia** *or* **ganglions**) **1** a small cyst on a joint or tendon. **2** a mass of nerve cells.

gangplank *n* a movable plank used to board a ship from a quay or another ship.

gangrene *n* the death of soft body tissues in a localized area, due to loss of blood supply. ➤ **gangrenous** *adj*.

gangster *n* a member of a criminal gang.

gang up *v* (*often* + on/against) to combine as a group, *esp* to attack somebody.

gangway *n* **1** a gangplank. **2** *Brit* a narrow passage, e.g. between sections of seats in a theatre.

gannet *n* **1** a large white fish-eating seabird. **2** *Brit, informal* a greedy person.

gantry *n* (*pl* **-ies**) a raised framework spanning something, which carries railway signals, a travelling crane, etc.

gaol *n and v Brit* see JAIL[1], JAIL[2].

gap *n* **1** a break in e.g. a wall or hedge. **2** an empty space between two objects. **3** an interval. **4** a disparity. ➤ **gappy** *adj*.

gape[1] *v* **1** to open or part widely. **2** to gaze openmouthed in surprise or wonder. ➤ **gaping** *adj*.

gape[2] *n* an act of gaping; *esp* an openmouthed stare.

gap year *n* a year's break between leaving school and starting further education.

garage[1] *n* **1** a building where motor vehicles are kept. **2** an establishment for providing essential services to motor vehicles, e.g. supplying fuel or carrying out repairs. **3** a style of house music with a soul influence.

garage[2] *v* to keep or put (a car) in a garage.

garb[1] *n* a style of clothing; dress.

garb[2] *v* to dress.

garbage *n* **1** *chiefly NAmer* rubbish or waste. **2** worthless writing or speech.

garble *v* to distort or confuse (a message, transmitted text).

garden[1] *n* **1** *Brit* a plot of ground, typically beside a house, where vegetables, flowers, etc are cultivated. **2** (*also in pl*) a public park. **✻ lead somebody up the garden path** to mislead or deceive somebody.

garden[2] *v* to work in a garden. ➤ **gardener** *n*.

gargantuan *adj* gigantic.

gargle¹ v to cleanse one's mouth or throat by blowing through a liquid held in it.

gargle² n **1** a liquid used in gargling. **2** an act or the sound of gargling.

gargoyle n a rainwater spout in the form of a grotesque human or animal figure projecting from a roof gutter.

garish adj excessively and gaudily bright. ➤ **garishly** adv.

garland¹ n a wreath of flowers or leaves worn as an ornament or trophy.

garland² v to crown with a garland.

garlic n the pungent compound bulb of a plant of the lily family, used as a flavouring in cookery.

garment n an article of clothing.

garner v to collect (e.g. evidence or information).

garnet n a transparent deep red semiprecious stone.

garnish¹ v to decorate or embellish (esp food).

garnish² n an embellishment, esp a decorative addition to a dish.

garret n a small room just under the roof of a house.

garrison¹ n a body of troops stationed in a town or fortress to defend it.

garrison² v to station troops in (a place).

garrotte¹ (NAmer **garotte** or **garrote**) n a wire or cord used for strangling somebody.

garrotte² (NAmer **garotte** or **garrote**) v to kill with a garrotte.

garrulous adj excessively talkative. ➤ **garrulity** n.

garter n a band worn to hold up a stocking or sock. ➤ **gartered** adj.

gas¹ n (pl **gases** or **gasses**) **1** a fluid substance, e.g. air, that tends to expand indefinitely. **2** a gas or gaseous mixture used as a fuel, anaesthetic, etc. **3** NAmer, informal petrol. **4** NAmer flatulence.

gas² v (**gassed, gassing**) **1** to poison or affect adversely with gas. **2** informal to talk idly.

gas chamber n a chamber in which prisoners are executed or animals killed by poison gas.

gaseous adj having the form or nature of a gas.

gash¹ v to injure with a deep long cut.

gash² n a deep long cut.

gasket n a piece of sealing material for ensuring that a joint does not leak liquid or gas.

gaslight n light from a gas lamp. ➤ **gaslit** adj.

gas mask n a mask with a chemical air filter, used as a protection against harmful gases.

gasoline or **gasolene** n NAmer petrol.

gasometer n a large cylindrical storage container for gas.

gasp¹ v **1** to catch the breath suddenly and audibly, e.g. with shock. **2** to breathe laboriously. **3** (+ for) to crave.

gasp² n an audible catching of the breath.

gassy adj (**-ier, -iest**) **1** containing or like gas. **2** informal talkative.

gastric adj relating to the stomach.

gastroenteritis n inflammation of the lining of the stomach and the intestines.

gastronomy n the art or science of good eating. ➤ **gastronomic** adj.

gasworks n (pl **gasworks**) a place where gas is manufactured.

gate n **1** the usu hinged frame that closes an opening in a wall or fence. **2** a numbered exit from an airport building to the airfield. **3** either of a pair of barriers that let water in and out of a lock or close a road at a level crossing. **4** the number of spectators at a sporting event.

gateau n (pl **gateaux** or **gateaus**) a rich elaborate cream cake.

gate-crash v to attend (a party) without a ticket or invitation. ➤ **gate-crasher** n.

gatefold n a large folded page inserted in a book, journal, etc.

gatehouse n a lodge at the entrance to the grounds of a large house.

gatekeeper n somebody who guards a gate.

gatepost n the post on which a gate is hung or against which it closes.

gateway n **1** an opening for a gate. **2** a point of entry or access.

gather¹ v **1** to bring (things) together; to collect. **2** to come together in a body. **3** to pick or harvest (flowers, crops, etc). **4** to accumulate (speed). **5** to prepare (e.g. oneself) for an effort. **6** to clasp (somebody), e.g. to oneself, in an embrace. **7** to pull (fabric) together to create small tucks. **8** to reach a conclusion from hints or through inferences.

gather² n a tuck in cloth made by gathering.

gathering n an assembly or meeting.

gauche adj lacking social experience or grace.

gaucho n (pl **-os**) a cowboy of the pampas regions in S America.

gaudy adj (**-ier, -iest**) ostentatiously or tastelessly and brightly ornamented. ➤ **gaudily** adv.

gauge¹ (NAmer **gage**) n **1** an instrument for measuring or testing something, e.g. a dimension or quantity. **2** a measure of the thickness of a thin sheet of metal, plastic, etc, the diameter of wire, or the bore of a shotgun. **3** the distance between the rails of a railway, etc.

gauge² (NAmer **gage**) v **1** to measure exactly the size, dimensions, or capacity of. **2** to estimate or judge.

Usage Note: Note the spelling with -au-.

gaunt adj **1** excessively thin and angular. **2** of a place: barren or desolate.

gauntlet¹ n **1** a strong protective glove with a wide extension above the wrist. **2** a glove formerly worn with medieval armour. ✳ **throw down the gauntlet** to issue a challenge.

gauntlet[2] *n* * **run the gauntlet** to have to suffer criticism or a testing experience in order to achieve something.

gauze *n* 1 a thin often transparent fabric. 2 a fine mesh of metal or plastic. ➤ **gauzy** *adj*.

gave *v* past tense of GIVE[1].

gavel *n* a small mallet with which a chairman, judge, or auctioneer commands attention or confirms a vote, sale, etc.

gavotte *n* a popular 18th-cent. French dance.

gawk *v* to gawp.

gawky *adj* (-**ier**, -**iest**) awkward and lanky.

gawp *v Brit, informal* to gape or stare stupidly.

gay[1] *adj* 1 homosexual. 2 for or relating to homosexuals. 3 *dated* bright or attractive. 4 *dated* happily excited; carefree.

gay[2] *n* a homosexual; *esp* a man.

gaze[1] *v* to look steadily.

gaze[2] *n* a fixed intent look.

gazebo *n* (*pl* -**os** *or* -**oes**) a summerhouse, placed to command a view.

gazelle *n* (*pl* **gazelles** *or* **gazelle**) a small, graceful antelope.

gazette *n* a newspaper or journal, *esp* an official one.

gazetteer *n* a dictionary of place names.

gazump *v Brit* to thwart (a would-be house purchaser) by raising the price after agreeing to sell at a lower one. ➤ **gazumper** *n*.

GB *abbr* 1 (*also* **Gb**) gigabyte(s). 2 Great Britain.

GBH *abbr Brit* grievous bodily harm.

GC *abbr* George Cross.

GCSE *abbr Brit* General Certificate of Secondary Education.

Gd *abbr* the chemical symbol for gadolinium.

Ge *abbr* the chemical symbol for germanium.

gear[1] *n* 1 a set of interlocking wheels in the transmission system of a vehicle that determines the direction of travel or ratio of engine speed to vehicle speed. 2 a particular adjustment of the transmission system: *second gear*. 3 equipment. 4 *informal* clothing.

gear[2] *v* 1 to connect (machinery) by gears. 2 (+ to) to adjust so as to match, blend with, or satisfy.

gearbox *n* a set of vehicle gears or the protective casing enclosing them.

gear lever *n* a control rod on a gear-changing mechanism, *esp* a vehicle's gearbox.

gear up *v* to make ready for effective operation.

gecko *n* (*pl* -**os** *or* -**oes**) a small tropical lizard able to walk on vertical or overhanging surfaces.

gee *interj NAmer, informal* used as an exclamation of surprise or enthusiasm.

geek *n informal* 1 somebody unfashionable or socially awkward. 2 somebody obsessively interested in computers and technology. ➤ **geeky** *adj*.

geese *n* pl of GOOSE.

gee up *v informal* 1 to stir to greater activity. 2 to encourage (e.g. a horse) to go faster.

geezer *n informal* a man.

Geiger counter *n* an instrument for detecting and measuring radioactivity.

geisha /'gaysha/ *n* (*pl* **geisha** *or* **geishas**) a Japanese woman trained to provide entertaining and light-hearted company for men.

gel[1] *n* a jelly-like substance, e.g. a hair gel or shaving gel.

gel[2] *v* (**gelled, gelling**) 1 of a liquid: to set. 2 (*NAmer* **jell**) of an idea, plan, etc: to become definite. 3 (*NAmer* **jell**) of a group of people: to get on well together. 4 to put gel on (the hair).

gelatin *or* **gelatine** *n* a glutinous material obtained from animal tissues by boiling and used in food, e.g. to set jellies, and photography.

geld *v* to castrate (a male animal).

gelding *n* a castrated male horse.

gelignite *n* a type of dynamite.

gem *n* 1 a precious stone. 2 somebody or something highly prized.

Gemini *n* the third sign of the zodiac (the Twins).

gemstone *n* a mineral or petrified material used as a gem.

gen *n Brit, informal* information.

gendarme /'zhondahm/ *n* a member of an armed police force, *esp* in France.

gender *n* 1 in some languages, a grammatical class, , labelled as masculine, feminine, or neuter, that determines the agreement of *esp* nouns with other words. 2 the state of being male or female, *esp* as regards cultural and social differences. 3 the members of either sex.

gene *n* a unit of DNA that is carried on a chromosome and controls transmission of hereditary characteristics.

genealogy *n* (*pl* -**ies**) 1 the descent of a person, family, or group from an ancestor. 2 the study of family pedigrees. ➤ **genealogical** *adj*, **genealogist** *n*.

genera *n* pl of GENUS.

general[1] *adj* 1 involving, or applicable to, all or most members of a class, kind, or group. 2 concerned with the main or universal aspects of something rather than particular details. 3 taking precedence over others similarly titled: *the general manager*. * **in general** usually; for the most part.

general[2] *n* 1 a commander of an army. 2 an officer in the British army ranking below a field marshal.

general anaesthetic *n* an anaesthetic that causes loss of consciousness and lack of sensation over the whole body.

general election *n* an election in which candidates are elected in all constituencies of a nation.

generalist *n* somebody whose skills, interests, etc extend to several different activities.

generality *n* (*pl* -**ies**) **1** a vague and unspecific statement. **2** the quality or state of being general.

generalize *or* -**ise** *v* **1** to make general or vague statements. **2** to make more general or widespread. ➤ **generalization** *n*.

generally *adv* **1** without regard to specific instances. **2** usually; as a rule. **3** as a whole.

general practitioner *n* a medical doctor who treats all types of disease for patients living in a particular area. ➤ **general practice** *n*.

general-purpose *adj* suitable for two or more basic purposes.

generate *v* **1** to create (e.g. energy) by a physical process. **2** to be the cause of (a situation, action, or state of mind).

generation *n* **1** a group of individuals born and living at the same time. **2** a group constituting a single step in the line of descent from an ancestor. **3** a class of objects developed from an earlier type. **4** the average time between the birth of parents and the birth of their offspring, usu about 30 years. **5** production or creation.

generator *n* a machine for producing electrical energy.

generic *adj* **1** characteristic of a whole group or class. **2** not having a trademark. **3** relating to a biological genus. ➤ **generically** *adv*.

generous *adj* **1** giving e.g. money or help freely and abundantly. **2** magnanimous and kindly. **3** marked by abundance or richness. ➤ **generosity** *n*.

Genesis *n* the first book of the Old Testament.

genesis *n* (*pl* **geneses**) the origin or coming into being of something.

genetic *adj* **1** relating to genetics. **2** relating to genes. ➤ **genetically** *adv*.

genetically modified *adj* of food: containing an ingredient that has had its genetic structure altered, e.g. to make it grow better.

genetic engineering *n* the artificial manipulation of the genetic material of living things for experimental or industrial purposes.

genetic fingerprint *n* a unique pattern of repeated DNA sequences in the genetic make-up of an individual that can be used to identify him or her. ➤ **genetic fingerprinting** *n*.

genetics *pl n* the branch of biology that deals with the ways in which hereditary characteristics are passed down. ➤ **geneticist** *n*.

genial *adj* cheerfully good-tempered. ➤ **geniality** *n*, **genially** *adv*.

genie *n* a spirit in Arabian folklore who can be summoned to grant wishes.

genital *adj* relating to or in the region of the genitalia.

genitalia *pl n* the external reproductive and sexual organs.

genitals *pl n* the genitalia.

genitive *adj* denoting a grammatical case expressing a relationship of possessor or source.

genius *n* (*pl* **geniuses**) **1** a person of a very high intelligence or skill. **2** extraordinary intellectual power.

genocide *n* the deliberate murder of a racial or cultural group. ➤ **genocidal** *adj*.

genre *n* a category of artistic, musical, or literary composition.

gent *n* *informal* a gentleman.

genteel *adj* showing, or trying to show, upper-class refinement or manners. ➤ **gentility** *n*.

gentile[1] *n* (*often* **Gentile**) a non-Jewish person.

gentile[2] *adj* (*often* **Gentile**) non-Jewish.

gentle *adj* **1** of a person: kind and mild. **2** soft or delicate. **3** of a breeze: moderate. **4** of a slope: gradual. ➤ **gentleness** *n*, **gently** *adv*.

gentleman *n* (*pl* **gentlemen**) **1** a man who is chivalrous and honourable. **2** a man belonging to the landed gentry or nobility. **3** in polite or formal use: a man. ➤ **gentlemanly** *adj*.

gentleman's agreement *n* an unwritten agreement secured only by the honour of the participants and not legally enforceable.

gentry *n* the upper class.

genuflect *v* to go down on one knee briefly, *esp* as a gesture of respect to sacred objects. ➤ **genuflection** *n*.

genuine *adj* **1** actually what it is claimed to be. **2** sincere. ➤ **genuinely** *adv*.

gen up *v* (**genned**, **genning**) *Brit, informal* (+ on) to find information or learn about something.

genus *n* (*pl* **genera**) a category in the classification of living things ranking between family and species.

geodesic *adj* relating to the plotting of straight lines on curved surfaces, or to a method of construction that uses light, straight structural elements to form a curved surface.

geographical *or* **geographic** *adj* to do with geography. ➤ **geographically** *adv*.

geography *n* **1** a science that deals with the earth, its physical features, and the distribution of plant, animal and human life over its surface. **2** the geographical features of an area. ➤ **geographer** *n*.

geology *n* **1** a science that deals with the structure and history of the earth, *esp* as recorded in rocks. **2** the geological features of an area. ➤ **geological** *adj*, **geologist** *n*.

geometric *adj* **1** relating to geometry. **2** using patterns formed from straight and curved lines. ➤ **geometrical** *adj*, **geometrically** *adv*.

geometry *n* (*pl* -**ies**) **1** a branch of mathematics that deals with the measurement, properties, and relationships of points, lines, angles, surfaces, and solids. **2** a surface shape, e.g. of a crystal.

Geordie *n Brit, informal* a native or inhabitant of Tyneside.

Georgian *adj* of the reigns of the first four King Georges of Britain (1714–1830).

geranium *n* a garden plant with red, pink or white flowers.

gerbil *n* a burrowing desert rodent with long hind legs.

geriatric[1] *adj* **1** relating to or for elderly people. **2** *informal, derog* aged or decrepit.

geriatric[2] *n* an elderly person.

germ *n* **1** a micro-organism, *esp* one that causes disease. **2** a small mass of cells capable of developing into an organism. **3** the rudimentary state from which something develops.

German *n* **1** a native or inhabitant of Germany. **2** the language of Germany, Austria, and parts of Switzerland. ➤ **German** *adj*.

germane *adj* relevant and appropriate.

Germanic *adj* **1** relating to a branch of the Indo-European language family containing English, German, Dutch, and the Scandinavian languages. **2** characteristic of the German people.

German measles *pl n* = RUBELLA.

German shepherd *n* = ALSATIAN.

germicide *n* a substance that kills germs. ➤ **germicidal** *adj*.

germinal *adj* **1** of or having the characteristics of a germ cell or early embryo. **2** in the earliest stage of development.

germinate *v* to begin to grow; to sprout. ➤ **germination** *n*.

gerontology *n* the study of ageing and the problems of old people.

gerrymander *v* to divide (an area) into election districts to give one political party an electoral advantage.

gerund *n* a noun ending in *-ing* that is formed from a verb and shows certain verbal features, e.g. *singing* in *He likes singing*.

Gestapo /ɡə'shtahpoh, ɡə'stahpoh/ *n* the secret police organization in Nazi Germany.

gestation *n* **1** the carrying or development of young in the uterus. **2** conception and development, *esp* in the mind.

gesticulate *v* to make expressive gestures, *esp* when speaking. ➤ **gesticulation** *n*.

gesture[1] *n* **1** a movement, usu of the body or limbs, that expresses an idea or attitude. **2** something said or done for its effect on the attitudes of others or to convey a feeling.

gesture[2] *v* to make a gesture.

get *v* (**getting**, *past tense* **got**, *past part.* **got** or *NAmer or archaic* **gotten**) **1** to gain possession of; to obtain or receive. **2** to fetch. **3** to capture. **4** to succeed in achieving. **5** to become affected by (an illness). **6** to suffer or undergo. **7** to cause (something or somebody) to come into a certain condition: *I must get my shoes mended.* **8** to persuade or induce. **9** to become: *to get drunk.*

10 to travel by (a form of public transport). **11** to succeed in coming or going: *Where did they get to?* **12** *informal* to hear or understand (something said). **13** *informal* to punish or harm (somebody). ✱ **get at 1** to reach. **2** *informal* to imply. **3** *informal* to criticize or tease. **4** *informal* to bribe.

getaway *n* a departure or escape.

get away *v* to escape. ✱ **get away with** to avoid punishment or blame for.

get by *v* to manage with difficulty or limited resources.

get down *v* to make dejected. ✱ **get down to** to start to give attention to (an activity).

get off *v* to escape punishment.

get on *v* **1** to be on friendly terms. **2** to succeed. ✱ **be getting on for** to be approaching (a specified age, time, distance, etc).

get over *v* **1** to overcome (a difficulty). **2** to recover from (something unpleasant). **3** to succeed in communicating (an idea, etc).

get round *v* to evade (a law or responsibility). ✱ **get round to** to make a start eventually on (a task, etc).

get through *v* **1** to reach the end of (an ordeal or difficulty). **2** to make contact by telephone. ✱ **get through to** to make oneself understood by.

get-together *n* an informal social gathering or meeting.

get up *v* to rise from a sitting or lying position, or from one's bed. ✱ **get up to** *Brit, informal* to be involved in (something wrong, mischievous, etc).

get-up *n informal* an outfit or costume.

geyser *n* a spring that intermittently throws out jets of heated water and steam.

ghastly *adj* (**-ier, -iest**) **1** terrifyingly horrible. **2** *informal* intensely unpleasant, disagreeable, or objectionable. **3** pale and wan. ➤ **ghastliness** *n*.

gherkin *n* a small pickled cucumber.

ghetto *n* (*pl* **-os** *or* **-oes**) **1** an area of a city in which a minority group live. **2** part of a city in which Jews formerly lived.

ghetto blaster *n informal* a large portable radio, usu incorporating a cassette or CD player.

ghost[1] *n* **1** a disembodied soul; *esp* the soul of a dead person haunting the living. **2** a faint shadowy trace.

ghost[2] *v* to ghostwrite (e.g. a book).

ghostly *adj* (**-ier, -iest**) of or like a ghost; spectral.

ghost town *n* a once-flourishing but now deserted town.

ghostwrite *v* (**ghostwrote, ghostwritten**) to write (e.g. a book) for another person, who is the presumed author. ➤ **ghostwriter** *n*.

ghoul *n* **1** an evil spirit or ghost. **2** a person with a morbid interest in fatal accidents, disasters, etc. ➤ **ghoulish** *adj*.

GI *n* (*pl* **GI's** *or* **GIs**) a member of the US army, *esp* a private.

giant[1] *n* **1** a legendary being, like a human in shape, but having great size and strength. **2** an extraordinarily large person, animal, or plant.

giant[2] *adj* extremely large.

gibber *v* to make rapid, inarticulate, and usu incomprehensible sounds.

gibberish *n* unintelligible or meaningless language.

gibbet *n* **1** a gallows. **2** an upright post with an arm, used formerly for displaying the bodies of executed criminals as a warning.

gibbon *n* a small tailless tree-dwelling ape of SE Asia.

gibe *v and n* see JIBE[1], JIBE[2].

giblets *pl n* a fowl's heart, liver, neck and other edible internal organs.

giddy *adj* (**-ier, -iest**) **1** feeling a sensation of unsteadiness and lack of balance as if everything is whirling round. **2** lightheartedly frivolous.

gift[1] *n* **1** something freely given by one person to another; a present or donation. **2** a natural capacity or talent. * **gift of the gab** *informal* the ability to talk persuasively.

gift[2] *v* to give as a gift.

gifted *adj* having great natural ability or intelligence.

gig[1] *n* a light two-wheeled carriage pulled by a horse.

gig[2] *n* *informal* a live performance by a singer, rock group, etc.

gigabyte *n* in computing, a quantity of data equal to one thousand million (10^9) bytes.

gigantic *adj* unusually great; enormous.

giggle[1] *v* to laugh in a silly or nervous manner.

giggle[2] *n* **1** an act of giggling. **2** *Brit, informal* something amusing. ➤ **giggly** *adj*.

gigolo *n* (*pl* **-os**) a man paid by a usu older woman for companionship or sex.

gild *v* (*past tense and past part.* **gilded** *or* **gilt**) **1** to overlay with a thin covering of gold. **2** to give an attractive but often deceptive appearance to.

gill[1] *n* **1** an organ, *esp* of a fish, for taking in oxygen dissolved in water. **2** a radiating plate on the undersurface of the cap of some fungi, e.g. mushrooms.

gill[2] *n* a unit of liquid capacity equal to a quarter of a pint.

gilt[1] *adj* covered with gold or gilt.

gilt[2] *n* gold leaf or gold paint laid on a surface.

gilt-edged *adj* of government securities: traded on the Stock Exchange and having a guaranteed fixed interest rate.

gimlet *n* a T-shaped tool for boring small holes in wood.

gimmick *n* a scheme or object devised to gain attention or publicity. ➤ **gimmickry** *n*, **gimmicky** *adj*.

gin[1] *n* a spirit made from distilled grain and flavoured with juniper berries.

gin[2] *n* **1** a machine for separating cotton fibre from seeds and waste material. **2** a machine for raising or moving heavy weights. **3** a snare for game.

ginger *n* **1** the rhizome of a tropical plant, which has a strong hot taste and is used in cooking or dried and ground to make a spice. **2** a reddish or yellowish brown colour.

ginger ale *n* a sweet carbonated non-alcoholic drink flavoured with ginger.

ginger beer *n* a weak fizzy alcoholic drink, made by fermenting ginger and syrup.

gingerbread *n* a thick cake made with treacle and flavoured with ginger.

gingerly *adv* very cautiously or carefully.

gingham *n* a lightweight cotton fabric with a checked pattern.

gingivitis *n* inflammation of the gums.

ginormous *adj* *Brit, informal* exceptionally large.

ginseng *n* the aromatic root of a Chinese or North American plant, widely valued as a tonic.

gipsy *n* see GYPSY.

giraffe *n* (*pl* **giraffes** *or* **giraffe**) a large African mammal with a very long neck.

gird *v* (*past tense and past part.* **girded** *or* **girt**) to encircle with a flexible band, e.g. a belt. * **gird (up) one's loins** to prepare for action.

girder *n* a strong horizontal metal beam.

girdle[1] *n* **1** a belt or cord encircling the body, usu at the waist. **2** a woman's tightly fitting undergarment that extends from the waist to below the hips.

girdle[2] *v* to encircle with , or as if with, a girdle.

girl *n* **1** a female child. **2** a young woman. **3** a girlfriend. ➤ **girlish** *adj*.

girlfriend *n* **1** a regular female companion with whom somebody is romantically or sexually involved. **2** a female friend.

girn *or* **gurn** *v* *Brit* to pull a grotesque face.

giro *n* (*pl* **-os**) **1** a computerized system of money transfer, comparable to a current account. **2** *informal* a giro cheque or payment, *esp* a social security benefit.

girt *v* past tense and past part. of GIRD.

girth *n* **1** a measurement round something, e.g. a tree trunk or somebody's waist. **2** a strap that passes under the body of a horse to fasten a saddle on its back.

gist *n* the main point of something said or written.

give[1] *v* (**gave, given**) **1** to transfer the possession or use of (something) to another person. **2** to offer (advice, a promise, etc). **3** to express or propose (a reason, argument, etc). **4** to provide or organize: *to give a party*. **5** to cause somebody to experience or suffer (something): *You gave me a fright.* **6** to utter (a sound). **7** to collapse or yield under physical pressure. ✳ **give or take** allowing for a specified margin of error. **give way 1** to allow someone to pass or go first. **2** to collapse under pressure. **give way to** to be replaced by. ➤ **giver** *n*.

give² *n* the capacity or tendency to yield to pressure.

give-and-take *n* the practice of making mutual concessions.

giveaway *n* **1** an unintentional revelation. **2** something given free or at a reduced price.

give away *v* **1** to make a present of. **2** to betray. **3** to reveal (a secret).

give in *v* to yield or surrender.

given¹ *v* past part. of GIVE¹.

given² *adj* **1** (+ to) prone; disposed. **2** fixed; specified.

given³ *prep* in view of.

given name *n chiefly NAmer* = FORENAME.

give off *v* to emit (something unpleasant).

give out *v* **1** to distribute. **2** of a supply: to come to an end.

give up *v* **1** to abandon an activity and concede failure. **2** to discontinue (a habit). **3** to surrender (somebody or oneself) as a prisoner.

gizmo *or* **gismo** *n* (*pl* **-os**) *informal* a gadget.

gizzard *n* an enlargement of the digestive tract of birds, with thick muscular walls for breaking up and grinding food.

glacé *adj* of fruit: coated with a glaze; candied.

glacial *adj* **1** of or produced by glaciers. **2** extremely cold.

glaciation *n* the process of forming ice or glaciers.

glacier *n* a large body of ice moving slowly down a slope.

glad *adj* (**gladder, gladdest**) **1** expressing or experiencing joy or delight. **2** causing happiness. **3** (+ of) grateful for; pleased to have. ➤ **gladly** *adv*.

gladden *v* to make glad.

glade *n* an open space in a wood or forest.

gladiator *n* a man trained to fight another man or wild animals in a public arena in ancient Rome. ➤ **gladiatorial** *adj*.

gladiolus *n* (*pl* **gladioli** *or* **gladioluses**) a plant of the iris family with sword-shaped leaves and spikes of brilliantly coloured flowers.

glad rags *pl n informal* smart clothes worn for a party or special occasion.

glamorize *or* **-ise** *or* **glamourize** *or* **-ise** *v* **1** to make glamorous. **2** to romanticize. ➤ **glamorization** *n*.

glamorous *adj* romantically or excitingly attractive.

glamour (*NAmer* **glamor**) *n* a romantic, exciting, and often illusory attractiveness.

glance¹ *v* **1** (*usu* + at) to take a quick look. **2** (*often* + off) to strike a surface obliquely and go off at an angle.

glance² *n* a quick or cursory look.

gland *n* an organ of the body that secretes chemical substances.

glandular *adj* relating to or affecting a gland or glands.

glandular fever *n* an acute infectious disease, characterized by fever and swollen and painful lymph glands.

glare¹ *v* **1** to stare angrily or fiercely. **2** to shine with a harsh light.

glare² *n* **1** an angry or fierce stare. **2** a harsh uncomfortably bright light.

glasnost *n esp* in the former USSR, openness about government affairs and policy.

glass *n* **1** a hard brittle transparent substance formed by melting sand with metallic oxides. **2** a glass drinking vessel. **3** a mirror. **4** a barometer. ➤ **glassy** *adj*.

glass-blowing *n* the process of shaping a mass of semi-molten glass by blowing air into it through a tube.

glass ceiling *n* a hypothetical barrier to career advancement, *esp* one caused by sexism or racism.

glasses *pl n* a pair of glass lenses in a frame, worn in front of the eyes to correct defects of vision or for protection.

glass fibre *n* = FIBREGLASS.

glasshouse *n chiefly Brit* a greenhouse.

glasspaper *n* paper covered with a thin layer of powdered glass for use as an abrasive.

glaucoma *n* increased pressure within the eyeball causing damage to the retina and gradual impairment of vision.

glaze¹ *v* **1** to fit (e.g. a window frame) with glass. **2** to coat (e.g. food or pottery) with a glaze. **3** (*often* + over) to become dull or lifeless. ➤ **glazing** *n*.

glaze² *n* **1** a liquid preparation that hardens to give a glossy coating to food. **2** a vitreous coating used to seal or decorate pottery.

glazier *n* a person who fits glass, *esp* into windows and doors.

gleam¹ *n* **1** a short-lived appearance of reflected or subdued light. **2** a brief or faint indication of emotion, etc.

gleam² *v* to shine, *esp* with reflected light.

glean *v* **1** to gather grain left by reapers. **2** to gather (e.g. information) bit by bit.

glee *n* a feeling of joy or delight.

gleeful *adj* merry or triumphant. ➤ **gleefully** *adv*.

glen *n* a narrow valley, *esp* in Scotland or Ireland.

glib *adj* (**glibber, glibbest**) fluent in speaking or writing, often to the point of being superficial or dishonest. ➤ **glibly** *adv*.

glide[1] v **1** to move noiselessly in a smooth, continuous, and effortless manner. **2** of an aircraft: to fly without the use of engines.

glide[2] n an act of gliding.

glider n a light aircraft without an engine.

glimmer[1] v to shine faintly or unsteadily.

glimmer[2] n **1** a feeble or unsteady light. **2** a small sign or amount.

glimpse[1] v to see briefly or partially.

glimpse[2] n a brief look or partial view.

glint[1] v to shine with tiny bright flashes.

glint[2] n a tiny bright flash of usu reflected light.

glisten v to shine with the lustre of a wet or oily surface.

glitch n informal a temporary malfunction or setback.

glitter[1] v to shine by reflection in bright flashes.

glitter[2] n **1** bright shimmering reflected light. **2** small sparkling particles used for ornamentation. **3** a brilliantly attractive, but sometimes superficial quality. ➤ **glittery** adj.

glitz n informal superficial glamour.

gloaming n (**the gloaming**) literary twilight or dusk.

gloat[1] v (often + over) to talk about something, esp one's own achievements or another person's misfortunes, with great and often malicious satisfaction. ➤ **gloating** adj.

gloat[2] n the act of gloating.

glob n chiefly informal a blob, esp of a semiliquid substance.

global adj **1** involving the entire world. **2** general; comprehensive. ➤ **globally** adv.

global village n the world viewed as an integrated community linked by modern technology.

global warming n an increase in the average temperature of the earth's atmosphere believed to be caused by the greenhouse effect.

globe n **1** a spherical representation of the earth. **2** (**the globe**) the world; the earth. **3** something spherical or rounded, e.g. a glass bowl or light.

globetrotter n informal somebody who travels widely. ➤ **globetrotting** n and adj.

globular adj **1** spherical. **2** consisting of globules.

glockenspiel /'glokənspeel, -shpeel/ n a percussion instrument consisting of a series of graduated metal bars played with two hammers.

gloom n **1** partial or total darkness. **2** despondency.

gloomy adj (-**ier**, -**iest**) **1** dismally or depressingly dark. **2** feeling or causing despondency. ➤ **gloomily** adv.

glorified adj made to appear more special, important, etc than is really the case.

glorify v (-**ies**, -**ied**) **1** to make (something) appear admirable or splendid. **2** to give glory to (God), e.g. in worship. ➤ **glorification** n.

glorious adj **1** possessing or conferring glory. **2** marked by great beauty, splendour, or excellence. ➤ **gloriously** adv.

glory[1] n (pl -**ies**) **1** praise, honour, or renown. **2** worshipful praise and thanksgiving. **3** something that is splendid or brings renown. **4** splendour or magnificence.

glory[2] v (-**ies**, -**ied**) informal (often + in) to take great pride or pleasure.

gloss[1] n **1** surface lustre or sheen. **2** something that gives this: lip gloss. **3** a deceptively attractive outer appearance. **4** paint that gives a shiny finish.

gloss[2] v to give a gloss to.

gloss[3] n a brief explanation or translation of a difficult word or expression.

gloss[4] v to supply a gloss for (a word, text, etc).

glossary n (pl -**ies**) a list of terms, esp those used in a particular text or a specialized field, with their meanings.

gloss over v to try to hide (something undesirable) by rapid or superficial treatment.

glossy[1] adj (-**ier**, -**iest**) **1** having a lustre or sheen. **2** superficially attractive in a sophisticated manner.

glossy[2] n (pl -**ies**) informal a magazine expensively produced on glossy paper with many colour photographs.

glottal adj of or produced by the glottis.

glottal stop n a speech sound produced by closure and sudden reopening of the glottis, as between the two syllables in a Cockney pronunciation of butter.

glottis n (pl **glottises** or **glottides** /'glotideez/) technical the slit-like space between the two vocal cords in the larynx.

glove n **1** a close-fitting covering for the hand with separate sections for each of the fingers and the thumb. **2** a padded covering for the fist worn by a boxer.

glove compartment n a small storage compartment in a car's dashboard.

glow[1] v **1** to shine with a steady light. **2** of the complexion, etc: to have a strong, healthy, esp red, colour. **3** to show great pleasure or satisfaction.

glow[2] n a steady light.

glower[1] v to stare with sullen annoyance or anger.

glower[2] n a sullen or angry look.

glowing adj highly appreciative or commendatory.

glow-worm n a type of beetle that emits light from its abdomen.

glucose n a simple natural sugar that is the usual form in which carbohydrate is absorbed and used in the body by animals.

glue[1] n a substance used for sticking things together.

glue[2] v (**glues**, **glued**, **gluing** or **glueing**) **1** to cause to stick tightly with glue. **2** (**be glued to**) to be unable to stop watching or listening to.

glum *adj* (**glummer, glummest**) sad; downcast. ➤ **glumly** *adv*.

glut[1] *n* an excessive supply of something.

glut[2] *v* (**glutted, glutting**) to fill or feed beyond capacity.

gluten *n* a protein substance, *esp* in wheat flour, that gives dough its cohesive and elastic properties.

glutinous *adj* resembling glue; sticky.

glutton *n* **1** a habitually greedy eater and drinker. **2** somebody who has a great liking for something. ➤ **gluttonous** *adj*.

gluttony *n* habitual greed in eating or drinking.

glycerin *or* **glycerine** *n* a sweet syrupy fluid obtained from fats and used as a solvent or in medicines.

GM *abbr* **1** genetically modified. **2** George Medal.

gm *abbr* gram.

GMT *abbr* Greenwich Mean Time.

gnarled *adj* **1** of a tree: covered with knots or lumps. **2** of hands, etc: rough and twisted, *esp* with age.

gnash *v* to grind (the teeth) together.

gnat *n* a small two-winged fly that bites.

gnaw *v* **1** to bite or chew on with the teeth, or wear away by persistent nibbling. **2** to cause continuous pain or anxiety.

gnocchi /'n(y)oki/ *pl n* small dumplings made from flour, semolina, or potatoes.

gnome *n* in folklore, a dwarf who lives under the earth and guards treasure.

gnomic /'nohmik, 'nomik/ *adj* mysterious or enigmatic.

GNP *abbr* gross national product.

gnu *n* (*pl* **gnus** *or* **gnu**) a large African antelope with an oxlike head and a short mane.

GNVQ *abbr Brit* General National Vocational Qualification.

go[1] *v* (**goes, going**, *past tense* **went**, *past part.* **gone**) **1** to proceed on a course; to travel. **2** to leave. **3** to make an expedition for a specified activity: *go fishing.* **4** to attend a specified institution habitually. **5** to extend. **6** to arrive at a specified state or condition. **7** to be consumed or spent. **8** to disappear. **9** to elapse. **10** to turn out in a specified manner. **11** to function *esp* in the proper way. **12** (+ an infinitive) to be about, intending, or destined: *Is it going to rain?* **13** (*often* + with) to be compatible or harmonize. **14** to be capable of passing, or of being contained or inserted. **15** to belong. **16** to be satisfactory or adequate. **17** to emit (a sound). **18** *Brit, informal* to say. ✳ **go about** to undertake or begin to tackle. **go ahead 1** to begin. **2** to continue or proceed. **go at** to undertake (e.g. a task) energetically. **go back on** to fail to keep (e.g. a promise). **go for 1** to try to gain. **2** to choose or accept. **3** to attack. **go into 1** of a

number: to be contained in (another number). **2** to investigate or explain in depth. **go over** to examine, inspect, or check. **go through 1** to subject to examination, study, or discussion. **2** to experience (something difficult or unpleasant). **3** to spend or use up. **go without** to be deprived of. **leave/let go** to stop holding.

go[2] *n* (*pl* **goes**) **1** a turn in an activity, e.g. a game. **2** an attempt, a try. **3** energy; vigour. ✳ **have a go at** to attack, *esp* verbally. **on the go** *informal* constantly or restlessly active.

goad[1] *n* **1** a pointed rod used to urge on an animal. **2** something that stimulates somebody into action.

goad[2] *v* **1** to drive (e.g. cattle) with a goad. **2** to incite by nagging or persistent annoyance.

go-ahead[1] *adj* energetic and progressive.

go-ahead[2] *n* (**the go-ahead**) permission to proceed.

goal *n* **1** in sport, an area or object into which players must put a ball, etc to score. **2** an instance of putting a ball, etc into a goal. **3** an aim or objective. **4** the destination of a journey. ➤ **goalless** *adj*.

goalkeeper *n* a player who defends the goal in football, hockey, lacrosse, etc.

go along *v* to go as a companion. ✳ **go along with** to agree or cooperate with.

goalpost *n* either of two vertical posts forming part of the goal in football, rugby, etc. ✳ **move the goalposts** to change the rules, conditions, etc that apply to something.

goat *n* a mammal with backward-curving horns and a straight thick coat, living wild or farmed for milk.

goatee *n* a small beard covering only the bottom of the chin.

goatherd *n* somebody who tends goats.

gob[1] *n* a shapeless or sticky lump.

gob[2] *v* (**gobbed, gobbing**) *chiefly Brit, informal* to spit.

gob[3] *n Brit, informal* the mouth.

gobbet *n* a piece or portion.

gobble[1] *v* **1** to eat greedily or noisily. **2** (*often* + up) to take over or use up quickly.

gobble[2] *v* to make the guttural sound of a male turkey. ➤ **gobbler** *n*.

gobbledygook *or* **gobbledegook** *n* unintelligible jargon.

go-between *n* an intermediary or agent.

goblet *n* a drinking vessel with a rounded bowl, a foot, and a stem.

goblin *n* a grotesque mischievous elf.

gobsmacked *adj Brit, informal* utterly taken aback.

gobstopper *n* a large round hard sweet.

goby *n* (*pl* **gobies** *or* **goby**) a small spiny-finned sea fish.

go-cart *n* see GO-KART.

god *n* **1** (**God**) the being worshipped as creator and ruler of the universe. **2** a being or object with supernatural attributes and powers.

godchild n (pl **godchildren**) somebody for whom another person becomes godparent.

goddaughter n a female godchild.

goddess n a female deity.

godfather n 1 a male godparent. 2 the leader of a criminal organization, esp the Mafia.

God-fearing adj devout.

godforsaken adj remote; desolate.

godhead n 1 divine nature or essence. 2 (**the Godhead**) God.

godless adj 1 not acknowledging a deity; atheistic. 2 wicked.

godly adj (-ier, -iest) pious; devout.

godmother n a female godparent.

go down v 1 to decrease. 2 to sink. 3 to be defeated. 4 of a computer system or program: to crash. 5 to be received in a specified way. 6 (often + with) to become ill.

godparent n somebody who undertakes responsibility for the religious education of another person at baptism.

godsend n something needed that comes at just the right time.

godson n a male godchild.

goes v third person present sing. of GO[1].

goggle v to stare with wide eyes.

goggles pl n protective glasses with a flexible, snugly fitting frame.

go in v to enter. ✴ **go in for 1** to engage in (an activity), esp for enjoyment. 2 to compete in (e.g. a test or race).

going[1] n 1 the condition of the ground, e.g. for horse racing. 2 the general conditions under which one tries to do something.

going[2] adj 1 living; existing: the best novelist going. 2 available; to be had. 3 current; prevailing.

going concern n a business that is operating and profitable.

going-over n (pl **goings-over**) 1 a thorough examination. 2 a severe beating.

goings-on pl n 1 actions or events. 2 dubious activities.

goitre (NAmer **goiter**) /ˈɡoɪtə/ n an abnormal enlargement of the thyroid gland visible as a swelling of the neck.

go-kart or **go-cart** n a small racing car used in karting.

gold n 1 a yellow precious metallic element, used esp in jewellery and as a currency reserve. 2 gold coins. 3 a deep metallic yellow colour.

golden adj 1 consisting of or containing gold. 2 of the colour of gold. 3 prosperous; flourishing. 4 favourable. 5 marking a 50th anniversary: golden jubilee.

golden age n 1 a period of great happiness, prosperity, or achievement. 2 a period when something, e.g. a particular art form, was flourishing.

golden boy n a man or boy who is very successful or popular.

golden eagle n a large eagle with brownish yellow tips on its head and neck feathers.

golden girl n a woman or girl who is very successful or popular.

golden handshake n informal a large sum of money given to an employee on leaving a company.

golden rule n a guiding principle.

goldfinch n a small red, black, yellow, and white European finch.

goldfish n (pl **goldfishes** or **goldfish**) a small orange-red fish related to the carps, kept in aquariums and ponds.

gold leaf n gold beaten into very thin sheets.

gold medal n a medal of gold awarded to the winner of a competition or race.

gold rush n a rush of people to a newly discovered goldfield in pursuit of riches.

goldsmith n somebody who makes articles of gold.

gold standard n a monetary system in which the basic unit of currency is defined by a stated quantity of gold.

golf n a game in which players using long-shafted clubs attempt to hit a small ball into each of the holes on a course. ➤ **golfer** n.

golliwog n a soft doll with a black face.

gonad /ˈɡohnad/ n a primary sex gland in which egg or sperm cells are produced, e.g. the ovaries or testes.

gondola n a long narrow flat-bottomed boat used on the canals of Venice.

gondolier n somebody who propels a gondola.

gone[1] v past part. of GO[1].

gone[2] adj 1 past; ended. 2 used up.

gone[3] adv Brit later or older than: It's gone three o'clock.

goner n informal 1 an irreparable or irretrievable thing. 2 a dead person.

gong n 1 a metal disc that produces a resounding tone when struck. 2 Brit, informal a medal or decoration.

gonorrhoea (NAmer **gonorrhea**) /ɡonəˈriːə/ n a sexually transmitted disease causing inflammation of the mucous membranes of the genital tracts.

goo n informal a sticky substance.

good[1] adj (**better**, **best**) 1 of a favourable or desirable character. 2 of a high standard. 3 agreeable; pleasant. 4 (+ for) beneficial to the health or character of. 5 morally commendable; virtuous. 6 well-behaved. 7 kind; benevolent. 8 (often + at) competent; skilful. 9 suitable; fit. 10 thorough; full. ✴ **as good as** virtually; in effect. **make good 1** to be successful in life. 2 chiefly Brit to repair. 3 to provide compensation for (a loss, expense, etc). 4 to fulfil (a promise, etc).

good² n 1 benefit; advantage. 2 (usu in pl) personal property. 3 (usu in pl) wares; merchandise. 4 Brit freight. ✻ **for good** forever; permanently.

goodbye¹ interj used to express farewell.

goodbye² n (pl **goodbyes**) a concluding remark or gesture at parting.

good faith n honest or sincere intentions.

good-for-nothing adj of no value; worthless.

Good Friday n the Friday before Easter Sunday, observed in the Christian Church as the anniversary of the crucifixion of Christ.

goodly adj (-ier, -iest) significantly large; considerable.

goodwill n 1 a kindly feeling of approval and support. 2 the prestige of a business above and beyond its financial value.

goody or **goodie** n (pl -ies) informal 1 (usu in pl) something particularly attractive or desirable. 2 a good person or hero, esp in a film or book.

goody-goody n (pl **goody-goodies**) informal somebody who is affectedly or ingratiatingly virtuous.

gooey adj (**gooier**, **gooiest**) soft and sticky.

goof¹ n chiefly NAmer, informal 1 a ridiculous or stupid person. 2 a blunder.

goof² v chiefly NAmer, informal 1 (often + about/around) to fool around. 2 to make a foolish mistake.

go off v 1 to explode. 2 of food: to begin to decompose. 3 informal to stop liking or begin to dislike.

goofy adj (-ier, -iest) informal 1 chiefly NAmer silly; foolish. 2 chiefly Brit of teeth: protruding.

goon n informal 1 a silly or foolish person. 2 chiefly NAmer a bully or thug.

go on v 1 to continue. 2 to take place. 3 to talk, esp effusively.

goose n (pl **geese**) 1 a large water bird with a long neck and webbed feet. 2 the female of such a bird. 3 informal a foolish person.

gooseberry n (pl -ies) a small round edible green or yellow fruit with soft prickly skin.

goose pimples pl n small bumps on the skin caused by cold or fear.

goose step n a straight-legged marching step with the legs swung high.

go out v 1 to go to social events, entertainments, etc. 2 (+ with) to spend time regularly with somebody in a romantic relationship. 3 to be extinguished.

gopher n an American burrowing rodent with large cheek pouches.

gore¹ n thick or clotted blood, esp when shed as a result of violence.

gore² v of e.g. a bull: to wound with a horn or tusk.

gore³ n a triangular piece of material used to give shape to e.g. a garment or sail.

gorge¹ n a narrow steep-walled valley.

gorge² v to eat hungrily or greedily.

gorgeous adj 1 splendidly beautiful. 2 informal very pleasant.

gorgon n 1 (**Gorgon**) any of three sisters in Greek mythology who had live snakes in place of hair and could turn anybody who looked at them to stone. 2 a repulsive or formidable woman.

gorilla n a large anthropoid ape of western equatorial Africa.

gormless adj Brit, informal slow to act or understand; stupid.

gorse n an evergreen shrub with yellow flowers and green spines.

gory adj (-ier, -iest) 1 full of violence and bloodshed. 2 covered with blood.

gosling /'gozling/ n a young goose.

gospel n 1 (often **Gospel**) the teachings of Jesus Christ. 2 (usu **Gospel**) any of the first four books of the New Testament relating these teachings. 3 something so authoritative as not to be questioned. 4 (also **gospel music**) a type of religious music rooted in black American culture.

gossamer n 1 a film of cobwebs floating in the air. 2 (used before a noun) light, delicate, or insubstantial.

gossip¹ n 1 a chatty talk. 2 talk or esp sensational allegations about other people. 3 somebody who habitually gossips. ➤ **gossipy** adj.

gossip² v (**gossiped**, **gossiping**) to engage in casual conversation or gossip.

got v past tense and past part. of GET.

Gothic adj 1 denoting a style of architecture of the 12th to the 16th centuries characterized by pointed arches. 2 (often **gothic** or **gothick**) of fiction: dealing with macabre or mysterious events.

gotten v NAmer past part. of GET.

gouache /goo'ahsh/ n 1 a method of painting using watercolours mixed with gum. 2 paint or a painting produced in this way.

gouge¹ /gowj/ v 1 to make (an uneven hole, dent, etc) in a surface. 2 (+ out) to force out roughly or violently.

gouge² n 1 a chisel with a concave blade. 2 a groove or cavity made by gouging.

goujon /'goohzhonh/ n a small strip of fish, chicken, etc, coated in batter or breadcrumbs and deep-fried.

goulash /'goohlash/ n a meat stew of Hungarian origin highly seasoned with paprika.

go up v 1 to increase. 2 to burst into flames.

gourd n the inedible fruit of a climbing plant, which has a hard rind used to make vessels and utensils.

gourmand n somebody who is excessively fond of food and drink.

gourmet /'gawmay, 'goosmay/ n 1 a connoisseur of food and drink. 2 (used before a noun) suitable for a gourmet.

gout /gowt/ n a disorder that results in the joints, *esp* of the big toe, becoming painfully inflamed.

govern v 1 to control the making and administration of policy in (a state, organization, etc). 2 to be a deciding influence on. 3 to restrain.

governance n *formal* the action or manner of governing.

governess n a woman entrusted with the teaching of a child in a private household.

government n 1 the body of people that governs a state. 2 the act of governing. 3 the system by which a state, organization, etc is governed. ➤ **governmental** adj.

governor n 1 a ruler or chief executive of a political unit. 2 the most senior administrator of an institution, e.g. a prison. 3 a member of a body that controls an institution, e.g. a school.

gown n 1 a loose flowing robe worn *esp* by a professional or academic person when acting in an official capacity. 2 a woman's dress, *esp* an elegant or formal one. 3 a protective outer garment worn in an operating theatre.

GP *abbr* 1 general practitioner. 2 Grand Prix.

gr. *abbr* 1 grain. 2 gram. 3 gross.

grab¹ v (**grabbed, grabbing**) 1 to seize hastily or roughly. 2 to obtain unscrupulously or opportunistically. 3 *informal* to impress: *It doesn't really grab me.*

grab² n a sudden snatch. ✳ **up for grabs** *informal* available for anyone to take or win.

grace¹ n 1 ease and suppleness of movement. 2 a charming or attractive trait. 3 a temporary exemption; a reprieve. 4 (*also in pl*) approval; favour. 5 unmerited divine assistance given to human beings. 6 a short prayer at a meal giving thanks. 7 (**Her/His/Your Grace**) used as a title for a duke, duchess, or archbishop.

grace² v 1 (+ with) to confer honour on with one's presence. 2 to adorn or embellish.

graceful adj having or displaying grace or elegance. ➤ **gracefully** adv.

graceless adj devoid of elegance or charm.

grace note n a musical note added as an ornament.

gracious adj 1 marked by kindness and courtesy. 2 having qualities, e.g. comfort and elegance, made possible by wealth. 3 showing divine grace. ➤ **graciously** adv.

gradation n 1 a series of successive stages. 2 a step in such a series.

grade¹ n 1 a position in a scale of ranks or qualities. 2 a mark indicating a degree of accomplishment at school. ✳ **make the grade** to succeed.

grade² v 1 to sort according to quality. 2 to assign a grade to (e.g. a student's work). 3 to pass from one stage or level to another *esp* gradually.

gradient n 1 the degree of inclination of a slope. 2 a sloping road or railway.

gradual adj 1 happening by small degrees, usu over a long period. 2 of a slope: not steep. ➤ **gradually** adv.

graduate¹ n the holder of a first academic degree.

graduate² v 1 to mark (e.g. an instrument or vessel) with degrees of measurement. 2 to receive an academic degree. 3 (*often* + to) to move up to a higher stage of proficiency or prestige. ➤ **graduation** n.

graffiti pl n unauthorized drawings or writing painted on a wall in a public place.

graft¹ v 1 to cause (a plant cutting) to unite with a growing plant. 2 to attach or add. 3 to implant (living tissue) surgically. ➤ **grafter** n.

graft² n 1 a grafted plant cutting. 2 a surgical operation in which living tissue is grafted. 3 the living tissue implanted. 4 the improper use of one's position to one's own advantage.

graft³ v Brit, informal to work hard.

graft⁴ n Brit, informal hard work.

Grail n the cup or platter used, according to medieval legend, by Christ at the Last Supper.

grain n 1 cereals or similar food plants. 2 the edible seeds of cereal plants. 3 a small hard particle, e.g. of sand or salt. 4 the least amount possible. 5 the arrangement of the fibres, particles, etc in wood, rock, fabric, etc. 6 a unit of weight equal to approximately 0.065 gram. ✳ **against the grain** contrary to one's disposition or feeling. ➤ **grainy** adj.

gram or **gramme** n a metric unit of mass equal to one thousandth of a kilogram (about 0.04oz).

grammar n 1 the study of the functions of words and their relations in sentences. 2 the characteristic system of inflections and syntax of a language. 3 a grammar textbook.

grammar school n Brit a usu selective secondary school providing an academic type of education.

grammatical adj 1 relating to grammar. 2 conforming to the rules of grammar. ➤ **grammatically** adv.

gramophone n Brit, dated a record player.

grampus n 1 a marine animal resembling a dolphin but with a bulbous head. 2 a killer whale.

gran n chiefly Brit, informal one's grandmother.

granary n (pl **-ies**) a storehouse for threshed grain.

granary bread n brown bread containing malted wheat grains.

grand¹ adj 1 large and striking in size or conception. 2 characterized by magnificence or opulence. 3 extremely dignified and proud. 4 having more importance than others; principal. 5 Brit, informal very good; wonderful. ➤ **grandly** adv.

grand² n informal a thousand pounds or dollars.

grandad or **granddad** n informal one's grandfather.

grandchild n a child of one's son or daughter.

granddaughter n a daughter of one's son or daughter.

grandee n 1 a Spanish or Portuguese nobleman. 2 any senior or high-ranking man.

grandeur n 1 the quality of being large or impressive. 2 personal greatness, dignity, or power.

grandfather n the father of one's father or mother.

grandiloquence n high-sounding or pompously eloquent speech or writing. ➤ **grandiloquent** adj

grandiose adj large-scale and intended to impress, but often overly ambitious or ostentatious.

grandma n informal one's grandmother.

grandmother n the mother of one's father or mother.

grandpa n informal one's grandfather.

grandparent n a parent of one's father or mother.

grand piano n a large piano with a horizontal frame and strings.

Grand Prix /,gronh 'pree/ n (pl **Grands Prix**) each of a series of world-championship motor races held in different countries.

grand slam n 1 the winning of all the major tournaments in a particular sport in a given year, or of all the games in a tournament. 2 in bridge, the winning of all 13 tricks by one player or side.

grandson n a son of one's son or daughter.

grandstand n the main stand at a racecourse or stadium, that gives the best view.

grand total n the final amount after lesser items have been added together.

grange n a large country house, often with many outbuildings.

granite n a very hard grey rock.

granny or **grannie** n (pl **-ies**) informal one's grandmother.

granny flat n Brit a part of a house converted into an independent dwelling to accommodate an elderly relative.

granny knot n a reef knot crossed the wrong way and therefore not secure.

grant[1] v 1 to consent to carry out (e.g. a wish or request). 2 to bestow or transfer (something, e.g. a title or property) formally. 3 to be willing to concede (something). ✻ **take for granted 1** to assume to be true, real, or certain to occur. 2 to value too lightly.

grant[2] n 1 an amount of money given by a government or other body for a particular purpose. 2 the act of granting.

granted adv admittedly.

granulated adj formed or crystallized into granules. ➤ **granulation** n.

granule n a small hard particle.

grape n a smooth-skinned juicy green or purple berry that grows in clusters on a grapevine, eaten as a fruit or fermented to produce wine.

grapefruit n a large round yellow citrus fruit with a somewhat acid juicy pulp.

grapeshot n ammunition for cannons, in the form of small iron balls shot in clusters.

grapevine n 1 a vine on which grapes grow. 2 (**the grapevine**) informal an unofficial means of circulating information or gossip.

graph n a diagram expressing a relation between quantities, typically a line joining points plotted relative to vertical and horizontal axes.

graphic or **graphical** adj 1 relating to drawing, pictures, or the pictorial arts. 2 marked by clear and vivid description; explicit. ➤ **graphically** adv.

graphic design n the art of combining text and illustration in the design of printed matter.

graphics pl n 1 designs (e.g. advertising posters) containing both typographical and pictorial elements. 2 the pictorial images on a computer screen. 3 the use of computers to create and manipulate images, e.g. in television and films.

graphite n a soft black form of carbon used in lead pencils, as a lubricant, and in lightweight sports equipment.

graphology n the study of handwriting, esp for character analysis. ➤ **graphologist** n.

graph paper n paper printed with small squares for drawing graphs and diagrams.

grapple v 1 (often + with) to engage in hand-to-hand fighting; to wrestle. 2 (+ with) to struggle to deal with.

grappling iron or **grappling hook** n a device like a small anchor with several radiating hooks, attached to a line and thrown to hook onto something.

grasp[1] v 1 to take hold of eagerly or firmly. 2 to take advantage of enthusiastically. 3 to succeed in understanding.

grasp[2] n 1 a firm hold. 2 the ability to seize or attain something. 3 ability to understand.

grasping adj eager for material possessions; greedy.

grass[1] n 1 vegetation in the form of low, spreading ground cover plants with slender green leaves. 2 an area covered in growing grass. 3 slang marijuana. 4 Brit, slang a police informer. ✻ **put/send out to grass** to cause to enter usu enforced retirement. ➤ **grassy** adj.

grass[2] v 1 to cover (an area) with grass. 2 Brit, slang (often + on/up) to inform on somebody to the police.

grasshopper n a plant-eating insect with hind legs that are adapted for leaping and produce a chirping noise when rubbed together.

grass roots *pl n* the ordinary members of society or an organization as opposed to the leadership.

grate[1] *n* **1** a frame of metal bars that holds the fuel in a fireplace or furnace. **2** = GRATING[1].

grate[2] *v* **1** to reduce (a hard food) to small particles by rubbing it on something rough. **2** to rub or rasp noisily. **3** to cause irritation; to jar.

grateful *adj* feeling or expressing thanks. ➤ **gratefully** *adv*.

grater *n* a tool with sharp-edged holes, used for grating food.

gratify *v* (**-ies, -ied**) **1** to give pleasure or satisfaction to. **2** to satisfy (an urge, whim, etc). ➤ **gratification** *n*.

grating[1] *n* a framework of parallel bars, e.g. covering a window.

grating[2] *adj* of sounds: annoyingly harsh; rasping.

gratis /'gratis, 'grah-/ *adv and adj* without charge; free.

gratitude *n* the state or feeling of being grateful; thankfulness.

gratuitous *adj* not called for by the circumstances; unwarranted. ➤ **gratuitously** *adv*.

gratuity *n* (*pl* **-ies**) a small sum of money given in return for a service; a tip.

grave[1] *n* **1** a pit excavated for the burial of a body. **2** (**the grave**) *literary* death.

grave[2] *adj* **1** serious; important. **2** causing concern. **3** solemn and dignified. ➤ **gravely** *adv*.

grave[3] *or* **grave accent** /grahv/ *n* a mark (`) placed over a vowel in some languages to show that it is pronounced in a particular way.

gravel *n* loose fragments of rock or small stones, used to surface roads and paths.

gravelly *adj* **1** like or covered with gravel. **2** harsh-sounding; grating.

graven image *n* an idol carved from wood or stone.

gravestone *n* a usu inscribed stone over or at one end of a grave.

graveyard *n* an area of ground used for burials.

gravitas /'gravitas/ *n* a solemn and serious manner.

gravitate *v* to move gradually and steadily.

gravitation *n* movement caused by gravity. ➤ **gravitational** *adj*.

gravity *n* **1** the force that attracts objects towards the earth, or towards any body that has mass. **2** dignity or solemnity of bearing. **3** seriousness.

gravy *n* the fat and juices from cooked meat, thickened and seasoned and used as a sauce.

gravy boat *n* a small boat-shaped vessel used for pouring gravy.

gray *adj, n, and v* NAmer = GREY[1], GREY[2], and GREY[3].

graze[1] *v* **1** of animals: to feed on growing grass and other green plants. **2** *informal* to eat snacks frequently, instead of eating meals at regular times.

graze[2] *v* **1** to scrape or scratch (*esp* the skin), usu by glancing contact. **2** to touch lightly in passing.

graze[3] *n* an abrasion, *esp* of the skin, made by a scraping along a surface.

grazing *n* vegetation or land for animals to feed on.

grease[1] *n* **1** a thick oily substance, *esp* one used as a lubricant. **2** animal fat used or produced in cooking.

grease[2] *v* to smear or lubricate with grease. ✱ **grease somebody's palm** to bribe somebody.

greasepaint *n* theatrical make-up.

greaseproof paper *n* paper resistant to grease, oil, etc, used for wrapping food.

greasy *adj* (**-ier, -iest**) **1** smeared with or containing grease. **2** oily in texture. **3** insincerely polite or fawning.

greasy spoon *n informal* a café serving cheap, mainly fried food.

great *adj* **1** above the norm in size, number, amount or degree. **2** significant; momentous. **3** eminent or distinguished. **4** aristocratic or grand. **5** (*chiefly in combination*) one stage further removed in family relationship: *great-grandfather; great-aunt.* **6** remarkably skilled: *a great organizer.* **7** enthusiastic: *a great fan.* **8** *informal* used as a generalized term of approval. ➤ **greatness** *n*.

greatcoat *n* a heavy overcoat.

Great Dane *n* a very large, long-legged dog of a smooth-coated breed.

greater *adj* (*often* **Greater**) consisting of a central city together with adjacent, geographically or administratively connected areas.

grebe *n* a diving bird with lobed rather than webbed toes.

Grecian *adj* relating to ancient Greece.

greed *n* **1** excessive desire for food. **2** excessive desire to acquire or possess things.

greedy *adj* (**-ier, -iest**) having an excessive desire or need for something, *esp* food. ➤ **greedily** *adv*.

Greek *n* **1** a native or inhabitant of Greece. **2** the language of the people of ancient or modern Greece. ➤ **Greek** *adj*.

green[1] *adj* **1** of the colour of grass, between blue and yellow. **2** covered by grass or other vegetation. **3** of a person: inexperienced or naive. **4** beneficial to the natural environment. **5** (*often* Green) concerned about environmental issues.

green[2] *n* **1** a green colour. **2** (*in pl*) green vegetables. **3** an area of open grass for public use. **4** a smooth area of grass for a special purpose, *esp* bowling or putting. **5** (*often* Green) a member or supporter of an environmentalist party or group.

green belt *n* an area of parks, farmland, etc encircling an urban area and usu subject to restrictions on new building.

green card *n* a permit allowing a foreign person to settle permanently and work in the USA.

greenery *n* green foliage or plants.

green-eyed monster *n* jealousy.

greenfield *adj* consisting of land not previously built on.

greenfinch *n* a common European finch with green and yellow plumage.

green fingers *pl n* an unusual ability to make plants grow.

greenfly *n* (*pl* **greenflies** *or* **greenfly**) *Brit* a green aphid that is destructive to plants.

greengage *n* a small greenish cultivated plum.

greengrocer *n* chiefly *Brit* a retailer of fresh vegetables and fruit.

greenhouse *n* a building with walls and roof of glass, for the cultivation or protection of plants.

greenhouse effect *n* the warming of the atmosphere that occurs when solar radiation reflected from the earth cannot escape because of a build-up of carbon dioxide and other pollutants in the air.

greenhouse gas *n* a gas, *esp* carbon dioxide or methane, that contributes to the greenhouse effect.

green light *n* authority or permission to undertake a project.

green pepper *n* a green unripe fruit of the sweet pepper plant, eaten as a vegetable.

greet *v* 1 to acknowledge the presence or arrival of with gestures or words. 2 to react to in a specified manner.

greeting *n* 1 a phrase or gesture expressing welcome or recognition. 2 (*usu in pl*) an expression of good wishes; regards.

gregarious *adj* 1 of people: having a liking for companionship; sociable. 2 of animals: tending to associate with others of the same kind.

Gregorian chant *n* a type of unaccompanied liturgical chant developed in the early Middle Ages.

gremlin *n* a mischievous creature said to cause the unexplained malfunctioning of machinery or equipment.

grenade *n* a small bomb that is thrown by hand or fired from a launcher.

grenadier *n* 1 a soldier formerly specially trained in the use of grenades. 2 (*often* **Grenadier**) in Britain, a member of the Grenadier Guards, the first regiment of the royal household infantry.

grew *v* past tense of GROW.

grey¹ (*NAmer* **gray**) *adj* 1 of a colour between black and white, like that of ash or a rain cloud. 2 lacking sunshine or brightness; dull. 3 of hair: turning white with age. 4 without colour or character; nondescript.

grey² (*NAmer* **gray**) *n* 1 a grey colour. 2 a horse with white hair but dark skin.

grey³ (*NAmer* **gray**) *v* to make or become grey.

grey area *n* a subject or situation that is imprecisely defined or difficult to categorize.

greyhound *n* a dog of a tall slender smooth-coated breed, used for racing.

grey matter *n* informal brains or intellect.

grid *n* 1 a framework of parallel or intersecting metal bars covering an opening; a grating. 2 a network of uniformly spaced intersecting horizontal and perpendicular lines, e.g. for locating points on a map. 3 a network of cables for the distribution of electricity.

griddle *n* a flat metal plate on which food is cooked by dry heat.

gridiron *n* a framework of metal bars on which food is placed to be cooked; a grill.

gridlock *n* a severe traffic jam affecting a whole area. ➤ **gridlocked** *adj*.

grief *n* 1 deep distress, *esp* caused by bereavement. 2 *informal* trouble of any kind. ✳ **come to grief** to end badly; to fail.

grievance *n* a cause of dissatisfaction, constituting grounds for complaint.

grieve *v* 1 (*often* + for) to feel or express grief. 2 to cause to suffer grief; to distress.

grievous *adj* 1 causing severe pain or sorrow. 2 very serious. ➤ **grievously** *adv*.

grievous bodily harm *n* serious physical harm done to a person in a criminal attack.

griffin *or* **griffon** *or* **gryphon** *n* a mythical animal with the head and wings of an eagle and the body and tail of a lion.

griffon *n* 1 see GRIFFIN. 2 a large vulture with brown plumage. 3 a small wire-haired terrier.

grill¹ *n* 1 a cooking utensil consisting of a set of parallel bars on which food is exposed to heat. 2 *Brit* an apparatus on a cooker under which food is cooked or browned. 3 a dish of grilled food. 4 see GRILLE.

grill² *v* 1 to cook (food) on or under a grill. 2 *informal* to subject to intense questioning.

grille *or* **grill** *n* a grating forming a barrier or screen; *esp* an ornamental metal one at the front end of a motor vehicle.

grim *adj* (**grimmer, grimmest**) 1 forbidding in disposition or appearance. 2 unyielding. 3 *informal* unpleasant; nasty. ➤ **grimly** *adv*.

grimace¹ *n* a distorted facial expression, usu of disgust, anger, or pain.

grimace² *v* to express pain, disapproval, or disgust by twisting one's face.

grime *n* dirt, *esp* when sticking to a surface. ➤ **grimy** *adj*.

grin¹ *v* (**grinned, grinning**) to smile broadly, usu showing the teeth. ✳ **grin and bear it** to put up with an unpleasant experience stoically.

grin² *n* a broad smile.

grind[1] v (*past tense and past part.* **ground**) **1** to reduce to powder or small fragments by crushing. **2** to polish, sharpen, or wear down by friction. **3** to rub, press, or twist harshly. **4** to move with friction, *esp* so as to make a grating noise. ➤ **grinder** n.

grind[2] n **1** dreary monotonous labour or routine. **2** an act of grinding.

grind down v to subject to domineering treatment.

grind out v *derog* to produce in a mechanical way.

grindstone n **1** a revolving stone or abrasive disc used for grinding, polishing, sharpening, etc. **2** a millstone.

grip[1] v (**gripped, gripping**) **1** to seize or hold firmly. **2** to attract and hold the interest of. **3** of an emotion: to take control of.

grip[2] n **1** a strong or tenacious grasp. **2** control, mastery, or power. **3** the ability to understand. **4** a part or device that grips. **5** a part by which something is grasped, *esp* a handle. **6** a travelling bag; a holdall. ✳ **come/get to grips with** to set about dealing with. **lose one's grip** to be unable any longer to deal with things effectively.

gripe[1] v **1** to cause to feel sharp intestinal pain. **2** *informal* to complain persistently.

gripe[2] n **1** (*usu in pl*) a stabbing spasmodic intestinal pain. **2** *informal* a grievance or complaint, *esp* a trivial or unjustified one.

gripping adj very exciting and absorbing.

grisly adj (**-ier, -iest**) inspiring horror, fear, or disgust. ➤ **grisliness** n.

grist n grain for grinding. ✳ **grist to the mill** something that can be put to use or profit.

gristle n tough cartilaginous matter in cooked meat. ➤ **gristly** adj.

grit[1] n **1** small hard particles of stone or coarse sand. **2** (*also* **gritstone**) coarse sandstone. **3** *informal* firmness of mind or spirit; determination.

grit[2] v (**gritted, gritting**) **1** to cover or spread (*esp* an icy road surface) with grit. **2** to clench (one's teeth) as a sign of determination.

gritty adj (**-ier, -iest**) **1** courageously determined. **2** not flinching from unpleasantness; uncompromising. **3** resembling or containing grit. ➤ **grittily** adv.

grizzle v *Brit, dated, informal* of a child: to cry quietly and fretfully.

grizzled adj streaked with grey.

grizzly *or* **grizzly bear** n (*pl* **-ies**) a very large bear that has brownish fur streaked with white.

groan[1] v to utter a deep moan.

groan[2] n a deep moaning sound.

groat n a former British coin worth four old pence.

grocer n a dealer in staple foodstuffs and household supplies.

grocery n a grocer's shop or business.

grog n an alcoholic spirit, usu rum, mixed with water.

groggy adj (**-ier, -iest**) weak and dazed.

groin n **1** the area of the body between the lower abdomen and the inner part of the thigh. **2** *euphem* the genitals. **3** *chiefly NAmer* = GROYNE.

grommet n **1** an eyelet to strengthen an opening. **2** a small plastic tube inserted in the ear to drain off fluid.

groom[1] n **1** somebody who takes care of horses. **2** a bridegroom.

groom[2] v **1** to clean and care for (e.g. a horse or dog), *esp* by brushing its coat. **2** to make (oneself or one's appearance) neat or attractive. **3** to get (somebody) ready for a specific role, e.g. by training.

groove[1] n **1** a long narrow channel cut into wood, stone, etc. **2** the continuous spiral track on a gramophone record. **3** a fixed routine.

groove[2] v **1** to make a groove in. **2** *dated, informal* to dance to or perform popular music.

groovy adj (**-ier, -iest**) *dated, informal* fashionably attractive or exciting.

grope[1] v **1** to search about blindly, *esp* with the hands. **2** to fondle for sexual pleasure.

grope[2] n an act of groping.

gross[1] adj **1** glaringly noticeable or objectionable; flagrant. **2** constituting an overall total before deductions (e.g. for taxes) are made. **3** of weight: including both the object in question and any incidentals, e.g. packaging or load. **4** coarse or vulgar. **5** *informal* disgustingly unpleasant; repulsive. **6** big or bulky, *esp* excessively overweight. ➤ **grossly** adv.

gross[2] n an overall total before deductions.

gross[3] v **1** to earn or bring in (an overall total) before deductions. **2** *informal* (+ out) to disgust or repel.

gross[4] n (*pl* **gross**) a group of twelve dozen (144) things.

grotesque[1] adj **1** amusingly or repellently ugly in appearance. **2** absurdly incongruous or inappropriate. ➤ **grotesquely** adv.

grotesque[2] n a grotesque person or thing.

grotto n (*pl* **-oes** *or* **-os**) a small natural or artificial cave.

grotty adj (**-ier, -iest**) *Brit, informal* **1** unpleasant. **2** of poor quality. **3** unwell.

grouch n **1** a bad-tempered complaint. **2** an irritable or complaining person. ➤ **grouchy** adj.

ground[1] n **1** the solid surface of the earth. **2** soil or earth. **3** an area of land used for a particular purpose. **4** (*in pl*) the area around and belonging to a large building. **5** (*also in pl*) a basis for belief, action, or argument. ✳ **gain ground** to become more widely accepted. **give ground** to retreat. **go to ground** to go into hiding. **off the ground** started and in progress.

ground[2] v **1** (*often* **be grounded in/on**) to provide a reason or justification for. **2** to forbid (a pilot or aircraft) to fly. **3** *informal* to give (a child) the punishment of having to stay at home. **4** of a ship: to run aground.

ground[3] *v* past tense and past part. of GRIND[1].

ground-breaking *adj* introducing entirely new methods; pioneering.

ground control *n* the equipment and operators that control aircraft from the ground.

ground floor *n* the floor of a house on a level with the ground.

ground frost *n* a temperature below freezing on the ground.

grounding *n* fundamental training in a field of knowledge.

groundless *adj* having no basis in fact or reason; unjustified.

groundnut *n chiefly Brit* = PEANUT.

ground rent *n* the rent paid by the owner of a building to the owner of the land that it is built on.

ground rule *n* a basic rule of procedure.

groundsel *n* a common weed with small yellow flower heads.

groundsheet *n* a waterproof sheet placed on the ground (e.g. in a tent).

groundsman *n* (*pl* **groundsmen**) somebody who tends a playing field.

groundswell *n* **1** a heavy sea swell caused by an often distant gale or ground tremor. **2** a spontaneous build-up of public opinion.

groundwork *n* work done to provide a foundation or basis.

group[1] *n* **1** a number of people or things gathered together or forming a single unit. **2** a small band of musicians, *esp* playing pop music.

group[2] *v* to form or combine in a group.

groupie *n* an ardent fan, *esp* one who follows a famous person, e.g. a rock star, on tour.

grouse[1] *n* (*pl* **grouse**) a game bird with a plump body.

grouse[2] *v informal* to complain, *esp* annoyingly or without reason.

grouse[3] *n informal* a complaint.

grout[1] *n* (*also* **grouting**) a thin mortar used for filling spaces, *esp* the gaps between tiles.

grout[2] *v* to fill up the spaces between (tiles) with grout.

grove *n* a small wood or group of trees.

grovel *v* (**grovelled, grovelling,** *NAmer* **groveled, groveling**) **1** to lie or creep on the ground *esp* to show subservience. **2** to abase oneself in order to earn forgiveness or favour.

grow *v* (**grew, grown**) **1** of an organism: to increase in size and develop to maturity. **2** to increase or expand. **3** to become gradually. **4** to cause (a plant, fruit, or vegetables, etc) to grow; to cultivate. ➤ **grower** *n*.

growl *v* **1** to utter a deep sound in the throat that expresses hostility. **2** to speak in an angry or hostile way. **3** to make a continuous low sound. ➤ **growl** *n*.

grown-up[1] *adj* fully mature; adult.

grown-up[2] *n* an adult.

grow on *v* to become gradually more pleasing to.

grow out of *v* **1** to become too big to fit (a piece of clothing). **2** to become too mature to get enjoyment from.

growth *n* **1** the process of growing. **2** an increase or expansion. **3** something that grows or has grown. **4** a tumour.

grow up *v* of a person: to become mature.

groyne (*NAmer* **groin**) *n* a wall-like structure built out from a shore, *esp* to check erosion of the beach.

grub[1] *v* (**grubbed, grubbing**) **1** to dig in the ground. **2** (*usu* + up) to dig up or out.

grub[2] *n* **1** a wormlike larva of an insect. **2** *informal* food.

grubby *adj* (**-ier, -iest**) **1** dirty; grimy. **2** disreputable or sordid.

grudge[1] *v* **1** to be unwilling to give or admit. **2** to feel resentful towards (somebody) who has something one envies.

grudge[2] *n* a feeling of deep-seated resentment or ill will.

grudging *adj* offered or given only unwillingly. ➤ **grudgingly** *adv*.

gruel *n* thin porridge.

gruelling (*NAmer* **grueling**) *adj* extremely taxing or demanding.

gruesome *adj* inspiring horror or repulsion; ghastly.

gruff *adj* **1** brusque or stern in manner or speech. **2** deep and harsh. ➤ **gruffly** *adv*.

grumble[1] *v* **1** to mutter discontentedly or in complaint. **2** to rumble.

grumble[2] *n* a complaint or cause of complaint.

grumpy *adj* (**-ier, -iest**) moodily cross; surly. ➤ **grumpily** *adv*.

grunge *n* **1** *informal* dirt. **2** a style of rock music featuring markedly discordant guitar sound. ➤ **grungy** *adj*.

grunt[1] *v* **1** to utter the deep short guttural sound of a pig. **2** to utter a similar sound, e.g. in reluctant agreement or during strenuous exertion.

grunt[2] *n* a grunting sound.

gryphon *n* see GRIFFIN.

G-string *n* a small piece of cloth, leather, etc covering the genitals and held in place by thongs etc passed round the hips and between the buttocks.

guano *n* the excrement of seabirds used as a fertilizer.

guarantee[1] *n* **1** an assurance of the quality of a product, work, etc, accompanied by a promise of replacement or compensation if it proves defective. **2** (*also* **guaranty**) an agreement by which one person accepts responsibility for another's obligations, *esp* debts, in case of default. **3** an assurance that something will happen.

guarantee² *v* (**guaranteed, guaranteeing**) **1** to provide a guarantee of replacement or repayment with respect to (a product, work, etc). **2** to give an assurance relating to. **3** to undertake to answer for the debt or default of.

Usage Note: Note the spelling with *-ua-*.

guarantor *n* somebody who makes or gives a guarantee.

guard¹ *n* **1** the duty of protecting or defending or of preventing escape. **2** a person or group who performs this duty. **3** a protective or safety device, e.g. on a machine to prevent injury. **4** a state of readiness to deal with adverse events; vigilance: *They caught me off guard.* **5** *Brit* the person in charge of the carriages, passengers, etc in a railway train.

guard² *v* **1** to protect from danger. **2** to watch over so as to prevent escape, entry, etc. ✳ **guard against** to attempt to prevent by taking precautions.

guarded *adj* marked by caution.

guardian *n* **1** somebody that guards or protects. **2** somebody entrusted by law with the care of a person who is of unsound mind, not of age, etc. ➤ **guardianship** *n*.

guardian angel *n* an angel who is thought to watch over a particular person.

guava /'gwahva/ *n* a tropical fruit with pink aromatic flesh.

gudgeon¹ *n* **1** a pivot or spindle. **2** the socket into which the pins of a hinge fit. **3** a socket into which the rudder of a boat fits. **4** a pin that holds two blocks together.

gudgeon² *n* (*pl* **gudgeons** *or* **gudgeon**) a small European freshwater fish.

guerrilla *or* **guerilla** *n* a member of a small independent fighting force which engages in sabotage, unexpected assaults, etc.

guess¹ *v* **1** to estimate or judge without sufficient knowledge or information for an accurate assessment. **2** to arrive at a correct conclusion about by conjecture, chance, or intuition.

guess² *n* an opinion or estimate arrived at by guessing.

guesswork *n* the act of guessing, or a judgment based on a guess.

guest *n* **1** a person entertained in another's home or at another's expense. **2** a person who pays to stay at a hotel, etc. **3** somebody who is present or takes part, e.g. in a show, by invitation.

guesthouse *n* a private house used to accommodate paying guests.

guffaw¹ *n* a loud or boisterous laugh.

guffaw² *v* to laugh loudly or boisterously.

guidance *n* advice or instructions on how to do something.

guide¹ *n* **1** somebody who leads, directs, or advises others. **2** a book providing information about a place, activity, etc. **3** a principle that directs somebody's conduct. **4** a device or mark for directing the motion of something. **5** (**Guide**) *chiefly Brit* a member of a worldwide movement of girls founded with the aim of forming character and teaching good citizenship.

guide² *v* **1** to lead or direct along a route or to a place. **2** to control and direct the movement of, e.g. a missile. **3** to give advice or instructions to regarding behaviour, an appropriate course of action, etc.

guidebook *n* a book of information for travellers.

guide dog *n* a dog trained to lead a blind person.

guideline *n* a recommendation as to policy or conduct.

guild *n* **1** an association of people with similar interests or pursuits. **2** a medieval association of merchants or craftsmen.

guilder *n* (*pl* **guilders** *or* **guilder**) the basic monetary unit of the Netherlands before the euro.

guildhall *n* **1** a hall where a guild or corporation meets. **2** in some British towns, the town hall.

guile *n* deceitful cunning.

guillemot /'gilimot/ *n* (*pl* **guillemots** *or* **guillemot**) a sea bird with black-and-white plumage.

guillotine¹ /'gilateen/ *n* **1** a machine for beheading with a heavy blade that slides down between grooved posts. **2** an instrument (e.g. a paper cutter) that works like a guillotine.

guillotine² *v* to behead with a guillotine.

guilt *n* **1** the fact of having committed an offence, *esp* a crime. **2** a feeling of being at fault or to blame. ➤ **guiltless** *adj*.

guilty *adj* (**-ier, -iest**) **1** responsible for an offence or wrongdoing. **2** found to have committed a crime by a judge, jury, etc after a trial. **3** suggesting guilt. **4** feeling guilt. ➤ **guiltily** *adv*.

guinea *n* a former British gold coin worth 21 shillings.

guinea fowl *n* a large African game bird with white-speckled slate-coloured plumage.

guinea pig *n* **1** a tailless South American rodent often kept as a pet. **2** somebody or something used as a subject of research or experimentation.

guise *n* **1** assumed appearance. **2** external appearance.

guitar *n* a stringed musical instrument played by plucking. ➤ **guitarist** *n*.

gulch *n* *chiefly NAmer* a ravine.

gulf *n* **1** a partially landlocked part of the sea, usu larger than a bay. **2** a deep chasm. **3** an unbridgeable gap e.g. between the attitudes or opinions of different people.

gull[1] n a sea bird with long wings, webbed feet, and largely white, grey, or black plumage.

gull[2] v dated to trick or deceive.

gull[3] n archaic a person who is easily tricked or deceived.

gullet n the oesophagus or throat.

gullible adj easily tricked or deceived. ➤ **gullibility** n.

gully or **gulley** n (pl **-ies** or **-eys**) **1** a trench worn in the earth by running water. **2** a deep gutter or drain.

gulp[1] v **1** (often + down) to swallow hurriedly or greedily. **2** to make a sudden swallowing movement as if surprised or nervous.

gulp[2] n **1** a swallowing sound or action. **2** the amount swallowed in a gulp.

gum[1] n the tissue that surrounds the teeth.

gum[2] n **1** a plant substance that is sticky when moist but hardens on drying. **2** a soft glue used for sticking paper and other lightweight materials. **3** informal chewing gum.

gum[3] v (**gummed, gumming**) to stick with gum.

gumboot n a waterproof rubber boot reaching usu to the knee.

gumdrop n a hard jellylike sweet.

gummy[1] adj (**-ier, -iest**) viscous or sticky.

gummy[2] adj (**-ier, -iest**) with no teeth.

gumption n the intelligence and courage to take action; initiative.

gun[1] n **1** a weapon that discharges a bullet or shell through a metal tube. **2** a device that releases a controlled amount of something, e.g. grease or glue. ✳ **jump the gun** to move or act before the proper time. **stick to one's guns** to refuse to change one's intentions or opinion in spite of opposition.

gun[2] v (**gunned, gunning**) ✳ **be gunning for** to be intent on criticizing, punishing, or killing.

gunboat n a heavily armed ship of shallow draught.

gundog n a dog trained to locate or retrieve game for hunters.

gun down v to kill (somebody) by shooting them, usu in cold blood.

gunge n Brit, informal an unpleasant, dirty, or sticky substance.

gung ho adj excessively enthusiastic, esp for fighting or warfare.

gunk n informal any unpleasant, dirty, or sticky substance; gunge.

gunman n (pl **gunmen**) a man armed with a gun, esp a professional killer.

gunmetal n **1** a greyish form of bronze. **2** a bluish grey colour.

gunnel n see GUNWALE.

gunner n a soldier who operates a gun, esp a private in the Royal Artillery.

gunnery n the science of the effective use of guns.

gunpoint ✳ **at gunpoint** while threatening somebody, or being threatened, with a gun.

gunpowder n an explosive mixture of potassium nitrate, charcoal, and sulphur.

gunrunner n somebody who imports or deals in contraband arms and ammunition. ➤ **gunrunning** n.

gunship n a heavily armed helicopter.

gunwale or **gunnel** n the upper edge of a ship's or boat's side.

guppy n (pl **guppies** or **guppy**) a small fish native to the West Indies and South America.

gurgle v to make a low-pitched bubbling sound. ➤ **gurgle** n.

Gurkha n a soldier of Nepalese origin serving in the British or Indian army.

gurn v see GIRN.

guru n (pl **gurus**) **1** a Hindu or Sikh religious teacher and spiritual guide. **2** a mentor. **3** informal an acknowledged leader or expert in a field.

gush[1] v **1** to flow out or emit copiously or violently. **2** to make an effusive display of sentiment or enthusiasm. ➤ **gushing** adj.

gush[2] n a sudden outpouring.

gushy adj (**-ier, -iest**) marked by effusive often affected sentiment or enthusiasm.

gusset n a piece of material inserted in a seam (e.g. the crotch of an undergarment) to provide reinforcement or allow for movement.

gust[1] n **1** a sudden brief rush of wind. **2** a sudden outburst. ➤ **gusty** adj.

gust[2] v to blow in gusts.

gusto n enthusiastic and vigorous enjoyment or vitality.

gut[1] n **1** (also in pl) the belly or abdomen. **2** (often in pl) the intestine. **3** (often used before a noun) the part of a person that responds emotionally or instinctively: a gut feeling. **4** informal (in pl) the inner essential parts. **5** informal (in pl) courage or determination. ✳ **hate somebody's guts** informal to hate somebody with great intensity.

gut[2] v (**gutted, gutting**) **1** to remove the intestines of (esp an animal). **2** to destroy the inside of (esp a building).

gutless adj informal lacking courage; cowardly.

gutsy adj (**-ier, -iest**) informal courageous.

gutted adj Brit, informal deeply disappointed or disheartened.

gutter[1] n **1** a trough just below the eaves of a roof or at the side of a street to carry off water. **2** (**the gutter**) the lowest level or condition of human life.

gutter[2] v of a flame: to burn fitfully or feebly.

guttering n the gutters on the roof of a building.

guttersnipe n dated a deprived and ill-bred child living in poverty.

guttural adj of a sound: pronounced in the throat.

guy¹ *n* a rope, chain, etc used to secure something (e.g. a tent).

guy² *v* to secure with guys.

guy³ *n* **1** *informal* a man. **2** *informal* (*in pl*) people of either sex. **3** a humorous effigy of a man burned in Britain on 5 November.

guy⁴ *v dated* to make fun of; to ridicule.

guzzle *v* to consume greedily.

gym *n* **1** a gymnasium. **2** gymnastics.

gymkhana *n* a local sporting event featuring competitions and displays relating to horse riding.

gymnasium *n* (*pl* **gymnasiums** *or* **gymnasia**) a large room or separate building used for indoor sports and gymnastic activities.

gymnast *n* somebody trained in gymnastics.

gymnastics *pl n* (*treated as sing.*) physical exercises to develop bodily strength and coordination. ➤ **gymnastic** *adj*.

gymslip *n chiefly Brit* a girl's tunic or pinafore dress worn, *esp* formerly, as part of a school uniform.

gynaecology (*NAmer* **gynecology**) /gienə'kolǝji/ *n* a branch of medicine that deals with diseases and disorders of women, *esp* of the female reproductive system. ➤ **gynaecological** *adj*, **gynaecologist** *n*.

gypsum *n* hydrated calcium sulphate occurring as a mineral and used *esp* in plaster of Paris.

gypsy *or* **gipsy** *n* (*pl* **-ies**) a member of the Romany people, who retain an itinerant lifestyle in modern societies.

gyrate *v* **1** to move with a circular or spiral motion. **2** to dance wildly or erotically. ➤ **gyration** *n*.

gyroscope *n* a device containing a wheel that is mounted to spin rapidly about an axis and is free to turn in any direction so that it maintains the same orientation.

H[1] or **h** *n* (*pl* **H's** *or* **Hs** *or* **h's**) the eighth letter of the English alphabet.

H[2] *abbr* the chemical symbol for hydrogen.

h *abbr* hour.

Ha *abbr* the chemical symbol for hahnium.

ha *abbr* hectare.

habeas corpus /ˌhaybi·əsˈkawpəs/ *n* a legal order requiring a detained person to be brought before a court.

haberdashery *n* (*pl* -**ies**) **1** articles used in sewing and dressmaking. **2** a shop selling these.

habit *n* **1** something a person does regularly. **2** an addiction to a drug. **3** a long dress-like garment worn by a monk or nun.

habitable *adj* suitable for living in.

habitat *n* the place where a plant or animal naturally grows or lives.

habitation *n* **1** the inhabiting of a place. **2** *formal* a residence or home.

habitual *adj* **1** done or doing something as a habit. **2** in accordance with habit; customary. ➤ **habitually** *adv*.

habituate *v* (+ to) to make or become used to something.

habitué /həˈbityooay/ *n* a person who frequents a place.

hacienda /hasiˈendə/ *n* in a Spanish-speaking country, a large house and estate.

hack[1] *v* **1** to cut with repeated rough blows. **2** to gain unauthorized access to a computer system. * **hacking cough** a hard dry cough. ➤ **hacker** *n*.

hack[2] *n* a rough hacking blow.

hack[3] *n* **1** a journalist or other writer who turns out a lot of mediocre work. **2** a riding horse let out for hire.

hack[4] *adj* hackneyed or trite.

hack[5] *v* to ride a horse at an ordinary pace, *esp* over roads. ➤ **hacker** *n*.

hackles *pl n* the hairs along the neck and back of an animal, which rise when it is roused.

hackney carriage *n esp* a taxi.

hackneyed *adj* of a phrase: overused and lacking originality.

hacksaw *n* a fine-toothed saw for cutting metal.

had *v* past tense and past part. of HAVE.

haddock *n* (*pl* **haddocks** *or* **haddock**) a silver-grey sea fish used for food.

hadn't *contraction* had not.

haematology (*NAmer* **hematology**) *n* the study of diseases of the blood. ➤ **haematologist** *n*.

haemoglobin (*NAmer* **hemoglobin**) *n* a protein of red blood cells that carries oxygen from the lungs to the body tissues.

haemophilia (*NAmer* **hemophilia**) *n* a disorder involving delayed clotting of the blood, causing difficulty in controlling bleeding. ➤ **haemophiliac** *n* and *adj*.

haemorrhage[1] (*NAmer* **hemorrhage**) *n* a loss of blood from a burst blood vessel.

haemorrhage[2] (*NAmer* **hemorrhage**) *v* to undergo a haemorrhage.

haemorrhoid (*NAmer* **hemorrhoid**) *n* (*usu in pl*) a mass of swollen veins round the anus.

haft *n* the handle of a weapon or tool.

hag *n* an ugly or ill-natured old woman. ➤ **haggish** *adj*.

haggard *adj* having a worn or gaunt appearance, *esp* from tiredness.

haggis *n* (*pl* **haggis** *or* **haggises**) a Scottish dish of minced sheep's or calf's offal mixed with suet, oatmeal, and seasonings, and boiled in the stomach of the animal or in a substitute bag.

haggle *v* to bargain or wrangle. ➤ **haggler** *n*.

hagiography *n* (*pl* -**ies**) **1** biography of saints or venerated people. **2** an idealizing biography.

ha-ha *n* a fence sunk into a ditch, forming a boundary to grounds without uninterrupting the view.

haiku /ˈhiekooh/ *n* (*pl* **haiku** *or* **haikus**) a Japanese poem of three lines containing five, seven, and five syllables.

hail[1] *n* **1** a fall of small particles of clear ice or compacted snow. **2** a large number of things coming at once.

hail[2] *v* to fall as hail.

hail[3] *v* **1** to salute or greet. **2** to greet with approval; to acclaim. **3** to summon (a taxi) by calling. * **hail from** to live in or come from (a place).

hailstone *n* a pellet of hail.

hair *n* **1** a slender threadlike strand growing from the skin of an animal. **2** a structure resembling a hair, e.g. on a plant. **3** a coating of hairs on the human head or an animal's body. * **let one's hair down** to relax and enjoy oneself.

not turn a hair to remain completely unmoved. ➤ **hairless** adj.

haircut n **1** the cutting and shaping of the hair. **2** the style in which hair is cut.

hairdo n (pl -os) informal a person's hairstyle.

hairdresser n a person who cuts and styles people's hair. ➤ **hairdressing** n.

hairdryer or **hairdrier** n an electrical device for drying the hair with warm air.

hairgrip n Brit a flat hairpin.

hairline n **1** the line formed by the edge of a person's hair. **2** of a crack: very thin.

hairnet n a loosely woven net worn over the hair to keep it in place.

hairpiece n a piece of false hair worn to fill a gap in a person's natural hair.

hairpin n a two-pronged pin of thin wire for holding the hair in place.

hairpin bend n a sharp U-shaped bend in a road.

hair-raising adj causing great fear or alarm.

hair shirt n a shirt of coarse cloth formerly worn next to the skin as a penance.

hairspray n a substance sprayed on the hair to hold it in place.

hairspring n a slender spiral spring regulating the balance wheel of a watch.

hairstyle n a way in which the hair is cut or arranged. ➤ **hairstylist** n.

hair trigger n a trigger adjusted so that very slight pressure will release it.

hairy adj (-ier, -iest) **1** covered with hair or material like hair. **2** informal alarmingly difficult or dangerous.

hake n a large seafish related to the cod.

halal or **hallal** /hə'lahl/ adj of meat: prepared according to Islamic law.

halberd n a former weapon combining a spear and battle-axe. ➤ **halberdier** n.

halcyon adj denoting an idyllic past time.

hale adj of a person: sound and healthy.

half[1] n (pl **halves**) **1** either of two equal parts into which something can be divided. **2** Brit, informal half a pint of beer. **3** informal a half-price fare or ticket. ✻ **go halves** informal to pay half each.

half[2] adj amounting to half, or one of two equal parts.

half[3] adv **1** in an equal part or degree. **2** to the extent of a half. **3** incompletely or almost. ✻ **half a chance** informal the slightest opportunity. **half past** thirty minutes past (an hour). **not half** informal very much so.

half-and-half adj and adv half one thing and half another.

halfback n a player in rugby, football, hockey, etc positioned immediately behind the forward line.

half-baked adj badly thought out or planned.

half-board n Brit provision of bed, breakfast, and an evening meal.

half brother n a brother related through one parent only.

half-caste n offensive a person with parents of different races.

half-cocked adj lacking adequate preparation or forethought.

half crown n a former British coin worth two shillings and sixpence (12.5p).

half-dozen or **half a dozen** n a set of six.

halfhearted adj lacking enthusiasm or effort. ➤ **halfheartedly** adv.

half hour n a period of thirty minutes. ➤ **half-hourly** adv and adj.

half-life n the time required for half of the atoms of a radioactive substance to become disintegrated.

half measures pl n an inadequate line of action.

half nelson n a wrestling hold in which one arm is thrust under the arm of an opponent and the hand placed on the back of their neck.

halfpenny or **ha'penny** /'haypni/ n (pl **halfpennies** or **halfpence** or **ha'pennies**) a former British coin worth one half of an old penny.

half sister n a sister related through one parent only.

half term n Brit a short holiday halfway through a school term.

half-timbered adj built of a timber framework filled in with brickwork or plaster.

halftime n a pause between the two halves of a game or contest.

halfway adj and adv **1** midway between two points. **2** in the least; minimally.

half-wit n informal a foolish or stupid person. ➤ **half-witted** adj.

halibut n (pl **halibut**) a large flatfish used for food.

halitosis n abnormally bad-smelling breath.

hall n **1** the entrance room or passage of a building. **2** a large room for public assembly or entertainment. **3** (also **hall of residence**) a residential building for students of a college or university. **4** Brit the manor house of a landed proprietor.

hallelujah or **alleluia** interj used to express praise or joy.

hallmark[1] n **1** an official mark stamped on gold and silver articles to show their purity. **2** a distinguishing characteristic.

hallmark[2] v to stamp with a hallmark.

hallo interj = HELLO.

hallowed adj **1** made sacred. **2** greatly respected.

Halloween or **Hallowe'en** n 31 October, the eve of All Saints' Day.

hallucinate v to have hallucinations. ➤ **hallucinator** n.

hallucination n the perception of something apparently real but having no objective reality. ➤ **hallucinatory** adj.

hallucinogen *n* a substance that induces hallucinations. ➤ **hallucinogenic** *adj*.

halo *n* (*pl* -**oes** *or* -**os**) **1** in art, a circle of light surrounding the head of a holy person. **2** a circle of light round the sun or moon.

halogen *n* any of the elements fluorine, chlorine, bromine, iodine, and astatine.

halt[1] *v* to come or bring to a stop.

halt[2] *n* **1** a stop or interruption. **2** *Brit* a minor stopping place on a railway. ✻ **call a halt** to demand a stop to an activity.

halter *n* a rope or strap for leading or tying an animal.

halter neck *n* a neckline on a woman's dress formed by a strap passing from the front of it round the neck.

halting *adj* hesitant or faltering.

halve *v* **1** to divide into two equal parts. **2** to reduce (an amount) to a half.

halyard *or* **halliard** *n* a rope or tackle for hoisting or lowering a sail or flag.

ham[1] *n* **1** meat from the rear thigh of a pig, cured with salt. **2** (*usu in pl*) a buttock with its associated thigh.

ham[2] *n* **1** a showy or clumsy performer or actor. **2** an amateur radio operator.

ham[3] *v* (**hammed, hamming**) *informal* to overact.

hamburger *n* a round flat cake of minced beef, fried or grilled and usu served in a bread roll.

ham-fisted *adj informal* clumsy with the hands.

hamlet *n* a small village.

hammer[1] *n* **1** a hand tool with a heavy solid head, used for driving in nails. **2** a lever with a striking head for ringing a bell or striking a gong. **3** the part of the mechanism of a modern gun whose action ignites the cartridge. **4** an auctioneer's mallet. **5** a heavy metal ball attached to a flexible wire to a handle and thrown as an athletic contest. ✻ **hammer and tongs** with great energy.

hammer[2] *v* **1** to beat or drive with a hammer. **2** (+ into) to make (somebody) learn or remember something by repetition. **3** *informal* to defeat decisively.

hammer away *v* **1** to work hard and persistently. **2** (+ at) to go on repeating an opinion or attitude.

hammerhead *n* a shark with projections on each side of a flattened head.

hammer out *v* to produce or bring about through lengthy discussion.

hammock *n* a strip of netting or canvas suspended by cords at each end and used to lie on.

hammy *adj* (-**ier, -iest**) *informal* characterized by clumsy overacting.

hamper[1] *v* to restrict the movement or progress of.

hamper[2] *n* **1** a large basket with a cover for packing, storing, or transporting food, etc. **2** a

selection of festive fare contained in a hamper, presented as a gift.

hamster *n* a small rodent with large cheek pouches.

hamstring[1] *n* any of the five tendons at the back of the knee.

hamstring[2] *v* (*past tense and past part.* **hamstrung**) **1** to cripple by cutting the leg tendons. **2** to restrict severely.

hand[1] *n* **1** the end of the arm beyond the wrist. **2** an indicator or pointer on a dial. **3** (*in pl*) possession. **4** (*in pl*) control or supervision. **5** a pledge of betrothal or marriage. **6** handwriting. **7** a unit of measure for a horse's height, equal to about 102mm (4in.). **8** a round of applause. **9** assistance or aid. **10** the cards or pieces held by a player in a game. **11** a person employed to work. ✻ **at hand** near in time or place. **by hand** with the hands, rather than mechanically. **give/lend a hand** to help. **go hand in hand** to be closely linked. **hand in glove** cooperating closely. **hand to mouth** satisfying one's immediate needs. **in hand** being done; in progress. **off hand** without checking or investigating. **on hand 1** ready to use. **2** present. **on one's hands** in one's possession or care. **out of hand 1** out of control. **2** without pause for consideration. **to hand** available and ready for use. **win hands down** *informal* to win with ease.

hand[2] *v* to give or pass (something) to somebody. ✻ **hand it to** to give credit to.

handbag *n Brit* a woman's bag for small personal articles and money.

handball *n* **1** a ball game played using the hands in a walled court. **2** the offence of handling the ball in football.

handbill *n* a small printed sheet of information handed out in the street.

handbook *n* a book giving information on a practical subject.

hand brake *n* a hand-operated brake used to hold a stationary motor vehicle.

handcuff *v* to put handcuffs on.

handcuffs *pl n* a pair of linked metal rings for locking round a prisoner's wrists.

hand down *v* **1** to pass on or bequeath. **2** to deliver (a judgment) in court.

handful *n* (*pl* **handfuls**) **1** an amount that can be held in the hand. **2** a small quantity or number. **3** *informal* a person who is difficult to control or deal with.

hand grenade *n* a grenade for throwing by hand.

handgun *n* a gun for holding and firing with one hand.

handhold *n* something to grasp for support in climbing.

handicap[1] *n* **1** a disability or disadvantage that makes a task unusually difficult. **2** an advantage or disadvantage given to contestants to even out the chances of winning. **3** the number of strokes by which a golfer on average exceeds par for a course. **4** the extra weight assigned to a racehorse as a handicap.

handicap² *v* (**handicapped, handicapping**) **1** to put at a disadvantage. **2** to assign handicaps to.

handicapped *adj* having a handicap or disadvantage.

handicraft *n* **1** a manual skill, or an occupation requiring it. **2** an article made by handicraft.

handiwork *n* **1** a person's own work or actions. **2** work done with the hands.

handkerchief *n* (*pl* **handkerchiefs** *or* **hand-kerchieves**) a small piece of cloth for wiping or blowing the nose.

handle¹ *n* **1** a part that is designed to be grasped by the hand. **2** *informal* a person's name or nickname. **3** *informal* a means of approaching or dealing with a situation.

handle² *v* **1** to touch or feel with the hands. **2** to deal with (a subject, idea, etc) in speech or writing, or as a work of art. **3** to manage or be in charge of. **4** to deal with (somebody or something). **5** to engage in buying, selling, or distributing (a commodity). **6** of a vehicle, etc: to respond to the controls in a specified way. ➤ **handler** *n*.

handlebar *n* (*also in pl*) a steering bar on a bicycle or motore cycle.

handmade *adj* made by hand rather than by machine.

handmaid *or* **handmaiden** *n* *archaic* a female servant.

hand-me-down *n* a piece of clothing that has been passed from an older to a younger member of a family.

handout *n* **1** an item of food, clothing, or money given free to people in need. **2** a sheet of information for free distribution.

hand out *v* to give (something) freely to a group of people.

handover *n* an act of transferring power or responsibility from one person or group to another.

hand over *v* to pass something officially to another person or organization.

handpick *v* to choose personally and carefully.

handset *n* **1** the part of a telephone that contains the mouthpiece and earpiece. **2** the remote-control device for a television set, video recorder, etc.

handshake *n* an act of shaking a person's hand in greeting or agreement.

hands-off *adj* keeping free of close involvement in an activity.

handsome *adj* **1** of a man: having a pleasing appearance; good-looking. **2** of a woman: attractive in a dignified way. **3** of a building,

room, etc: well-proportioned; stately. **4** large or generous. ➤ **handsomely** *adv*.

hands-on *adj* taking a direct involvement in an activity.

handspring *n* a movement turning the body in a circle and landing first on the hands and then on the feet.

handstand *n* an act of balancing the body upside down on the hands with the legs in the air.

hand-to-hand *adj* involving physical contact; very close.

handwriting *n* **1** writing done with a pen or pencil. **2** a person's particular style of writing. ➤ **handwritten** *adj*.

handy *adj* (**-ier, -iest**) **1** convenient to use; useful. **2** conveniently near. **3** clever in practical ways. ➤ **handily** *adv*.

handyman *n* (*pl* **handymen**) a man who does various minor building and repair tasks.

hang¹ *v* (*past tense and past part.* **hung**) **1** to fasten or be fastened at the top so that the lower part is free. **2** (*past tense and past part.* **hanged**) to suspend (somebody) by the neck until dead, usu as a form of capital punishment. **3** to attach (a door, window, etc) to its frame so that it can be opened and closed freely. **4** to paste (wallpaper) to a wall. **5** to display (a picture). **6** to remain poised or stationary in the air. **7** to stay on; to persist. **8** (+ over) to be imminent or threatening. **9** (+ up) to depend on something.

hang² *n* the way in which something hangs. ✴ **get the hang of** *informal* to learn how to use or deal with (something).

hang about *v* *Brit* to wait or stay without purpose or activity.

hangar *n* a shed; *esp* a large shed for housing aircraft.

hangdog *adj* ashamed or abject.

hanger *n* **1** a piece of shaped material with a hook, for hanging clothes on. **2** a person who hangs something.

hanger-on *n* (*pl* **hangers-on**) a fawning associate of a person or group.

hang-glider *n* a glider controlled by the movements of the person harnessed beneath it. ➤ **hang-gliding** *n*.

hanging *n* a tapestry or other decorative covering for a wall.

hangman *n* (*pl* **hangmen**) an executioner who hangs condemned prisoners.

hangnail *n* a piece of skin hanging loose at the side or root of a fingernail.

hang on *v* **1** to keep hold; to hold onto something. **2** *informal* to persist. **3** *informal* to wait for a short time.

hang out *v* *informal* to spend time in a leisurely or idle way.

hangover *n* **1** the unpleasant physical effects of heavy consumption of alcohol. **2** a custom that remains from the past.

hang up v to end a telephone conversation by replacing the receiver.

hang-up n informal a source of mental or emotional difficulty.

hank n a coil or loop of yarn, rope, wool, etc.

hanker v (+ after/for) to want something strongly or persistently. ➤ **hankering** n.

hankie or **hanky** n (pl -**ies**) informal a handkerchief.

hanky-panky n informal mildly improper behaviour.

hansom n a light two-wheeled covered carriage for two people.

Hanukkah or **Chanukah** n an eight-day Jewish festival in December.

haphazard adj lacking any method or order; aimless. ➤ **haphazardly** adv.

hapless adj unlucky or unfortunate.

happen v 1 to take place; to occur. 2 to occur by chance. * **happen on** literary to encounter by chance. **happen to** to do or be the case by chance.

happening[1] n something that happens; an event.

happening[2] adj informal exciting and fashionable.

happy adj (-**ier**, -**iest**) 1 enjoying or expressing pleasure and contentment. 2 glad; pleased. 3 favoured by luck or fortune. 4 well adapted or fitting. 5 impulsively quick to do or use something: trigger-happy. ➤ **happily** adv, **happiness** n.

happy-go-lucky adj cheerfully unconcerned; carefree.

happy hour n a period of the day during which drinks are sold at a reduced price in a bar, pub, etc.

hara-kiri n suicide by ritual disembowelment with a sword, formerly practised by Japanese samurai when disgraced.

harangue[1] n a lengthy critical speech or piece of writing.

harangue[2] v to criticize (somebody) at tedious length.

harass v to annoy or worry persistently. ➤ **harassed** n.

Usage Note: Note the spelling with -r- and -ss.

harbinger n literary a person or thing that signals a future event or change.

harbour[1] (NAmer **harbor**) n a port or coastal inlet providing safe anchorage for ships.

harbour[2] (NAmer **harbor**) v 1 to have or keep (thoughts or feelings) in the mind. 2 to give shelter or refuge to. 3 to be the habitat of (something unpleasant).

hard[1] adj 1 not easily penetrated or yielding to pressure; firm. 2 physically fit and tough. 3 revealing no weakness. 4 difficult to understand or explain. 5 demanding energy or stamina. 6 of currency: stable in value or soundly backed. 7 harsh or severe. 8 forceful or violent. 9 lacking consideration or compassion. 10 difficult to endure. 11 not speculative or conjectural; factual. 12 close or searching. 13 firm or definite. 14 of a drink: containing a high percentage of alcohol. 15 of water: containing salts that inhibit lathering. 16 of a drug: addictive and harmful. * **hard feelings** offence or resentment. **hard going** arduous or difficult. **hard of hearing** rather deaf. ➤ **hardness** n.

hard[2] adv 1 with great effort or energy; strenuously. 2 in a firm manner; tightly. * **be hard put to it** to have difficulty. **hard done by** harshly or unfairly treated.

hardback n a book bound in stiff covers.

hard-bitten adj steeled by difficult experience.

hardboard n board made by compressing shredded wood chips.

hard-boiled adj 1 of an egg: boiled until the yolk has solidified. 2 of a person: tough and insensitive.

hard cash n coins and bank notes as opposed to cheques or credit.

hard copy n a paper copy of data held on computer.

hard core n the most committed members of a group.

hard-core adj of pornography: extremely explicit.

hard disk or **hard drive** n a rigid high-capacity disk permanently installed in a computer.

harden v to make or become hard or harder.

hardheaded adj sober and realistic.

hardhearted adj severe and unsympathetic. ➤ **hardheartedly** adv.

hard-line adj strict and unyielding. ➤ **hard-liner** n.

hardly adv 1 not in the least. 2 used as a response: certainly not! 3 only just; barely.

hard-nosed adj informal sober and realistic.

hardship n suffering or privation.

hard shoulder n Brit a strip alongside a motorway, for use in an emergency.

hard up adj informal short of money.

hardware n 1 household tools and gardening equipment. 2 the physical components of a computer or other electronic device. 3 heavy military equipment such as tanks and missiles.

hardwood n 1 a broad-leaved as distinguished from a coniferous tree. 2 the wood of such a tree.

hardy adj (-**ier**, -**iest**) 1 inured to hardship; tough. 2 of a plant: capable of withstanding adverse conditions. ➤ **hardiness** n.

hare[1] n a mammal like a large rabbit with long ears and long hind legs.

hare[2] v informal to run fast.

harebell n a plant with blue bell-shaped flowers.

harebrained adj flighty or foolish.

harelip n a split in the upper lip occurring as a congenital deformity.

harem n 1 a secluded part of a house reserved for women in a Muslim household. 2 the women occupying a harem.

haricot n a type of French bean with white seeds.

hark v literary to listen. * **hark at** used to draw attention to a foolish or pompous comment.

harken v see HEARKEN.

Harlequin n a mute pantomime character, wearing a mask and diamond-patterned costume.

harlequin adj of a pattern: brightly coloured.

harlot n archaic a prostitute.

harm¹ n 1 physical or mental damage or injury. 2 mischief or wrong. ➤ **harmful** adj, **harmfully** adv.

harm² v 1 to damage or injure. 2 to have a bad effect on.

harmless adj not likely to cause harm. ➤ **harmlessly** adv.

harmonic¹ adj 1 relating to musical harmony. 2 pleasing to the ear.

harmonic² n a flutelike overtone produced on a stringed instrument.

harmonica n a small rectangular wind instrument with a row of reeds recessed in air slots for blowing through to produce different notes.

harmonious adj 1 musically tuneful or pleasing. 2 having the parts arranged so as to produce a pleasing effect. 3 free from argument or conflict. ➤ **harmoniously** adv.

harmonium n a musical instrument of the reed organ family in which pedals operate a bellows that forces air through free reeds.

harmonize or **-ise** v 1 to play or sing in harmony. 2 (often + with) to be in harmony or keeping. 3 to provide (a tune) with harmony. 4 to make harmonious. ➤ **harmonization** n.

harmony n (pl **-ies**) 1 a pleasing combination of musical notes in a chord. 2 the structure of music with respect to the composition and progression of chords. 3 a pleasing arrangement of parts. 4 agreement or accord.

harness¹ n 1 a system of straps for attaching a horse or other draught animal to the thing it is pulling. 2 something that resembles a harness, e.g. in holding or fastening something. * **in harness** in one's usual work or routine.

harness² v 1 to put a harness on. 2 to attach by means of a harness. 3 to make use of (a natural source of energy).

harp¹ n a musical instrument with strings stretched across an open triangular frame, plucked with the fingers. ➤ **harpist** n.

harp² v (+ on) to keep talking about something tediously or monotonously.

harpoon¹ n a barbed spear used in hunting large fish or whales.

harpoon² v to spear with a harpoon.

harpsichord n a keyboard instrument with a horizontal frame and strings that are plucked when keys are pressed. ➤ **harpsichordist** n.

harpy n (pl **-ies**) 1 (**Harpy**) a vicious creature of Greek mythology with the head of a woman and the body of a bird. 2 a cruel or spiteful woman.

harridan n a bad-tempered old woman.

harrier n 1 a hunting dog used for catching hares. 2 a slender hawk with long angled wings.

harrow¹ n a cultivating implement set with teeth or discs and drawn over the ground to break up or smooth the soil.

harrow² v to cultivate with a harrow.

harrowing adj causing distress.

harry v (**-ies, -ied**) 1 to attack (an enemy) repeatedly. 2 to harass or torment.

harsh adj 1 disagreeable or painful to the senses. 2 unduly exacting or severe. 3 of a climate or conditions: difficult to endure. ➤ **harshly** adv.

hart n an adult male red deer.

harvest¹ n 1 the gathering in of an agricultural crop. 2 a year's mature crop or yield.

harvest² v 1 to gather in (a crop). 2 to gather (a natural product) as if by harvesting. ➤ **harvester** n.

has v third person sing. present of HAVE.

has-been n informal a person or thing that is no longer important.

hash¹ n 1 a dish of reheated chopped food. 2 informal a muddle or jumble. * **make a hash of something** informal to do something badly.

hash² v to chop (food) into small pieces.

hash³ n informal hashish.

hash⁴ n the symbol #.

hashish n cannabis.

hasn't contraction has not.

hasp n a hinged metal strip that fits over a metal loop and is secured by a pin or padlock as a fastening.

hassle¹ n informal 1 a difficult or trying situation. 2 harassment.

hassle² v informal to subject to persistent harassment.

hassock n a cushion for kneeling on in church.

haste n speedy or rash action.

hasten v 1 to make (something) happen more quickly. 2 to move or act quickly.

hasty adj (**-ier, -iest**) rash or hurried. ➤ **hastily** adv.

hat n a covering to fit the head. ➤ **hatless** adj.

hatch¹ n 1 a small door or opening. 2 an opening in the deck of a ship or in an aircraft.

hatch² v 1 of young: to emerge from an egg or pupa. 2 of an egg: to open and release young. 3 to incubate (an egg). 4 to devise (a plot or plan).

hatch³ v to mark (a map or drawing) with fine closely spaced parallel lines. ➤ **hatching** n.

hatchback *n* a car with a large upward-opening door at the back.

hatchet *n* an axe with a short handle.

hatchling *n* a newly hatched animal.

hate[1] *v* to feel extreme dislike or hostility towards.

hate[2] *n* 1 intense dislike or hostility. 2 *informal* an object of hatred.

hateful *adj* deserving or arousing hate. ➤ **hatefully** *adv.*

hatred *n* intense dislike or hate.

hat trick *n* three successes by one person or side.

haughty *adj* (-ier, -iest) disdainfully proud or arrogant. ➤ **haughtily** *adv*, **haughtiness** *n.*

haul[1] *v* 1 to pull or drag with an effort. 2 to transport (goods) in a commercial vehicle.

haul[2] *n* 1 an amount gathered or acquired, *esp* illegally. 2 the fish taken in a single spell of fishing.

haulage *n* the act or process of hauling.

haulier *n* a person or establishment that transports goods commercially.

haulm *n* a plant stem.

haunch *n* 1 the human hip. 2 the hindquarters of a four-legged animal. 3 the back half of the side of a slaughtered animal.

haunt[1] *v* 1 of a ghost: to be present in (a place) regularly. 2 of a person: to visit (a place) often. 3 of a thought: to recur constantly and disturb (somebody).

haunt[2] *n* a place habitually frequented.

haunted *adj* 1 inhabited by a ghost. 2 worried or anguished.

haunting *adj* 1 of thoughts or memories: constantly recurring and evocative. 2 of music: poignant. ➤ **hauntingly** *adv.*

haute couture /ˌoht kooh'tyooa/ *n* the designing and making of fashionable clothes by leading fashion houses.

haute cuisine /kwi'zeen/ *n* cooking of a high standard and following French methods.

have *v* (*third person sing. present* **has**, *past tense and past part.* **had**) 1 to own or possess. 2 to display (a feeling or quality). 3 to experience or undergo (an illness). 4 to engage in (an activity). 5 to eat or drink. 6 to receive or be given. 7 to get (something) done or to get (somebody) to do something. 8 to accommodate or be the host of. 9 to arrange or organize. 10 used to form the perfect, pluperfect, and future perfect tenses of verbs. ✳ **have had it** *informal* to have failed or be useless. **have it out** *informal* to settle a disagreement. **have to** must.

haven *n* 1 a place of safety. 2 a harbour or port.

haven't *contraction* have not.

have on *v* 1 to be wearing. 2 to have planned or organized (an event). 3 *informal* to deceive or tease (somebody).

haver *v* 1 *Scot* to talk nonsense. 2 *chiefly Brit* to be indecisive.

haversack *n* a strong bag carried on the back.

havoc *n* 1 widespread destruction or devastation. 2 great confusion and disorder. ✳ **play havoc with** to disrupt.

hawk[1] *n* 1 a bird of prey with short rounded wings and a long tail. 2 a supporter of an aggressive policy. ➤ **hawkish** *adj.*

hawk[2] *v* to hunt game with a trained hawk.

hawk[3] *v* to offer (goods) for sale in the street. ➤ **hawker** *n.*

hawk[4] *v* 1 to clear the throat with a harsh noise. 2 to produce (phlegm) by hawking.

hawser *n* a large rope used on a ship.

hawthorn *n* a spiny shrub with white or pink flowers and small red fruits.

hay *n* grass that has been mown and dried for fodder.

hay fever *n* an allergy to pollen causing nasal catarrh and conjunctivitis.

haystack *n* a large pile of stacked hay.

haywire *adj informal* out of control; erratic.

hazard[1] *n* 1 a risk or peril. 2 a source of danger. 3 a bunker or other obstacle on a golf course.

hazard[2] *v* 1 to venture (an estimate or guess). 2 to expose to danger.

hazardous *adj* involving or causing danger.

haze *n* 1 a light mist caused by vapour, dust, etc in the air. 2 mental vagueness or confusion.

hazel *n* 1 a small tree bearing nuts in autumn and catkins in spring. 2 a yellowish brown colour.

hazy *adj* (-ier, -iest) 1 obscured or cloudy. 2 vague or indefinite. ➤ **hazily** *adv.*

H-bomb *n* a hydrogen bomb.

He *abbr* the chemical symbol for helium.

he *pron* 1 used to refer to a male person or animal previously mentioned. 2 used to refer to a person of either sex.

head[1] *n* 1 the upper or front part of the body containing the brain, mouth, and sense organs. 2 (*in pl*) the side of a coin bearing the head of a monarch or president. 3 a person or individual. 4 a specified number of livestock. 5 the end that is upper, higher, or opposite the foot. 6 the source of a stream, river, etc. 7 a director or leader. 8 a school principal. 9 a cluster of flowers or leaves. 10 the operational part of a weapon, tool, or device. 11 the flattened or rounded end of a nail or screw. 12 the pressure of a fluid. 13 the foam at the top of a glass of beer. ✳ **come to a head** to reach a crisis. **a head start** an initial advantage over competitors. **keep one's head** to retain one's composure. **lose one's head** to panic or behave irrationally. ➤ **headless** *adj.*

head[2] *adj* principal or chief.

head[3] *v* 1 to lead or be at the head of. 2 to put as the heading to. 3 to stand as the first item of. 4 to drive (a ball) with the head. 5 to move in a specified direction.

headache n **1** a prolonged pain in the head. **2** informal something that causes worry.

headband n a band of stretch fabric worn round the head.

headboard n an upright board at the head of a bed.

headbutt[1] v to hit (somebody) with the front of the head.

headbutt[2] n a blow with the head.

headdress n a decorative or ceremonial covering for the head.

header n **1** a shot or pass in football made with the head. **2** informal a headfirst fall or dive. **3** a raised water tank that maintains pressure in a system. **4** a line of text at the top of each page of a book or document.

headfirst adv and adj with the head foremost; headlong.

headgear n clothing for the head.

headhunt v to find and recruit personnel to fill business vacancies. ➤ **headhunter** n.

heading n **1** a title at the top of a letter, chapter, etc. **2** a compass direction. **3** the top edge of a curtain above the hooks.

headland n a point of high land jutting into the sea.

headlight or **headlamp** n a main light at the front of a motor vehicle.

headline[1] n **1** a title printed in large type above a newspaper story or article. **2** Brit (in pl) a summary at the beginning or end of a news broadcast.

headline[2] v **1** to provide (an article or story) with a headline. **2** to be a star performer in (a show).

headlock n a hold in which one arm is locked around a person's head.

headlong adv and adj **1** headfirst. **2** without pause or delay.

headmaster or **headmistress** n chiefly Brit a head teacher of a school.

head off v to stop and turn aside.

head of state n the official leader of a state.

head-on adv and adj **1** with the front making the initial contact. **2** in direct opposition.

headphones pl n a pair of earphones held over the ears by a band worn on the head.

headquarters n (pl **headquarters**) **1** a place from which a military commander directs operations. **2** the administrative centre of an enterprise.

headset n a set of earphones and microphone worn on the head.

head start n an initial advantage over competitors.

headstone n a memorial stone placed at the head of a grave.

headstrong adj wilful or obstinate.

head teacher n chiefly Brit the teacher in charge of a school.

headway n **1** advance or progress. **2** motion in a forward direction.

headwind n a wind blowing against the progress of a ship or aircraft.

headword n a word placed at the beginning of an encyclopedia or dictionary entry.

heady adj (-**ier**, -**iest**) **1** of alcoholic drinks: strong and intoxicating. **2** exciting or exhilarating.

heal v **1** to make healthy after an illness or injury. **2** to make (a wound) sound or whole. **3** to mend (a breach in relations).

health n **1** soundness of body or mind. **2** the general condition of the body.

health farm n a residential establishment providing treatment for people wishing to improve their health.

health food n organically grown food eaten for its health-giving properties.

healthful adj good for the health of body or mind.

healthy adj (-**ier**, -**iest**) **1** enjoying or enhancing good health. **2** prosperous or flourishing. **3** sufficient or substantial. ➤ **healthily** adv.

heap[1] n **1** a collection of things lying one on top of another. **2** informal (in pl) a large quantity. **3** informal a dilapidated vehicle or building.

heap[2] v **1** (often + up) to put or throw in a heap. **2** to form a heap. **3** (often + with) to supply with a lot of something. **4** to bestow (things) lavishly or in large quantities on somebody.

hear v (past tense and past part. **heard**) **1** to perceive (sound) with the ear. **2** to learn of by hearing. **3** (also + out) to listen to (somebody) with attention. **4** to give a legal or official hearing to (a case, complaint, etc). **5** (+ of/about) to gain information about; to learn. ✻ **hear from** to receive a communication from. **hear! hear!** an expression of agreement. **hear of** (in negative contexts) to entertain the idea of (something). ➤ **hearer** n.

hearing n **1** the faculty of perceiving sound. **2** earshot. **3** an opportunity to be heard. **4** a review of evidence in a court.

hearing aid n a device worn by a deaf person to enable them to hear better.

hearken or **harken** v archaic (usu + to) to listen.

hearsay n something heard from another person.

hearse n a vehicle for transporting a coffin at a funeral.

heart n **1** the organ that maintains the circulation of blood in the body. **2** the essential or most vital part of an organization or enterprise. **3** (in pl) the suit in a pack of cards that is marked with red figures in the shape of a heart. **4** tenderness or compassion. **5** love or affections. **6** courage or spirit. **7** one's innermost character or feelings. ✻ **by heart** from memory. **take**

heart to gain confidence. **take to heart** to be deeply affected by.

heartache *n* mental anguish or sorrow.

heart attack *n* a sudden failure of the heart.

heartbeat *n* 1 a single pulsation of the heart. 2 a driving impulse. 3 a brief moment.

heartbreak *n* intense grief or distress. ➤ **heartbreaking** *adj*.

heartbroken *adj* overcome by sorrow.

heartburn *n* indigestion in the form of a burning pain in the chest.

hearten *v* to cheer or encourage. ➤ **heartening** *adj*.

heart failure *n* a sudden failure of the heart to continue working.

heartfelt *adj* earnest or sincere.

hearth *n* the area in front of a fireplace.

hearthrug *n* a rug placed in front of a fireplace.

heartily *adv* 1 wholeheartedly or vigorously. 2 thoroughly.

heartless *adj* unfeeling or cruel.

heart-rending *adj* causing great sorrow.

heart-searching *n* close examination of one's motives or feelings.

heart-throb *n* informal a good-looking man.

heart-to-heart *adj* of talk: sincere and intimate.

heart-warming *adj* cheering or uplifting.

hearty *adj* (-ier, -iest) 1 vigorous or enthusiastic. 2 sincere or heartfelt. 3 robustly healthy. 4 of a meal: substantial or abundant.

heat[1] *n* 1 the state of being hot. 2 a form of energy associated with the motion of the molecules and atoms of matter. 3 intensity of feeling or reaction. 4 a preliminary round of a contest. 5 informal pressure or criticism. * **on heat** of a female mammal: ready for mating.

heat[2] *v* 1 (*often* + up) to make or become hot. 2 (+ up) to make or become more exciting or intense.

heater *n* a device for heating air or water.

heath *n* an area of level uncultivated land, usu with heather and gorse.

heathen *n* archaic somebody who does not belong to any of the main religions. ➤ **heathen** *adj*.

heather *n* a shrub with purplish pink flowers.

heating *n* a system for supplying heat to a building.

heatstroke *n* a disorder caused by overheating of the body from prolonged exposure to high temperature.

heat wave *n* a prolonged period of unusually hot weather.

heave[1] *v* (*past tense and past part.* heaved or hove) 1 to lift or pull with great effort. 2 informal to throw (something heavy). 3 to utter (a loud sigh). 4 to rise and fall rhythmically. 5 to retch. * **heave in sight/into view** to come into view.

heave[2] *n* an act of heaving.

heaven *n* 1 in some beliefs, the dwelling place of God or the gods, where good people go when they die. 2 (**the heavens**) literary the sky. 3 informal a place or state of complete happiness. * **move heaven and earth** to do all one can.

heavenly *adj* 1 relating to heaven or the sky. 2 informal delightful.

heavenly body *n* a planet, star, or other body in space.

heavy[1] *adj* (-ier, -iest) 1 having great weight; difficult to carry, move, or lift. 2 large or heavy of its kind. 3 thick or solid. 4 of food: rich and difficult to digest. 5 of soil: full of clay and inclined to hold water. 6 not delicate. 7 slow or sluggish; clumsy. 8 falling with force, powerful. 9 loud and dull in sound. 10 of an unusually large amount, degree, or force: *heavy traffic*. 11 of rock music: loud and having a strong rhythm. 12 needing physical effort and strength. 13 needing considerable mental effort; serious or important. * **heavy going** difficult to understand or deal with. ➤ **heavily** *adv*, **heaviness** *n*.

heavy[2] *n* (*pl* -ies) 1 informal a large intimidating man. 2 informal a powerful or important person.

heavy-duty *adj* designed to withstand unusual strain or wear.

heavy industry *n* production of large or heavy articles in large numbers.

heavy metal *n* 1 a metal with a high relative density or high relative atomic weight. 2 a type of highly amplified rock music.

heavyweight *n* 1 the heaviest weight in boxing and wrestling. 2 informal an important or influential person.

Hebrew *n* 1 a member of an ancient Semitic people. 2 the language of the Hebrews, or the modern form of it.

heckle[1] *v* to interrupt (a speaker) with shouts or jeers. ➤ **heckler** *n*.

heckle[2] *n* a heckling comment or jeer.

hectare *n* a metric unit of area equal to 10,000 square metres (2.471 acres).

hectic *adj* filled with excitement or feverish activity. ➤ **hectically** *adv*.

hector *v* to intimidate in a bullying way.

he'd contraction he had or he would.

hedge[1] *n* 1 a boundary formed by a dense row of shrubs or bushes. 2 a means of protection or defence. 3 an evasive use of language.

hedge[2] *v* 1 to enclose with a hedge. 2 to avoid saying anything definite. * **hedge one's bets** to avoid committing oneself.

hedgehog *n* a small mammal covered in spines and able to roll into a ball when threatened.

hedgerow *n* a row of shrubs or trees surrounding a field.

hedonism *n* the pursuit of sensual pleasure. ➤ **hedonist** *n*, **hedonistic** *adj*.

heebie-jeebies *pl n* (**the heebie-jeebies**) *informal* a state of nervous anxiety.

heed[1] *v* to pay close attention to.

heed[2] *n* careful attention; notice. ✳ **pay/take heed** to take notice or care. ➤ **heedful** *adj*.

heedless *adj* thoughtless or reckless.

heel[1] *n* **1** the back of the foot below the ankle. **2** the part of the palm of the hand nearest the wrist. **3** the part of a shoe or boot that covers or supports the heel. ✳ **down at heel** run-down or shabby. **take to one's heels** to run away.

heel[2] *v* **1** to supply (a shoe) with a new heel. **2** of a dog: to walk close behind the person in charge of it.

heel[3] *v* of a ship: to tilt to one side.

heft *v* to hoist or to heave up.

hefty *adj* (**-ier, -iest**) large, heavy, or powerful.

hegemony *n* (*pl* **-ies**) domination or leadership of a nation or group.

heifer *n* a young cow.

height *n* **1** the distance from the top to the bottom. **2** the elevation above a level. **3** the quality of being tall or high. **4** a high point or position. **5** the most extreme or intense point.

heighten *v* **1** to increase the amount or degree of. **2** to deepen or intensify. **3** to make higher. **4** to become greater in extent or intensity.

heinous *adj* shockingly wicked. ➤ **heinously** *adv*.

heir *n* **1** a person who inherits property or rank. **2** a person who receives a position or role from a predecessor.

heir apparent *n* (*pl* **heirs apparent**) **1** an heir who cannot be displaced by the birth of another heir. **2** a person who seems most likely to succeed to the position of another.

heiress *n* a female heir.

heirloom *n* a piece of valuable property handed down within a family for generations.

heist[1] *n* chiefly *NAmer, informal* a robbery.

heist[2] *v* chiefly *NAmer, informal* to steal (something).

held *v* past tense and past part. of HOLD[1].

helical *adj* having the form of a helix; spiral.

helicopter *n* an aircraft which derives lift and power from a set of horizontally rotating rotors.

helium *n* a natural gas used *esp* for inflating large balloons.

helix *n* (*pl* **helices** or **helixes**) an object that is spiral in form.

hell *n* **1** in some beliefs, a place of torment and punishment for the dead. **2** a place or state of suffering or misery. ✳ **for the hell of it** *informal* just for fun. **give somebody hell** *informal* to scold them severely.

he'll *contraction* he shall or he will.

hell-bent *adj* stubbornly or recklessly determined.

Hellenic *adj* Greek.

hellhole *n* a place of extreme discomfort or squalor.

hellish *adj* **1** of or resembling hell; diabolical. **2** *informal* extremely difficult or unpleasant. ➤ **hellishly** *adv*.

hello or **hallo** or **hullo** *interj* **1** used as a greeting. **2** *Brit* used to express surprise or attract attention.

hellraiser *n* a person who acts in a wild or drunken manner.

helm *n* **1** a tiller or wheel for steering a ship. **2** (**the helm**) the position of control or leadership.

helmet *n* a protective head covering.

helmsman *n* (*pl* **helmsmen**) a person who steers a ship.

help *v* **1** to give assistance or support to. **2** to be of use or benefit to. **3** to promote or further the advancement of. **4** to refrain from (doing something). **5** to keep from occurring; to prevent. **6** to restrain (oneself) from taking action. **7** to remedy or improve (a situation). **8** to serve with food or drink. ✳ **help oneself** to take without permission or dishonestly. ➤ **helper** *n*.

helpful *adj* **1** ready to help. **2** useful. ➤ **helpfully** *adv*.

helping *n* a serving of food.

helpless *adj* **1** lacking protection or support. **2** powerless to act. **3** lacking control or restraint. ➤ **helplessly** *adv*.

helpmate *n* a companion and helper.

helter-skelter[1] *adj and adv* in a hurried and disorderly manner.

helter-skelter[2] *n Brit* a spiral slide at a fairground.

hem *n* the border of a cloth article when turned back and stitched down.

hematology *n NAmer* see HAEMATOLOGY.

hemisphere *n* **1** a half sphere. **2** the northern or southern half of the earth divided by the equator. ➤ **hemispherical** *adj*.

hemline *n* the line formed by the hem of a skirt or dress.

hemlock *n* a poison made from a plant with small white flowers.

hemp *n* **1** the fibre of an Asian plant, used for making rope and fabrics. **2** the drug cannabis.

hen *n* **1** a female bird, *esp* a domestic fowl. **2** (*in pl*) domestic fowls of both sexes.

hence *adv* **1** for this reason. **2** from this time.

henceforth *adv* from this time or point on.

henchman *n* (*pl* **henchmen**) a follower or supporter, *esp* an unscrupulous one.

henna *n* a reddish brown dye obtained from the leaves of a tropical shrub.

hen night *n Brit, informal* a party for women, held for a woman who is about to get married.

henpecked *adj* persistently nagged by a woman.

hepatitis *n* a disease marked by inflammation of the liver.

heptagon *n* a figure with seven angles and seven sides.

heptathlon *n* an athletic contest for women with seven events. ➤ **heptathlete** *n*.

her[1] *adj* belonging to or associated with a female person or animal already mentioned.

her[2] *pron* used as the objective case: she.

herald[1] *n* **1** formerly, an official crier or messenger. **2** somebody or something that is a sign of the arrival of something.

herald[2] *v* **1** to announce or give notice of. **2** to be a sign of the arrival of.

heraldic *adj* relating to heraldry.

heraldry *n* the system of designing and using coats of arms.

herb *n* **1** a plant used to flavour food or in medicine. **2** in botany, a plant that bears seeds and dies down at the end of a growing season. ➤ **herby** *adj*.

herbaceous *adj* relating to a herb (in the botanical sense).

herbaceous border *n* a permanent border of perennial flowering plants.

herbage *n* herbaceous plants used for grazing.

herbalist *n* somebody who grows or sells herbs for medicines. ➤ **herbalism** *n*.

herbivore *n* a plant-eating animal. ➤ **herbivorous** *adj*.

Herculean *adj* requiring or showing great effort or strength.

herd[1] *n* **1** a number of animals of one kind kept together or living as a group. **2** *derog* a large group of people.

herd[2] *v* **1** to keep or move (animals) together. **2** to assemble or move in a herd or group.

here *adv* in, at, or to this place or position. ✳ **neither here nor there** of no consequence.

hereabouts *or* **hereabout** *adv* in this vicinity.

hereafter[1] *adv formal* **1** after this. **2** in some future time or state. **3** after death.

hereafter[2] *n* (**the hereafter**) life after death.

hereby *adv formal* by this means.

hereditary *adj* **1** based on inheritance. **2** genetically transmitted from parent to offspring.

heredity *n* **1** the transmission of characteristics from one generation to the next. **2** the qualities genetically derived from ancestors.

herein *adv formal* in this document, matter, etc.

hereof *adv formal* of this document.

heresy *n* (*pl* **-ies**) **1** a belief or doctrine contrary to established doctrine. **2** a markedly unorthodox opinion.

heretic *n* a person who subscribes to a heresy. ➤ **heretical** *adj*.

hereto *adv formal* to this matter or document.

heretofore *adv formal* up to this time.

herewith *adv formal* with this.

heritable *adj* capable of being inherited.

heritage *n* **1** property that is inherited. **2** something valuable acquired from predecessors.

hermaphrodite *n* a person, animal, or plant having both male and female reproductive organs or characteristics.

hermetic *adj* **1** of a seal: airtight. **2** impervious to external influences. ➤ **hermetically** *adv*.

hermit *n* a person who lives in solitude, *esp* for religious reasons.

hernia *n* a protrusion of part of the intestine through the wall of its enclosing cavity.

hero *n* (*pl* **-oes**) **1** a person admired for special courage or achievements. **2** the principal male character in a literary or dramatic work.

heroic *adj* **1** showing great courage. **2** grand or impressive. ➤ **heroically** *adv*.

heroin *n* a strongly addictive narcotic drug made from morphine.

heroine *n* **1** a woman admired for special courage or great achievements. **2** the principal female character in a literary or dramatic work.

heroism *n* great courage.

heron *n* (*pl* **herons** *or* **heron**) a wading bird with a long neck, long legs, and a tapering bill.

hero worship *n* excessive admiration for somebody.

herpes *n* a viral disease of the skin, causing blisters.

herring *n* (*pl* **herrings** *or* **herring**) a silvery food fish common in the North Atlantic.

herringbone *n* a pattern made up of rows of parallel lines slanting in opposite directions on adjacent rows.

hers *pron* the one or ones that belong to or are associated with a female person or animal already mentioned.

Usage Note: Note that there is no apostrophe in *hers*.

herself *pron* used reflexively or for emphasis to refer to a female person or animal that is the subject of the clause.

hertz *n* (*pl* **hertz**) the SI unit of frequency, equal to one cycle per second.

he's *contraction* he is or he has.

hesitant *adj* tending to hesitate; irresolute. ➤ **hesitancy** *n*, **hesitantly** *adv*.

hesitate *v* **1** to pause in doubt or indecision. **2** to be reluctant or unwilling to do something. ➤ **hesitation** *n*.

hessian *n* a coarse heavy fabric.

heterogeneous *adj* varied or disparate. ➤ **heterogeneity** *n*.

heterosexual[1] *adj* having a sexual preference for members of the opposite sex. ➤ **heterosexuality** *n*.

heterosexual[2] *n* a heterosexual person.

het up *adj informal* angry or upset.

hew *v* (*past part.* **hewed** *or* **hewn**) to chop or fell (wood) with a heavy cutting instrument.

hex[1] *v chiefly NAmer* to cast a spell on.

hex[2] *n chiefly NAmer* a magic spell or jinx.

hexagon *n* a figure with six angles and six sides. ➤ **hexagonal** *adj.*

hexameter *n* a line of verse consisting of six metrical feet.

heyday *n* the period of one's greatest vigour or prosperity.

Hf *abbr* the chemical symbol for hafnium.

Hg *abbr* the chemical symbol for mercury.

HGV *abbr Brit* heavy goods vehicle.

hiatus *n* (*pl* **hiatuses**) a break or gap in continuity.

hibernate *v* of an animal or plant: to pass the winter in a dormant or resting state. ➤ **hibernation** *n.*

hibiscus *n* a plant or shrub with large showy flowers.

hiccup[1] *or* **hiccough** *n* **1** an involuntary spasm in the glottis (opening between the throat and windpipe) accompanied by a sharp sound. **2** a brief interruption or setback.

hiccup[2] *or* **hiccough** *v* (**hiccuped** *or* **hiccupped, hiccuping** *or* **hiccupping**) to make the sound of a hiccup, or be affected with hiccups.

hickory *n* (*pl* **hickories** *or* **hickory**) a hardwood tree with sweet edible nuts and tough pale wood.

hide[1] *v* (**hid, hidden**) **1** to put out of sight; to conceal. **2** to conceal oneself. **3** to keep secret.

hide[2] *n* the skin of an animal.

hide-and-seek *n* a children's game in which a player hides and is sought by the others.

hideaway *n* a retreat or hideout.

hidebound *adj* narrow or inflexible in character or outlook.

hideous *adj* **1** extremely ugly or repulsive. **2** very unpleasant. ➤ **hideously** *adv.*

hideout *n* a hiding place used by a criminal.

hiding[1] *n* **1** a beating or thrashing. **2** a severe defeat. ✳ **on a hiding to nothing** *Brit* bound to fail.

hiding[2] *n* a state or place of concealment.

hierarchy *n* (*pl* **-ies**) **1** a system in which people or groups are ranked according to their status or authority. **2** a system in which things are ranked according to importance. ➤ **hierarchical** *adj.*

hieroglyphic *adj* relating to or using a system of writing in which pictures represent a word or sound. ➤ **hieroglyphics** *pl n.*

hi-fi *n* (*pl* **hi-fis**) *informal* a set of equipment for the high-fidelity reproduction of sound.

higgledy-piggledy *adv and adj* in confusion; disordered.

high[1] *adj* **1** extending upwards for a considerable distance. **2** situated at a considerable distance above the ground or above sea level. **3** having a specified elevation. **4** of greater degree, or amount than average. **5** foremost in rank, dignity, or standing. **6** near the upper end of a sound range. **7** forceful or strong. **8** of food:

beginning to go bad. **9** *informal* elated or excited, *esp* as an effect of drugs or alcohol. ✳ **high time** time for something that should have happened already.

high[2] *adv* **1** at or to a high place or altitude. **2** highly. **3** of a sound: at or to a high pitch.

high[3] *n* **1** a high point or level. **2** a region of high atmospheric pressure. **3** *informal* a state of ecstasy or euphoria. ✳ **on high** in or to a high place.

highbrow *adj* refined in intellectual and cultural interests.

High Church *n* a movement or tendency in the Anglican Church that favours aspects of Roman Catholicism in liturgy and dogma.

high commissioner *n* an ambassador of one Commonwealth country stationed in another.

high court *n* a supreme judicial court.

higher education *n* education beyond the secondary level, at a college or university.

high explosive *n* a powerful explosive, e.g. TNT.

highfalutin *or* **highfaluting** *adj informal* pretentious or pompous.

high fidelity *n* sound reproduction that is close to the original.

high-flier *or* **high-flyer** *n* an ambitious or successful person.

high-flown *adj* **1** excessively ambitious or extravagant. **2** of language: pretentious.

high gear *n* a gear used for a high speed of travel.

high-handed *adj* overbearing or inconsiderate.

high jinks *pl n* high-spirited fun and games.

high jump *n* an athletic field event in which contestants jump over a high bar.

highland *n* **1** (*also in pl*) high or mountainous land. **2** (**the Highlands**) the mountainous northern part of Scotland. ➤ **highlander** *n.*

highlight *n* **1** an event or detail of special importance. **2** a light area in a painting or photograph. **3** (*usu in pl*) contrasting bright tints in the hair.

highly *adv* **1** to a high degree; extremely. **2** favourably.

highly-strung *adj Brit* extremely nervous or sensitive.

high-minded *adj* having elevated principles and feelings.

Highness *n* used as a title for a person of royal rank.

high-rise *adj* of a building: having a large number of storeys.

high school *n* a secondary school.

high seas *pl n* (**the high seas**) the part of a sea outside territorial waters.

high-spirited *adj* bold or lively.

high tea *n Brit* an early evening meal including a drink of tea.

high-tech *or* **hi-tech** *adj* using or requiring advanced technology.

high technology *n* advanced technological processes.

high-tension *adj* having or using a high voltage.

high tide *n* the time when the sea reaches its highest level.

highway *n* **1** a public road. **2** *chiefly NAmer* a main road.

highwayman *n* (*pl* **highwaymen**) formerly, a mounted robber of travellers on a road.

hijack *v* **1** to seize control of (a vehicle or aircraft) while it is in transit. **2** to steal or appropriate. ➤ **hijacker** *n*.

hike[1] *n* **1** a long walk in the country. **2** a big increase or rise.

hike[2] *v* **1** to go on a hike. **2** (*usu* + up) to pull or lift up. **3** (*usu* + up) to raise (prices, wages, etc). ➤ **hiker** *n*.

hilarious *adj* extremely funny. ➤ **hilariously** *adv*, **hilarity** *n*.

hill *n* a natural rise of land lower than a mountain. ✻ **over the hill** *informal* old and past one's prime. ➤ **hilly** *adj*.

hillock *n* a small hill.

hilt *n* the handle of a sword, dagger, or knife. ✻ **to the hilt** completely.

him *pron* used as the objective case: he.

himself *pron* used reflexively or for emphasis to refer to a male person or animal that is the subject of the clause.

hind[1] *adj* situated at the back or behind.

hind[2] *n* (*pl* **hinds** *or* **hind**) a female deer.

hinder *v* to retard or obstruct.

Hindi *n* the language of northern India.

hindmost *adj* furthest back.

hindquarters *pl n* the hind legs and adjoining parts of a four-legged animal.

hindrance *n* **1** the act of hindering. **2** an impediment or obstacle.

hindsight *n* understanding of a situation only after the event.

Hindu *n* an adherent of Hinduism.

Hinduism *n* a religion of the Indian subcontinent, including reincarnation and the worship of many gods.

hinge[1] *n* a device that enables a door, gate, lid, etc to turn.

hinge[2] *v* (**hingeing** *or* **hinging**) **1** to attach with a hinge. **2** (+ on) to depend on.

hint[1] *n* **1** a brief suggestion or piece of advice. **2** an indirect or veiled statement. **3** a slight indication or trace.

hint[2] *v* (*often* + at) to indicate indirectly or by allusion.

hinterland *n* **1** a region lying inland from a coast. **2** a region remote from a town or city.

hip[1] *n* the projecting part at each side of the body, formed by the pelvis and upper thigh.

hip[2] *n* the ripened fruit of a rose.

hip[3] *interj* used to begin a cheer.

hip[4] *adj* (**hipper, hippest**) *informal* fashionable.

hip hop *n* a style of popular music with spoken words and music having a regular heavy beat.

hippie *or* **hippy** *n* (*pl* **-ies**) a person who rejects established values and dresses unconventionally.

hippo *n* (*pl* **hippos** *or* **hippo**) *informal* a hippopotamus.

hippopotamus *n* (*pl* **hippopotamuses** *or* **hippopotami**) a large African mammal with an extremely large head and mouth, thick skin, and short legs, living partly in the water.

hippy *n* (*pl* **-ies**) see HIPPIE.

hipsters *pl n* *Brit* trousers that start at the hips rather than the waist.

hire[1] *v* **1** to pay to obtain the temporary use of. **2** (+ out) to allow (something) to be used for a time in return for payment. ➤ **hirer** *n*.

hire[2] *n* **1** payment for the temporary use of something. **2** hiring or being hired.

hireling *n* *derog* a person who is hired for dull or routine work.

hire purchase *n* *Brit* a system by which a customer pays for goods in instalments while having ownership of them.

hirsute *adj* *formal* hairy.

his[1] *adj* belonging to or associated with a male person or animal already known or mentioned.

his[2] *pron* the one or ones that belong to or are associated with a male person or animal already mentioned.

Hispanic *adj* relating to Spain or Spanish-speaking people.

hiss[1] *v* **1** to make a sharp sound like a prolonged *s*. **2** to utter angrily with a hiss.

hiss[2] *n* a hissing sound.

histamine *n* a chemical compound released in the body after injury or in the presence of an allergen.

historian *n* a student of or expert in history.

historic *adj* famous or important in history.

historical *adj* **1** relating to history and past events. **2** belonging to the past. ➤ **historically** *adv*.

history *n* (*pl* **-ies**) **1** the study of past events. **2** past events as a whole. **3** an account of past events. **4** a person's medical, sociological, etc background. **5** an unusual or interesting past.

histrionic *adj* deliberately affected or theatrical. ➤ **histrionics** *pl n*.

hit[1] *v* (**hitting**, *past tense and past part.* **hit**) **1** to aim a blow at with the hand or an implement. **2** to come or bring into violent contact with. **3** to propel (a ball, etc) with a blow. **4** to reach (a target). **5** to harm or have a bad effect on. **6** *informal* to arrive at (a place). ✻ **hit it off** *informal* to enjoy one another's company. **hit on** to arrive at (a solution) unexpectedly. **hit the roof** *informal* to become extremely angry.

hit² n **1** a blow, esp one that meets its target. **2** a popular or successful person or thing. **3** a successful match when a database is being searched. **4** informal a dose of a substance, e.g. a drug.

hit-and-miss adj = HIT-OR-MISS.

hit-and-run adj of a road accident: involving a driver who does not stop after causing damage or injury.

hitch¹ v **1** to move (something) by jerks. **2** to catch or fasten by a hook or knot. **3** informal to request and obtain (a free lift) in a passing vehicle. ✳ **get hitched** informal to get married.

hitch² n **1** a temporary setback. **2** a knot used for a temporary fastening. **3** informal an act of hitchhiking.

hitchhike v to travel by obtaining free lifts in passing vehicles. ➤ **hitchhiker** n.

hither adv archaic to or towards this place.

hitherto adv up to this time.

hit list n a list of criminal targets.

hit-or-miss adj inconsistent or haphazard.

hit out v to act or speak violently or aggressively.

HIV abbr human immunodeficiency virus, the virus that causes Aids.

hive n **1** a beehive. **2** a place full of busy people.

hive off v chiefly Brit to separate from a group or larger unit.

hives pl n an allergic rash on the skin.

HM abbr His/Her Majesty.

HMS abbr His/Her Majesty's Ship.

HND abbr Brit Higher National Diploma.

Ho abbr the chemical symbol for holmium.

hoard¹ n **1** a supply of money or food stored up for future use. **2** a store of useful information.

Usage Note: Do not confuse this word with horde, which is a large disorganized group of people (hordes of tourists).

---

hoard² v to accumulate (a hoard). ➤ **hoarder** n.

hoarding n Brit **1** a large board for displaying advertisements. **2** a temporary fence put round a building site.

hoarfrost n a covering of minute ice crystals on the ground, trees, etc.

hoarse adj of a voice: rough or harsh in sound. ➤ **hoarsely** adv.

hoary adj (-ier, -iest) **1** grey or white with age. **2** having greyish or whitish hair. **3** venerably old. **4** hackneyed.

hoax¹ n a trick or practical joke.

hoax² v to deceive or trick. ➤ **hoaxer** n.

hob n Brit the top surface of a cooker, with hotplates for pans.

hobble¹ v **1** to walk unsteadily. **2** to fasten together the legs of (a horse) to prevent it from straying.

hobble² n **1** a hobbling movement. **2** a rope used to hobble a horse.

hobby n (pl -ies) a leisure activity or pastime.

hobbyhorse n **1** a toy consisting of an imitation horse's head attached to one end of a stick. **2** a favourite topic or preoccupation.

hobgoblin n a mischievous goblin.

hobnail n a short nail for studding the soles of shoes or boots. ➤ **hobnailed** adj.

hobnob v (hobnobbed, hobnobbing) informal to socialize or chat with.

hobo n (pl -oes or -os) NAmer a tramp or vagrant.

Hobson's choice n an apparently free choice that offers no real alternative.

hock¹ n **1** the middle joint of an animal's hind leg. **2** a knuckle of meat.

hock² n Brit a medium-dry white German wine.

hock³ v informal to pawn.

hock⁴ ✳ **in hock 1** having been pawned. **2** in debt.

hockey n a team game played with long hooked sticks and a small hard ball.

hocus-pocus n **1** nonsensical words uttered by a conjurer. **2** obscure or misleading nonsense.

hod n **1** a trough mounted on a pole handle for carrying mortar, bricks, etc. **2** a tall coal scuttle.

hoe¹ n an implement with a long handle and a flat blade, used for tilling, weeding, etc.

hoe² v **1** to weed or cultivate (land or a crop) with a hoe. **2** to remove (weeds) with a hoe.

hoedown n NAmer a lively square dance.

hog¹ n **1** a castrated male pig raised for slaughter. **2** informal a greedy person. ✳ **go the whole hog** informal to do something thoroughly.

hog² v (hogged, hogging) informal to take too much of (something); to monopolize. ➤ **hogger** n.

Hogmanay n in Scotland, New Year's Eve.

hogshead n a large cask or barrel.

hogwash n informal nonsensical talk.

hoick v Brit, informal to lift or pull abruptly.

hoi polloi pl n the common people.

hoist¹ v to raise into position by means of tackle.

hoist² n an apparatus for hoisting something.

hoity-toity adj haughty or self-important.

hokey cokey n a dance performed by a large group of people in a circle.

hokum n informal **1** nonsense. **2** the use of sentimentality to captivate the audience of a play, film, etc.

hold¹ v (past tense and past part. **held**) **1** to have or support something in the hands or arms. **2** to embrace. **3** to detain (somebody). **4** of a container: to contain or be able to contain. **5** to keep in a specified position. **6** to occupy (a position or job). **7** to maintain (a belief). **8** to consider (somebody) to be to blame for something. **9** to organize (a meeting, party, etc). **10** to take part in (a conversation). **11** to maintain a condition or position. **12** to keep a telephone connection. * **hold forth** to speak at length. **hold one's own** to maintain one's position in the face of opposition. **hold somebody to something** to make somebody honour a commitment. **hold something against somebody** to have a grudge against somebody. **hold to** to remain faithful to (a principle). ➤ **holder** n.

hold² n **1** a manner of grasping something or somebody; a grip. **2** something for grasping as a support. **3** influence or control. **4** the cargo compartment of a ship or aircraft. * **no holds barred** with no limits or restrictions. **on hold** postponed or temporarily suspended. **take hold 1** to grasp, or seize. **2** to take effect.

holdall n *Brit* a large bag for miscellaneous articles.

hold back v **1** to keep in check. **2** to hesitate.

hold down v to keep and manage well in (a job).

holding n **1** a piece of land held by a tenant. **2** (*in pl*) financial assets in the form of land or securities.

hold off v **1** to keep (an attacker or challenge) at a distance. **2** to delay (action). **3** of bad weather: not to occur.

hold on v **1** to persevere despite difficulties. **2** to wait. * **hold on to** to keep possession of.

hold out v **1** to persevere despite difficulties. **2** to offer (hope). **3** to continue to be enough.

hold over v to postpone (an event).

holdup n **1** an armed robbery. **2** a delay.

hold up v **1** to delay (a person or activity). **2** to rob at gunpoint. **3** to retain force or value.

hole¹ n **1** a hollow in something solid. **2** a gap or opening through something. **3** in golf, a cylindrical cavity in a putting green into which the ball is played. **4** *informal* a small or unpleasant place. **5** *informal* an awkward situation. * **make a hole in** to use up a lot of (a supply).

hole² v **1** to make a hole in. **2** in golf, to hit (the ball) into a hole.

hole up v *informal* (*usu* + in) to hide oneself in a confined place.

holiday¹ n **1** *Brit* an extended period taken as leave or a break from one's normal occupation. **2** an official day of leave from work.

holiday² v to take or spend a holiday.

holidaymaker n a person on holiday away form home.

holiness n **1** the quality of being holy. **2** (**His/Your Holiness**) a title for the Pope and other religious leaders.

holistic adj in alternative medicine, treating the whole person, not merely the symptoms. ➤ **holism** n.

holler v *NAmer* to shout loudly.

hollow¹ adj **1** having a recessed surface; curved inwards. **2** having a cavity within. **3** of a sound: echoing or muffled. **4** lacking in real value or

significance. **5** insincere. * **beat hollow** to defeat thoroughly. ➤ **hollowly** adv.

hollow² v (*usu* + out) to make hollow.

hollow³ n **1** a small valley or basin. **2** an unfilled space or cavity.

holly n a shrub with thick glossy spiny-edged leaves and bright red berries.

hollyhock n a tall plant with large rounded leaves and tall spikes of showy flowers.

holocaust n **1** an instance of wholesale destruction or loss of life. **2** (**the Holocaust**) the persecution of European Jews by the Nazis during World War II.

hologram n a photograph that produces a three-dimensional image when illuminated. ➤ **holographic** adj, **holography** n.

holster n a holder for a pistol, usu worn on a belt.

holy adj (**-ier, -iest**) **1** set apart to the service of God or a god; sacred. **2** spiritually pure; godly.

holy of holies n a place considered sacred.

Holy Spirit n (**the Holy Spirit**) the third person of the Trinity.

holy war n a war undertaken in the name of religion.

Holy Week n the week before Easter.

homage n public honour or deference to a person.

homburg n a man's felt hat with a stiff curled brim and a high crown.

home¹ n **1** the place where one lives. **2** a place of origin. **3** an establishment providing residential care. **4** the finishing point in a race. * **at home** relaxed and comfortable. ➤ **homeless** adj, **homeward** adj and adv.

home² adv **1** to or at one's home or family. **2** into place. * **bring home to somebody** to make somebody aware of (a fact or circumstance). **home and dry** having reached one's objective.

home³ adj **1** relating to one's home. **2** relating to one's own country. **3** denoting the headquarters or centre of operations. **4** of a match: played on a team's own ground.

home⁴ v of a bird or animal: to return to its base by instinct. * **home in on** to move towards or concentrate on.

home economics pl n the study of cookery and household management.

home help n *Brit* a person employed to carry out household chores.

homeland n one's native land.

homely adj (**-ier, -iest**) **1** commonplace or familiar. **2** simple and unpretentious. **3** affectionate and sympathetic. **4** *chiefly NAmer* plain or unattractive. ➤ **homeliness** n.

homeopathy or **homoeopathy** n a system of treating diseases by administering minute doses of substances that produce symptoms like those of the disease. ➤ **homeopathic** adj.

home page *n* the page of a website with general information, which is accessed first.

home rule *n* self-government by the people of a dependent political unit.

home run *n* in baseball, a hit that enables the batter to make a complete circuit of the bases and score a run.

homesick *adj* missing one's home while absent from it. ➤ **homesickness** *n*.

homespun *adj* lacking sophistication; simple.

homestead *n* a house with adjoining land.

home truth *n* (*also in pl*) an unpleasant fact about one's character or situation, heard from another person.

homework *n* **1** school work that a pupil is given to do at home. **2** preparatory reading or research.

homicide *n* murder. ➤ **homicidal** *adj*.

homily *n* (*pl* **-ies**) a talk on a religious or moral subject.

homoeopathy *n* see HOMEOPATHY.

homogeneous /homə'jeeni-əs/ *adj* **1** of the same or a similar kind. **2** of uniform structure or composition. ➤ **homogeneity** *n*.

homogenize *or* **-ise** *v* **1** to make or become uniform. **2** to break up the fat globules of (milk) so that the cream does not rise. ➤ **homogenized** *adj*.

homonym *n* a word that has the same spelling and pronunciation as another but a different meaning and origin, as with the noun and the verb *bear*.

homophobia *n* hostility to or fear of homosexuality and homosexuals. ➤ **homophobic** *adj*.

homophone *n* a word that is pronounced like another but has a different meaning, origin, or spelling, e.g. *to*, *too*, and *two*.

Homo sapiens *n* the species that includes humans.

homosexual[1] *adj* having a sexual preference for members of the same sex. ➤ **homosexuality** *n*.

homosexual[2] *n* a homosexual person.

Hon. *abbr* used as a title: Honourable.

hone *v* **1** to sharpen (a tool) with a stone. **2** to make keener or more effective.

honest *adj* **1** sincere and truthful. **2** earned fairly. **3** simple and unpretentious. ➤ **honestly** *adv*.

honesty *n* **1** sincerity and truthfulness. **2** upright and straightforward conduct.

honey *n* a sweet sticky golden liquid made by bees from the nectar of flowers and used as a food.

honeybee *n* a honey-producing bee.

honeycomb *n* **1** a mass of six-sided wax cells built by bees to contain their brood and stores of honey. **2** a cellular structure resembling this. ➤ **honeycombed** *adj*.

honeydew *n* a sweet deposit secreted on the leaves of plants by insects.

honeyed *or* **honied** *adj literary* of words: sweet and soothing.

honeymoon *n* **1** a holiday taken by a married couple immediately after their marriage. **2** a period of harmony and goodwill at the start of a new relationship.

honeypot *n* a place with attractions that draw many visitors.

honeysuckle *n* a climbing shrub with showy sweet-smelling flowers.

honk[1] *v* **1** to sound a car's horn. **2** to make the cry of a goose. ➤ **honker** *n*.

honk[2] *n* a honking sound.

honky-tonk *n* **1** ragtime piano playing. **2** *chiefly NAmer, informal* a cheap nightclub or dance hall.

honorary *adj* **1** of a title or award: conferred in recognition of achievement. **2** unpaid or voluntary.

honorific *adj* conferring or conveying honour.

honour[1] (*NAmer* **honor**) *n* **1** public recognition or fame. **2** a privilege. **3** a person who brings credit or recognition. **4** an award for achievement or excellence. **5** a sense of morality and justice. **6** a good name or reputation. **7** (*in pl*) the highest academic standard in a degree course or examination. **8** (**Your/His Honour**) used as a title for a judge in court. ✴ **in honour of** as a mark of respect for.

honour[2] (*NAmer* **honor**) *v* **1** to regard with deep respect. **2** to confer a mark of distinction on. **3** to fulfil (an obligation or commitment).

honourable (*NAmer* **honorable**) *adj* **1** characterized by a sense of honour. **2** worthy of respect. **3** (*often* **Honourable**) used as a title for Members of Parliament.

hooch *or* **hootch** *n NAmer, informal* a cheap or illicit alcoholic drink.

hood[1] *n* **1** a covering for the top and back of the head and neck. **2** a folding waterproof cover for an open car, pram, etc. **3** a cover or canopy. **4** *NAmer* the bonnet of a vehicle. ➤ **hooded** *adj*.

hood[2] *n NAmer, informal* a hoodlum or gangster.

hoodlum *n* a thug or gangster.

hoodoo *n* (*pl* **-os**) **1** voodoo. **2** a malign influence that haunts one.

hoodwink *v* to deceive or delude.

hoof[1] *n* (*pl* **hooves** *or* **hoofs**) a horny casing on the foot of a horse, cow, etc. ➤ **hoofed** *adj*.

hoof[2] *v informal* to kick (a ball, etc) firmly. ✴ **hoof it** *informal* to go on foot.

hook[1] *n* **1** a curved device for hanging things on or attaching things to. **2** a repeated melodic phrase in a song. **3** a sickle. **4** a short blow delivered with a circular motion while the elbow remains bent and rigid. ✴ **by hook or by crook** by any possible means. **hook, line, and**

243 | horror

sinker completely. **off the hook** *informal* freed from a difficulty.

hook² *v* **1** to attach with a hook. **2** (+ round/over) to crook or bend (an arm or leg) round something. **3** to get hold of with a hooked implement. ✻ **be hooked** *informal* to be addicted or infatuated.

hookah *n* an oriental tobacco pipe in which the smoke is drawn through a container of water by means of a flexible tube.

hooker *n* **1** in rugby, the player in the middle of the front row of the scrum. **2** *informal* a woman prostitute.

hook up *v* to link or be linked to (electronic equipment).

hookworm *n* a parasitic worm with strong mouth hooks for attaching to the host's intestinal lining.

hooligan *n* a violent young troublemaker. ➤ **hooliganism** *n*.

hoop *n* **1** a large circular strip of rigid material. **2** a circular figure or object. **3** an arch through which balls are hit in croquet. **4** a horizontal band of contrasting colour round a cap or sports shirt. ✻ **go through the hoops** to undergo difficult tests. ➤ **hooped** *adj*.

hoop-la *n* **1** *Brit* a fairground game in which rings are thrown over prizes to win them. **2** *NAmer* fuss or noise.

hooray *interj* = HURRAY.

hoot¹ *v* **1** to make the cry of an owl. **2** to sound the horn of a vehicle. **3** to shout or laugh derisively.

hoot² *n* **1** a hooting sound. **2** *informal* a source of laughter or amusement.

hooter *n* **1** *chiefly Brit* a device for producing a loud hooting noise. **2** *informal* the nose.

Hoover *n trademark* a vacuum cleaner.

hooves *n* pl of HOOF¹.

hop¹ *v* (**hopped, hopping**) **1** to jump repeatedly on one foot. **2** of an animal: to move with a quick springy leap. **3** of a bird: to jump with both feet. **4** to make a quick trip by air. **5** to jump over. ✻ **hop it!** *Brit, informal* go away! **hopping mad** *informal* extremely angry.

hop² *n* **1** a hopping leap or movement. **2** a short journey by air. **3** *informal* a dance. ✻ **on the hop** *informal* unprepared.

hop³ *n* **1** a climbing plant with cone-shaped catkins. **2** (*in pl*) the ripe dried catkins of a hop used to give a bitter taste in brewing.

hope¹ *v* **1** to desire or trust that something is or may be the case. **2** to desire and expect (to do something). **3** (+ for) to be eager for.

hope² *n* **1** (*also in pl*) the feeling that what one wants to happen can happen. **2** a chance that a desired thing may happen. **3** (*in pl*) the things one wants to happen. **4** a person or thing that one is depending on.

hopeful¹ *adj* feeling or inspiring hope.

hopeful² *n* a person hoping or likely to succeed.

hopefully *adv* **1** in a hopeful manner. **2** *informal* it is hoped; I hope.

Usage Note: The second meaning, as in *hopefully, I'll be home before dark*, is controversial.

hopeless *adj* **1** having no expectation of success. **2** unable to be dealt with or resolved. **3** incompetent or useless. ➤ **hopelessly** *adv*, **hopelessness** *n*.

hopper *n* a funnel-shaped receptacle for storing and dispensing grain, coal, etc.

hopscotch *n* a children's game in which players hop through a figure marked on the ground.

horde *n* a large disorganized group of people.

Usage Note: Do not confuse this word with *hoard*, which is a supply of something (*a hoard of money*).

horizon *n* **1** the line in the distance where the land and the sky appear to meet. **2** (*also in pl*) one's range of perception, experience, or knowledge.

horizontal *adj* parallel to the earth's surface; level. ➤ **horizontally** *adv*.

hormone *n* **1** a substance produced in the body, creating a specific effect on the activity of cells. **2** a synthetic substance that imitates a natural hormone. ➤ **hormonal** *adj*.

horn *n* **1** a bony projection on the head of cattle, deer, and other animals. **2** the tough fibrous material forming the horns and hooves of animals. **3** a brass instrument with a coiled tube that flares out at the end. **4** a device on a vehicle, for making loud warning noises. ✻ **draw in one's horns** to reduce one's activities or spending. ➤ **horned** *adj*.

hornblende *n* a dark mineral consisting chiefly of silicates of calcium, magnesium, and iron.

hornet *n* a large wasp.

hornpipe *n* a lively sailors' dance.

horny *adj* (**-ier, -iest**) **1** made of or resembling horn. **2** *informal* sexually aroused.

horology *n* **1** the science of measuring time. **2** the art of making clocks and watches.

horoscope *n* a forecast of a person's future, based on the relative positions of planets and signs of the zodiac at the time of birth.

horrendous *adj* dreadful or horrible. ➤ **horrendously** *adv*.

horrible *adj* **1** causing horror. **2** *chiefly informal* extremely unpleasant. ➤ **horribly** *adv*.

horrid *adj* horrible or shocking.

horrific *adj* causing horror; horrifying. ➤ **horrifically** *adv*.

horrify *v* (**-ies, -ied**) to cause to feel horror.

horror *n* **1** intense fear or dread. **2** intense aversion or repugnance. **3** the quality of inspiring horror. **4** *informal* an unpleasant or ugly person or thing.

hors d'oeuvre /ˌaw 'duhv/ *n* (*pl* **hors d'oeuvres** *or* **hors d'oeuvre**) a savoury appetizer.

horse[1] *n* **1** a large four-footed mammal, used for riding or as a beast of burden. **2** (*treated as sing. or pl*) cavalry. **3** a wooden block for vaulting over in gymnastics. ✻ **from the horse's mouth** first-hand.

horse[2] *v informal* (*usu* + around/about) to fool about.

horseback *n* ✻ **on horseback** riding a horse.

horsebox *n* a lorry or trailer for transporting horses.

horse chestnut *n* **1** a large tree with five-lobed leaves and nuts enclosed in a spiny case. **2** a nut of this tree, a conker.

horsefly *n* (*pl* **-ies**) a large fly, the females of which suck blood.

horse laugh *n* a loud boisterous laugh.

horseman *n* (*pl* **horsemen**) a skilled rider on horseback. ➤ **horsemanship** *n*.

horseplay *n* rough or boisterous play.

horsepower *n* a unit of power equal to about 746 watts.

horseradish *n* a plant with a pungent root from which a sauce is made.

horse sense *n* ordinary common sense.

horseshoe *n* a U-shaped metal shoe for horses.

horsewhip[1] *n* a long whip used for controlling horses.

horsewhip[2] *v* (**horsewhipped, horsewhipping**) to beat with a horsewhip.

horsewoman *n* (*pl* **horsewomen**) a skilled female rider on horseback.

hortative *or* **hortatory** *adj formal* giving encouragement.

horticulture *n* the science of growing fruits, vegetables, and flowers. ➤ **horticultural** *adj*.

hosanna *interj* and *n* a cry of acclamation and adoration.

hose[1] *n* **1** a flexible tube for conveying fluids. **2** tights or stockings.

hose[2] *v* (*often* + down) to spray or water with a hose.

hosepipe *n* a length of hose for conveying water.

hosiery *n* socks, stockings, and tights.

hospice *n* a nursing home for terminally ill patients.

hospitable *adj* **1** offering a generous welcome to guests or strangers. **2** of an environment: pleasant and sustaining. ➤ **hospitably** *adv*.

hospital *n* a place where sick or injured people are given medical care.

hospitality *n* friendly treatment of guests and visitors.

hospitalize *or* **-ise** *v* to admit to a hospital as a patient. ➤ **hospitalization** *n*.

host[1] *n* **1** a person who receives or entertains guests socially. **2** an establishment that provides facilities for an event or function. **3** a compere on a radio or television programme. **4** a living animal or plant on or in which a parasite or smaller organism lives.

host[2] *v* to act as host at or of.

host[3] *n* **1** a very large number; a multitude. **2** *chiefly literary or archaic* an army.

host[4] *or* **Host** *n* the bread consecrated in the Christian Eucharist.

hostage *n* a person held captive to ensure that demands are met by another party. ✻ **hostage to fortune** a commitment that lays one open to the risk of failure or criticism.

hostel *n* an establishment providing accommodation for a particular group of people.

hostelry *n* (*pl* **-ies**) *archaic* an inn or hotel.

hostess *n* **1** a woman host. **2** a woman who welcomes male patrons at a bar or nightclub.

hostile *adj* **1** relating to an enemy. **2** aggressive and unfriendly.

hostility *n* (*pl* **-ies**) **1** hostile action or attitudes. **2** (*in pl*) overt acts of warfare.

hot[1] *adj* (**hotter, hottest**) **1** having a relatively high temperature. **2** uncomfortable from excessive heat. **3** of a taste: pungent or spicy. **4** interesting or exciting. **5** currently popular or retailing fast. **6** *informal* of goods: stolen and difficult to dispose. **7** (+ on) knowledgeable about. **8** (+ on) strict about rules, standards, etc. ✻ **hot under the collar** *informal* angry or irritated. **in hot water** in trouble. **not so hot** *informal* not very good.

hot[2] *v* (**hotted, hotting**) *informal* (+ up) to become more intense or exciting.

hot air *n informal* empty talk.

hotbed *n* a place of intense or exciting activity of a particular kind.

hot-blooded *adj* excitable or passionate.

hotchpotch (*NAmer* **hodgepodge**) *n* a random mixture or jumble.

hot cross bun *n* a spicy bun with a pastry cross on top, eaten on Good Friday.

hot dog *n* a hot sausage served in a bread roll.

hotel *n* an establishment that provides meals and accommodation for the public, in return for payment.

hotelier *n* the proprietor or manager of a hotel.

hotfoot[1] *adv* in haste.

hotfoot[2] *v* ✻ **hotfoot it** *informal* to hurry.

hothead *n* an impetuous or hot-tempered person.

hothouse *n* a heated greenhouse.

hotly *adv* keenly or passionately.

hot plate *n* a metal plate on an electric cooker, for heating food.

hot pot *n Brit* a stew of meat and vegetables with sliced potatoes.

hot rod *n* a car modified for high speed.

hotshot *n informal* a showily successful or important person.

hot spot *n* a place of excitement or potential danger.

hot-tempered *adj* inclined to lose one's temper easily.

hot-water bottle *n* a rubber container filled with hot water and used to warm a bed.

hot-wire *v* to start (a vehicle) by bypassing the ignition switch.

hound[1] *n* a hunting dog.

hound[2] *v* to pursue or harass persistently.

hour *n* **1** the 24th part of a day; a period of 60 minutes. **2** a particular point in time. **3** a period of time set aside for a specified purpose. **4** (*in pl*) the period during which a business, etc is operational. ✱ **on the hour** at an exact hour. **till all hours** until very late at night.

hourglass *n* a device consisting of two glass bulbs joined by a narrow neck, with sand taking one hour to run from the top bulb to the lower.

hourly *adj and adv* **1** at or during every hour. **2** by the hour. **3** constant or constantly.

house[1] /hows/ *n* (*pl* **houses** /'howziz/) **1** a building for people to live in. **2** a building or establishment with a particular purpose: *an opera house; a boathouse.* **3** a specific type of business: *a publishing house.* **4** a legislative or deliberative assembly. **5** a division of pupils in a school. **6** an important or ancient family. **7** the area occupied by the audience in a theatre or cinema. ✱ **on the house** at the expense of the management. ➤ **houseful** *n*.

house[2] /howz/ *v* to provide with accommodation or storage.

house arrest *n* confinement in one's home instead of prison.

houseboat *n* a moored boat fitted out as a home.

housebound *adj* confined to one's house.

housebreaking *n* an act of breaking into a building with a criminal purpose. ➤ **housebreaker** *n*.

household *n* a dwelling and all the people who live in it.

household name *or* **household word** *n* a person or thing everyone has heard of.

housekeeper *n* a person employed to take charge of running a house.

housemaid *n* a female servant employed to do housework.

housemaster *or* **housemistress** *n* a teacher in charge of a house at a boarding school.

house music *n* dance music with a strong fast beat.

House of Commons *n* the lower house of the British Parliament.

House of Lords *n* the upper house of the British Parliament, including lords and bishops.

house-proud *adj* careful about the management and appearance of one's home.

houseroom ✱ **not give something houseroom** *Brit* to have no interest in something.

housetrain *v* to train (a pet) to defecate and urinate outdoors.

housewarming *n* a party to celebrate moving into a new house.

housewife *n* (*pl* **housewives**) a woman who runs her family's home.

housework *n* the work involved in running a home.

housing *n* **1** houses or living-places collectively. **2** a protective cover for machinery or instruments.

hove *v* past tense and past part. of HEAVE[1].

hovel *n* a small squalid dwelling.

hover *v* **1** to stay motionless in the air. **2** to linger or wait restlessly. **3** to be in a state of uncertainty or suspense. ➤ **hoverer** *n*.

hovercraft *n* (*pl* **hovercraft**) a vehicle supported on a cushion of air for travelling over land and water.

how *adv* **1** in what way or by what means. **2** in what state or condition. **3** to what extent or degree. **4** used in exclamations: *how odd!*

howdah *n* a seat for riding on the back of an elephant or camel.

however *adv* **1** be that as it may; nevertheless. **2** in whatever manner or way. **3** no matter how.

howitzer *n* a short cannon with a high trajectory.

howl[1] *v* **1** of a dog: to make a loud sustained cry. **2** to yell or cry loudly. **3** of wind: to make a sustained wailing sound.

howl[2] *n* a howling sound.

howler *n* *informal* a careless blunder.

HP *or* **hp** *abbr* **1** hire purchase. **2** horsepower.

HQ *abbr* headquarters.

HRH *abbr* His/Her Royal Highness.

HTML *abbr* hypertext markup language, a system for presenting computer text for use on a network.

hub *n* **1** the central part of a wheel, propeller, or fan. **2** the focal point of an activity.

hubbub *n* a noisy confusion or uproar.

hubris *n* excessive pride leading to retribution. ➤ **hubristic** *adj*.

huckster *n* **1** a hawker or pedlar. **2** a person who uses aggressive selling methods.

huddle[1] *v* **1** (*often* + together) to gather in a close group. **2** to curl up or crouch.

huddle[2] *n* **1** a crowded group. **2** a secretive meeting.

hue *n* **1** a colour or shade. **2** a complexion or aspect.

hue and cry *n* a loud public outcry.

huff[1] *v* **1** to emit loud puffs of breath. **2** to make empty threats.

huff[2] ✱ **in a huff** sulky and resentful. ➤ **huffy** *adj*.

hug[1] *v* (**hugged, hugging**) **1** to hold tightly in one's arms. **2** to keep close to.

hug[2] *n* an act of hugging.

huge *adj* very large. ➤ **hugely** *adv*.

hugger-mugger *adj and adv* confused or muddled.

hula *or* **hula-hula** /'hoohlə/ *n* a Polynesian dance involving swaying of the hips.

hula hoop *n* a large light hoop spun round the waist by movement of the body.

hulk *n* **1** the stripped hull of a disused ship. **2** a bulky or clumsy person or thing.

hulking *adj informal* bulky; massive.

hull *n* **1** the main body of a ship. **2** the outer covering of a fruit or seed. **3** the calyx that surrounds a strawberry or raspberry.

hullabaloo *n* (*pl* **-os**) *informal* a confused noise or uproar.

hullo *interj chiefly Brit* see HELLO.

hum[1] *v* (**hummed, humming**) **1** to utter a prolonged /m/ sound. **2** to make the droning noise of an insect in flight. **3** to sing with the lips closed. **4** *informal* to be lively or active. * **hum and haw** to be indecisive.

hum[2] *n* a humming sound.

human[1] *adj* **1** relating to people. **2** having the good attributes thought to be characteristic of people. ➤ **humanly** *adv.*

human[2] *n* a man, woman, or child.

humane *adj* marked by compassion or consideration for others. ➤ **humanely** *adv.*

humanism *n* a philosophy that asserts the intrinsic worth of human beings and rejects religious belief. ➤ **humanist** *n and adj,* **humanistic** *adj.*

humanitarian[1] *adj* relating to or promoting human welfare.

humanitarian[2] *n* a humanitarian person; a philanthropist.

humanity *n* (*pl* **-ies**) **1** human beings collectively. **2** the quality of being human or humane. **3** (*in pl*) the cultural branches of learning.

humanize *or* **-ise** *v* **1** to give (something) a human quality. **2** to make (a person) humane.

humankind *n* human beings collectively.

humanoid[1] *adj* having human form or characteristics.

humanoid[2] *n* a humanoid being.

human rights *pl n* the basic rights that all human beings are entitled to.

humble[1] *adj* **1** having a low opinion of oneself. **2** marked by deference or submission. **3** ranking low in a hierarchy or scale. **4** modest or unpretentious. ➤ **humbly** *adv.*

humble[2] *v* **1** to make humble in spirit or manner. **2** to destroy the power or importance of. **3** to sacrifice one's pride and abase (oneself).

humbug *n* **1** pretentious or deceptive talk. **2** an impostor or sham. **3** *Brit* a hard peppermint-flavoured striped sweet.

humdrum *adj* monotonous or dull.

humerus *n* (*pl* **humeri**) the bone of the upper arm, extending from the shoulder to the elbow.

humid *adj* of the atmosphere: warm and moist. ➤ **humidity** *n.*

humiliate *v* to make (somebody) feel foolish or unworthy. ➤ **humiliation** *n.*

humility *n* the quality of being humble.

hummingbird *n* a small brightly coloured bird with narrow wings that it beats rapidly making a humming sound.

hummock *n* a mound or hillock.

hummus *or* **hoummous** *n* a puree made from chick-peas and sesame seed paste.

humorist *n* a person noted for humour.

humorous *adj* characterized by or expressing humour. ➤ **humorously** *adv.*

humour[1] (*NAmer* **humor**) *n* **1** a comic or amusing quality. **2** a state of mind; temper. * **out of humour** in a bad temper. ➤ **humourless** *adj.*

humour[2] (*NAmer* **humor**) *v* to comply with the mood or wishes of.

hump[1] *n* **1** a humped or crooked back. **2** a fleshy lump on the back of a camel, bison, etc. **3** a mound or knoll. ➤ **humped** *adj.*

hump[2] *v* to carry with difficulty.

humus *n* an organic substance resulting from partial decomposition of plant or animal matter.

hunch[1] *v* **1** to assume a bent or crooked posture. **2** to arch (one's shoulders).

hunch[2] *n* a strong intuitive feeling.

hunchback *n offensive* a person with a humped back.

hundred *n* (*pl* **hundreds** *or* **hundred**) **1** (**a/one hundred**) the number 100. **2** (*in pl*) the numbers 100 to 999. **3** *informal* (*in pl*) a large number. ➤ **hundredth** *adj and n.*

hundredweight *n* (*pl* **hundredweights** *or* **hundredweight**) **1** a British unit of weight equal to 112lb (about 50.80kg). **2** *NAmer* a US unit of weight equal to 100lb (about 45.36kg).

hung *v* past tense and past part. of HANG[1]. * **hung up** *informal* emotionally anxious. **hung up on** *informal* obsessed with.

hunger[1] *n* **1** an unpleasant feeling caused by a need for food. **2** a strong desire or craving.

hunger[2] *v* (**hungered, hungering**) **1** to feel or suffer hunger. **2** (+ for/after) to have a strong desire for something.

hunger strike *n* refusal to eat, as an act of protest.

hung over *adj* suffering from a hangover.

hung parliament *n* a parliament in which no party holds an overall majority.

hungry *adj* (**-ier, -iest**) **1** feeling hunger. **2** eager or avid for something. ➤ **hungrily** *adv.*

hunk *n* **1** a large lump or piece of something. **2** *informal* an attractive muscular man. ➤ **hunky** *adj.*

hunky-dory *adj informal* pleasing or satisfactory.

hunt[1] *v* **1** to chase and kill (a wild animal) for food or enjoyment. **2** of an animal: to chase and kill (prey). **3** to pursue (a suspect). **4** (+ for) to attempt to find something. **5** of a device, machine, etc: to run alternately fast and slowly. ➤ **hunter** n.

hunt² n **1** the act or an instance of hunting. **2** a group of mounted hunters and their hounds. **3** an area where people hunt.

hunt down v to pursue to capture or kill.

huntsman n (pl **huntsmen**) a person who hunts.

hurdle¹ n **1** a framework used for enclosing land or livestock. **2** a light barrier jumped by athletes or horses in a race. **3** an obstacle or testing experience.

hurdle² v to jump over (a barrier) while running. ➤ **hurdler** n.

hurdy-gurdy n (pl **-ies**) a musical instrument played by turning a handle.

hurl v **1** to throw forcefully. **2** to shout (abuse or insults) at somebody.

hurling n an Irish team game resembling hockey.

hurly-burly n an uproar or commotion.

hurrah interj = HURRAY.

hurray or **hooray** interj used as a cheer to express joy, approval, or encouragement.

hurricane n a cyclone with a wind speed greater than 117km/h (73mph).

hurry¹ v (**-ies, -ied**) **1** (often + up) to act or move quickly. **2** (often + up) to make (a person or process) go faster. ➤ **hurried** adj, **hurriedly** adv.

hurry² n haste or rush. ✳ **in a hurry** in haste; rushed.

hurt¹ v (past tense and past part. **hurt**) **1** to cause pain or injury to. **2** to be painful. **3** to offend or upset.

hurt² adj **1** injured. **2** upset or offended.

hurt³ n emotional distress caused by being offended or upset.

hurtful adj unkind or likely to upset. ➤ **hurtfully** adv.

hurtle v to move rapidly or precipitately.

husband¹ n the man to whom a woman is married.

husband² v to make economical use of (a resource).

husbandry n **1** farming. **2** economical use of resources.

hush¹ v to quieten or become quiet. ➤ **hushed** adj.

hush² n a silence or calm.

husk¹ n the dry outer covering of a seed or fruit.

husk² v to strip the husk from.

husky¹ adj (**-ier, -iest**) **1** of a voice: hoarse and rough. **2** burly or hefty. ➤ **huskily** adv.

husky² n (pl **-ies**) a powerful sledge dog native to Greenland and Labrador.

hussar n a member of a cavalry regiment.

hussy n (pl **-ies**) derog an impudent or promiscuous woman or girl.

hustings pl n the speeches and campaigning of a political election.

hustle¹ v **1** to push or convey roughly or forcibly. **2** to force (somebody) into doing something. **3** informal to swindle or cheat (somebody) out of something. ➤ **hustler** n.

hustle² n the act of hustling.

hut n a small simple dwelling or shelter.

hutch n a pen or cage for a small animal.

hyacinth n a plant with blue, pink, or white flowers growing in spikes.

hyaena n see HYENA.

hybrid n **1** an offspring of two animals or plants of different breeds or varieties. **2** something formed from two or more different things.

hydrangea n a shrub with large clusters of white, pink, or pale blue flowers.

hydrant n a pipe with a valve and nozzle from which water may be drawn from a main.

hydrate v to cause (a substance) to absorb or combine with water. ➤ **hydration** n.

hydraulic adj operated by pressure in a liquid being forced through pipes, tubes, etc. ➤ **hydraulically** adv.

hydraulics pl n a branch of physics dealing with the uses of liquid in motion.

hydrocarbon n an organic compound containing only carbon and hydrogen.

hydrocephalus or **hydrocephaly** n an abnormal increase in fluid in the brain cavity.

hydrochloric acid n a solution of hydrogen and chlorine in water that is a strong corrosive acid.

hydroelectric adj relating to the production of electricity by water power. ➤ **hydroelectricity** n.

hydrofoil n a boat fitted with an aerofoil that lifts the hull out of the water at speed.

hydrogen n a flammable gas that is the simplest and lightest of the chemical elements.

hydrogen bomb n a bomb with enormous power due to the sudden release of atomic energy from the fusion of hydrogen nuclei.

hydrogen sulphide n an inflammable poisonous gas with a smell of rotten eggs.

hydrophobia n **1** abnormal dread of water. **2** rabies.

hydroplane n a speedboat that is raised out of the water when moving at speed.

hydrous adj containing water.

hydroxide n a compound of hydrogen and oxygen with an element or radical.

hyena or **hyaena** n a doglike nocturnal animal of Asia and Africa, with front legs longer than the rear legs.

hygiene n conditions and practices that encourage and maintain good health.

hygienic adj clean and conducive to good health. ➤ **hygienically** adv.

hygienist n a person who is trained in hygiene.

hymen *n* a membrane partly closing the opening of the vagina until it is broken, usu on the first occurrence of sexual intercourse.

hymn[1] *n* **1** a song of praise to God. **2** a song of praise or joy.

hymn[2] *v* to praise or worship with hymns.

hymnal *n* a book of hymns.

hype[1] *v informal* (*also* + up) to publicize or promote intensively or in an exaggerated way.
∗ **be hyped up** to be stimulated or excited.

hype[2] *n informal* intensive or exaggerated advertising or publicity.

hyper *adj informal* over-excited; overwrought.

hyperactive *adj* excessively or abnormally active. ➤ **hyperactivity** *n*.

hyperbola *n* (*pl* **hyperbolas** *or* **hyperbolae**) a plane curve generated by a point moving so that the difference of its distances from two fixed points is a constant.

hyperbole *n* deliberate exaggeration for special effect, as in *It took me years to finish*. ➤ **hyperbolic** *adj*.

hyperlink *n* a link to another location from a hypertext document.

hypermarket *n* a very large supermarket.

hypersensitive *adj* abnormally sensitive. ➤ **hypersensitivity** *n*.

hypersonic *adj* **1** denoting a speed more than five times that of sound. **2** denoting sound frequencies above a thousand million hertz.

hypertension *n* abnormally high blood pressure. ➤ **hypertensive** *adj*.

hypertext *n* a type of computerized document that contains active links from one part to another.

hyperventilate *v* to breathe excessively fast and deeply. ➤ **hyperventilation** *n*.

hyphen *n* a punctuation mark (-) used to join words or to divide a word at the end of a line. ➤ **hyphened** *adj*.

hyphenate *v* to join or separate (words) with a hyphen. ➤ **hyphenation** *n*.

hypnosis *n* (*pl* **hypnoses**) a condition resembling sleep, in which a person is susceptible to suggestions made to them.

hypnotherapy *n* the treatment of disease using hypnosis.

hypnotic *adj* **1** relating to hypnosis. **2** tending to produce sleep. ➤ **hypnotically** *adv*.

hypnotism *n* the study or practice of hypnosis. ➤ **hypnotist** *n*.

hypnotize *or* **-ise** *v* **1** to induce hypnosis in. **2** to fascinate.

hypoallergenic *adj* of cosmetics: unlikely to cause an allergic reaction.

hypochondria *n* excessive concern about one's health.

hypochondriac *n* a person who is affected by hypochondria.

hypocrisy *n* (*pl* **-ies**) the advocacy to others of principles or qualities that one does not practise oneself.

hypocrite *n* a person given to hypocrisy. ➤ **hypocritical** *adj*.

hypodermic[1] *adj* of a syringe or needle: used to inject drugs beneath the skin.

hypodermic[2] *n* a hypodermic syringe or injection.

hypotension *n* abnormally low blood pressure. ➤ **hypotensive** *adj*.

hypotenuse *n* the longest side of a right-angled triangle, opposite the right angle.

hypothermia *n* abnormally low body temperature. ➤ **hypothermic** *adj*.

hypothesis *n* (*pl* **hypotheses**) a proposed explanation for a phenomenon, set of circumstances, etc, as a basis for argument.

hypothesize *or* **-ise** *v* to propose as a hypothesis.

hypothetical *adj* **1** involving hypothesis or a condition. **2** depending on supposition; conjectural. ➤ **hypothetically** *adv*.

hysterectomy *n* (*pl* **-ies**) surgical removal of the womb.

hysteria *n* **1** a mental disorder marked by extreme emotional excitability. **2** unmanageable emotional excess.

hysterical *adj* **1** relating to or affected by hysteria. **2** *informal* very funny.

hysterics *pl n* **1** a fit of hysteria. **2** *informal* uncontrollable laughter or crying.

Hz *abbr* hertz.

I¹ or **i** *n* (*pl* **I's** or **Is** or **i's**) **1** the ninth letter of the English alphabet. **2** the Roman numeral for one.

I² *pron* the word used by a speaker or writer to refer to himself or herself.

I³ *abbr* the chemical symbol for iodine.

iambic *adj* in a poetic metre that consists of feet containing one unstressed syllable followed by one stressed syllable.

ibex *n* (*pl* **ibexes** or **ibices** or **ibex**) a wild mountain goat with large backward-curving horns.

ibid. *abbr* to be found in the same book, chapter, article, etc, as the quotation immediately preceding this one.

ibis *n* (*pl* **ibises** or **ibis**) a long-legged, long-necked wading bird with a slender downward-curving bill.

ice¹ *n* **1** frozen water. **2** *chiefly Brit* an ice cream. * **on ice** in abeyance; in reserve for later use. **on thin ice** in danger of getting into trouble.

ice² *v* **1** to cover (e.g. a cake) with icing. **2** to chill (e.g. a drink) with ice. **3** (*often* + over/up) to become covered with ice.

ice age *n* a period when much of the earth's surface was covered in ice.

iceberg *n* a large mass of ice floating in the sea. * **the tip of the iceberg** the small visible or known part of something much larger, *esp* of something potentially troublesome.

icebox *n* **1** *Brit* the freezing compartment of a refrigerator. **2** *NAmer* a refrigerator. **3** a container chilled by ice and used for keeping food and drink, etc cold.

icebreaker *n* a ship equipped to make a channel through ice.

ice cap *n* a permanent covering of ice, *esp* over a polar region of a planet.

ice cream *n* a sweet flavoured frozen food made from milk, cream, or custard.

iced *adj* **1** covered with icing. **2** cooled or mixed with ice.

ice hockey *n* a game resembling hockey played on an ice rink by two teams of six players.

ice pack *n* a bag of ice applied to part of the body to reduce swelling or lower temperature.

ice skate *n* a shoe with a metal runner attached for skating on ice.

ichthyology *n* the branch of zoology that deals with fish. ➤ **ichthyologist** *n*.

icicle *n* a hanging tapering mass of ice formed by the freezing of dripping water.

icing *n chiefly Brit* a sweet coating for cakes, biscuits, etc, usu made by mixing icing sugar with water, butter, or egg white. * **the icing on the cake** a final addition that perfects something already good.

icing sugar *n chiefly Brit* finely powdered sugar used in making icing.

icon *n* **1** (*also* **ikon**) a religious image, *esp* a small painting of Christ, the Virgin Mary, or a saint, used as an aid to devotion in the Eastern Orthodox churches. **2** an image or symbol. **3** a revered or idolized person, *esp* one regarded as symbolizing something. **4** in computing, a symbol displayed on a screen, representing or providing access to a program or facility. ➤ **iconic** *adj*.

iconify *v* (**-ies, -ied**) in computing, to reduce a screen window to an icon.

iconoclast *n* a person who attacks established beliefs or institutions. ➤ **iconoclasm** *n*, **iconoclastic** *adj*.

iconography *n* (*pl* **-ies**) **1** pictorial material relating to or illustrating a subject. **2** the use, or study, of imagery or symbolism in works of art. ➤ **iconographic** *adj*.

icy *adj* (**-ier, -iest**) **1** covered with or full of ice. **2** intensely cold. **3** extremely unwelcoming, unfriendly, or hostile. ➤ **icily** *adv*.

ID¹ *abbr* **1** identification. **2** identity.

ID² *v* (**IDs, IDed, IDing**) *informal* to identify or check the identity of.

I'd *contraction* **1** I had. **2** I should. **3** I would.

id *n* in psychoanalytic theory, the division of the mind that is completely unconscious and comprises a person's instinctual needs and drives.

idea *n* **1** a thought, concept, or image present in the mind. **2** an opinion or belief. **3** an indefinite or vague impression. **4** a plan of action. **5** (**the idea**) the central meaning or aim of a particular action. * **have no idea** not to know at all.

ideal¹ *n* **1** a principle or standard of excellence to be aspired to. **2** a person or thing that is regarded as perfect.

ideal² *adj* **1** perfect. **2** existing only in the mind. ➤ **ideally** *adv*.

idealism *n* **1** the practice of striving to live according to one's ideals. **2** the belief that ideals represent true reality. ➤ **idealist** *n*, **idealistic** *adj*.

idealize *or* **-ise** *v* to attribute excellence or perfection to, often unjustifiably. ➤ **idealization** *n*.

identical *adj* **1** the very same. **2** (*often* + to/with) exactly alike. **3** of twins, triplets, etc: derived from a single ovum and therefore very similar in appearance. ➤ **identically** *adv*.

identification *n* **1** the act of identifying. **2** evidence of identity.

identify *v* (**-ies, -ied**) **1** to establish the identity of. **2** to discover by observation or analysis. **3** (+ with) to equate or link (somebody, oneself, or something) with another person or thing. **4** (*usu* + with) to consider that one shares the same qualities or experiences as somebody else. ➤ **identifiable** *adj*.

identity *n* (*pl* **-ies**) **1** who or what somebody or something is. **2** the individual characteristics that define a person. **3** the condition of being exactly alike; sameness.

identity parade *n chiefly Brit* a line-up of people assembled by the police to see whether a witness can identify a suspect.

ideology *n* (*pl* **-ies**) **1** a systematic body of ideas underlying a social, political, or cultural programme. **2** a manner of thinking characteristic of an individual, group, or culture. ➤ **ideological** *adj*.

idiocy *n* (*pl* **-ies**) **1** foolishness. **2** something very stupid or foolish.

idiom *n* **1** an established expression in a language, which has a meaning that cannot be deduced from the meanings of its individual elements, e.g. *in hot water* meaning in serious trouble. **2** the words and expressions characteristically used by a particular group of people. **3** a characteristic style of artistic expression.

idiomatic *adj* **1** relating to idioms. **2** using a language in the way its native speakers naturally do.

idiosyncrasy *n* (*pl* **-ies**) **1** a characteristic of thought or behaviour peculiar to an individual; an eccentricity. **2** a characteristic peculiarity. ➤ **idiosyncratic** *adj*.

idiot *n* a silly or foolish person.

idiotic *adj* extremely foolish. ➤ **idiotically** *adv*.

idle[1] *adj* **1** lazy. **2** not occupied or employed. **3** not in use or operation. **4** having no purpose, effect, or foundation in reality. ➤ **idleness** *n*, **idly** *adv*.

idle[2] *v* **1** to spend time doing nothing. **2** *esp* of an engine: to run without being connected to the part that it drives. ➤ **idler** *n*.

idol *n* **1** an image of a god used as an object of worship. **2** a person who is the object of passionate or excessive devotion.

idolatry *n* **1** the worship of idols. **2** excessive attachment or devotion to somebody or something.

idolize *or* **-ise** *v* to love or admire to excess.

idyll *or* **idyl** *n* **1** a time or situation of peace and happiness. **2** a simple work in poetry or prose describing peaceful rustic life.

idyllic *adj* wonderfully happy, peaceful, or beautiful. ➤ **idyllically** *adv*.

i.e. *abbr* that is to say.

if *conj* **1** in the event that. **2** supposing. **3** on condition that. **4** whether. **5** although.

igloo *n* (*pl* **igloos**) an Inuit dwelling, usu made of snow blocks and in the shape of a dome.

igneous *adj* of rocks: formed by the solidification of molten rock from the earth's core.

ignite *v* **1** to set fire to, or to catch fire. **2** to arouse (an emotion). **3** to cause or start (e.g. a riot or protest).

ignition *n* **1** the act of igniting. **2** the process of igniting a fuel mixture, e.g. in an internal-combustion engine, or a device that does this.

ignoble *adj* base; dishonourable.

ignominious *adj* causing disgrace or discredit; humiliating. ➤ **ignominiously** *adv*.

ignominy *n* (*pl* **-ies**) deep humiliation and disgrace.

ignoramus *n* (*pl* **ignoramuses**) an ignorant or stupid person.

ignorant *adj* **1** having a general lack of knowledge or education. **2** (*often* + of) uninformed about or unaware of. **3** *chiefly informal* lacking social training; impolite. ➤ **ignorance** *n*, **ignorantly** *adv*.

ignore *v* to refuse or fail to take notice of.

iguana *n* a large tropical American lizard with a serrated crest on its back.

ikon *n* see ICON.

ilk *n* sort or kind.

I'll *contraction* I will or I shall.

ill[1] *adj* **1** not in good health. **2** nauseated. **3** causing discomfort or inconvenience; disagreeable: *ill effects*. **4** malevolent; hostile. **5** unlucky or disadvantageous. **6** harsh. ✳ **ill at ease** uneasy or uncomfortable.

ill[2] *adv* (**worse, worst**) **1** hardly; scarcely: *can ill afford*. **2** in a faulty, imperfect, or unpleasant manner.

ill[3] *n* **1** misfortune or trouble. **2** evil.

ill-advised *adj* **1** unwise. **2** showing lack of proper thought or planning.

ill-bred *adj* showing bad upbringing; impolite. ➤ **ill-breeding** *n*.

ill-disposed *adj* (*often* + to/towards) unfriendly; unsympathetic.

illegal *adj* not authorized by law. ➤ **illegality** *n*, **illegally** *adv*.

illegible *adj* unable to be read or deciphered. ➤ **illegibility** *n*.

illegitimate adj **1** not allowed by law or rules. **2** of a child: born to parents who are not lawfully married to each other. ➤ **illegitimacy** n.

ill-fated adj destined for misfortune; unlucky.

ill-favoured (NAmer **ill-favored**) adj unattractive in physical appearance.

ill-gotten adj acquired by illicit or improper means.

illiberal adj **1** not broad-minded; bigoted. **2** not generous; mean.

illicit adj not permitted by law, rules, or custom. ➤ **illicitly** adv.

illiterate adj **1** unable to read or write. **2** showing a lack of education, esp through poor grammar and spelling. **3** lacking knowledge in a particular field. ➤ **illiteracy** n.

illness n a disease or period of sickness.

illogical adj **1** contrary to logic. **2** not well reasoned; senseless. ➤ **illogicality** n, **illogically** adv.

ill-starred adj ill-fated; unlucky.

ill-treat v to treat cruelly or improperly. ➤ **ill-treatment** n.

illuminate v **1** to cast light on; to fill with light. **2** to elucidate or clarify. **3** to decorate (a manuscript) with elaborate and colourful initial letters or marginal designs. ➤ **illuminating** adj.

illumination n **1** the act of illuminating. **2** (also in pl) decorative lighting, e.g. on a building or street.

illumine v literary to illuminate.

illusion n **1** a false impression or belief. **2** something that deceives or misleads, either visually or intellectually. ✳ **be under the illusion that** to have the mistaken belief that.

illusionist n a conjuror or magician.

illusory or **illusive** adj deceptive; unreal.

illustrate v **1** to provide (e.g. a book) with pictures. **2** to clarify, explain, or demonstrate, esp by using examples, analogy, etc. **3** to be an example of. ➤ **illustrative** adj, **illustrator** n.

illustration n **1** a picture or diagram illustrating the text of a book, magazine, etc. **2** an example that explains or clarifies something. **3** the act of illustrating.

illustrious adj **1** admired and well-known, esp for something done in the past. **2** of an action, etc: impressive and publicly acclaimed.

ill will n unfriendly feeling.

I'm contraction I am.

image¹ n **1** a picture or statue of a person or thing. **2** the optical counterpart of an object produced by a lens, mirror, etc, or on a screen, or in a photograph. **3** a mental picture of something not actually present. **4** a conception of the nature or character of a person or organization created in the minds of the general public. **5** a person who strikingly resembles another specified person. **6** a figure of speech, esp a metaphor or simile.

image² v to create or form an image of.

imagery n (pl **-ies**) **1** figurative language. **2** visual symbols.

imaginary adj existing only in imagination; lacking factual reality.

imagination n **1** the part of the mind that can form mental images of things not present to the senses or never before perceived in reality. **2** creative ability. **3** resourcefulness; inventiveness.

imaginative adj **1** having a lively imagination. **2** creative. **3** resourceful; inventive. ➤ **imaginatively** adv.

imagine v **1** to form a mental image of (something not present). **2** to suppose or think. **3** to believe (something) without sufficient basis.

imam n the person who leads the prayers in a mosque.

imbalance n a lack of proportion or balance.

imbecile n informal a fool or idiot. ➤ **imbecilic** adj, **imbecilically** adv, **imbecility** n.

imbed v see EMBED.

imbibe v **1** chiefly formal or humorous. **2** to drink (esp alcohol). **3** to receive (e.g. ideas) into the mind.

imbroglio n (pl **-os**) an intricate or complicated situation or misunderstanding.

imbue v (**imbues, imbued**) of a feeling, principle, etc: to be a pervasive presence in.

imitate v **1** to follow as a pattern, model, or example. **2** to mimic, esp for humorous effect. ➤ **imitator** n.

imitation n **1** the act of imitating. **2** a copy or counterfeit. **3** (used before a noun) not genuine; fake.

imitative adj imitating or copying something.

immaculate adj **1** spotlessly clean and very tidy. **2** free from flaw or error. ➤ **immaculately** adv.

immanent adj **1** existing within something; indwelling; inherent. **2** of God: always present in nature or the universe. ➤ **immanence** n.

immaterial adj **1** unimportant or not relevant. **2** not consisting of matter; incorporeal; spiritual.

immature adj **1** not yet full-grown or fully developed. **2** lacking the wisdom, good sense, etc, associated with adulthood. ➤ **immaturity** n.

immeasurable adj too vast to be measured. ➤ **immeasurably** adv.

immediate adj **1** occurring at once or likely to occur very shortly. **2** current; most in need of attention or action. **3** closest in space, time, or relationship. **4** acting without any intervening agency or factor; direct. ➤ **immediacy** n.

immediately¹ adv **1** at once; without delay. **2** in direct relation or proximity; directly.

immediately² conj chiefly Brit as soon as.

immemorial adj extending beyond the reach of memory, record, or tradition.

immense *adj* very great in size, degree, or extent. ➤ **immensely** *adv*, **immenseness** *n*, **immensity** *n*.

immerse *v* **1** to plunge completely into a fluid. **2** to engross (oneself) in something.

immersion *n* **1** the act of immersing. **2** intensive involvement in an activity or situation.

immersion heater *n* an electric water-heater fixed inside a domestic hot-water storage tank.

immigrant *n* a person who comes to a country to take up permanent residence.

immigrate *v* to come into a country of which one is not a native to take up permanent residence. ➤ **immigration** *n*.

imminent *adj* about to take place. ➤ **imminence** *n*, **imminently** *adv*.

immiscible *adj* of liquids: incapable of being mixed together.

immobile *adj* **1** incapable of being moved. **2** motionless. ➤ **immobility** *n*.

immobilize *or* **-ise** *v* **1** to prevent from moving freely or normally. **2** to prevent (somebody or a body part) from moving to encourage healing. ➤ **immobilization** *n*.

immoderate *adj* lacking moderation; excessive.

immodest *adj* **1** not conforming to accepted standards of sexual propriety. **2** bold; shameless.

immolate *v* to kill or offer as a sacrificial victim, *esp* by burning. ➤ **immolation** *n*.

immoral *adj* not conforming to accepted moral standards, e.g. in sexual matters or business: compare AMORAL. ➤ **immorality** *n*.

immortal[1] *adj* **1** living for ever. **2** enduring for ever; imperishable. ➤ **immortality** *n*.

immortal[2] *n* **1** a person or being that lives for ever, *esp* a classical god. **2** a person of lasting fame.

immortalize *or* **-ise** *v* to give everlasting existence or fame to.

immovable *or* **immoveable** *adj* **1** not able to be moved. **2** not able to be changed or persuaded. ➤ **immovably** *adv*.

immune *adj* **1** (*often* + to) not susceptible to something, *esp* having high resistance to a disease. **2** (*often* + to/from) not liable to be affected by something bad. **3** (*often* + from) free or exempt.

immunity *n* (*pl* **-ies**) **1** (*often* + from/to) the state of being immune. **2** (*often* + against/to) the ability to resist the effects of a disease-causing micro-organism.

immunize *or* **-ise** *v* to make immune, *esp* by inoculation. ➤ **immunization** *n*.

immunology *n* the branch of biology and medicine that deals with immunity to disease. ➤ **immunological** *adj*, **immunologist** *n*.

immure *v* to enclose within walls; to shut away or imprison.

immutable *adj* unchangeable or unchanging.

imp *n* **1** a small demon. **2** a mischievous child.

impact[1] /'impakt/ *n* **1** an *esp* violent contact or collision between one body and another. **2** a powerful effect or impression.

impact[2] /im'pakt/ *v* **1** to fix or press firmly. **2** to make contact, *esp* forcefully. **3** (*often* + on) to affect, *esp* strongly.

impacted *adj* of a tooth: unable to grow properly because of a lack of space in the jaw or obstruction by other teeth.

impair *v* to damage, spoil, or weaken. ➤ **impairment** *n*.

impale *v* to pierce with something pointed.

impalpable *adj* **1** incapable of being sensed by the touch. **2** not easily discerned by the mind.

impart *v* **1** to make known or disclose (information, etc). **2** to give or bestow.

impartial *adj* not showing any favouritism; unbiased. ➤ **impartiality** *n*, **impartially** *adv*.

impassable *adj* of a road, etc: blocked or unable to be travelled along.

impasse *n* a deadlock or stalemate.

impassioned *adj* showing great intensity of feeling.

impassive *adj* **1** incapable of emotion. **2** showing no emotion. ➤ **impassively** *adv*.

impasto *n* (*pl* **-os**) in art, the process of applying paint so thickly that it stands out from the canvas, etc.

impatient *adj* **1** lacking patience; quickly roused to anger or exasperation. **2** (+ of) intolerant. **3** (*often* + to/for) eagerly desirous; anxious. ➤ **impatience** *n*, **impatiently** *adv*.

impeach *v* **1** *Brit* to charge with a serious crime against the state. **2** *NAmer* to charge (a serving public official) with misconduct. ➤ **impeachment** *n*.

impeccable *adj* free from fault or blemish; flawless. ➤ **impeccably** *adv*.

impecunious *adj* having very little or no money.

impedance *n* the opposition in an electrical circuit to the flow of an alternating current.

impede *v* to interfere with or retard the progress of.

impediment *n* **1** (*often* + to) something that impedes. **2** a physiological speech defect, e.g. a stammer or lisp.

impel *v* (**impelled**, **impelling**) to urge forward or force into action.

impending *adj* about to happen.

impenetrable *adj* **1** incapable of being penetrated or pierced. **2** incapable of being understood. ➤ **impenetrability** *n*.

impenitent *adj* feeling or showing no regret or shame. ➤ **impenitence** *n*.

imperative[1] *adj* **1** very urgent or important. **2** commanding; showing authority. **3** denoting the grammatical mood that expresses command, e.g. the verb *stop* in *Stop that at once!*

impossible

imperative² *n* **1** a necessary or urgent act or duty. **2** the imperative mood or a verb form expressing this mood.

imperceptible *adj* too small, slight, or gradual to be perceived. ➤ **imperceptibly** *adv*.

imperfect *adj* **1** flawed, defective, or incomplete. **2** denoting a verb tense expressing a continuing state or an incomplete action in the past. ➤ **imperfection** *n*, **imperfectly** *adv*.

imperial *adj* **1** relating to an empire, emperor, or empress. **2** belonging to an official nonmetric British series of weights and measures such as the pound and the pint.

imperialism *n* the policy of extending the power and dominion of a nation over other nations, *esp* by territorial acquisition. ➤ **imperialist** *n and adj*, **imperialistic** *adj*.

imperil *v* (**imperilled, imperilling,** *NAmer* **imperiled, imperiling**) to put in danger or at risk of harm.

imperious *adj* marked by arrogant assurance; domineering. ➤ **imperiously** *adv*.

impermanent *adj* not permanent or lasting. ➤ **impermanence** *n*.

impermeable *adj* not permitting something, *esp* a fluid, to pass through.

impersonal *adj* **1** not influenced by or involving personal feelings or opinions; objective or unbiased. **2** cold, formal, or detached. **3** denoting a verb used with *it* because it has no identifiable subject, e.g. *rained* in *it rained*. **4** of a pronoun: not referring to a particular person, e.g. *it* in *it rained*. ➤ **impersonality** *n*, **impersonally** *adv*.

impersonate *v* to pretend to be (somebody), either for entertainment or as an act of deception. ➤ **impersonation** *n*, **impersonator** *n*.

impertinent *adj* rude; insolent. ➤ **impertinence** *n*.

imperturbable *adj* marked by great calm and composure.

impervious *adj* **1** (+ to) not capable of being affected or disturbed by something. **2** (*often* + to) not allowing a fluid to pass through.

impetuous *adj* acting or done hastily and without thinking things through. ➤ **impetuously** *adv*.

impetus *n* **1** a driving force. **2** an incentive or stimulus. **3** in physics, the energy possessed by a moving body.

impinge *v* **1** to encroach on something. **2** (+ on/upon) to make an impression.

impious *adj* lacking in reverence or proper respect, e.g. for God.

implacable *adj* **1** not capable of being appeased or pacified. **2** never stopping, weakening, or changing. ➤ **implacably** *adv*.

implant¹ *v* **1** to fix securely or deeply. **2** to set (e.g. an idea or principle) permanently in somebody's consciousness. **3** to insert (e.g. artificial tissue, a hormone, etc) in a living organism. ➤ **implantation** *n*.

implant² *n* something implanted *esp* in tissue.

implausible *adj* unlikely to be true. ➤ **implausibility** *n*, **implausibly** *adv*.

implement¹ *n* a utensil or tool, *esp* one with a specified purpose.

implement² *v* to put (plans, orders, etc) into effect. ➤ **implementation** *n*.

implicate *v* **1** (*often* + in) to show that (a person) is involved in a crime, wrongdoing, etc. **2** (**be implicated in**) to play a part in making something the way it is.

implication *n* **1** (*usu* + in) involvement *esp* in something incriminating. **2** a possible result or effect. **3** something implied. ➤ **implicative** *adj*.

implicit *adj* **1** implied rather than directly stated. **2** (+ in) present but underlying rather than explicit. **3** unquestioning; absolute. ➤ **implicitly** *adv*.

implode *v* to collapse inwards suddenly. ➤ **implosion** *n*.

implore *v* to beg (somebody) to do something. ➤ **imploring** *adj*.

imply *v* (**-ies, -ied**) **1** to express indirectly; to hint at. **2** to involve as a necessary or potential consequence.

impolite *adj* not having or showing good manners.

impolitic *adj* unwise or ill-advised.

imponderable¹ *adj* incapable of being precisely evaluated or assessed.

imponderable² *n* something whose effect is hard or impossible to calculate.

import¹ *v* **1** to bring in (*esp* goods) from a foreign or external source. **2** to transfer (a file, data, etc) from one computer or database into another. ➤ **importation** *n*, **importer** *n*.

import² *n* **1** something imported, *esp* goods from abroad. **2** the act of importing. **3** *formal* meaning or significance. **4** *formal* importance.

important *adj* **1** of considerable significance or consequence. **2** having great influence or responsibility, or high rank. ➤ **importance** *n*, **importantly** *adv*.

importunate *adj* **1** very persistent in making requests or demands. **2** made persistently.

importune *v* to make persistent demands of.

impose *v* **1** (*often* + on/upon) to make (a tax, fine, rule, etc) compulsory. **2** to force (oneself) into the company or on the attention of another. **3** (*often* + on/upon) to cause excessive trouble or inconvenience.

imposing *adj* large and impressive.

imposition *n* **1** the act of imposing. **2** a cause of excessive trouble or inconvenience.

impossible *adj* **1** incapable of existing or occurring. **2** extremely undesirable or difficult to deal with. ➤ **impossibility** n, **impossibly** adv.

impostor or **imposter** n a person who assumes a false identity for fraudulent purposes.

imposture n a fraud or deception.

impotent adj 1 lacking in efficacy or strength; powerless. 2 of a man: unable to have sexual intercourse through an inability to maintain an erection. ➤ **impotence** n.

impound v 1 to shut up (an animal) in a pound. 2 to take legal possession of (e.g. evidence from a crime scene or an illegally parked vehicle).

impoverish v 1 to make poor. 2 to deprive of strength, richness, or fertility. ➤ **impoverishment** n.

impracticable adj incapable of being carried out.

impractical adj 1 of a person: not good at doing practical tasks or dealing with everyday matters. 2 of an idea or plan: unrealistic. ➤ **impracticality** n.

imprecation n a curse.

imprecise adj vague or inaccurate. ➤ **imprecision** n.

impregnable adj 1 too strongly fortified to be taken by assault. 2 strong or unassailable.

impregnate v 1 to make (a female person or animal) pregnant. 2 (+ with) to soak or saturate with something. 3 of a quality, emotion, etc: to be a dominant presence in (speech or writing). ➤ **impregnation** n.

impresario n (pl -os) a person who organizes and finances a public entertainment, e.g. a concert.

impress v 1 (often + by/with) to produce a deep and usu favourable impression on. 2 (usu + on) to fix (e.g. an idea or thought) firmly in the mind or memory. 3 to apply (something) with pressure so as to imprint it on something.

impression n 1 an influence or effect on the mind or senses. 2 a thought or opinion. 3 a notion or recollection, esp one that is vague or subjective. 4 an imitation of a person, animal, etc; esp as a form of entertainment. 5 a mark produced by impressing something onto a surface. 6 all the copies of a book printed for issue at a single time.

impressionable adj easily influenced.

impressionism n (often **Impressionism**) a late 19th-cent. French art movement that aimed to reproduce images as they were actually seen by the artist at a particular moment.

impressionist n 1 (often **Impressionist**) a painter working in the style of impressionism. 2 an entertainer who does impressions.

impressionistic adj 1 based on subjective impression rather than knowledge or research. 2 (usu **Impressionistic**) relating to Impressionism.

impressive adj large, good, or skilful enough to arouse admiration. ➤ **impressively** adv.

imprimatur n sanction or approval.

imprint[1] n 1 a mark made by pressure. 2 a publisher's name or brand name under which a range of books is published.

imprint[2] v to make a mark on something by pressure.

imprison v to put in prison or confine as if in a prison. ➤ **imprisonment** n.

improbable adj unlikely to be true or to occur. ➤ **improbability** n, **improbably** adv.

impromptu adj and adv made or done on the spur of the moment.

improper adj 1 not in accordance with propriety; indecent. 2 inappropriate. 3 not in accordance with normal or correct procedure. ➤ **improperly** adv.

impropriety n (pl -ies) an absence of accepted standards of decency.

improve v 1 to make or become better. 2 (usu + on/upon) to produce something better than a previous version, result, etc. ➤ **improvement** n.

improvident adj not providing for the future; wasteful.

improvise v 1 to make or provide (something) using what is available. 2 to compose or perform (music, poetry, drama, etc) without a set script or musical score. ➤ **improvisation** n.

imprudent adj lacking discretion or caution.

impudent adj showing contemptuous disrespect. ➤ **impudence** n, **impudently** adv.

impugn v to dispute the validity or integrity of.

impulse n 1 a sudden spontaneous desire to do something. 2 a force that produces motion suddenly.

impulsive adj acting or done on the basis of a sudden whim or desire. ➤ **impulsively** adv.

impunity n freedom from punishment, harm, or retribution.

impure adj 1 not pure, esp as a result of contamination. 2 morally wrong.

impurity n (pl -ies) 1 the state of being impure. 2 something that makes something else impure.

impute v to attribute (esp something bad) to somebody, often unjustly. ➤ **imputation** n.

In abbr the chemical symbol for indium.

in[1] prep 1 used to indicate location within or inside an area or object. 2 used to indicate location in time. 3 = INTO. 4 used to indicate a means, instrument, or medium of expression: in pencil. 5 used to indicate a circumstance or condition: in public; in pain. 6 used to indicate the larger member of a ratio: 40p in the £. * **in that** for the reason that; because.

in[2] adv 1 used to indicate movement towards the inside or centre. 2 used to indicate movement to or towards home, the shore, a destination, etc. 3 used to indicate presence at one's home or business. ✳ **be in for** to be certain to experience (usu something undesirable). **in on** having a share in or knowledge of something.

in³ *adj* extremely fashionable.

in. *abbr* inch or inches.

in- or **il-** or **im-** or **ir- prefix 1** not: *inaccurate*. **2** in, into, or towards: *influx*.

inability *n* lack of sufficient power, skill, intelligence, etc to do something.

in absentia *adv* in the absence of the specified person.

inaccessible *adj* **1** difficult or impossible to reach. **2** difficult or impossible to understand.

inaccurate *adj* faulty or imprecise. ➤ **inaccuracy** *n*. **inaccurately** *adv*

inaction *n* lack of action or activity.

inactive *adj* **1** not moving or doing anything. **2** not functioning. ➤ **inactivity** *n*.

inadequate *adj* **1** not of the required quantity or quality. **2** unable to cope with people or situations. ➤ **inadequacy** *n*, **inadequately** *adv*.

inadmissible *adj esp* of evidence in a court: invalid. ➤ **inadmissibility** *n*.

inadvertent *adj* unintentional. ➤ **inadvertently** *adv*.

inadvisable *adj* likely to have unwanted consequences; unwise.

inalienable *adj* incapable of being removed or surrendered.

inane *adj* senseless or unintelligent. ➤ **inanely** *adv*, **inaneness** *n*, **inanity** *n*.

inanimate *adj* **1** not alive. **2** unconscious and apparently lifeless.

inapplicable *adj* not appropriate or relevant.

inappropriate *adj* not appropriate or suitable. ➤ **inappropriately** *adv*.

inarticulate *adj* **1** unable to express oneself coherently or effectively. **2** not coherently or effectively expressed. **3** not understandable as spoken words.

inasmuch as *conj* **1** = INSOFAR AS. **2** *formal* in view of the fact that.

inattention *n* failure to pay attention; disregard. ➤ **inattentive** *adj*.

inaudible *adj* unable to be heard. ➤ **inaudibly** *adv*.

inaugural *adj* **1** marking a beginning. **2** first in a series.

inaugurate *v* **1** to open (e.g. a new building) ceremonially. **2** to begin or introduce (a new system, project, etc). ➤ **inauguration** *n*.

inauspicious *adj* not promising future success.

inauthentic *adj* not genuine.

inborn *adj* **1** forming part of somebody's natural make-up. **2** existing from birth; congenital.

inbred *adj* **1** deeply ingrained in somebody's nature. **2** produced by inbreeding.

inbreeding *n* breeding involving closely related individuals.

inbuilt *adj* built-in; inherent or integral.

Inc. *abbr chiefly NAmer* incorporated.

incalculable *adj* **1** too great or numerous to be calculated. **2** unable to be predicted or estimated.

incandescent *adj* **1** glowing white with intense heat. **2** *informal* extremely angry.

incantation *n* a formula used in magic rituals. ➤ **incantatory** *adj*.

incapable *adj* **1** (*usu* + of) lacking the capacity, ability, etc to do something. **2** unfit, *esp* because of illness or the effects of alcohol or drugs. ➤ **incapability** *n*.

incapacitate *v* to prevent from functioning or operating properly. ➤ **incapacitation** *n*.

incapacity *n* (*pl* **-ies**) lack of ability or power.

incarcerate *v* to imprison. ➤ **incarceration** *n*.

incarnate *adj* invested with a human nature and form.

incarnation *n* **1** the human embodiment of a deity, spirit, or abstract quality. **2** (**Incarnation**) in Christian belief, the manifestation of Christ in human form.

incautious *adj* lacking care or caution; rash.

incendiary¹ *adj* **1** tending to inflame or stir up trouble. **2** *esp* of a bomb: designed to start fires.

incendiary² *n* (*pl* **-ies**) an incendiary bomb.

incense¹ *n* a substance that produces a fragrant smell when burned.

incense² *v* to make extremely angry or indignant.

incentive *n* something that motivates somebody.

inception *n* the beginning of a process or undertaking.

incessant *adj* continuing without interruption. ➤ **incessantly** *adv*.

incest *n* sexual intercourse between people so closely related that they are forbidden by law to marry.

incestuous *adj* **1** involving incest. **2** unhealthily close or shut off from outside influences. ➤ **incestuously** *adv*.

inch¹ *n* **1** a unit of length equal to one twelfth of a foot (about 2.54cm). **2** a small amount or distance.

inch² *v* to move slowly.

incidence *n* **1** the rate of occurrence of something. **2** the arrival of e.g. a projectile or a ray of light at a surface.

incident *n* **1** something that happens. **2** an occurrence that involves violence or is a cause of conflict.

incidental *adj* **1** occurring merely by chance. **2** (*often* + to) occurring as a minor consequence or accompaniment.

incidentally *adv* **1** by the way. **2** by chance.

incidental music *n* background music in a play, film, etc.

incinerate *v* to burn to ashes. ➤ **incineration** *n*.

incinerator n a furnace or container for incinerating waste.

incipient adj just beginning to emerge or develop.

incise v to carve letters, designs, etc into a surface.

incision n 1 a cut, esp one made in a surgical operation. 2 the act of cutting into something.

incisive adj 1 showing sharp intelligence. 2 impressively direct and decisive.

incisor n a cutting tooth at the front of the mouth.

incite v to encourage (violence, unlawful behaviour, etc), or encourage (somebody) to commit this. ➤ **incitement** n.

incivility n (pl -ies) discourtesy.

inclement adj of the weather: unpleasant, esp cold and wet. ➤ **inclemency** n.

inclination n 1 a particular, esp natural tendency or urge. 2 a liking. 3 a deviation from the vertical or horizontal.

incline[1] v 1 to influence (somebody) to a specified action or way of thinking. 2 to slope or slant. 3 to nod or bend (the head). ✳ **inclined to 1** having a tendency to (do or be something). 2 in favour of (doing something).

incline[2] n a slope.

include v 1 to take in, contain, or consider as a part of a larger whole. 2 to add or put in.

including prep with the inclusion of.

inclusion n 1 the act of including. 2 something or somebody that is included.

inclusive adj 1 including everything or the items specified. 2 including the stated limits. 3 broad in scope.

incognito adv and adj in disguise or under a false name.

incoherent adj 1 too confused and disordered to be clearly intelligible. 2 lacking logical connection. ➤ **incoherence** n, **incoherently** adv.

incombustible adj incapable of being burned.

income n money received from work, property, or investment.

incomer n a person who moves into an area.

income tax n a tax levied on personal income.

incoming adj 1 arriving or coming in. 2 about to take on a role or office.

incommensurable adj incapable of being compared.

incommensurate adj (usu + with) disproportionate to.

incommode v formal to inconvenience.

incommunicado adv and adj without means of communication with other people, e.g. while in solitary confinement.

incomparable adj incapable of being compared with anything else, esp because too good. ➤ **incomparably** adv.

incompatible adj 1 of people: unable to live or work together, because of opposing views, temperaments, etc. 2 unable to exist together. 3 unsuitable for use together. ➤ **incompatibility** n.

incompetent adj 1 lacking the skill, experience, etc needed for effective action. 2 not legally qualified. ➤ **incompetence** n, **incompetently** adv.

incomplete adj not complete. ➤ **incompletely** adv.

incomprehensible adj impossible to understand. ➤ **incomprehensibility** n.

inconceivable adj unimaginable or unbelievable. ➤ **inconceivably** adv.

inconclusive adj leading to no conclusion or definite result. ➤ **inconclusively** adv.

incongruous adj out of place. ➤ **incongruity** n, **incongruously** adv.

inconsequential adj 1 irrelevant. 2 unimportant. ➤ **inconsequentiality** n.

inconsiderable adj small in size, amount, etc.

inconsiderate adj showing a lack of care for others.

inconsistent adj 1 containing conflicting or contradictory elements. 2 (often + with) not in agreement. ➤ **inconsistency** n.

inconsolable adj incapable of being consoled; brokenhearted.

inconspicuous adj not readily noticeable. ➤ **inconspicuously** adv.

inconstant adj 1 likely to change without apparent reason. 2 literary unfaithful; unreliable.

incontestable adj indisputable. ➤ **incontestably** adv.

incontinent adj 1 unable to control urination or defecation. 2 lacking self-restraint, esp sexually. ➤ **incontinence** n.

incontrovertible adj not able to be denied or disputed. ➤ **incontrovertibly** adv.

inconvenience[1] n 1 the fact of being rather difficult or troublesome. 2 a cause of trouble or unnecessary effort to somebody. ➤ **inconvenient** adj, **inconveniently** adv.

inconvenience[2] v to cause inconvenience.

incorporate v to make (something) a usu indistinguishable part of a larger whole. ➤ **incorporation** n.

incorporated adj formed into a legal corporation.

incorporeal adj having no material body or form.

incorrect adj 1 inaccurate; factually wrong. 2 not in accordance with an established norm; improper. ➤ **incorrectly** adv.

incorrigible adj incapable of being corrected or improved, esp incurably bad.

incorruptible adj 1 incapable of being bribed or morally corrupted. 2 not subject to decay.

increase[1] v to make or become progressively greater in size, amount, number, or intensity. ➤ **increasing** adj.

increase² *n* an amount by which something increases.

increasingly *adv* to an ever greater extent.

incredible *adj* **1** too extraordinary and improbable to be believed. **2** *informal* excellent; outstanding. ➤ **incredibly** *adv*.

incredulity *n* unwillingness or inability to believe something.

incredulous *adj* unwilling or unable to believe something.

increment *n* an increase, *esp* a regular consecutive increase. ➤ **incremental** *adj*.

incriminate *v* to suggest or demonstrate that (somebody) is guilty of a crime. ➤ **incriminating** *adj*.

incubate *v* **1** of a bird: to sit on (eggs) to hatch them by the warmth of the body. **2** to keep (e.g. bacteria, cells) under conditions favourable for their development. **3** to develop (a disease) without any noticeable symptoms. ➤ **incubation** *n*.

incubator *n* **1** an apparatus in which a premature or sick baby is kept under controlled conditions. **2** an apparatus in which eggs are hatched artificially.

inculcate *v* to teach (something) by frequent repetition.

incumbency *n* the period of office of an incumbent.

incumbent¹ *n* the current holder of an office.

incumbent² *adj* **1** (+ on/upon) imposed as a duty on somebody. **2** currently holding a specified office.

incur *v* (**incurred, incurring**) to become liable or subject to (something unpleasant).

incurable *adj* not able to be cured. ➤ **incurably** *adv*.

incurious *adj* lacking curiosity; uninterested.

incursion *n* a sudden or brief invasion.

indebted *adj* **1** owing gratitude to somebody. **2** owing money. ➤ **indebtedness** *n*.

indecent *adj* **1** improper or unseemly. **2** morally offensive. ➤ **indecency** *n*, **indecently** *adv*.

indecipherable *adj* **1** illegible. **2** of a code: unable to be solved or understood.

indecisive *adj* **1** incapable of making quick or definite decisions. **2** giving an uncertain result. ➤ **indecision** *n*, **indecisively** *adv*, **indecisiveness** *n*.

indeed *adv* **1** used as an intensifier or for emphasis: *It has been very cold indeed.* **2** used to introduce additional information: actually.

indefatigable *adj* tireless or unflagging.

indefensible *adj* incapable of being justified or excused.

indefinable *adj* incapable of being precisely described or analysed.

indefinite *adj* **1** not precise; vague or unsettled. **2** lasting for an unspecified length of time. ➤ **indefinitely** *adv*.

indefinite article *n* the word *a* or *an*.

indelible *adj* **1** of a mark, stain, ink, etc: incapable of being removed or erased. **2** of a memory: not able to be forgotten. ➤ **indelibly** *adv*.

indelicate *adj* **1** almost indecent or offensive. **2** lacking in good manners or sensitivity.

indemnify *v* (**-ies, -ied**) **1** to exempt in advance from legal liability. **2** to compensate for harm or loss.

indemnity *n* (*pl* **-ies**) **1** exemption from incurred penalties or liabilities. **2** compensation for harm, loss, or damage.

indent¹ *v* **1** to set (a line of text, a paragraph, etc) in from the margin. **2** to notch the edge of (something).

indent² *n* *chiefly Brit* an official requisition or order.

indentation *n* **1** an angular cut in an edge. **2** a dent or depression. **3** the act of indenting.

indenture *n* **1** an official agreement or contract. **2** (*also in pl*) a contract binding an apprentice to work for an employer.

independent¹ *adj* **1** not connected with or relying on something else. **2** not controlled by others. **3** having or providing enough money to live on, *esp* without working. **4** of a country: self-governing. ➤ **independence** *n*, **independently** *adv*.

independent² *n* somebody who is independent.

in-depth *adj* comprehensively detailed and thorough.

indescribable *adj* unable to be put into words. ➤ **indescribably** *adv*.

indestructible *adj* impossible to destroy.

indeterminate *adj* not definitely or precisely fixed; vague.

index¹ *n* (*pl* **indexes** *or* **indices**) **1** an alphabetical list of names, topics, etc mentioned in a printed work. **2** a systematic guide or list to aid reference, e.g. a catalogue of publications. **3** an indicator of a fact or circumstance. **4** a number or scale used as an indicator or measure, e.g. of the cost of living.

index² *v* **1** to provide (e.g. a book) with an index. **2** to list (an item) in an index.

index finger *n* = FOREFINGER.

index-linked *adj* increasing or decreasing in proportion to a rise or fall in an index, *esp* the cost-of-living index.

Indian *n* **1** a native or inhabitant of India. **2** *dated, offensive* a member of an indigenous people of North, Central, or South America. ➤ **Indian** *adj*.

Indian ink *n Brit* an ink made from a solid black pigment and used in drawing and lettering.

Indian summer *n* a period of warm weather in late autumn or early winter.

indicate *v* **1** to point to or point out. **2** to be a sign or symptom of. **3** (**be indicated**) to be necessary or advisable. **4** to state briefly; to suggest. ➤ **indication** *n*.

indicative *adj* **1** (*usu* + of) serving to indicate. **2** in grammar, representing the act or state in question as an objective fact.

indicator *n* **1** a device that shows a measurement, level, etc, or gives information. **2** a flashing light on a vehicle, used to show that the driver intends to change direction.

indict *v* to charge with an offence, *esp* a serious crime. ➤ **indictable** *adj*.

indictment *n* **1** a formal written accusation by a prosecuting authority. **2** grounds for severe censure or condemnation of something.

indifferent *adj* **1** mediocre or poor. **2** (*often* + to) not interested or concerned. ➤ **indifference** *n*, **indifferently** *adv*.

indigenous *adj* growing or living naturally in a particular place.

indigent *adj* very needy or poor.

indigestible *adj* **1** difficult or impossible to digest. **2** difficult to understand, read, etc.

indigestion *n* pain or discomfort from difficulty in digesting something.

indignant *adj* filled with or marked by indignation. ➤ **indignantly** *adv*.

indignation *n* anger aroused by something unjust or mean.

indignity *n* (*pl* -ies) something that causes loss of dignity or self-respect.

indigo *n* a dark greyish blue colour or dye.

indirect *adj* **1** deviating from a direct line or course. **2** not going straight to the point. **3** not being a direct cause or consequence of something. ➤ **indirectly** *adv*.

indirect question *n* in grammar, a question in indirect speech, e.g. *He asked if I'd ever been to New York before.*

indirect speech *n* in grammar, the reporting of something previously said, e.g. *I told him I'd never been to New York.*

indiscipline *n* lack of discipline.

indiscreet *adj* not discreet, *esp* in revealing secret or private things. ➤ **indiscreetly** *adv*.

indiscretion *n* **1** lack of discretion. **2** an indiscreet act or remark.

indiscriminate *adj* **1** showing a lack of care in choosing or making distinctions. **2** random. ➤ **indiscriminately** *adv*.

indispensable *adj* not able to be done without.

indisposed *adj* **1** slightly ill. **2** (*usu* + to) unwilling to do something.

indisposition *n* a slight illness.

indisputable *adj* not able to be denied or called into question. ➤ **indisputably** *adv*.

indissoluble *adj* incapable of being dissolved or annulled.

indistinct *adj* not sharply outlined; not clearly visible, audible, etc. ➤ **indistinctly** *adv*.

indistinguishable *adj* (*usu* + from) incapable of being clearly identified as different; identical.

individual¹ *adj* **1** relating to or intended for a single person or thing. **2** existing as a distinct entity; separate. **3** having unusual or distinctive characteristics. ➤ **individually** *adv*.

individual² *n* **1** a particular person or thing, *esp* as distinguished from a group. **2** a person who has unusual or distinctive characteristics.

individualism *n* **1** independence and self-reliance. **2** a social theory stressing the political and economic independence of the individual. ➤ **individualist** *n and adj*, **individualistic** *adj*.

individuality *n* the quality of being distinctive or unique.

individualize *or* -ise *v* to make different or distinctive.

indivisible *adj* not able to be separated or divided.

indoctrinate *v* to teach (a person or group) to accept a view, ideology, etc uncritically. ➤ **indoctrination** *n*.

Indo-European *n* a family of languages containing those spoken in most of Europe and in Asia as far as North India. ➤ **Indo-European** *adj*.

indolent *adj* lazy. ➤ **indolence** *n*.

indomitable *adj* incapable of being subdued.

indoor *adj* done, situated, or belonging inside a building.

indoors *adv* inside or into a building.

indubitable *adj* too evident to be doubted or called into question. ➤ **indubitably** *adv*.

induce *v* **1** to persuade or influence to do something. **2** to cause or bring about. **3** to cause (labour) to begin, *esp* by the use of drugs.

inducement *n* **1** something that motivates or encourages somebody to do something. **2** *euphem* a bribe.

induct *v* to install formally into office or as a member of an organization.

inductance *n* a property of an electric circuit by which an electromotive force is induced in it by a variation of current.

induction *n* **1** the act of inducting, *esp* into office. **2** a method of reasoning that proceeds from particular premises to reach a general conclusion. **3** the act of inducing. **4** the production of an electric charge or magnetism in an object by its being close to, but not in contact with, a similarly energized body.

indulge *v* **1** to give free rein to (a taste, desire, etc). **2** (*often* + in) to allow oneself to do or have something pleasurable. **3** to treat with excessive leniency or generosity; to spoil.

indulgence *n* **1** the act of indulging. **2** something indulged in; a luxury. **3** leniency or tolerance.

indulgent *adj* characterized by indulgence. ➤ **indulgently** *adv*.

industrial *adj* relating to or used in industry. ➤ **industrially** *adv*.

industrial action *n* a strike, go-slow, work-to-rule, etc by a body of workers.

industrial estate *n chiefly Brit* an area designed for industries and businesses.

industrialist *n* somebody who is engaged in the management of an industry.

industrialize *or* **-ise** *v* to develop industries extensively in (a region). ➤ **industrialization** *n*.

industrious *adj* conscientious and hard-working. ➤ **industriously** *adv*.

industry *n* (*pl* **-ies**) **1** economic activity concerned with the manufacture of goods, the processing of raw materials, construction work, etc. **2** a specified branch of this. **3** hard work.

inebriate *v esp* of alcohol: to intoxicate. ➤ **inebriation** *n*.

inedible *adj* not fit to be eaten.

ineffable *adj* too great or intense to be expressed.

ineffective *adj* **1** not producing an effect or the intended effect. **2** not capable of performing efficiently or achieving results. ➤ **ineffectively** *adv*.

ineffectual *adj* **1** unable to get things done; weak in character. **2** ineffective. ➤ **ineffectually** *adv*.

inefficient *adj* failing to work, operate, etc in a capable or economical way. ➤ **inefficiency** *n*, **inefficiently** *adv*.

inelegant *adj* lacking in refinement, grace, or good taste. ➤ **inelegance** *n*, **inelegantly** *adv*.

ineligible *adj* not qualified to receive or do something.

ineluctable *adj formal* unavoidable; inescapable.

inept *adj* incompetent or clumsy. ➤ **ineptitude** *n*, **ineptly** *adv*.

inequality *n* (*pl* **-ies**) the state of being unequal.

inequitable *adj* unfair or unjust.

inequity *n* (*pl* **-ies**) injustice or unfairness.

ineradicable *adj* incapable of being eradicated.

inert *adj* **1** lacking the power to move. **2** lacking active chemical or biological properties. **3** inactive or indolent.

inertia *n* **1** a tendency to resist exertion or change. **2** in physics, a property of matter by which it remains at rest or in uniform motion in a straight line unless acted on by some external force.

inescapable *adj* incapable of being avoided, ignored, or denied.

inessential[1] *adj* not absolutely necessary.

inessential[2] *n* something that is not absolutely necessary.

inestimable *adj* too great, valuable, or excellent to be measured.

inevitable *adj* incapable of being avoided; bound to happen. ➤ **inevitability** *n*, **inevitably** *adv*.

inexact *adj* not precisely correct or true.

inexcusable *adj* too bad to be excused or justified.

inexhaustible *adj* **1** of a supply: incapable of being used up. **2** of a person: tireless.

inexorable *adj* **1** unable to be persuaded or moved by entreaty. **2** unable to be averted. ➤ **inexorably** *adv*.

inexpensive *adj* reasonable in price; cheap.

inexperience *n* lack of experience. ➤ **inexperienced** *adj*.

inexpert *adj* unskilled or lacking knowledge. ➤ **inexpertly** *adv*.

inexplicable *adj* incapable of being explained. ➤ **inexplicably** *adv*.

inexpressive *adj* lacking expression or meaning.

in extremis *adv* **1** in extremely difficult circumstances. **2** at the point of death.

inextricable *adj* incapable of being disentangled or separated. ➤ **inextricably** *adv*.

infallible *adj* **1** incapable of error. **2** known to be effective. ➤ **infallibility** *n*.

infamous *adj* **1** having a bad reputation; notorious. **2** disgraceful. ➤ **infamously** *adv*, **infamy** *n*.

infancy *n* (*pl* **-ies**) **1** early childhood. **2** an early period of existence or development.

infant *n* **1** a very young child. **2** *Brit* a schoolchild between the ages of five and seven.

infanticide *n* the act of killing an infant.

infantile *adj* **1** relating to infants. **2** *derog* childish or immature.

infantry *n* soldiers trained and equipped to fight on foot.

infatuate *v* (**be infatuated with**), to have powerful but often superficial feelings of love for. ➤ **infatuation** *n*.

infect *v* **1** to contaminate (e.g. air or food) with an agent that causes disease. **2** to pass on a disease to.

infection *n* **1** an infectious disease. **2** the act of infecting.

infectious *adj* **1** of a disease: communicable to others. **2** capable of causing or spreading disease. **3** readily spread or communicated to others. ➤ **infectiously** *adv*.

infer *v* (**inferred, inferring**) to deduce (something) from available evidence or from what is suggested rather than explicitly stated.

inference *n* **1** the act of inferring. **2** a conclusion arrived at from the available evidence or from indirect hints.

inferior[1] *adj* of low or lower rank, quality, or importance. ➤ **inferiority** *n*.

inferior[2] *n* a person who is lower in rank, standing, ability, etc than another.

infernal *adj* 1 relating to hell. 2 *informal* dreadful; damned.

inferno *n* (*pl* -os) a raging fire.

infertile *adj* 1 not capable of producing offspring. 2 of land: not capable of sustaining vegetation, *esp* crops. ➤ **infertility** *n*.

infest *v* of insects or vermin, etc: to spread or swarm over causing damage or disease. ➤ **infestation** *n*.

infidel *n* 1 somebody who does not believe in a particular religion, *esp* Christianity or Islam. 2 an atheist.

infidelity *n* (*pl* -ies) unfaithfulness *esp* in marital or sexual matters.

infighting *n* dissension among members of a group or organization.

infiltrate *v* 1 to enter or become established in (e.g. an organization) gradually or unobtrusively, often to spy on it. 2 of a fluid: to filter or permeate into. ➤ **infiltration** *n*, **infiltrator** *n*.

infinite *adj* 1 having no limitations or boundaries in time, space, number, etc. 2 great, immense, or extreme. ➤ **infinitely** *adv*.

infinitesimal *adj* immeasurably or incalculably small. ➤ **infinitesimally** *adv*.

infinitive *n* the base form of a verb, without inflections, in English often preceded by *to* (e.g. *go* or *to go*).

infinity *n* (*pl* -ies) 1 unlimited time or space, etc. 2 an immeasurably distant point, e.g. where parallel lines are supposed to meet. 3 a very great number or amount.

infirm *adj* physically feeble, *esp* from age.

infirmary *n* (*pl* -ies) a hospital or sick room.

infirmity *n* (*pl* -ies) a disease or mental weakness.

inflame *v* 1 to arouse passion or strong feeling in. 2 to make (e.g. an emotion or dispute) more violent. 3 to cause inflammation in (body tissue).

inflammable *adj* easily set on fire; flammable.

inflammation *n* redness, heat, swelling, and pain in an area of body tissue as a result of injury or infection.

inflammatory *adj* 1 tending to arouse strong feeling, *esp* anger. 2 accompanied by or causing inflammation.

inflatable¹ *adj* capable of being inflated.

inflatable² *n* an inflatable boat, toy, etc.

inflate *v* 1 to swell (e.g. a balloon or tyre) by filling it with air or gas. 2 to increase abnormally or excessively. 3 to cause inflation in (e.g. prices or the economy).

inflated *adj* 1 exaggerated. 2 swollen or distended.

inflation *n* 1 a substantial and continuing rise in prices, e.g. caused by an increase in the supply of money and credit. 2 the act of inflating. ➤ **inflationary** *adj*.

inflect *v* 1 to change the form or ending of (a word). 2 to vary the pitch of (a voice).

inflection *or* **inflexion** *n* 1 in grammar, a change in the form of a word to show its case, gender, number, tense, etc. 2 variation in pitch or loudness of the voice.

inflexible *adj* 1 incapable of or resistant to change. 2 not variable to suit a particular circumstance. 3 not able to be bent.

inflict *v* (*usu* + on) to impose (something unpleasant or painful) on somebody. ➤ **infliction** *n*.

influence¹ *n* 1 the power or capacity to produce an effect on somebody or something, *esp* in indirect or intangible ways. 2 power resulting from wealth or position. 3 somebody or something that has or exerts influence. ✷ **under the influence** *informal* drunk.

influence² *v* to affect, *esp* by indirect or intangible means.

influential *adj* exerting or possessing influence.

influenza *n* a highly infectious viral disease characterized by fever, severe aches and pains, and catarrh.

influx *n* an arrival of people or things in large numbers.

inform *v* 1 to communicate knowledge or information to. 2 (*usu* + against/on) to give the police information about a criminal or crime.

informal *adj* 1 marked by an absence of formality or ceremony. 2 of clothes: suitable for a friendly and relaxed occasion. 3 of language: in a style appropriate to conversation rather than formal writing. ➤ **informality** *n*, **informally** *adv*.

informant *n* 1 a person who gives somebody information about something. 2 = INFORMER.

information *n* facts or data obtained from investigation, study, or instruction.

information technology *n* the use of computers, telecommunications, etc to store, retrieve, and send information.

informative *adj* conveying information; instructive.

informed *adj* 1 based on possession of information. 2 knowledgeable, *esp* about matters of contemporary interest.

informer *n* a person who gives information about a criminal or crime to the police.

infraction *n* an infringement, *esp* of a law or agreement.

infra dig *adj informal* beneath one's dignity.

infrared *adj* of electromagnetic radiation: lying outside the visible spectrum, with a wavelength between red light and microwaves.

infrastructure *n* the permanent features, e.g. road and rail networks, power supplies, etc, necessary for a country's economic well-being.

infrequent *adj* not occurring often. ➤ **infrequency** *n*, **infrequently** *adv*.

infringe v **1** to encroach on (a right or privilege). **2** to violate (a law, agreement, etc). ➤ **infringement** n.

infuriate v to make furious. ➤ **infuriating** adj.

infuse v **1** to steep (tea, herbs, etc) in liquid so as to extract the flavour, soluble properties, etc. **2** to imbue or pervade.

infusion n **1** the process of infusing. **2** an extract or drink obtained by infusing.

ingenious adj original, resourceful, and clever. ➤ **ingeniously** adv.

ingenue or **ingénue** /anzhay'nooh/ n a naive or artless young woman.

ingenuity n resourcefulness, cleverness, or inventiveness.

ingenuous adj showing innocent or childlike simplicity.

ingest v to take (food or drink) into the body.

inglenook n an alcove by a large open fireplace.

inglorious adj shameful; ignominious.

ingoing adj entering.

ingot n a mass of cast metal in the shape of a bar or brick.

ingrained or **engrained** adj **1** of a habit, moral value, etc: firmly and deeply implanted. **2** of dirt, stains, etc: thoroughly worked into something.

ingratiate v to gain favour for (e.g. oneself) by deliberate effort. ➤ **ingratiating** adj.

ingratitude n failure to appreciate kindness received.

ingredient n a component part of a compound or mixture, esp an edible substance combined in the preparation of food.

ingress n **1** the act of entering. **2** a way in; an entrance.

ingrown or **ingrowing** adj esp of a toenail: with the free end embedded in the flesh.

inhabit v (**inhabited, inhabiting**) to live in (a place). ➤ **inhabitable** adj.

inhale v to breathe in.

inhaler n a device used for inhaling a medication, e.g. to relieve asthma.

inherent adj forming an essential and indivisible part of something. ➤ **inherently** adv.

inherit v (**inherited, inheriting**) **1** to receive (property) from somebody at his or her death. **2** to receive (something, e.g. a physical attribute) by genetic transmission. **3** to come to possess (something) left by a predecessor.

inheritance n **1** the act of inheriting. **2** property that is inherited.

inhibit v (**inhibited, inhibiting**) **1** to discourage (somebody) from behaving freely or spontaneously. **2** to restrain (e.g. an impulse). ➤ **inhibited** adj.

inhibition n a psychological restraint on the way somebody thinks or behaves.

inhospitable adj **1** of a person: not friendly or welcoming. **2** of a place, climate, etc: hard to live in.

in-house adj and adv within a group or organization.

inhuman adj **1** extremely cruel; barbarous. **2** not human in nature or quality.

inhumane adj completely lacking in kindness or compassion.

inhumanity n (pl -**ies**) pitilessness or cruelty.

inimical adj adverse in influence or effects; harmful; hostile.

inimitable adj so good that no others can match it; unique. ➤ **inimitably** adv.

iniquity n (pl -**ies**) **1** wickedness. **2** a wicked act; a sin. ➤ **iniquitous** adj.

initial[1] adj **1** existing at the beginning. **2** placed at the beginning; first. ➤ **initially** adv.

initial[2] n the first letter of a name.

initial[3] v (**initialled, initialling**, NAmer **initialed, initialing**) to put one's initials on (something), usu to indicate ownership or authorization.

initiate v **1** to cause or allow to begin. **2** to introduce (somebody) to a new subject or activity, esp a complex one. **3** to grant (somebody) membership of an organization, traditionally by formal rites. ➤ **initiation** n.

initiative n **1** energy or resourcefulness displayed in acting without being prompted. **2** a new plan, strategy, or programme of action. **3** the opportunity to act first.

inject v **1** to force a fluid into the body using a syringe. **2** to introduce as an element or factor.

injection n **1** the act of injecting something, esp a medication, into a person's body. **2** the introduction of a new element or factor.

in-joke n a joke understood only by the members of a particular group.

injudicious adj showing a lack of judgment. ➤ **injudiciously** adv, **injudiciousness** n.

injunction n **1** a court order requiring somebody to do or refrain from doing a particular act. **2** a firm warning or an order.

injure v **1** to inflict bodily harm on. **2** to inflict damage or loss on.

injurious adj inflicting injury or harm.

injury n (pl -**ies**) **1** a physical hurt caused to somebody. **2** damage or loss.

injustice n **1** unfairness. **2** an unjust act or state of affairs.

ink[1] n **1** a coloured liquid used for writing and printing. **2** the black secretion of a squid, octopus, etc. ➤ **inky** adj.

ink[2] v to apply ink to.

inkling n **1** a slight knowledge or vague idea. **2** a hint.

inland adj and adv in or towards the interior part of a country.

Inland Revenue n the government department responsible for collecting taxes in Britain.

in-law *n informal* a relative by marriage.

inlay¹ *v* (*past tense and past part.* **inlaid**) **1** to set into a surface *esp* for decoration. **2** to decorate with inlaid material.

inlay² *n* a decorative inlaid pattern.

inlet *n* **1** a usu long and narrow recess in a shoreline. **2** a means of entry, *esp* for fluids.

in loco parentis *adv* having the responsibilities of a parent.

inmate *n* a resident of an institution, *esp* a prison or hospital.

inn *n* a pub.

innards *pl n informal* **1** the internal organs, *esp* the intestines. **2** the internal parts or mechanism.

innate *adj* belonging to an individual from birth. ➤ **innately** *adv*.

inner *adj* **1** situated inside something or near its centre. **2** relating to the mind or soul. **3** unexpressed; private.

inner city *n* the usu older and more densely populated central section of a city.

innermost *adj* **1** most inward or central. **2** most secret and private.

inner tube *n* an inflatable tube inside the casing of a tyre.

innings *n* (*pl* **innings**) in cricket, a division of a match during which one side bats and the other bowls.

innkeeper *n* the landlord or landlady of an inn.

innocent¹ *adj* **1** free from guilt or sin, *esp* not guilty of a crime. **2** harmless in effect or intention. **3** knowing little of life and human nature. ➤ **innocence** *n*, **innocently** *adv*.

innocent² *n* somebody who is innocent.

innocuous *adj* **1** having no harmful effects. **2** unlikely to offend.

innovate *v* to introduce new practices or ideas. ➤ **innovative** *adj*, **innovator** *n*.

innovation *n* **1** the act of innovating. **2** a change that introduces a new idea or practice.

innuendo *n* (*pl* **-os** or **-oes**) an obliquely worded comment, *esp* a suggestive or subtly disparaging one.

innumerable *adj* too many to be counted.

innumerate *adj Brit* not able to use numbers effectively or do basic arithmetic.

inoculate *v* to introduce a disease-causing organism into the body in order to induce immunity. ➤ **inoculation** *n*.

inoffensive *adj* not intended or intending to cause harm or offence.

inoperable *adj* **1** not suitable for treatment by surgery. **2** impracticable. **3** unable to be operated.

inoperative *adj* not functioning, or having no effect.

inopportune *adj* happening at an awkward time; inconvenient.

inordinate *adj* going beyond reasonable limits; excessive. ➤ **inordinately** *adv*.

inorganic *adj* **1** composed of or relating to matter that is not plant or animal. **2** not arising through natural growth.

inpatient *n* a patient who lives at a hospital while undergoing treatment.

input¹ *n* **1** something, e.g. energy, material, or data, supplied to a machine or system. **2** the entry point for an input into a system, machine, etc. **3** the act of putting something in. **4** work, suggestions, advice, etc that somebody contributes.

input² *v* (**inputting**, *past tense and past part.* **input** or **inputted**) to enter (data) into a computer.

inquest *n* **1** a judicial enquiry, *esp* by a coroner, into the cause of a death. **2** an investigation, *esp* into something that has failed.

inquire *v* see ENQUIRE.

inquiry *n* see ENQUIRY.

inquisition *n* a ruthless investigation or examination.

inquisitive *adj* **1** unduly curious about the affairs of others. **2** eager for knowledge or understanding. ➤ **inquisitively** *adv*.

inquisitor *n* somebody who conducts an inquisition.

inroad *n* ✳ **make inroads into** to have made progress in dealing with or reducing.

inrush *n* a crowding or flooding in.

insalubrious *adj* unhealthy.

ins and outs *pl n* characteristic peculiarities and complexities; ramifications.

insane *adj* **1** *dated, offensive* suffering from a mental illness. **2** utterly absurd. ➤ **insanely** *adv*, **insanity** *n*.

insanitary *adj* unclean enough to endanger health.

insatiable *adj* incapable of being satisfied. ➤ **insatiably** *adv*.

inscribe *v* **1** to write, engrave, or print, *esp* on a hard surface. **2** to dedicate (*esp* a book) to somebody by a handwritten note.

inscription *n* any written or engraved form of words, e.g. on a statue or a coin or as a dedication in a book.

inscrutable *adj* hard to interpret or understand. ➤ **inscrutably** *adv*.

insect *n* a small invertebrate animal with three pairs of legs.

insecticide *n* a substance that destroys insects.

insectivore *n* an insect-eating plant or animal. ➤ **insectivorous** *adj*.

insecure *adj* **1** lacking in self-confidence. **2** not firmly fixed or supported. ➤ **insecurity** *n*.

inseminate *v* to introduce semen into (a woman or female animal). ➤ **insemination** *n*.

insensate *adj* **1** not capable of feeling. **2** lacking in human feeling; insensitive. **3** senseless; foolish. ➤ **insensately** *adv*.

insensible adj **1** unconscious. **2** numb. **3** formal (+ of) unaware or heedless.

insensitive adj **1** unsympathetic to the needs or feelings of others; callous; tactless. **2** (+ to) not physically or chemically sensitive. ➤ **insensitively** adv, **insensitiveness** n, **insensitivity** n.

inseparable adj **1** incapable of being separated. **2** always seen or found together. ➤ **inseparably** adv.

insert[1] v **1** to put in through an opening. **2** to introduce into the body of something, e.g. text. ➤ **insertion** n.

insert[2] n a piece of written or printed material placed between the pages of a book or magazine.

inset[1] n **1** a small illustration set within a larger one. **2** a piece of cloth set into a garment for decoration, shaping, etc.

inset[2] v (**insetting**, past tense and past part. **inset** or **insetted**) to insert.

inshore adj and adv **1** towards the shore. **2** at sea but near the shore.

inside[1] n **1** an inner side or surface. **2** an interior or internal part. **3** (usu in pl) the stomach or the intestines. ✳ **inside out** with the inner surface on the outside.

inside[2] adj **1** of, on, near, or towards the inside. **2** carried out by somebody within an organization: an inside job.

inside[3] prep **1** in or into the interior of. **2** closer to the centre than. **3** in less than a particular period of time.

inside[4] adv **1** in or into the interior. **2** indoors. **3** within somebody's body or mind. **4** chiefly Brit, informal in or into prison.

insider n somebody accepted as a member of a group, esp somebody with access to confidential information.

insidious adj acting gradually but with very harmful consequences. ➤ **insidiously** adv.

insight n **1** the ability to discern the true nature of something. **2** an explanation that displays this ability.

insignia n (pl **insignia**, **insignias**) a badge of authority or honour.

insignificant adj **1** too unimportant to be worth consideration. **2** very small in size, amount, or number. ➤ **insignificance** n, **insignificantly** adv.

insincere adj not expressing feelings or opinions honestly. ➤ **insincerely** adv, **insincerity** n.

insinuate v **1** to suggest (something unpleasant) in a subtle or oblique manner. **2** (+ into) to gain acceptance for (e.g. oneself) by crafty means. **3** to squeeze in somewhere. ➤ **insinuating** adj.

insinuation n a sly and usu derogatory reference.

insipid adj **1** lacking flavour. **2** with no interesting or stimulating qualities.

insist v **1** to persist in maintaining that something is the case. **2** (usu + on/upon) to state wishes or requirements forcefully, accepting no refusal. **3** (+ on/upon) to refuse to stop doing something.

insistent adj **1** insisting forcefully or repeatedly. **2** demanding attention. ➤ **insistence** n, **insistently** adv.

in situ adv and adj in the natural or original position.

insofar as conj to the extent or degree that.

insole n **1** a shaped strip placed inside a shoe for e.g. a better fit. **2** a fixed inside sole of a shoe.

insolent adj showing disrespectful rudeness. ➤ **insolence** n, **insolently** adv.

insoluble adj **1** incapable of being dissolved in liquid. **2** impossible to solve or explain.

insolvent adj unable to pay one's debts. ➤ **insolvency** n.

insomnia n prolonged inability to sleep. ➤ **insomniac** adj and n.

insomuch as conj to the degree that.

insouciance n light-hearted unconcern; nonchalance. ➤ **insouciant** adj.

inspect v **1** to examine closely and critically. **2** to view or examine officially. ➤ **inspection** n.

inspector n **1** an official who assesses whether standards are being met or established rules followed. **2** a police officer ranking immediately above a sergeant.

inspiration n **1** the act of stimulating the intellect or emotions. **2** an inspiring agent or influence. **3** an inspired idea. ➤ **inspirational** adj.

inspire v **1** to have an animating or uplifting influence on. **2** to act as a stimulus for. **3** (+ with) to cause to feel a particular emotion. ➤ **inspiring** adj.

inspired adj **1** created by inspiration. **2** especially clever or effective.

instability n (pl **-ies**) lack of stability.

install (NAmer **instal**) v **1** to place in position for use. **2** to establish (somebody) in a specified place, office, or rank.

Usage Note: Note the spelling with -all.

---

installation n **1** the act of installing. **2** a usu large piece of equipment installed to perform some specified function. **3** a military base or establishment. **4** a large-scale work of art assembled in the gallery where it is exhibited.

instalment (NAmer **installment**) n **1** a part into which a debt is divided for repayment. **2** each of a series of parts, e.g. of a publication or broadcast, presented at intervals.

instance[1] n an example or occurrence of something. ✳ **for instance** as an example.

instance[2] v to put forward as a case or example.

instant[1] n **1** a very brief period of time; a second. **2** a precise point in time.

instant² *adj* **1** immediate. **2** of food: prepared for easy final preparation.

instantaneous *adj* occurring or acting instantly. ➤ **instantaneously** *adv.*

instead *adv* as a substitute or alternative.

instep *n* the arched middle portion of the human foot.

instigate *v* to initiate or bring about (a course of action or procedure). ➤ **instigation** *n.*

instil (*NAmer* **instill**) *v* (**instilled, instilling**) (+ in/into) to cause to become firmly fixed in someone's mind over time.

instinct *n* a natural or inherent way of acting or thinking. ➤ **instinctual** *adj.*

instinctive *adj* arising spontaneously and independent of judgment or will. ➤ **instinctively** *adv.*

institute¹ *n* an organization for research or education in a particular field.

institute² *v* to originate and establish.

institution *n* **1** an established organization or body, e.g. a university or hospital. **2** an established practice in a culture. **3** *dated* a psychiatric hospital or unit. ➤ **institutional** *adj.*

institutionalize *or* **-ise** *v* **1** to establish as a custom or regular practice. **2** to put or keep in an institution, *esp* a psychiatric hospital. **3** to cause to acquire personality traits typical of people in an institution, *esp* a lack of independent thought or action.

instruct *v* **1** to teach. **2** to command. **3** to engage (a lawyer) for a case. **4** to inform of something.

instruction *n* **1** (*usu in pl*) an order or command. **2** (*usu in pl*) a direction or piece of advice on how to do something. **3** teaching or training.

instructive *adj* giving useful information or advice. ➤ **instructively** *adv.*

instructor *n* a teacher.

instrument *n* **1** an implement, tool, or device *esp* for delicate work or measurement. **2** a device used to produce music. **3** a device used in navigating an aircraft or ship. **4** a formal legal document.

instrumental¹ *adj* **1** (+ in) serving as a means or agent. **2** composed for or performed on a musical instrument.

instrumental² *n* a musical composition for instruments but not voice.

instrumentalist *n* a player of a musical instrument.

instrumentation *n* **1** the instruments specified for the performance of a musical composition. **2** the navigation instruments on an aeroplane, ship, etc.

insubordinate *adj* disobedient. ➤ **insubordination** *n.*

insubstantial *adj* lacking firmness or solidity.

insufferable *adj* too bad, unpleasant, or annoying to put up with. ➤ **insufferably** *adv.*

insufficient *adj* not enough; inadequate. ➤ **insufficiency** *n,* **insufficiently** *adv.*

insular *adj* **1** relating to islands. **2** cut off from other people. **3** narrow-minded. ➤ **insularity** *n.*

insulate *v* **1** to separate from conducting bodies by means of nonconductors so as to prevent loss of electricity, heat, or sound. **2** to protect (somebody) from harsh realities. ➤ **insulator** *n.*

insulation *n* **1** material used in insulating. **2** the act of insulating.

insulin *n* a hormone that regulates the level of glucose in the blood.

insult¹ *v* to speak about or treat with insolence or contempt.

insult² *n* a remark, gesture, etc that insults.

insuperable *adj* incapable of being surmounted or overcome.

insupportable *adj* **1** unendurable. **2** incapable of being supported or sustained.

insurance *n* **1** a contract whereby one party undertakes to indemnify another against a particular type of loss, or the protection offered by such a contract. **2** the premium demanded under such a contract. **3** the sum for which something is insured. **4** the business of insuring people or property.

insure *v* **1** to procure insurance on (a property, etc) or for (an owner). **2** (+ against) to protect from something unpleasant. **3** *chiefly NAmer* to ensure.

Usage Note: Do not confuse this word with *ensure,* which means 'to make sure'.

insurgent¹ *n* somebody who revolts against civil authority or an established government. ➤ **insurgency** *n.*

insurgent² *adj* rebellious.

insurmountable *adj* too great or difficult to overcome.

insurrection *n* a revolt against civil authority or established government.

intact *adj* not harmed or damaged.

intake *n* an amount or number taken in, *esp* the number of students entering a school or college in any one year.

intangible *adj* **1** not able to be perceived by touch. **2** not clear or definite. ➤ **intangibly** *adv.*

integer *n* a whole number.

integral *adj* **1** essential to completeness; constituent. **2** lacking nothing essential; whole.

integrate *v* **1** to form or blend (separate elements) into a whole. **2** (+ into) to incorporate into a larger unit.

integrity *n* **1** uncompromising adherence to a code of *esp* moral or artistic values. **2** the state of being complete or undivided. **3** *formal* an unimpaired condition; wholeness.

intellect *n* the capacity for intelligent thought.

intellectual[1] *adj* **1** of the intellect. **2** using or requiring the intellect for understanding, often in preference to emotion or experience. ➤ **intellectually** *adv*.

intellectual[2] *n* an intellectual person.

intellectualize *or* **-ise** *v* to consider in an intellectual way.

intelligence *n* **1** the ability to learn, apply knowledge, or think abstractly. **2** information concerning an enemy or competitor, or an organization with the task of gathering such information.

intelligence quotient *n* a number expressing the ratio of somebody's intelligence to the average for his or her age.

intelligent *adj* having or indicating the ability to learn and apply knowledge effectively. ➤ **intelligently** *adv*.

intelligentsia *n* intellectuals considered as a social or political class.

intelligible *adj* capable of being understood. ➤ **intelligibility** *n*, **intelligibly** *adv*.

intemperate *adj* going beyond the bounds of reasonable behaviour. ➤ **intemperance** *n*.

intend *v* **1** to have in mind as a purpose or goal. **2** to design for a specified use or destine for a particular future.

intended[1] *adj* planned; future.

intended[2] *n informal* somebody's future spouse.

intense *adj* **1** existing or occurring in an extreme degree. **2** feeling emotion deeply. ➤ **intensely** *adv*, **intensity** *n*.

intensify *v* (**-ies, -ied**) to make or become more intense.

intensive *adj* **1** very thorough and concentrated within a short time. **2** using a specified factor to a greater extent than others: *labour-intensive*. **3** designed to maximize productivity: *intensive farming*. ➤ **intensively** *adv*.

intensive care *n* continuous care and special treatment given to a seriously ill patient.

intent[1] *n* intention. ✳ **to all intents and purposes** in every practical or important respect.

intent[2] *adj* **1** (+ on/upon) having the mind or attention concentrated on. **2** (+ on/upon) determined to. **3** directed with strained or eager attention. ➤ **intently** *adv*.

intention *n* **1** what somebody intends to do; an aim. **2** a determination to act in a certain way. **3** (*in pl*) purpose with respect to proposal of marriage.

intentional *adj* deliberate. ➤ **intentionally** *adv*.

inter *v* (**interred, interring**) to place (a dead body) in the earth or a tomb.

inter- *prefix* **1** between; among: *intercity; interstellar*. **2** reciprocally: *interact*.

interact *v* to produce an effect upon each other. ➤ **interaction** *n*.

interactive *adj* **1** characterized by interaction. **2** involving the exchange of information between a computer and user while a program is being run.

interbreed *v* (*past tense and past part*. **interbred**) to crossbreed.

intercede *v* to plead with somebody on behalf of another person.

intercept *v* to stop (something or somebody) reaching the place they are going to. ➤ **interception** *n*, **interceptor** *n*.

intercession *n* the act of interceding, *esp* by prayer.

interchange[1] *v* **1** to put each of (two things) in the place of the other. **2** of two people: to give each other (a thing of the same kind). ➤ **interchangeability** *n*, **interchangeable** *adj*.

interchange[2] *n* **1** a junction of two or more roads at different levels. **2** the act of interchanging.

intercity *adj* existing or travelling between cities.

intercom *n* an internal communication system, e.g. in a building.

interconnect *v* to connect with one another.

intercontinental *adj* carried on, or capable of travelling, between continents.

intercourse *n* **1** = SEXUAL INTERCOURSE. **2** *formal* communication or dealings between people.

intercut *v* (**intercutting**, *past tense and past part*. **intercut**) to alternate shots from (one cinematic scene) with shots from a contrasting scene.

interdependent *adj* depending one on the other. ➤ **interdependence** *n*.

interest[1] *n* **1** readiness to be concerned with something. **2** a subject or activity that one is concerned with and enthusiastic about. **3** a quality in a thing that arouses interest. **4** a charge for borrowed money, generally a percentage of the amount borrowed. **5** benefit or advantage to somebody. **6** a right, title, or legal share in something, e.g. a business.

interest[2] *v* **1** to engage the attention or arouse the interest of. **2** (+ in) to persuade (somebody) to do or buy something. ➤ **interesting** *adj*.

interested *adj* **1** having the curiosity aroused or attention engaged. **2** involved; not impartial.

interface[1] *n* **1** the place at which independent systems meet and act on each other. **2** a piece of computer hardware or software that allows a user to communicate with a computer.

interface[2] *v* **1** to connect by means of an interface. **2** to interact.

interfere *v* **1** (+ with) to get in the way or be a hindrance. **2** (+ with) to handle or adjust without authorization. **3** (*often* + in) to take a part in matters that do not concern one. **4** *informal* (+ with) to carry out a sexual assault.

interference *n* **1** the act of interfering. **2** disturbance to received radio signals by other unwanted signals or noise.

interferon *n* a protein that inhibits the development of viruses.

intergalactic *adj* existing or operating between galaxies.

interim[1] *n* an intervening time.

interim[2] *adj* temporary or provisional.

interior[1] *adj* **1** lying or occurring inside something. **2** away from the border or shore. **3** relating to the domestic affairs of a country. **4** of the mind or soul.

interior[2] *n* **1** the internal or inner part of a thing. **2** the part of a country that lies away from the border or the shore. **3** the internal affairs of a country.

interject *v* to say something abruptly while something else is being said.

interlace *v* **1** to interweave. **2** to intersperse among other things.

interleave *v* **1** to intersperse (e.g. blank pages or protective sheets) between the pages of (a book). **2** to insert between layers.

interlock *v* to become firmly connected by parts designed to fit together.

interlocutor *n formal* somebody who takes part in dialogue or conversation.

interloper *n* somebody who interferes or encroaches.

interlude *n* **1** an intervening period or event, *esp* of a contrasting character. **2** a break between parts of a play or other performance. **3** a musical composition inserted between the parts of a longer composition.

intermarry *v* (-ies, -ied) to become connected by marriage with another group.

intermediary *n* (*pl* -ies) somebody acting as a mediator or go-between.

intermediate *adj* **1** existing or occurring in the middle or between two extremes. **2** involving a level of skill or knowledge greater than that of a beginner, but not yet considered advanced.

interment *n* the placing of a corpse in a grave.

intermezzo /inta'metsoh/ *n* (*pl* **intermezzi** or **intermezzos**) a movement that comes between the major sections of an extended musical work, e.g. an opera.

interminable *adj* seeming to have no end; wearisomely long. ➤ **interminably** *adv*.

intermingle *v* to mingle (things) together or combine (something) with something else.

intermission *n* **1** a break between the acts of a performance. **2** a pause or respite.

intermittent *adj* occurring at irregular intervals. ➤ **intermittently** *adv*.

intern[1] *v* to confine e.g. in prison or a concentration camp, *esp* during a war. ➤ **internment** *n*.

intern[2] *n chiefly NAmer* **1** a person receiving practical training in the workplace. **2** a junior doctor working under supervision in a hospital.

internal *adj* **1** existing or situated within the limits or surface of something. **2** present within the body. **3** operative within a state or an organization. **4** existing within the mind. ➤ **internally** *adv*.

internal-combustion engine *n* an engine in which the combustion that generates energy takes place inside, e.g. in a cylinder, as opposed to in a separate furnace.

internalize or **-ise** *v* to incorporate (e.g. learned values) within the self and use them as guiding principles.

international[1] *adj* **1** affecting or involving two or more nations. **2** known or recognized in more than one country. ➤ **internationally** *adv*.

international[2] *n* **1** a sporting or other contest between two national teams. **2** a player who has taken part in such a contest.

internationalism *n* support for cooperation among nations. ➤ **internationalist** *n*.

internationalize or **-ise** *v* to become or make international.

internecine *adj* involving conflict within a group.

Internet *n* (**the Internet**) the worldwide computer network for the exchange of information via telephone lines and satellite links.

interpersonal *adj* involving relations between people.

interplanetary *adj* existing or operating between planets.

interplay *n* the effect that two or more things have on each other; interaction.

interpolate *v* to insert (words) into a text or conversation. ➤ **interpolation** *n*.

interpose *v* **1** to place (something) between two things. **2** to interrupt with (words) during a conversation or argument.

interpret *v* (**interpreted, interpreting**) **1** to understand the meaning of (something), often in the light of one's beliefs or circumstances. **2** to explain the meaning of. **3** to give an oral translation of somebody's words. ➤ **interpretation** *n*, **interpreter** *n*.

interracial *adj* involving members of different races.

interregnum *n* (*pl* **interregnums** or **interregna**) the time during which a throne is vacant between reigns or normal government is suspended.

interrelate *v* to relate to one another. ➤ **interrelation** *n*.

interrogate *v* to question formally, exhaustively, or aggressively. ➤ **interrogation** *n*, **interrogator** *n*.

interrogative[1] *adj* **1** questioning. **2** used in a question. ➤ **interrogatively** *adv*.

interrogative[2] *n* a word, *esp* a pronoun, used in asking questions.

interrupt *v* **1** to break the flow of (a speaker or speech). **2** to break the uniformity or continuity of (something). ➤ **interruption** *n*.

intersect *v* **1** to divide (e.g. a line or area) by passing through or across it. **2** of lines, roads, etc: to meet and cross at a point.

intersection *n* a place where two or more things, e.g. streets, roads, etc, intersect.

intersperse *v* **1** to insert at intervals among other things. **2** (+ with) to vary with scattered things.

interstate *adj* between two or more states, *esp* of the USA or Australia.

interstellar *adj* existing or operating between the stars.

interstice *n formal* a small space between adjacent things.

intertwine *v* to twine together or join twisting round each other.

interval *n* **1** an intervening space, e.g. a time between events or states. **2** the difference in pitch between two notes. **3** *Brit* a break in the presentation of an entertainment, e.g. a play.

intervene *v* **1** to occur or come between two things. **2** to become involved so as to change a situation, e.g. to settle a dispute. ➤ **intervention** *n*.

interview[1] *n* **1** a formal consultation to evaluate e.g. a prospective student or employee. **2** a meeting at which information is obtained from somebody. ➤ **interviewee** *n*, **interviewer** *n*.

interview[2] *v* to invite or subject to an interview.

interweave *v* (**interwove**, **interwoven**) to weave together.

intestate *adj* having made no valid will.

intestine *n* (*also in pl*) the tubular organ connecting the stomach to the anus. ➤ **intestinal** *adj*.

intimacy *n* (*pl* **-ies**) **1** familiarity, *esp* close friendship. **2** an intimate remark.

intimate[1] *adj* **1** marked by a warm friendship developing through long association. **2** suggesting informal warmth or privacy. **3** of a very personal or private nature. **4** of knowledge: derived from a very close association or long familiarity. **5** *euphem* involved in a sexual relationship. ➤ **intimately** *adv*.

intimate[2] *v* **1** to make known, e.g. by a formal announcement. **2** to hint at or imply. ➤ **intimation** *n*.

intimate[3] *n* a close friend or confidant.

intimidate *v* **1** to frighten or unnerve. **2** to compel or deter with threats. ➤ **intimidation** *n*.

into *prep* **1** so as to be inside. **2** so as to become or find oneself in: *Don't get into trouble.* **3** used in division: *Divide 35 into 70.* **4** in the direction of. **5** *informal* involved with or keen on.

intolerable *adj* too bad or unpleasant to endure. ➤ **intolerably** *adv*.

intolerant *adj* **1** unwilling to accept others' views or allow others their own views, lifestyles, etc. **2** (+ of) unable to endure. ➤ **intolerance** *n*.

intonation *n* the rise and fall of the voice in speech.

intone *v* to recite or say in a monotonous tone.

intoxicate *v* **1** to excite or stupefy with alcohol or drugs, *esp* so that physical and mental control is markedly diminished. **2** to make very excited or elated. ➤ **intoxicating** *adj*, **intoxication** *n*.

intra- *prefix* inside; within: *intrauterine*.

intractable *adj* **1** not easily solved or dealt with. **2** stubborn.

intranet *n* an internal computer network that operates by using Internet protocols.

intransigent *adj* refusing to compromise or to abandon a position or attitude. ➤ **intransigence** *n*.

intransitive *adj* of a verb: not having a direct object.

intrauterine *adj* within the uterus.

intravenous *adj* in or by way of a vein. ➤ **intravenously** *adv*.

intrepid *adj* fearless and bold. ➤ **intrepidity** *n*.

intricacy *n* (*pl* **-ies**) **1** the quality of being intricate. **2** a detail or complexity.

intricate *adj* having many complexly interrelating parts. ➤ **intricately** *adv*.

intrigue[1] *v* **1** to arouse the interest or curiosity of. **2** to develop a secret or underhand scheme. ➤ **intriguer** *n*, **intriguing** *adj*.

intrigue[2] *n* **1** a secret scheme or plot. **2** the use of scheming or underhand plots in pursuit of an end. **3** a clandestine love affair.

intrinsic *adj* belonging to the essential nature of something. ➤ **intrinsically** *adv*.

introduce *v* **1** to bring into use or into play, *esp* for the first time. **2** to cause (somebody or oneself) to be acquainted with another person. **3** (+ to) to call somebody's attention to a subject for the first time. **4** to make preliminary remarks about (e.g. a speaker). **5** to occur at the beginning of. **6** to place or insert somewhere.

introduction *n* **1** the act of introducing or process of being introduced. **2** a formal presentation of one person to another. **3** a part of a book, lecture, etc that is preliminary to the main part. **4** a book or course of study that gives a basic grounding in a subject. **5** something introduced, e.g. a plant or animal new to an area.

introductory *adj* serving as an introduction; preliminary.

introspection *n* the examining of one's own mind or its contents. ➤ **introspective** *adj*.

introvert *n* a shy person whose attention is often directed to his or her own mental life: compare EXTROVERT. ➤ **introvert** *adj*, **introverted** *adj*.

intrude *v* **1** to thrust oneself into a situation or a place without invitation or welcome. **2** to force (something) in or on something, *esp* without permission.

intruder *n* **1** somebody who intrudes. **2** somebody who trespasses on or breaks into somebody's property.

intrusion *n* **1** the act of intruding. **2** something or somebody that intrudes.

intrusive *adj* constituting an intrusion; unwelcome.

intuit *v* (**intuited**, **intuiting**) to apprehend by intuition.

intuition *n* the power of attaining knowledge without evident rational thought.

intuitive *adj* **1** known or perceived by intuition. **2** possessing intuition or insight. ➤ **intuitively** *adv*.

Inuit *n* (*pl* **Inuits** *or* **Inuit**) **1** a member of the indigenous peoples inhabiting northern Canada, Alaska, and Greenland. **2** the language spoken by these peoples.

inundate *v* **1** to flood (an area). **2** to overwhelm with demands, offers, etc. ➤ **inundation** *n*.

inure *or* **enure** *v* (+ to) to accustom to something undesirable.

invade *v* **1** to enter (e.g. a country) for hostile purposes. **2** to encroach on. **3** to spread over or into (something) as if invading it. ➤ **invader** *n*.

invalid[1] *n* somebody who is unwell or disabled.

invalid[2] *adj* **1** without legal force. **2** logically inconsistent.

invalid[3] *v* (*usu* + out) to remove from active duty because of sickness or disability.

invalidate *v* to make invalid. ➤ **invalidation** *n*.

invalidity *n* **1** *Brit* the fact of being an invalid. **2** lack of validity.

invaluable *adj* very useful.

invariable *adj* not changing; constant.

invariably *adv* always.

invasion *n* **1** a hostile attack on a foreign territory by an army. **2** the incoming or spread of something harmful, e.g. a tumour.

invasive *adj* **1** involving an invasion or intrusion. **2** of medical treatment: involving the insertion of an instrument or other object into the body.

invective *n* abusive or insulting language.

inveigh *v* (+ against) to speak or protest bitterly or vehemently.

inveigle *v* (*usu* + into) to persuade to do something by ingenuity or flattery. ✳ **inveigle oneself into** to gain access to (a place or situation) by ingenuity or trickery.

invent *v* **1** to produce (e.g. a device or machine) for the first time. **2** to think up, *esp* in order to deceive. ➤ **inventor** *n*.

invention *n* **1** something invented. **2** productive imagination; inventiveness. **3** the act of inventing.

inventive *adj* showing original thought or ingenuity; creative. ➤ **inventively** *adv*.

inventory *n* (*pl* **-ies**) **1** an itemized list, e.g. of the contents of a building or stock in a warehouse. **2** *NAmer* the quantity of goods in stock.

inverse[1] *adj* opposite in order, direction, nature, or effect. ➤ **inversely** *adv*.

inverse[2] *n* **1** a direct opposite. **2** in mathematics: a reciprocal quantity. ➤ **inversion** *n*.

invert *v* **1** to turn inside out or upside down. **2** to reverse the position, order, or relationship of.

invertebrate *n* an animal without spinal column, such as an insect, mollusc or worm.

inverted comma *n* = QUOTATION MARK.

invest[1] *v* **1** (*often* + in) to commit money to a particular use in order to earn a financial return. **2** (*often* + in) to devote (e.g. time or effort) to something for future advantages. **3** *informal* (+ in) to buy (*esp* something expensive). ➤ **investor** *n*.

invest[2] *v* **1** (+ in/with) to confer authority, office, or rank on. **2** (+ with) to endow with something.

investigate *v* **1** to make a systematic examination or study of. **2** to conduct an official enquiry into. ➤ **investigation** *n*, **investigative** *adj*, **investigator** *n*.

investiture *n* a formal ceremony conferring an office or honour on somebody.

investment *n* **1** a sum of money invested for income or profit. **2** an asset, e.g. property, purchased for its future usefulness or profitability. **3** the act of investing.

inveterate *adj* **1** firmly and persistently established. **2** confirmed in a habit; habitual.

invidious *adj* tending to cause discontent, ill will, or envy.

invigilate *v* *Brit* to supervise candidates at an examination. ➤ **invigilation** *n*, **invigilator** *n*.

invigorate *v* to give life and energy to. ➤ **invigorating** *adj*.

invincible *adj* incapable of being defeated or overcome. ➤ **invincibility** *n*.

inviolable *adj* that must not be violated or degraded.

inviolate *adj* not violated or profaned.

invisible *adj* **1** incapable of being seen, either by nature or because of concealment. **2** not included in statistics, financial statements, etc: *invisible earnings.* ➤ **invisibility** *n*, **invisibly** *adv*.

invitation *n* **1** the act of inviting. **2** a request to be present or participate. **3** something that induces somebody to behave in a particular way.

invite[1] *v* **1** to request (somebody) to be present at or take part in something. **2** to ask. *esp* formally, for (e.g. tenders, comments). **3** to increase the likelihood of.

invite[2] *n informal* an invitation.

inviting *adj* attractive or tempting. ➤ **invitingly** *adv*.

in vitro *adv and adj* outside the living body and in an artificial environment such as a test tube.

invocation *n* **1** the act of invoking. **2** a prayer asking a deity or spirit for help or support.

invoice[1] *n* a list of goods or services provided, together with a note of the sum owed.

invoice[2] *v* to submit an invoice to or for.

invoke *v* **1** to appeal to (an authority) for help, a judgment, etc. **2** to call forth (e.g. a spirit) by uttering a spell or magical formula. **3** to make an earnest request for.

involuntary *adj* **1** not subject to conscious control; reflex. **2** done against one's will. ➤ **involuntarily** *adv*.

involve *v* **1** to cause to be associated or take part. **2** to absorb (oneself) mentally or to commit (oneself) emotionally. **3** to require as a necessary accompaniment. ➤ **involvement** *n*.

involved *adj* **1** needlessly complex. **2** taking part. **3** connected with something, *esp* emotionally.

invulnerable *adj* incapable of being injured or harmed. ➤ **invulnerability** *n*.

inwards (*NAmer* **inward**) *adv* **1** towards the interior. **2** towards the mind or spirit.

iodine *n* **1** a blackish grey non-metallic chemical element. **2** a solution of iodine in alcohol, used as an antiseptic.

ion *n* an atom or group of atoms that carries a positive or negative electric charge through having lost or gained electrons.

ionize *or* **-ise** *v* to convert into ions. ➤ **ionization** *n*.

ionizer *n* a machine that emits ions into the air to improve air quality.

ionosphere *n* an upper layer of the earth's atmosphere extending from an altitude of about 60km to at least 480km.

iota *n* **1** the ninth letter of the Greek alphabet (I, ι). **2** an infinitesimal amount; a bit.

IOU *n* a written acknowledgment of a debt.

ipso facto *adv* by that very fact, or by the very nature of the case.

IQ *abbr* intelligence quotient.

Ir *abbr* the chemical symbol for iridium.

IRA *abbr* Irish Republican Army.

irascible *adj* easily provoked to anger; irritable.

irate *adj* extremely angry.

ire *n literary* anger.

iridescent *adj* displaying a shimmering shift of colours. ➤ **iridescence** *n*.

iris *n* **1** (*pl* **irises** *or* **irides**) the round coloured portion of the eye with the pupil in the centre. **2** (*pl* **irises** *or* **iris**) a plant with long straight leaves and large showy flowers.

Irish[1] *adj* of Ireland, its people, or the Irish language.

Irish[2] *n* **1** (**the Irish**) the people of Ireland. **2** (*also* **Irish Gaelic**) the Celtic language of the people of Ireland.

irk *v* to irritate or annoy.

irksome *adj* troublesome or annoying.

iron[1] *n* **1** a silver-white magnetic metal that is heavy and malleable, readily rusts in moist air. **2** a metal implement with a smooth flat heated base, used to smooth or press clothing. **3** (*usu in pl*) a device, *esp* fetters, used to bind or restrain. **4** a golf club with metal heads. **5** a tool, implement, or device made of iron.

iron[2] *adj* **1** made of iron. **2** resembling iron, e.g. in strength or durability.

iron[3] *v* to smooth (e.g. a garment) with a heated iron.

Iron Age *n* (**the Iron Age**) the period of human culture, dating from before 1000 BC, characterized by the widespread use of iron for making tools and weapons.

Iron Curtain *n* (**the Iron Curtain**) the political and ideological barrier formerly separating the Communist and non-Communist countries of Europe.

ironic *adj* **1** containing or constituting irony. **2** tending to use irony. ➤ **ironically** *adv*.

ironmonger *n* **Brit** a dealer in hardware. ➤ **ironmongery** *n*.

ironwork *n* **1** articles made of iron. **2** (*in pl*) a place where iron or steel is smelted or iron or steel products are made.

irony /'ierəni/ *n* (*pl* **-ies**) **1** the *esp* humorous use of words to express a meaning opposite to their literal meaning. **2** incongruity between actual and the expected results of a particular event or course of action.

irradiate *v* **1** to expose (food) to radiation in order to kill bacteria and prolong its shelf life. **2** to cast rays of light on. ➤ **irradiation** *n*.

irrational *adj* not governed by or according to reason; illogical. ➤ **irrationality** *n*, **irrationally** *adv*.

irreconcilable *adj* **1** impossible to reconcile. **2** incompatible. ➤ **irreconcilably** *adv*.

irrecoverable *adj* not capable of being recovered or put right.

irredeemable *adj* too bad to be saved or improved. ➤ **irredeemably** *adv*.

irreducible *adj* impossible to reduce, *esp* to a simpler state.

irrefutable *adj* not able to be denied or disproved.

irregular *adj* 1 lacking continuity or occurring unpredictably. 2 lacking symmetry or evenness. 3 contrary to rules, customs, or moral principles. 4 of a word: not inflected in the normal manner. 5 of troops: not belonging to the regular army organization. ➤ **irregularity** *n*.

irrelevant *adj* not relevant; inapplicable. ➤ **irrelevance** *n*, **irrelevantly** *adv*.

irreligious *adj* hostile to or disrespectful of religion.

irremediable *adj* impossible to remedy; incurable.

irreparable *adj* not able to be repaired or set to rights. ➤ **irreparably** *adv*.

irreplaceable *adj* having no adequate substitute.

irrepressible *adj* impossible to restrain or control.

irreproachable *adj* beyond criticism or blame.

irresistible *adj* too attractive or powerful to resist. ➤ **irresistibly** *adv*.

irresolute *adj* lacking decisiveness or a firm purpose.

irrespective *adv* ✳ **irrespective of** without regard to.

irresponsible *adj* showing no regard for the consequences of one's actions. ➤ **irresponsibly** *adv*.

irretrievable *adj* not retrievable or recoverable. ➤ **irretrievably** *adv*.

irreverence *n* lack of respect. ➤ **irreverent** *adj*, **irreverently** *adv*.

irreversible *adj* unable to be changed back into a previous state. ➤ **irreversibly** *adv*.

irrevocable *adj* incapable of being revoked or altered. ➤ **irrevocably** *adv*.

irrigate *v* 1 to supply (land) with water by means of channels. 2 to flush (e.g. an eye or wound) with a stream of liquid. ➤ **irrigation** *n*.

irritable *adj* 1 easily angered or exasperated. 2 abnormally sensitive to stimuli. ➤ **irritability** *n*, **irritably** *adv*.

irritant *n* something that irritates.

irritate *v* 1 to make impatient or angry. 2 to cause (a part of the body) to become sore or inflamed. ➤ **irritating** *adj*, **irritatingly** *n*.

is *v* third person sing. present tense of BE.

ISA /ˈiesə/ *n* an individual savings account, a tax-free savings scheme.

-ise *suffix* see -IZE.

-ish *suffix* 1 denoting a particular quality: *childish*. 2 denoting nationality: *Finnish*. 3 slightly; somewhat: *biggish*. 4 approximately: *fortyish*.

Islam *n* 1 the religious faith of Muslims including belief in Allah as the sole deity and in Muhammad as his prophet. 2 the civilization based on Islam. ➤ **Islamic** *adj*.

island *n* 1 an area of land surrounded by water. 2 something that is isolated or surrounded. ➤ **islander** *n*.

isle *n* an island.

islet *n* a little island.

-ism *suffix* 1 denoting an act or practice: *cannibalism*. 2 denoting a state or a pathological condition: *magnetism; alcoholism*. 3 denoting a doctrine or cult: *Buddhism*. 4 denoting prejudice: *sexism*.

isn't *contraction* is not.

isobar *n* a line on a chart connecting places where the atmospheric pressure is the same.

isolate *v* 1 to set apart from others. 2 to separate out (a substance) in its pure form. ➤ **isolation** *n*.

isolated *adj* 1 cut off from others; remote; lonely. 2 single or exceptional.

isolationism *n* a policy of refraining from engaging in international relations. ➤ **isolationist** *n* and *adj*.

isomer *n* a chemical compound with the same chemical formula as another but a different arrangement of atoms.

isometric *adj* having equal dimensions or measurements.

isosceles /ieˈsosəleez/ *adj* of a triangle: having two equal sides.

isotope *n* any of two or more forms of a chemical element that have the same atomic number but differ in atomic mass and physical properties.

Israeli *n* (*pl* **Israelis**) a native or inhabitant of modern Israel. ➤ **Israeli** *adj*.

Israelite *n* a native or inhabitant of the ancient kingdom of Israel.

issue[1] *n* 1 a matter or topic, *esp* one that is in dispute. 2 any of a series of e.g. magazines regularly published under the same title. 3 the act of issuing something. ✳ **at issue** under discussion or in dispute. **take issue with** to disagree or argue with.

issue[2] *v* 1 to send (e.g. a newspaper) out for sale or circulation. 2 to give (e.g. a statement) out officially. 3 to go, come, or flow out.

isthmus *n* a narrow strip of land connecting two larger land areas.

IT *abbr* information technology.

it *pron* 1 that thing, animal, etc. 2 used as subject of an impersonal verb: *It's raining*. 3 used to refer to a state of affairs: *How's it going?* 4 the important or appropriate thing.

Italian *n* 1 a native or inhabitant of Italy. 2 the language of Italy. ➤ **Italian** *adj*.

italic[1] *n* a printed character that slants upwards to the right, like the labels *n*, *adj*, etc in this dictionary.

italic[2] *adj* of a printed character: in italic.

itch[1] *n* **1** an irritating sensation in the skin that makes one want to scratch. **2** *informal* a restless desire.

itch[2] *v* **1** to have or produce an itch. **2** *informal* to have a restless desire to do something.

it'd *contraction* **1** it had. **2** it would.

item *n* **1** a separate piece of news or information. **2** a separate article or unit in a series. **3** (**an item**) *informal* two people in a romantic relationship.

itemize *or* **-ise** *v* to set down in a list of individual elements.

itinerant[1] *adj* travelling from place to place.

itinerant[2] *n* somebody who moves from place to place.

itinerary *n* (*pl* **-ies**) the proposed route of a journey, usu including a list of stops on the way.

it'll *contraction* **1** it will. **2** it shall.

its *adj* belonging to or associated with a thing, animal, etc already mentioned.

Usage Note: Do not confuse *its* , the possessive form of *it* with no apostrophe, and *it's*, a shortened form of *it is* or *it has*.

it's *contraction* **1** it is. **2** it has.

itself *pron* used reflexively or for emphasis to refer to a thing, animal, etc that is the subject of the clause.

ITV *abbr* Independent Television.

IUD *abbr* intrauterine device.

I've *contraction* I have.

IVF *abbr* in vitro fertilization.

ivory *n* (*pl* **-ies**) **1** the hard creamy-white substance of which the tusks of elephants are made. **2** a creamy white colour. **3** (**the ivories**) *informal* the keys of a piano.

ivory tower *n* a place or situation remote from everyday life or practical concerns.

ivy *n* a common climbing plant with evergreen leaves.

-ize *or* **-ise** *suffix* **1** to become or become like: *liquidize; Americanize*. **2** to subject to: *criticize*.

Usage Note: Either spelling is correct, in British English, for most verbs: *criticize* or *criticise; organize* or *organise; privatise* or *privatize*. There are, however, a number of verbs which must end in *-ise*, e.g. *advertise, advise, chastise, comprise, compromise, despise, devise, enfranchise, excise, exercise, franchise, improvise, merchandise, revise, supervise, surmise, surprise*, and *televise*.

J or **j** *n* (*pl* **J's** or **Js** or **j's**) the tenth letter of the English alphabet.

jab¹ *v* (**jabbed, jabbing**) **1** to pierce or poke sharply. **2** to strike with a short straight blow.

jab² *n* **1** an act of jabbing. **2** *informal* an injection.

jabber *v* to talk rapidly and unintelligibly.

jack¹ *n* **1** a mechanism for lifting a vehicle on one side, e.g. to replace a tyre. **2** a playing card ranking below the queen. **3** an electrical connection. **4** a small target ball in the game of bowls. **5** a small national flag flown at the bow of a ship.

jack² *v* **1** (*usu* + up) to move or lift with a jack. **2** (+ up) to raise the level or quality of.

jackal *n* a wild dog that scavenges or hunts in packs.

jackass *n* **1** a male ass. **2** a stupid person.

jackdaw *n* a black and grey bird related to the crow.

jacket¹ *n* **1** an outer garment for the upper body opening down the front. **2** a protective or insulating covering. **3** the skin of a baked potato.

jacket² *v* (**jacketed, jacketing**) to enclose in a jacket.

jacket potato *n* (*pl* **-oes**) *Brit* a potato baked and served in its skin.

jack-in-the-box *n* a toy consisting of a small box out of which a figure springs when the lid is raised.

jackknife¹ *n* (*pl* **jackknives**) **1** a large pocket knife with a folding blade. **2** a dive in which the body is bent from the waist and then straightened before hitting the water.

jackknife² *v* **1** to double up like a jackknife. **2** to cause to jackknife. **3** of an articulated lorry: to form a V-shape in an uncontrolled skid.

jack plug *n* a single-pronged electrical plug.

jackpot *n* the largest prize in a lottery or on a fruit machine.

Jacobean *adj* of the reign of James I of England (1603–25).

Jacobite *n* a supporter of James II of England or of the Stuarts after 1688.

jacquard *n* **1** an apparatus for a loom holding punched cards that enable decorated and patterned fabrics to be woven. **2** a fabric made with this.

Jacuzzi /jə'koohzi/ *n trademark* a large bath with underwater jets that massage the body.

jade *n* a hard green mineral used as a stone.

jaded *adj* weary or bored by a surfeit of something.

jagged *adj* having a sharply indented or uneven edge or surface.

jaguar *n* a large wild cat having a brownish yellow coat with black spots.

jail¹ (*Brit* **gaol**) or **gaol** *n* a place where people are confined when accused or convicted of a crime.

jail² (*Brit* **gaol**) or **gaol** *v* to confine in a jail.

jalopy *n* (*pl* **-ies**) *informal* a dilapidated old car.

jam¹ *v* (**jammed, jamming**) **1** to squeeze or pack closely or tightly into a space. **2** to fill or overfill. **3** to fill (a street) so that passage along it is blocked. **4** to cause to become stuck so that it does not work or move. **5** to send out interfering signals to suppress (a radio signal). **6** (+ on) to apply (brakes) suddenly. **7** *informal* to take part in an improvised jazz session.

jam² *n* **1** a crowd or mass that impedes or blocks something. **2** the pressure or congestion of a crowd. **3** an instance of jamming. **4** *informal* a difficult or awkward situation. **5** an improvised jazz session.

jam³ *n* a preserve made by boiling fruit and sugar.

jamb *n* a straight vertical post forming the side of a door or window opening.

jamboree *n* a large festive party or gathering.

jammy *adj* (**-ier, -iest**) **1** covered or filled with jam. **2** *Brit, informal* lucky.

jam-packed *adj* full to overflowing.

jangle *v* **1** to make or cause to make a harsh, ringing noise. **2** of the nerves: to be tense.
➤ **jangly** *adj*.

janitor *n* a caretaker of a large building.

January *n* the first month of the year.

Japanese *n* (*pl* **Japanese**) **1** a native or inhabitant of Japan. **2** the language of Japan. ➤ **Japanese** *adj*.

jape *n* a jest or joke.

jar¹ *n* a cylindrical container made of glass.

jar² *v* (**jarred, jarring**) **1** to give (something or somebody) a shock or jolt. **2** to have a disagreeable or incongruous effect. **3** to make a harsh or discordant noise. **4** to jolt or vibrate.

jar³ *n* **1** a sudden or unexpected jolt or shake. **2** an unsettling shock.

jargon *n* the terminology or idiom of a particular activity or group. ➤ **jargonistic** *adj*.

jasmine *n* a shrub or climbing plant with fragrant yellow or white flowers.

jasper *n* an opaque reddish brown quartz used as a gemstone.

jaundice *n* **1** an abnormal condition marked by yellowing of the skin. **2** a state of bitterness or resentment. ➤ **jaundiced** *adj*.

jaunt *n* a short journey for pleasure.

jaunty *adj* (**-ier, -iest**) having or showing lively self-confidence. ➤ **jauntily** *adv*.

javelin *n* a light spear thrown in an athletic field event or as a weapon.

jaw¹ *n* **1** each of two bony structures that form a framework above and below the mouth and in which the teeth are set. **2** (*in pl*) the two parts of a tool or machine that grips or crushes. **3** *informal* a long chat.

jaw² *v informal* to talk for a long time.

jawbone *n* the lower bone of a jaw.

jay *n* a bird of the crow family with strongly patterned plumage.

jaywalk *v* to cross a street carelessly without regard for traffic. ➤ **jaywalker** *n*.

jazz *n* music developed from ragtime and blues and characterized by syncopated rhythms and improvisation.

jazz up *v informal* to make more lively or interesting.

jazzy *adj* (**-ier, -iest**) **1** having the characteristics of jazz. **2** *informal* bright or showy. ➤ **jazzily** *adv*.

jealous *adj* **1** resentful and envious of an advantage enjoyed by somebody else. **2** apprehensive and suspicious of romantic or sexual rivalry. **3** vigilant in guarding a possession or right. ➤ **jealously** *adv*, **jealousy** *n*.

jeans *pl n* casual trousers made of denim.

jeep *n trademark* a small rugged motor vehicle with four-wheel drive.

jeer¹ *v* to speak or laugh mockingly or rudely.

jeer² *n* a jeering remark or taunt.

Jehovah *n* a Hebrew name for God.

jejune *adj* **1** lacking maturity; puerile. **2** lacking interest or significance.

jell *v chiefly NAmer* see GEL².

jelly *n* **1** a soft fruit-flavoured transparent dessert set with gelatin. **2** a substance resembling jelly in consistency. ➤ **jellied** *adj*.

jelly baby *n* (*pl* **-ies**) a soft sweet made of gelatin in the shape of a baby.

jellyfish *n* (*pl* **-ies** or **jellyfish**) a sea animal with a soft nearly transparent saucer-shaped body and stinging tentacles.

jemmy¹ *n* (*pl* **-ies**) a short crowbar.

jemmy² (*NAmer* **jimmy**) *v* (**-ies, -ied**) to force open with a jemmy.

je ne sais quoi /ˌʒhə nə say 'kwah/ *n* a quality that cannot be readily described or expressed.

jenny *n* (*pl* **-ies**) a female donkey or ass.

jeopardize *or* **-ise** *v* to put in danger.

jeopardy *n* risk of death, loss, or harm.

jerboa *n* a desert rodent with long back legs adapted for jumping.

jerk¹ *v* to move with a short sudden movement.

jerk² *n* **1** a short sudden movement. **2** *chiefly NAmer, informal* a foolish or irritating person.

jerkin *n* a close-fitting sleeveless jacket.

jerky *adj* (**-ier, -iest**) marked by irregular or spasmodic movements. ➤ **jerkily** *adv*.

jerry-built *adj* built cheaply and flimsily.

jerry can *or* **jerrican** *n* a narrow flat-sided container for liquids.

jersey *n* **1** a knitted garment with sleeves. **2** a shirt worn by a footballer or other sports player. **3** a knitted fabric used for clothing. **4** (**Jersey**) a breed of cattle noted for rich milk.

Jerusalem artichoke *n* the edible sweet-tasting tubers of a sunflower.

jest¹ *n* a joke.

jest² *v* to make a joke or witty remark.

jester *n* a clown formerly employed in royal or noble households.

Jesuit /'jezyoo·it/ *n* a member of the Society of Jesus, a Roman Catholic order.

jet¹ *n* **1** a stream of liquid or gas forced out under pressure from a narrow opening or nozzle. **2** an aircraft powered by jet engines.

jet² *v* (**jetted, jetting**) **1** to spurt out. **2** to travel by jet aircraft.

jet³ *n* **1** a hard black polished mineral used for jewellery. **2** (**jet black**) an intense black colour.

jet engine *n* an aircraft engine that produces motion by discharging hot gases produced by burning fuel.

jet lag *n* a temporary disruption of normal bodily rhythms after a long flight from one time zone to another. ➤ **jet-lagged** *adj*.

jetsam *n* goods thrown overboard from a ship and washed up on shore.

jet set *n* wealthy people who frequently travel by air. ➤ **jetsetter** *n*.

jet-ski *n* a small motorized vehicle ridden over water for sport.

jettison *v* **1** to discard or abandon. **2** to throw (goods) overboard to lighten the load of a ship or aircraft.

jetty *n* (*pl* **-ies**) a small landing pier for boats.

Jew *n* **1** a member of a Semitic people living in ancient Israel, or a modern descendant of this people. **2** a person whose religion is Judaism.

jewel *n* **1** a precious stone. **2** a piece of jewellery. **3** a highly valued person or thing. ➤ **jewelled** *adj*.

jeweller (*NAmer* **jeweler**) *n* a person who makes or deals in jewellery.

jewellery (*NAmer* **jewelry**) *n* personal ornaments such as rings and necklaces.

Jewish *adj* relating to Jews or Judaism.

Jewry *n* the Jewish people collectively.

Jew's harp n a small lyre-shaped instrument placed between the teeth and sounded by striking a metal tongue with the finger.

Jezebel n a shameless or immoral woman.

jib¹ n **1** a triangular sail at the front of a ship. **2** the projecting arm of a crane.

jib² v (**jibbed, jibbing**) of a horse: to refuse to go on. ✳ **jib at** to take fright or balk at.

jibe¹ or **gibe** v to make jibes.

jibe² or **gibe** n a taunting or insulting remark.

jiffy or **jiff** n informal a moment or instant.

jig¹ n **1** a lively springy dance in triple time. **2** a device used to hold a piece of work in position and guide the tools working on it.

jig² v (**jigged, jigging**) **1** to dance a jig. **2** to move up and down in a rapid and jerky fashion.

jiggle v informal to move or cause to move with quick short jerks. ➤ **jiggle** n, **jiggly** adj.

jigsaw n **1** a puzzle consisting of small irregularly cut pieces of wood or card that are fitted together to form a picture. **2** a power-driven fretsaw.

jihad /jiˈhad/ n a holy war waged by Muslims against their enemies.

jilt v to break off a romantic relationship with (somebody) suddenly.

jingle¹ v to make or cause to make a light clinking or tinkling sound.

jingle² n **1** a light clinking or tinkling sound. **2** a short catchy song or tune. ➤ **jingly** adj.

jingoism n excessive patriotism; chauvinism. ➤ **jingoistic** adj.

jink¹ n a quick turn or sidestep while running.

jink² v to move quickly with sudden turns and shifts.

jinx¹ n informal somebody or something that brings bad luck.

jinx² v to bring bad luck to.

jitterbug n a lively swinging dance popular in the 1940s.

jitters pl n a feeling of extreme agitation. ➤ **jittery** adj.

jive¹ n a style of lively dancing popular in the 1940s and 1950s, performed to swing music and rock and roll.

jive² v to dance the jive.

job¹ n **1** a regular paid position of employment. **2** a piece of work. **3** a task. **4** a specific duty or function. **5** informal a crime. ✳ **just the job** exactly what is needed. ➤ **jobless** adj.

job² v (**jobbed, jobbing**) to do occasional work. ➤ **jobber** n.

jobcentre n a government office where unemployed people can get information about jobs.

job lot n a miscellaneous collection of goods sold as one item.

job share n an arrangement by which two or more part-time employees share a single full-time job.

jockey¹ n (pl **-eys**) a professional rider in a horse race.

jockey² v (**-eys, -eyed**) to act deftly or deviously to get an advantage.

jockstrap n a support for a man's genitals.

jocose adj formal playfully humorous. ➤ **jocosity** n.

jocular adj jolly or joking. ➤ **jocularity** n, **jocularly** adv.

jocund adj literary cheerful and good-humoured.

jodhpurs pl n riding trousers made close-fitting below the knee.

jog¹ v (**jogged, jogging**) **1** to shake or push gently. **2** to prompt (the memory). **3** to run at a slow steady pace. **4** of a horse: to move at a slow trot. **5** (+ along) to progress slowly.

jog² n **1** a gentle shake or push. **2** a period of steady running. **3** a jogging pace.

joggle v informal to move or shake slightly.

joie de vivre /ˌzhwah də ˈveevrə/ n keen enjoyment of life.

join¹ v **1** to put (two or more things) together to form a unit, or to come together in this way. **2** to connect, meet, or merge with. **3** to enter into the company of. **4** (usu + in) to associate oneself with (another or others) in an activity. **5** to become a member or employee of (a club, organization, etc). ✳ **join forces** to form an alliance or combine efforts.

join² n a place where two parts are joined.

joiner n somebody who constructs or repairs wooden furniture or structures.

joinery n **1** the craft of a joiner. **2** woodwork done or made by a joiner.

joint¹ n **1** a place where two parts are joined. **2** a point of contact between two or more bones of the body. **3** a large piece of meat for roasting. **4** a point on a plant stem where a leaf or branch emerges. **5** informal a place of entertainment, café, etc. **6** slang a cannabis cigarette.

joint² adj **1** united or combined. **2** shared by or affecting two or more people. **3** sharing with another. ➤ **jointly** adv.

joint³ v **1** to provide with a joint or joints. **2** to cut (meat) into joints.

join up v **1** to enlist in the armed forces. **2** to come together.

joist n a timber or beam that helps to support a floor or ceiling.

jojoba /həˈhohbə/ n a North American shrub with edible seeds that yield an oil used in cosmetics.

joke¹ n **1** a brief story told to provoke laughter. **2** a trick played on somebody for fun. **3** something or somebody that is ridiculously unsuitable or inadequate. ➤ **jokey** adj, **joky** adj.

joke² v to make jokes.

joker n **1** somebody who likes joking. **2** a playing card with a picture of a jester, used as a wild card. **3** informal a foolish or incompetent person.

jollification n merrymaking or a celebration.

jollity *n* the quality or state of being jolly; merriment.

jolly¹ *adj* (**-ier, -iest**) **1** cheerful and good-humoured. **2** lively and amusing. ➤ **jolliness** *n*.

jolly² *adv informal* very.

jolly³ *v* (**-ies, -ied**) (+ along) to encourage (somebody) cheerfully.

jolt¹ *v* **1** to move with a jerky motion. **2** to give a sudden knock to. **3** to disconcert (somebody) abruptly.

jolt² *n* **1** an act of jolting. **2** a surprise or shock.

josh *v* to tease or make fun of.

joss stick *n* a thin stick of incense for burning.

jostle *v* **1** to push and shove roughly. **2** to vie with other people.

jot¹ *n* the least bit.

jot² *v* (**jotted, jotting**) (*usu* + down) to write briefly or hurriedly.

jotter *n* a small notebook or pad.

joule *n* the SI unit of work or energy.

journal *n* **1** a periodical dealing with a particular subject. **2** a daily record or diary.

journalese *n* a style of writing characteristic of newspapers.

journalism *n* the work of newspapers and journalists.

journalist *n* a person who writes about news and current affairs for a newspaper or broadcasting outlet. ➤ **journalistic** *adj*.

journey¹ *n* (*pl* **-eys**) **1** an act of travelling from one place to another. **2** the distance or time involved in travelling.

journey² *v* (**-eys, -eyed**) to travel.

journeyman *n* (*pl* **journeymen**) a reliable but not exceptional worker or performer.

joust¹ *n* a medieval combat on horseback between knights armed with lances.

joust² *v* **1** to fight in a joust or tournament. **2** (*often* + with) to engage in a contest or argument.

jovial *adj* good-humoured and cheerful. ➤ **joviality** *n*, **jovially** *adj*.

jowl *n* the lower jaw or cheek.

joy *n* **1** a feeling of great happiness or pleasure. **2** a cause of delight. **3** *Brit, informal* success or satisfaction. ➤ **joyless** *adj*.

joyful *adj* causing or feeling joy. ➤ **joyfully** *adv*.

joyous *adj literary* joyful. ➤ **joyously** *adv*.

joyride *n* a reckless ride in a stolen car. ➤ **joyrider** *n*, **joyriding** *n*.

joystick *n* **1** a lever used to control an aircraft. **2** a lever for controlling the position of an image on a computer screen.

JP *abbr* Justice of the Peace.

jubilant *adj* filled with or expressing great joy or triumph. ➤ **jubilantly** *adv*.

jubilation *n* great joy and satisfaction; rejoicing.

jubilee *n* a special anniversary of a major event such as a sovereign's accession.

Judaism *n* **1** the religious faith developed among the ancient Jews and characterized by belief in one God. **2** the cultural and social practices of the Jews. ➤ **Judaic** *adj*.

Judas *n* somebody who betrays a friend.

judder¹ *v chiefly Brit* to vibrate jerkily.

judder² *n* a sharp vibrating movement.

judge¹ *v* **1** to form or express an opinion about. **2** to give a legal verdict on. **3** to decide the result of (a competition).

judge² *n* **1** a public official who decides cases in a law court. **2** somebody appointed to decide the winner of a competition or contest. **3** somebody who is qualified to give an opinion.

judgment or **judgement** *n* **1** the capacity for forming good opinions or making wise decisions. **2** an opinion or evaluation. **3** a formal decision by a court or judge.

judgmental or **judgemental** *adj* **1** given to making moral judgments about other people. **2** relating to the use of judgment.

Judgment Day *n* in some beliefs, the day of judgment at the end of the world.

judicature *n* **1** the administration of justice. **2** judges collectively.

judicial *adj* relating to justice or a court of law. ➤ **judicially** *adv*.

judiciary *n* (*pl* **-ies**) judges collectively. ➤ **judiciary** *adj*.

judicious *adj* having or characterized by sound judgment. ➤ **judiciously** *adv*.

judo *n* a martial art using quick movement and leverage to throw an opponent.

jug *n* a rounded container with a handle and a lip, for holding and pouring liquids. ➤ **jugful** *n*.

juggernaut *n* **1** *chiefly Brit* a very large articulated transport vehicle. **2** an inexorable force or influence.

juggle¹ *v* **1** to keep several objects in motion in the air at the same time by alternately tossing and catching them. **2** to deal with (several activities) at the same time. **3** to manipulate (facts or figures). ➤ **juggler** *n*.

juggle² *n* an act of juggling.

jugular *adj* relating to the throat or neck.

juice¹ *n* **1** the liquid contained in a fruit or vegetable. **2** a drink made from fruit or vegetable juice. **3** (*in pl*) the natural fluids of an animal body. **4** *informal* an electric current.

juice² *v* to extract the juice from.

juicy *adj* (**-ier, -iest**) **1** succulent; full of juice. **2** *informal* titillatingly or scandalously interesting. **3** *informal* financially profitable.

ju-jitsu or **jiu-jitsu** /jooh'jitsooh/ *n* a Japanese martial art.

jukebox *n* a coin-operated machine that plays pop music.

julep *n* a drink made from a spirit and sugar poured over crushed ice.

July *n* the seventh month of the year.

jumble¹ *v* (*often* + up) to mix up in a confused manner.

jumble² *n* **1** a confused mass of things mingled together. **2** *Brit* articles for a jumble sale.

jumble sale *n Brit* a sale of secondhand articles to raise money for charity.

jumbo *n* (*pl* -os) **1** a very large example of its kind. **2** a jumbo jet. ➤ **jumbo** *adj*.

jumbo jet *n* a large jet passenger aircraft.

jump¹ *v* **1** to spring into the air using the feet and legs. **2** to pass over (an obstacle) by jumping. **3** to move quickly or energetically. **4** to move suddenly from shock or surprise. **5** to pass rapidly or abruptly from one point or state to another. **6** to undergo a sudden sharp increase. **7** (+ on) to make a sudden verbal or physical attack. **8** (**be jumping**) to bustle with activity. **9** to fail to stop at (a traffic light). ✳ **jump at** to accept eagerly. **jump ship** of a sailor: to leave a ship without authority. **jump the queue** to move in front of others in a queue. **jump to it 1** to make an enthusiastic start. **2** to hurry.

jump² *n* **1** an act of jumping; a leap. **2** an obstacle to be jumped over. **3** a sudden involuntary movement. **4** a descent by parachute from an aircraft. **5** a sudden sharp increase.

jumped-up *adj derog* arrogantly displaying a rise in wealth or status.

jumper *n* **1** *Brit* a knitted garment worn on the upper body. **2** *NAmer* a pinafore dress.

jump-jet *n chiefly Brit* a jet aircraft able to take off and land vertically.

jump leads *pl n* a pair of thick cables used to start a vehicle's engine from another battery.

jump-off *n* an extra deciding round of a show-jumping competition.

jump seat *n* a small folding seat in a vehicle or aircraft.

jump-start *v* to start (a motor vehicle) with jump leads. ➤ **jump start** *n*.

jumpsuit *n* a one-piece garment combining top and trousers.

jumpy *adj* (-ier, -iest) **1** nervous or jittery. **2** moving irregularly.

junction *n* **1** a place where things meet or join. **2** a place where roads or railway lines meet. **3** a point of contact or interface between dissimilar metals or semiconductor regions.

juncture *n* **1** a particular or significant point of time. **2** an instance or place of joining.

June *n* the sixth month of the year.

jungle *n* **1** a tropical area overgrown with trees and other vegetation. **2** a confused or complex mass. **3** a place of ruthless struggle for survival. **4** a type of fast electronic dance music.

junior¹ *n* **1** a person who is younger than another by a stated amount: *He is three years her junior*. **2** a person holding a lower or subordinate rank. **3** a member of a junior school, sports team, etc.

junior² *adj* **1** used after a name to distinguish a son with the same name as his father. **2** lower in standing or rank. **3** comprising younger pupils, players, etc. **4** of or for juniors.

juniper *n* an evergreen shrub with small purple cones resembling berries.

junk¹ *n* useless or discarded articles.

junk² *v informal* to get rid of (something) as worthless.

junk³ *n* a flat-bottomed sailing ship in the Far East.

junket *n* **1** a dish of sweetened milk curdled with rennet. **2** *informal* an extravagant business trip or entertainment.

junk food *n* unhealthy processed food.

junkie or **junky** *n* (*pl* -ies) *informal* a drug addict.

junk mail *n* unsolicited advertising material received by post.

junta *n* (*treated as sing. or pl*) a group controlling a government after a revolution.

jurisdiction *n* **1** the power or authority to apply the law. **2** the limits within which authority may be exercised.

jurisprudence *n* the study of the law.

jurist *n* **1** an expert in law. **2** *NAmer* a lawyer or a judge. ➤ **juristic** *adj*.

juror *n* a member of a jury.

jury *n* (*pl* -ies) **1** a body of people who give a verdict based on evidence heard in court. **2** a committee judging a competition.

just¹ *adj* **1** conforming with what is morally upright. **2** being what is merited; appropriate. **3** legally correct. **4** of an opinion: well-founded. ➤ **justly** *adv*.

just² *adv* **1** exactly or precisely. **2** immediately or soon: *I'm just coming.* **3** by a very small margin. **4** only or simply. **5** *informal* very or completely. ✳ **just about 1** almost. **2** not more than.

justice *n* **1** the quality or principle of being just. **2** the just administration of the law. **3** a judge or magistrate. ✳ **do justice to** to appreciate or represent in the best light.

justice of the peace *n* a lay magistrate authorized to hear minor cases.

justifiable *adj* able to be justified; defensible. ➤ **justifiably** *adv*.

justify *v* (-ies, -ied) **1** to prove or show to be right or reasonable. **2** to space out (a line of printed text) so that it is flush with a margin. ➤ **justification** *n*.

jut *v* (**jutted, jutting**) (*often* + out) to extend beyond a normal line or limit; to project.

jute *n* the fibre of an Indian plant used for making rope or sacking.

juvenile[1] *adj* **1** relating to or suitable for young people. **2** physiologically immature or undeveloped.

juvenile[2] *n* **1** a young person, *esp* one under the age of 18. **2** a young bird or animal.

juvenile delinquent *n* a young person who has committed a criminal offence. ➤ **juvenile delinquency** *n*.

juxtapose *v* to place side by side. ➤ **juxtaposition** *n*.

K or **k** *n* (*pl* **K's** or **Ks** or **k's**) the eleventh letter of the English alphabet.

K² *abbr informal* thousand.

K³ *abbr* the chemical symbol for potassium.

kaftan or **caftan** *n* a long loose garment worn by men in Arab countries.

kaiser /ˈkiezə/ *n* a former German or Austrian emperor.

kale or **kail** *n* a cabbage with curled leaves.

kaleidoscope *n* **1** a tube with mirrors inside and pieces of coloured glass that form different patterns as the tube is rotated. **2** a pattern that is continually changing. ➤ **kaleidoscopic** *adj*.

kamikaze¹ /kamiˈkahzi/ *n* in World War II, a Japanese pilot who crashed an aircraft laden with explosives suicidally on a target.

kamikaze² *adj* reckless or self-destructive.

kangaroo *n* (*pl* **kangaroos**) an Australian animal that hops on its long powerful hind legs and has a long thick tail.

kangaroo court *n* an unofficial or irregular court in which justice is disregarded or perverted.

kaolin *n* a fine white clay used in ceramics and medicine.

kapok *n* a mass of silky fibres that surround the seeds of a tropical tree, used as a soft padding.

kappa *n* the tenth letter of the Greek alphabet (Κ, κ).

kaput *adj informal* broken or useless.

karaoke /karaˈohki/ *n* singing against a backing of recorded music from a machine.

karate /kaˈrahti/ *n* a martial art using the hands and feet.

karma *n* in Hinduism and Buddhism, the force generated by a person's actions that is believed to influence their destiny.

karst *n* a limestone region with underground streams, caverns, and potholes.

kart *n* = GO-KART.

karting *n* racing in go-karts.

kasbah or **casbah** *n* the older Arab section of a North African city, or a market in this.

kayak /ˈkie(y)ak/ *n* a canoe made of a frame covered with a water-resistant covering.

kazoo *n* (*pl* **kazoos**) a musical instrument consisting of a tube that produces a humming sound when blown into.

kebab *n* **1** cubes of meat, vegetables, etc, grilled on a skewer. **2** = DONER KEBAB.

kedgeree *n* a dish of rice, flaked smoked fish, and chopped hard-boiled eggs.

keel¹ *n* a structure that runs along the bottom of a ship and improves its stability.

keel² *v* **1** (*usu* + over) to capsize or turn over. **2** *informal* (+ over) to fall over.

keelhaul *v* to drag (somebody) under the keel of a ship as punishment.

keen¹ *adj* **1** enthusiastic and eager. **2** of emotion or feeling: intense. **3** of a blade: sharp. **4** intellectually alert. **5** *Brit* of prices: competitively low. ✳ **keen on** attracted to or fond of. ➤ **keenly** *adv*, **keenness** *n*.

keen² *v* to wail loudly in lamentation for the dead.

keep¹ *v* (*past tense and past part.* **kept**) **1** to retain possession or control of. **2** to cause to remain in a specified place or condition. **3** to retain or store for future use. **4** to record (notes, accounts). **5** to defend or guard. **6** to support or provide for. **7** to obey or honour (a law, promise, etc). **8** to delay or detain (somebody). **9** to refrain from revealing (a secret). **10** to continue or persist in doing something. **11** to remain in a specified situation or condition: *keep calm.* **12** *esp* of food: to remain in good condition. ✳ **keep from** to refrain from (doing something). **keep to 1** to stay in or on (a place, path, etc). **2** not to deviate from (a commitment).

keep² *n* **1** the fortified tower of a castle. **2** food and other essentials of living. ✳ **for keeps** permanently.

keeper *n* **1** a protector or custodian. **2** somebody who looks after animals in a zoo. **3** a goalkeeper or wicketkeeper.

keep fit *n* physical exercises done for personal fitness.

keeping *n* **1** custody or care. **2** conforming or clashing with something implied or specified. ✳ **in keeping with** conforming to or consistent with.

keepsake *n* something kept as a memento of the giver.

keep up *v* **1** to persist in (an activity). **2** (*often* + with) to maintain an equal pace or rate of progress.

keg *n Brit* a small barrel.

kelim *n* see KILIM.

kelp *n* a large brown seaweed.

kelvin *n* an SI unit of temperature.

ken[1] v (**kenned** or **kent, kenning**) chiefly Scot to know or recognize.

ken[2] n range of perception or knowledge.

kennel n 1 a shelter for a dog. 2 (also in pl) an establishment for breeding or boarding dogs.

kept v past tense and past part. of KEEP[1].

keratin n a protein that forms the chemical basis of nails, claws, hooves, horns, feathers, and hair.

kerb (NAmer **curb**) n a stone edging to a pavement or path.

kerb crawling n driving slowly by a pavement looking for a prostitute.

kerbstone n a block of stone or concrete forming a kerb.

kerchief n (pl **kerchiefs** or **kerchieves**) a piece of cloth worn on the head.

kerfuffle n Brit, informal a fuss or commotion.

kernel n 1 the inner soft part of a seed, fruit stone, or nut. 2 a whole seed of a cereal. 3 a central or essential part of something.

kerosene or **kerosine** n = PARAFFIN.

kestrel n a small falcon that hovers in the air against the wind.

ketch n a small sailing vessel with two masts.

ketchup (NAmer **catchup**) n a sauce made from tomatoes, vinegar, and seasonings.

kettle n a vessel with a lid, handle, and spout, used for boiling water.

kettledrum n a large bowl-shaped drum with a covering stretched across it.

key[1] n 1 a metal instrument used to operate a lock. 2 a device used to wind a clock. 3 a small button on a panel or keyboard. 4 a lever of a musical instrument that is pressed to produce notes. 5 a small switch for opening or closing an electric circuit. 6 a means of gaining or preventing entrance or control. 7 an instrumental or deciding factor. 8 something that gives an explanation or solution. 9 in music, a system of seven notes based on their relationship to the first and lowest note. ➤ **keyed** adj, **keyless** adj.

key[2] v 1 (often + in) to enter (data) by means of a keyboard or keypad. 2 to roughen (a surface) to receive plaster or paint. 3 to bring into harmony or conformity. ✷ **be keyed into** to appreciate or sympathize with. **be keyed up** to be tense or excited.

key[3] adj of great importance.

keyboard[1] n 1 a set of keys on a piano or other musical instrument. 2 (also in pl) an electronic musical instrument having keys. 3 a set of keys for operating a computer or typewriter.

keyboard[2] v to enter (data) by means of a keyboard. ➤ **keyboarder** n.

keyhole n a hole in a lock into which the key is put.

keyhole surgery n surgery performed through a very small incision.

keynote n 1 a fundamental or central principle or idea. 2 of a speech: presenting the main theme of a conference. 3 the base note of a musical scale.

keypad n a small keyboard or set of buttons for operating a portable electronic device.

keystone n 1 the central locking piece at the top of an arch. 2 something on which associated things depend for support.

keystroke n a single act of pressing a key on a keyboard.

kg abbr kilogram.

khaki n 1 a dull yellowish brown colour. 2 cloth of this colour used for military uniforms.

khan /kahn/ n a medieval ruler over the Turkish, Tartar, and Mongol peoples.

kHz abbr kilohertz.

kibble v to grind (grain) coarsely.

kibbutz /ki'boots/ n a farm or settlement in Israel run as a cooperative.

kibosh or **kybosh** ✷ **put the kibosh on** to ruin or put an end to.

kick[1] v 1 to strike forcefully with the foot. 2 to strike out with the foot or feet. 3 informal to free oneself of (a habit). 4 to show opposition; to rebel. 5 of a gun: to recoil when fired. ✷ **kick oneself** to reprove oneself with hindsight. **kick one's heels** to be idle or kept waiting. **kick the bucket** informal to die. ➤ **kicker** n.

kick[2] n 1 an act of kicking. 2 a stimulating effect. 3 a pleasurable experience or feeling.

kickback n 1 a sharp violent reaction. 2 an illicit payment for help or favours given.

kickboxing n a martial art using gloved hands and the bare feet. ➤ **kickboxer** n.

kick in v to start functioning or taking effect.

kickoff n the start of a football game.

kick off v 1 in ball games, to start or resume play with a kickoff. 2 informal to begin proceedings.

kick-start v 1 to start (a motorcycle engine) by kicking down a lever. 2 to take swift action to resume (a process). ➤ **kick-start** n.

kick up v informal to stir up (a row or fuss).

kid[1] n 1 a young goat or related animal. 2 informal a child or young person. ✷ **with kid gloves** with great care.

kid[2] v (**kidded, kidding**) informal 1 to fool or deceive. 2 to tease playfully.

kidnap v (**kidnapped, kidnapping**, NAmer **kidnaped, kidnaping**) to seize and detain (a person) by force. ➤ **kidnap** n, **kidnapper** n.

kidney n (pl **-eys**) 1 either of a pair of organs that excrete urine. 2 the kidney of an animal eaten as food.

kidney bean n a dark red kidney-shaped bean.

kidney machine n a machine that purifies the blood when the kidneys do not function properly.

kidney stone n a hard stony mass formed abnormally in the kidney.

kilim or **kelim** n a pileless woven rug from Turkey or Iran.

kill[1] v **1** to deprive of life. **2** to put an end to. **3** to destroy or neutralize the effect of. **4** to pass (time). **5** informal to switch off or cause to stop. **6** informal to cause extreme pain to. **7** informal to exhaust or overwhelm.

kill[2] n **1** an act of killing. **2** something killed as game or prey.

killer n **1** a person or thing that kills. **2** informal something that is extremely arduous or exhausting.

killer whale n a flesh-eating black-and-white whale.

killing[1] n **1** an act of causing death. **2** informal a sudden huge gain or profit.

killing[2] adj **1** causing death. **2** informal extremely exhausting or difficult to endure. **3** informal highly amusing.

killjoy n somebody who spoils the pleasure of others.

kiln n an oven for burning, firing, or drying a substance, e.g. clay.

kilo /'keeloh/ n (pl -os) a kilogram.

kilobyte n in computing, a unit of memory or information equal to 1024 bytes.

kilogram n the basic metric SI unit of mass equal to the weight of one litre of water (about 2.205lb).

kilometre (NAmer **kilometer**) n a metric unit of length equal to 1000m (about 0.62mi).

kiloton n a unit of explosive force equivalent to 1000 tons of TNT.

kilovolt n 1000 volts.

kilowatt n 1000 watts.

kilowatt-hour n a unit of energy equal to that expended by one kilowatt in one hour.

kilt n a tartan pleated skirt worn as traditional dress by Scottish Highlanders.

kilter ✷ **out of kilter** not in proper working order or balance.

kimono n (pl -os) a loose Japanese robe with wide sleeves and a broad sash.

kin n one's relatives.

kind[1] n **1** fundamental nature or quality. **2** a group of people or things having common features. **3** a member of a category. ✷ **in kind** in goods or services as distinct from money.

kind[2] adj **1** considerate or compassionate. **2** helpful or generous.

kindergarten /'kindəgahtn/ n a school for young children.

kindle v **1** to cause to start burning. **2** to arouse (an emotion).

kindling n small sticks for lighting a fire.

kindly[1] adj (-ier, -iest) sympathetic or generous. ➤ **kindliness** n.

kindly[2] adv in a kind or appreciative manner.

kindness n **1** the quality of being kind. **2** a kind act.

kindred[1] n **1** one's relatives. **2** family relationship.

kindred[2] adj **1** similar in nature or character. **2** related.

kindred spirit n somebody with similar interests or opinions.

kinetic adj relating to motion. ➤ **kinetically** adv.

king n **1** the male ruler of a state. **2** the holder of a preeminent position within a particular sphere. **3** in chess, the principal piece on each side, which the opposing side tries to trap. **4** a playing card normally ranking below the ace. ➤ **kingly** adv, **kingship** n.

kingdom n **1** a country ruled by a king or queen. **2** a primary division in the classification of natural objects.

kingfisher n a brightly-coloured fish-eating bird with a large head and a long stout sharp bill.

kingpin n **1** the key person or thing in a group or undertaking. **2** a pin connecting two pivoting parts, e.g. on a hinge joint.

king-size or **king-sized** adj larger than the standard size.

kink[1] n **1** a short twist or curl. **2** an eccentricity or quirk. **3** an imperfection likely to cause difficulties.

kink[2] v to make or become twisted or curled.

kinky adj (-ier, -iest) **1** twisted or curled. **2** informal sexually deviant or unusual.

kinsfolk pl n one's relatives.

kinship n **1** blood relationship. **2** similarity.

kinsman n (pl **kinsmen**) a male relative.

kinswoman n (pl **kinswomen**) a female relative.

kiosk n **1** a small stall or stand for the sale of newspapers, cigarettes, and sweets. **2** Brit a public telephone box.

kip[1] n chiefly Brit, informal a short sleep.

kip[2] v (**kipped, kipping**) chiefly Brit, informal to sleep.

kipper n a fish, esp a herring that has been split open, salted, and smoked.

kipper tie n a very wide tie.

kirk n chiefly Scot a church.

kismet n fate or destiny.

kiss[1] v **1** to touch with the lips as a mark of affection or greeting. **2** to touch gently or lightly.

kiss[2] n an act of kissing.

kiss-curl n a small curl of hair falling on the forehead or cheek.

kiss of life n artificial respiration using mouth-to-mouth contact.

kit[1] n **1** a set of tools or implements. **2** a set of clothes or equipment for a particular activity.

kit[2] v (**kitted, kitting**) chiefly Brit (+ out/up) to provide with suitable clothes or equipment.

kitbag n a large cylindrical shoulder bag used by soldiers to carry their possessions.

kitchen *n* a room where food is prepared and cooked.

kitchenette *n* a small kitchen or part of a room containing cooking facilities.

kitchen garden *n* a garden in which vegetables and herbs are grown.

kite *n* 1 a light frame covered with thin material that is flown in the air at the end of a long string. 2 a hawk with long narrow wings and a forked tail. 3 a quadrilateral with two pairs of equal adjacent sides.

kith ∗ kith and kin one's friends and relatives.

kitsch *n* sentimentally pretentious or inferior artistic or literary material. ► **kitschy** *adj*.

kitten *n* 1 a young cat. 2 the young of some other animals, e.g. the beaver. ∗ **have kittens** *Brit, informal* to be extremely worried or upset.

kittenish *adj* coyly playful or flirtatious.

kitty¹ *n* (*pl* -ies) a cat or kitten.

kitty² *n* (*pl* -ies) 1 a jointly held fund of money. 2 a fund in a card game.

kiwi *n* (*pl* **kiwis**) 1 a flightless bird of New Zealand. 2 (**Kiwi**) *informal* a person from New Zealand.

kiwi fruit *n* the oval fruit of an Asian climbing plant with a brown hairy skin, green flesh, and black seeds.

Klaxon *n trademark* a powerful electrical horn or warning signal.

kleptomania *n* a recurrent desire to steal. ► **kleptomaniac** *n*.

km *abbr* kilometre.

knack *n* a special skill or aptitude.

knacker¹ *n Brit* somebody who buys and slaughters worn-out horses and other animals.

knacker² *v chiefly Brit, informal* to exhaust (somebody).

knacker's yard *n Brit* a slaughterhouse for old animals.

knapsack *n* a bag strapped on the back for carrying supplies or personal belongings.

knave *n* 1 *archaic* a wicked or unprincipled man. 2 a jack in a pack of playing cards. ► **knavish** *adj*.

knead *v* 1 to work and press (something soft) with the hands. 2 to manipulate as if by kneading.

knee¹ *n* 1 a joint in the leg between the thighbone and the shinbone. 2 the upper surface of a seated person's thigh.

knee² *v* to hit with the knee.

kneecap¹ *n* a thick flat bone that protects the front of the knee joint.

kneecap² *v* (**kneecapped, kneecapping**) to shoot the kneecap of (somebody) as a punishment.

knee-deep *adj* 1 immersed up to the knees. 2 deeply engaged or occupied.

knee-jerk *adj* occurring as a conditioned response; automatic.

kneel *v* (*past tense and past part.* **knelt** or **kneeled**) to be in a position supported by the knees.

knees-up *n Brit, informal* a lively celebration with dancing.

knell¹ *v* of a bell: to ring for a death, funeral, etc.

knell² *n* the sound of a bell rung slowly.

knew *v* past tense of KNOW¹.

knickerbockers *pl n* short baggy trousers gathered at the knee.

knickers *pl n Brit* women's or girls' underpants.

knick-knack or **nicknack** *n informal* a small trivial ornament or trinket.

knife¹ *n* (*pl* **knives**) a cutting implement consisting of a blade fixed in a handle.

knife² *v* to cut or stab with a knife.

knife-edge *n* an uncertain or precarious situation.

knifepoint *n* ∗ **at knifepoint** under a threat of injury by being knifed.

knight *n* 1 in medieval times, a mounted armed soldier serving a feudal superior. 2 in Britain, a man honoured by a sovereign for merit, bearing the title 'Sir'. 3 in chess, either of two pieces of each colour, usu in the shape of a horse's head, that move diagonally from one corner to another of a rectangle of three by two squares. ► **knighthood** *n*.

knight² *v* to make a knight of (somebody).

knit¹ *v* (**knitted** or **knit, knitting**) 1 to form (a fabric or garment) by working yarn into a series of interlocking loops using needles or a machine. 2 to make (stitches or rows) in this way. 3 to link or join together. 4 to contract (the brow) into wrinkles.

knit² *n* a fabric or garment made by knitting.

knitwear *n* knitted clothing.

knob *n* 1 a rounded protuberance or ornament. 2 a small rounded handle or control. 3 a small piece or lump.

knobble *n* a small knob or lump. ► **knobbly** *adj*.

knock¹ *v* 1 to strike (a surface) sharply with the knuckles or a hard object. 2 to strike a door to gain admission. 3 to drive, make, or remove by striking. 4 to collide or cause to collide. 5 *informal* to find fault with. 6 *informal* to have sexual intercourse with. 7 of an engine: to make a metallic rapping noise when faulty. ∗ **knock spots off** *informal* to surpass or outdo with ease. **knock together** to make hurriedly.

knock² *n* 1 a sharp blow or collision. 2 the sound of knocking. 3 a setback or minor misfortune.

knockabout *adj* of comedy: characterized by boisterous antics.

knocker *n* a metal object hinged to a door for use in knocking.

knock-knees *pl n* a condition in which the legs curve inward at the knees. ► **knock-kneed** *adj*.

knock off v **1** to stop work. **2** to do or produce hurriedly. **3** to deduct (an amount). **4** *informal* to steal.

knock-on effect n an effect one action or situation has on the next in a series.

knockout n **1** knocking out or being knocked out. **2** in boxing, a blow that knocks an opponent down and ends the match. **3** a competition with successive rounds in which losing competitors are eliminated. **4** *informal* a striking person or thing.

knock out v **1** to make unconscious. **2** to eliminate from a knockout competition. **3** *informal* to impress or amaze greatly.

knoll n a small hill or mound.

knot¹ n **1** a looping of string, thread, etc pulled tight to form a fastening. **2** a tangled mass of hair or wool. **3** a sense of tight constriction in the stomach. **4** a lump or swelling in tissue. **5** the base of a woody branch enclosed in the stem from which it arises, or a hard mass this causes in timber. **6** a cluster of people or things. **7** a unit of speed equal to one nautical mile per hour. ✳ **tie in knots** to confuse or bewilder. **tie the knot** to get married.

knot² v (**knotted, knotting**) **1** to tie with a knot. **2** to cause (hair or wool) to become tangled. **3** to cause (a muscle) to become tense or constricted.

knotty adj (**-ier, -iest**) **1** full of knots. **2** complicated or difficult to solve.

know v (**knew, known**) **1** to be aware of or have information about. **2** to be convinced or certain of. **3** to have a practical understanding of. **4** to recognize or identify. **5** to be acquainted or familiar with. **6** to have experience of. ✳ **be known as** to be called, e.g. as a nickname. **know the ropes** to be familiar with a routine or procedure. ➤ **knowable** adj.

know² ✳ **in the know** having exclusive knowledge or information.

know-all n somebody who behaves as if they know everything.

know-how n expertise in a particular field.

knowing adj **1** implying knowledge of a secret. **2** shrewd or astute. **3** deliberate or conscious. ➤ **knowingly** adv.

knowledge n **1** information or understanding acquired through learning or experience. **2** the total of known facts about a subject.

knowledgeable adj having knowledge or intelligence; well-informed. ➤ **knowledgeably** adv.

known¹ v past part. of KNOW¹.

known² adj **1** generally recognized. **2** identified.

knuckle n **1** each of the joints between the hand and the fingers or between the bones of the fingers. **2** a cut of meat consisting of the lowest leg joint with the adjoining flesh. ✳ **near the knuckle** almost improper or indecent.

knuckle down v to apply oneself earnestly.

knuckle-duster n a metal device worn over the knuckles as a weapon.

knuckle under v to give in or submit.

koala /koh'ahlə/ n an Australian tree-dwelling mammal with large ears and grey fur.

kohl n a black powder used to darken the eyelids.

kohlrabi /kohl'rahbi/ n (pl **kohlrabies**) a cabbage with a fleshy stem resembling a turnip.

kookaburra n a large Australian kingfisher with a call resembling loud laughter.

Koran /kaw'rahn, kə'rahn/ or **Qur'an** /koo'rahn/ n the sacred book of Islam, believed by Muslims to contain revelations made to Muhammad by Allah.

kosher /'kohshə/ adj **1** of food: prepared according to Jewish law. **2** *informal* proper or legitimate.

kowtow¹ n a former Chinese gesture of respect by kneeling and touching the ground with the forehead.

kowtow² v to show obsequious deference.

Kr abbr the chemical symbol for krypton.

kraal n **1** an enclosed village in southern Africa. **2** an enclosure for domestic animals.

krill pl n small sea animals that resemble shrimps and constitute the chief food of whales and other sea creatures.

krona n (pl **kronor**) the basic monetary unit of Sweden.

krone /'krohnə/ n (pl **kroner**) the basic monetary unit of Denmark and Norway.

krypton n a colourless gaseous element used in fluorescent lights.

Ku abbr the chemical symbol for kurchatovium.

kudos /'kyoohdos/ n renown and prestige resulting from achievement.

kumquat or **cumquat** n a small orange citrus fruit.

kung fu n a Chinese martial art resembling karate.

Kurd n a member of a pastoral people inhabiting adjoining parts of Turkey, Iran, and Iraq. ➤ **Kurdish** adj.

kV abbr kilovolt.

kW abbr kilowatt.

L¹ or **l** n (pl **L's** or **Ls** or **l's**) **1** the twelfth letter of the English alphabet. **2** the Roman numeral for 50.

L² abbr Brit learner driver.

l abbr **1** litre(s). **2** archaic pound(s).

La abbr the chemical symbol for lanthanum.

lab n informal a laboratory.

label¹ n **1** a slip, e.g. of paper or cloth, attached to something to give information about it. **2** a brand name, esp the name of a fashion house or a record company. **3** a descriptive or identifying word or phrase.

label² v (**labelled, labelling,** NAmer **labeled, labeling**) **1** to fasten a label to (an item). **2** to describe or categorize, esp unfairly or sweepingly.

labia pl n the outer and inner folds of the vulva.

labor¹ n NAmer, Aus see LABOUR¹.

labor² v NAmer, Aus see LABOUR².

laboratory n (pl **-ies**) **1** a place equipped for scientific experiment, testing, or analysis. **2** a place where chemicals and chemical products are developed.

laborious adj **1** requiring a lot of time or effort. **2** lacking grace and ease; laboured. ➤ **laboriously** adv.

labour¹ (NAmer, Aus **labor**) n **1** work, esp when difficult or done for wages. **2** workers collectively. **3** (**Labour**) the Labour Party. **4** the process of childbirth.

labour² (NAmer, Aus **labor**) v **1** to work hard. **2** to do unskilled manual work. **3** to struggle to do something difficult. **4** to move with diffi-

culty. **5** (+ under) to be misled by (something). **6** to deal with or explain in laborious detail.

labour camp n a prison camp in which inmates are forced to work.

laboured (NAmer **labored**) adj showing signs of effort; lacking natural grace or easy fluency.

labourer (NAmer **laborer**) n a person who does unskilled manual work, esp outdoors.

labour force n people in work.

labour-intensive adj using many workers in the process of production.

Labour Party n in Britain, a political party founded to represent working people and based on socialist principles.

Labrador n a dog of a gold-coloured or black breed, often employed as a retriever or guide dog.

laburnum n a shrub or tree with bright yellow flowers that hang in clusters.

labyrinth n **1** a place that is a network of intricate passageways. **2** something perplexingly complex or tortuous. ➤ **labyrinthine** adj.

lace¹ n **1** a fine decorative fabric made by twisting or looping thread in symmetrical patterns. **2** a cord or string used for drawing together two edges, e.g. of a garment or shoe.

lace² v **1** to fasten (e.g. a shoe) by means of a lace. **2** to entwine or interlace (esp the fingers). **3** to add a dash of a stronger ingredient, esp an alcoholic drink, to (a drink or dish).

lacerate v to tear or cut (skin or flesh) roughly. ➤ **laceration** n.

lachrymal or **lacrimal** adj **1** formal or literary causing or marked by the shedding of tears. **2** (**lacrimal**) relating to the glands that produce tears.

lachrymose adj formal or literary **1** tearful. **2** mournful.

lack¹ v **1** to suffer from an absence or deficiency of. **2** (often + in/for) to be deficient in.

lack² n an absence or shortage of something.

lackadaisical adj **1** lacking enthusiasm or zest. **2** casual or negligent.

lackey n (pl **-eys**) **1** a servant, esp a liveried footman. **2** a servile follower.

lacklustre (NAmer **lackluster**) adj **1** lacking in vitality or enthusiasm; uninspired. **2** lacking in sheen or radiance.

laconic adj using a minimum of words. ➤ **laconically** adv.

lacquer¹ n **1** a clear or coloured varnish for wood. **2** decorative wooden articles that have been coated with lacquer. **3** Brit a substance sprayed onto the hair to fix it in place.

lacquer² v to coat or spray with lacquer.

lacrimal adj see LACHRYMAL.

lacrosse n an outdoor team game played with a long-handled stick with a loose mesh pouch for throwing and catching the ball.

lactate *v* of a female mammal: to produce milk. ➤ **lactation** *n*.

lactic *adj* relating to or obtained from milk.

lactic acid *n* an organic acid formed in the muscles during strenuous exercise and found in sour milk.

lactose *n* a sugar present in milk.

lacuna *n* (*pl* **lacunae** *or* **lacunas**) a blank space or missing part.

lacy *adj* (**-ier, -iest**) resembling, consisting of, or trimmed with lace.

lad *n* 1 *informal* a boy or young man. 2 *Brit, informal* a boisterous or macho man.

ladder[1] *n* 1 a structure for climbing up or down that has two long sidepieces joined at intervals by crosspieces on which one steps. 2 a hierarchical structure with stages allowing for promotion. 3 *Brit* a vertical line in hosiery or knitting caused by stitches becoming unravelled.

ladder[2] *v Brit* to cause a ladder to develop in (e.g. tights).

laddish *adj* irritatingly rowdy or macho.

laden *adj* carrying a heavy load.

la-di-da *or* **lah-di-dah** *adj informal* affectedly refined, *esp* in pronunciation.

ladies *n Brit* a public lavatory for women.

ladle[1] *n* a deep-bowled long-handled spoon.

ladle[2] *v* to serve with a ladle.

lady *n* (*pl* **-ies**) 1 a woman of refinement or superior social position. 2 in polite or formal use: a woman. 3 (**Lady**) a title given to a peeress or to the wife of a knight or peer. ✳ **my Lady** used as a form of address to women judges and noblewomen.

ladybird *n* a small beetle that has red wing cases with black spots.

lady-in-waiting *n* (*pl* **ladies-in-waiting**) a woman appointed to wait on a queen or princess.

lady-killer *n informal* a man who captivates women.

ladylike *adj* befitting a well-bred woman or girl; refined and dignified.

lag[1] *v* (**lagged, lagging**) (*often* + behind) to fall behind.

lag[2] *n* a delay between two events.

lag[3] *v* (**lagged, lagging**) to cover (e.g. pipes) with lagging.

lager *n* a light beer usu served chilled.

laggard *n* a person who lags or lingers.

lagging *n* material for thermal insulation, e.g. wrapped round pipes.

lagoon *n* a shallow saltwater pool separated from the sea by a sand bank, reef, etc.

lah-di-dah *adj* see LA-DI-DA.

laid *v* past tense and past part. of LAY[1].

laid back *adj informal* relaxed or casual.

lain *v* past part. of LIE[1].

lair *n* 1 the resting or living place of a wild animal. 2 a person's den.

laird *n Scot* a person who owns a large country estate.

laissez-faire /ˌlesay ˈfeə/ *n* 1 a doctrine opposing government interference in economic affairs. 2 deliberate non-interfererence in the freedom and choices of others.

laity *n* (**the laity**) lay people.

lake *n* a large inland body of water.

lam *v* (**lammed, lamming**) *informal* to hit hard.

lama *n* 1 a title given to a Tibetan Buddhist spiritual leader. 2 a Tibetan or Mongolian Buddhist monk.

lamb[1] *n* 1 a young sheep. 2 a meek or innocent person.

lamb[2] *v* 1 of a ewe: to give birth to lambs. 2 to tend (ewes) at lambing time.

lambada /lamˈbahdə/ *n* a fast ballroom dance of Brazilian origin.

lambaste *or* **lambast** *v* to criticize severely.

lambda *n* the eleventh letter of the Greek alphabet (Λ, λ).

lambent *adj literary* softly bright, radiant, or flickering.

lame[1] *adj* 1 having a leg or foot so disabled as to impair freedom of movement. 2 of a story or excuse: weak and unconvincing. ➤ **lamely** *adv*, **lameness** *n*.

lamé *n* a brocaded fabric interwoven with gold or silver threads.

lame[2] *v* to make (a person or animal) lame.

lame duck *n* a weak or incapable person or thing.

lament[1] *n* 1 an expression of grief. 2 a song or poem expressing grief.

lament[2] *v* 1 to feel or express grief for (a person's loss or death); to mourn. 2 to express regret or disappointment over something. ➤ **lamentation** *n*.

lamentable *adj* 1 woefully bad or inadequate. 2 regrettable. ➤ **lamentably** *adv*.

laminate[1] *v* 1 to overlay with a thin sheet of e.g. metal or plastic. 2 to make (e.g. a building material) by bonding superimposed layers of one or more materials. 3 to separate (a substance) into layers. 4 to roll (e.g. metal) into a thin plate. ➤ **lamination** *n*.

laminate[2] *n* a product made by laminating.

lamp *n* a device using electricity, oil, or gas to give out artificial light.

lampoon[1] *v* to satirize or ridicule.

lampoon[2] *n* a satirical attack on a person, literary work, etc.

lamprey *n* (*pl* **-eys**) an eel-like fish that has a large sucking mouth with no jaws.

lance[1] *n* a weapon with a long shaft and a sharp steel head, carried by horsemen.

lance[2] *v* to open (e.g. a boil) with a lancet or other sharp instrument.

lance corporal *n* a non-commissioned officer of the lowest rank in the British army.

lancer *n* a member of a regiment armed with lances.

lancet *n* a sharp-pointed, two-edged surgical instrument used to make small incisions.

land[1] *n* **1** the solid part of the earth's surface, as distinct from seas, lakes, rivers, etc. **2** ground owned as property or attached to a building. **3** (**the land**) ground used for agriculture. **4** a particular country or state.

land[2] *v* **1** to bring (e.g. an aircraft) to a surface from the air. **2** of an aircraft, bird, etc: to alight on a surface. **3** to set on shore, or go ashore, from a ship. **4** of a boat, ship, etc: to reach shore or a port. **5** *informal* to gain or secure. **6** to catch and bring in (a fish). **7** *informal* (+ in) to put (somebody) in a usu undesirable place or situation. **8** *informal* to cause (a blow) to hit somebody. **9** *informal* (+ with) to burden with something unwanted.

landau *n* a four-wheeled carriage with a folding top.

landed *adj* owning land.

landfall *n* an instance of sighting or reaching land after a voyage or flight.

landfill *n* **1** the disposal of rubbish by burying it in a pit. **2** rubbish disposed of in this way.

landing *n* **1** the act of coming or bringing to land. **2** a place for discharging and taking on passengers and cargo. **3** a level space at the top of a flight of stairs.

landing craft *n* a naval craft designed for putting troops and equipment ashore.

landing gear *n* the undercarriage of an aircraft.

landlady *n* (*pl* **-ies**) **1** a woman who owns and rents out land, buildings, or accommodation. **2** a woman who keeps a guesthouse or pub.

landless *adj* owning no land.

landlocked *adj* of e.g. a country: with no access to the sea; completely enclosed by land.

landlord *n* **1** a person, usu a man, who owns and rents out land, buildings, or accommodation. **2** a person, usu a man, who keeps a guesthouse or pub.

landlubber *n* *informal* a person unacquainted with the sea or seamanship.

landmark *n* **1** a conspicuous object that can be used to identify a locality. **2** an event that marks a turning point or new development.

landmine *n* an explosive mine hidden just below the surface of the ground.

landscape[1] *n* **1** an expanse of natural inland scenery. **2** a picture, drawing, etc of a landscape.

landscape[2] *v* to improve the look of (a garden, park, etc) by reshaping or adding natural features, planting trees, etc.

landslide *n* **1** a movement of a mass of rock, earth, etc down a slope. **2** an overwhelming victory in an election.

land up *v* to end up in a place or situation.

lane *n* **1** a narrow passageway or road. **2** a strip of road for a single line of vehicles. **3** any of several marked parallel courses for competitors in a running or swimming race. **4** a fixed route used by ships or aircraft.

language *n* **1** a means of communicating ideas or feelings by the use of sounds, gestures, or signs that have understood meanings. **2** the words, grammatical constructions, etc used and understood by a particular community or group. **3** a formal system of signs and symbols used in programming a computer. ✻ **speak the same language** to have the same interests, ideas, etc.

languid *adj* **1** without energy; spiritless or apathetic. **2** weak or drooping from fatigue. ➤ **languidly** *adv*.

languish *v* **1** to be or become feeble. **2** to suffer hardship or neglect.

languor *n* a feeling of not unpleasant weariness or drowsiness. ➤ **languorous** *adj*.

lank *adj* of hair: straight and limp.

lanky *adj* (**-ier**, **-iest**) tall, thin, and ungraceful.

lanolin or **lanoline** *n* wool grease, *esp* when refined for use in ointments and cosmetics.

lantern *n* a light in a portable protective case with transparent windows.

lanthanum *n* a soft, silver-white metallic chemical element of the rare-earth group.

lanyard or **laniard** *n* **1** a piece of rope for fastening something on board ship. **2** a cord worn round the neck to hold something, e.g. a whistle.

lap[1] *n* the front part of the lower trunk and thighs of a seated person. ✻ **in the lap of luxury** in an environment of great comfort and wealth. **in the lap of the gods** beyond human influence or control.

lap[2] *n* **1** one circuit round a course or track. **2** one stage of a journey. **3** a part of an object that overlaps another.

lap[3] *v* (**lapped**, **lapping**) to overtake (another contestant in a race) and lead them by a full circuit of a track.

lap[4] *v* (**lapped**, **lapping**) **1** of an animal: to take in (liquid) with the tongue. **2** of water: to splash against (something) in little waves.

lapdog *n* **1** a small, *esp* docile or pampered, pet dog. **2** somebody who is completely controlled by somebody else.

lapel *n* a fold of the top front edge of a coat or jacket.

lapidary *adj* **1** relating to the cutting, polishing, and engraving of stones and gems. **2** of a literary style: elegant and dignified.

lapis lazuli *n* a rich blue semiprecious stone, used in making jewellery.

Lapp *n* a member of a nomadic people of Lapland, a region of northern Scandinavia.

lapse[1] *n* **1** a slight error, e.g. of memory or in manners. **2** a decline in standards, *esp* of morality. **3** an elapsed period of time; an interval.

lapse[2] *v* **1** of e.g. a right: to become invalid, *esp* because it has not been exercised. **2** to abandon a religion or doctrine. **3** to decline from a higher to a lower level, e.g. of morals. **4** (+ into) to pass gradually into a particular state, way of behaving, etc.

laptop *n* a portable computer with an integral keyboard and a flat screen that folds down.

lap up *v* **1** to drink (a liquid). **2** to take in eagerly or uncritically.

lapwing *n* a crested plover with a shrill wailing cry.

larboard *n archaic* port.

larceny *n* (*pl* -ies) *dated* theft of personal property.

larch *n* a tree of the pine family with short deciduous needles.

lard[1] *n* soft white solid fat from a pig, used in cooking.

lard[2] *v* **1** to insert strips of fat or bacon into (meat) before cooking. **2** (+ with) to intersperse or embellish (speech or writing) with something.

larder *n* a room or cupboard where food is stored.

large *adj* **1** relatively great in size, quantity, extent, etc. **2** operating on an extensive scale, or having more than usual power or scope. ✲ **at large 1** not imprisoned or restrained. **2** as a whole.

largely *adv* to a large extent; mostly.

largesse or **largess** *n* **1** generosity. **2** something, e.g. money, given generously.

largo *adj and adv* of a piece of music: performed in a very slow and broad manner.

lariat *n* a rope used as a lasso or for tethering animals.

lark[1] *n* a brown singing bird, e.g. a skylark.

lark[2] *n informal* **1** a prank or light-hearted adventure. **2** *Brit* an activity regarded as misguided or foolish.

lark[3] *v informal* (+ about/around) to have fun in a playful or mischievous way.

larva *n* (*pl* **larvae**) the immature, often worm-like form of an insect that hatches from an egg.

laryngitis *n* inflammation of the larynx.

larynx *n* (*pl* **larynges** or **larynxes**) the upper part of the throat, containing the vocal cords.

lasagne /lə'zanyə/ *n* **1** pasta in the form of broad flat sheets. **2** a baked dish of minced meat or vegetables layered with lasagne, white sauce, and cheese.

lascivious *adj* showing unseemly or offensive sexual interest. ➤ **lasciviously** *adv*, **lasciviousness** *n*.

laser *n* a device that generates an intense narrow beam of light.

laserdisc *n* a multimedia storage medium that looks like a large compact disc.

lash[1] *v* **1** to strike with a whip or similar object. **2** to beat hard against. **3** of an animal: to flick (the tail) quickly or sharply.

lash[2] *n* **1** a blow with a whip. **2** the flexible part of a whip. **3** an eyelash.

lash[3] *v* to bind or fasten with a cord, rope, etc.

lashings *pl n Brit, informal* (+ of) an abundance of something.

lash out *v* **1** to make a sudden physical attack. **2** *Brit, informal* to spend money freely.

lass or **lassie** *n chiefly Scot, N Eng* a girl or young woman.

lassitude *n* physical or mental fatigue.

lasso[1] *n* (*pl* **-os** or **-oes**) a rope with a running noose, used *esp* in North America for catching horses and cattle.

lasso[2] *v* (**lassoes** or **lassos**, **lassoed**, **lassoing**) to catch with a lasso.

last[1] *adj* **1** following all the rest in time, place, or order. **2** lowest in rank or importance. **3** most up-to-date; latest. **4** next before the present. **5** being the only remaining. **6** (**the last**) least suitable or likely. ✲ **on one's last legs** on the verge of failure, exhaustion, etc.

last[2] *adv* **1** on the most recent occasion. **2** after all others. **3** in conclusion.

last[3] *n and pron* (*pl* **last**) somebody or something that is last. ✲ **at last/at long last** after a long time or much delay. **the last of** the remaining part, amount, etc of something.

last[4] *v* **1** to continue in time; to go on. **2** to remain in good or adequate condition. **3** to be enough for the needs of (somebody) during a particular length of time.

last[5] *n* a shoemaker's model of the human foot, on which a shoe is shaped or repaired.

Last Judgment *n* the final judgment of humankind before God at the end of the world.

last rites *pl n* rites performed by a Roman Catholic priest for somebody who is about to die.

latch[1] *n* **1** a fastener, e.g. for a gate, with a pivoted bar that falls into a notch. **2** a type of doorlock with a spring-loaded bolt that can only be opened from outside with a key.

latch[2] *v* to fasten (e.g. a door) with a latch.

latchkey *n* a key to an outside door, *esp* the front door of a house.

latch on *v* **1** to understand. **2** to attach oneself to somebody or something.

late[1] *adj* **1** occurring or arriving after the expected time. **2** happening far on in a particular period. **3** far on in the day or night. **4** (**the late**) recently deceased. **5** very recent. ➤ **lateness** *n*.

late[2] *adv* **1** after the usual or proper time. **2** at or near the end of a period of time or a process. **3** far on in the day or night. ✲ **of late** recently.

lately *adv* recently.

latent *adj* present but not manifest or active. ➤ **latency** *n*.

later *adv* **1** afterwards. **2** at some time in the future.

lateral *adj* situated on, directed towards, or coming from the side. ➤ **laterally** *adv*.

lateral thinking *n* chiefly *Brit* thinking that concentrates on unexpected aspects of a problem to find a fresh approach to it.

latest[1] *adj* most recent; most up-to-date. * **at the latest** no later than the specified time.

latest[2] *n* (**the latest**) the most recent news.

latex *n* (*pl* **latices** or **latexes**) **1** a milky usu white fluid from various plants that is the source of rubber and chewing gum. **2** a water emulsion of a synthetic rubber or plastic, used e.g. in paints.

lath *n* a thin narrow strip of wood.

lathe *n* a machine for shaping wood or metal by rotating it against a fixed cutting tool.

lather[1] *n* **1** a foam or froth formed when a detergent, e.g. soap, is agitated in water. **2** foam or froth on a horse's skin from profuse sweating.

lather[2] *v* **1** to form or cover with a lather. **2** (+ with) to spread something with (a substance).

Latin[1] *n* the language of ancient Rome and the Roman Empire.

Latin[2] *adj* of or relating to Latin.

Latin America *n* the parts of the American continent where Spanish or Portuguese is spoken. ➤ **Latin American** *adj*.

Latino /la'teenoh/ *n* (*pl* **-os**) *NAmer* a person of Latin American or Spanish American descent.

latitude *n* **1** the angular distance of a place north or south of the equator. **2** (*in pl*) an area of the earth's surface between particular latitudes. **3** freedom of action or choice.

latrine *n* a small pit used as a toilet, *esp* in a military camp or barracks.

latter *adj* **1** near the end; later. **2** recent or present. **3** (**the latter**) denoting the second of two things mentioned or understood. ➤ **latterly** *adv*.

latter-day *adj* of present or recent times.

lattice *n* a framework of crossed wooden or metal strips with open spaces between.

laud *v* formal to praise enthusiastically.

laudable *adj* worthy of praise; commendable.

laudanum *n* a preparation of opium formerly used in medicine as a sedative.

laudatory *adj* expressing praise.

laugh[1] *v* **1** to make explosive vocal sounds expressing amusement. **2** (+ at) to ridicule; to make fun of. * **laugh on the other side of one's face** to be embarrassed after feeling confident or proud.

laugh[2] *n* an act of laughing. * **a laugh 1** *informal* a bit of fun. **2** *informal* a joke. **have the last laugh** to be proved right, successful, etc.

laughable *adj* ridiculous. ➤ **laughably** *adv*.

laughing gas *n* = NITROUS OXIDE.

laughing stock *n* an object of ridicule.

laugh off *v* to minimize or dismiss (something) by treating it as amusingly trivial.

laughter *n* the act or sound of laughing.

launch[1] *v* **1** to set (a boat or ship) afloat. **2** to send (e.g. a rocket) up into the air. **3** to initiate (something), or set (somebody) on e.g. a course or career. **4** to introduce (a new product) onto the market. **5** to throw (oneself) forward. **6** (+ into) to begin to do something energetically.

launch[2] *n* an act of launching something.

launch[3] *n* a large motorboat.

launder *v* **1** to wash and iron (dirty clothes, etc). **2** *informal* to pass (money obtained illegally) through a bank or legal business to disguise its origins.

launderette or **laundrette** *n* a self-service laundry providing coin-operated machines.

laundry *n* (*pl* **-ies**) **1** clothes and linen that have been, or are to be, washed and dried. **2** a place where laundering is done.

laurel *n* **1** an evergreen tree or shrub that has smooth shiny leaves. **2** (*in pl*) a crown of laurel awarded as a token of victory or preeminence. **3** distinction or honour. * **rest on one's laurels** to become complacent after previous successes or achievements.

lava *n* molten rock flowing from a volcano, or this same rock after it has cooled and solidified.

lavatorial *adj* **1** relating to lavatories. **2** of humour: characterized by excessive reference to bodily functions.

lavatory *n* (*pl* **-ies**) a toilet.

lavender *n* **1** a shrub with narrow aromatic leaves and spikes of lilac or purple flowers. **2** a pale purple colour.

lavish[1] *adj* **1** abundant or extravagant and sumptuous. **2** giving or spending in large quantities. ➤ **lavishly** *adv*.

lavish[2] *v* to spend or give in large quantities.

law *n* **1** a rule of conduct, recognized as binding or enforced by authority within a community. **2** the whole body of such rules. **3** a statement of scientific fact, e.g. describing the workings of a natural phenomenon. **4** a rule of procedure in a sport. **5** (**the law**) *informal* the police. * **be a law unto oneself** to be unconventional. **lay down the law** to give orders or express opinions forcefully.

lawful *adj* constituted or allowed by law; rightful or legal. ➤ **lawfully** *adv*.

lawless *adj* not regulated or restrained by law. ➤ **lawlessness** *n*.

lawn[1] *n* an area of ground covered with mown grass.

lawn[2] *n* a fine sheer linen or cotton fabric.

lawn mower *n* a machine for cutting grass on lawns.

lawsuit *n* a non-criminal case in a court of law.

lawyer *n* a person whose profession is to advise on legal matters and represent people in court.

lax *adj* **1** not strict or conscientious; negligent. **2** relaxed or slack. ➤ **laxity** *n*.

laxative *n* a medicinal preparation that relaxes the bowels to relieve constipation. ➤ **laxative** *adj*.

lay[1] *v* (*past tense and past part.* **laid**) **1** to put down on or spread over a surface. **2** to set in order or position for use: *to lay the table*. **3** to impose as a duty or burden. **4** to make (a charge or accusation). **5** to assign (blame, emphasis, etc). **6** of a bird: to produce (an egg). **7** to place (a bet). **8** *coarse slang* to have sexual intercourse with. ✳ **lay into** *informal* to attack or criticize fiercely. **lay to rest 1** to dispel (a fear or anxiety). **2** to bury (a body) in a grave.

lay[2] *v* past tense of LIE[1].

lay[3] *adj* **1** not belonging to the clergy. **2** not having expert or professional knowledge.

lay[4] *n* a simple poem intended to be sung.

layabout *n* a lazy shiftless person.

lay-by *n* (*pl* **lay-bys**) an area at the side of a road where vehicles can stop without obstructing traffic.

lay down *v* **1** to formulate (e.g. a rule). **2** to store (wine) in a cellar. **3** to sacrifice (one's life).

layer[1] *n* a single thickness of some substance lying over or under another.

layer[2] *v* to arrange in layers.

layman *n* (*pl* **laymen**) a male layperson.

layoff *n* **1** the laying off of an employee. **2** a period of unemployment or inactivity.

lay off *v* **1** to cease to employ (a worker) because of a shortage of work. **2** *informal* to give up: *lay off the beer*. **3** *informal* to leave (somebody) alone.

layout *n* the plan or arrangement of something laid out, e.g. rooms in a building or material to be printed.

lay out *v* **1** to arrange according to a plan. **2** *informal* to make unconscious. **3** *informal* to spend (an amount of money). **4** to prepare (a body) for burial.

layperson *n* (*pl* **laypeople**) **1** a person who is not a member of the clergy. **2** a person without special or professional knowledge of some field.

lay up *v* ✳ **be laid up** to be incapacitated by illness or injury.

laze *v* to act or rest lazily.

lazy *adj* (**-ier, -iest**) **1** disinclined or averse to activity. **2** not energetic or vigorous. ➤ **lazily** *adv*, **laziness** *n*.

lazybones *n* (*pl* **lazybones**) *informal* a lazy person.

lb *abbr* pound.

lbw *abbr* in cricket, leg before wicket.

lea *n* *chiefly literary* an area of grassland or pasture.

leach *v* to separate out from e.g. soil by the action of a liquid passing through it.

lead[1] *v* (*past tense and past part.* **led**) **1** to guide (a person or an animal) along a way, *esp* by going in front. **2** to go or be at the head of. **3** to be first or ahead, e.g. in a race. **4** to direct the operations or activities of. **5** to carry on (a specified kind of life or existence). **6** (*often* + to) to serve as an entrance or passage. **7** (*often* + to) to result in. **8** to influence (somebody) to do or believe something. ✳ **lead astray** to encourage somebody to behave badly. **lead on** to deceive (somebody). **lead up to** to be a preliminary to.

lead[2] *n* **1** a position at the front or ahead. **2** a position of advantage or superiority. **3** guidance or example. **4** an indication or clue. **5** a principal role in a play or film. **6** *Brit* a line or strap for leading or restraining a dog. **7** an insulated wire that conducts an electrical current.

lead[3] *n* **1** a bluish white metal that is heavy and soft. **2** a thin stick of graphite in a pencil.

leaded *adj* **1** of petrol: containing lead. **2** covered or framed with lead.

leaden *adj* **1** heavy, sluggish, or dull. **2** lacking spirit or animation; sluggish. **3** dull grey. ➤ **leadenly** *adv*.

leader *n* **1** somebody or something that guides, precedes, or holds an advantage over all others. **2** somebody who has commanding authority or influence. **3** the principal player among a group of musicians. **4** *Brit* a newspaper editorial. ➤ **leadership** *n*.

leading *adj* coming or ranking first; foremost.

leading article *n Brit* a newspaper editorial.

leading light *n* a prominent and influential person.

leading question *n* a question so phrased as to suggest the desired answer.

leaf[1] *n* (*pl* **leaves**) **1** a flat, usu green outgrowth from the stem of a plant. **2** the state of having foliage. **3** a sheet of paper, *esp* in a book, with a page on each side. **4** a part *esp* of a table that slides or is hinged. **5** metal, e.g. gold or silver, in very thin sheets. ✳ **take a leaf out of somebody's book** to copy somebody's behaviour. **turn over a new leaf** to make a change for the better, *esp* in one's way of living. ➤ **leafy** *adj*.

leaf[2] *v* ✳ **leaf through** to turn over the pages of (a book, magazine, etc) quickly while glancing at the contents.

leaflet[1] *n* **1** a single sheet of paper or small pamphlet containing advertisements or information. **2** a small leaf.

leaflet[2] *v* (**leafleted, leafleting**) to distribute leaflets to.

league[1] *n* **1** an association of nations, groups, or people for a common purpose. **2** an association of sports clubs that organizes a competi-

tion for an overall title. **3** a class or category.
✳ **in league** in alliance or conspiracy.

league[2] *n* a former unit of distance equal to about 3mi (5km).

leak[1] *v* **1** of a liquid, gas, etc: to enter or escape through a crack or hole, usu accidentally. **2** of a container: to let something enter or escape in this way. **3** (*often* + *out*) of information: to become known despite efforts at concealment. **4** to give out (information) surreptitiously. ➤ **leakage** *n*, **leaky** *adj*.

leak[2] *n* **1** a crack or hole through which something leaks. **2** information that becomes known despite efforts at concealment.

lean[1] *v* (*past tense and past part.* **leaned** *or* **leant**) **1** to incline from a vertical position. **2** (+ *on/against*) to rest for support against something. **3** (+ *on/upon*) to rely on for support. **4** (+ *towards*) to be inclined to favour a particular opinion, course of action, etc. **5** *informal* (+ *on*) to exert pressure on somebody to do something.

lean[2] *adj* **1** of a person or animal: deficient in flesh or bulk; thin. **2** of meat: containing little or no fat. **3** unproductive or unremunerative.

leaning *n* an attraction, tendency, or partiality.

lean-to *n* (*pl* **-os**) a small building with a roof that rests on the side of a larger building.

leap[1] *v* (*past tense and past part.* **leaped** *or* **leapt**) **1** to jump in or through the air. **2** to pass over (something) by leaping. **3** to move abruptly from one state, topic, etc to another. **4** (+ *at*) to seize an opportunity, offer, etc eagerly.

leap[2] *n* **1** a jump. **2** a sudden transition or increase. ✳ **by/in leaps and bounds** very rapidly.

leapfrog[1] *n* a game in which one player bends down and another leaps over them with legs apart.

leapfrog[2] *v* (**leapfrogged, leapfrogging**) **1** to leap over in leapfrog. **2** to progress rapidly by passing over (rivals, obstacles, etc).

leap year *n* a year with an extra day added, occurring every fourth year.

learn *v* (*past tense and past part.* **learned** *or* **learnt**) **1** to gain knowledge of or skill in. **2** to memorize. **3** to come to be able (to do something). **4** to come to realize or know. ➤ **learner** *n*.

learned *adj* having acquired great knowledge through study.

learning *n* knowledge or skills acquired by study.

lease[1] *n* a contract putting the land or property of one party at the disposal of another, usu for a stated period and rent. ✳ **new lease of life** a renewed period of healthy activity or usefulness.

lease[2] *v* to grant or hold (property) by lease.

leasehold *n* tenure by lease.

leash *n* a lead for a dog.

least[1] *adj* **1** smallest in quantity or extent. **2** lowest in or importance. ✳ **at least 1** as a minimum. **2** if nothing else. **3** anyway.

least[2] *adv* to the smallest degree or extent. ✳ **least of all** especially not. **not least** especially.

leather[1] *n* tanned animal skin used in clothing, upholstery, etc.

leather[2] *v* (**leathered, leathering**) **1** to cover (something) with leather. **2** *informal* to beat (a person or animal) with a strap; to thrash (them).

leathery *adj* resembling leather; tough.

leave[1] *v* (*past tense and past part.* **left**) **1** to go away from (a place, person, etc). **2** to desert or abandon (somebody). **3** to withdraw from (an organization, institution, etc). **4** to allow to remain in a specified place or condition: *She left her notes at home.* **5** (*also* + *off/out*) to fail to include. **6** to allow to do or continue something without interference. **7** to put or deposit (something) where it can be collected or dealt with. **8** to bequeath (property). **9** to have (a quantity) as a remainder: *Ten from twelve leaves two.* ✳ **leave alone/be** *informal* to refrain from interfering with, annoying, or disturbing. **leave off** to stop (doing something).

leave[2] *n* **1** authorized absence, e.g. from employment. **2** *formal* permission. ✳ **take one's leave** (*often* + *of*) to say farewell.

leaven[1] *n* **1** a substance, e.g. yeast, used to lighten dough and make it rise. **2** something that modifies or enlivens something.

leaven[2] *v* to modify or enliven with an additional element.

leaves *n pl* of LEAF[1].

lecher *n* a lecherous man.

lecherous *adj* showing inordinate or offensive sexual desire. ➤ **lechery** *n*.

lectern *n* a tall stand with a sloping top designed to hold an open book, papers etc from which a person can read aloud, e.g. in church.

lecture[1] *n* **1** a discourse on an educational subject read aloud to an audience. **2** a lengthy reprimand.

lecture[2] *v* **1** to deliver a lecture. **2** to reprimand at length or severely.

led *v* past tense and past part. of LEAD[1].

ledge *n* a narrow horizontal surface projecting from e.g. a wall or rock face.

ledger *n* a book recording financial accounts.

lee *n* the side, e.g. of a ship, that is sheltered from the wind.

leech *n* **1** a bloodsucking freshwater worm. **2** a person who tries to extract as much of another's wealth or resources from them as possible.

leek *n* a plant with a white cylindrical stalk and bulb, used as a vegetable.

leer[1] *v* to give a lascivious or sly look.

leer[2] *n* a lascivious or sly look.

leery *adj* (**-ier, -iest**) (*often* + of) suspicious or wary.

lees *pl n* the sediment left in a barrel or bottle of wine.

leeward *adj and adv* in or facing the direction towards which the wind is blowing: compare WINDWARD.

leeway *n* an allowed margin of freedom or variation.

left¹ *adj* **1** on the side of somebody or something that is nearer the west when the front faces north. **2** (*often* **Left**) of the left wing in politics.

left² *adv* on or towards the left.

left³ *n* **1** the part, direction, etc on the left side. **2** the left hand, or a blow struck with it. **3** *informal* a left turn. **4** (*often* **the Left**) those professing socialist or radical political views.

left⁴ *v* past tense and past part. of LEAVE¹.

left-field *adj* unorthodox; not mainstream.

leftover¹ *n* (*also in pl*) something, *esp* food, that is left unused or unconsumed.

leftover² *adj* remaining unused or unconsumed.

left wing *n* **1** (*often* **Left Wing**) the more socialist or reformist division of a political party. **2** in sport, the left side of the field when facing towards the opposing team. ➤ **left-wing** *adj*, **left-winger** *n*.

lefty *n* (*pl* **-ies**) *informal* a left-wing person.

leg *n* **1** a limb of a person or animal used for supporting the body and walking. **2** an upright pole serving as a support, e.g. for a a table. **3** a portion of a trip or race; a stage. **4** a round of a competition, or one of two or more events constituting a round. ✻ **leg it** *informal* to run away. **not have a leg to stand on** to have no basis for one's position, *esp* in a controversy.

legacy *n* (*pl* **-ies**) **1** money or property received under a will. **2** something passed on by a predecessor or remaining from the past.

legal *adj* **1** relating to law. **2** permitted by law. ➤ **legally** *adv*.

legal aid *n* money from public funds to pay for legal advice for those who cannot afford it.

legalize *or* **-ise** *v* to make legal. ➤ **legalization** *n*.

legal tender *n* currency, usu coins and banknotes, acceptable as payment of a debt.

legate *n* a representative of the Pope.

legation *n* **1** a diplomatic mission headed by a minister rather than an ambassador. **2** the official residence of a diplomat.

legato /li'gahtoh/ *adj and adv* of a piece of music: performed in a smooth and connected manner.

legend *n* **1** a popular story coming down from the past that is not historically verifiable. **2** a very famous person, act, or thing. **3** an inscription on an object, e.g. a coin. **4** a caption. **5** the key to a map, chart, etc.

legendary *adj* **1** described in legends. **2** very famous.

leggings *pl n* **1** close-fitting stretchy trousers worn by women or children. **2** close-fitting protective garments for the legs.

leggy *adj* (**-ier, -iest**) **1** having long legs. **2** of a plant: having unnaturally long thin stems.

legible *adj* capable of being read or deciphered. ➤ **legibility** *n*, **legibly** *adv*.

legion¹ *n* **1** the principal unit of the ancient Roman army comprising 3000–6000 soldiers. **2** (*also in pl*) a very large number.

legion² *adj* many or numerous.

legionnaire *n* a member of a legion or ex-servicemen's association.

legionnaire's disease *n* a serious infectious disease resembling pneumonia.

legislate *v* **1** to make laws. **2** (+ for/against) to make preparations to deal with.

legislation *n* laws.

legislative *adj* **1** having the power to make laws. **2** relating to legislation.

legislature *n* a body of people with the power to make laws.

legitimate¹ *adj* **1** in accordance with law, or accepted rules and standards. **2** genuine. **3** of a child: born in wedlock. **4** in accordance with reason or logic. ➤ **legitimacy** *n*, **legitimately** *adv*.

legitimate² *v* = LEGITIMIZE.

legitimize *or* **-ise** *v* **1** to give legal status to. **2** to justify. ➤ **legitimization** *n*.

legume *n* a member of a large family of plants that have pods containing seeds, e.g. peas and beans. ➤ **leguminous** *adj*.

leisure *n* time free from work or duties. ✻ **at leisure** free; not working. **at one's leisure 1** at an unhurried pace. **2** at one's convenience.

leisurely *adj* unhurried; relaxed.

lemming *n* **1** a small furry Arctic rodent with a short tail, which periodically undertakes mass migrations resulting in the death of many through drowning in the sea. **2** a member of a group mindlessly risking self-destruction through their actions.

lemon *n* **1** an oval yellow citrus fruit with a thick rind and acid flesh. **2** a pale yellow colour. **3** *informal* a feeble or useless person or thing.

lemonade *n* a soft drink, often carbonated, flavoured with lemon.

lemon curd *n* a thick buttery lemon-flavoured conserve.

lemur *n* a tree-dwelling mammal of Madagascar with large eyes and a long furry tail.

lend *v* (*past tense and past part.* **lent**) **1** to give (something) to somebody for temporary use on condition that it is returned. **2** to give (money) to somebody on condition of repayment, usu with interest. **3** to add or contribute. **4** (**lend itself to**) to be suitable for. ➤ **lender** *n*.

length n **1** the quality of being long. **2** a measurement of how long something is. **3** the longest dimension of an object. **4** the extent from end to end, or from beginning to end. **5** duration or extent in time. **6** a piece of something long and narrow. ∗ **at length 1** comprehensively. **2** for a long time. **3** at last. **go to great/any lengths** to make a great/every effort or use any means.

lengthen v to become or make longer.

lengthways or **lengthwise** adv and adj in the direction of the length.

lengthy adj (-ier, -iest) long. ➤ **lengthily** adv.

lenient adj merciful or tolerant. ➤ **leniency** n.

lens n **1** a piece of transparent material with a curved surface, used to form an image by focusing rays of light, e.g. in a camera or microscope. **2** a transparent, nearly spherical body in the eye that focuses light rays on the retina.

Lent n the 40 weekdays preceding Easter Saturday, observed by Christians as a time of penitence and fasting.

lent v past tense and past part. of LEND.

lentil n a small flattish seed of a plant of the pea family, used as a vegetable.

lento adj and adv of a piece of music: performed slowly.

Leo n the fifth sign of the zodiac (the Lion).

leonine adj of or resembling a lion.

leopard or **leopardess** n a big cat of South Asia and Africa that has a tawny coat with black spots.

leotard n a close-fitting stretchy one-piece garment worn for dance, gymnastics, etc.

leper n **1** a person suffering from leprosy. **2** a person shunned for moral or social reasons.

leprechaun n a mischievous elf of Irish folklore.

leprosy n a contagious bacterial disease affecting the skin that can cause wasting of muscle and disfigurement.

lesbian n a homosexual woman. ➤ **lesbian** adj, **lesbianism** n.

lesion n an area of an organ, the skin, etc, structurally damaged by injury or disease.

less¹ adj **1** smaller in quantity or extent. **2** informal fewer.

Usage Note: Strictly, *less* should be used only with a singular mass noun: *less tea. Fewer* should be used with a plural noun: *fewer teacups.*

---

less² adv to a smaller degree or extent.

less³ prep minus.

less⁴ n a smaller portion or quantity.

-less suffix **1** not having: *childless.* **2** free from: *painless.*

lessee n somebody who holds property under a lease.

lessen v to decrease in size, extent, etc.

lesser adj and adv less in size, quality, or significance.

lesson n **1** a period of instruction. **2** an instructive or warning example. **3** something learned by study or experience. **4** a passage from the Bible read during a church service.

lessor n somebody who lets property by lease.

lest conj **1** so that not; to avoid the possibility of. **2** used after an expression of fear, anxiety, etc: that.

let¹ v (**letting,** past tense and past part. **let**) **1** to allow. **2** used to introduce request or proposal: *Let's go now.* **3** to allow somebody the use of (accommodation) for rent or lease. ∗ **let alone** and definitely not. **let alone/be** to leave alone. **let go 1** to stop holding. **2** to release (somebody captured). **let oneself go 1** to abandon self-restraint. **2** to allow one's appearance or habits to deteriorate.

let² n Brit a period for which premises are let.

let³ n a serve or shot in tennis, squash, etc that does not count and must be replayed.

letdown n informal a disappointment or disillusionment.

let down v **1** to fail to support or assist (somebody). **2** to disappoint (somebody) by not keeping a promise, appointment, etc. **3** to deflate (e.g. a tyre).

lethal adj **1** capable of causing death. **2** seriously damaging or destructive. ➤ **lethally** adv.

lethargic adj slow moving, usu through lack of energy or interest. ➤ **lethargically** adv.

lethargy n **1** lack of energy or interest. **2** abnormal drowsiness.

let off v **1** to excuse from punishment or a responsibility. **2** to cause (a bomb or firework) to explode or (a gun) to fire.

let's contraction let us.

letter¹ n **1** a symbol representing a speech sound, forming part of an alphabet. **2** a written or printed message sent through the post. **3** literary (in pl) literature. **4** (**the letter**) the strict or literal meaning. ∗ **to the letter** precisely or literally.

letter² v to mark with letters.

letter bomb n an explosive device concealed in an envelope or package.

letter box n Brit a hole in a door to receive material delivered by post.

letterhead n a printed heading on stationery showing the name, address, etc of a person or organization.

lettering n the letters used in an inscription.

lettuce n a common garden plant with edible leaves eaten raw in salads.

letup n informal a cessation or lessening of effort or intensity.

let up v to diminish or become less intense.

leucocyte (NAmer **leukocyte**) n a white blood cell.

leukaemia (*NAmer* **leukemia**) *n* a type of cancer characterized by an abnormal increase in white blood cells in the body tissues.

levee *n chiefly NAmer* an embankment constructed to prevent flooding.

level[1] *n* **1** a horizontal line, surface, or state. **2** height, *esp* in relation to the ground. **3** a layer in a vertical structure, e.g. a floor in a building. **4** a position in a scale or rank. ✳ **on the level** *informal* honest; genuine.

level[2] *adj* **1** having no part higher than another. **2** (*often* + with) of or at the same height. **3** equal in quantity, position, or standing. ✳ **a level playing field** a situation in which nobody has an unfair advantage. ➤ **levelly** *adv*.

level[3] *v* (**levelled, levelling**, *NAmer* **leveled, leveling**) **1** (*also* + off) to make (a line or surface) horizontal. **2** (*often* + at) to bring (a weapon) to a horizontal aiming position. **3** (+ at/against) to aim direct (criticism, an accusation, etc). **4** to equalize. **5** to raze. **6** *informal* (+ with) to deal frankly and openly with somebody.

level crossing *n Brit* a place where a railway crosses a road on the same level.

levelheaded *adj* calm and sensible.

lever[1] *n* **1** a bar used for prising up or dislodging something. **2** a projecting part by which a mechanism is operated or adjusted.

lever[2] *v* to raise or move with a lever.

leverage *n* **1** the force exerted when using a lever. **2** power or influence.

leveret *n* a young hare.

leviathan *n* **1** (*often* **Leviathan**) a biblical sea monster. **2** something very large or powerful.

levitate *v* to rise or float in the air. ➤ **levitation** *n*.

levity *n* lack of seriousness or unseemly frivolity when dealing with a serious subject.

levy[1] *n* (*pl* -**ies**) **1** the imposing of a tax, fine, etc. **2** an amount levied. **3** *archaic* (*often pl*) troops enlisted for military service.

levy[2] *v* (-**ies, -ied**) **1** to impose (e.g. a tax) by legal authority. **2** *archaic* to enlist for military service.

lewd *adj* sexually coarse or suggestive.

lexical *adj* **1** relating to the words or the vocabulary of a language. **2** relating to dictionaries.

lexicography *n* the compiling of dictionaries. ➤ **lexicographer** *n*.

lexicon *n* **1** the vocabulary of a language, individual, or subject. **2** a dictionary.

ley line *n* a line linking ancient sites, supposed by some people to be a source of energy and connected with paranormal phenomena.

liability *n* (*pl* -**ies**) **1** the fact of being liable. **2** something for which one is liable, *esp* a debt. **3** a hindrance or drawback.

liable *adj* **1** legally responsible. **2** (+ to) subject to or punishable for something. **3** (+ to) likely to do something.

liaise *v* **1** (*often* + with) to establish a connection and cooperate. **2** to maintain communication and act as a go-between.

liaison *n* **1** communication and usu cooperation. **2** an illicit sexual relationship.

Usage Note: Note the spelling with two *i*'s and one *a*.

liana *n* a climbing plant that attaches itself to trees *esp* in tropical rain forests.

liar *n* a person who tells lies.

libation *n* **1** a drink poured out in sacrifice to a god.

libel[1] *n* **1** defamation of somebody by published writing as opposed to spoken words. **2** a false defamatory written statement. ➤ **libellous** *adj*.

libel[2] *v* (**libelled, libelling**, *NAmer* **libeled, libeling**) to publish a libel about.

liberal[1] *adj* **1** broad-minded or tolerant. **2** advocating individual rights and freedom and moderate reform. **3** (**Liberal**) in Britain, of, belonging to, or supporting the Liberal Democrats. **4** generous. **5** ample. **6** not strict or literal. ➤ **liberalism** *n*, **liberality** *n*, **liberally** *adv*.

liberal[2] *n* somebody with liberal views.

liberalize *or* -**ise** *v* to make less strict or restrictive. ➤ **liberalization** *n*.

liberate *v* **1** to set free. **2** to free from social conventions. ➤ **liberated** *adj*, **liberation** *n*, **liberator** *n*.

libertine *n* a person who leads a dissolute life.

liberty *n* (*pl* -**ies**) **1** the power to do as one pleases. **2** freedom from physical restraint or dictatorial control. **3** the power of choice. **4** a right or privilege. **5** *informal* (*also in pl*) a breach of etiquette or propriety. ✳ **take liberties 1** to show disrespect or be overfamiliar. **2** to disregard requirements for strict accuracy.

libidinous *adj* marked by strong sexual desire.

libido *n* (*pl* -**os**) sexual drive.

Libra *n* the seventh sign of the zodiac (the Scales).

librarian *n* a person who manages or works in a library.

library *n* (*pl* -**ies**) **1** a room or building in which books, periodicals, etc are kept for reference or for borrowing by the public. **2** a person's collection of books.

libretto *n* (*pl* **libretti** *or* **librettos**) the text of an opera. ➤ **librettist** *n*.

lice *n* pl of LOUSE.

licence (*NAmer* **license**) *n* **1** an official document showing that the holder is authorized to do something. **2** freedom of action. **3** unrestrained and usu immoral behaviour.

Usage Note: In British English the noun is spelled -*ence* and the verb -*ense*.

license *v* to give official permission to (somebody) to do something or for (something) to take place.

licensee *n* the holder of a licence, *esp* to sell alcoholic drink.

license plate *n NAmer* a numberplate.

licentious *adj* sexually unrestrained.

lichen *n* a plant that grows in flat, greyish patches on rocks and tree trunks.

lich-gate *n* see LYCHGATE.

lick¹ *v* **1** to pass the tongue over. **2** to touch lightly, *esp* with a darting movement. **3** *informal* to defeat, *esp* decisively. ✻ **lick into shape** to put into proper form or condition.

lick² *n* **1** an act of licking. **2** *informal* a small amount. ✻ **a lick and a promise** *informal* a quick wash. **at a lick** *informal* at a fast speed.

licorice *n NAmer* see LIQUORICE.

lid *n* **1** a hinged or detachable cover for a receptacle. **2** an eyelid.

lido *n* (*pl* -**os**) a public open-air swimming pool.

lie¹ *v* (**lying**, *past tense* **lay**, *past part.* **lain**) **1** to be or rest in a horizontal position. **2** (*often* + down) to assume a horizontal position. **3** to be in a specified state or condition: *The machinery was lying idle.* **4** to be located. ✻ **lie low** to stay in hiding or avoid notice. **the lie of the land 1** the contours and geographical features of an area. **2** the current nature of the situation.

lie² *n* an untrue statement, *esp* one made with intent to deceive.

lie³ *v* (**lies, lied, lying**) to make an untrue statement or statements.

lie detector *n* an instrument that detects physical evidence, e.g. a change in pulse rate, of the mental tension that accompanies telling lies.

liege¹ *adj* **1** of a lord: entitled to feudal allegiance. **2** of a vassal: owing feudal allegiance.

liege² *n* **1** a feudal lord. **2** a feudal vassal.

lieu ✻ **in lieu of** instead of.

lieutenant *n* **1** a deputy or representative. **2** an officer in the Royal Navy ranking below a lieutenant commander. **3** an officer in the British army ranking below a captain.

life *n* (*pl* **lives**) **1** the quality that distinguishes living beings from dead or inanimate ones. **2** the period of existence of an individual. **3** a way or manner of living. **4** living beings, e.g. of a specified kind or environment: *forest life.* **5** the period of usefulness of e.g. a machine. **6** vitality or excitement. **7** *informal* a sentence of life imprisonment.

life assurance *n chiefly Brit* = LIFE INSURANCE.

lifebelt *n chiefly Brit* a buoyant ring for keeping a person afloat.

lifeblood *n* a vital or life-giving force.

lifeboat *n* **1** a shore-based boat for saving lives at sea. **2** a boat carried by a ship for use in an emergency.

lifeguard *n* a person employed to safeguard others at a swimming pool or beach.

life insurance *n* insurance providing for payment of a stipulated sum on the death of the insured person or at the end of a fixed period.

life jacket *n* an inflatable or buoyant jacket designed to keep a person afloat.

lifeless *adj* **1** dead. **2** inanimate. **3** having no living beings. **4** dull.

lifelike *adj* accurately representing or imitating real life.

lifeline *n* **1** a rope used to pull a person to safety from water. **2** something, *esp* a sole means of communication, indispensable for the protection of life. **3** a line on the palm of the hand, taken to be an indication of the length of a person's life.

lifelong *adj* lasting or continuing throughout life.

life peer *or* **life peeress** *n* a British peer whose title is not hereditary.

life raft *n* a usu inflatable raft for use in an emergency at sea.

life span *n* **1** the duration of existence of an individual. **2** the average length of life of a kind of organism or of a material object, *esp* in a particular environment or in specified circumstances.

lifestyle *n* an individual's way of life, or the activities, possessions, etc associated with this.

lifetime *n* the length of time for which a living being exists or a thing remains useful, valid, etc.

lift¹ *v* **1** to raise to a higher position. **2** to pick (something or somebody) up in order to move them. **3** to put an end to (e.g. a blockade). **4** to revoke (a restriction).

lift² *n* **1** *Brit* a device for conveying people or objects from one level to another, *esp* in a building. **2** a free ride as a passenger in a motor vehicle. **3** a feeling of cheerfulness or encouragement. **4** the upward force acting on an aircraft or wing that opposes the pull of gravity.

ligament *n* a tough band of tissue connecting two or more bones or cartilages or supporting an organ.

ligature *n* something that is used to bind; *esp* a thread used in surgery to tie off a severed artery.

light¹ *n* **1** natural radiation that makes vision possible by stimulating the sense of sight. **2** a source of light, e.g. a lamp or a candle. **3** daylight. **4** a flame lighting *esp* a cigarette. **5** (*also in pl*) a traffic light. **6** understanding or knowledge. **7** a particular aspect in which something is viewed. ✻ **bring to light** to disclose or reveal. **come to light** to be revealed or disclosed. **in the light of** with the insight provided by. **see the light 1** to understand suddenly. **2** to undergo conversion.

light² *adj* **1** having plenty of light; bright. **2** pale in colour. ➤ **lightness** *n*.

light³ *v* (*past tense* **lit**, *past part.* **lit** *or* **lighted**) **1** to provide light in. **2** to catch fire. **3** to set fire to.

light⁴ *adj* **1** having little weight; not heavy. **2** designed to carry a comparatively small load. **3** insufficient in weight. **4** not abundant or intense. **5** gentle or soft. **6** requiring little effort. **7** graceful, deft, or nimble. **8** intended chiefly to entertain: *light reading.* ➤ **lightly** *adv*, **lightness** *n*.

light⁵ *v* (*past tense and past part.* **lit** *or* **lighted**) (+ on/upon) to find by chance.

lighten¹ *v* **1** to make or become lighter or less burdensome. **2** to make or become more cheerful.

lighten² *v* **1** to make (a colour, hair, etc) paler. **2** to brighten.

lighter¹ *n* a device for lighting a cigarette, cigar, etc.

lighter² *n* a large flat-bottomed barge used in unloading or loading ships.

light-fingered *adj* expert at or given to stealing.

light-headed *adj* faint or dizzy.

light-hearted *adj* **1** free from care or worry. **2** playful or amusing.

lighthouse *n* a tower equipped with a powerful light to warn or guide shipping.

lighting *n* **1** the apparatus providing a supply of light. **2** the arrangement of lights to produce a particular effect.

lightning *n* **1** the flash produced by a discharge of atmospheric electricity between two clouds or between a cloud and the earth. **2** (*used before a noun*) very quick, short, or sudden.

lightning conductor (*NAmer* **lightning rod**) *n* a metal rod fixed to the highest point of a building to carry lightning safely to earth.

light pen *n* **1** a pen-shaped photoelectric device moved over a VDU screen to communicate with a computer. **2** a pen-shaped device used to read bar codes.

lights *pl n* the lungs of a slaughtered sheep, pig, etc, used as food.

light up *v* **1** to illuminate or become illuminated. **2** to make or become more animated or cheerful. **3** to start smoking a cigarette, pipe, etc.

lightweight¹ *n* **1** a weight in boxing between welterweight and featherweight. **2** *informal* somebody of little ability or importance.

lightweight² *adj* **1** of less than average weight. **2** *informal* lacking in seriousness or profundity.

light-year *n* the distance that light travels in one year, approximately 9460 thousand million km (about 5878 thousand million mi).

ligneous *adj* of or resembling wood.

likable *or* **likeable** *adj* pleasant or agreeable.

like¹ *prep* **1** similar to. **2** typical of. **3** in the manner of. **4** such as.

like² *conj informal* **1** in the same way as. **2** as if.

like³ *n* somebody or something that is similar. ✳ **the like** similar things.

like⁴ *adj* similar in appearance, character, or quantity.

like⁵ *v* **1** to find (something or somebody) agreeable or acceptable. **2** to wish or choose (to have, be, or do something).

like⁶ *n* a liking or preference.

likeable *adj* see LIKABLE.

likelihood *n* probability.

likely¹ *adj* (**-ier, -iest**) **1** probable. **2** promising.

likely² *adv* probably.

liken *v* (+ to) to point out the resemblance of (a person or thing) to another.

likeness *n* **1** resemblance. **2** a portrait. **3** an appearance or semblance.

likewise *adv* **1** moreover; in addition. **2** similarly.

liking *n* **1** favourable regard. **2** taste or fondness.

lilac *n* **1** a shrub with heart-shaped leaves and large clusters of fragrant white or pale purple flowers. **2** a pale pinkish purple colour.

Li-Lo *n* (*pl* **-os**) *trademark* an airbed.

lilt *n* a rhythmic swing, flow, or rising and falling inflection in music or speech.

lily *n* (*pl* **-ies**) a plant that grows from bulbs and has showy trumpet-shaped flowers.

lily-livered *adj* cowardly.

lily of the valley *n* (*pl* **lilies of the valley**) a low-growing plant with fragrant bell-shaped white flowers.

limb *n* **1** a leg or arm of a human being. **2** a large branch of a tree. ✳ **out on a limb** in an exposed and unsupported position.

limber up *v* to prepare for physical action by gentle exercise.

limbo¹ *n* an intermediate or transitional state.

limbo² *n* (*pl* **-os**) an acrobatic West Indian dance that involves bending backwards to pass under a horizontal pole.

lime¹ *n* an alkaline substance used in building and in fertilizers.

lime² *n* a tree with heart-shaped leaves and clusters of yellow flowers.

lime³ *n* **1** a small green citrus fruit with acid juicy pulp. **2** a bright greenish yellow colour.

limelight *n* (**the limelight**) the centre of public attention.

limerick *n* a humorous verse form of five lines with a rhyme scheme of aabba.

limestone *n* rock consisting mainly of calcium carbonate.

limit¹ *n* **1** a line or point that cannot or should not be passed. **2** the furthest point or extreme degree of something. **3** a prescribed maximum or minimum amount, quantity, or number. ➤ **limitless** *adj*.

limit² *v* (**limited, limiting**) to restrict to specific bounds or limits.

limitation n 1 a restriction. 2 a defect or weak point.

limited adj 1 restricted in size or scope. 2 lacking the ability to grow or do better. 3 (often **Limited**) Brit of a company: in which individual shareholders' responsibility for the company's debts is limited.

limo n (pl -os) informal = LIMOUSINE.

limousine n a large luxurious motor car.

limp[1] v 1 to walk with an uneven step, usu because of an injured leg. 2 to proceed slowly or with difficulty.

limp[2] n a limping gait.

limp[3] adj 1 lacking firmness and stiffness. 2 lacking energy. ► **limply** adv.

limpet n a shellfish with a large suction foot that enables it to cling very tightly to rock.

limpid adj transparent or clear.

linchpin or **lynchpin** n 1 a pin inserted crosswise through the end of an axle to hold a wheel in place. 2 somebody or something regarded as vital.

linctus n a syrupy usu medicated liquid used to relieve throat irritation and coughing.

line[1] n 1 a long narrow mark across a surface. 2 a narrow crease, e.g. on the face; a wrinkle. 3 a boundary, border, or defining outline. 4 a row or queue. 5 a horizontal row of written or printed characters. 6 (in pl) all of the text making up a particular role in a play. 7 Brit (in pl) a specified number of lines of writing to be copied as a school punishment. 8 a thread, string, cord, or rope. 9 a conducting wire or cable conveying electrical power or a telecommunications signal. 10 a telephone connection. 11 a railway track or route. 12 a related series of people or things coming one after the other in time. 13 a particular type of merchandise, product, or service. 14 a field of activity, interest, or business. 15 a linked series of trenches and fortifications, esp facing the enemy. ✳ **draw the line** to set a limit as to what is acceptable. **in line for** likely to get. **in line with** conforming to. **on the line** at risk. **out of line** informal behaving in an unacceptable fashion.

line[2] v 1 to form a line along. 2 to mark or cover with lines.

line[3] v to cover the inner surface of.

lineage n a line of descent from a common ancestor or source.

lineal adj 1 in a direct line of ancestry or descent. 2 arranged in lines. ► **lineally** adv.

lineament n (also in pl) a distinctive outline or feature, esp of the face.

linear adj 1 arranged in a straight line. 2 consisting of lines. 3 involving a single dimension. 4 showing a straightforward progression through a sequence of stages. ► **linearity** n.

line dancing n a type of dancing to country and western music, performed by people in rows executing a sequence of steps simultaneously.

linen n 1 cloth made from flax. 2 household articles, e.g. sheets and tablecloths, made, esp formerly, of linen.

line-out n in Rugby Union, a method of restarting play after the ball has crossed a touchline by throwing it in between two lines of opposing forwards.

liner[1] n 1 a large passenger ship. 2 something, e.g. a cosmetic, used to draw lines.

liner[2] n something used to line clothing or a container.

linesman n (pl **linesmen**) in sport: an official who assists the referee or umpire in determining if a ball or player is out of the playing area.

line up v 1 to arrange in or form a line. 2 to put into alignment. 3 to assemble or organize in readiness for something.

line-up n 1 an identity parade. 2 a group of people or items assembled for a particular purpose.

ling[1] n a long-bodied sea fish.

ling[2] n = HEATHER.

linger v 1 to delay going or be reluctant to leave. 2 to be slow in disappearing. 3 (+ over/on/upon) to spend a long time doing, dealing with, or looking at. ► **lingering** adj.

lingerie n women's underwear and nightclothes.

lingo n (pl -**oes** or -**os**) informal 1 a foreign language. 2 the special vocabulary of a particular subject; jargon.

lingua franca n (pl **lingua francas** or **linguae francae**) a language used as a common tongue among people not speaking the same native language.

linguini or **linguine** /ling'gweeni/ pl n pasta in the form of flat strands.

linguist n 1 somebody accomplished in languages. 2 somebody who studies linguistics.

linguistic adj relating to language or linguistics. ► **linguistically** adv.

linguistics pl n the scientific study of language.

liniment n a liquid medication applied to the skin, esp to relieve pain.

lining n a layer of a different material used to cover the inside of something, e.g. a garment.

link[1] n 1 a single ring of a chain. 2 a connection or relationship between people or things. 3 a system that enables people, machines, etc to communicate. 4 a means of transportation between one place and another.

link[2] v 1 (often + up) to join, connect, or to become connected. 2 to suggest that (people or things) are significantly associated.

linkage n 1 the act of linking. 2 a system of links.

links pl n a golf course, esp along the seashore.

linnet n a finch with a red breast and forehead.

lino *n* (*pl* -**os**) *chiefly Brit, informal* = LINOLEUM.

linoleum *n* a usu patterned floor covering made of hardened linseed oil and a filler, e.g. cork dust.

linseed *n* the seed of flax that is the source of linseed oil, which is used in paints, varnishes, linoleum, etc.

lint *n* **1** a soft absorbent material used chiefly for surgical dressings. **2** fluff or shreds of fibre from cloth.

lintel *n* a horizontal support above an opening, *esp* a door.

lion *or* **lioness** *n* **1** a flesh-eating African big cat with a tawny body and, in the male, a shaggy blackish mane. **2** a courageous or ferocious person. ✳ **the lion's share** the largest portion or share.

lionize *or* -**ise** *v* to treat (somebody) as a celebrity.

lip *n* **1** either of the two fleshy folds that surround the mouth. **2** the edge of a hollow vessel or cavity. **3** *informal* impudent or insolent talk.

liposuction *n* a technique in plastic surgery for removing excess body fat by vacuum suction.

lippy *adj* (-**ier**, -**iest**) *informal* cheeky or impudent.

lip-read *v* (*past tense and past part.* **lip-read**) to understand speech by watching the movements of a person's lips.

lipstick *n* a stick of waxy solid cosmetic for colouring the lips.

lip-synch *or* **lip-sync** *v* to match one's lip movements to the words of a recorded speech or song.

liquefy *v* (-**ies**, -**ied**) to become or make liquid. ➤ **liquefaction** *n*.

Usage Note: Note the spelling -*efy* not -*ify*.

liqueur *n* a strong usu sweet alcoholic drink.

liquid[1] *adj* **1** flowing freely like water. **2** shining and clear. **3** of sounds: flowing and free of harshness. **4** of assets: consisting of, or readily convertible into, cash.

liquid[2] *n* a substance that is liquid.

liquidate *v* **1** to settle (a debt). **2** to end the commercial activities of (a business) and use its assets to pay off its debts. **3** to convert (assets) into cash. **4** *informal* to kill. ➤ **liquidation** *n*.

liquidity *n* the liquid assets of a company.

liquidize *or* -**ise** *v* to mash (e.g. fruit or vegetables) into a liquid.

liquor *n* **1** alcoholic drink, *esp* spirits. **2** a liquid produced by cooking food or in which food has been cooked.

liquorice (*NAmer* **licorice**) *n* an extract from the black thick root of a plant of the pea family, used in sweets and as a laxative.

lira /ˈliərə/ *n* (*pl* **lire** *or* **liras**) the basic monetary unit of Turkey and formerly of Italy (replaced by the euro in 2002).

lisp[1] *n* a speech defect in which /s/ is pronounced as /th/.

lisp[2] *v* to speak with a lisp.

lissom *or* **lissome** *adj* slim, supple, and graceful.

list[1] *n* a series of words or numbers arranged in order usu down a page.

list[2] *v* **1** to make a list of. **2** to include on a list.

list[3] *v* of a ship: to lean to one side.

listed *adj* **1** *Brit* of a building: protected as being historically or architecturally important. **2** of a company: having its shares quoted on the main market of the London Stock Exchange.

listen *v* **1** to pay attention to sound. **2** (*often* + to) to hear and give thoughtful consideration to; to heed. **3** (*often* + out/for) to be alert to catch an expected sound. ➤ **listener** *n*.

listeria *n* a rod-shaped bacterium that causes sometimes fatal food poisoning.

listing *n* **1** an entry in a list. **2** a list or catalogue.

listless *adj* characterized by indifference and lack of energy. ➤ **listlessly** *adv*.

list price *n* the basic price of an item as published in a manufacturer's catalogue, etc.

lit *v* past tense and past part. of LIGHT[3], LIGHT[5].

litany *n* (*pl* -**ies**) **1** a prayer consisting of a series of petitions by the leader, each followed by a response from the congregation. **2** a repetitive recital.

liter *n NAmer* see LITRE.

literacy *n* **1** the ability to read and write. **2** knowledge of a particular subject: *computer literacy*.

literal *adj* **1** denoting the factual or primary meaning of a word or expression. **2** keeping strictly to the straightforward meaning of a written text. **3** reproduced or translated word for word.

literally *adv* **1** in the literal sense. **2** *informal* used to intensify a metaphorical expression.

literary *adj* **1** relating to literature. **2** of language: characteristic of literature; formal or picturesque.

literate *adj* **1** able to read and write. **2** possessing knowledge in a particular field of activity: *computer literate*.

literati /litəˈrahtee/ *pl n* educated people with an interest in literature.

literature *n* **1** writings in prose or verse, *esp* those having artistic value. **2** the body of writings on a particular subject. **3** printed matter, e.g. leaflets or circulars.

lithe *adj* supple and athletic.

lithium *n* a light soft silver-white metallic element used in alloys.

lithograph /ˈlithəgrahf, -graf/ *n* a print made by lithography.

lithography *n* the process of printing from a metal surface treated so that the image to be printed is ink-receptive and the blank area ink-repellent.

litigation *n* the use of the courts or lawsuits to settle issues.

litigious *adj* inclined to take legal action frequently.

litmus *n* a colouring matter that turns red in acid solutions and blue in alkaline solutions.

litmus paper *n* paper coloured with litmus, used as an indicator of acidity or alkalinity.

litmus test *n* a sure test of something's worth.

litre (*NAmer* **liter**) *n* a metric unit of capacity equal to 1000 cubic centimetres (about 1.75 pints).

litter[1] *n* **1** scattered rubbish, *esp* in a public place. **2** an untidy accumulation of things. **3** a group of animal offspring born at one birth. **4** absorbent material placed in a location where a cat, urinates and defecates. **5** straw or similar material used as bedding for animals. **6** the uppermost slightly decayed layer of organic matter on a forest floor. **7** a covered and curtained couch carried by people or animals.

litter[2] *v* to strew (an area) with litter.

little[1] *adj* **1** small in size or extent. **2** of a person: young or younger. **3** not much. **4** short in duration or distance.

little[2] *adv* (**less, least**) **1** not much: *little-known.* **2** hardly or not at all.

little[3] *n* not much. ✳ **a little 1** to a small extent or degree. **2** a small amount or portion. **3** a short time or distance.

liturgy *n* (*pl* **-ies**) a prescribed form of public worship.

live[1] *v* **1** to be alive, or to be alive for or during a particular period of time. **2** to continue alive. **3** to have a particular way of life, aim in life, etc. **4** to maintain oneself or earn a living. **5** to have a home. ✳ **live it up** *informal* to live or celebrate lavishly. **live off** to rely on for subsistence. **live together** of two people: to share a home and have a sexual relationship without being married. **live up to** to achieve (an expected standard).

live[2] *adj* **1** having life. **2** connected to a source of electric power. **3** unexploded or unfired. **4** of continuing or current interest. **5** performed, performing, or recorded in the presence of an audience. **6** broadcast as it happens.

live[3] *adv* **1** in person and in front of an audience. **2** simultaneously as it happens.

live down *v* to overcome the shame or embarrassment caused by (a mistake or offence).

livelihood *n* something, *esp* a job, that provides a person with the means to support themselves.

lively *adj* (**-ier, -iest**) **1** active and energetic. **2** full of life, movement, or incident. ➤ **liveliness** *n*.

liven *v* (*often* + up) to make or become more lively.

live out *v* **1** to live to the end of (a period of time). **2** to carry out (something imagined) in real life.

liver *n* **1** a large glandular organ that secretes bile. **2** the liver of an animal eaten as food.

liverish *adj* **1** suffering from liver disorder; bilious. **2** peevish or irascible.

livery *n* (*pl* **-ies**) **1** a distinctive uniform worn by servants, employees, officials, etc. **2** a distinctive colour scheme, e.g. on a vehicle, distinguishing an organization. ➤ **liveried** *adj*.

lives *n* pl of LIFE.

livestock *n* farm animals.

live wire *n* *informal* a very dynamic or lively person.

livid *adj* **1** *informal* very angry. **2** discoloured by bruising.

living[1] *adj* **1** alive. **2** still in use, *esp* still spoken. ✳ **in living memory** in a time that people who are alive now can remember.

living[2] *n* **1** a means of subsistence; a livelihood. **2** the condition of being alive.

living room *n* a room in a home used for everyday activities.

living wage *n* a wage sufficient to provide an acceptable standard of living.

lizard *n* a small four-legged reptile with a long body and tail.

llama *n* a usu domesticated South American mammal with a woolly fleece.

lo *interj archaic* used to call attention or to express wonder.

loach *n* a small slender freshwater fish with spines round the mouth.

load[1] *n* **1** an amount, *esp* a large or heavy one, that is carried or supported. **2** a quantity carried at one time by a specified means. **3** a burden of responsibility, anxiety, etc. **4** *informal* (*also in pl*) a large quantity; a lot.

load[2] *v* **1** to put a load in or on e.g. a vehicle or ship. **2** to put ammunition into (a gun). **3** to insert (e.g. a film or tape) in a device or piece of equipment.

loaded *adj* **1** carrying a load. **2** of a question, argument, etc: biased, *esp* so as to produce a particular result. **3** having hidden implications. **4** of a dice: weighted so that it falls in a particular way. **5** *informal* having a large amount of money. **6** *informal* drunk.

loaf[1] *n* (*pl* **loaves**) a shaped mass of baked bread.

loaf[2] *v* to spend time in idleness.

loafer *n* **1** an idler or slacker. **2** *trademark* a low leather shoe with a broad flat heel.

loam *n* rich crumbly soil consisting of clay, silt, and sand.

loan[1] *n* **1** something lent, *esp* money lent at interest. **2** the act of lending. ✳ **on loan** being temporarily used by a borrower.

loan[2] *v* to lend.

loan shark *n informal* a person who lends money at exorbitant rates of interest.

loath or **loth** *adj* (*usu* + to) unwilling to do something; reluctant.

Usage Note: Do not confuse this word with *loathe*, which is a verb.

---

loathe *v* to dislike intensely.

Usage Note: Do not confuse this word with *loath*, which is an adjective.

---

loathsome *adj* hateful or disgusting.

loaves *n* pl of LOAF¹.

lob¹ *v* (**lobbed, lobbing**) to throw or hit (e.g. a ball) in a high arc.

lob² *n* in sports, a ball or shot that is lobbed.

lobby¹ *n* (*pl* **-ies**) **1** a porch or entrance hall. **2** an anteroom of a legislative chamber, *esp* one where Members of Parliament go to vote during a division or where they meet members of the public. **3** a group of people engaged in lobbying.

lobby² *v* (**-ies, -ied**) to try to influence members of a legislative body with respect to a particular issue. ➤ **lobbyist** *n*.

lobe *n* **1** a flat, curved projection, e.g. of the ear. **2** a rounded section of an organ, *esp* the brain.

lobelia *n* a plant with clusters of small blue, red, or white flowers.

lobotomy *n* (*pl* **-ies**) a brain operation in which nerve fibres in the cerebral cortex are cut, used formerly in the treatment of some mental disorders.

lobster *n* (*pl* **lobsters** or **lobster**) a large ten-legged shellfish with a pair of large claws.

lobster pot *n* a basket used as a trap for catching lobsters.

local¹ *adj* **1** relating to a particular place; not general or widespread. **2** serving the needs of a particular area. **3** affecting only a restricted part of a living organism. ➤ **locally** *adv*.

local² *n* **1** a local person or thing. **2** *Brit, informal* the neighbourhood pub.

locale /loh'kahl/ *n* a place, *esp* the setting for a particular event.

locality *n* (*pl* **-ies**) a particular area or neighbourhood.

localize or **-ise** *v* to restrict to a particular place. ➤ **localization** *n*.

locate *v* **1** to determine the position of. **2** to establish in a particular place. **3** (**be located**) to be sited or situated.

location *n* **1** a particular place or position. **2** a place outside a studio where a broadcast or film is made. **3** the act of locating.

loch /lokh/ *n* a lake or nearly landlocked arm of the sea in Scotland.

loci *n* pl of LOCUS.

lock¹ *n* **1** a fastening that can be opened only by means of a particular key or combination. **2** an enclosed section of a river or canal with gates at each end, in which the water level can be raised or lowered as boats pass through. **3** in wrestling, etc, a hold secured on a usu specified body part. **4** *chiefly Brit* the extent to which the front wheels of a vehicle are turned.

lock² *v* **1** to fasten with a lock. **2** to shut in or make inaccessible by locking a door, lid, etc. **3** become fixed or jammed immovably. ➤ **lockable** *adj*.

lock³ *n* **1** a curl, tuft, etc of hair. **2** *literary* (*in pl*) the hair of the head.

locker *n* **1** a cupboard or compartment that can be locked. **2** a storage compartment on a boat or ship.

locket *n* a small gold or silver case with space for a memento, usu worn on a chain round the neck.

lockjaw *n* **1** an early symptom of tetanus characterized by an inability to open the jaws. **2** = TETANUS.

lockout *n* a temporary closing of a workplace by an employer in order to gain concessions from employees.

locksmith *n* somebody who makes or mends locks.

lock, stock, and barrel *adv* wholly or completely.

lockup *n* **1** a prison, *esp* a small or temporary one. **2** *Brit* a shop or garage that can be locked up.

lock up *v* **1** to lock all the doors of a building. **2** to put in prison.

locomotion *n* the act of moving from place to place.

locomotive¹ *n* a powered vehicle that pulls railway carriages and wagons.

locomotive² *adj* relating to movement from place to place.

locum *n informal* a doctor or cleric temporarily taking the place of another.

locus /'lohkəs, 'lokəs/ *n* (*pl* **loci** /'lohsie, 'lohkie/) a place or position.

locust *n* a large grasshopper that travels in vast swarms through tropical areas, stripping them of all vegetation.

locution *n* **1** a word or expression. **2** a style or manner of speaking.

lode *n* an ore deposit.

lodestone *n* a piece of magnetized mineral.

lodge¹ *n* **1** a house lived in during a particular season, e.g. the hunting season. **2** a small house at the gates or in the grounds of a country estate. **3** a porter's room, e.g. at the entrance to a college, block of flats, etc. **4** a branch of a fraternal organization such as the Freemasons. **5** a beaver's or otter's den. **6** a Native American tent or dwelling.

lodge² *v* **1** to reside temporarily as a lodger. **2** to fix or become fixed firmly in place. **3** to lay (e.g. a complaint) before an authority. **4** to deposit (e.g. money) for safekeeping.

lodger *n* somebody who occupies a rented room in somebody else's house.

lodging *n* 1 a temporary place to live. 2 (*in pl*) a rented room or rooms, usu in a private house.

loft[1] *n* 1 an attic. 2 a gallery in a church or hall. 3 an upper floor in a barn or warehouse used for storage. 4 a warehouse loft converted into an open-plan flat. 5 a shed or coop for pigeons.

loft[2] *v* to propel (e.g. a ball) high up into the air.

lofty *adj* (**-ier, -iest**) **1** impressively high. **2** showing high ideals or moral principles. **3** having a haughty overbearing manner. ➤ **loftily** *adv*.

log[1] *n* 1 a piece of unshaped timber ready for sawing or use as firewood. 2 the full record of a ship's voyage or an aircraft's flight. 3 an apparatus for measuring the speed of a ship.

log[2] *v* (**logged, logging**) **1** to enter in a log. **2** to attain (e.g. an indicated distance, speed, or time). **3** (*often* + up) to have to one's credit. **4** to cut down trees for timber. ➤ **logger** *n*.

log[3] *n* = LOGARITHM.

loganberry *n* (*pl* **-ies**) a sweet red edible berry, similar to a raspberry.

logarithm *n* a number expressed as the mathematical exponent of a base number. Adding and subtracting logarithms produces the same results respectively as multiplying and dividing ordinary numbers. ➤ **logarithmic** *adj*.

logbook *n* 1 a book recording the details of a ship's voyage or an aircraft's flight. 2 *Brit* an official document recording details of a motor vehicle and its ownership.

loggerheads *pl n* * **at loggerheads** in quarrelsome disagreement.

loggia /ˈlɒj(i)ə/ *n* a roofed open gallery behind a colonnade or arcade.

logic *n* 1 a science that deals with the principles of reasoning. 2 rationality in thought or argument. 3 an inevitable progression of cause and effect. 4 the principles underlying the connection of circuit elements for performing operations in a computer. ➤ **logician** *n*.

logical *adj* 1 conforming with logic. 2 using or based on sound reasoning. 3 to be expected under the circumstances. ➤ **logically** *adv*.

log in *v* = LOG ON.

logistics *pl n* the work of planning and organizing a large and complex operation. ➤ **logistic** *adj*.

logjam *n* a deadlock or impasse.

logo *n* (*pl* **-os**) an identifying symbol used by a company.

log off *v* to end a session at a computer terminal.

log on *v* to begin a session at a computer terminal.

log out *v* = LOG OFF.

-logy *or* **-ology** *suffix* 1 denoting a doctrine, theory, or science: *archaeology*. 2 oral or written expression: *phraseology*. 3 writings of a specified kind: *trilogy*. ➤ **-logist** *suffix*.

loin *n* 1 the part of the body between the hipbone and the lower ribs. 2 a cut of meat comprising this part of a carcass. 3 (*in pl*) the genitals.

loincloth *n* a cloth worn round the hips and covering the genitals.

loiter *v* 1 to remain in an area for no obvious reason. 2 to dawdle. ➤ **loiterer** *n*.

loll *v* 1 to recline or move in a lazy manner. 2 to hang down loosely.

lollipop *n* a large round sweet of boiled sugar on the end of a stick.

lollop *v* (**lolloped, lolloping**) to move with an ungainly loping motion.

lolly *n* (*pl* **-ies**) 1 a lollipop. 2 (*also* **ice lolly**) a flavoured piece of ice or ice cream on a stick. 3 *Brit, informal* money.

lone *adj* 1 single or sole. 2 isolated.

lonely *adj* (**-ier, -iest**) **1** sad from being alone or without friends. **2** cut off from others; solitary. **3** not frequented by people. ➤ **loneliness** *n*.

loner *n* a person who prefers solitude.

lonesome *adj chiefly NAmer* = LONELY.

lone wolf *n* a person who prefers to work, act, or live alone.

long[1] *adj* 1 extending for a considerable distance. 2 having a specified length. 3 extending over a considerable or specified time. 4 containing a large or specified number of items: *a long list*. 5 of betting odds: greatly differing in the amounts wagered on each side and reflecting the unlikelihood of success. * **be long** *informal* to take a long time. **in the long run** in the course of prolonged time, trial, or experience. **long in the tooth** old. **long on** *informal* having a large amount of. **not by a long chalk** see CHALK[1]. **the long and (the) short** the gist; the outline.

long[2] *adv* (**longer, longest**) **1** for a long time. **2** throughout a specified period: *all night long*. **3** far in the past. * **no longer** not now, though usu previously. **so/as long as 1** during and up to the end of the time that; while. **2** on condition that. **so long** *informal* goodbye.

long[3] *v* (*often* + for) to feel a strong desire or craving.

longboat *n* the largest boat carried by a sailing vessel.

longbow *n* a medieval English bow of about 2m (6ft) in length.

longevity /lɒnˈjevitɪ, long-/ *n* great length of life.

long face *n* a sad facial expression.

longhand *n* handwriting.

long haul *n* 1 a lengthy period of time. 2 the transport of goods or passengers over long distances.

longing *n* a strong desire, *esp* for something difficult to attain. ➤ **longing** *adj,* **longingly** *adv.*

longitude *n* the angular distance of a place east or west of the Greenwich meridian.

longitudinal *adj* 1 extending lengthways. 2 relating to longitude. ➤ **longitudinally** *adv.*

long johns *pl n informal* underpants with legs extending to the ankles.

long jump *n* an athletic event consisting of a jump for distance from a running start.

long-range *adj* 1 fit for long distances. 2 involving a long period of time.

longship *n* a long open Viking warship propelled by oars and a sail.

long shot *n* a venture that involves considerable risk and has little chance of success.

longsighted *or* **long-sighted** *adj* unable to see things that are close to the eyes clearly.

long-suffering *adj* patiently enduring pain, difficulty, or provocation.

longways *adv* = LENGTHWAYS.

long-winded *adj* tediously long in speaking or writing.

loo *n Brit, informal* = TOILET.

loofah *n* a dried seed pod of a plant used as a bath sponge.

look[1] *v* 1 to direct one's sight in a specified direction. 2 to appear or seem. 3 to have a specified outlook. * **look after** to take care of. **look back** to think about the past. **look down on** to regard as inferior. **look for** to try to find. **look into** to investigate.

look[2] *n* 1 an act of looking; a glance. 2 (*in pl*) physical appearance. 3 the general appearance of somebody or something. 4 a style or fashion.

lookalike *n* somebody or something that looks like another.

looking glass *n* = MIRROR[1].

look on *v* to be a spectator at an event.

lookout *n* 1 a place or structure affording a wide view for observation. 2 somebody engaged in keeping watch. 3 a careful watch.

look out *v* to remain alert in case of trouble.

look up *v* 1 to improve in prospects. 2 to search for in a source of reference. 3 *informal* to visit or make contact with. * **look up to** to have great respect for.

loom[1] *n* a machine for weaving thread into cloth.

loom[2] *v* 1 to come into sight indistinctly, often in menacing form. 2 to be about to happen.

loony[1] *adj* (**-ier, -iest**) *informal* crazy or foolish.

loony[2] *n* (*pl* **-ies**) *informal* a crazy or foolish person.

loop[1] *n* 1 a shape formed when a line is drawn in an elongated circle and its ends are crossed. 2 a manoeuvre in which an aircraft flies in a vertical circle. 3 a piece of film or magnetic tape whose ends are spliced together so as to reproduce the same material continuously. 4 a closed electric circuit.

loop[2] *v* to form or move in a loop. * **loop the loop** to perform a loop in an aircraft.

loophole *n* 1 an ambiguity or omission in a text through which its intent may be evaded. 2 a small opening through which missiles may be discharged.

loopy *adj* (**-ier, -iest**) *informal* slightly crazy or foolish.

loose[1] *adj* 1 not tightly fastened or securely attached. 2 not tight-fitting. 3 free from confinement or restraint. 4 not kept together in a bundle, container, etc. 5 not dense or compact in structure or arrangement. 6 not tightly drawn or stretched. 7 lacking in precision or exactness. 8 careless or irresponsible. 9 *dated* dissolute or promiscuous. * **on the loose** free, *esp* having escaped. ➤ **loosely** *adv,* **looseness** *n.*

Usage Note: Do not confuse this word with *lose*, which is a verb.

loose[2] *v* 1 to release. 2 to unfasten or detach. 3 (*often* + off) to fire (e.g. a bullet or a volley).

loose cannon *n* somebody who acts independently and disruptively in an organization.

loose end *n* an incomplete or unexplained detail. * **at a loose end** bored or unoccupied.

loose-leaf *adj* of an album or book: bound so that individual leaves can be detached or inserted.

loosen *v* to make or become loose or looser.

loosen up *v* 1 to become more relaxed. 2 to warm up one's muscles before exercising.

loot[1] *n* 1 goods taken as plunder in war or illegally by force or deception. 2 *informal* money.

loot[2] *v* to steal goods from a place during a war or public disturbance. ➤ **looter** *n.*

lop *v* (**lopped, lopping**) 1 to cut off branches or twigs from a tree. 2 (+ off/away) to remove (something unnecessary or undesirable).

lope[1] *n* an easy bounding gait.

lope[2] *v* to move at a lope.

lop-eared *adj* of an animal: having ears that droop.

lopsided *adj* having one side heavier or lower than the other.

loquacious *adj formal* = TALKATIVE. ➤ **loquacity** *n.*

Lord *n* 1 God. 2 Jesus Christ. 3 (**the Lords**) the House of Lords. 4 used as the title of a lord or a prefix to some official titles. * **my Lord** used as a form of address to judges, bishops, and noblemen.

lord[1] *n* 1 a nobleman. 2 a ruler or leader.

lord[2] *v* * **lord it over** to behave domineeringly towards.

Lord Chancellor *n* a British officer of state who presides over the House of Lords and serves as head of the judiciary.

Lord Chief Justice *n* the president of the Queen's Bench Division of the High Court.

lordly *adj* (**-ier, -iest**) **1** dignified or noble. **2** disdainful and arrogant. ➤ **lordliness** *n*.

Lord Mayor *n* the mayor of the City of London and other large British cities.

Lord's Day *n* (*usu* **the Lord's Day**) = SUNDAY.

Lordship *n* used as a title for a bishop, a High Court Judge, or a peer.

lore *n* a specified body of knowledge or tradition.

lorgnette /law'nyet/ *n* (*also in pl*) a pair of glasses or opera glasses with a handle.

lorry *n* (*pl* **-ies**) *Brit* a large motor vehicle for carrying loads by road.

lose *v* (*past tense and past part.* **lost**) **1** to miss from one's possession and fail to find. **2** to cease to have or fail to keep. **3** to suffer loss through the death of. **4** to fail to win (a contest). **5** to fail to use (e.g. an opportunity). **6** *informal* to escape from (a pursuer). **7** to withdraw (oneself) from immediate reality. **8** (**be lost**) to be destroyed or killed. **9** to make less money from something than one has spent on it. ✴ **lose face** to lose one's dignity or reputation. **lose heart** to become dispirited. **lose it** *informal* to lose control of oneself. **lose one's way 1** to be unable to find the correct direction to go in. **2** to go astray intellectually or morally.

Usage Note: Do not confuse this word with *loose*, which is an adjective.

lose out *v* **1** (*often* + on) to make a loss. **2** to be denied an opportunity, advantage, etc.

loser *n* **1** somebody who loses a contest. **2** somebody who loses consistently.

loss *n* **1** the act of losing possession of something. **2** the harm or privation resulting from loss. **3** a person, thing, or amount lost. **4** failure to gain or use something. **5** an amount by which cost exceeds revenue. ✴ **at a loss 1** uncertain or puzzled. **2** not making enough money to cover costs.

loss leader *n* an article sold at a loss to draw customers.

lost[1] *adj* **1** unable to find the way. **2** bewildered or helpless. **3** (*usu* + in) rapt or absorbed. ✴ **be lost for words** to be unable to think what to say, e.g. because of shock. **be lost on** to be unnoticed or unappreciated by. **get lost** *informal* to go away.

lost[2] *v* past tense and past part. of LOSE.

lost cause *n* a cause that has no prospect of success.

lost generation *n* a generation considered socially and emotionally disadvantaged.

lot *n* **1** (**a lot** or **lots**) *informal* a considerable amount or number. **2** (**the lot**) *chiefly Brit* the whole amount or number. **3** *informal* a number of associated people or things. **4** an article or a number of articles offered as one item in an auction sale. **5** one's fate. **6** *chiefly NAmer* a portion of land. ✴ **a lot 1** *informal* much or considerably. **2** *informal* often. **draw lots** to decide an issue by asking people to choose e.g. a slip of paper at random from among several such slips.

loth *adj* see LOATH.

Lothario /lə'thahrioh/ *n* (*pl* **-os**) a man whose chief interest is seducing women.

lotion *n* a medicinal or cosmetic liquid for external use.

lottery *n* (*pl* **-ies**) **1** a way of raising money by selling tickets bearing numbers, some of which are later randomly selected to entitle the holder to a prize. **2** an event whose outcome is decided by chance.

lotus *n* a water lily.

lotus position *n* a yoga position in which one sits with legs folded, the feet resting on the thighs.

louche /loohsh/ *adj* morally dubious; disreputable.

loud *adj* **1** producing a high volume of sound. **2** obtrusively or tastelessly bright in colour. ➤ **loudly** *adv*, **loudness** *n*.

loud-hailer *n* *chiefly Brit* = MEGAPHONE.

loudmouth *n* *informal* a person who talks in a loud offensive way. ➤ **loudmouthed** *adj*.

loudspeaker *n* a device that converts electrical energy into acoustic energy and that is used to reproduce sounds.

lough /lokh/ *n* a loch in Ireland.

lounge[1] *v* to sit, lie, or stand in a lazy or relaxed way.

lounge[2] *n* **1** a sitting room in a private house. **2** a room in a public building providing comfortable seating.

lounge bar *n* *Brit* a more comfortable and usu more expensive bar in a pub or hotel.

lounger *n* a comfortable extended chair for relaxing outdoors.

lounge suit *n* *Brit* a man's suit for wear during the day.

lour or **lower** /'lowə/ *v* **1** to scowl or look sullen. **2** of the sky or weather: to become dark and threatening.

louse *n* (*pl* **lice**) **1** a small wingless insect parasitic on animals, fish, or plants. **2** (*pl* **louses**) *informal* a contemptible person.

louse up *v* *informal* to spoil or make a mess of.

lousy *adj* (**-ier, -iest**) *informal* very bad, unpleasant, useless, etc.

lout *n* a rough ill-mannered man or boy. ➤ **loutish** *adj*.

louvre (*NAmer* **louver**) /'loohvə/ *n* a set of slanted strips fitted across an opening to allow air, light, or sound to enter while providing privacy.

lovable

lovable or **loveable** adj having qualities that inspire affection.

lovage n an aromatic plant cultivated as a herb.

love[1] n **1** a strong feeling of attachment, tenderness, and protectiveness for another person. **2** attraction or devotion based on sexual desire. **3** warm interest in and enjoyment of something. **4** an object of love. **5** a score of zero in tennis, squash, etc. ✳ **make love** to have sexual intercourse. ➤ **loveless** adj.

love[2] v **1** to feel love for. **2** to have a great liking for. ➤ **lover** n, **loving** adj, **lovingly** adv.

love affair n **1** a sexual liaison or romantic attachment between people. **2** a lively enthusiasm.

lovebird n **1** a small usu grey or green parrot that shows great affection for its mate. **2** (in pl) an affectionate couple.

love child n euphem an illegitimate child.

lovelorn adj sad because of unrequited love.

lovely adj (-ier, -iest) **1** delightfully beautiful. **2** very pleasing; fine. ➤ **loveliness** n.

lovesick adj languishing with love.

low[1] adj **1** not high or tall. **2** situated or rising only a little above the ground. **3** of less than the usual degree, size, amount, or value. **4** considered comparatively unimportant. **5** of sound: soft or deep. **6** weak or depressed. **7** morally reprehensible or vulgar. **8** unfavourable. **9** humble in character or status.

low[2] n **1** a low point or level. **2** a region of low atmospheric pressure.

low[3] adv **1** at or to a low position. **2** softly or at a low pitch.

low[4] v to make the deep sound characteristic of a cow.

lowbrow adj informal, derog having unsophisticated or unintellectual tastes. ➤ **lowbrow** n.

Low Church adj tending to minimize emphasis on the priesthood, sacraments, and ceremonial in the Anglican Church.

lowdown n (**the lowdown**) informal useful information.

lower[1] adj **1** relatively low in position, rank, or order. **2** denoting the southern part of a specified area.

lower[2] v **1** to cause to descend. **2** to reduce in height, value, amount, pitch, etc. **3** to degrade.

lower[3] v see LOUR.

lower case n small letters, e.g. a, b, c rather than A, B, C. ➤ **lower-case** adj.

lowest common denominator n **1** the lowest number that two or more denominators can be exactly divided by. **2** derog something acceptable or comprehensible to the greatest possible number of people.

low gear n a gear designed for slow speed.

low-key adj of low intensity; restrained.

lowland n **1** (also in pl) low or level country. **2** (**the Lowlands**) the part of Scotland lying south and east of the Highlands. ➤ **lowlander** n.

lowlife n (pl **lowlifes**) informal a criminal or immoral person, or criminal and worthless people collectively.

lowly adj (-ier, -iest) low-ranking; humble. ➤ **lowliness** n.

low tide n the time when the sea reaches its lowest level.

loyal adj showing unswerving support for a person, country, or cause. ➤ **loyally** adv.

loyalist n **1** somebody loyal to a government or sovereign, esp in time of revolt. **2** (**Loyalist**) in Northern Ireland: a supporter of continued union with the United Kingdom.

loyalty n (pl -ies) **1** being loyal. **2** a feeling of allegiance or duty.

loyalty card n Brit a card issued by e.g. a supermarket to reward regular customers by giving them points towards discounts on future purchases.

lozenge n **1** a small medicated sweet. **2** a diamond or rhombus.

LP n a long-playing gramophone record.

Lr abbr the chemical symbol for lawrencium.

LSD n lysergic acid diethylamide, an illegal drug with a potent mind-altering effect.

Ltd abbr Brit Limited.

Lu abbr the chemical symbol for lutetium.

lubricant n a lubricating substance, e.g. grease or oil. ➤ **lubricant** adj.

lubricate v to apply a greasy substance to (something) to reduce friction and wear between its surfaces. ➤ **lubrication** n.

lubricious adj formal lecherous or salacious.

lucid adj **1** clear to the understanding; plain. **2** having full use of one's faculties; sane. ➤ **lucidity** n, **lucidly** adv.

Lucifer n the Devil.

luck n **1** whatever good or bad events happen to a person by chance. **2** good fortune. ✳ **try one's luck** attempt to do something that may or may not succeed.

luckless adj unlucky or unfortunate.

lucky adj (-ier, -iest) having, resulting from, or bringing good luck.

lucky dip n Brit an attraction, e.g. at a fair, in which small prizes can be drawn unseen from a receptacle.

lucrative adj producing wealth; profitable.

lucre n money.

Luddite n **1** a member of a group of early 19th-cent. English workmen who destroyed labour-saving machinery to protect their jobs. **2** somebody opposed to technological progress.

ludicrous adj amusingly absurd. ➤ **ludicrously** adv.

ludo n a simple board game played with counters and dice.

lug¹ v (**lugged, lugging**) to drag or carry with great effort.

lug² n **1** something, e.g. a handle, that projects like an ear. **2** Brit, dialect or humorous an ear.

luggage n cases, bags, etc containing a traveller's belongings.

lugubrious adj mournful, esp exaggeratedly so.

lukewarm adj **1** moderately warm; tepid. **2** lacking enthusiasm.

lull¹ v **1** to calm with soothing sounds, motion, etc. **2** to cause to relax vigilance, esp by deception.

lull² n a temporary pause in activity.

lullaby n (pl **-ies**) a song used to lull children to sleep.

lumbago n muscular pain in the lower back.

lumbar adj relating to the region of the lower back.

lumber¹ v to move heavily or clumsily.

lumber² n **1** surplus or disused articles. **2** NAmer timber or logs.

lumber³ v Brit, informal to encumber or saddle (somebody) with something.

lumberjack n a person engaged in logging.

luminary n (pl **-ies**) a brilliantly outstanding or important person.

luminescence n light produced at low temperatures e.g. by physiological processes or chemical action. ➤ **luminescent** adj.

luminous adj emitting or full of light; bright. ➤ **luminosity** n.

lump¹ n **1** a compact mass of indefinite size and shape. **2** an abnormal swelling. ➤ **lumpy** adj.

lump² v (usu + together) to group without discrimination. ✳ **lump it** informal to put up with it.

lumpen adj informal stupid or unenlightened.

lumpish adj **1** dull or sluggish. **2** heavy or awkward.

lump sum n a large sum of money given in a single payment.

lunacy n **1** wild foolishness. **2** insanity.

lunar adj of the moon.

lunar eclipse n an eclipse in which the moon passes through the earth's shadow.

lunar month n the period of time, averaging 29½ days, between two successive new moons.

lunatic n **1** a mentally ill person. **2** a foolish or foolhardy person.

lunch¹ n a midday meal. ✳ **out to lunch** informal crazy.

lunch² v to eat lunch.

luncheon n formal = LUNCH¹.

lung n either of the paired respiratory organs in the chest of air-breathing vertebrates.

lunge¹ v to make a sudden forward movement or thrust.

lunge² n a sudden forward movement or thrust.

lupin or **lupine** /'loohpin/ n a plant with long spikes of flowers.

lupine /'loohpien/ adj relating to or resembling a wolf.

lurch¹ n an abrupt, uncontrolled, and jerky movement.

lurch² v to move in an abrupt, uncontrolled, and jerky manner.

lurch³ n ✳ **in the lurch** in a vulnerable and unsupported position.

lurcher n a dog that is a cross between a greyhound and another breed, e.g. the collie or terrier.

lure¹ n **1** something used to entice or decoy. **2** the power to appeal or attract.

lure² v to attract with something that promises pleasure, food, or gain.

Lurex n trademark a type of thread that is partly coated to give a metallic appearance.

lurid adj **1** unnaturally or unattractively bright in colour. **2** sensational or shocking. ➤ **luridly** adv.

lurk v **1** to lie hidden in wait, esp with evil intent. **2** to be present but undetected.

luscious adj **1** having a delicious taste or smell. **2** esp of a woman: extremely attractive.

lush¹ adj **1** producing or covered by luxuriant growth. **2** opulent or sumptuous. ➤ **lushly** adv, **lushness** n.

lush² n chiefly NAmer, informal a heavy drinker.

lust¹ n **1** strong sexual desire. **2** an intense longing; a craving. ➤ **lustful** adj.

lust² v (usu + for/after) to have an intense esp sexual desire for.

lustre (NAmer **luster**) n **1** a glow of reflected light; a sheen. **2** glory or distinction. ➤ **lustrous** adj.

lusty adj (**-ier, -iest**) full of vitality; healthy and vigorous. ➤ **lustily** adv.

lute n a plucked stringed musical instrument with a large pear-shaped body and long neck.

luxuriant adj characterized by abundant growth. ➤ **luxuriance** n, **luxuriantly** adv.

luxuriate v (often + in) to enjoy the delights of something unrestrainedly.

luxurious adj extremely comfortable and usu expensive and elegant. ➤ **luxuriously** adv.

luxury n (pl **-ies**) **1** great ease or comfort based on the use of expensive items. **2** something desirable or expensive but not essential.

-ly suffix **1** having the characteristics of: fatherly. **2** recurring at intervals of: hourly. **3** in such a manner: slowly.

lychee or **litchi** n a small oval fruit with a scaly skin and soft white fragrant pulp.

lychgate or **lichgate** n a roofed gate at the entrance to a churchyard.

Lycra n trademark a synthetic stretchy yarn used chiefly in tight-fitting sportswear and swimwear.

lye *n* a strong alkaline solution, used e.g. in oven and drain cleaners.

lying[1] *v* present part. of LIE[1].

lying[2] *v* present part. of LIE[3].

lymph *n* a pale body fluid containing white blood cells.

lymph node *n* a rounded mass of tissue in which white blood cells are formed.

lynch *v* to put (an alleged offender) to death illegally by mob action.

lynchpin *n* see LINCHPIN.

lynx *n* (*pl* **lynxes** *or* **lynx**) a wildcat with a short tail, mottled coat, and tufted ears.

lyre *n* a stringed instrument of the harp family with a U-shaped frame, used by the ancient Greeks.

lyric[1] *n* **1** (*in pl*) the words of a popular song. **2** a lyric poem.

lyric[2] *adj* of poetry: expressing direct personal emotion.

lyrical *adj* **1** having a beautiful, songlike quality. **2** = LYRIC[2]. ✳ **wax lyrical** talk with great admiration or enthusiasm about something. ➤ **lyrically** *adv*.

lyricism *n* **1** a pleasantly melodious and songlike quality, *esp* in music. **2** a directly personal style in art, literature, etc.

lyricist *n* a writer of song lyrics.

M¹ or **m** n (pl **M's** or **Ms** or **m's**) **1** the 13th letter of the English alphabet. **2** the Roman numeral for 1000.

M² abbr **1** Monsieur. **2** motorway.

m abbr **1** metre. **2** mile. **3** million. **4** minute.

MA abbr Master of Arts.

ma'am n madam.

mac or **mack** n Brit, informal a raincoat.

macabre /mə'kahb(r)ə/ adj gruesome in relating to or depicting unpleasant aspects of death.

macadam n broken stones compacted into a solid mass to make a road surface.

macadamia n the edible round nut of an Australian evergreen tree.

macaroni pl n pasta shaped in hollow tubes.

macaroon n a cake or biscuit made with ground almonds or coconut.

macaw n a large brightly coloured parrot of South and Central America.

mace¹ n **1** a heavy medieval spiked staff or club. **2** an ornamental staff used as a symbol of authority.

mace² n an aromatic spice made from the dried external covering of a nutmeg.

macerate v to make (food) soft by soaking it in liquid. ➤ **maceration** n.

Mach /mak, mahk/ n used to show a speed relative to the speed of sound: Mach 1 is the speed of sound, Mach 2 is twice that, and so on.

machete /mə'sheti/ n a large heavy knife used for cutting vegetation or as a weapon.

Machiavellian adj cunning and opportunist.

machination n a scheming move or plot.

machine¹ n **1** a mechanical apparatus for performing a task. **2** an efficient and controlling person or organization.

machine² v to make or operate on with a machine. ➤ **machinability** n.

machine gun n an automatic gun for rapid continuous fire.

machine-readable adj in a form that can be processed by a computer.

machinery n **1** machines in general. **2** the working parts of a machine. **3** the system or organization controlling an activity or process.

machinist n a person who operates a machine or repairs machinery.

machismo /mə'kizmoh, mə'chizmoh/ n an assertion of masculinity.

macho /'machoh/ adj toughly or aggressively virile.

mackerel n (pl **mackerels** or **mackerel**) a food fish of the North Atlantic.

mackintosh or **macintosh** n chiefly Brit a raincoat.

macramé /mə'krahmi/ n the art of tying threads or cords in patterns to make decorative articles.

macrobiotic adj of a diet: consisting chiefly of whole grains and vegetables.

macrocosm n **1** the universe. **2** a complex that is a large-scale reproduction of one of its constituents.

mad adj (**madder, maddest**) **1** mentally disordered; insane. **2** utterly foolish. **3** very angry. **4** obsessively enthusiastic. **5** of a dog: affected with rabies. **6** distraught or frantic. ✳ **like mad** informal very hard, fast, loud, etc. ➤ **madly** adv, **madness** n.

madam n **1** a form of respectful address to a woman. **2** the female head of a brothel. **3** Brit, informal a conceited or petulant young girl.

madame /'madəm/ n (pl **mesdames** /'maydam, may'dam/) a title of or form of address to a French woman.

madcap adj impulsive or reckless.

mad cow disease n informal BSE (bovine spongiform encephalopathy).

madden v **1** to drive mad. **2** to exasperate or enrage. ➤ **maddening** adj.

madder n a red dye prepared from the root of a Eurasian plant.

made v past tense and past part. of MAKE¹.

Madeira n a fortified wine from Madeira.

Madeira cake n Brit a rich sponge cake.

madeleine n a small rich sponge cake baked in a mould.

mademoiselle /,madmwə'zel/ n (pl **mademoiselles** or **mesdemoiselles** /,maydmwa'zel/) a title of or form of address to an unmarried French woman.

made-to-measure adj of a garment: made according to an individual's measurements.

made-up adj **1** wearing make-up. **2** fictional or invented.

Madonna n (**the Madonna**) the Virgin Mary.

madrigal n **1** an unaccompanied secular song for several voices. **2** a short medieval love poem. ➤ **madrigalist** n.

maelstrom /'maylstrohm, 'maylstrəm/ *n* **1** a powerful whirlpool. **2** a turbulent or violent upheaval.

maestro /'miestroh/ *n* (*pl* **maestros** *or* **maestri** /'miestree/) a master in an art; *esp* an eminent musician.

Mafia *n* **1** (**the Mafia**) a secret international criminal organization originating in Sicily. **2** (**mafia**) an excessively influential coterie of a usu specified kind.

mafioso /mafi'ohsoh/ *n* (*pl* **mafiosi** /-see/) a member of the Mafia.

magazine *n* **1** an illustrated periodical containing miscellaneous pieces. **2** a holder from which cartridges can be fed into a gun chamber automatically. **3** a storeroom for arms, ammunition, or explosives.

magenta *n* a deep purplish red colour.

maggot *n* the soft-bodied larva of a fly. ➤ **maggoty** *adj.*

magi /'mayjie/ *n* the three wise men from the East who traditionally paid homage to the infant Jesus.

magic[1] *n* **1** the use of supernatural powers over natural forces. **2** the art of producing illusions by sleight of hand. **3** an extraordinary power or influence.

magic[2] *adj* **1** relating to magic. **2** having supernatural qualities. **3** *informal* very good or exciting. ➤ **magical** *adj*, **magically** *adv.*

magic[3] *v* (**magicked, magicking**) *informal* to create or affect by magic.

magician *n* **1** a person skilled in magic. **2** a conjurer.

magisterial *adj* **1** authoritative or masterly. **2** relating to the office of a magistrate.

magistracy *n* (*pl* **-ies**) **1** the office or power of a magistrate. **2** magistrates as a group.

magistrate *n* a local judicial officer who tries minor cases and holds preliminary hearings.

magma *n* molten rock material from within the earth.

magnanimous *adj* showing nobility of feeling and generosity of mind. ➤ **magnanimity** *n*, **magnanimously** *adv.*

magnate *n* a prominent and wealthy business person.

magnesium *n* a light silver-white metallic element which burns with an intense white light.

magnet *n* **1** a piece of iron or steel that has the property of attracting iron and producing a magnetic field outside itself. **2** a person or thing that attracts.

magnetic *adj* **1** relating to magnetism. **2** capable of being magnetized. **3** possessing an extraordinary ability to attract or charm. ➤ **magnetically** *adv.*

magnetic pole *n* either of two small regions in the North and South geographical polar areas of the earth towards which a magnetic needle points.

magnetic storm *n* a marked local disturbance of the earth's magnetic field.

magnetic tape *n* a ribbon of magnetizable tape used in recording sound or video signals.

magnetism *n* **1** the phenomenon by which magnets attract or repel metal objects. **2** an ability to attract or charm.

magnetize *or* **-ise** *v* to make magnetic. ➤ **magnetizable** *n.*

magneto /mag'neetoh/ *n* (*pl* **-os**) an alternator with permanent magnets formerly used to generate a high voltage for an engine's ignition.

magnification *n* **1** the process of magnifying. **2** the degree to which something is magnified.

magnificent *adj* **1** strikingly beautiful or impressive. **2** exceptionally fine. ➤ **magnificence** *n*, **magnificently** *adv.*

magnify *v* (**-ies, -ied**) **1** to enlarge in appearance by optical means. **2** to increase or exaggerate the significance of.

magnifying glass *n* a single lens for magnifying objects or print.

magnitude *n* **1** size or extent. **2** a numerical quantity or value. **3** importance or significance.

magnolia *n* **1** a shrub or tree with large white, yellow pink, or purple flowers. **2** a pale creamy white colour.

magnum *n* (*pl* **magnums**) a wine bottle holding twice the usual amount (about 1.5l).

magpie *n* **1** a large bird with a long tail and black-and-white plumage. **2** a person who collects objects randomly.

maharajah *or* **maharaja** *n* formerly, an Indian prince.

mah-jong *or* **mah-jongg** *n* a Chinese game played with small tiles.

mahogany *n* **1** the dark-coloured wood of a tropical tree. **2** a reddish brown colour.

mahout /mə'howt/ *n* a keeper and driver of an elephant.

maid *n* **1** a female servant. **2** *archaic* an unmarried girl or young woman.

maiden[1] *n* **1** *archaic or literary*. **2** an unmarried girl or young woman. **3** (*also* maiden over) in cricket, an over in which no runs are scored. ➤ **maidenhood** *n*, **maidenly** *adj.*

maiden[2] *adj* denoting the first instance of something: *a maiden voyage.*

maidenhead *n* *archaic* a woman's virginity.

maiden name *n* the surname of a woman before she is married.

mail[1] *n* **1** letters and parcels sent by post. **2** the postal system. **3** email.

mail[2] *v* **1** to send by post. **2** to contact by email.

mail[3] *n* armour made of interlocking metal rings or plates.

mail order *n* a system of ordering goods and receiving them by post.

maim *v* to injure or wound permanently.

main[1] *adj* chief or principal.

main² n **1** a principal pipe or cable carrying gas, electricity, or water. **2** (**the mains**) the central source of water, gas, or electricity supplied to an area. * **in the main** generally; on the whole.

mainframe n a large computer linked to a number of workstations.

mainland n the largest land area of a continent or country, considered apart from any offshore islands.

mainly adv in most cases or for the most part; chiefly.

mainspring n **1** the chief spring of a watch or clock. **2** the chief cause of or influence on something.

mainstay n **1** the chief support or main part of something. **2** a stretched rope or wire supporting the mainmast of a sailing ship.

mainstream n the prevailing influences, values, and activities of a group or society.

maintain v **1** to keep (something) in its normal state of operation or repair. **2** to sustain or defend. **3** to continue or keep up (something). **4** to support or provide for (e.g. dependants). **5** to assert.

maintenance n **1** the action of maintaining. **2** chiefly Brit payments for the support of one spouse by another after legal separation.

maisonette n a part of a house, usu on two floors, let or sold separately.

maize n a tall cereal grass bearing seeds on elongated ears.

majestic adj showing great grandeur or beauty. > **majestically** adv.

majesty n (pl **-ies**) **1** impressive grandeur or beauty. **2** (**Majesty**) used in addressing or referring to a king or queen.

major¹ adj **1** notable in effect or scope; considerable. **2** greater in importance, size, rank, or degree. **3** of a musical scale: having semitones between the third and fourth and the seventh and eighth notes.

major² n **1** an army officer ranking below a lieutenant colonel. **2** NAmer a student specializing in a specified subject.

major³ v chiefly NAmer (+ in) to take courses in a particular subject.

major-domo n (pl **major-domos**) the head steward of a large household.

major general n an army officer ranking below a lieutenant general.

majority n (pl **-ies**) **1** a number greater than half of a total. **2** the number by which the votes cast for the winning party in an election exceed those for its nearest rival or its rivals together. **3** the age, usu 18 or 21, at which full legal rights are acquired.

make¹ v (past tense and past part. **made**) **1** to form or put together from ingredients or parts. **2** to produce or bring about by work or effort. **3** to perform or carry out. **4** to cause to be in a particular state or act in a certain way. **5** (+ into)

to change (something) so that it becomes something different. **6** to have as a possible function; to serve as. **7** to compel (somebody) to do something. **8** to earn (money) as income. **9** to achieve or reach. **10** to estimate as an amount or total. **11** to arrange (a bed) to be ready for use. **12** (+ for) to attempt to move in a particular direction. * **make away with** to take or steal. **make believe** to pretend. **make do** to manage with limited resources. **make something of 1** to attribute significance to. **2** to understand. **make way** to give room or allow somebody to pass. > **maker** n.

make² n a manufacturer or brand. * **on the make** informal seeking a higher social or financial status.

make-believe n imagination or fantasy.

make off v to leave in haste. * **make off with** to take or steal.

make out v **1** to manage with difficulty to perceive or understand. **2** to claim or pretend. **3** to write out (a document). **4** informal to fare or manage.

makeover n **1** the refurbishing or renovation of a building, piece of clothing, etc. **2** the remodelling of a person's appearance.

make over v **1** to transfer the title of (property). **2** to refurbish or remodel.

makeshift adj crudely improvised.

make up v **1** to invent (a story or excuse). **2** to assemble or form (a whole). **3** to be reconciled. **4** (+ for) to compensate for a disadvantage or loss. **5** to apply cosmetics. * **make it up to** to compensate (somebody) for a disappointment or unfairness.

make-up n **1** cosmetics applied to the face. **2** the way in which the parts of something are put together.

makeweight n something added to bring a weight to the required value.

malachite n a green mineral used for ornaments.

maladjusted adj unable to cope with the normal conditions of life.

maladroit adj clumsy or inept.

malady n (pl **-ies**) a disease or disorder.

malaise n **1** a vague feeling of being unwell or dissatisfied. **2** social or economic disquiet.

malapropism n the wrong use of a word instead of another like it, as in 'polo bears'.

malaria n a disease caused by mosquito bites, with attacks of chills and fever. > **malarial** adj.

malarkey n informal nonsense.

malcontent n an aggressively discontented person.

male¹ adj **1** relating to the sex that fertilizes or inseminates the female to produce offspring. **2** of a plant or flower: having stamens but no ovaries. **3** designed for fitting into a corresponding hollow part.

male² n a male person, animal, or plant.

malediction *n formal* a curse. ➤ **maledictory** *adj.*

malefactor *n formal* a person who commits a crime or does wrong.

malevolent *adj* intending to do harm to others. ➤ **malevolence** *n*, **malevolently** *adv.*

malformation *n* abnormal formation or structure. ➤ **malformed** *adj.*

malfunction *v* to fail to operate in the normal manner. ➤ **malfunction** *n.*

malice *n* a desire to do harm to others.

malicious *adj* intended to cause harm to others. ➤ **maliciously** *adv.*

malign[1] *adj* evil in nature or effect. ➤ **malignity** *n.*

malign[2] *v* to speak ill of.

malignancy *n* (*pl* -ies) 1 a malignant tumour. 2 being malevolent or malign.

malignant *adj* 1 harmful; malevolent. 2 of a tumour: tending to spread.

malinger *v* to pretend to be ill or injured to avoid work. ➤ **malingerer** *n.*

mall *n* 1 a large covered shopping precinct. 2 a public promenade.

mallard *n* a large wild duck with a shiny green head.

malleable *adj* 1 able to be beaten or rolled into shape. 2 easily influenced or persuaded. ➤ **malleability** *n.*

mallet *n* 1 a hammer with a large wooden head. 2 a long-handled implement with a wooden head for striking the ball in croquet or polo.

mallow *n* a plant with showy pink, purple, or white flowers.

malnourished *adj* suffering from malnutrition.

malnutrition *n* ill health caused by a faulty or inadequate diet.

malodorous *adj formal* smelling bad.

malpractice *n* failure to exercise due professional skill or care.

malt *n* softened and roasted grain used in brewing and distilling. ➤ **malted** *adj.*

maltreat *v* to treat cruelly or roughly. ➤ **maltreatment** *n.*

mama *or* **mamma** *n informal* one's mother.

mamba *n* a tropical African poisonous snake.

mammal *n* a warm-blooded animal that has mammary glands and nourishes the young with milk. ➤ **mammalian** *adj.*

mammary *adj* relating to the breasts or milk-producing organs.

Mammon *n* material wealth or possessions, considered as an evil.

mammoth[1] *n* an extinct hairy elephant with a long tail and long tusks.

mammoth[2] *adj* huge.

man[1] *n* (*pl* **men**) 1 an adult human male. 2 an individual or person. 3 the human race. 4 a piece in a board game.

man[2] *v* (**manned, manning**) to provide (a machine or a place) with the people needed to run it.

manacle[1] *n* (*usu in pl*) a shackle or handcuff.

manacle[2] *v* to confine with manacles.

manage *v* 1 to conduct the running of (an organization or group of people). 2 to use (money) economically. 3 to succeed in achieving (something difficult). 4 to be able to cope with a difficult situation. ➤ **manageable** *adj.*

management *n* 1 the activity of managing. 2 the people who manage an organization.

manager *n* 1 a person who manages an organization or group of people. 2 a person who manages a sports team or individual. ➤ **manageress** *n*, **managerial** *adj.*

manatee *n* a tropical plant-eating sea mammal with a broad tail.

mandarin *n* 1 (**Mandarin**) the official dialect of Chinese. 2 formerly, a senior Chinese official. 3 a person of position and influence. 4 a yellowish orange citrus fruit with a loose skin.

mandate[1] *n* 1 an authoritative command from a superior. 2 an authorization to act on behalf of another. 3 the authority granted by the electorate to the winner of an election to carry out a policy.

mandate[2] *v* to give a mandate to.

mandatory *adj* 1 constituting a command. 2 compulsory or obligatory.

mandible *n* 1 the lower jaw together with its surrounding soft parts. 2 the upper or lower part of a bird's bill. 3 an insect's mouth part for holding or biting food.

mandolin *or* **mandoline** *n* a musical instrument of the lute family with four pairs of strings and a fretted neck.

mandrake *n* a plant with a large forked root formerly used in medicine.

mandrill *n* a large baboon with red and blue striped cheeks and hindquarters.

mane *n* 1 a growth of thick hair growing on the neck of a horse, male lion, etc. 2 long thick hair on a person's head.

maneuver *n and v NAmer see* MANOEUVRE[1], MANOEUVRE[2].

manful *adj* showing courage and resolution. ➤ **manfully** *adv.*

manganese *n* a greyish white brittle metallic element.

mange *n* a contagious skin disease affecting domestic animals.

mangel-wurzel *n* a large type of beet grown as food for livestock.

manger *n* a trough or open box in a stable for holding feed.

mangetout /'monzhtooh/ *n* (*pl* **mangetouts** *or* **mangetout**) a variety of pea with thin flat edible pods.

mangle[1] *v* 1 to hack or crush. 2 to spoil by inept rendering.

mangle² n a machine with rollers for squeezing water from laundry.

mangle³ v to squeeze (laundry) with a mangle.

mango n (pl -oes or -os) a yellowish red tropical fruit with a juicy pulp.

mangrove n a tropical tree or shrub with roots that form dense masses above ground.

mangy or **mangey** adj (-ier, -iest) 1 of an animal: suffering from mange. 2 badly worn or shabby. ➤ **manginess** n.

manhandle v 1 to move (a large or heavy object) by human force. 2 to handle (somebody or something) roughly.

manhole n a covered opening giving access to a sewer or other underground system.

mania n 1 abnormal excitement with hyperactivity and disorganization of behaviour. 2 an extreme enthusiasm or obsession.

maniac n 1 a person who behaves in a violent or uncontrolled way. 2 a person with an extreme enthusiasm for something.

manic adj of or affected by mania. ➤ **manically** adv.

manic depression n a mental disorder characterized by alternating periods of exhilaration and depression. ➤ **manic-depressive** adj and n.

manicure¹ n a treatment for the care of the hands and fingernails.

manicure² v to give a manicure to. ➤ **manicurist** n.

manifest¹ adj readily perceived; obvious. ➤ **manifestly** adv.

manifest² v 1 to show or display. 2 of a spirit, etc: to appear in visible form.

manifest³ n a list of passengers and cargo on a ship.

manifestation n 1 something that provides evidence or proof. 2 a sign of the presence of a spirit.

manifesto n (pl -os or -oes) a public declaration of intentions by a political party before an election.

manifold¹ adj many and varied.

manifold² n a hollow fitting with several outlets or inlets for connecting one pipe with other pipes.

manikin or **mannikin** n 1 a little man. 2 an anatomical model of the body.

manioc n = CASSAVA.

manipulate v 1 to handle or operate skilfully. 2 to control or influence by artful or insidious means. ➤ **manipulation** n, **manipulative** adj, **manipulator** n.

mankind n the human race.

manky adj (-ier, -iest) Brit, informal nasty or dirty.

manly adj (-ier, -iest) having the qualities traditionally thought to befit a man, e.g. courage or strength. ➤ **manliness** n.

man-made adj made or produced by human beings rather than nature.

manna n in the Bible, food miraculously given to the Israelites on their journey through the wilderness.

mannequin n a model of the human figure used for displaying clothes in a shop.

manner n 1 the way in which something is done. 2 a characteristic or distinctive bearing or air. 3 (in pl) polite social behaviour.

mannered adj 1 having manners of the kind specified: well-mannered. 2 artificial or stilted.

mannerism n a characteristic gesture or idiosyncrasy.

mannerly adj having good manners; polite.

mannish adj of a woman: like a man in appearance or manner.

manoeuvre¹ (NAmer **maneuver**) n 1 a movement requiring skill and dexterity. 2 a deft or well-planned social or political action. 3 (in pl) a large-scale military training exercise.

manoeuvre² (NAmer **maneuver**) v 1 to perform a manoeuvre. 2 to use stratagems. 3 to guide carefully into position. ➤ **manoeuvrable** adj.

man of letters n 1 a scholar. 2 a distinguished male scholar or author.

man of straw n an unreliable or insignificant person.

man of the cloth n a clergyman.

man-of-war or **man-o'-war** n (pl **men-of-war** or **men-o'-war**) formerly, an armed sailing ship.

manometer n an instrument used for measuring the pressure of gases and vapours.

manor n a large country house with an estate. ➤ **manorial** adj.

manpower n the supply of people available for work.

manse n the house of a clergyman in Scotland.

mansion n a large imposing house.

manslaughter n the unlawful killing of somebody without malicious intent.

mantel or **mantle** n a mantelpiece or mantelshelf.

mantelpiece or **mantlepiece** n 1 an ornamental structure round a fireplace. 2 a mantelshelf.

mantelshelf or **mantleshelf** n a shelf forming the top of a mantelpiece.

mantilla n a light scarf worn over the head and shoulders by Spanish and Latin-American women.

mantis n (pl **mantises** or **mantes**) an insect that clasps its prey in forelimbs held as if in prayer.

mantle¹ n 1 a loose sleeveless cloak. 2 something that covers or conceals. 3 a role adopted or taken over from somebody else. 4 a sheath placed over the flame of a gas or oil lamp to increase the light given off. 5 the part of the earth that lies between the crust and the central core.

mantle² *n* see MANTEL.

mantra *n* a word or sound used in meditation to focus the mind and help concentration.

manual¹ *adj* **1** of or involving the hands. **2** worked or done by hand rather than by machine. ➤ **manually** *adv*.

manual² *n* **1** a book of instructions or information. **2** a keyboard of an organ played with the hands.

manufacture¹ *n* **1** the large-scale making of products by machinery. **2** the act or process of producing something.

manufacture² *v* **1** to make (products) on a large scale by machinery. **2** to invent or fabricate. ➤ **manufacturer** *n*.

manure *n* animal dung used to fertilize land.

manuscript *n* a book or document written by hand or in a form prior to publication.

Manx *n* the Celtic language of the Isle of Man. ➤ **Manx** *adj*.

Manx cat *n* a cat of a short-haired breed with no tail.

many¹ *adj* (**more, most**) amounting to a large number.

many² *pron* a large number of people or things.

many³ *n* (**the many**) *literary* the great majority.

Maori *n* (*pl* **Maoris** *or* **Maori**) **1** a member of the aboriginal people of New Zealand. **2** the language of this people.

map¹ *n* a reduced representation on a flat surface of part of the earth's surface, showing geographical features, towns, roads, etc.

map² *v* (**mapped, mapping**) **1** to make a map of. **2** (*often* + out) to plan in detail. ➤ **mapping** *n*.

maple *n* a tree having broad leaves with pointed lobes.

maple syrup *n* syrup made by concentrating the sap of sugar maple trees.

map reference *n* a pair of coordinates for finding a point on a map.

mar *v* (**marred, marring**) to spoil the perfection or wholeness of.

maraca /mə'rakə/ *n* each of a pair of rattles used as a percussion instrument.

marathon *n* **1** a long-distance running race, usu of 42.2km (about 26mi 385yd). **2** a lengthy or strenuous activity.

maraud *v* to roam about in search of plunder. ➤ **marauder** *n*.

marble *n* **1** a hard stone with a veined or mottled appearance that can be polished to a very smooth finish. **2** a small glass ball used in children's games. **3** *informal* (*in pl*) one's sanity or common sense. ➤ **marbly** *adj*.

marbled *adj* marked with a mottled or streaked pattern.

March *n* the third month of the year.

march¹ *v* **1** to move along with a steady pace. **2** to walk in a direct purposeful manner. **3** to make steady progress. **4** to take part in a protest march. **5** to make (somebody) march. ➤ **marcher** *n*.

march² *n* **1** the action of marching. **2** a regular step used in marching. **3** a musical composition suitable to accompany marching. **4** a procession organized as a demonstration of support or protest.

march³ *n* (*often* **the Marches**) a border region between two countries.

marchioness *n* **1** the wife or widow of a marquess. **2** a woman having the rank of a marquess.

Mardi Gras /ˌmahdi'grah/ *n* a Shrove Tuesday carnival.

mare¹ *n* the female of a horse or other animal.

mare² /'mahray/ *n* (*pl* **maria** /'mahri-ə/) a large dark area on the surface of the moon or Mars.

margarine *n* a substitute for butter made from vegetable oils.

margin *n* **1** the edge or outside limit of an area. **2** a rim or border. **3** the part of a page outside the main area of text. **4** (*usu in pl*) the fringes of a movement, organization, etc. **5** an extreme limit of tolerance or practicability. **6** the difference between one amount and another. * **margin of error** an amount allowed for possible mistakes or miscalculation.

marginal *adj* **1** placed in the margin. **2** only just qualifying or acceptable. **3** denoting a parliamentary constituency where the MP has a small majority. ➤ **marginally** *adv*.

marginalize *or* **-ise** *v* to treat as peripheral or unimportant. ➤ **marginalization** *n*.

marigold *n* a plant of the daisy family with yellow or red flowers.

marijuana *or* **marihuana** /mari'(h)wahnə/ *n* a mild form of cannabis.

marina *n* a dock or basin providing moorings for yachts and small boats.

marinade¹ *n* a mixture in which food is soaked before cooking to enrich its flavour or make it tender.

marinade² *v* to soak in a marinade.

marinate *v* = MARINADE².

marine¹ *adj* **1** of the sea. **2** relating to the navigation or commerce of the sea.

marine² *n* a soldier able to serve at sea as well as on land.

mariner *n* *formal or literary* a sailor.

marionette *n* a small-scale figure operated by strings or wires.

marital *adj* relating to marriage or the relations between husband and wife.

maritime *adj* **1** relating to navigation or commerce on the sea. **2** associated with or found near the sea. **3** of a climate: having small variations in seasonal temperatures because of the influence of the sea.

marjoram *n* **1** a fragrant aromatic plant of the mint family with leaves used as a herb. **2** = OREGANO.

mark¹ *n* **1** a spot, scratch, etc on the surface of something. **2** a line, notch, etc designed to record position. **3** an identifying symbol. **4** a distinguishing characteristic. **5** a written or printed symbol. **6** a sign or token. **7** a point or level reached or achieved. **8** a symbol or figure indicating an assessment of merit. **9** a particular model of a vehicle, weapon, machine, etc. **10** a goal or target in a game. **11** the starting line or position in a track event. ✷ **make one's mark** to make a good impression. **near the mark** not far from the truth. **on your marks** used to instruct runners in a race to take starting positions. **quick off the mark** reacting promptly. **up to the mark** reaching the desired standard. **wide of the mark** not accurate or relevant.

mark² *v* **1** to make a mark on. **2** to evaluate or give a mark to (a piece of work). **3** to add appropriate symbols to (a text). **4** to indicate or identify by a mark or symbol. **5** to register or record. **6** to characterize or distinguish. **7** to be a sign of. **8** to be the occasion of (something notable). **9** (*usu* + off) to set apart or delineate. **10** to observe or take notice of. **11** in a team game, to stay close to (an opponent) to prevent them from getting or passing the ball. ✷ **mark time 1** to move the feet in march time without moving forward. **2** to pass time unproductively while waiting.

mark³ *n* the former basic monetary unit of Germany (replaced by the euro in 2002).

mark down *v* to put a lower price on.

marked *adj* **1** having natural marks. **2** made identifiable by marking. **3** distinct and noticeable. **4** being an object of attack or suspicion. ➤ **markedly** /'mahkidli/ *adv*.

marker *n* **1** something used to mark a position, place, or direction. **2** a felt-tip pen with a broad tip. **3** a person who marks something. **4** in a team game, a player who marks an opponent.

market¹ *n* **1** a meeting of people for trading. **2** a place where provisions, livestock, etc are sold. **3** an opportunity for selling particular goods, or a section of the community offering this. **4** commercial activity or demand. ✷ **on the market** available for buying.

market² *v* (**marketed, marketing**) to sell or offer for sale. ➤ **marketable** *adj*.

market garden *n* a plot in which fruit and vegetables are grown for market. ➤ **market gardening** *n*, **market gardener** *n*.

marketing *n* the promotion and advertising of goods or services for sale.

marketplace *n* **1** an open place where markets are held. **2** an opportunity for selling.

market research *n* the collection information about consumer demand and preferences.

market town *n* a town that holds a regular public market.

market value *n* the value of something in a free market.

marking *n* **1** a mark or marks. **2** an arrangement or pattern of marks.

marksman *n* (*pl* **marksmen**) a person skilled in shooting. ➤ **marksmanship** *n*.

markup *n* an amount added to the price of something to guarantee the seller a profit.

mark up *v* to put a higher price on.

marl *n* a crumbly deposit of silt or clay, used as a fertilizer.

marmalade *n* a sweetened preserve made from oranges.

marmoreal *adj literary* made of or resembling marble.

marmoset *n* a small American monkey with a long tail and silky fur.

marmot *n* a burrowing rodent with short legs and coarse fur.

maroon¹ *v* to abandon (somebody) in a desolate place.

maroon² *n* a dark brownish red colour.

marque *n* a make of vehicle, as distinct from a particular model.

marquee *n* **1** a large tent for outdoor social events. **2** *NAmer* a canopy over an entrance to a large building.

marquess *n* a member of the British peerage ranking below a duke and above an earl.

marquetry or **marqueterie** *n* decorative work made from coloured pieces of wood, ivory, etc inlaid in the surface of furniture.

marquis *n* **1** a nobleman in Europe ranking above a count and below a duke. **2** a marquess.

marquise *n* a marchioness.

marriage *n* **1** the union of a man and woman in a special kind of social and legal dependence. **2** the state of being husband and wife. ➤ **marriageable** *adj*.

married *adj* joined in marriage.

marrow *n* **1** a fruit of a gourd, used as a vegetable. **2** a soft tissue inside bones, in which blood cells are produced.

marrowbone *n* a bone rich in marrow.

marry *v* (**-ies, -ied**) **1** to take as a husband or wife. **2** to join in marriage. **3** to bring (two or more things) together closely.

marsh *n* an area of soft continuously wet land. ➤ **marshy** *adj*.

marshal¹ *n* **1** an officer of the highest military rank. **2** a district law officer in the USA. **3** an official who organizes a public occasion.

marshal² *v* (**marshalled, marshalling**, *NAmer* **marshaled, marshaling**) **1** to place in proper rank or position. **2** to order (information) in an effective way. **3** to lead or usher (a group of people) ceremoniously.

marshmallow *n* **1** a pink-flowered marsh

plant. **2** a light spongy confection made from sugar, albumen, and gelatin.

marsupial *n* a mammal the females of which have a pouch on the abdomen for carrying young.

mart *n* a market or other place of trade.

marten *n* (*pl* **martens** *or* **marten**) a tree-dwelling mammal with a slender body.

martial *adj* relating to war.

martial art *n* an art of combat practised as a sport.

martial law *n* government by military forces in occupied territory or in an emergency.

Martian[1] *adj* relating to or coming from the planet Mars.

Martian[2] *n* a supposed inhabitant of Mars.

martin *n* a small swallow with a short tail.

martinet *n* a strict disciplinarian.

martyr[1] *n* **1** a person who is put to death because of their religious beliefs. **2** any person who suffers for any cause or set of beliefs. **3** a person who behaves in a deliberately self-sacrificing manner. ➤ **martyrdom** *n*.

martyr[2] *v* to put to death as a martyr.

marvel[1] *n* something or somebody amazing.

marvel[2] *v* (**marvelled, marvelling,** *NAmer* **marveled, marveling**) (+ at) to be filled with wonder or amazement.

marvellous (*NAmer* **marvelous**) *adj* **1** causing wonder. **2** extremely good. ➤ **marvellously** *adv*.

Marxism *n* the principles and policies of Karl Marx (d.1883), on which communism was based. ➤ **Marxist** *n and adj*.

marzipan *n* a paste made from ground almonds, sugar, and egg whites.

mascara *n* a cosmetic for darkening the eyelashes.

mascot *n* a person, animal, or object thought to bring good luck.

masculine *adj* **1** male. **2** characteristic of men. **3** of the gender that includes most words or grammatical forms referring to males. ➤ **masculinity** *n*.

mash[1] *n* **1** a soft pulpy mass produced by crushing a substance. **2** *Brit, informal* mashed potatoes.

mash[2] *v* to crush or pound to a soft pulpy state.

mask[1] *n* **1** a covering for all or part of the face, worn for disguise or protection. **2** a copy of a face made by sculpting or by means of a mould.

mask[2] *v* **1** to cover or conceal with a mask. **2** to disguise or conceal. **3** to make indistinct or imperceptible. **4** to cover for protection. ➤ **masked** *adj*.

masochism *n* the deriving of pleasure from being physically or mentally abused. ➤ **masochist** *n*, **masochistic** *adj*.

mason *n* **1** a skilled worker with stone. **2** (**Mason**) a Freemason.

Masonic *adj* relating to Freemasons.

masonry *n* stonework.

masque *n* a dramatic entertainment performed by masked actors.

masquerade[1] *n* **1** a social gathering of people wearing masks. **2** a show or pretence.

masquerade[2] *v* (+ as) to pretend to be something that one is not.

mass[1] *n* **1** (**Mass**) the Roman Catholic celebration of the Eucharist. **2** a musical setting for the fixed parts of the Mass.

mass[2] *n* **1** a quantity of matter irrespective of its shape. **2** in physics, the resistance of a body to a change in its speed or position, taken as a measure of the amount of material it contains. **3** the principal part or main body. **4** *informal* (*in pl*) a large quantity or amount. **5** a large body of people in a compact group. **6** (**the masses**) the ordinary people.

mass[3] *v* to assemble into a single mass.

mass[4] *adj* involving a lot of people.

massacre[1] *v* **1** to kill (a large number of people) brutally. **2** *informal* to defeat (an opponent) overwhelmingly.

massacre[2] *n* the brutal killing of large numbers of people.

massage[1] *n* the action of kneading and rubbing the body to relieve aches and give relaxation.

massage[2] *v* **1** to give a massage to. **2** (+ in/into) to rub a substance into (the skin or the scalp). **3** to adjust (data) to present a particular appearance.

massage parlour *n* **1** an establishment where professional massage is provided. **2** a brothel.

masseur /ma'suh/ *or* **masseuse** /ma'suhz/ *n* a person who provides professional massage.

massif /'maseef, ma'seef/ *n* a group of mountains with tall peaks.

massive *adj* **1** large and heavy. **2** unusually large or intense. ➤ **massively** *adv*.

mass-market *adj* of a product: intended for a wide range of people.

mass-produce *v* to produce (goods) in large quantities. ➤ **mass-produced** *adj*.

mast[1] *n* **1** a tall pole on a ship, for carrying sails. **2** a vertical pole or framework carrying a radio or television aerial.

mast[2] *n* nuts that have fallen on the forest floor and are eaten by animals.

mastectomy *n* (*pl* **-ies**) the amputation of a breast.

master[1] *n* **1** a person having control or authority over another. **2** the owner of a slave or animal. **3** a male teacher. **4** the head of a college. **5** a person holding an academic degree higher than a bachelor's but lower than a doctor's. **6** a skilled exponent of an art or activity. **7** an original film or recording from which copies can be made.

master[2] *v* **1** to acquire complete knowledge or skill in. **2** to gain control of.

master[3] *adj* principal or controlling.

master class *n* a class in which an eminent performer instructs advanced pupils.

masterful *adj* **1** inclined to take control and dominate. **2** having great artistic or intellectual skill. ➤ **masterfully** *adv.*

master key *n* a key designed to open several different locks.

masterly *adj* demonstrating exceptional expertise.

mastermind[1] *n* a person who plans and implements a complex project.

mastermind[2] *v* to plan and implement (a complex project).

master of ceremonies *n* a person who directs the proceedings at a public entertainment or other event.

masterpiece *n* a work of exceptional skill.

mastery *n* **1** complete control or authority. **2** extensive skill or knowledge in a subject.

masthead *n* **1** the top of a ship's mast. **2** the name of a newspaper displayed on the top of the first page.

mastic *n* **1** an aromatic resin from an evergreen tree, used in varnishes. **2** a waterproof substance like putty used in building.

masticate *v* to grind or crush (food) before swallowing. ➤ **mastication** *n.*

mastiff *n* a large smooth-coated dog of a breed used as guard dogs.

mastodon *n* an extinct mammal similar to an elephant.

mastoid *or* **mastoid process** *n* a conical projecting part of the bone behind the ear.

masturbate *v* to stimulate one's genitals for sexual pleasure. ➤ **masturbation** *n,* **masturbatory** *adj.*

mat[1] *n* **1** a piece of thick fabric used as a floor covering. **2** a flat piece of material used to protect a surface from heat, moisture, etc. **3** a thick pad used as a surface for wrestling and gymnastics. **4** a mass of intertwined or tangled strands.

mat[2] *v* (**matted, matting**) of fibres, hair, etc: to become tangled.

matador *n* a principal bullfighter.

match[1] *n* **1** a contest between two or more teams or individuals. **2** a person or thing that is the equal of another. **3** one thing that corresponds exactly to another. **4** a pair of things that correspond exactly. **5** a prospective partner in marriage. **6** a marriage union.

match[2] *v* **1** to correspond or suit. **2** to be the exact counterpart of. **3** to be equal to. **4** to place (a person or thing) in competition with another.

match[3] *n* a short thin piece of wood or cardboard tipped with a mixture that ignites when rubbed against a rough surface.

matchbox *n* a small box that contains matches.

matchless *adj* having no equal.

matchmaker *n* a person who arranges marriages or romantic relationships.

match point *n* a point in tennis the winning of which also wins the match.

matchstick *n* the stem of a match.

mate[1] *n* **1** a friend or companion. **2** an assistant to a more skilled worker. **3** an officer on a merchant ship ranking below captain. **4** a marriage partner. **5** either member of a breeding pair of animals.

mate[2] *v* of animals: to come together to breed.

mate[3] *v* in chess, to checkmate (an opponent).

mate[4] *n* in chess, checkmate.

matelot *n Brit, informal* a sailor.

material[1] *n* **1** the substances of which something is made. **2** cloth or fabric. **3** (*in pl*) things needed for doing or making something.

material[2] *adj* **1** important or significant. **2** (+ to) relevant. **3** concerned with physical rather than spiritual things. ➤ **materially** *adv.*

materialism *n* **1** an interest in or emphasis on physical rather than spiritual things. **2** a theory that only physical matter is real. ➤ **materialist** *n and adj,* **materialistic** *adj.*

materialize *or* **-ise** *v* **1** to assume a bodily form. **2** to become reality.

maternal *adj* **1** relating to or characteristic of a mother. **2** related through one's mother. ➤ **maternally** *adv.*

maternity *n* motherhood.

matey *or* **maty** *adj* (**-ier, -iest**) *informal* friendly.

mathematics *pl n* the science of numbers and using them to make calculations and measurements. ➤ **mathematical** *adj,* **mathematically** *n.*

maths *pl n Brit* mathematics.

matinée *n* an afternoon performance in a theatre or cinema.

matins *pl n* a morning prayer service.

matriarch *n* a woman who is the head of her family.

matriarchy *n* (*pl* **-ies**) a system of social organization in which the female is the head of the family. ➤ **matriarchal** *adj.*

matricide *n* **1** the act of killing one's mother. **2** somebody who does this. ➤ **matricidal** *adj.*

matriculate *v* to admit be admitted as a member of a college or university. ➤ **matriculation** *n.*

matrimony *n* marriage. ➤ **matrimonial** *adj.*

matrix *n* (*pl* **matrices** *or* **matrixes**) **1** a substance, environment, etc within which something develops. **2** a mould in which something is cast. **3** a rectangular array of mathematical elements treated as a unit. **4** an arrangement of elements into rows and columns.

matron *n* **1** a woman in charge of living arrangements in a school or residential home. **2** *Brit* a woman in charge of the nursing in a hospital. **3** a mature or dignified married woman >. ➤ **matronly** *adj*.

matron of honour *n* a bride's principal married wedding attendant.

matt *or* **matte** *adj* lacking gloss; not shiny.

matted *adj* of fibres, hair, etc: tangled.

matter¹ *n* **1** the physical substance of an object. **2** a subject of interest or concern. **3** something to be considered or proved. **4** something written or printed. ✳ **for that matter** so far as that is concerned. **no matter 1** that is of no importance. **2** regardless of a certain thing.

matter² *v* to be important or relevant.

matter-of-fact *adj* practical and unimaginative.

mattock *n* a digging tool with a head like a pick and a blade like an axe.

mattress *n* a fabric case filled with resilient material or a set of springs, used on a bed.

mature¹ *adj* **1** fully grown. **2** physically, emotionally, or mentally advanced. **3** having completed natural growth; ripe. **4** sensible and well considered. ➤ **maturely** *adv*.

mature² *v* **1** to become mature. **2** of an insurance policy: to become due for payment.

maturity *n* **1** the quality or state of being mature. **2** the date when an insurance policy becomes due.

maudlin *adj* weakly sentimental.

maul *v* **1** of an animal: to attack and tear the flesh of. **2** to handle roughly.

maunder *v* **1** to act or wander idly. **2** to speak in a rambling or indistinct manner.

mausoleum *n* (*pl* **mausoleums**) a large elaborate tomb.

mauve *n* a pinkish purple colour.

maverick *n* an independent and nonconformist individual.

maw *n* the throat or jaws of a flesh-eating animal.

mawkish *adj* feebly sentimental.

max. *abbr* maximum.

maxim *n* a succinct expression of a general truth or principle.

maximize *or* **-ise** *v* **1** to make as large or numerous as possible. **2** to use to best advantage.

maximum¹ *n* (*pl* **maxima** *or* **maximums**) the greatest amount, number, or degree possible or recorded. ➤ **maximal** *adj*.

maximum² *adj* greatest in amount or number.

May *n* the fifth month of the year.

may¹ *v aux* (*third person sing. present tense* **may**, *past tense* **might**) **1** expressing permission. **2** expressing possibility. **3** expressing a wish or hope.

may² *n* hawthorn or hawthorn blossom.

maybe *adv* perhaps.

Mayday *n* an international radio distress signal.

mayhem *n* a state of great confusion or disorder.

mayn't *contraction* may not.

mayonnaise *n* a thick dressing made with egg yolks, vegetable oil, and vinegar or lemon juice.

mayor *n* the head of a city or borough council. ➤ **mayoral** *adj*.

mayoralty *n* (*pl* **-ies**) the term of office of a mayor.

mayoress *n* **1** the wife of a mayor. **2** a woman mayor.

maypole *n* a tall pole with ribbons hanging from the top, for dancing round on May Day.

maze *n* **1** a complex network of paths through which people have to find a way to the centre. **2** something very complicated.

mazurka *n* a Polish folk dance in moderate triple time.

Mb *abbr* megabyte(s).

MBA *abbr* Master of Business Administration.

MBE *abbr* Member of the Order of the British Empire.

MC *abbr* **1** Master of Ceremonies. **2** *Brit* Military Cross.

MD *abbr* **1** Doctor of Medicine. **2** *Brit* Managing Director.

Md *abbr* the chemical symbol for mendelevium.

ME *abbr* myalgic encephalomyelitis, a condition causing intense tiredness and aching joints.

me *pron* used as the objective case: I.

mead¹ *n* a fermented alcoholic drink made of water and honey.

mead² *n archaic* a meadow.

meadow *n* an area of level grassland.

meagre (*NAmer* **meager**) *adj* deficient in quality or quantity. ➤ **meagreness** *n*.

meal¹ *n* **1** the portion of food eaten at one time. **2** the time of eating a meal. ✳ **make a meal of** *informal* to deal laboriously with.

meal² *n* the ground seeds of a cereal grass or pulse.

mealy *adj* (**-ier**, **-iest**) **1** soft and crumbly. **2** containing meal. **3** pale.

mealy-mouthed *adj* unwilling to speak plainly or directly.

mean¹ *adj* **1** not generous; stingy. **2** unpleasant and spiteful. **3** inferior in quality or status. **4** merely ordinary. **5** *informal* excellent or impressive. ➤ **meanly** *adv*, **meanness** *n*.

mean² *v* (*past tense and past part.* **meant**) **1** to have in mind as a purpose. **2** of a word or statement: to have as its explanation or significance. **3** to intend for a particular use or purpose. **4** (*usu* + to) to have significance or importance.

mean³ *n* **1** a middle point between extremes. **2** a value that is the average of a range of values.

mean⁴ *adj* **1** midway between extremes. **2** average or intermediate.

meander¹ *v* **1** of a river or road: to follow a winding course. **2** to wander aimlessly.

meander² n 1 a turn or winding of a stream. 2 a winding path or pattern.

meaning n 1 what a word is intended to convey or signify. 2 sense or significance.

meaningful adj 1 having meaning. 2 having a special significance; expressive. 3 worthwhile. ➤ **meaningfully** adv.

meaningless adj having no meaning or purpose. ➤ **meaninglessly** adv.

means pl n 1 a method or way that enables a purpose to be achieved. 2 money or other resources available. * **by all means** of course; certainly. **by means of** with the help or use of. **by no means** not at all; in no way.

means test n an examination into somebody's financial state to determine their eligibility for public assistance.

meant v past tense and past part. of MEAN².

meantime n * **in the meantime** meanwhile.

meanwhile adv 1 during the intervening time. 2 during the same period.

measles pl n an infectious disease marked by a red rash and high fever.

measly adj (-ier, -iest) informal very small or few; worthless or insignificant.

measure¹ v 1 to find out the size, amount, or degree in terms of a standard unit. 2 to have (a specified measurement). 3 (+ out) to take in measured amounts. 4 (+ up) to have the necessary ability or qualities. ➤ **measurable** adj, **measurably** adv.

measure² n 1 a step planned or taken to achieve an end. 2 a proposed legislative act or bill. 3 a standard or unit of measurement. 4 an instrument or utensil for measuring. 5 an appropriate or due portion. 6 a moderate extent, amount, or degree. 7 poetic rhythm or metre. 8 a metrical unit. * **for good measure** in addition to what is strictly necessary. **get the measure of** to understand the character or nature of.

measured adj 1 rhythmically slow and regular. 2 carefully thought out.

measurement n 1 the act of measuring. 2 a figure or amount obtained by measuring.

meat n animal flesh used as food.

meatball n a ball of minced meat for cooking.

meaty adj (-ier, -iest) 1 like meat. 2 fleshy or heavily built. 3 offering plenty to think about or discuss.

Mecca n a place that attracts a particular group of people.

mechanic n a skilled worker who repairs or maintains machinery.

mechanical adj 1 relating to or operated by machinery or machines. 2 done spontaneously or without thought. 3 in accordance with the principles of mechanics. ➤ **mechanically** adv.

mechanics pl n 1 the branch of science that deals with energy and forces and their effect on

movement. 2 the working parts of something. 3 the functional details of something.

mechanism n 1 a set of moving parts designed to perform a function. 2 a process or technique for achieving a result.

mechanize or **-ise** v to equip with machines of mechanical equipment. ➤ **mechanization** n.

medal n a stamped metal disc commemorating a person or event or awarded for an achievement.

medallion n 1 a pendant in the shape of a medal. 2 a decorative tablet or panel bearing a figure or portrait in relief.

medallist (NAmer **medalist**) n a person who has been awarded a medal for a sporting achievement.

meddle v (usu + in/with) to interfere in the concerns of others. ➤ **meddler** n.

meddlesome adj interfering in other people's concerns.

media n 1 pl of MEDIUM¹. 2 the press and television as a source of news and information for the public.

Usage Note: The word *media* is plural, and should be followed by a plural verb: *The media have shown little interest in this event.*

mediaeval adj see MEDIEVAL.

median¹ adj technical positioned in the middle.

median² n 1 a statistical value midway in a range of values. 2 a line from a point where two sides of a triangle meet to the midpoint of the opposite side.

mediate v to intervene to settle a dispute. ➤ **mediation** n, **mediator** n.

medic n informal a medical doctor or student.

medical¹ adj relating to physicians or to medicine. ➤ **medically** adv.

medical² n an examination to determine a person's physical fitness.

medicament n a medicine.

medicate v 1 to treat with a medicine. 2 to impregnate with a medicinal substance.

medication n 1 a medicine or drug. 2 treatment with drugs.

medicinal adj 1 used to cure disease or relieve pain. 2 relating to medicines or drugs. ➤ **medicinally** adv.

medicine n 1 the science and practice of maintaining or restoring health and preventing disease. 2 a substance used in treating or preventing disease.

medicine man n a healer believed to have supernatural powers.

medieval or **mediaeval** adj dating from or typical of the Middle Ages.

medievalist n a specialist in medieval history or culture.

mediocre adj of ordinary or average quality.

meditate v 1 to fix the mind on one matter, as a religious or spiritual exercise. 2 (often + on) to consider or plan in the mind. ➤ **meditation** *n*, **meditative** *adj*.

Mediterranean *adj* of the Mediterranean Sea or the region round it.

Usage Note: Note the spelling with *-t-* and *-rr-*.

medium[1] *n* (*pl* **media** *or* **mediums**) **1** a means of doing something. **2** a channel or means of large-scale communication. **3** a means of artistic expression. **4** (*pl* **mediums**) a person through whom others seek to communicate with the spirits of the dead. **5** a middle position or state.

medium[2] *adj* intermediate between extremes.

medlar *n* a small brown fruit like a crab apple.

medley *n* (*pl* **-eys**) **1** a varied or confused mixture. **2** a musical composition made up of short pieces.

meek *adj* timid or submissive. ➤ **meekly** *adv*.

meerkat *n* a small flesh-eating South African mammal related to the mongoose.

meet[1] *v* (*past tense and past part.* **met**) **1** to come into the presence of (somebody) by accident or design. **2** to become acquainted with (somebody). **3** (*often* + with) to encounter or experience. **4** to come into contact with. **5** to satisfy or conform to (a requirement).

meet[2] *n* a gathering or assembly of people.

meeting *n* **1** an assembly of people for formal discussion or business. **2** a coming together of two or more people.

mega *adj informal* very large or important.

megabyte *n* a unit of computer storage equal to one million bytes.

megalith *n* a large block of stone forming part or whole of a prehistoric monument. ➤ **megalithic** *adj*.

megalomania *n* an obsessive craving for or belief in power over others. ➤ **megalomaniac** *adj and n*.

megaphone *n* a funnel-shaped device for amplifying the voice.

megaton *n* an explosive force equivalent to one million tons of TNT.

megawatt *n* a unit of power equal to one million watts.

melamine *n* a hard plastic used for coatings.

melancholia *n* melancholy or depression.

melancholy[1] *n* deep sadness or depression. ➤ **melancholic** *adj*.

melancholy[2] *adj* **1** depressed or dejected. **2** causing sadness.

melanin *n* a dark pigment in the hair and skin, responsible for tanning when the skin is exposed to sunlight.

melanoma *n* (*pl* **melanomas** *or* **melanomata**) a tumour of the skin cells that produce melanin.

meld *v* to combine or blend.

melee *n* a confused or riotous fight or struggle.

mellifluous *adj* sounding sweet and smooth. ➤ **mellifluously** *adv*.

mellow[1] *adj* **1** rich and soft in colour or taste. **2** made gentle by age or experience. **3** relaxed and genial.

mellow[2] *v* to make or become mellow.

melodic *adj* **1** relating to or having melody. **2** melodious. ➤ **melodically** *adv*.

melodious *adj* having a pleasant sound or tune.

melodrama *n* **1** a film or play with an exciting plot and exaggerated emotions. **2** sensational or dramatic behaviour. ➤ **melodramatic** *adj*, **melodramatically** *adv*.

melody *n* (*pl* **-ies**) **1** a simple or basic tune. **2** the principal part in a harmonic composition.

melon *n* a large round fruit with sweet juicy flesh.

melt *v* **1** to change from a solid to a liquid state by heating. **2** to dissolve or disintegrate. **3** (+ away) to disappear gradually. **4** to become tender or gentle.

meltdown *n* **1** the overheating of the uranium fuel in the core of a nuclear reactor, so that it burns through its container. **2** a catastrophic collapse or failure.

melting pot *n* **1** a place where diverse peoples, traditions, etc influence each other. **2** an unstable situation.

member *n* **1** an individual or unit belonging to a group or organization. **2** *archaic* a limb or other part of the body. ➤ **membership** *n*.

membrane *n* **1** a thin layer covering, lining, or connecting organs or cells in animals and plants. **2** a thin pliable sheet of material. ➤ **membranous** *adj*.

memento *n* (*pl* **-os** *or* **-oes**) something kept as a reminder of the past.

memo *n* (*pl* **-os**) *informal* a brief note sent from one person to another in an organization.

memoir *n* **1** an account or narrative written from personal experience. **2** (*in pl*) the published reminiscences of a public figure.

memorabilia *pl n* objects valued because of their connection with people or events.

memorable *adj* **1** worth remembering; notable. **2** easy to remember. ➤ **memorably** *adv*.

memorandum *n* (*pl* **memorandums** *or* **memoranda**) **1** *formal* a memo. **2** a written reminder.

memorial[1] *n* a monument or occasion that commemorates a person or event.

memorial[2] *adj* serving to commemorate a person or event.

memorize *or* **-ise** *v* to commit (facts) to memory; to learn by heart.

memory *n* (*pl* **-ies**) **1** the ability of the mind to retain and recall facts and experiences. **2** the store of things learned and retained from an individual's experience. **3** an image or impression stored in the mind. **4** the time within which past events are remembered. **5** a computer's facility or capacity for storing data.

men *n* pl of MAN[1].

menace[1] *n* **1** a threatening or dangerous person or thing. **2** a threatening atmosphere or tone.

menace[2] *v* to threaten. ➤ **menacing** *adj*.

ménage à trois /me'nahzh ah 'trwah/ *n* a situation in which a third person lives with a married couple and shares their sexual life.

menagerie *n* a collection of animals for exhibition.

mend[1] *v* **1** to restore to good condition or working order. **2** to improve or rectify. **3** to improve in health.

mend[2] *n* a mended place or part. ✱ **on the mend** improving in health.

mendacious *adj* lying or untruthful. ➤ **mendacity** *n*.

mendicant[1] *n* **1** a friar living off alms. **2** a beggar.

mendicant[2] *adj* **1** dependent on alms or begging. **2** given to begging.

menhir *n* a prehistoric monument consisting of a single upright stone.

menial[1] *adj* of work: routine and involving little skill.

menial[2] *n* somebody with a menial job.

meningitis *n* a disease involving inflammation of the membranes enveloping the brain and spinal cord.

meniscus *n* (*pl* **menisci** or **meniscuses**) **1** the curved upper surface of a column of liquid. **2** a lens that is concave on one side and convex on the other.

menopause *n* the natural cessation of menstruation occurring between the ages of 45 and 50. ➤ **menopausal** *adj*.

menorah *n* a branched candelabrum, a symbol of Judaism.

menstrual *adj* relating to menstruation.

menstruate *v* of a woman: to discharge blood from the womb about once a month. ➤ **menstruation** *n*.

-ment *suffix* forming nouns: *development*; *encampment*.

mental *adj* **1** relating to or experienced by the mind. **2** relating to disorders of the mind. **3** *informal* mad. ➤ **mentally** *adv*.

mentality *n* (*pl* **-ies**) **1** a way of thinking. **2** mental power or capacity.

menthol *n* an alcohol that occurs in mint oils, with the properties of peppermint. ➤ **mentholated** *adj*.

mention[1] *n* **1** a brief reference to somebody or something. **2** a formal citation for outstanding achievement.

mention[2] *v* **1** to refer to briefly. **2** to cite for outstanding achievement.

mentor *n* a wise and trusted adviser or teacher.

menu *n* (*pl* **menus**) **1** a list of the dishes available in a restaurant. **2** the dishes to be served at a meal. **3** a list of available programs, functions, commands, etc, displayed on a computer screen.

meow *v* see MIAOW.

MEP *abbr* Member of the European Parliament.

mercantile *adj* relating to merchants or trading.

mercenary[1] *n* (*pl* **-ies**) a soldier who is hired to fight for a foreign country.

mercenary[2] *adj* acting primarily for financial reward.

merchandise[1] *n* goods for sale.

merchandise[2] *or* **-ize** *v* to promote the sale of.

merchant *n* **1** a wholesale trader. **2** *informal* a person who indulges in a specified unwelcome activity.

merchantable *adj* of a quality acceptable for sale.

merchant bank *n* a banking firm dealing with large corporations. ➤ **merchant banker** *n*.

merchant navy *n* the commercial shipping of a nation.

merciful *adj* **1** showing mercy. **2** affording relief from suffering. ➤ **mercifully** *adv*.

merciless *adj* showing no mercy; pitiless. ➤ **mercilessly** *adv*.

mercurial *adj* **1** having constant changes of mood. **2** of or containing mercury.

mercury *n* a heavy silver-white liquid metallic element used in thermometers and barometers.

mercy *n* (*pl* **-ies**) **1** compassion or forbearance shown to an offender or enemy. **2** a fortunate circumstance. ✱ **at the mercy of** wholly in the power of.

mere[1] *adj* **1** being what is specified and nothing else. **2** (**the merest**) the slightest.

mere[2] *n* literary a lake.

merely *adv* only; simply.

meretricious *adj* attractive in a showy or tawdry way.

merge *v* **1** to combine or unite. **2** to blend or come together gradually.

merger *n* a combining of two organizations to form one.

meridian *n* a circle on the earth's surface passing through both poles.

meringue *n* a mixture of stiffly beaten egg whites and sugar baked until crisp.

merino *n* (*pl* **-os**) **1** a sheep of a breed originating in Spain. **2** a soft wool obtained from this sheep.

merit[1] *n* **1** worth or excellence. **2** a good or praiseworthy quality.

merit[2] *v* (**merited, meriting**) to be worthy of.

meritocracy *n* (*pl* **-ies**) a society in which people hold power on the basis of their ability. ➤ **meritocratic** *adj*.

meritorious *adj* deserving reward or honour.

mermaid n a mythical sea creature having a woman's head and trunk and a fish's tail.

merriment n light-hearted fun.

merry adj (-ier, -iest) 1 cheerful and lively. 2 Brit, informal slightly drunk. ➤ **merrily** adv.

merry-go-round n a revolving fairground machine with model horses or vehicles that people ride on.

merrymaking n festive activity or fun.

Mesdames /may'dahm/ n pl of Mrs.

mesdemoiselles /ˌmaydəmwah'zel/ n pl of MADEMOISELLE.

mesh¹ n 1 the cords, wires, etc that make up a net. 2 an open space in a net or network. 3 an interlocking construction.

mesh² v 1 of a gearwheel: to link with another gearwheel. 2 to become entangled. 3 to coordinate or harmonize.

mesmeric adj totally absorbing or hypnotic. ➤ **mesmerically** adv.

mesmerism n hypnotism.

mesmerize or **-ise** v to engross or fascinate totally.

mess¹ n 1 an untidy or dirty state or condition. 2 a state of confusion or disorder. 3 the excrement of a domestic animal. 4 a prepared dish of soft or liquid food. 5 a place where members of the armed forces eat their meals.

mess² v 1 to make untidy or dirty. 2 informal (+ with) to meddle with. 3 (+ about/around) to behave in a silly way.

message n 1 a written or spoken communication. 2 a central theme or idea. ＊ **get the message** informal to understand what somebody is saying.

messenger n a person who carries a message.

messiah n 1 (**the Messiah**) a name for Jesus Christ in Christianity. 2 a professed leader of a cause.

messianic adj associated with a messiah.

messieurs /me'syuh, mə'syuhz/ n pl of MONSIEUR.

Messrs n pl of Mr.

messy adj (-ier, -iest) 1 untidy or dirty. 2 awkward or difficult to deal with. ➤ **messily** adv, **messiness** n.

met v past tense and past part. of MEET¹.

metabolism n the process in living cells by which energy is provided and new material is assimilated. ➤ **metabolic** adj.

metabolize or **-ise** v to process by metabolism.

metal n 1 a hard shiny substance capable of being melted and fused, and a good conductor of electricity and heat. 2 broken stones used in making roads.

metalled (NAmer **metaled**) adj of a road: covered with a hard surface.

metallic adj 1 containing or like metal. 2 of a sound: sharp and ringing.

metallurgy n the branch of science concerned with the properties of metals. ➤ **metallurgical** adj, **metallurgist** n.

metamorphic adj of rock: having undergone change resulting from heat and pressure.

metamorphosis n (pl **metamorphoses**) 1 a natural change in the form or structure of an insect or amphibian, e.g. the change from a tadpole to a frog. 2 a change of form, structure, or substance.

metaphor n a word or phrase literally denoting one kind of object or idea and applied to another to suggest an analogy, e.g. in the ship ploughs the sea. ➤ **metaphorical** adj, **metaphorically** adv.

metaphysical adj 1 relating to metaphysics. 2 beyond what is physical; supernatural. ➤ **metaphysically** adv.

metaphysics pl n the branch of philosophy concerned with ultimate causes and the underlying nature of things.

mete v (+ out) to allot or inflict (something unpleasant).

meteor n a small particle of matter from space that falls into the earth's atmosphere and is heated by friction so that it glows.

meteoric adj 1 associated with a meteor or meteorite. 2 rapidly and brilliantly successful.

meteorite n a rock from space that reaches the surface of the earth.

meteorology n the science of the atmosphere and its phenomena, esp the weather. ➤ **meteorological** adj, **meteorologist** n.

meter¹ n an instrument for measuring and recording the amount of something used.

meter² v to measure by means of a meter.

meter³ n NAmer see METRE¹, METRE².

methadone n a synthetic drug used as a substitute narcotic in the treatment of heroin addiction and as a painkiller.

methane n a flammable gas that is a product of decomposition of plant or animal matter in marshes and mines, and is used as a fuel.

methanol n a flammable poisonous liquid alcohol that is added to ethyl alcohol to make it unfit to drink.

methinks v (past tense **methought**) archaic it seems to me.

method n 1 a systematic procedure for doing something. 2 an orderly arrangement or system. 3 the habitual practice of orderliness and regularity.

methodical adj done with method or order; systematic. ➤ **methodically** adv.

Methodist n a member of a Christian denomination having an evangelical character. ➤ **Methodism** n.

methodology n (pl **-ies**) a particular set of methods and rules. ➤ **methodological** adj.

meths n Brit, informal methylated spirits.

methylated spirits or **methylated spirit** n alcohol mixed with methanol to make it unfit for drinking.

meticulous adj marked by extreme care over detail. ➤ **meticulously** adv.

métier /'maytyay/ n a person's trade or special talent.

metre¹ (NAmer **meter**) n the basic metric SI unit of length equal to 100 centimetres (about 39.37in.).

metre² (NAmer **meter**) n the rhythm of verse.

metric adj using decimal units of measure.

metrical adj relating to or composed in poetic metre. ➤ **metrically** adv.

metricate v to change (measurements) to the metric system. ➤ **metrication** n.

metric system n a decimal system of weights and measures based on the metre, the litre, and the kilogram.

metric ton or **metric tonne** n a metric unit of weight equal to 1000 kilograms; a tonne.

metro n (pl **-os**) an underground railway system in a city.

metronome n a musicians' device marking the speed of a beat with a regular tick. ➤ **metronomic** adj.

metropolis n the chief city of a country or region.

metropolitan adj relating to a metropolis or a large urban area.

mettle n 1 strength of spirit or temperament. 2 stamina. ✳ **on one's mettle** ready to do one's best.

mew v to utter the high-pitched cry of a cat or gull.

mewl v 1 to cry weakly. 2 to mew.

mews n (pl **mews**) Brit a street or row of houses converted from former stables.

mezzanine n a storey situated between two main storeys of a building.

mezzo /'metsoh/ or **mezzo-soprano** n (pl **-os**) a female singer with a range between soprano and contralto.

Mg abbr the chemical symbol for magnesium.

mg abbr milligram(s).

MHz abbr megahertz.

miaow or **meow** v to make the cry of a cat. ➤ **miaow** n.

miasma n 1 a heavy or foul-smelling vapour. 2 an unhealthy or unpleasant influence or atmosphere.

mica n a silicate material occurring as crystals that separate into thin flexible leaves.

mice n pl of MOUSE.

mickey ✳ **take the mickey** chiefly Brit, informal to tease or ridicule somebody.

microbe n a bacterium or other microorganism. ➤ **microbial** adj.

microbiology n the biology of viruses, bacteria and other microscopic organisms.

microchip n a miniature integrated circuit made with a thin piece of silicon.

microclimate n the climate of a small area or habitat.

microcosm n something regarded as having the characteristics of a larger whole.

microfiche n a sheet of microfilm containing rows of very small images of printed pages.

microfilm n a photographic film on which printed material can be recorded in miniature form.

microlight n chiefly Brit a very small light aircraft for one or two people.

micrometer n an instrument for measuring very small distances.

micro-organism n a bacterium or other organism of microscopic size.

microphone n a device that converts sounds into electrical signals, for transmission or recording.

microprocessor n an integrated circuit forming the central processing unit of a computer.

microscope n an optical instrument used to magnify minute objects.

microscopic adj needing a microscope to be visible or distinguishable. ➤ **microscopically** adv.

microscopy n the use of a microscope.

microsurgery n surgery done under a microscope with very small instruments.

microwave¹ n 1 a band of very short electromagnetic waves of between 0.001m and 0.3m in wavelength. 2 (also **microwave oven**) an oven in which food is heated by means of microwaves.

microwave² v to cook or heat in a microwave oven.

mid¹ adj 1 being in the middle. 2 occupying a middle position.

mid² prep literary amid.

Midas touch n a talent for producing wealth from any activity one takes on.

midday n the middle part of the day; noon.

midden n a pile of dung.

middle¹ adj 1 equally distant from the extremes of something; central. 2 intermediate in rank or quality.

middle² n 1 a middle point or position. 2 informal the waist and abdomen.

middle age n the period of life from about 40 to about 60. ➤ **middle-aged** adj.

Middle Ages pl n (usu **the Middle Ages**) the period of European history from about 1000 to 1500.

middle class n the social class consisting of business and professional people. ➤ **middle-class** adj.

middle ear n a cavity through which sound waves are transmitted from the eardrum to the inner ear.

Middle East n the countries of southwest Asia and northern Africa, including Libya, Egypt, Lebanon, Syria, Israel, Jordan, the states of the Arabian Peninsula, Iran, and Iraq. ➤ **Middle Eastern** adj.

middleman *n* (*pl* **middlemen**) a dealer intermediate between the producer of goods and the retailer or consumer.

middling *adj and adv* of middle or moderate size or degree.

midfield *n* the central part of a playing field between the goals. ➤ **midfielder** *n*.

midge *n* a small fly often found near water.

midget *n* 1 a very small person. 2 (*used before a noun*) smaller than usual.

midland *n* 1 the central region of a country. 2 (**the Midlands**) the central inland region of England.

midnight *n* twelve o'clock at night.

midriff *n* the middle part of the human torso.

midship *n* the middle section of a ship or boat.

midshipman *n* (*pl* **midshipmen**) a person training to become a naval officer in the Royal Navy.

midships *adv and adj* amidships.

midst¹ *n archaic* the inner or central part of something.

midst² *prep archaic* amid.

midstream *n* the part of a stream towards the middle. ✳ **in midstream** in the middle of a process.

midsummer *n* 1 the period around the middle of summer. 2 the summer solstice.

Midsummer Day *or* **Midsummer's Day** *n* 24 June.

midterm *n* the period around the midpoint of an academic term, a term of office, or a pregnancy.

midway *adv and adj* halfway.

midweek *n* the middle of the week. ➤ **midweek** *adj and adv.*

midwife *n* (*pl* **midwives**) a nurse trained to assist women in childbirth. ➤ **midwifery** *n*.

midwinter *n* 1 the period around the middle of winter. 2 the winter solstice.

mien *n* a person's air or bearing.

miff *v informal* to annoy or upset slightly. ➤ **miffed** *adj.*

might¹ *v past tense of* MAY¹ 1 used to express permission or possibility. 2 used to express a polite question.

might² *n* great power or strength.

mightn't *contraction* might not.

mighty *adj* (**-ier, -iest**) very powerful or strong. ➤ **mightily** *adv*, **mightiness** *n*.

migraine *n* a recurrent severe headache usu associated with nausea and disturbances of vision.

migrant *n* 1 an animal that migrates. 2 a person who moves regularly to find seasonal work. ➤ **migrant** *adj.*

migrate *v* 1 of an animal: to pass seasonally from one region to another for feeding or breeding. 2 of a person: to move from one country or locality to another. ➤ **migration** *n*, **migratory** *adj.*

mike *n informal* a microphone.

milch *adj* of a domestic animal: bred or used for its milk.

mild¹ *adj* 1 gentle in nature or manner. 2 not severe. 3 not strong in flavour or effect. 4 not acutely felt or strongly expressed. 5 of the weather: quite warm. ➤ **mildly** *adv*, **mildness** *n*.

mild² *n Brit* a dark-coloured beer not flavoured with hops.

mildew *n* a whitish fungal growth on the surface of organic matter, e.g. paper or leather, ➤ **mildewed** *adj.*

mile *n* 1 (*also* **statute mile**) a unit of distance equal to 1760yd (about 1.61km). 2 = NAUTICAL MILE. 3 (*often in pl*) a large distance. ✳ **be miles away** to be inattentive.

mileage *or* **milage** *n* 1 a distance covered in miles. 2 *informal* an advantage or benefit.

mileometer *or* **milometer** *n Brit* an instrument fitted in vehicle to record its mileage.

miles *adv informal* very much: *That's miles better.*

milestone *n* 1 a stone serving as a milepost. 2 a significant stage in development.

milieu /'meelyuh, meel'yuh/ *n* (*pl* **milieus** *or* **milieux**) a person's social environment.

militant *adj* forcefully or aggressively active in a cause. ➤ **militancy** *n*, **militant** *n*, **militantly** *adv.*

militarism *n* a policy of aggressive military preparedness. ➤ **militarist** *n*, **militaristic** *adj.*

militarize *or* **-ise** *v* to equip with military forces and defences.

military¹ *adj* relating to soldiers and warfare. ➤ **militarily** *adv.*

military² *n* (**the military**) a country's armed forces.

militate *v* (*usu* + against) to have a significant effect in preventing or countering.

Usage Note: Do not confuse this word with *mitigate*, which means 'to make less harsh or intense'.

militia *n* a body of people who are not professional soldiers but are called on to fight in an emergency. ➤ **militiaman** *n*.

milk¹ *n* 1 a white liquid produced by female mammals to feed their young. 2 the milk of cows, goats, etc used as food for humans. 3 the juice of a plant or a coconut.

milk² *v* 1 to draw milk from (an animal). 2 to draw full advantage from (a situation or person). 3 to extract money from (somebody) over a period of time.

milk chocolate *n* solid chocolate made with added milk.

milk float *n Brit* a light electrically powered vehicle for carrying milk for domestic delivery.

milkmaid *n archaic* a girl or woman who works in a dairy.

mindless

milkman n (pl **milkmen**) a man who sells or delivers milk.

milk round n Brit a regular route for delivering milk.

milk shake n a drink made from milk blended or whisked with a flavouring syrup.

milksop n a weak and timid person.

milk tooth n a first tooth of a child, replaced when it is older.

milky adj (-ier, -iest) **1** containing milk. **2** resembling milk in colour or consistency. **3** cloudy or semi-opaque. ➤ **milkily** adv, **milkiness** n.

Milky Way n the galaxy of which the earth is a part, seen as a broad band of faint light stretching across the sky.

mill[1] n **1** a machine or building for grinding grain into flour. **2** a device for crushing or grinding coffee beans or peppercorns. **3** a building with machinery for manufacturing. * **go/be put through the mill** to undergo a trying experience.

mill[2] v **1** to grind in a mill. **2** to shape or dress (metal) by means of a rotary cutter. **3** to give a raised rim or a ridged edge to (a coin). **4** (+ about/around) to move in a confused mass.

millenary[1] n (pl **-ies**) **1** a period of a thousand years. **2** a thousandth anniversary.

millenary[2] adj consisting of a thousand.

millennium n (pl **millennia** or **millenniums**) **1** a period of a thousand years. **2** a thousandth anniversary. **3** the date on which one period of a thousand years ends and another begins. ➤ **millennial** adj.

Usage Note: Millennium is spelt with two l's and two n's.

miller n a person who owns or works a grain mill.

millet n a cereal cultivated for grain and used as food.

millibar n a unit of pressure equal to 1000th of a bar.

milligram or **milligramme** n one thousandth of a gram.

millilitre (NAmer **milliliter**) n one thousandth of a litre (0.002 pints).

millimetre (NAmer **millimeter**) n one thousandth of a metre (about 0.039in.).

milliner n a person who makes or sells women's hats. ➤ **millinery** n.

million n (pl **millions** or **million**) **1** the number 1,000,000 (10^6). **2** informal (also in pl) a very large number. ➤ **millionth** adj and n.

millionaire or **millionairess** n a person whose wealth is estimated at a million or more pounds or dollars.

millipede n an invertebrate animal with a segmented body and two pairs of legs on each segment.

millisecond n one thousandth of a second.

millpond n a pond produced by damming a stream to produce a head of water for operating a mill.

millstone n **1** each of a pair of circular stones that rotate against each other to grind grain. **2** a heavy responsibility.

mill wheel n a water-powered wheel that drives a mill.

milometer n see MILEOMETER.

mime[1] n **1** the art of portraying a character or telling a story by gesture and body movement. **2** a performance of mime.

mime[2] v **1** to act a part with mime. **2** to pretend to sing or play a musical instrument against a recording.

mimic[1] v (**mimicked, mimicking**) **1** to imitate (a person or their mannerisms). **2** to ridicule by imitation. **3** to simulate (something). **4** in biology, to resemble (something) by mimicry.

mimic[2] n somebody or something that mimics others.

mimosa n an acacia tree with sweetly scented yellow flowers in compact globular clusters.

minaret n a slender tower attached to a mosque, with balconies from which Muslims are summoned to prayer.

minatory adj formal menacing; threatening.

mince[1] v **1** to cut or chop (meat) into very small pieces. **2** to walk with short steps in an affected manner. * **not mince one's words** to speak honestly and frankly. ➤ **mincer** n.

mince[2] n chiefly Brit minced meat.

mincemeat n a mixture of dried fruit, suet, and spices, used as a pie filling.

mind[1] n **1** the conscious and unconscious mental processes of an organism that result in reasoning, thinking, perceiving, etc. **2** recollection or memory. **3** an intention or desire. **4** an opinion or view. * **bear/keep in mind** to think of or remember (something). **change one's mind** to alter a decision or opinion. **on one's mind** occupying or troubling one. **out of one's mind** insane or overcome with worry.

mind[2] v **1** to be concerned or care about. **2** to give protective care to. **3** to object to. **4** to attend to (something) closely. **5** to pay attention to or follow (advice or orders). **6** to be careful or sure to do (something). **7** to be cautious about (something). **8** (often + out) to be attentive or wary.

minded adj inclined or disposed.

minder n **1** a person who looks after somebody or something. **2** chiefly Brit, informal a bodyguard.

mindful adj (often + of) keeping something in mind; aware of something.

mindless adj **1** involving no proper thought or concentration. **2** (+ of) inattentive to or heedless of something. ➤ **mindlessly** adv.

mindset n a habitual way of thinking about something.

mine[1] pron the one or ones that belong to or are associated with the speaker or writer.

mine[2] n 1 an excavation from which mineral substances are taken. 2 a rich source of something. 3 an encased explosive placed in the ground or sea and detonated by contact. 4 an underground passage beneath an enemy position.

mine[3] v 1 to obtain (ore, coal, etc) from a mine. 2 to dig into (the earth) for ore, coal, etc. 3 to place military mines in or on. ➤ **miner** n.

minefield n 1 an area where explosive mines have been laid. 2 a highly fraught or hazardous situation.

miner n a person who works in a mine.

mineral n 1 a solid inorganic substance. 2 any of various naturally occurring substances, e.g. stone, coal, or petroleum.

mineralogy n the scientific study of minerals. ➤ **mineralogical** adj, **mineralogist** n.

mineral water n water impregnated with mineral salts or gases.

minestrone /mini'strohni/ n a rich Italian soup containing vegetables and pasta.

minesweeper n a ship designed for removing or neutralizing explosive mines.

mingle v 1 to bring or mix together. 2 to go among a group of people.

mingy adj (-ier, -iest) informal mean or miserly.

mini[1] n (pl minis) a miniskirt.

mini[2] adj small of its kind; miniature.

miniature[1] n 1 a much smaller copy or representation. 2 something that is small of its kind. 3 a tiny portrait on ivory or metal. ➤ **miniaturist** n.

miniature[2] adj much smaller than the usual size.

miniaturize or **-ise** v 1 to design or construct as a small copy. 2 to reduce in scale.

minibar n a small refrigerator containing drinks in a hotel room.

minibus n a small bus for about ten passengers.

minicab n a taxi that can be hired by telephone but not hailed in the street.

MiniDisc n trademark a small CD for recording sound or data.

minim n a musical note with the time value of two crotchets.

minimal adj being a minimum; constituting the least possible. ➤ **minimally** adv.

minimalism n the use of minimal devices or resources in art, music, and design. ➤ **minimalist** n and adj.

minimize or **-ise** v 1 to reduce to a minimum. 2 to represent at less than true importance or value.

minimum[1] n (pl minima or minimums) the least possible quantity or value.

minimum[2] adj least in amount or number.

minion n derog a minor employee or official.

miniskirt n a very short skirt.

minister[1] n 1 a member of the clergy in a Protestant or nonconformist Church. 2 a head of a government department. 3 a diplomatic representative accredited to a foreign state. ➤ **ministerial** adj.

minister[2] v (+ to) to give assistance or care to.

ministrations pl n provision of assistance or care.

ministry n (pl -ies) 1 a government department headed by a minister. 2 the period of government of one Prime Minister. 3 the office or functions of a minister of religion.

mink n (pl minks or mink) a small mammal having a thick coat of soft fur.

minnow n (pl minnows or minnow) a small dark-coloured freshwater fish.

minor[1] adj 1 inferior in importance, size, or rank. 2 not serious or dangerous. 3 esp of a musical scale: having semitones between the second and third, fifth and sixth, or seventh and eighth notess.

minor[2] n a person who has not reached the age of legal responsibility.

minority n (pl -ies) 1 the smaller of two groups forming a whole. 2 a group of people sharing characteristics or interests that differ from those of the majority.

minster n a large or important church.

minstrel n a medieval singer, poet, or musician.

mint[1] n 1 a plant with a characteristic strong taste and smell, used as a flavouring. 2 the flavour of mint. 3 a sweet flavoured with peppermint. ➤ **minty** adj.

mint[2] n 1 a place where coins or medals are made. 2 informal a large sum of money. * **in mint condition** new and unblemished.

mint[3] v to make (coins or medals) by stamping metal.

minuet n a slow graceful dance in triple time.

minus[1] prep 1 reduced or subtracted by. 2 informal without.

minus[2] n (pl minuses) 1 (also minus sign) the symbol (–) used to indicate subtraction or a negative quantity. 2 a deficiency or defect.

minus[3] adj 1 less than zero; negative. 2 involving a disadvantage. 3 falling lower than the specified grade. 4 of or having a negative electric charge.

minuscule adj very small.

Usage Note: The spelling is minuscule, not mini-.

---

minute[1] n 1 a unit of time equal to one sixtieth of an hour. 2 a unit of angular measurement equal to one sixtieth of a degree. 3 informal a short space of time. 4 a short note or memorandum. 5 (in pl) the official record of the proceedings of a meeting.

minute² v 1 to make a summary of (a meeting). 2 to send a minute to.

minute³ adj 1 extremely small. 2 painstaking and careful over details. ➤ **minutely** adv.

minutiae pl n small or precise details.

minx n a flirtatious or cheeky girl or young woman.

miracle n 1 an extraordinary event that is attributed to divine intervention. 2 a remarkable example or instance of something.

miracle play n a medieval drama based on episodes from the Bible.

miraculous adj 1 of the nature of a miracle. 2 evoking wonder; marvellous. ➤ **miraculously** adv.

mirage n 1 an optical illusion appearing esp as a pool of water or as the reflection of distant objects and caused by the reflection of rays of light by a layer of heated air. 2 something illusory and unattainable.

mire¹ n 1 a tract of soft waterlogged ground. 2 a situation of great difficulty or complexity. ➤ **miry** adj.

mire² v 1 to sink or stick fast in a mire. 2 to be in a difficult or complex situation.

mirror¹ n 1 a surface that forms images by reflection. 2 something that gives a true representation.

mirror² v 1 to reflect in a mirror. 2 to represent or correspond to exactly.

mirror image n something that has its parts arranged in reverse in comparison with an otherwise identical thing.

mirth n cheerful amusement. ➤ **mirthful** adj.

mis- prefix 1 bad or badly; wrong or wrongly: misbehave. 2 not: misunderstand.

misadventure n 1 a misfortune or mishap. 2 (also **death by misadventure**) in law, death due to an action not intended to cause harm.

misalliance n an unsuitable alliance or marriage.

misanthrope or **misanthropist** n a person who hates or distrusts other people. ➤ **misanthropic** adj, **misanthropy** n.

misapprehend v to misunderstand. ➤ **misapprehension** n.

misappropriate v to take (something) dishonestly. ➤ **misappropriation** n.

misbegotten adj not well thought out or planned.

misbehave v to behave badly. ➤ **misbehaviour** n.

miscalculate v to calculate or assess wrongly. ➤ **miscalculation** n.

miscarriage n the expulsion of a human foetus before it is able to survive outside the womb. * **miscarriage of justice** a failure to achieve justice in a law court.

miscarry v (-ies, -ied) 1 to have a miscarriage. 2 to fail or go wrong.

miscast v (past tense and past part. **miscast**) to cast (an actor) in an unsuitable role.

miscellaneous adj consisting of diverse items.

miscellany n (pl -ies) a collection of various things.

mischance n bad luck.

mischief n 1 playful or disruptive misbehaviour. 2 a person who misbehaves. 3 something that causes inconvenience or disruption.

mischievous adj 1 disruptively playful. 2 playfully provocative; arch. 3 able or tending to cause annoyance or minor injury. ➤ **mischievously** adv.

Usage Note. Note the spelling with -ie-, and -ous not -ious.

---

miscible adj of liquids: capable of being mixed together.

misconceive v to fail to understand correctly.

misconception n a false or mistaken idea or understanding.

misconduct n bad or improper behaviour.

misconstrue v (**misconstrues**, **misconstrued**, **misconstruing**) to misinterpret or misunderstand. ➤ **misconstruction** n.

miscreant n a person who behaves badly or criminally.

misdeed n a wrong deed; an offence.

misdemeanour (NAmer **misdemeanor**) n a minor offence or wrongdoing that does not amount to a crime.

misdiagnose v to diagnose wrongly.

misdirect v to direct wrongly or inappropriately. ➤ **misdirection** n.

miser n a person who hoards money and lives meanly.

miserable adj 1 pitifully unhappy and distressed. 2 habitually gloomy or morose. 3 wretchedly inadequate or meagre. 4 causing great discomfort or unhappiness. 5 shameful or contemptible. ➤ **miserably** adv.

misericord n a ledge on the underside of the hinged seat of a choir stall to support the occupant in a standing position when the seat is turned up.

miserly adj 1 characteristic of a miser; mean. 2 of an amount: small and inadequate. ➤ **miserliness** n.

misery n (pl -ies) 1 great unhappiness or distress. 2 a cause of this. 3 chiefly Brit, informal a gloomy or morose person.

misfire v 1 of an engine: to fail to ignite the fuel at the proper time. 2 of a gun: to fail to fire. 3 to fail to have the intended effect.

misfit n 1 a person who is poorly adjusted to their environment. 2 something that fits badly.

misfortune n 1 bad luck. 2 an unfortunate incident or event.

misgiving n a feeling of doubt or suspicion.

misguided adj directed by mistaken ideas or motives.

mishandle v 1 to treat roughly; to maltreat. 2 to mismanage (a situation).

mishap n an unfortunate accident.

mishear v (*past tense and past part.* **misheard**) to hear wrongly.

mishit v (**mishitting**, *past tense and past part.* **mishit**) to hit or kick (a ball) badly.

mishmash n *informal* a hotchpotch or jumble.

misinform v to give untrue or misleading information to. ➤ **misinformation** n.

misinterpret v (**misinterpreted**, **misinterpreting**) to understand or explain wrongly. ➤ **misinterpretation** n.

misjudge v 1 to estimate wrongly. 2 to have an unjustly bad opinion of. ➤ **misjudgment** n.

mislay v (*past tense and past part.* **mislaid**) to put or leave (something) in a place that you later forget.

mislead v (*past tense and past part.* **misled**) to lead (somebody) into a mistaken action or belief. ➤ **misleading** adj.

mismanage v to manage wrongly or incompetently. ➤ **mismanagement** n.

mismatch[1] v to match (people or things) incorrectly or unsuitably, e.g. in marriage.

mismatch[2] n a poor or unsuitable match.

misnomer n 1 an incorrect or inappropriate name. 2 the wrong use of a name.

misogynist n a man who hates women. ➤ **misogynistic** adj, **misogyny** n.

misplace v to put in the wrong place.

misplaced adj 1 directed towards an unsuitable object or outcome. 2 wrong or inappropriate.

misprint[1] n a printing error.

misprint[2] v to print incorrectly.

mispronounce v to pronounce wrongly. ➤ **mispronunciation** n.

misquote v to quote or repeat incorrectly. ➤ **misquotation** n.

misread v (*past tense and past part.* **misread**) to read or interpret incorrectly.

misrepresent v to give an untrue or misleading account of. ➤ **misrepresentation** n.

misrule[1] v to rule (a nation, etc) incompetently; to misgovern.

misrule[2] n lack of government or of good government.

miss[1] v 1 to fail to hit, reach, meet, catch, or attain. 2 to feel the absence of. 3 to escape or avoid. 4 (*often* + out) to leave out; to omit. 5 to fail to understand. 6 to fail to attend or be present at. 7 to be too late to catch (a bus, train, etc). * **miss out on** to fail to have or experience. **miss the boat** *informal* to fail to take advantage of an opportunity.

miss[2] n a failure to hit, catch, or achieve something.

Miss n 1 used as a form of address to a girl or unmarried woman. 2 used as a term of address to a female schoolteacher.

missal n a book containing the liturgy for the Roman Catholic mass for the year.

misshapen adj unnaturally shaped; deformed.

missile n 1 an object thrown or projected so as to hit something. 2 a self-propelled weapon that travels through the air.

missing adj 1 absent or lost. 2 not confirmed as alive or dead.

mission n 1 a specific task assigned to a person or group. 2 a group sent to a foreign country to negotiate or advise. 3 a permanent embassy or legation. 4 a military or scientific task or undertaking. 5 a religious ministry propagating its faith abroad. 6 a calling or vocation.

missionary[1] n (pl **-ies**) a person in charge of a religious mission.

missionary[2] adj relating to or engaged in a religious mission.

missive n *formal* a letter.

misspell v (*past tense* **misspelt**, *past part.* **misspelt** *or* **misspelled**) to spell incorrectly. ➤ **misspelling** n.

misspend v (*past tense and past part.* **misspent**) to spend (money or time) wrongly or unwisely.

missus *or* **missis** n 1 *informal* a person's wife. 2 *informal* a form of address to a married woman.

mist[1] n 1 water in the form of tiny particles in the atmosphere. 2 condensed water vapour on a surface.

mist[2] v to cover or be covered with mist.

mistake[1] v (**mistook**, **mistaken**) 1 to misunderstand the meaning or significance of. 2 to estimate wrongly. 3 to identify wrongly. 4 to confuse (somebody or something) with another.

mistake[2] n 1 an incorrect action, statement, or conclusion. 2 a misunderstanding of the meaning or significance of something.

mistaken adj 1 based on wrong thinking; incorrect. 2 of a person: wrong in opinion. ➤ **mistakenly** adv.

mister n 1 (**Mister**) = MR. 2 (*often* **Mister**) a generalized informal form of address to a man.

mistime v to do or say at a wrong or inappropriate time.

mistletoe n a shrub that grows as a parasite on trees and has thick leaves and waxy white berries.

mistreat v to treat badly or unkindly. ➤ **mistreatment** n.

mistress n 1 a woman in a position of power or authority. 2 a woman who has achieved mastery of a subject. 3 a woman with whom a married man has a sexual relationship outside marriage. 4 *chiefly Brit* a female schoolteacher.

mistrial n a trial declared void because of an error in the proceedings.

mistrust[1] v to have no trust in.

mistrust[2] n a lack of trust. ➤ **mistrustful** adj.

misty adj (**-ier**, **-iest**) 1 covered with or

obscured by mist. **2** consisting of or marked by mist. **3** indistinct or blurred.

misunderstand v (*past tense and past part.* **misunderstood**) to fail to understand correctly.

misuse[1] v **1** to use wrongly. **2** to abuse or maltreat.

misuse[2] n **1** incorrect or improper use. **2** abuse.

mite n **1** a minute invertebrate animal related to the spiders and ticks. **2** a small child or animal. **3** a very small amount. ✳ **a mite** *informal* slightly, somewhat.

mitigate v to make less harsh or intense. ➤ **mitigation** n.

Usage Note: Do not confuse this word with *militate*, which means 'to have a significant effect in preventing or counteracting'.

---

mitre[1] (*NAmer* **miter**) n **1** a tall pointed divided hat worn by bishops. **2** a joint made by cutting two pieces of wood to form a right angle when fitted together.

mitre[2] (*NAmer* **miter**) v **1** to cut (wood) to form a mitre. **2** to join in a mitre.

mitt n **1** a glove that leaves the ends of the fingers uncovered. **2** a mitten. **3** *informal* a person's hand.

mitten n a covering for the hand and wrist that has one section for all four fingers and another for the thumb.

mix[1] v **1** to combine or blend into one mass. **2** to combine (one ingredient) with others. **3** to prepare by mixing ingredients. **4** to control the balance of (various sounds) during a recording. **5** to enjoy a varied social life.

mix[2] n **1** a mixture or combination. **2** a commercially prepared mixture of food ingredients. **3** the proportion in which elements are mixed. **4** a version of a musical recording that has been mixed to produce a different type of sound from the original.

mixed *adj* **1** combining diverse elements. **2** involving people of different sexes or races. **3** including or accompanied by conflicting or dissimilar elements.

mixed bag n a miscellaneous assortment.

mixer n **1** a device or machine for mixing something. **2** a soft drink for mixing with an alcoholic one. **3** an electronic device for combining sound from several sources in a recording.

mixture n **1** the act or an instance of mixing. **2** a combination or blend produced by mixing. **3** a combination of components that retain their own properties. **4** the proportion of fuel to air supplied to an engine.

mix up v **1** to mistake or confuse (somebody or something) for another. **2** to make untidy or disordered. ✳ **be/get mixed up in** to be involved in an illegal or suspect activity.

mix-up n *informal* a state or instance of confusion.

mizzen *or* **mizen** n the mast behind the mainmast in a sailing vessel.

ml *abbr* **1** mile(s). **2** millilitre.

mm *abbr* millimetre.

MMR *abbr* measles, mumps, and rubella (vaccination).

Mn *abbr* the chemical symbol for manganese.

mnemonic[1] *adj* helping to remember something.

mnemonic[2] n a word or code that helps to remember something.

mnemonics *pl* n a system for improving the memory.

Mo *abbr* the chemical symbol for molybdenum.

moan[1] n **1** a low prolonged sound of pain or grief. **2** a mournful sound made by the wind. **3** *informal* a minor complaint.

moan[2] v **1** to produce a moan. **2** *informal* to complain or grumble.

moat n a deep trench, usu filled with water, round a castle or fortified place.

mob[1] n **1** (*also before a noun*) a disorderly or riotous crowd. **2** *Brit, informal* a particular group of people. **3** (**the mob**) the ordinary populace. **4** (*usu* **the Mob**) *chiefly NAmer* the Mafia.

mob[2] v (**mobbed, mobbing**) **1** to attack in a large crowd or group. **2** to crowd round (somebody).

mobile[1] *adj* **1** capable of moving or being moved. **2** of a library, shop, etc: set up in a vehicle and able to move from place to place. **3** *informal* having the use of a vehicle for transport. **4** of people: able to move to a different location or job. **5** of features: readily expressing different moods. ➤ **mobility** n.

mobile[2] n **1** a decoration with suspended parts moved by air currents. **2** (*also* **mobile phone**) a portable telephone for use in a cellular radio system.

mobilize *or* **-ise** v **1** to prepare and assemble (troops) for active service. **2** to organize (people or resources) for action. ➤ **mobilization** n.

mobster n *informal* a member of a criminal gang.

moccasin n a soft leather shoe with the sole brought up the sides of the foot and joined to a U-shaped top piece.

mocha n **1** a coffee of fine quality. **2** a flavouring obtained from coffee or from coffee and chocolate.

mock[1] v **1** to ridicule or deride. **2** to copy or mimic in fun or derision.

mock[2] n (*also in pl*) a school examination used as practice for a public one.

mock[3] *adj* **1** not real; imitation. **2** of a battle, examination, etc: simulated for practice or training.

mockery n (pl -ies) **1** contemptuous words or ridicule. **2** an object of derision or ridicule. **3** a deceitful imitation; a travesty. ✳ **make a mockery of something** to make something look foolish or pointless.

mockingbird n an American songbird that imitates the calls of other birds.

mock-up n a full-sized model or representation for study or testing.

modal adj relating to form or structure, as opposed to substance or content.

modal auxiliary verb n in grammar, a verb that helps another verb to express what is possible or necessary, e.g. will, shall, should, would, may, might.

mode n **1** a way of doing something. **2** a prevailing fashion or style.

model[1] n **1** a three-dimensional replica of something. **2** an example used for reproducing or copying. **3** an outstanding example to be followed. **4** a person who poses for an artist or photographer. **5** a person who displays clothing by wearing it. **6** a type or design of an article or product.

model[2] v (**modelled, modelling**, NAmer **modeled, modeling**) **1** to shape in a mouldable material. **2** to produce a model of. **3** (often + on) to plan or construct(something) in imitation of something else. **4** to work as a fsahion model.

modem n a device that connects a computer to a telephone line.

moderate[1] adj **1** calm, mild, or temperate. **2** avoiding extreme political or social measures; not radical. **3** average in quality, amount, degree, or extent. ➤ **moderately** adv.

moderate[2] v **1** to decrease in violence or severity. **2** to ensure consistency of grading in (examination papers or results).

moderate[3] n a person who holds moderate views.

moderation n **1** the process of moderating. **2** the avoidance of extremes in behaviour and attitudes.

moderator n **1** a person who resolves disagreements. **2** a person who presides over an assembly or debate. **3** a person who moderates examination papers.

modern adj **1** relating to the present or immediate past. **2** involving recent techniques or ideas. ➤ **modernity** n.

modernism n **1** modern ideas practices, or styles. **2** a new direction in the arts or religion involving a break with the past. ➤ **modernist** n and adj, **modernistic** adj.

modernize or **-ise** v to adapt to modern ideas or practices. ➤ **modernization** n.

modest adj **1** showing a moderate estimate of one's abilities or worth. **2** small or limited in size, amount, or aim. **3** observant of proprieties; decent. ➤ **modestly** adv, **modesty** n.

modicum n a small or limited amount.

modification n **1** a small or limited change. **2** the making of a change.

modifier n **1** a word that qualifies the meaning of another, e.g. horror in horror film. **2** somebody or something that modifies.

modify v (**-ies, -ied**) to make minor changes in.

modish adj fashionable or stylish.

modular adj consisting of or made from separate parts.

modulate v **1** to vary (the voice) in tone, pitch, etc. **2** to keep in proper measure or proportion. **3** to vary the amplitude, frequency, or phase of (a wave) to match the variations of another. **4** in music, to pass from one key to another. ➤ **modulation** n.

module n **1** any of a set of standardized units that are combined to form a structure. **2** a unit of an educational course, treating a specific subject or topic. **3** an independent unit forming part of a space vehicle.

moggie or **moggy** n (pl -ies) Brit, informal a cat.

mogul n informal a wealthy or powerful person.

mohair n a fabric or yarn made from the hair of the Angora goat.

Mohican n a hairstyle in which the head is shaved except for a central strip of erect hair.

moiety n (pl -ies) a half.

moist adj slightly wet; damp. ➤ **moisten** v.

moisture n liquid diffused as vapour or condensed as tiny droplets.

moisturize or **-ise** v to add moisture to. ➤ **moisturizer** n.

molar n a grinding tooth towards the back of the jaw.

molasses n **1** a dark syrup left after refining raw sugar. **2** NAmer treacle or golden syrup.

mold[1] n NAmer see MOULD[1].

mold[2] v NAmer see MOULD[2].

mold[3] n NAmer see MOULD[3].

mold[4] n NAmer see MOULD[4].

mole[1] n **1** a small burrowing mammal with tiny eyes, concealed ears, and soft fur. **2** a spy operating from a well-established position of trust within an organization.

mole[2] n a dark spot on the skin.

mole[3] n **1** a solid structure laid in the sea as a pier or breakwater. **2** a harbour formed by a mole.

mole[4] or **mol** n the SI unit equal to the amount of a substance that contains the same number of atoms, molecules, ions, etc as there are atoms in 0.012kg of carbon.

molecule n the smallest unit of a substance, usu consisting of two or more bonded atoms.

molehill n a mound of earth thrown up by a burrowing mole.

moleskin n **1** the skin of a mole used as fur. **2** a heavy cotton fabric with a velvety nap on one side.

molest v **1** to pester unpleasantly. **2** to abuse sexually. ➤ **molestation** n, **molester** n.

moll n informal a gangster's female companion.

mollify v (-ies, -ied) **1** to lessen the anger or hostility of. **2** to reduce in intensity or severity. ➤ **mollification** n.

mollusc (NAmer **mollusk**) n an animal with a soft unsegmented body often enclosed in a shell, e.g. snails, shellfish, and squids.

mollycoddle v to treat with excessive indulgence or protection.

molt v NAmer see MOULT.

molten adj liquefied by heat; melted.

molto adv in music: very.

molybdenum n a hard silver-white metallic element.

mom n NAmer, informal = MUM[1].

moment n **1** a brief interval of time. **2** a specific point in time. **3** formal importance. **4** a tendency to produce rotational motion.

momentarily adv **1** for a short time. **2** chiefly NAmer very soon or immediately.

momentary adj lasting a short time; transitory.

momentous adj of great consequence or significance.

momentum n (pl **momenta**) the tendency to continue onwards possessed by a moving object.

mommy n (pl **-ies**) = MOM.

monarch n a person who reigns over a kingdom or empire. ➤ **monarchical** adj.

monarchism n the principle of monarchy, or support for it. ➤ **monarchist** n and adj.

monarchy n (pl **-ies**) **1** a state with a monarch as head of state. **2** the institution of a sovereign and royal family.

monastery n (pl **-ies**) a community of monks or the buildings they occupy.

monastic adj **1** relating to monks or nuns. **2** resembling life in a monastery. ➤ **monasticism** n.

Monday n the day of the week following Sunday.

monetarism n an economic theory that the best way of controlling the economy is by restricting the money supply. ➤ **monetarist** n and adj.

monetary adj relating to money.

money n (pl **-eys** or **-ies**) **1** coins or paper currency used as a means of payment. **2** payment. **3** wealth. **4** (in pl) a sum or sums of money.

moneyed or **monied** adj having a lot of money.

money order n a postal order issued by a bank.

money spider n a tiny spider supposedly bringing good fortune.

Mongol n a member of certain peoples of Mongolia, northern China, and central Asia.

mongoose n (pl **mongooses**) an African and Asian mammal with grey-brown fur, short legs, and a long tail.

mongrel n a dog of no recognized breed.

moniker or **monicker** n informal a name or nickname.

monitor[1] n **1** a pupil appointed to help a teacher. **2** a person or machine that monitors. **3** a receiver with a screen used to view data from a television or computer. **4** a large tropical lizard.

monitor[2] v to observe or record over a period of time.

monk n a male member of a religious order living under vows of poverty and chastity.

monkey[1] n **1** a primate with a long tail living in trees in tropical countries. **2** informal a mischievous child.

monkey[2] v informal **1** (often + about/around) to act in a silly or mischievous manner. **2** to meddle or tamper with.

monkey business n informal mischievous or underhand activity.

monkey nut n Brit a peanut.

monkey-puzzle n a South American evergreen tree with a network of branches covered with spirals of stiff sharp leaves.

monkey wrench n a large spanner with adjustable jaws.

mono n monophonic sound reproduction.

monochrome adj **1** reproduced in shades of black and white, or of a single colour. **2** lacking in variety or interest. ➤ **monochromatic** adj.

monocle n a single lens for one eye.

monogamy n the practice of being married to one person at any time. ➤ **monogamous** adj.

monogram n a design formed of the interwoven initials of a name. ➤ **monogrammed** adj.

monograph n a short book on a specialized subject.

monolingual adj knowing or using only one language.

monolith n **1** a single large block of stone. **2** a complex structure or organization.

monolithic adj **1** formed of a single large block of stone. **2** forming a large complex whole.

monologue n **1** a long speech by an actor alone on stage. **2** a long tedious speech that monopolizes a conversation.

monomania n an obsessive preoccupation with a single idea. ➤ **monomaniac** n and adj.

monomer n any of the identical units that combine to form a polymer. ➤ **monomeric** adj.

monophonic adj denoting a sound system using only one channel.

monoplane n an aeroplane with one main pair of wings.

monopolize or **-ise** v to assume exclusive control or use of.

monopoly n (pl **-ies**) **1** exclusive ownership or control of a commodity or market. **2** a person or group having a monopoly. **3** something controlled by a monopoly. **4** exclusive control or use of something.

monorail *n* a single rail serving as a track for a wheeled vehicle.

monosyllabic *adj* **1** consisting of one syllable. **2** of a person: using only short words. **3** brief or terse.

monosyllable *n* a word of one syllable.

monotheism *n* the belief that there is only one God. ➤ **monotheistic** *adj*.

monotone *n* **1** a single unvaried musical note. **2** a tedious sameness or repetition.

monotonous *adj* tediously uniform or repetitive. ➤ **monotonously** *adv*, **monotonousness** *n*, **monotony** *n*.

monoxide *n* an oxide containing one atom of oxygen.

monsieur /mə'syuh/ *n* (*pl* **messieurs** /mə'syuh, mə'syuhz/) a title of or form of address to a French man.

monsignor /mon'seenyə, monsee'nyaw/ *n* (*pl* **monsignori** /-'nyawree/) a title for certain high-ranking Roman Catholic priests.

monsoon *n* **1** a seasonal wind of southest Asia blowing from the southwest in summer and the northeast in winter. **2** the season of a monsoon, marked by heavy rains.

monster *n* **1** a terrifying imaginary creature. **2** something exceptionally large of its kind. **3** a wicked or cruel person.

monstrosity *n* (*pl* **-ies**) **1** something deviating wildly from the normal; a monster or freak. **2** an excessively bad or shocking example; a hideous thing.

monstrous *adj* **1** having the qualities or appearance of a monster. **2** extraordinarily large. **3** extraordinarily ugly or vicious. **4** outrageously wrong or ridiculous. **5** shocking; appalling. ➤ **monstrously** *adv*, **monstrousness** *n*.

montage /monh'tahzh/ *n* **1** a picture made by combining or overlapping several separate pictures. **2** a method of film editing in which the chronological sequence of events is interrupted by juxtaposed or rapidly succeeding shots. **3** a film sequence using montage.

month *n* **1** each of the twelve named periods into which the year is divided. **2** a period of four weeks. **3** the interval between the same date in successive months. ✻ **a month of Sundays** *informal* a very long period of time.

monthly[1] *adj* of or occurring every month.

monthly[2] *adv* every month.

monthly[3] *n* (*pl* **-ies**) a periodical published monthly.

monument *n* **1** a memorial stone, or sculpture erected to commemorate a person or event. **2** a structure or site of historical importance. **3** a lasting evidence or reminder of something important.

monumental *adj* **1** serving as a monument. **2** imposing or outstanding. ➤ **monumentally** *adv*.

moo[1] *v* to make the deep noise of a cow.

moo[2] *n* a mooing sound.

mooch *v* *informal* (+ around/about/along) to wander aimlessly or disconsolately.

mood *n* **1** a predominant emotion or frame of mind. **2** a bout of bad temper. **3** a form of a verb used to express a fact, possibility, wish, command, or question.

moody *adj* (**-ier, -iest**) **1** sullen or gloomy. **2** subject to changing moods; temperamental. ➤ **moodily** *adv*, **moodiness** *n*.

moon[1] *n* **1** (**the Moon**) the earth's natural satellite. **2** a satellite of any planet. **3** *literary* a month. ✻ **over the moon** *informal* delighted. ➤ **moonless** *adj*.

moon[2] *v* **1** *informal* (*often* + around/about) to behave or move about listlessly. **2** *informal* to expose one's buttocks to somebody as a joke or insult.

moonlight[1] *n* the light of the moon. ➤ **moonlit** *adj*.

moonlight[2] *v* (*past tense and past part.* **moonlighted**) *informal* to hold a second job in addition to one's regular work, without declaring it to the tax authorities. ➤ **moonlighter** *n*.

moonscape *n* the surface of the moon as a landscape.

moonshine *n* **1** empty talk; nonsense. **2** *NAmer, informal* illegally distilled or smuggled whisky.

moonstone *n* a milky-white translucent feldspar with a pearly lustre.

moony *adj* (**-ier, -iest**) *informal* inanely dreamy.

Moor *n* a member of an African Muslim people. ➤ **Moorish** *adj*.

moor[1] *n* an expanse of open land overgrown by heathers, grasses, etc.

moor[2] *v* to secure (a boat or buoy) in position.

moorhen *n* a blackish bird that nests near fresh water.

mooring *n* **1** (*also in pl*) a place where a ship or boat can be made fast. **2** (*usu in pl*) a rope or chain used to moor a vessel.

moose *n* (*pl* **moose**) a large North American deer related to the elk.

moot[1] *v* to put forward for discussion.

moot[2] *adj* open to question; debatable.

mop[1] *n* **1** a long handle with a head of absorbent material, used for cleaning floors. **2** a shock of untidy hair.

mop[2] *v* (**mopped, mopping**) **1** to clean or wipe with a mop. **2** (*often* + up) to soak up (water or other liquid) with a mop.

mope *v* to become listless or dejected. ➤ **mopy** *adj*.

moped *n* a low-powered motorcycle.

moraine n earth and stones deposited by a glacier.

moral[1] adj 1 relating to the principles of right and wrong in human behaviour. 2 conforming to a standard of right behaviour. ➤ **morally** adv.

moral[2] n 1 a moral or practical lesson to be learned from a story or experience. 2 (in pl) standards of behaviour.

morale n the degree or enthusiasm and loyalty shown by an individual or group.

moralist n a person who is srict about moral principles. ➤ **moralistic** adj.

morality n (pl -ies) 1 right behaviour or moral correctness. 2 degree of conformity to moral standards. 3 a system of moral values or principles.

moralize or **-ise** v to talk tediously or sanctimoniously about matters of morality.

morass n 1 a marsh or swamp. 2 a confused and disorganized situation.

moratorium n (pl **moratoriums** or **moratoria**) a temporary suspension of or ban on an activity or commitment.

morbid adj 1 having an unnatural interest in death or disease. 2 relating to disease. ➤ **morbidity** n, **morbidly** adv.

mordant adj caustic or sharply critical in manner or style.

more[1] adj 1 greater in amount or degree. 2 additional; further.

more[2] adv 1 as an additional amount. 2 to a greater degree, extent, or amount. 3 again: once more. 4 used with an adjective or adverb to form the comparative. ✳ **more or less** somewhat, approximately.

more[3] n a greater or additional amount or part.

morello n (pl -os) a sour cherry with a dark-red skin.

moreover adv in addition to what has been said.

mores pl n the customs of a particular group.

morgue n 1 a mortuary. 2 a collection of information used for writing obituaries in a newspaper office.

moribund adj 1 dying. 2 nearing the end of existence.

Mormon n a member of the Church of Jesus Christ of Latter-Day Saints. ➤ **Mormonism** n.

morn n literary morning.

morning n 1 the time from midnight to noon or sunrise to noon. 2 the dawn.

morning sickness n nausea and vomiting occurring during the earlier months of pregnancy.

moron n informal a stupid person. ➤ **moronic** adj.

morose adj gloomy and bad-tempered. ➤ **morosely** adv.

morph v in cinematography, to change gradually from one image to another.

morphine n a drug made from opium, used as a powerful painkiller.

morris dance n a traditional English dance performed by a group of people wearing costumes and carrying handkerchiefs or small sticks. ➤ **morris dancing** n.

morrow n (usu **the morrow**) archaic or literary the next day.

Morse or **Morse code** n a signalling code in which letters are represented by combinations of short and long sounds or flashes of light.

morsel n a small piece of food.

mortal[1] adj 1 subject to death. 2 of human existence. 3 causing death. 4 of an enemy: relentless until death. 5 intense or severe. ➤ **mortally** adv.

mortal[2] n a human being.

mortality n (pl -ies) 1 the state of being mortal. 2 the death people or animals in large numbers. 3 the number of deaths in a given time or place.

mortal sin n in Christian belief, a serious sin that can lead to damnation.

mortar n 1 a mixture of cement and lime with sand and water, used to join bricks, stones, etc or for plastering. 2 a bowl in which substances are ground with a pestle. 3 a light artillery gun used for firing shells at high angles.

mortarboard n 1 a square board with a handle underneath, used by bricklayers for holding mortar. 2 an academic cap consisting of a close-fitting crown with a stiff flat square on top.

mortgage[1] n 1 an agreement for borrowing money to buy a property, with the property as security. 2 a loan received by this agreement.

mortgage[2] v to assign the ownership of (property) to the lender in a mortgage. ➤ **mortgageable** adj.

mortician n chiefly NAmer an undertaker.

mortify v (-ies, -ied) 1 to subject to feelings of shame or embarrassment. 2 to subdue (bodily desires) by abstinence. ➤ **mortification** n, **mortifying** adj.

mortise[1] or **mortice** n a cavity cut into a piece of wood for receiving the end of another piece.

mortise[2] or **mortice** v 1 to join by a mortise joint. 2 to cut a mortise in.

mortise lock n a lock fitted into a mortise in the edge of a door.

mortuary[1] n (pl -ies) a room or building in which dead bodies are kept before burial or cremation.

mortuary[2] adj of death or the burial of the dead.

mosaic n a pattern or picture made from small pieces of glass or stone.

mosey v (-eys, -eyed) informal (usu + along/around/off) to go in a leisurely or aimless way.

Moslem n see MUSLIM.

mosque n a place of worship for Muslims.

mosquito n (pl -oes or -os) a small two-winged fly which can transmit diseases when sucking the blood of animals and humans.

moss n a mass or small green plants covering a surface. ➤ **mossy** adj.

most¹ adj greatest in amount or degree.

most² adv **1** (often **the most**) to the greatest degree or extent. **2** used with an adjective or adverb to form the superlative. **3** very.

most³ n the greatest amount or part.

mostly adv **1** for the greatest part; mainly. **2** in most cases; usually.

mote n a particle of dust in the air.

motel n a roadside hotel for motorists.

motet n a choral composition on a sacred text.

moth n a flying insect similar to a butterfly, active at night.

mothball¹ n a ball of naphthalene or camphor, used to keep moths from stored clothing, linen, etc. ✽ **in mothballs** suspended or postponed.

mothball² v to set aside or postpone.

moth-eaten adj **1** damaged by moth larvae. **2** worn-out or shabby.

mother¹ n **1** a female parent. **2** a female acting as the parent of a child or offspring. **3** a woman considered as the originator or founder of something. **4** a source, origin, or producer of something. ➤ **motherhood** n.

mother² v often derog to care for or protect lovingly.

mother-in-law n (pl **mothers-in-law**) the mother of one's husband or wife.

mother-of-pearl n a hard pearly substance forming the inner layer of the shells of certain molluscs.

mother tongue n one's native language.

motif n **1** a recurring theme in a work of art, music, or literature. **2** a design or pattern.

motion¹ n **1** the act of changing position; a movement. **2** the way in which a person or thing moves. **3** a gesture. **4** a moving part or mechanism. **5** a formal proposal made for discussion at a meeting. **6** (also in pl) an evacuation of the bowels. ✽ **go through the motions** to carry out an activity half-heartedly or mechanically. ➤ **motionless** adj.

motion² v to direct by a gesture.

motion picture n chiefly NAmer a cinema film.

motivate v to provide with a motive to do something. ➤ **motivator** n.

motivation n **1** something that motivates. **2** enthusiasm or drive. ➤ **motivational** adj.

motive¹ n **1** a need or desire that causes somebody to act. **2** a motif.

motive² adj of or causing motion.

motley¹ adj (-ier, -iest) **1** composed of varied elements. **2** multicoloured.

motley² n **1** the characteristic clothing of mixed colours worn by a jester. **2** a haphazard mixture.

motocross n cross-country motorcycle racing.

motor¹ n **1** any of various machines or devices that transform energy into motion. **2** chiefly Brit a car. **3** (used before a noun) conveying motion or impulses.

motor² v **1** to travel by car. **2** informal to make rapid progress.

motor bike n informal a motorcycle.

motorboat or **motor boat** n a small boat propelled by a motor.

motorcade n a procession of motor vehicles.

motorcycle n a two-wheeled motor vehicle. ➤ **motorcyclist** n.

motorist n somebody who drives a car.

motor vehicle n a road vehicle powered by a motor.

motorway n Brit a major road for high-speed traffic, having separate carriageways each with several lanes.

mottled adj marked with spots or patches of a different colour.

motto n (pl -oes or -os) **1** a short expression of a principle or belief. **2** a humorous or sentimental saying.

mould¹ (NAmer **mold**) n **1** a dish for shaping an object from hot liquid poured into it. **2** a fixed pattern or form. **3** distinctive character or type.

mould² (NAmer **mold**) v **1** to give shape to. **2** to form in a mould. **3** to exert a steady formative influence on.

mould³ (NAmer **mold**) n a growth of minute fungi that forms on the surface of damp or decaying organic matter.

mould⁴ (NAmer **mold**) n crumbling soft soil rich in humus.

moulder (NAmer **molder**) v (often + away) to decay or crumble.

moulding (NAmer **molding**) n a band or strip with moulded designs used for decoration in a building.

moult (NAmer **molt**) v of birds or animals: to shed (hair, feathers, or skin) periodically.

mount¹ v **1** to go up or climb. **2** to seat oneself on a horse or bicycle to ride it. **3** (often + up) to increase in amount or degree. **4** to attach to a support or backing. **5** to organize (a plan or activity).

mount² or **mounting** n **1** something on which a picture or other object is mounted for display or use. **2** a horse for riding.

mount³ n **1** literary a hill. **2** a hill or mountain.

mountain n **1** a tall landmass that is higher than a hill. **2** (also in pl) a vast amount or quantity.

mountaineer n a person who climbs mountains.

mountaineering n the pastime or technique of climbing mountains.

mountainous adj **1** containing many mountains. **2** huge.

mountebank n a swindler or charlatan.

muddle

mourn v to feel or express great sorrow at the death of. ➤ **mourner** n.

mournful adj expressing great sorrow; gloomy or sad. ➤ **mournfully** adv.

mourning n 1 the expression of great sorrow for somebody who has died. 2 black clothes worn while formally mourning.

mouse n (pl **mice**) 1 a small rodent with a pointed snout and a long thin tail. 2 (pl also **mouses**) in computing, a small device operated by hand to direct the cursor on a VDU screen and execute commands by clicking buttons. 3 a shy or timid person.

moussaka or **mousaka** n a Greek dish of minced lamb with aubergines, tomatoes, and a cheese topping.

mousse n 1 a sweet or savoury dish made with whipped egg whites. 2 a frothy cosmetic applied to the hair to hold it in position.

moustache (NAmer **mustache**) n a band of hair growing on a man's upper lip.

mousy or **mousey** adj (-ier, -iest) 1 quiet or stealthy. 2 timid. 3 light greyish brown.

mouth[1] n (pl **mouths**) 1 the opening on the face into which food is put and from which sounds are made. 2 an opening or entrance. 3 the place where a river enters a sea or lake.

mouth[2] v 1 to say insincerely or pompously. 2 to form (words) soundlessly.

mouthful n (pl **mouthfuls**) 1 an amount of food or drink put into the mouth. 2 a long or difficult word or phrase.

mouth organ n a harmonica.

mouthpiece n 1 a part of a musical instrument or a telephone that is put into or next to the mouth. 2 somebody who speaks on another's behalf.

mouthwash n a preparation for cleansing the mouth.

mouth-watering adj 1 appetizing. 2 extremely attractive.

mouthy adj (-ier, -iest) inclined to talk impudently or boastfully.

movable or **moveable** adj 1 capable of being moved. 2 of a church festival: changing date from year to year.

move[1] v 1 to go or move in a particular direction. 2 to change position or shape. 3 to change one's home or place of work. 4 to change to a new activity, topic, etc. 5 to take action or prompt (somebody) to take action. 6 to spend one's time in a particular social environment. 7 to affect emotionally. 8 to propose formally for discussion or consideration. 9 of the bowels: to discharge faeces. ➤ **mover** n.

move[2] n 1 an act of moving; a movement. 2 a step taken to achieve something. 3 a change of home or work. 4 the act of moving a piece in a game. * **get a move on** to hurry up.

movement n 1 the act or process of moving. 2 a particular manner of moving. 3 (in pl) the

activities of a person during a specified time. 4 an organization for achieving a particular objective. 5 a trend or change. 6 the moving parts of a mechanism. 7 a distinct section of a musical composition. 8 an act of emptying the bowels.

move on v to change to a new location, job, etc.

move out v to leave one's home or place of work.

movie n a cinema film.

moving adj causing a strong emotional response. ➤ **movingly** adv.

mow v (past tense **mowed**, past part. **mowed** or **mown**) 1 to cut or trim (grass, hay, etc). 2 to cut down the growth in (a field). ➤ **mower** n.

mow down v to kill or knock down in large numbers.

mozzarella n a moist white Italian curd cheese.

MP abbr Member of Parliament.

Mr n a title used before a man's name.

MRI abbr magnetic resonance imaging, a process for scanning an image of a part of the body.

Mrs n a title used before a married woman's name.

MS abbr 1 manuscript. 2 multiple sclerosis.

Ms n a title used before the name of a woman regardless of her marital status.

MSc abbr Master of Science.

MSP abbr Member of the Scottish Parliament.

Mt[1] abbr Mount.

Mt[2] abbr the chemical symbol for meitnerium.

mu n the twelfth letter of the Greek alphabet (M, μ).

much[1] adj and n 1 a large amount or or extent. 2 used in questions about quantity or extent: how much? * **a bit much** informal rather excessive or unreasonable. **not up to much** not very good.

much[2] adv to a great degree or extent.

muck n 1 moist dirt or filth. 2 soft moist manure. ➤ **mucky** adj.

muck about or **muck around** v Brit, informal 1 to waste time or act in a silly way. 2 (+ with) to interfere with or spoil.

muck in v Brit, informal to share a task or accommodation.

muck out v to remove manure or filth from an animal's quarters.

muck up v informal to bungle or spoil.

mucous adj of or covered with mucus.

mucous membrane n a membrane that secretes mucus, lining the nose and other body passages.

mucus n a thick slimy secretion produced by the mucous membranes.

mud n soft wet or sticky earth. * **sling/throw mud at** to be abusive about.

muddle[1] v 1 to confuse. 2 (often + up) to confuse (two or more people or things) in one's mind. 3 (often + up) to get (things) confused or

muddle

out of order. **4** (+ along/through) to manage with difficulty. ➤ **muddled** adj, **muddly** adj.

muddle² n a state of confusion.

muddleheaded adj mentally confused.

muddy¹ adj (-ier, -iest) **1** covered with mud. **2** obscure or unclear.

muddy² v (-ies, -ied) to make muddy or confused.

mudflap n a flap hung behind the wheel of a vehicle to prevent mud and splashes being thrown up.

mudflat n a muddy area of ground exposed at low tide.

mudguard n a guard over a vehicle wheel to deflect or catch mud.

muesli n (pl mueslis) a breakfast dish of rolled oats, dried fruit, and nuts.

muezzin n a mosque official who calls Muslims to prayer.

muff¹ n a warm cylindrical wrap in which both hands are placed.

muff² v to handle clumsily; to bungle.

muffin n **1** a light round bun, eaten toasted and buttered. **2** NAmer a small round cake.

muffle v **1** (often + up) to wrap up so as to conceal or keep warm. **2** to deaden the sound of.

muffler n **1** a scarf worn round the neck. **2** a device for deadening sound.

mufti¹ n (pl muftis) a professional Muslim jurist.

mufti² n civilian clothes worn by somebody who is normally in uniform.

mug¹ n **1** a large cylindrical drinking cup with a handle. **2** informal the face or mouth. **3** Brit, informal a foolish or gullible person.

mug² v (mugged, mugging) to assault and rob in a public place. ➤ **mugger** n.

muggins n informal oneself, regarded as foolish or gullible.

muggy adj (-ier, -iest) of the weather: warm and close.

mug shot n informal a police photograph of a person's face.

mug up v Brit, informal to study something intensively, e.g. for an exam.

mulatto n (pl -oes or -os) a person who has one black and one white parent.

mulberry n (pl -ies) **1** an edible red, purple, or white fruit resembling a raspberry. **2** a dark purple colour.

mulch¹ n a covering of leaves and compost spread on the ground to enrich the soil.

mulch² v to cover or treat with mulch.

mule¹ n the offspring of female horse and a male donkey.

mule² n a backless shoe or slipper.

mulish adj obstinate.

mull¹ v to sweeten and flavour (warmed wine or beer) with spices.

mull² n crumbly soil humus forming a layer on top of mineral soil.

mullah n a Muslim trained in traditional Islamic law and doctrine.

mullet n (pl mullets or mullet) a food fish with barbels on the chin.

mulligatawny n a rich Indian meat soup seasoned with curry.

mullion n a slender vertical bar between panes of a window. ➤ **mullioned** adj.

mull over v to consider at length.

multicoloured (NAmer **multicolored**) adj having many colours.

multicultural adj relating to or composed of several cultural groups. ➤ **multiculturalism** n.

multifaceted adj having several facets or aspects.

multifarious adj diverse.

multilateral adj **1** involving more than two participants. **2** having many sides. ➤ **multilaterally** adv.

multilingual adj using or speaking several languages.

multimillionaire n a person whose wealth is estimated at several million pounds or dollars.

multinational¹ adj involving more than two countries.

multinational² n a company operating in several countries.

multiple¹ adj **1** involving more than one part or element. **2** many and varied. **3** of a disease: affecting several parts of the body.

multiple² n a number that can be divided exactly by a given number.

multiple-choice adj of an examination question: giving several choices from which the correct answer had to be chosen.

multiple sclerosis n a chronic condition with progressive paralysis resulting from the formation of hardened tissue in nerves of the brain and spinal cord.

multiplex n **1** a cinema with several auditoriums. **2** a multiplex communications system.

multiplication n the process of multiplying.

multiplication sign n the symbol (×) denoting quantities to be multiplied together.

multiplicity n (pl -ies) a great number or variety.

multiply v (-ies, -ied) **1** to increase in number. **2** to add a number to itself a specified number of times to produce a larger number. **3** to breed or propagate.

multiracial adj involving several racial groups.

multistorey¹ adj of a building: having several storeys.

multistorey² n (pl -eys) a multistorey car park.

multitude n **1** a great number or crowd. **2** (**the multitude**) the ordinary people.

multitudinous adj formal very numerous.

mum¹ n Brit, informal one's mother.

mum² *adj* not divulging information.

mumble¹ *v* to speak or say in a low indistinct voice.

mumble² *n* words said in a low indistinct voice.

mumbo jumbo *n* elaborate but meaningless language.

mummify *v* (-ies, -ied) to embalm and dry (a dead body). ➤ **mummification** *n*.

mummy¹ *n* (*pl* -ies) *informal* one's mother.

mummy² *n* (*pl* -ies) a body embalmed and wrapped for burial in the manner of the ancient Egyptians.

mumps *pl n* a disease marked by swelling of the glands in the sides of the face.

munch *v* to eat ponderously and noisily.

mundane *adj* dully practical or ordinary. ➤ **mundanity** *n*.

municipal *adj* of a municipality.

municipality *n* (*pl* -ies) a a town, city, or district having some self-government.

munificent *adj formal* generous. ➤ **munificence** *n*, **munificently** *adv*.

munitions *pl n* military weapons, ammunition, and equipment.

mural¹ *n* painting done directly on a wall.

mural² *adj* relating to a wall or walls.

murder¹ *n* **1** the crime of intentionally killing a person. **2** *informal* something very difficult or dangerous.

murder² *v* to kill unlawfully and intentionally. ➤ **murderer** *n*, **murderess** *n*.

murderous *adj* **1** capable of murder. **2** causing murder or bloodshed. **3** *informal* extremely difficult or dangerous.

murk *or* **mirk** *n* **1** gloom or darkness. **2** fog.

murky *adj* (-ier, -iest) **1** dark and gloomy. **2** of water: cloudy or dirty. **3** obscure or unknown.

murmur¹ *n* **1** a low indistinct sound or utterance. **2** a half-suppressed complaint. **3** an unusual heartbeat indicating an abnormality.

murmur² *v* **1** to say in a murmur. **2** to make a murmur.

muscle *n* **1** a tissue of cells that contract and relax when stimulated to produce motion. **2** an organ consisting of this tissue that moves a part of the body. **3** muscular strength. **4** power or force. ➤ **muscly** *adj*.

muscular *adj* **1** of or affecting the muscles. **2** having well-developed muscles.

muscular dystrophy *n* a hereditary disease with progressive wasting of the muscles.

musculature *n* the system of muscles in the body.

muse¹ *v* **1** to become absorbed in thought. **2** to think or say reflectively.

muse² *n* **1** (**Muse**) each of the nine goddesses in Greek mythology who were the patrons of the arts and sciences. **2** a woman who is a source of inspiration to a creative artist.

museum *n* an institution displaying objects of historical or cultural interest.

mush *n* **1** a soft mass of semiliquid material. **2** mawkish sentimentality. ➤ **mushy** *adj*.

mushroom¹ *n* a fungus consisting of a stem bearing a flattened or domed cap.

mushroom² *v* to grow or multiply rapidly.

mushroom cloud *n* a mushroom-shaped cloud of dust that forms above a nuclear explosion.

music *n* **1** the sounds of voices and instruments made to have rhythm, melody, or harmony. **2** the art of writing music. **3** a musical accompaniment. **4** the score of a musical composition set down on paper.

musical¹ *adj* **1** relating to music or musicians. **2** having the harmonious qualities of music. **3** having a talent for music. **4** accompanied by music. ➤ **musically** *adv*.

musical² *n* a film or play with songs and dances.

music hall *n* **1** formerly, entertainment consisting of a comedy acts, singing, and dancing. **2** a theatre where this was performed.

musician *n* a composer or performer of music. ➤ **musicianship** *n*.

musicology *n* the study of musical theory and history. ➤ **musicologist** *n*.

musk *n* a strong-smelling substance obtained from a gland of the male musk deer and used in perfume. ➤ **musky** *adj*.

musk deer *n* a small hornless deer of central Asia.

musket *n* a long-barrelled gun fired from the shoulder.

musketeer *n* formerly, a soldier armed with a musket.

musk ox *n* a wild ox of Greenland and North America.

muskrat *n* (*pl* **muskrats** *or* **muskrat**) a rodent of North America with glands at the base of its tail.

Muslim *or* **Moslem** *n* a follower of Islam.

muslin *n* a delicate plain-woven cotton fabric.

musquash *n archaic* = MUSKRAT.

mussel *n* a mollusc with a dark elongated shell.

must¹ *v aux* (*third person sing. present tense* **must**, *past tense in reported speech* **must**) **1** to have to; to be obliged to. **2** to be required or necessary. **3** to be supposed or likely. **4** used to express insistence.

must² *n* an essential or prerequisite.

must³ *n* grape juice before fermentation.

mustache *n* see MOUSTACHE.

mustang *n* a small wild horse of the western plains of the USA.

mustard *n* **1** a pungent yellow or brown paste made from the seeds of a plant of the cabbage family. **2** a brownish yellow colour.

mustard gas *n* an irritant oily liquid used as a poison gas.

muster¹ *v* **1** to assemble (troops) for fighting.

2 of people: to come together. **3** (*often* + up) to summon (courage) to meet a need.

muster² *n* an assembling of troops for fighting.
* **pass muster** to be acceptable or satisfactory.

mustn't *contraction* must not.

musty *adj* (**-ier, -iest**) **1** affected by mould or damp. **2** tasting or smelling of damp and decay.

mutable *adj* capable of or liable to change. ➤ **mutability** *n*.

mutant¹ *n* an animal or organism that has undergone mutation.

mutant² *adj* relating to or affected by mutation.

mutate *v* to undergo mutation.

mutation *n* **1** the act or an instance of changing. **2** a relatively permanent change in an organism's hereditary material. **3** an individual or strain resulting from such a change.

mute¹ *adj* **1** not speaking. **2** unable to speak. **3** felt but not expressed. **4** in law, refusing to plead. **5** of a letter: used in the spelling of a word but not pronounced. ➤ **mutely** *adv*.

mute² *n* **1** a person who cannot speak. **2** a device attached to a musical instrument to soften its tone.

mute³ *v* **1** to muffle or reduce the sound of. **2** to reduce the strength of (a colour).

mutilate *v* to injure or damage severely. ➤ **mutilation** *n*.

mutineer *n* somebody who mutinies.

mutinous *adj* tending to mutiny; rebellious.

mutiny¹ *n* (*pl* **-ies**) open resistance to authority, *esp* an organized revolt of soldiers or sailors against their commanders.

mutiny² *v* (**-ies, -ied**) to take part in a mutiny; to rebel.

mutt *n informal* **1** a mongrel dog. **2** a dull or foolish person.

mutter¹ *v* **1** to utter sounds in a low indistinct voice. **2** to utter muffled complaints.

mutter² *n* muttered sounds or words.

mutton *n* the flesh of a mature sheep used as food.

mutual *adj* **1** directed by two people or groups towards the other. **2** having the same specified feeling for each other. **3** shared by two or more people or groups. **4** of a building society: owned by its members. ➤ **mutuality** *n*, **mutually** *adv*.

muzzle¹ *n* **1** the jaws and nose of an animal. **2** a covering for the mouth of an animal. **3** the discharging end of a gun barrel.

muzzle² *v* **1** to put a muzzle on (an animal). **2** to restrain from free expression.

muzzy *adj* (**-ier, -iest**) **1** mentally confused; befuddled. **2** blurred or unclear. ➤ **muzziness** *n*.

my *adj* belonging to or associated with the person speaking or writing.

myalgia *n* pain in the muscles. ➤ **myalgic** *adj*.

mycology *n* the scientific study of fungi. ➤ **mycologist** *n*.

mynah *or* **myna** *or* **mina** *n* an Asian bird that can imitate sounds of human speech.

myopia *n* shortsightedness. ➤ **myopic** *adj*.

myriad¹ *n* (*also in pl*) an indefinitely large number.

myriad² *adj* innumerable; countless.

myrrh *n* an aromatic gum resin obtained from various African and Asian trees, used in perfumes and incense.

myrtle *n* an evergreen shrub with fragrant white or rosy flowers and black berries.

myself *pron* used reflexively or for emphasis to refer to the person speaking or writing.

mysterious *adj* difficult to understand or explain. ➤ **mysteriously** *adv*.

mystery *n* (*pl* **-ies**) **1** something or somebody not easily understood or explained. **2** a secretive quality or character. **3** a fictional work dealing with the solution of a mysterious crime. **4** a religious truth disclosed by revelation alone.

mystery play *n* a medieval drama based on biblical episodes or the lives of the saints.

mystic¹ *n* a person who believes that God or ultimate reality can be apprehended by direct personal experience.

mystic² *adj* = MYSTICAL.

mystical *adj* **1** having a sacred or spiritual meaning not understood by normal thought. **2** relating to mysticism. **3** mysterious or esoteric. **4** arousing awe and wonder. ➤ **mystically** *adv*.

mysticism *n* **1** the belief that direct knowledge of God or ultimate reality can be attained through prayer and meditation. **2** a vague belief without sound basis.

mystify *v* (**-ies, -ied**) **1** to perplex or bewilder. **2** to make mysterious or obscure. ➤ **mystifying** *adj*.

mystique *n* **1** a reverential quality associated with a person or thing. **2** an aura of secrecy and special skill surrounding an activity.

myth *n* **1** a traditional story, often involving gods and heroes, that embodies popular beliefs or explains a natural phenomenon. **2** = MYTHOLOGY. **3** a fictional person or thing. **4** a widely believed but false notion.

mythical *adj* **1** based on or described in a myth. **2** invented or imagined.

mythology *n* (*pl* **-ies**) **1** a body of myths. **2** a set of attractive and widely held but essentially false beliefs. ➤ **mythological** *adj*, **mythologist** *n*.

myxomatosis *n* a severe and usu fatal viral disease of rabbits.

N¹ or **n** *n* (*pl* **N's** or **Ns** or **n's**) the 14th letter of the English alphabet.

N² *abbr* **1** north. **2** northern.

N³ *abbr* the chemical symbol for nitrogen.

Na *abbr* the chemical symbol for sodium.

n/a *abbr* **1** not applicable. **2** not available.

naan *n* see NAN².

nab *v* (**nabbed, nabbing**) *informal* **1** to arrest. **2** to catch hold of.

nacho *n* (*pl* **-os**) a piece of tortilla covered with melted cheese, chopped peppers, etc.

nadir *n* **1** in astronomy, the point of the celestial sphere directly opposite the ZENITH and vertically downward from the observer. **2** the lowest or worst point.

naff *adj Brit, informal* lacking sophistication, coolness, or style.

nag¹ *n* a horse, *esp* an old or inferior one.

nag² *v* (**nagged, nagging**) **1** to subject to constant scolding or urging. **2** to be a persistent source of annoyance or discomfort.

nag³ *n* **1** a person who nags habitually. **2** a nagging feeling.

naiad *n* (*pl* **naiads** or **naiades**) (*often* **Naiad**) a water nymph in classical mythology.

nail¹ *n* **1** a slender pointed and headed spike designed to be hammered into a surface. **2** a horny sheath protecting the upper end of each finger and toe. ✳ **hit the nail on the head** to describe or explain the situation exactly. **on the nail** of payment: immediate.

nail² *v* **1** (*often* + down/together) to fasten with nails. **2** *informal* to detect or arrest (a criminal, etc). **3** *informal* to expose (a lie or liar).

nail-biting *adj informal* characterized by or causing emotional tension.

naive or **naïve** *adj* lacking in worldly wisdom or sophistication; ➤ **naively** *adv*.

naivety or **naïvety** or **naiveté** *n* naive behaviour; lack of sophistication or worldliness.

naked *adj* **1** having no clothes on. **2** of a plant, animal, or object: without its usual covering. **3** of a light: not shaded. **4** of a feeling: open and undisguised. ✳ **the naked eye** eyesight unaided by a magnifying glass, telescope, etc. ➤ **nakedness** *n*.

namby-pamby *adj* weak, cowardly, and soft.

name¹ *n* **1** a word or phrase by which a person, place, or thing is known and referred to. **2** a famous or important person. **3** one's reputation. ✳ **call somebody names** to insult somebody verbally. **in name only** officially, but not in reality. **in the name of 1** reserved, intended, etc, for (somebody). **2** for the sake of (a cause, etc). **the name of the game** *informal* the main feature or purpose of some activity.

name² *v* **1** to give a name to. **2** to identify or mention by name. **3** to appoint. **4** to specify (a sum, date, etc). ✳ **name after** (*NAmer* **name for**) to give (somebody or something) the same name as somebody or something else.

name-dropping *n* the practice of trying to impress others by mentioning prominent people as if they were one's acquaintances or contacts.

nameless *adj* **1** without a name. **2** not named, e.g. to avoid embarrassment. **3** too vague or too terrible to describe.

namely *adv* that is to say.

namesake *n* somebody or something with the same name as the person or thing in question.

nan¹ *n Brit, informal* used by children: one's grandmother.

nan² or **naan** *n* a traditional Indian type of bread, usu formed into flat leaf-shaped pieces.

nanny or **nannie** *n* (*pl* **-ies**) *chiefly Brit* a woman employed to look after children in their own home.

nanny goat *n informal* a female domestic goat.

nanosecond *n* one thousand-millionth of a second.

nap¹ *v* (**napped, napping**) to take a short sleep, *esp* during the day. ✳ **catch somebody napping** to catch somebody unprepared.

nap² *n* a short sleep, *esp* during the day.

nap³ *n* a hairy or downy surface on a woven fabric.

napalm *n* jellied petrol used in incendiary bombs and flamethrowers.

nape *n* the back of the neck.

naphtha *n* a liquid hydrocarbon mixture extracted from petroleum, coal, etc, used chiefly as a solvent.

napkin *n* **1** a square piece of material, e.g. linen or paper, used at table to wipe the lips or fingers and protect the clothes. **2** *chiefly Brit, formal* a baby's nappy. **3** *chiefly NAmer* a sanitary towel.

nappy *n* (*pl* **-ies**) *chiefly Brit* a shaped pad or a square piece of towelling worn by babies to absorb urine and faeces.

narcissism *n* abnormal interest in oneself or one's appearance. ➤ **narcissist** *n and adj*, **narcissistic** *adj*.

narcissus *n* (*pl* **narcissi** *or* **narcissuses**) a daffodil with pale outer petals and an orange or bright yellow centre.

narcotic[1] *n* **1** a drug that induces drowsiness or unconsciousness, and relieves pain. **2** any drug, *esp* an illegal or addictive one, that affects mood and behaviour.

narcotic[2] *adj* relating to narcotics.

nark[1] *n informal* Brit, Aus, NZ a police informer.

nark[2] *v informal* to annoy or offend.

narrate *v* **1** to tell (a story). **2** to give a spoken commentary for (a film, etc). ➤ **narration** *n*, **narrator** *n*.

narrative[1] *n* something that is narrated; a story.

narrative[2] *adj* relating to narration.

narrow[1] *adj* **1** of little width, *esp* in comparison with height or length. **2** limited in size or scope. **3** only just sufficient or successful. ➤ **narrowly** *adv*, **narrowness** *n*.

narrow[2] *n* (*in pl*) a narrow sea passage; = STRAIT 1.

narrow[3] *v* **1** to make or become narrower. **2** (*often* + down) to restrict the scope of (research, an enquiry, etc).

narrowboat *n* a canal barge with a width of 2.1m (7ft) or less.

narrow-minded *adj* lacking tolerance of, or openness to, others and their views. ➤ **narrow-mindedness** *n*.

NASA *abbr NAmer* National Aeronautics and Space Administration.

nasal *adj* **1** relating to the nose. **2** of somebody's speech: characterized by resonance produced through the nose. ➤ **nasally** *adv*.

nascent *adj formal* in the process of being born; just beginning to develop.

nasturtium *n* a common garden plant with circular leaves and bright orange, red, or yellow flowers.

nasty *adj* (**-ier, -iest**) **1** unpleasant, repugnant, or disgusting. **2** of people or their behaviour: spiteful, bad-tempered, or vicious. **3** harmful or dangerous. ➤ **nastily** *adv*, **nastiness** *n*.

natal *adj* associated with one's birth.

nation *n* **1** a people with a common origin, tradition, and language. **2** a community of people possessing a defined territory and government.

national[1] *adj* **1** relating or belonging to a nation. **2** of national, etc: run by the central government. ➤ **nationally** *adv*.

national[2] *n* a citizen of a specified nation.

national curriculum *n* a curriculum designed to operate throughout the state-maintained school system in England and Wales.

national debt *n* the amount of money owed by the government of a country.

national grid *n* **1** in Britain, a country-wide network of high-voltage cables between major power stations. **2** in Britain, the system of coordinates used for map reference by the Ordnance Survey.

National Insurance *n Brit* a compulsory social-security scheme, funded by employers, employees, and the government, which insures individuals against sickness, retirement, and unemployment.

nationalism *n* **1** excessive devotion to and admiration for one's nation. **2** the pursuit of political independence for one's nation. ➤ **nationalist** *n and adj*, **nationalistic** *adj*.

nationality *n* (*pl* **-ies**) **1** the status of belonging to a particular nation. **2** an ethnic group.

nationalize *or* **-ise** *v* to transfer control or ownership of (an industry) to the state government. ➤ **nationalization** *n*.

national park *n* an area of countryside, maintained by the government for public enjoyment or the preservation of wildlife, etc.

national service *n* a period of compulsory service in one's country's armed forces.

nationwide *adj and adv* throughout the whole country.

native[1] *adj* **1** relating to the place of one's birth. **2** belonging to a particular place by birth. **3** of a plant, etc: living or growing naturally in a particular region. **4** characteristic of a particular locality or its indigenous population. **5** inborn; innate.

native[2] *n* **1** a person born or reared in a particular place. **2** *dated, offensive* an original or indigenous inhabitant, *esp* of a country colonized by Europeans. **3** a plant, animal, etc living or growing in a particular locality. **4** *chiefly humorous* a local resident.

Native American *n* a member of any of the indigenous races of North, South, or Central America.

native speaker *n* a person who speaks the language in question as their native language.

nativity *n* (*pl* **-ies**) **1** one's birth. **2** (**the Nativity**) the birth of Jesus Christ.

NATO *or* **Nato** *abbr* North Atlantic Treaty Organization.

natter[1] *v chiefly Brit, informal* to chatter or gossip.

natter[2] *n chiefly Brit, informal* a chat.

natterjack *n* a common brownish yellow toad that runs rather than hops.

natty *adj* (**-ier, -iest**) *informal* of clothes or their wearer: neat and stylish.

natural[1] *adj* **1** existing in or produced by nature without human intervention. **2** happening in accordance with the ordinary course of nature. **3** normal; to be expected. **4** innate; inherent. **5** not affected or forced; easy and

relaxed. **6** related by blood rather than adoption. **7** of musical notes: neither sharp nor flat.
➤ **naturally** *adv*.

natural² *n* **1** *informal* a person having natural skills, talents, or abilities. **2** an off-white or creamy beige colour. **3** in music, a natural note, or a sign (♮) indicating that a note is not sharp or flat.

natural childbirth *n* the management of labour by the mother, through special breathing and relaxation techniques, so that the use of drugs is kept to a minimum.

natural gas *n* gas occurring naturally underground and used chiefly as a fuel.

natural history *n* the study of plants and animals.

naturalism *n* extreme realism in art or literature, without concealment of the ugly and distasteful.

naturalist *n* a person who studies animals and plants.

naturalistic *adj* **1** very true to life. **2** in accordance with the principles of naturalism in art or literature. ➤ **naturalistically** *adv*.

naturalize *or* **-ise** *v* **1** to make (a foreigner) a citizen of a country. **2** to establish (a plant or animal) in an area where it is not indigenous.

natural selection *n* a natural process of evolution that tends to result in the survival of organisms best adapted to their environment.

nature *n* **1** the physical world of landscape, plants, and animals, as distinct from human creations. **2** the inherent character of a person or thing. **3** a kind or class of thing.

nature reserve *n* an officially protected area of great botanical or zoological interest.

naturism *n* = NUDISM. ➤ **naturist** *adj and n*.

naught *n archaic or literary* nothing.

naughty *adj* (**-ier, -iest**) **1** of a child: badly behaved; disobedient. **2** *euphem or humorous* slightly improper. ➤ **naughtiness** *n*.

nausea *n* **1** a feeling of discomfort in the stomach and an urge to vomit. **2** extreme disgust.

nauseate *v* to affect with nausea or disgust. ➤ **nauseating** *adj*, **nauseatingly** *adv*.

nauseous *adj* **1** feeling nausea or disgust. **2** disgusting.

nautical *adj* relating to sailors, navigation, or ships.

nautical mile *n* a unit of distance used for sea and air navigation, equal to 1852m (about 6076.17ft).

naval *adj* relating to a navy.

nave *n* the main long central space of a church.

navel *n* the depression in the middle of the abdomen marking the point where the umbilical cord was attached.

navel orange *n* a seedless orange with a pit at the top.

navigable *adj* **1** suitable for ships to pass through or along. **2** of e.g. a website: containing hypertext links for access to other information.

navigate *v* **1** to plan or direct the course of a ship or aircraft. **2** in computing, to explore (the Internet) using hypertext links. **3** of a car passenger: to advise the driver about the route.

navigation *n* **1** the science of determining the position, course, etc of a ship or aircraft. **2** traffic on any stretch of water. ➤ **navigational** *adj*.

navvy *n* (*pl* **-ies**) *Brit* an unskilled labourer.

navy *n* (*pl* **-ies**) **1** (*often* **Navy**) the branch of a country's armed services supplying crews and supporting personnel for warships. **2** = NAVY BLUE.

navy blue *n* a deep dark blue colour. ➤ **navy blue** *adj*.

nay *adv archaic* no.

Nazi /'nahtsi/ *n* (*pl* **Nazis**) a member of the National Socialist German Workers' Party, which controlled Germany from 1933 to 1945. ➤ **Nazi** *adj*, **Nazism** *n*.

NB *abbr* (Latin) nota bene: note well.

Nb *abbr* the chemical symbol for niobium.

Nd *abbr* the chemical symbol for neodymium.

NE *abbr* **1** northeast. **2** northeastern.

Ne *abbr* the chemical symbol for neon.

Neanderthal *n* an extinct species of human that inhabited Europe between 120,000 and 35,000 years ago.

neap tide *n* a tide at the time when the difference between high and low tide is at its smallest.

near¹ *adv* **1** (*often* + to) at or to only a short distance away. **2** almost: *with near-disastrous results*.

near² *prep* a short distance or time from.

near³ *adj* **1** close in place or time. **2** almost but not quite a particular thing: *a near disaster*. **3** closely related. ➤ **nearness** *n*.

near⁴ *v* to approach (a place or point).

nearby *adv and adj* close at hand.

Near East *n* the countries of Southwest Asia between the Mediterranean coast and India.

nearly *adv* **1** almost but not quite. **2** closely.

nearside *n Brit* the side of a vehicle nearest the kerb.

nearsighted *adj* able to see near things more clearly than distant ones.

neat *adj* **1** tidy or orderly. **2** well-defined or precise. **3** *NAmer, informal* excellent. **4** of spirits: without addition or dilution. ➤ **neatly** *adv*, **neatness** *n*.

neaten *v* to make neat.

nebula *n* (*pl* **nebulas** *or* **nebulae**) an immense body of highly rarefied gas or dust in interstellar space.

nebulous *adj* of ideas, etc: indistinct or vague.

necessarily adv as a necessary consequence; inevitably.

necessary[1] adj 1 essential; indispensable. 2 inevitable; inescapable.

necessary[2] n (pl -ies) an indispensable item. * **the necessary** 1 informal the action required. 2 Brit, informal money.

necessitate v to make necessary or unavoidable.

necessity n (pl -ies) 1 the quality of being necessary. 2 pressing need or desire. 3 something indispensable. * **of necessity** necessarily.

neck[1] n 1 the part of a person or animal that connects the head with the body. 2 the constricted end of a bottle. 3 the part of a stringed musical instrument extending from the body and supporting the fingerboard and strings. 4 Brit, informal insolent boldness; cheek. * **catch/get it in the neck** informal to be severely rebuked or punished. **neck and neck** keeping abreast in a race. **neck of the woods** usu humorous a district or locality. **up to one's neck** deeply involved in (some business).

neck[2] v informal to kiss and caress in sexual play.

neckerchief n a square of fabric folded and worn round the neck.

necklace n a string of jewels, beads, etc worn round the neck as an ornament.

necklet n a rigid, close-fitting ornament for wearing round the neck.

neckline n the upper edge of a garment that forms the opening for the neck and head.

necromancy n 1 the conjuring up of the spirits of the dead in order to predict the future. 2 magic or sorcery generally. ➤ **necromancer** n.

necrophilia n obsession with, erotic interest in, or sexual intercourse with corpses. ➤ **necrophiliac** adj and n.

necropolis n a cemetery, esp a large and elaborate one.

necrosis n (pl **necroses**) the death of living tissue through disease, injury, or interruption of the blood supply.

nectar n 1 a sweet liquid secreted by plants and made into honey by bees. 2 in classical mythology, the drink of the gods.

nectarine n a type of peach with a smooth thin skin.

née or **nee** /nay/ adj used to identify a married woman by her maiden name: born as: Mary Thomson, née Wilkinson.

need[1] v 1 to have to have (something or somebody) in order to function, be complete, be happy, etc. 2 to be in a position where it is essential to do something: We need to discuss this urgently. 3 to be compelled or obliged to do something: She need not decide straight away.

need[2] n 1 obligation. 2 sufficient reason. 3 (also in pl) something one requires. 4 poverty; want.

needful adj necessary.

needle[1] n 1 a small slender pointed instrument with an eye for thread at one end, used for sewing. 2 a thin rod used in crocheting or knitting. 3 the hollow pointed end of a hypodermic syringe. 4 a slender pointed indicator on a dial or compass. 5 a stylus for playing records. 6 a needle-shaped leaf, esp of a conifer.

needle[2] v informal to provoke by persistent teasing or gibes.

needlecord n a fine corduroy with close ribs.

needlepoint n embroidery worked on canvas usu in a simple even stitch.

needless adj not needed; unnecessary. * **needless to say** naturally; of course. ➤ **needlessly** adv.

needlework n sewing or embroidery.

needn't contraction need not.

needy adj (-ier, -iest) in want; impoverished. ➤ **neediness** n.

ne'er adv literary never.

ne'er-do-well n an idle worthless person.

nefarious adj highly suspect or criminal.

negate v 1 to make ineffective or invalid. 2 to deny the existence or truth of. ➤ **negation** n.

negative[1] adj 1 expressing denial, prohibition, or refusal. 2 denoting the absence of something. 3 having a critical, unfavourable, or discouraging attitude or qualities. 4 of a number: less than zero. 5 having lower electric potential and constituting the part towards which the current flows from the external circuit. 6 of a photographic image: having the light and dark parts or the colours of the subject reversed. ➤ **negatively** adv, **negativity** n.

negative[2] n 1 in grammar, etc, a word, e.g. no, not, or never, or a statement that negates something. 2 a negative photographic image used for printing positive pictures.

neglect[1] v 1 to fail to give (a person, animal, or thing) proper care and attention. 2 to fail (to do something required of one).

neglect[2] n 1 lack of proper care and attention. 2 the act of neglecting something.

neglectful adj (often + of) careless, heedless, or forgetful.

negligee or **negligé** /'neglizhay/ n a woman's light decorative dressing gown.

negligence n 1 carelessness or forgetfulness. 2 in law, the offence of failing to take due care, so that damage or harm results. ➤ **negligent** adj.

negligible adj so slight or insignificant as to be not worth considering.

negotiable adj 1 transferable to another person. 2 of a road, route, etc: capable of being passed along. 3 capable of being dealt with through discussion.

negotiate v 1 to confer with others with the aim of reaching agreement over a disputed issue. **2** to achieve (a settlement, etc) by discussion with others. **3** to succeed in passing (an obstacle en route). **4** to transfer (a cheque or bill of exchange) to somebody else's legal possession. ➤ **negotiator** *n*, **negotiation** *n*.

Negro *n* (*pl* **-oes**) *offensive* a black person. ➤ **Negro** *adj*.

neigh *v* to make the characteristic cry of a horse. ➤ **neigh** *n*.

neighbour (*NAmer* **neighbor**) *n* a person who lives next door, or very close, to one. ➤ **neighbourly** *adj*.

neighbourhood (*NAmer* **neighborhood**) *n* **1** the area surrounding one's own home. **2** the area around the person or thing specified. **3** a particular area of a town.

neighbouring (*NAmer* **neighboring**) *adj* adjoining, or situated near to, a place.

neither[1] *adj and pron* not the one or the other of two.

neither[2] *conj* used used before the first of two or more alternatives that are part of the same negative statement: *Neither Janet nor her sister is coming.*

neither[3] *adv* similarly not; also not: *'I can't understand it.' 'Neither can I'.*

nemesis *n* (*pl* **nemeses**) a person or thing that brings deserved retribution to somebody.

neoclassical *adj* relating to a revival of classical forms in the arts. ➤ **neoclassicism** *n*, **neoclassicist** *n and adj*.

Neolithic *adj* of the last period of the Stone Age.

neologism *n* a new word or expression.

neon *n* a gaseous chemical element that glows when electricity passes through it, used in fluorescent signs and lighting.

neonate *n technical* a newborn child less than a month old. ➤ **neonatal** *adj*.

neophyte *n* **1** a beginner in a subject, skill, etc. **2** a recently ordained priest or a novice in a religious order.

nephew *n* the son of one's brother or sister.

nephritis *n* inflammation of the kidneys.

nepotism *n* favouritism shown to a relative.

nerd or **nurd** *n informal* a person who is obsessed with a technical subject, *esp* computing, and is often boring or socially inept.

nerve[1] *n* **1** a threadlike band of fibrous tissue that conducts the impulses that transmit sensations and messages to the brain and other organs. **2** a combination of courage, self-discipline, and tenacity. **3** *informal* cheek; audacity. **4** (*in pl*) feelings of acute nervousness or anxiety. ✱ **get on somebody's nerves** to annoy somebody.

nerve[2] *v* (*also* + up/for) to prepare (oneself) psychologically for a challenge.

nerve cell *n* = NEURON.

nerve gas *n* a deadly gas that interferes with nerve transmission and disrupts the vital functions.

nerveless *adj* **1** lacking strength or vigour. **2** not agitated or afraid.

nerve-racking or **nerve-wracking** *adj* causing great tension and anxiety.

nervous *adj* **1** relating to the nerves. **2** anxious or apprehensive. **3** constitutionally anxious or easily upset. ➤ **nervously** *adv*, **nervousness** *n*.

nervous breakdown *n* a mental and emotional disorder in which depression, severe tiredness, etc prevent one from coping with one's responsibilities.

nervous system *n* the brain, spinal cord, and nerves together forming a system for interpreting stimuli from the sense organs and transmitting impulses to muscles, glands, etc.

nervy *adj* (**-ier, -iest**) *chiefly Brit* suffering from nervousness or anxiety.

-ness *suffix* **1** denoting a state or quality: *goodness.* **2** happiness.

nest[1] *n* **1** a structure built by a bird to lay eggs in and shelter its young. **2** a structure where other creatures, e.g. insects, breed or shelter. **3** a set of things in a range of sizes, that fit one inside the other.

nest[2] *v* **1** of birds: to construct or occupy a nest. **2** to fit (a set of tables, etc) one inside the other.

nest egg *n* an amount of money saved up as a reserve.

nestle *v* **1** to settle snugly or comfortably. **2** of a place: to lie in a sheltered position.

nestling *n* a young bird that has not abandoned the nest.

net[1] *n* **1** a fabric of threads, etc, twisted, knotted, or woven together at regular intervals to leave square spaces in between. **2** a device made of net for catching fish, birds, or insects. **3** a net barricade which divides a tennis, badminton, etc court in half. **4** a football, hockey, etc goal. **5** (**the Net**) the Internet.

net[2] *v* (**netted, netting**) **1** to catch (a fish, etc) in a net. **2** to hit or kick (a ball or puck) into the goal in hockey, football, etc.

net[3] or *Brit* **nett** *adj* **1** remaining after all deductions, e.g. for taxes, outlay, or loss. **2** excluding the weight of the packaging or container. **3** final; overall.

net[4] or *Brit* **nett** *v* (**netted, netting**) to make (a sum) as clear profit.

netball *n* a game played between teams of seven players who try to score goals by tossing an inflated ball through a high horizontal ring on a post.

nether *adj formal* lower or under.

nettle[1] *n* a plant with jagged leaves covered with stinging hairs. ✱ **grasp the nettle** to tackle a problem with bold determination.

nettle² *v* of a remark, etc: to goad or annoy.

network¹ *n* **1** a structure of crisscrossing horizontal and vertical lines, cords, wires, etc. **2** a system of interconnected railways, roads, etc. **3** a group of broadcasting stations linked together for a simultaneous broadcast. **4** a set of interconnected computers or terminals. **5** a group of people who maintain contact with each other and exchange information.

network² *v* to create useful contacts for oneself by talking and interacting with others. ➤ **networker** *n*.

neural *adj* relating to a nerve or the nervous system. ➤ **neurally** *adv*.

neuralgia *n* intense pain radiating along a nerve, *esp* in the head or face. ➤ **neuralgic** *adj*.

neurology *n* the study of the nervous system, its structure, and function. ➤ **neurological** *adj*, **neurologist** *n*.

neuron *or* **neurone** *n* a specialized type of cell that transmits impulses through the nervous system.

neurosis *n* (*pl* **neuroses**) a nervous disorder in which phobias, compulsions, anxiety, and obsessions make normal life difficult.

neurotic *adj* **1** relating to or caused by a neurosis. **2** hypersensitive or obsessive about something. **3** *informal* unduly anxious. ➤ **neurotic** *n*, **neurotically** *adv*.

neuter¹ *adj* **1** of nouns: neither masculine nor feminine. **2** lacking sexual or reproductive organs.

neuter² *v* to spay or castrate (a domestic animal).

neutral¹ *adj* **1** of a country or a person: not engaged on either side of a war, dispute, etc. **2** impartial or unbiased. **3** having no strongly distinctive characteristics. **4** denoting a colour that is any shade of beige or grey. **5** denoting chemical substances having a pH value of about 7, so neither acid nor alkaline. **6** not electrically charged. ➤ **neutrality** *n*, **neutrally** *adv*.

neutral² *n* **1** a neutral person or state. **2** the gear position in which no gear is engaged.

neutralize *or* **-ise** *v* **1** to counteract or nullify by having the opposite effect. **2** to make neutral. ➤ **neutralization** *n*.

neutrino *n* (*pl* **-os**) an uncharged elementary particle that is created in the process of particle decay and is believed to be massless.

neutron *n* an uncharged elementary particle with a mass about that of the proton.

never *adv* **1** not ever; at no time. **2** used emphatically for *not*.

nevermore *adv literary* never again.

never-never *or* **the never-never** *n Brit, informal* = HIRE PURCHASE.

nevertheless *adv* in spite of that; however.

new¹ *adj* **1** recently bought, made, built, invented, etc. **2** fresh; unused. **3** doing something for the first time. **4** replacing the previous one. **5** fresh; unfamiliar; different. **6** refreshed; regenerated. ➤ **newness** *n*.

new² *adv* newly or recently.

New Age *n* a cultural movement of the late 1980s, characterized by enthusiasm for alternative beliefs, environmentalism, and holistic medicine.

newborn *adj* just born.

newcomer *n* **1** a recent arrival. **2** a beginner or novice.

newel *n* an upright post supporting either end of a staircase handrail.

newfangled *adj derog* modern and unnecessarily complicated or gimmicky.

newly *adv* **1** lately; recently. **2** anew.

newlywed *n* a recently married person.

new moon *n* the phase of the moon when its dark side is towards the earth or it reappears as a thin crescent.

news *n* **1** information about something that has recently happened. **2** (**the news**) a broadcast report of recent events.

newsagent *n chiefly Brit* a retailer of newspapers and magazines.

newscast *n* a broadcast news report. ➤ **newscaster** *n*.

newsflash *n* a brief broadcast reporting an important item of news, *esp* one that interrupts a programme.

newsgroup *n* a forum of Internet users who exchange news and views about topics of mutual interest.

newsletter *n* a publication containing news relevant to a particular group, association, etc, for circulation to its members.

newspaper *n* a printed daily or weekly publication containing news reports and articles.

newsprint *n* cheap paper used mostly for newspapers.

newsreader *n* a broadcaster who reads the news.

newsreel *n* a short film dealing with current events.

newsroom *n* a place, e.g. an office, where news is prepared for publication or broadcast.

newsworthy *adj* (**-ier, -iest**) sufficiently interesting to warrant reporting.

newt *n* a small amphibian with a long slender body and tail and short legs.

New Testament *n* the second part of the Christian Bible, comprising the Gospels and Epistles, the books of Acts, and the book of Revelation.

newton *n* the SI unit of force.

New World *n* (**the New World**) North and South America.

New Year *n* **1** the first day or days of a calendar year. **2** the festive period around 31 December and 1 January.

next[1] *adj* immediately adjacent or following, in place, time, or order.

Usage Note: When used of days of the week, *next* usually refers to the relevant day in the following week, so that on Monday 1st *next Wednesday* more often means Wednesday 10th than Wednesday 3rd.

next[2] *adv* **1** in the time, place, or position immediately following. **2** on the following occasion.

next[3] *n* a person or thing that is next.

next door *adv* in or to the next building, room, etc.

next-door *adj* situated or living in the next building, room, etc.

next of kin *n* (*pl* **next of kin**) the person most closely related to oneself.

nexus *n* (*pl* **nexuses** *or* **nexus**) **1** a connection. **2** a connected group or series.

NHS *abbr Brit* National Health Service.

Ni *abbr* the chemical symbol for nickel.

nib *n* the pointed end of a pen, from which the ink is distributed.

nibble[1] *v* **1** to bite cautiously, gently, or playfully. **2** to eat or chew in small bites.

nibble[2] *n* **1** an act of nibbling. **2** a very small amount, e.g. of food. **3** *informal* (*in pl*) savoury snacks served at a reception, etc.

nice *adj* **1** pleasant or agreeable. **2** of a person: kind, considerate, or accommodating. **3** socially respectable. **4** satisfactorily performed. **5** subtle. ▶ **nicely** *adv*, **niceness** *n*.

nicety *n* (*pl* **-ies**) **1** a fine point or distinction. **2** subtlety or precision.

niche *n* **1** a recess in a wall. **2** a place or activity for which a person is best suited.

nick[1] *n* **1** a small cut or notch. **2** (**the nick**) *Brit, informal* a prison or police station. ✳ **in good/bad nick** *Brit, informal* in good or bad condition. **in the nick of time** just before it would be too late.

nick[2] *v* **1** to make a nick in. **2** *Brit, informal* to steal. **3** *Brit, informal* to arrest.

nickel *n* **1** a silver-white metallic element, used in coins and in alloys. **2** a US coin worth five cents.

nickname[1] *n* a familiar or humorous name used in place of a proper name.

nickname[2] *v* to give (a person or thing) a nickname.

nicotine *n* a poisonous chemical compound that occurs in tobacco.

niece *n* the daughter of one's brother or sister.

Usage Note: Note the spelling with *-ie-*.

niff[1] *n Brit, informal* an unpleasant smell.

niff[2] *v Brit, informal* to smell unpleasant.

nifty *adj* (**-ier**, **-iest**) *informal* **1** very good or effective. **2** quick or deft.

niggardly *adj* grudgingly mean; miserly.

nigger *n offensive or derog* a black person.

niggle[1] *v* **1** to cause minor but persistent discomfort or anxiety. **2** to find fault constantly in a petty way.

niggle[2] *n* **1** a petty criticism. **2** a minor cause of anxiety.

nigh *adv, adj, and prep archaic* near.

night *n* **1** the period of darkness from dusk to dawn. **2** an evening characterized by a specified event or activity.

nightcap *n* **1** formerly, a cloth cap worn in bed. **2** a drink taken at bedtime.

nightclub *n* a place of entertainment open at night, usu with a disco and a bar.

nightdress *n* a woman's or girl's nightgown.

nightfall *n* dusk.

nightgown *n* a loose garment for sleeping in.

nightie *or* **nighty** *n* (*pl* **-ies**) *informal* a nightdress.

nightingale *n* a small thrush with brown plumage, noted for its sweet song, typically heard at night.

nightjar *n* an insect-eating bird with large eyes and greyish brown plumage that is active at night.

nightlife *n* late-evening entertainment or social life.

nightly *adj and adv* happening every night.

nightmare *n* **1** a frightening or distressing dream. **2** a very unpleasant or terrifying experience or situation. ▶ **nightmarish** *adj*.

night owl *n informal* somebody who tends to be most active at night.

nightshade *n* a poisonous rambling plant with purple flowers and black (*deadly nightshade*) or red (*woody nightshade*) berries.

nightshirt *n* a long loose shirt for sleeping in.

nightspot *n informal* a nightclub.

nihilism *n* a view that rejects all values and beliefs as meaningless or unfounded. ▶ **nihilist** *n*, **nihilistic** *adj*.

nil *n* nothing; zero.

nimble *adj* **1** quick and light in movement. **2** quick and clever in thinking and understanding. ▶ **nimbly** *adv*.

nimbus *n* (*pl* **nimbi** *or* **nimbuses**) a heavy grey rain-bearing cloud.

Nimby *n* (*pl* **Nimbys** *or* **Nimbies**) a person who is not against something in principle, but objects when it happens in their immediate vicinity.

nincompoop *n* a silly or foolish person.

nine *n* the number 9. ✳ **dressed to/up to the nines** *informal* dressed very smartly or elaborately. ▶ **nine** *adj*.

nineteen *adj and n* the number 19. ✳ **talk nineteen to the dozen** *informal* to talk or converse volubly. ▶ **nineteenth** *adj and n*.

ninety *adj and n* (*pl* **-ies**) **1** the number 90. **2** (*in pl*) the numbers 90 to 99. ▶ **ninetieth** *adj and n*.

ninny *n* (*pl* **-ies**) *informal* a silly or weak person.

ninth *adj and n* **1** having the position in a sequence corresponding to the number nine. **2** one of nine equal parts of something. ➤ **ninthly** *adv.*

nip[1] *v* (**nipped, nipping**) **1** to bite, squeeze, or pinch sharply. **2** *chiefly Brit, informal* to go quickly or briefly; to hurry. * **nip something in the bud** to prevent the growth or development of something at an early stage.

nip[2] *n* **1** a sharp chill in the air. **2** a sharp squeeze, pinch, or bite.

nip[3] *n* a small measure or drink of spirits.

nipper *n* **1** (*in pl*) pincers or pliers. **2** *chiefly Brit, informal* a child.

nipple *n* the small protuberance of a mammary gland, e.g. a breast, from which milk is drawn.

nippy *adj* (**-ier, -iest**) **1** nimble and lively. **2** of the weather: chilly.

nirvana /nuh'vahna/ *n* (*often* **Nirvana**) a Hindu and Buddhist state of final bliss and freedom from the cycle of rebirth.

nit[1] *n* the egg of a louse.

nit[2] *n* *chiefly Brit, informal* a nitwit.

nit-picking *n* petty and often unjustified criticism.

nitrate *n* a salt or ester of nitric acid.

nitric acid *n* a corrosive liquid acid.

nitrite *n* a salt or ester of nitrous acid.

nitrogen *n* a gas that constitutes about 78% of the atmosphere.

nitroglycerine *or* **nitroglycerin** *n* an oily explosive liquid used in making dynamite.

nitrous oxide *n* a gas used as a general anaesthetic.

nitty-gritty *n* *informal* the important basic realities.

nitwit *n* *informal* a scatterbrained or stupid person.

No *abbr* the chemical symbol for nobelium.

no[1] *interj* used in answers expressing negation, dissent, denial, or refusal.

no[2] *adv* not in any respect or degree.

no[3] *adj* **1** not any. **2** not a: *He's no expert*. * **no way** *informal* certainly not!

no[4] *n* (*pl* **noes** *or* **nos**) a negative reply or vote.

no. *abbr* number.

nob *n* *chiefly Brit, informal* a wealthy or influential person.

no-ball *n and interj* an illegal delivery of the ball in cricket that counts one run to the batsman's side.

nobble *v* *informal* **1** to incapacitate (a racehorse), *esp* by drugging. **2** to win over to one's side, *esp* by dishonest means.

nobility *n* (*pl* **-ies**) **1** the quality of being noble. **2** the class of people who have aristocratic rank and titles.

noble[1] *adj* **1** having a title such as duke, earl, etc. **2** imposing; stately. **3** having or showing a magnanimous character or high ideals. ➤ **nobly** *adv.*

noble[2] *n* a person of noble rank or birth.

nobleman *n* (*pl* **noblemen**) a man of noble rank.

noblewoman *n* (*pl* **noblewomen**) a woman of noble rank.

nobody[1] *pron* no person.

nobody[2] *n* (*pl* **-ies**) a person of no influence or consequence.

no-claims bonus *n Brit* a discount allowed in an insurance premium when no claim has been made in previous years.

nocturnal *adj* occurring or active at night.

nocturne *n* a work of art dealing with evening or night, *esp* a dreamy pensive composition for the piano.

nod[1] *v* (**nodded, nodding**) **1** to make a short downward movement of the head, e.g. in assent, understanding, or greeting. **2** to make repeated down-and-up movements with the head. **3** to become drowsy or sleepy.

nod[2] *n* an act of nodding.

node *n* **1** in anatomy, any normal or abnormal knot, thickness, or swelling. **2** in a plant, the point on a stem at which one or more leaves are attached. **3** a point in a network where lines cross or branch.

nod off *v* to fall asleep, *esp* unintentionally while in a sitting position.

nodule *n* any small hardish rounded mass, e.g. of cells in the body. ➤ **nodular** *adj.*

Noel *or* **Noël** *n* Christmas.

noggin *n* a small measure of spirits, usu 0.142 litres (¼pt).

Noh *n* classic Japanese dance-drama.

noise *n* **1** loud confused or discordant sound. **2** a sound, *esp* if sudden or harsh. **3** unwanted signals or fluctuations in an electrical circuit. ➤ **noiseless** *adj.*

noisome *adj* *literary* repellent; offensive.

noisy *adj* (**-ier, -iest**) **1** making a lot of noise. **2** full of noise. ➤ **noisily** *adv,* **noisiness** *n.*

nomad *n* **1** a member of a people that wanders from place to place, e.g. to find grazing for its animals. **2** a person who has an unsettled or wandering lifestyle. ➤ **nomadic** *adj.*

nom de plume /ˌnom də 'ploohm/ *n* (*pl* **noms de plume**) a pseudonym under which an author writes.

nomenclature *n* a system of terms used in a particular science, discipline, or art.

nominal *adj* **1** in name only. **2** of a sum of money: very small. ➤ **nominally** *adv.*

nominate *v* **1** to recommend for an appointment, award, etc. **2** *literary* to designate or specify by name. ➤ **nomination** *n,* **nominee** *n.*

nominative *n* the case used for the subject of a verb.

non- *prefix* **1** not of the class or category specified: *non-alcoholic*. **2** the reverse or absence of the thing specified: *nonconformity*.

nonagenarian *n* a person between 90 and 99 years old.

nonchalant *adj* giving an impression of easy unconcern or indifference. ➤ **nonchalance** *n*, **nonchalantly** *adv*.

non-commissioned officer *n* a subordinate officer, e.g. a sergeant, in the armed forces who does not hold a commission.

non-committal *adj* giving no clear indication of attitude or feeling. ➤ **non-committally** *adv*.

non compos mentis *adj* not of sound mind; insane.

nonconformist *n* **1** a person who does not conform to a generally accepted pattern of thought or behaviour. **2** (*often* **Nonconformist**) a member of a Protestant Church separated from the Church of England. ➤ **Nonconformism** *n*, **nonconformity** *n*.

nondescript *adj* lacking distinctive or interesting qualities; dull.

none¹ *pron* **1** not any. **2** *literary* nobody.

none² *adv* not in the least; not at all.

nonentity *n* (*pl* **-ies**) **1** somebody or something of little importance or interest. **2** nonexistence.

nonetheless *or* **none the less** *adv* nevertheless.

non-event *n* an event that turns out to be much duller or less important than expected.

non-existent *adj* **1** not real. **2** totally absent.

no-nonsense *adj* serious, businesslike, or straightforward.

nonplus *v* (**nonplussed, nonplussing,** *NAmer* **nonplused, nonplusing**) to perplex or disconcert.

non-profitmaking *adj* not run with the intention of making a profit.

non-proliferation *n* action to stop something, *esp* nuclear weapons, becoming more widespread.

nonsense *n* **1** meaningless words or language. **2** frivolous or insolent behaviour. ➤ **nonsensical** *adj*.

non sequitur *n* a statement that does not follow logically from anything previously said.

non-starter *n* **1** somebody or something that is sure to fail. **2** a competitor, racehorse, etc that fails to take part in a race.

non-stick *adj* of a pan: having a surface treated so that food does not stick to it during cooking.

non-stop *adj* **1** continuous. **2** of a journey: with no intermediate stops. ➤ **non-stop** *adv*.

noodle *n* (*usu in pl*) a narrow flat ribbon of pasta made with egg.

nook *n* a small secluded or sheltered place; a corner or recess. ❋ **every nook and cranny** everywhere possible.

noon *n* twelve o'clock in the day; midday.

noonday *adj literary* occurring in the middle of the day.

no one *or* **no-one** *pron* nobody.

noose *n* a loop with a running knot that tightens as the rope is pulled.

nor *adv and conj* and not; neither.

Nordic *adj* characteristic of Scandinavia, Finland, and Iceland and their peoples.

norm *n* **1** (**the norm**) the average or usual level or situation. **2** an authoritative standard; a model.

normal¹ *adj* conforming to ordinary expectations; usual or typical. ➤ **normality** *n*, **normally** *adv*.

normal² *n* the normal condition or state of affairs.

normalize *or* **-ise** *v* to make (something abnormal or irregular) normal. ➤ **normalization** *n*.

Norman¹ *n* a member of a people of mixed Frankish and Scandinavian stock who settled in Normandy in the tenth century and conquered England in 1066.

Norman² *adj* relating to the Normans or Normandy.

normative *adj* serving as or prescribing a norm.

Norse¹ *n* = OLD NORSE.

Norse² *adj* of ancient or medieval Scandinavia or Norway.

north¹ *n* **1** the direction in which a compass needle normally points, 90° anticlockwise from east. **2** regions or countries lying to the north. ➤ **northbound** *adj and adv*.

north² *adj and adv* **1** at or towards the north. **2** of the wind: blowing from the north.

northeast¹ *n* **1** the direction midway between north and east. **2** regions lying to the northeast. ➤ **northeastern** *adj*.

northeast² *adj and adv* **1** at or towards the northeast. **2** of the wind: blowing from the northeast.

northeasterly *adj and adv* **1** in a northeastern position or direction. **2** of the wind: blowing from the northeast.

northerly *adj and adv* **1** in a northern position or direction. **2** of the wind: blowing from the north.

northern *adj* in or towards the north.

Northerner *n* a person from the northern part of a country.

northern lights *pl n* = AURORA BOREALIS.

northward *adj and adv* towards the north; in a direction going north. ➤ **northwards** *adv*.

northwest¹ *n* **1** the direction midway between north and west. **2** regions lying to the northwest. ➤ **northwestern** *adj*.

northwest² *adj and adv* **1** at or towards the northwest. **2** of the wind: blowing from the northwest.

northwesterly *adj and adv* **1** in a northwestern position or direction. **2** of the wind: blowing from the northwest.

nose¹ *n* **1** the projecting part of the face above the mouth, containing the nostrils and used for breathing and smelling. **2** the front end of a vehicle. **3** the aroma or bouquet of wine. **4** an instinct for detecting a certain thing. ∗ **get up somebody's nose** *informal* to annoy somebody. **keep one's nose clean** *informal* to stay out of trouble. **keep one's nose out of** *informal* to refrain from interfering in (e.g. somebody else's business). **look down one's nose at** *informal* to show or express disdain for. **nose to tail** of vehicles: in a long slowly-moving queue. **pay through the nose** *informal* to pay exorbitantly. **turn one's nose up at** *informal* to show or express disdain for (a person or thing).

nose[2] *v* **1** of an animal: to push its nose into or against. **2** (*often* + about/around) to pry. **3** of a vehicle or driver: to move slowly forward.

nose bag *n* a bag for feeding a horse or other animal that covers its muzzle.

nosebleed *n* an attack of bleeding from the nose.

nose dive *n* **1** a downward nose-first plunge of an aircraft. **2** a sudden dramatic drop.

nose-dive *v* to make a nose dive.

nosegay *n* a small bunch of flowers.

nosh[1] *n informal* food; a meal.

nosh[2] *v informal* to eat.

nostalgia *n* a wistful yearning for something past or irrecoverable. ➤ **nostalgic** *adj*.

nostril *n* either of the two external openings of the nose.

nostrum *n* (*pl* **nostrums**) a medicine or remedy favoured by somebody, which is often of questionable effectiveness.

nosy or **nosey** *adj* (**-ier, -iest**) *informal* inquisitive; prying.

not *adv* **1** used to express a negative. **2** less than (a surprisingly small amount).

notable[1] *adj* worthy of note; remarkable or distinguished. ➤ **notably** *adv*.

notable[2] *n* a prominent person.

notary *n* (*pl* **-ies**) a legal official appointed to administer oaths and draw up and authenticate documents.

notation *n* a system of marks, signs, symbols, etc used in e.g. mathematics, music, or choreography.

notch[1] *n* **1** a V-shaped indentation or cut. **2** a degree or point on a scale.

notch[2] *v* **1** to make a notch in. **2** (+ up) to score or achieve (e.g. a success).

note[1] *n* **1** (*also in pl*) a short written record. **2** a brief comment or explanation. **3** a short informal letter. **4** a piece of paper money. **5** a sound having a definite pitch and length, made by a musical instrument or the human voice. **6** a written symbol used to indicate such a sound. **7** a feeling or element of something. ∗ **of note 1** distinguished. **2** significant. **take note** (*often* + of) to pay attention.

note[2] *v* **1** to pay due attention to. **2** (*often* + down) to record (information) in writing.

notebook *n* **1** a book for notes or memoranda. **2** a small portable computer.

noted *adj* well-known; famous.

notepaper *n* paper for letter-writing.

noteworthy *adj* worthy of or attracting attention.

nothing *pron and noun* **1** not anything. **2** a thing of no consequence or significance. **3** nought. ∗ **for nothing 1** without pay or without paying. **2** to no purpose. **nothing but** only. **sweet nothings** *humorous* affectionate exchanges between lovers.

nothingness *n* **1** nonexistence. **2** a void; emptiness.

notice[1] *n* **1** attention or observation. **2** advance warning. **3** *formal* notification of one's intention to terminate an agreement, typically relating to employment or tenancy. **4** a placard or poster displaying information. **5** a brief announcement in a newspaper, etc. **6** a short critical review of a play, etc. ∗ **at short notice** with little or no warning. **take no notice of** to disregard or pay no heed to.

notice[2] *v* to become aware of.

noticeable *adj* capable of being noticed; perceptible. ➤ **noticeably** *adv*.

notifiable *adj* of a disease: required by law to be reported to the health authorities.

notify *v* (**-ies, -ied**) (*also* + of) to let (somebody) know about something, *esp* formally or officially. ➤ **notification** *n*.

notion *n* **1** a broad general concept. **2** an idea or belief, *esp* a fanciful one.

notional *adj* theoretical, speculative, or imaginary. ➤ **notionally** *adv*.

notoriety *n* the fact of being notorious.

notorious *adj* well-known for something bad or unfavourable. ➤ **notoriously** *adv*.

notwithstanding[1] *prep* in spite of.

notwithstanding[2] *adv* nevertheless.

nougat *n* a sweet consisting of nuts or fruit pieces in a semisolid sugar paste.

nought *n and pron* **1** the arithmetical symbol 0; zero. **2** nothing.

noun *n* a word that is a name or term identifying a person, thing, animal, quality, or state.

nourish *v* **1** to provide (a person, animal, or plant) with the substances needed for healthy growth and development. **2** to cherish or entertain (an idea, feeling, etc). ➤ **nourishing** *adj*.

nourishment *n* food or nutriment.

nous *n chiefly Brit* practical common sense.

nouveau riche /ˌnoohvoh'reesh/ *n* (*pl* **nouveaux riches**) a person who has recently become rich.

nouvelle cuisine /noohˈvel kwiˈzeen/ *n* a style of cooking that emphasizes the natural flavours and textures of the food and attractive presentation.

nova n (pl **novas** or **novae**) a double star system that becomes suddenly much brighter as a result of a thermonuclear explosion and then fades away.

novel[1] n an invented prose narrative of book length.

novel[2] adj new and unlike anything previously known.

novelist n a writer of novels.

novella n (pl **novellas** or **novelle**) a short novel or substantial short story.

novelty n (pl **-ies**) **1** something new and unusual. **2** the quality of being novel. **3** a small ornament or toy.

November n the eleventh month of the year.

novice n **1** a new or inexperienced person in a job, etc; a beginner. **2** a person admitted to probationary membership of a religious community.

novitiate or **noviciate** n **1** the period of being a novice in a religious order. **2** a house where novices are trained.

now[1] adv **1** at the present time. **2** immediately. **3** in the light of recent developments. * **now and again/then** occasionally.

now[2] conj (often + that) as a result of the circumstance that; since.

nowadays adv in these modern times, in contrast to the past.

nowhere adv and pron not anywhere.

noxious adj harmful to living things.

nozzle n a projecting part with a usu adjustable outlet for liquid or gas.

Np abbr the chemical symbol for neptunium.

nu n the 13th letter of the Greek alphabet (N, ν).

nuance n a subtle but distinct gradation in colour, meaning, or tone.

nub n **1** a knob, lump, or protuberance. **2** (**the nub**) the crux of a matter.

nubile adj **1** of a girl: **2** of marriageable age. **3** young and sexually attractive.

nuclear adj **1** relating to a nucleus. **2** relating to or using the energy released when atomic nuclei are split or fused. **3** possessing nuclear weapons.

nuclear family n a family unit that consists of husband, wife, and children.

nuclear physics n the branch of physics concerned with atomic nuclei and their interactions, esp as a source of energy.

nucleic acid n a complex organic substance such as DNA or RNA, present in living cells.

nucleus n (pl **nuclei** or **nucleuses**) **1** the central and main part of esp a group. **2** a specialized structure within a cell containing the chromosomes and surrounded by a membrane. **3** the positively charged central part of an atom.

nude[1] adj without clothing; naked. ➤ **nudity** n.

nude[2] n a painting or sculpture of a nude human figure.

nudge[1] v **1** to poke (somebody) gently with one's elbow, esp to draw their attention to something. **2** to push or move gently in a certain direction.

nudge[2] n **1** the act of nudging. **2** a gentle hint or reminder.

nudism n the cult or practice of going nude as much as possible. ➤ **nudist** n.

nugatory adj formal trifling; inconsequential.

nugget n a solid lump of a precious metal in its natural state.

nuisance n a person or thing that is a source of annoyance or inconvenience.

nuke[1] n informal a nuclear weapon.

nuke[2] v informal to attack with nuclear weapons.

null adj having no force in law; invalid.

nullify v (**-ies, -ied**) **1** to make legally null and void. **2** to render ineffective or cancel out. ➤ **nullification** n.

nullity n (pl **-ies**) **1** in law, something that is legally null and void. **2** the state of being legally null and void.

numb[1] adj **1** devoid of sensation, esp as a result of cold or anaesthesia. **2** unable to feel emotion or react. ➤ **numbly** adv, **numbness** n.

numb[2] v **1** to make (a person or a body part) numb. **2** to reduce the sharpness of (a pain).

number[1] n **1** a word, numeral, or other symbol used in counting or calculating quantities. **2** a numeral or set of digits used to identify something. **3** a quantity or total. **4** (**a number of**) several. **5** a single issue of a periodical. **6** a song or a piece of pop or jazz music. * **somebody's number is up** informal somebody's doomed. ➤ **numberless** adj.

number[2] v **1** to amount to (a certain total). **2** to assign numbers to (things in a series). **3** (usu + among) to regard (a person or thing) as being included in a certain group.

numberplate n chiefly Brit a rectangular plate on a vehicle showing its registration number.

numbskull n see NUMSKULL.

numeral n a symbol that represents a number or zero.

numerate adj understanding basic mathematics; able to use numbers in calculation. ➤ **numeracy** n.

numeration n **1** counting. **2** designating by a number.

numerator n the part of a fraction that is above the line.

numerical adj relating to, expressed in, or involving numbers. ➤ **numerically** adv.

numerous adj **1** many. **2** consisting of many units or individuals. ➤ **numerously** adv.

numinous adj awe-inspiring or mysterious; suggesting the presence of a god.

numismatics pl n the study or collection of coins or medals. ➤ **numismatic** adj, **numismatist** n.

numskull *or* **numbskull** *n* a stupid person.

nun *n* a female member of a religious order living in a convent under vows of chastity, poverty, and obedience.

nuncio *n* (*pl* **-os**) a papal ambassador to a civil government.

nunnery *n* (*pl* **-ies**) a convent of nuns.

nuptial[1] *adj* relating to marriage.

nuptial[2] *n* (*usu in pl*) a wedding.

nurse[1] *n* a person trained to care for the sick or injured.

nurse[2] *v* **1** to tend (e.g. a sick person). **2** to suckle (a baby). **3** to hold or handle carefully. **4** to harbour (a feeling) in one's mind.

nursemaid *n* a girl or woman employed to look after children.

nursery *n* (*pl* **-ies**) **1** a child's bedroom or play-room. **2** = NURSERY SCHOOL. **3** an area where plants, trees, etc are grown for sale or trans-planting.

nursery rhyme *n* a short traditional story in rhyme for children.

nursery school *n* a school for children aged usu from three to five.

nursing home *n* a usu private hospital or home, where care is provided for the aged, chronically ill, etc.

nurture[1] *n* the provision of food, care, and the means for growth and development.

nurture[2] *v* **1** to provide with food, care and the means for growth and development. **2** to encourage and develop (an interest, talent, etc). **3** to cherish (a hope, ambition, etc).

nut *n* **1** a dry fruit or seed consisting of a hard separable rind or shell and an often edible kernel. **2** the kernel of such a fruit. **3** a small metal block with a threaded central hole, which can be screwed onto something, *esp* a bolt. **4** *informal* a person's head. **5** *informal*. **6** an

insane or wildly eccentric person. **7** an ardent enthusiast. ➤ **nutty** *adj*.

nutcase *n informal* a mad person.

nutcracker *n* (*also in pl*) an implement for cracking nuts.

nutmeg *n* the round hard seed of an Indone-sian tree, used as a spice.

nutrient *n* something that provides nourish-ment.

nutriment *n* something that nourishes or pro-motes growth.

nutrition *n* the processes by which an organ-ism takes in and uses food. ➤ **nutritional** *adj*, **nutritionist** *n*.

nutritious *adj* nourishing.

nutritive *adj* **1** relating to nutrition. **2** nourish-ing.

nuts *adj informal* crazy; mad.

nuts and bolts *n informal* **1** the basic practical issues. **2** the practical workings (e.g. of a busi-ness or enterprise).

nutshell *n* the hard outside covering of a nut. ✴ **in a nutshell** in brief; in essence.

nutter *n chiefly Brit, informal* a crazy fool.

nuzzle *v* to rub (something or somebody) affec-tionately with the nose or face.

NVQ *abbr Brit* National Vocational Qualifica-tion.

NW *abbr* **1** northwest. **2** northwestern.

nylon *n* **1** a strong light synthetic material, used *esp* in textiles and plastics. **2** (*in pl*) stockings made of nylon.

nymph *n* **1** a minor female spirit of nature in classical mythology. **2** an immature insect; *esp* a larva of a dragonfly.

nymphet *or* **nymphette** *n* a sexually desirable girl in early adolescence.

nymphomania *n* excessive sexual desire in a female. ➤ **nymphomaniac** *n*.

O¹ or **o** *n* (*pl* **O's** or **Os** or **o's**) **1** the 15th letter of the English alphabet. **2** a representation in speech of zero.

O² *abbr* the chemical symbol for oxygen.

oaf *n* a clumsy, slow-witted, or boorish person. ➤ **oafish** *adj.*

oak *n* a tree with a tough hard wood and lobed leaves, which produces acorns.

oaken *adj* made of oak wood.

OAP *abbr Brit* old age pensioner.

oar *n* a long usu wooden shaft with a broad blade at one end, used for propelling a boat.

oarsman or **oarswoman** *n* (*pl* **oarsmen** or **oarswomen**) somebody who rows a boat.

oasis *n* (*pl* **oases**) **1** a fertile area in a desert or other dry region. **2** a place or time affording relaxation or relief.

oast house *n* a usu circular building housing a kiln for drying hops.

oat *n* (*usu in pl*) a cereal grass with a loosely branched flower head, producing grain used mainly to feed livestock. ✳ **sow one's wild oats** to enjoy a wild youth.

oatcake *n* a savoury biscuit made of oatmeal.

oath *n* (*pl* **oaths**) **1** a form of words by which one solemnly swears to do something *esp* to tell the truth. **2** a swearword. ✳ **on/under oath** bound by a solemn promise to tell the truth.

oatmeal *n* meal made from oats, used *esp* in porridge and oatcakes.

obdurate *adj* stubbornly refusing to change opinions, decisions, etc. ➤ **obduracy** *n.*

OBE *abbr* Officer of the Order of the British Empire.

obedient *adj* willingly carrying out the commands of another person. ➤ **obedience** *n,* **obediently** *adv.*

obeisance /oh'bay(i)səns/ *n* **1** a gesture made as a sign of respect or submission. **2** deference or homage.

obelisk *n* an upright four-sided pillar that tapers towards the top.

obese *adj* very overweight. ➤ **obesity** *n.*

obey *v* **1** to submit to the commands or authority of. **2** to comply with (instructions, the law, etc).

obfuscate *v* to make difficult to understand. ➤ **obfuscation** *n.*

obituary *n* (*pl* **-ies**) a short biography of a recently dead person, printed in a newspaper, etc.

object¹ *n* **1** something that can be seen and touched. **2** something that is being considered or examined. **3** something or somebody that arouses an emotion or provokes a reaction. **4** a goal or purpose. **5** a noun following a preposition or representing the recipient of the action of a verb.

object² *v* (*often* + to) to feel or express dislike or disapproval. ➤ **objector** *n.*

objectify *v* (**-ies, -ied**) **1** to represent (something abstract) as a concrete thing. **2** to reduce to the status of a mere object.

objection *n* a feeling or statement of dislike, disapproval, or opposition.

objectionable *adj* unpleasant or offensive.

objective¹ *adj* **1** dealing with facts without distortion by personal feelings or prejudices. **2** existing independently of the mind; belonging to the external world and observable or verifiable. ➤ **objectively** *adv,* **objectivity** *n.*

objective² *n* a goal or aim.

objet d'art /ˌobzhay'dah/ *n* (*pl* **objets d'art** /ˌobzhay/) a usu small article of some artistic value.

oblate *adj* of a spheroid: flattened at the poles.

oblation *n* an offering made for religious purposes.

obligate *v* to compel legally or morally.

obligation *n* **1** something one is bound to do; a duty. **2** indebtedness for a service or favour.

obligatory *adj* compulsory.

oblige *v* **1** to compel by force, law, or circumstance. **2** to do a favour for. **3** (**be obliged**) to be grateful or indebted.

obliging *adj* eager to help; accommodating. ➤ **obligingly** *adv.*

oblique *adj* **1** sloping. **2** not straightforward or explicit; indirect. ➤ **obliquely** *adv.*

obliterate *v* **1** to destroy all trace of. **2** to make illegible. ➤ **obliteration** *n.*

oblivion *n* **1** the state of being oblivious. **2** the state of being forgotten or no longer existing.

oblivious *adj* (+ of/to) completely unaware.

oblong¹ *adj* rectangular with adjacent sides of unequal length.

oblong² *n* something that is oblong in shape.

obloquy *n* (*pl* **-ies**) **1** strongly worded condemnation. **2** discredit or disgrace.

obnoxious *adj* highly offensive or repugnant.

oboe *n* a woodwind musical instrument with a double reed. ➤ **oboist** *n*.

obscene *adj* **1** offending standards of sexual propriety or decency. **2** morally repugnant. ➤ **obscenely** *adv*.

obscenity *n* (*pl* **-ies**) **1** the state of being obscene. **2** an obscene act or utterance.

obscure¹ *adj* **1** hard to understand. **2** not well-known. **3** difficult to see or identify. ➤ **obscurely** *adv*.

obscure² *v* **1** to prevent from being seen, identified, or discovered. **2** to make indistinct or unintelligible.

obscurity *n* **1** the state of being little known. **2** the state of being difficult to understand.

obsequies /'obsikwiz/ *pl n formal* funeral rites.

obsequious *adj* excessively respectful and eager to oblige or admire; fawning. ➤ **obsequiously** *adv*, **obsequiousness** *n*.

observance *n* **1** (*usu in pl*) a customary *esp* religious rite or ceremony. **2** compliance with a custom, rule, or law.

observant *adj* **1** quick to notice. **2** paying close attention; watchful.

observation *n* **1** the act of observing, or the condition of being observed. **2** the gathering of information by noting facts or occurrences. **3** a remark or comment.

observatory *n* (*pl* **-ies**) a building containing a telescope for the observation of astronomical phenomena.

observe *v* **1** to perceive or take note of. **2** to keep a close watch on. **3** to act in conformity with (e.g. a law). **4** to celebrate or follow the traditional procedures for (e.g. a ceremony or festival). **5** to remark or comment. ➤ **observable** *adj*, **observer** *n*.

obsess *v* to preoccupy intensely or abnormally. ➤ **obsessed** *adj*.

obsession *n* **1** a persistent and usu excessive preoccupation with something or somebody. **2** something that preoccupies somebody. ➤ **obsessional** *adj*.

obsessive *adj* **1** suffering from an obsession. **2** excessive to the point of abnormality. ➤ **obsessively** *adv*, **obsessiveness** *n*.

obsessive-compulsive *adj* denoting a psychiatric disorder in which a particular type of behaviour is frequently repeated as a means of keeping fears or other unwelcome thoughts at bay.

obsidian *n* a usu black volcanic glass-like rock.

obsolescent *adj* becoming obsolete. ➤ **obsolescence** *n*.

obsolete *adj* **1** no longer in use. **2** outmoded.

obstacle *n* something that hinders or obstructs.

obstetrician *n* a doctor who specializes in obstetrics.

obstetrics *pl n* a branch of medicine dealing with the treatment of women during childbirth. ➤ **obstetric** *adj*.

obstinate *adj* **1** clinging stubbornly to an opinion, decision, or course of action. **2** not easily remedied or removed. ➤ **obstinacy** *n*, **obstinately** *adv*.

obstreperous *adj* noisy and unruly.

obstruct *v* **1** to block or close with an obstacle. **2** to impede the progress of; to hinder.

obstruction *n* **1** something that obstructs. **2** the act of deliberately hindering or delaying somebody or something.

obstructive *adj* deliberately hindering or delaying somebody or something.

obtain *v* **1** to gain by effort or request. **2** *formal* to be generally accepted or practised. ➤ **obtainable** *adj*.

obtrude *v* to thrust oneself or itself forward with unwelcome assertiveness. ➤ **obtrusion** *n*.

obtrusive *adj* unduly or irritatingly noticeable.

obtuse *adj* **1** lacking sensitivity or mental alertness. **2** of an angle: greater than 90° but less than 180°. **3** not pointed or sharp.

obverse *n* **1** the side of a coin, medal, etc that bears the principal design and lettering. **2** a counterpart or opposite.

obviate *v* to anticipate and dispose of (a difficulty, etc) in advance.

obvious *adj* **1** very easily perceived by the senses or understanding; clear. **2** lacking subtlety. ➤ **obviously** *adv*.

ocarina *n* a simple egg-shaped wind instrument with finger holes in its body.

occasion¹ *n* **1** a time at which something occurs. **2** a suitable opportunity. **3** *formal* a reason or grounds. **4** a special event or ceremony. * **on occasion** from time to time. **rise to the occasion** to perform well when a situation demands it.

occasion² *v formal* to cause.

occasional *adj* **1** occurring at irregular or infrequent intervals. **2** acting in a specified capacity from time to time. ➤ **occasionally** *adv*.

occidental or **Occidental** *adj* of or situated in the countries of the West.

occlude *v* to stop up or block (a passage or opening).

occult¹ *n* (**the occult**) matters involving the action or influence of supernatural agencies or some secret knowledge of them. ➤ **occultism** *n*, **occultist** *n*.

occult² *adj* **1** involving supernatural powers. **2** known only to the initiated few; esoteric.

occupancy *n* (*pl* **-ies**) **1** the act of occupying land, a property, etc. **2** the proportion of a building, e.g. a hotel, that is occupied.

occupant *n* somebody who occupies a particular building.

occupation *n* **1** an activity by which one earns a living. **2** an activity in which one engages. **3** the act of taking possession or control of a place, *esp* by a foreign military force.

occupational *adj* of or resulting from a particular job or profession.

occupational therapy *n* creative activity used as therapy for promoting recovery or rehabilitation.

occupy *v* (**-ies, -ied**) **1** to engage the attention or energies of. **2** to fill up (a portion of space or time). **3** to take or maintain possession of (e.g. land). **4** to reside in or use (a building) as owner or tenant. ➤ **occupier** *n*.

occur *v* (**occurred, occurring**) **1** to happen. **2** to be found; to exist. **3** (+ to) to come to mind.

occurrence *n* **1** something that takes place; an event. **2** the act of occurring.

ocean *n* **1** any or all of the large expanses of salt water that cover much of the earth's surface. **2** *informal* (*in pl*) a huge amount.

oceanic /ohshi'anik/ *adj* relating to the oceans.

oceanography *n* the science dealing with oceans and their biology and resources. ➤ **oceanographer** *n*.

ocelot *n* a medium-sized wildcat of Central and South America with a dotted and striped coat.

ochre (*NAmer* **ocher**) *n* an earthy usu red or yellow pigment.

o'clock *adv* used in specifying the exact hour when telling the time.

octagon *n* a polygon with eight angles and eight sides. ➤ **octagonal** *adj*.

octahedron *n* (*pl* **octahedrons** *or* **octahedra**) a polyhedron with eight faces.

octane *n* a colourless liquid chemical compound occurring *esp* in petroleum.

octave *n* **1** a musical interval of eight notes on the diatonic scale. **2** the whole series of notes within this interval.

octavo /ok'tayvoh/ *n* (*pl* **-os**) a size of book page that is created when a standard sheet is folded into 8 leaves or 16 pages.

octet *n* **1** a group of eight instruments, voices, or performers. **2** a musical composition for an octet.

October *n* the tenth month of the year.

octogenarian *n* a person between 80 and 89 years old.

octopus *n* (*pl* **octopuses** *or* **octopi**) a sea creature with eight muscular arms equipped with suckers.

ocular *adj* of the eye.

oculist *n* an ophthalmologist or optician.

OD *v* (**OD's, OD'd, OD'ing**) to take an overdose of a drug.

odalisque *n* a female slave or concubine in a harem.

odd *adj* **1** different from the usual or conventional; strange. **2** left over when others are paired or grouped. **3** not matching. **4** of a number: not divisible by two without leaving a remainder. **5** occasional; spare: *at odd moments*. **6** somewhat more than the specified number: *300-odd pages*. ➤ **oddly** *adv*, **oddness** *n*.

oddball *n informal* an eccentric or peculiar person.

oddity *n* (*pl* **-ies**) **1** an odd person, thing, or event. **2** strangeness.

odd man out *n* somebody or something that differs from all the others in a group.

oddment *n* **1** something left over; a remnant. **2** (*in pl*) miscellaneous things.

odds *pl n* **1** the ratio between the amount to be paid for a winning bet and the amount of the bet. **2** (**the odds**) the probability, often expressed as a ratio, that one thing will happen rather than another. **3** (**the odds**) a difference in terms of advantage or disadvantage. ✳ **at odds** in disagreement or at variance.

odds and ends *pl n* miscellaneous items or remnants.

odds-on *adj* **1** viewed as having a better than even chance to win. **2** likely to succeed, happen, etc.

ode *n* a poem of medium length, often addressed to a particular person or thing or celebrating an event, and usu marked by an exalted tone.

odious *adj* arousing hatred or revulsion.

odium *n formal* general condemnation or disgrace.

odoriferous *adj* giving off an odour.

odour (*NAmer* **odor**) *n* a scent or smell. ➤ **odorous** *adj*, **odourless** *adj*.

odyssey *n* (*pl* **-eys**) a long and wandering journey or quest.

OED *abbr* Oxford English Dictionary.

oedema (*NAmer* **edema**) *n* abnormal swelling caused by an accumulation of liquid between tissue cells.

oesophagus (*NAmer* **esophagus**) /ee'sofəgəs/ *n* (*pl* **oesophagi** /-gie/) the muscular tube leading from the back of the mouth to the stomach; the gullet.

oestrogen (*NAmer* **estrogen**) *n* a steroid hormone that stimulates the development of secondary sex characteristics in females.

oeuvre /'uhvrə/ *n* all the works produced by a writer, artist, or composer, considered as a body.

of *prep* **1** used to indicate origin or derivation. **2** composed or made from. **3** containing. **4** from among. **5** belonging or related to. **6** possessing or characterized by. **7** connected with.

of course *adv* **1** as might be expected. **2** used in reply to express agreement or permission.

off[1] *adv* **1** from a place or position. **2** away in space or ahead in time. **3** away from a course or direction. **4** so as not to be in contact or attached. **5** to or in a state of non-operation or suspension. **6** away from work. **7** into sleep or unconsciousness.

off² *prep* **1** used to indicate physical separation or distance from. **2** lying or turning aside from. **3** so as to become detached from. **4** not occupied in. **5** no longer interested in or using. **6** below the usual standard or level of.

off³ *adj* **1** started on a journey or race. **2** cancelled. **3** not busy; slack. **4** no longer fresh; beginning to decay. **5** provided: *How are you off for socks?* **6** *informal* of behaviour: not what one has a right to expect.

off⁴ *n* the start or outset.

offal *n* the inner organs, e.g. liver, kidney, etc, of an animal used as food.

offbeat *adj informal* unusual or unconventional.

off chance *n* a remote possibility. ✳ **on the off chance** just in case.

off-colour *adj* unwell.

offcut *n* a piece of e.g. fabric or wood left after the required amount has been cut.

offence (*NAmer* **offense**) *n* **1** a breach of a law, rule, etc; a crime. **2** a feeling of displeasure or resentment.

offend *v* **1** to cause pain or displeasure to; to hurt or insult. **2** to cause to feel indignation or disgust. **3** to commit a crime or wrongdoing. ➤ **offender** *n*.

offensive¹ *adj* **1** causing indignation, outrage, or disgust. **2** of or designed for attack. ➤ **offensively** *adv*.

offensive² *n* **1** an attacking attitude or position. **2** a large-scale military attack or non-military campaign.

offer¹ *v* **1** to present for acceptance, rejection, or consideration. **2** to make available; to provide. **3** to declare one's willingness (to do something).

offer² *n* **1** an undertaking to do or give something. **2** a price named by a prospective buyer. **3** an article on sale at a reduced price. ✳ **on offer 1** available. **2** for sale at a reduced price.

offering *n* something offered or presented, e.g. a sacrifice or donation.

offertory *n* (*pl* **-ies**) **1** the offering of the Communion bread and wine to God before consecration. **2** the collection of money from the congregation at public worship.

offhand¹ *or* **offhanded** *adj* **1** without proper courtesy or warmth. **2** informal or casual.

offhand² *adv* without forethought or preparation.

office *n* **1** a room in which administrative or clerical work is done. **2** a building where the business of a particular organization is carried out. **3** a position giving authority or having special responsibilities. **4** *formal* (*in pl*) services carried out for other people.

officer *n* **1** somebody who holds a position of authority in the armed forces. **2** a member of a police force. **3** somebody who holds a position with special duties or responsibilities, e.g. in a government or business.

official¹ *adj* **1** sanctioned or carried out by people in authority. **2** holding a position of authority. **3** suitable for or characteristic of people in authority. ➤ **officially** *adv*.

official² *n* somebody who holds a position of authority, *esp* in a public organization or institution. ➤ **officialdom** *n*.

officiate *v* **1** to perform an *esp* religious ceremony. **2** to act as an official.

officious *adj* overzealous in exercising authority, and tending to interfere in other people's affairs.

offing *n* ✳ **in the offing** likely to happen in the near future.

off-licence *n Brit* a shop licensed to sell alcoholic drinks to be consumed off the premises.

off-line *adv and adj* not connected to or controlled by a computer.

off-load *v* **1** to unload (cargo). **2** to get rid of (something unwanted).

off-peak *adj and adv* at a time of relatively light demand or activity.

off-putting *adj chiefly Brit, informal* disagreeable or disconcerting.

offset *v* (**offsetting**, *past tense and past part.* **offset**) to balance or compensate for.

offshoot *n* something that develops out of something else.

offshore *adj and adv* **1** away from the shore. **2** at a distance from the shore. **3** located or operating abroad.

offside *adv and adj* illegally in advance of the ball or puck in a team game.

offspring *n* (*pl* **offspring**) the progeny of a person, animal, or plant.

offstage *adv and adj* not visible to the audience in a theatre.

off-white *adj* of a yellowish or greyish white colour. ➤ **off-white** *n*.

often *adv* **1** at many times. **2** in many cases.

ogle *v* to stare at with sexual interest, *esp* offensively.

ogre *or* **ogress** *n* **1** a hideous giant of folklore believed to feed on human beings. **2** a dreaded person or thing.

ohm *n* the SI unit of electrical resistance.

oik *n slang* a vulgar, loud, or otherwise obnoxious person.

oil¹ *n* **1** a smooth greasy liquid substance, obtained from plants or animals, that is not soluble in water. **2** = PETROLEUM. **3** a substance derived from petroleum, used for fuel, lubrication, etc. **4** (*also in pl*) = OIL PAINT.

oil² *v* to apply oil to, *esp* for lubrication.

oilfield *n* a region rich in petroleum deposits.

oil paint *n* artist's paint consisting of ground pigment mixed with oil. ➤ **oil painting** *n*.

oilskin *n* **1** an oiled waterproof cloth. **2** an outer garment made of oilskin or other waterproof material.

oily *adj* (**-ier, -iest**) **1** resembling, containing, or covered with oil. **2** too eager to please or flatter. ➤ **oiliness** *n*.

oink *v* of a pig: to make a characteristic grunting noise. ➤ **oink** *n*.

ointment *n* a soothing or healing oily cream applied to the skin.

OK[1] or **okay** *interj* an expression of agreement or permission.

OK[2] or **okay** *adj* **1** quite good, but not outstanding. **2** permissible; acceptable. **3** unharmed or in good health.

OK[3] *adv* quite well; adequately or satisfactorily.

OK[4] or **okay** *v* (**OK's, OK'd, OK'ing** or **okays, okayed, okaying**) to give approval or authorization to.

OK[5] or **okay** *n* (*pl* **OK's** or **okays**) an approval or endorsement.

okapi /oh'kahpi/ *n* (*pl* **okapis** or **okapi**) an African mammal closely related to the giraffe but with a shorter neck and ring marks on the upper legs.

okra *n* the long green pods of a tropical plant, used as a vegetable.

old *adj* **1** having lived or existed for many years. **2** having lived or existed for a specified period of time. **3** dating from the past, *esp* the remote past. **4** persisting from an earlier time. **5** of long standing. **6** former.

old age *n* the final stage of the normal life span.

old boy *n chiefly Brit* **1** a former pupil of a particular school. **2** *informal* an old man.

olden *adj literary* of a bygone era.

Old English *n* the earliest form of the English language, dating from around the seventh to the eleventh centuries; Anglo-Saxon.

old-fashioned *adj* belonging to a past era; outdated.

old girl *n chiefly Brit* **1** a former pupil of a particular school. **2** *informal* an old woman.

old guard *n* the conservative members of a group.

old hand *n* somebody with a great deal of experience.

old hat *adj* tediously familiar or old-fashioned.

old maid *n derog* a single woman of advanced age.

old master *n* **1** a distinguished European painter of the 16th to early 18th cents. **2** a painting produced by an old master.

Old Nick *n informal* the devil.

Old Norse *n* the ancient or medieval language of Scandinavia and Iceland.

Old Testament *n* a collection of writings forming the Jewish canon of Scripture and the first part of the Christian Bible.

old wives' tale *n* a traditional superstitious notion.

Old World *n* (**the Old World**) Europe, Asia, and Africa.

oleaginous *adj* **1** oily. **2** obsequious or unctuous in manner.

O level *n* a former secondary school examination in England and Wales, replaced by the GCSE.

olfactory *adj* relating to the sense of smell.

oligarch *n* a member of the ruling group in an oligarchy.

oligarchy *n* (*pl* **-ies**) **1** a state or organization in which a small group exercises control. **2** a small group governing or exercising control. ➤ **oligarchic** *adj*.

olive *n* **1** a small green or purplish black fruit with a stone, used as a food and a source of oil. **2** the small evergreen tree that bears this fruit. **3** (*also* **olive green**) a dull greyish green colour. ➤ **olive** *adj*.

olive branch *n* an offer or gesture of conciliation.

olive oil *n* oil obtained from ripe olives, used in cooking and salad dressings.

Olympiad *n* a holding of the Olympic Games.

Olympian[1] *adj* **1** of or dwelling on Mount Olympus. **2** of the Olympic Games.

Olympian[2] *n* **1** any of the ancient Greek deities dwelling on Olympus. **2** a participant in the Olympic Games.

Olympic *adj* relating to the Olympic Games.

Olympic Games *pl n* **1** an international sports meeting held once every four years in a different host country. **2** an ancient Greek festival held every four years with athletic, literary, and musical contests.

Olympics *pl n* (**the Olympics**) the modern Olympic Games.

ombudsman *n* (*pl* **ombudsmen**) a government official appointed to investigate complaints made by individuals against government or public bodies.

omega *n* the 24th and last letter of the Greek alphabet (Ω, ω).

omelette (*NAmer* **omelet**) *n* a mixture of beaten eggs cooked in a shallow pan until set.

omen *n* an event believed to be a sign of some future occurrence.

omicron *n* the 15th letter of the Greek alphabet (O, o).

ominous *adj* suggesting future disaster or evil. ➤ **ominously** *adv*.

omission *n* **1** the act of omitting. **2** something omitted. **3** failure to do something.

omit *v* (**omitted, omitting**) **1** to leave out or unmentioned. **2** to fail to do.

omni- *comb. form* all or universally: *omniscient*.

omnibus *n* **1** a book containing reprints of a number of works originally published separately. **2** a television or radio programme consisting of two or more episodes of a series, originally broadcast separately. **3** *formal, dated* a bus.

omnipotent *adj* having unlimited or very great power. ➤ **omnipotence** *n*.

omnipresent *adj* **1** present in all places at all times. **2** very widespread or frequently encountered. ➤ **omnipresence** *n*.

omniscient *adj* knowing everything. ➤ **omniscience** *n*.

omnivorous *adj* **1** feeding on both animal and vegetable substances. **2** avidly taking in, *esp* reading, everything.

on¹ *prep* **1** in contact with or supported from below by. **2** attached or fastened to. **3** carried on the person of. **4** positioned at or towards. **5** with regard to; concerning. **6** belonging to (e.g. a team). **7** paid for by. **8** in the specified state, process, manner, etc: *on fire*. **9** using by way of transport. **10** regularly taking (a drug). **11** indicating a time, *esp* a day of the week, when something happens. **12** in the course of. **13** broadcast by or recorded with.

on² *adv* **1** so as to be supported from below. **2** so as to be worn. **3** so as to be attached. **4** ahead or forwards in space or time. **5** with the specified part forward. **6** without interruption. **7** in or into operation.

on³ *adj* **1** taking place. **2** performing or broadcasting. **3** operating. **4** *chiefly Brit* possible or practicable.

onanism *n* masturbation.

once¹ *adv* **1** one time and no more. **2** at some indefinite time in the past; formerly. ✻ **at once 1** immediately. **2** simultaneously. **once again/more 1** now again as before. **2** for one more time. **once in a while** occasionally. **once or twice** a few times. **once upon a time** used as a traditional formula to begin a children's story: at some time in the past.

once² *conj* from the moment when; as soon as.

once-over *n informal* a swift appraising glance.

oncoming *adj* approaching from the front.

one¹ *adj* **1** being a single unit or thing. **2** being a particular but unspecified instance. **3** the same; identical. **4** in a state of agreement; united. **5** being some unspecified future time. **6** being a particular object or person.

one² *pron* (*pl* **ones**) **1** an indefinitely indicated person; anybody at all. **2** used to refer to a noun or noun phrase previously mentioned or understood.

one³ *n* **1** the number 1. **2** the first in a set or series. **3** a particular example or instance. ✻ **at one** in agreement or harmony. **one after another/the other** in succession. **one by one** singly or successively. **one or other** either; any. **one or two** a few.

one-armed bandit *n* a fruit machine that is operated by a lever on one side.

one-liner *n* a short funny remark.

oneness *n* the state of being whole, identical, or in agreement.

one-off¹ *adj chiefly Brit* intended as a single and unrepeated item or occurrence.

one-off² *n* a unique person or thing.

onerous *adj* representing or involving a burden. ➤ **onerousness** *n*.

oneself *pron* used reflexively or for emphasis to refer to an indefinitely indicated person or to people in general.

one-upmanship *n* the art of gaining a psychological advantage over others.

ongoing *adj* **1** actually in progress. **2** growing or developing.

onion *n* a pungent smelling, strong tasting edible bulb that is used as a vegetable.

on-line *adv and adj* connected to or controlled by a computer or network.

onlooker *n* a passive spectator.

only¹ *adj* **1** alone in its class or kind; sole. **2** without a brother or sister.

only² *adv* **1** nothing more than; merely. **2** solely or exclusively. **3** with nevertheless the final result. **4** no earlier than.

only³ *conj informal* **1** but or however. **2** were it not for the fact that.

onomatopoeia *n* the use of words intended to be a vocal imitation of the sound associated with the thing or action designated, e.g. *buzz*. ➤ **onomatopoeic** *adj*.

onrush *n* a forceful rushing forwards.

onset *n* a time or point at which something begins.

onshore *adj and adv* **1** towards the shore. **2** on or near the shore.

onside *adv and adj* **1** in a position permitted by the rules of the game; not offside. **2** in a position of agreement or support.

onslaught *n* a fierce attack.

onstage *adj and adv* on or onto the stage; in view of the audience.

onto *or* **on to** *prep* **1** to a position on. **2** in or into a state of awareness about. **3** *chiefly Brit* in or into contact with.

ontology *n* a branch of philosophy concerned with the nature of being. ➤ **ontological** *adj*.

onus *n* a duty or responsibility.

onward¹ *adj* directed or moving forwards.

onward² *adv* = ONWARDS.

onwards *adv* towards a point lying ahead in space or time.

onyx *n* a translucent semiprecious stone with layers of different colours.

oodles *pl n informal* a great quantity; a lot.

oomph *n informal* vitality or enthusiasm.

ooze¹ *v* **1** of a liquid: to move or be emitted slowly. **2** to display (a quality) in abundance.

ooze² *n* the act of oozing.

op *n informal* a military or surgical operation.

opacity *n* the quality of being opaque.

opal *n* a semitransparent iridescent mineral used as a gem.

opalescent *adj* reflecting a milky iridescent light.

opaque *adj* **1** not able to be seen through. **2** hard to understand; unintelligible.

op. cit. *abbr* (Latin) opere citato = in the work cited.

open¹ *adj* **1** allowing access or passage; not shut or locked. **2** not fastened or sealed. **3** not covered or protected. **4** not enclosed, blocked, or restricted. **5** having the parts or surfaces spread out or unfolded. **6** in operation, *esp* ready for business or use. **7** not disguised, concealed, or kept secret. **8** (+ to) liable to undergo (e.g. attack or criticism). **9** (*often* + to) available or remaining available. **10** not finally decided or settled. **11** (+ to) willing to receive and consider. **12** candid or frank. **13** unprejudiced: *an open mind.* ➤ **opener** *n*, **openly** *adv*, **openness** *n*.

open² *v* **1** to make or become open. **2** to unfold or spread out. **3** to start operating for business. **4** to begin an activity. **5** to declare to be available for use, especially in a ceremony. **6** (+ into/onto) to give access.

open³ *n* **1** (**the open**) a large outdoor space, *esp* in the countryside. **2** (*often* **Open**) a contest in which anybody can compete.

open air *n* (**the open air**) a large outdoor space; outdoors. ➤ **open-air** *adj*.

open-and-shut *adj* easily settled.

opencast *adj* of a mine or mining: worked from or carried out on the earth's surface by removing material covering the mineral.

open-heart surgery *n* surgery in which the heart is actually exposed.

open house ✳ **keep open house** to be ready to receive visitors at all times.

opening¹ *n* **1** a space through which something can pass; a gap. **2** a beginning or first part. **3** a ceremony marking the first time a building, exhibition, etc can be visited by the public. **4** a first performance. **5** a favourable opportunity; a chance. **6** an opportunity for employment; a vacancy.

opening² *adj* coming at or marking the beginning of something.

open letter *n* a letter addressed to an individual but published so that it can be read by the general public.

open market *n* a market based on free competition and an unrestricted flow of goods.

open-minded *adj* receptive to new arguments or ideas. ➤ **open-mindedness** *n*.

open-plan *adj* having no or few internal dividing walls.

open verdict *n* a verdict at an inquest that does not state the cause of death.

opera¹ *n* a drama set to music and made up of vocal pieces and orchestral music.

opera² *n* pl of OPUS.

operable *adj* **1** suitable for surgical treatment. **2** fit or possible to use.

opera glasses *pl n* small binoculars suitable for use at the opera or theatre.

operate *v* **1** to function or cause (e.g. a machine) to function. **2** to act or produce a desired effect. **3** to be in effect. **4** to carry out trade or business. **5** to carry on a military or naval action. **6** (*often* + on) to perform surgery.

operatic *adj* **1** of opera. **2** overtly theatrical in behaviour. ➤ **operatically** *adv*.

operation *n* **1** the act of operating. **2** the state of being functional or operative. **3** an action or manoeuvre, *esp* an organized or complex one, e.g. by the military. **4** a surgical procedure carried out on a living body with special instruments. **5** a single step performed by a computer in executing a program. **6** a business organization.

operational *adj* **1** relating to or involved in the operations of an organization. **2** currently functioning or able to function. ➤ **operationally** *adv*.

operative¹ *adj* **1** in force or operation. **2** significant or relevant. **3** of or using a surgical operation.

operative² *n* a worker.

operator *n* **1** somebody who operates a machine or device. **2** somebody who owns or runs a business, organization, etc. **3** somebody who works at a telephone switchboard. **4** *informal* somebody who manipulates people or situations shrewdly.

operetta *n* a less formal or serious opera, usu on a romantic or humorous theme.

ophthalmic *adj* relating to the eye and diseases of the eye.

ophthalmology *n* the branch of medical science dealing with the structure, functions, and diseases of the eye. ➤ **ophthalmologist** *n*.

opiate *n* a preparation or derivative of opium.

opine *v formal* to state as an opinion.

opinion *n* **1** a view or judgment formed about a particular matter. **2** a belief that is not supported by positive knowledge. **3** a generally held view. **4** a formal expression by an expert of his or her professional judgment or advice. ✳ **matter of opinion** something that cannot be decided objectively or proved conclusively.

opinionated *adj* having strong opinions and always ready to express them.

opinion poll *n* a survey conducted by questioning a selected number of people to establish public opinion on some matter.

opium *n* an addictive drug derived from the juice of poppy seeds.

opossum n (pl **opossums** or **opossum**) **1** an American tree-dwelling marsupial with a prehensile tail. **2** = POSSUM.

opponent n **1** somebody who takes the opposite side in a contest, conflict, etc. **2** somebody who opposes something, e.g. a plan or proposal.

opportune adj **1** suitable for a particular occurrence or action. **2** occurring at an appropriate time.

opportunist n somebody who takes advantage of opportunities with little regard for principles or consequences. ➤ **opportunist** adj, **opportunistic** adj.

opportunity n (pl **-ies**) **1** a favourable set of circumstances. **2** a chance for advancement or progress.

oppose v **1** to be hostile to; to resist. **2** to fight or compete with. **3** to place opposite or against something else, e.g. as a contrast or counterbalance. ✳ **as opposed to** in contrast to. ➤ **opposing** adj.

opposite[1] adj **1** positioned at a distance from and facing somebody or something else, often on the other side of something. **2** diametrically different; contrary. **3** being the other of a matching or contrasting pair: *the opposite sex*.

opposite[2] prep **1** across from and usu facing. **2** in a role in a play or film complementary to that of.

opposite[3] adv on or to an opposite side.

opposite[4] n an opposite person or thing.

opposition n **1** hostility or resistance. **2** the state of being opposed or opposite. **3** a body of people opposing something. **4** (often **Opposition**) the main political party opposing the party in power. ➤ **oppositional** adj.

oppress v **1** to treat in a harsh or authoritarian manner. **2** to be a heavy burden on the mind or spirit of. ➤ **oppression** n, **oppressor** n.

oppressive adj **1** unreasonably harsh or severe. **2** causing a sense of being mentally weighed down. **3** of the weather: stiflingly warm and windless; close. ➤ **oppressively** adv.

opprobrious adj formal sharply critical, scornful, or abusive.

opprobrium n formal **1** scornful criticism. **2** the public disgrace that results from shameful behaviour.

opt v to make a choice.

optic[1] adj of vision or the eye.

optic[2] n Brit a device fitted to the neck of an inverted bottle to deliver a measure of alcoholic spirit.

optical adj relating to optics, vision, or light.

optical fibre n a very thin glass fibre used to transmit light.

optical illusion n something that makes observers believe they are seeing something that they are not.

optician n somebody who examines eyes and prescribes correctional lenses for eye defects.

optics pl n the science of the nature, properties, and uses of light.

optimal adj most satisfactory. ➤ **optimally** adv.

optimism n a tendency to emphasize favourable aspects of situations or events or to expect the best possible outcome. ➤ **optimist** n.

optimistic adj emphasizing favourable aspects or expecting a successful outcome. ➤ **optimistically** adv.

optimize or **-ise** v to make as effective or advantageous as possible. ➤ **optimization** n.

optimum[1] adj most favourable or desirable.

optimum[2] n (pl **optima** or **optimums**) the most favourable or desirable condition.

option n **1** an alternative course of action; a choice. **2** the right to choose. **3** a right to buy or sell something at a specified price during a stipulated period.

optional adj available as a choice; not compulsory. ➤ **optionally** adv.

optometry n the profession of examining the eye for defects and prescribing correctional lenses or exercises. ➤ **optometrist** n.

opt out v to choose not to participate in something.

opulent adj rich or luxurious. ➤ **opulence** n, **opulently** adv.

opus n (pl **opera** or **opuses**) **1** a musical composition or set of compositions. **2** an artistic work of any kind.

or conj **1** used to join two or more alternatives. **2** used to introduce a word or phrase that defines or explains a preceding word or phrase. **3** otherwise.

-or suffix denoting somebody or something that performs an action: *vendor*.

oracle n a priest or priestess of ancient Greece or Rome who delivered answers, purporting to come from a god and often cryptically worded, to questions regarding the future.

oracular adj resembling an oracle in authority or obscurity of expression.

oral[1] adj **1** involving speech rather than writing. **2** of, taken through, or affecting the mouth. ➤ **orally** adv.

oral[2] n an oral examination.

orange n **1** a spherical fruit with a reddish yellow rind and sweet juicy edible pulp. **2** the colour of oranges, between red and yellow in the spectrum.

orangeade n sweetened orange juice mixed with carbonated water.

orang-utan or **orang-utang** n a tree-dwelling anthropoid ape with orange-brown skin and hair and very long arms.

oration n a formal speech.

orator n a skilled public speaker.

oratorio n (pl -os) a large-scale choral work usu with orchestral accompaniment and based on a religious subject.

oratory[1] n (pl -ies) a place of prayer, esp a private or institutional chapel.

oratory[2] n 1 the art of public speaking. 2 impressive or eloquent speech. ➤ **oratorical** adj.

orb n 1 a golden globe surmounted by a cross, symbolizing royal power. 2 a spherical object.

orbit[1] n 1 a path followed regularly by a moon, spacecraft or satellite round a celestial body. 2 a sphere of activity or influence.

orbit[2] v (orbited, orbiting) to revolve in an orbit round (e.g. a celestial body).

orbital adj 1 relating to an orbit in space. 2 of a road: bypassing and circling a major city.

orca n = KILLER WHALE.

orchard n a usu enclosed area in which fruit trees are planted.

orchestra n 1 a large group of musicians, esp one comprising string, woodwind, brass, and percussion sections. 2 = ORCHESTRA PIT. ➤ **orchestral** adj.

orchestra pit n in a theatre, the space in front of the stage where the members of the orchestra sit.

orchestrate v 1 to arrange (music) for an orchestra. 2 to arrange cleverly to achieve the desired outcome. ➤ **orchestration** n.

orchid n a plant having colourful flowers with an enlarged liplike middle petal.

ordain v 1 to invest with the authority of a priest or minister. 2 to order by decree or law.

ordeal n a severe or testing experience.

order[1] n 1 a command. 2 a request for goods to be supplied, food to be served, work to be done, etc. 3 regular, correct, or harmonious arrangement. 4 an arrangement of objects, people, etc according to sequence in space, time, value or importance. 5 a proper, orderly, or functioning condition. 6 the rule of law or proper authority. 7 the customary procedure, e.g. for a debate or a religious service. 8 a category or kind. 9 a rank or group in a community. 10 a category in the classification of living things ranking above the family and below the class. 11 a religious body or community living under a specific rule. 12 (in pl) the office of a person in the Christian ministry. 13 a group of people who have been awarded a specific type of honour, esp a knighthood: the Order of the Bath. * **in/of the order of** approximately. **out of order 1** not in the correct sequence. 2 not in working condition. 3 informal not acceptable or appropriate.

order[2] v 1 to put in order; to arrange. 2 to give a command to or for. 3 to place an order for (e.g. goods).

orderly[1] adj 1 arranged or carried out in a neat and methodical way. 2 well behaved or peaceful. ➤ **orderliness** n.

orderly[2] n (pl -ies) 1 a soldier assigned to carry messages, relay orders, etc for a superior officer. 2 a hospital attendant who does routine or heavy work.

ordinal adj of a specified order or rank in a series.

ordinal number n a number, e.g. first, second, or third, designating the place occupied by an item in a series.

ordinance n 1 an authoritative order or regulation. 2 a prescribed practice or ceremony.

ordinary adj 1 routine or usual. 2 not exceptional; commonplace. * **out of the ordinary** not usual or customary. ➤ **ordinarily** adv, **ordinariness** n.

Ordinary level n = O LEVEL.

ordination n the act of ordaining somebody as a priest or minister.

ordnance n 1 military supplies. 2 heavy artillery.

ordure n formal excrement.

ore n a mineral containing a metal or other valuable constituent.

oregano /ori'gahnoh, ə'regənoh/ n a bushy plant whose leaves are used as a herb in cooking.

organ n 1 a musical instrument with a keyboard and sets of pipes activated by compressed air. 2 an electronic keyboard instrument producing a similar sound. 3 a specialized biological structure, e.g. the heart or a leaf, performing some specific function in an organism. 4 formal a newspaper or periodical. ➤ **organist** n.

organic adj 1 of or derived from living organisms. 2 of food, farming, etc: produced or carried out without the aid of chemical fertilizers, pesticides, etc. 3 of or arising in a bodily organ. 4 of e.g. development: proceeding in a natural and usu gradual and unforced manner. 5 containing, or dealing with materials containing, carbon compounds. ➤ **organically** adv.

organism n 1 an individual member of a biological species; a being. 2 a complex structure of interdependent elements.

organization or **-isation** n 1 the act of organizing. 2 the state of being arranged or proceeding in an orderly manner. 3 an association of people undertaking a particular activity, e.g. a business or a political party. ➤ **organizational** adj.

organize or **-ise** v 1 to arrange in an orderly way or so as to form a functioning whole. 2 to plan and make the necessary preparations for (an event). ➤ **organizer** n.

orgasm n the climax of sexual excitement. ➤ **orgasmic** adj.

orgy n (pl -ies) 1 a wild party characterized by sexual promiscuity, drunken revelry, etc. 2 an excessive indulgence in a specified activity. ➤ **orgiastic** adj.

oriel window *n* a bay window projecting from an upper storey.

orient[1] *n* (**the Orient**) *dated* the countries of eastern Asia, *esp* China, Japan, and their neighbours.

orient[2] *v* = ORIENTATE.

oriental *adj* (*often* **Oriental**) from or characteristic of the Orient.

orientate *v chiefly Brit* **1** to set in position in relation to the points of the compass. **2** to adjust to a particular environment or situation. * **orientate oneself** to ascertain one's position in unfamiliar surroundings.

orientation *n* **1** the act of orientating. **2** an arrangement, alignment, or relative position. **3** a lasting tendency of thought, inclination, or interest.

orienteering *n* a sport in which contestants have to cross unfamiliar country on foot using a map and compass.

orifice *n* an opening.

origami /ori'gahmi/ *n* the Japanese art of folding paper into complex shapes.

origin *n* **1** a source or starting-point. **2** ancestry or parentage.

original[1] *adj* **1** initial or earliest. **2** not secondary, derivative, or imitative. **3** inventive or creative. ➤ **originality** *n*, **originally** *adv*.

original[2] *n* something from which a copy, reproduction, or translation is made.

original sin *n* in Christianity, the innate sinfulness of all human beings that resulted from Adam's disobedience to God.

originate *v* **1** to begin or come into existence. **2** to bring into existence. ➤ **origination** *n*, **originator** *n*.

ormolu *n* gilded brass or bronze used to decorate furniture, ornaments, etc.

ornament[1] *n* **1** something that adds beauty to a person or thing. **2** a small decorative object. **3** decoration or embellishment. ➤ **ornamental** *adj*.

ornament[2] *v* to decorate or embellish. ➤ **ornamentation** *n*.

ornate *adj* elaborately or excessively decorated. ➤ **ornately** *adv*.

ornithology *n* a branch of zoology dealing with birds. ➤ **ornithological** *adj*, **ornithologist** *n*.

orphan[1] *n* a child whose parents are dead.

orphan[2] *v* to make (somebody) an orphan.

orphanage *n* an institution for the care of orphans.

orthodontics *pl n* a branch of dentistry dealing with the correction of irregularities of the teeth. ➤ **orthodontic** *adj*, **orthodontist** *n*.

orthodox *adj* **1** conforming to established or official doctrine or practice. **2** conventional or normal. **3** (**Orthodox**) of or denoting any of the Eastern Churches, e.g. in Greece or Russia, headed by the patriarch of Constantinople.

orthodoxy *n* (*pl* **-ies**) **1** being orthodox. **2** an orthodox belief or practice.

orthography *n* (*pl* **-ies**) the spelling system of a language. ➤ **orthographic** *adj*.

orthopaedics (*NAmer* **orthopedics**) *pl n* a branch of medicine dealing with the correction of skeletal and muscular deformities. ➤ **orthopaedic** *adj*.

Os *abbr* the chemical symbol for osmium.

Oscar *n* a gold statuette awarded for outstanding achievement in the cinema.

oscillate *v* **1** to swing backward and forward like a pendulum. **2** to vary between opposing beliefs, feelings, courses of action, etc. ➤ **oscillation** *n*, **oscillator** *n*.

osier *n* a willow with pliable twigs that are used for furniture and basketry.

osmium *n* a hard brittle blue-grey metallic element.

osmosis *n* **1** movement of a solvent through a membrane into a solution of higher concentration. **2** a process of gradual assimilation, e.g. of knowledge. ➤ **osmotic** *adj*, **osmotically** *adv*.

osprey *n* (*pl* **-eys**) a large fish-eating hawk with dark brown and white plumage.

osseous *adj technical* consisting of bone.

ossify *v* (**-ies**, **-ied**) **1** to change into bone. **2** to become inflexible in habit or attitude. ➤ **ossification** *n*.

ostensible *adj* seeming to be so, but not necessarily true or real. ➤ **ostensibly** *adv*.

ostentation *n* unnecessary display of wealth, knowledge, etc designed to attract attention.

ostentatious *adj* designed to impress or attract attention. ➤ **ostentatiously** *adv*.

osteoarthritis *n* a degenerative form of arthritis usu associated with increasing age. ➤ **osteoarthritic** *adj*.

osteopathy *n* a system of treatment of disease based on the manipulation of bones or other parts of the body. ➤ **osteopath** *n*.

osteoporosis *n* a disease that causes the bones to become thin, brittle, and porous.

ostinato *n* (*pl* **-os**) a musical figure repeated persistently throughout a composition.

ostler (*NAmer* **hostler**) *n* formerly, a groom or stableman at an inn.

ostracize *or* **-ise** *v* to exclude from a group or society over a period of time and have nothing to do with. ➤ **ostracism** *n*.

ostrich *n* a large flightless African bird that has dark plumage, a long neck, and long legs.

other[1] *adj* **1** distinct from that or those previously mentioned. **2** not the same; different. **3** additional or further. **4** second; alternate: *every other Tuesday*. **5** far or opposite. **6** recently past: *the other day*.

other[2] *pron* **1** the remaining or opposite one. **2** a different or additional one.

otherness *n* the state of being other or different.

otherwise adv 1 in different circumstances. 2 in other respects. 3 in a different way. 4 if not; or else.

otherworldly adj 1 suggestive of a spiritual or non-terrestrial realm of existence. 2 concerned with spiritual or intellectual matters and ignoring practical realities.

otiose adj formal futile or pointless.

OTT abbr over the top.

otter n (pl **otters** or **otter**) an aquatic fish-eating mammal with webbed feet and a long streamlined body.

ottoman n (pl **ottomans**) a low upholstered seat without a back or arms.

oubliette /oohblï'et/ n a dungeon with an opening only at the top.

ought v aux (third person sing. present tense **ought**, past tense in reported speech **ought**) 1 used to express moral obligation. 2 used to express what is advisable or recommended. 3 used to express probability or expectation.

oughtn't contraction ought not.

Ouija board /'weeja, 'weeji/ n trademark a board with letters around the edge and a moving pointer, used to produce messages in spiritualistic seances.

ounce n 1 a unit of weight equal to one sixteenth of a pound (about 28.35g). 2 the least amount.

our adj 1 belonging to or associated with me and one or more other people. 2 belonging to or associated with people in general.

ours pron the one or ones that belong to or are associated with us.

Usage Note: Note that there is no apostrophe in *ours*.

ourselves pron used reflexively or for emphasis to refer to the people speaking or to a person speaking and associated people.

-ous suffix full of or characterized by: *envious*. ➤ **-ously** suffix.

oust v to remove esp from a position of authority, or supplant.

out¹ adv 1 away from the inside or centre. 2 away from a place. 3 away from one's home or business. 4 clearly in or into view or public knowledge. 5 inaccurate in reckoning. 6 no longer in vogue or fashion. 7 to the fullest extent or degree; completely. 8 aloud. 9 so as to be eliminated, esp from a game. 10 in or into a state of unconsciousness. ✳ **have it out** informal to settle a matter of contention by discussion or a fight. **out of 1** from within to the outside of. 2 beyond the range or limits of. 3 away from. 4 used to indicate a position or state that is not correct or desirable: *out of alignment*. 5 used to indicate origin or cause. 6 using the specified material. 7 used to indicate exclusion from or deprivation of. 8 from among.

out² v informal to reveal that (somebody) is homosexual.

out³ adj 1 directed outwards. 2 not permissible, possible, or worth considering. 3 in cricket, baseball, etc, not allowed to continue batting. 4 of a ball, shot, etc: landing outside the prescribed area. 5 informal open about one's homosexuality.

out⁴ prep non-standard or NAmer out of.

outback n (**the outback**) remote rural areas, esp in Australia.

outbid v (**outbidding**, past tense and past part. **outbid**) to make a higher bid than.

outboard¹ adv and adj on or towards the outside of a ship or an aircraft.

outboard² n an outboard motor.

outboard motor n a motor, propeller, and rudder attached as a unit to the stern of a small boat.

outbreak n a sudden or violent occurrence of something.

outbuilding n a smaller building separate from but belonging to a main building.

outburst n 1 a violent expression of feeling. 2 a surge of activity or growth.

outcast n a person who is rejected by society.

outclass v to far surpass in quality, skill, etc.

outcome n a result.

outcrop n the part of a rock formation that appears at the surface of the ground.

outcry n (pl **-ies**) a public expression of anger or disapproval.

outdated adj old-fashioned or obsolete.

outdistance v to go far ahead of (somebody), e.g. in a race.

outdo v (**outdoes**, past tense **outdid**, past part. **outdone**) to surpass in action or performance.

outdoor adj 1 situated, performed, or used outdoors. 2 fond of open-air activities.

outdoors¹ adv in or into the open air.

outdoors² n a place or the whole area outside buildings; the open air.

outer adj 1 external. 2 situated farther out.

outermost adj farthest from the centre.

outface v to cause (somebody) to waver or submit by confronting them unflinchingly.

outfall n the outlet for a river, lake, drain, sewer, etc.

outfit¹ n 1 a set of garments worn together. 2 informal a group that works as a team.

outfit² v (**outfitted, outfitting**) to provide with an outfit. ➤ **outfitter** n.

outflank v 1 to outmanoeuvre (an opposing force) by going round their flank. 2 to gain an advantage over (somebody) by doing something unexpected.

outfox v to get the better of by cunning.

outgoing adj 1 about to give up a position or office. 2 going away; departing. 3 friendly or sociable.

outgoings pl n expenditure.

outgrow v (**outgrew, outgrown**) **1** to grow too large for (e.g. clothes). **2** to lose (e.g. a habit) as one grows older.

outhouse n an outbuilding.

outing n a short pleasure trip.

outlandish adj strikingly unusual; bizarre.

outlast v to last longer than.

outlaw[1] n a fugitive from the law.

outlaw[2] v to make illegal; to ban.

outlay n expenditure or a payment.

outlet n **1** a place or opening through which something, esp a liquid or gas, is let out. **2** a means of release or expression for e.g. an emotion or talent. **3** a shop or other agency through which a product is sold.

outline[1] n **1** a line around the outer edge of something, indicating its shape. **2** a drawing showing the outline of something with no shading or detail. **3** a plan, draft, summary showing the main features only.

outline[2] v **1** to draw the outline of. **2** to summarize, or indicate the principal features of.

outlive v to live longer than.

outlook n **1** a view from a particular place. **2** an attitude or point of view. **3** a prospect for the future.

outlying adj remote from a centre or main point.

outmanoeuvre (NAmer **outmaneuver**) v to defeat by more skilful manoeuvring.

outmoded adj no longer in fashion; obsolete.

outnumber v to exceed in number.

out of bounds adv outside the prescribed boundaries or limits.

out-of-date adj **1** old-fashioned or obsolete. **2** no longer valid or usable.

outpace v to surpass in speed, growth, development, etc.

outpatient n a patient who visits a hospital for treatment but does not stay there overnight.

outperform v to perform better than.

outplay v to play better than.

outpost n **1** a post established at a distance from a main body of troops. **2** an outlying or frontier settlement.

outpouring n **1** an outburst of powerful emotion. **2** something that pours out.

output[1] n **1** something produced, or the amount produced, by somebody or something. **2** the process of producing. **3** power or energy produced by a machine or system. **4** the terminal for the output on an electrical device.

output[2] v (**outputting**, past tense and past part. **output**) to produce as output.

outrage[1] n **1** anger and resentment aroused by injury or insult. **2** an act of shocking violence, criminality, or immorality.

outrage[2] v to arouse intense anger or resentment in.

outrageous adj **1** shocking or offensive. **2** not conventional or moderate; extravagant.
➤ **outrageously** adv.

outran v past tense of OUTRUN.

outrank v to rank higher than.

outré /'oohtray/ adj rather shockingly unconventional or bizarre.

outreach n involvement with and education of people in the community.

outrider n a mounted attendant or motorcyclist escorting a carriage or car.

outrigger n a projecting framework, often with a float, attached to the side of a boat.

outright[1] adv **1** completely; altogether. **2** instantaneously; on the spot. **3** without reservation or restrictions.

outright[2] adj **1** utter; complete. **2** without reservation or restrictions.

outrun v (**outrunning**, past tense **outran**, past part. **outrun**) to run or travel faster than.

outsell v (past tense and past part. **outsold**) to exceed in numbers sold.

outset n (**the outset**) the beginning or start.

outshine v (past tense and past part. **outshone**) **1** to shine brighter than. **2** to outdo or surpass.

outside[1] n **1** the outer side or surface of something. **2** the outward appearance of something or somebody. **3** the part surrounding or beyond the boundaries of something. **4** the side of a curve or bend that has the longer edge.
✻ **at the outside** at the most.

outside[2] adj **1** of, on, or near the outside. **2** originating elsewhere. **3** not belonging to one's regular occupation or duties. **4** maximum. **5** barely possible; remote: an outside chance.

outside[3] adv **1** on or to the outside. **2** outdoors.

outside[4] prep **1** on or to the outside of. **2** beyond the limits of.

outsider n **1** somebody who does not belong to a particular group. **2** a competitor who has only a remote chance of winning.

outsize adj of an exceptionally large size.

outskirts pl n the parts of a town or city that are farthest from the centre.

outsmart v to get the better of by superior cleverness.

outsold v past tense and past part. of OUTSELL.

outspoken adj direct and open in speech or expression; frank.

outstanding adj **1** conspicuously good; excellent. **2** conspicuous. **3** unpaid. **4** continuing or unresolved. ➤ **outstandingly** adv.

outstay v to stay beyond the time or limits of.

outstrip v (**outstripped, outstripping**) **1** to go faster or farther than. **2** to do better than.

out-take n a section of film, recording, etc that is cut out during editing.

outvote v to defeat by a majority of votes.

outward adj **1** situated on or directed towards the outside. **2** being or going away from a place.

3 relating to external appearances. ➤ **out-wardly** adv.

outwards or **outward** adv towards the outside; away from the centre.

outweigh v to exceed in weight, value, or importance.

outwit v (**outwitted, outwitting**) to get the better of by superior cleverness.

ouzo /'oohzoh/ n an unsweetened Greek spirit flavoured with aniseed.

ova n pl of OVUM.

oval[1] adj having the shape of an egg or ellipse.

oval[2] n an oval figure or object.

ovary n (pl **-ies**) **1** a female reproductive organ that produces eggs and female sex hormones. **2** the base of the female reproductive organ of a flowering plant. ➤ **ovarian** adj.

ovation n a burst of sustained and enthusiastic applause.

oven n an enclosed compartment or chamber used for baking, heating, or drying, esp one used in a kitchen for cooking food.

ovenproof adj sufficiently heat-resistant for use in an oven.

ovenware n heat-resistant dishes for cooking food in an oven.

over[1] adv **1** across a barrier or intervening space. **2** to a particular place. **3** downwards from an upright position. **4** so as to be inverted or reversed. **5** beyond some quantity or limit. **6** in excess; remaining. **7** so as to cover the whole surface. **8** at an end. **9** used to show repetition.

over[2] prep **1** higher than. **2** vertically above but not touching. **3** across. **4** so as to cover. **5** used to indicate authority, power, or preference. **6** more than. **7** by means of (a medium or channel of communication). **8** during. **9** used to indicate an object of care, reference, occupation, or activity. ✱ **over and above** besides; in addition to.

over[3] n in cricket, a series of six balls bowled by one bowler from the same end of the pitch.

over- prefix **1** outer or covering: overcoat. **2** excessive or excessively: overactive. **3** above: overarching.

overact v to speak and gesture in an exaggerated way while acting.

overactive adj too active, esp restless or uncontrollable.

overall[1] n chiefly Brit a usu loose-fitting protective coat or suit worn over other clothing.

overall[2] adj and adv including or considering everything.

overarching adj **1** forming an arch overhead. **2** dominating or embracing everything else.

overarm adj and adv with the hand and arm brought forward and down from above shoulder level.

overawe v to make nervous or silent with respect or fear.

overbalance v **1** to lose balance and fall. **2** to cause to overbalance.

overbearing adj harshly masterful or domineering.

overblown adj inflated or pretentious.

overboard adv over the side of a ship or boat into the water. ✱ **go overboard 1** to be very enthusiastic. **2** to go to extremes.

overcast adj cloudy.

overcharge v to charge (a customer) too much.

overcoat n **1** a warm coat for wearing outdoors over other clothing. **2** a protective coat of paint or varnish.

overcome v (**overcame, overcome**) **1** to deal with (a problem, handicap, etc) successfully. **2** to overpower or overwhelm.

overcommit ✱ **overcommit oneself** to take on more work or responsibilities than one can handle.

overcompensate v to try to make up for a weakness or failing by exaggerating some other trait.

overcrowded adj containing too many people or things for the available space.

overdo v (**overdoes,** past tense **overdid,** past part. **overdone**) **1** to do or use to excess. **2** to exaggerate. **3** to cook (food) too much. ✱ **overdo it** to exhaust oneself, esp through overwork.

overdose[1] n a dangerously excessive dose of drugs, medicine, etc.

overdose[2] v to take an overdose.

overdraft n **1** permission from a bank to take more money out of one's account than has been credited to it. **2** the amount by which an account is overdrawn.

overdrawn adj **1** of a bank account: in deficit. **2** of a person: having an overdrawn account.

overdress v to dress too elaborately or formally.

overdrive n a gear in a motor vehicle that provides a higher ratio than top gear. ✱ **go into/be in overdrive** to be extremely active.

overdue adj **1** unpaid when due. **2** delayed beyond the proper or appointed time.

overestimate v **1** to estimate as being more than the actual amount or size. **2** to overrate. ➤ **overestimate** n.

overexpose v **1** to expose (photographic film) to too much light. **2** (**be overexposed**) to receive too much attention from the media. ➤ **overexposed** adj, **overexposure** n.

overflow[1] v **1** to flow over or beyond a brim or edge. **2** to be too numerous, large, etc to be contained in. **3** to be filled with an emotion.

overflow[2] n **1** an excess of people, things, etc that cannot be accommodated. **2** an outlet for surplus liquid.

overground adj and adv on the surface; not underground.

overgrown *adj* 1 covered or choked with vegetation. 2 grown too large.

overhang[1] *v* (*past tense and past part.* **overhung**) to project over or beyond.

overhang[2] *n* something that overhangs.

overhaul *v* 1 to examine (e.g. a machine) thoroughly and carry out any necessary repairs. 2 to overtake. ➤ **overhaul** *n*.

overhead *adv and adj* above one's head.

overheads *pl n* business expenses, e.g. rent, insurance, or heating, that are not chargeable to a particular part of the work or product.

overhear *v* (*past tense and past part.* **overheard**) to hear without the speaker's knowledge or intention.

overheat *v* to make or become excessively hot.

overindulge *v* 1 to indulge in something to an excessive degree. 2 to indulge (somebody) to an excessive degree. ➤ **overindulgence** *n*.

overjoyed *adj* extremely pleased.

overkill *n* an amount or effort beyond what is required for a particular purpose.

overland *adv and adj* by land rather than sea or air.

overlap[1] *v* (**overlapped, overlapping**) 1 to extend over and cover a part of. 2 to coincide partly; to have something in common.

overlap[2] *n* a part or amount that overlaps.

overlay[1] *v* (*past tense and past part.* **overlaid**) 1 (+ with) to cover or decorate (a surface) with something laid over it. 2 to superimpose another feeling, quality, etc on.

overlay[2] *n* something laid or spread over something else.

overleaf *adv* on the other side of the page.

overload *v* to load to excess. ➤ **overload** *n*.

overlook *v* 1 to fail to notice. 2 to ignore or excuse. 3 to have or provide a view of from above.

overlord *n* an absolute or supreme ruler.

overly *adv* to an excessive degree.

overmuch *adj and adv and n* too much.

overnight[1] *adv* 1 during or throughout the night. 2 for a single night. 3 suddenly.

overnight[2] *adj* 1 occurring, operating, or used during the night. 2 lasting for a single night. 3 sudden.

overpass *n* = FLYOVER.

overplay *v* to give too much emphasis to.

overpower *v* 1 to defeat by superior force. 2 to be so strong or intense as to overwhelm. ➤ **overpowering** *adj*.

overprice *v* to price too high.

overqualified *adj* having more education, training, or experience than a job calls for.

overrate *v* to consider (something or somebody) to be better than they actually are.

overreach *v* ✳ **overreach oneself** to fail by trying to do or gain too much.

overreact *v* to show an excessive or exaggerated reaction. ➤ **overreaction** *n*.

override[1] *v* (**overrode, overridden**) 1 to be more important than. 2 to use one's superior authority to set aside or annul (e.g. a decision by somebody else). 3 to take manual control of (e.g. an automatic control).

override[2] *n* a device or system used to override a control.

overrule *v* to use one's superior authority to reject or disallow (a decision, judgment, objection, etc). 2 to overrule the decision, argument, objection, etc of (somebody).

overrun *v* (**overrunning,** *past tense* **overran,** *past part.* **overrun**) 1 to invade and occupy (a place) in large numbers. 2 to go beyond or past. 3 to exceed (e.g. an allowed cost or time). ➤ **overrun** *n*.

overseas *adv and adj* beyond or across the sea; abroad; foreign.

oversee *v* (**oversaw, overseen**) to watch and supervise (a task, operation, etc). ➤ **overseer** *n*.

oversexed *adj* having an abnormally strong sexual drive.

overshadow *v* 1 to cast a shadow over. 2 to exceed in importance. 3 to cause (an occasion) to be less happy than it should have been.

overshoot *v* (*past tense and past part.* **overshot**) 1 to pass over or beyond (e.g. a target) and miss it. 2 of an aircraft: to fly or taxi beyond the end of a runway. ➤ **overshoot** *n*.

oversight *n* an inadvertent omission or error.

oversimplify *v* (**-ies, -ied**) to simplify to such an extent as to cause distortion, misunderstanding, or error. ➤ **oversimplification** *n*.

oversized or **oversize** *adj* of above average or normal size.

oversleep *v* (*past tense and past part.* **overslept**) to sleep beyond the intended time for waking.

overspend[1] *v* (*past tense and past part.* **overspent**) to spend too much.

overspend[2] *n* an amount spent that exceeds the available budget.

overspill *n chiefly Brit* the movement of excess urban population into less crowded areas, e.g. new towns, or the excess population itself.

overstate *v* to state in too strong terms; to exaggerate. ➤ **overstatement** *n*.

overstay *v* to stay beyond the time or limits of.

overstep *v* (**overstepped, overstepping**) to go beyond (a limit). ✳ **overstep the mark** to go beyond what is acceptable.

overstretch *v* to make too many demands on (e.g. resources).

oversubscribed *adj* having more applicants than there are e.g. places or shares available.

overt *adj* not concealed or disguised. ➤ **overtly** *adv*.

overtake *v* (**overtook, overtaken**) 1 to catch up with and move past (e.g. a vehicle going in the same direction). **2** to catch up with and do better than. **3** to happen to (somebody) suddenly.

overthrow[1] *v* (**overthrew, overthrown**) to remove from power.

overthrow[2] *n* **1** removal from power. **2** in cricket, a run scored when a fielder returns the ball inaccurately.

overtime *n* working time in excess of a standard working day or week.

overtone *n* (*also in pl*) a secondary effect, quality, or meaning.

overture *n* **1** the orchestral introduction to a musical dramatic work. **2** an orchestral concert piece written as a single movement. **3** (*also in pl*). **4** an initiative towards an agreement, negotiation, or relationship.

overturn *v* **1** to upset, capsize, or invert, or become upset or inverted. **2** to cancel or reverse (e.g. a decision).

overuse[1] *n* excessive use.

overuse[2] *v* to use excessively.

overview *n* a usu brief general survey.

overweening *adj* arrogant or presumptuous.

overweight *adj* exceeding the expected, normal, or proper weight.

overwhelm *v* **1** to defeat by superior force or numbers. **2** to affect with intense emotion. **3** to cover over completely; to submerge. ➤ **overwhelming** *adj*.

overwork *v* **1** to work or cause to work too hard or too long. **2** to make excessive use of. ➤ **overwork** *n*.

overwrite *v* (**overwrote, overwritten**) **1** to write on top of (existing writing). **2** to destroy (existing data) in a computer file by replacing it with new data. **3** to write in an inflated or pretentious style.

overwrought *adj* **1** extremely excited or agitated. **2** too elaborate in construction or design.

ovulate *v* to produce eggs or discharge them from an ovary. ➤ **ovulation** *n*.

ovum *n* (*pl* **ova**) a female reproductive cell in animals that when fertilized can develop into a new individual.

owe *v* **1** to be under obligation to pay (money) to somebody. **2** to be under obligation to give or show (an explanation, respect, etc) to somebody. **3** (*usu* + to) to have as a result of the

action or existence of something or somebody else: *He owes his success to luck*.

owing *adj* unpaid; due. ✳ **owing to** because of.

owl *n* a nocturnal bird of prey with large eyes and a short hooked bill.

owlish *adj* having a round face or a wide-eyed stare.

own[1] *adj* used after a possessive: belonging to, relating to, or done by oneself or itself.

own[2] *v* **1** to possess. **2** *literary* to acknowledge or admit.

own[3] *pron* used after a possessive: one or ones belonging to oneself or itself. ✳ **come into one's own** to begin to be fully effective. **get one's own back** to have revenge. **on one's own 1** in solitude; alone. **2** without assistance or control.

owner *n* the person who owns something. ➤ **ownership** *n*.

own up *v* to confess to a fault or wrongdoing.

ox *n* (*pl* **oxen** *or* **ox**) **1** a domestic bovine mammal. **2** an castrated bull.

Oxbridge *n* the universities of Oxford and Cambridge.

oxidation *n* **1** the process of oxidizing. **2** the state of being oxidized.

oxide *n* a compound of oxygen with a chemical element or group.

oxidize *or* **-ise** *v* to combine with oxygen.

oxtail *n* the tail of an ox, used *esp* in making soup.

oxygen *n* a colourless odourless gas that forms about 21% of the atmosphere and is essential for the life of most organisms.

oxygenate *v* to combine or supply (e.g. blood) with oxygen.

oxymoron *n* a combination of contradictory or incongruous words, e.g. *cruel kindness*.

oyster *n* **1** an edible marine invertebrate animal with a rough irregular hinged shell. **2** a pinkish or greyish white colour.

oz *abbr* ounce.

ozone *n* **1** a poisonous form of oxygen with three atoms in each molecule, which has a pungent smell. **2** *informal* pure and refreshing air.

ozone layer *n* an atmospheric layer at heights of approximately 30–50km (20–30mi) that has a high ozone content and protects the earth by absorbing ultraviolet radiation from the sun.

P¹ or **p** *n* (*pl* **P's** or **Ps** or **p's**) the 16th letter of the English alphabet.

P² *abbr* **1** parking. **2** the chemical symbol for phosphorus.

PA *abbr* **1** personal assistant. **2** public address.

Pa *abbr* **1** pascal. **2** the chemical symbol for protactinium.

p.a. *abbr* per annum (= every year).

pace¹ *n* **1** a step taken in walking. **2** the rate or speed of moving, working, or developing. ✳ **keep pace with** to progress at the same speed as. **put somebody through their paces** to test somebody by making them demonstrate their abilities.

pace² *v* **1** to walk with a steady tread. **2** (*often* + out/off) to measure (a distance) by pacing. **3** to set (oneself) a steady rate of working or doing something.

pacemaker *n* **1** a person who sets the pace or leads by example. **2** an electronic device implanted in the body to stimulate or steady the heartbeat.

pachyderm *n* an elephant, rhinoceros, or other animal with a thick skin.

pacific *adj* **1** tending to bring about peace. **2** (**Pacific**) of or found near the Pacific Ocean.

pacifism *n* opposition to war and violence as means of settling disputes. ➤ **pacifist** *n and adj*.

pacify *v* (**-ies, -ied**) **1** to make less angry or agitated. **2** to restore (a country) to a peaceful state.

pack¹ *n* **1** a light paper or cardboard container for goods. **2** a knapsack or rucksack. **3** a set of playing cards. **4** a number of animals kept or grouping together for hunting. **5** an organized group of Cub Scouts or Brownie Guides. **6** the forwards in a rugby team. **7** the main group of competitors running close together in a race behind the leaders. **8** a concentrated mass of snow or ice. **9** an absorbent pad for applying to the body for therapeutic purposes.

pack² *v* **1** to place in a container for transportation or storage. **2** to cover or surround with packing material for protection. **3** (*often* + away) to be collapsible for storage or transport. **4** (*often* + with) to fill with a large quantity of material or things. **5** (+ in/into) to fit (a large number of people) into a small space. **6** *informal* (+ in) to attract a large number of (people). **7** to influence the composition of (a jury) so as to influence the verdict. ✳ **pack a punch 1** to be capable of hitting hard. **2** to be very strong or effective. **send packing** *informal* to dismiss (somebody) abruptly. ➤ **packable** *adj*, **packer** *n*.

package¹ *n* **1** an object or number of objects wrapped or packed up together. **2** a group of proposals or terms offered together.

package² *v* **1** to enclose in a package or covering. **2** to group (various items) together for sale as a whole. **3** to present in an appealing way.

package deal *n* an offer or agreement which has to be accepted in its entirety.

package holiday *n* a holiday organized by an agent who is responsible for all aspects of travel and accommodation.

packed *adj* full or crowded.

packet *n* **1** a paper or cardboard container. **2** a parcel. **3** *Brit, informal* a large sum of money.

packhorse *n* a horse used to carry loads.

pack ice *n* a large mass of ice floating in the sea.

pack in *informal* to end (an activity).

pack off *v informal* to send (somebody) away abruptly or unceremoniously.

pack up *v informal* to break down.

pact *n* an agreement or treaty.

pacy or **pacey** *adj* (**-ier, -iest**) *Brit* fast or speedy.

pad¹ *n* **1** a thick piece of soft or absorbent material. **2** a piece of padding used to shield parts of the body against impact. **3** the thickened underside of an animal's foot. **4** a number of sheets of paper fastened together at one edge. **5** a flat surface for a helicopter to land on or for launching a rocket. **6** *informal* the place where a person lives.

pad² *v* (**padded, padding**) **1** to provide with a pad or padding. **2** (*often* + out) to fill out (speech or writing) with superfluous matter. **3** to walk with a muffled step.

padding *n* material with which something is padded.

paddle¹ *n* **1** a wooden implement like a small oar, used to propel a boat. **2** an implement with a broad flat blade used for stirring and mixing. **3** a flattened limb or flipper of a swimming bird or mammal. **4** a spell of paddling in water.

paddle² *v* **1** to propel (a boat) with a paddle.

2 to swim with short strokes like an animal. **3** to walk or wade in shallow water. ➤ **paddler** n.

paddle steamer n a boat driven by steam-powered paddle wheels.

paddle wheel n a power-driven wheel with paddles round its circumference, used to propel a boat.

paddock n **1** a small enclosed field for horses. **2** an area where racehorses or racing cars are paraded before a race.

paddy¹ n (pl **-ies**) (also **paddyfield**) a field of wet ground for growing rice.

paddy² n (pl **-ies**) Brit, informal a temper tantrum.

padlock¹ n a detachable lock with a shackle that can be passed through a link and secured.

padlock² v to secure using a padlock.

paean n a song of praise or tribute.

paediatrician n a specialist in paediatrics.

paediatrics (NAmer **pediatrics**) pl n the branch of medicine dealing with the diseases of children. ➤ **paediatric** adj.

paedophile (NAmer **pedophile**) n a person who is sexually attracted to children. ➤ **paedophilia** n.

paella /pie'ela/ n a Spanish dish of rice, meat, seafood, and vegetables.

pagan n a follower of a religion that is not one of the main religions. ➤ **pagan** adj, **paganism** n.

page¹ n **1** a leaf of a book or periodical, or a single side of a leaf. **2** an Internet document.

page² v (often + through) to turn pages in a haphazard manner.

page³ n **1** a boy attending the bride at a wedding. **2** a young man or boy employed to deliver messages or run errands. **3** formerly, a boy being trained for the rank of knight.

page⁴ v to summon over a public-address system or with a pager.

pageant n **1** an entertainment with dramatic presentations or a procession. **2** an ostentatious display.

pageantry n colourful or elaborate display.

pager n a small electronic device that emits an audible tone or receives a text message, as a means of communication or alert.

paginate v to number the pages of (a book or periodical). ➤ **pagination** n.

pagoda n a Buddhist temple with upturned projecting roofs at the division of each storey.

paid v past and past part. of PAY¹. ✱ **put paid to** to bring to an abrupt end.

pail n a bucket.

pain¹ n **1** an unpleasant bodily sensation induced by injury or illness. **2** mental or emotional distress. **3** informal an annoyance or nuisance. **4** (in pl) trouble or care taken. ✱ **on pain of** subject to penalty of.

pain² v to cause pain or distress to.

painful adj **1** causing or feeling pain or distress. **2** proceeding with great effort. **3** informal very bad. ➤ **painfully** adv.

painkiller n a drug that relieves pain.

painless adj **1** not causing any pain. **2** easy or effortless. ➤ **painlessly** adv.

painstaking adj showing diligence and effort. ➤ **painstakingly** adv.

paint¹ v **1** to apply paint or cosmetics to. **2** to apply with a movement resembling that used in painting. **3** to represent on a surface by applying paint. **4** to describe vividly.

paint² n a mixture of a pigment and liquid which forms a coloured coating on a surface.

painter¹ n **1** an artist who paints pictures. **2** somebody who applies paint to buildings.

painter² n a line used for securing or towing a boat.

painting n **1** a painted work of art. **2** the art or occupation of painting.

paintwork n a painted surface of a building or vehicle.

pair¹ n **1** two corresponding things used or considered together. **2** an implement or piece of clothing made up of two connected pieces. **3** two people in a marriage or partnership. **4** two mated animals.

pair² v (often + up) to arrange in pairs.

pair off v to form a couple or a group of two.

paisley n a pattern of colourful abstract curved figures.

pajamas pl n NAmer = PYJAMAS.

pakora n an Indian savoury snack of diced vegetables or meat fried in batter.

pal n informal a friend.

palace n **1** a large stately house or public building. **2** the official residence of a sovereign or bishop.

Palaeolithic adj (NAmer **Paleolithic**) of the earliest period of the Stone Age.

palaeontology (NAmer **paleontology**) n the study of geological periods as discovered from fossil remains. ➤ **palaeontologist** n.

palatable adj **1** pleasant to the taste. **2** acceptable.

palate n **1** the roof of the mouth. **2** the sense of taste. **3** an intellectual taste or liking.

palatial adj grand and spacious. ➤ **palatially** adv.

palaver n a fuss or bother.

pale¹ adj **1** lacking intensity of colour. **2** not bright or brilliant. **3** feeble or faint. **4** of a colour: light in shade. ➤ **palish** adj.

pale² v **1** to become pale. **2** to seem less important by comparison.

pale³ n **1** an upright post forming part of a fence. **2** formerly, a district within a boundary. ✱ **beyond the pale** not socially acceptable.

palette n **1** a thin board on which a painter mixes pigments. **2** a particular range or use of colour.

palette knife n a knife with a blunt flexible blade, used for mixing paints.

palimpsest n a parchment or tablet, reused over earlier writing.

palindrome n a word or phrase that reads the same backwards or forwards, e.g. *radar*.

paling n 1 a fence made of stakes. 2 a stake used in such a fence.

palisade n a fence of stakes for defence.

pall[1] n 1 a heavy cloud of smoke or dust that covers or conceals. 2 a heavy cloth draped over a coffin or tomb.

pall[2] v to cease to be interesting or attractive.

palladium n a silver-white metallic element.

pallbearer n a person who helps to carry the coffin at a funeral.

pallet[1] n 1 a portable platform for storing or moving materials. 2 a tool with a flat blade for shaping clay.

pallet[2] n 1 a straw-filled mattress. 2 a makeshift bed.

palliate v 1 to lessen the bad effects of (a disease). 2 to moderate the intensity or gravity of. ➤ **palliative** n and adj.

pallid adj 1 pale or lacking colour. 2 lacking liveliness.

pallor n paleness in the face.

pally adj (-ier, -iest) informal friendly.

palm[1] n 1 a tropical or subtropical tree with a crown of large leaves. 2 a palm leaf representing distinction.

palm[2] n the inside of the human hand between the fingers and the wrist.

palm[3] v (often + off) to get rid of (something unwanted), or persuade (somebody) to take something awkward or unwanted.

palmistry n the activity of reading a person's character or future from markings on the palms. ➤ **palmist** n.

palmtop n a small computer that can be held in the hand.

palmy adj (-ier, -iest) prosperous or flourishing.

palomino n (pl -os) a light tan horse with slender legs.

palpable adj 1 capable of being touched or felt. 2 easily perceptible; obvious. ➤ **palpably** adv.

palpate v to examine (a part of the body) medically by touching it. ➤ **palpation** n.

palpitate v 1 of the heart: to beat rapidly and strongly. 2 to tremble or flutter. ➤ **palpitation** n.

palsy n (pl -ies) dated uncontrollable tremor of the body. ➤ **palsied** adj.

paltry adj (-ier, -iest) 1 very small or insignificant. 2 mean and petty. ➤ **paltriness** n.

pampas n an extensive area of grassy plains in South America.

pamper v to treat with excessive care and attention.

pamphlet[1] n a small printed publication with a paper cover.

pamphlet[2] v (**pamphleted, pamphleting**) to hand out pamphlets to.

pan[1] n 1 a metal container with a long handle, used for cooking food. 2 any shallow open receptacle for various uses. 3 each of the receptacles in a pair of scales. 4 Brit the bowl of a toilet. 5 a hollow in land.

pan[2] v (**panned, panning**) 1 to wash earth or gravel in a pan in search of gold. 2 informal to criticize harshly.

pan[3] v (**panned, panning**) to rotate (a film or television camera) horizontally so as to keep a moving object in view or for a panoramic effect.

pan- comb. form all or completely: *Pan-American*.

panacea n a remedy for all diseases or difficulties.

panache n dash or flamboyance in style and action.

panama n a lightweight hat of plaited straw.

panatella n a long slender cigar.

pancake n a thin flat cake of batter fried in an open pan.

pancake landing n an emergency landing by an aircraft descending level with the undercarriage retracted.

pancreas n a large gland that secretes digestive enzymes into the intestines. ➤ **pancreatic** adj.

panda n 1 (also **giant panda**) a large black-and-white mammal of China resembling a bear but related to the raccoons. 2 (also **red panda**) a long-tailed Himalayan mammal resembling the American raccoon and having long chestnut fur.

pandemic[1] adj of a disease: affecting a high proportion of the population.

pandemic[2] n an outbreak of a pandemic disease.

pandemonium n a scene of confusion or uproar.

pander v (+ to) to provide gratification for the desires of.

pane n a framed sheet of glass in a window or door.

panegyric n a speech or piece of writing in praise of somebody or something.

panel n 1 a flat section of a door or other surface. 2 a mounting for a set of controls or instruments. 3 a group of people brought together to consider a matter or take part in a broadcast game or quiz. 4 a list of people summoned for jury service. ➤ **panelled** adj, **panellist** n.

pang n a brief spasm of pain or fear.

panic[1] n a sudden frenzied feeling of fear or anxiety. ➤ **panicky** adj.

panic[2] v (**panicked, panicking**) to feel or cause to feel panic.

pannier n each of a pair of baskets or boxes carried on both sides of an animal, bicycle, or motorcycle.

panoply n a magnificent or impressive array of things.

panorama n 1 an open view of a landscape or area. 2 a comprehensive survey of a topic or series of events. ➤ **panoramic** adj.

pan out v to turn out in a particular way.

panpipes pl n a wind instrument consisting of a row of vertical pipes varying in length.

pansy n (pl -ies) 1 a garden plant with flowers having rounded velvety petals. 2 informal, derog an effeminate or homosexual man.

pant v to breathe quickly or in a laboured manner. ➤ **pant** n.

pantaloons pl n 1 women's loose-fitting trousers gathered at the ankles. 2 formerly, men's tight-fitting trousers fastened with straps under the feet.

pantechnicon n Brit a large van for transporting furniture.

pantheism n a belief that God exists in nature. ➤ **pantheist, pantheistic** adj.

pantheon n 1 the gods of a people collectively. 2 a building containing memorials to famous dead. 3 a group of famous people.

panther n 1 a black leopard. 2 NAmer a puma.

panties pl n short underpants for women or girls.

pantile n a roofing tile with an S-shape that fits over the tile next to it.

panto n (pl -os) Brit, informal a pantomime.

pantomime n Brit a slapstick musical entertainment based on a nursery story.

pantry n (pl -ies) a room or cupboard for storing food.

pants pl n 1 Brit underpants or knickers. 2 NAmer trousers.

pantyhose or **pantihose** pl n NAmer women's tights.

pap n 1 soft food for babies or invalids. 2 feeble fiction or drama.

papa n informal one's father.

papacy n (pl -ies) the office of pope.

papal adj relating to a pope or the papacy.

paparazzo n (pl **paparazzi**) a news photographer who seeks out celebrities to photograph.

papaya n a large oval tropical fruit with a yellow skin, orange flesh, and round black seeds.

paper¹ n 1 a material for writing, printing on, etc made from compacted vegetable fibres in the form of thin sheets. 2 (also in pl) a written or printed document. 3 (in pl) an individual's personal documents and records, diaries, etc. 4 a newspaper. 5 a written composition designed for publication or to be read aloud. 6 a government report or discussion document. 7 a set of questions to be answered in an examination. ✳ **on paper 1** in writing. **2** in theory.

paper² v to cover (a wall) with wallpaper.

paperback n a book with a flexible paper binding.

paper clip n a small clip made from two loops of wire, used for holding sheets of paper together.

paperknife n (pl **paperknives**) a blunt knife for slitting envelopes open.

paper over v to conceal or suppress (differences or weaknesses) for the sake of appearances.

paper round n a round of delivering newspapers to people's houses.

paper tiger n a person or power that appears threatening, but is actually ineffectual.

paperweight n a small heavy object used to hold down loose papers.

paperwork n routine clerical or work.

papery adj thin and light like paper.

papier-mâché n a light strong moulding material made of paper pulped with glue.

papist or **Papist** n derog a Roman Catholic.

paprika n a powdered red spice made from sweet peppers.

papyrus n (pl **papyri**) a writing material made in antiquity from the pith of a sedge plant of the Nile valley.

par n 1 in golf, the standard score of a good player for each hole of a course. 2 an amount taken as an average or norm. 3 a usual standard of physical condition or health. ✳ **on a par with** equal to. **par for the course** what is to be expected in a particular situation.

parable n a short story illustrating a moral or religious principle.

parabola n a symmetrical curve of the kind generated when a cone is intersected by a plane parallel to its side.

paracetamol n a chemical compound used as a painkiller.

parachute¹ n a folding expanse of light fabric attached by lines to a harness, that opens out into an umbrella shape to slow the descent of a person or thing dropped from a great height. ➤ **parachutist** n.

parachute² v to drop by means of a parachute.

parade¹ n 1 a public procession. 2 a formal assembly or march past by a troops. 3 a succession of things or people on display. 4 an ostentatious display. 5 chiefly Brit a row of shops. 6 a place for walking along.

parade² v 1 to march in a procession. 2 to walk up and down. 3 to display ostentatiously.

paradigm n 1 a clear or typical example of something. 2 a model used in science as a framework for ideas. ➤ **paradigmatic** adj.

paradise n 1 (often **Paradise**) heaven. 2 (often **Paradise**) the Garden of Eden. 3 an idyllic place or state.

paradox n 1 a true statement that seems contradictory or absurd. 2 a person or thing with

paraffin

seemingly contradictory features. ➤ **para-doxical** *adj*, **paradoxically** *adv*.

paraffin *n* **1** a waxy mixture of hydrocarbons obtained from coal, petroleum, etc and used in candles, chemical synthesis, and cosmetics. **2** *Brit* an inflammable liquid hydrocarbon obtained from petroleum and used as a fuel.

paragliding *n* the sport of travelling through the air with a rectangular parachute after being released at a height. ➤ **paraglider** *n*.

paragon *n* a model of excellence or of a particular quality.

paragraph *n* a division of a piece of writing, starting on a new line.

parakeet *or* **parrakeet** *n* a small slender parrot with a long tail.

parallax *n* the apparent difference in position or direction of an object as seen from different points not on the same straight line.

parallel[1] *adj* **1** extending in the same direction at a constant distance apart. **2** occurring simultaneously. **3** analogous or comparable.

parallel[2] *n* **1** somebody or something equal or similar to another. **2** a comparison that shows a resemblance. **3** a line representing any of the imaginary circles on the surface of the earth parallel to the equator.

parallel[3] *v* (**paralleled**, **paralleling**) **1** to run parallel to. **2** to equal or match. **3** to correspond to.

Usage Note: Note the spelling with *-ll-* followed by *-l*.

parallel bars *pl n* a pair of horizontal bars supported on a base, used in gymnastics.

parallelogram *n* a four-sided figure with opposite sides parallel and equal.

paralyse (*NAmer* **paralyze**) *v* **1** to affect with paralysis. **2** to make powerless or ineffective. **3** to make immobile.

paralysis *n* (*pl* **paralyses**) **1** total or partial loss of movement or sensation in a part of the body. **2** loss of the ability to move or to act.

paralytic *adj* **1** of paralysis. **2** *informal* very drunk.

paramedic *n* a member of a medical team who is not a qualified doctor. ➤ **paramedical** *adj*.

parameter *n* **1** a property whose value determines the characteristics or behaviour of something. **2** *informal* a limiting factor or characteristic.

paramilitary[1] *adj* organized on military principles.

paramilitary[2] *n* (*pl* **-ies**) a member of a paramilitary organization.

paramount *adj* superior to or more powerful than all others.

paramour *n archaic* a lover.

paranoia *n* a mental disorder characterized by delusions of persecution. ➤ **paranoiac** *adj and n*, **paranoid** *adj and n*.

paranormal *adj* not scientifically explainable; supernatural.

parapet *n* **1** a wall, rampart, or mound of earth to protect soldiers. **2** a low wall along the edge of a platform, roof, or bridge.

paraphernalia *n* the things needed for a particular pursuit or production.

paraphrase[1] *n* a restatement of a text or statement giving the meaning in another form.

paraphrase[2] *v* to make a paraphrase of.

paraplegia *n* paralysis of the lower half of the body. ➤ **paraplegic** *adj and n*.

paraquat *n* a poisonous weedkiller.

parasite *n* **1** an organism living in or on another organism and drawing its nourishment from it. **2** a person who depends on somebody else without making a useful return. ➤ **parasitic** *adj*, **parasitical** *adj*, **parasitism** *n*.

parasol *n* a lightweight umbrella used for protection from the sun.

paratroops *pl n* troops equipped to parachute from aircraft. ➤ **paratrooper** *n*.

parboil *v* to boil (vegetables) until partly cooked.

parcel[1] *n* **1** an object wrapped in paper for sending by post. **2** a plot of land. **3** a collection or group of people or things.

parcel[2] *v* (**parcelled**, **parcelling**, *NAmer* **parceled**, **parceling**) **1** (*often* + up) to make up into a parcel. **2** (+ out) to divide or distribute.

parch *v* to make or become dry or scorched.

parched *adj* **1** of land: dry from lack of rain. **2** *informal* of a person: extremely thirsty.

parchment *n* **1** the skin of a sheep or goat formerly used as writing material. **2** strong paper resembling parchment.

pardon[1] *n* **1** forgiveness for a fault or offence. **2** a release from legal penalties.

pardon[2] *v* **1** to absolve from the consequences of a fault or crime. **2** to allow (an offence) to pass without punishment. ➤ **pardonable** *adj*.

pare *v* **1** to cut or shave off the outer surface or edges of. **2** (*often* + down/away) to diminish gradually. ➤ **parer** *n*.

parent[1] *n* **1** a father or mother. **2** an animal or plant regarded in relation to its offspring. **3** the material or source from which something is derived. ➤ **parental** *adj*, **parenthood** *n*.

parent[2] *v* to be or act as the parent of.

parentage *n* descent from parents or ancestors.

parenthesis *n* (*pl* **parentheses**) **1** an extra or explanatory word or phrase inserted in a passage and set off, in writing, by punctuation. **2** either or both of the curved marks (or) used in writing and printing to enclose a parenthesis. ➤ **parenthetic** *adj*, **parenthetical** *adj*.

par excellence *adj* (*used after a noun*) the best of its kind: *a poet par excellence*.

pariah *n* a rejected person or outcast.

paring *n* a thin piece cut off from a surface.

parish *n* **1** a district of a diocese served by a single church or clergyman. **2** a unit of local government in rural England.

parishioner *n* a member or inhabitant of a church parish.

parity *n* the state of being equal or equivalent.

park[1] *n* **1** an area of land for recreation in a city or town. **2** an area maintained in its natural state as a public property. **3** an enclosed area of lawns, woodland, etc attached to a country house. **4** a site for a number of buildings housing establishments of a similar type. **5** an area for parking vehicles.

park[2] *v* **1** to leave (a vehicle) for a time. **2** *informal* to leave (somebody or something) temporarily.

parka *n* a weatherproof jacket with a hood.

Parkinson's disease *or* **Parkinsonism** *n* a progressive nervous disease, marked by tremor and weakness of the muscles.

parky *adj* (**-ier, -iest**) *Brit, informal* chilly.

parlance *n* a manner of speaking.

parley[1] *v* to discuss terms with an enemy.

parley[2] *n* (*pl* **-eys**) a meeting under truce to discuss terms with an enemy.

parliament *n* **1** the supreme legislative body of the UK, consisting of the House of Commons and the House of Lords and summoned and dissolved by the sovereign. **2** a similar body in other countries.➤ **parliamentary** *adj*.

Usage Note: Note the spelling with an *-a-* in the middle.

parliamentarian *n* a member of a parliament.

parlour (*NAmer* **parlor**) *n* **1** *dated* a sitting room in a private house. **2** a shop or business specializing in a special line.

parlous *adj formal* giving cause for concern or alarm.

Parma ham *n* Italian cured ham in thin slices.

Parmesan *n* a hard strongly flavoured Italian cheese.

parochial *adj* **1** relating to a church parish. **2** limited or provincial in outlook. ➤ **parochialism** *n*.

parody[1] *n* (*pl* **-ies**) **1** a literary or musical work in which a particular style is imitated for comic effect. **2** a feeble or ridiculous imitation.

parody[2] *v* (**-ies, -ied**) to imitate for comic effect.

parole[1] *n* the early release of a prisoner on condition of good behaviour.

parole[2] *v* to release (a prisoner) on parole.

paroxysm *n* **1** a sudden attack of pain or convulsions. **2** a sudden violent emotion. ➤ **paroxysmal** *adj*.

parquet *n* a floor or flooring made of wood blocks arranged in patterns.

parricide *n* **1** the act of murdering one's father or mother. **2** a person who commits parricide. ➤ **parricidal** *adj*.

parrot[1] *n* a large tropical bird with brightly coloured plumage and a hooked beak, some of which can mimic human speech.

parrot[2] *v* (**parroted, parroting**) to repeat or imitate without understanding or thought.

parrot-fashion *adv* repeated without regard for meaning.

parry[1] *v* (**-ies, -ied**) **1** to ward off (a blow). **2** to avoid answering (a question or accusation) directly.

parry[2] *n* (*pl* **-ies**) **1** an act of parrying a blow. **2** an evasive reply.

parse *v* to explain (a sentence) in terms of its grammatical parts.

parsimony *n* a tendency to be careful with money. ➤ **parsimonious** *adj*.

parsley *n* a plant of the carrot family with leaves used in cooking.

parsnip *n* a plant of the carrot family used as a vegetable.

parson *n* a clergyman in charge of an Anglican parish.

parsonage *n* a house provided for a parson.

parson's nose *n* a fatty extension of the rump of a cooked fowl.

part[1] *n* **1** a piece or section which along with others forms the whole of something. **2** a certain amount of something but not the whole. **3** a separable piece in a machine. **4** an organ or member of a plant or animal body. **5** the music for a particular voice or instrument in a group. **6** an actor's role in a play. **7** somebody's contribution to an action or event. **8** (*in pl*) an unspecified territorial area. ✻ **in part** partially. **on the part of** by or on behalf of. **take part** (*often* + in) to join in.

part[2] *v* **1** to separate from somebody. **2** to separate into parts or sections. **3** (+ with) to relinquish possession of. ✻ **part company** to leave in different directions.

partake *v* (**partook, partaken**) *formal* (+ in/of) to participate in. ➤ **partaker** *n*.

partial *adj* **1** not whole or total. **2** inclined to favour one side over another. **3** (+ to) markedly fond of. ➤ **partiality** *n*, **partially** *adv*.

participate *v* to join with others in doing something. ➤ **participant** *n*, **participation** *n*, **participator** *n*, **participatory** *adj*.

participle *n* a verbal form, e.g. *singing* or *sung*, that has the function of an adjective and can also be used in compound verb forms. ➤ **participial** *adj*.

particle *n* **1** a minute quantity or fragment of something. **2** a minute subdivision of matter, *esp* at subatomic level, e.g. an electron or proton.

particular[1] *adj* **1** relating to a single person or thing. **2** worthy of notice; special, unusual. **3** detailed or exact. **4** meticulous or exacting.

particular[2] *n* an individual fact, point, or detail. ∗ **in particular** specifically or especially.

particularly *adv* 1 to an unusual degree. 2 in detail; specifically.

parting *n* 1 the act of parting from somebody. 2 *Brit* the line where the hair is parted.

partisan *n* 1 a firm adherent to a party or cause, or person. 2 a member of a guerrilla band operating behind enemy lines. ➤ **partisan** *adj*.

partition[1] *n* 1 division into parts. 2 a part or section of a whole. 3 a light interior dividing wall. ➤ **partitioner** *n*, **partitionist** *n*.

partition[2] *v* 1 to divide (a country or region) into parts. 2 to divide (a room) with a partition.

partly *adv* not completely; to some extent or degree.

partner[1] *n* 1 a member of a partnership. 2 an associate in a joint venture. 3 each of two people in a joint activity. 4 a spouse or lover.

partner[2] *v* to act as a partner to.

part of speech *n* a class of words having a particular type of meaning and grammatical function, e.g. noun, verb, and adjective.

partook *v* past of PARTAKE.

partridge *n* (*pl* **partridges** *or* **partridge**) a game bird with variegated plumage.

part song *n* an unaccompanied song consisting of two or more voice parts.

part-time *adj and adv* involving less than the normal working hours. ➤ **part-timer** *n*.

parturition *n formal* childbirth.

party[1] *n* (*pl* **-ies**) 1 an informal social gathering with food and drink. 2 a political group representing a particular standpoint and putting up candidates for election. 3 a group of people carrying out an activity together. 4 a person or group taking one side of a dispute or contest. ∗ **be party to** to be involved in (an activity, decision, etc).

party[2] *v* (**-ies, -ied**) *informal* to celebrate with a party.

party line *n* the official principles of a political party.

party wall *n* a wall dividing two adjoining properties.

parvenu *n* a person of low social position who has recently acquired wealth or power.

pascal *n* the SI unit of pressure.

pass[1] *v* 1 to move or proceed past or in a specified direction. 2 to transfer or be transferred to another person. 3 to go past (another vehicle) in the same direction. 4 of time: to elapse. 5 of a situation or event: to complete its course. 6 to spend (time). 7 to go from one quality or state to another. 8 to be successful in (an examination or test). 9 to declare to be successful or satisfactory. 10 to approve or enact (a law or proposal). 11 in a team game, to hit, throw, or kick (the ball) to another player. 12 to pronounce (a judgment or sentence). 13

to utter (a remark). 14 to decline an opportunity or offer. ∗ **pass as/for** resemble or qualify as.

pass[2] *n* 1 the act of passing. 2 a written permission for somebody to go somewhere or to go on leave. 3 a ticket allowing free travel or admission. 4 the passing of an examination. 5 *informal* a sexual approach. 6 a single complete operation in a process. 7 an act of passing a ball to a teammate.

pass[3] *n* a narrow route through a mountain range.

passable *adj* 1 barely acceptable; tolerable. 2 capable of being travelled on. ➤ **passably** *adv*.

passage *n* 1 the action or process of passing from one place or condition to another. 2 a way through or along which one can move. 3 a corridor or lobby. 4 an act of travelling by sea or air. 5 a right or permission to pass. 6 a brief portion of a text or musical composition.

passageway *n* a narrow passage or corridor between rooms or buildings.

pass away *v* to die.

passé *adj* no longer fashionable.

passenger *n* 1 somebody, other than the driver or crew, who travels in a vehicle. 2 a member of a group who contributes little to its functioning.

passer-by *n* (*pl* **passers-by**) a person who happens to pass by a particular place.

passim *adv* occurring at various points throughout the text.

passing[1] *adj* 1 having a brief duration. 2 carried out quickly or casually.

passing[2] *n* a person's death.

passion *n* 1 intense or uncontrollable feeling. 2 an outbreak of anger. 3 ardent affection; love. 4 a strong liking or interest. 5 strong sexual desire. 6 (*usu* **Passion**) the sufferings and death of Christ.

passionate *adj* 1 expressing intense love, hatred, or anger. 2 extremely enthusiastic. ➤ **passionately** *adv*.

passionflower *n* a tropical plant with showy flowers.

passionfruit *n* a fruit from a passionflower.

passion play *n* a dramatic representation of Christ's Passion and crucifixion.

passive[1] *adj* 1 lacking in energy or initiative. 2 offering no resistance; submissive. 3 acted on by external forces or impressions. 4 in grammar, of a verb: having as the subject the person or thing affected by the action, e.g. *was hit* in *the ball was hit*. ➤ **passively** *adv*, **passiveness** *n*, **passivity** *n*.

passive[2] *n* a passive verb form or voice.

passive resistance *n* nonviolent forms of resistance.

passive smoking *n* the inhalation of tobacco smoke from other people's cigarettes.

pass off v **1** (+ off) to represent falsely in order to deceive. **2** to take place successfully.

pass out v to lose consciousness.

Passover n the Jewish festival celebrating the liberation of the Israelites from slavery in Egypt.

passport n an official document issued by a government as proof of identity and nationality to its citizens for use when leaving or reentering the country.

pass up v to decline or reject (an opportunity).

password n a word or phrase to be uttered or entered before being admitted.

past[1] adj **1** just gone or elapsed. **2** having gone by; earlier. **3** finished or ended. **4** of the verb tense that expresses action or state in time gone by. **5** preceding or former.

past[2] prep **1** beyond the age of or for. **2** subsequent to. **3** at the farther side of. **4** up to and then beyond. **5** beyond the capacity or scope of. * **past it** informal no longer in one's prime.

past[3] n **1** time gone by. **2** a verb form expressing past events. **3** a person's earlier life.

past[4] adv so as to pass by the speaker.

pasta n dough formed into various shapes and boiled in water.

paste[1] n **1** an adhesive made from starch and water. **2** a clay mixture used in making pottery or porcelain. **3** a soft smooth substance. **4** a brilliant glass used in making imitation gems.

paste[2] v **1** to cover or stick with paste. **2** in computing, to insert (a piece of text) into a document.

pastel[1] n **1** a crayon made from a paste of powdered pigment mixed with gum. **2** a drawing in pastels. **3** a pale colour.

pastel[2] adj pale in colour.

pasteurize or **-ise** v to sterilize (milk) by heating and cooling it. ➤ **pasteurization** n.

pastiche n an artistic or musical work that imitates the style of a previous work.

pastille or **pastil** n an aromatic or medicated lozenge.

pastime n a hobby or game undertaken for enjoyment.

past master n an expert in a particular activity.

pastor n the minister in charge of a church congregation. ➤ **pastorate** n.

pastoral[1] adj **1** used for livestock rearing. **2** of or relating to the countryside. **3** peaceful and innocent; idyllic. **4** providing spiritual care or guidance for a church congregation. **5** providing personal guidance for students. ➤ **pastoralism** n, **pastorally** adv.

pastoral[2] n a pastoral description, portrayal, or piece of music.

past participle n a participle, e.g. taken, used to form the perfect tense and passive voice.

pastrami n a highly seasoned smoked beef.

pastry n (pl **-ies**) **1** a fatty dough used to make pies, flans, and tarts. **2** a sweet tart or small cake.

pasture[1] n land used for grazing cattle or sheep.

pasture[2] v to feed (animals) on pasture.

pasty[1] n (pl **-ies**) a small savoury pastry case with a filling.

pasty[2] adj (**-ier, -iest**) **1** pallid and unhealthy in appearance. **2** having the consistency of paste.

pat[1] n **1** a light tap with the hand or a flat instrument. **2** a light tapping sound. **3** a small mass of butter. * **a pat on the back** an informal compliment.

pat[2] v (**patted, patting**) **1** to strike lightly with the open hand. **2** to put into place or shape with light blows.

pat[3] adj **1** prompt or immediate. **2** suspiciously appropriate or contrived.

pat[4] adv aptly or promptly. * **have something off pat** to have memorized something so that one can say it without hesitation.

patch[1] n **1** a piece of material used to mend a hole or reinforce a weak spot. **2** a shield worn over an injured eye. **3** a small area distinct from its surroundings. **4** a small piece of land used for growing. **5** a piece of medicated adhesive plaster worn on the skin to allow the drug to be absorbed. **6** a small file supplied to correct a fault in a computer program. **7** Brit, informal an area for which a particular person or group has responsibility. * **not a patch on** Brit, informal not nearly as good as.

patch[2] v **1** to mend with a patch. **2** to mend hastily or temporarily. **3** informal (+ up) to end (a quarrel or disagreement).

patchwork n **1** pieces of coloured cloth sewn together. **2** something made of incongruous parts.

patchy adj (**-ier, -iest**) **1** uneven in quality. **2** occurring in some areas and not others. ➤ **patchily** adv.

pate n archaic or humorous the head.

pâté n a rich savoury paste of spiced meat, fish, etc.

patella n (pl **patellae**) the kneecap.

patent[1] n an official licence allowing somebody the exclusive right to make, use, or sell an invention for a specified period.

patent[2] adj **1** readily visible or intelligible. **2** protected by or made under a patent. ➤ **patently** adv.

patent[3] v to obtain a patent for.

patent leather n leather with a hard glossy surface.

paterfamilias n the male head of a household.

paternal adj **1** typical of or characteristic of a father. **2** related through one's father. ➤ **paternally** adv.

paternalism n a system of dealing with subjects or employees in an authoritarian but protective way. ➤ **paternalistic** adj.

paternity n fatherhood.

paternoster n the Latin form of the Lord's Prayer.

path n 1 a track made for walking on or worn by walking. 2 a course or route. 3 in computing, the sequence of directories giving the location of a file.

pathetic adj 1 arousing pity; pitiful. 2 informal feeble or inadequate. ➤ **pathetically** adv.

pathological (NAmer **pathologic**) adj 1 involving or caused by disease. 2 informal irrationally habitual. ➤ **pathologically** adv.

pathology n 1 the study of the causes and nature of diseases. 2 the processes that characterize a particular disease. ➤ **pathologist** n.

pathos n a quality evoking pity or compassion.

pathway n a path or course.

patience n 1 the capacity to bear pains or trials without complaint. 2 Brit a card game played by one person.

patient[1] adj having or showing patience. ➤ **patiently** adv.

patient[2] n a person awaiting or receiving medical care.

patina n 1 a green or brown film formed by weathering on copper and bronze. 2 a surface shine developed on old polished wood.

patio n (pl **-os**) a paved area adjoining a house.

patisserie n an establishment where pastries and cakes are sold.

patois n (pl **patois**) 1 the local dialect of a region. 2 the jargon of a particular group.

patriarch n 1 a man who is head of a family or social group. 2 any of the biblical fathers of the human race. 3 a venerable old man. 4 a bishop in Orthodox and Eastern churches. ➤ **patriarchal** adj.

patriarchy n (pl **-ies**) a system of social organization with the father as head of the family and descent through the male line.

patrician n a person of high birth; an aristocrat. ➤ **patrician** adj.

patricide n 1 the act of killing one's father. 2 somebody who does this. ➤ **patricidal** adj.

patrimony n (pl **-ies**) property inherited from one's father or male ancestor.

patriot n a person who strongly supports their country. ➤ **patriotic** adj, **patriotism** n.

patrol[1] n a person or group sent to monitor or observe and area.

patrol[2] v (**patrolled, patrolling**) to carry out a patrol of (an area). ➤ **patroller** n.

patron n 1 a person who gives financial support to an individual or institution. 2 a regular customer of a hotel, restaurant, etc.

patronage n 1 support given by a patron. 2 the power to control political appointments. 3 custom provided by patrons of an establishment.

patronize or **-ise** v 1 to adopt an air of condescension towards. 2 to be a regular customer of. ➤ **patronizing** adj.

patron saint n a saint regarded as protecting a particular person, group, etc.

patter[1] v 1 to strike lightly and rapidly. 2 to run with quick light steps.

patter[2] n a quick succession of taps or pats.

patter[3] n rapid glib talk or jargon.

pattern[1] n 1 a repeated decorative design. 2 a regular arrangement or sequence. 3 a design, model, or set of instructions for making something. 4 an example or model for imitation.

pattern[2] v 1 to decorate with a pattern. 2 (+ on/after) to make according to a pattern.

patty n (pl **-ies**) a small pie or pasty.

paucity n smallness of number or quantity.

paunch n a large or protruding stomach. ➤ **paunchy** adj.

pauper n a very poor person.

pause[1] n a temporary stop in a process or activity.

pause[2] v to stop talking or doing something briefly.

pave v to cover (a piece of ground) with a flat surface of stones or concrete. ➤ **paving** n.

pavement n 1 Brit a raised walk for pedestrians at the side of a road. 2 NAmer the covered surface of a road. 3 a level area of bare rock.

pavilion n 1 Brit a building on a sports ground containing changing rooms, etc. 2 a light ornamental structure in a garden or park. 3 a temporary structure for an individual exhibitor at an exhibition.

pavlova n a dessert made of meringue topped with cream and fruit.

paw[1] n the clawed foot of an animal.

paw[2] v 1 to touch or scrape with a paw or hoof. 2 informal to touch (somebody) clumsily or indecently.

pawn[1] n 1 each of eight chess pieces of each colour of least value. 2 somebody who is exploited for another's purpose.

pawn[2] v to deposit (something) with a pawnbroker as security.

pawn[3] n the state of being pledged.

pawnbroker n a person who lends money on the security of personal property pledged, which can be sold if the money is not repaid.

pawnshop n a pawnbroker's shop.

pawpaw or **papaw** n a papaya.

pay[1] v (past and past part. **paid**) 1 to give money to in return for goods or services. 2 to give (money required or owed). 3 to discharge a debt on (a bill or account). 4 to give or forfeit (something) in reparation or retribution. 5 to give or offer (attention, one's respects, etc). 6 to make (a visit). 7 to make amends or be punished. ➤ **payable** adj.

pay[2] n money paid as a salary or wage.

pay back *v* **1** to repay (money owed). **2** to get revenge on.

PAYE *abbr Brit* pay as you earn, a system by which an employer deducts income tax from pay.

payee *n* a person receiving payment.

paymaster *n* an official whose duty it is to pay salaries or wages.

payment *n* **1** the act of paying. **2** a sum of money paid.

payoff *n informal* **1** a profit or reward. **2** a decisive factor resolving a situation.

payola *n chiefly NAmer* an undercover payment for unofficial promotion of a commercial product.

payroll *n* a list of employees of a company and of the amounts due to them in pay.

Pb *abbr* the chemical symbol for lead.

PC *abbr* **1** personal computer. **2** police constable. **3** political correct or correctness.

Pd *abbr* the chemical symbol for palladium.

PE *abbr* physical education.

pea *n* the rounded green seed of a climbing plant used as a vegetable.

peace *n* **1** a state of tranquillity or quiet. **2** freedom from anxiety. **3** public order and security. **4** freedom from hostility between countries. **5** an agreement to end hostilities.

peaceable *adj* **1** wanting to avoid hostility or conflict. **2** free from strife or disorder. ➤ **peaceably** *adv*.

peaceful *adj* **1** untroubled by noise or conflict; tranquil. **2** not involving violence or force. **3** not inclined to dispute or quarrel. ➤ **peacefully** *adv*.

peach *n* **1** a fruit with downy skin and sweet yellow flesh. **2** a light yellowish pink colour. **3** *informal* a fine or beautiful person or thing.

peacock *n* a large bird with a small head and brightly coloured tail feathers that can be spread in a fan.

peahen *n* a female bird of the peacock.

peak¹ *n* **1** a mountain or its pointed top. **2** a projecting part on the front of a cap. **3** a high point in a course of development. **4** the highest level or greatest degree. ➤ **peaked** *adj*.

peak² *v* to reach a maximum or high point.

peal¹ *n* **1** the loud ringing of bells. **2** a set of tuned bells. **3** a loud prolonged sound, e.g. of thunder or laughter.

peal² *v* to ring or sound loudly.

peanut *n* **1** a small oval seed that grows in a pod. **2** *informal* (*in pl*) a trifling amount of money.

peanut butter *n* a spread made from ground peanuts.

pear *n* a yellowish brown fruit, with a rounded shape narrowing towards the stalk.

pearl *n* **1** a hard round milky-white ball that forms in the shell of some molluscs and is used as a gem. **2** something very rare or precious. ➤ **pearly** *adj*.

pearl barley *n* barley that has been ground into medium-sized grains.

pearlescent *adj* having a shiny finish like a pearl.

peasant *n* **1** a member of a class of poor farm labourers or owners of smallholdings, having low social status. **2** *informal* an uneducated or rude person. ➤ **peasantry** *n*.

pease pudding *n* a puree of boiled split peas.

peat *n* partially carbonized vegetable tissue formed by partial decomposition in water of plants found in large bogs. ➤ **peaty** *adj*.

pebble *n* **1** a small rounded stone. **2** *informal* (*used before a noun*) very thick. ➤ **pebbly** *adj*.

pebbledash *n chiefly Brit* small pebbles embedded in a stucco base, used to coat exterior walls.

pecan *n* a smooth oblong edible nut.

peccadillo *n* (*pl* **-oes** *or* **-os**) a slight or trifling offence.

peck¹ *v* **1** of a bird: to strike or pierce with its beak. **2** to kiss (somebody) gently. **3** *informal* to eat reluctantly in small bites.

peck² *n* **1** an act of pecking. **2** a quick sharp stroke. **3** a light kiss.

peck³ *n* a unit of volume or capacity equal to 2 gallons (9.092l).

pecker *n* ✻ **keep one's pecker up** *Brit, informal* to stay cheerful despite difficulty.

pecking order *n* a hierarchy of importance in a group of animals or people.

peckish *adj chiefly Brit, informal* slightly hungry.

pectin *n* a substance in fruit that acts as a setting agent in jams and jellies. ➤ **pectic** *adj*.

pectoral¹ *adj* relating to the chest.

pectoral² *n* each of the muscles connecting the front walls of the chest with the bones of the upper arm and shoulder.

peculiar *adj* **1** different from the usual; strange. **2** (+ to) belonging exclusively to. ➤ **peculiarly** *adv*.

peculiarity *n* (*pl* **-ies**) **1** a distinguishing characteristic. **2** the state of being peculiar.

pecuniary *adj formal* relating to money.

pedagogue *n formal* a teacher. ➤ **pedagogy** *n*.

pedal¹ *n* a lever operated by the foot, e.g. on a bicycle or in a motor vehicle, or one pressed in playing a musical instrument.

pedal² *v* (**pedalled, pedalling,** *NAmer* **pedaled, pedaling**) to work the pedals of (a bicycle).

pedalo *n* (*pl* **-os** *or* **-oes**) *Brit* a small pleasure boat with paddles turned by pedals.

pedant *n* a person who is excessively concerned with detail. ➤ **pedantic** *adj*, **pedantry** *n*.

peddle v 1 to sell (goods) as a pedlar. 2 to sell (illegal drugs). 3 *derog* to seek to disseminate (ideas or opinions).

peddler n 1 a person who peddles something. 2 *NAmer* see PEDLAR.

pederast or **paederast** n a man who has sexual intercourse with a boy. ➤ **pederasty** n.

pedestal n 1 a base supporting a column or statue. 2 a supporting column of a washbasin or a toilet.

pedestrian[1] n a person going on foot.

pedestrian[2] adj dull or commonplace.

pedicure n a treatment for the care of the feet and toenails.

pedigree n 1 the record of an animal's line of descent. 2 the distinguished ancestral line of a person. 3 the origin and history of something.

pediment n in a classical building, the triangular piece of wall in the angle formed by the two slopes of the roof.

pedlar (*NAmer* **peddler**) n a person who travels about offering small wares for sale.

pedometer n an instrument that records the distance a walker covers by responding to body motion at each step.

pee[1] v *informal* to urinate.

pee[2] n *informal* 1 an act of urinating. 2 urine.

peek[1] v 1 to take a brief look. 2 to be just visible behind something else.

peek[2] n a brief look.

peel[1] v 1 to strip the skin or rind off (a fruit or vegetable). 2 to remove (something) by stripping it. 3 to lose an outer layer.

peel[2] n the skin or rind of a fruit or vegetable.

peep[1] v 1 to look cautiously or slyly. 2 (*often* + out) to begin to emerge from concealment.

peep[2] n 1 a brief or furtive look. 2 the first faint appearance of something.

peep[3] v to make a short shrill sound. ➤ **peep** n.

peephole n a hole in a door through which callers can be observed.

peeping Tom n a voyeur.

peep show n a sequence of pictures viewed through a small hole.

peer[1] v 1 to look curiously or searchingly at something. 2 to be partially visible.

peer[2] n 1 a member of the British nobility. 2 a person of the same age or social group as another.

peerage n 1 the rank or title of a peer. 2 (**the peerage**) the body of peers.

peeress n 1 a woman having the rank of a peer. 2 the wife or widow of a peer.

peer group n a group of people of approximately the same age or status.

peerless adj matchless or incomparable.

peeve[1] v *informal* to annoy.

peeve[2] n *informal* a grievance or grudge.

peevish adj querulous or fretful. ➤ **peevishly** adv.

peewit or **pewit** n *Brit* a lapwing.

peg[1] n 1 a small pointed or tapered piece of hard material used to hang things on or hold things down. 2 a clip for holding washing on a line for drying. ✻ **off the peg** *chiefly Brit* of clothes: ready-made.

peg[2] v (**pegged, pegging**) 1 to fix or mark with pegs. 2 to hold (prices, etc) at a certain level.

peg out v *chiefly Brit, informal* to die.

peignoir n a woman's loose negligee.

pejorative adj expressing criticism; disparaging. ➤ **pejoratively** adv.

Pekinese n a small dog with a snub nose and a thick soft coat.

pelican n a bird with a pouch hanging from its bill for catching and keeping fish.

pelican crossing n a pedestrian crossing controlled by traffic lights.

pellagra n a disease associated with a deficiency in the diet, marked by inflammation of the skin, diarrhoea, and disorders of the central nervous system.

pellet n 1 a small rounded mass of a substance. 2 a piece of small shot.

pell-mell adv and adj in confusion or disorder.

pellucid adj 1 clear or transparent. 2 easy to understand.

pelmet n a length of board or fabric placed above a window to conceal curtain fixtures.

pelt[1] v 1 to throw things at. 2 of rain: to fall heavily. 3 to run fast.

pelt[2] ✻ **at full pelt** with great speed.

pelt[3] n an undressed animal skin with its hair, wool, or fur.

pelvis n a basin-shaped structure at the base of the spine. ➤ **pelvic** adj.

pen[1] n an implement for writing or drawing with ink.

pen[2] v (**penned, penning**) to write.

pen[3] n a small enclosure for farm animals.

pen[4] v (**penned, penning**) to shut in a pen.

pen[5] n a female swan.

penal adj 1 relating to or prescribing punishment. 2 of an offence: liable to punishment. 3 harsh.

penalize or **-ise** v 1 to inflict a penalty on. 2 to put at a disadvantage.

penalty n (pl **-ies**) 1 a punishment imposed for doing wrong or breaking a rule. 2 a penalty kick. 3 disadvantage, loss, or suffering due to some action.

penalty area n a rectangular area in front of each goal on a football pitch.

penalty kick n in football, a free kick at goal in football or rugby.

penance n 1 a penalty or personal sacrifice undertaken to show repentance for sin. 2 a sacramental rite of some Churches involving confession and performance of a penance.

pence n pl of PENNY.

penchant n a strong liking.

pencil[1] *n* an implement for writing or drawing consisting of a slender strip of graphite in a wooden case.

pencil[2] *v* (**pencilled, pencilling,** *NAmer* **penciled, penciling**) to draw or write with a pencil. * **pencil in** to record a provisional appointment.

pencil skirt *n* a narrow straight skirt.

pendant *n* **1** an ornament hanging from a chain worn round the neck. **2** an electric light fitting suspended from the ceiling.

pending[1] *prep* while awaiting; until.

pending[2] *adj* **1** not yet decided or dealt with. **2** about to happen.

pendulous *adj* hanging down.

pendulum *n* a weight suspended from a fixed point so as to swing freely, used to regulate the mechanism of a clock.

penetrate *v* **1** to pass into or through. **2** to enter (an organization or a market) by overcoming resistance. **3** to insert the penis into the vagina or anus of (a sexual partner). **4** to see into or through. **5** to discover the inner contents or meaning of. **6** to diffuse through or into. **7** to be understood. ➤ **penetration** *n*.

pen-friend *n* a person with whom a friendship is made by exchanging letters.

penguin *n* a flightless sea bird of the southern hemisphere, with a dark back and white belly, wings resembling flippers, and webbed feet.

penicillin *n* an antibiotic originally obtained from moulds.

penile *adj* relating to the penis.

peninsula *n* a narrow strip of land almost surrounded by water. ➤ **peninsular** *adj*.

penis *n* (*pl* **penises** *or* **penes**) the male organ used for sexual intercourse and urination.

penitent[1] *adj* feeling sorrow for sins or offences. ➤ **penitence** *n*, **penitential** *adj*.

penitent[2] *n* somebody who repents of sin.

penitentiary *n* (*pl* -**ies**) *NAmer* a prison for people convicted of serious crimes.

penknife *n* (*pl* **penknives**) a small knife with a blade that folds into the handle.

pennant *n* a flag that tapers to a point or divides into two points.

penne *pl n* pasta in short tubes with diagonally cut ends.

penniless *adj* having no money.

penny *n* (*pl* **pennies** *or* **pence**) **1** a unit of currency worth 100th of a pound. **2** formerly in Britain, a bronze coin worth 240th of a pound.

penny-farthing *n Brit* an early type of bicycle with a small rear wheel and a large front wheel.

penny-pinching *adj* mean or stingy. ➤ **penny-pincher** *n*.

penny whistle *n* a simple whistle with finger holes.

pension[1] *n* a fixed sum paid regularly to a retired person.

pension[2] *v* to pay a pension to. ➤ **pensionable** *adj*.

pension[3] /'ponhsyonh/ *n* a hotel or boarding house in a European country.

pensioner *n* a person who receives a retirement pension.

pension off *v* to retire (somebody) from service with a pension.

pensive *adj* deeply thoughtful. ➤ **pensively** *adv*.

pentacle *n* a pentagram.

pentagon *n* a figure with five angles and five sides. ➤ **pentagonal** *adj*.

pentagram *n* a five-pointed star used as a magical symbol.

pentameter *n* a line of verse consisting of five metrical feet.

pentathlon *n* an athletic contest consisting of five events.

Pentecost *n* a Christian festival commemorating the descent of the Holy Spirit on the apostles, observed on the seventh Sunday after Easter.

Pentecostal *adj* **1** of evangelical Christian bodies that lay emphasis on the gifts of the Holy Spirit, e.g. healing the sick. **2** relating to Pentecost. ➤ **Pentecostalism** *n*.

penthouse *n* an apartment on the roof or top floor of a building.

penultimate *adj* last but one.

penumbra *n* **1** a region of partial darkness in a shadow surrounding the umbra. **2** a less dark region surrounding the dark centre of a sunspot. ➤ **penumbral** *adj*.

penurious *adj formal* very poor.

penury *n* severe poverty.

peony *or* **paeony** *n* (*pl* -**ies**) a plant with large showy flowers.

people[1] *pl n* **1** human beings in general. **2** one's family. **3** (**the people**) the inhabitants or citizens of a state. **4** a body of persons forming a politically organized group.

people[2] *v* **1** to fill (a place) with people. **2** to dwell in or inhabit (a place).

pep[1] *n informal* energy or high spirits.

pep[2] *v* (**pepped, pepping**) (*usu* + up) to fill with energy or enthusiasm.

pepper[1] *n* **1** a hot-tasting ground black or white powder obtained from peppercorns, used for flavouring. **2** any of various fruits of tropical plants. ➤ **peppery** *adj*.

pepper[2] *v* **1** to season with pepper. **2** to cover extensively with many instances of a thing. **3** to shower (somebody or something) with shot or other missiles.

peppercorn *n* a dried berry of a plant, used as a spice or ground as powder.

peppercorn rent *n Brit* a very low or nominal rent.

peppermint n 1 a mint plant with dark green tapering leaves and whorls of small pink flowers. 2 an aromatic essential oil obtained from this. 3 a sweet flavoured with peppermint oil.

pepperoni or **peperoni** n a spicy Italian beef and pork sausage.

pep talk n informal a talk designed to encourage morale.

peptic adj of or promoting digestion.

peptic ulcer n an ulcer in the mucous membranes of the digestive tract.

per prep 1 for each. 2 by the means of.

perambulate v formal to travel on foot. ➤ **perambulation** n.

perambulator n formal a pram.

per annum adv for each year.

per capita adv and adj for each person.

perceive v 1 to become aware of (something) through the senses. 2 to regard in the specified way. ➤ **perceivable** adj.

Usage Note: Note the spelling with -ei-.

per cent[1] adv for each hundred.

per cent[2] n (pl **per cent**) 1 one part in a hundred. 2 a percentage.

percentage n 1 a proportion expressed as per cent of a whole. 2 a share or proportion of a whole.

percentile n each of the 100 groups of individuals comprising a part of a population for statistical purposes.

perceptible adj able to be perceived by the senses. ➤ **perceptibly** adv.

perception n 1 an awareness of one's surroundings produced by the senses. 2 a result of perceiving; an observation. 3 intuitive discernment; insight.

perceptive adj showing keen perception; observant or discerning. ➤ **perceptively** adv.

perceptual adj relating to perception or sensory experience. ➤ **perceptually** adv.

perch[1] n 1 a roost for a bird. 2 a seat or resting place.

perch[2] v 1 to settle briefly or precariously. 2 to place in a high or precarious spot.

perch[3] n (pl **perches** or **perch**) a freshwater fish with vertical stripes and spiny fins.

perchance adv archaic perhaps or possibly.

percipient adj perceptive or discerning. ➤ **percipience** n.

percolate v 1 of a liquid or gas: to pass through a porous substance. 2 of information: to spread gradually through a group or area. 3 to prepare (coffee) in a percolator. 4 of coffee: to be prepared in a percolator. ➤ **percolation** n.

percolator n a coffee pot in which boiling water passes through a perforated basket containing ground coffee beans.

percussion n musical instruments played by striking or shaking them. ➤ **percussionist** n.

perdition n in Christianity, eternal damnation.

peregrination n archaic a long and wandering journey.

peregrine n a falcon with dark grey wings and back.

peremptory adj aggressively or unreasonably insistent. ➤ **peremptorily** adv.

perennial[1] adj 1 lasting throughout the year or for several years. 2 of a plant: living for several years with new growth each year. ➤ **perennially** adv.

perennial[2] n a perennial plant.

perestroika n the political and social reform of the communist system of the former Soviet Union.

perfect[1] adj 1 entirely without fault or defect; flawless or entirely satisfactory. 2 lacking in no essential detail; complete. 3 absolute or utter. 4 of the verb tense that expresses an action or state completed at the time of speaking or at a time spoken of. ➤ **perfectly** adv.

perfect[2] v to make perfect. ➤ **perfectible** adj.

perfection n 1 making or being perfect. 2 something or somebody that is perfect.

perfectionism n a wish for everything one does to be perfect. ➤ **perfectionist** adj and n.

perfect pitch n the ability to sing or identify a note of a given pitch.

perfidious adj treacherously disloyal.

perfidy n literary faithlessness or disloyalty.

perforate v to make a hole or holes in. ➤ **perforation** n.

perforce adv formal by necessity.

perform v 1 to do or carry out. 2 to give a rendering of (a dramatic or musical piece). ➤ **performer** n.

performance n 1 the act or an instance of performing. 2 a presentation to an audience of a play, piece of music, dance, etc. 3 the ability of a machine to operate. 4 informal a tedious process or piece of behaviour.

performing arts pl n arts that are performed to an audience, e.g. music, dance, and drama.

perfume[1] n 1 a pleasant-smelling liquid preparation applied to the skin. 2 a sweet or pleasant smell. ➤ **perfumery** n.

perfume[2] v 1 to give a sweet smell to. 2 to apply perfume to.

perfunctory adj mechanical or cursory. ➤ **perfunctorily** adv.

pergola n an arched framework for training plants over.

perhaps adv possibly but not certainly; maybe.

peril n exposure to the risk of being injured or lost. ➤ **perilous** adj, **perilously** adv.

perimeter n 1 the boundary of a closed plane figure. 2 an outer edge or limit. ➤ **perimetric** adj.

period n 1 a portion of time. 2 a stage of history. 3 (used before a noun) of a particular historical time: *period costume.* **4** any of the divisions of the school day. **5** an occurrence of menstruation. **6** *chiefly NAmer* a full stop.

periodic *adj* recurring at regular intervals.

periodical¹ *adj* **1** recurring at regular intervals. **2** of a magazine or journal: published at fixed intervals. ➤ **periodically** *adv.*

periodical² *n* a periodical publication.

periodic table *n* a listing of the chemical elements by their atomic numbers.

period piece *n* a piece of furniture or work of art that evokes a historical period.

peripatetic *adj* travelling or itinerant.

peripheral¹ *adj* **1** of or forming an outer limit or boundary. **2** of relatively minor significance. **3** auxiliary or supplementary. ➤ **peripherally** *adv.*

peripheral² *n* a printer or other device connected to a computer.

periphery *n* (*pl* -ies) **1** the outer limits or edge of something. **2** a less important or central position.

periscope *n* a tubular optical instrument containing mirrors or prisms for seeing objects not in the direct line of sight.

perish *v* **1** to die. **2** to be ruined or destroyed. **3** to deteriorate or rot. **4** of cold or exposure: to weaken or numb (somebody). ✻ **perish the thought** *informal* used to express horror at an idea.

perishable *adj* of food: liable to rot or decay.

peristalsis *n* successive waves of involuntary contraction passing along the walls of the intestine and forcing the contents onward.

peritoneum *n* (*pl* **peritoneums** or **peritonea**) a smooth transparent membrane lining the cavity of the abdomen. ➤ **peritoneal** *adj.*

peritonitis *n* inflammation of the peritoneum.

periwinkle *n* **1** a trailing evergreen plant with blue or white flowers. **2** a marine snail with a spiral shell.

perjure *v* to make (oneself) guilty of perjury.

perjury *n* (*pl* -ies) the deliberate violation of an oath in a court of law.

perk *n* *informal* an extra privilege or benefit.

perk up *v* to become more lively or cheerful.

perky *adj* (-ier, -iest) lively and cheerful.

perm¹ *n* a long-lasting arrangement of the hair by using chemicals.

perm² *v* to give a perm to (the hair).

perm³ *n* *Brit, informal* a permutation of the teams in a football pool.

permafrost *n* a layer of permanently frozen ground in cold regions.

permanent *adj* lasting or stable. ➤ **permanence** *n,* **permanently** *adv.*

permeable *adj* having pores or openings that permit liquids or gases to pass through.

permeate *v* to spread throughout.

permissible *adj* allowed.

permission *n* formal consent or authorization to do something.

permissive *adj* tolerant with regard to social or sexual morality. ➤ **permissiveness** *n.*

permit¹ *v* (**permitted, permitting**) **1** to give authorization to do something. **2** to consent to. **3** *formal* (+ of) to make possible.

permit² *n* an official document allowing somebody to do or keep something.

permutation *n* each of various possible arrangements of things.

pernicious *adj* highly injurious or destructive.

pernickety *adj* **1** fussy about details. **2** requiring precision and care.

peroration *n* the concluding part of a speech.

peroxide *n* **1** an oxide containing a high proportion of oxygen. **2** a chemical used in bleaching hair.

perpendicular¹ *adj* at right angles to the plane of the horizon or a given line or plane.

perpendicular² *n* a perpendicular line, plane, or surface.

perpetrate *v* to be guilty of (something wrong). ➤ **perpetration** *n,* **perpetrator** *n.*

perpetual *adj* **1** continuing for all time. **2** repeated or constant. ➤ **perpetually** *adv.*

perpetuate *v* to cause to last indefinitely. ➤ **perpetuation** *n.*

perpetuity *n* (*pl* -ies) the state of being perpetual.

perplex *v* to puzzle or confuse. ➤ **perplexity** *n.*

perquisite *n* *formal* an extra privilege or benefit.

per se *adv* in itself.

persecute *v* **1** to harass or harm (somebody) because of their religion, political beliefs, etc. **2** to annoy or pester. ➤ **persecution** *n,* **persecutor** *n.*

persevere *v* (*often* + in/with) to persist in an undertaking in spite of difficulties. ➤ **perseverance** *n.*

Persian *n* **1** a native or inhabitant of ancient Persia or modern Iran. **2** the language of ancient Persia and modern Iran. **3** a short-nosed cat with a long silky coat. ➤ **Persian** *adj.*

persimmon *n* a round fruit with flesh that is sweet when ripe.

persist *v* **1** (*often* + in/with) to continue resolutely in spite of difficulty. **2** to continue to exist.

persistent *adj* **1** persisting in a course of action. **2** continuing or recurring. ➤ **persistence** *n,* **persistently** *adv.*

person *n* (*pl* **people** or *formal* **persons**) **1** a distinct human being. **2** a living human body. **3** any of three forms of a verb or pronoun that indicate reference to the speaker, to somebody or something spoken to, or to somebody or something spoken of: compare FIRST PERSON, SECOND PERSON, THIRD PERSON. ✴ **in person** physically present oneself.

persona *n* (*pl* **personas** *or* **personae**) a role or character adopted by a person.

personable *adj* pleasing in person; attractive. ➤ **personably** *adv*.

personage *n* a person of rank or distinction.

personal *adj* **1** affecting a particular person; private. **2** done in person without the intervention of another. **3** carried on between individuals directly. **4** of the person or body. **5** relating to the private affairs of an individual. **6** referring offensively to the character, appearance, or private affairs of an individual.

personal column *n* a section of a newspaper containing personal messages and advertisements.

personality *n* (*pl* **-ies**) **1** the behavioural and emotional tendencies that an individual person has. **2** distinction or excellence of personal and social traits. **3** an important or celebrated person.

personalize *or* **-ise** *v* **1** to mark (something) as the property of a particular person. **2** to design or make (something) to fit in with a person's wishes or needs. **3** to focus (an argument, etc) on personalities rather than issues.

personal pronoun *n* a pronoun, e.g. *I, you, he, she,* or *they,* that relates to the speaker, the person addressed, or a person or people reffered to.

personal stereo *n* a small cassette player or CD player used with earphones or headphones.

persona non grata /puh,sohnə non 'grahtə/ *n* a person who is unwelcome at a particular place.

personify *v* (**-ies, -ied**) **1** to conceive of or represent (something not human) as having human qualities or human form. **2** to be the embodiment of (a quality) in human form. ➤ **personification** *n*.

personnel *n* a body of people employed by an organization.

perspective *n* **1** the relationship of solid objects to each other in space as they appear to the eye, or the technique of showing this on a flat surface. **2** the aspect of an object of thought from a particular standpoint. **3** the capacity to understand the true relationship or relative importance of things. **4** a picture showing a vista.

Perspex *n trademark* a transparent acrylic plastic.

perspicacious *adj* having acute mental vision or discernment. ➤ **perspicacity** *n*.

perspicuous *adj* clear and precise and easy to understand. ➤ **perspicuity** *n*.

perspiration *n* **1** the process of sweating. **2** sweat.

perspire *v* to sweat.

persuade *v* to make (somebody) believe or do something by argument, reasoning, or entreaty. ➤ **persuadable** *adj*.

persuasion *n* **1** the process of persuading or being persuaded. **2** a particular belief or system of beliefs.

persuasive *adj* tending or able to persuade. ➤ **persuasively** *adv*.

pert *adj* **1** impudent and forward; saucy. **2** trim and chic; jaunty.

pertain *v* to belong to or be appropriate to.

pertinacious *adj formal* clinging resolutely to an opinion or purpose. ➤ **pertinacity** *n*.

pertinent *adj* relevant to the matter in hand. ➤ **pertinence** *n*, **pertinently** *adv*.

perturb *v* to disturb greatly in the mind; to trouble. ➤ **perturbation** *n*.

peruse *v formal* to read or examine in detail. ➤ **perusal** *n*.

pervade *v* to become diffused through every part of. ➤ **pervasive** *adj*.

perverse *adj* **1** obstinate in opposing what is reasonable or accepted. **2** arising from stubbornness or obstinacy. **3** uncooperative or contrary. ➤ **perversely** *adv*, **perverseness** *n*, **perversity** *n*.

perversion *n* **1** the act of perverting. **2** abnormal sexual behaviour.

pervert[1] *v* **1** to cause (somebody) to turn away from what is true or morally right. **2** to divert to a wrong use or purpose. **3** to twist the meaning or sense of.

pervert[2] *n* a person who enjoys abnormal sexual behaviour.

perverted *adj* sexually abnormal.

pervious *adj* allowing liquid to pass through.

peseta /pə'sayta/ *n* the former basic monetary unit of Spain (replaced by the euro in 2002).

pesky *adj* (**-ier, -iest**) *informal* troublesome or annoying.

pessary *n* (*pl* **-ies**) a device worn in the vagina to support the uterus or prevent conception.

pessimism *n* a tendency to stress the worst aspects of something to expect the worst outcome. ➤ **pessimist** *n*, **pessimistic** *adj*, **pessimistically** *adv*.

pest *n* **1** a nuisance. **2** an animal or insect that causes damage or carries disease.

pester *v* to harass or annoy with petty irritations and demands.

pesticide *n* a chemical used to destroy insects and other pests.

pestilence *n* a virulent epidemic disease.

pestilential *adj* **1** destructive of life; deadly. **2** morally harmful; pernicious. **3** *informal* annoying or irritating.

pestle *n* an implement with a rounded tip for pounding substances in a mortar.

pesto *n* a paste made from crushed basil leaves, garlic, pine nuts, olive oil, and Parmesan cheese.

pet[1] *n* **1** an animal, bird, etc kept for pleasure. **2** somebody who is treated with special favour.

pet[2] *adj* **1** favourite. **2** special or strongest.

pet[3] *v* (**petted, petting**) **1** to stroke (an animal) in a gentle or loving manner. **2** to engage in amorous caressing.

pet[4] *n* a fit of sulkiness or anger.

petal *n* any of the outer parts that form a flower.

peter out *v* to diminish gradually and come to an end.

petite *adj* of a woman: having a small trim figure.

petit four /ˌpeti ˈfaw/ *n* (*pl* **petits fours** or **petit fours** /ˌpeti ˈfawz/) a small fancy cake or biscuit.

petition[1] *n* **1** a formal written request made to somebody in authority by a large number of people. **2** an earnest request.

petition[2] *v* to present a petition to. ➤ **petitioner** *n*.

petit point /ˌpeti ˈpoynt/ *n* embroidery on canvas across single threads in tent stitch.

pet name *n* an informal name used for endearment.

petrel *n* a sea bird that comes inland to breed.

petri dish or **Petri dish** *n* a small shallow glass or plastic dish with a loose cover, used in laboratories.

petrify *v* (**-ies, -ied**) **1** to paralyse with fear or amazement. **2** to convert into stone or a hard or stony substance.

petrochemical[1] *n* a chemical obtained from petroleum or natural gas.

petrochemical[2] *adj* relating to petrochemicals or the properties of petroleum and natural gas.

petrol *n* *chiefly Brit* a mixture refined from petroleum and used as a fuel for internal-combustion engines.

petroleum *n* an inflammable liquid composed of a mixture of hydrocarbons, refined for use as petrol, naphtha, etc.

petticoat *n* a woman's light undergarment hanging from the waist or shoulders.

pettifogging *adj archaic* quibbling or trivial.

pettish *adj* peevish or petulant. ➤ **pettishly** *adv.*

petty *adj* (**-ier, -iest**) **1** trivial. **2** having little importance. **3** small-minded. **4** of a crime: minor. ➤ **pettiness** *n.*

petty cash *n* an amount of cash kept for payment of minor items.

petty officer *n* a rank of non-commissioned naval officer.

petulant *adj* childishly bad-tempered or peevish. ➤ **petulance** *n,* **petulantly** *adv.*

petunia *n* a plant with large brightly coloured funnel-shaped flowers.

pew *n* **1** a bench fixed in a row for the use of the congregation in a church. **2** *Brit, informal* a seat.

pewter *n* an alloy of tin and lead or one containing copper and antimony.

pfennig /ˈ(p)fenig, ˈ(p)fenikh/ *n* a former unit of currency in Germany, worth 100th of a mark (replaced by the euro in 2002).

PFI *abbr* Private Finance Initiative.

PG *adj* in Britain, a classification of cinema films for which parental guidance is recommended.

pH *n* a figure used to show how acid or alkaline a solution is.

phalanx *n* **1** a close arrangement of people, animals, or things. **2** a body of troops in close array behind a wall of shields.

phallic *adj* of or resembling a phallus.

phallus *n* (*pl* **phalli** or **phalluses**) a representation of an erect penis.

phantasm *n literary* **1** an illusion or figment. **2** a ghost or spectre.

phantasmagoria *n* a confused succession of things imagined in a dream or feverish state.

phantom[1] *n* **1** a ghost. **2** something existing only in the imagination.

phantom[2] *adj* non-existent.

pharaoh *n* a ruler of ancient Egypt. ➤ **pharaonic** *adj.*

Usage Note: Note the spelling *-aoh* not *-oah.*

pharisee *n* a member of a Jewish party that interpreted religious law strictly.

pharmaceutical[1] *adj* relating to medicinal substances.

pharmaceutical[2] *n* a medicinal drug.

pharmacology *n* the science of drugs and their effect on living things. ➤ **pharmacological** *adj,* **pharmacologist** *n.*

pharmacy *n* (*pl* **-ies**) **1** a place where medicines are prepared and dispensed. **2** a chemist's shop. **3** the preparation and dispensing of medicinal drugs. ➤ **pharmacist** *n.*

pharynx *n* (*pl* **pharynges** or **pharynxes**) the part of the alimentary canal between the mouth cavity and the throat.

phase[1] *n* a distinct part or stage in a process or activity.

phase[2] *v* to carry out (an activity) in planned phases.

phase in *v* to introduce in gradual stages.

phase out *v* to discontinue in gradual stages.

PhD *abbr* Doctor of Philosophy.

pheasant *n* (*pl* **pheasants** or **pheasant**) a large long-tailed game bird.

phenomenal *adj* extraordinary or remarkable. ➤ **phenomenally** *adv.*

phenomenon *n* (*pl* **phenomena**) **1** an observable fact or event. **2** an exceptional or unusual person, thing, or event.

Usage Note: Phenomenon is a singular noun, and *phenomena* is the plural.

pheromone *n* a chemical substance produced by an animal that stimulates responses in the same species.

phi *n* the 21st letter of the Greek alphabet (Φ, φ).

phial *n* a small bottle for holding liquid medicine.

philander *v* of a man: to have many casual love affairs. ➤ **philanderer** *n*.

philanthropy *n* active effort to promote the welfare of others. ➤ **philanthropic** *adj*, **philanthropist** *n*.

philately *n* the study and collection of postage stamps. ➤ **philatelist** *n*.

philharmonic *adj* used *esp* in the names of choirs and orchestras: devoted to music.

philippic *n literary* an attacking speech or declamation.

philistine *n* **1** (**Philistine**) a member of a people of ancient Palestine. **2** a person who has no interest in intellectual or aesthetic values. ➤ **philistinism** *n*.

philology *n* the study of the development and structure of languages. ➤ **philological** *adj*, **philologist** *n*.

philosopher *n* **1** somebody who studies philosophy. **2** a scholar or thinker.

philosophical *adj* **1** of philosophers or philosophy. **2** calm in the face of trouble. ➤ **philosophically** *adv*.

philosophize *or* **-ise** *v* to engage in philosophical reasoning.

philosophy *n* (*pl* **-ies**) **1** the study of the nature of knowledge and existence. **2** a specific set of philosophical principles.

phlegm *n* thick mucus in the nose and throat.

phlegmatic *adj* having a calm temperament. ➤ **phlegmatically** *adv*.

phobia *n* an irrational fear of something. ➤ **phobic** *adj* and *n*.

phoenix (*NAmer* **phenix**) *n* a mythical bird believed to burn itself on a pyre and rise alive from the ashes.

phone[1] *n* a telephone.

phone[2] *v* to make a telephone call.

phonecard *n* a plastic card used to make telephone calls from a public telephone.

phonetic *adj* **1** of spoken language or speech sounds. **2** representing speech sounds by symbols that each have one value only. ➤ **phonetically** *adv*.

phonetics *pl n* the study and classification of speech sounds.

phoney[1] *or* **phony** *adj* (**-ier, -iest**) *informal* not genuine or real.

phoney[2] *or* **phony** *n* (*pl* **-eys** *or* **-ies**) a phoney person or thing.

phonic *adj* **1** of or producing sound; acoustic. **2** relating to speech sounds. ➤ **phonically** *adv*.

phonics *pl n* a system of teaching reading through the phonetic value of syllables.

phonograph *n* **1** an early device for recording and reproducing sound. **2** *NAmer* a record player.

phosphate *n* a salt or ester of a phosphoric acid.

phosphorescence *n* **1** light emission caused by the absorption of radiation and continuing after the radiation has stopped. **2** lasting emission of light without noticeable heat. ➤ **phosphorescent** *adj*.

phosphoric acid *n* an acid used in preparing phosphates, used in fertilizers and as a flavouring.

phosphorus *n* a non-metallic element that occurs as phosphates. ➤ **phosphorous** *adj*.

photo *n* (*pl* **-os**) a photograph.

photocall *n* a session at which a famous person is photographed publicity.

photocopy[1] *n* (*pl* **-ies**) a reproduction of written or printed text, photographs, etc by a process involving photography.

photocopy[2] *v* (**-ies, -ied**) to make a photocopy of. ➤ **photocopiable** *adj*, **photocopier** *n*.

photoelectric *adj* involving electrical effects caused by the interaction of radiation with matter.

photo finish *n* a close finish to a race with the winner decided from a photograph.

photofit *n* a likeness of a person's face constructed from photographs.

photogenic *adj* looking attractive in photographs.

photograph[1] *n* a picture or likeness obtained by photography.

photograph[2] *v* to take a photograph of. ➤ **photographer** *n*, **photographic** *adj*.

photography *n* the process of producing images on a sensitized surface by the action of light.

photogravure *n* a process for making prints from an engraving produced from photographic negatives, or a picture produced in this way.

photometer *n* an instrument for measuring light intensity or brightness. ➤ **photometric** *adj*, **photometry** *n*.

photon *n* a very small quantity of electromagnetic radiation.

photosensitive *adj* sensitive to light.

Photostat *n* **1** *trademark* a device for making a photographic copy of documents. **2** (**photostat**) a copy made in this way.

photostat *v* (**photostatted, photostatting**) to copy on a Photostat or similar device.

photosynthesis *n* the process by which plants synthesize organic chemical compounds from carbon dioxide using light. ➤ **photosynthetic** *adj*.

phrase[1] *n* **1** a group of words that go together in a sentence but do not form a clause. **2** in music, a group of notes forming a unit of melody. ➤ **phrasal** *adj*.

phrase² v to express in a particular form of words.

phrase book n a book containing words and phrases in a foreign language with their translation.

phraseology n (pl -ies) a manner of putting words and phrases together.

phrenology n the former study of the shape of the skull as a supposed indicator of mental faculties and character. ➤ **phrenologist** n.

phylum n (pl **phyla**) a major group of related species in the classification of plants and animals.

physical¹ adj **1** having material existence; perceptible through the senses. **2** relating to material things. **3** relating to the body: *a physical examination*. **4** concerned with or preoccupied with the body and its needs, as opposed to spiritual matters. **5** involving bodily contact. **6** relating to sciences such as physics, chemistry, and astronomy. ➤ **physicality** n, **physically** adv.

physical² n a medical examination to determine a person's health and fitness.

physical education n instruction in sports, athletics, and gymnastics.

physician n a person skilled in medicine.

physics pl n the branch of science that deals with matter and energy and their properties. ➤ **physicist** n.

physiognomy n (pl -ies) a person's face and facial features.

physiology n the branch of biology that deals with the functions and activities of life or of living matter. ➤ **physiological** adj, **physiologist** n.

physiotherapy n the treatment of disease or injury by massage and regulated exercise. ➤ **physiotherapist** n.

physique n the form or structure of a person's body.

pi n **1** the 16th letter of the Greek alphabet (Π, π). **2** the ratio of the circumference of a circle to its diameter with a value of 3.14159265.

pianissimo adj and adv of a piece of music: performed very softly.

piano¹ n (pl -os) a standing keyboard instrument with strings stretched across a frame and struck by hammers when keys are pressed. ➤ **pianist** n.

piano² adj and adv of a piece of music: performed in softly or quietly.

pianoforte /pi͡aˌnohˈfawti/ n formal a piano.

piazza /piˈatsə/ n an open square in a town.

picador n (pl **picadors** or **picadores**) in bullfighting, a horseman who prods the bull with a lance to weaken its neck and shoulder muscles.

picaresque adj of a type of fiction narrating the adventures of a likeable rogue.

piccalilli n (pl **piccalillies** or **piccalillis**) a hot relish of chopped vegetables, mustard, and spices.

piccaninny (NAmer **picaninny** or **pickaninny**) n (pl -ies) offensive a small black child.

piccolo n (pl -os) a small flute with a range an octave higher than an ordinary flute.

pick¹ v **1** to choose from a number of choices or possibilities. **2** to remove (a fruit or flower) by pulling it from a tree or plant. **3** to remove (unwanted matter) with a finger or pointed instrument. **4** to steal from (a person's pocket). **5** to provoke (a quarrel or fight). **6** to unlock (a lock) with a wire or other device other than the key. * **pick at** to eat (food) sparingly and with little appetite. **pick holes in** to find fault or weaknesses in. **pick on** to single out for unpleasant treatment. **pick one's way** to go forward carefully or with difficulty. **pick somebody's brains** to get ideas from them. **pick through/over** to sort (a number of items). ➤ **picker** n.

pick² n **1** the act of choosing; a choice. **2** the best or choicest.

pick³ or **pickaxe** n a heavy iron or steel tool with a long wooden handle and a head that is pointed at one or both ends.

picket¹ n **1** a person or group of people posted at a place of work affected by a strike to try to persuade workers not to work. **2** a pointed stake or post.

picket² v (**picketed, picketing**) to be a picket outside (a place of work).

pickings pl n **1** eatable fragments or scraps. **2** gains or rewards obtained by dubious means.

pickle¹ n **1** a brine or vinegar solution in which foods are preserved. **2** a mixture of chopped vegetables preserved in a brine or vinegar solution. **3** informal a difficult or confused situation.

pickle² v to preserve in pickle.

pick off v to shoot at (a target in a group).

pick out v **1** to select (one person or thing) in a group. **2** to play the notes of (a tune) by ear.

pickpocket n a person who steals from pockets or bags.

pickup n **1** the act or an instance of picking up. **2** a light motor truck having an open body with low sides and tailboard. **3** the device on a record player that holds the stylus. **4** a device on a guitar that converts the vibrations of the strings into electrical signals.

pick up v **1** to take hold of and lift. **2** to collect or take in a vehicle. **3** to acquire or learn casually. **4** to begin a casual relationship with. **5** to receive (a radio signal). **6** to become aware of (another person's feeling, etc). **7** to recover or improve. * **pick up on** to criticize (a previous speaker).

picky adj (-ier, -iest) fussy or choosy.

picnic¹ n an informal meal eaten in the open. * **no picnic** informal something by no means straightforward or pleasant.

picnic[2] *v* (**picnicked, picnicking**) to have or go on a picnic. ➤ **picnicker** *n*.

Pict *n* a member of a Celtic people of northern Britain in Roman times.

pictograph *n* **1** an ancient or prehistoric drawing or painting, often on a rock wall. **2** a small picture used as a symbol in some writing systems. ➤ **pictographic** *adj*.

pictorial *adj* consisting of or illustrated by pictures. ➤ **pictorially** *adv*.

picture[1] *n* **1** a design or representation made by painting, drawing, or photography. **2** a vivid description. **3** an image on a television screen. **4** a cinema film. **5** *chiefly Brit, informal* (*in pl*) the cinema. * **in the picture** *informal* fully informed.

picture[2] *v* **1** to depict or represent in a picture. **2** to form a mental image of.

picturesque *adj* quaintly or charmingly attractive.

picture window *n* a large single-paned window.

piddle *v informal* **1** (*usu* + about/around) to act in an idle or trifling manner. **2** to urinate.

piddling *adj informal* trivial or paltry.

pidgin *n* a language based on two or more languages and used between people with different native languages.

pie *n* a baked dish with a sweet or savoury filling covered by pastry. * **pie in the sky** *informal* an illusory hope or prospect.

piebald *adj* of a horse: spotted with different colours.

piece[1] *n* **1** a part detached from a whole, or forming one element of it. **2** a distinct separate bit or item of something. **3** a literary or musical work. **4** a coin of a specified value. **5** a small object used in playing a board game. * **go to pieces** to lose control of oneself.

piece[2] *v* (*often* + together) to join into a whole.

pièce de résistance /ˌpyes də rəˈzistanhs/ *n* (*pl* **pièces de résistance**) the most outstanding item.

piecemeal *adj and adv* **1** done gradually or one piece at a time. **2** in pieces or fragments.

piecework *n* work that is paid for at a set rate per unit.

pie chart *n* a chart in which each component of a whole is represented by a sector of a circle.

pied *adj* having patches of two or more colours.

pied-à-terre /ˌpyay dah ˈteə/ *n* (*pl* **pieds-à-terre**) a second lodging kept for occasional use.

pie-eyed *adj informal* drunk.

pier *n* **1** a structure extending into a sea or lake and used as a landing place or promenade. **2** a support for a bridge or wall.

pierce *v* **1** to make a hole in or through. **2** to force or make a way into or through.

piercing *adj* **1** very loud or shrill. **2** penetratingly cold.

piety *n* (*pl* **-ies**) the quality of being pious or religious.

piffle *n informal* trivial nonsense.

piffling *adj informal* trivial or derisory.

pig[1] *n* **1** an animal with a thick bristly skin and a long snout. **2** *informal* a dirty, greedy, or disagreeable person. **3** a shaped mass of cast crude metal. ➤ **piggish** *adj*, **piglet** *n*.

pig[2] *v* (**pigged, pigging**) *informal* **1** to eat (food) greedily. **2** to overindulge (oneself).

pigeon *n* a bird with a stout body and smooth plumage.

pigeonhole[1] *n* **1** a small open compartment for letters or documents. **2** a convenient but often oversimplified category. **3** a hole for a pigeon to nest in.

pigeonhole[2] *v* to assign to a particular category.

pigeon-toed *adj* having the toes turned in.

piggery *n* (*pl* **-ies**) a place where pigs are kept.

piggy[1] *n* (*pl* **-ies**) used by or to children: a pig.

piggy[2] *adj* (**-ier, -iest**) resembling a pig.

piggyback *n* a ride on somebody's back and shoulders.

piggy bank *n* a money box in the shape of a pig.

pigheaded *adj* obstinate or stubborn.

pig iron *n* crude iron from a blast furnace, before refining.

pigment[1] *n* **1** a powdered substance mixed with a liquid to colour paints, inks, plastics, etc. **2** any of various colouring matters in animals and plants. ➤ **pigmentation** *n*.

pigment[2] *v* to colour with pigment.

pigskin *n* leather made from the skin of a pig.

pigsty *n* (*pl* **-ies**) **1** an enclosure for pigs. **2** a dirty or untidy place.

pigswill *n* waste food fed to pigs.

pigtail *n* a tight plait of hair worn at the back of the head. ➤ **pigtailed** *adj*.

pike[1] *n* (*pl* **pikes** or **pike**) a long bony food fish.

pike[2] *n* a long wooden shaft with a pointed steel head, formerly used by foot soldiers.

pikestaff *n* the staff of a foot soldier's pike. * **plain as a pikestaff** very plain or obvious.

pilaster *n* a shallow pier or column projecting slightly from a wall.

pilchard *n* a food fish of the herring family.

pile[1] *n* **1** a quantity of things heaped together. **2** *informal* a large quantity or amount. **3** *informal* a large building.

pile[2] *v* **1** (*often* + up) to lay or place (things) in a pile. **2** to put or heap (things) in large quantities. **3** (+ into/out of) to get into or out of a vehicle in a confused rush. * **pile into** of a vehicle: to crash into.

pile[3] *n* a soft raised surface on a fabric or carpet, consisting of cut threads or loops.

pile[4] *n* a beam driven into the ground to carry a vertical load.

pile-driver *n* a machine for driving piles into the ground.

piles *pl n* haemorrhoids.

pile up *v* to accumulate.

pile-up *n informal* a collision involving several vehicles.

pilfer *v* to steal (items of little value).

pilgrim *n* 1 a person making a pilgrimage. 2 *archaic or literary* a traveller.

pilgrimage *n* a journey to a shrine or sacred place as an act of devotion.

pill *n* 1 a small solid mass of medicine to be swallowed whole. 2 (**the Pill**) an oral contraceptive.

pillage[1] *n* the act of looting or plundering.

pillage[2] *v* to plunder or loot (a place).

pillar *n* 1 a firm upright support for a structure. 2 a supportive and helpful person. * **from pillar to post** hurriedly from one place or one situation to another.

pillar box *n* a red pillar-shaped public postbox.

pillbox *n* 1 a small box for pills. 2 a small low concrete weapon emplacement. 3 a small round brimless hat with a flat crown and straight sides.

pillion *n* a seat for a passenger on a motorcycle.

pillory[1] *n* (*pl* **-ies**) a device for publicly punishing offenders, consisting of a wooden frame with holes to hold the head and hands.

pillory[2] *v* (**-ies, -ied**) 1 to put in a pillory. 2 to expose to public ridicule.

pillow *n* a cloth container filled with soft material to support the head when lying down.

pillowcase *n* a removable cover for a pillow.

pillow talk *n* intimate conversation between two people in bed.

pilot[1] *n* 1 a person who flies an aircraft or spacecraft. 2 a person qualified to conduct a ship into and out of a port. 3 a trial of a project or broadcast programme, e.g. to test public opinion.

pilot[2] *v* (**piloted, piloting**) 1 to act as a pilot of (an aircraft or ship). 2 to test (a product, programme, etc) by means of a pilot.

pilot light *n* a small permanent flame used to ignite gas in a cooker or boiler.

pimento *or* **pimiento** *n* (*pl* **-os**) a mild sweet pepper.

pimp[1] *n* a man who solicits clients for prostitutes and takes some of their earnings.

pimp[2] *v* to act as a pimp.

pimple *n* a small solid inflamed elevation of the skin. > **pimply** *adj*.

PIN *or* **PIN number** *abbr* personal identification number, a four-digit security code used with a bank card.

pin[1] *n* 1 a small thin pointed piece of metal with a head used for fastening cloth, paper, etc. 2 an ornament or badge fastened with a pin. 3 a slender piece of wood or metal, used for fastening, as a safety catch, or as a support. 4 a skittle

or other target. 5 a projecting metal bar on an electrical plug. 6 *informal* (*usu in pl*) a leg.

pin[2] *v* (**pinned, pinning**) 1 to fasten or attach with a pin or pins. 2 to hold (somebody) so they cannot move. * **pin something on somebody** to blame them for it.

pinafore *n Brit* 1 an apron with a bib. 2 a sleeveless dress worn over a blouse or sweater.

pinball *n* a game in which balls are shot across a sloping surface at pins and score points if they hit them.

pince-nez /'pans nay, 'pins/ *n* glasses clipped to the nose by a spring.

pincer *n* 1 (*in pl*) a tool with two strong jaws for gripping things. 2 the front claw of a lobster, crab, etc. 3 each part of a two-pronged attack.

pinch[1] *v* 1 to squeeze tightly between the finger and thumb or between the jaws of an instrument. 2 to squeeze or compress painfully. 3 *informal* to steal. 4 to cause physical or mental pain to.

pinch[2] *n* 1 an act of pinching; a squeeze. 2 as much as may be held between the finger and thumb. * **at a pinch** in an emergency. **feel the pinch** to be short of money.

pinched *adj* of the face: thin or shrunken from cold or illness.

pincushion *n* a small cushion in which pins are stuck ready for use.

pin down *v* 1 to force (somebody) to be decisive or explicit about their intentions. 2 to trap (an enemy or fugitive) by surrounding them or firing on them.

pine[1] *n* an evergreen tree with cones and long slender needles.

pine[2] *v* 1 to lose vigour or health. 2 (+ for) to yearn intensely for somebody or something.

pineapple *n* a large oval prickly fruit with succulent yellow flesh.

pine nut *n* the edible seed of a pine tree.

ping *v* to make a sharp ringing sound. > **ping** *n*, **pinger** *n*.

Ping-Pong *n trademark* table tennis.

pinion[1] *n* the section of a bird's wing where the flight feathers grow.

pinion[2] *v* 1 to restrain (somebody) by holding their arms. 2 to restrain (a bird) from flight by cutting off the pinion of a wing.

pinion[3] *n* a gear with a small number of teeth designed to mesh with a larger gear wheel or rack.

pink[1] *adj* of a colour midway between red and white.

pink[2] *n* a colour midway between red and white. * **in the pink** flourishing or in good health.

pink[3] *n* a plant with scented pink or white flowers.

pink[4] *v* to cut a zigzag pattern on the edge of (fabric) to prevent fraying.

pink⁵ *v* of an engine: to make rattling noises when the mixture of fuel and air is faulty.

pinkie *or* **pinky** *n* (*pl* **-ies**) *informal* the little finger.

pinking shears *pl n* scissors with a saw-toothed inner edge on the blades, used for pinking cloth.

pin money *n* money for casual spending.

pinnacle *n* **1** the most successful point in an activity. **2** a mountain peak or similar structure. **3** an ornament like a small spire crowning a buttress.

pinpoint¹ *v* to locate precisely.

pinpoint² *adj* extremely precise.

pinpoint³ *n* a very small point or area.

pinprick *n* a small puncture made by a pin.

pins and needles *pl n* a pricking tingling sensation in a part of the body recovering from numbness.

pinstripe *n* **1** a very thin stripe on a fabric. **2** (*usu in pl*) a suit or trousers with pinstripes. ➤ **pinstriped** *adj*.

pint *n* **1** a unit of capacity equal to one eighth of a gallon (0.568l in Britain). **2** *Brit, informal* a pint of beer.

pint-sized *adj informal* small.

pin tuck *n* a very narrow tuck in a garment.

pin-up *n* a picture or poster of a sexually attractive person.

pinwheel *n* a type of cogwheel with pins projecting from its rim.

pioneer¹ *n* **1** any of the first people to settle in a territory. **2** a person or group that helps open up a new line of thought or activity.

pioneer² *v* to originate or take part in the development of.

pious *adj* **1** devout; deeply religious. **2** dutiful; reverential. **3** marked by sham or hypocritical virtue; sanctimonious. ➤ **piously** *adv*.

pip¹ *n* a small fruit seed of a fruit.

pip² *n* (*usu in pl*) a short high-pitched tone given as a radio or telephone signal.

pip³ *n* a symbol or dot indicating value on a playing card or domino.

pip⁴ *v* (**pipped, pipping**) *informal* to beat by a narrow margin. ✴ **pip at the post** to beat at the very last minute.

pipe¹ *n* **1** a long tube through which a liquid or gas can flow. **2** a tube of wood or clay with a mouthpiece at one end and a small bowl at the other, for smoking tobacco. **3** a simple wind instrument consisting of a tube with holes in it, the holes being covered by the fingers to produce different notes. **4** (**the pipes**) bagpipes. **5** each of several cylindrical tubes that produce sound on an organ.

pipe² *v* **1** to convey (a liquid or gas) along a pipe. **2** to transmit (a broadcast, music, or electrical signal) along wires or cables. **3** to put (a decoration) on a cake in icing or cream using a bag with a nozzle. **4** to trim with decorative cord. **5** to say or sing in a shrill voice. **6** to play (a tune) on a pipe.

pipe cleaner *n* a piece of wire covered with tufted fabric, used to clean a tobacco pipe.

piped music *n* recorded music played through loudspeakers in public places.

pipe down *v informal* to stop talking or making noise.

pipe dream *n* an unattainable plan or hope.

pipeline *n* a line of pipe for conveying a liquid or gas over a long distance. ✴ **in the pipeline** in the process of being developed or received.

piper *n* somebody who plays a pipe or bagpipes.

pipette (*NAmer* **pipet**) *n* a narrow tube into which a liquid is drawn by suction for measuring or transferring small quantities.

pipe up *v* to begin to speak suddenly.

piping *n* **1** a quantity or system of pipes. **2** a narrow cord trimming. **3** a thin line of icing or cream used to decorate cakes.

piping hot *adj* of food: hot and ready to eat.

pipistrelle *n* a small insect-eating bat.

pipit *n* a small songbird with brown streaked plumage.

pippin *n* an eating apple with a yellow skin flushed with red.

pipsqueak *n* *informal* a small or insignificant person.

piquant *adj* having an agreeably sharp taste. ➤ **piquancy** *n*, **piquantly** *adv*.

pique¹ *n* resentment or bad temper resulting from wounded pride.

pique² *v* (**piques, piqued, piquing**) **1** to arouse anger or resentment in (somebody). **2** to arouse (curiosity or interest).

piracy *n* **1** the act of committing robbery at sea. **2** the infringement of copyright on published books or recordings.

piranha /pi'rahn(y)ə/ *n* a small freshwater fish with strong jaws and sharp teeth.

pirate¹ *n* **1** somebody who commits robbery at sea. **2** (*used before a noun*) violating copyright: *pirate videos*. ➤ **piratic** *adj*.

pirate² *v* to reproduce (copyright material) without authorization.

pirouette¹ *n* in ballet, a fast spin of the body on one foot.

pirouette² *v* to perform a pirouette.

piscatorial *adj* relating to fishing.

Pisces *n* the twelfth sign of the zodiac (the Fish).

piss¹ *v coarse slang* to urinate.

piss² *n coarse slang* **1** urine. **2** an act of urinating.

pissed *adj* **1** *Brit, coarse slang* drunk. **2** *NAmer, slang* angry or upset.

pistachio *n* (*pl* **-os**) a pale green nut.

piste /peest/ *n* a prepared slope for skiing.

pistil *n* the female parts of a flowering plant, comprising the ovary, style, and stigma.

pistol *n* a small gun for firing with one hand.

piston *n* a sliding disc or cylinder fitted closely

in a tube in which it moves up and down in an internal-combustion engine.

pit[1] *n* **1** a hole or shaft in the ground. **2** a mine where coal or minerals are excavated. **3** an area at the side of a motor-racing track for servicing and refuelling during a race. **4** a natural hollow in the surface of the body. **5** the hollow of the stomach. **6** a sunken area in a garage or workshop where mechanics can work on the underside of vehicles. **7** the area in front of a theatre stage where the orchestra plays. **8** (**the pits**) *informal* the worst imaginable.

pit[2] *v* (**pitted, pitting**) **1** to make small holes in the surface of. **2** (+ against) to set (a person or oneself) in competition with another person.

pit-a-pat *or* **pitapat** *n* a series of light tapping sounds.

pit bull terrier *n* a breed of short-haired terrier with a stocky muscular body.

pitch[1] *n* **1** *Brit* a piece of ground marked out for playing a team sport. **2** the distinctive quality that a sound has according to the frequency of the vibrations that produce it. **3** the slope of a roof. **4** a level or degree, *esp* an advanced or extreme one. **5** *informal* a way of speaking or arguing. **6** *Brit* a place regularly used by a a street vendor or performer. **7** the up-and-down movement of a ship or aircraft.

pitch[2] *v* **1** to throw in a rough or casual way. **2** to move or fall heavily forwards or downwards. **3** of a ship or aircraft: to move with a rocking motion. **4** to express or adapt (speech or writing) for a particular audience. **5** to set at a specified level. **6** to erect (a tent) temporarily.

pitch[3] *n* a black or dark viscous substance made from tar.

pitch-black *adj* completely black or dark.

pitched *adj* of a roof: sloping.

pitched battle *n* a battle between armies fought on previously chosen ground.

pitcher *n* a large jug.

pitchfork *n* a long-handled fork with two long curved prongs used for lifting hay.

piteous *adj* causing or deserving pity. ➤ **piteously** *adv*.

pitfall *n* a hidden danger or difficulty.

pith *n* **1** a white tissue directly below the skin of a citrus fruit. **2** spongy cellular tissue in the stems of some plants. **3** the essential part or susbstance of something.

pithead *n* the top of a mining pit and the ground around it.

pith helmet *n* a hat made from the pith of swamp plants and worn in tropical regions as protection from the sun.

pithy *adj* (**-ier, -iest**) **1** of language: full of meaning concisely expressed. **2** of a plant fruit: having a lot of pith. ➤ **pithily** *adv*.

pitiable *adj* **1** deserving or arousing pity. **2** contemptibly inadequate.

pitiful *adj* **1** deserving or arousing pity. **2** very small or inadequate. ➤ **pitifully** *adv*.

pitiless *adj* showing no pity. ➤ **pitilessly** *adv*.

piton *n* a spike or peg driven into a rock or ice surface as a support in mountaineering.

pitta (*NAmer* **pita**) *n* slightly leavened bread that can be split open to hold a filling.

pittance *n* a small amount or allowance of money.

pitter-patter *n* a rapid succession of light tapping sounds.

pituitary gland *n* an organ attached to the brain which secretes hormones controlling growth and metabolism.

pity[1] *n* (*pl* **-ies**) **1** sympathetic sorrow for the suffering of others. **2** a cause of regret or disappointment.

pity[2] *v* (**-ies, -ied**) to feel pity for.

pivot[1] *n* a shaft or pin on which a mechanism turns.

pivot[2] *v* (**pivoted, pivoting**) **1** to turn on a pivot, or as if on a pivot. **2** (*usu* + on) to depend on.

pivotal *adj* vitally important.

pixel *n* each of thousands of tiny spots on a computer screen that together form an image.

pixie *or* **pixy** *n* (*pl* **-ies**) a little person depicted in folklore as a small human with pointed ears.

pizza *n* a round base of baked dough spread with tomatoes, cheese, herbs, etc.

pizzeria /peetsə'riə/ *n* a restaurant providing pizzas.

pizzicato /pitsi'kahtoh/ *adj and adv* of a piece of music for strings: performed by plucking instead of bowing. ➤ **pizzicato** *n*.

placard *n* a sign or notice for display, placed on a wall or carried in a demonstration.

placate *v* to soothe or mollify by making concessions. ➤ **placatory** *adj*.

place[1] *n* **1** a position or point in space. **2** a city, town, or other geographical location. **3** a right or duty. **4** an appropriate occasion for something. **5** a position in a sequence, e.g. of winners in a competition or race. **6** a short residential street or square. * **in place of** as a substitute for. **take place** to happen.

place[2] *v* **1** to put in a specified position or condition. **2** to cause to be in a specified position or condition. **3** to assert or assign a role to (a quality, etc). **4** to remember or identify. **5** to find employment or a home for. **6** to submit or confirm (a bet, order, etc).

placebo *n* (*pl* **-os**) a medication that has no physiological effect and is prescribed for the patient's psychological benefit.

placement *n* **1** the act or result of putting somebody or something in a specified place. **2** a temporary spell of work offered for practical experience.

placenta n (pl **placentas** or **placentae**) an organ that develops in the womb during pregnancy and provides the foetus with oxygen and nourishment.

placid adj not easily upset or excited. ➤ **placidly** adv.

placket n a flap of fabric covering a slit in a piece of clothing.

plagiarize or **-ise** v to appropriate and pass off (the ideas or words of another) as one's own. ➤ **plagiarism** n, **plagiarist** n.

plague¹ n **1** an epidemic disease caused by a bacterium carried by rat fleas and transmitted to humans via their bite. **2** a large destructive influx of insects or animals causing widespread damage.

plague² v (**plagues, plagued, plaguing**) **1** to annoy or harass continually. **2** to infest or afflict with disease or calamity.

plaice n (pl **plaice**) a large flatfish with a brown skin flecked with orange.

plaid n a woollen fabric with a tartan pattern.

plain¹ adj **1** simple, ordinary, or without decoration. **2** without a pattern. **3** consisting of a single colour. **4** obvious; easy to understand. **5** of speech: candid. **6** of a person: unattractive. **7** utter; absolute. ➤ **plainly** adv, **plainness** n.

plain² n a large area of level country with few trees.

plain³ adv totally; utterly.

plain chocolate n Brit dark chocolate with no added milk.

plain clothes pl n ordinary civilian dress as opposed to uniform.

plain sailing n easy or steady progress.

plainsong n unaccompanied vocal music of the medieval church.

plaintiff n somebody who brings a civil legal action against another in a court of law.

plait¹ n a length of interwoven strands of hair or rope.

plait² v to form into a plait or plaits.

plan¹ n **1** a detailed proposal of how something can be done. **2** (also in pl) a proposed course of action. **3** a financial arrangement designed to give security in the future. **4** a detailed diagram or map.

plan² v (**planned, planning**) **1** to arrange in advance. **2** (+ to/on) to intend to do something. **3** to design. ➤ **planner** n.

plane¹ n **1** a flat or level physical surface. **2** a level of existence or development. **3** informal an aeroplane.

plane² adj **1** having no elevations or depressions; flat. **2** of or dealing with geometric planes. **3** lying in a plane.

plane³ v **1** of a bird: to fly with the wings still. **2** to skim across the surface of water.

plane⁴ n a cutting tool for smoothing a wooden surface by removing thin shavings.

plane⁵ v to smooth (a surface) with a plane.

plane⁶ n a large tree with lobed leaves and thin bark that is shed in flakes.

planet n a large celestial body that orbits a star. ➤ **planetary** adj.

planetarium n (pl **planetariums** or **planetaria**) a building or room with a domed ceiling for showing images of stars and planets.

plangent adj literary of a sound: having an expressive plaintive quality.

plank n a long flat piece of sawn timber. * **walk the plank** formerly, to be made to walk off the end of a plank jutting out from a ship.

plankton n minute animals and plants that float near the surface of seas and lakes.

plant¹ n **1** a living organism such as a tree or flower, with root systems for absorbing water and leaves that manufacture nutrients. **2** a place where large-scale manufacturing or processing takes place. **3** machinery used in manufacturing or processing. **4** a person placed in an organization as a spy. **5** something placed surreptitiously in a person's belongings in order to incriminate them.

plant² v **1** to put (a seed, plant, bulb, etc) in the ground for it to grow. **2** to put or settle firmly in a specified place. **3** to place (somebody) as a spy in an organization. **4** to place or hide (an explosive device). **5** to establish (an idea, etc) in somebody's mind. **6** to put (something incriminating) surreptitiously in somebody's belongings. ➤ **planter** n.

Plantagenet n a member of the English royal house that ruled from 1154 to 1485.

plantain¹ n a short-stemmed plant with dense spikes of flowers and a rosette of oval or sword-shaped leaves.

plantain² n a green-skinned fruit resembling a banana.

plantation n **1** a large estate where commercial crops, such as coffee, tea, tobacco, and rubber, are grown. **2** an area where trees are grown.

plaque n **1** an inscribed tablet fixed to a wall. **2** a film of mucus on teeth where bacteria multiply.

plasma n **1** the fluid part of blood, lymph, or milk in which corpuscles, fat globules, and other cells are suspended. **2** a highly ionized gas containing approximately equal numbers of positive ions and electrons.

plaster¹ n **1** a mixture of lime, water, and sand that hardens on drying and is used to form a surface on walls and ceilings. **2** an adhesive strip used for covering and protecting small cuts. **3** a rigid dressing made from plaster of Paris and used for setting a broken bone.

plaster² v **1** to coat (a surface) with plaster. **2** to coat or cover thickly. **3** to cause to lie flat or stick to another surface. ➤ **plasterer** n.

plasterboard n a board with a plaster core used as a lining for interior walls.

plaster of Paris *n* a white powder made from gypsum and forming a quick-hardening paste when mixed with water, used in setting bones and in sculpture.

plastic[1] *n* **1** a synthetic substance that can be moulded while soft and set to have a rigid or slightly elastic form. **2** *informal* credit cards.

plastic[2] *adj* **1** made of plastic. **2** soft and pliable. **3** *derog* artificial. ➤ **plasticity** *n*.

Plasticine *n trademark* a soft substance used for modelling.

plastic surgery *n* surgery done to repair or restore parts of the body.

plate[1] *n* **1** a flat dish from which food is eaten or served. **2** a thin flat sheet or strip of metal used to coat another metal. **3** metal or plastic objects coated in this. **4** tableware and other household articles made of gold or silver. **5** a thin piece of metal or plastic bearing an inscription. **6** any of the rigid but mobile blocks that together form the earth's crust. **7** a full-page illustration in a book. ✻ **on a plate** without having to make any great effort. **on one's plate** to be dealt with.

plate[2] *v* to coat (a metal) with a thin layer of rolled or hammered gold, silver, or steel.

plateau[1] *n* (*pl* **plateaus** *or* **plateaux**) **1** a flat area of high ground. **2** a state of stability after a period of activity.

plateau[2] *v* (**plateaus, plateaued, plateauing**) to reach a stable stage after a period of activity.

plate glass *n* thick sheet glass used for shop and office windows.

platelet *n* any of the minute discs in the blood of vertebrates that assist in blood clotting.

platen *n* **1** a flat plate in a printing press that holds the paper against the type. **2** the roller of a typewriter against which the paper is held.

platform *n* **1** a raised area where a speaker or performer can be seen by the audience. **2** a level horizontal surface that is raised above the area around it. **3** a raised area by the track at a railway station where passengers stand. **4** a raised structure housing the equipment used for drilling for oil and gas. **5** a declared political policy that distinguishes one party or group from others. **6** an opportunity or place for expressing opinions. **7** (*usu in pl*) a shoe with a built-up sole.

platinum *n* a greyish white precious metallic element.

platitude *n* a trite remark stating the self-evident. ➤ **platitudinous** *adj*.

platonic *adj* **1** (**Platonic**) relating to the Greek philosopher Plato (d.349 BC). **2** of friendship or love: close but not sexual. ➤ **platonically** *adv*.

platoon *n* (*treated as sing. or pl*) a subdivision of a military company.

platter *n* a large plate for serving food.

platypus *n* (*pl* **platypuses**) a small aquatic egg-laying mammal with a bill like a duck's, webbed feet, and a broad flattened tail.

plaudit *n* (*usu in pl*) an expression of approval.

plausible *adj* **1** apparently fair or reasonable. **2** of a person: persuasive or believable. ➤ **plausibility** *n*, **plausibly** *adv*.

play[1] *v* **1** to take part in activities for enjoyment or recreation. **2** (+ with) to use something for amusement or fun. **3** to take part in (a sport or game). **4** to compete with (an opponent) in a game. **5** to make use of (a card or piece) at one's turn in a game. **6** to perform music on a musical instrument. **7** to make (a radio, etc) produce music or sounds. **8** to perform (a role) in a drama or film. **9** (+ on) to take advantage of (a weakness or opportunity). ✻ **play ball** *informal* to cooperate. **play the game** to behave fairly. **play with** to treat frivolously or unfairly.

play[2] *n* **1** activity that is done for recreation or amusement. **2** a piece of dramatic literature for acting on stage or broadcast on television or radio. **3** taking part in sports or games. **4** in a sport or game, a move or the action. **5** ease of movement of a machine part. **6** freedom or scope. ✻ **make a play for** to try to obtain.

play about *v* **1** to behave irresponsibly. **2** *informal* to have a sexual affair.

play-act *v* **1** to pretend or make believe. **2** to behave in a misleading or insincere manner.

play along *v* to pretend to cooperate.

playboy *n* a wealthy man who devotes himself to enjoyment.

play down *v* to minimize the importance of.

player *n* **1** a person who takes part in a sport or game. **2** a person who plays a musical instrument. **3** a device for playing music, videos, etc. **4** a person or group taking part in some activity.

playful *adj* **1** full of fun; high-spirited. **2** humorously light-hearted or good-natured. ➤ **playfully** *adv*.

playground *n* a piece of land for children to play on.

playgroup *n chiefly Brit* a supervised play activity for children below school age.

playhouse *n* **1** a theatre. **2** a toy house for children to play in.

playing card *n* each of a set of small cards with numbers and symbols on them, used in playing games.

playmate *n* a friend with whom a child regularly plays.

play off *v* **1** to bring (other people) into conflict for one's own advantage. **2** of two teams or players: to take part in a play-off.

play-off *n* a final contest or an extra match played to determine a winner.

playpen *n* a portable enclosure in which a baby or young child can play safely.

plaything *n* **1** a toy. **2** a person regarded or treated dismissively.

play up v **1** to emphasize the importance of. **2** *Brit, informal.* **3** to cause distress to. **4** to be troublesome or mischievous. **5** to be not working properly. ✻ **play up to** to flatter.

playwright n a writer of plays.

plaza n **1** a public square in a city or town. **2** *NAmer* a shopping complex.

plc *abbr* (*also* **PLC**) public limited company.

plea n **1** an earnest or emotional request or appeal. **2** an accused person's answer to an indictment.

plead v (*past tense and past part.* **pleaded** or **plead** or *NAmer, Scot* **pled**) **1** to make an impassioned request or appeal. **2** to give or offer (a specified condition) as an excuse or reason. **3** of an accused person in a court of law: to answer an accusation in a specified way. **4** to argue (a case) or put forward (a point of law).

pleasant *adj* **1** having qualities that tend to give pleasure. **2** likable and friendly. ➤ **pleasantly** *adv.*

pleasantry n (*pl* **-ies**) a polite but trivial remark.

please[1] v **1** to give a feeling of satisfaction or pleasure to. **2** *formal* to be the wish or will of (somebody or something). ✻ **please oneself** to do as one likes. ➤ **pleasing** *adj.*

please[2] *adv* used in a polite request or an urgent appeal.

pleased *adj* **1** satisfied or contented. **2** glad or willing (to do something).

pleasurable *adj* pleasant or enjoyable. ➤ **pleasurably** *adv.*

pleasure n **1** a feeling of satisfaction or contentment. **2** a source of enjoyment. **3** enjoyment or recreation. **4** sensual gratification or indulgence.

pleat[1] n a fold in cloth made by doubling material over on itself and stitching or pressing it in place.

pleat[2] v to make pleats in.

pleb n *chiefly Brit, informal, derog* a member of the ordinary people. ➤ **plebby** *adj.*

plebeian[1] n a member of the ordinary people.

plebeian[2] *adj* **1** of plebeians. **2** ordinary or common.

plebiscite n a vote by the people of a country for or against an important proposal.

plectrum n (*pl* **plectra** or **plectrums**) a thin flat piece of plastic, metal, etc used to pluck the strings of a guitar.

pled v *NAmer, Scot* past tense and past part. of PLEAD.

pledge[1] n **1** a solemn promise or undertaking. **2** something given as a token of love or remembrance. **3** something handed over to an authority as security.

pledge[2] v **1** to promise solemnly. **2** to deposit as security.

plenary *adj* **1** absolute; unqualified. **2** of a meeting: attended by all entitled to be present.

plenipotentiary[1] n (*pl* **-ies**) a diplomat invested with full power to transact business.

plenipotentiary[2] *adj* having full power to act.

plenitude n *formal* **1** an abundance. **2** the condition of being full or complete.

plenteous *adj literary* plentiful.

plentiful *adj* producing or existing in large quantities. ➤ **plentifully** *adv.*

plenty[1] n (*pl* **-ies**) **1** a full or more than adequate amount or supply. **2** a large number or amount. **3** ample supplies.

plenty[2] *adv informal* quite or abundantly.

plenum n (*pl* **plenums**) an assembly or meeting at which all the people eligible to attend are present.

plethora n a large or excessive quantity.

pleurisy n inflammation of the membranes that line the chest, causing fever and painful breathing.

plexus n (*pl* **plexus** or **plexuses**) a network of parts or elements in a structure or system.

pliable *adj* **1** easily bent. **2** yielding readily to others. ➤ **pliability** n.

pliant *adj* pliable.

pliers *pl* n pincers with flattened jaws for gripping small objects or for bending and cutting wire.

plight[1] n a condition of extreme hardship or danger.

plight[2] v *archaic* to promise solemnly.

plimsoll n *Brit* a sports shoe with a rubber sole and canvas top.

plink v to make a quick sharp tinkling noise. ➤ **plink** n.

plinth n a square block serving as a base for a column or statue.

PLO *abbr* Palestine Liberation Organization.

plod[1] v (**plodded, plodding**) **1** to walk heavily or slowly. **2** to work laboriously and monotonously.

plod[2] n a slow heavy walk.

plonk[1] v to put (something) down heavily or carelessly.

plonk[2] n *Brit, informal* cheap or inferior wine.

plonker n *informal* a foolish or useless person.

plop v (**plopped, plopping**) to drop suddenly with a sound like something dropping into water. ➤ **plop** n.

plot[1] n **1** a secret plan to do something illegal or harmful. **2** the main sequence of events of a literary work, film, etc. **3** a small piece of land makred out for a specific purpose.

plot[2] v (**plotted, plotting**) **1** to plan a plot to do (something illegal or harmful). **2** to mark or note on a map or chart. ➤ **plotter** n.

plough[1] (*NAmer* **plow**) n **1** a device used to cut, lift, and turn over soil in preparation for sowing. **2** (**the Plough**) a formation of seven stars in the northern sky.

plough[2] (*NAmer* **plow**) v **1** to turn or work (earth or land) with a plough. **2** (*often* + into) to force a way violently. **3** (*often* + *through*) to proceed steadily and laboriously. **4** (*often* + *in/into*) to invest (money or resources).

plough back *v* to reinvest (profits) in an industry.

ploughman's lunch *n Brit* a lunch of bread, cheese, and pickle.

plover *n* (*pl* **plovers** *or* **plover**) a stout wading bird with a short beak.

ploy *n* a cunningly devised plan or act.

pluck¹ *v* **1** to take a firm hold of (something) and remove it. **2** to pick (a flower, fruit, etc). **3** to pull out (hairs or feathers). **4** to remove the feathers from (a bird's carcass). **5** to produce sounds from (a stringed instrument) using the fingers or a plectrum.

pluck² *n* courage.

pluck up *v* to find (the necessary courage) to do something difficult or frightening.

plucky *adj* (**-ier, -iest**) showing spirited courage and determination. ➤ **pluckily** *adv*.

plug¹ *n* **1** a piece of solid material used to seal a hole. **2** an insulated device with metal prongs that connects an appliance to an electricity supply at a socket. **3** *informal* a publicity boost.

plug² *v* (**plugged, plugging**) **1** to block or close (a hole or gap) with a plug. **2** *informal* to publicize (a book, film, etc). **3** *informal* to shoot (somebody or something). **4** (*usu* + *away*) to work doggedly and persistently. ➤ **plugger** *n*.

plughole *n Brit* a hole in a sink or bath through which the water drains away.

plug in *v* to connect (an electrical appliance) to a power point.

plum *n* **1** an oval fruit with yellow, purple, red, or green skin and an oblong seed. **2** a dark reddish purple colour. **3** *informal* (*used before a noun*) excellent or desirable: *a plum job*.

plumage *n* a bird's feathers.

plumb¹ *n* a lead weight attached to a cord to gauge the depth of water or to establish a vertical line.

plumb² *adv informal* exactly.

plumb³ *v* **1** to measure (the depth of water) with a plumb. **2** to examine minutely and critically. **3** to test (a surface) for being vertial with a plumb line.

plumb⁴ *adj* exactly vertical or true.

plumber *n* a person who installs and repairs water piping and fittings.

plumbing *n* **1** a plumber's occupation or trade. **2** the system of pipes, tanks, and fixtures installed for a water supply and heating in a building.

plumb line *n* a line with a weight at one end, used to determine whether a surface is vertical.

plume *n* **1** a long attractive and brightly coloured feather or group of feathers. **2** a cloud of smoke or vapour reaching high into the sky. ➤ **plumed** *adj*.

plummet¹ *v* (**plummeted, plummeting**) to fall sharply and rapidly.

plummet² *n* a rapid fall or drop.

plummy *adj* (**-ier, -iest**) of a voice: resembling that associated with the English upper classes.

plump¹ *adj* having a full rounded form; slightly fat.

plump² *v* (*also* + *up*) to make or become rounder or fatter.

plump³ *v* **1** (*usu* + *down/into*) to drop or sink suddenly or heavily. **2** (+ *for*) to make a choice of.

plunder¹ *v* **1** to pillage or sack (a place). **2** to take (goods) by force.

plunder² *n* **1** goods taken by plundering. **2** the act of plundering.

plunge¹ *v* **1** to fall or move rapidly or unexpectedly. **2** (*usu* + *into*) to jump or dive in water. **3** to cause (a place) to be in an unwelcome condition. **4** to immerse in a liquid.

plunge² *n* **1** an act of plunging. **2** a sudden decline in value. ✳ **take the plunge** *informal* to decide to do something after some consideration.

plunge pool *n* a small deep pool of cold water, for use after a sauna.

plunger *n* **1** a device that acts with a plunging or thrusting motion. **2** a rubber suction cup on a handle used for clearing blocked pipes or drains.

plunk *v* to play (a keyboard instrument) so as to produce a hollow metallic sound.

pluperfect *n* of the verb tense, usually formed with *had*, that expresses an action or state completed before a past time spoken of.

plural¹ *adj* **1** consisting of more than one. **2** in grammar, of a word or word form: denoting more than one. ➤ **plurally** *adv*.

plural² *n* in grammar, a plural number or word.

pluralism *n* **1** the existence in a society of diverse social groups with their own cultures or special interests. **2** the holding of two or more offices at the same time. ➤ **pluralist** *adj and n*.

plurality *n* (*pl* **-ies**) **1** the state of being plural or numerous. **2** a large number or quantity.

plus¹ *prep* **1** increased by; with the addition of. **2** and also.

plus² *n* (*pl* **pluses** *or* **plusses**) **1** a positive factor, quantity, or quality. **2** (*also* **plus sign**) a sign (+) denoting addition or a positive value

plus³ *adj* **1** of a number: having a positive value. **2** having a positive electric charge. **3** additional and welcome: *a plus factor*. **4** of a grade: slightly higher than that specified: *B plus*.

plus⁴ *conj* and moreover.

plus fours *pl n* loose wide trousers gathered on a band and finishing just below the knee.

plush¹ *n* a fabric with a soft even pile.

plush² *adj* luxurious or lavish.

plutocracy *n* (*pl* **-ies**) **1** government by the

wealthy. **2** a state that is governed by wealthy people. ➤ **plutocratic** adj.

plutocrat n a person whose power is based on wealth.

plutonium n a radioactive metallic element used in weapons and as a fuel for atomic reactors.

ply¹ n (pl **-ies**) **1** a strand in a yarn, wool, etc. **2** a layer of a material forming a whole with others.

ply² v (**-ies, -ied**) **1** to use (a tool) carefully. **2** to perform (a job) steadily and diligently. **3** to keep supplying something to (somebody). **4** to keep asking (somebody) questions. **5** to go over (a specified route) regularly.

plywood n a a board made from thin sheets of wood glued together with the grains arranged crosswise.

Pm abbr the chemical symbol for promethium.

p.m. abbr post meridiem, after midday.

PMT abbr premenstrual tension.

pneumatic adj operated by or containing gas or air under pressure. ➤ **pneumatically** adv.

pneumonia n an infection causing inflammation of the lungs.

Po abbr the chemical symbol for polonium.

poach¹ v to cook in a simmering liquid.

poach² v **1** to take (game or fish) illegally by hunting or fishing without permission. **2** to entice (employees, customers, etc) away from their present loyalties. ➤ **poacher** n.

pock n a pockmark. ➤ **pocked** adj.

pocket¹ n **1** a small bag sewn in clothing and open at the top or side. **2** financial resources. **3** a pouchlike compartment for storage. **4** an opening at the corner or side of a billiard or snooker table into which balls are struck. **5** a small isolated area or group. ＊ **in pocket** having made a profit. **out of pocket** having lost money. ➤ **pocketful** n.

pocket² v **1** to put in one's pocket. **2** to steal or appropriate.

pocket money n **1** money regularly given to a child by its parents. **2** money for small personal expenses.

pockmark n a mark or pit in the skin left by smallpox, chickenpox, etc. ➤ **pockmarked** adj.

pod¹ n **1** a long seed case of a pea or bean. **2** a detachable compartment on a spacecraft or aircraft.

pod² v (**podded, podding**) **1** of a plant: to produce pods. **2** to remove (peas or beans) from their pods.

pod³ n a small group of whales, seals, or other sea mammals.

podgy adj (**-ier, -iest**) short and plump.

podium n (pl **podiums** or **podia**) a small raised platform for giving a speech or conducting an orchestra.

poem n a literary composition in verse.

poesy n archaic or literary poetry.

poet n **1** a person who writes poetry. **2** a very imaginative or sensitive person with considerable powers of expression.

poetic adj **1** relating to poets or poetry. **2** having qualities associated with poetry. ➤ **poetically** adv.

poetic justice n an outcome of appropriate punishment and reward.

poetic licence n freedom to depart from the normal rules of language or accuracy for a particular literary effect.

Poet Laureate n (pl **Poets Laureate**) in Britain, a poet appointed for life to write poetry to celebrate important events.

poetry n **1** literary writing in the form of poems. **2** a quality of beauty and grace.

po-faced adj Brit, informal looking affectedly serious or disapproving.

pogo stick n a toy consisting of a pole on a spring for jumping about on.

pogrom n an organized massacre of people from an ethnic group, esp of Jews in eastern Europe and Russia.

poignant adj of memories etc: causing distress or pity; painfully sad. ➤ **poignancy** n, **poignantly** adv.

point¹ n **1** the sharp, tapering, or narrow and rounded end of something; a tip. **2** a very small mark; a dot. **3** a full stop. **4** a decimal point. **5** a precisely indicated position. **6** an exact moment. **7** an end or object to be achieved; a purpose. **8** (often **the point**) the most important element of a discussion or matter. **9** an individual detail; an item. **10** a unit of counting, e.g. in scoring a game. **11** each of 32 compass directions. **12** a projecting piece of land. **13** Brit (in pl) a device with movable rails that joins two railway lines. **14** Brit an electric socket. **15** a contact in the distributor of a motor vehicle. ＊ **beside the point** irrelevant. **make a point of** to take particular care to. **on the point of** just about to. **to the point** relevant. **up to a point** to a certain extent.

point² v **1** to indicate the position or direction of something, esp by directing a finger. **2** to cause to be turned in a particular direction. **3** to face a particular direction. **4** (+ to) to indicate the fact or probability of. **5** to fill the joints of (brickwork) with mortar.

pointed adj **1** having a point. **2** esp of a remark: aimed at a particular person or group. **3** conspicuous.

pointer n **1** a needle indicating a reading on a dial or scale. **2** a useful suggestion or hint. **3** a large strong gundog of a smooth-haired breed that indicates the presence of game by pointing its head and body towards it.

pointless adj devoid of meaning or purpose. ➤ **pointlessly** adv.

point of order n (pl **points of order**) a question of procedure in an official meeting.

point of view n (pl **points of view**) a particular opinion or attitude.

point out v to direct somebody's attention to.

point-to-point n a cross-country race for riders on hunting horses.

point up v to emphasize or show the importance of.

poise[1] n **1** easy self-possessed assurance of manner. **2** a graceful manner of carrying oneself.

poise[2] v **1** to hold or carry in equilibrium. **2** to hold (something) supported or suspended in a steady position. **3** to be poised.

poison[1] n **1** a substance that through its chemical action kills or harms a living organism. **2** something that destroys or corrupts.

poison[2] v **1** to harm or kill with poison. **2** to contaminate with poison. **3** to have a harmful influence on. ➤ **poisoner** n.

poisonous adj **1** having the properties or effects of poison. **2** malicious or spiteful.

poke[1] v **1** to strike or prod with a fingertip or something sharp. **2** to protrude or cause to protrude. **3** (+ about/around) to look about or through something.

poke[2] n **1** a prod or jab. **2** informal a punch.

poke[3] n NAmer, Scot a bag or sack.

poker[1] n a metal rod for poking a fire.

poker[2] n a card game in which players bet on the value of their hands.

poker face n an inscrutable face that conceals thoughts or feelings. ➤ **poker-faced** adj.

poky or **pokey** adj (-**ier**, -**iest**) informal of a space: small and cramped.

polar adj **1** in the region near a geographical pole. **2** of the poles of a magnet. **3** in chemistry, having groups with opposing properties at opposite ends. **4** completely opposite in nature or action.

polar bear n a large white Arctic bear.

polarity n (pl -**ies**) **1** the condition of having properties or powers in opposite directions. **2** magnetic attraction in a specific direction. **3** the state of having a positive or negative electrical charge.

polarize or -**ise** v **1** to cause (light waves) to vibrate in a definite pattern or direction. **2** to give (something) electrical or magnetic polarity. **3** to divide (people or their opinions) into two opposing groups. ➤ **polarization** n.

Polaroid n **1** trademark. **2** a material used in sunglasses to polarize the light and prevent glare. **3** a camera that produces a finished print after each exposure.

Pole n a native or inhabitant of Poland. ➤ **Polish** adj.

pole[1] n a long thin piece of wood, metal, etc, used as a support.

pole[2] n **1** either of the two points at the northern and southern extremities of the earth's axis. **2** either of the terminals of an electric cell or battery. **3** any of two or more regions in a magnetized body at which the magnetism is concentrated. ✳ **be poles apart** to have no connection or similarity.

poleaxe[1] (NAmer **poleax**) n an axe with a short handle and a large head.

poleaxe[2] (NAmer **poleax**) v **1** to attack or knock down with a heavy blow. **2** informal to give (somebody) a great shock.

polecat n **1** an animal like a weasel with dark brown fur, noted for its unpleasant smell. **2** NAmer a skunk.

polemic n **1** an aggressive attack on or refutation of somebody's opinions or principles. **2** (in pl) the art of discussion or argument. ➤ **polemic** adj, **polemical** adj, **polemicist** n.

pole vault n an athletic event consisting of a jump over a high bar using a long flexible pole. ➤ **pole-vault** v.

police[1] n a body of trained people entrusted with maintaining public order and enforcing the law.

police[2] v to enforce law and order in (an area, event, etc).

policeman or **policewoman** n (pl **policemen** or **policewomen**) a man or woman police officer.

police officer n a member of the police.

police state n a country or state with repressive governmental control of political and and social life, enforced by secret police.

police station n the headquarters of a local police force.

policy[1] n (pl -**ies**) **1** a definite course of action proposed or adopted. **2** an overall plan for guiding and determining decisions. **3** wise or sensible procedure.

policy[2] n (pl -**ies**) a contract of insurance.

polio or **poliomyelitis** n an infectious disease with inflammation of the nerve cells of the spinal cord, causing paralysis.

Polish n the Slavonic language of Poland. ➤ **Polish** adj.

polish[1] v **1** to make smooth and glossy by rubbing. **2** to make more refined. **3** (often + up) to bring (knowledge or a skill) to a more highly developed level. ➤ **polisher** n.

polish[2] n **1** a special cream or liquid rubbed on a surface to give it a shine. **2** the act of polishing. **3** a smooth glossy surface. **4** refinement or social grace.

polish off v to consume or dispose of rapidly.

polite adj **1** considerate and respectful in speech or manner. **2** showing correct social usage; refined. ➤ **politely** adv, **politeness** n.

politic adj **1** wise or expedient. **2** shrewd in dealing with people and situations.

political adj **1** relating to government or public affairs. **2** relating to politics. ➤ **politically** adv.

political correctness n the practice of avoiding offence to particular groups of people by choice of language or behaviour. ➤ **politically correct** adj.

political prisoner n a person imprisoned for their political beliefs.

politician n **1** a person who is engaged in politics, *esp* as an elected representative. **2** *NAmer, derog* somebody who uses underhand methods for personal advancement.

politicize or **-ise** v **1** to give a political character to. **2** to make politically aware or active. **3** to discuss or engage in politics. ➤ **politicization** n.

politics pl n **1** the art or practice of government. **2** the activities associated with government; political affairs. **3** political life as a profession. **4** a person's political sympathies. **5** the relations and use of power between individuals within an organization or group.

polity n (pl **-ies**) **1** a state regarded as a political unit. **2** a form of government or social organization.

polka n a lively dance with two beats to the bar.

polka dot n each of a pattern of distributed dots in a design.

poll[1] n **1** the casting or recording of votes. **2** the number of votes recorded. **3** a survey of people questioned at random or by quota.

poll[2] v **1** to receive (a specified number of votes). **2** to record the votes of (a constituency or an electorate). **3** to question (people) in a poll.

pollard[1] n a tree cut back to the main stem to promote growth of foliage.

pollard[2] v to make a pollard of (a tree).

pollen n a fine dust of granules discharged from the male reproductive organ of a flower to fertilize the ovules.

pollen count n a measure of the amount of pollen in the air.

pollinate v to place pollen on the female reproductive organ of (a flower or plant) and so fertilize it. ➤ **pollination** n.

pollster n somebody who conducts opinion polls.

poll tax n a fixed tax levied on every adult.

pollute v **1** to contaminate with toxic substances. **2** to corrupt or defile. ➤ **pollutant** n, **polluter** n.

pollution n **1** the act of polluting or the state of being polluted. **2** material that pollutes.

polo n a team game played on horseback using long mallets to drive a wooden ball into the opponents' goal.

polo neck n chiefly Brit a high folded over collar on a jumper.

polo shirt n a casual cotton shirt with a soft collar and buttons at the neck.

poltergeist n a ghost said to make loud noises and throw objects about.

poly- comb. form many or much: *polyphonic*.

polychrome adj having several colours. ➤ **polychromatic** adj.

polyester n **1** a polymer used in making fibres or plastics. **2** a synthetic fibre made from polyester.

polygamy n the practice of being married to more than one person at a time. ➤ **polygamist** n, **polygamous** adj.

polyglot adj speaking several languages.

polygon n a two-dimensional figure with three or more straight sides. ➤ **polygonal** adj.

polygraph n an instrument recording the pulse rate, used as a lie detector.

polyhedron n (pl **polyhedrons** or **polyhedra**) a solid figure with four or more faces.

polymath n somebody who has a wide range of knowledge.

polymer n a chemical compound consisting of repeating structural units and formed by chemical combination of many molecules. ➤ **polymeric** adj, **polymerize** v.

polymorphic adj having various forms.

polyp n **1** a sea organism with a hollow cylindrical body that is attached at one end and has a central mouth surrounded by tentacles at the other. **2** a small abnormal growth projecting from a mucous membrane.

polyphony n in music, the harmonic combination of different parts played simultaneously. ➤ **polyphonic** adj.

polystyrene n a rigid light transparent material made from a polymer.

polysyllabic adj having two or more syllables.

polytheism n the worship of more than one god. ➤ **polytheistic** adj.

polythene n a tough lightweight plastic.

polyunsaturated adj of a fat or oil: having a chemical structure that is thought to be less conducive to the formation of cholesterol.

polyurethane n any of various polymers used in foams, paints, and resins.

pomade n a perfumed ointment for the hair or scalp.

pomander n a bag of aromatic substances used to scent clothes or perfume a room.

pomegranate n a thick-skinned reddish fruit containing many seeds and a crimson pulp.

pommel n **1** the raised part at the front and top of a saddle. **2** a knob on the hilt of a sword.

Pommy or **Pommie** n (pl **-ies**) Aus, NZ, informal, chiefly derog a British person.

pomp n **1** a stately or ceremonial display; splendour. **2** ostentatious boastful display.

pompom n an ornamental ball or tuft used on clothing.

pompous adj **1** affectedly self-important and opinionated. **2** excessively elevated or ornate. ➤ **pomposity** n, **pompously** adv.

ponce[1] n Brit, informal **1** a pimp for a prostitute. **2** derog an effeminate man. ➤ **poncey** adj, **poncy** adj.

ponce² v Brit, informal (+ around/about) to act in a silly or effeminate manner.

poncho n (pl **ponchos**) a cloak resembling a blanket with a slit in the middle for the head.

pond n a small body of fresh water.

ponder v to think about carefully.

ponderous adj **1** heavy and unwieldy. **2** oppressively dull. ➤ **ponderously** adv.

pondweed n a water plant with spikes of greenish flowers.

pong¹ v Brit, informal to emit a strong unpleasant smell.

pong² n a strong unpleasant smell.

pontiff n the Pope.

pontifical adj of the pope; papal.

pontificate¹ v to express opinions in a pompous or dogmatic way.

pontificate² n the office or term of office of a pope.

pontoon¹ n **1** a flat-bottomed boat or portable float used in building a temporary bridge or in salvage work. **2** a floating landing stage, e.g. in a marina.

pontoon² n a card game in which players try to achieve a score as close as possible to 21.

pony n (pl **-ies**) a small horse, esp of a breed under 14.2 hands in height.

ponytail n a hairstyle in which the hair is drawn back tightly and tied at the back of the head.

poo¹ n informal faeces.

poo² v (**poos, pooed, pooing**) informal to defecate.

pooch n informal a dog.

poodle n **1** a dog of a breed with a thick curly coat that is often clipped and shaved. **2** a servile person.

poof or **pouf** n Brit, informal, offensive an effeminate or homosexual man.

pooh interj used to express contempt or disgust.

pooh-pooh v to disparage or belittle.

pool¹ n **1** a small body of standing water. **2** a small deep body of still water in a stream or river. **3** = SWIMMING POOL.

pool² n **1** players' combined stakes in a gambling game. **2** (in pl) a form of organized gambling based on forecasting football results. **3** a game similar to billiards. **4** an amount of money, vehicles, etc for general use.

pool³ v to combine (resources or effort) for a common purpose.

poop n a raised deck at the back of a ship.

poor adj **1** not having much money. **2** inferior or inadequate. **3** (+ in) lacking in something specified. **4** inspiring pity.

poorhouse n a workhouse.

poorly¹ adv in a poor or inferior manner.

poorly² adj unwell.

pootle v Brit, informal to go in a leisurely fashion.

pop¹ v (**popped, popping**) **1** to make a sharp explosive sound. **2** to cause to burst open. **3** informal to go or come suddenly or quickly. **4** informal to put quickly or for a short time. **5** of the eyes: to appear to stick out, e.g. in amazement. ✳ **pop the question** informal to propose marriage.

pop² n **1** a popping sound. **2** a flavoured fizzy soft drink.

pop³ n chiefly NAmer, informal an affectionate name for one's father.

pop⁴ adj **1** of pop music. **2** popularized by the media.

pop⁵ n (also **pop music**) a modern popular music having a strong beat.

pop art n art incorporating items from popular culture and the mass media.

popcorn n maize kernels that swell and burst when heated to form a white starchy mass.

pope n (often **Pope**) the bishop of Rome as head of the Roman Catholic Church.

popery n derog Roman Catholicism. ➤ **popish** adj.

pop-eyed adj having staring or bulging eyes.

popinjay n archaic a conceited or supercilious person.

poplar n a tall slender tree of the willow family.

poplin n a plain cotton fabric with fine crosswise ribs.

poppadom or **poppadum** n in Indian cookery, a crisp wafer-thin pancake of deep-fried dough.

popper n Brit, informal a press-stud.

poppet n chiefly Brit, informal a lovable or enchanting person.

poppy n (pl **-ies**) a plant with bright flowers and a large seed case.

poppycock n informal nonsense.

populace n the general public.

popular adj **1** generally liked or admired. **2** liked or favoured by a particular person or group. **3** suited to the needs or tastes of ordinary people. **4** of or used by the general public. ➤ **popularity** n, **popularly** adv.

popularize or **-ise** v **1** to make popular. **2** to present in a generally understandable or interesting form. ➤ **popularization** n.

populate v **1** to occupy or inhabit (a place). **2** to provide (a place) with inhabitants.

population n the people living in a place, or their total number.

populist n somebody who aims to represent or appeal to ordinary people. ➤ **populism** n, **populist** adj.

populous adj having many inhabitants.

porcelain n a hard translucent white ceramic material.

porch n **1** a covered entrance to a building. **2** NAmer a veranda.

porcine adj like a pig or pigs.

porcupine n a rodent with stiff protective bristles.

pore¹ n each of many minute openings in the skin or other surface.

pore² v (+ over/through) to study closely or attentively.

Usage Note: Do not confuse this word with the verb *pour*.

pork n the flesh of a pig used as food.

porker n a young pig fattened for food.

porn n informal pornography.

pornography n books, photographs, and films intended to cause sexual excitement. ➤ **pornographic** adj.

porous adj allowing liquids and gases to pass through. ➤ **porosity** n.

porpoise n (pl **porpoises** or **porpoise**) a small whale with a blunt snout.

porridge n a soft food made by boiling oatmeal in milk or water.

port¹ n a town or city with a harbour for ships.

port² n the left side of a ship or aircraft looking forward.

port³ n a fortified sweet wine made in Portugal.

port⁴ n 1 an opening in machinery, allowing liquid or gas to pass. 2 a socket in a computer for connecting a device to it. 3 an opening in a ship's side for loading and unloading cargo. 4 an opening in an armoured vehicle or fortification through which guns can be fired.

portable¹ adj small and light enough to be carried about. ➤ **portability** n.

portable² n a portable device.

portal n a grand door or gateway.

portcullis n a heavy grating that can be lowered to prevent passage through a gateway.

portend v to be a warning or sign of (something unpleasant or momentous).

portent n a sign or warning of something unpleasant or momentous.

portentous adj 1 being a portent; ominous. 2 self-consciously solemn. ➤ **portentously** adv.

porter¹ n chiefly Brit an official who regulates entry at the entrance to a large building.

porter² n 1 somebody employed to carry luggage. 2 somebody employed to move patients or equipment in a hospital. 3 a heavy dark brown beer.

portfolio n (pl -os) 1 a flexible case for carrying loose papers, pictures, etc. 2 a set of drawings, photographs, etc presented as evidence of creative talent. 3 the office or responsibilities of a government minister. 4 the securities held by an investor.

porthole n a small window in the side of a ship or aircraft.

portico n (pl -oes or -os) a roof supported by columns at the entrance to a building.

portion¹ n 1 a part or share of something. 2 a helping of food.

portion² v to share out in portions.

portly adj (-ier, -iest) rather fat.

portmanteau n (pl **portmanteaus** or **portmanteaux**) a large bag that opens into two parts.

port of call n 1 a port where ships call during a voyage. 2 a stop in an itinerary.

portrait n 1 a painting or drawing of a person. 2 a description of a person in a novel, film, etc. ➤ **portraiture** n.

portray v 1 to make a picture of. 2 to describe in words. 3 to represent in a particular way. ➤ **portrayal** n.

Portuguese n (pl **Portuguese**) 1 a native or inhabitant of Portugal. 2 the language of Portugal and Brazil. ➤ **Portuguese** adj.

Usage Note: Note the spelling with a second *u* after the *g*.

pose¹ v 1 to assume a certain position to be painted or photographed. 2 to constitute (a problem or threat). 3 to present (a question) for attention. 4 (+ as) to pretend to be. 5 Brit, informal to behave in an affectedly stylish way to impress others.

pose² n 1 a position adopted to be painted or photographed. 2 an affected manner intended to impress others.

poser n 1 a puzzling or baffling question. 2 somebody who poses to impress others.

poseur n somebody who is insincere or affects a style of behaviour to impress others.

posh adj informal exclusive or luxurious.

posit v (**posited, positing**) to put forward as fact or basis for argument.

position¹ n 1 the place occupied by somebody or something. 2 the proper place for something. 3 the way in which somebody or something is disposed or arranged. 4 a condition or situation. 5 social or official rank or status. 6 formal a post or job. ➤ **positional** adj.

position² v to put in a proper or specified position.

positive¹ adj 1 concentrating on what is good or beneficial; optimistic. 2 capable of being constructively applied; helpful. 3 indicating acceptance or approval. 4 showing the presence of something. 5 confident or certain. 6 utter, complete. 7 greater than zero. 8 of a photographic image: having the light and dark parts corresponding to those of the original subject. 9 having higher electric potential and constituting the part from which the current flows to the external circuit. ➤ **positively** adv.

positive² n 1 a positive state or quality. 2 a positive photograph or a print.

positive discrimination n a bias in favour of members of a group that is discriminated against or inadequately represented.

positive vetting n thorough investigation into the character of a candidate for the civil service.

positivism n a theory of knowledge based on the scientific observation of natural phenomena. ➤ **positivist** adj and n.

positron n a positively charged elementary particle that has the same mass and magnitude of electrical charge as the electron.

posse n 1 formerly, a body of men summoned by a sheriff to assist in enforcing the law. 2 a large group of people.

possess v 1 to have as property; to own. 2 to have as an attribute or skill. 3 to influence or dominate (somebody). ➤ **possessor** n.

possession n 1 the state of having or owning something. 2 something owned.

possessive[1] adj 1 demanding undivided love or attention. 2 reluctant to share or give up possessions. 3 in grammar, denoting ownership or a similar relation. ➤ **possessively** adv.

possessive[2] n the possessive case or a word in this case.

possibility n (pl -ies) 1 the condition or fact of being possible. 2 something possible. 3 a person or thing worth considering. 4 (usu in pl) potential or prospective value.

possible[1] adj 1 within the limits of ability or realization. 2 that may or may not occur.

possible[2] n 1 something possible. 2 somebody or something that may be chosen.

possibly adv 1 it is possible that; maybe. 2 used as an intensifier with can or could.

possum n 1 an opossum. 2 an Australian tree-dwelling marsupial animal. * **play possum** informal to pretend to be asleep or unaware.

post[1] n 1 a fixed upright piece of timber or metal forming a stay or support. 2 a pole marking the start or finish of a race.

post[2] v 1 to display (a notice) in a public place. 2 to announce or advertise.

post[3] n chiefly Brit 1 the dispatch and delivery of letters, parcels, etc. 2 a single collection or delivery of post. 3 letters and parcels dispatched or received.

post[4] v 1 to send by post. 2 to enter (an item) in a ledger. * **keep posted** to provide with any news or information.

post[5] n 1 the place at which somebody is stationed. 2 an office to which a person is appointed.

post[6] v 1 to station (a sentry or police officer) somewhere. 2 chiefly Brit to send (somebody) to work in a different unit or location.

post- prefix after or later (than): postdate; postscript.

postage n the charge for sending something by post.

postal adj relating to the sending of things by post. ➤ **postally** adv.

postal order n Brit an order issued by a post office and sent to another person who can exchange it for money.

postbox n a box for the posting of mail.

postcard n a card for sending a message by post without an envelope.

postcode n a combination of letters and numbers that identifies a postal address.

postcode lottery n Brit disparities in medical treatment or social care in different parts of the country.

postdate v 1 to put a future date on (a cheque). 2 to follow (something) in time.

poster n a large picture or sign put up for advertisement or decoration.

poste restante /,pohst 'restont/ n chiefly Brit a service by which mail is kept for collection by the recipient at a post office.

posterior[1] adj 1 later in time or order. 2 situated towards the back.

posterior[2] n informal the buttocks.

posterity n future generations.

postgraduate n a student continuing higher education after completing a first degree.

posthaste adv with all possible speed.

posthumous adj occurring or published after a person's death. ➤ **posthumously** adv.

posting n an appointment to a position abroad.

postman n (pl **postmen**) a man who delivers the post.

postmark[1] n a cancellation mark showing the date and place of posting of a piece of mail.

postmark[2] v to stamp with a postmark.

postmaster or **postmistress** n a person in charge of a post office.

postmodernism n an artistic movement advocating a reinterpretation of classical ideas and forms. ➤ **postmodern** adj, **postmodernist** n and adj.

postmortem n an examination of a dead body to determine the cause of death.

postnatal adj relating to the period after childbirth.

post office n 1 a national organization that runs a postal system. 2 a local branch of a national post office.

postpone v to move to a later time; to defer. ➤ **postponement** n.

postscript n a note added at the end of a letter.

postulant n a person seeking admission to a religious order.

postulate v to assume (something) to be true for the purposes of argument.

posture[1] n 1 a position in which the body is held. 2 an attitude or frame of mind. ➤ **postural** adj.

posture[2] v to assume an affected posture designed to impress others.

posy n (pl -ies) a small bouquet of flowers.

pot[1] *n* **1** a rounded container for holding liquids or solids. **2** a flowerpot. **3** the total of the bets taken in a gambling game. ✳ **go to pot** *informal* to deteriorate or collapse. ➤ **potful** *n*.

pot[2] *v* (**potted, potting**) **1** to preserve (food) in a sealed pot or jar. **2** to plant in a flowerpot. **3** to shoot or kill (an animal or person). **4** in billiards or snooker, to send (a ball) into a pocket.

pot[3] *n informal* cannabis.

potable *adj* of water: suitable for drinking.

potash *n* potassium or a potassium compound, *esp* as used in agriculture or industry.

potassium *n* a silver-white metallic element.

potato *n* (*pl* **-oes**) a starchy edible tuber used as a vegetable.

potbelly *n* (*pl* **-ies**) a protruding abdomen. ➤ **potbellied** *adj*.

potent *adj* **1** strong and powerful. **2** of a man: able to achieve an erection. ➤ **potency** *n*.

potentate *n* a ruler or monarch.

potential[1] *adj* capable of coming into being or developing further. ➤ **potentiality** *n*, **potentially** *adv*.

potential[2] *n* **1** capacity to develop in a particular way. **2** qualities that indicate future achievements or benefits.

pothole[1] *n* **1** a hole in a road surface. **2** a deep hole in the ground or in the floor of a cave. ➤ **potholed** *adj*.

pothole[2] *v* to explore underground pothole systems as a leisure activity. ➤ **potholer** *n*, **potholing** *n*.

potion *n* a dose of medicine, poison, etc in liquid form.

pot-luck *n* whatever happens to be available.

potpourri *n* **1** a mixture of dried flowers, herbs, and spices, kept for their fragrance. **2** a miscellaneous collection.

potshot *n* a casual shot at an easy target.

pottage *n* a thick soup or stew.

potted *adj* **1** planted or grown in a flowerpot. **2** preserved in a sealed pot. **3** *chiefly Brit* abridged or summarized.

potter[1] *n* somebody who makes pottery.

potter[2] *v* **1** (*often* + around/about) to spend time aimlessly. **2** to move in a random fashion.

pottery *n* (*pl* **-ies**) **1** articles made of baked clay. **2** the craft of making pottery. **3** a place where pottery is made.

potting shed *n* a garden shed for potting plants and storing tools.

potty[1] *adj* (**-ier, -iest**) *Brit, informal* **1** slightly crazy. **2** foolish or silly. **3** (*usu* + about) having a great liking for something or somebody.

potty[2] *n* (*pl* **-ies**) a bowl-shaped receptacle used as a toilet by a small child.

pouch *n* **1** a small bag made of flexible material. **2** a pocket of skin in the abdomen of marsupials for carrying their young.

pouf *n* see POOF.

pouffe *or* **pouf** *n* a large firmly stuffed cushion used to sit on or rest the feet on.

poulterer *n* somebody who deals in poultry or game.

poultice *n* a soft moist mass of clay, bread, mustard, etc spread on cloth and applied to inflamed or injured parts of the body.

poultry *n* chickens, ducks, and other domestic fowl kept for eggs or meat.

pounce[1] *v* **1** to spring forward down to seize something. **2** (*often* + on) to react swiftly to criticize a mistake.

pounce[2] *n* the act of pouncing.

pound[1] *n* (*pl* **pounds** *or* **pound**) **1** a unit of weight equal to 16oz (about 0.454kg) avoirdupois or 12oz (about 0.373kg) troy. **2** the basic monetary unit of the UK.

pound[2] *v* **1** to reduce to powder or pulp by beating or crushing. **2** to strike heavily or repeatedly. **3** to move along with heavy steps. **4** to beat or throb with a heavy rhythm.

pound[3] *n* an enclosure for stray animals or lost property.

pour *v* **1** to flow or cause to flow in a stream. **2** to dispense (a drink) into a container. **3** to supply or produce freely or copiously. **4** to move or go with a continuous flow and in large quantities. **5** (*often* + down) to rain hard. **6** (+ out) to express (feelings) at length. ✳ **pour cold water on** to be unenthusiastic about.

Usage Note: Do not confuse this word with the verb *pore*, which means 'to study closely'.

---

pout[1] *v* to thrust out the lips to show displeasure or in a sexually provocative way. ➤ **pouty** *adj*.

pout[2] *n* an act of pouting.

poverty *n* **1** the state of being poor. **2** a deficiency.

powder[1] *n* **1** a mass of dry loose particles. **2** a cosmetic or medicine produced as fine particles. ➤ **powdery** *adj*.

powder[2] *v* **1** to sprinkle or cover with powder. **2** to reduce to powder.

powder blue *n* pale blue.

power[1] *n* **1** the ability to do something. **2** legal authority or right. **3** the possession of control over others. **4** somebody or something that possesses authority or influence. **5** a sovereign state having military strength and international influence. **6** physical strength. **7** mental or moral effectiveness. **8** electricity or another form of energy. **9** the energy or driving force generated by a motor or a similar machine. **10** in physics, the amount of work done or energy emitted or transferred per unit of time. **11** the number of times a given number is to be multiplied by itself.

power[2] *v* **1** to supply with power. **2** (*often* +

down/up) to switch an electrical device off or on. **3** to move in a forceful manner.

powerboat *n* a powerful motorboat.

power cut *n* a failure in the supply of electric power to an area.

power dressing *n* a formal style of dressing as an expression of status by professional women.

powerful *adj* **1** having great power or influence. **2** very strong or forceful. **3** extremely effective. ➤ **powerfully** *adv*.

powerhouse *n informal* a person or thing having great energy and force.

powerless *adj* lacking the authority or capacity to act.

power station *n* an electricity generating station.

power steering *n* steering reinforced by power from the engine.

powwow[1] *n* **1** a traditional Native American ceremony with feasting and dancing. **2** *informal* a meeting for discussion.

powwow[2] *v* to hold a powwow.

pox *n* **1** a disease causing the formation of spots on the skin that may leave pockmarks after healing. **2** *informal* syphilis.

poxy *adj* (-**ier**, -**iest**) *chiefly Brit, informal* of poor quality or value.

pp *abbr* **1** pages. **2** Latin *per procurationem*: used to indicate that a person is signing on behalf of somebody else.

PPS *abbr* **1** Parliamentary Private Secretary. **2** Latin *post postscriptum*: used to introduce a second or further postscript.

PR *abbr* **1** proportional representation. **2** public relations.

Pr *abbr* the chemical symbol for praseodymium.

practicable *adj* capable of being done. ➤ **practicability** *n*, **practicably** *adv*.

practical[1] *adj* **1** relating to actual performance and experience rather than theory. **2** suitable for real situations. **3** adapted or suitable for a particular use. **4** realistic in dealing with problems or situations. **5** good at carrying out ordinary tasks. **6** very nearly as described: *a practical certainty*.

practical[2] *n* an examination or lesson that tests or teaches the ability to put theory into practice.

practicality *n* (*pl* -**ies**) **1** the practical nature of something or somebody. **2** (*in pl*) the practical aspects of a situation or question.

practical joke *n* a trick played on somebody to make them appear foolish.

practically *adv* **1** almost; nearly. **2** in a practical manner.

practice *n* **1** regular or repeated exercise to acquire skill. **2** the actual carrying out of tasks as opposed to theory. **3** a habit. **4** the usual way something is done. **5** work in a profession, e.g. law or medicine. **6** the business or premises of a

professional person. * **In practice** in real situations.

Usage Note: In British English *practice* is the correct spelling for the noun and *practise* for the verb.

practise (*NAmer* **practice**) *v* **1** to perform (an activity) repeatedly so as to become skilled in it. **2** to carry out or apply (something) in fact or in real situations. **3** to be a member of (a particular religion). **4** to be professionally engaged in (a particular type of work).

practitioner *n* somebody who practises a profession or art.

pragmatic *adj* concerned with practicalities rather than theory; realistic. ➤ **pragmatically** *adv*.

pragmatism *n* a practical approach to problems and affairs. ➤ **pragmatist** *n*.

prairie *n* an extensive area of treeless grassland in North America.

praise[1] *v* **1** to express approval or admiration of. **2** to glorify or extol (God or a god).

praise[2] *n* words expressing admiration and approval.

praiseworthy *adj* deserving praise; commendable.

praline *n* a sweet substance made from nuts heated in boiling sugar.

pram *n Brit* a four-wheeled carriage for a baby, pushed by a person on foot.

prance *v* to walk in a silly and affected manner.

prang[1] *v Brit, informal* to crash (a vehicle or aircraft).

prang[2] *n Brit, informal* a crash involving a vehicle or aircraft.

prank *n* a mischievous act or trick.

prankster *n* somebody who plays pranks.

prat *n Brit, informal* a foolish person.

prate *v* (*often* + about) to talk foolishly and excessively; to chatter.

prattle *v* to chatter in silly or inconsequential manner.

prawn *n* a crustacean like a large shrimp.

pray[1] *v* **1** to say a prayer. **2** (*usu* + for) to wish or hope fervently.

pray[2] *adv formal* please.

prayer *n* **1** a personal request or expression of praise or thanksgiving addressed to God or a god. **2** (*in pl*) a religious service consisting chiefly of prayers. **3** an earnest request or devout wish.

praying mantis *n* = MANTIS.

pre- *prefix* before or earlier (than): *prehistoric*.

preach *v* **1** to deliver a sermon. **2** (*often* + at) to give advice or warnings in a tiresome or highly moral manner. **3** to advocate (something) earnestly. ➤ **preacher** *n*.

preamble *n* an introductory statement.

prearrange *v* to arrange beforehand.

precarious *adj* **1** likely to fall or collapse. **2** dependent on chance. ➤ **precariously** *adv*.

precaution n 1 a measure taken to avoid undesirable consequences. 2 informal (in pl) contraceptive measures. ➤ **precautionary** adj.

precede v to go or happen before something or somebody else.

precedence n greater importance or priority in status or treatment.

precedent n an earlier similar occurrence of something under consideration, esp a judicial decision that serves as a rule for similar cases.

precept n a principle serving as a general rule of conduct.

precinct n 1 (in pl) the region immediately surrounding a place. 2 an enclosure surrounded by buildings. 3 an area of a town closed to traffic. 4 NAmer an administrative district.

precious adj 1 of great value or high price. 2 highly esteemed or cherished. 3 excessively refined; affected. 4 used as an ironic intensifier: Precious help you were!

precious metal n a valuable metal, e.g. gold, silver, or platinum.

precious stone n a valuable stone used as a jewel, e.g. a diamond, ruby, or emerald.

precipice n a sheer rockface or cliff.

precipitate[1] v 1 to hurl or throw violently. 2 to bring about (an event or action) suddenly or unexpectedly. 3 to separate out, or cause (a substance) to separate out, from a solution or suspension. 4 to cause (vapour) to condense and fall as rain, snow, etc.

precipitate[2] n a substance separated from a solution by chemical or physical change.

precipitate[3] adj acting or carried out suddenly or with undue haste. ➤ **precipitately** adv.

precipitation n 1 rain, snow, etc falling in the atmosphere. 2 the process of precipitating something.

precipitous adj 1 dangerously steep or high. 2 extremely sudden and severe in effect.

precis[1] /'praysee/ n (pl precis) a concise summary.

precis[2] v (precising, precised) to make a precis of.

precise adj 1 specific or detailed. 2 carried out with attention to accuracy. 3 taking great care to be accurate; punctilious. 4 particular; very. ➤ **precisely** adv.

precision n the quality of being precise and careful.

preclude v to make impossible in advance. ➤ **preclusion** n.

precocious adj showing mature qualities at an unusually early age. ➤ **precociously** adv, **precocity** n.

precognition n the apparent ability to foresee future events.

preconceived adj of an opinion: reached without actual knowledge or experience.

preconception n 1 a preconceived idea. 2 a prejudice.

precondition n something that must happen or exist to enable something else to happen or exist.

precursor n somebody or something that precedes and prepares the way for somebody or something similar.

predate v to exist or occur earlier than.

predator n an animal that lives by hunting and killing other animals.

predatory adj 1 of an animal: hunting and killing other animals. 2 taking advantage of other people.

predecease v to die before (another person).

predecessor n 1 the previous occupant of a job or position. 2 a person or thing that has been replaced or superseded by something else.

predestination n the religious doctrine that God has decided all events in advance, including matters of salvation.

predestined adj decided by God or by fate in advance.

predetermine v to decide on or arrange beforehand.

predeterminer n in grammar, an adjective or adverb that can occur before a determiner, e.g. both in both her hands.

predicament n a difficult or trying situation.

predicate[1] n the part of a sentence or clause that contains the verb and says something about the subject.

predicate[2] v formal to base or found on something else.

predicative adj contained in the predicate of a sentence, e.g. red in the dress is red. ➤ **predicatively** adv.

predict v to assert in advance the likelihood of (something happening). ➤ **predictor** n.

predictable adj 1 capable of being predicted. 2 always behaving in an expected way. ➤ **predictability** n, **predictably** adv.

prediction n 1 a statement of what will happen. 2 the act of predicting. ➤ **predictive** adj.

predilection n a liking or preference.

predispose v 1 to make more likely or willing to do something. 2 (+ to) to make susceptible to something. ➤ **predisposition** n.

predominant adj 1 constituting the largest part of something. 2 having greater strength or influence. ➤ **predominance** n, **predominantly** adv.

predominate v 1 to be the main part of. 2 to exert a controlling power. ➤ **predomination** n.

preeminent adj superior to all others. ➤ **preeminence** n, **preeminently** adv.

preempt v 1 to take action to prevent. 2 to take (something) over, esp to prevent others having it. ➤ **preemption** n, **preemptive** adj.

preponderant

preen v **1** of a bird: to clean and smooth its feathers with its beak. **2** to make oneself look attractive. **3** usu derog to pride or congratulate (oneself) on something.

preexist v to exist at a previous time. ➤ **preexistence** n.

prefab n a prefabricated structure or building.

prefabricated adj of a building: manufactured in parts ready for assembly on site.

preface[1] n an introduction to a book.

preface[2] v (usu + by/with) to say or write by way of introduction to.

prefect n **1** Brit a senior pupil in a secondary school with some authority over other pupils. **2** the chief administrative officer of a region in some countries.

prefecture n a district governed by a prefect.

prefer v (**preferred, preferring**) **1** (often + to) to like better than. **2** formal to bring (a charge) against somebody. **3** archaic to give promotion or advancement to.

preferable adj more desirable or suitable. ➤ **preferably** adv.

preference n **1** (usu + for) greater liking for one thing over another. **2** a person or thing preferred. **3** special favour or consideration.

preferential adj showing special or undue favour. ➤ **preferentially** adv.

preferment n promotion to a higher rank or office.

prefigure v to represent or suggest in advance.

prefix[1] n **1** a group of letters placed at the beginning of a word and affecting its meaning, e.g. un- in unhappy. **2** a title used before a person's name.

prefix[2] v to add a prefix to.

pregnancy n (pl **-ies**) the state or period of being pregnant.

pregnant adj **1** of a woman: having an unborn child in the womb. **2** rich in meaning.

prehensile adj of a tail: adapted for seizing or grasping.

prehistoric adj dating from the period of time before written records.

prehistory n the time before the existence of written records.

preindustrial adj prior to the development of large-scale industry.

prejudge v to pass judgment on prematurely.

prejudice[1] n **1** an opinion formed without sufficient reason or knowledge. **2** preconceived or biased judgments generally. **3** irrational hostility against an individual or group.

prejudice[2] v **1** to cause to have a prejudice. **2** to cause harm to or put at a disadvantage. ➤ **prejudiced** adj.

prejudicial adj **1** harmful or disadvantageous. **2** leading to prejudiced judgments.

prelate n a bishop or other clergyman of high rank.

preliminary[1] n (pl **-ies**) something that is preparatory to something else.

preliminary[2] adj preparing for what is to follow.

prelude n **1** an introductory performance, action, or event. **2** an introductory piece of music. ➤ **preludial** adj.

premarital adj occurring before marriage.

premature adj **1** happening or done before the proper time. **2** of a baby: born before the end of the normal gestation period. ➤ **prematurely** adv.

premeditated adj considered and planned beforehand. ➤ **premeditation** n.

premenstrual adj occurring in the period before menstruation.

premier[1] adj first in position, rank, or importance.

premier[2] n a head of government. ➤ **premiership** n.

premiere[1] n a first public performance of a play, film, etc.

premiere[2] v to give the premiere of.

premise or **premiss** n a proposition used as a basis of argument.

premises pl n a piece of land with the buildings on it.

premium n **1** a sum paid to obtain insurance. **2** an extra sum added to a standard price. **3** a high value. **4** (used before a noun) of exceptional quality or amount. ✳ **at a premium** valuable because rare or difficult to obtain.

premonition n a strong feeling that something is going to happen. ➤ **premonitory** adj.

prenatal adj before birth.

preoccupation n **1** complete mental absorption or obsession. **2** something that absorbs one's attention.

preoccupy v (**-ies, -ied**) to engage all the attention of.

preordain v to decree or decide in advance.

prep n Brit school work done outside ordinary lessons.

prepaid v paid for in advance.

preparation n **1** the activity of preparing for something. **2** (usu in pl) a preparatory act or measure. **3** a medicine or other prepared substance.

preparatory adj **1** intended to prepare for something. **2** (+ to) in preparation for something.

preparatory school n Brit a private school for pupils from the age of seven.

prepare v **1** to make ready for some purpose or activity. **2** to put into a suitable frame of mind. **3** to work out the details of. **4** to put together from various ingredients. ✳ **to be prepared to** to be willing to do something.

preparedness n a state of readiness to act.

preponderant adj **1** occurring in greater number or quantity. **2** having superior force or influence. ➤ **preponderance** *n,* **preponderantly** *adv.*

preposition *n* a word used to link a noun, pronoun, etc to another part of the sentence, e.g. *in, by.* ➤ **prepositional** *adj.*

prepossessing *adj* attractive or appealing.

preposterous *adj* ridiculous and absurd. ➤ **preposterously** *adv.*

prep school *n* a preparatory school.

prepubescent *adj* in the period before puberty.

prerequisite *n* a requirement that must be satisfied in advance.

prerogative *n* 1 an exclusive right or privilege. 2 a discretionary power.

presage *v* to be an omen or warning of.

Presbyterian[1] *adj* denoting a Christian Church governed by elected representative bodies. ➤ **Presbyterianism** *n.*

Presbyterian[2] *n* a member of a Presbyterian Church.

presbytery *n* (*pl* **-ies**) 1 a local ruling body in Presbyterian Churches. 2 the house of a Roman Catholic parish priest. 3 the part of a church reserved for the clergy.

prescience *n* foreknowledge of events. ➤ **prescient** *adj.*

prescribe *v* 1 of a doctor: to order or recommend (a medicine or treatment) as a remedy. 2 to recommend as beneficial. 3 to give specific instructions regarding.

prescription *n* 1 a written direction for the preparation and use of a medicine. 2 an authoritative ruling.

prescriptive *adj* giving instructions or laying down rules.

presence *n* 1 the fact or condition of being present. 2 the immediate proximity of a person. 3 something non-physical that is felt to be present. 4 a body of people playing an influential role. 5 impressive personal distinction or magnetism. 6 a dignified bearing or appearance. ✶ **presence of mind** composure in difficult circumstances.

present[1] *n* something presented; a gift.

present[2] *v* 1 to give formally or ceremonially. 2 (+ with) to allow (somebody) to gain something without effort. 3 to introduce (somebody) formally. 4 to bring before the public. 5 to introduce (a television or radio programme). 6 to offer (a particular type of appearance) to the view of others; to show or exhibit. 7 to submit for approval or consideration. 8 to describe or explain (a plan, idea, etc) in a particular way. 9 to constitute or pose (a problem or difficulty). ✶ **present oneself** to be present; to attend. ➤ **presenter** *n.*

present[3] *adj* 1 in or at a place. 2 existing in something mentioned or understood. 3 now existing or in progress. 4 currently doing something or being considered. 5 of the verb tense that expresses present time or the time of speaking.

present[4] *n* (**the present**) the time now in progress. ✶ **at present** now. **for the present** for the time being.

presentable *adj* 1 fit to be seen or inspected. 2 smart enough to appear in company.

presentation *n* 1 the manner in which something is presented. 2 the act or process of presenting something. 3 an informative talk or lecture.

presentiment *n* a feeling that something is about to happen.

presently *adv* 1 before long; soon. 2 now.

present participle *n* a participle, e.g. *dancing, being,* expressing a current event or state.

preservative *n* a substance that helps to preserve food.

preserve[1] *v* 1 to keep in its original condition. 2 to keep in existence. 3 to maintain (an appearance or type of behaviour) in spite of adverse circumstances or provocation. 4 to keep safe from injury or harm. 5 to treat and store (food) for future use. ➤ **preservation** *n.*

preserve[2] *n* 1 a jam, jelly, or other food preserved by cooking with sugar. 2 an area restricted for the preservation of natural resources. 3 a sphere of activity reserved for certain people.

preset *v* (**presetting,** *past tense and past part.* **preset**) to set the controls on (a device) so that it operates in a certain way.

preside *v* 1 to have charge of a meeting or court. 2 (+ over) to exercise guidance or control.

presidency *n* (*pl* **-ies**) 1 the office of president. 2 the period during which a president holds office.

president *n* 1 the elected head of state in a republic. 2 the chief officer of a business. ➤ **presidential** *adj.*

presidium *or* **praesidium** *n* (*pl* **presidia** *or* **presidiums**) a permanent executive committee in a communist country.

press[1] *v* 1 to push firmly and steadily against (something). 2 to move (something) in this way. 3 to flatten or mould to a particular shape by pressing. 4 to iron (clothes). 5 to squeeze. 6 to squeeze the juice from (a fruit). 7 to try to persuade (somebody) to do something. 8 (+ for) to make vigorous efforts to obtain or bring about. 9 to put forward (e.g. a claim) forcefully. 10 (*often* + ahead/forward) to make one's way determinedly. ✶ **be pressed for time** to have little time available. **be pressed to do** to have difficulty in doing.

press[2] *n* 1 a device for shaping material, extracting liquid, or compressing something. 2 a printing press. 3 a publishing house or printing firm. 4 (**the press**) newspapers and magazines collectively. 5 a crowd of people.

press[3] v formerly, to force into military service. * **press into service** to use (something) temporarily for a makeshift purpose.

press conference n an interview given by a public figure to journalists.

press gang n a body of men who forced people into military service.

press-gang v to force (somebody) to do something unwillingly.

pressing[1] adj 1 needing immediate action or attention. 2 earnest or insistent.

pressing[2] n an object produced from a mould or matrix.

press on v to continue or proceed resolutely.

press release n a prepared statement released to the news media.

press-stud n Brit a fastener consisting of two parts joined by pressing.

press-up n an exercise performed in a prone position by raising and lowering the body with the arms while supporting it only on the hands and toes.

pressure[1] n 1 the application of force to something by something else in direct contact with it. 2 influence or compulsion directed towards achieving a particular end. 3 demands needing a quick response or a sustained effort. 4 distress or difficulty resulting from domestic, social, or economic factors. 5 in physics, the force or thrust exerted over a surface divided by its area.

pressure[2] v to try to persuade (somebody) to do something.

pressure cooker n an airtight saucepan used to cook food quickly in steam heated under pressure. > **pressure-cook** v.

pressure group n a group organized to influence government policy or public opinion.

pressurize or **-ise** v 1 to maintain near-normal atmospheric pressure in (an aircraft cabin). 2 to subject to strong persuasion or coercion.

prestige n high standing based on achievement or success.

prestigious adj enjoying or bringing prestige.

presto adj and adv of a piece of music: performed at a fast tempo.

prestressed adj of a beam: having internal stresses introduced in it to counteract external stresses in use.

presumably adv as one may reasonably assume.

presume v 1 to suppose or assume with some degree of certainty. 2 to take for granted. 3 to undertake (to do something) without justification. 4 (+ on/upon) to take advantage unfairly. > **presumable** adj, **presumer** n.

presumption n 1 overconfident or forward conduct. 2 an attitude or belief based on reasonable grounds. 3 a ground or reason for presuming something.

presumptuous adj overconfident or forward. > **presumptuously** adv.

presuppose v 1 to suppose beforehand, usu without proof or justification. 2 to require (something) to exist or be the case in order that something else may exist or be true or valid. > **presupposition** n.

pretence (NAmer **pretense**) n 1 an act of pretending. 2 (+ to) a claim made or implied, when not supported by fact.

pretend v 1 to act as if something were the case that is not. 2 to make it appear that one has a particular feeling. 3 (+ to) to claim to have something.

pretender n somebody who lays claim to a title or position.

pretension n 1 an unjustified claim to a status or quality. 2 an ambition or aspiration. 3 vanity; pretentiousness.

pretentious adj trying to impress by a false display of importance or some other quality. > **pretentiousness** n.

preternatural adj 1 beyond what is natural. 2 extraordinary. > **preternaturally** adv.

pretext n a false reason or excuse.

prettify v (-ies, -ied) to make pretty or depict prettily.

pretty[1] adj (-ier, -iest) attractive or aesthetically pleasing. > **prettily** adv, **prettiness** n.

pretty[2] adv 1 to some degree; moderately. 2 very. * **be sitting pretty** to be in an advantageous position. **pretty much/nearly/well** informal almost; very nearly.

pretty[3] v (-ies, -ied) informal (usu + up) to make pretty.

pretzel n a brittle glazed and salted biscuit in the shape of a knot.

prevail v 1 (often + against/over) to defeat or subdue from superior strength. 2 (+ on/upon/with) to persuade somebody successfully. 3 to be frequent or widespread.

prevalent adj widely occurring or existing; widespread. > **prevalence** n.

prevaricate v to speak or act evasively. > **prevarication** n.

prevent v 1 to stop from happening or existing. 2 (often + from) to stop (somebody) from doing something. > **preventable** adj, **prevention** n.

preventive or **preventative** adj intended to prevent something.

preview[1] v 1 to view or show (a film or exhibition) before its public presentation. 2 to report on (events, films, programmes, etc) that are to be presented in the near future.

preview[2] n 1 an advance showing of a film or exhibition. 2 a description of coming events or entertainments.

previous adj 1 going before in time or order. 2 informal acting too soon; premature. * **previous to** before; prior to. > **previously** adv.

prey[1] n 1 an animal killed by another animal

for food. **2** somebody or something that is unable to resist attack; a victim.

prey² v **1** (often + on/upon) to seize and devour prey. **2** (often + on/upon) to live by deception or taking advantage. **3** (+ on/upon) to preoccupy (one's mind). ➤ **preyer** n.

price¹ n **1** the amount of money for which something is bought or sold. **2** something unpleasant suffered in order to achieve something. **3** the odds in betting. * **at any price** whatever the cost or sacrifice.

price² v to set a price for.

priceless adj **1** so valuable it cannot be priced. **2** informal highly amusing.

pricey or **pricy** adj (**-ier, -iest**) informal expensive.

prick¹ v **1** to pierce slightly with a sharp point. **2** to make a small hole in by piercing. **3** to feel or cause discomfort as if from being pricked. **4** (often + up). **5** (usu + out) to transplant (seedlings). * **prick up one's ears 1** of an animal: to raise its ears when alert. **2** to start to listen intently.

prick² n **1** the act of pricking or the sensation of being pricked. **2** a hole made by pricking. **3** coarse slang the penis. **4** coarse slang a disagreeable person.

prickle¹ n **1** a small sharp pointed spike on a plant or animal. **2** a pricking or tingling sensation.

prickle² v to feel a pricking or tingling sensation.

prickly adj (**-ier, -iest**) **1** full of or covered with prickles. **2** causing a prickling sensation. **3** easily irritated.

prickly pear n a cactus that produces a prickly oval fruit.

pride¹ n **1** a feeling of satisfaction arising from some action, achievement or possession. **2** a consciousness of one's own worth and dignity; self-respect. **3** an excessive sense of one's own importance; conceit. **4** a source of pride. **5** the best in a group or class. **6** a group of lions. * **pride of place** the most prominent position.

pride² v * **pride oneself on** to be particularly proud of.

priest n **1** a person authorized to perform the sacred rites of a religion. **2** a Christian clergyman ranking below a bishop and above a deacon. ➤ **priesthood** n, **priestly** adj.

prig n somebody who is excessively self-righteous. ➤ **priggish** adj.

prim adj (**primmer, primmest**) **1** stiffly formal and proper. **2** prudish. ➤ **primly** adv.

prima ballerina n (pl **prima ballerinas**) the principal female dancer in a ballet company.

primacy n formal the state of being first or most important.

prima donna n (pl **prima donnas**) **1** the prin-

cipal female singer in an opera company. **2** an extremely temperamental person.

primaeval adj see PRIMEVAL.

prima facie adj and adv valid from a first impression until disproved.

primal adj **1** original or primitive. **2** first in importance; fundamental.

primarily adv **1** for the most part; chiefly. **2** in the first place; originally.

primary¹ adj **1** first in importance or value. **2** basic or fundamental. **3** first in order of time or development. **4** preparatory to something else. **5** relating to the education of children from five to eleven.

primary² n (pl **-ies**) in the USA, an election to choose a candidate for political office or to select delegates for a party convention.

primary care n the first level of health care provided by general practitioners and clinics.

primary colour n each of the three coloured pigments red, yellow, and blue that are mixed to produce other pigments.

primate n **1** any of an order of mammals, including human beings, apes, and monkeys. **2** a bishop who has precedence in a province or nation.

prime¹ n the most active stage of one's life.

prime² adj **1** first in importance. **2** first-rate or excellent. **3** of the highest grade or quality. **4** not deriving from something else; primary. **5** of a number: that can only be divided by itself and 1. ➤ **primely** adv, **primeness** n.

prime³ v **1** to make ready for use or action. **2** to give (somebody) information or instructions beforehand. **3** to put (primer) on a surface.

prime minister n the chief minister of a government.

primer n **1** a book with basic information on a subject. **2** a type of paint used as a first coat on some surfaces.

prime time n the time when a television or radio audience is at its highest.

primeval or **primaeval** adj relating to the earliest times.

primitive adj **1** characteristic of an early stage of development; crude or rudimentary. **2** characteristic of a relatively simple people or culture. **3** of accommodation or facilities: of a low or basic standard. **4** of behaviour: lacking in good manners or sophistication. ➤ **primitively** adv.

primordial adj existing from the beginning of time.

primp v chiefly NAmer to arrange (one's appearance) fastidiously.

primrose n a plant with pale yellow flowers.

primula n any of a genus of plants that includes the primrose and cowslip.

Primus n trademark a portable oil-burning stove.

prince n 1 the son or grandson of a monarch. 2 a sovereign ruler of a principality.

prince consort n the husband of a reigning queen.

princeling n a petty or insignificant prince.

princely adj 1 relating to or befitting a prince. 2 lavish or generous.

princess n 1 a daughter or granddaughter of a sovereign. 2 the wife or widow of a prince.

princess royal n the eldest daughter of a reigning king or queen.

principal[1] adj most important or influential; chief. ➤ **principally** adv.

Usage Note: Do not confuse this word with *principle*, which is a noun only.

---

principal[2] n 1 the person in charge of an organization. 2 the head of an educational institution. 3 *NAmer* a headteacher. 4 the peron for whom somebody acts. 5 a leading performer in a group. 6 a capital sum earning interest or due as a debt. ➤ **principalship** n.

principal boy n the role of the hero in British pantomime, played by a woman.

principality n (pl -**ies**) the office or territory of a prince.

principle n 1 a rule or law on which action or behaviour is based. 2 a rule or code of conduct. 3 devotion to the rules of right morality. 4 the basic idea behind something. 5 a law or fact of nature underlying the working of a natural phenomenon. 6 a chemical that imparts a characteristic quality. * **in principle** in theory. **on principle** on the basis of one's beliefs or moral code.

Usage Note: Do not confuse this word with *principal*.

---

principled adj based on moral principles.

print[1] n 1 printed words or text. 2 a copy made by printing. 3 an impression or mark made by pressure. * **in/out of print** of a book: obtainable (or no longer obtainable) from the publisher.

print[2] v 1 to stamp or impress with a mark, design, etc. 2 to make a copy of by transferring ink to paper automatically. 3 to publish (e.g. a book or newspaper). 4 to make (a positive image) from a negative or transparency. 5 to write with each letter produced separately. ➤ **printable** adj.

printing n 1 reproduction in printed form. 2 handwriting with unjoined letters.

printing press n a machine that produces printed matter by pressing paper against an inked surface.

printout n a printed record produced by a computer.

prion n a protein particle thought to be responsible for brain diseases such as BSE and CJD.

prior[1] adj 1 earlier in time or order. 2 taking precedence. * **prior to** before in time.

prior[2] n 1 the deputy head of a monastery, ranking below abbot. 2 the head of a religious house.

prioritize or -**ise** v 1 to give priority to. 2 to arrange in order of priority. ➤ **prioritization** n.

priority n (pl -**ies**) 1 the fact of being considered more important. 2 the right to go first. 3 something meriting prior attention. 4 (in pl) the relative importance attached to various things.

prise or **prize** v 1 to press or force open or apart. 2 to remove with difficulty.

prism n 1 a three-dimensional figure with ends that are equal and parallel and sides that are parallelograms. 2 a piece of glass having this form with triangular ends, used to deflect or disperse light.

prison n a building in which people are confined while awaiting trial or for punishment after conviction.

prisoner n 1 somebody kept in enforced confinement. 2 somebody who is trapped by circumstances.

prisoner of conscience n a person imprisoned for political or religious beliefs.

prisoner of war n somebody captured in war.

prissy adj (-**ier**, -**iest**) prim and prudish in a fussy way. ➤ **prissily** adv, **prissiness** n.

pristine adj 1 in its original unspoilt state. 2 fresh and clean as if new.

privacy n 1 a state of being apart from other people. 2 freedom from undesirable intrusions.

private[1] adj 1 restricted to the use of a particular person or group. 2 owned or run by an independent individual or company. 3 not intended to be known by others. 4 not wishing for the company of others. 5 of a person: not holding public office or employment. 6 of a place: where one is likely to be alone or undisturbed. 7 of a soldier: having the rank of private.

private[2] n a soldier of the lowest rank in the army.

private company n a company whose shares cannot be offered for sale to the general public.

private detective n a detective who acts privately and is not a member of a police force.

private enterprise n business undertaken by privately owned companies.

privateer n formerly, a privately owned warship commissioned by a government in wartime.

private eye n *informal* a private detective.

private means n income derived from investments or inheritance rather than earnings.

private member n a Member of Parliament who does not hold a government appointment.

private parts pl n *euphem* a person's genitalia.

private practice *n* medical practice outside a state system.

private school *n Brit* a school supported by payment of fees.

private secretary *n* **1** a secretary employed to assist with a person's confidential business matters. **2** a civil servant who advises a senior government official.

private sector *n* the part of the economy that is not controlled by the state.

privation *n* lack of the basic necessities of life.

privatize *or* **-ise** *v* to transfer (a business or industry) to private ownership. ➤ **privatization** *n*.

privet *n* an ornamental shrub with small white flowers, used in hedges.

privilege *n* **1** a special right or advantage granted to a particular person or group. **2** the possession of privileges conferred by rank or wealth. **3** immunity from normal legal sanctions.

privileged *adj* **1** having one or more privileges. **2** of information: not subject to public disclosure.

privy[1] *adj* (+ to) sharing in the knowledge of something secret.

privy[2] *n* (*pl* **-ies**) a toilet in a small outside building.

Privy Council *n* an advisory council to the monarch.

prize[1] *n* **1** something offered as a reward for success or achievement. **2** something exceptionally desirable or precious.

prize[2] *v* to value highly.

prize[3] *v* see PRISE.

pro[1] *n* (*pl* **pros**) ❊ **pros and cons** the arguments for and against something.

pro[2] *prep* for; in favour of.

pro[3] *n* (*pl* **pros**) *informal* a professional.

pro[4] *adj* professional.

pro- *prefix* **1** before in time or order: *prologue*. **2** favouring; supporting: *pro-European*.

proactive *adj* taking the initiative rather than just reacting.

probability *n* (*pl* **-ies**) **1** the state of being probable. **2** something that is probable.

probable *adj* **1** supported by strong evidence but not certain. **2** likely to be or occur. ➤ **probably** *adv*.

probate *n* the judicial process of declaring a will to be valid.

probation *n* **1** a method of dealing with offenders by which sentence is suspended subject to good behaviour under supervision. **2** a period of testing of a new recruit to a job. ➤ **probationary** *adj*, **probationer** *n*.

probe[1] *n* **1** a surgical instrument used to examine a cavity. **2** a device inserted in something to be monitored or measured. **3** an unmanned spacecraft used for exploring. **4** a penetrating or critical investigation.

probe[2] *v* **1** to examine with a probe. **2** to investigate thoroughly. ➤ **probing** *adj*.

probity *n formal* honesty and integrity.

problem *n* **1** a situation or question that is difficult to understand or resolve. **2** something or somebody that is difficult to deal with.

problematic *or* **problematical** *adj* presenting a problem.

proboscis /prə'bosis/ *n* (*pl* **proboscises** /-seez/ *or* **proboscides** /-deez/) **1** an animal's long flexible snout, e.g. the trunk of an elephant. **2** an elongated sucking tube extending from the mouth of some insects.

procedure *n* **1** a particular or established way of doing something. **2** a series of ordered steps. ➤ **procedural** *adj*.

proceed *v* **1** to begin and carry on an action. **2** to move along a course. **3** to continue after a pause or interruption. **4** to arise from a source.

proceedings *pl n* **1** the events involved in an established procedure. **2** legal action. **3** an official record of things said or done.

proceeds *pl n* money earned or obtained.

process[1] *n* **1** a series of actions or operations designed to achieve an end. **2** a natural series of changes: *the growth process*.

process[2] *v* **1** to subject to a special process or treatment. **2** to take appropriate action on. ➤ **processor** *n*.

process[3] *v chiefly Brit* to move in a procession.

procession *n* **1** a group of people, vehicles, etc, moving in an orderly way. **2** the action of moving along. **3** a succession or sequence.

proclaim *v* **1** to declare publicly and officially. **2** to show clearly. ➤ **proclamation** *n*.

proclivity *n* (*pl* **-ies**) an inclination to do something undesirable.

procrastinate *v formal* to delay until a later time. ➤ **procrastination** *n*.

procreate *v formal* to conceive or produce offspring. ➤ **procreation** *n*.

proctor *n* an officer in charge of student discipline at certain universities.

procurator *n* an agent or attorney.

procurator fiscal *n* a local coroner and public prosecutor in Scotland.

procure *v* to obtain by special care and effort. ➤ **procurement** *n*.

prod[1] *v* (**prodded, prodding**) **1** to poke or jab with a finger or pointed instrument. **2** to incite to action.

prod[2] *n* **1** a prodding action or jab. **2** a pointed instrument. **3** an incitement to act.

prodigal[1] *adj* **1** recklessly extravagant or wasteful. **2** lavish. ➤ **prodigally** *adv*.

prodigal[2] *n* **1** an extravagant or wasteful person. **2** a repentant sinner or reformed spendthrift.

prodigious *adj* remarkable in size or achievement. ➤ **prodigiously** *adv*.

prodigy *n* (*pl* **-ies**) an exceptionally talented child.

produce[1] *v* 1 to give being, form, or shape to; to make or manufacture. 2 to make happen or exist. 3 to offer to view or notice. 4 to supervise the making of (a film, play, piece of recorded music, etc). ➤ **producer** *n*.

produce[2] *n* 1 agricultural products, *esp* fresh fruit and vegetables. 2 a product or products.

product *n* 1 a commodity made available for sale. 2 something produced by a process. 3 a result of a combination of causes. 4 the result of multiplying numbers together.

production *n* 1 the act of producing something. 2 the total output of a commodity or an industry. 3 something produced; a product. 4 a theatrical or broadcast work.

production line *n* an assembly line.

productive *adj* 1 producing large quantities of something. 2 yielding significant results or benefits. ➤ **productively** *adv*.

productivity *n* 1 the quality of being productive. 2 the effectiveness of labour in terms of industrial output.

profane[1] *adj* 1 not concerned with religion or religious purposes. 2 debasing or defiling what is holy.

profane[2] *v* to treat irreverence or contempt. ➤ **profanation** *n*.

profanity *n* (*pl* **-ies**) 1 profane language. 2 a swear word.

profess *v* 1 to declare openly or freely. 2 to claim or pretend. 3 to declare one's allegiance to (a religion).

profession *n* 1 an occupation requiring special training and qualifications. 2 the people engaged in such an occupation. 3 an act of declaring a faith, opinion, etc. 4 a declaration or claim.

professional[1] *adj* 1 relating or belonging to a profession. 2 conforming to the standards associated with a profession. 3 of a person: taking part in an activity as a paid occupation. ➤ **professionally** *adv*.

professional[2] *n* 1 a professional person. 2 a person having the qualifications of a profession.

professionalism *n* the knowledge and standards associated with professional people.

professor *n* 1 an acaedmic of the highest academic rank at a university. 2 *NAmer* a university teacher. ➤ **professorial** *adj*, **professorship** *n*.

proffer *v* to present for acceptance.

proficient *adj* competent or skilled. ➤ **proficiency** *n*.

profile[1] *n* 1 a side view of the human face. 2 an outline seen in sharp relief. 3 a concise biographical or descriptive outline. 4 the extent to which somebody attracts public attention.

✳ **keep a low profile** to avoid attracting attention.

profile[2] *v* to produce a profile of.

profit[1] *n* 1 the excess of income over expenditure. 2 a gain or benefit. ➤ **profitless** *adj*.

profit[2] *v* (**profited, profiting**) 1 (*often* + from/by) to derive benefit; to gain. 2 to be of service to.

profitable *adj* producing a profit. ➤ **profitability** *n*, **profitably** *adv*.

profiteer *v* to make an excessive or unreasonable profit. ➤ **profiteering** *n*.

profiterole *n* a small ball of choux pastry filled with cream and covered with a chocolate sauce.

profit margin *n* the difference between the selling price of a product and its cost price.

profligate[1] *adj* 1 utterly dissolute; immoral. 2 wildly extravagant; prodigal. ➤ **profligacy** *n*.

profligate[2] *n* a profligate person.

profound *adj* 1 having intellectual depth and insight. 2 difficult to fathom or understand. 3 extending far below a surface. 4 of a feeling: strongly felt. ➤ **profoundly** *adv*, **profundity** *n*.

profuse *adj* 1 extravagant. 2 abundant. ➤ **profusely** *adv*, **profusion** *n*.

progenitor *n* 1 a parent or direct ancestor. 2 a precursor or originator.

progeny *n* descendants or children.

progesterone *n* a steroid hormone that causes changes in the uterus in preparation for pregnancy.

prognosis *n* (*pl* **prognoses**) 1 an assessment of how an illness is likely to develop. 2 a forecast or prediction.

programmatic *adj* resembling or having a programme.

programme[1] (*NAmer* **program**) *n* 1 a systematic plan of action. 2 a radio or television broadcast. 3 a list of features to be presented in a public performance. 4 (**program**) a sequence of coded instructions for a computer to follow to perform a function.

programme[2] (*NAmer* **program**) *v* (**programmed, programming,** *NAmer* **programed, programing**) 1 to arrange or provide a programme for. 2 to enter in a programme. 3 to condition (something or somebody). 4 (**program**) to provide (a computer) with a program. ➤ **programmable** *adj*, **programmer** *n*.

progress[1] *n* 1 forward movement towards a destination or objective. 2 development towards a better or more complete state.

progress[2] *v* 1 to move forward. 2 to develop or improve.

progression *n* 1 the act of progressing; an advance. 2 a continuous and connected series.

progressive[1] *adj* 1 characterized by progress or progression. 2 making use of or interested in new ideas or opportunities. 3 moving forward

in stages. **4** of a disease: increasing in severity.
➤ **progressively** adv.

progressive² n somebody who advocates progressive political or social ideas.

prohibit v (**prohibited, prohibiting**) **1** to forbid formally. **2** to prevent (something) from happening.

prohibition n **1** the act of prohibiting something. **2** an order that forbids something.

prohibitive adj **1** tending to prohibit or restrain. **2** of a cost: unreasonably high. ➤ **prohibitively** adv.

project¹ n **1** a specific plan or design; a scheme. **2** a piece of research with a definite plan. **3** a task or problem engaged in usu by a group of pupils.

project² v **1** to devise in the mind; to design. **2** to calculate or estimate on the basis of known data or trends. **3** to cause (light or an image) to fall on a surface. **4** to protrude or cause to protrude. **5** to cause (the voice) to be heard at a distance. **6** to present or express (oneself) in a manner that wins approval.

projectile n a missile or other object fired at a target.

projector n an apparatus for projecting films or slides onto a surface.

prolapse n a condition in which a body part has slipped from its usual position.

proletarian n a member of the proletariat. ➤ **proletarian** adj.

proletariat n the working people of a community.

proliferate v **1** to grow or reproduce rapidly. **2** to increase rapidly in number or quantity. ➤ **proliferation** n.

prolific adj **1** producing offspring, fruit, etc freely. **2** highly inventive or productive. ➤ **prolifically** adv.

prolix adj tediously prolonged or repetitious. ➤ **prolixity** n.

prologue (NAmer **prolog**) n **1** the introductory part of a literary or musical work. **2** an introductory event or development.

prolong v to lengthen in time or space. ➤ **prolongation** n, **prolonged** adj.

prom n **1** a promenade concert. **2** a promenade for walking. **3** NAmer a formal dance at a high school or college.

promenade¹ n a paved walk by the sea.

promenade² v to take a leisurely walk.

promenade concert n a concert of classical music at which some of the audience stand.

prominence n **1** the state or quality of being prominent. **2** something that sticks out.

prominent adj **1** famous and eminent. **2** readily noticeable. **3** projecting beyond a surface or line. ➤ **prominently** adv.

promiscuous adj having many casual sexual relationships. ➤ **promiscuity** n.

promise¹ n **1** a declaration that one will or will not do something. **2** grounds for expecting success or excellence.

promise² v **1** to make a promise. **2** to give grounds for expecting something.

promising adj showing signs of success. ➤ **promisingly** adv.

promissory note n a written promise to pay a specified sum of money.

promo n (pl **-os**) informal an advertising video or film.

promontory n (pl **-ies**) a high point of land projecting into the sea.

promote v **1** to contribute to the start or development of. **2** to advertise or publicize. **3** to contribute to in a beneficial way. **4** to give (somebody) a higher position or rank. ➤ **promoter** n.

promotion n **1** being raised in position or rank. **2** the advertising and marketing of a product. **3** a concession intended to promote a product or increase sales. ➤ **promotional** adj.

prompt¹ v **1** to move (somebody) to action; to incite. **2** to serve as the cause of; to urge. **3** to remind (an actor) of the next words to be spoken.

prompt² adj **1** done readily or immediately. **2** ready and quick to act. **3** happening or arriving on time. ➤ **promptly** adv, **promptness** n.

prompt³ n **1** an instance of prompting. **2** somebody or something that prompts. **3** a symbol on a VDU screen marking the place where a command will take effect.

prompt⁴ adv informal exactly; punctually: six o'clock prompt.

promulgate v **1** to make known openly. **2** to put (a law, decree, etc) into force. **3** to promote publicly. ➤ **promulgation** n.

prone adj **1** (+ to) having a tendency or inclination to something. **2** lying flat or face downward.

prong¹ n **1** each of the sharp-pointed parts of a fork. **2** a distinct part of an attack.

prong² v to pierce with a prong.

pronominal adj of a pronoun.

pronoun n a word used as a substitute for a noun already mentioned, e.g. I, he, these.

pronounce v **1** to utter the sound or sounds of (a word). **2** to declare officially. ➤ **pronounceable** adj, **pronouncement** n.

pronounced adj strongly marked or conspicuous.

pronto adv informal without delay.

pronunciation n the act or manner of pronouncing a word.

Usage Note: Note the spelling -nunc- not -nounc-.

proof¹ n **1** evidence that establishes a truth or fact. **2** the process of establishing the truth or validity of something. **3** an operation designed to establish a fact or the truth. **4** a sample printing of a piece of text for correction. **5** a test of the quality of an article or substance. **6** the alcoholic content of a drink.

proof² adj resisting or repelling: soundproof.

prop¹ n **1** a rigid vertical support, e.g. a pole. **2** a source of strength or support.

prop² v (**propped, propping**) **1** to support with a prop. **2** to place against a vertical surface for support.

prop³ n an object used in a play or film other than painted scenery or costumes.

prop⁴ n informal a propeller.

propaganda n the systematic spreading of ideas and information to promote an institution or point of view. ➤ **propagandist** n.

propagate v **1** to cause (a plant) to reproduce or multiply. **2** to publicize (information). ➤ **propagation** n.

propane n a gas found in crude petroleum and natural gas and used as a fuel.

propel v (**propelled, propelling**) **1** to drive (something) forward. **2** to urge (somebody) on.

propellant n a gas that releases the contents from a pressurized container.

propeller n a device with radiating twisted blades, used to propel a ship or aircraft.

propensity n (pl -ies) formal a natural inclination or tendency.

proper adj **1** suitable; appropriate. **2** strictly accurate; correct. **3** decorous or genteel. **4** being strictly so-called: the city proper. **5** (+ to) belonging characteristically to.

proper fraction n a fraction in which the number above the line is less than the number below the line.

proper noun n a noun with a capital initial that denotes a particular person, place, or thing.

property n (pl -ies) **1** something owned or possessed. **2** a piece of land and the buildings on it. **3** a quality or attribute.

prophecy n (pl -ies) a prediction of what will happen.

prophesy v (-ies, -ied) to predict that something will happen at a certain time.

prophet or **prophetess** n **1** a person who claims to utter divinely inspired revelations. **2** somebody who foretells future events.

prophetic adj **1** characteristic of a prophet or prophecy. **2** foretelling events.

prophylactic¹ adj protecting from or preventing disease.

prophylactic² n a prophylactic drug.

propinquity n nearness in place or time.

propitiate v to gain or regain the favour of. ➤ **propitiation** n, **propitiatory** adj.

propitious adj **1** boding well. **2** opportune.

proponent n somebody who argues in favour of something.

proportion n **1** the relation of one part to another or to the whole. **2** harmonious relation

of parts. **3** a relationship of constant ratio. **4** a proper or equal share. **5** a fraction or percentage. **6** (in pl) size or dimensions. ＊ **sense of proportion** an ability to assess the relative importance of things.

proportional or **proportionate** adj corresponding in size, shape, etc. ➤ **proportionally** adv.

proportional representation n an electoral system in which political groups gain seats in proportion to the number of votes they receive.

proposal n **1** a proposed idea or plan of action. **2** an offer of marriage. **3** the act of putting something forward for consideration.

propose v **1** to present for consideration or adoption. **2** to establish as an aim or intention. **3** to recommend or nominate. **4** to announce (a toast). **5** to make an offer of marriage. ➤ **proposer** n.

proposition¹ n **1** something offered for consideration. **2** a formal mathematical statement to be proved. **3** somebody or something to be dealt with. ➤ **propositional** adj.

proposition² v to propose sexual intercourse to (somebody).

propound v formal to offer for consideration.

proprietary adj **1** characteristic of a proprietor. **2** made and marketed under a patent or trademark. **3** privately owned and managed.

proprietor or **proprietress** n a person with a legal right or exclusive title to something. ➤ **proprietorial** adj.

propriety n (pl -ies) **1** the quality or state of being proper. **2** correctness of behaviour. **3** (in pl) the conventions and manners of polite society.

propulsion n the action or process of propelling. ➤ **propulsive** adj.

prop up v to give support to.

pro rata /ˌproh 'rahtə/ adj and adv proportional or proportionally.

prosaic adj **1** characteristic of prose. **2** dull or commonplace. ➤ **prosaically** adv.

proscenium n (pl **proscenia** or **prosceniums**) the part of a theatre stage in front of the curtain.

proscenium arch n the arch in a conventional theatre through which the spectator sees the stage.

proscribe v **1** to condemn or forbid something harmful); to prohibit. **2** to outlaw or exile. ➤ **proscription** n.

prose n ordinary language as spoken or written.

prosecute v **1** to pursue criminal proceedings against. **2** formal to follow (something) through, to pursue. ➤ **prosecutor** n.

prosecution n **1** the formal institution of a criminal charge. **2** the party that institutes criminal proceedings.

proselyte *n* a person who has been newly converted to a religion or cause.

proselytize *or* **-ise** *v* to convert to a new religion or cause.

prosody *n* **1** the patterns of rhythm and metre used in poetry. **2** the study of verse structure.

prospect[1] *n* **1** a mental picture of something to come. **2** the expectation or possibility of something happening. **3** (*in pl*) financial and social expectations. **4** (*in pl*) chances, *esp* of success. **5** a potential client, candidate, etc.

prospect[2] *v* to explore (an area) for mineral deposits. ➤ **prospector** *n*.

prospective *adj* likely to be or happen. ➤ **prospectively** *adv*.

prospectus *n* (*pl* **prospectuses**) a printed brochure describing an organization or enterprise.

prosper *v* to succeed or thrive.

prosperous *adj* financially successful. ➤ **prosperity** *n*.

prostate *n* in male mammals, a gland situated round the neck of the bladder and secreting most of the volume of semen.

prostitute[1] *n* a person who engages in sexual activities for money.

prostitute[2] *v* **1** to make a prostitute of. **2** to devote (something) to unworthy purposes. ➤ **prostitution** *n*.

prostrate[1] *adj* **1** lying full-length face downwards. **2** overcome with exhaustion.

prostrate[2] *v* **1** to put into a prostrate position. **2** to humble (oneself). **3** to reduce to submission or helplessness. ➤ **prostration** *n*.

protagonist *n* **1** the leading part in a drama or film. **2** a notable supporter of a cause.

protean *adj* able to change or adapt readily.

protect *v* **1** to cover or shield from injury or destruction. **2** to guard or defend against attack or harm. ➤ **protector** *n*.

protection *n* **1** the act of protecting. **2** something that protects. **3** immunity from threatened violence, in exchange for payment.

protectionism *n* the shielding of the producers of a country from foreign competition by import tariffs. ➤ **protectionist** *adj and n*.

protective *adj* providing or able to provide protection.

protectorate *n* a state that is partly controlled by and dependent on the protection of another.

protégé *or* **protégée** /'protizhay/ *n* somebody under the protection and guidance of a more experienced person.

protein *n* a naturally occurring chemical compound that is an important part of the human diet.

Usage Note: Note the spelling with *-ei-*.

---

protest[1] *v* **1** to express strong disagreement or objection. **2** to take part in a public demonstration of disapproval. **3** to declare formally: *He*

protested his innocence. ➤ **protester** *n*, **protestor** *n*.

protest[2] *n* **1** a formal declaration of disapproval or objection. **2** a public demonstration of disapproval.

Protestant *n* a member of any of the Western Christian Churches that are separate from the Roman Catholic Church. ➤ **Protestant** *n*.

protestation *n* **1** the act or an instance of protesting. **2** a solemn declaration or avowal.

protocol *n* **1** a code or system of conduct on official occasions. **2** the correct way to behave in a particular situation. **3** a signed record of agreement made at a diplomatic conference.

proton *n* an elementary particle that carries a single positive electrical charge.

prototype *n* an original model from which later versions are developed.

protozoan *or* **protozoon** *n* a minute single-celled animal.

protract *v* to prolong in time or space. ➤ **protracted** *adj*.

protractor *n* a flat semicircular instrument marked with degrees, used for measuring angles.

protrude *v* to project from or extend beyond a surface. ➤ **protrusion** *n*.

protuberance *n* something that projects from a surrounding or adjacent surface. ➤ **protuberant** *adj*.

proud *adj* **1** pleased or satisfied with an achievement or possession. **2** having excessive self-esteem. **3** having proper self-respect. **4** stately or magnificent. **5** giving reason for pride. **6** projecting slightly from a surface. ✻ **do somebody proud 1** to treat somebody very well. **2** to give somebody cause for pride. ➤ **proudly** *adv*.

prove *v* (*past part*. **proved** *or* **proven**) **1** to establish the truth or validity of by evidence or demonstration. **2** to show (oneself) to have the required qualities. **3** to turn out to be. ➤ **provable** *adj*.

proven *adj* known from experience to be sound or reliable.

provenance *n* the place of origin of a work of art or other object.

provender *n* dry food for domestic animals.

proverb *n* a brief pithy saying embodying a truth or belief.

proverbial *adj* **1** of or resembling a proverb. **2** characteristic or well-known. ➤ **proverbially** *adv*.

provide *v* **1** to give or make available. **2** (+ with) to supply (somebody) with. **3** (+ for) to supply what is needed for sustenance. **4** (+ for) to take action in relation to a possible event.

provided *or* **providing** *conj* on condition that.

providence *n* **1** (**Providence**) God or nature as the power guiding human destiny. **2** adequate preparation for the future.

provident *adj* careful in providing for the future.

providential *adj* happening by good fortune; lucky. ➤ **providentially** *adv*.

province *n* **1** an administrative district or division of a country. **2** (**the provinces**) all of a country outside the capital. **3** a field of knowledge or activity.

provincial[1] *adj* **1** of a province or the provinces. **2** limited in outlook; narrow-minded. ➤ **provincialism** *n*.

provincial[2] *n* somebody living in the provinces.

provision[1] *n* **1** the act of providing something. **2** a preparation or precaution. **3** (*in pl*) a stock of food or other supplies. **4** a proviso or stipulation in a legal document.

provision[2] *v* to supply with provisions.

provisional *adj* serving for the time being and requiring later confirmation. ➤ **provisionally** *adv*.

proviso *n* (*pl* **-os** *or* **-oes**) a condition in an agreement.

provocation *n* **1** the act of provoking. **2** something that angers or irritates.

provocative *adj* **1** tending to provoke or make indignant. **2** sexually stimulating. ➤ **provocatively** *adv*.

provoke *v* **1** to incite to anger; to incense. **2** to cause to behave in a specified way. **3** to stir up or evoke. **4** to provide the needed stimulus for.

provost *n* **1** the head of certain university colleges and public schools. **2** the head of certain Scottish district councils. **3** the head of the assembly of canons in a cathedral or other church.

prow *n* the bow of a ship or boat.

prowess *n* **1** outstanding ability. **2** military valour.

prowl[1] *v* to move about in a stealthy or predatory manner. ➤ **prowler** *n*.

prowl[2] *n* the act of prowling.

proximity *n* nearness in space, time, or association.

proxy *n* (*pl* **-ies**) **1** a deputy authorized to act for another. **2** authority to act or vote for another.

prude *n* a person who affects extreme modesty or propriety in sexual matters. ➤ **prudish** *adj*.

prudent *adj* acting with good sense and caution. ➤ **prudence** *n*.

prudential *adj* exercising prudence in business matters.

prune[1] *n* a dried plum.

prune[2] *v* **1** to remove unwanted parts of (a plant or shrub). **2** to remove as superfluous.

prurient *adj* having or arousing an excessive interest in sexual matters. ➤ **prurience** *n*.

pry *v* (**-ies, -ied**) (*usu* + into) to show an excessively eager interest in.

PS *abbr* postscript.

psalm *n* a sacred song or poem used in worship.

Psalter *n* a book of biblical psalms.

pseudo *adj* **1** apparent rather than actual. **2** *informal* false; pretentious.

pseudonym *n* a fictitious name used by an author.

psi /sie, psie/ *n* the 23rd letter of the Greek alphabet (Ψ, ψ).

psoriasis *n* a skin condition with red patches covered by white scales.

psych *or* **psyche** *v informal* **1** (+ out) to intimidate psychologically. **2** (+ up) to prepare (oneself) mentally.

psyche *n* the soul, mind, or spirit.

psychedelia *n* art, music, etc, associated with psychedelic drugs.

psychedelic *adj* **1** of drugs: producing hallucinations. **2** having strong colours and a swirling pattern. ➤ **psychedelically** *adv*.

psychiatry *n* a branch of medicine that deals with mental disorders. ➤ **psychiatric** *adj*, **psychiatrist** *n*.

psychic *adj* **1** lying outside the sphere of physical science or knowledge. **2** sensitive to supernatural forces or influences. **3** of or originating in the mind. ➤ **psychical** *adj*, **psychically** *adv*.

psycho *n* (*pl* **-os**) *informal* a psychopath.

psychoanalyse (*NAmer* **psychoanalyze**) *v* to treat by means of psychoanalysis.

psychoanalysis *n* a method of analysing unconscious mental processes to treat mental disorders. ➤ **psychoanalyst** *n*, **psychoanalytic** *adj*.

psychological *adj* **1** relating to psychology. **2** of the mind. ➤ **psychologically** *adv*.

psychology *n* **1** the study of the mind. **2** a person's mental or behavioural characteristics. ➤ **psychologist** *n*.

psychopath *n* a person suffering from a disorder with violent antisocial tendencies. ➤ **psychopathic** *adj*.

psychosis *n* (*pl* **psychoses**) a mental disorder leading to loss of contact with reality.

psychosomatic *adj* resulting from the interaction of psychological and physical factors. ➤ **psychosomatically** *adv*.

psychotherapy *n* treatment of mental disorders by psychological methods. ➤ **psychotherapist** *n*.

psychotic *adj* relating to or suffering from a psychosis.

PT *abbr* physical training.

Pt *abbr* the chemical symbol for platinum.

pt *abbr* **1** pint. **2** point.

PTA *abbr* Parent-Teacher Association.

Pte *abbr* Private.

pterodactyl *n* a flying dinosaur with toothed jaws and a long neck.

PTO *abbr* please turn over.

pub *n Brit* an establishment where alcoholic beverages are sold and consumed.

puberty *n* the period during which adolescents become sexually mature.

pubes *n* the lower front part of the abdomen.

pubescence *n* the beginning of puberty. ➤ **pubescent** *adj*.

pubic *adj* in the region of the pubis or pubes.

pubis *n* (*pl* **pubes**) the bottom front of the three principal bones that form either half of the pelvis.

public[1] *adj* **1** of or affecting all the people. **2** of or being in the service of the community. **3** general or popular. **4** of national or community concerns. **5** accessible to all members of the community. **6** exposed to general view; open. ➤ **publicly** *adv*.

public[2] *n* (**the public**) people as a whole. ✳ **in public** in the presence of strangers.

public-address system *n* an apparatus including a microphone and loudspeakers used to address a large audience.

publican *n chiefly Brit* a person who owns or runs as pub.

publication *n* **1** the act or process of publishing. **2** a published work.

public company *n* a company whose shares can be traded on the stock exchange.

public house *n Brit* an establishment where alcoholic beverages are sold and consumed.

publicist *n* a person whose job is to publicize a product or organization.

publicity *n* **1** information issued as a means of gaining public attention or support. **2** public attention or acclaim.

publicize or **-ise** *v* to give publicity to.

public limited company *n* a company whose shareholders have only a limited liability for any debts or losses created by the company.

public prosecutor *n* an official who conducts criminal prosecutions on behalf of the state.

public relations *pl n* the business of informing the public about an organization so as to secure their goodwill.

public school *n* in Britain, an independent fee-paying school.

public sector *n* the part of the economy owned or controlled by the state.

publish *v* **1** to produce (a book, newspaper, etc) for sale. **2** to print (information) in a book, newspaper, etc. **3** to announce publicly. ➤ **publisher** *n*.

puce *n* a brownish purple colour.

puck *n* a hard rubber disc used in ice hockey.

pucker[1] *v* to become wrinkled or creased.

pucker[2] *n* a crease or wrinkle.

pudding *n* **1** a sweet dish eaten at the end of a meal. **2** a sweet or savoury dish made from flour, suet, etc.

puddle *n* a small pool of liquid, *esp* of rainwater on the ground.

pudgy *adj* (**-ier**, **-iest**) short and plump.

puerile *adj* childish or silly.

puff[1] *v* **1** to exhale or blow forcibly. **2** to breathe hard and quickly. **3** to emit small whiffs of smoke or steam. **4** to move while emitting puffs of smoke. **5** (*usu* + out/up) to become distended; to swell. **6** (*usu* + out/up) to inflate. **7** to smoke (a pipe, cigarette, etc).

puff[2] *n* **1** the act of puffing. **2** a slight explosive sound accompanying a puff. **3** a small cloud of smoke emitted in a puff. **4** a draw on a pipe or cigarette. **5** a light round hollow pastry made of puff pastry. **6** *chiefly Brit, informal* one's breath.

puffball *n* a fungus that discharges a cloud of ripe spores when pressed or struck.

puffin *n* a seabird with a short neck and a deep brightly coloured bill.

puff pastry *n* a type of light flaky pastry made with a rich dough.

puffy *adj* (**-ier**, **-iest**) *esp* of the eyes or cheeks: swollen.

pug *n* a dog of a breed with a small sturdy compact body and a broad wrinkled face.

pugilism *n formal* boxing. ➤ **pugilist** *n*, **pugilistic** *adj*.

pugnacious *adj* inclined to fight or quarrel; belligerent. ➤ **pugnacity** *n*.

puke[1] *v informal* (*often* + up) to vomit.

puke[2] *n informal* vomit.

pukka *adj* **1** *informal*. **2** genuine or authentic. **3** first-class or excellent.

pulchritude *n formal* physical beauty.

pull[1] *v* **1** to exert a force on (somebody or something) so as to make it move towards oneself. **2** to move (something) in this way. **3** to make something come apart by force. **4** to remove or detach by pulling. **5** to strain (a muscle, tendon, etc). **6** to move steadily. **7** *informal* to attract (somebody) sexually. ✳ **pull a face** to grimace. **pull oneself together** to regain one's self-control. **pull one's punches** to be more restrained than one might. **pull one's weight** to do one's full share of work. **pull somebody's leg** to deceive or tease somebody. **pull strings** to use one's influence to achieve something.

pull[2] *n* **1** the act of pulling. **2** a force that attracts or influences. **3** a deep draught of liquid. **4** an inhalation of smoke.

pull apart *v* **1** to separate into pieces. **2** to criticize harshly.

pull back *v* to withdraw or retreat.

pull down *v* to demolish or destroy.

pullet *n* a young female domestic fowl.

pulley *n* (*pl* **-eys**) a wheel round which a rope or chain passes to lift heavy loads.

pull in *v* of a vehicle: to stop by the side of the road.

pull off *v* to achieve (something difficult).

pull out *v* **1** of a vehicle: to move out into a stream of traffic. **2** to withdraw from an undertaking.

pullover n a sweater put on by being pulled over the head.

pull up v to come to a stop.

pulmonary adj in the region of the lungs.

pulp[1] n **1** the soft fleshy part of a fruit or vegetable. **2** a soft mass of vegetable matter. **3** a soft shapeless mass produced by crushing or beating. **4** (used before a noun) cheap and sensational: pulp fiction. ➤ **pulpy** adj.

pulp[2] v to reduce to pulp.

pulpit n a raised platform in a church, from which sermons are preached.

pulsar n a celestial source of frequent intermittent bursts of radio waves.

pulsate v **1** to beat with a pulse. **2** to throb or move rhythmically; to vibrate. **3** in physics and astronomy, to vary in brightness, magnitude, etc. ➤ **pulsation** n.

pulse[1] n **1** a regular throbbing caused in the arteries by the contractions of the heart. **2** rhythmical vibrating or sounding. **3** a single beat or throb. **4** a short-lived variation of electrical current, voltage, etc whose value is normally constant. **5** an electromagnetic wave or sound wave of brief duration.

pulse[2] v to pulsate or throb.

pulse[3] n the edible seeds of various crops, e.g. peas, beans, or lentils.

pulverize or **-ise** v **1** to reduce to very small particles. **2** informal to defeat utterly.

puma n (pl **pumas** or **puma**) a large American wild cat with a tawny coat.

pumice n a light volcanic rock used as an abrasive.

pummel v (**pummelled, pummelling**, NAmer **pummeled, pummeling**) to pound or strike repeatedly with the fists.

pump[1] n a device that moves liquids or gases by suction and pressure.

pump[2] v **1** to move (air, water, etc) with a pump. **2** to raise (water, etc) with a pump. **3** (often + out) to draw a gas or liquid out of (a container) with a pump. **4** (usu + up) to inflate (a tyre, etc) with a pump. **5** to move rapidly up and down. **6** informal to question persistently.

pump[3] n a light flat shoe.

pumpkin n the large round fruit of the gourd family, used as a vegetable.

pun[1] n a humorous use of a word with more than one meaning.

pun[2] v (**punned, punning**) to make puns. ➤ **punster** n.

punch[1] v **1** to hit with a hard thrust of the fist. **2** to push (a button or key).

punch[2] n **1** a blow with the fist. **2** informal energy or forcefulness.

punch[3] n **1** a tool for perforating, embossing, cutting, or driving the heads of nails below a surface. **2** a device for cutting holes in paper.

punch[4] v to make a hole in or a pattern on.

punch[5] n a drink made from wine or spirits mixed with fruit, spices, and water.

punchbag n an inflated or stuffed bag punched with the fists as a form of exercise.

punch bowl n **1** a large bowl for mixing and serving punch. **2** Brit a bowl-shaped hollow among hills.

punch-drunk adj **1** suffering brain damage as a result of repeated blows to the head. **2** confused or dazed.

punch line n a sentence or phrase that forms the climax to a joke or story.

punchy adj (**-ier, -iest**) effective or forceful.

punctilious adj **1** strict or precise in observing codes of behaviour. **2** paying careful attention to detail. ➤ **punctiliously** adv.

punctual adj arriving or happening at the exact or agreed time. ➤ **punctuality** n, **punctually** adv.

punctuate v **1** to mark with punctuation marks. **2** to interrupt at intervals.

punctuation n **1** the use of marks such as commas, colons, and full stops, to clarify a piece of writing. **2** the marks used in punctuation.

puncture[1] n a hole made by piercing with a pointed object.

puncture[2] v to pierce with a pointed object.

pundit n a person who gives opinions in an authoritative manner.

pungent adj **1** having a strong sharp smell or taste. **2** of remarks: to the point, highly expressive. ➤ **pungency** n.

punish v **1** to impose a penalty on. **2** to impose a penalty for (an offence). **3** informal to treat roughly or damagingly. ➤ **punishable** adj.

punishment n **1** the act of punishing. **2** something done in order to punish. **3** informal rough or damaging treatment.

punitive adj inflicting or intended to inflict punishment.

punk n **1** (also **punk rock**) a loud aggressive style of rock music. **2** somebody who listens to or plays punk rock. **3** NAmer, informal a worthless person.

punnet n Brit a small basket for soft fruit or vegetables.

punt[1] n a long narrow flat-bottomed boat propelled with a pole.

punt[2] v to travel in a punt.

punt[3] v Brit, informal to bet or gamble.

punt[4] n Brit, informal a bet.

punt[5] v to kick (a ball) after dropping it onto the foot.

punt[6] n the act of punting a ball.

punt[7] /poont/ n the former basic monetary unit of the Republic of Ireland (replaced by the euro in 2002).

punter n informal **1** a person who gambles. **2** Brit a client or customer.

puny *adj* (**-ier, -iest**) **1** small and weak. **2** insignificant.

pup[1] *n* **1** a young dog. **2** a young seal, rat, or other animal.

pup[2] *v* (**pupped, pupping**) to give birth to a pup or pups.

pupa *n* (*pl* **pupae**) an insect at the stage between larva and adult. ➤ **pupal** *adj*.

pupate *v* of an insect: to become a pupa. ➤ **pupation** *n*.

pupil[1] *n* a child or young person who is being taught.

pupil[2] *n* the round dark opening in the centre of the iris of the eye.

puppet *n* **1** a toy figure that is moved by strings, wires, or rods, or by movements of the hand and fingers inside the body. **2** a person controlled by somebody else. ➤ **puppeteer** *n*, **puppetry** *n*.

puppy *n* (*pl* **-ies**) a young dog. ➤ **puppyish** *adj*.

puppy fat *n* temporary plumpness in children.

puppy love *n* short-lived love between adolescents.

purblind *adj* **1** partly blind. **2** lacking in vision or insight.

purchase[1] *v* to buy. ➤ **purchaser** *n*.

purchase[2] *n* **1** something bought. **2** the act of buying. **3** a firm grip or contact.

purdah *n* the seclusion of women from public view among some Muslims and Hindus.

pure *adj* **1** not mixed with any other matter. **2** free from anything that spoils or weakens. **3** free from contamination. **4** free from moral fault; innocent. **5** sheer or unmitigated: *pure folly*. **6** abstract or theoretical: *pure mathematics*. **7** of a sound: in tune and free from harshness. ➤ **purely** *adv*.

puree[1] *or* **purée** /'pyooəray/ *n* a thick pulp of fruit or vegetables produced by blending or crushing.

puree[2] *or* **purée** *v* (**purees** *or* **purées, pureed** *or* **puréed, pureeing** *or* **puréeing**) to make into a puree.

purgative[1] *adj* causing evacuation of the bowels.

purgative[2] *n* a purgative substance or medicine.

purgatory *n* (*pl* **-ies**) in Roman Catholic doctrine, a place of punishment in which the souls of sinners may make amends for past sins and so become fit for heaven.

purge[1] *v* **1** to rid of impurities. **2** to rid a nation, party, etc) of unwanted or undesirable members. **3** to get rid of (undesirable people) by means of a purge. **4** to cause evacuation of faeces from (the bowels).

purge[2] *n* an instance of purging.

purify *v* (**-ies, -ied**) to make pure. ➤ **purification** *n*.

purist *n* a person who keeps strictly to established or traditional usage, *esp* in language. ➤ **purism** *n*.

puritan *n* **1** (**Puritan**) a member of a 16th- and 17th-cent. Protestant group that wished to purify the Church of England of all elaborate forms of worship. **2** a person who preaches a rigorous or severe moral code. ➤ **Puritan** *adj*, **puritan** *adj*, **puritanical** *adj*.

purity *n* the state of being pure.

purl[1] *n* a basic knitting stitch made by inserting the needle into the back of a stitch that produces a raised pattern on the back of the work.

purl[2] *v* to knit (a stitch) in purl.

purlieu *n* (*pl* **purlieus**) (*in pl*) the environs or neighbourhood of a place.

purloin *v* *formal* to steal.

purple *n* **1** the colour between red and blue. **2** the red robes of a cardinal.

purple patch *n* **1** a piece of obtrusively ornate writing. **2** *informal* a period of good luck or success.

purport[1] *n* *formal* **1** professed or implied meaning. **2** purpose or intention.

purport[2] *v* to seem or claim to be. ➤ **purportedly** *adv*.

purpose[1] *n* **1** the object for which something exists or is done. **2** resolution or determination. **3** use or value. * **on purpose** intentionally. ➤ **purposeless** *adj*.

purpose[2] *v* *formal* to have as a purpose.

purposeful *adj* **1** full of determination. **2** having a purpose or aim. ➤ **purposefully** *adv*.

purposely *adv* with a deliberate or express purpose.

purposive *adj* *formal* **1** serving or effecting a useful. **2** having or tending to fulfil a conscious purpose.

purr *v* **1** of a cat: to make a low vibratory murmur. **2** of an engine: to run smoothly. ➤ **purr** *n*.

purse[1] *n* **1** a small bag for holding money. **2** *NAmer* a handbag. **3** resources or funds. **4** a sum of money offered as a prize or present.

purse[2] *v* to pucker or knit (the lips).

purser *n* an officer on a ship who has charge of documents and accounts.

purse strings *pl n* control over expenditure.

pursuance *n* *formal* the act of carrying out a plan or order.

pursuant to *prep* *formal* in accordance with.

pursue *v* (**pursues, pursued, pursuing**) **1** to follow in order to overtake or capture. **2** to try to accomplish (a goal). **3** to engage in (an activity). **4** to follow up (an argument). ➤ **pursuer** *n*.

pursuit *n* **1** the act of pursuing. **2** an activity engaged in as a pastime.

purulent *adj* of or containing pus. ➤ **purulence** *n*.

purvey v to supply (provisions, etc) by way of business. ➤ **purveyor** n.

purview n *informal* **1** the range or limit of authority or concern. **2** the range of vision or understanding.

pus n thick yellowish or greenish fluid matter formed in an abscess or other infected part of the body.

push[1] v **1** to exert a force on (somebody or something) so as to make it move away from oneself. **2** to move (something) in this way. **3** to urge (somebody or oneself) to do something. **4** to develop or promote (an idea or argument). **5** to make strong efforts to sell (a product). **6** *informal* to engage in the illicit sale of (drugs). **7** to approach in age or number. **8** to press forward energetically. ✶ **be pushed** *informal* have too little time. **push for** to demand strenuously. **push one's luck** *informal* to risk having continuing luck after initial success. ➤ **pusher** n.

push[2] n **1** the act of pushing. **2** a vigorous effort. ✶ **at a push** *Brit, informal* if really necessary.

push-bike n *Brit, informal* a pedal cycle.

pushchair n *Brit* a light folding chair on wheels in which a young child can be pushed.

push in v to force one's way into a queue.

push off v *Brit, informal* to leave hastily.

pushover n *informal* **1** a person who is easily defeated or persuaded. **2** something accomplished easily.

push through v to force acceptance of (a proposal).

pushy adj (**-ier, -iest**) very self-assertive. ➤ **pushiness** n.

pusillanimous adj lacking courage or resolution. ➤ **pusillanimity** n.

pussy n (pl **-ies**) *informal* a cat.

pussyfoot v to move or act warily or stealthily.

pussy willow n a willow having grey silky catkins.

pustule n a small raised spot on the skin containing pus. ➤ **pustular** adj.

put[1] v (**putting**, *past tense and past part.* **put**) **1** to place in or move to a specified position. **2** to bring into a specified condition: *He tried to put us right.* **3** to devote or apply to some purpose. **4** to assign to do something. **5** to estimate or set a value on. **6** to present (an idea or proposal) for consideration. **7** to throw (a shot or weight) in athletics. **8** of a ship: to take a specified course.

put[2] n the act of putting the shot.

putative adj *formal* commonly accepted or supposed.

put by v to save (money) for future use.

put down v **1** to suppress or bring to an end. **2** to kill (a sick or injured animal) painlessly. **3** to pay (a sum of money) as a deposit. **4** *informal* to disparage publicly.

put off v **1** to disconcert or discourage. **2** to postpone.

put on v **1** to assume (an attitude or feeling). **2** to increase in weight by a specified amount. **3** to present (a performance).

put out v **1** to annoy or irritate. **2** to inconvenience. **3** of a ship: to set out from shore.

putrefy v (**-ies, -ied**) to become rotten or putrid. ➤ **putrefaction** n.

putrid adj decaying or rotten and foul-smelling.

putsch /pooch/ n a secret plot to overthrow a government.

putt[1] n a gentle golf stroke.

putt[2] v to hit (a golf ball) gently towards or into the hole.

putter[1] n a golf club used for putting.

putter[3] n a rapidly repeated popping sound made by a small motor.

putter[3] v of a motor: to make a rapidly repeated popping sound.

putting green n an area of smooth grass round each hole on a golf course.

putty n (pl **-ies**) a soft building paste used for fixing glass in windows and filling gaps in woodwork.

put up v **1** to build or erect. **2** to accommodate for a short time. **3** to offer or present. ✶ **put up to** to encourage (somebody) to do something wrong or unwise. **put up with** to tolerate.

puzzle[1] v **1** to confuse or perplex with a problem or difficulty that is hard to understand. **2** to make (oneself) think hard about something. **3** (*usu* + about/over) to be uncertain about an action or choice. ➤ **puzzlement** n, **puzzling** adj.

puzzle[2] n **1** somebody or something that is difficult to understand. **2** a problem, toy, etc designed to test one's ingenuity. ➤ **puzzler** n.

PVC abbr polyvinyl chloride, a plastic vinyl.

pygmy or **pigmy** n (pl **-ies**) **1** (**Pygmy**) a member of an African people short in height. **2** a very small person or thing. **3** (*used before a noun*) being a small variety of something.

pyjamas (*NAmer* **pajamas**) pl n a loose jacket and trousers for sleeping in.

pylon n a tower for supporting electricity power cables.

pyramid n a massive stone structure with walls in the form of four triangles that meet in a point at the top. ➤ **pyramidal** adj.

pyre n a heap of combustible material for ritually burning a dead body.

pyrites n (pl **pyrites**) a metallic-looking sulphide mineral that is a compound of iron and sulphur.

pyromania n a compulsive urge to start fires. ➤ **pyromaniac** n.

pyrotechnics pl n **1** a display of fireworks. **2** the art of making fireworks. ➤ **pyrotechnic** adj.

Pyrrhic victory n a victory won at so great a cost as to be worthless.

python n a large snake that kills its prey by crushing it.

Q¹ or **q** *n* (*pl* **Q's** or **Qs** or **q's**) the 17th letter of the English alphabet.

Q² *abbr* question.

QC *abbr* Queen's Counsel.

QED *abbr* (Latin) quod erat demonstrandum = which was to be demonstrated, used at the conclusion of a proof.

qt *abbr* quart.

qua *prep* in the capacity or character of.

quack¹ *v* to make the cry of a duck.

quack² *n* **1** somebody who pretends to have medical skills or qualifications. **2** *informal* a doctor. ➤ **quackery** *n*.

quad *n* **1** a quadrangle. **2** a quadruplet.

quad bike *n* an off-road vehicle, resembling a motorcycle, with four large wheels.

quadrangle *n* **1** = QUADRILATERAL¹. **2** a courtyard, with buildings on all four sides. ➤ **quadrangular** *adj*.

quadrant *n* **1** a quarter of the circumference or area of a circle. **2** formerly, a navigational or astronomical instrument for measuring angles.

quadraphonic or **quadrophonic** *adj* recording or reproducing sound using four channels.

quadrate *adj* square or approximately square.

quadratic *adj* in mathematics, relating to the power of two, but no higher power.

quadrennial *adj* occurring every four years.

quadriceps *n* (*pl* **quadriceps**) the large muscle at the front of the thigh that straightens the leg.

quadrilateral¹ *n* a polygon having four sides.

quadrilateral² *adj* having four straight sides.

quadrille *n* a square dance for four couples.

quadriplegia *n* paralysis of both arms and both legs. ➤ **quadriplegic** *adj and n*.

quadruped *n* an animal that walks on four legs.

quadruple¹ *adj* **1** having four parts. **2** being four times as great or as many.

quadruple² *v* to become or make four times as great or as many.

quadruplet *n* any of four offspring born at one birth.

quaff *v* to drink, *esp* in long draughts.

quagmire *n* **1** an area of soft boggy land. **2** a predicament from which it is difficult to extricate oneself.

quail¹ *n* (*pl* **quails** or **quail**) a small game bird with a rounded body and short tail.

quail² *v* to shrink back in fear.

quaint *adj* pleasingly old-fashioned or unusual. ➤ **quaintly** *adv*.

quake¹ *v* **1** to shake or vibrate. **2** to tremble or shudder, *esp* from fear.

quake² *n informal* an earthquake.

Quaker *n* a member of a pacifist Christian sect, the Society of Friends, that rejects sacraments and a formal ministry. ➤ **Quakerism** *n*.

qualification *n* **1** an official record that a person has completed a course or passed an examination. **2** a quality or skill that makes a person suitable for a particular task or appointment. **3** a restriction in meaning or application. **4** the act of qualifying.

qualifier *n* **1** a contestant or team that qualifies in e.g. a tournament. **2** a preliminary heat or contest; a qualifying round. **3** in grammar, a word that restricts the meaning of another.

qualify *v* (**-ies, -ied**) **1** to be, or to make (somebody), fit for or entitled to something, e.g. a job or position. **2** to obtain a qualification or reach an accredited level of competence in a profession. **3** to become eligible for the higher rounds of a contest by succeeding in a preliminary round. **4** to restrict the meaning or application of (a statement). **5** (*often = as*) to characterize or describe.

qualitative *adj* relating to, or involving the assessment of, quality. ➤ **qualitatively** *adv*.

quality *n* (*pl* **-ies**) **1** degree of excellence in comparison to others of the kind. **2** superior nature or standard. **3** a distinguishing attribute; a characteristic. **4** peculiar and essential character; nature.

qualm *n* a scruple or feeling of uneasiness.

quandary *n* (*pl* **-ies**) a state of perplexity or doubt.

quango *n* (*pl* **-os**) *Brit* an autonomous body set up by the government and having statutory powers in a specific field.

quantify *v* (**-ies, -ied**) to express or measure the quantity of. ➤ **quantifiable** *adj*.

quantitative *adj* relating to, or involving the measurement of, quantity. ➤ **quantitatively** *adv*.

quantity *n* (*pl* **-ies**) **1** a specified or unspecified amount or number. **2** (*also in pl*) a considerable amount or number. **3** the aspect in which something is measurable in terms of magnitude.

quantity surveyor n somebody who estimates quantities of materials and labour needed for a building project.

quantum n (pl **quanta**) in physics, the smallest discrete unit of quantity into which energy can be subdivided or by which it can increase or decrease.

quantum leap n a sudden large increase or major advance.

quantum mechanics pl n a branch of mechanics that deals with the physical behaviour of atoms and particles of matter, for which the laws of classical mechanics are inapplicable.

quarantine[1] n a state or period of isolation for people or animals, designed to prevent the spread of disease.

quarantine[2] v to put into quarantine.

quark n in physics, a hypothetical particle that carries a fractional electric charge and is held to be a constituent of known elementary particles, e.g. the proton or neutron.

quarrel[1] n 1 a usu verbal conflict between people; an argument. 2 a reason for dispute or complaint.

quarrel[2] v (**quarrelled, quarrelling,** NAmer **quarreled, quarreling**) 1 to have a quarrel. 2 (+ with) to find fault with.

quarrelsome adj inclined or quick to quarrel.

quarry[1] n (pl **-ies**) an open excavation from which building materials are obtained.

quarry[2] v (**-ies, -ied**) to obtain (e.g. stone) from a quarry.

quarry[3] n (pl **-ies**) 1 the prey of a predator or hunter. 2 somebody or something pursued.

quart n a unit of liquid capacity equal to 2 pints (about 1.136l in Britain), (about 0.946l in the USA).

quarter[1] n 1 any of four equal parts into which something can be divided. 2 a quarter of a pound or hundredweight. 3 any of four three-month divisions of a year. 4 a point of time 15 minutes before or after the hour. 5 a coin worth a quarter of a US or Canadian dollar. 6 a person, group, direction, or place not specifically identified: *We had financial help from many quarters.* 7 a district of a town or city. 8 (in pl) living accommodation or lodgings. 9 mercy for a defeated enemy.

quarter[2] v 1 to divide into four equal parts. 2 to provide (somebody) with lodgings or shelter. 3 formerly, to divide (a criminal's body) into four parts after execution by hanging.

quarterdeck n the stern area of a ship's upper deck.

quarterfinal n any of four matches in the round that is second from last in a knockout competition.

quarterly[1] adv and adj at three-monthly intervals.

quarterly[2] n (pl **-ies**) a periodical published at three-monthly intervals.

quartermaster n an army officer who provides supplies and quarters for a body of troops.

quarter tone n in music, an interval of half a semitone.

quartet or **quartette** n 1 a group of four instruments, voices, or performers. 2 a musical composition for a quartet.

quarto n (pl **-os**) a size of book page that is created when a standard sheet is folded into 4 leaves or 8 pages.

quartz n a crystalline mineral consisting of silicon dioxide, found in many rocks, e.g. granite and sandstone.

quasar n a very distant and very compact celestial object that emits enormous amounts of energy and is thought to be a supermassive black hole in the centre of a galaxy.

quash v 1 to annul (e.g. a law or judgment). 2 to suppress or crush (e.g. a rumour or rebellion).

quasi- prefix 1 to some degree; partly: *quasi-officially.* 2 seemingly: *quasi-stellar object.*

quatrain n a stanza of four lines.

quaver[1] v esp of the voice: to tremble or shake. ➤ **quavery** adj.

quaver[2] n 1 a musical note with the time value of half a crotchet. 2 a tremulous sound.

quay n a landing place for loading and unloading ships.

quayside n a quay or the land bordering a quay.

queasy adj (**-ier, -iest**) suffering from nausea. ➤ **queasiness** n.

queen n 1 a female monarch. 2 the wife or widow of a king. 3 a woman who is preeminent in a specified sphere. 4 in chess, the most powerful piece of each colour, which has the power to move any number of squares in any direction. 5 a playing card marked with a picture of a queen and ranking below the king. 6 the fertile fully developed female in a colony of bees, wasps, ants, or termites. 7 informal an effeminate male homosexual. ➤ **queenly** adj.

queen mother n a woman who is the widow of a king and the mother of the reigning sovereign.

Queensberry rules pl n the basic rules of boxing.

queer[1] adj 1 odd or strange. 2 informal slightly unwell; faint or queasy. 3 informal, derog homosexual.

queer[2] v informal to spoil or thwart. ✳ **queer somebody's pitch** to prejudice or ruin somebody's chances in advance.

queer[3] n informal, derog a male homosexual.

quell v 1 to overwhelm (e.g. a rebellion) thoroughly; to suppress or subdue. 2 to overcome or alleviate (e.g. a feeling).

quench v **1** to relieve or satisfy (thirst) with liquid. **2** to bring to an end, *esp* by satisfying, damping, or decreasing. **3** to put out (e.g. a fire).

querulous *adj* complaining, *esp* habitually. ➤ **querulously** *adv*.

query[1] n (pl **-ies**) a question, *esp* one expressing doubt or uncertainty.

query[2] v (**-ies, -ied**) **1** to question the accuracy of (e.g. a statement). **2** to express doubt or uncertainty about.

quest[1] n a search, *esp* a long or arduous one, or one involving a journey.

quest[2] v *literary* to search for something.

question[1] n **1** a word, phrase, or sentence used to elicit information or test knowledge. **2** a subject that is in dispute or at issue. **3** a thing on which the outcome of a situation depends: *It's simply a question of availability.* **4** a problem to be resolved. **5** doubt or objection. **6** chance or possibility. ✷ **in question** under discussion. **out of the question** preposterous or impossible.

question[2] v **1** to ask (somebody) a question or a series of questions. **2** to doubt or dispute (something). ➤ **questioner** n.

questionable *adj* **1** open to doubt or challenge. **2** of doubtful morality or propriety. ➤ **questionably** *adv*.

question mark n a punctuation mark (?) used at the end of a sentence to indicate a direct question.

questionnaire n a set of questions, usu on a form, used to obtain statistically useful information.

queue[1] n a line of *esp* people or vehicles waiting.

queue[2] v (**queues, queued, queuing** or **queueing**) to line up or wait in a queue.

queue-jump v to join a queue at a point in front of those already waiting.

quibble[1] n a minor objection or criticism.

quibble[2] v to make minor or trivial objections.

quiche n a pastry shell filled with a rich savoury egg and cream custard and other ingredients.

quick[1] *adj* **1** fast in development or occurrence. **2** marked by speed, readiness, or promptness of physical movement. **3** lasting a short time. **4** inclined to hastiness, e.g. in action or response: *quick to find fault.* **5** fast in understanding, thinking, or learning. **6** of e.g. temper: aroused immediately and intensely. ➤ **quickly** *adv*.

quick[2] *adv informal* fast; soon.

quick[3] n **1** painfully sensitive flesh, *esp* under a fingernail or toenail. **2** somebody's emotional centre or most sensitive feelings.

quicken v **1** to become or make more rapid. **2** to enliven or stimulate. **3** of a foetus: to begin to show signs of life.

quicklime n = LIME[1].

quicksand n a deep mass of loose wet sand into which heavy objects easily sink.

quicksilver[1] n liquid mercury.

quicksilver[2] *adj* changeable in mood or rapid in movement.

quickstep n a ballroom dance with short rapid steps.

quick-tempered *adj* easily angered.

quick-witted *adj* quick in understanding or response.

quid n (pl **quid**) *Brit, informal* a pound sterling. ✷ **quids in** *Brit, informal* having made a profit.

quid pro quo n (pl **quid pro quos**) something given or received in exchange for something else.

quiescent *adj* at rest; inactive. ➤ **quiescence** n.

quiet[1] *adj* (**quieter, quietest**) **1** making little or no noise. **2** free from noise, activity, or excitement; peaceful. **3** gentle or reserved. **4** private or discreet: *a quiet word.* **5** informal and usu involving small numbers of people: *a quiet wedding.* ➤ **quietly** *adv,* **quietness** n.

quiet[2] n tranquillity or silence. ✷ **on the quiet** without telling anyone.

quiet[3] *adv* in a quiet manner.

quieten (*NAmer* **quiet**) v to become or make quiet.

quietude n *formal* being quiet; repose.

quiff n *Brit* a lock of hair brushed so that it stands up over the forehead.

quill n **1** the hollow horny barrel of a feather. **2** any of the large stiff feathers of a bird's wing or tail. **3** any of the hollow sharp spines of a porcupine, hedgehog, etc. **4** a bird's feather made into a writing pen.

quilt[1] n a thick warm top cover for a bed consisting of padding held in place between two layers of cloth by lines of stitching.

quilt[2] v to stitch or sew (fabric) together in layers with padding in between. ➤ **quilted** *adj,* **quilter** n.

quin n *Brit* a quintuplet.

quince n a yellow round or pear-shaped fruit, used for making marmalade, jelly, and preserves.

quinine n a bitter-tasting chemical compound obtained from cinchona bark, formerly used to treat malaria.

quintessence n **1** the pure and concentrated essence. **2** the most typical example or perfect embodiment.

quintessential *adj* representing a perfect example or embodiment. ➤ **quintessentially** *adv*.

quintet n **1** a group of five instruments, voices, or performers. **2** a musical composition for a quintet.

quintuple[1] *adj* **1** having five parts. **2** being five times as great or as many.

quintuple[2] *v* to become or make five times as great or as many.

quintuplet *n* any of five offspring born at one birth.

quip[1] *n* a clever, witty, or sarcastic remark.

quip[2] *v* (**quipped, quipping**) to make a quip.

quire *n* **1** 24 or 25 sheets of paper; one twentieth of a ream. **2** four sheets of paper folded to form eight leaves or sixteen pages.

quirk *n* **1** an odd or peculiar trait. **2** an accident or vagary. ➤ **quirky** *adj*.

quisling *n* a traitor who collaborates with invaders.

quit *v* (**quitting,** *past tense and past part.* **quitted** *or* **quit**) **1** to leave (a person or place). **2** to give up (e.g. an activity or employment). **3** *informal* to admit defeat. ➤ **quitter** *n*.

quite[1] *adv* **1** wholly or completely. **2** certainly: *It's quite the best I've seen.* **3** more than usually; rather: *It took quite a while.* **4** *chiefly Brit* to only a moderate degree.

quite[2] *interj* used to express agreement.

quits *adj* on even terms as a result of repaying a debt or retaliating for an injury.

quiver[1] *n* a case for carrying or holding arrows.

quiver[2] *v* to shake with a slight rapid trembling motion.

quiver[3] *n* the act of quivering; a tremor.

quixotic *adj* idealistic in a rash or impractical way. ➤ **quixotically** *adv*.

quiz[1] *n* (*pl* **quizzes**) a test of knowledge, *esp* a form of entertainment.

quiz[2] *v* (**quizzes, quizzed, quizzing**) to question closely.

quizzical *adj* indicating a state of puzzlement; questioning. ➤ **quizzically** *adv*.

quoin *n* **1** a solid exterior corner of a building. **2** a block used to form a quoin.

quoit *n* **1** a ring used in a throwing game. **2** (*in pl*) a game in which quoits are thrown at an upright pin.

quorate *adj formal* having a quorum.

quorum *n* (*pl* **quorums**) the minimum number of members of a body that must be assembled for proceedings to be constitutionally valid.

quota *n* **1** the share or proportion to be either contributed or received by an individual. **2** a numerical limit set on a particular kind of people or things.

quotation *n* **1** something quoted. **2** the act of quoting. **3** a statement of the expected cost of a service or commodity.

quotation mark *n* (*usu in pl*) either of a pair of punctuation marks (" " or ' ') used to indicate the beginning and end of a direct quotation or to enclose a word or phrase, e.g. a title or definition.

quote[1] *v* **1** to repeat (something previously said or written, *esp* by somebody else) in writing or speech. **2** to give a quotation for a service or commodity. **3** to name the current buying or selling price of (a commodity, stock, share, etc). **4** to quote the shares of (a company) on a stock exchange.

quote[2] *n informal* **1** = QUOTATION 1, 3. **2** = QUOTATION MARK.

quoth *v archaic* said.

quotidian *adj* **1** occurring every day. **2** commonplace or ordinary.

quotient *n* the result of dividing one number by another.

q.v. *abbr* (Latin) quod vide = which see, used to indicate a cross-reference.

qwerty *adj* of computer and typewriter keyboards: having the conventional arrangement of keys for English, with *q,w,e,r,t,y* on the left side of the top row of letters.

R¹ or **r** *n* (*pl* **R's** or **Rs** or **r's**) the eighteenth letter of the alphabet.

R² *abbr* **1** (Latin) Regina = Queen. **2** (Latin) Rex = King. **3** river.

Ra *abbr* the chemical symbol for radium.

rabbi *n* (*pl* **rabbis**) **1** a Jewish scholar qualified to teach Jewish law. **2** the official leader of a Jewish congregation.

rabbit¹ *n* (*pl* **rabbits** or **rabbit**) a small long-eared short-tailed mammal that lives in a burrow.

rabbit² *v* (**rabbited, rabbiting**) *Brit, informal* (*often* + on) to talk aimlessly or inconsequentially.

rabbit punch *n* a short chopping blow to the back of the neck.

rabble *n* **1** a disorderly crowd of people. **2** (**the rabble**) the lowest class of society.

rabid *adj* **1** unreasoning or fanatical. **2** affected with rabies. ➤ **rabidly** *adv*.

rabies *n* a usu fatal viral disease of mammals, transmitted through the bite of an affected animal and characterized by convulsions and extreme fear of water.

raccoon or **racoon** *n* (*pl* **raccoons** or **racoons** or **raccoon** or **racoon**) a small North American mammal that has a bushy ringed tail and lives in trees.

race¹ *n* **1** a contest of speed, e.g. in running or riding. **2** a contest for a prize or position. **3** a strong or rapid current of water. **4** a swift-flowing watercourse used industrially, e.g. to turn a mill wheel. ➤ **racer** *n*.

race² *v* **1** to compete in a race. **2** to have a race with. **3** to go or move at top speed. **4** of a motor, engine, etc: to run at a very high speed.

race³ *n* **1** a division of humankind having physical characteristics that are transmissible by descent, e.g. skin colour. **2** an ethnic group. **3** a subspecies of plants or animals.

racecourse *n* a place or track where races, *esp* horse races, are held.

racehorse *n* a horse bred or kept for racing.

raceme *n* a simple stalk of flowers in which the flowers are borne on short side-stalks along a tall main stem.

race relations *pl n* relations between members of a country's different racial communities.

racetrack *n* a track on which races, e.g. between cars or runners, are held.

racial *adj* **1** relating to race or based on distinctions of race. **2** existing between people of different races. ➤ **racially** *adv*.

racialism *n* = RACISM. ➤ **racialist** *n and adj*.

racism *n* **1** the belief that race is the main source of human traits and abilities. **2** hostility towards or discrimination against people of races other than one's own. ➤ **racist** *n and adj*.

rack¹ *n* **1** a framework or stand on which articles are placed. **2** (**the rack**) an instrument of torture formerly used to stretch the victim's body. **3** a triangular frame for arranging pool balls at the beginning of a game. **4** the front rib section of lamb used for chops or as a roast. ✴ **rack/wrack and ruin** a state of destruction or extreme neglect.

rack² *v* **1** (*also* **wrack**) to cause to suffer torture, pain, or anguish. **2** to place (an object) in a rack. ✴ **rack/wrack one's brains** to make a great mental effort.

racket¹ or **racquet** *n* **1** a lightweight bat with netting stretched across an open frame, used in tennis, squash, badminton, etc. **2** (*in pl*) a game similar to squash, played on a four-walled court.

racket² *n* **1** a loud and confused noise. **2** *informal* a fraudulent scheme engaged in profit.

racketeer *n* a person who makes money through fraudulent schemes. ➤ **racketeering** *n*.

raconteur *n* a person who is good at telling anecdotes.

racoon *n* see RACCOON.

racy *adj* (**-ier, -iest**) **1** slightly indecent; risqué. **2** full of zest or vigour. ➤ **racily** *adv*, **raciness** *n*.

radar *n* an electronic system that detects nearby ships, aircraft, etc by generating high-frequency radio waves and analysing those reflected back from objects they strike.

raddled *adj* haggard with age and the effects of a dissipated lifestyle.

radial *adj* **1** arranged like rays emerging from a central point or axis. **2** of a tyre: having the cords of its fabric running at right angles to the circumference of the tyre. ➤ **radially** *adv*.

radian *n* a unit equal to the angle at the centre of a circle formed by a part of the circumference equal in length to the radius, 57.3°.

radiant *adj* **1** vividly bright and shining. **2** expressing love or happiness, health, etc. **3** transmitted by radiation. ➤ **radiance** *n*, **radiantly** *adv*.

radiate *v* **1** to send (energy) out, or to be given out, in rays or waves. **2** to show or display (a quality, feeling, etc) clearly. **3** to proceed outwards in straight lines from a central point.

radiation *n* **1** the process of radiating. **2** energy radiated in the form of waves or particles.

radiator *n* **1** a room heater with a large surface area, *esp* one through which hot water circulates as part of a central heating system. **2** a device for cooling an internal-combustion engine.

radical[1] *adj* **1** involving the basic nature or composition of something; fundamental. **2** marked by a considerable departure from the usual or traditional. **3** favouring or making extreme changes in existing conditions or institutions. **4** of surgery: designed to remove the root of a disease or all diseased tissue. **5** of a mathematical root. ➤ **radicalism** *n*, **radically** *adj*.

radical[2] *n* **1** a person who who holds radical views. **2** in chemistry, a group of atoms that is capable of remaining unchanged during a series of reactions.

radii *n* pl of RADIUS.

radio[1] *n* (*pl* -os) **1** the transmission and reception of sound signals by means of electromagnetic waves. **2** a device designed to receive sound broadcasts. **3** the radio broadcasting industry.

radio[2] *v* (**radios, radioed, radioing**) to send a message to somebody by radio.

radioactive *adj* emitting harmful rays or particles.

radioactivity *n* the spontaneous emission of harmful rays or particles by the disintegration of the atomic nuclei of some elements, e.g. uranium.

radiocarbon *n* a radioactive isotope of carbon, used in carbon dating.

radiography *n* the production of images by a form of radiation other than light, *esp* X-rays. ➤ **radiographer** *n*.

radioisotope *n* a radioactive isotope.

radiology *n* the study and use of radioactive substances and X-rays in the diagnosis and treatment of disease. ➤ **radiologist** *n*.

radiotherapy *n* the treatment of disease, e.g. cancer, by means of X-rays.

radish *n* the dark red root of a plant of the mustard family, eaten as a salad vegetable.

radium *n* an intensely radioactive metallic element.

radius *n* (*pl* **radii** *or* **radiuses**) **1** a straight line extending from the centre of a circle or sphere to the circumference or surface. **2** the circular

area defined by a stated radius. **3** the bone on the thumb side of the human forearm.

radon *n* a radioactive gas.

RAF *abbr Brit* Royal Air Force.

raffia *n* fibre from the leaves of a Madagascan palm tree used for making baskets, etc.

raffish *adj* not entirely respectable or honest, but not unattractive.

raffle[1] *n* a lottery in which the prizes are usually goods.

raffle[2] *v* to offer as a prize in a raffle.

raft[1] *n* **1** a flat usu wooden floating structure used as a platform or vessel. **2** an inflatable boat or mat.

raft[2] *v* to travel or transport by raft. ➤ **rafting** *n*.

raft[3] *n* a large collection or quantity.

rafter *n* any of the parallel beams that form the framework of a roof.

rag[1] *n* **1** a piece of old worn cloth. **2** (*in pl*) clothes that are in poor or ragged condition. **3** *informal* a newspaper, *esp* one that is sensational or poorly written. ✳ **lose one's rag** *informal* to lose one's temper.

rag[2] *n* a series of processions and stunts organized by students to raise money for charity.

rag[3] *v* (**ragging, ragged**) *Brit* to tease.

rag[4] *n* ragtime music, or a ragtime tune.

ragamuffin *n* a ragged often disreputable person, *esp* a child.

ragbag *n* a miscellaneous collection.

rage[1] *n* **1** violent and uncontrolled anger. **2** a fashionable and temporary enthusiasm, or the object of it.

rage[2] *v* **1** to be in a rage. **2** to be unchecked in violence or effect.

ragged /'ragid/ *adj* **1** of clothes: torn or worn to tatters. **2** wearing tattered clothes. **3** having an irregular edge or outline; jagged. **4** performed in an irregular, faulty, or uneven manner. ➤ **raggedly** *adv*.

ragout /ra'gooh/ *n* a thick well-seasoned stew of meat and vegetables.

ragtag *adj* consisting of a varied or odd mixture.

ragtime *n* music with a strongly syncopated rhythm, developed in America in about 1900 and usu played on the piano.

rag trade *n informal* the clothing trade.

ragwort *n* a yellow-flowered plant with deeply cut leaves.

raid[1] *n* **1** a surprise attack or incursion by a small force, often to seize somebody or something. **2** a sudden invasion by the police, e.g. in search of criminals or stolen goods. **3** an act of robbery.

raid[2] *v* **1** to make a raid on. **2** to take or steal something from (a place). ➤ **raider** *n*.

rail[1] *n* **1** a fixed horizontal bar, serving as a barrier or from which something may be hung. **2** either of a pair of lengths of steel forming the running surface for trains or other wheeled vehicles. **3** the railway. ✳ **go off the rails 1** *informal* to behave strangely or become mentally unbalanced. **2** *informal* to be misguided or mistaken.

rail² *v* (*often* + off) to enclose or separate (an area) with a rail or rails.

rail³ *v* (*often* + against/at) to utter angry complaints or abuse.

railhead *n* the farthest point reached by a railway.

railing *n* a fence or similar barrier made of rails.

raillery *n* good-humoured teasing.

railroad¹ *n NAmer* a railway.

railroad² *v informal* to hustle into taking action or making a decision.

railway *n chiefly Brit* **1** a track usu having two parallel rails on which trains run. **2** a railway network or the organization that runs it.

raiment *n archaic or literary* clothing.

rain¹ *n* **1** water falling in drops condensed from vapour in the atmosphere. **2** rainy weather. **3** (*in pl*) the rainy season. **4** a dense flow or fall of something.

rain² *v* **1** of rain: to fall in drops from the clouds. **2** to fall or bestow in profusion. ✳ **rain cats and dogs** to rain heavily.

rainbow *n* a multicoloured arch in the sky formed by the refraction of the sun's rays in raindrops, spray, etc.

raincoat *n* a coat made from waterproof material.

rainfall *n* the amount of rain that has fallen.

rainforest *n* a dense tropical woodland with a heavy annual rainfall.

rain off *v* (*usu* **be rained off**) to be prevented or interrupted by rain.

rainy *adj* (-ier, -iest) characterized by heavy rainfall.

rainy day *n* a future time when money or other things may be in short supply.

raise¹ *v* **1** to lift to a higher position. **2** to bring to an upright position. **3** to increase the amount, level, strength, intensity, etc of. **4** to bring up (a subject) for consideration or debate. **5** to express (*esp* a doubt or objection). **6** to collect (e.g. money). **7** to cause to occur or appear. **8** to rear (a child or an animal). **9** to grow or cultivate (crops or other plants). **10** to multiply (a quantity) by itself a number of times so as to produce a specified power. **11** *Brit, informal* to establish radio or telephone communication with (a person or place). ✳ **raise hell 1** *informal* to create a disturbance. **2** *informal* to complain angrily about something. **raise the roof** *informal* to make a loud noise, *esp* by cheering.

raise² *n chiefly NAmer* an increase in salary; a rise.

raisin *n* a dried grape.

raison d'être /ˌrayzon(h) 'detrə/ *n* (*pl* **raisons d'être** /ˌrayzon(h) 'detrə/) the main reason that something or somebody exists.

Raj *n* (**the Raj**) British rule in India before 1947.

rajah *or* **raja** *n* an Indian or Malayan prince or chief.

rake¹ *n* a long-handled implement with a row of prongs on the head for gathering grass, leaves etc or for loosening or levelling the ground.

rake² *v* **1** to gather or level with a rake. **2** to scrape, e.g. in passing. **3** to sweep the length of, e.g. with gunfire. **4** (+ through) to search through.

rake³ *n* inclination from the perpendicular; a sloping angle.

rake⁴ *v* to set at an angle from the perpendicular.

rake⁵ *n* a dissolute man, *esp* in fashionable society.

rake in *v informal* to earn or gain (money) rapidly or in abundance.

rake up *v* to revive (something long and often best forgotten).

rakish *adj* **1** of a car, boat, etc: smart, stylish, and suggestive of speed. **2** suggestive of a lively or rather disreputable personality.

rally¹ *v* (-ies, -ied) **1** to bring or come together for a common cause. **2** to come or bring together again to renew an effort. **3** to recover from illness, a state of depression, etc. **4** of e.g. shares: to recover value after a fall. **5** to drive in a rally. ✳ **rally round** to give practical or emotional support.

rally² *n* (*pl* **-ies**) **1** a mass meeting of people supporting a common cause. **2** a motor race over public roads or countryside tracks, designed to test driving and navigational skills. **3** a recovery of strength, courage, value, etc. **4** a series of strokes interchanged between players, e.g. in tennis.

ram¹ *n* **1** an uncastrated male sheep. **2** a battering ram. **3** the weight that strikes the blow in a pile driver.

ram² *v* (**rammed, ramming**) **1** to force down or in by driving, pressing, or pushing. **2** to strike against (something) violently and usu head-on. ✳ **ram something down somebody's throat** to force somebody to accept or listen to something.

Ramadan *n* the ninth month of the Muslim year, during which Muslims fast daily from dawn to sunset.

ramble¹ *v* **1** to walk for pleasure in the countryside. **2** to talk or write in a disconnected long-winded fashion. ➤ **rambler** *n*, **rambling** *adj and n*.

ramble² *n* a leisurely walk taken for pleasure in the countryside.

ramekin *or* **ramequin** *n* an individual baking and serving dish.

ramification *n* (*usu in pl*) a wide-reaching and complex consequence.

ramp *n* **1** a slope leading from one level to another. **2** a stairway for entering or leaving an aircraft. **3** *Brit* a point where roadworks cause a rise or fall in the level of the road.

rampage[1] *v* to rush about wildly or violently.

rampage[2] *n* * **on the rampage** behaving in a wild or violent way.

rampant *adj* **1** spreading or growing unchecked. **2** of a heraldic animal: rearing up on one hind leg with forelegs extended.

rampart *n* a broad embankment or wall built as a fortification.

ram raid *n* a robbery in which entrance is gained to a building by driving a vehicle through the front window. ➤ **ram-raider** *n*.

ramrod *n* a rod for ramming home the charge in a muzzle-loading firearm.

ramshackle *adj* badly constructed or needing repair.

ran *v* past tense of RUN[1].

ranch *n* a large farm for raising livestock, *esp* in North America. ➤ **rancher** *n*.

rancid *adj* of food: smelling or tasting unpleasantly sour.

rancour (*NAmer* **rancor**) *n* bitter and deep-seated ill will or hatred. ➤ **rancorous** *adj*.

rand *n* (*pl* **rand**) the basic monetary unit of South Africa.

R & B *abbr* rhythm and blues.

random *adj* lacking a definite plan, purpose, or pattern; occurring or selected by chance. * **at random** without a definite aim, rule, or method; unpredictably. ➤ **randomly** *adv*, **randomness** *n*.

randy *adj* (**-ier**, **-iest**) *chiefly Brit, informal* sexually aroused; lustful.

rang *v* past tense of RING[3].

range[1] *n* **1** a sequence or series between limits. **2** a number of individual people or objects forming a distinct class or series. **3** the distance or extent covered or within which something functions. **4** the distance between a weapon and target, a camera and subject, etc. **5** a large connected group of mountains. **6** an open region over which livestock may roam and feed, *esp* in North America. **7** a place where something, *esp* shooting, is practised. **8** a large cooking stove with one or more ovens and a flat metal top for heating pans.

range[2] *v* **1** to change or differ within limits. **2** to travel or roam at large or freely. **3** to include a large number of topics. **4** to set in a particular order or position. * **be ranged against** to oppose.

ranger *n* a keeper of a park or forest.

rangy *adj* (**-ier**, **-iest**) **1** of a person: tall and slender. **2** of an animal: long-limbed and long-bodied.

rank[1] *n* **1** a degree or position in a hierarchy or order, *esp* in the armed forces. **2** high social position. **3** a row or series of people or things, *esp* a line of soldiers standing side by side. **4** (**the ranks**) the ordinary members of an armed force as distinguished from the officers. * **close ranks** to unite to resist a threat. **pull rank** to make use of one's senior position to compel somebody to do something.

rank[2] *v* **1** to have a position in relation to others. **2** to arrange in lines. **3** to determine the relative position of; to rate.

rank[3] *adj* **1** offensive in odour or flavour. **2** of vegetation: excessively vigorous in growth. **3** absolute or complete.

rank and file *n* the ordinary members of an organization, etc as distinguished from the leaders.

rankle *v* to cause continuing anger, irritation, or bitterness.

ransack *v* **1** to go through (a place) stealing things and causing general chaos. **2** to search thoroughly.

ransom[1] *n* a price paid or demanded for the release of a captured or kidnapped person. * **hold to ransom 1** to kidnap (somebody) and demand money for their release. **2** to try to make somebody do something by threatening to cause harm.

ransom[2] *v* to free from captivity by paying a ransom.

rant *v* to talk in a wild or declamatory manner.

rap[1] *n* **1** a sharp blow or knock, or the sound made by it. **2** a sharp rebuke or criticism. **3** (**the rap**) *informal* the responsibility for or adverse consequences of an action. **4** *chiefly NAmer, informal* a criminal charge. * **a rap on/over the knuckles** *informal* a scolding.

rap[2] *v* (**rapped, rapping**) **1** to strike with a sharp blow. **2** to strike against something hard. **3** (+ out) to utter (e.g. a command) abruptly and forcibly. **4** *informal* to criticize sharply.

rap[3] *n* a type of pop music characterized by rapidly chanted lyrics accompanied by electronic music with a heavy beat. ➤ **rapper** *n*.

rapacious *adj* ferociously grasping or covetous. ➤ **rapaciously** *adv*, **rapacity** *n*.

rape[1] *n* **1** the crime of forcing somebody to have sexual intercourse against their will. **2** the act of despoiling: *the rape of the countryside*.

rape[2] *v* **1** of a man: to commit rape on. **2** to treat in a violent or destructive way.

rape[3] *n* a plant with bright yellow flowers grown for its oil-rich seeds.

rapid[1] *adj* moving, acting, or occurring with speed. ➤ **rapidity** *n*, **rapidly** *adv*.

rapid[2] *n* (*usu in pl*) a part of a river where the water flows swiftly over a rocky slope.

rapier *n* a straight sword with a narrow pointed blade.

rapist *n* a man who commits rape.

rapport /ra'paw/ *n* a sympathetic or harmonious relationship.

rapprochement /ra'proshmonh/ *n* the re-establishment of cordial relations.

rapscallion *n archaic* a rascal.

rapt *adj* completely engrossed.

rapture *n* **1** great joy; ecstasy. **2** (*usu in pl*) an expression of extreme happiness or enthusiasm.

rapturous *adj* feeling or expressing great joy or pleasure. ➤ **rapturously** *adv*.

rare¹ *adj* **1** seldom occurring or found. **2** marked by unusual quality or appeal. ➤ **rareness** *n*.

rare² *adj* of red meat: cooked lightly so that the inside is still red.

rarebit *n* = WELSH RAREBIT.

rare earth *n* any of a series of metallic elements with atomic numbers from 58 to 71, e.g. lanthanum.

rarefied *adj* **1** of air or the atmosphere: of a density that is lower than normal; thin. **2** distant from ordinary reality and practical concerns; esoteric or abstruse.

raring *adj informal* full of enthusiasm or eagerness to do something.

rarity *n* (*pl* **-ies**) **1** the state of being rare. **2** a rare person or thing.

rascal *n* **1** a mischievous person. **2** an unprincipled or dishonest person. ➤ **rascally** *adj*.

rash¹ *adj* acting with or resulting from undue haste or impetuosity. ➤ **rashly** *adv*, **rashness** *n*.

rash² *n* **1** an outbreak of red spots or patches on the body. **2** a large number of instances of something during a short period.

rasher *n* a thin slice of bacon.

rasp¹ *v* **1** to file with a rasp. **2** to utter in a harsh tone. **3** to make a grating sound.

rasp² *n* **1** a coarse file. **2** a grating sound.

raspberry *n* (*pl* **-ies**) **1** a reddish pink edible berry. **2** *informal* a rude sound made by sticking the tongue out and blowing noisily.

Rasta *n and adj informal* = RASTAFARIAN.

Rastafarian *n* a member of a religious and political movement among black West Indians that takes the former Emperor of Ethiopia, Haile Selassie, to be God. ➤ **Rastafarianism** *n*.

rat¹ *n* **1** a rodent resembling but considerably larger than a mouse. **2** *informal* a contemptible person, *esp* somebody who betrays or deserts friends or associates.

rat² *v* (**ratted, ratting**) **1** to catch or hunt rats. **2** *informal* to desert one's party or cause. **3** *informal* (+ on) to betray or inform on one's associates. **4** *informal* (+ on) to default on an agreement. ➤ **ratting** *n*.

ratatouille /ratə'tooh-i/ *n* a vegetable stew typically containing tomatoes, onions, aubergines, courgettes, and peppers.

ratchet *n* a mechanism that consists of a bar or wheel with angled teeth into which a cog, etc drops so that motion is allowed in one direction only.

rate¹ *n* **1** a quantity or frequency of something measured per unit of something else. **2** a fixed charge, payment, or price. **3** speed of movement, change, development, etc. **4** (*usu in pl*) a tax based on property values, levied by a British local authority formerly on domestic and business premises, now only on businesses. ✻ **at any rate** in any case; anyway.

rate² *v* **1** to assign a relative rank or class to. **2** to consider to be of a particular standard. **3** to be worthy of. **4** *informal* to think highly of.

rate³ *v archaic* to scold angrily; to berate.

rateable or **ratable** *adj* capable of being rated or estimated.

rather *adv* **1** more readily or willingly; sooner: *I'd rather not go*. **2** to some degree; somewhat. **3** more properly, reasonably, or truly. **4** on the contrary; instead.

ratify *v* (**-ies, -ied**) to approve or confirm (e.g. a treaty) formally, so that it can come into force. ➤ **ratification** *n*.

rating *n* **1** a classification according to grade. **2** (*in pl*) an index that lists television programmes, etc in order of popularity. **3** *Brit* a noncommissioned sailor, *esp* an ordinary seaman.

ratio *n* (*pl* **-os**) the relationship in quantity or degree between one thing and another; proportion.

ratiocinate *v formal* to reason logically. ➤ **ratiocination** *n*.

ration¹ *n* **1** a share or amount, e.g. of food in short supply, that somebody is allowed. **2** (*in pl*) regular supplies of food given to troops.

ration² *v* **1** to limit (a person or commodity) to a fixed ration. **2** to use sparingly.

rational *adj* **1** based on or compatible with reason; reasonable. **2** endowed with the ability to think logically. ➤ **rationality** *n*, **rationally** *adv*.

rationale /rashə'nahl/ *n* a logical basis for or explanation of beliefs, actions, or phenomena.

rationalism *n* the belief that reason, not emotion, intuition, religion, etc, should govern the actions that people take. ➤ **rationalist** *adj* and *n*, **rationalistic** *adj*.

rationalize or **-ise** *v* **1** to attribute (e.g. one's actions) to rational and creditable motives in order to justify conduct. **2** to increase the efficiency of (e.g. an industry) by more effective organization. ➤ **rationalization** *n*.

rat race *n informal* a fiercely competitive struggle, e.g. to progress in a career or survive the pressures of modern life.

rat run *n Brit, informal* a minor road used by drivers to avoid congestion.

rattan n a tropical climbing palm tree with long tough stems used for furniture and wickerwork.

rattle[1] v 1 to make a succession of short sharp knocking or jangling sounds when shaken. 2 informal to upset or make anxious. 3 (+ off) to say or perform in a brisk lively fashion. 4 (often + on) to chatter incessantly and aimlessly.

rattle[2] n 1 a rattling sound. 2 a device or toy that produces a rattling sound.

rattlesnake n an American poisonous snake with horny joints at the end of its tail that rattle when shaken.

ratty adj (-ier, -iest) 1 Brit, informal irritable. 2 informal dilapidated or shabby.

raucous adj disagreeably harsh or strident. ➤ **raucously** adv.

raunchy adj (-ier, -iest) informal sexually suggestive.

ravage[1] v to wreak havoc on; to devastate.

ravage[2] n (usu in pl) damage resulting from ravaging.

rave[1] v 1 to talk irrationally, esp in delirium. 2 to talk or write with passionate enthusiasm.

rave[2] n chiefly Brit, informal a very large organized party with dancing to loud electronic music.

raven[1] n a very large black bird of the crow family.

raven[2] adj of a glossy black colour.

ravening adj literary fiercely greedy or predatory.

ravenous adj extremely hungry. ➤ **ravenously** adv.

raver n informal an uninhibited person who enjoys a wild social life.

rave-up n Brit, informal a wild party.

ravine n a narrow steep-sided valley.

raving[1] n (usu in pl) a burst of irrational or incoherent speech.

raving[2] adj and adv informal used as an intensifier: great or greatly.

ravioli /ravi'ohli/ pl n pasta in the form of little cases containing meat, cheese, etc.

ravish v archaic or literary 1 to fill with joy, delight, etc. 2 to rape.

ravishing adj extremely beautiful.

raw[1] adj 1 not cooked. 2 not processed or purified; still in its natural state. 3 of data: not analysed or modified. 4 having the surface abraded or chafed. 5 sensitive. 6 of emotion: not refined or disguised in the least; crude. 7 lacking experience, training, etc. 8 disagreeably damp or cold. ➤ **rawness** n.

raw[2] n (**the raw**) a sensitive place or state.

rawboned adj lean and having prominent bones.

ray[1] n 1 a narrow beam of radiant energy, e.g. light or X-rays. 2 a slight manifestation or trace: a ray of hope.

ray[2] n a fish with a flat body, winglike pectoral fins, and a long narrow tail.

rayon n a fabric made from cellulose fibre.

raze or **rase** v to destroy (e.g. a town or building) completely.

razor n a sharp-edged cutting implement for shaving hair.

razzle * **on the razzle** informal enjoying a spell of partying or drinking.

razzmatazz or **razzamatazz** n informal a noisy, colourful, and showy atmosphere or activity.

Rb abbr the chemical symbol for rubidium.

RC abbr Roman Catholic.

Re abbr the chemical symbol for rhenium.

re prep with regard to.

re- prefix 1 again or anew: reprint. 2 back or to a previous state: recede; restore.

reach[1] v 1 to make a stretch with one's hand. 2 to touch or grasp by extending a part of the body. 3 to extend to. 4 to achieve or arrive at. 5 to contact or communicate with. ➤ **reachable** adj.

reach[2] n 1 the extent of somebody's ability to reach. 2 range, e.g. of somebody's comprehension. 3 (often in pl) a continuous stretch or expanse, esp a straight portion of a river.

react v 1 to respond to something in a particular way. 2 to undergo chemical reaction or physical change.

reaction n 1 a mental or emotional response to circumstances. 2 a bodily response to a stimulus. 3 tendency towards a former and usu outmoded political or social order. 4 a chemical transformation, esp interaction between atoms, molecules, etc to form new substances. 5 in physics, the equal and opposing force exerted by something subjected to the action of a force.

reactionary[1] adj opposing social or political change.

reactionary[2] n (pl -ies) a reactionary person.

reactivate v to make active again. ➤ **reactivation** n.

reactor n an apparatus in which a controlled chain reaction takes place, esp for the production of nuclear power.

read[1] v (past tense and past part. **read**) 1 to look at and understand (e.g. words). 2 to utter aloud (printed or written words). 3 to be worded or phrased in a particular way. 4 to understand the nature of by observing outward expression or signs. 5 (often + into) to attribute a sometimes non-existent meaning to; to interpret. 6 to look at the measurement shown on (e.g. a dial or gauge). 7 to indicate (a specified measurement). 8 chiefly Brit to study (a subject), esp for a degree. * **read between the lines** to work out the implicit meaning of something, rather than what is actually written. **take**

something as read to accept something as agreed. ➢ **reader** n.

read² n *informal* something to read considered in terms of the interest, enjoyment, etc it provides.

readership n the readers of a particular publication or author.

readily adv 1 without hesitating; willingly. 2 easily.

reading n 1 an event at which something is read to an audience. 2 material read or intended for reading. 3 a particular interpretation. 4 the value indicated by an instrument.

readjust v 1 to adapt to new or changing circumstances. 2 to adjust (e.g. a control) to a new setting. ➢ **readjustment** n.

ready¹ adj (-ier, -iest) 1 prepared for an experience or action. 2 prepared or available for immediate use. 3 willing. 4 likely or about to do the specified thing. 5 spontaneously prompt. ➢ **readiness** n.

ready² v (-ies, -ied) to prepare.

ready³ n (pl -ies) (readies *or* the ready) *Brit, informal* available money. * **at the ready** available for immediate use.

reagent n a substance that takes part in or brings about a particular chemical reaction.

real¹ adj 1 actual, genuine, or authentic. 2 significant. 3 used chiefly for emphasis: complete or great: *Her visit was a real surprise.*

real² adv *chiefly NAmer, Scot, informal* very.

real estate n *chiefly NAmer* property in the form of buildings and land.

realign v 1 to align again or in a different way. 2 to become part of a different *esp* political grouping. ➢ **realignment** n.

realism n 1 concern for fact or reality and rejection of the impractical or visionary. 2 representation of things in art and literature in a way that is true to nature. ➢ **realist** adj and n.

realistic adj 1 basing aims or opinions on known facts or reasonable expectations. 2 depicting things in a way that seems real. ➢ **realistically** adv.

reality n (pl -ies) 1 the state of being real. 2 a real entity or state of affairs. 3 the totality of real things and events.

reality TV *or* **reality television** n television programmes whose entertainment value is based on the spontaneous reactions of a group of real people placed in a particular situation.

realize *or* **-ise** v 1 to be or become fully aware of. 2 to cause to become a reality; to accomplish. 3 to convert (property, assets, etc) into actual money. 4 to earn (money) by sale, investment, or effort. ➢ **realization** n.

really¹ adv 1 in reality; actually. 2 without question; thoroughly.

really² interj used as an expression of surprise or indignation.

realm n 1 a kingdom. 2 (*also in pl*) a domain or sphere.

real tennis n an early form of tennis, played with a racket and a solid ball in an irregularly-shaped indoor court.

ream n 1 a quantity of paper equal to 500 sheets. 2 (*usu in pl*) a great amount, e.g. of something written or printed.

reap v 1 to cut or harvest (a crop). 2 to obtain or win, *esp* as the reward for effort.

reaper n a person or machine that harvests crops. * **the reaper/grim reaper** death, *esp* personified as a skeleton wielding a scythe.

rear¹ n 1 the back part of something. 2 *informal* the buttocks. * **bring up the rear** to be the last in a group, series, etc.

rear² adj at the back.

rear³ v 1 to breed (an animal) for use or sale. 2 to bring up (a child). 3 (*often + up*) *esp* of a horse: to rise up on the hind legs. 4 (+ up) to react with anger, indignation, or resentment. 5 *literary* (*usu + up/over*) to rise to a height.

rear admiral n a naval officer ranking below a vice admiral.

rear guard n a military detachment for guarding the rear of a main force.

rearm v to arm (e.g. a nation or military force) again, *esp* with new or better weapons. ➢ **rearmament** n.

rearrange v to arrange differently. ➢ **rearrangement** n.

reason¹ n 1 an explanation or justification. 2 a rational ground or motive. 3 a cause. 4 the power of thinking, *esp* in an orderly rational way. 5 sanity. 6 sensible or logical thinking. * **it stands to reason** it is obvious or reasonable. **listen to reason** to be willing to accept advice to act sensibly. **within reason** within reasonable limits.

reason² v 1 to use the faculty of reason to arrive at conclusions. 2 (+ with) to talk or argue with another person so as to influence or persuade them. ➢ **reasoning** n.

reasonable adj 1 moderate or fair; not extreme or excessive. 2 in accord with reason; logical. 3 sensible. ➢ **reasonably** adv.

reassure v to restore confidence to; to calm. ➢ **reassurance** n, **reassuring** adj.

rebarbative adj *formal* repellent or unattractive.

rebate n 1 a return of part of a payment. 2 a deduction from a sum before payment.

rebel¹ n somebody who rebels against a government, authority, convention, etc.

rebel² v (rebelled, rebelling) 1 to oppose or disobey authority or control. 2 to carry out armed resistance to a government. 3 to feel or show opposition or revulsion.

rebellion n 1 opposition to authority or dominance. 2 a campaign of open armed resistance to an established government.

rebellious adj given to or engaged in rebellion.
➤ **rebelliously** adv.

rebirth n a renaissance or revival.

reborn adj 1 brought back to life. 2 regenerated or spiritually renewed.

rebound[1] v 1 to spring back on collision or impact with another body. 2 to return to an original strong or healthy state after a setback, illness, etc. 3 (often + on) to have unexpected adverse effects.

rebound[2] n a shot or ball that rebounds. * **on the rebound** while in an unsettled or emotional state resulting from a setback, the end of a relationship, etc.

rebuff[1] v to reject or refuse sharply.

rebuff[2] n a curt rejection or refusal.

rebuild v (past tense and past part. **rebuilt**) 1 to build again, esp after damage or destruction. 2 to make extensive changes to.

rebuke[1] v to criticize severely; to reprimand.

rebuke[2] n a reprimand.

rebus n a representation of words or syllables by pictures that suggest the same sound.

rebut v (**rebutted, rebutting**) to disprove or expose the falsity of (e.g. a claim). ➤ **rebuttal** n.

recalcitrant adj defiant of authority or restraint; uncooperative. ➤ **recalcitrance** n.

recall[1] v 1 to remember. 2 to make somebody think of. 3 to summon (somebody) back officially. 4 to request the return of (a faulty product) to the manufacturer.

recall[2] n 1 a summons to return or a request to return something. 2 remembrance or ability to remember.

recant v to withdraw or renounce (a statement or belief). ➤ **recantation** n.

recap v (**recapped, recapping**) Informal = RECAPITULATE.

recapitulate v to repeat the principal points of (an argument, discourse, etc); to sum up.

recapture v 1 to capture again. 2 to recreate or experience again. ➤ **recapture** n.

recast v (past tense and past part. **recast**) to remodel or refashion.

recce n chiefly Brit, informal a reconnaissance.

recede v 1 to move back or away. 2 to slant backwards: a receding chin. 3 of hair or a hairline: to stop growing around the temples and above the forehead. 4 to diminish.

receipt n 1 a written acknowledgment of having received goods or money. 2 the act of receiving. 3 (usu in pl) something, esp money, received.

receive v 1 to acquire or be given. 2 to take delivery of. 3 chiefly Brit, informal to buy and sell (stolen goods). 4 to convert (an incoming signal, esp radio waves) into a form suitable for human perception. 5 to act in response to. 6 to elicit (a particular response). 7 to suffer or be

forced to experience. 8 to admit, greet, or entertain formally.

received adj accepted as authoritative or true: received wisdom.

Received Pronunciation n the form of British English pronunciation used by many educated people in southeastern England and widely regarded as standard.

receiver n 1 a radio, television, or other part of a communications system that receives the signal. 2 the part of a telephone that contains the mouthpiece and earpiece. 3 a person appointed to administer the affairs of a business that is being wound up. 4 somebody who or something that receives. ➤ **receivership** n.

recent adj 1 of a time not long past. 2 having lately come into existence. ➤ **recently** adv.

receptacle n an object that receives and contains something.

reception n 1 the act of receiving. 2 a formal social gathering during which guests are received. 3 an office or desk where visitors or clients are received on arrival. 4 a response or reaction. 5 the quality of the radio or television signal received.

receptionist n a person employed to greet and assist callers or clients, e.g. at an office or hotel.

receptive adj able or inclined to receive, esp open and responsive to ideas, impressions, or suggestions. ➤ **receptivity** n.

receptor n a cell or group of cells in the body that receives stimuli from the environment, e.g. light, sound, etc, which are then transmitted as nerve impulses.

recess[1] n 1 an alcove or niche. 2 (in pl) hidden, secret, or secluded places. 3 a suspension of business or activity, e.g. of a legislative body or law court, usu for a period of rest.

recess[2] v to make a recess in (e.g. a wall).

recession n a period of reduced economic activity and prosperity.

recessive adj of a gene or inherited characteristic: suppressed if the contrasting dominant gene or characteristic is present.

recharge v to charge (esp a battery) again. ➤ **rechargeable** adj.

recherché /rəˈsheashay/ adj 1 obscure or rare. 2 pretentious or affected.

recidivist n somebody who relapses, esp into criminal behaviour. ➤ **recidivism** n.

recipe /ˈresipi/ n 1 a list of ingredients and instructions for making a food dish. 2 a procedure likely to result in the specified thing: a recipe for success.

recipient n somebody who receives something.

reciprocal adj 1 felt or shown by both sides; mutual. 2 given or done in return. ➤ **reciprocally** adv.

reciprocate *v* to return (a thing, feeling, treatment, etc of the same kind as has been previously given or shown to one). ➤ **reciprocation** *n*.

reciprocity *n* a situation in which help, privileges, etc are mutually exchanged.

recital *n* **1** a concert given by a musician or a small group of musicians. **2** a detailed account.

recite *v* **1** to repeat from memory or read aloud. **2** to relate in detail; to enumerate. ➤ **recitation** *n*.

reckless *adj* marked by lack of proper caution; careless of consequences. ➤ **recklessly** *adv*, **recklessness** *n*.

reckon *v* **1** to estimate or calculate. **2** to consider or think of in a specified way. **3** *informal* to suppose or think. **4** (+ on) to expect or rely on.
✳ **reckon with** to take into account. **reckon without** to fail to take into account. **to be reckoned with** of considerable power or importance.

reckoning *n* **1** the act of calculating or estimating. **2** *archaic* an account or bill. **3** events regarded as retribution for earlier behaviour.
✳ **into/out of the reckoning** included among/omitted from the things or people to be considered.

reclaim *v* **1** to get back; to recover. **2** to make (e.g. submerged or waste land) available for human use. **3** to obtain (a useful substance) from a waste product. ➤ **reclamation** *n*.

recline *v* **1** to lean backwards. **2** to be in a relaxed position.

recluse *n* somebody who deliberately avoids company and leads a solitary life. ➤ **reclusive** *adj*.

recognition *n* **1** the act of recognizing. **2** acknowledgment or reward for one's efforts, talents, etc.

recognize *or* **-ise** *v* **1** to perceive to be something or somebody previously known or encountered. **2** to acknowledge the status, validity, independence, etc of. **3** to show appreciation of, e.g. by praise or reward. ➤ **recognizable** *adj*.

recoil[1] *v* **1** to shrink back physically or emotionally: e.g. in horror, fear, or disgust. **2** of a firearm: to move backwards sharply when fired. **3** (+ on/upon) to have unexpected adverse effects on the doer.

recoil[2] *n* the act of recoiling.

recollect *v* **1** to remember. **2** to bring (oneself) back to a state of composure or concentration. ➤ **recollection** *n*.

recommend *v* **1** to declare to be suitable, competent, etc or worth trying. **2** to advise (a course of action). **3** to make acceptable or desirable: *The school has other things to recommend it.* ➤ **recommendation** *n*.

recompense[1] *v* **1** to pay or reward , e.g. for a service rendered. **2** to compensate for damage incurred.

recompense[2] *n* a return for something done, suffered, or given.

reconcile *v* **1** to restore (e.g. opposing factions) to friendship or harmony. **2** to settle or resolve (e.g. differences of opinion). **3** (+ with) to make (something) consistent or compatible with something else. **4** (+ to) to persuade (somebody) to submit to or accept something.

reconciliation *n* **1** a return to friendly relations after conflict. **2** the act of reconciling e.g. differences of opinion or opposing ideas.

recondite *adj* known only by a few people; obscure.

recondition *v* *Brit* to restore to good working condition, e.g. by replacing parts.

reconnaissance /ri'konəs(ə)ns/ *n* an exploratory military survey of enemy territory or positions.

reconnoitre (*NAmer* **reconnoiter**) /rekə'nɔɪtə/ *v* (**reconnoitres, reconnoitred, reconnoitring,** *NAmer* **reconnoiters, reconnoitered, reconnoitering**) to make a reconnaissance of (e.g. an enemy position or a region of land).

reconsider *v* to consider again, *esp* with a view to changing the original decision. ➤ **reconsideration** *n*.

reconstitute *v* **1** to reestablish or thoroughly reorganize. **2** to restore (dried food, etc) to its natural state by adding water. ➤ **reconstitution** *n*.

reconstruct *v* **1** to rebuild. **2** to reorganize or reestablish. **3** to build up a mental image of or reenact (e.g. a crime or a battle) on the basis of available evidence. ➤ **reconstruction** *n*.

record[1] *v* **1** to commit (something) to writing, film, etc so as to supply evidence of it. **2** to register by mechanical or other means. **3** to indicate (a measurement on a scale). **4** to give evidence of; to show. **5** to convert (e.g. sound) into a permanent form for reproduction.

record[2] *n* **1** a permanent account of something that serves as evidence of it. **2** a body of known or recorded facts regarding something or somebody. **3** a list of previous criminal convictions. **4** a performance, occurrence, etc that goes beyond all others of its kind; *esp* the best recorded performance in a competitive sport. **5** a flat plastic disc with a spiral groove encoding musical or other sounds for reproduction.
✳ **for the record** to be reported as official. **off the record** not for publication. **put/set the record straight** to correct a mistake or misapprehension.

recorder *n* **1** something that records. **2** a person who keeps official records. **3** a simple woodwind instrument consisting of a tube with usu eight finger holes and a mouthpiece.

recording *n* something, e.g. sound or a television programme, that has been recorded.

record player *n* an apparatus for playing records.

recount[1] *v* to relate in detail.

recount[2] *v* to count again.

recount[3] *n* a second or fresh counting, *esp* of votes.

recoup *v* to regain or make up for (something lost).

recourse *n* **1** a source of help or strength. **2** (+ to) the use of somebody or something for help or protection.

recover *v* **1** to regain possession or use of. **2** to regain a normal or stable condition, *esp* of health. **3** to make up for (e.g. losses). ➤ **recoverable** *adj*.

recovery *n* (*pl* **-ies**) **1** a return to normal health. **2** a regaining of balance or control, e.g. after a stumble or mistake. **3** an economic upturn, e.g. after a depression. **4** the act of recovering something.

recreate *v* to reproduce exactly.

recreation *n* pleasurable activity engaged in for relaxation or enjoyment. ➤ **recreational** *adj*.

recrimination *n* (*usu in pl*) an accusation of wrongdoing made against somebody who has made a similar accusation.

recrudescence *n formal* a new outbreak or recurrence.

recruit[1] *n* a newcomer to an occupation or activity, *esp* a newly enlisted member of the armed forces.

recruit[2] *v* to enlist (a person) as a new member of the armed forces or a workforce. ➤ **recruitment** *n*.

rectal *adj* relating to the rectum.

rectangle *n* a polygon with four right angles and four sides, *esp* one with adjacent sides of different lengths. ➤ **rectangular** *adj*.

rectify *v* (**-ies, -ied**) **1** to put right; to remedy or correct. **2** to convert (alternating current) to direct current. ➤ **rectification** *n*.

rectilinear *adj* **1** moving in a straight line. **2** characterized by straight lines.

rectitude *n formal* moral integrity.

recto *n* (*pl* **-os**) a right-hand page.

rector *n* **1** a priest in charge of a parish. **2** the head of a university or college.

rectory *n* (*pl* **-ies**) a rector's residence.

rectum *n* (*pl* **rectums** *or* **recta**) the last part of the intestine, ending at the anus.

recumbent *adj* lying down or reclining.

recuperate *v* **1** to regain a former healthy state or condition. **2** to regain (something lost). ➤ **recuperation** *n*.

recur *v* (**recurred, recurring**) to occur again, *esp* repeatedly or after an interval. ➤ **recurrence** *n*.

recurrent *adj* happening repeatedly or periodically.

recycle *v* **1** to convert (sewage, waste paper, glass, etc) back into a useful product. **2** to reuse. ➤ **recyclable** *adj*.

red[1] *adj* (**redder, reddest**) **1** of the colour of blood or a ruby. **2** of hair or fur: of a colour between orange and brown. **3** of the face: flushed, *esp* with anger or embarrassment. **4** of wine: made from dark grapes and coloured by their skins. **5** *informal, derog* communist or socialist. ➤ **reddish** *adj*.

red[2] *n* **1** a red colour. **2** *informal, derog* a communist or socialist. ✳ **in the red** not in credit; insolvent. **see red** *informal* to become angry suddenly.

red-blooded *adj* full of vigour; virile.

red card *n* a red card held up by a football referee to indicate the sending-off of a player.

red carpet *n* a long piece of red carpet for an important guest to walk on.

redcurrant *n* a small red edible berry.

redden *v* to make or become red.

redeem *v* **1** to offset the bad effect of. **2** to atone for (a mistake, error of judgment, etc). **3** to release from blame or debt. **4** to free from the consequences of sin or evil. **5** to make up for an earlier poor performance or wrongdoing by (oneself). **6** to get or buy back, e.g. by repaying a loan or debt. **7** to convert (trading stamps, tokens, etc) into money or goods. **8** to fulfil (e.g. a promise).

Redeemer *n* **1** (**the Redeemer**) Jesus Christ. **2** (**redeemer**) a person who redeems somebody or something.

redemption *n* the act of redeeming or the fact of being redeemed.

redeploy *v* to transfer (e.g. troops or workers) from one area or activity to another. ➤ **redeployment** *n*.

red-faced *adj* flushed with embarrassment.

red-handed *adj* in the act of committing a crime or misdeed.

redhead *n* a person with red hair.

red herring *n* something irrelevant that distracts attention from the real issue.

red-hot *adj* **1** glowing red with heat. **2** very intense, exciting, or popular.

Red Indian *n dated, offensive* a Native American.

red-letter day *n* a day of special significance, *esp* a particularly happy occasion.

red-light district *n* a district that has many brothels.

redneck *n NAmer, informal, derog* **1** a white rural working-class person from the southern USA. **2** a bigoted reactionary.

redolent *adj* **1** (+ of/with) suggestive; evocative. **2** (+ of/with) having a specified smell. ➤ **redolence** *n*.

redouble v to make or become greater or more intense.

redoubt n a small usu temporary fortified structure.

redoubtable adj arousing fear or respect; formidable.

redound v formal (+ to) to lead or contribute to something.

redress[1] v 1 to set right. 2 to adjust and make equal again.

redress[2] n action or payment to compensate for wrong or loss.

redskin n dated, offensive a Native American.

red tape n excessively complex bureaucratic routines that result in delay.

reduce v 1 to make or become less. 2 to lower the price of. 3 (+ to) to bring or force to a specified state or condition. 4 (+ to) to change to a simpler or more basic form. 5 to make more concentrated, e.g. by boiling. ➤ **reducible** adj.

reduction n 1 the act of reducing. 2 the amount by which something is reduced.

reductive adj expressing complex data or phenomena in simplified or oversimplified terms.

redundant adj 1 no longer useful or necessary. 2 excessive, esp excessively wordy. 3 chiefly Brit no longer required for a job. ➤ **redundancy** n.

redwood n a very tall American pine tree with reddish wood.

reed n 1 a tall grass that grows in wet or marshy areas. 2 a thin piece of cane, metal, or plastic, fastened over an air opening in e.g. an oboe or clarinet, which produces a sound by vibration.

reedy adj (-ier, -iest) 1 full of of reeds. 2 of a voice: thin and high.

reef[1] n a ridge of rocks, sand, or coral at or near the surface of water.

reef[2] n a part of a sail taken in or let out to regulate the area exposed to the wind.

reef[3] v to reduce the area of (a sail) by taking in a portion.

reefer n informal a cannabis cigarette.

reefer jacket n a close-fitting double-breasted jacket of thick cloth.

reef knot n a secure symmetrical knot.

reek[1] v 1 to have a strong or offensive smell. 2 (+ of/with) to give a strong impression of some undesirable quality or feature.

reek[2] n a strong or disagreeable smell.

reel[1] n 1 a spool for thread, film, tape, cable, etc. 2 a quantity of something wound on a reel.

reel[2] v (+ in) to draw (something) towards one by turning a reel.

reel[3] v 1 to be giddy or bewildered. 2 to walk or move unsteadily.

reel[4] n a lively Scottish or Irish dance.

reel off v to recite or repeat readily and without pause.

re-entry n (pl -ies) 1 the return to the earth's atmosphere by a space vehicle. 2 a second or new entry, e.g. to a country.

refectory n (pl -ies) a dining hall in an institution, e.g. a monastery or college.

refer v (referred, referring) 1 (+ to) to direct attention to something by mentioning it. 2 (+ to) to describe or relate to. 3 (+ to) to have recourse to something, e.g. for information. 4 (often + to) to send (somebody) for treatment, aid, information, etc.

referee[1] n 1 an official who supervises the play and enforces the rules in a sport, e.g. football or boxing. 2 a person who reviews an academic paper before publication. 3 a person who gives a professional or character reference to a candidate's prospective employer.

referee[2] v (referees, refereed, refereeing) to act as a referee for.

reference n 1 the act of referring to or consulting something or somebody. 2 bearing on or connection with a matter. 3 an allusion or mention. 4 a source of information to which somebody is referred. 5 a statement of the character, ability, or qualifications of a person seeking employment. 6 a standard for measuring, evaluating, etc.

referendum n (pl referendums or referenda) a vote by the whole electorate on a single question or measure.

referral n the act of referring somebody to another person, esp a medical specialist.

refine v 1 to free (a raw material) from impurities. 2 to improve or perfect (e.g. a method) by making small adjustments.

refined adj 1 without crudeness or vulgarity; elegant or cultivated. 2 subtle and sophisticated. 3 processed industrially to remove impurities.

refinement n 1 the act of refining or the state of being refined. 2 a subtle feature or improvement.

refinery n (pl -ies) a plant where raw materials, e.g. oil or sugar, are refined.

refit[1] v (refitted, refitting) to fit out (e.g. a ship) again with new fixtures and equipment.

refit[2] n a repair or replacement of parts, fittings, etc.

reflect v 1 to send (light, sound, etc) back from a surface. 2 to show the image or likeness of. 3 to make manifest or apparent. 4 (often + on) to think quietly and calmly. 5 (+ on) to give people a specified impression of something: The results reflect unfavourably on the department.

reflection n 1 the reflecting of light, sound, etc. 2 an image given back by a reflecting surface. 3 an effect produced by a particular state of affairs. 4 (usu + on) an indirect criticism. 5 thought or consideration.

reflective adj 1 capable of reflecting light, etc. 2 thoughtful. ➤ **reflectively** adv.

reflector n something intended to reflect light, etc.

reflex[1] *n* an action that takes place automatically in response to a stimulus and involves no conscious thought.

reflex[2] *adj* **1** produced without intervention of consciousness. **2** of an angle: greater than 180° but less than 360°.

reflexive *adj* referring back to the subject of a clause or sentence, e.g. *herself* in *she blames herself*.

reflexology *n* a therapy that involves massaging nerve endings in the feet to relieve tension or to treat disorders. ➤ **reflexologist** *n*.

refocus *v* (**refocused** *or* **refocussed**, **refocusing** *or* **refocussing**) **1** to focus (a lens or the eyes) again. **2** to change the emphasis or direction of.

reform[1] *v* **1** to change for the better. **2** to cause (somebody) to adopt a more virtuous, healthier, etc way of life.

reform[2] *n* the act of reforming.

reformation *n* **1** the act of reforming. **2** (**the Reformation**) a 16th-century religious movement marked ultimately by the rejection of papal authority and the establishment of the Protestant Churches.

reformism *n* a doctrine, policy, or movement of reform. ➤ **reformist** *n and adj*.

refract *v* to deflect (e.g. light) from a straight path when it enters another medium at an angle.

refractory *adj* **1** *formal* resisting control or authority. **2** resistant to treatment or cure.

refrain[1] *v* (+ from) to keep oneself from doing, feeling, or indulging in something.

refrain[2] *n* a regularly recurring phrase, *esp* at the end of each verse of a poem or song.

refresh *v* **1** to restore strength, vigour, or freshness to. **2** to arouse or stimulate (e.g. the memory). **3** in computing, to update the data in (a file, web page, etc).

refresher *n* a course of instruction designed to keep one abreast of developments in one's field.

refreshing *adj* **1** cooling and restorative. **2** agreeably stimulating because of freshness or newness. ➤ **refreshingly** *adv*.

refreshment *n* **1** the act of refreshing. **2** something, e.g. food or drink, that refreshes. **3** (*in pl*) assorted food and drink, *esp* for a light snack.

refrigerant *n* a substance used in refrigeration.

refrigerate *v* to make or keep cold or cool, *esp* to freeze or chill (e.g. food) for preservation. ➤ **refrigeration** *n*.

refrigerator *n* an insulated appliance for keeping food, drink, etc cool.

refuel *v* (**refuelled**, **refuelling**, *NAmer* **refueled**, **refueling**) to provide with or take on additional fuel.

refuge *n* **1** a place that provides protection. **2** a

person, thing, or course of action that is resorted to in difficulties.

refugee *n* somebody who flees to a foreign country to escape danger or persecution.

refund[1] *v* **1** to return (money) to somebody. **2** to pay (somebody) back. ➤ **refundable** *adj*.

refund[2] *n* **1** the act of refunding. **2** a sum refunded.

refurbish *v* to repair, redecorate, and usu re-equip (e.g. a house). ➤ **refurbishment** *n*.

refuse[1] *v* **1** to show unwillingness to accept or do (something). **2** to be unwilling to allow or grant (something) to (somebody).

refuse[2] *n* rubbish.

refusenik *n* **1** formerly, a Soviet Jew who was refused permission to emigrate, *esp* to Israel. **2** somebody who refuses to accept a situation or proposal.

refute *v* to prove wrong by argument or evidence. ➤ **refutation** *n*.

Usage Note: To *refute* statements, accusations, or people is to prove them wrong, not merely to assert that they are wrong.

regain *v* **1** to recover possession of. **2** to reach (a place) again.

regal *adj* **1** of a king or queen. **2** stately or splendid. ➤ **regally** *adv*.

regale *v* **1** to entertain sumptuously. **2** to give pleasure or amusement to.

regalia *pl n* **1** the ceremonial emblems of royalty. **2** special dress, *esp* official finery.

regard[1] *n* **1** attention or consideration. **2** a protective interest; care. **3** esteem. **4** (*in pl*) friendly greetings. **5** an aspect or respect: *We were fortunate in that regard.* **6** a gaze or look. ✳ **in/with regard to** concerning.

regard[2] *v* **1** (*usu* + as/with) to think of or feel about in a specified way. **2** to look steadily at. ✳ **as regards** in so far as it concerns.

regarding *prep* about; on the subject of.

regardless[1] *adj* (+ of) heedless or careless.

regardless[2] *adv* despite everything.

regatta *n* a sports event consisting of a series of boat races.

regency *n* (*pl* **-ies**) **1** the period of rule of a regent. **2** (**Regency**) the period (1811–1820) when George, Prince of Wales (later George IV) was regent of Great Britain.

regenerate *v* **1** to replace (a body part or tissue) by new growth. **2** to change radically and for the better. ➤ **regeneration** *n*.

regent *n* somebody who governs a kingdom in the minority, absence, or disability of the sovereign.

reggae /'regay/ *n* popular music of West Indian origin, combining elements of rock, soul, and calypso.

regicide *n* **1** the act of murdering a king. **2** a person who commits regicide.

regime

regime /ray'zheem/ *n* **1** a form of management or government. **2** a government in power. **3** = REGIMEN.

regimen *n* a systematic plan, e.g. of diet, exercise, or medical treatment.

regiment[1] *n* **1** a permanent military unit. **2** a large number or group. ➤ **regimental** *adj*.

regiment[2] *v* to subject (people or things) to strict organization or control. ➤ **regimentation** *n*, **regimented** *adj*.

Regina /ri'jiena/ *n* **1** a title given to a reigning queen. **2** used in legal cases, when the British monarch is a queen, to denote the Crown as a party to the action.

region *n* **1** an indefinite area of the world or universe. **2** a broadly uniform geographical or ecological area. **3** an administrative area. **4** an indefinite area surrounding a specified body part. * **in the region of** approximately. ➤ **regional** *adj*, **regionally** *adv*.

register[1] *n* **1** an official written record of items, names, transactions, etc. **2** a part of the range of a human voice or musical instrument. **3** the language style and vocabulary appropriate to particular circumstances.

register[2] *v* **1** to enter (information) officially in a register. **2** to put one's name in a register. **3** to record automatically; to indicate. **4** to show (an emotion) through facial expression or body language. **5** to become aware of. **6** to make or convey an impression.

register office *n Brit* a place where births, marriages, and deaths are recorded and civil marriages are conducted.

registrar *n* **1** an official keeper of records. **2** a senior administrative officer of a university. **3** *Brit* a senior hospital doctor ranking below a consultant.

registration *n* **1** the act of registering. **2** (*also* **registration number**) the identifying set of letters and numbers on a vehicle's number-plate.

registry *n* (*pl* **-ies**) **1** a place where registers are kept. **2** registration.

registry office *n* = REGISTER OFFICE.

regress *v* to revert to an earlier or less advanced state. ➤ **regression** *n*.

regressive *adj* **1** characterized by regression. **2** of a tax: decreasing in rate as the amount taxed increases.

regret[1] *v* (**regretted, regretting**) to be very sorry about.

regret[2] *n* **1** grief or sorrow tinged with disappointment, longing, or remorse. **2** (*in pl*) a conventional expression of disappointment or apology. ➤ **regretful** *n*.

regrettable *adj* not as one would wish; unwelcome.

regular[1] *adj* **1** done or recurring at fixed or uniform intervals. **2** following or arranged according to a discernible pattern. **3** steady or

uniform in practice or occurrence; habitual, usual, or constant. **4** done in conformity with established or prescribed usages, rules, etc. **5** in grammar, of a word, *esp* a verb: conforming to the normal pattern of inflection. **6** of a polygon: having sides of equal length and angles of equal size. **7** belonging to a permanent standing army. ➤ **regularity** *n*, **regularly** *adv*.

regular[2] *n* somebody who is usu present or participating, *esp* a habitual customer.

regularize *or* **-ise** *v* to make regular. ➤ **regularization** *n*.

regulate *v* **1** to control or direct according to rules. **2** to fix or adjust the amount, degree, or rate of. ➤ **regulator** *n*, **regulatory** *adj*.

regulation[1] *n* **1** the act of regulating. **2** an authoritative rule dealing with details or procedure.

regulation[2] *adj* **1** official. **2** *informal* standard; usual.

regurgitate *v* **1** to bring (incompletely digested food) back from the stomach to the mouth. **2** to reproduce (information) with little or no alteration. ➤ **regurgitation** *n*.

rehabilitate *v* **1** to restore to a condition of health or useful activity, e.g. after illness or imprisonment. **2** to reestablish the good name of. ➤ **rehabilitation** *n*.

rehash[1] *v* to present or use again without substantial change or improvement.

rehash[2] *n* something rehashed.

rehearsal *n* a practice session, *esp* of a play, concert, etc preparatory to a public performance.

rehearse *v* **1** to hold a rehearsal of (a play, piece of music, etc). **2** to recount or repeat (something) in order, *esp* tediously.

rehydrate *v* to restore fluid to (something dehydrated).

Reich /riekh/ *n* the German empire.

reign[1] *n* the time during which somebody or something reigns.

reign[2] *v* **1** to exercise sovereign power; to rule. **2** to be predominant or prevalent. **3** to be the current holder of a trophy or title: *the reigning champion*.

reimburse *v* to pay back (money) to (somebody). ➤ **reimbursement** *n*.

rein[1] *n* **1** (*usu in pl*) a long strap by which a rider or driver controls an animal. **2** (*in pl*) controlling or guiding power. * **give free rein to** to allow to proceed or function freely.

rein[2] *v* **1** (*often* + in) to check or stop (a horse) by pulling on the reins. **2** (*often* + in) to restrain or stop.

reincarnate *v* (**be reincarnated**) to be reborn in another body after death. ➤ **reincarnation** *n*.

reindeer *n* (*pl* **reindeers** *or* **reindeer**) a deer with large antlers that inhabits cold northern regions.

reinforce v 1 to strengthen with additional material or support. 2 to strengthen (e.g. an army) with additional forces.

reinforcement n 1 the act of reinforcing. 2 (in pl) additional military personnel sent to strengthen an existing force.

reinstate v to restore to a former position or status. ➤ **reinstatement** n.

reiterate v to say or do again or repeatedly. ➤ **reiteration** n.

reject[1] v 1 to refuse to accept, consider, or submit to. 2 to refuse love or care to (somebody). 3 to fail to accept (e.g. a skin graft or transplanted organ). ➤ **rejection** n.

reject[2] n a rejected person or thing.

rejig v (**rejigged, rejigging**) to rearrange or reorganize.

rejoice v 1 to feel or express joy or great delight. 2 (+ in) to have or enjoy (something noteworthy).

rejoin[1] v to say in response, esp in a sharp or critical way.

rejoin[2] v 1 to return to. 2 to join (two things) together again.

rejoinder n a reply, esp a sharp or critical answer.

rejuvenate v 1 to make young or youthful again. 2 to restore to a more vigorous state. ➤ **rejuvenation** n.

rekindle v 1 to arouse (e.g. an emotion) again. 2 to light (a fire) again.

relapse[1] n a recurrence of symptoms of a disease after a period of improvement.

relapse[2] v to slip or fall back into a former worse state.

relate v 1 to give an account of. 2 to show a logical or causal connection between (two or more things). 3 (often + to) to have reference or connection. 4 (+ to) to sympathize with or respond to. 5 (**be related to**) to have a relationship by blood or marriage with.

relation n 1 a person connected by blood, marriage, or adoption. 2 relationship by blood, marriage, or adoption. 3 (in pl) the attitude or behaviour which people or groups show towards one another. 4 euphem (in pl) sexual intercourse. 5 an aspect or quality that connects two or more things. ＊ **in/with relation to** with regard to; concerning.

relationship n 1 the way in which people or things are related. 2 the relations or dealings that exist between people, groups, organizations, etc. 3 a close friendship or love affair.

relative[1] n = RELATION (1).

relative[2] adj 1 considered in comparison with something else; not absolute. 2 existing only in connection with, or measurable only by reference to, something else. 3 of a pronoun, adverb, etc: introducing a subordinate clause qualifying a preceding word. 4 of a clause: introduced in this way. ＊ **relative to** with regard to.

relatively adv 1 in comparison with other things. 2 quite; fairly.

relativism n a theory that knowledge and moral principles are relative and have no objective standard. ➤ **relativist** n.

relativity n 1 the state of being dependent on or determined by a relation to something else. 2 in physics: a theory, formulated by Albert Einstein, that asserts that mass, dimension, and time will change with increased velocity.

relax v 1 to make or become less tense or rigid. 2 to refrain from work or rest and enjoy leisure. 3 to make (e.g. a rule) less severe or stringent. ➤ **relaxation** n.

relay[1] n 1 a number of people or animals that relieve others in some work. 2 a race between teams in which each team member covers a set portion of the course and then is replaced by another. 3 a device set in operation by variation in an electric circuit and operating other devices in turn. 4 a device that receives and retransmits a signal.

relay[2] v 1 to pass (e.g. information) along by relay. 2 to broadcast (a radio or television signal) by means of a relay.

release[1] v 1 to set free from restraint or confinement. 2 to free from an obligation or responsibility. 3 to give permission for the publication, performance, or sale of. 4 to publish or issue. 5 to move (e.g. a handle or catch) in order to allow a mechanism free movement.

release[2] n 1 the act of releasing. 2 relief from sorrow, suffering, or trouble. 3 a newly issued film, CD, etc.

relegate v 1 to remove to an inferior or insignificant status. 2 Brit to demote (a team) to a lower division of a sporting competition. ➤ **relegation** n.

relent v 1 to become less severe, harsh, or strict. 2 to become less intense or violent.

relentless adj 1 of a person: showing no sign of stopping or becoming less determined. 2 remaining constant at the same demanding level. ➤ **relentlessly** adv.

relevant adj having a significant bearing on the matter at hand. ➤ **relevance** n.

reliable adj able to be relied on. ➤ **reliability** n, **reliably** adv.

reliance n the act of relying; dependence or trust. ➤ **reliant** adj.

relic n 1 an object left behind after something has decayed or disappeared. 2 an outmoded custom, belief, or practice. 3 an object, e.g. part of the body of a saint, preserved as an object of religious reverence.

relief n 1 the removal or lightening of something oppressive, painful, or distressing. 2 a feeling of happiness or comfort brought about by the removal of a burden. 3 a means of breaking monotony or boredom. **4** aid in the form of money or necessities. **5** somebody who takes over from somebody else who has been on duty. **6** the liberation of a besieged city, castle, etc. **7** a method of sculpture in which forms stand out from a flat surface.

relief map *n* a map showing the differences in height of a land surface by shading, etc.

relieve *v* **1** (*often* + of) to free from a burden, obligation, or restriction. **2** to remove or alleviate (e.g. pain). **3** (**be relieved**) to stop feeling anxious or distressed. **4** to release (somebody) from a post or duty by taking their place. **5** to lessen the monotony of. ✳ **relieve oneself** to urinate or defecate.

Usage Note: Note the spelling with *-ie-*.

religion *n* **1** the organized belief in and worship of a god or gods. **2** a particular system of religious beliefs.

religious *adj* **1** relating to religion. **2** pious or devout. **3** scrupulously and conscientiously faithful. ➤ **religiously** *adv.*

relinquish *v* to renounce or abandon; to give up. ➤ **relinquishment** *n.*

reliquary *n* (*pl* **-ies**) a container in which sacred relics are kept.

relish¹ *n* **1** enjoyment of or delight in something. **2** a highly seasoned sauce, e.g. of pickles or mustard, eaten with plainer food.

relish² *v* **1** to enjoy greatly. **2** to anticipate with pleasure.

relive *v* to experience again in the imagination.

reload *v* to load (*esp* a firearm) again.

relocate *v* to establish one's home or business in a new place. ➤ **relocation** *n.*

reluctant *adj* not eager to do something; unwilling. ➤ **reluctance** *n*, **reluctantly** *adv.*

rely *v* (**-ies, -ied**) **1** (+ on/upon) to have confidence in; to trust. **2** (+ on/upon) to be dependent.

remain *v* **1** to stay in the same place. **2** to continue to be. **3** to survive unchanged. **4** to be left over.

remainder *n* **1** a group, part, number, etc that is left over or yet to appear. **2** the final undivided part left after division.

remains *pl n* **1** a remaining part or trace. **2** a dead body.

remand¹ *v* to place (a defendant or prisoner) in custody or on bail until they appear again in court.

remand² *n* ✳ **on remand** in custody awaiting trial.

remark¹ *v* **1** to express as an observation or comment. **2** *formal* to notice.

remark² *n* an expression of an opinion or judgment.

remarkable *adj* striking or extraordinary. ➤ **remarkably** *adv.*

rematch *n* a second match between the same contestants or teams.

remedial *adj* **1** intended as a remedy. **2** designed to help people with learning difficulties.

remedy¹ *n* (*pl* **-ies**) **1** a medicine or treatment that relieves or cures a disease. **2** something that counteracts an evil or deficiency.

remedy² *v* (**-ies, -ied**) to provide or serve as a remedy for.

remember *v* **1** to bring to mind or think of again. **2** to retain in the memory. **3** to not forget or fail to do something. **4** to convey greetings from (somebody) to somebody.

remembrance *n* **1** the act of remembering. **2** an important memory. **3** a commemoration.

remind *v* **1** to cause (somebody) to remember something. **2** (+ of) to appear to (somebody) to be like somebody or something else.

reminder *n* a thing that helps somebody to remember for.

reminisce *v* to talk or write about events or people from one's past.

reminiscence *n* **1** the process of reminiscing. **2** (*usu in pl*) an account of a memorable experience.

reminiscent *adj* tending to remind one of something seen or known before.

remiss *adj* negligent in the performance of work or duty.

remission *n* **1** the act of remitting. **2** a period during which something, e.g. a disease, is remitted. **3** *Brit* reduction of a prison sentence.

remit¹ *v* (**remitted, remitting**) **1** to refrain from inflicting or exacting (e.g. a debt or punishment). **2** to pardon (a sin). **3** to send (money) in payment. **4** to refer (something) for consideration or judgment.

remit² *n* the area of responsibility or concern assigned to a person or organization.

remittance *n* **1** a sum of money remitted. **2** the act of remitting money.

remix¹ *v* to change the balance of sounds of (a recording).

remix² *n* a remixed recording.

remnant *n* a usu small part or trace remaining.

remonstrate *v* (*usu* + with) to make one's objections or opposition to somebody's conduct, opinions, etc known forcefully. ➤ **remonstration** *n.*

remorse *n* deep distress arising from a sense of guilt for past wrongdoing. ➤ **remorseful** *adj*, **remorsefully** *adv.*

remorseless *adj* **1** having no remorse; merciless. **2** continuing without letup. ➤ **remorselessly** *adv.*

remote *adj* **1** far removed in space or time. **2** situated far away from the main centres of activity or population. **3** not belonging to one's close family. **4** controlling something, or being controlled, from a distance, *esp* by an infrared or radio signal. **5** small in degree; slight. **6** distant in manner; aloof. ➤ **remotely** *adv*, **remoteness** *n*.

remote control *n* **1** control over e.g. a machine or weapon exercised from a distance, usu by means of an electrical circuit or radio waves. **2** a device by which this is carried out. ➤ **remote-controlled** *adj*.

removal *n* **1** the act of removing. **2** *Brit* the moving of household goods from one residence to another.

remove[1] *v* **1** to move by lifting, pushing aside, or taking away or off. **2** to get rid of. **3** to dismiss from office. ➤ **removable** *adj*, **remover** *n*.

remove[2] *n* a degree or stage of separation.

removed *adj* **1** separated by a specified degree of relationship: *my first cousin once removed*. **2** very different in character.

remunerate *v* to pay (somebody) for work done. ➤ **remuneration** *n*.

remunerative *adj* profitable or well-paid.

renaissance *n* **1** (**Renaissance**) the revival of classical influence in Europe from the 14th to the 17th century. **2** a rebirth or revival.

renal *adj* relating to or in the region of the kidneys.

rename *v* to give a different name to.

renascence *n* a rebirth or revival.

rend *v* (*past tense and past part.* **rent**) **1** to pull or tear apart or in pieces. **2** to cause mental or emotional pain to.

render *v* **1** to cause to be or become. **2** to submit (e.g. an opinion) for consideration, approval, etc. **3** to do (a service) for or give (assistance) to somebody. **4** to reproduce by artistic or verbal means. **5** to give a performance of (e.g. a piece of music). **6** to translate. **7** to melt down (fat). **8** to apply a coat of plaster or cement directly to (brickwork, stone, etc). ➤ **rendering** *n*.

rendezvous[1] /'rondayvooh/ *n* (*pl* **rendezvous** /-vooh/) **1** a meeting at an appointed place and time. **2** a place appointed for meeting.

rendezvous[2] *v* (**rendezvouses** /-voohz/, **rendezvoused** /-voohd/, **rendezvousing** /-vooh-ing/) to come together at a rendezvous.

rendition *n* a performance or interpretation.

renegade *n* a deserter from one faith, cause, or allegiance to another.

renege *v* (+ on) to go back on a commitment.

renew *v* **1** to begin (something) again. **2** to restore to freshness, vigour, or perfection. **3** to grant or obtain an extension of (e.g. a subscription or licence). **4** to replace or replenish. ➤ **renewal** *n*.

rennet *n* a preparation containing an extract from the stomach lining of a young calf, used in cheese-making.

renounce *v* **1** to state, usu by formal declaration, that one is giving up (something that one formerly possessed, believed, practised, etc). **2**

to break off, usu formally, one's connection with or allegiance to (somebody).

renovate *v* to restore to a better state, e.g. by cleaning, repairing, or rebuilding. ➤ **renovation** *n*.

renown *n* the state of being widely known and admired; fame.

renowned *adj* celebrated or famous.

rent[1] *n* **1** a periodical payment made by a tenant of property to the owner. **2** a similar payment for the use of goods, equipment, etc.

rent[2] *v* **1** to take and use (e.g. property or equipment) under an agreement to pay rent. **2** to grant the use of (e.g. property or equipment) for rent.

rent[3] *n* a split or tear.

rent[4] *v* past tense and past part. of REND.

rental *n* **1** an amount paid or collected as rent. **2** the act of renting.

rent boy *n* *Brit, informal* a young male prostitute.

renunciation *n* the act of renouncing.

reorganize or **-ise** *v* to organize again or in a different way. ➤ **reorganization** *n*.

rep[1] *n* *informal* a sales representative.

rep[2] *n* *informal* a repertory theatre or company.

repaid *v* past tense and past part. of REPAY.

repair[1] *v* to restore (something damaged or worn) to a sound or working condition. ➤ **repairable** *adj*, **repairer** *n*.

repair[2] *n* **1** the act of repairing. **2** an instance or result of repairing. **3** the condition of something with respect to its soundness or need of repair: *in good repair*.

repair[3] *v* *formal* to go.

reparable *adj* capable of being repaired.

reparation *n* **1** the act of making amends for a wrong or injury. **2** (*usu in pl*) compensation payable by a defeated nation for war damages.

repartee *n* the exchange of amusing and witty remarks.

repast *n* *formal* a meal.

repatriate *v* to send (somebody or something) back to their country of origin. ➤ **repatriation** *n*.

repay *v* (*past tense and past part.* **repaid**) **1** to pay back. **2** to do something in return for (a previous kindness or injury). **3** to reward or be worthy of (e.g. investigation). ➤ **repayment** *n*.

repeal[1] *v* to revoke (a law).

repeal[2] *n* the act of repealing.

repeat[1] *v* **1** to say or state again. **2** to make, do, experience, etc again. **3** to express (oneself) again in the same words. **4** to present (itself) again in the same form. ➤ **repeated** *adj*, **repeatedly** *adv*.

repeat[2] *n* **1** the act of repeating. **2** something repeated, e.g. a television or radio programme that has previously been broadcast at least once.

repel v (**repelled, repelling**) **1** to drive back or away. **2** to disgust. **3** to be incapable of sticking to, mixing with, etc. **4** of a magnetic pole: to tend to force (e.g. another magnet) away.

repellent[1] or **repellant** adj **1** serving to repel something. **2** repulsive. ➤ **repellently** adv.

repellent[2] or **repellant** n something that repels, e.g. a substance used to prevent insect attacks.

repent v to feel regret or contrition. ➤ **repentance** n, **repentant** adj.

repercussion n a widespread, indirect, or unforeseen effect of an action or event.

repertoire n **1** a list of works or parts that a company or person is prepared to perform. **2** a range of skills, techniques, etc.

repertory n (pl **-ies**) **1** the presentation of several different plays, in alternation or for short periods, in one season at a theatre. **2** = REPERTOIRE.

repetition n **1** the act of repeating. **2** a repeat or copy.

repetitious adj characterized by esp tedious repetition. ➤ **repetitiously** adv.

repetitive adj **1** done, uttered, etc repeatedly. **2** = REPETITIOUS. ➤ **repetitively** adv.

rephrase v to put in different words.

repine v formal or literary to feel dejection or discontent.

replace v **1** to restore to a former place or position. **2** to take the place of. **3** (often + with) to put something new in the place of (something). ➤ **replaceable** adj.

replacement n **1** the process of replacing or being replaced. **2** something or somebody that replaces something or somebody else.

replay[1] v to play (something) again.

replay[2] n **1** the act of replaying. **2** the playing of a tape, e.g. a videotape. **3** a repetition or re-enactment. **4** a match played to resolve a tie in an earlier match.

replenish v to stock or fill up again. ➤ **replenishment** n.

replete adj **1** (+ with) abundantly provided or filled. **2** full with food. ➤ **repletion** n.

replica n an accurate reproduction, copy, or model.

replicate v **1** to duplicate or repeat. **2** to make an exact copy of. ➤ **replication** n.

reply[1] v (**-ies, -ied**) **1** to respond in words or writing. **2** to do something in response.

reply[2] n (pl **-ies**) something said, written, or done in answer.

report[1] n **1** a usu detailed account or statement. **2** Brit a statement of a pupil's performance at school. **3** a loud explosive noise.

report[2] v **1** (often + on) to make or submit a report. **2** (often + on) to give news of or information about. **3** to make a formal complaint about, esp to the authorities. **4** to present oneself, esp on arrival somewhere. **5** chiefly Brit (+ to) to be responsible to somebody superior.

reportage n writing intended to give a usu factual account of events.

reporter n a journalist who reports news for the press, radio, or television.

repose[1] n the state of resting after exertion or strain.

repose[2] v **1** to lie resting. **2** formal (+ in) to place (e.g. confidence or trust) in someone or something.

repository n (pl **-ies**) **1** a place or container where something is stored. **2** somebody or something that contains something, e.g. knowledge or secrets, esp in large quantities.

repossess v to resume possession of (goods) when the due payments are not made. ➤ **repossession** n.

reprehensible adj deserving censure; culpable.

represent v **1** to act for or in the place of. **2** to serve as the elected member of a legislative body for (a particular constituency or electorate). **3** to serve as a specimen, example, or instance of. **4** to serve as a sign or symbol of. **5** to have the nature or effect of; to constitute. **6** to portray in art. **7** to attribute a specified character or identity to, esp falsely.

representation n **1** a likeness or image. **2** the act of representing. **3** (in pl) statements made to influence opinion or express a protest.

representational adj **1** relating to representation. **2** in the graphic or plastic arts, involving realistic depiction of physical objects or appearances.

representative[1] adj **1** serving as a typical or characteristic example. **2** containing typical examples. **3** acting on behalf of somebody else. **4** based on representation of the people in government or lawmaking. **5** serving to represent.

representative[2] n **1** somebody who represents another person or a group; an agent or delegate. **2** somebody who represents a business organization, esp a sales representative. **3** a typical example of a group, class, or quality.

repress v **1** to subdue by force. **2** to prevent the natural or normal expression of (e.g. an emotion). **3** to prevent the normal activity or development of. ➤ **repressed** adj, **repression** n.

repressive adj unjustly or unduly restricting people's freedom.

reprieve[1] v **1** to delay or cancel the punishment of (e.g. a condemned prisoner). **2** to remove the threat of an unpleasant fate, e.g. demolition, closure, etc, from.

reprieve[2] n **1** a suspension or cancellation of a punishment. **2** a temporary removal of a threat.

reprimand[1] n a formal expression of disapproval.

reprimand² *v* to criticize formally, usu from a position of authority.

reprint¹ *n* **1** the act of reprinting (e.g. a book). **2** a reprinted copy of something.

reprint² *v* to print again.

reprisal *n* a retaliatory act.

reproach¹ *v* to express disappointment and displeasure with (somebody) for blameworthy conduct.

reproach² *n* an expression of rebuke or disapproval. ➤ **reproachful** *adj*, **reproachfully** *adv*.

reprobate¹ *n* somebody who is morally dissolute or unprincipled.

reprobate² *adj* morally dissolute; unprincipled.

reproduce *v* **1** to repeat, copy, or emulate. **2** to make an image or copy of. **3** to produce offspring.

reproduction *n* **1** the sexual or asexual process by which plants and animals give rise to offspring. **2** a copy, *esp* of a work of art. ➤ **reproductive** *adj*.

reproof *n* criticism for a fault.

reprove *v* to express disapproval of. ➤ **reproving** *adj*.

reptile *n* a cold-blooded vertebrate of a class that includes crocodiles, lizards, snakes, turtles, and extinct related forms, e.g. dinosaurs. ➤ **reptilian** *adj*.

republic *n* a state whose head is not a monarch and in which supreme power resides in the people and is exercised by their elected representatives.

republican¹ *adj* **1** relating to or belonging to a republic. **2** advocating a republic. **3** (**Republican**) denoting a political party in the USA favouring a restricted governmental role in social and economic life. ➤ **republicanism** *n*.

republican² *n* **1** somebody who favours republican government. **2** (**Republican**) a member of the US Republican party. **3** (**Republican**) a supporter of the union of Northern Ireland with the Irish Republic.

repudiate *v* **1** to refuse to have anything to do with; to disown. **2** to reject as unauthorized or invalid or as untrue or unjust. ➤ **repudiation** *n*.

repugnance *n* strong dislike or antipathy; disgust.

repugnant *adj* arousing strong dislike.

repulse¹ *v* **1** to drive (attackers) back. **2** to reject or rebuff. **3** to cause repulsion in.

repulse² *n* the act of repelling.

repulsion *n* **1** a feeling of strong aversion. **2** in physics, a force, e.g. between like magnetic poles, tending to produce separation.

repulsive *adj* arousing strong aversion or disgust. ➤ **repulsively** *adv*.

reputable *adj* held in good repute; well regarded.

reputation *n* overall quality or character as seen or judged by others.

repute¹ *n* **1** the character or status commonly ascribed to somebody or something. **2** the state of being favourably known or spoken of.

repute² *v* (*usu* **be reputed**) to be believed or considered to be as specified.

request¹ *n* **1** an instance of asking for something, *esp* politely or formally. **2** something asked for.

request² *v* **1** to make a request to (somebody). **2** to ask for (something), *esp* politely or formally.

requiem *n* **1** a mass for the dead. **2** (*often* **Requiem**) a musical setting of the mass for the dead.

require *v* **1** to have to have (something) because it is necessary or essential. **2** to call for as suitable or appropriate. **3** to impose an obligation on.

requirement *n* **1** something wanted or needed. **2** a necessary precondition for something.

requisite¹ *adj* necessary or required.

requisite² *n* **1** something that is required or necessary. **2** an article of the specified sort.

requisition¹ *n* **1** the act of compulsorily taking over goods or property for official use. **2** an authoritative written demand or application.

requisition² *v* to demand the use or supply of officially.

rerun *v* (**rerunning**, *past tense* **reran**, *past part*. **rerun**) **1** to run (something, e.g. a race) again. **2** to show (e.g. a film or television programme) again. ➤ **rerun** *n*.

resat *v* past tense and past part. of RESIT.

reschedule *v* **1** to change the time that (an event) is to take place. **2** to set a new timetable for the repayment of (a debt).

rescind *v* to cancel (e.g. an order).

rescue¹ *v* to free from confinement, danger, or difficulty; to save. ➤ **rescuer** *n*.

rescue² *n* the act of rescuing somebody or something.

research¹ *n* study, investigations, experiments, etc aimed at making discoveries, establishing facts, or enabling new conclusions.

research² *v* to engage in research on (a subject) or for (e.g. a book or television programme). ➤ **researcher** *n*.

resemblance *n* **1** the state of resembling somebody or something else. **2** a point on which two people or things are similar.

resemble *v* to be similar to, *esp* in appearance.

resent *v* to harbour or express ill will at (something considered wrong or unfair). ➤ **resentful** *adj*, **resentfully** *adv*.

resentment *n* a feeling of bitterness caused by something considered wrong or unfair.

reservation *n* **1** the act of reserving something, e.g. a seat or hotel room, or a record of this. **2** (*usu in pl*) a doubt or objection with regard to something. **3** an area of land set aside, *esp* one designated for the use of Native Americans.

reserve¹ *v* **1** to retain for future use. **2** to arrange that (a seat, hotel room, etc) be kept for one's own or another's use at a specified future time. **3** to hold over (*esp* a judgment) until later. **4** to retain (e.g. a right).

reserve² *n* **1** a supply of something retained for future use or need. **2** *chiefly Brit* an area of land set apart for the conservation of natural resources or rare plants and animals. **3** = RESERVATION 3. **4** caution or lack of openness in one's words and actions; reticence. **5** a qualification or doubt. **6** (*usu in pl*) a military force available as a support for regular forces when needed. **7** in sport, a player who has been selected to substitute for another if the need should arise. **8** (**the reserves**) a team made up of players who do not currently form part of the first team. **9** (*also in pl*) money, gold, foreign exchange, etc kept in hand usu to meet liabilities. ✴ **in reserve** held back ready for use if needed.

reserved *adj* restrained in speech and behaviour.

reservist *n* a member of a military reserve.

reservoir *n* **1** a natural or artificial lake where water is collected for use by a community. **2** a place or part in which fluid gathers or is stored. **3** an available extra source or supply.

reshuffle *v* **1** to rearrange (something) by altering the relative positions of its elements. **2** to reorganize (a group *esp* of government ministers) by a redistribution of roles. ➤ **reshuffle** *n*.

reside *v* **1** to occupy a place as one's permanent home. **2** (+ in) to lie in, or be associated with, a certain thing. **3** (+ in) to be vested as a right in a certain personage, etc.

residence *n* **1** the fact of living in a place. **2** a dwelling, *esp* a large and impressive house or a dignitary's official home. ✴ **in residence** of a writer, artist, etc: working in e.g. a college or gallery, and available to give instruction, advice, etc.

residency *n* (*pl* -**ies**) **1** = RESIDENCE 1. **2** a period of time spent as a writer or artist in residence.

resident¹ *adj* **1** living in a place, *esp* for some length of time. **2** serving in a regular or full-time capacity.

resident² *n* **1** somebody who lives in a place. **2** a guest staying at a hotel.

residential *adj* **1** used as a residence or by residents. **2** relating to or involving residence. **3** given over to private housing as distinct from industry or commerce.

residual *adj* remaining as a residue.

residue *n* something that remains after a part, *esp* the greater part, has been taken away or used up.

resign *v* **1** to give up one's job or position. **2** (+ to) to reconcile (oneself) to an unpleasant fact, circumstance, etc.

resignation *n* **1** the act of resigning. **2** a formal notification of resigning. **3** the state of being resigned to something.

resilient *adj* **1** able to withstand shocks or return to shape after bending, stretching, etc. **2** *esp* of a person: able to recover from or adjust to misfortune or change. ➤ **resilience** *n*.

resin *n* **1** a sticky plant secretion that is used *esp* in varnishes, inks, and plastics. **2** a synthetic substance that has the qualities of natural resin.

resist *v* **1** to withstand the force or effect of. **2** to strive against or oppose. **3** to refrain from (something tempting).

resistance *n* **1** the act of resisting. **2** the ability to resist e.g. infection or the effects of drugs, etc. **3** an opposing or retarding force. **4** in physics, the opposition offered to the passage of a steady electric current through a body, circuit, etc. **5** (*often* **Resistance**) an underground organization operating against occupying forces in a country or those in power. ➤ **resistant** *adj*.

resistor *n* a component included in an electrical circuit to provide resistance.

resit *v* (**resitting**, *past tense and past part.* **resat**) *Brit* to take (an examination) again after failing.

resolute *adj* firmly resolved. ➤ **resolutely** *adv*.

resolution *n* **1** the process of resolving, e.g. a problem or dispute. **2** courageous firmness of purpose. **3** a formal expression of opinion or intent by a body or group. **4** the capability, e.g. of a television or computer screen, to produce a clear and detailed image, or the degree of clarity produced.

resolve¹ *v* **1** to find a solution to (a problem). **2** to reach a firm decision to do something. **3** to decide by a formal resolution and vote. **4** to break up or separate into constituent parts.

resolve² *n* **1** the state of being determined or decided. **2** a firm decision.

resonant *adj* **1** of a sound: rich or echoing. **2** of a space, object, etc: tending to intensify and enrich sound. **3** suggesting meanings or associations other than those that are immediately present. ➤ **resonance** *n*.

resonate *v* to resound or reverberate.

resort¹ *n* **1** a frequently visited place providing accommodation and recreation, *esp* for holidaymakers. **2** somebody or something turned to for help or protection. **3** recourse.

resort² *v* **1** (+ to) to turn to somebody or something in order to achieve an end. **2** *formal* to go.

resound *v* **1** to become filled with sound. **2** to produce a sonorous or echoing sound.

resounding *adj* clear; unqualified.

resource¹ *n* **1** (*usu in pl*) an available means of support or provision. **2** (*usu in pl*) a source of wealth or revenue, e.g. minerals. **3** a source of information or expertise. **4** (*usu in pl*) the ability to deal with a difficult situation.

resource² *v* to supply with resources.

resourceful *adj* good at devising ways of dealing with difficult situations. ➤ **resourcefully** *adv*, **resourcefulness** *n*.

respect¹ *n* **1** high or special regard; esteem. **2** politeness or deference. **3** (*in pl*) expressions of respect or politeness. **4** an aspect or detail. ✳ **with respect to** in relation to; concerning.

respect² *v* **1** to consider worthy of respect. **2** to refrain from violating or interfering with. **3** to recognize and abide by (e.g. a decision).

respectable *adj* **1** decent or conventional in character or conduct. **2** acceptable in size or quantity. ➤ **respectability** *n*, **respectably** *adv*.

respectful *adj* showing respect or deference. ➤ **respectfully** *adv*.

respecting *prep* with regard to; concerning.

respective *adj* belonging or relating to each.

respectively *adv* separately and in the order given.

respiration *n* **1** the act of breathing. **2** a single breath.

respirator *n* **1** a device worn over the mouth or nose to prevent the breathing of poisonous gases, etc. **2** a device for maintaining artificial respiration.

respiratory *adj* relating to breathing.

respire *v formal* to breathe.

respite *n* a period of rest or relief.

resplendent *adj* shining brilliantly; splendid.

respond *v* to write, speak, or act in reply.

respondent *n* **1** a defendant, *esp* in an appeal or divorce case. **2** a person who replies to a survey, advertisement, etc.

response *n* a reply or reaction.

responsibility *n* (*pl* -ies) **1** the state of being responsible. **2** something or somebody for which one is responsible. **3** the opportunity to act, take decisions, etc independently.

responsible *adj* **1** liable to be called to account as the person who did something. **2** constituting the reason or cause of something. **3** (*usu* + for) having control or care of. **4** involving important duties, decision-making, accountability, etc. **5** trustworthy, reliable, or sensible. **6** (+ to) required to answer to the specified person or body. ➤ **responsibly** *adv*.

responsive *adj* quick to respond appropriately or sympathetically.

rest¹ *n* **1** freedom or a break from activity or work. **2** a state of motionlessness or inactivity. **3** repose, relaxation, or sleep. **4** in music, a silence of a specified duration. **5** something used for support.

rest² *v* **1** to relax the body or mind, e.g. by lying down or sleeping. **2** to stop working or exerting oneself. **3** to lie supported. **4** to place on a support. **5** (+ on) to be based or founded. **6** (+

with) to depend for action or accomplishment. **7** to remain as specified. ✳ **rest on one's laurels** see LAUREL.

rest³ *n* **1** (**the rest**) the part, amount, or number that remains. **2** (**the rest**) the other people or things.

restaurant *n* a place where meals are sold, usu to be eaten on the premises.

restaurateur *n* the manager or proprietor of a restaurant.

restful *adj* quiet, peaceful, or soothing.

restitution *n* **1** the returning of something, e.g. property, to its rightful owner. **2** compensation given for an injury or wrong.

restive *adj* **1** resisting authority or control. **2** restless and uneasy.

restless *adj* **1** unable to rest, *esp* due to mental agitation. **2** giving no rest. **3** continuously moving or active. ➤ **restlessly** *adv*.

restorative *adj* capable of restoring health or vigour. ➤ **restorative** *n*.

restore *v* **1** to bring back to a former or original state, e.g. by repairing damage. **2** to bring back into existence, force, or use. **3** *formal* to give back. **4** *formal* to put (somebody) in possession of something again. ➤ **restoration** *n*, **restorer** *n*.

restrain *v* **1** to keep under control. **2** to hold onto and physically prevent (a person or animal) from moving.

restrained *adj* characterized by restraint, *esp* not extravagant or emotional.

restraint *n* **1** moderation of one's behaviour. **2** the absence of extravagance or indulgence. **3** the act of restraining. **4** a restraining force or influence. **5** a device that prevents freedom of movement.

restrict *v* **1** to prevent from moving or acting freely. **2** to limit.

restricted *adj* **1** not general; limited. **2** available only to particular groups or for a particular purpose. **3** narrow or confined.

restriction *n* **1** a regulation that restricts or restrains. **2** the act of restricting.

restrictive *adj* limiting freedom of action or movement.

restrictive practice *n* **1** an anti-competitive trading agreement between companies. **2** a practice by a trade union that limits the freedom of action of other workers or management.

rest room *n NAmer* public toilet facilities in a building.

result¹ *v* **1** to proceed or arise as an effect or conclusion. **2** (+ in) to have the specified outcome.

result² *n* **1** a consequence, effect, or conclusion. **2** something obtained by calculation, experiment, or investigation. **3** the outcome or final score, mark, etc of a contest or examination. **4** *informal* a win in a sporting contest or successful conclusion to an operation.

resultant *adj* resulting from something else.

resume *v* **1** to take or occupy (e.g. a position) again. **2** to continue or begin again after an interruption. ➤ **resumption** *n*.

résumé *n* **1** a summary. **2** *NAmer* = CURRICULUM VITAE.

resurgence *n* a rising again into life, activity, or influence. ➤ **resurgent** *adj*.

resurrect *v* **1** to bring back to life from the dead. **2** to bring back into use.

resurrection *n* **1** (**the Resurrection**) the rising of Christ from the dead. **2** a resurgence, revival, or restoration.

resuscitate *v* **1** to revive from unconsciousness or apparent death. **2** to revitalize. ➤ **resuscitation** *n*.

retail[1] *v* **1** to sell (goods) to final consumers who will not resell them. **2** (*often* + at/for) to be sold , *esp* at a specified price. ➤ **retailer** *n*.

retail[2] *n* the sale of goods in small quantities to final consumers who will not resell them.

retain *v* **1** to continue to have or hold. **2** to keep in one's mind or memory. **3** to have the ability to hold or contain. **4** to hold in place.

retainer *n* **1** a fee paid to a lawyer for access to their services whenever required. **2** an old and trusted domestic servant.

retake[1] *v* (**retook, retaken**) **1** to recapture. **2** to sit (a test or examination) again.

retake[2] *n* a retaken test or examination.

retaliate *v* to take action that repays somebody for some wrong they have done. ➤ **retaliation** *n*.

retard[1] *v* to hinder the progress, development, or accomplishment of something. ➤ **retardation** *n*.

retard[2] *n* *offensive* a person with learning difficulties.

retarded *adj* slow in intellectual or emotional development.

retch *v* to experience a vomiting spasm without actually vomiting anything. ➤ **retch** *n*.

retention *n* the act of retaining.

retentive *adj* able to retain something, *esp* knowledge.

rethink *v* (*past tense and past part.* **rethought**) to reconsider (a plan, attitude, etc) with a view to changing it. ➤ **rethink** *n*.

reticent *adj* inclined to be uncommunicative or reluctant to speak openly. ➤ **reticence** *n*.

retina *n* (*pl* **retinas** *or* **retinae**) the light-sensitive membrane at the back of the eye that is connected with the brain by the optic nerve.

retinue *n* a group of attendants accompanying an important person.

retire *v* **1** to give up one's position or occupation permanently, *esp* at the end of one's working life. **2** to cause or force to retire from a position or occupation. **3** *formal* to withdraw

from a place. **4** *formal* to go to bed. **5** of troops: to fall back or retreat. **6** to withdraw from a sporting contest. **7** of a jury: to leave the court to consider their verdict. ➤ **retired** *adj*.

retirement *n* **1** permanent withdrawal from active working life. **2** the age at which one normally retires from work. **3** the state or period of being retired. **4** *literary* seclusion.

retiring *adj* tending to avoid contact with other people; shy.

retook *v* past tense of RETAKE[1].

retort[1] *v* to answer back sharply or tersely.

retort[2] *n* a witty, angry, or cutting reply.

retouch *v* to restore or improve the appearance of with small additions or changes.

retrace *v* **1** to go over (e.g. footsteps or a route) again, often in the opposite direction. **2** to go back over (something) e.g. for purposes of clarification.

retract *v* **1** to draw back or in. **2** to withdraw (something said or written). **3** to refuse to abide by (e.g. a promise or agreement). ➤ **retractable** *adj*, **retraction** *n*.

retreat[1] *n* **1** the forced withdrawal of troops *esp* after losing a battle. **2** the act of withdrawing, *esp* from something difficult or dangerous. **3** a place of peace, privacy, or safety. **4** a period of withdrawal for prayer, meditation, and study.

retreat[2] *v* to make a retreat.

retrench *v* **1** to reduce (*esp* costs or expenses). **2** to economize. ➤ **retrenchment** *n*.

retrial *n* a second or subsequent legal trial.

retribution *n* punishment or retaliation for an insult or injury.

retrieve *v* **1** to get back again. **2** to rescue or save. **3** of a dog: to find and bring in (killed or wounded game). **4** to recover (e.g. data) from a computer memory. ➤ **retrieval** *n*.

retriever *n* a dog of a breed used to retrieve game.

retrograde *adj* **1** resulting in a worse or less advanced state. **2** moving or directed backward.

retrogress *v* to return to an earlier usu worse state. ➤ **retrogression** *n*, **retrogressive** *adj*.

retrorocket *n* a rocket used to slow down an aircraft, spacecraft, etc by producing thrust in a direction opposite to its motion.

retrospect *n* ✻ **in retrospect** when considering the past or a past event, *esp* in the light of present knowledge or experience.

retrospective[1] *adj* **1** relating to or affecting things in the past. **2** of an art exhibition: showing the evolution of an artist's work over a period. ➤ **retrospectively** *adv*.

retrospective[2] *n* a retrospective exhibition.

retroussé /rǝ'troohsay/ *adj* of a nose: turned up at the end.

retsina *n* a white Greek wine flavoured with resin.

return[1] v **1** to go back or come back. **2** (+ to) to go back to something in thought, conversation, or practice. **3** to put back in a former place or state. **4** to give or send back, *esp* to its owner. **5** to elect (a candidate). **6** to state or present (a verdict). **7** to bring in (e.g. a profit). **8** to repay (e.g. a compliment or favour). **9** in sport, to play (a ball) hit by an opponent.

return[2] n **1** the act of returning. **2** *Brit* a ticket bought for a trip to a place and back again: compare. **3** (*also in pl*) the profit from work, investment, or business. ✶ **in return** in compensation or repayment.

reunify v (**-ies, -ied**) to restore the unity of (e.g. a previously divided country). ➢ **reunification** n.

reunion n **1** a gathering of people after a period of separation. **2** the act of reuniting.

reunite v to come or bring together again.

reuse v to use again. ➢ **reusable** adj, **reuse** n, **reuser** n.

Rev. abbr Reverend.

rev[1] n *informal* (*usu in pl*) a revolution per minute of an engine.

rev[2] v (**revved, revving**) *informal* (*often* + up) to increase the number of revolutions per minute of (an engine).

revamp[1] v to change and improve the appearance or structure of.

revamp[2] n a modified or improved version.

reveal v **1** to make known (something secret or hidden). **2** to open (something) up to view.

revealing adj **1** exposing something, *esp* part of the body, usu concealed from view. **2** providing significant or interesting information.

reveille n a signal, *esp* a military bugle call, to get up in the morning.

revel[1] v (**revelled, revelling**, *NAmer* **reveled, reveling**) **1** (+ in) to derive intense satisfaction from. **2** to enjoy oneself in a noisy and exuberant way. ➢ **reveller** n, **revelry** n.

revel[2] n (*also in pl*) a riotous party or celebration.

revelation n **1** the act of revealing something. **2** something revealed, *esp* a sudden and illuminating disclosure.

revelatory adj serving to reveal something.

revenge[1] n **1** the act of retaliating in order to get even for a wrong or injury. **2** a desire to retaliate in this way.

revenge[2] v **1** to retaliate for (an insult, injury, etc). **2** to take revenge on behalf of (oneself or somebody else).

revenue n the total income produced by a given source or received by a business, government, etc.

reverberate v **1** of a sound: to continue in a series of echoes. **2** to have a continuing and powerful effect. ➢ **reverberation** n.

revere v to regard with deep and devoted respect.

reverence n profound respect, *esp* accorded to something sacred.

Reverend adj used as a title for a member of the clergy.

reverend n *informal* a member of the clergy.

reverent adj characterized by reverence. ➢ **reverently** adv.

reverie n a daydream.

reversal n the act of reversing, *esp* a change to an opposite direction, position, policy, etc.

reverse[1] adj **1** contrary to a previous or usual condition or direction. **2** causing backward movement.

reverse[2] v **1** to go or drive backward. **2** to change to an opposite position or direction. **3** to turn upside down or inside out. **4** to annul (a legal judgment). **5** to change (e.g. a decision or policy) to the contrary. ✶ **reverse the charges** *Brit* to arrange for the recipient of a telephone call to pay for it. ➢ **reversible** adj.

reverse[3] n **1** the opposite of something. **2** the side of a coin, medal, etc that does not bear the principal design and lettering. **3** a gear that causes backward motion. **4** a change for the worse; a setback. ✶ **in reverse 1** backward. **2** in the opposite direction.

reversion n a return to an earlier inferior state.

revert v to return to a former state, practice, belief, etc.

review[1] n **1** an act of inspecting or examining something, *esp* in order to decide if changes need to be made. **2** a critical evaluation of a book, play, etc. **3** a magazine or newspaper, or part of one, devoted chiefly to critical articles. **4** a general survey, e.g. of current affairs. **5** a formal military or naval inspection. **6** = REVUE.

review[2] v **1** to make, write, etc a review of. **2** to examine or study again. ➢ **reviewer** n.

revile v to criticize very harshly or abusively.

revise v **1** to make an amended version of (a text). **2** *Brit* to refresh one's knowledge of (a subject), *esp* before an examination. **3** to change (e.g. an opinion), *esp* in the light of further consideration or new information. ➢ **revision** n.

revisionism n *chiefly derog* a movement in Marxist socialism favouring an evolutionary rather than a revolutionary transition to socialism. ➢ **revisionist** adj and n.

revitalize or **-ise** v to give new life or vigour to. ➢ **revitalization** n.

revival n **1** a return or bringing back to life, vigour, popularity, etc. **2** a new presentation or production, e.g. of a play. **3** a period of renewed religious fervour.

revivalism n efforts to bring about a return to religious faith. ➢ **revivalist** n and adj.

revive v **1** to return to a state of consciousness, health, or strength. **2** to bring back into an active state or current use.

revivify v (**-ies, -ied**) to revitalize.

revoke *v* to declare to be no longer valid or operative. ➤ **revocation** *n*.

revolt[1] *v* **1** to rebel. **2** to cause to feel disgust or loathing.

revolt[2] *n* a rebellion, *esp* a determined and armed one.

revolting *adj* extremely offensive; nauseating.

revolution *n* **1** the overthrow of one government and the substitution of another. **2** a sudden or far-reaching change. **3** one complete turn of an object round a central point or axis.

revolutionary[1] *adj* **1** completely new and different. **2** promoting or engaging in revolution.

revolutionary[2] *n* (*pl* **-ies**) somebody who advocates or is engaged in a revolution.

revolutionize *or* **-ise** *v* to change fundamentally or completely.

revolve *v* **1** to move in a circular course or round a central point or axis. **2** (+ around) to be centred on or a specified theme or main point. ➤ **revolving** *adj*.

revolver *n* a handgun with revolving chambers each holding one cartridge.

revue *n* a theatrical production consisting typically of brief often satirical sketches, songs, and dances.

revulsion *n* a feeling of utter distaste or repugnance.

reward[1] *n* **1** something offered or given for service, effort, or achievement. **2** a sum of money offered for the capture of a criminal or the recovery of lost or stolen property.

reward[2] *v* to give a reward to (somebody) or for (something).

rewarding *adj* personally satisfying.

rewind *v* (*past tense and past part.* **rewound**) to wind (film, tape, etc) back to the beginning or to an earlier point.

rewire *v* to provide (e.g. a house) with new electric wiring.

rework *v* to revise, alter, or make suitable for a different purpose.

Rf *abbr* the chemical symbol for rutherfordium.

Rh[1] *abbr* rhesus (factor).

Rh[2] *abbr* the chemical symbol for rhodium.

rhapsodize *or* **-ise** *v* to speak or write with ardent enthusiasm.

rhapsody *n* (*pl* **-ies**) **1** an expression of ardent enthusiasm. **2** a musical composition in one continuous movement. ➤ **rhapsodic** *adj*.

rheostat *n* a device that regulates an electric current by varying resistance.

rhesus baby *n* a baby born with a blood disease because the rhesus factor of its mother's blood is incompatible with that of its own blood.

rhesus factor *n* a substance present in red blood cells that defines blood groups and can provoke intense allergic reactions when incompatible blood types are mixed.

rhesus monkey *n* a small pale brown monkey of southern Asia.

rhetoric *n* **1** the art of effective public speaking. **2** impressive language that may be insincere or exaggerated.

rhetorical *adj* **1** relating to or involving rhetoric. **2** of language: impressive or used merely to impress. ➤ **rhetorically** *adv*.

rhetorical question *n* a question to which no answer is expected, used to make a statement with dramatic effect.

rheumatic *adj* relating to or suffering from rheumatism.

rheumatism *n* a condition characterized by inflammation and pain in muscles, joints, or fibrous tissue.

rhinestone *n* an imitation diamond.

rhino *n* (*pl* **rhinos** *or* **rhino**) *informal* a rhinoceros.

rhinoceros *n* (*pl* **rhinoceroses** *or* **rhinoceros**) a large plant-eating mammal of Africa and Asia with a very thick skin and either one or two horns on its snout.

rhizome *n* a horizontal underground plant stem that produces both roots and buds.

rho *n* the 17th letter of the Greek alphabet (P, ρ).

rhododendron *n* a shrub with clusters of showy red, pink, purple, or white flowers and leathery evergreen leaves.

rhombus *n* (*pl* **rhombuses** *or* **rhombi**) a parallelogram with equal sides but unequal angles; a diamond-shaped figure.

rhubarb *n* a plant with large fleshy leaves and edible stalks that are cooked and eaten as a dessert.

rhumba *n* see RUMBA.

rhyme[1] *n* **1** correspondence in the sound of words or their final syllables, *esp* those at the ends of lines of verse. **2** a word that corresponds with another in this way. **3** rhyming verse or a rhyming poem. * **rhyme or reason** reasonableness or logic.

rhyme[2] *v* **1** of a word: (*often* + with) to correspond in sound. **2** of verse: to have lines ending with a rhyming word or syllable.

rhyming slang *n* slang in which a word is replaced by a rhyming phrase often subsequently reduced to the first element, e.g. *head* becomes *loaf of bread* and then *loaf*.

rhythm *n* **1** a repeated pattern in the flow of sound, e.g. in music or poetry. **2** movement or fluctuation marked by a regular recurrence of particular elements.

rhythm and blues *n* a type of popular music with elements of blues and jazz.

rhythmic *adj* **1** of or involving rhythm. **2** regularly recurring. ➤ **rhythmically** *adv*.

rib[1] *n* **1** any of the paired curved rods of bone that stiffen the body walls of most vertebrate animals and protect the heart, lungs, etc. **2** a structural member in the framework of a ship or the wing of an aircraft. **3** a rod supporting the fabric of an umbrella. **4** an arched support in architectural vaulting. **5** a vein of a leaf. **6** a narrow ridge in a knitted or woven fabric.

rib² v (**ribbed, ribbing**) *informal* to tease (somebody). ➤ **ribbing** n.

ribald adj crudely or obscenely humorous. ➤ **ribaldry** n.

riband n a ribbon.

ribbon n **1** a narrow band of fabric used for decorative effect or as a fastening. **2** a long narrow strip. **3** a strip of inked material used in a typewriter or computer printer. **4** (*in pl*) tatters or shreds.

ribcage n the enclosing wall of the chest consisting chiefly of the ribs and their connective tissue.

riboflavin n a yellow chemical compound of the vitamin B complex occurring *esp* in green vegetables, milk, eggs, and liver.

rice n **1** a cereal grass widely cultivated in warm climates. **2** the grains of this plant used as food.

rice paper n a very thin edible material resembling paper, usu made from plant pith and used in baking and for oriental painting.

rich adj **1** having a great deal of money and possessions. **2** of a country or area: having abundant natural resources, successful industries, a strong economy, etc. **3** having high worth, value, or quality. **4** (*often* + in) well supplied or endowed. **5** vivid and deep in colour. **6** full and mellow in tone or quality. **7** of soil: having abundant plant nutrients. **8** of food: highly seasoned, fatty, oily, or sweet.

riches pl n great wealth.

richly adv **1** in a rich manner. **2** in full measure; amply.

Richter scale n a scale for expressing the magnitude of earthquakes.

rick¹ n a stack of hay, corn, etc in the open air.

rick² v *chiefly Brit* to wrench or sprain (e.g. one's neck).

rickets pl n a disease, *esp* of children, characterized by softening and deformation of bones.

rickety adj likely to collapse, *esp* because badly made or old and worn.

rickshaw or **ricksha** n a small covered two-wheeled vehicle pulled by one or more people, used *esp* in Southeast Asia.

ricochet¹ n **1** the rebound of a projectile (e.g. a bullet) that strikes a hard or flat surface at an angle. **2** something that ricochets.

ricochet² v (**ricocheted, ricocheting**) of e.g. a bullet: to rebound off a surface.

rictus n an unnatural gaping grin or grimace.

rid v (**ridding**, *past tense and past part.* **rid** or **ridded**) to relieve of something unwanted. ✳ **get rid of** to free oneself of (something unwanted).

riddance n ✳ **good riddance** an expression of relief at becoming free of something or somebody unwanted.

-ridden comb. form **1** afflicted or excessively concerned with: *guilt-ridden*. **2** excessively full of: *priest-ridden*.

riddle¹ n **1** a short and *esp* humorous verbal puzzle. **2** something or somebody difficult to understand.

riddle² n a large coarse sieve.

riddle³ v **1** to pierce with many holes. **2** (**be riddled with**) to have (something undesirable) spread throughout itself.

ride¹ v (**rode, ridden**) **1** to travel mounted on and controlling an animal, bicycle, etc. **2** to travel in a vehicle. **3** to be borne up or supported by. **4** (usu + out) to survive (e.g. a storm) without great damage or loss. **5** (usu + up) of clothing: to work its way up the body as one moves. ✳ **be riding for a fall** to act in such a way as to make disaster seem inevitable. **ride high** to experience success. **ride on** to be dependent on.

ride² n **1** an outing or journey by horseback or by vehicle. **2** any of various mechanical devices, e.g. at a funfair, for riding on. **3** a path used for riding. ✳ **take for a ride** *informal* to deceive or trick (somebody).

rider n **1** somebody who rides a horse, a bicycle, or a motorcycle. **2** a clause appended to a legal document.

ridge n **1** a long narrow stretch of elevated land or mountain range. **2** the top of a roof at the point where the two sloping sides meet. **3** an elongated part raised above a surrounding surface. ➤ **ridged** adj.

ridicule¹ n scornful or contemptuous words or actions.

ridicule² v to mock.

ridiculous adj deserving ridicule; absurd. ➤ **ridiculously** adv.

riding n (*often* **Riding**) any of three former administrative jurisdictions of Yorkshire.

rife adj **1** occurring everywhere or to a great degree. **2** (+ with) full of.

riff n a constantly repeated phrase in jazz or rock music.

riffle v **1** to leaf through (something) rapidly. **2** to search through (something) rapidly.

riffraff n disreputable or worthless people.

rifle¹ n a firearm with a long barrel with spiral grooves cut inside it.

rifle² v **1** to cut spiral grooves inside the barrel of (a rifle, cannon, etc). **2** to propel (e.g. a ball) with great force or speed.

rifle³ v to search through (e.g. a drawer or safe) in order to find and steal something.

rift n **1** a fissure or crack. **2** a disruption of friendly relations.

rig¹ v (**rigged, rigging**) **1** to fit out (e.g. a ship) with rigging, sails, etc. **2** (usu + out) to clothe or dress. **3** (often + out) to supply with equipment for a particular use. **4** (often + up) to assemble or erect. **5** to manipulate or control for dishonest purposes.

rig² *n* **1** an outfit of clothing worn for a particular activity. **2** equipment or machinery fitted for a usu specified purpose, e.g. for extracting oil or gas.

rigging *n* the ropes and chains used aboard a ship for controlling sails and supporting masts.

right¹ *adj* **1** in accordance with what is morally good, just, or proper. **2** conforming to facts or truth. **3** suitable or appropriate. **4** in a correct, proper, or healthy state. **5** on the side of somebody or something that is nearer the east when the front faces north. **6** (*often* **Right**) of the right wing in politics. **7** *chiefly Brit, informal* real or utter. ✳ **on the right side of 1** in favour with. **2** less than the specified age. ➤ **rightly** *adv.*

right² *n* **1** qualities that together merit moral approval. **2** a power, privilege, etc to which one has a just claim. **3** (*in pl*) entitlement to publish, perform, film, etc a work. **4** the part, direction, etc on the right side. **5** the right hand, or a blow struck with it. **6** *informal* a right turn. **7** (*often* **the Right**) those professing conservative or reactionary political views. ✳ **by rights** with reason or justice; properly. **in one's own right** by virtue of one's own qualifications or attributes. **in the right** correct in what one says or does. **to rights** into proper order.

right³ *adv* **1** on or towards the right. **2** in a proper or correct manner. **3** exactly. **4** in a direct line; straight. **5** all the way; completely.

right⁴ *v* **1** to correct. **2** to restore (e.g. a boat) to an upright position. **3** to compensate for or avenge (a wrong, an injustice, etc).

right angle *n* an angle of 90°, e.g. at the corner of a square. ➤ **right-angled** *adj.*

righteous *adj* morally right or justified. ➤ **righteously** *adv*, **righteousness** *n.*

rightful *adj* **1** having a just claim; legitimate. **2** held by right; legal. **3** fitting or proper. ➤ **rightfully** *adv.*

right of way *n* (*pl* **rights of way**) **1** a legal right to pass over another person's property. **2** a public path along which a right of way exists. **3** precedence accorded to one vehicle, vessel, etc over another.

right wing *n* **1** (*often* **Right Wing**) the more conservative division of a political party. **2** in sport, the right side of the field when facing towards the opposing team. ➤ **right-wing** *adj*, **right-winger** *n.*

rigid *adj* **1** unable to bend or be bent; stiff. **2** inflexibly set in opinions or habits. **3** unable to be changed. ➤ **rigidity** *n*, **rigidly** *adv.*

rigmarole *n* **1** an absurdly long and complex procedure. **2** a nonsensical account or explanation.

rigor mortis *n* the temporary rigidity of muscles that occurs after death.

rigorous *adj* **1** very strict. **2** harsh or severe. **3** scrupulously accurate; precise. ➤ **rigorously** *adv.*

rigour (*NAmer* **rigor**) *n* **1** strictness. **2** (*in pl*) conditions that make life difficult or unpleasant.

rile *v* to make angry or resentful.

rill *n* a small brook.

rim¹ *n* **1** an outer edge of something circular. **2** an outer edge or boundary.

rim² *v* (**rimmed, rimming**) to serve as a rim for; to border.

rime *n* a thin coating of frost.

rind *n* a tough outer layer of fruit, cheese, bacon, etc.

ring¹ *n* **1** a circular band usu of precious metal, worn on the finger. **2** a circular line, figure, arrangement, or object. **3** a circular electric element or gas burner set into the top of a cooker. **4** a space, often a circular one, for shows, competitions, or *esp* a circus. **5** a square enclosure in which boxing or wrestling matches are held. **6** an exclusive association of people, often for a corrupt purpose. ✳ **hold the ring** to act as a neutral umpire in a dispute. **run rings round somebody** *informal* to outdo or outwit somebody completely.

ring² *v* (*past tense and past part.* **ringed**) to place, form, draw, etc a ring round; to encircle. ➤ **ringed** *adj.*

ring³ *v* (**rang, rung**) **1** to make, or cause to make, a resonant sound like that of a bell. **2** (+ for) to sound a bell as a summons. **3** (*often* + with) to be filled with resonant sound. **4** of one's ears: to have the sensation of a continuous humming sound. **5** *chiefly Brit* (*often* + up) to telephone. ✳ **ring a bell** to sound familiar. **ring the changes** to vary the manner of doing or arranging something. **ring true** to appear to be true or authentic.

ring⁴ *n* **1** a clear resonant sound as made by vibrating metal. **2** the act of ringing. **3** *Brit, informal* a telephone call. **4** a sound or character suggestive of a particular quality or feeling: *This story has a familiar ring to it.*

ring binder *n* a loose-leaf binder with split metal rings to hold the paper.

ringing *adj* **1** resounding. **2** unequivocal.

ringleader *n* a leader of a group engaged in illegal or objectionable activities.

ringlet *n* a lock of hair curled in a spiral.

ringmaster *n* the person in charge of a circus performance.

ring off *v Brit* to end a telephone conversation.

ring out *v* to sound resonantly.

ring-pull *n* a built-in ring-shaped device for opening a tin.

ring road *n* a road round a town or town centre designed to relieve traffic congestion.

ring up *v* **1** to record (a sale) by means of a cash register. **2** to telephone.

ringworm n a contagious fungal disease in which itchy ring-shaped patches form on the skin.

rink n **1** a surface of ice for ice-skating, ice hockey, or curling. **2** an enclosure for roller-skating. **3** part of a bowling green being used for a match.

rinse[1] v **1** (often + out) to remove soap from (washed clothing) with clean water. **2** (often + out) to remove (dirt, impurities, or unwanted matter) by washing lightly.

rinse[2] n **1** an act of rinsing. **2** liquid used for rinsing. **3** a solution that temporarily tints the hair.

riot[1] n **1** a violent public disturbance caused by a large crowd of people. **2** a profuse and random display. **3** informal somebody or something wildly funny. ✳ **run riot** to act wildly or without restraint.

riot[2] v (**rioted, rioting**) to participate in a riot. ➤ **rioter** n.

riotous adj **1** wild and disorderly; constituting a riot. **2** profuse and brightly coloured.

RIP abbr rest in peace.

rip[1] v (**ripped, ripping**) **1** to tear or become torn. **2** (+ out/off) to remove by force. ✳ **let rip** informal to do something without restraint.

rip[2] n a tear or torn split.

rip[3] n a body of rough water formed by the meeting of opposing currents, winds, etc.

riparian adj of or occurring on the bank of a river.

ripcord n a cord for releasing a parachute from its pack.

ripe adj **1** of fruit or grain: fully developed and ready for harvesting or eating. **2** of a cheese or wine: aged to full flavour. **3** (+ for) fully prepared or ready for. ✳ **a ripe old age** a very great age. ➤ **ripely** adv, **ripeness** n.

ripen v to make or become ripe.

rip off v informal **1** to rob or defraud. **2** to steal.

rip-off n informal **1** an instance of financial exploitation, esp overcharging. **2** an act of stealing.

riposte n a quick-witted reply or retort.

ripple[1] n **1** a small wave or a succession of small waves. **2** a sound like that of rippling water. **3** a feeling or emotion that spreads through a person, place, etc. **4** ice cream with coloured and flavoured bands of syrup running through it.

ripple[2] v **1** to stir up small waves on (water). **2** to flow in small waves. **3** to spread irregularly outwards, esp from a central point.

rip-roaring adj noisily excited or exciting; exuberant.

riptide n **1** = RIP[3]. **2** a strong surface current flowing outwards from a shore.

rise[1] v (**rose, risen**) **1** to move upwards. **2** to slope upwards. **3** to assume an upright position, esp from lying, kneeling, or sitting. **4** to get up from sleep or from one's bed. **5** of the

sun, moon, etc: to appear above the horizon. **6** to increase in amount, number, volume, or intensity. **7** to attain a higher office or rank. **8** (+ to) to show oneself equal to (a challenge). **9** (often + up) to rebel; to take up arms. **10** of a river: to have its source. ✳ **rise above** to overcome or not be affected by (difficulties, unworthy feelings, etc).

rise[2] n **1** a movement upwards. **2** an upward slope. **3** an increase. **4** Brit an increase in pay. ✳ **give rise to** to be the origin or cause of.

riser n **1** somebody who rises in a specified manner: an early riser. **2** the upright part between two consecutive stair treads.

risible adj arousing laughter; ridiculous. ➤ **risibility** n.

rising[1] adj **1** approaching a specified age. **2** achieving a higher rank or greater influence.

rising[2] n an insurrection or uprising.

rising damp n Brit moisture that has entered the floor of a building and moved up a wall.

risk[1] n **1** a dangerous element or factor. **2** a possibility of loss, injury, or damage. **3** somebody or something that is a hazard. ✳ **at risk** (often + of) in danger. **at somebody's (own) risk** with the person concerned accepting responsibility for any possible harm or loss to themselves.

risk[2] v **1** to expose (e.g. one's life) to danger. **2** to incur the possibility of (something unpleasant happening).

risky adj (**-ier, -iest**) involving danger or the possibility of loss or failure. ➤ **riskily** adv, **riskiness** n.

risotto n (pl **-os**) an Italian dish of rice flavoured with vegetables, shellfish, etc.

risqué adj verging on impropriety or indecency.

rissole n a small fried cake of cooked minced food, esp meat.

rite n a ceremonial, esp religious act or procedure.

rite of passage n a ritual associated with a change of status, e.g. assuming adult responsibilities.

ritual[1] n **1** a solemn or religious ceremony involving a series of actions carried out in a set order. **2** an action habitually carried out in a set order.

ritual[2] adj relating to rituals; ceremonial. ➤ **ritually** adv.

ritzy adj (**-ier, -iest**) informal ostentatiously smart.

rival[1] n **1** any of two or more people competing for a single goal. **2** somebody or something that equals another in desirable qualities. ➤ **rivalry** n.

rival[2] v (**rivalled, rivalling**, NAmer **rivaled, rivaling**) to possess qualities that approach or equal (those of another).

rive v (*past part.* **riven**) (*usu* **be riven**) to be torn apart.

river n 1 a natural stream of water of considerable volume. 2 (*often in pl*) a copious or overwhelming quantity.

rivet[1] n a headed metal pin used to join two metal plates.

rivet[2] v (**riveted, riveting**) 1 to fasten with rivets. 2 to attract and hold (the attention, etc) completely.

riveting *adj* holding the attention; fascinating.

riviera n (*also* **Riviera**) a coastal region, usu with a mild climate, frequented as a resort.

rivulet n a small stream.

RN *abbr Brit* Royal Navy.

Rn *abbr* the chemical symbol for radon.

RNA n a nucleic acid similar to DNA that is associated with the control of cellular chemical activities.

roach[1] n (*pl* **roaches** or **roach**) a silver-white European freshwater fish of the carp family.

roach[2] n *chiefly NAmer, informal* a cockroach.

road n 1 an open, usu paved way for the passage of vehicles, people, and animals. 2 a route or path: *the road to ruin.*

roadblock n a road barricade set up by an army, the police, etc.

roadholding n the ability of a moving vehicle to remain stable, *esp* when cornering.

roadie n *informal* a person who looks after the transport and setting up of equipment of a rock group.

road map n 1 a map showing the roads of an area. 2 a plan of action for achieving a particular result.

road rage n violent and aggressive behaviour by a motorist towards another road user.

road show n 1 a public-relations or government information unit that travels from place to place to give displays. 2 a radio or television programme broadcast from different locations.

roadster n an open sports car.

road test n a test of a vehicle, or other piece of equipment, under practical operating conditions. ➤ **road-test** v.

roadway n the part of a road used by vehicles.

roadworks *pl* n *Brit* the repair or construction of roads.

roadworthy *adj* of a vehicle: in a fit condition to be used on the roads.

roam v 1 to wander. 2 to wander over (an area).

roan *adj* of horses and cattle: having a reddish brown coat lightened by some white hairs.

roar[1] n 1 the deep prolonged cry of a wild animal, e.g. a lion. 2 a loud cry of pain, anger, or laughter. 3 a loud continuous confused sound.

roar[2] v 1 to give a roar. 2 to laugh loudly. 3 of a fire: to burn fiercely and noisily. 4 to happen or progress rapidly.

roaring *adj informal* marked by energetic or successful activity: *a roaring trade.*

roast[1] v 1 to cook (*esp* meat) by exposing it to dry heat, e.g. in an oven. 2 to be excessively hot.

roast[2] n a piece of meat roasted or suitable for roasting.

roast[3] *adj* of food, *esp* meat: roasted.

roasting[1] *adj informal* extremely hot.

roasting[2] n *informal* a severe scolding.

rob v (**robbed, robbing**) 1 to steal something from (a person or place), *esp* by violence or threat. 2 (+ of) to deprive of. 3 *informal* to overcharge. ➤ **robber** n.

robbery n (*pl* **-ies**) the act of robbing.

robe[1] n 1 a long flowing outer garment, esp one used for ceremonial occasions or as a symbol of office. 2 *NAmer* a dressing gown.

robe[2] v to clothe or cover with a robe.

robin n a small brownish bird with an orange-red throat and breast.

robot n 1 a machine programmed to carry out a sequence of actions automatically. 2 *esp* in science fiction, a machine that carries out human functions.

robotic *adj* 1 relating to robots. 2 stiff and mechanical; lacking human warmth.

robotics *pl* n the study of the construction and behaviour of robots.

robust *adj* 1 exhibiting vigorous health or stamina. 2 strongly formed or constructed. 3 forceful and determined. ➤ **robustly** *adv.*

rock[1] n 1 hard solid mineral matter forming the earth's crust. 2 a particular form of this, e.g. granite or limestone. 3 a large mass of rock forming an outcrop, cliff, etc. 4 a boulder. 5 *NAmer* a stone. 6 *Brit* a sweet in the form of a hard and brittle cylindrical stick. 7 *informal* a gem, *esp* a diamond. * **on the rocks 1** *informal* in difficulties. 2 of a drink: served over ice cubes.

rock[2] v 1 to move gently back and forth or from side to side. 2 to sway or cause to sway rapidly or violently. 3 to disturb or upset. 4 to dance to or play rock music. * **rock the boat** to cause problems for one's colleagues, etc.

rock[3] n a style of popular music played on electronically amplified instruments and with a persistent, heavily accented beat.

rock and roll n SEE ROCK 'N' ROLL.

rock bottom n the lowest level.

rocker n 1 a rock musician or fan. 2 a curved piece of wood or metal on which an object, e.g. a cradle, rocks. * **off one's rocker** *informal* crazy.

rockery n (*pl* **-ies**) a bank of rocks and earth where rock plants are grown.

rocket[1] n 1 a firework with a guiding stick that shoots high into the air before bursting. 2 a spacecraft, missile, etc propelled by a jet engine that operates independently of the oxygen in the air. 3 *Brit, informal* a sharp reprimand.

rocket² v (**rocketed, rocketing**) **1** of prices, etc: to increase rapidly or spectacularly. **2** to travel with the speed of a rocket.

rocket³ n a Mediterranean plant of the cabbage family, used in salad.

rocking chair n a chair mounted on rockers.

rocking horse n a toy horse mounted on rockers.

rock music n = ROCK³.

rock 'n' roll or **rock and roll** n a style of popular music, originating in the 1950s, characterized by a heavy beat, simple melodies, and often country, folk, and blues elements.

rock salt n common salt occurring as a solid mineral.

rock solid adj **1** completely firm, fixed, or stable. **2** completely reliable or committed.

rocky¹ adj (**-ier, -iest**) **1** full of or consisting of rocks. **2** filled with obstacles; difficult.

rocky² adj (**-ier, -iest**) unsteady; tottering.

rococo adj of an 18th-century style of architecture and decoration characterized by elaborate curved forms and shell motifs.

rod n **1** a slender bar, e.g. of wood or metal. **2** a pole with a line for fishing.

rode v past tense of RIDE¹.

rodent n any of an order of gnawing mammals including the mice, rats, squirrels, and beavers.

rodeo n (pl **-os**) a public performance featuring the riding skills of cowboys.

roe n the eggs or sperm of a fish.

roebuck n (pl **roebucks** or **roebuck**) a male roe deer.

roe deer n a small graceful deer with erect cylindrical antlers.

roentgen n see RÖNTGEN.

roger interj used in radio communications to indicate that a message has been received and understood.

rogue n **1** a wilfully dishonest or corrupt person. **2** a mischievous person. **3** an animal roaming alone and vicious and destructive.

roguish adj mischievous.

roister v archaic to engage in noisy revelry.

role or **rôle** n **1** a part played by an actor. **2** the function or expected contribution to a job, situation, etc of a person or thing.

role model n somebody who serves as an example to others of how to behave.

role playing n behaving in a way typical of another person or of a stereotype.

roll¹ v **1** to move along by turning over and over. **2** of a vehicle: to move on wheels. **3** to rotate (the eyes) in their sockets. **4** to move steadily onward or pass in succession. **5** of a ship, aircraft, etc: to rock from side to side as it moves forward. **6** to begin operating, or to cause (a machine) to begin operating. **7** (often + up) to wrap (something) round itself to form a cylinder or ball. **8** (often + up) to curl or wind itself into a cylindrical shape. **9** to shape or

flatten by rolling. **10** of thunder: to make a long reverberating sound. * **be rolling in it/in money** informal to be very wealthy.

roll² n **1** something rolled up to resemble a cylinder. **2** a small round or cylindrical loaf of bread. **3** an official list of people's names.

roll³ n **1** a rolling or swaying movement. **2** a gymnastic manoeuvre in which the body is tucked up and rolled completely over forwards or backwards. **3** a sound produced by rapid strokes on a drum. **4** a prolonged reverberating sound of thunder. * **on a roll** informal having a period of success.

roll call n the calling out of a list of names, e.g. for checking attendance.

roller n **1** a revolving cylinder used to move, press, shape, or apply something. **2** a hair curler. **3** a long heavy wave.

Rollerblade n trademark (usu in pl) a roller skate with a single central line of wheels.

roller coaster n **1** an elevated railway in a funfair, constructed with steep curves and inclines. **2** a situation in which one experiences highs and lows.

roller skate n a boot with four small wheels attached to the sole that allow the wearer to glide over hard surfaces. ➤ **roller-skate** v, **roller skater** n, **roller skating** n.

rollicking¹ adj boisterously carefree.

rollicking² n Brit, informal a severe scolding.

rolling pin n a long cylinder for rolling out dough.

rolling stock n the vehicles owned and used by a railway.

rollmop n a herring fillet rolled up and pickled.

roll neck n a loose high collar, esp on a jumper, worn rolled over.

roll-on adj of e.g. deodorant: applied to the skin by means of a rolling ball.

roll up v **1** to roll into a cylinder. **2** informal to arrive.

roly-poly¹ n (pl **-ies**) a pudding consisting of suet pastry spread with jam, rolled, and baked or steamed.

roly-poly² adj informal short and plump.

Roman¹ adj **1** of Rome or the Romans. **2** (**roman**) of type: not slanted; perpendicular.

Roman² n **1** a native or inhabitant of ancient or modern Rome. **2** (**roman**) roman letters or type.

Roman alphabet n the alphabet used for writing most European languages, including English.

Roman candle n a cylindrical firework that discharges balls of fire at intervals.

Roman Catholic¹ n a member of the Roman Catholic Church. ➤ **Roman Catholicism** n.

Roman Catholic² adj relating or belonging to the Roman Catholic Church.

Roman Catholic Church n a Christian episcopal church headed by the pope and having a form of service centred on the Mass.

Romance *n* the family of languages developed from Latin that includes e.g. French, Spanish, and Italian.

romance[1] *n* **1** romantic love, or the feelings and behaviour usually associated with it. **2** a love affair. **3** a story or film about romantic love. **4** an emotional aura attaching to an enthralling era, adventure, or pursuit.

romance[2] *v* to court (somebody).

Romanesque *n* a style of architecture developed in western Europe between c.AD 900 and 1200 and characterized by the use of round arches. ➤ **Romanesque** *adj*.

Roman numeral *n* a numeral in the ancient Roman system of numbering using the symbols I, V, X, L, C, D, and M.

romantic[1] *adj* **1** involving sexual attraction accompanied by tender, loving feelings and elaborate courtship. **2** associated with or conducive to love. **3** impractical or overly idealistic. **4** (*often* **Romantic**) of or having the characteristics of romanticism. ➤ **romantically** *adv*.

romantic[2] *n* **1** a romantic person. **2** (**Romantic**) a Romantic writer, artist, or composer.

romanticism *n* (*also* **Romanticism**) a late 18th- and early 19th-century literary and artistic movement that emphasized individual aspirations, nature, and the emotions.

romanticize *or* **-ise** *v* to present (a person or incident) in a misleadingly romantic way.

Romany *n* (*pl* **-ies**) **1** the Indic language of the gypsies. **2** a gypsy.

Romeo *n* (*pl* **-os**) a romantic male lover.

romp[1] *v* **1** to play in a boisterous manner. **2** *informal* to engage in light-hearted sexual activity. ✳ **romp home** *informal* to win easily. **romp through** to accomplish very easily.

romp[2] *n* **1** boisterous or bawdy entertainment or play. **2** *informal* a period of light-hearted sexual activity.

rompers *pl n* a one-piece child's garment.

rondo *n* (*pl* **-os**) an instrumental composition with an opening section that recurs in the form ABACADA.

röntgen *or* **roentgen** *n* a unit of ionizing radiation.

rood screen *n* a large crucifix on a screen at the entrance to the chancel of a church.

roof[1] *n* (*pl* **roofs**) **1** the upper rigid cover of a building, vehicle, etc. **2** the vaulted or covering part of the mouth, skull, etc. **3** a ceiling. ✳ **go through the roof 1** of e.g. prices: to reach extraordinarily high levels. **2** hit the roof (see HIT[1]).

roof[2] *v* to cover with a roof. ➤ **roofed** *adj*, **roofer** *n*, **roofing** *n*.

roofer *n* a person who builds or repairs roofs.

roof rack *n chiefly Brit* a metal carrying frame fixed on top of a car.

rook[1] *n* a common bird with black plumage, similar to a crow but nesting in colonies and having a bare grey face.

rook[2] *v informal* to defraud, cheat, or overcharge.

rook[3] *n* in chess, a castle-shaped piece that can move in a straight line across any number of squares.

rookery *n* (*pl* **-ies**) **1** the nests, usu built in the upper branches of trees, of a colony of rooks. **2** a breeding ground of a colony of penguins, seals, etc.

rookie *n informal* a new recruit.

room[1] *n* **1** a partitioned part of the inside of a building. **2** (*also in pl*) a set of rooms used as a separate lodging. **3** an extent of space sufficient or available for something.

room[2] *v NAmer* (*often* + with) to share lodgings.

roomy *adj* (**-ier**, **-iest**) having ample room; spacious.

roost[1] *n* a support or place where birds roost.

roost[2] *v* of a bird: to settle down for rest or sleep.

rooster *n* = COCK[1].

root[1] *n* **1** the underground part of a flowering plant that anchors it and absorbs food. **2** the part of a tooth, hair, the tongue, etc by which it is attached to the body. **3** an underlying cause or basis. **4** (*in pl*) family background or origin, or a feeling of belonging established through familiarity with a particular place. **5** a number which produces a given number when multiplied by itself an indicated number of times. ✳ **take root 1** of a plant: to become rooted. **2** to become fixed or established.

root[2] *v* **1** to enable (a plant) to develop roots. **2** to fix or implant as if by roots. **3** (**be rooted in**) to originate or have developed from. ➤ **rooted** *adj*.

root[3] *v* **1** of a pig: to dig with the snout. **2** (+ about/in) to search unsystematically.

root[4] *v informal* (+ for) to lend vociferous or enthusiastic support to.

rootless *adj* having no established home or attachment to a particular place.

root out *v* to get rid of or destroy completely.

rootstock *n* **1** an underground plant part formed from several stems. **2** a plant onto which a scion is grafted.

rope[1] *n* **1** a strong thick cord composed of strands of fibres or wire twisted together. **2** a row or string of things. **3** (**the ropes**) the sides of a boxing ring. **4** (**the ropes**) the methods or procedures used in a job or activity. ✳ **on the ropes** close to defeat.

rope[2] *v* **1** to fasten or tie with a rope. **2** (*usu* + off) to enclose or separate off with a rope.

rope in *v* to persuade (somebody) to join in or help with an activity.

rope ladder *n* a ladder having rope sides.

ropy *or* **ropey** *adj* (**-ier**, **-iest**) *Brit, informal* **1** of poor quality; shoddy. **2** somewhat unwell.

rosary *n* (*pl* **-ies**) a string of beads used in counting prayers while they are being recited.

rose[1] *n* **1** a prickly shrub with showy fragrant flowers. **2** a flower of this shrub. **3** a perforated outlet for water, e.g. from a shower or watering can. **4** a circular fitting that anchors the flex of a light bulb to a ceiling. **5** a pale to dark pinkish colour.

rosé *n* a light pink table wine.

rose[2] *v* past tense of RISE[1].

rosehip *n* see HIP[2].

rosemary *n* a shrubby plant with fragrant leaves that are used as a cooking herb.

rosette *n* **1** an ornament made of material gathered to resemble a rose and worn as a badge, trophy, or trimming. **2** a stylized carved or moulded rose used as a decorative motif in architecture.

rosewood *n* the valuable dark red or purplish wood of a tropical tree.

Rosh Hashanah or **Rosh Hashana** *n* the Jewish New Year.

rosin *n* a translucent resin used for rubbing on violin bows.

roster[1] *n* **1** a list giving the order in which personnel are to perform a duty, go on leave, etc. **2** a list of people available for a particular task or duty.

roster[2] *v* to place on a roster.

rostrum *n* (*pl* **rostra** or **rostrums**) a raised platform, *esp* for making a speech.

rosy *adj* (**-ier, -iest**) **1** rose-pink. **2** characterized by or encouraging optimism.

rot[1] *v* (**rotted, rotting**) to decompose, *esp* by the action of bacteria or fungi.

rot[2] *n* **1** the state of being rotten. **2** *informal* nonsense or rubbish.

rota *n* *chiefly Brit* a list specifying a fixed order of rotation, e.g. of people or duties.

rotary *adj* **1** characterized by rotation. **2** having a principal part that turns on an axis.

rotate *v* **1** to turn about an axis or a centre. **2** to take turns at performing an act or operation. **3** to cause (a crop or crops) to grow in rotation. **4** to exchange (individuals or units) with others. ➤ **rotatory** *adj*.

rotation *n* **1** movement on or around an axis. **2** one complete turn. **3** recurrence in a regular series. **4** the growing of different crops in succession in one field.

rote *n* the mechanical repetition of something to implant it in the memory.

rotisserie *n* a rotating spit on which meat is cooked.

rotor *n* **1** a part that revolves, *esp* in an electrical machine. **2** the system of a hub and horizontal blades that enables a helicopter to fly.

rotten *adj* **1** having rotted. **2** morally corrupt. **3** *informal* extremely unpleasant. **4** *informal* unhappy; ashamed. **5** *informal* inferior; useless.

rotter *n* *informal, dated* an objectionable or unprincipled person.

Rottweiler *n* a tall strongly-built black-and-tan dog with short hair.

rotund *adj* **1** markedly plump. **2** rounded.

rouble or **ruble** *n* the basic monetary unit of Russia.

roué *n* a debauched man.

rouge *n* a red cosmetic, *esp* for the cheeks or lips.

rough[1] *adj* **1** having an irregular or uneven surface; not smooth. **2** not gentle; harsh or violent. **3** of the sea: moving violently, with large waves. **4** of the weather: unpleasant; stormy. **5** lacking finish or refinement. **6** crudely or hastily made. **7** not thoroughly worked out; approximate. **8** of a voice: harsh-sounding. **9** *informal* difficult or unpleasant.

rough[2] *n* **1** *chiefly Brit, informal* a hooligan or ruffian. **2** (**the rough**) uneven ground covered with high grass, brush, and stones bordering a golf fairway. **3** a quick preliminary drawing or layout.

rough[3] *adv Brit* in want of material comforts; without proper lodging.

rough[4] *v* ✳ **rough it** *informal* to live in uncomfortable or primitive conditions.

roughage *n* coarse bulky food, e.g. bran, that is relatively high in fibre.

rough diamond *n* **1** an uncut diamond. **2** a person without social graces but of an upright or amiable nature.

roughen *v* to make or become rough.

rough justice *n* harsh or unfair treatment.

roughly *adv* **1** with insolence or violence. **2** crudely. **3** approximately.

roughneck *n* **1** *informal* a tough. **2** a worker who handles heavy drilling equipment on an oil rig.

rough out *v* to shape or plan in a preliminary way.

roughshod ✳ **ride roughshod over** to treat (a person or their rights) without justice or consideration.

rough up *v informal* to beat up.

roulette *n* a gambling game in which players bet on which compartment of a revolving wheel a small ball will come to rest in.

round[1] *adj* **1** circular. **2** cylindrical. **3** spherical. **4** shaped in a smooth curve. **5** of a voice: richly resonant in tone. **6** of a number: approximately correct; expressed as the nearest large unit. ➤ **roundness** *n*.

round[2] *adv chiefly Brit* **1** in a circular or curved path. **2** with revolving or rotating motion. **3** in circumference. **4** in an encircling position. **5** in or to the other or a specified direction. **6** in the specified order or relationship: *the right way round*. **7** to a particular person or place: *invite somebody round*. **8** back to consciousness or awareness. **9** from beginning to end: *all year* *round.* ✻ **round about 1** approximately; more or less. **2** in a ring round; on all sides of.

round³ *prep chiefly Brit* **1** so as to revolve or progress about (a centre). **2** so as to encircle or enclose. **3** so as to avoid or get past. **4** in a position on the other side of: *round the corner.* **5** near to: *somewhere round here.*

round⁴ *n* **1** a circular piece or spherical mass. **2** a route regularly travelled, e.g. by a person making deliveries. **3** a recurring sequence of events or tasks: *the weekly round.* **4** an event or series of events constituting a single stage in a larger process, *esp* in sport. **5** a division of a boxing or wrestling match. **6** in music, an unaccompanied song for three or more voices in which each sings the same tune starting one after the other. **7** a set of drinks served at one time to each person in a group. **8** a unit of ammunition enabling a gun to fire one shot. **9** *Brit* a sandwich made with two whole slices of bread.

round⁵ *v* **1** to go round (a bend or corner). **2** (*often* + off/up/down) to express (a figure) as a round number. **3** (*often* + off) to make round or rounded. **4** (*often* + off/out) to bring to completion or perfection.

roundabout¹ *n* **1** a road junction with a central island about which traffic moves in one direction only. **2** *Brit* a merry-go-round. **3** *Brit* a rotatable platform that is an amusement in a children's playground.

roundabout² *adj* circuitous; indirect.

rounded *adj* **1** smoothly curved. **2** fully developed in all respects.

roundel *n* **1** a circular panel, window, etc. **2** a circular mark identifying the nationality of a warplane.

rounders *n* a team game with bat and ball, where players try to score by running round all four bases before the ball is fielded.

Roundhead *n* an adherent of Parliament in the English Civil War.

roundly *adv* **1** in a blunt or severe manner. **2** thoroughly.

round on *v* to attack or scold (somebody) suddenly.

round robin *n* **1** a tournament in which every contestant plays every other contestant in turn. **2** a written petition or protest.

round-the-clock *adj* lasting or continuing 24 hours a day; constant.

round trip *n* a trip to a place and back.

round up *v* to gather in or bring together (people or things) from various quarters.

roundworm *n* a round-bodied parasitic worm that infests the intestines of people and animals.

rouse *v* **1** to wake up. **2** to make active. **3** to stimulate or excite (e.g. one's curiosity).

rousing *adj* stirring.

rout¹ *n* **1** a confused retreat. **2** a disastrous defeat.

rout² *v* to defeat (an army, team, etc) decisively or disastrously.

route¹ *n* a course planned or taken to get from a starting point to a destination.

route² *v* (**routeing** *or* **routing**) to send by a selected route.

routine¹ *n* **1** a sequence of actions performed regularly or habitually in the same order. **2** a fixed piece of entertainment often repeated. **3** a sequence of computer instructions for carrying out a given task.

routine² *adj* **1** in accordance with established procedure. **2** commonplace or repetitious in character. ➤ **routinely** *adv.*

roux /rooh/ *n* (*pl* **roux**) a cooked mixture of fat and flour used as a thickening agent in a sauce.

rove *v* **1** to wander aimlessly or idly. **2** of the eyes: to look around at one object after the other. ➤ **rover** *n.*

row¹ /roh/ *n* a number of objects or people arranged in a straight line. ✻ **in a row** *informal* one after another.

row² /roh/ *v* to propel a boat by means of oars. ➤ **rower** *n.*

row³ /row/ *n informal* **1** *chiefly Brit* a noisy quarrel. **2** *chiefly Brit* excessive or unpleasant noise.

row⁴ /row/ *v chiefly Brit, informal* to quarrel.

rowan *n* a small tree with white flowers and red berries.

rowdy¹ *adj* (**-ier, -iest**) rough or boisterous.

rowdy² *n* (*pl* **-ies**) a rowdy person.

rowlock *n* a device on the side of a boat for holding an oar in place.

royal¹ *adj* **1** relating, related, or belonging to a monarch. **2** suitable for royalty; regal or magnificent. **3** of superior size or quality. ➤ **royally** *adv.*

royal² *n informal* a member of a royal family.

royal blue *n* rich purplish blue.

royalist *n* (*also* **Royalist**) a supporter of a king or queen or of monarchical government, e.g. a Cavalier. ➤ **royalist** *adj.*

royal jelly *n* a highly nutritious secretion of the honeybee fed to larvae that will develop into queens.

royalty *n* (*pl* **-ies**) **1** people of royal blood. **2** regal character or bearing. **3** a payment made to an author or composer each time a work of theirs is performed or a copy of it is sold.

RSPCA *abbr Brit* Royal Society for the Prevention of Cruelty to Animals.

RSVP *abbr* (French) répondez s'il vous plaît = please reply.

Rt Hon. *abbr Brit* Right Honourable.

Ru *abbr* the chemical symbol for ruthenium.

rub¹ *v* (**rubbed, rubbing**) **1** to move over the surface of (something), *esp* with a back-and-forth motion, while pressing down on it. **2** to move along a surface while pressing against it. **3** to apply (a substance) to a surface by rubbing.

✱ **rub shoulders** to mix socially. **rub up the wrong way** to irritate or displease.

rub² n 1 an act of rubbing. 2 a cream or ointment for rubbing on a painful body part. 3 (**the rub**) an obstacle or difficulty.

rub along v Brit, informal 1 to continue coping in a difficult situation. 2 to remain on friendly terms.

rubber¹ n 1 an elastic substance obtained by coagulating the juice of a tropical tree and used in car tyres, waterproof materials, etc. 2 Brit a small piece of rubber or plastic used for rubbing out pencil marks. 3 NAmer, informal a condom. ➤ **rubbery** adj.

rubber² n in bridge or whist, a unit of play consisting of three or five games.

rubber band n a loop of rubber used for holding small objects together.

rubberneck v informal 1 to show exaggerated curiosity. 2 to engage in sightseeing.

rubber plant n a plant of the fig family with glossy leathery leaves, grown as a houseplant.

rubber stamp n 1 a stamp of rubber for making imprints. 2 a routine endorsement or approval.

rubber-stamp v to approve (a plan, etc) as a matter of routine or at the dictate of somebody else.

rubbing n an image of a raised surface obtained by placing paper over it and rubbing the paper with charcoal, chalk, etc.

rubbish¹ n 1 chiefly Brit worthless or rejected articles. 2 nonsense. ➤ **rubbishy** adj.

rubbish² v Brit, informal to condemn as rubbish.

rubble n broken fragments of building material, e.g. brick or stone.

rub down v to clean, smooth, or dry by rubbing. ➤ **rubdown** n.

rubella n a virus disease, similar to but milder than measles.

rubicund adj ruddy.

ruble n see ROUBLE.

rub off v 1 to remove by rubbing, or disappear through rubbing. 2 (often + on) to be transferred to somebody through contact or example.

rub out v to remove or be removable with a rubber.

rubric n 1 a heading, e.g. in a book or manuscript. 2 an authoritative rule, esp for the conduct of church ceremonial.

ruby n (pl -ies) 1 a red precious stone. 2 the dark red colour of the ruby. 3 (used before a noun) marking a 40th anniversary.

RUC abbr Royal Ulster Constabulary.

ruche n a pleated or gathered strip of fabric used for trimming. ➤ **ruched** adj.

ruck¹ n 1 in rugby, a loose scrum formed round the ball when it is on the ground. 2 an indistin-

guishable mass of people or things. 3 Brit, informal a fight.

ruck² v in rugby, to be part of a ruck.

ruck³ v (often + up) to wrinkle or crease.

ruck⁴ n a wrinkle or crease.

rucksack n a lightweight bag carried on the back by shoulder straps.

ruckus n a row or disturbance.

ruction n informal 1 (in pl) a violent dispute. 2 a disturbance or uproar.

rudder n 1 a flat hinged piece attached vertically to a ship's stern and used for steering. 2 a movable piece attached to the tailfin of an aircraft to enable it to turn horizontally.

ruddy adj (-ier, -iest) 1 said of a complexion: having a healthy reddish colour. 2 red; reddish. 3 Brit, euphem = BLOODY 4.

rude adj 1 discourteous. 2 vulgar; indecent. 3 sudden and unpleasant; abrupt. 4 robust; vigorous. ➤ **rudely** adv, **rudeness** n.

rudiment n 1 (usu in pl) a basic principle or element, or a fundamental skill. 2 (usu in pl) something in its earliest stage of development.

rudimentary adj 1 basic and simple. 2 undeveloped or only partly developed.

rue v to feel bitter regret for (e.g. a past deed).

rueful adj expressing regret, often mixed with self-deprecating humour. ➤ **ruefully** adv.

ruff n 1 a broad starched collar of fluted linen or muslin. 2 a fringe of long hairs or feathers growing round the neck of a bird or animal.

ruffian n a brutal and lawless person.

ruffle¹ v 1 to disturb the smoothness of. 2 to trouble or vex. 3 to make (fabric) into a ruffle. ➤ **ruffled** adj.

ruffle² n a strip of fabric gathered or pleated on one edge.

rug n 1 a small carpet. 2 chiefly Brit a woollen blanket used as a wrap.

rugby or **Rugby** n a team game played with an oval ball, which features kicking, hand-to-hand passing, and tackling.

rugged adj 1 of terrain: having a rough uneven surface or outline. 2 strongly built or constituted; sturdy. 3 of a man: having attractively strong masculine features. ➤ **ruggedly** adv, **ruggedness** n.

rugger n Brit, informal rugby.

ruin¹ n 1 destruction or spoiling. 2 (often in pl) the remains of something dilapidated or destroyed. 3 a person's downfall, or the cause of it. 4 the total loss of one's money and other assets.

ruin² v 1 to damage irreparably. 2 to reduce to financial ruin. 3 to make thoroughly unpleasant or unenjoyable; to spoil.

ruination n the act of ruining, or a cause of ruin.

ruinous adj 1 causing ruin or the likelihood of ruin. 2 ruined. ➤ **ruinously** adv.

rule[1] *n* **1** a statement of what constitutes right conduct that people are expected to obey. **2** the exercise of sovereign authority, or the period during which a particular ruler or government exercises it. **3** (**the rule**) what happens normally or customarily. **4** a printed or written line or dash. ＊ **as a rule** generally; for the most part.

rule[2] *v* **1** to have sovereign power over (a nation or people). **2** to exercise control over. **3** to keep under control; to restrain. **4** to make a judicial decision. **5** to draw (a line) with a ruler. **6** to mark (paper) with parallel lines.

rule in *v* to consider as a possibility.

rule of thumb *n* a rough practical or common-sense method.

rule out *v* **1** to exclude. **2** to deny the possibility of. **3** to make impossible.

ruler *n* **1** somebody who rules. **2** a smooth-edged strip of wood, plastic, etc that is marked off in units, e.g. centimetres, and is used for drawing straight lines or measuring.

ruling *n* an official or authoritative decision.

rum[1] *n* an alcoholic spirit made by distilling molasses.

rum[2] *adj* (**rummer, rummest**) *Brit, informal, dated* peculiar; strange.

rumba *or* **rhumba** *n* a ballroom dance of Cuban origin marked by pronounced hip movements.

rumble[1] *v* **1** to make a low heavy rolling sound. **2** *Brit, informal* to discover the true character of.

rumble[2] *n* **1** a rumbling sound. **2** *NAmer, informal* a street fight, *esp* between gangs.

rumbustious *adj chiefly Brit, informal* irrepressibly exuberant.

ruminant *n* a mammal, e.g. a cow, sheep, or camel, that chews the cud.

ruminate *v* **1** to engage in deep thought. **2** of a ruminant: to chew the cud.

rummage[1] *v* to engage in a haphazard search.

rummage[2] *n* **1** a search, *esp* among a jumbled assortment of objects. **2** *chiefly NAmer* = JUMBLE[2].

rummy *n* a card game in which each player tries to assemble combinations of related cards.

rumour[1] (*NAmer* **rumor**) *n* a statement circulated without confirmation of its truth.

rumour[2] (*NAmer* **rumor**) *v* (**be rumoured**) to be said, according to rumour, to be.

rump *n* **1** the rear part of a mammal, bird, etc. **2** *humorous* a person's buttocks. **3** a small or inferior remnant of a larger group.

rumple *v* to make or become wrinkled, crumpled, or dishevelled. ➤ **rumpled** *adj*.

rumpus *n* a noisy commotion.

run[1] *v* (**running**, *past tense* **ran**, *past part.* **run**) **1** to go at a speed faster than a walk, with only one foot on the ground at any time. **2** to hasten or move quickly. **3** to cause to move lightly or freely: *She ran a comb through her hair.* **4** of a bus or train: to operate on a regular route. **5** to

convey (somebody) a short distance in a vehicle. **6** to take part in a race. **7** to be a candidate in an election. **8** to manage or carry on (a business, enterprise, etc). **9** to operate (a vehicle, machine, etc). **10** of a machine: to function. **11** of an agreement etc: to continue in force. **12** to continue or extend over a specified period or length. **13** (+ in) of a characteristic: to be prevalent. **14** to cause (water, etc) to flow. **15** of a liquid: to flow. **16** of a colour: to spread or dissolve when wet. **17** to be at a specified level: *Inflation is running at 4 per cent.* **18** to publish (a story in a newspaper, etc). **19** to smuggle (e.g. guns or drugs). **20** (+ by/past) to outline (an idea, plan, etc) to somebody in order to ascertain their opinion of it. ＊ **run across** to meet with or discover by chance. **run after** to pursue or chase. **run into 1** to encounter (somebody) by chance. **2** to collide with. **run short of** to have little left of (a supply).

run[2] *n* **1** an act of running. **2** a journey or excursion in a car. **3** a regularly travelled course or route. **4** an inclined course, e.g. for skiing. **5** a continuous period or sequence: *a run of bad luck.* **6** (**the run of**) free access to every part of a place. **7** general tendency or direction. **8** the average or prevailing kind or class: *the general run of students.* **9** an enclosure for domestic animals. **10** a unit of scoring in cricket or baseball. **11** a ladder in tights or a stocking. ＊ **give somebody a run for their money** to present a serious challenge to somebody. **on the run 1** without pausing. **2** trying to avoid arrest or capture, *esp* after escaping from custody.

run along *v informal* to leave.

runaround *n* (**the runaround**) *informal* delaying action, *esp* in response to a request: *When I phoned to complain, they just gave me the runaround.*

runaway[1] *n* a fugitive.

runaway[2] *adj* **1** running out of control. **2** of a victory, success, etc: decisive.

run away *v* **1** to flee or escape. **2** to avoid responsibilities. ＊ **run away with 1** to go beyond the control of. **2** to believe too easily.

rundown *n* an itemized report or summary.

run down *v* **1** to knock down with a vehicle. **2** to criticize or disparage. **3** to reduce or be reduced in size or strength. **4** to deteriorate.

run-down *adj* **1** in a state of disrepair. **2** in poor health.

rune *n* **1** a character from an ancient Germanic alphabet. **2** a magical or cryptic utterance or inscription. ➤ **runic** *adj*.

rung[1] *n* **1** any of the crosspieces of a ladder. **2** a level or stage in something.

rung[2] *v* past part. of RING[3].

run in *v* **1** to use (a vehicle) carefully when it is new. **2** *informal* to arrest (somebody).

runnel *n* **1** a small stream; a brook. **2** a gutter.

runner *n* **1** a person who runs in a race or for exercise. **2** an entrant for a race that actually competes in it. **3** a messenger. **4** somebody who smuggles illicit or contraband goods. **5** a groove or bar on which something, e.g. a drawer, a sledge, or an ice skate, slides. **6** a horizontal stem from the base of a plant that buds to produce new plants. **7** a long narrow carpet. * **do a runner** *Brit, informal* to leave in haste or escape.

runner bean *n chiefly Brit* the long green pod of a climbing bean, used as a vegetable.

runner-up *n* (*pl* **runners-up**) a competitor or team that comes second in a contest.

running[1] *n* **1** the act of running. **2** management; operation. * **in/out of the running** having a good/poor chance of winning. **make the running** to set the pace.

running[2] *adj* **1** of water: flowing in a stream, etc or available through pipes. **2** of e.g. a sore: producing pus. **3** having stages that follow in rapid succession. **4** made during the course of a process or activity: *a running commentary*.

running[3] *adv* in succession.

running board *n* a footboard along the side of a car.

runny *adj* (**-ier, -iest**) **1** of a thinner or more liquid consistency than usual. **2** of the nose: continuously producing mucus.

run off *v* **1** to compose or produce quickly. **2** to decide a competition with an extra contest.

run-of-the-mill *adj* average; commonplace.

run out *v* **1** to become used up. **2** to come to an end; to expire. **3** in cricket: to dismiss a batsman by breaking the wicket while the batsman is making a run. * **run out of** to finish the available supply of. **run out on** *informal* to desert (somebody).

run over *v* **1** to injure or kill with a motor vehicle. **2** to read through quickly.

runt *n* an unusually small animal, *esp* the smallest of a litter.

run through *v* **1** to pierce with a weapon. **2** to read through quickly.

run up *v* **1** to accumulate (debts). **2** to make or erect quickly. * **run up against** to experience (an unexpected difficulty).

run-up *n* **1** a period that immediately precedes an action or event. **2** an approach run to provide momentum, e.g. for a jump or throw.

runway *n* an strip of ground on which aircraft land and take off.

rupee /rooh'pee/ *n* **1** the basic monetary unit of India, Pakistan, and Sri Lanka.

rupture[1] *n* **1** the act of breaking apart or bursting. **2** a hernia.

rupture[2] *v* **1** to break or burst. **2** to cause a hernia in (oneself or a body part).

rural *adj* relating to the country, country people, or country life. ➤ **rurally** *adv*.

ruse *n* a wily scheme or trick.

rush[1] *v* **1** to move forward, progress, or act quickly or eagerly or without preparation. **2** to perform or finish in a short time or at high speed. **3** to urge (somebody) to an excessive speed. **4** to attack with a sudden charge.

rush[2] *n* **1** a rapid and violent forward motion. **2** a sudden onset of emotion. **3** a surge of busy or hurried activity. **4** a sudden demand for something. **5** a great movement of people, *esp* in search of wealth. **6** (*in pl*) the unedited print of a film scene processed directly after shooting. **7** an immediate brief pleasurable feeling after taking a drug such as heroin.

rush[3] *n* a tufted marsh plant with leaves used to make the seats of chairs, mats, etc.

rush hour *n* a period of the day when traffic is at a peak.

rusk *n* a dry and crisp piece of twice-baked bread, or a light dry biscuit.

russet *n* **1** a reddish to yellowish brown colour. **2** a russet-coloured eating apple.

Russian roulette *n* an act of bravado consisting of spinning the cylinder of a revolver loaded with one cartridge, pointing the muzzle at one's own head, and pulling the trigger.

rust[1] *n* **1** brittle reddish coating formed on iron by contact with moist air. **2** a destructive fungal disease of plants. **3** a reddish brown to orange colour.

rust[2] *v* to form rust.

rustic[1] *adj* characteristic of the countryside, *esp* in being simple or unsophisticated. ➤ **rusticity** *n*.

rustic[2] *n* *often derog* an unsophisticated rural person.

rustle[1] *n* a quick succession of faint crackling sounds.

rustle[2] *v* **1** to make or cause a rustle. **2** to steal cattle or horses. ➤ **rustler** *n*.

rustle up *v* *informal* to produce (food, etc) at short notice.

rusty *adj* (**-ier, -iest**) **1** affected by rust. **2** of the colour of rust. **3** slow or inexpert through lack of practice.

rut[1] *n* **1** a groove in a track worn by a wheel. **2** a tedious routine. ➤ **rutted** *adj*.

rut[2] *n* **1** an annually recurrent state of readiness to copulate, in the male deer or other mammals. **2** (*often* **the rut**) the period during which rut normally occurs.

rut[3] *v* (**rutted, rutting**) to be in a state of rut.

ruthless *adj* showing no pity or compassion. ➤ **ruthlessly** *adv*, **ruthlessness** *n*.

rye *n* **1** a hardy grass widely grown for grain. **2** whisky made from rye.

ryegrass *n* a type of grass used *esp* for pasture and lawns.

S¹ or **s** *n* (*pl* **S's** or **Ss** or **s's**) the 19th letter of the English alphabet.

S² *abbr* **1** South. **2** Southern.

S³ *abbr* the chemical symbol for sulphur.

sabbath *n* (*usu* **the Sabbath**) a day observed for rest and worship.

sabbatical *n* a period of paid leave granted to academics for study or travel.

sable¹ *n* (*pl* **sables** or **sable**) a mammal like a marten, found in the forests of northern Asia and having a valuable dark brown fur.

sable² *adj* **1** (*often used after a noun*) in heraldry, black. **2** *literary* black, dark, or gloomy.

sabotage¹ *n* **1** deliberate damage done to military or industrial installations. **2** deliberate subversion of a plan or project.

sabotage² *v* to destroy or subvert by sabotage.

saboteur *n* somebody who commits sabotage.

sabre (*NAmer* **saber**) *n* **1** a heavy sword with a curved blade. **2** a light fencing sword with an arched guard and a tapering blade.

sabre-toothed tiger *n* an extinct wild cat with long curved upper canine teeth.

sac *n* a pouch, often filled with fluid, in an animal or plant.

saccharin *n* a sweet-tasting compound that is used as a substitute for sugar.

saccharine *adj* sentimental or mawkish.

sacerdotal *adj* of priests or the priesthood.

sachet *n* a small sealed bag or packet containing a small amount of something.

sack¹ *n* **1** a large bag of plastic or thick material. **2** (**the sack**) *informal* dismissal from employment. **3** (**the sack**) *informal* bed. * **hit the sack** *informal* to go to bed.

sack² *v* *informal* to dismiss (somebody) from employment. ➤ **sackable** *adj*.

sack³ *n* the destruction of a place captured in war.

sack⁴ *v* to plunder and destroy (a place) after capturing it.

sackcloth *n* a coarse fabric used as sacking.

sacra *n* pl of SACRUM.

sacrament *n* **1** a formal religious act regarded as conferring divine grace on the recipient. **2** (**the Sacrament**) the bread and wine used in the Eucharist. **3** something considered to have sacred or religious significance.

sacred *adj* **1** dedicated or set apart for the worship of a god or gods. **2** dedicated as a memorial. **3** worthy of religious veneration; holy. **4** commanding reverence and respect. **5** relating to or used in religion.

sacred cow *n* something regarded as beyond criticism.

sacrifice¹ *n* **1** the killing of a victim on an altar as an offering to a deity. **2** a person or animal offered in sacrifice. **3** the losing of one thing for the sake of a greater. **4** something forgone or done without.

sacrifice² *v* **1** to offer as a sacrifice. **2** to give up (something) for the sake of an ideal or end. ➤ **sacrificial** *adj*.

sacrilege *n* an improper use of or attitude to something sacred. ➤ **sacrilegious** *adj*.

sacristan or **sacrist** *n* an official in charge of the sacristy of a church.

sacristy *n* (*pl* **-ies**) a room in a church where the clergy put on their vestments.

sacrosanct *adj* accorded the highest reverence and respect.

sacrum *n* (*pl* **sacra**) the part of the spinal column that is directly connected with or forms part of the pelvis.

sad *adj* (**sadder, saddest**) **1** affected with or expressing unhappiness. **2** causing unhappiness. **3** *informal* pathetic or contemptible. ➤ **sadly** *adv*, **sadness** *n*.

sadden *v* to make sad.

saddle¹ *n* **1** a padded seat secured to the back of a horse for the rider to sit on. **2** a seat on a bicycle or motorcycle. **3** a ridge connecting two peaks. **4** a cut of meat from the back of an animal.

saddle² *v* **1** to put a saddle on (a horse). **2** to burden with a task or responsibility.

saddlebag *n* a bag attached to the back of a saddle.

saddler *n* somebody who makes and sells saddles and other equipment for horses.

saddlery *n* (*pl* **-ies**) **1** saddles, bridles, etc, used for riding a horse. **2** the making, repair, or sale of saddlery. **3** a saddler's place of work or trade.

sadism *n* the act of obtaining sexual gratification by inflicting physical pain and humiliation on another person. ➤ **sadist** *n*, **sadistic** *adj*.

sadomasochism *n* the act obtaining sexual gratification through sadism and masochism. ➤ **sadomasochist** *n*, **sadomasochistic** *adj*.

safari n (pl **safaris**) an expedition to observe wild animals in their natural habitat.

safari park n a large area of land where wild animals are kept for visitors to observe as they drive through.

safe[1] adj **1** secure from threat of danger or loss. **2** no longer in danger. **3** providing protection from danger. **4** not threatening or involving danger. **5** unlikely to cause controversy. **6** not liable to take risks. **7** trustworthy; reliable. ➤ **safely** adv.

safe[2] n a reinforced room or cabinet, often with a complex lock, for keeping money and valuables.

safeguard[1] n a precautionary measure or stipulation.

safeguard[2] v to provide a safeguard for.

safe house n a place of concealment and safety for people threatened with violence.

safekeeping n protection or the state of being kept safe.

safe sex n sexual activity in which precautions are taken to prevent the transmission of diseases.

safety n (pl **-ies**) the condition of being safe.

safety belt n a seat belt in a vehicle.

safety net n **1** a net designed to protect acrobats by catching them if they fall. **2** a protective measure.

safety pin n a pin in the form of a clasp with a guard covering its point when fastened.

saffron n a yellow spice made from the dried stigmas of a type of crocus, used to colour and flavour food.

sag v (**sagged**, **sagging**) **1** to drop or sink from weight or pressure. **2** to lose strength.

saga n **1** a medieval narrative dealing with historic or legendary figures and events. **2** a long detailed account of successive events.

sagacious adj having sound judgment. ➤ **sagacity** n.

sage[1] n a person renowned for great wisdom.

sage[2] adj having or showing great wisdom. ➤ **sagely** adv.

sage[3] n a plant of the mint family with aromatic leaves used as a herb.

Sagittarius n the ninth sign of the zodiac (the Archer).

sago n a dry powdered starch made from the pith of a palm and used as a food.

sahib n a respectful term of address to a man, used in India.

said[1] v past tense and past part. of SAY[1].

said[2] adj mentioned previously.

sail[1] n **1** an expanse of fabric spread to catch the wind as a means of propelling a ship or boat. **2** a flat board forming an arm of a windmill. **3** a voyage by ship or boat.

sail[2] v **1** to travel in a boat or ship. **2** to handle a sailing boat as a sport. **3** to travel on water by the action of wind on sails. **4** to move in a stately manner. **5** to begin a journey by water. **6** to direct the movement of (a ship or boat). ✳ **sail close to the wind** to take risks. **sail through** to succeed in (something) with ease.

sailboard n a flat board with a mast and a sail, used in windsurfing.

sailcloth n **1** a heavy canvas used for making sails. **2** a lightweight canvas used for clothing.

sailing boat n a boat propelled by sails.

sailor n **1** somebody who sails a ship or boat. **2** a member of a ship's crew. **3** somebody who sails for sport. **4** a person considered in terms of their likelihood to be seasick.

saint[1] n **1** a person officially recognized by the Christian Church as being holy and worthy of veneration. **2** any of the spirits of the dead in heaven. **3** a person of outstanding piety or virtue. ➤ **sainthood** n, **saintly** adj.

saint[2] v to recognize or designate as a saint.

Saint Elmo's fire n an electrical discharge seen as flame in stormy weather at prominent points.

Saint George's Cross n a red cross on a white background, esp on the national flag of England.

Saint John's wort n a preparation made from a plant and used to relieve depression.

saint's day n in the Christian Church, a day on which a particular saint is commemorated each year.

sake[1] n benefit, purpose, or interest. ✳ **for goodness sake** used as an exclamation of protest or impatience. **for the sake of 1** for the benefit of. **2** in the interest of.

sake[2] or **saki** /'sahki/ n a Japanese alcoholic drink made from fermented rice.

salaam[1] n a ceremonial greeting performed in Muslim countries by bowing low and placing the right palm on the forehead.

salaam[2] v to make a salaam.

salacious adj **1** arousing sexual desire. **2** lecherous or lustful.

salad n a dish of mixed raw vegetables.

salad days pl n a time of youthful inexperience.

salamander n **1** an amphibian resembling a lizard but covered with a soft moist skin. **2** a mythical animal that can withstand the effects of fire.

salami /sə'lahmi/ n (pl **salamis**) a highly seasoned sliced sausage.

salary n (pl **-ies**) a fixed monthly payment made to an employee. ➤ **salaried** adj.

sale n **1** the act or an instance of selling. **2** an event at which goods are sold or auctioned. **3** a period in which goods are sold at reduced prices. ✳ **for sale** available to be bought. ➤ **saleable** adj.

saleroom n chiefly Brit a place where goods are displayed for sale, esp by auction.

salesman or **saleswoman** n (pl **salesmen** or **saleswomen**) a man or woman employed to sell goods. ➤ **salesmanship** n.

salesperson n (pl **salespersons** or **salespeople**) a person employed to sell goods.

salient¹ adj most noticeable or important. ➤ **salience** n.

salient² n a piece of land or part of a fortification that projects from its surroundings.

saline adj **1** containing salt. **2** esp of a laxative: containing salts of potassium, sodium, or magnesium. ➤ **salinity** n.

saliva n a mixture of water, protein, salts, and enzymes that is secreted into the mouth by glands, to help with chewing and digesting food. ➤ **salivary** adj.

salivate v to have a flow of saliva in the mouth. ➤ **salivation** n.

sallow adj of a sickly yellowish colour.

sally¹ n (pl **-ies**) **1** a sortie of troops from a besieged position. **2** a witty remark or retort.

sally² v (**-ies, -ied**) (usu + forth) to set out with determination.

salmon n (pl **salmons** or **salmon**) a large food fish of the North Atlantic that is highly valued for its pink flesh.

salmonella n (pl **salmonellae**) a bacterium that causes food poisoning.

salon n **1** an establishment where hairdressers, beauticians, couturiers, etc work. **2** an elegant reception room or living room. **3** formerly, a gathering of writers and artists in a fashionable home.

saloon n **1** Brit a more comfortable bar in a pub. **2** NAmer a bar. **3** Brit an enclosed car with a separate boot. **4** a well-appointed railway carriage.

salopettes pl n high-waisted padded or quilted trousers with shoulder straps, worn for skiing.

salsa n **1** a lively and rhythmic type of Latin American popular music. **2** a spicy Mexican sauce.

salt¹ n **1** sodium chloride occurring naturally, and used in the form of white powder or crystals for seasoning or preserving food. **2** a chemical compound resulting from replacement of all or part of the hydrogen atoms of an acid by a metal atom or other chemical group. ✳ **the salt of the earth** a person noted for goodness, kindness, honesty, etc. **take something with a pinch/grain of salt** to have doubts or reservations about it.

salt² v **1** to season or preserve with salt. **2** to sprinkle salt on (a road or path) to melt ice or snow.

salt³ adj **1** containing salt. **2** growing in salt water.

saltcellar n a small open dish or shaker for salt.

saltings pl n a marshy coastal area flooded regularly by tides.

saltpetre (NAmer **saltpeter**) n a white powder (potassium nitrate) used in making gunpowder.

salty adj (**-ier, -iest**) **1** seasoned with or containing salt. **2** piquant or witty. **3** earthy or coarse. ➤ **saltiness** n.

salubrious adj **1** promoting health or wellbeing. **2** of a place: pleasant and respectable.

salutary adj of a bad experience: offering an opportunity to learn or improve.

salutation n an expression of greeting.

salute¹ v **1** to address (somebody) with expressions of greeting or respect. **2** to show recognition to (a superior) by raising the hand to the side of the head. **3** to honour (somebody) by the firing of a guns into the air. **4** to praise or admire. ➤ **saluter** n.

salute² n **1** a greeting or salutation. **2** a sign or ceremony expressing goodwill or respect. **3** an act of saluting somebody. **4** a ceremonial firing of guns into the air.

salvage¹ n **1** the act of rescuing a ship or its cargo from loss at sea. **2** property saved or rescued from a wreck or fire.

salvage² v **1** to rescue (a ship or its cargo) from loss at sea. **2** to extract or preserve (something of use or value) from destruction or failure. ➤ **salvageable** adj.

salvation n **1** deliverance from danger or destruction. **2** somebody or something that brings about salvation. **3** in Christian theology, deliverance from sin brought about by faith.

salve¹ n **1** an ointment for soothing wounds or sores. **2** a soothing influence or agency.

salve² v to soothe or assuage.

salver n an ornamental tray.

salvo n (pl **-os** or **-oes**) **1** a simultaneous discharge of guns. **2** a sudden or emphatic burst of criticism or applause.

Samaritan n **1** a native or inhabitant of Samaria in ancient Palestine. **2** somebody who gives aid to those in distress.

samba¹ n a Brazilian dance of African origin.

samba² v (**sambas, sambaed, sambaing**) to dance the samba.

same¹ adj **1** being one single thing, person, or group. **2** identical in appearance, quantity, type, etc.

same² pron **1** the same thing, person, or group. **2** something previously mentioned. ✳ **all/just the same** nevertheless.

same³ adv (usu **the same**) in the same manner: two words spelt the same.

samey adj (**samier, samiest**) Brit, informal lacking in individuality or originality.

samovar n a Russian tea urn with a tap at its base and an interior heating tube.

sample¹ n **1** a part or item serving to show the character or quality of a larger whole or group. **2** a selection of individuals used as a basis for statistical analysis. **3** a specimen taken for scientific testing or analysis.

sample² v **1** to take a sample of. **2** to experience or get a taste of. **3** to take an extract from (a recording) and mix it into a new recording.

sampler n **1** a piece of needlework embroidered in various stitches as an example of skill. **2** a piece of equipment used for sampling a recording.

samurai /'sam(y)oorie/ n (pl **samurai**) a member of the warrior class of feudal Japan.

sanatorium n (pl **sanatoriums** or **sanatoria**) **1** a medical establishment for treating people with long-term illnesses. **2** Brit a room in a boarding school where sick pupils are looked after.

sanctify v (**-ies, -ied**) **1** to set apart for a sacred purpose. **2** to give moral, social, or religious sanction to. ➤ **sanctification** n, **sanctifier** n.

sanctimonious adj making a show or pretence of piety.

sanction¹ n **1** official permission or authoritative ratification. **2** a penalty attached to an offence. **3** (in pl) economic or military measures adopted to force a nation to comply with a requirement.

sanction² v **1** to give approval or consent to. **2** to make valid or binding.

sanctity n (pl **-ies**) the quality or state of being holy.

sanctuary n (pl **-ies**) **1** a consecrated place. **2** a place of refuge and protection. **3** a wildlife refuge. **4** a refuge for animals that have been injured or ill-treated. **5** immunity from the law formerly extended to somebody taking refuge in a church.

sanctum n (pl **sanctums** or **sancta**) **1** a sacred place. **2** a private or secluded place.

sand¹ n **1** loose granular particles formed from the disintegration of rock, forming the main constituent of beaches and the beds of seas and rivers. **2** (usu in pl) an area of sand.

sand² v to smooth or prepare (a surface) by rubbing with sandpaper.

sandal n a light shoe consisting of a sole held on the foot by straps.

sandalwood n the fragrant yellowish wood of an Asian tree.

sandbag¹ n a bag filled with sand and used as ballast or to form a barrier.

sandbag² v (**sandbagged, sandbagging**) to support or protect with sandbags.

sandbank n a large deposit of sand that becomes visible at low tide.

sandbar n a ridge of sand built up by currents in a river or sea.

sandblast v to clean (stone or glass) with a high-speed jet of sand.

sandcastle n a model of a castle made from sand.

sander n a power tool used for smoothing a surface.

sandpaper¹ n paper with a thin layer of sand glued to it, used for smoothing wood.

sandpaper² v to rub or smooth (a surface) with sandpaper.

sandpit n an enclosure containing sand for children to play in.

sandstone n a rock consisting of compressed sand grains.

sandstorm n a strong wind driving clouds of sand in a desert.

sandwich¹ n **1** two slices of bread with a filling between. **2** a sponge cake with jam or cream between its layers.

sandwich² v **1** (+ between) to insert (something) between two things of a different kind. **2** (+ together) to put together in layers.

sandwich board n a pair of boards hung in front of and behind the body of a walking person, used for advertising.

sandwich course n Brit a vocational course including periods of practical experience.

sandy adj (**-ier, -iest**) **1** consisting of or sprinkled with sand. **2** yellowish brown.

sane adj **1** mentally sound. **2** sensible or rational.

sang v past tense of SING.

sangfroid /song'frwah/ n self-possession or coolness under strain.

sanguinary adj formal bloodthirsty or murderous.

sanguine adj cheerfully confident and optimistic.

sanitarium n (pl **sanitariums** or **sanitaria**) NAmer = SANATORIUM.

sanitary adj **1** of or promoting health. **2** hygienic.

sanitary towel n a pad worn by a woman during menstruation to absorb the flow of blood.

sanitation n facilities and measures involved in the promotion of hygiene and prevention of disease, e.g. the disposal of sewage and collection of rubbish.

sanitize or **-ise** v **1** to make hygienic. **2** to make (something unpleasant) more acceptable. ➤ **sanitization** n.

sanity n **1** the state of being sane. **2** rational behaviour or judgment.

sank v past tense of SINK¹.

Sanskrit n an ancient language of the people of India.

Santa Claus or **Santa** n Father Christmas.

sap¹ n **1** a watery solution that circulates through a plant bringing nourishment. **2** vitality or vigour.

sap² v (**sapped, sapping**) to drain of vitality.

sapling n a young tree.

sapper n a soldier who digs trenches, lays mines, and does other engineering work.

sapphic adj relating to lesbians.

sapphire n **1** a transparent blue gem. **2** a brilliant blue colour.

saprophyte n a plant or fungus that lives on dead or decaying plant and animal tissues. ➤ **saprophytic** adj.

Saracen n a Muslim at the time of the Crusades.

sarcasm n the use of caustic and ironic language to express contempt or bitterness.

sarcastic adj using sarcasm. ➤ **sarcastically** adv.

sarcophagus n (pl **sarcophagi**) a large decorated stone coffin.

sardine n (pl **sardines** or **sardine**) a small fish of the herring family.

sardonic adj derisively mocking. ➤ **sardonically** adv.

sari or **saree** /'sahri/ n (pl **saris** or **sarees**) a length of cloth draped over the body, worn by women from the Indian subcontinent.

sarky adj (-ier, -iest) Brit, informal sarcastic. ➤ **sarkily** adv.

sarnie n Brit, informal a sandwich.

sarong n a long strip of cloth wrapped round the body, worn in parts of SE Asia.

sartorial adj relating to tailoring or clothing. ➤ **sartorially** adv.

sash[1] n a band of cloth worn round the waist or over one shoulder.

sash[2] n a frame holding a pane of glass in a window.

sashay /'sashay/ v informal to walk with exaggerated swaying movements of the hips and shoulders.

sash window n a window having two sashes that slide up and down.

Sassenach n Scot, Irish, derog an English person.

sassy adj informal cheeky or impudent.

SAT abbr standard assessment task.

sat v past tense and past part. of SIT[1].

Satan n the Devil.

satanic adj of Satan or satanism.

satanism n the worship of Satan. ➤ **satanist** n and adj.

satchel n a bag with a shoulder strap.

sated adj having as much as, or more than, one wants.

satellite n **1** a celestial body orbiting another of larger size. **2** an artificial device that orbits the earth or another planet, used for collecting scientific information or in communications. **3** somebody or something that is dependent on and controlled by another.

satellite dish n a dish-shaped aerial used to transmit and receive signals in satellite communications.

satellite television n television broadcasting using satellites to transmit and receive signals.

satiate v to give as much as or more than somebody wants. ➤ **satiation** n.

satiety n the state of being sufficiently or excessively fed or gratified.

satin n a smooth silky fabric. ➤ **satiny** adj.

satire n **1** the use of wit, irony, or sarcasm to expose foolishness or vice. **2** a literary work that uses satire. ➤ **satirist** n.

satirical or **satiric** adj involving the use of satire. ➤ **satirically** adv.

satirize or **-ise** v to censure or ridicule with satire.

satisfaction n **1** the fulfilment of something that is necessary or the good feeling arising from this. **2** compensation for a loss or injury. **3** the discharge of a legal obligation.

satisfactory adj fulfilling a need; acceptable. ➤ **satisfactorily** adv.

satisfy v (-ies, -ied) **1** to fulfil the needs or expectations of. **2** to meet or comply with (requirements). **3** to provide with reassurance.

satsuma n a sweet type of tangerine with a loose skin.

saturate /'sachoorayt/ v **1** to provide or fill (a substance) with another substance to the point where no more of it can be absorbed. **2** to cause (two or more substances) to combine chemically until there is no further ability or tendency to combine. **3** to make thoroughly wet. **4** to supply (a market) with all the goods it will absorb. **5** to overwhelm (an area) with military forces or firepower. ➤ **saturation** n.

saturated adj **1** of a solution: not capable of absorbing any more of the substance it contains. **2** of a chemical compound: unable to form products by chemical addition or by uniting directly with another compound. **3** of a colour: bright and rich.

Saturday n the day of the week following Friday.

saturnine adj **1** of a person or their temperament: gloomy or sullen. **2** dark and brooding.

satyr n (also **Satyr**) in classical mythology, a lustful woodland god represented as a man with the ears, legs, and tail of a horse or goat.

sauce n **1** a thick liquid used as a relish to food. **2** informal cheek or impudence.

sauce boat n a shallow jug for serving sauce, gravy, etc.

saucepan n a deep cooking pan with a long handle and a lid.

saucer n a small shallow dish on which a cup is placed.

saucy adj (-ier, -iest) informal **1** cheeky. **2** mildly titillating or sexually suggestive. ➤ **saucily** adv.

sauerkraut /'sowǝkrowt/ n finely chopped pickled cabbage.

sauna n a small room for invigorating the body in hot dry air or steam.

saunter[1] v to walk about in an idle or casual manner.

saunter[2] n a casual stroll.

sausage n **1** a food consisting of a tubular skin filled with finely chopped meat, eaten grilled or fried. **2** a food made from cooked or cured meat and spices, eaten cold in thin slices. * **not a sausage** Brit, informal nothing at all.

sausage dog n Brit, informal a dachsund.

sausage meat n seasoned minced meat used in sausages or as a stuffing.

sausage roll n a piece of sausage meat wrapped in pastry.

sauté /'sawtay, 'sohtay/ v (**sautés, sautéed** or **sautéd, sautéing**) to fry (potatoes) in oil or fat.

sauté² adj fried quickly in shallow oil or fat.

savage¹ adj **1** not domesticated; untamed. **2** very severe. **3** brutal or cruel and violent. ➤ **savagely** adv, **savagery** n.

savage² n **1** a member of a people regarded as lacking a developed culture. **2** a brutal person.

savage³ v **1** to attack or treat brutally or ferociously. **2** to criticize ruthlessly.

savanna or **savannah** n a tropical grassland with scattered trees.

savant or **savante** /'sav(ə)nt/ n a person with exceptional knowledge.

save¹ v **1** to rescue or deliver from danger or harm. **2** to prevent (somebody) from dying. **3** to preserve or guard from injury or loss. **4** in Christianity, to preserve (a soul) from damnation. **5** to put aside for future use. **6** in computing, to preserve (data) by storing it in the computer's memory. **7** to conserve or avoid use of (a resource). **8** to prevent an opponent from scoring or winning (a goal or point). * **save face** to avoid being humiliated. **save the day** to find a solution against expectation.

save² n in sport, an act of preventing an opponent from scoring.

save³ prep and conj except or other than.

saveloy n Brit a smoked pork sausage.

saving¹ n **1** an economy or reduction in money or time. **2** (in pl) money that has been put aside for future use.

saving² prep except.

saving grace n a redeeming or compensatory quality.

saviour (NAmer **savior**) n **1** a person who saves somebody or something from danger or harm. **2** (**Saviour**) in Christianity, Jesus Christ or God.

savoir faire /,savwah 'feə/ n the ability to behave appropriately in social situations.

savour¹ (NAmer **savor**) v **1** to appreciate (food or drink) with relish. **2** to enjoy and appreciate to the full.

savour² (NAmer **savor**) n a characteristic taste or smell.

savoury¹ (NAmer **savory**) adj **1** of food: having a salty or spicy flavour. **2** morally wholesome or respectable.

savoury² (NAmer **savory**) n (pl **-ies**) Brit a savoury snack or dish.

savvy¹ v (**-ies, -led**) informal to know or understand.

savvy² n informal practical knowledge or judgment.

savvy³ adj (**-ier, -iest**) informal shrewd or knowledgeable.

saw¹ v past tense of SEE¹.

saw² n a tool with a long toothed blade, used for cutting wood by passing it back and forth.

saw³ v (past part. **sawn**, NAmer **sawed**) **1** to cut with a saw. **2** to cut through or off with a saw.

saw⁴ n a maxim or proverb.

sawdust n wood powder produced in sawing.

sawmill n a factory where wood is cut into logs or planks.

sawtooth or **sawtoothed** adj shaped or arranged like the teeth of a saw.

sawyer n a person who saws timber.

sax n informal a saxophone.

Saxon n **1** a member of a Germanic people that settled in southern England in the fifth and sixth cents. **2** the language of the ancient Saxons. ➤ **Saxon** adj.

saxophone n a brass instrument with a single reed like a clarinet and a conical bore like an oboe. ➤ **saxophonist** n.

say¹ v (third person sing. present tense **says**, past tense and past part. **said**) **1** to state in spoken words. **2** to utter or pronounce (a sound, word, sentence, etc). **3** to recite or repeat. **4** of a clock or watch: to indicate or show. **5** (usu in passive) to report or allege. **6** to assume for the purposes of discussion.

say² n a chance to speak or give one's opinion.

saying n a maxim or proverb.

Sc abbr the chemical symbol for scandium.

scab¹ n **1** a crust of hardened blood that forms over a wound. **2** informal, offensive a person who declines to take part in a strike. ➤ **scabby** adj.

scab² v (**scabbed, scabbing**) to become covered with a scab.

scabbard n a sheath for a sword or dagger.

scabies n a skin disease with intense itching and inflammation.

scabrous adj **1** covered with scabs. **2** indecent or salacious.

scaffold n **1** a raised platform formerly used for executions. **2** a structure made from scaffolding.

scaffolding n **1** a temporary structure of poles and planks, erected on the outside of a building that is being built or repaired. **2** the poles and planks used for this.

scald¹ v **1** to injure or burn with hot liquid or steam. **2** to bring (a liquid) almost to boiling point. **3** to dip briefly in boiling water.

scald² n an injury or burn caused by scalding.

scale¹ n **1** each of the overlapping plates that cover and protect the skin of fish and reptiles. **2** a dry flake of dead skin. **3** a white deposit of lime formed on the inside of a kettle or pipe caused by hard water. **4** a hard deposit on the teeth.

scale² v **1** to remove the scales from. **2** to come off in scales or flakes.

scale³ n **1** (usu in pl) an instrument for weighing. **2** either pan or tray of a balance. * **tip the scales** to be a deciding factor.

scale⁴ n **1** a graduated range of values used in measuring. **2** a measuring instrument marked with a range of values. **3** the relative size or extent of something. **4** the ratio of the size of an object to a representation of it. **5** in music, a series of regularly rising or falling notes. * **to scale** reduced or enlarged by a constant factor.

scale⁵ v **1** to climb up or over (something high). **2** to make a model or representation of (something) using a uniform size ratio. **3** to regulate or estimate according to a rate or standard. **4** (+ down/up) to decrease or increase in size or amount.

scallion n an onion with a small bulb, e.g. a spring onion or shallot.

scallop¹ n **1** an edible mollusc with a shell consisting of two fan-shaped halves having wavy edges. **2** each of a series of rounded projections forming a decorative border.

scallop² v (**scalloped, scalloping**) to shape or finish with decorative scallops.

scallywag (NAmer **scalawag**) n informal a mischievous but likable person.

scalp¹ n **1** the skin at the top and back of the human head. **2** a part of this with the hair attached, formerly cut from an enemy as a battle trophy by Native American warriors.

scalp² v to remove the scalp of (an enemy).

scalpel n a small sharp knife with a thin blade, used in surgery.

scaly adj (**-ier, -iest**) **1** covered with scales. **2** dry and flaky.

scam n informal a dishonest scheme for obtaining money.

scamp n a mischievous child.

scamper¹ v to run nimbly and lightly.

scamper² n a dash or scurry.

scampi n (treated as sing. or pl) large prawns prepared and cooked.

scan¹ v (**scanned, scanning**) **1** to glance at (something) hastily or in search of a particular item. **2** to examine the whole of (an object) with a sensing device. **3** to make a detailed examination of (part or all of the body) using ultrasonic waves, X-rays, etc. **4** to change (an image) into an electrical signal by moving an electron beam across it according to a predetermined pattern for television transmission. **5** to convert (data) into a digital format for electronic purposes. **6** to examine or search (an object or region) using a radar scanner. **7** to read or mark (a piece of verse) in order to show

metrical structure. **8** of verse: to conform to a metrical pattern. ➤ **scannable** adj.

scan² n **1** the act of scanning. **2** a medical examination using a scanner. **3** an image produced by a scanner.

scandal n **1** an act or event that causes great public indignation. **2** rumour or that arises from this.

scandalize or **-ise** v to shock or offend by immoral or disgraceful behaviour.

scandalous adj **1** causing public indignation. **2** offensive to propriety. ➤ **scandalously** adv.

scanner n **1** a device used to scan the human body with X-rays, ultrasonic waves, etc. **2** a device that converts data into a digital format for electronic purposes.

scansion n **1** the analysis of verse to show its metre. **2** the rhythm of a particular piece of verse.

scant adj barely sufficient; inadequate.

scanty adj (**-ier, -iest**) small or insufficient in quantity. ➤ **scantily** adv.

scapegoat¹ n a person who is blamed for the wrongdoing of another.

scapegoat² v to make a scapegoat of.

scapula n (pl **scapulae** or **scapulas**) the shoulder blade.

scar¹ n **1** a mark left on the skin or body tissue by a healed injury. **2** a mark left on a plant stem where a leaf formerly grew. **3** a psychological ill effect caused by trauma.

scar² v (**scarred, scarring**) to form or mark with a scar.

scar³ n a steep rocky cliff or outcrop.

scarab n **1** a large dung beetle held sacred by the ancient Egyptians. **2** a gemstone representation of this.

scarce adj **1** not plentiful or sufficient to meet demand. **2** few in number. ➤ **scarcity** n.

scarcely adv **1** only just. **2** almost not. **3** certainly or probably not.

scare¹ v **1** to frighten suddenly. **2** (+ off/away) to drive (a person or animal) away by frightening them. **3** to become afraid.

scare² n **1** a sudden fright. **2** a widespread state of alarm.

scarecrow n an object made to look like a person set up to frighten birds away from crops.

scarf n (pl **scarves** or **scarfs**) a strip or square of cloth worn round the neck or head.

scarify v (**-ies, -ied**) **1** to scrape (a lawn) to remove moss, dead leaves, and other debris. **2** to break up and loosen the surface of (soil). **3** to make scratches or small cuts in (the skin). **4** to criticize hurtfully.

scarlatina n scarlet fever.

scarlet n a vivid red colour.

scarlet fever n an infectious disease with a fever and a red rash.

scarp n a steep slope.

scarper v Brit, informal to run away.

scarves *n* pl of SCARF.

scary *adj* (**-ier, -iest**) *informal* causing fear or alarm ➤ **scarily** *adv*.

scat¹ *v* (**scatted, scatting**) *informal* to leave hurriedly.

scat² *n* jazz singing with improvised vocals sounding like an instrument.

scathing *adj* bitterly severe; scornful. ➤ **scathingly** *adv*.

scatology *n* an obsession with excrement or excretion. ➤ **scatological** *adj*.

scatter *v* **1** to cause to separate widely. **2** to throw in all directions or at random. **3** to separate and go in various directions.

scattered *adj* found in various places over an area.

scatty *adj* (**-ier, -iest**) *Brit, informal* forgetful and disorganized.

scavenge *v* **1** to search for (something useful) among discarded items. **2** of animals: to search for and feed on (carrion or refuse).

scenario *n* (pl **-os**) **1** an outline of a dramatic work, novel, or film. **2** an account of a projected course of action.

scene *n* **1** a setting in which something real or imaginary happens. **2** a landscape or view. **3** an episode or sequence in a play, film, etc. **4** a stage setting. **5** a public display of strong feeling. **6** a sphere of activity or interest. **7** *informal* something in which a person is particularly interested. ✲ **behind the scenes** out of public view.

scenery *n* **1** the natural features of a landscape. **2** the painted scenes or hangings used on a theatre stage or film set.

scenic *adj* having attractive natural scenery. ➤ **scenically** *adv*.

scent¹ *n* **1** a pleasant characteristic smell. **2** a light perfume worn on the skin. **3** a smell left by an animal, by which it can be traced.

scent² *v* **1** to give a pleasant smell to. **2** to perceive by smell. **3** to get an inkling of. ➤ **scented** *adj*.

sceptic (*NAmer* **skeptic**) *n* a person who doubts accepted opinions or beliefs. ➤ **scepticism** *n*.

sceptical (*NAmer* **skeptical**) *adj* doubtful about accepted opinions or beliefs.

sceptre (*NAmer* **scepter**) *n* a staff carried by a ruler as a symbol of sovereignty. ➤ **sceptred** *adj*.

schedule¹ *n* **1** a plan of things to be done and the order in which to do them. **2** a timetable. ✲ **on schedule** as planned or on time.

schedule² *v* **1** to plan for (something) to occur at a fixed time. **2** to include in a schedule.

scheduled *adj* of a flight: operating as part of a regular timetable, not chartered.

schema *n* (pl **schemata** or **schemas**) an outline or diagram of a plan or theory.

schematic *adj* **1** representing something in a simplified way. **2** of understanding or an idea:

unsophisticated or formulaic. ➤ **schematically** *adv*.

scheme¹ *n* **1** a systematic plan for putting something into effect. **2** a systematic arrangement or design. **3** a secret or dishonest plan.

scheme² *v* to make a dishonest plan. ➤ **schemer** *n*.

scherzo /'skeətsoh/ *n* (pl **scherzos** or **scherzi**) a lively instrumental piece of music.

schism *n* a fundamental disagreement or split between parts of an institution or organization.

schist *n* a metamorphic rock made of thin layers of different minerals.

schizoid *adj* **1** of a person: extremely shy and unable to cope in social situations. **2** *informal* suffering from schizophrenia.

schizophrenia *n* a mental disorder characterized by loss of contact with reality and disintegration of personality. ➤ **schizophrenic** *adj and n*.

schmaltz or **schmalz** *n* excessive sentimentality. ➤ **schmaltzy** *adj*.

schnapps /shnaps/ *n* (pl **schnapps**) a strong alcoholic drink resembling gin.

scholar *n* **1** a person who specializes in a particular academic subject. **2** a student holding a scholarship.

scholarly *adj* characteristic of or suitable for advanced academic study.

scholarship *n* **1** academic learning and work. **2** a grant of money awarded to a student to pay for education and upkeep.

scholastic *adj* relating to education or schools.

school¹ *n* **1** a building or organization for educating children. **2** an establishment that teaches a specific subject or skill. **3** a department or faculty in a university. **4** *NAmer, informal* a university. **5** a group of philosophers, artists, etc, who share the same approach to a subject or follow the same principles.

school² *v* **1** *NAmer or formal* to educate. **2** to train in a specific subject or skill.

school³ *n* a large number of fish or sea animals swimming together.

schooling *n* education received in school.

schooner *n* **1** a sailing ship with two or more masts. **2** *Brit* a large sherry glass.

sciatic *adj* relating to the hip or the nerves that run from the lower spine down the back of each thigh.

sciatica *n* pain in the back of the thigh and lower back caused by pressure on the sciatic nerve.

science *n* **1** the study of the nature and behaviour of phenomena in the physical and natural world. **2** a branch of knowledge and study.

science fiction *n* fiction involving the imaginative use of science, set in the future.

science park *n* an area where businesses involved in scientific and technological research and manufacturing are based.

scientific adj 1 relating to or based on science. 2 systematic. ➤ **scientifically** adv.

scientist n a person who studies or is an expert in one of the natural or physical sciences.

sci-fi n informal science fiction.

scimitar n a short sword with a curved blade.

scintillating adj 1 shining or sparkling. 2 lively or witty.

scion n 1 a detached living part of a plant. 2 a descendant of a notable family.

scissors pl n a cutting instrument with two blades pivoted so that their cutting edges slide past each other.

sclerosis n 1 abnormal hardening of body tissue. 2 a disease involving this, esp multiple sclerosis.

scoff[1] v (often + at) to speak contemptuously about something.

scoff[2] v chiefly Brit, informal to eat greedily or rapidly.

scold v to reprove angrily.

sconce n a wall bracket for holding a candle or light.

scone n a small lightly sweetened cake made from a dough or batter.

scoop[1] n 1 a large ladle with a deep bowl. 2 a utensil for spooning out ice cream. 3 a deep bucket forming part of a mechanical digger. 4 informal a news item published by a newspaper ahead of its competitors.

scoop[2] v 1 to take out or up with a scoop. 2 (often + out) to make (a hollow). 3 to pick up as if with a scoop. 4 informal to report a news item in advance of (a competitor). 5 informal to obtain (something, esp money) by swift action or sudden good fortune.

scoot v informal to go or move suddenly and swiftly.

scooter n 1 a child's toy consisting of a narrow board with a wheel at each end and an upright steering handle, propelled by pressing one foot against the ground. 2 a light motorcycle.

scope n 1 space or opportunity for action, thought, or development. 2 extent of treatment, activity, or responsibility.

scorch[1] v 1 to burn or become burned in a way that causes a change in colour. 2 to cause (land or vegetation) to become dried up from the effects of heat. 3 informal to move or travel at great speed.

scorch[2] n a mark resulting from scorching.

scorcher n informal a very hot day or period.

score[1] n 1 the number of points, goals, etc a team or individual makes in a game. 2 (pl **score**) a group of twenty people or things. 3 an unspecified large quantity. 4 (**the score**) informal the present state of affairs. 5 the written or printed music of a composition. 6 a scratch or incision. ✻ **settle the score** to take revenge.

score[2] v 1 to gain (points, etc) in a game. 2 to keep score in a game or contest. 3 to mark (a surface) with lines or scratches. 4 (+ out/through) to delete or cancel something written or printed. 5 to arrange (music) for an orchestra. ➤ **scorer** n.

scoreline n the result of a game or match.

scorn[1] n strong contempt or disdain.

scorn[2] v 1 to treat with angry contempt. 2 to refuse or reject contemptuously.

scornful adj feeling or expressing scorn. ➤ **scornfully** adv.

Scorpio n the eighth sign of the zodiac (the Scorpion).

scorpion n an arachnid with an elongated body and a narrow tail bearing a poisonous sting at the tip.

Scot n a native or inhabitant of Scotland.

Scotch n (also **Scotch whisky**) whisky distilled in Scotland.

scotch v 1 to put an end to. 2 archaic to temporarily disable or make harmless.

Scotch egg n a hard-boiled egg covered with sausage meat.

scot-free adj without any penalty or injury.

Scots[1] adj Scottish.

Scots[2] n the form of English used in Scotland.

Scottish adj relating to Scotland.

scoundrel n an unscrupulous or dishonest person.

scour[1] v 1 to clean by vigorous rubbing with abrasive material. 2 of running water or a glacier: to create an eroded channel in.

scour[2] v to search thoroughly.

scourge[1] n 1 a cause of trouble or distress. 2 a whip.

scourge[2] v 1 to whip. 2 to cause great distress to.

Scouse n Brit, informal 1 the dialect or accent of Liverpool. 2 (also **Scouser**) a native or inhabitant of Liverpool. ➤ **Scouse** adj.

scout[1] n 1 a person sent forward to survey land or assess an enemy's position or strength. 2 (**Scout**) a member of the Scout Association, a worldwide movement for young people. 3 a talent scout.

scout[2] v 1 to make an advance survey to obtain information. 2 to look for something. 3 to explore (a place) to obtain information.

scowl[1] v to frown in an angry or displeased way.

scowl[2] n an angry frown.

scrabble v 1 to scratch or scrape about to find or catch hold of something. 2 to scramble or clamber.

scraggy adj (-ier, -iest) lean and lanky.

scram v (scrammed, scramming) informal to leave hurriedly.

scramble[1] v 1 to move or climb using the hands and feet. 2 to compete chaotically for something. 3 to make or become muddled. 4 esp of a fighter aircraft: to take off quickly in response to an alert. 5 to cook (eggs) beaten in a pan. **6** to put (a message) into a form that needs decoding by the recipient.

scramble[2] *n* **1** the act of scrambling. **2** *Brit* a motorcycle race over rough ground. **3** a muddle or jumble.

scrap[1] *n* **1** a small detached fragment of something. **2** (*in pl*) discarded or leftover food. **3** discarded metal suitable for reprocessing.

scrap[2] *v* (**scrapped, scrapping**) **1** to discard or get rid of. **2** to convert into scrap.

scrap[3] *v* (**scrapped, scrapping**) *informal* to fight or quarrel.

scrap[4] *n informal* a fight or quarrel.

scrapbook *n* a blank book for pasting pictures or cuttings.

scrape[1] *v* **1** to grate harshly over or against. **2** to damage or injure by contact with a rough surface. **3** to draw roughly over a surface. **4** to remove (matter) from a surface with an edged instrument. **5** to achieve (an exam grade or a pass) by a narrow margin.

scrape[2] *n* **1** an act or sound of scraping. **2** an injury or mark caused by scraping. **3** *informal* an awkward predicament.

scrappy *adj* (**-ier, -iest**) disjointed or incomplete. ➤ **scrappily** *adv*.

scrapyard *n Brit* a yard where scrap metal is collected.

scratch[1] *v* **1** to mark or cut the surface of (something) with a sharp object. **2** to make a superficial wound on. **3** to scrape or rub (a body part) to relieve itching. **4** to cancel or erase with or as if with a line. **5** to withdraw from a competition. **6** to abandon or cancel (an event or project).

scratch[2] *n* **1** a mark or injury produced by scratching. **2** *informal* a slight wound. **3** an act or sound of scratching. ✻ **from scratch** from the very beginning. **up to scratch** satisfactory or adequate.

scratch[3] *adj* put together haphazardly or hastily.

scratchcard *n* a small card with a coated section to be scratched off to reveal whether a prize has been won.

scrawl[1] *v* to write or draw awkwardly or hastily.

scrawl[2] *n* an untidy piece of writing or drawing.

scrawny *adj* (**-ier, -iest**) thin and bony.

scream[1] *v* **1** to make a loud piercing cry in fear or pain. **2** to move with great speed.

scream[2] *n* **1** a loud shrill cry or noise. **2** *informal* a highly amusing person or thing.

scree *n* loose stones or rocky debris on a hillside or mountain slope.

screech[1] *v* to make a shrill piercing cry or sound.

screech[2] *n* a shrill sound or cry.

screed *n* **1** a long speech or piece of writing. **2** a mixture applied to a floor to give it a level surface.

screen[1] *n* **1** the part of a television set or computer monitor on which images or data are displayed. **2** a blank surface for projecting photographs or films. **3** the medium of films or television. **4** a partition or curtain used to divide a room or provide privacy. **5** something that protects or conceals.

screen[2] *v* **1** to shelter or protect with a screen. **2** to guard from injury or danger. **3** (*also* + off) to separate or enclose with a screen. **4** to show or broadcast (a film or broadcast) on a screen. **5** to carry out a test on (somebody) for the presence of disease.

screenplay *n* the script of a film with stage directions.

screen saver *n* a computer program that generates a blank screen or moving screen images after a period of inactivity.

screen test *n* an audition to assess an actor's suitability for a film role.

screenwriter *n* a writer of screenplays. ➤ **screenwriting** *n*.

screw[1] *n* **1** a metal pin with a spiral thread running round it and a slotted head turned by a screwdriver to fasten parts together. **2** the propeller of a ship or aircraft. **3** *informal* a prison warder. **4** *coarse slang* an act of sexual intercourse. ✻ **have a screw loose** *informal* to be eccentric.

screw[2] *v* **1** to fasten, close, or tighten with a screw. **2** to join or assemble (parts) by means of a screw. **3** to cause to rotate spirally about an axis. **4** *informal* to cheat or defraud. **5** *coarse slang* to have sexual intercourse with.

screwdriver *n* a tool with a tip that fits into the head of a screw to turn it.

screw up *v* **1** to crush or crumple. **2** *informal* to make emotionally disturbed. **3** *informal* to bungle or cause to go wrong.

screwy *adj informal* odd or eccentric.

scribble[1] *v* to write or draw hurriedly or carelessly.

scribble[2] *n* a scribbled drawing or piece of writing.

scribe *n* formerly, a person who copied manuscripts. ➤ **scribal** *adj*.

scrimmage *n* a disorderly struggle or fight.

scrimp *v* (*often* + on) to be frugal or sparing; to skimp.

script[1] *n* **1** the written text of a stage play, film, or broadcast. **2** written characters; handwriting.

script[2] *v* to write a script for.

scripture *n* **1** (*also in pl*) the sacred writings of Christianity as contained in the Bible. **2** the sacred writings of another religion. ➤ **scriptural** *adj*.

scrofula *n* a former name for tuberculosis of the lymph glands. ➤ **scrofulous** *adj*.

scroll[1] *n* **1** a roll of parchment with writing or

drawing on it. **2** a stylized ornamental design imitating the spiral curves of a scroll.

scroll[2] *v* to move (text on a computer screen) up and down to view different parts of it.

Scrooge *n* a mean or miserly person.

scrotum *n* (*pl* **scrota** or **scrotums**) the pouch of skin that contains the testicles.

scrounge *v informal* to try to get or be given (something) for nothing. ➤ **scrounger** *n*.

scrub[1] *v* (**scrubbed, scrubbing**) **1** to clean by hard rubbing. **2** *informal* to cancel or abandon.

scrub[2] *n* an act of scrubbing.

scrub[3] *n* **1** vegetation consisting chiefly of stunted trees or shrubs. **2** an area covered with such vegetation. ➤ **scrubby** *adj*.

scruff[1] *n* the back of the neck.

scruff[2] *n Brit, informal* an untidy or grubby person.

scruffy *adj* (-ier, -iest) slovenly and untidy in personal appearance. ➤ **scruffily** *adv*.

scrum *n* **1** in rugby, a set piece in which the forwards of each side crouch in a tight formation and push against each other as the ball is put into play between them. **2** *Brit, informal* a disorderly crowd.

scrummy *adj* (-ier, -iest) *informal* delicious.

scrump *v Brit, informal* to steal (fruit) from an orchard or garden.

scrumptious *adj informal* delicious or delightful.

scrumpy *n Brit* dry rough cider brewed in the English West Country.

scrunch *v* to crunch or crush.

scruple[1] *n* a feeling of doubt about the morality of an action.

scruple[2] *v* to hesitate on grounds of conscience.

scrupulous *adj* **1** painstakingly exact. **2** eager to avoid doing anything wrong or immoral. ➤ **scrupulously** *adv*.

scrutinize or **-ise** *v* to examine in detail.

scrutiny *n* (*pl* -ies) a searching study or inspection.

scuba-dive *v* to swim underwater with an aqualung. ➤ **scuba-diving** *n*.

scud *v* (**scudded, scudding**) to move or run swiftly.

scuff[1] *v* **1** to scrape or damage the surface of (a shoe or other object). **2** to drag or shuffle (the feet) while walking.

scuff[2] *n* a mark or damage caused by scuffing.

scuffle[1] *n* a brief confused fight.

scuffle[2] *v* to engage in a scuffle.

scull[1] *n* **1** either of a pair of light oars used by a single rower. **2** a narrow light racing boat propelled by a scull or sculls.

scull[2] *v* to propel a boat with sculls.

scullery *n* (*pl* -ies) a small kitchen used mainly for washing dishes.

sculpt *v* to create by sculpture.

sculptor *n* an artist who makes sculptures.

sculpture[1] *n* **1** the art of making three-dimensional works of art by carving or modelling. **2** a piece of work produced in this way. ➤ **sculptural** *adj*.

sculpture[2] *v* **1** to make (a work of art) by sculpture. **2** to form (wood or stone) into a work of art. **3** to shape by carving or moulding.

scum *n* **1** impurities that have collected on the surface of a liquid. **2** *informal* a despicable person or group of people. ➤ **scummy** *adj*.

scupper *v* **1** *Brit, informal* to prevent (something) from working, happening, etc. **2** to sink (a ship) deliberately.

scurf *n* thin dry flakes of skin. ➤ **scurfy** *adj*.

scurrilous *adj* offensive and defamatory.

scurry *v* (-ies, -ied) to move with short hurried steps.

scurvy *n* a disease caused by a lack of vitamin C.

scut *n* the short erect tail of a rabbit, hare, or deer.

scuttle[1] *n* a container used for carrying or storing coal indoors.

scuttle[2] *v* to run hurriedly or furtively.

scuttle[3] *v* **1** to sink (one's own ship) deliberately. **2** to destroy or wreck.

scythe[1] *n* a tool with a long curving blade for cutting grass or corn.

scythe[2] *v* to cut with a scythe.

SE *abbr* **1** Southeast. **2** Southeastern.

Se *abbr* the chemical symbol for selenium.

sea *n* **1** the salt water that covers much of the earth. **2** a large body of salt water. **3** something vast or overwhelming. ✳ **at sea** lost or confused.

sea anemone *n* a brightly coloured sea creature with a cluster of tentacles resembling a flower.

seabird *n* a bird that lives on the sea or coast.

seaboard *n* an area beside or near the sea.

sea change *n* a complete transformation.

sea cow *n* a manatee or other plant-eating sea animal.

seafaring *n* travel by sea. ➤ **seafarer** *n*.

seafood *n* edible sea fish, shellfish, etc.

seafront *n* the part of a seaside town facing the sea.

seagoing *adj* designed for travel on the sea.

sea gull *n* a gull.

sea horse *n* a small upright fish with a head like that of a horse.

seal[1] *n* **1** a closure that has to be broken in order to give access. **2** a tight closure preventing the passage of air, water, etc. **3** a guarantee or assurance. **4** an emblem or word stamped in wax on a document as a mark of authenticity.

seal[2] *v* **1** to fasten or close tightly. **2** to close (a container) in a way that prevents unauthorized opening. **3** to cover (a porous surface) with a coating of a nonporous substance. **4** to confirm (an arrangement) or make it secure. **5** to set or affix an authenticating seal to (e.g a document). **6** to authenticate or ratify. **7** to mark with a stamp or seal.

seal³ *n* (*pl* **seals** *or* **seal**) a sea animal with webbed flippers for swimming.

sealant *n* a sealing agent for making something watertight or airtight.

sea legs *pl n* the ability to walk steadily and avoid being seasick when on a ship at sea.

sea level *n* the mean level of the sea's surface midway between high and low tides.

sealing wax *n* a wax that becomes soft when heated, used for sealing letters, parcels, etc.

sea lion *n* a large seal with short coarse fur and large flippers.

seal off *v* to close an area to prevent movement in or out.

seam¹ *n* **1** a line of stitching joining two pieces of fabric. **2** a line or ridge formed at the meeting of two edges. **3** a layer of coal or rock.

seam² *v* to join with a seam.

seaman *n* (*pl* **seamen**) a sailor or mariner. ➤ **seamanship** *n*.

sea mile *n* a nautical mile.

seamless *adj* **1** without seams. **2** without breaks or gaps; continuous.

seamy *adj* (**-ier**, **-iest**) unpleasant or sordid.

séance *or* **seance** /'sayons, 'sayonhs/ *n* a meeting at which people attempt to communicate with the dead.

seaplane *n* an aeroplane designed to take off from and land on the water.

seaport *n* a port or town accessible to seagoing ships.

sear *v* **1** to burn or scorch with a sudden intense heat. **2** of heat or pain: to be felt as a burning sensation.

search¹ *v* **1** (*usu* + for) to look or enquire carefully or thoroughly. **2** (*often* + for) to look through thoroughly to find or discover something. **3** to examine (a person) for concealed articles. **4** to investigate (a computer file, database, etc) to find information. ➤ **searcher** *n*.

search² *n* the act of searching.

searching *adj* seeking to obtain detailed or personal information.

searchlight *n* an apparatus for projecting a movable beam of light.

search party *n* a group of people organized to search for a missing person.

search warrant *n* a warrant authorizing police to search premises.

seascape *n* a picture representing a view of the sea.

seashell *n* the empty shell of a sea mollusc.

seashore *n* sandy or stony land next to the sea.

seasick *adj* suffering from sickness caused by the motion of a ship. ➤ **seasickness** *n*.

seaside *n* land bordering the sea, *esp* a holiday resort or beach.

season¹ *n* **1** each of the four parts into which the year is divided (spring, summer, autumn, and winter). **2** a period characterized by a particular kind of weather or activity: *the dry season; the holiday season*. * **in season 1** of food: readily available for eating. **2** of a female animal: ready to mate.

season² *v* **1** to add spices or flavouring to (food). **2** to enliven or make more interesting. **3** to treat or expose (timber) to prepare it for use.

seasonable *adj* **1** suitable to the season or circumstances. **2** *archaic* occurring in good or proper time.

seasonal *adj* **1** occurring or produced at a particular season. **2** determined by seasonal need or availability. ➤ **seasonally** *adv*.

seasoned *adj* fit or expert from experience.

seasoning *n* salt, pepper, or spices added to food to give it flavour.

season ticket *n* a ticket allowing repeated travel or admission over a period.

seat¹ *n* **1** a piece of furniture for sitting on. **2** the part of something on which one rests when sitting. **3** the buttocks. **4** a place for sitting, e.g. in a vehicle, or the right to this. **5** a right of sitting in parliament or on an elected committee. **6** *Brit* a parliamentary constituency. **7** a place where something is established or practised: *a seat of learning*. **8** a large country mansion.

seat² *v* **1** to provide a seat or seats for. **2** to have sitting accommodation for. ➤ **seating** *n*.

seat belt *n* a belt for securing a person in a seat in a vehicle or aircraft.

sea urchin *n* a sea creature with a thin shell covered with movable spines.

seaweed *n* thick slimy plants growing in the sea.

seaworthy *adj* of a ship: fit or safe for travel at sea. ➤ **seaworthiness** *n*.

sebaceous *adj* secreting fatty material.

secateurs *pl n chiefly Brit* small pruning shears.

secede *v* to withdraw from an organization or federation.

secession *n* the act of seceding.

secluded *adj* screened or hidden from view.

seclusion *n* the condition of being private or secluded.

second¹ *adj* **1** having the position in a sequence corresponding to the number two. **2** next to the first in value, quality, or degree. **3** (+ to) inferior or subordinate. **4** next below the top in authority or importance. **5** alternate: *every second year*. ➤ **secondly** *adv*.

second² *n* **1** somebody or something that is second. **2** an assistant to someone boxing or fighting a duel. **3** a slightly flawed or inferior article for sale. **4** *informal* (*in pl*) a second helping of food.

second³ *n* **1** a 60th part of a minute. **2** a brief moment.

second[4] *v* **1** to give support or encouragement to. **2** to endorse (a motion or nomination). ➤ **seconder** *n*.

second[5] *v* chiefly Brit to release (an employee) for temporary duty elsewhere. ➤ **secondment** *n*.

secondary *adj* **1** of second or lesser rank or importance. **2** of a level of education following primary. ➤ **secondarily** *adv*.

second best *n* not quite the best in quality or worth.

second class *n* the second and next to highest group in a classification.

second-class *adj* **1** of a second class. **2** inferior or mediocre.

second cousin *n* a child of a first cousin of either of one's parents.

second-degree *adj* of a burn: causing blisters and surface damage to the skin.

second fiddle *n* a secondary or subordinate role or function.

second-guess *v* to try to guess the actions of.

secondhand *adj* **1** acquired after being owned by another. **2** dealing in secondhand goods. **3** received from an intermediary.

second-in-command *n* an officer immediately below a commander.

second nature *n* an action or ability that has become instinctive.

second person *n* in grammar, the term used to refer to a person or thing addressed, represented by the pronoun *you*.

second-rate *adj* of inferior quality.

second sight *n* the ability to see future events.

second thoughts *pl n* a reconsideration of a previous decision.

second wind *n* renewed energy after a period of exertion.

secret[1] *adj* **1** kept or hidden from knowledge or view. **2** secretive. ➤ **secrecy** *n*, **secretly** *adv*.

secret[2] *n* **1** something kept hidden or unexplained. **2** a special and not commonly known way of achieving something.

secret agent *n* a spy.

secretariat *n* a government administrative department or its staff.

secretary *n* (*pl* **-ies**) **1** a person who is employed to handle correspondence and manage routine administrative work. **2** an official of an organization responsible for its records and correspondence. **3** in Britain, a senior civil servant. ➤ **secretarial** *adj*.

secretary of state *n* **1** in Britain, a government minister who is the head of a department. **2** in the USA, the government official responsible for foreign affairs.

secrete[1] *v* to form and give off (a substance). ➤ **secretion** *n*.

secrete[2] *v* to put in a secret place.

secretive *adj* inclined to say little and hide one's feelings. ➤ **secretively** *adv*.

secret police *n* a police organization operating secretly for the political purposes of a government.

secret service *n* a government agency concerned with national security and intelligence.

sect *n* a small group within a religious or political organization that differs in its beliefs from the main body.

sectarian *adj* of or characteristic of a sect. ➤ **sectarianism** *n*.

section[1] *n* **1** a distinct part or division of something. **2** a distinct part of a community or group of people. **3** the action of cutting or separating by cutting in surgery. **4** a shape or figure resulting from cutting through a solid form.

section[2] *v* to cut or separate into sections.

sector *n* **1** a distinct part or division. **2** a part of a circle between two lines joining the centre to the circumference.

secular *adj* **1** of this world rather than the heavenly or spiritual. **2** not overtly or specifically religious. ➤ **secularism** *n*.

secure[1] *adj* **1** free from danger or risk of loss. **2** firmly fixed or fastened. **3** calm in mind. **4** assured or certain. ➤ **securely** *adv*.

secure[2] *v* **1** to fix or fasten firmly. **2** to make safe from risk or danger. **3** to obtain by effort.

security *n* (*pl* **-ies**) **1** freedom from danger, fear, or anxiety. **2** the safety of a state or organization against attack or subversion. **3** something pledged to guarantee the fulfilment of an obligation.

sedan *n* **1** NAmer a saloon car. **2** a portable enclosed chair carried on poles by two people.

sedate[1] *adj* calm and even in temper or pace. ➤ **sedately** *adv*.

sedate[2] *v* to give a sedative to.

sedation *n* the act of sedating somebody, or the condition of being sedated.

sedative[1] *adj* tending to calm or to tranquillize somebody.

sedative[2] *n* a sedative drug.

sedentary *adj* **1** doing or involving much sitting. **2** of birds: that do not migrate. **3** of animals: permanently attached to a surface.

sedge *n* a marsh plant having a solid stem.

sediment *n* **1** matter that settles at the bottom of a liquid. **2** material deposited by water, wind, or glaciers. ➤ **sedimentary** *adj*.

sedition *n* incitement to defy or rise up against the government. ➤ **seditious** *adj*.

seduce *v* **1** to persuade (somebody) to have sexual intercourse. **2** to incite to wrongdoing or disloyalty. ➤ **seduction** *n*.

seductive *adj* tending to seduce; alluring or attractive. ➤ **seductively** *adv*.

sedulous *adj* formal diligent and careful. ➤ **sedulously** *adv*.

see[1] *v* (**saw, seen**) **1** to perceive with the eyes. **2** to perceive or deduce by thinking. **3** to imagine or envisage. **4** to determine or decide. **5** to make sure of. **6** to call on or visit. **7** to consult professionally. **8** to keep company with. **9** to escort (somebody) to a specified place. ∗ **see about** to deal with or consider. **see the back of** to be rid of. **see through 1** to undergo or endure to the end. **2** to be aware of (a deception). **see to** to attend to or take care of.

see² n the area over which a bishop has authority.

seed¹ n (pl **seeds** or **seed**) **1** the fertilized ovule of a flowering plant or conifer that contains an embryo and can produce a new plant. **2** the grains or fertilized ovules of plants used for sowing. **3** a source of development or growth. **4** a competitor who has been seeded in a tournament. **5** something that resembles a seed in shape or size. **6** archaic semen. **7** archaic offspring. ➤ **seedless** adj.

seed² v **1** of a plant: to produce or shed seeds. **2** to plant seeds in (a field, plot, etc). **3** to extract the seeds from. **4** to schedule (tournament players or teams) so that strong ones will not meet each other in early rounds.

seedling n a plant grown from seed.

seedy adj (**-ier, -iest**) **1** shabby or grubby. **2** disreputable or run-down. ➤ **seediness** n.

seeing conj (often + that) because; since.

seek v (past tense and past part. **sought**) **1** (often + out) to go in search of. **2** to try to discover. **3** to ask for (advice, etc). **4** to try to acquire or gain. **5** to make an effort (to do something). ➤ **seeker** n.

seem v to give the impression of being or doing something. ∗ **not seem** used for 'seem not': *He doesn't seem to understand.*

seeming adj apparent rather than real.

seemly adj (**-ier, -iest**) in accord with good taste or propriety. ➤ **seemliness** n.

seen v past part. of SEE¹.

see off v **1** to accompany (somebody) to the place where they are leaving. **2** informal to chase away.

see out v **1** to escort out of a room or building. **2** to last until the end of.

seep v to pass slowly through fine pores or small openings. ➤ **seepage** n.

seer n a person who predicts future events.

seersucker n a light slightly puckered fabric.

seesaw¹ n a plank balanced in the middle so that one end goes up as the other goes down, used for amusement.

seesaw² v **1** to move backward and forward or up and down. **2** to alternate or vacillate.

seethe v **1** to feel suppressed anger. **2** to be in a state of agitated movement.

see-through adj esp of clothing: transparent or nearly so.

segment¹ n each of the parts into which something is divided or marked off. ➤ **segmental** adj.

segment² v to separate or divide into segments.

segregate v **1** to keep separate from others; to set apart. **2** to cause or force the separation of (racial groups, religions, or sexes) from the rest of a community. ➤ **segregation** n.

segue /'segway, 'saygway/ v (**segues, segued, segueing**) to pass directly from one musical number or theme to another.

seine n a large fishing net with floats at one end that hangs vertically in the water.

seismic adj **1** of or caused by an earthquake. **2** very great in importance or effect.

seismology n the study of earthquakes. ➤ **seismological** adj, **seismologist** n.

seize v **1** to take hold of abruptly or forcefully. **2** to confiscate by legal authority. **3** (+ on) to use or take advantage of eagerly. **4** (often + up) of machinery: to become locked and fail to work.

Usage Note: Note the spelling with *-ei-*

seizure n **1** the act of seizing. **2** a sudden attack of a fit or other illness.

seldom adv rarely or infrequently.

select¹ adj **1** picked out in preference to others. **2** of special value or quality. **3** socially exclusive.

select² v to pick out or choose carefully.

select committee n a committee appointed by a legislative body to examine a particular matter.

selection n **1** the act of selecting. **2** somebody or something selected. **3** a collection of selected items. **4** a range of things from which to choose.

selective adj **1** using or involving selection. **2** tending to choose carefully. **3** affecting only some in a group. ➤ **selectively** adv, **selectivity** n.

selenium n a grey chemical element used in electronic devices.

self n (pl **selves**) **1** the entire being of an individual. **2** a person's individual character. **3** the physical and emotional elements that make up the particular identity of a person.

self-absorbed adj preoccupied with one's own thoughts or activities. ➤ **self-absorption** n.

self-abuse n masturbation.

self-addressed adj addressed for return to the sender.

self-appointed adj assuming a position of authority not approved by others.

self-assessment n **1** assessment of one's own performance. **2** a system of calculating one's own liability for income tax.

self-assurance n confidence in oneself. ➤ **self-assured** adj.

self-catering adj of holiday accommodation: including kitchen facilities.

self-centred *adj* preoccupied with one's own wishes or needs.

self-certification *n* in Britain, a system by which an employee who has been absent from work for a short period can declare the reason in writing without needing a doctor's certificate.

self-confessed *adj* openly acknowledged.

self-confidence *n* confidence in oneself and one's abilities. ➤ **self-confident** *adj*.

self-congratulation *n* a complacent acknowledgment of one's own superiority or achievements. ➤ **self-congratulatory** *adj*.

self-conscious *adj* uncomfortably conscious of oneself as an object of attention. ➤ **self-consciously** *adv*.

self-contained *adj* complete in itself.

self-control *n* the ability to control one's own impulses or emotions. ➤ **self-controlled** *adj*.

self-defeating *adj* of a plan or action: preventing its own success.

self-defence *n* the act of defending or justifying oneself.

self-denial *n* the limitation of one's desires or their gratification.

self-deprecating *adj* critical of oneself. ➤ **self-deprecation** *n*.

self-destruct *v* to destroy itself automatically. ➤ **self-destructive** *adj*.

self-determination *n* the right of a person or country to manage their affairs without interference.

self-discipline *n* the ability to control one's thoughts and actions. ➤ **self-disciplined** *adj*.

self-doubt *n* a lack of confidence in oneself.

self-effacement *n* the act of avoiding attention. ➤ **self-effacing** *adj*.

self-employed *adj* working for oneself and not an employer. ➤ **self-employment** *n*.

self-esteem *n* confidence and satisfaction in oneself.

self-evident *adj* requiring no proof; obvious. ➤ **self-evidently** *adv*.

self-explanatory *adj* capable of being understood without explanation.

self-expression *n* the expression of one's own thoughts and feelings, e.g. by painting or poetry.

self-fulfilling *adj* of a prediction: bound to come true because it causes people to behave in a way that causes this.

self-help *n* dependence on one's own efforts.

self-importance *n* an exaggerated sense of one's own importance. ➤ **self-important** *adj*.

self-indulgence *n* excessive gratification of one's own appetites or desires. ➤ **self-indulgent** *adj*.

self-interest *n* a concern for one's own advantage and well-being. ➤ **self-interested** *adj*.

selfish *adj* concerned chiefly with one's own advantage or needs. ➤ **selfishly** *adv*, **selfishness** *n*.

selfless *adj* having more concern for others than for oneself.

self-made *adj* having achieved success by one's own efforts.

self-pity *n* a self-indulgent dwelling on one's own misfortunes. ➤ **self-pitying** *adj*.

self-portrait *n* a portrait in which the artist is the subject.

self-possessed *adj* composed in mind or manner; calm. ➤ **self-possession** *n*.

self-preservation *n* an instinctive tendency to protect oneself.

self-raising flour (*NAmer* **self-rising flour**) *n* a form of flour with its own raising agent.

self-regard *n* **1** concern or consideration for oneself. **2** self-respect. ➤ **self-regarding** *adj*.

self-reliance *n* reliance on one's own efforts and resources. ➤ **self-reliant** *adj*.

self-respect *n* confidence in and respect for oneself. ➤ **self-respecting** *adj*.

self-restraint *n* restraint imposed on oneself and one's feelings.

self-righteous *adj* sure that one is right or morally superior.

self-sacrifice *n* sacrifice of oneself or one's well-being for the sake of others. ➤ **self-sacrificing** *adj*.

selfsame *adj* precisely the same.

self-satisfied *adj* smugly satisfied with oneself or one's achievements. ➤ **self-satisfaction** *n*.

self-seeking *adj* seeking only to safeguard one's own interests. ➤ **self-seeker** *n*.

self-service *adj* of a shop, cafeteria, etc: where customers serve themselves.

self-styled *adj* called by oneself, *esp* without justification: *a self-styled expert*.

self-sufficient *adj* able to provide for one's own needs without outside help. ➤ **self-sufficiency** *n*.

self-worth *n* self-esteem.

sell *v* (*past tense and past part.* **sold**) **1** to give (goods or property) in exchange for money. **2** to achieve a sale of (a certain number). **3** to be sold or achieve sales. **4** to persuade somebody of the worth of (an idea, etc). ✳ **sell short** to belittle or disparage. ➤ **seller** *n*.

selling point *n* a particularly good feature that makes something desirable.

sell off *v* to sell all of (something) quickly and cheaply. ➤ **sell-off** *n*.

Sellotape *n trademark* a transparent adhesive tape.

sell out *v* **1** to sell all of (something). **2** to be sold entirely. **3** to betray or be unfaithful to.

sell-out *n* **1** an event for which all tickets or seats are sold. **2** *informal* a betrayal.

selvage *or* **selvedge** *n* the edge on a woven fabric, finished to prevent unravelling.

selves n pl of SELF.

semantic adj relating to meaning in language. ➤ **semantically** adv.

semantics pl n **1** the branch of linguistics concerned with meaning. **2** the meaning of a sentence, word, etc. ➤ **semanticist** n.

semaphore n a system of visual signalling with the arms or a pair of flags held one in each hand.

semblance n the way something seems or appears.

semen n a fluid containing sperm, produced by the male reproductive glands.

semester n an academic term lasting half a year.

semi n (pl **semis**) informal **1** Brit a semidetached house. **2** a semifinal.

semiautomatic adj of a gun: equipped to load each cartridge in turn, but needing manual release of the trigger for each shot.

semibreve n a musical note with the time value of two minims or four crotchets.

semicircle n a half circle. ➤ **semicircular** adj.

semicolon n a punctuation mark (;) used to indicate a break or pause that is more marked than one indicated by a comma.

semiconductor n a substance that conducts electricity in proportion to temperature or the presence of certain impurities.

semidetached adj of a house: joined to another house by a common wall.

semifinal n a match or round that is next to the last in a knockout competition. ➤ **semifinalist** n.

seminal adj **1** originating and influencing future development. **2** relating to seed or semen.

seminar n **1** a meeting of university students with a teacher for discussion. **2** a meeting for exchanging and discussing information.

seminary n (pl **-ies**) an institution for the training of the clergy.

semiotics pl n the study of signs and symbols as a feature of language. ➤ **semiotic** adj.

semiprecious adj of a gemstone: of less value than a precious stone.

semiquaver n a musical note with the time value of half a quaver.

semiskimmed adj of milk: with some of its cream removed.

semitone n a musical interval equal to half a tone.

semolina n the purified hard parts left after milling of wheat, used to make pasta and puddings.

senate n (treated as sing. or pl) **1** the upper chamber in some legislatures. **2** the supreme council of ancient Rome. **3** the governing body of some universities.

senator n a member of a senate. ➤ **senatorial** adj.

send v (past tense and past part. **sent**) **1** to cause or direct to go to a place. **2** to cause to move quickly or violently. **3** (often + out) to emit or discharge. **4** to cause (somebody) to be in a specified state. **5** (usu + for) to summon or order somebody or something. ➤ **sender** n.

send down v **1** Brit to suspend or expel (a student) from a university. **2** informal to sentence (somebody) to a term in prison.

send off v of a referee: to order (a player) to leave the field.

send-off n a gathering of people to say goodbye to somebody starting a journey.

send up v chiefly Brit to imitate mockingly.

senile adj losing mental or physical faculties through old age. ➤ **senility** n.

senior¹ adj **1** higher in standing or rank. **2** older. **3** relating to old age and older people. **4** Brit relating to students in the upper years of secondary school. **5** NAmer relating to students in the final year of higher education. **6** used to distinguish a father with the same name as his son; elder. ➤ **seniority** n.

senior² n **1** a person who is older than another person by a specified amount. **2** in sporting competitions, an adult or more advanced competitor. **3** Brit a student in the upper years of secondary school. **4** NAmer a student in the final year of higher education.

senior citizen n an old age pensioner.

senna n the dried pods of certain plants, used as a laxative.

sensation n **1** a mental process resulting from stimulation of a sense organ. **2** a general state of awareness of something external. **3** a surge of interest or excitement, or the cause of this.

sensational adj **1** arousing great general interest or excitement. **2** informal exceptionally fine or impressive. ➤ **sensationally** adv.

sensationalize or **-ise** v to report (a story, etc) in sensationalist terms.

sense¹ n **1** any of the faculties of perceiving things by touching, hearing, seeing, smelling, or tasting. **2** an ability to use the senses for a specified purpose: a sense of balance. **3** a vague awareness or impression. **4** an awareness that motivates action or judgment: a sense of justice. **5** a capacity for appreciating something: a sense of humour. **6** (usu in pl, but treated as sing.) soundness of mind or judgment. **7** the use of practical intelligence. **8** a meaning conveyed by a word or expression. * **make sense** to be understandable or reasonable.

sense² v **1** to perceive by the senses. **2** to become vaguely aware of. **3** to grasp or comprehend. **4** to detect automatically.

senseless adj **1** unconscious. **2** foolish or stupid. **3** having no meaning or purpose.

sensibility n (pl **-ies**) **1** (usu in pl) the degree of being sensitive to feelings and tastes. **2** the ability to discern or appreciate emotion in others.

sensible *adj* **1** having or showing good sense or sound reason. **2** plain and practical. **3** (+ of/to) capable of feeling something: *sensible to pain.* ➤ **sensibly** *adv.*

sensitive *adj* **1** (+ to) capable of being stimulated by external agents such as light, gravity, or contact. **2** (*often* + to) easily affected emotionally. **3** (*often* + to) finely aware of the feelings of others. **4** controversial and needing tactful handling. **5** of information: secret or classified. ➤ **sensitively** *adv*, **sensitivity** *n.*

sensitize *or* **-ise** *v* to make sensitive to or aware of something.

sensor *n* a device that responds to heat, light, sound, or other physical attributes.

sensory *adj* of sensation or the senses.

sensual *adj* relating to the gratification of the physical senses. ➤ **sensuality** *n*, **sensually** *adv.*

sensuous *adj* **1** relating or appealing to the senses rather than the intellect. **2** producing rich imagery or sense impressions. ➤ **sensuously** *adv.*

sent *v* past tense and past part. of SEND.

sentence[1] *n* **1** a group of words that is grammatically complete and expresses a statement, question, command, wish, or exclamation. **2** a punishment pronounced by a law court.

sentence[2] *v* (*often* + to) to impose a judicial sentence on.

sententious *adj* given to pompous moralizing.

sentient *adj* capable of perceiving through the senses.

sentiment *n* **1** strong or exaggerated emotion or feeling. **2** a specific view or opinion. **3** a feeling or attitude.

sentimental *adj* **1** appealing to or resulting from feeling rather than reason. **2** having an excess of superficial sentiment. ➤ **sentimentality** *n*, **sentimentally** *adv.*

sentinel *n* somebody that keeps guard; a sentry.

sentry *n* (*pl* **-ies**) a soldier standing guard at a gate, door, etc.

sepal *n* any of the modified leaves forming the green outer part of a flower.

separable *adj* capable of being separated or dissociated. ➤ **separability** *n.*

separate[1] *v* **1** to move or come apart. **2** to stop living together as spouses or partners. **3** to divide or stand between (two or more people or things). **4** (*often* + from) to make a distinction between. **5** to detach from a larger group. **6** (*often* + out) to divide into constituent parts or types. ➤ **separative** *adj.*

separate[2] *adj* **1** set or kept apart; detached or separated. **2** not shared with another. **3** existing independently. **4** different in kind; distinct. ➤ **separately** *adv.*

Usage Note: Note the spelling with *-ar-.*

separation *n* **1** the act of separating. **2** the living apart of a husband and wife while still married.

separatism *n* a belief or movement advocating separation from a main group. ➤ **separatist** *n and adj.*

sepia *n* a rich dark brown.

sepoy *n* an Indian soldier serving with the British army.

sepsis *n* (*pl* **sepses**) the spread of bacteria from a focus of infection.

September *n* the ninth month of the year.

septet *n* **1** a group of seven instruments, voices, or performers. **2** a musical composition for a septet.

septic *adj* infected with bacteria. ➤ **septically** *adv*, **septicity** *n.*

septicaemia (*NAmer* **septicemia**) *n* blood poisoning caused by micro-organisms.

septic tank *n* an underground tank in which sewage is disintegrated by bacteria.

septuagenarian *n* a person between 70 and 79 years old.

septum *n* (*pl* **septa**) a membrane between bodily spaces or masses of soft tissue.

septuple *adj* **1** having seven parts. **2** being seven times as great or as many.

septuplet *n* any of seven offspring born at one birth.

sepulchral *adj* **1** having to do with a tomb or burial. **2** sombre or dismal. ➤ **sepulchrally** *adv.*

sepulchre (*NAmer* **sepulcher**) *n* a tomb or place of burial.

sequel *n* **1** a play, film, or literary work continuing the story of a previous one. **2** a subsequent development or course of events.

sequence[1] *n* **1** a continuous or connected series. **2** a continuous progression. **3** the order of succession of things, events, etc.

sequence[2] *v* to place in a sequence.

sequential *adj* **1** of or arranged in a sequence. **2** following in sequence. ➤ **sequentially** *adv.*

sequester *v* **1** to segregate from the company of others. **2** in law, to seize (property) until a debt is paid.

sequestrate *v* in law, to sequester (property). ➤ **sequestration** *n*, **sequestrator** *n.*

sequin *n* a small shining disc used on clothing for ornamentation.

sequoia *n* a tall coniferous Californian tree.

seraglio /se'rahlioh, -lyoh/ *n* (*pl* **-os**) **1** a harem. **2** the women's apartments in a sultan's palace.

seraph *n* (*pl* **seraphim** *or* **seraphs**) any of the six-winged angels standing in the presence of God. ➤ **seraphic** *adj.*

serenade[1] *n* a piece of music played outdoors at night by a man for a woman he is courting.

serenade[2] *v* to perform a serenade for.

serendipity *n* the discovery of pleasing or interesting things by chance. ➤ **serendipitous** *adj*.

serene *adj* calm and tranquil. ➤ **serenely** *adv*, **serenity** *n*.

serf *n* an agricultural labourer in a feudal society, bound in service to a lord. ➤ **serfdom** *n*.

serge *n* a durable woollen fabric.

sergeant *or* **serjeant** *n* **1** a British police officer ranking below an inspector. **2** a non-commissioned officer in the army, ranking above a corporal.

sergeant major *n* (*pl* **sergeant majors**) a non-commissioned officer in the British army or Royal Marines.

serial[1] *n* a story published or broadcast in parts at intervals.

serial[2] *adj* **1** of or constituting a series, rank, or row. **2** appearing in successive instalments. **3** repeating the same offence several times: *a serial rapist*. ➤ **serially** *adv*.

serialism *n* music based on a series of notes in an arbitrary but fixed order without traditional tonality.

serialize *or* **-ise** *v* to publish or broadcast in serial form. ➤ **serialization** *n*.

serial number *n* a number used as a means of identifying an object.

series *n* (*pl* **series**) **1** a number of things or events of the same kind following one another. **2** a number of radio or television programmes of the same type or on the same theme. **3** a mathematical sequence whose terms are to be added together.

serious *adj* **1** grave or thoughtful in appearance or manner. **2** sincere and in earnest. **3** deeply interested or committed. **4** severe or dangerous. **5** requiring careful attention. ➤ **seriously** *adv*, **seriousness** *n*.

sermon *n* a religious talk given as a part of a church service.

serpent *n literary* a large snake.

serpentine *adj* winding or twisting.

serrated *adj* having projections like the teeth of a saw.

serration *n* each of the points of a serrated edge.

serried *adj* of rows or ranks: crowded or pressed together.

serum *n* (*pl* **serums** *or* **sera**) the protein-rich fluid constituent of blood.

servant *n* a person employed to perform personal or domestic duties.

serve[1] *v* **1** to perform duties or obligations for. **2** to be a member of the armed forces of (a country). **3** to be imprisoned for (a period of time). **4** to attend to (a customer) in a shop, bar, etc. **5** to provide with (food or drinks). **6** to fulfil a particular purpose; to help or benefit. **7** to be adequate or satisfactory. **8** in tennis and other games, to begin a period of play by hitting the ball or shuttlecock. ✻ **serve somebody right** to be their just deserts.

serve[2] *n* the act of serving in tennis, badminton, etc.

server *n* **1** the player who serves, e.g. in tennis. **2** a person or thing that serves. **3** a computer or program that connects users in a network to a centralized store of data.

service[1] *n* **1** work or duty carried out for a person, organization, country, etc. **2** a system or facility designed to meet a public need. **3** the work of attending to customers in a shop, bar, etc. **4** a helpful action or favour. **5** a religious ceremony in a Christian church. **6** a routine inspection and repair of a machine or motor vehicle. **7** a set of matching tableware for serving food. **8** (*usu in pl*) any of a nation's military forces. **9** *Brit* (*in pl*) facilities provided for the users of a motorway. **10** (*in pl*) gas, water, and other utilities connected to a building. **11** a serve in tennis, badminton, etc. ✻ **in service** working as a domestic servant. **out of service** not currently being used or operated.

service[2] *v* **1** to provide a service or services for. **2** to carry out routine repairs and maintenance on. **3** to meet interest payments on (a debt).

serviceable *adj* **1** in good working order. **2** reliable and durable.

service industry *n* an industry that provides a service and does not produce goods.

serviceman *or* **servicewoman** *n* (*pl* **servicemen** *or* **servicewomen**) a member of the armed forces.

service station *n* a roadside garage selling petrol, oil, etc.

serviette *n chiefly Brit* a table napkin.

servile *adj* **1** slavishly willing to please or satisfy others. **2** characteristic of a slave or menial. ➤ **servility** *n*.

serving *n* a single portion of food.

servitude *n* the state of being a slave or completely subject to somebody.

servo *n* (*pl* **-os**) a device that converts a low power input into a much larger power output.

sesame *n* a tropical plant with seeds used as a source of oil and as a flavouring.

session *n* **1** a period devoted to a particular activity. **2** a meeting or series of meetings of a court or council.

set[1] *v* (**setting**, *past tense and past part.* **set**) **1** to put in a particular place or position. **2** to put in a specified condition. **3** to decide on and fix (an amount, etc). **4** to give somebody (a task) to perform. **5** to prepare or adjust (a device) for use. **6** to prepare (a table) for use at a meal. **7** to describe (an event, story, etc) as taking place at a particular place and time. **8** to provide music for (a text). **9** to arrange (type) for printing. **10** to fix (wet hair) in the right style after washing.

11 to put (a dislocated or fractured bone or limb) into its normal position for healing. **12** to fix (a gem) in a border of metal. **13** to become solid or thickened. **14** of the sun, moon, etc: to go down below the horizon. ✳ **set on** to attack suddenly and violently. **set sail** to begin a voyage by sea. **set to work** to start to do something.

set² adj **1** arranged or fixed in advance. **2** (usu + on) resolutely determined. **3** unchanging and immovable. **4** prepared and ready.

set³ n **1** a number of things of the same kind belonging or used together. **2** a radio or television apparatus. **3** in tennis and similar sports, a number of games forming a unit for scoring. **4** the artificial scenery used for a play. **5** bearing or posture.

set about v **1** to start doing something. **2** to attack.

set aside v **1** to discard or put to one side. **2** to override (a decision).

setback n a problem or difficulty that causes a delay or interruption.

set forth v **1** to start on a journey. **2** to give an account of.

set off v **1** to start on a journey. **2** to cause (a bomb) to explode.

set out v **1** to start on a journey. **2** to have as an intention. **3** to state or describe in detail.

set square n chiefly Brit a flat triangular instrument with a right angle, used to mark out angles.

sett n the burrow of a badger.

settee n a long upholstered seat for more than one person.

setting n **1** the physical or historical background for an object or event. **2** the way in which something is set. **3** the music composed for a text. **4** a set of cutlery, glasses, etc for one person at a meal. **5** the frame in which a gem is mounted.

settle¹ v **1** to find an acceptable answer or solution to. **2** (often + down) to make or become calm or orderly. **3** (usu + down) to adopt an ordered or stable lifestyle. **4** to place or arrange firmly or comfortably. **5** to become established in a particular place or position. **6** to establish a home or a colony. **7** to come to rest. **8** to pay (a debt). **9** (+ on) to make a decision or choice. **10** (+ for) to accept something less than one hoped for. ✳ **settle down to** to begin (an activity) in a purposeful way.

settle² n a wooden bench with arms and a high back.

settle in v to become comfortably established in a new environment.

settlement n **1** the process of settling. **2** an agreement resolving differences. **3** a place where a new community has been established. **4** the act of leaving property or money to somebody in a will.

set-to n (pl **-os**) informal a brief and vigorous conflict.

set up v **1** to raise into position. **2** to establish or found.

seven n the number 7. ➤ **seven** adj.

seventeen adj and n the number 17. ➤ **seventeenth** adj and n.

seventh adj and n **1** having the position in a sequence corresponding to the number seven. **2** one of seven equal parts of something.

seventy adj and n (pl **-ies**) **1** the number 70. **2** (in pl) the numbers 70 to 79. ➤ **seventieth** adj and n.

sever v **1** to divide by cutting. **2** to put or keep apart. **3** to terminate. ➤ **severable** adj.

several adj and n **1** more than two but not many. **2** formal separate or distinct.

severance n **1** the act of separating by cutting. **2** the state of being separated. **3** the ending of a relationship.

severe adj **1** stern or austere. **2** strict or stringent. **3** restrained in decoration or manner. **4** of something difficult or unwelcome: great or extreme. ➤ **severely** adv, **severity** n.

sew v (past tense **sewed**, past part. **sewn** or **sewed**) **1** to join or attach by stitches made with a needle and thread. **2** to make or mend by sewing.

sewage n waste matter carried off by sewers.

sewer n an underground channel or pipe used to carry off waste matter from drains. ➤ **sewerage** n.

sewing machine n a machine for sewing, with a motor or handle that moves the needle.

sex n **1** either of two categories, male or female, into which organisms are divided. **2** the characteristics that distinguish males and females. **3** sexual intercourse or activity.

sexagenarian n a person between 60 and 69 years old.

sex appeal n the quality of being sexual attractive.

sexism n discrimination or prejudice, esp against women, on the basis of a person's sex. ➤ **sexist** adj and n.

sexless adj **1** lacking sex appeal or the sexual urge. **2** not male or female.

sex symbol n a famous person noted for sex appeal.

sextant n an instrument for measuring angles and distances in surveying and navigation.

sextet n **1** a group of six instruments, voices, or performers. **2** a musical composition for a sextet.

sexton n an official in charge of church property.

sextuple adj **1** having six parts. **2** being six times as much or as many.

sextuplet n any of six offspring born at one birth.

sexual *adj* **1** relating to sex and to physical attraction and contact between individuals. **2** relating to male and female or to relations between the two sexes. **3** of reproduction: involving the fusion of male and female reproductive cells. ➤ **sexually** *adv*.

sexual harassment *n* repeated unwelcome physical contact or sexual suggestions directed at somebody, *esp* in the workplace.

sexual intercourse *n* sexual activity with penetration of the vagina by the erect penis.

sexuality *n* (*pl* **-ies**) **1** the condition of experiencing sexual desires. **2** a person's sexual orientation or preference.

sexy *adj* (**-ier, -iest**) **1** sexually attractive or stimulating. **2** sexually aroused. **3** *informal* interesting or fashionable. ➤ **sexily** *adv*, **sexiness** *n*.

shabby *adj* (**-ier, -iest**) **1** worn or threadbare. **2** shameful or despicable. ➤ **shabbily** *adv*.

shack *n* a small crudely built hut or shelter.

shackle[1] *n* **1** a pair of metal rings joined by a chain used to fasten a prisoner's hands or legs. **2** (*usu in pl*) something that restricts or prevents free action.

shackle[2] *v* **1** to chain or fasten with shackles. **2** to restrain or handicap.

shack up *v informal* (*usu* + together/with) to live with as a sexual partner.

shad *n* (*pl* **shads** *or* **shad**) a fish of the herring family.

shade[1] *n* **1** partial darkness caused when sunlight is obstructed. **2** a place sheltered from the rays of the sun. **3** a lampshade. **4** *informal* (*in pl*) sunglasses. **5** a particular variety of a colour. **6** a small amount. **7** a ghost. ✳ **a shade** slightly; somewhat. **shades of** reminiscent of.

shade[2] *v* **1** to shelter or screen from light or heat. **2** to cover or darken with a shade. **3** to mark (a picture or drawing) with shading or darker colour. **4** to change gradually. **5** (+ into) to pass imperceptibly into a different state. ➤ **shaded** *adj*.

shading *n* lines, dots, or colour used to represent degrees of light and dark.

shadow[1] *n* **1** a dark shape made on a surface by an object that is between it and a source of light. **2** partial darkness caused when light is interrupted. **3** the slightest trace trace: *not a shadow of doubt*. **4** a much reduced and weakened form of a person or thing. **5** a source of gloom or disquiet. **6** a person who accompanies or follows somebody else. **7** (*used before a noun*) denoting a member of the opposition who speaks on matters for which the corresponding government minister is responsible. ➤ **shadowy** *adj*.

shadow[2] *v* **1** to cast a shadow over. **2** to follow or keep under surveillance.

shadow-box *v* to box with an imaginary opponent as a form of training.

shady *adj* (**-ier, -iest**) **1** producing or giving shade. **2** sheltered from the sun. **3** *informal* of questionable legality or integrity.

shaft[1] *n* **1** the long narrow body of a spear or arrow or handle of a tool. **2** a rotating cylindrical bar used to transmit power or motion in a machine. **3** an opening to a mine, well, etc. **4** a vertical passage through the floors of a building. **5** a beam of light shining from an opening. **6** either of two poles between which a horse is hitched to a vehicle.

shaft[2] *v informal* to treat unfairly or harshly.

shag[1] *n* **1** long coarse or matted fibre. **2** a strong coarse tobacco. **3** a bird similar to a cormorant but smaller.

shag[2] *v* (**shagged, shagging**) *Brit, coarse slang* to have sexual intercourse with.

shag[3] *n Brit, coarse slang* an act of sexual intercourse.

shaggy *adj* (**-ier, -iest**) **1** having long, coarse, or matted hair. **2** unkempt.

shah *n* formerly, a sovereign of Iran.

shake[1] *v* (**shook, shaken**) **1** to move back and forth or up and down with short rapid movements. **2** to tremble. **3** to shock or upset. **4** to weaken (somebody's confidence). ✳ **shake a leg** *informal* to hurry up. **shake hands** to clasp hands in greeting or agreement. **shake on it** to shake hands as a sign of agreement. **shake one's head** to move one's head from side to side to express refusal or disagreement.

shake[2] *n* **1** an act of shaking. **2** a milk shake.

Shakespearean *or* **Shakespearian** *adj* relating to the English dramatist and poet William Shakespeare (d.1616).

shake up *v* **1** to rouse from inactivity or complacency. **2** *informal* to reorganize drastically.

shaky *adj* (**-ier, -iest**) **1** not firm or stable; unsteady. **2** precarious or uncertain. ➤ **shakily** *adv*.

shale *n* a finely stratified or laminated rock formed by the consolidation of clay, mud, or silt.

shall *v aux* (*third person sing. present tense* **shall,** *past tense* **should**) **1** used in the first person to express a future action or state: *We shall try to be there.* **2** used to express determination or insistence: *They shall not stop us.* **3** used to express a polite request or suggestion: *Shall I leave?*

shallot *n* an edible bulb like a small onion.

shallow *adj* **1** having little depth. **2** superficial in knowledge or thought. ➤ **shallowly** *adv*.

shallows *pl n* a shallow area in a body of water.

sham[1] *n* **1** something that is not genuine or what it seems to be. **2** a person who pretends or makes false claims.

sham[2] *adj* **1** not genuine; imitation. **2** pretended or feigned.

sham[3] *v* (**shammed, shamming**) to pretend.

shaman *n* (*pl* **shamans**) a priest believed to exercise magic powers of healing and divination. ➤ **shamanism** *n*.

shamble *v* to walk awkwardly with dragging feet.

shambles *n* (*pl* **shambles**) a state of complete chaos or confusion.

shambolic *adj* *Brit, informal* completely chaotic or confused.

shame[1] *n* **1** an unpleasant feeling caused by awareness of having done something wrong or foolish. **2** humiliating disgrace or ignominy. **3** a cause of disgrace. **4** a cause of regret. ✳ **put to shame** to show obvious superiority over.

shame[2] *v* to cause to feel shame.

shamefaced *adj* showing shame. ➤ **shamefacedly** *adv*.

shameful *adj* **1** bringing disgrace or ignominy. **2** causing a feeling of shame. ➤ **shamefully** *adv*.

shameless *adj* not feeling any shame. ➤ **shamelessly** *adv*.

shammy *n* (*pl* **-ies**) *informal* a chamois leather.

shampoo[1] *n* (*pl* **shampoos**) **1** a liquid soap for washing the hair. **2** a similar cleaning agent used on a carpet, car, etc. **3** an act of washing with shampoo.

shampoo[2] *v* (**shampoos, shampooed, shampooing**) to wash or clean with shampoo.

shamrock *n* a clover with three-part leaves, the national emblem of Ireland.

shandy *n* (*pl* **-ies**) beer mixed with lemonade or ginger beer.

shanghai *v* (**shanghais, shanghaied, shanghaiing**) *informal* to trick or force (somebody) into doing something.

shank *n* **1** the leg between the knee and the ankle. **2** a straight narrow part of an object.

shanks's pony *n* one's own legs as a means of transport.

shan't *contraction* shall not.

shantung *n* a silk fabric in plain weave with a slightly irregular surface.

shanty[1] *n* (*pl* **-ies**) a small crudely built hut or shelter.

shanty[2] *n* (*pl* **-ies**) a song sung by sailors in rhythm with their work.

shantytown *n* a poor area of a town consisting mainly of shanties.

shape[1] *v* **1** to give a particular shape to. **2** to determine the nature or course of. **3** (*often* + up) to develop or proceed. ➤ **shaper** *n*.

shape[2] *n* **1** the form of something determined by its outline and outer surface. **2** a circle, square, or other standard geometrical form. **3** a piece of paper or material cut into a particular form. **4** definite physical or mental form. **5** the condition of a person or thing at a particular time. ✳ **in shape** in good physical condition. **take shape** to take on a definite form.

shapeless *adj* having no definite shape.

shapely *adj* (**-ier, -iest**) having a pleasing shape.

shape up *v* **1** to develop in a particular way. **2** of a person: to become physically fit.

shard *n* a piece of broken glass or earthenware.

share[1] *n* **1** a portion belonging to or contributed by an individual. **2** the part belonging to any member of a group owning property together. **3** any of the equal portions into which the invested capital of a company is divided.

share[2] *v* **1** to use or experience (something) with others. **2** (+ out) to divide and distribute in shares. ➤ **sharer** *n*.

shareholder *n* an owner of shares in a company. ➤ **shareholding** *n*.

shark[1] *n* a large sea fish with a tall fin on its back and its mouth on the under part of its body.

shark[2] *n* a person who extorts money dishonestly from others.

sharp[1] *adj* **1** having a thin edge or fine point for cutting or piercing. **2** characterized by hard lines and angles. **3** involving an abrupt change in direction. **4** clear or distinct. **5** sudden and forceful. **6** capable of reacting quickly. **7** able to perceive clearly or understand quickly. **8** causing sudden strong anguish. **9** pungent, tart, or acid in flavour. **10** of a sound: shrill or piercing. **11** intensely cold. **12** of a musical note: raised one semitone in pitch. **13** slightly higher than the true or desired pitch. ➤ **sharply** *adv*, **sharpness** *n*.

sharp[2] *adv* **1** in an abrupt manner. **2** exactly or precisely.

sharp[3] *n* **1** a musical note one semitone higher than the note at that position on the staff. **2** the character (#) that indicates such a note.

sharpen *v* to make or become sharp. ➤ **sharpener** *n*.

sharpish *adv* *Brit, informal* promptly; without delay.

sharpshooter *n* a person skilled in shooting.

shatter *v* **1** to break apart suddenly and violently. **2** to break (something) into pieces, e.g. by a sudden blow. **3** to cause (something) to break down; to impair or destroy. **4** to have a forceful effect on the feelings of. **5** *informal* to make exhausted. ➤ **shattered** *adj*.

shave[1] *v* (*past part.* **shaved** *or* **shaven**) **1** to cut off hair close to the skin with a razor. **2** to cut or trim closely. **3** (*often* + off) to remove in thin layers or slices. **4** to reduce (e.g. a price) by a small amount. **5** to brush against in passing.

shave[2] *n* the process of shaving.

shaven *v* past part. of SHAVE[1].

shaver *n* an electric razor.

shaving *n* a thin layer or shred shaved off.

shawl *n* a piece of fabric worn to cover the head or shoulders.

she *pron* **1** used to refer to a female person or animal previously mentioned. **2** used to refer to something regarded as female, e.g. a vehicle or ship.

sheaf *n* (*pl* **sheaves**) **1** a bundle of stalks and ears of a cut cereal grass. **2** a collection of papers.

shear *v* (*past part.* **sheared** *or* **shorn**) **1** to cut off the wool from (a sheep). **2** to cut with shears. **3** (*often* + off) to cut or break (something) off something else. ✳ **be shorn of** to be deprived of. ➤ **shearer** *n*.

shears *pl n* a cutting implement like a large pair of scissors.

sheath *n* (*pl* **sheaths**) **1** a cover for the blade of a knife or sword. **2** a close-fitting casing or covering. **3** a condom.

sheathe *v* **1** to insert (a knife or sword) into a sheath **2** to enclose in a protective covering.

shebang *n informal* an affair or business.

shed[1] *v* (**shedding**, *past tense and past part.* **shed**) **1** to cast off or let fall (leaves, hair, skin, etc). **2** to take off (an item of clothing). **3** to get rid of. **4** to allow to flow or spill. **5** to cast or spread (light). **6** to drop (a load) accidentally. ✳ **shed tears** to cry.

shed[2] *n* **1** a simple garden building for storage. **2** a large building for storing or repairing vehicles, machinery, etc.

she'd *contraction* **1** she had. **2** she would.

sheen *n* **1** brightness or lustre. **2** a subdued surface shine.

sheep *n* (*pl* **sheep**) an animal with a thick woolly coat, kept for its flesh and wool.

sheep-dip *n* a liquid in which sheep are dipped to destroy parasites.

sheepdog *n* a breed of dog used for guarding and driving sheep.

sheepish *adj* embarrassed by shame or shyness. ➤ **sheepishly** *adv.*

sheepskin *n* **1** the skin of a sheep with the wool on. **2** the skin of a sheep or leather made from it.

sheer[1] *adj* **1** absolute or utter. **2** forming a vertical or almost vertical surface from a great height. **3** of fabric: transparently fine. ➤ **sheerly** *adv.*

sheer[2] *adv* **1** altogether or completely. **2** straight up or down.

sheer[3] *v* to change or move from a course.

sheet[1] *n* **1** a broad piece of cotton or other fabric used on a bed. **2** a rectangular piece of paper. **3** a piece of thin flat material such as glass or metal. **4** a broad flat expanse. **5** a suspended or moving mass of flame, water, etc.

sheet[2] *n* a rope controlling the angle at which a sail is set in relation to the wind.

sheet music *n* music printed on sheets of paper.

sheikh *or* **sheik** /shayk, sheek/ *n* an Arab or Muslim leader. ➤ **sheikhdom** *n.*

shekel /'shekl/ *n* the basic monetary unit of Israel.

shelf *n* (*pl* **shelves**) **1** a flat long piece of a solid material fastened horizontally to hold objects. **2** a partially submerged sandbank or ledge of rocks. **3** a flat projecting layer of rock. ✳ **off the shelf** available from stock. **on the shelf** of a woman: unlikely or too old to marry.

shelf-life *n* the length of time for which an item for sale can be kept in a shop.

shell[1] *n* **1** a hard rigid covering of an animal, e.g. a turtle or beetle. **2** the hard outer covering of an egg, nut, or seed. **3** a seashell. **4** a framework or exterior structure. **5** a projectile filled with an explosive charge for firing from a large gun. **6** a hollow metal or paper case. ➤ **shelly** *adj.*

shell[2] *v* **1** to take (something) out of its shell. **2** to fire shells at.

she'll *contraction* **1** she will. **2** she shall.

shellfish *n* a water animal with a shell, *esp* an edible mollusc or crustacean.

shell shock *n* a mental disorder resulting from the stress of continued wartime combat.

shell suit *n* a lightweight top and trousers with a soft lining and a shiny covering.

shelter[1] *n* **1** a structure providing cover or protection. **2** the state of being protected.

shelter[2] *v* **1** to serve as a shelter for. **2** to keep concealed or protected. **3** to take cover or find refuge.

sheltered *adj* **1** protected from hardship or unpleasantness. **2** of accommodation: designed for elderly or disabled people to live in, and having a resident warden.

shelve *v* **1** to provide with shelves. **2** to place on a shelf. **3** to postpone or discontinue for a time. **4** of ground: to slope gently.

shelves *n* pl of SHELF.

shenanigans *pl n* **1** deliberate deception or trickery. **2** lively mischief.

shepherd[1] *n* somebody who tends sheep. ➤ **shepherdess** *n.*

shepherd[2] *v* **1** to tend (sheep) as a shepherd. **2** to guide or conduct.

shepherd's pie *n* a dish of minced meat covered with mashed potato.

sherbet *n* **1** a sweet effervescent powder, eaten dry or used to make fizzy drinks. **2** a Middle Eastern cold drink of sweetened diluted fruit juice.

sheriff *n* **1** the chief executive officer in an English or Welsh county, with mainly judicial and ceremonial duties. **2** the chief judge of a Scottish county or district. **3** a county law enforcement officer in the USA.

Sherpa *n* (*pl* **Sherpa** *or* **Sherpas**) a member of a Tibetan people living on the southern slopes of the Himalayas.

sherry *n* (*pl* **-ies**) a blended fortified wine from southern Spain.

she's *contraction* **1** she is. **2** she has.

Shetland pony *n* a small shaggy pony originating in the Shetland Islands.

shiatsu *n* a medical treatment involving the application of pressure with the hands to particular points of the body.

shibboleth *n* a custom or belief that characterizes the members of a particular group.

shied *v* past tense and past part. of SHY², SHY³.

shield¹ *n* **1** a piece of armour carried as protection against blows. **2** somebody or something that protects or defends. **3** a guard or device protecting people from injury from moving parts of machinery. **4** an armoured screen protecting an otherwise exposed gun. **5** a defined area on which heraldic arms are displayed. **6** a sports trophy in the form of a small mounted shield. **7** a decorative or identifying emblem.

shield² *v* to protect or conceal.

shift¹ *v* **1** to change or move from a place, position, or direction. **2** *Brit, informal* to move fast. **3** *Brit* to remove (e.g. a stain) by hard cleaning. **4** *informal* to sell or dispose of.

shift² *n* **1** a change in place, position, or direction. **2** a change in emphasis, judgment, or attitude. **3** a group who work together in alternation with other groups, or the period of their work. **4** a key on a computer keyboard that changes the characters entered from small to capital letters, and changes other functions. **5** a loose dress or slip.

shiftless *adj* lacking ambition; lazy.

shifty *adj* (**-ier, -iest**) appearing to be dishonest or untrustworthy. ➤ **shiftily** *adv*.

Shiite /'shee-iet/ *n* an adherent of the branch of Islam tracing its authority to Muhammad's son-in-law Ali.

shilling *n* **1** a former British monetary unit, worth one 20th of a pound or twelve old pence. **2** the basic monetary unit of Kenya, Somalia, Tanzania, and Uganda.

shilly-shally *v* (**-ies, -ied**) to be indecisive.

shimmer¹ *v* to shine with a softly wavering light.

shimmer² *n* a shimmering light. ➤ **shimmery** *adj*.

shimmy *v* (**-ies, -ied**) **1** to dance a body-shaking jazz dance. **2** to shake or tremble.

shin¹ *n* the front part of the leg below the knee.

shin² *v* (**shinned, shinning**) (*usu* + up/down) to climb by gripping with the arms and the legs and moving oneself up or down.

shindig *n* *informal* a lively social gathering.

shine¹ *v* (*past tense and past part.* **shone**) **1** to give out or reflect light. **2** to be outstanding or distinguished. **3** to have a radiant or lively appearance. **4** to direct the light of (a lamp or torch). **5** (*past tense and past part.* **shined**) to polish.

shine² *n* **1** brightness from light. **2** brilliance or splendour. **3** an act of polishing. * **take a shine to** *informal* to like immediately.

shiner *n* *informal* a black eye.

shingle¹ *n* a wooden tile laid in overlapping rows as a roof or wall covering.

shingle² *n* a mass of small rounded pebbles on the seashore. ➤ **shingly** *adj*.

shingles *pl n* a disease affecting the nerve endings, caused by a virus and involving a rash of painful blisters.

shin pad *n* a pad worn to protect the shin in ball games.

shiny *adj* (**-ier, -iest**) **1** bright or glossy in appearance. **2** reflecting light.

ship¹ *n* a large floating vessel for travelling by sea.

ship² *v* (**shipped, shipping**) **1** to transport (goods) by ship or by other means. **2** of a boat or ship: to take in (water) over the side.

-ship *suffix* forming nouns: *friendship*; *scholarship*; *membership*.

shipbuilder *n* a person or company that designs or builds ships. ➤ **shipbuilding** *n*.

shipment *n* **1** the process of transporting goods. **2** a quantity of goods transported.

shipping *n* **1** the ships of a particular country or route. **2** the business of transporting goods.

shipshape *adj* neat and tidy.

shipwreck¹ *n* **1** the destruction or loss of a ship at sea. **2** a wrecked ship or its remains.

shipwreck² *v* to cause to undergo shipwreck.

shipyard *n* a place where ships are built or repaired.

shire *n* **1** an English county. **2** (*usu* **the Shires**) conservative rural areas of England.

shire horse *n* a large powerful draught horse.

shirk *v* to evade (a duty or responsibility). ➤ **shirker** *n*.

shirt *n* a piece of clothing for the upper body, with sleeves and a collar, and buttons down the front. * **keep one's shirt on** *informal* to remain calm.

shirtsleeves *pl n* * **in shirtsleeves** wearing a shirt without a jacket.

shirty *adj* (**-ier, -iest**) *informal* bad-tempered.

shish kebab *n* a kebab cooked on a skewer.

shiver¹ *v* to shake or tremble with cold or fever.

shiver² *n* an act of shivering or trembling. ➤ **shivery** *adj*.

shiver³ *n* a small piece of something shattered.

shoal¹ *n* **1** an underwater sandbank exposed at low tide. **2** an area of shallow water.

shoal² *v* of water: to become shallow or less deep.

shoal³ *n* a large group of fish.

shock¹ *n* **1** a sudden disturbance of a person's thoughts or emotions. **2** something that disturbs or upsets in this way. **3** a state in which bodily functions temporarily cease to operate as normal, caused usu by severe injury or trauma. **4** sudden stimulation of the nerves and convulsive contraction of the muscles caused by electricity passing through the body. **5** a violent impact or collision. **6** a violent shaking or jarring.

shock² v **1** to cause to feel sudden surprise, alarm, or offence. **2** to cause to undergo a physical or nervous shock. ➤ **shockproof** adj.

shock³ n a thick bushy mass of hair.

shock absorber n a device on a vehicle for absorbing sudden jolts or shocks.

shocking adj **1** causing shock or indignation. **2** Brit, informal very bad. ➤ **shockingly** adv.

shock troops pl n troops trained and selected for sudden assault.

shock wave n a high-pressure wave formed by an explosion or by a body exceeding the speed of sound.

shod v past tense and past part. of SHOE².

shoddy adj (**-ier, -iest**) **1** hastily or poorly done; inferior. **2** discreditable or despicable. ➤ **shoddily** adv.

shoe¹ n **1** an outer covering for the foot, having a stiff sole. **2** a horseshoe. **3** the part of a vehicle's brake that presses on the drum. ✳ **be in somebody's shoes** to be in their position.

shoe² v (**shoes, shoed, shoeing,** past tense and past part. **shod**) **1** to fit (a horse) with a shoe. **2** (usu in passive) to equip with shoes.

shoehorn¹ n a curved piece of metal or plastic used to ease the heel into the back of a shoe.

shoehorn² v to force into a tight space.

shoelace n a lace or string for fastening a shoe.

shoestring n NAmer a shoelace. ✳ **on a shoestring** informal with very little money available

shogun /'shohgən/ n formerly, a Japanese military governor.

shone v past tense and past part. of SHINE¹.

shook v past tense of SHAKE¹.

shoot¹ v (past tense and past part. **shot**) **1** to wound or kill (a person or animal) with a bullet, arrow, or similar missile. **2** to fire (a gun) or release an arrow from (a bow). **3** to move suddenly or rapidly. **4** to drive (a ball or puck) towards a goal or hole. **5** to direct (a sudden glance or question) at somebody. **6** to photograph or film (a person or scene). **7** to push or slide (a bolt) into or out of a fastening. **8** of a boat: to pass swiftly over (rapids). **9** to produce a piercing sensation through part of the body. **10** of a plant: to put out shoots.

shoot² n **1** a new stem or branch of a plant. **2** a shooting trip or party. **3** a session of photography or filming.

shooter n **1** somebody who uses a gun. **2** informal a gun.

shooting star n a meteor appearing as a temporary streak of light in the sky.

shooting stick n a spiked stick with a handle that opens into a seat.

shop¹ n **1** a building or room for the sale of goods. **2** a place where things are manufactured or repaired. ✳ **talk shop** to talk about one's work outside working hours.

shop² v (**shopped, shopping**) **1** to visit a shop to buy goods. **2** informal to inform on. ➤ **shopper** n, **shopping** n.

shop around v to look around for the best price for something.

shopfloor n **1** Brit the area of a factory where machinery or workbenches are located. **2** workers as distinct from management.

shopkeeper n somebody who runs a retail shop.

shoplift v to steal from a shop. ➤ **shoplifter** n, **shoplifting** n.

shopping n **1** the buying of goods from a shop **2** things bought from a shop.

shopping centre n a group of shops in one place.

shopsoiled adj chiefly Brit dirty or worn from handling or display in a shop.

shop steward n a union member elected to represent workers in dealings with the management.

shore¹ n **1** the land bordering the sea or another body of water. **2** land as distinguished from the sea.

shore² v (often + up) to support with a beam or prop to prevent sinking or sagging.

shoreline n the line where a body of water and the shore meet.

shorn v past part. of SHEAR.

short¹ adj **1** having little or insufficient length or height. **2** not extended in time; brief. **3** limited in distance. **4** not meeting a requirement: in short supply. **5** not reaching far enough. **6** (often + of) insufficiently supplied with. **7** (often + for) abbreviated from. **8** abrupt or curt. **9** of betting odds: almost even. **10** of pastry: crisp and crumbly from containing a high proportion of fat. ✳ **in the short run** for the immediate future. ➤ **shortness** n.

short² adv **1** abruptly or suddenly. **2** not as far as intended or required. ✳ **be taken/caught short** Brit, informal to need suddenly to defecate or urinate. **bring/pull somebody up short** to make somebody stop or pause suddenly.

short³ n **1** Brit, informal a drink of spirits. **2** a brief film or documentary. **3** a short circuit. ✳ **for short** as an abbreviation. **in short** briefly.

short⁴ v to short-circuit.

shortage n a lack or deficit.

shortbread or **shortcake** n a thick crumbly biscuit made from flour, sugar, and fat.

shortchange v to give less than the due change or amount to.

short circuit n the joining of two parts of an electric circuit, allowing an excessive current to flow.

short-circuit v (**short-circuited, short-circuiting**) to cause a short circuit in.

shortcoming n a deficiency or defect.

shortcrust pastry *n* a pastry used for pies and tarts, made with half as much fat as flour.

shortcut *n* a route or procedure that is more direct than the usual one.

shorten *v* to make or become shorter.

shortening *n* fat used in making pastry.

shortfall *n* a state of not being enough; a deficit.

shorthand *n* a method of rapidly writing down what somebody is saying by use of special symbols and abbreviations.

shorthanded *adj* not having enough staff or help.

short list *n* Brit a list of selected candidates from which a final choice is made.

short-list *v* Brit to place on a short list.

short-lived *adj* not living or lasting long.

shortly *adv* **1** in a short time; soon. **2** abruptly or curtly.

shorts *pl n* knee-length or thigh-length trousers.

short shrift *n* summary or inconsiderate treatment.

short-sighted *adj* **1** unable to see distant objects clearly. **2** not taking likely consequences into account.

short-staffed *adj* not having enough staff.

short-tempered *adj* quickly or easily made angry.

shot[1] *n* **1** the act of firing a gun or other weapon. **2** somebody who shoots, *esp* with regard to their ability. **3** a stroke, throw, or kick in a game when attempting to score. **4** *informal* an attempt or try. **5** a wild guess. **6** (*pl* **shot**) a small pellet fired from a shotgun. **7** a heavy metal ball thrown as an athletic field event. **8** a single photographic exposure. **9** a single sequence of a film taken by one camera. **10** an injection of a drug or vaccine. **11** *informal* a single drink of spirits. **12** the launch of a rocket into space. ✱ **a shot in the dark** a wild guess. **a shot in the arm** *informal* a stimulus or boost. **like a shot** *informal* very rapidly.

shot[2] *adj* (+ with) permeated with a quality or element. ✱ **be/get shot of** Brit, *informal* to be or get rid of.

shot[3] *v* past tense and past part. of SHOOT[1].

shotgun *n* a gun for firing metal shot at short range.

shotgun wedding *n* *informal* a wedding that is forced by the bride's pregnancy.

shot put *n* an athletic field event involving the throwing of a heavy metal ball. ➤ **shot-putter** *n*.

should *v aux* past tense of SHALL, used: **1** with *if* to introduce a possibility: *I should be surprised if he came.* **2** to express obligation or recommendation: *You should apologize.* **3** to express probability: *They should be here soon.* **4** to express a polite form of direct statement: *I should try if I were you.*

shoulder[1] *n* the joint linking the upper arm to the trunk. ✱ **shoulder to shoulder** side by side or united.

shoulder[2] *v* **1** to carry on one's shoulders. **2** to assume the burden or responsibility of. **3** to push or thrust with one's shoulder.

shoulder blade *n* each of two flat triangular bones at the top of the back.

shouldn't *contraction* should not.

shout[1] *v* **1** to utter a sudden loud cry. **2** to utter in a loud voice.

shout[2] *n* **1** a loud cry or call. **2** Brit, *informal* a person's turn to buy a round of drinks.

shove[1] *v* **1** to push along steadily or forcefully. **2** to put roughly or carelessly.

shove[2] *n* a hard push.

shovel[1] *n* an implement like a spade with a broad dished blade, used to lift and throw loose material.

shovel[2] *v* (**shovelled, shovelling**, *NAmer* **shoveled, shoveling**) **1** to dig or clear with a shovel. **2** to convey clumsily or in a mass.

show[1] *v* (*past part.* **shown** *or* **showed**) **1** to cause or permit to be seen. **2** to be visible. **3** to exhibit or put on display. **4** to present (a film or broadcast) for people to watch. **5** to display (a feeling or reaction). **6** to indicate or point out. **7** to explain. **8** to establish or prove. **9** to conduct to a specified place. **10** *informal* to arrive as expected. ✱ **show one's face** to let oneself be seen. **show somebody the door** to ask somebody to leave.

show[2] *n* **1** a presentation or entertainment in a theatre. **2** a light radio or television programme. **3** a large display or exhibition. **4** a competitive exhibition of animals, plants, etc. **5** a demonstration of something; a sign or display. **6** a false appearance; a pretence. ✱ **for show** just to impress or attract attention. **on show** being displayed.

show biz *n* *informal* = SHOW BUSINESS.

show business *n* the entertainment industry, including the theatre, films, pop music, and broadcasting.

showcase *n* **1** a case with a glass front or top used for displaying articles. **2** a setting for exhibiting something to best advantage.

showdown *n* a final confrontation to settle a disagreement.

shower[1] *n* **1** a brief fall of rain, snow, etc. **2** a large number of things arriving or presented together. **3** an apparatus that sprays water over the body for washing. **4** an act of washing oneself in this way. ➤ **showery** *adj*.

shower[2] *v* **1** to fall or cause to fall in a shower. **2** to wash in a shower. **3** to present (somebody) with a lot of of things at once.

showgirl *n* a young woman who dances or sings in a musical show.

showing *n* **1** a display or presentation. **2** a performance in competing.

showjumping *n* the competitive sport of riding horses over a course of obstacles.

shown *v* past part. of SHOW[1].

show off *v* **1** to behave boastfully or ostentatiously. **2** to display proudly.

show-off *n* somebody who shows off; an exhibitionist.

showpiece *n* an outstanding example used for exhibition.

showroom *n* a room where goods for sale are displayed.

show trial *n* a trial conducted by a state to make an impression rather than to see justice done.

show up *v* **1** to be evident or conspicuous. **2** *informal* to arrive. **3** to reveal the shortcomings of (something) by comparison. **4** *informal* to embarrass.

showy *adj* (**-ier, -iest**) **1** making an attractive show. **2** bright and colourful.

shrank *v* past tense of SHRINK[1].

shrapnel *n* fragments of metal thrown out in the explosion of a bomb or shell.

shred[1] *n* **1** a narrow strip cut or torn off. **2** a fragment or scrap.

shred[2] *v* (**shredded, shredding**) to cut or tear into shreds. ➤ **shredder** *n*.

shrew *n* **1** a small mammal with a long pointed snout and small eyes. **2** a bad-tempered nagging woman.

shrewd *adj* marked by keen discernment and judgment. ➤ **shrewdly** *adv*, **shrewdness** *n*.

shrewish *adj* of a woman: bad-tempered and nagging.

shriek *v* to make a shrill piercing cry. ➤ **shriek** *n*.

shrike *n* a grey or brownish songbird that impales its prey on thorns.

shrill[1] *adj* making a high-pitched sound; piercing. ➤ **shrilly** *adv*.

shrill[2] *v* to make a shrill sound.

shrimp[1] *n* (*pl* **shrimps** or **shrimp**) **1** a small edible crustacean with a long slender body. **2** *informal* a very small person.

shrimp[2] *v* to fish for shrimps.

shrine *n* **1** a place where people pray to a saint or deity. **2** a place for sacred images or relics.

shrink[1] *v* (**shrank, shrunk** or **shrunken**) **1** to make or become smaller or shorter. **2** to draw back or cower away in fear or revulsion. **3** (*usu* + from) to be reluctant to accept or do something.

shrink[2] *n* *informal* a psychiatrist.

shrinkage *n* the process or degree of shrinking.

shrinking violet *n* *informal* a meek or shy person.

shrink wrap *n* tough plastic film used as a tight-fitting wrapping. ➤ **shrink-wrap** *v*.

shrivel *v* (**shrivelled, shrivelling**, *NAmer* **shriveled, shriveling**) to shrink and become wrinkled through loss of moisture.

shroud[1] *n* **1** a piece of cloth for wrapping a corpse for burial. **2** something that covers or conceals. **3** any of the ropes supporting a ship's mast.

shroud[2] *v* **1** to conceal or disguise. **2** to wrap (a corpse) in a shroud.

shrub *n* a woody plant with several stems. ➤ **shrubby** *adj*.

shrubbery *n* (*pl* **-ies**) a planting or growth of shrubs.

shrug[1] *v* (**shrugged, shrugging**) to lift and contract (the shoulders) to express uncertainty or lack of concern.

shrug[2] *n* a shrugging of the shoulders.

shrug off *v* to disregard or belittle.

shudder *v* to tremble with a sudden convulsive movement. ➤ **shudder** *n*.

shuffle[1] *v* **1** to walk by moving the feet without lifting them. **2** to fidget restlessly. **3** to rearrange (playing cards) to produce a random order. **4** to rearrange in different positions or locations. **5** (*usu* + off) to avoid or get rid of.

shuffle[2] *n* **1** a shuffling, e.g. of cards. **2** an act of shuffling. **3** a dragging movement of the feet.

shun *v* (**shunned, shunning**) to avoid deliberately.

shunt *v* **1** *Brit* to move (railway vehicles) to different positions on the same or another track. **2** to move (something or somebody) to a less important position. **3** to travel back and forth. ➤ **shunter** *n*.

shut[1] *v* (**shutting**, *past tense and past part.* **shut**) **1** to move into a position to close an opening. **2** to fasten with a lock or bolt. **3** to close by bringing parts together. **4** (+ out) to prevent entrance to (a building or street). **5** (+ in) to confine in a space. **6** to suspend operation, or cause to do this.

shut[2] *adj* **1** in the closed position. **2** not open for business.

shutdown *n* the stopping of work or other activity.

shut down *v* to stop work or cease business.

shut off *v* to stop (something) flowing or working.

shutter[1] *n* **1** each of a pair of hinged outside covers for a window. **2** a device that opens and closes the lens aperture of a camera.

shutter[2] *v* to provide or close with shutters.

shuttle[1] *n* **1** a device in weaving that passes the thread of the weft between the threads of the warp. **2** a public-transport vehicle that travels back and forth over a regular route. **3** a space vehicle that travels from and back to earth.

shuttle[2] *v* **1** to travel back and forth on a regular route. **2** to transport in a shuttle.

shuttlecock *n* a rounded cork or plastic piece with projecting feathers, struck with rackets in badminton.

shut up *v* **1** to lock and prevent access to. **2** to imprison or confine. **3** *informal* to stop talking.

shy¹ *adj* (**-er, -est**) **1** easily alarmed; timid. **2** reserved or retiring. **3** (*often* + of) circumspect or reluctant. ➤ **shyly** *adv*, **shyness** *n*.

shy² *v* (**-ies, -ied**) **1** *esp* of a horse: to start in fright. **2** (*usu* + away/from) to avoid through nervousness.

shy³ *v* (**-ies, -ied**) *dated* to throw with a jerking movement.

shy⁴ *n* (*pl* **-ies**) a toss or throw.

shyster *n informal* a dishonest lawyer or other professional person.

SI *n abbr* Système International (d'Unités), an international system of units for measurement.

Si *abbr* the chemical symbol for silicon.

Siamese *n* (*pl* **Siamese**) **1** *dated* a native or inhabitant of Siam (now Thailand). **2** *dated* the Thai language. ➤ **Siamese** *adj*.

Siamese cat *n* a cat of a breed having blue eyes and short pale fur with a darker face.

Siamese twin *n* each of a pair of twins joined at birth.

sibilant¹ *adj* producing a hissing sound. ➤ **sibilance** *n*.

sibilant² *n* in phonetics, a sibilant speech sound.

sibling *n* a brother or sister.

sibyl *n* an ancient Greek or Roman female prophet. ➤ **sibylline** *adj*.

sic *adv* actually so written: used when copying a piece of text that is apparently misspelt or inappropriate.

sick¹ *adj* **1** affected by a disease; ill. **2** likely or about to vomit. **3** (+ of) having had too much of. **4** disgusted. **5** *informal* disappointed or upset. **6** mentally or emotionally disturbed. **7** of humour: macabre or morbid. ✴ **be sick** to be ill. **2** *Brit* to vomit.

sick² *n Brit, informal* vomit.

sick³ *v Brit, informal* (*usu* + up) to vomit.

sickbay *n* a room where sick people are treated.

sickbed *n* the bed on which somebody lies sick.

sicken *v* **1** to become ill. **2** to cause to feel disgust or loathing.

sickle *n* an implement with a curved blade, for cutting plants or hedges.

sick leave *n* absence from work because of illness.

sickly *adj* (**-ier, -iest**) **1** often unwell. **2** feeble or weak. **3** producing sickness or disease. **4** tending to produce nausea. **5** mawkish or sentimental.

sickness *n* **1** ill health. **2** a particular illness. **3** nausea or vomiting.

side¹ *n* **1** a surface forming a face of an object, usually not the front, back, top, or bottom. **2** either surface of a thin object. **3** a boundary line of a geometrical figure. **4** a position to the right or left of a person, object, or point. **5** a region or direction considered in relation to a centre or line of division. **6** the right or left part of the body. **7** a sports team. **8** a person or group in

competition or dispute with another. **9** the opinion or point of view of such a person or group. **10** an aspect or part of something or somebody. **11** *Brit, informal* a television channel. ✴ **on the side** in addition to a principal occupation. **take sides** to support one of the people or parties in a dispute.

side² *adj* additional or subordinate.

side³ *v* (+ with/against) to support or oppose in a dispute.

side⁴ *n Brit, informal* a self-important manner.

sideboard *n* **1** a piece of furniture with cupboards and drawers for storing crockery, cutlery, etc. **2** *Brit* (*in pl*) sideburns.

sideburns *pl n* a strip of hair on each side of a man's face in front of the ears.

sidecar *n* a small vehicle with a single wheel, attached to the side of a motorcycle to carry passengers.

side effect *n* a secondary effect of a drug.

sidekick *n informal* a person's helper or assistant.

sidelight *n* a small extra light beside the headlight on a motor vehicle.

sideline¹ *n* **1** a business or activity additional to a main occupation. **2** a line marking a side of a court or playing field. **3** (**the sidelines**) the standpoint of people not directly involved in something.

sideline² *v* to remove (somebody) from action or participation.

sidelong *adj and adv* directed to or from one side.

sidereal /sie'diəri·əl/ *adj* of, or expressed in relation to, stars or constellations.

sidesaddle *adj and adv* of a woman: riding a horse with both legs on the same side.

sideshow *n* a small show or stall at a circus or fairground.

sidestep *v* (**sidestepped, sidestepping**) **1** to avoid by stepping to one side. **2** to evade (an issue or question).

side street *or* **side road** *n* a minor street or road branching off a main road.

sideswipe *n* an incidental critical remark.

sidetrack¹ *v* to divert from a course or purpose.

sidetrack² *n* an unimportant line of thought.

sidewalk *n NAmer* a pavement.

sideways *adv and adj* **1** to or from the side. **2** with one side forward.

siding *n* a short length of railway track connected with a main track.

sidle *v* to walk timidly or furtively.

siege *n* **1** a military operation in which a place is surrounded and blockaded to compel it to surrender. **2** a similar operation by police to force somebody to surrender.

Usage Note: Note the spelling with *-ie-*.

sienna *n* an earthy substance used as a brownish yellow or reddish brown pigment.

siesta *n* an afternoon nap or rest.

sieve[1] *n* a device with a mesh for straining liquids or separating coarse from fine solids.

sieve[2] *v* to filter with a sieve.

sift *v* 1 to put through a sieve. 2 (*often* + out) to separate or remove from a mixture using a sieve. 3 to study or examine thoroughly.

sigh[1] *v* to take a deep audible breath in relief, weariness, or grief.

sigh[2] *n* an act or sound of sighing.

sight[1] *n* 1 the process or power of seeing. 2 the perception of an object by the eye. 3 the distance or area one can see. 4 something interesting to be seen. 5 (*in pl*) the things regarded as worth seeing in a particular place. 6 *informal* something ridiculous or displeasing in appearance. 7 an aiming device on a gun. 8 an observation to determine direction or position. 9 *informal* a great deal; a lot. * **a sight for sore eyes** *informal* somebody or something one is delighted to see. **at first sight** when first considered. **out of sight** hidden or not visible. **raise/lower one's sights** to become more (or less) ambitious. **set one's sights on** to aim to have or achieve.

sight[2] *v* to see or have a glimpse of.

sighted *adj* 1 able to see. 2 having sight of a specified kind: *short-sighted*.

sightless *adj* unable to see; blind.

sight-read *v* (*past tense and past part.* **sight-read**) to read and perform (music) without previous study.

sightsee *v* to make a tour of interesting sights. ➢ **sightseeing** *n*, **sightseer** *n*.

sigma *n* the 18th letter of the Greek alphabet (Σ, σ, or at the end of a word ς).

sign[1] *n* 1 something that indicates the presence or existence of something. 2 a presage or portent. 3 a board or notice giving information, direction, etc. 4 a motion or gesture by which a thought or wish is made known. 5 a mark with a conventional meaning, e.g. in music or mathematics. 6 any of the twelve divisions of the zodiac.

sign[2] *v* 1 to put a signature to (a letter, cheque, etc). 2 to write (one's name). 3 (*often* + over) to assign formally. 4 to engage or hire with a contract of employment. 5 to indicate or express by a sign. 6 to make a sign or signal. 7 to use sign language. ➢ **signer** *n*.

signal[1] *n* 1 an action, gesture, or word with an agreed meaning. 2 anything that prompts a particular action or event to take place. 3 a conventional sign, sound, etc that conveys information or gives a warning. 4 a set of coloured lights that regulates the flow of road or rail traffic. 5 the sound or image conveyed by telephone, radio, radar, or television.

signal[2] *v* (**signalled, signalling,** *NAmer* **signaled, signaling**) 1 to make or send a signal. 2 to warn or order (somebody) to do something

by a signal. 3 to communicate (something) by signals. 4 to be a sign of. ➢ **signaller** *n*.

signal[3] *adj* conspicuous or outstanding. ➢ **signally** *adv*.

signal box *n Brit* a building by a railway line from which signals and points are worked.

signatory *n* (*pl* **-ies**) somebody who has signed a document.

signature *n* 1 the name of a person written distinctively to serve as identification or authorization. 2 the act of signing one's name. 3 a distinguishing or identifying mark, feature, or quality.

signature tune *n* an identifying tune used at the beginning of a television or radio programme.

signet *n* an official seal formerly used instead of a signature.

signet ring *n* a ring engraved with a seal or monogram.

significance *n* 1 something conveyed as a meaning. 2 importance or consequence.

significant *adj* 1 having meaning or importance. 2 suggesting or containing a veiled or special meaning. 3 having or likely to have influence or effect; important. ➢ **significantly** *adv*.

signify *v* (**-ies, -ied**) 1 to mean or denote. 2 to be an indication of or imply. 3 to show by a word, signal, or gesture. 4 to be important. ➢ **signification** *n*.

signing *n* 1 somebody who has recently signed a contract with a sports team. 2 sign language. 3 an event at which copies of a book are signed by the author for publicity.

sign language *n* a system of hand gestures and other signs used by deaf people.

sign off *v* 1 to end a letter, message, or broadcast. 2 of a doctor: to declare (somebody) unfit for work.

sign on *v* 1 to commit oneself to a job by signature or agreement. 2 to give a job to. 3 *Brit* to register as unemployed.

sign out *v* 1 to indicate departure by signing a register. 2 to record the release or withdrawal of.

signpost[1] *n* a post by the road with signs on it to direct travellers.

signpost[2] *v* 1 to give information about (a road or place) with a signpost. 2 to indicate or mark.

sign up *v* to join an organization or accept an obligation by signing a contract.

Sikh /seek/ *n* an adherent of a religion of India combining aspects of Hinduism and Islam. ➢ **Sikhism** *n*.

silage *n* fodder stored in a silo and converted into feed for livestock.

silence[1] *n* 1 absence of sound or noise. 2 a state of being unable or unwilling to speak.

silence² v **1** to make silent or much quieter. **2** to prevent from speaking or expressing an opinion.

silencer n a device for muffling the noise made by a gun or vehicle exhaust.

silent adj **1** free from sound or noise. **2** saying nothing. **3** not talkative. **4** of a letter: not pronounced, e.g. the b in doubt. **5** of a film: without spoken dialogue. ➤ **silently** adv.

silhouette¹ n the shape of somebody or something as it appears against a lighter background.

silhouette² v to show in silhouette.

silica n silicon dioxide occurring in many rocks and minerals, e.g. quartz, opal, and sand.

silicon n a non-metallic element that is used in alloys, as a semiconductor, and in the manufacture of glass.

silicone n an organic silicon compound used for lubricants, varnishes, electrical insulators, etc.

silk n **1** a tough shiny fibre produced by silkworms and used for textiles. **2** thread or fabric made from silk filaments. **3** Brit, informal a King's or Queen's Counsel. ＊ **take silk** Brit to become a King's or Queen's Counsel.

silken adj **1** made of silk. **2** silky.

silkworm n the larva of a silk moth, which spins strong silk in making its cocoon.

silky adj (**-ier, -iest**) **1** resembling silk in softness or shine. **2** consisting of silk.

sill n a narrow shelf projecting from the base of a window frame or doorway.

silly adj (**-ier, -iest**) **1** showing a lack of common sense or sound judgment. **2** trifling or frivolous. ➤ **silliness** n.

silo n (pl **-os**) **1** a sealed trench, pit, or tower used for making and storing silage. **2** an underground structure for housing a guided missile.

silt¹ n a deposit of sediment at the bottom of a river. ➤ **silty** adj.

silt² v (often + up) to make or become choked or obstructed with silt.

silver¹ n **1** a soft white metal used in jewellery, ornaments, etc. **2** coins made of silver or a silver-like metal. **3** tableware made of or plated with silver. **4** a shiny whitish grey colour. ➤ **silvery** adj.

silver² adj **1** resembling silver in colour or sheen. **2** marking a 25th anniversary: silver jubilee.

silver³ v to cover or coat with silver.

silver birch n a birch tree with silvery peeling bark.

silverfish n (pl **silverfishes** or **silverfish**) a small silvery wingless insect found in houses.

silver medal n a medal of silver awarded for second place in a competition or race.

silver plate n **1** a coating of silver on another metal. **2** tableware and cutlery of silver or coated with silver.

silverside n Brit a cut of beef from the outer part of the top of the leg.

silversmith n somebody who makes objects of silver.

simian¹ adj of or resembling a monkey or ape.

simian² n a monkey or ape.

similar adj having a general resemblance but not identical. ➤ **similarity** n, **similarly** adv.

simile /'simili/ n a figure of speech comparing two different things, e.g. bold as brass.

simmer v **1** of a liquid: to bubble gently just below boiling point. **2** to cook in a simmering liquid. **3** to be agitated by suppressed emotion. ➤ **simmer** n.

simmer down v to become calm or less excited.

simper¹ v to smile in a foolish self-conscious manner.

simper² n a foolish self-conscious smile.

simple adj **1** easily understood or done. **2** basic or plain. **3** free from showiness; unpretentious. **4** lacking intelligence. **5** of humble birth or position. **6** not compound or subdivided.

simple fracture n a bone fracture in which the skin and tissue are undamaged.

simpleton n somebody who lacks common sense or intelligence.

simplicity n the state or quality of being simple.

simplify v (**-ies, -ied**) to make simple or simpler. ➤ **simplification** n.

simplistic adj presenting a complex matter as if it were simple; oversimplified. ➤ **simplistically** adv.

simply adv **1** without ambiguity; clearly. **2** without ornamentation or show. **3** solely or merely. **4** without any question.

simulacrum /simyoo'laykrəm/ n (pl **simulacra** or **simulacrums**) formal **1** an image or representation. **2** a vague or superficial likeness.

simulate v **1** to assume the outward qualities or appearance of. **2** to make a functioning model of (a system or device). ➤ **simulation** n, **simulator** n.

simultaneous adj existing or happening at the same time. ➤ **simultaneously** adv.

sin¹ n **1** an offence against moral or religious law. **2** an action considered to be wrong.

sin² v (**sinned, sinning**) to commit a sin.

since¹ adv **1** continuously or at a point between a time in the past and now. **2** before now; ago.

since² prep in the period between a time in the past and now.

since³ conj **1** in or during the time after. **2** because.

sincere adj free from deceit or hypocrisy; honest or genuine. ➤ **sincerely** adv, **sincerity** n.

sine n in mathematics, the ratio in a right-angled triangle between the side opposite a particular angle and the hypotenuse.

sinecure /'sinikyooə, 'sie-/ *n* a paid job that involves little or no work.

sine qua non /ˌsini kwah 'non/ *n* an absolutely essential thing.

sinew *n* tissue that connects a muscle with a bone. ➤ **sinewy** *adj.*

sinful *adj* being a sin; wicked. ➤ **sinfully** *adv*, **sinfulness** *n.*

sing *v* (**sang, sung**) **1** to produce musical sounds with the voice. **2** to perform (a song) by singing. **1** to make a shrill whistling sound. **2** *esp* of a bird: to produce melodious sounds. **3** (*usu* + out) to make a loud clear utterance. **4** to express enthusiastically. ➤ **singer** *n.*

singalong *n* an informal gathering for singing.

singe[1] *v* (**singed, singeing**) to burn superficially or slightly.

singe[2] *n* a superficial burn.

single[1] *adj* **1** not accompanied by others. **2** individual or distinct: *every single one*. **3** suitable for or involving only one person. **4** consisting of or having only one part. **5** having only one aspect; uniform. **6** not married. **7** *Brit* of a ticket: valid for a journey to a place but not back again. ➤ **singly** *adv.*

single[2] *n* **1** a CD or record with one short track or a small amount of music. **2** a single thing or amount.

single[3] *v* (+ out) to select specially from a number or group.

single-breasted *adj* of a coat, jacket, etc: having a centre fastening with one row of buttons.

single cream *n* light thin cream suitable for pouring.

single file *n* a line of people moving one behind the other.

single-handed *adj* done by one person alone or without help. ➤ **single-handedly** *adv.*

single-minded *adj* having a single overriding purpose. ➤ **single-mindedly** *adv.*

single parent *n* a person bringing up a child without a partner.

singlet *n* chiefly *Brit* a vest or a similar garment without sleeves.

singleton *n* an individual as opposed to a pair or group.

singsong *n* **1** a monotonous way of speaking like the rhythm of song. **2** *Brit* an informal gathering for singing.

singular[1] *adj* **1** superior; exceptional. **2** very unusual or strange. **3** in grammar, of a word or word form: denoting more than one person or thing. ➤ **singularity** *n*, **singularly** *adv.*

singular[2] *n* in grammar, a singular number or word.

sinister *adj* **1** darkly or frighteningly evil. **2** threatening evil or ill fortune. ➤ **sinisterly** *adv.*

sink[1] *v* (**sank, sunk**) **1** to go down below the surface of liquid. **2** of a ship: to fall or cause to fall to the bottom of the sea. **3** (*usu* + in/into) to

penetrate or cause to penetrate the surface of something soft. **4** to dig or bore (a well or shaft) in the earth. **5** to fall or drop to a lower place or level. **6** to disappear below the horizon. **7** to pass into a specified state. **8** to worsen or deteriorate. **9** to invest (money or energy) in something.

sink[2] *n* a basin connected to a drain and a water supply.

sinker *n* a weight for sinking a fishing line.

sink hole *n* a hollow through which surface water disappears into an underground area.

sink in *v* of information etc: to be understood.

sinner *n* a person who commits sins.

sinuous *adj* **1** having a wavy form; winding. **2** lithe or supple. **3** intricate or tortuous. ➤ **sinuously** *adv.*

sinus *n* a cavity in the bones of the skull that connects with the nostrils.

sinusitis *n* inflammation of a nasal sinus.

sip[1] *v* (**sipped, sipping**) to drink delicately or a little at a time.

sip[2] *n* a small amount of a drink taken by sipping.

siphon[1] *or* **syphon** *n* a tube for transferring liquid up over the side of a container and down to a lower level by atmospheric pressure.

siphon[2] *or* **syphon** *v* **1** to draw off (liquid) with a siphon. **2** (+ off) to take (money) in small amounts.

sir *n* **1** a form of respectful address to a man. **2** (**Sir**) used as a title of a knight or baronet.

sire[1] *n* **1** the male parent of an animal. **2** a father or male ancestor. **3** *archaic* a form of address to a king.

sire[2] *v* esp of a male animal: to beget (offspring).

siren *n* **1** a device that makes a loud wailing sound as a warning. **2** (**Siren**) in Greek mythology, each of a group of winged women who lured sailors to destruction by their singing. **3** a dangerously seductive woman.

sirloin *n* a cut of beef from the upper part of the hind loin.

sisal *n* a strong fibre obtained from the leaves of a Mexican plant, used for ropes, matting, etc.

sissy *n* (*pl* **-ies**) *informal* an effeminate or effete man.

sister *n* **1** a woman or girl having the same parents as another person. **2** a female colleague. **3** a female member of a religious order. **4** *Brit* a senior female nurse. ➤ **sisterly** *adj.*

sisterhood *n* **1** the state of being sisters. **2** a community of women bound by religious vows. **3** a group of women bound by a common interest.

sister-in-law *n* (*pl* **sisters-in-law**) **1** the sister of one's husband or wife. **2** the wife of one's brother.

sit[1] *v* (**sitting**, *past tense and past part.* **sat**) **1** to rest in a position supported by the buttocks and with the back upright. **2** of an animal: to rest with its body close to the ground. **3** to be a member of an official body. **4** of a political body, etc: to be in session for official business. **5** to lie or stand in a particular position. **6** of a bird: to cover eggs for hatching. **7** to pose as a model for an artist or photographer. **8** *Brit* to be a candidate in (an examination). **9** to have enough seats for. ✻ **sit tight** *informal* to maintain one's position.

sit² *n* a period of sitting.

sitar *n* an Indian lute with a long neck. ➤ **sitarist** *n*.

sitcom *n informal* a situation comedy.

site¹ *n* **1** an area of ground occupied by a building, town, etc. **2** a scene of a specified activity. **3** a website.

site² *v* to place or build in a particular position.

sit in *v* **1** to be present as a visitor or observer. **2** to be a substitute.

sit-in *n* the occupation of a building by a body of people as a protest.

sitter *n* **1** a person who sits as an artist's model. **2** a babysitter.

sitting *n* **1** a period of posing for a portrait. **2** a period when a group of people are served a meal. **3** a session of an official body.

sitting duck *n informal* an easy target for attack or criticism.

sitting room *n chiefly Brit* a room for sitting and relaxing.

sitting tenant *n Brit* a tenant who is occupying a property with the legal right to remain.

situate *v* to place in a particular location or situation.

situation *n* **1** the way in which something is placed in relation to its surroundings. **2** the conditions and circumstances at a particular time or place. **3** a job or post. ➤ **situational** *adj*.

situation comedy *n* a broadcast comedy series involving characters in successive episodes.

six *n* **1** the number 6. **2** a shot in cricket that crosses the boundary before it bounces and scores six runs. ✻ **at sixes and sevens** in confusion or disorder. **knock for six** *Brit, informal* to overwhelm or astonish. ➤ **six** *adj*.

sixpence *n* a former silver-coloured coin worth six old pence (2.5p).

sixteen *adj and n* the number 16. ➤ **sixteenth** *adj and n*.

sixth *adj and n* **1** having the position in a sequence corresponding to the number six. **2** one of six equal parts of something.

sixth-form college *n Brit* a state school for pupils above GCSE level.

sixth sense *n* a keen intuitive power independent of the five physical senses.

sixty *adj and n* (*pl* -**ies**) **1** the number 60. **2** (*in pl*) the numbers 60 to 69. ➤ **sixtieth** *adj and n*.

sizable *or* **sizeable** *adj* fairly large.

size¹ *n* **1** the overall dimensions or measurement of something. **2** each of a series of graduated measurements in which items of clothing are made. ✻ **the size of it** *informal* the actual state of affairs.

size² *v* to arrange or grade according to size.

size³ *n* a thick sticky material used for preparing surfaces of paper or plaster in decorating.

size⁴ *v* to treat with size.

sizeable *adj* SEE SIZABLE.

size up *v* **1** to form an opinion or estimate of. **2** to alter the size of according to requirements.

sizzle¹ *v* **1** to make the hissing sound of frying food. **2** *informal* to be very hot. ➤ **sizzling** *adj*.

sizzle² *n* a sizzling sound.

skate¹ *n* an ice skate or a roller skate. ✻ **get/ put one's skates on** *informal* to hurry.

skate² *v* to glide along on skates. ✻ **skate over/round** to avoid dealing with (something difficult or awkward). ➤ **skater** *n*.

skate³ *n* (*pl* **skates** *or* **skate**) a food fish of the ray family.

skateboard¹ *n* a narrow board mounted on small wheels for riding on.

skateboard² *v* to ride on a skateboard. ➤ **skateboarder** *n*.

skedaddle *v informal* to leave hurriedly.

skein *n* a loosely coiled length of yarn or thread.

skeletal *adj* **1** attached to or resembling a skeleton. **2** of an idea: existing only in outline.

skeleton *n* **1** a framework of an organism, *esp* the bones of a vertebrate animal. **2** something reduced to its bare essentials. **3** an emaciated person or animal. **4** a basic framework. **5** (*used before a noun*) reduced to a minimum: *a skeleton staff*. ✻ **skeleton in the cupboard** a secret cause of shame.

skeleton key *n* a key that is able to open several locks.

skeptic *n NAmer* SEE SCEPTIC.

sketch¹ *n* **1** a rough drawing. **2** a brief description or outline. **3** a short comic act.

sketch² *v* **1** to make a sketch of. **2** (*often* + out) to describe briefly.

sketchbook *n* a pad of plain paper for sketching.

sketchy *adj* (-**ier**, -**iest**) lacking detail; superficial or scanty. ➤ **sketchily** *adv*.

skew¹ *adj* placed or running obliquely.

skew² *n* **1** obliqueness or slant. **2** distortion or bias.

skew³ *v* **1** to take an oblique course; to twist or swerve. **2** to distort or give a bias to.

skewbald *adj* of a horse: marked with patches of white and brown.

skewer¹ *n* a long wooden or metal pin for holding food together while cooking.

skewer² *v* to hold or pierce with a skewer.

ski *n* (*pl* **skis**) each of a pair of long narrow strips of wood, metal, or plastic attached to the feet for gliding over snow.

ski² *v* (**skis, skied, skiing**) to travel on skis.
➤ **skier** *n*.

skid¹ *v* (**skidded, skidding**) **1** of a vehicle: to slide sideways out of control. **2** to slip or slide.

skid² *n* **1** an act of skidding. **2** a runner used as part of the landing gear of an aircraft.

skiff *n* a light rowing or sailing boat.

ski jump *n* a steep ramp overhanging a slope, used for jumping on skis. ➤ **ski-jump** *v*.

skilful (*NAmer* **skillful**) *adj* having or showing skill; expert. ➤ **skilfully** *adv*.

Usage Note: Note the spelling with one *l* and then *-ful*.

---

ski lift *n* a series of seats suspended from an overhead cable, used for transporting skiers up and down a mountainside.

skill *n* **1** special ability in a particular field. **2** a task or technique requiring skill.

skilled *adj* **1** having skill. **2** requiring trained workers.

skillet *n* a small frying pan.

skim *v* (**skimmed, skimming**) **1** to clear (a liquid) of floating matter. **2** to remove (fat or scum) from the surface of a liquid. **3** to pass swiftly or lightly over. **4** to read over quickly. **5** (*usu* + through/over) to consider briefly.

skimmed milk *n* milk with the cream removed.

skimp *v* (*usu* + on) to devote too little time, money, or effort to.

skimpy *adj* (**-ier, -iest**) inadequate in quality, size, etc; scanty. ➤ **skimpily** *adv*.

skin¹ *n* **1** the external covering of the body. **2** an outer covering, e.g. the peel or rind of a fruit or vegetable or the casing of a sausage. **3** the external covering of an animal, prepared and used e.g. for clothing. **4** a film that forms on the surface of a liquid. ✳ **by the skin of one's teeth** only just; barely. **get under somebody's skin** *informal* to irritate or interest somebody intensely. **no skin off somebody's nose** *informal* no disadvantage to somebody. **skin and bone** thin and emaciated.

skin² *v* (**skinned, skinning**) **1** to remove the skin of. **2** to scrape or graze (part of the body).

skin-deep *adj* transitory or superficial.

skin diving *n* swimming under water with flippers and an aqualung.

skinflint *n* *informal* a mean or niggardly person.

skinhead *n* a member of a group of young people with extremely short hair.

skinny *adj* (**-ier, -iest**) *informal* very thin. ➤ **skinniness** *n*.

skint *adj* *Brit, informal* having no money.

skintight *adj* of a piece of clothing: fitting close to the body.

skip¹ *v* (**skipped, skipping**) **1** to move with light leaps, or by hopping on alternate feet. **2** to jump repeatedly over a rope swung over the head and under the feet. **3** to pass over or omit.

4 (+ through) to deal with hastily or cursorily. **5** to fail to attend.

skip² *n* a skipping movement.

skip³ *n* a large open container for waste or rubble, removed when full.

skipper¹ *n* *informal* the captain of a ship, aircraft, or sports team.

skipper² *v* to be captain of.

skipper³ *n* **1** somebody or something that skips. **2** a small butterfly with a stout hairy body and a darting flight.

skirl *v* to emit the high shrill sound of bagpipes. ➤ **skirl** *n*.

skirmish¹ *n* a brief clash or fight.

skirmish² *v* to engage in a skirmish.

skirt¹ *n* a women's and girls' piece of clothing that hangs from the waist.

skirt² *v* **1** to extend along the edge of. **2** (*also* + round) to avoid through difficulty or danger.

skirting or **skirting board** *n* a strip of board fixed along the base of an interior wall.

skit *n* a humorous sketch or story.

skitter *v* to move lightly or swiftly.

skittish *adj* **1** of an animal: nervous and easily frightened. **2** lively or frisky. ➤ **skittishly** *adv*.

skittle *n* **1** (*in pl*) a game played by rolling a wooden ball at a group of pins in order to knock them over. **2** a pin used in skittles.

skive *v* *Brit, informal* (*often* + off) to avoid work or duty. ➤ **skiver** *n*.

skivvy *n* (*pl* **-ies**) *Brit, informal* a female domestic servant.

skua *n* a large dark-coloured seabird.

skulduggery or **skullduggery** *n* underhand or unscrupulous behaviour.

skulk *v* to move stealthily or furtively.

skull *n* a bony case forming the skeleton of the head and enclosing the brain.

skull and crossbones *n* a representation of a human skull over two crossed thigh bones, used as a warning of danger and formerly shown on pirate flags.

skullcap *n* a close-fitting cap without a peak.

skunk *n* an American mammal that can eject a foul-smelling liquid in self-defence.

sky *n* (*pl* **-ies**) the upper atmosphere seen from the earth.

sky blue *n* a light blue colour.

skydiving *n* the sport of jumping from an aircraft and executing body manoeuvres in the air before opening a parachute. ➤ **skydiver** *n*.

skylark¹ *n* a lark that sings in flight.

skylark² *v* to behave in a high-spirited or mischievous manner.

skylight *n* a window in a roof or ceiling.

skyline *n* an outline of buildings or landscape seen against the the sky.

skyrocket¹ *n* a rocket fired high into the air as a flare or firework.

skyrocket² *v* (**skyrocketed, skyrocketing**) to increase rapidly or suddenly.

skyscraper *n* a very tall building with many storeys.

slab *n* **1** a large thick flat piece of stone. **2** a thick slice of cheese, cake, etc.

slack[1] *adj* **1** not taut; loose. **2** lazy or sluggish. **3** negligent or lax. **4** lacking in activity; not busy. ➤ **slackly** *adv*, **slackness** *n*.

slack[2] *n* **1** the part of a rope or string that is not held taut. **2** (*in pl*) casual trousers. **3** *informal* a lull in activity.

slack[3] *v* **1** to work sluggishly or carelessly. **2** (*often + off*) to release tension in; to loosen. **3** to lessen or moderate. **4** (*+ off/up*) to be or become slack. ➤ **slacker** *n*.

slack[4] *n* coal in very small pieces.

slacken *v* **1** to make or become less taut. **2** to make or become less active, rapid, or intense.

slag[1] *n* **1** waste matter from the smelting of metal ores. **2** *Brit* waste material from coal mining. **3** *Brit, informal, derog* a promiscuous woman or girl.

slag[2] *v* (**slagged, slagging**) *Brit, informal* (*also + off*) to criticize abusively.

slagheap *n* *Brit* a mound of waste material from a mine.

slain *v* past part. of SLAY.

slake *v* to satisfy or quench (a thirst or desire).

slalom *n* a skiing or canoeing race on winding course between obstacles.

slam[1] *v* (**slammed, slamming**) **1** to shut forcibly and noisily. **2** to put or throw down noisily. **3** (*usu + into*) to crash into violently. **4** *informal* to criticize harshly. **5** *informal* to defeat easily.

slam[2] *n* a banging noise as made by a door in closing.

slam[3] *n* in bridge, the winning of all tricks or all tricks but one.

slander[1] *n* **1** the crime of saying untrue things that damage a person's reputation. **2** something said that is untrue and defamatory. ➤ **slanderous** *adj*.

slander[2] *v* to utter slander about. ➤ **slanderer** *n*.

slang *n* informal spoken words and phrases, often of a kind associated with a particular group of people. ➤ **slangy** *adj*.

slanging match *n* *chiefly Brit, informal* an angry and abusive argument between two or more people.

slant[1] *v* **1** to lean or slope. **2** to interpret or present (information) from a particular point of view.

slant[2] *n* **1** a slanting direction, line, or plane. **2** a particular point of view. ➤ **slantwise** *adv and adj*.

slap[1] *n* **1** a sharp blow with the open hand. **2** a noise that suggests a slap. ✻ **slap in the face** a rebuff or insult.

slap[2] *v* (**slapped, slapping**) **1** to hit with the open hand or a flat object. **2** to hit with the

sound of a slap. **3** (*usu + on*) to apply hastily or carelessly.

slap[3] *adv* *informal* directly or with force.

slap-bang *adv* *informal* **1** in an abrupt or forceful manner. **2** precisely.

slapdash *adj and adv* done in a haphazard or slipshod manner.

slap down *v* to criticize or reprimand abruptly.

slapstick *n* comedy characterized by farce and horseplay.

slap-up *adj* *chiefly Brit, informal* of a meal: lavish or extravagant.

slash[1] *v* **1** to cut with violent sweeping strokes. **2** to cut slits in. **3** *informal* to reduce (a price) drastically.

slash[2] *n* **1** a cut or stroke made by slashing. **2** a stroke (/) used to show alternatives or elements of a fraction.

slat *n* a thin narrow flat strip of wood or metal forming an overlapping series. ➤ **slatted** *adj*.

slate[1] *n* **1** a fine-grained rock that is easily split into thin layers. **2** a piece of this used as roofing material. **3** a tablet of slate or similar material for writing on. ➤ **slaty** *adj*.

slate[2] *v* to cover with slates. ➤ **slater** *n*.

slate[3] *v* *chiefly Brit, informal* to criticize severely.

slattern *n* *dated* an untidy slovenly woman. ➤ **slatternly** *adj*.

slaughter[1] *n* **1** the killing of livestock for food. **2** the violent killing of many people.

slaughter[2] *v* **1** to kill (animals) for food. **2** to kill (people) violently or in large numbers.

slaughterhouse *n* a place where animals are killed for food.

Slav *n* a member of a group of peoples of eastern Europe who speak a Slavonic language.

slave[1] *n* **1** a person held as the property of another and bound to obey them. **2** a person who is dominated by a specified thing: *a slave to fashion*.

slave[2] *v* to work very hard.

slave driver *n* *informal* a harsh taskmaster.

slave labour *n* hard work for little reward.

slaver[1] /'slavə/ *v* to drool or slobber.

slaver[2] *n* saliva dribbling from the mouth.

slavery *n* **1** the state of being a slave. **2** the practice of owning slaves.

slavish *adj* **1** imitative; having no originality. **2** excessively servile. ➤ **slavishly** *adv*.

Slavonic *adj* of a group of lanuages including Bulgarian, Czech, Polish, Russian, and Serbo-Croatian.

slay *v* (**slew, slain**) **1** *archaic* to kill violently or with great bloodshed. **2** *NAmer* to murder.

sleaze *n* *informal* corrupt or immoral behaviour.

sleazy *adj* (**-ier, -iest**) **1** of a place: squalid and disreputable. **2** of behaviour: corrupt or immoral.

sled[1] *n* *NAmer* = SLEDGE[1].

sled[2] *v* (**sledded, sledding**) *NAmer* = SLEDGE[2].

sledge[1] n 1 a vehicle with runners for travelling over snow or ice, often pulled by dogs. 2 *Brit* a toboggan.

sledge[2] v to ride or carry on a sledge.

sledgehammer n a large heavy hammer.

sleek[1] adj 1 smooth and glossy. 2 smart and well-groomed. 3 looking prosperous. ➤ **sleekly** adv.

sleek[2] v to make (the hair) sleek or smooth.

sleep[1] n 1 a natural state of unconsciousness with the eyes closed and the body relaxed. 2 a period spent sleeping. ✳ **go to sleep** 1 to fall asleep. 2 to become numb. **put to sleep** to kill (an animal) humanely. ➤ **sleepless** adj.

sleep[2] v (*past tense and past part.* **slept**) 1 to rest in a state of sleep. 2 *informal* (+ with/together) to have sexual relations with. 3 to provide sleeping accommodation for (a specified number of people).

sleep around v to be sexually promiscuous.

sleeper n 1 a sleeping car. 2 *Brit* a ring or stud worn in a pierced ear to keep the hole open. 3 each of a series of wooden or concrete supports on which railway rails are laid.

sleeping bag n a padded bag for sleeping in when camping.

sleeping car n a railway carriage having berths for sleeping.

sleeping partner n a partner who takes no active part in the running of a business.

sleeping pill n a tablet or capsule taken to induce sleep.

sleeping policeman n a hump in a road designed to slow traffic down.

sleeping sickness n a tropical disease marked by prolonged lethargy.

sleepwalk v to walk in one's sleep. ➤ **sleepwalker** n.

sleepy adj (-**ier**, -**iest**) 1 ready to fall asleep. 2 sluggish or lethargic. 3 of a place: quiet and inactive. ➤ **sleepily** adv, **sleepiness** n.

sleet[1] n partly frozen falling rain, or snow and rain falling together.

sleet[2] v to fall as sleet.

sleeve n 1 the part of a garment covering the arm or upper arm. 2 a covering for a record. 3 a tubular machine part designed to fit over another part. ✳ **up one's sleeve** kept hidden for future use. ➤ **sleeveless** adj.

sleigh n a large sledge pulled by horses or reindeer.

sleight n *literary* deceitful craftiness.

sleight of hand n 1 skilful use of the hands in conjuring or juggling. 2 shrewd deception.

slender adj 1 gracefully slim. 2 flimsy or meagre.

slept v past tense and past part. of SLEEP[2].

sleuth[1] n *informal* a detective.

sleuth[2] v *informal* to act as a detective.

slew[1] v to slide or swing about out of control.

slew[2] v past tense of SLAY.

slice[1] n 1 a thin broad flat piece cut from a larger whole. 2 a portion or share. 3 an implement with a broad blade for lifting food. 4 in sports, the flight of a ball that deviates from a straight course.

slice[2] v 1 to cut with a knife. 2 to cut into slices. 3 to hit (a ball) so that it deviates from a straight course. 4 to move rapidly or effortlessly.

slick[1] adj 1 deft or skilful. 2 superficially plausible or impressive; glib. 3 smooth or slippery. ➤ **slickly** adv.

slick[2] n a film of oil floating on water.

slick[3] v to make (hair) sleek or smooth.

slide[1] v (*past tense and past part.* **slid**) 1 to move over a smooth surface in continuous contact with it. 2 to glide over a slippery surface. 3 to pass quietly and unobtrusively. 4 to move smoothly and easily. 5 to pass gradually to a lower level or worse state.

slide[2] n 1 a structure with a sloping smooth surface down which children slide in play. 2 the act of sliding. 3 a sliding part or mechanism. 4 a flat piece of glass for mounting an object to be examined under a microscope. 5 a photographic transparency viewed with a projector.

slide rule n a ruler with a central sliding strip for making calculations.

sliding scale n a scale of fees or payments that changes according to the variation in some other factor.

slight[1] adj 1 small in amount or degree. 2 having a slim or frail build. 3 lacking strength or bulk; flimsy. 4 unimportant; trivial. 5 not serious; minor. ➤ **slightly** adv.

slight[2] v to treat with disdain or indifference; to snub.

slight[3] n a humiliating affront.

slim[1] adj (**slimmer**, **slimmest**) 1 attractively thin. 2 small in width in relation to length or height. 3 scanty or slight: *a slim chance.*

slim[2] v (**slimmed**, **slimming**) 1 to make or become thinner. 2 (*often* + down) to reduce the number of. ➤ **slimmer** n.

slime n an unpleasantly thick and slippery substance.

slimy adj (-**ier**, -**iest**) 1 resembling or covered with slime. 2 *informal* obsequious or ingratiating in a repellent way.

sling[1] n 1 a looped line used to raise or support something. 2 a bandage suspended from the neck to support an injured arm. 3 a short strap used as a simple weapon for throwing stones.

sling[2] v (*past tense and past part.* **slung**) 1 to throw carelessly. 2 to throw (a stone) with a sling. 3 to raise or carry in a sling. 4 *Brit, informal* (+ out) to expel unceremoniously.

slingback n a shoe held on by a strap passing round the ankle.

slingshot n *NAmer* a catapult.

slink v (past tense and past part. **slunk**) to move gracefully or stealthily.

slinky adj (-ier, -iest) informal sleek and flowing in movement or outline.

slip[1] v (**slipped, slipping**) 1 to slide out of place or away from one's grasp. 2 to slide on a slippery surface. 3 to decline from a standard or accustomed level by degrees. 4 to move or cause to move smoothly. 5 to move quietly and cautiously. 6 to pass imperceptibly from one state into another. 7 of time: to elapse. 8 to free oneself from (a restraint). 9 (+ on/off) to put on or take off (clothing) quickly or easily. 10 to place or pass quietly or secretly. 11 to leave (the clutch of a vehicle) partially engaged. ✱ **let slip** 1 to say casually or accidentally. 2 to fail to take (a chance). **slip one's mind** to be forgotten or overlooked. ➤ **slippage** n.

slip[2] n 1 an instance of slipping. 2 a minor mistake. 3 a woman's short undergarment. 4 in cricket, a fielding position close to the batsman. ✱ **give somebody the slip** informal to elude or evade somebody.

slip[3] n 1 a small piece of paper. 2 a small young person: a slip of a girl. 3 a shoot cut for planting or grafting.

slipknot n a knot that can be untied by pulling or that slides along the line it is tied to.

slip-on adj esp of shoes: having no fastenings.

slipped disc n a displaced disc in the spine, producing pressure on the nerves and causing pain.

slipper n a flat comfortable shoe for wearing indoors.

slippery adj (-ier, -iest) 1 tending to cause sliding from being icy, greasy, wet, or polished. 2 tending to slip from the grasp. 3 of a person: not to be trusted.

slippy adj (-ier, -iest) informal slippery.

slip road n Brit a road providing access to or exit from a major road or motorway.

slipshod adj careless or slovenly.

slipstream n 1 a stream of air or water driven backward by a propeller. 2 an area of reduced air pressure immediately behind a moving vehicle.

slip up v to make a careless mistake.

slip-up n informal a mistake or oversight.

slipway n a ramp sloping down into water, for launching or landing ships or boats.

slit[1] v (**slitting**, past tense and past part. **slit**) to make a narrow cut in.

slit[2] n a long narrow cut or opening.

slither v 1 to move smoothly with a sliding or twisting motion. 2 to slide unsteadily on a slippery surface. ➤ **slither** n, **slithery** adj.

sliver[1] n a small slender piece cut or broken off something.

sliver[2] v to cut or break into slivers.

slob n informal a lazy slovenly person.

slobber[1] v 1 to let saliva dribble from the mouth. 2 (often + over) to express excessive emotion about.

slobber[2] n saliva dribbled from the mouth. ➤ **slobbery** adj.

sloe n the small blue-black fruit of the blackthorn.

slog[1] v (**slogged, slogging**) 1 to move slowly and laboriously. 2 to work laboriously. 3 to hit hard and wildly. ✱ **slog it out** to compete fiercely.

slog[2] n 1 a spell of hard work. 2 an arduous march. 3 a hard blow.

slogan n a brief catchy phrase used in advertising or to characterize a particular point of view.

sloop n a sailing boat with one mast.

slop v (**slopped, slopping**) 1 of a liquid: to spill over the side of a container. 2 to serve or apply messily.

slope[1] v 1 to lie at a slant; to incline. 2 to cause to incline or slant. ➤ **sloping** adj.

slope[2] n 1 a strip or area that is lower at one end than the other. 2 (usu in pl) the side of a mountain or hill.

slop out v to empty the contents of a chamber pot.

sloppy adj (-ier, -iest) 1 wet so as to splash. 2 disagreeably wet or watery. 3 slovenly or careless. 4 excessively sentimental. ➤ **sloppily** adv, **sloppiness** n.

slops pl n 1 waste food or thin gruel fed to animals. 2 liquid household refuse. 3 tasteless drink or liquid food.

slosh[1] n 1 the sound of splashing liquid. 2 Brit, informal a heavy blow. ➤ **sloshy** adj.

slosh[2] v 1 of liquid: to move with a splashing motion or sound. 2 to flounder or splash through water, mud, etc. 3 to move or splash about in liquid. 4 Brit, informal to hit heavily. ➤ **sloshy** adj.

sloshed adj informal drunk.

slot[1] n 1 a narrow opening for inserting something. 2 a place in an organization or scheme.

slot[2] v (**slotted, slotting**) (often + in/into) to fit or place in a slot or position.

sloth n 1 laziness. 2 a slow-moving mammal that hangs from the branches of trees. ➤ **slothful** adj.

slot machine n 1 Brit = VENDING MACHINE. 2 a machine operated by inserting a coin in a slot.

slouch[1] v to sit, stand, or walk limply or lazily.

slouch[2] n a limp or drooping gait or posture. ✱ **no slouch** informal able or competent.

slough[1] /slow/ n 1 a swamp. 2 a state of dejection or hopelessness.

slough[2] /sluf/ v of an animal: to cast off a skin or shell.

slovenly adj 1 untidy or dirty, esp in personal appearance. 2 lazy and careless. ➤ **slovenliness** n.

slow[1] *adj* **1** moving or only able to move at a low speed. **2** marked by lack of speed or haste. **3** requiring or taking a long time. **4** of a clock or watch: showing a time earlier than the actual time. **5** not quickly learning or understanding. **6** lacking in activity. **7** of an oven: set at a low temperature. ➤ **slowly** *adv,* **slowness** *n.*

slow[2] *adv* slowly.

slow[3] *v* (*often* + down/up) to make or become slow or slower.

slowcoach *n Brit, informal* a person who moves or acts slowly.

slow motion *n* the playing back of a video recording at less than the standard speed.

slow puncture *n* a puncture that causes a tyre to deflate gradually.

slowworm *n* a small lizard with a snakelike body.

sludge *n* soft wet mud or slimy substance. ➤ **sludgy** *adj.*

slug[1] *n* a small slimy animal like a snail with no shell.

slug[2] *n* **1** a quantity of alcoholic drink swallowed in one gulp. **2** a bullet.

slug[3] *v* (**slugged, slugging**) to swallow in one gulp.

slug[4] *v* (**slugged, slugging**) *informal* to hit hard. ✳ **slug it out** to compete fiercely.

sluggard *n* a lazy person.

sluggish *adj* **1** slow in movement or action. **2** lacking energy or activity. ➤ **sluggishly** *adv.*

sluice[1] *n* **1** (*also* **sluice gate**) a gate or other device for controlling the flow of water. **2** a channel for draining or carrying off surplus water.

sluice[2] *v* **1** to wash in running water. **2** to drench or flush.

slum[1] *n* **1** a poor run-down area in a city. **2** a squalid place to live. ➤ **slummy** *adj.*

slum[2] *v* (**slummed, slumming**) to live in squalor or poverty. ✳ **slum it** *informal* to live temporarily in poor conditions.

slumber[1] *v literary* to sleep.

slumber[2] *n literary* sleep.

slump[1] *v* **1** to sit or drop down heavily. **2** to decline rapidly.

slump[2] *n* **1** an instance of slumping. **2** a marked decline.

slung *v* past tense and past part. of SLING[2].

slunk *v* past tense and past part. of SLINK.

slur[1] *v* (**slurred, slurring**) **1** to pronounce (words or sounds) unclearly. **2** (+ over) to pass over without due mention or consideration. **3** in music, to perform (successive notes of different pitch) in a smooth or connected manner.

slur[2] *n* **1** a slurred utterance or manner of speech. **2** in music, a curved line connecting notes to be slurred.

slur[3] *v* (**slurred, slurring**) to insult or disparage.

slur[4] *n* an insulting remark.

slurp[1] *v* to eat or drink with a loud sucking sound.

slurp[2] *n* a slurping sound.

slurry *n* (*pl* **-ies**) a watery mixture of mud, manure, or lime.

slush *n* **1** partly melted or watery snow. **2** liquid mud. **3** *informal* excessively sentimental language. ➤ **slushy** *adj.*

slush fund *n* a fund for dishonest uses.

slut *n* a promiscuous or slovenly woman. ➤ **sluttish** *adj.*

sly *adj* (**-er, -est**) **1** cunning and furtive. **2** humorously mischievous; roguish. ✳ **on the sly** secretly. ➤ **slyly** *adv.*

smack[1] *n* **1** a sharp blow with the open hand. **2** the sound of such a blow. **3** a loud kiss. ✳ **smack in the eye** *informal* a setback or rebuff.

smack[2] *v* **1** to hit with the open hand. **2** to strike or collide with sharply. **3** to put down forcefully or noisily. **4** to open (the lips) with a sudden sharp sound.

smack[3] *adv informal* squarely or directly.

smack[4] *v* **1** (+ of) to taste or smell of. **2** (+ of) to have a trace of (something unwelcome).

smack[5] *n* a small fishing vessel.

smack[6] *n slang* heroin.

smacker *n informal* **1** a loud kiss. **2** *Brit* a pound sterling.

small[1] *adj* **1** of less than normal size. **2** young or immature. **3** not great in quantity, value, importance, etc. **4** operating on a limited scale. **5** mean or petty. **6** humiliated. ➤ **smallness** *n.*

small[2] *n* **1** the narrowest part of the back. **2** *Brit, informal* (*in pl*) small articles of underwear.

small arms *pl n* (*usu in pl*) guns that can be carried about.

small beer *n chiefly Brit* unimportant matters.

small change *n* **1** coins of low denomination. **2** something unimportant.

small fry *pl n* **1** small fish. **2** young or insignificant people or things.

smallholding *n Brit* a small farm. ➤ **smallholder** *n.*

small hours *pl n* (**the small hours**) the hours after midnight.

smallpox *n* an infectious disease with fever and pustules that form scabs, usually leaving permanent scars.

small print *n* a part of a document with unattractive conditions, often printed in small type.

small talk *n* light or casual conversation.

small-time *adj informal* insignificant or petty.

smarmy *adj* (**-ier, -iest**) *informal* obsequiously friendly or polite.

smart[1] *adj* **1** neat or elegant in dress or appearance. **2** of a place: frequented by fashionable society. **3** *informal* mentally alert; clever. ➤ **smartly** *adv,* **smartness** *n.*

smart[2] *v* **1** to have or give a sharp stinging pain. **2** to feel upset or angry.

smart card n a plastic card with a memory chip that holds information.

smarten v (often + up) to make or become smarter.

smartish adv chiefly Brit, informal promptly and quickly.

smash¹ v **1** to break violently into pieces. **2** to drive, throw, or hit violently. **3** in sports, to hit (a ball) downward forcefully. **4** to destroy or defeat. **5** (+ into) to collide with.

smash² n **1** the action or sound of smashing. **2** a violent blow or collision. **3** informal a smash hit.

smash hit n informal a very successful song, show, etc.

smashing adj Brit, informal excellent.

smattering n **1** a small amount. **2** a slight knowledge of a subject.

smear¹ v **1** to spread or mark with a sticky or greasy substance. **2** to obscure or blur. **3** to blacken the reputation of. ➤ **smeary** adj.

smear² n **1** a sticky or greasy mark. **2** an unsupported accusation. **3** material smeared on a slide for examination under a microscope.

smear test n a test for cervical cancer.

smell¹ v (past tense and past part. **smelt** or **smelled**) **1** to perceive the odour of. **2** to sniff (something) in order to perceive its odour. **3** to detect or become aware of by instinct. **4** to have a specified smell. **5** (+ of) to be suggestive of. **6** to have an unpleasant smell. * **smell a rat** informal to suspect that something is wrong.

smell² n **1** the sense by which odours are perceived through sensitive areas in the nose. **2** the quality of something as perceived by this sense; an odour. **3** an unpleasant odour. **4** a pervading quality or aura. **5** the act of smelling.

smelling salts pl n a preparation sniffed as a stimulant to relieve faintness.

smelly adj (-ier, -iest) having a strong unpleasant smell.

smelt¹ n (pl **smelts** or **smelt**) a small fish with a delicate oily flesh.

smelt² v **1** to melt (ore) to separate the metal. **2** to separate (metal) by smelting ore. ➤ **smelter** n.

smelt³ v past part. of SMELL¹.

smidgin or **smidgen** n informal a small amount; a bit.

smile¹ v to form the face into an expression in which the corners of the mouth curve upwards to express amusement, friendliness, pleasure, etc.

smile² n an act of smiling.

smirk¹ v to smile in a fatuous or smug manner.

smirk² n an act of smirking.

smite v (**smote**, **smitten**) archaic **1** to strike sharply or heavily. **2** to kill, injure, or damage. * **be smitten by/with** to be attracted to or emotionally affected by.

smith n a person who works in metal, esp a blacksmith.

smithereens pl n small fragments.

smithy n (pl -ies) a blacksmith's forge.

smock n **1** a protective garment worn over clothes. **2** a garment like a long loose shirt or dress gathered into a yoke and decorated with smocking.

smocking n a decorative effect made by gathering cloth in regularly spaced tucks held in place with ornamental stitching.

smog n a fog made heavier and darker by smoke and fumes. ➤ **smoggy** adj.

smoke¹ n **1** the visible gaseous products of burning. **2** an act or spell of smoking tobacco. **3** informal something, e.g. a cigarette, that is smoked. * **go up in smoke** to come to nothing.

smoke² v **1** to emit smoke. **2** to inhale and exhale the smoke of (a cigarette, pipe, etc). **3** to smoke cigarettes, cigars, a pipe, etc, esp habitually. **4** to cure (meat or fish) by exposure to smoke. **5** to colour or darken (glass). ➤ **smoked** adj, **smoker** n.

smokeless adj producing little or no smoke.

smoke out v to drive out or away with smoke.

smoke screen n **1** a screen of smoke produced to conceal a military position or activity. **2** something said or done to conceal or confuse.

smokestack n a chimney or funnel through which smoke and gases are discharged, e.g. from a ship or factory.

smoking jacket n a man's loosely fitting jacket formerly worn while smoking after a meal.

smoky adj (-ier, -iest) **1** filled with or producing a lot of smoke. **2** like smoke in form or appearance.

smolder v NAmer see SMOULDER.

smooch v informal to kiss and cuddle. ➤ **smoochy** adj.

smooth¹ adj **1** having a continuous even surface. **2** of liquid: free from lumps. **3** free from difficulties or obstructions. **4** even and uninterrupted in movement or flow. **5** urbane and courteous. **6** excessively suave or ingratiating. **7** of a flavour: not sharp or acid. ➤ **smoothly** adv, **smoothness** n.

smooth² v **1** to make or become smooth. **2** (often + out) to press flat. **3** (often + down) to cause to lie evenly. **4** to free from obstruction or difficulty.

smoothie or **smoothy** n (pl -ies) informal a suave or ingratiating person.

smooth-talking adj ingratiating and persuasive in speech. ➤ **smooth-talk** v.

smorgasbord n a variety of foods and dishes, e.g. hors d'oeuvres, hot and cold meat or fish, cheeses, salads, etc.

smote v past tense of SMITE.

smother v **1** to suffocate by covering the nose and mouth. **2** to extinguish (a fire) by excluding oxygen. **3** to prevent the growth or development of. **4** to cause to feel overwhelmed or oppressed. **5** to cover thickly.

smoulder (NAmer **smolder**) v **1** to burn with smoke but no flame. **2** to show suppressed anger, hate, jealousy, etc.

smudge[1] v **1** to smear or daub. **2** to make indistinct; to blur.

smudge[2] n a blurry mark or streak. ➤ **smudgy** adj.

smug adj (**smugger, smuggest**) excessively pleased with oneself; self-satisfied. ➤ **smugly** adv, **smugness** n.

smuggle v **1** to import or export (goods) illegally without paying duties. **2** to convey secretly. ➤ **smuggler** n.

smut n **1** a particle of soot or dirt. **2** indecent language, writing, or pictures. ➤ **smutty** adj.

Sn abbr the chemical symbol for tin.

snack[1] n a light meal eaten between regular meals.

snack[2] v to eat a snack.

snaffle[1] n a simple jointed bit for a bridle.

snaffle[2] v informal to take secretly.

snag[1] n **1** a hidden or unexpected difficulty. **2** a sharp or jagged projecting part. **3** an irregular tear or flaw.

snag[2] v (**snagged, snagging**) to catch or tear on a snag.

snaggle-toothed adj having irregular or broken teeth.

snail n a small slow-moving animal with a soft body and a hard shell that it can contract into.

snake[1] n **1** a reptile with a long tapering body and no legs. **2** a sly treacherous person. ✳ **snake in the grass** a secretly treacherous friend or associate. ➤ **snaky** adj.

snake[2] v to move silently with a twisting motion.

snakes and ladders pl n a board game in which players move counters along squares, advancing up a ladder or going back down a snake.

snap[1] v (**snapped, snapping**) **1** to break with a sharp cracking sound. **2** to bite or close the jaws with force. **3** to close or fit in place with a sharp sound. **4** to reply irritably. **5** to lose self-control suddenly. **6** (+ up) to acquire (something) suddenly or eagerly. **7** to take a snapshot of. ✳ **snap out of** informal to free oneself from a mood, habit, etc with an effort.

snap[2] n **1** the act or sound of snapping. **2** a sudden spell of harsh weather. **3** a thin brittle biscuit. **4** a snapshot. **5** a card game in which players try to be the first to shout '*snap*' when two cards of identical value are laid successively.

snap[3] adj done suddenly or unexpectedly.

snapdragon n a plant with bright white, red, or yellow two-lipped flowers.

snapper n (pl **snappers** or **snapper**) a flesh-eating sea fish.

snappy adj (**-ier, -iest**) **1** curt and irritable. **2** stylish or smart. ✳ **make it snappy** informal be quick. ➤ **snappily** adv.

snapshot n a casual photograph taken quickly.

snare[1] n **1** a trap for catching small animals, consisting of a noose that is pulled tight. **2** something likely to trap or deceive. **3** a string or metal spiral placed over the skin of a snare drum to produce a rattling sound.

snare[2] v to catch in a snare.

snare drum n a small double-headed drum with snares stretched across its lower head.

snarl[1] v (often + up) to make or become tangled or confused.

snarl[2] v **1** to growl with bared teeth. **2** to speak in an aggressive or bad-tempered manner.

snarl-up n informal a traffic jam.

snatch[1] v **1** to seize or grab suddenly and forcibly. **2** to take or grasp abruptly or hastily. **3** (often + at) to attempt to seize something suddenly.

snatch[2] n **1** an act of snatching. **2** a brief period of time or activity. **3** a fragment of music or conversation.

snazzy adj (**-ier, -iest**) informal attractive and stylish.

sneak[1] v (past tense and past part. **sneaked** or NAmer informal **snuck**) **1** to go stealthily or furtively. **2** Brit, informal to tell somebody in authority of another's wrongdoing. **3** to put, bring, or take in a furtive or devious manner.

sneak[2] n **1** somebody who acts in a stealthy or furtive manner. **2** Brit, informal somebody who informs on others. **3** (used before a noun) done secretly or unofficially: a sneak preview.

sneaker n chiefly NAmer (usu in pl) a soft casual or sports shoe.

sneaking adj **1** not openly expressed; secret. **2** of a feeling: instinctively felt but unconfirmed.

sneaky adj unpleasantly furtive or secretive. ➤ **sneakily** adv.

sneer[1] v to smile or speak in a scornfully jeering manner.

sneer[2] n a sneering expression or remark.

sneeze[1] v to expel air suddenly from the nose and mouth, as a reflex caused by irritation in the nasal passages. ✳ **not to be sneezed at** not to be underestimated.

sneeze[2] n an act or sound of sneezing.

snick[1] v to cut slightly; to nick.

snick[2] n a small cut or nick.

snicker[1] v **1** to snigger. **2** of a horse: to whinny.

snicker[2] n a snigger or whinny.

snide adj slyly disparaging or insinuating.

sniff[1] v **1** to draw air audibly up the nose. **2** to smell (something). **3** (+ out) to detect or seek.

＊ **sniff at** to regard with contempt or disdain. ➤ **sniffer** n.

sniff² n **1** an act or sound of sniffing. **2** informal a trace or hint.

sniffle¹ v to sniff repeatedly, e.g. when crying. ➤ **sniffler** n.

sniffle² n **1** an act or sound of sniffling. **2** a slight cold. ➤ **sniffly** adj.

sniffy adj (-ier, -iest) informal haughty or supercilious. ➤ **sniffily** adv.

snifter n informal a small drink of spirits.

snigger¹ v to laugh in a partly suppressed or derisive manner.

snigger² n an act or sound of sniggering.

snip¹ n **1** a small piece, esp one snipped off. **2** a cut made by snipping. **3** an act or sound of snipping. **4** Brit, informal a bargain. **5** Brit, informal something easy to do; a cinch. **6** (in pl) shears used esp for cutting sheet metal by hand.

snip² v (**snipped, snipping**) to cut with shears or scissors with short rapid strokes.

snipe¹ n (pl **snipes** or **snipe**) a wading bird with a long straight bill.

snipe² v **1** (often + at) to shoot at people from a hiding place at long range. **2** (usu + at) to criticize in a sly or bad-tempered manner. ➤ **sniper** n.

snippet n a small piece from writing or conversation.

snitch¹ v **1** informal to inform on somebody. **2** informal to steal.

snitch² n informal an informer.

snivel v (**snivelled, snivelling,** NAmer **sniveled, sniveling**) **1** to have a runny nose. **2** to complain in a whining way. ➤ **snivel** n.

snob n **1** somebody who looks down on social inferiors. **2** somebody with an air of superiority in matters of knowledge or taste. ➤ **snobbery** n, **snobbish** adj, **snobby** adj.

snog¹ v (**snogged, snogging**) Brit, informal to kiss and cuddle.

snog² n informal an act or spell of snogging.

snood n **1** a net worn at the back of a woman's head to hold the hair. **2** a knitted garment worn as a hood or scarf.

snooker¹ n **1** a game played on a billiard table with cues, a white ball, and 21 coloured balls. **2** a position of the balls in snooker in which a legal direct shot cannot be made.

snooker² v **1** to position the cue ball in snooker to prevent (an opponent) from making a direct shot. **2** informal to present an obstacle or difficulty to.

snoop¹ v to look or pry in an interfering manner. ➤ **snooper** n.

snoop² n **1** somebody who snoops. **2** an act of snooping.

snooty adj (-ier, -iest) informal snobbish or supercilious.

snooze¹ v informal to sleep lightly for a short time.

snooze² n informal a short light sleep.

snore¹ v to breathe with a hoarse noise during sleep.

snore² n an act or sound of snoring.

snorkel n a tube allowing a swimmer to breathe while under water. ➤ **snorkelling** n.

snort¹ v **1** to force air through the nose with a rough harsh sound. **2** informal to inhale (a drug).

snort² n **1** an act or sound of snorting. **2** informal a small drink of spirits. **3** informal an amount of a drug for inhaling.

snot n informal mucus from the nose.

snotty adj (-ier, -iest) informal **1** covered with nasal mucus. **2** arrogantly unpleasant.

snout n **1** the projecting nose of a pig or other animal. **2** informal a cigarette or tobacco. **3** informal an informer.

snow¹ n **1** ice crystals formed in the atmosphere and falling as light white flakes. **2** (in pl) falls of snow.

snow² v **1** to fall as snow. **2** (+ in/up) to shut in or block with snow. ＊ **be snowed under** to have a lot of work to do.

snowball¹ n a round mass of compressed snow.

snowball² v to increase or expand rapidly.

snowboard n a board resembling a short wide ski, used to slide down over snow. ➤ **snowboarder** n, **snowboarding** n.

snowbound adj confined or surrounded by snow.

snowdrift n a deep bank of snow formed by the wind.

snowdrop n a plant that bears white flowers in late winter.

snowfall n the amount of snow falling at one time or in a given period.

snowflake n a flake or crystal of snow.

snow line n the height above which land is permanently covered in snow.

snowman n (pl **snowmen**) a pile of snow shaped to resemble a human figure.

snowplough (NAmer **snowplow**) n a vehicle or device for clearing snow.

snowshoe n a flat frame attached to a boot or shoe for walking over soft snow.

snowstorm n a storm with snow driven by the wind.

snowy adj (-ier, -iest) **1** covered with snow. **2** white like snow.

snub¹ v (**snubbed, snubbing**) to ignore or reject (somebody) ostentatiously.

snub² n an act of snubbing.

snub nose n a short and slightly turned-up nose.

snuck v NAmer, informal past tense and past part. of SNEAK¹.

snuff¹ v **1** to extinguish (a flame or candle). **2** (+ out) to put a sudden end to. ＊ **snuff it** informal to die.

snuff² n powdered tobacco inhaled through the nostrils. ✴ **up to snuff** informal good enough.

snuff³ v to inhale or sniff at.

snuffle¹ v **1** to sniff audibly and repeatedly. **2** to breathe noisily through a partially blocked nose.

snuffle² n **1** an act or sound of snuffling. **2** (**the snuffles**) a cold in the nose. ➤ **snuffly** adj.

snug¹ adj (**snugger, snuggest**) **1** warm and comfortable. **2** fitting closely. ➤ **snugly** adv.

snug² n Brit a small comfortable bar in a pub.

snuggle v **1** to curl up comfortably. **2** to draw close for comfort or in affection.

so¹ adv **1** in this or the same way. **2** used as a substitute for a word or phrase: Do you think so? **3** correspondingly. **4** to such an extreme degree. **5** very. **6** to a limited degree: We can only do so much. **7** most certainly; indeed. **8** therefore; consequently. ✴ **and so forth/and so on** and more or further. **or so** approximately. **so as to/so that** having as a purpose or result.

so² conj **1** with the result that. **2** in order that. **3** for that reason.

soak¹ v **1** to immerse or lie immersed in liquid. **2** to make thoroughly wet. **3** of a liquid: to spread over or pass through (something) completely. **4** (often + up) to absorb (a liquid, information, etc). **5** to immerse the mind and feelings of.

soak² n **1** an act or period of soaking. **2** informal a person who drinks a lot of alcohol.

so-and-so n (pl **so-and-sos**) **1** an unnamed or unspecified person or thing. **2** a disliked or unpleasant person.

soap¹ n **1** a substance used with water to produce a lather for washing or cleaning. **2** a soap opera. ➤ **soapy** adj.

soap² v to wash with soap.

soapbox n an improvised platform used for standing on by a speaker outdoors.

soap opera n a radio or television serial dealing with the lives of a group of characters.

soapstone n a soft stone having a soapy feel.

soar v **1** to fly or rise high into the air. **2** to increase rapidly.

sob¹ v (**sobbed, sobbing**) **1** to cry convulsively. **2** to express or utter with sobs.

sob² n an act or sound of sobbing.

sober¹ adj **1** not drunk. **2** serious. **3** subdued in tone or colour. ➤ **soberly** adv.

sober² v (usu + up) to make or become sober or serious.

sobriety n the state of being sober.

sobriquet /'sohbrikay/ or **soubriquet** /'sooh-, 'soh-/ n a nickname.

so-called adj commonly or wrongly named.

soccer n a football game with a round ball that must not be handled during play except by the goalkeepers.

sociable adj **1** eager to seek or enjoy companionship. **2** encouraging friendliness and good social relations. ➤ **sociability** n, **sociably** adv.

social¹ adj **1** relating to human society. **2** of or based on status in a particular society. **3** involving or promoting friendly interaction with others. **4** seeking the company of others; gregarious. **5** of animals: living and breeding in organized communities. ➤ **socially** adv.

social² n a social gathering or party.

socialism n a political theory advocating state ownership of the means of production and distribution of goods. ➤ **socialist** adj and n.

socialite n somebody who is active in fashionable society.

socialize or **-ise** v **1** to mix socially with other people. **2** to make (somebody) fit for life in society.

social science n **1** the study of human society and relationships. **2** a subject dealing with a particular aspect of this. ➤ **social scientist** n.

social security n a system of financial benefits provided by the state for those in need.

social services pl n public services provided by the state, e.g. education, housing, and health care.

social worker n a state employee concerned with supporting the poor, elderly, disadvantaged, etc. ➤ **social work** n.

society n (pl **-ies**) **1** the human race as a structure of social institutions. **2** a community of people with common traditions, institutions, and interests. **3** wealthy or privileged people regarded as arbiters of fashion or manners. **4** an organized group working or meeting together because of common interests, beliefs, etc. **5** companionship or association with others. ➤ **societal** adj.

sociology n the study of social institutions and relations. ➤ **sociological** adj, **sociologist** n.

sock¹ n a knitted covering for the foot extending above the ankle. ✴ **pull one's socks up** informal to make an effort to do better.

sock² v informal to hit forcefully. ✴ **sock it to** informal to impress with an achievement.

sock³ n informal a forceful blow or punch.

socket n **1** an opening or hollow into which something fits. **2** an electrical device into which a plug, bulb, etc can be fitted.

sod¹ n **1** a clump of grass together with roots and soil. **2** literary grass-covered ground.

sod² n Brit, informal **1** an objectionable person. **2** a person of a specified kind: a lucky sod. ✴ **sod all** Brit, informal nothing at all.

soda n **1** a chemical compound containing sodium. **2** soda water. **3** chiefly NAmer a sweet fizzy drink.

soda water n water made fizzy with carbon dioxide.

sodden adj 1 full of moisture; saturated. 2 having drunk too much alcohol: whisky-sodden.

sodium n a soft silver-white metallic element.

sodium bicarbonate n a white chemical compound used in baking powder and medicine.

sodium chloride n salt as a chemical compound.

sodium hydroxide n a white caustic chemical compound used in making soap, rayon, and paper.

sod off v Brit, slang to go away.

sodomite n somebody who practises sodomy.

sodomy n anal intercourse.

sofa n a long upholstered seat with a back and arms or raised ends.

soft adj 1 yielding to physical pressure. 2 easily shaped, spread, or cut. 3 smooth or delicate in texture. 4 of light or colour: not bright or glaring. 5 quiet in pitch or volume. 6 of a drink: non-alcoholic. 7 of water: free from chemical compounds that prevent lathering. 8 of a drug: not of the most addictive or harmful kind. 9 gentle or mild. 10 kind or lenient. 11 informal silly or foolish. 12 informal demanding little effort; easy. 13 of a target: not well protected; vulnerable. 14 not sharply outlined: soft focus. ✱ **have a soft spot for** to be sentimentally fond of. **soft on** amorously attracted to. ➤ **softly** adv, **softness** n.

softball n a game similar to baseball played with a larger softer ball.

soft-core adj of pornography: mildly titillating and not highly explicit.

soften v 1 to make or become soft or softer. 2 (often + up) to reduce the strength or resistance of.

soft-hearted adj kind and understanding.

softly-softly adj Brit patient and cautious.

soft sell n the use of gentle persuasion in selling.

soft-soap v informal to persuade with flattery or guile.

soft-top n a car with a top that can be folded back.

soft touch n informal a person who is easily imposed on or taken advantage of.

software n the programs and procedures used by a computer.

softwood n the wood of a coniferous tree.

soggy adj (-ier, -iest) 1 soaked or waterlogged. 2 heavy and damp.

soil¹ n 1 the upper layer of the surface of the earth, in which plants grow. 2 a nation's territory or land. 3 (**the soil**) agriculture.

soil² v 1 to make or become dirty. 2 to blacken or tarnish (a reputation).

soiree or **soirée** /'swahray/ n (pl **soirees** or **soirées**) an evening party or reception.

sojourn¹ n formal a temporary stay.

sojourn² v formal to stay temporarily.

solace¹ n consolation or comfort in grief or difficulty.

solace² v to give comfort to.

solar adj relating to the sun or its light or heat.

solar cell n a device that converts sunlight into electrical energy.

solar eclipse n an eclipse in which the moon wholly or partially obscures the sun.

solarium n (pl **solaria** or **solariums**) a room equipped with sunbeds, sunlamps, etc.

solar panel n a collection of solar cells providing energy.

solar plexus n a network of nerves in the abdomen behind the stomach.

solar system n the sun together with the planets and other bodies that revolve round it.

sold v past tense and past part. of SELL.

solder¹ n a soft alloy used to join metal surfaces.

solder² v to join with solder.

soldering iron n an electrical device for melting and applying solder.

soldier¹ n 1 a person who is serving in an army. 2 an enlisted man or woman. ➤ **soldierly** adj.

soldier² v 1 to serve as a soldier. 2 (+ on) to persevere.

soldier of fortune n a mercenary.

soldiery n (pl -ies) a body of soldiers.

sole¹ n the underside of the foot, or of a shoe or boot.

sole² v to provide (a shoe) with a sole.

sole³ n (pl **soles** or **sole**) a sea flatfish used for food.

sole⁴ adj 1 being the only one; only. 2 belonging or relating to one individual or group only. ➤ **solely** adv.

solecism /'solisiz(ə)m/ n 1 a minor grammatical error. 2 a breach of etiquette.

solemn adj 1 said or done formally. 2 marked by established form or ceremony. 3 serious. 4 sombre or gloomy. ➤ **solemnly** adv.

solemnity n (pl -ies) 1 the state of being solemn. 2 formal or ceremonious observance. 3 a solemn event or occasion.

solemnize or **-ise** v 1 to observe with solemnity. 2 to perform (a marriage) with ceremony. 3 to make solemn or serious.

solenoid /'solənoyd/ n a coil of wire that produces a magnetic field when an electric current passes through it. ➤ **solenoidal** adj.

solicit v (**solicited**, **soliciting**) 1 to make a formal request to. 2 to try to obtain by formal request. 3 to approach (somebody) to be a prostitute's client. ➤ **solicitation** n.

solicitor n a qualified lawyer who advises clients, represents them in the lower courts, and prepares cases for barristers to try in the higher courts.

solicitous adj showing care or concern about somebody. ➤ **solicitously** adv.

solicitude n care or concern.

solid[1] *adj* **1** without an internal cavity. **2** having no opening or division. **3** having a single substance or character. **4** three-dimensional. **5** retaining shape without needing external support. **6** hard, dense, or compact. **7** without break or interruption. **8** reliable or sound; of good quality. **9** united or unanimous. ➤ **solidity** *n,* **solidly** *adv.*

solid[2] *n* **1** a solid substance. **2** (*in pl*) solid food. **3** a three-dimensional figure.

solidarity *n* unity based on shared interests, objectives, and standards.

solidify *v* (**-ies, -ied**) to make or become solid. ➤ **solidification** *n.*

solid-state *adj* **1** relating to semiconductors. **2** using the electric or magnetic properties of solid materials and not thermionic valves.

soliloquy *n* (*pl* **-ies**) a speech expressing thoughts aloud while alone, especially on stage.

solipsism *n* the belief that the self is the only thing that can be known to exist. ➤ **solipsist** *n,* **solipsistic** *adj.*

solitaire *n* **1** a game for one person in which pieces are removed from a board by jumping one over another until only one piece remains. **2** *NAmer* = PATIENCE 2. **3** a single gem set alone in a ring.

solitary *adj* **1** liking to be alone. **2** lonely. **3** done or used by itself. **4** single; sole. **5** of a place: unfrequented or remote.

solitary confinement *n* the isolation of a prisoner as a punishment.

solitude *n* the state of being alone.

solo[1] *n* (*pl* **solos** *or* **soli**) **1** a musical composition, song, or dance for one performer. **2** a flight by one person alone in an aircraft. ➤ **soloist** *n.*

solo[2] *adj and adv* done or performed by one person.

solo[3] *v* (**soloes, soloed, soloing**) to perform or fly solo.

so long *interj informal* goodbye.

solstice *n* each of two occasions each year when the sun is furthest from the celestial equator and highest or lowest in the sky at noon.

soluble *adj* **1** of a substance: able to be dissolved in liquid. **2** capable of being solved. ➤ **solubility** *n.*

solution *n* **1** an answer to a problem. **2** the means or process of solving a problem. **3** a mixture formed when a substance is distributed in a solvent.

solve *v* to find an answer to or explanation for (a problem, mystery, etc).

solvent[1] *adj* **1** having enough money to pay all debts. **2** of a substance: able to dissolve other substances. ➤ **solvency** *n.*

solvent[2] *n* a liquid that is capable of dissolving other substances.

sombre (*NAmer* **somber**) *adj* **1** dark and gloomy. **2** of a dull or dark colour. **3** serious or grave. ➤ **sombrely** *adv.*

sombrero *n* (*pl* **-os**) a felt or straw hat with a wide brim.

some[1] *adj* **1** unspecified in amount or number. **2** unknown or unspecified. **3** being an unspecified member of a class. **4** appreciable or considerable. **5** *chiefly informal* striking or excellent.

some[2] *pron* some part, amount, or number but not all.

some[3] *adv* approximately; about.

somebody *pron* some person.

some day *adv* at some future time.

somehow *adv* **1** by some unknown means. **2** no matter how. **3** for some unknown reason.

someone *pron* some person.

someplace *adv NAmer* somewhere.

somersault[1] *n* a movement in which a person turns forward or backward in a complete revolution bringing the feet over the head.

somersault[2] *v* to perform a somersault.

something[1] *pron* **1** some unspecified or unknown thing. **2** a certain amount.

something[2] *adv* in some degree; somewhat.

sometime[1] *adv* at some unknown or unspecified time.

sometime[2] *adj* having been formerly.

sometimes *adv* at intervals; occasionally.

somewhat *adv* to some degree.

somewhere[1] *adv* **1** in or to some unknown or unspecified place. **2** at an unspecified point.

somewhere[2] *n* an unspecified place.

somnambulist *n* somebody who walks in their sleep. ➤ **somnambulism** *n.*

somnolent *adj* **1** sleepy; drowsy. **2** tending to induce sleep. ➤ **somnolence** *n.*

son *n* **1** a boy or man having the relation of child to parent. **2** a male descendant. **3** (**Son** *or* **the Son**) the second person of the Trinity.

sonar *n* a system for detecting an object under water by means of reflected sound waves.

sonata *n* a musical composition for one instrument, often with piano accompaniment.

son et lumière *n* an entertainment held in the dark at a noteworthy site, with lighting and recorded sound to describe its history.

song *n* **1** a set of words sung to a musical tune. **2** the act of singing. **3** the melodious sounds made by birds and some other animals. **4** *literary* poetry or a poem. * **for a song** for very little money. **on song** *Brit, informal* performing well.

song and dance *n Brit, informal* a fuss or commotion.

songbird *n* a bird that utters musical tones.

songster *n* a skilled singer or writer of songs.

sonic *adj* using or relating to sound waves. ➤ **sonically** *adv.*

sonic boom *n* an explosive sound produced by an aircraft travelling at supersonic speed.

son-in-law n (pl **sons-in-law**) the husband of one's daughter.

sonnet n a poem of 14 lines having a fixed rhyme scheme.

sonorous adj **1** pleasantly rich or deep in sound. **2** impressive in effect or style. ➤ **sonority** n, **sonorously** adv.

soon adv **1** after a short time. **2** promptly. **3** in comparisons: rather: I'd sooner stay here. ✳ **sooner or later** eventually.

soot n a fine black powder formed by the incomplete burning of coal or other organic matter. ➤ **sooty** adj.

soothe v **1** to calm (somebody) by comforting. **2** to relieve (pain). ➤ **soothing** adj.

soothsayer n somebody who predicts the future.

sop[1] n something offered or done as a concession or appeasement.

sop[2] v (**sopped, sopping**) (usu + up) to mop up (liquid).

sophism n a false or deceptive argument.

sophist n a person who uses false or deceptive reasoning. ➤ **sophistic** adj.

sophisticate n a sophisticated person.

sophisticated adj **1** highly developed or complex. **2** having refined tastes; cultured. **3** intellectually subtle or refined. ➤ **sophistication** n.

sophistry n (pl **-ies**) plausible but unsound reasoning.

sophomore n NAmer a second-year student at university or high school.

soporific adj tending to cause sleep.

sopping adj wet through; soaking.

soppy adj (**-ier, -iest**) informal **1** weakly sentimental; mawkish. **2** chiefly Brit, informal feeble or silly. ➤ **soppily** adv, **soppiness** n.

soprano n (pl **-os**) a female singer with the highest singing voice.

sorbet n a water ice.

sorcerer or **sorceress** n a man or woman who uses magic. ➤ **sorcery** n.

sordid adj **1** dirty or squalid. **2** base or immoral. ➤ **sordidly** adv.

sore[1] adj **1** causing or suffering pain. **2** painful or tender. **3** severe; urgent. **4** chiefly NAmer angry or upset. ➤ **soreness** n.

sore[2] n a painful area on the body.

sore[3] adv archaic greatly or extremely.

sorely adv much; extremely.

sore point n a cause of irritation or distress.

sorghum n a tropical grass similar to maize.

sorority n (pl **-ies**) a club for female students at some US universities.

sorrel n **1** a plant with bitter-flavoured leaves eaten in salads. **2** a brownish orange to light brown colour.

sorrow[1] n **1** deep distress caused by a loss or failure. **2** a cause of sorrow.

sorrow[2] v to feel or express sorrow.

sorry adj (**-ier, -iest**) **1** full of regret or pity. **2** inspiring sorrow, pity, or scorn. **3** bad or regrettable.

sort[1] n **1** a group having some common characteristic; a class or kind. **2** informal a person: a cheerful sort. **3** a process of arranging in a certain order. ✳ **out of sorts** slightly unwell or disgruntled. **sort of** informal somewhat; in a way.

sort[2] v to arrange in order or in groups. ➤ **sortable** adj, **sorter** n.

sorted adj Brit, informal **1** organized or ready. **2** emotionally well-adjusted.

sortie n **1** a sudden attack by troops from a defensive position. **2** a mission or attack by one aircraft. **3** a brief trip to an unfamiliar place.

sort out v **1** to deal with (a difficulty) effectively. **2** to separate from a mass or group. **3** to clear up or tidy.

SOS n **1** an internationally recognized signal of distress. **2** a call for help.

so-so adj neither very good nor very bad.

sot n a habitual drunkard. ➤ **sottish** adj.

sotto voce adv and adj in a quiet voice.

soubriquet n see SOBRIQUET.

soufflé n a light fluffy baked dish made by folding egg yolks into stiffly beaten whites.

sought v past tense and past part. of SEEK.

sought-after adj much in demand.

souk n an open-air market in an Arab country.

soul n **1** the spiritual part of a human being, believed by some to be immortal. **2** the essential character of a person, group, or thing. **3** emotional sensitivity or depth. **4** a person: a dear old soul. **5** exemplification or personification: the soul of tact. **6** a kind of music originating in black American gospel singing, characterized by intensity of feeling.

soul-destroying adj esp of a task, job, etc: very dull and uninteresting.

soulful adj expressing intense feeling. ➤ **soulfully** adv.

soulless adj **1** lacking sensitivity or compassion. **2** bleak or uninviting.

soul mate n a person with whom one has a close affinity.

soul-searching n close scrutiny of one's feelings and motives.

sound[1] n **1** the sensation perceived by the sense of hearing, caused by vibrations travelling through the air. **2** something heard; a noise or tone. **3** an impression conveyed by being heard. **4** recorded sounds or radio broadcasting. ➤ **soundless** adj.

sound[2] v **1** to make or cause to make a sound. **2** to give a specified impression; to seem. **3** to test the condition of (the chest or lungs) by tapping.

sound[3] adj **1** healthy or in good condition. **2** free from error or fallacy. **3** having good knowledge and judgment. **4** financially secure. **5** of sleep: deep and undisturbed. **6** thorough or severe. ➤ **soundly** *adv*, **soundness** *n*.

sound⁴ *n* a long passage of water connecting two larger bodies or separating a mainland and an island.

sound⁵ *v* **1** to measure the depth of (water). **2** to explore (a body cavity) with a probe.

sound barrier *n* the point at which an aircraft nears the speed of sound.

sound bite *n* a short pithy or apt excerpt from a speech or statement.

sound effect *n* a sound other than speech or music used to create an effect in a play, film, etc.

sounding *n* **1** the act of measuring the depth of water. **2** a measurement taken by sounding **3** (*also in pl*) a test or sampling of opinion.

sounding board *n* someone whose reaction serves as a test for new ideas.

sound off *v informal* to voice opinions freely and vigorously.

sound out *v* to seek the views or intentions of.

soundproof¹ *adj* preventing or minimizing the penetration of sound.

soundproof² *v* to make soundproof.

sound track *n* the dialogue and sounds accompanying a film.

sound wave *n* a wave by which sound is transmitted.

soup *n* a liquid food made from stock and often containing pieces of solid food. ✳ **in the soup** *informal* in an awkward predicament.

soupçon /'soohpson, 'soohpsonh/ *n* a very small amount of something.

soup kitchen *n* a place where free food is provided for the poor or homeless.

soup up *v informal* to increase the power of (an engine or car).

sour¹ *adj* **1** having an acid taste like vinegar or lemons. **2** rancid or rotten. **3** disenchanted or embittered. ➤ **sourly** *adv*, **sourness** *n*.

sour² *v* to make or become sour.

source¹ *n* **1** a place, person, or thing from which something is obtained. **2** an origin or cause. **3** the point of origin of a river or stream. **4** a person, publication, etc that supplies information.

source² *v* **1** to obtain (materials or components) for a manufacturing process. **2** to trace to a source.

sour cream *n* cream made sour with added bacteria.

sour grapes *pl n* an attitude of disparagement towards something one is unable to have or achieve oneself.

sourpuss *n informal* a bitter or bad-tempered person.

souse *v* **1** to pickle. **2** to plunge in liquid. **3** to drench or saturate.

south¹ *n* **1** the direction 90° clockwise from east. **2** regions or countries lying to the south. ➤ **southbound** *adj and adv*.

south² *adj and adv* **1** at or towards the south. **2** of the wind: blowing from the south.

southeast¹ *n* **1** the direction between south and east. **2** regions lying to the southeast. ➤ **southeastern** *adj*.

southeast² *adj and adv* **1** at or towards the southeast. **2** of the wind: blowing from the southeast.

southeasterly *adj and adv* **1** in a southeastern position or direction. **2** of a wind: blowing from the southeast.

southerly *adj and adv* **1** in a southern position or direction. **2** of a wind: blowing from the south.

southern *adj* in or towards the south.

Southerner *n* (*also* **southerner**) a person from the southern part of a country.

southpaw *n* **1** a left-handed boxer who leads with the right hand and guards with the left. **2** *chiefly NAmer* a left-handed person.

southward *adj and adv* towards the south; in a direction going south. ➤ **southwards** *adv*.

southwest¹ *n* **1** the direction between south and west. **2** regions lying to the southwest. ➤ **southwestern** *adj*.

southwest² *adj and adv* **1** at or towards the southwest. **2** of the wind: blowing from the southwest.

southwesterly *adj and adv* **1** in a southwestern position or direction. **2** of a wind: blowing from the southwest.

souvenir *n* something one keeps as a reminder of a person, place, or event.

sou'wester *n* a waterproof hat with a brim extended at the back.

sovereign¹ *n* **1** somebody possessing supreme power, *esp* a king or queen. **2** a former British gold coin worth one pound.

sovereign² *adj* **1** possessing supreme power. **2** of a country: politically independent.

sovereignty *n* (*pl* -**ies**) **1** supreme power over a politically organized body. **2** freedom from external influence or control. **3** an autonomous state.

soviet *n* **1** an elected council in the former USSR. **2** (**Soviets**) the people of the former USSR. ➤ **Soviet** *adj*.

sow¹ /sow/ *n* an adult female pig.

sow² /soh/ *v* (*past part.* **sown** *or* **sowed**) **1** to put (seed) in the ground to grow into plants. **2** to plant (an area) with seed. **3** to implant or initiate (something unwelcome). ➤ **sower** *n*.

soya bean (*NAmer* **soybean**) *n* a bean high in protein, obtained from an Asian plant.

soy sauce *n* a sauce made from fermented soya beans.

sozzled *adj informal* very drunk.

spa *n* **1** a spring of mineral water. **2** a resort with mineral springs.

space[1] *n* **1** the three-dimensional extent in which objects and events occur and have position. **2** the region beyond the earth's atmosphere. **3** a continuous unoccupied area or volume. **4** an amount of room set apart or available for something. **5** freedom for personal development and fulfilment. **6** a period of time. **7** a blank area separating words or lines on a page.

space[2] *v* (*often* + out) to place (two or more things) at intervals or with space between them.

spacecraft *n* (*pl* **spacecraft**) a vehicle for travelling beyond the earth's atmosphere.

spaced out *adj informal* dazed or stupefied.

spaceman *or* **spacewoman** *n* (*pl* **spacemen** *or* **spacewomen**) a man or woman who travels in space.

spaceship *n* a manned spacecraft.

space shuttle *n* a vehicle for making repeated journeys into space and back to earth.

space station *n* a manned artificial satellite serving as a base for manned travel in space.

space suit *n* a suit equipped to make life in space possible for an astronaut.

spacial *adj* see SPATIAL.

spacious *adj* containing ample space; roomy.

spade *n* a digging implement with a flat metal blade and a long handle. ✳ **call a spade a spade** to speak frankly and plainly. **in spades** *informal* in the extreme.

spades *pl n* the suit in a pack of playing cards that is marked with black heart-shaped figures.

spadework *n* hard or routine preparatory work.

spaghetti *pl n* pasta in thin solid strings.

spake *v archaic* past tense of SPEAK.

Spam *n trademark* tinned meat made from pork and ham.

spam *n* unsolicited email messages sent to multiple addresses.

span[1] *n* **1** an extent or distance from one side to the other. **2** a length of time. **3** the full reach or extent. **4** a part of a bridge between supports. **5** the distance from the end of the thumb to the end of the little finger of a spread hand.

span[2] *v* (**spanned, spanning**) to extend across.

spangle *n* **1** a sequin. **2** a small glittering object or particle. ➤ **spangly** *adj*.

Spaniard *n* a native or inhabitant of Spain.

spaniel *n* a dog of a breed with short legs, long wavy hair, and large drooping ears.

Spanish *n* the chief language of Spain and many Central and South American countries. ➤ **Spanish** *adj*.

spank[1] *v* to slap on the buttocks with the open hand or something flat.

spank[2] *n* a slap or a series of slaps.

spanking[1] *adj* **1** vigorous or brisk. **2** remarkable or striking.

spanking[2] *n* a series of spanks.

spanner *n Brit* a tool shaped for turning nuts or bolts. ✳ **spanner in the works** *informal* an obstruction or hindrance to a plan or operation.

spar[1] *n* **1** a stout pole. **2** a thick bar or pole used to support the sail of a ship.

spar[2] *v* (**sparred, sparring**) **1** to box without putting full force into the blows. **2** to argue or wrangle.

spar[3] *n* a sparring match or session.

spare[1] *adj* **1** not in use. **2** in excess of what is required; surplus. **3** plain and unelaborate. **4** healthily lean or thin. ✳ **go spare** *Brit, informal* to become extremely angry.

spare[2] *v* **1** to make available for use by others. **2** to refrain from killing or harming. **3** to refrain from using. **4** to relieve of the need to experience something unpleasant. ✳ **spare no expense** to pay whatever is needed.

spare[3] *n* **1** a spare or duplicate item or part, e.g. for a machine or vehicle. **2** a spare tyre.

sparerib *n* a pork rib with most of the meat removed for bacon.

spare tyre *n* **1** an extra tyre carried by a motor vehicle. **2** *informal* a roll of fat at the waist.

sparing *adj* not wasteful; frugal. ➤ **sparingly** *adv*.

spark[1] *n* **1** a small burning particle thrown out by something on fire or left among its ashes. **2** a luminous electrical discharge of short duration. **3** a sparkle or flash. **4** something that starts an event or development. **5** a trace that may develop.

spark[2] *v* **1** to produce or give off sparks. **2** (+ off) to prompt or precipitate (something).

sparking plug *n* = SPARK PLUG.

sparkle[1] *v* **1** to give off or reflect glittering points of light. **2** to show brilliance or animation.

sparkle[2] *n* **1** a little spark or flash of light. **2** liveliness and fun. ➤ **sparkly** *adj*.

sparkler *n* a hand-held firework that gives out sparks.

spark plug *n* a device that produces the electric spark to ignite the fuel in an internal-combustion engine.

sparrow *n* a small dull-coloured songbird.

sparrow hawk *n* a small hawk that preys on smaller birds.

sparse *adj* few and scattered; not thickly grown or settled. ➤ **sparsely** *adv*, **sparseness** *n*.

spartan *adj* not comfortable or pleasant; austere.

spasm *n* **1** an involuntary muscular contraction. **2** a sudden strong effort or emotion.

spasmodic *adj* occurring unpredictably at intervals. ➤ **spasmodically** *adv*.

spastic[1] *adj* **1** of or characterized by spasm. **2** *dated, offensive* affected by cerebral palsy. ➤ **spasticity** *n*.

spastic² *n dated, offensive* somebody who has cerebral palsy.

spat¹ *v* past tense and past part. of SPIT¹.

spat² *n* a cloth or leather gaiter covering the instep and ankle.

spat³ *n informal* a petty quarrel or disagreement.

spat⁴ *v* (**spatted, spatting**) to quarrel pettily.

spate *n* **1** a large number or amount in a short space of time. **2** a state of flood.

spathe *n* a sheath enclosing the cluster of flowers on some plants.

spatial *or* **spacial** *adj* relating to or occurring in space. ➤ **spatially** *adv*.

spatter¹ *v* (**spattered, spattering**) **1** to splash or sprinkle with drops of liquid. **2** to scatter by splashing or sprinkling. **3** to spurt out in scattered drops.

spatter² *n* the act or sound of spattering.

spatula *n* an implement with a thin flat blade, used for spreading, mixing, etc.

spawn¹ *v* **1** of a water animal: to produce or deposit (eggs). **2** to produce abundantly.

spawn² *n* eggs produced by frogs, oysters, fish, etc.

spay *v* to remove the ovaries of (a female animal).

speak *v* **1** to utter words with the voice. **2** to make a speech. **3** to use or be able to use (a language) for oral communication. **4** to be indicative or suggestive of. * **speak one's mind** to say frankly what one thinks. **speak volumes** to communicate or reveal a great deal.

speakeasy *n* (*pl* **-ies**) *informal* a place where alcoholic drinks were illegally sold during Prohibition in the USA.

speaker *n* **1** somebody who speaks, *esp* in public. **2** somebody who speaks a specified language. **3** the presiding officer of a legislative assembly. **4** a loudspeaker.

speak out *v* to speak loudly or boldly; to state one's opinion frankly.

speak up *v* **1** to speak more loudly. **2** to state one's opinion frankly. **3** (+ for) to speak in defence of.

spear¹ *n* a weapon with a long shaft and pointed head, for thrusting or throwing.

spear² *v* to pierce or strike with a spear.

spear³ *n* a young blade or sprout of asparagus or broccoli.

spearhead¹ *n* a leading element or force in a development or course of action.

spearhead² *v* to lead (an attack or initiative).

spearmint *n* a common mint grown for its aromatic oil.

spec¹ *n* * **on spec** *informal* in the hope of finding or obtaining something wanted.

spec² *n informal* a specification or description.

special¹ *adj* **1** superior or distinguished in some way from others. **2** held in particular esteem. **3** other than or in addition to the usual. **4** meant for particular purpose or need.

special² *n* **1** a special person or thing. **2** a dish in a restaurant that is not on the regular menu. **3** a special offer in a shop.

Special Branch *n* in Britain, the branch of the police force concerned with political security.

special constable *n Brit* somebody trained as an extra policeman for particular circumstances.

special effects *pl n* unusual visual or sound effects introduced into a film or television recording by special processing.

specialist *n* somebody who specializes in a special field or branch of knowledge. ➤ **specialism** *n*.

speciality (*NAmer* **specialty**) *n* (*pl* **-ies**) **1** a special aptitude or skill. **2** a particular occupation or branch of knowledge. **3** a product, service, etc that a person or place specializes in.

specialize *or* **-ise** *v* **1** (*often* + in) to concentrate on a special activity or field. **2** to adapt to a particular mode of life or environment. ➤ **specialization** *n*.

specialized *or* **-ised** *adj* designed for a specific purpose or occupation.

specially *adv* **1** for a particular purpose. **2** in a special way.

special pleading *n* an argument that ignores the damaging or unfavourable aspects of a case.

species *n* (*pl* **species**) **1** a class of organisms having common attributes and designated by a common name. **2** a kind or sort.

specific *adj* **1** clearly and individually identified. **2** free from ambiguity; explicit or particular. **3** (*usu* + to) confined to a particular individual, group, or circumstance. **4** having a particular rather than a general influence. ➤ **specifically** *adv*.

specification *n* **1** the act of specifying. **2** a detailed description of the structure and design of something. **3** a standard required in the workmanship and materials used in making something.

specifics *pl n* the exact particulars.

specify *v* (**-ies, -ied**) **1** to identify clearly and individually. **2** to state explicitly or in detail.

specimen *n* **1** an item or part typical of a group or whole. **2** a sample taken for medical examination. **3** an individual typical of a particular category. **4** *informal* a person of a particular kind: *an unfortunate specimen*.

specious *adj* **1** seeming to be persuasive or sound but in fact wrong. **2** having a deceptive attraction or fascination.

speck¹ *n* **1** a small spot or blemish. **2** a small particle.

speck² *v* to mark with specks.

speckle¹ *n* a little speck of colour.

speckle² *v* to mark with speckles. ➤ **speckled** *adj*.

specs pl n informal spectacles.

spectacle n a striking or dramatic public display or show.

spectacles pl n a pair of glasses.

spectacular[1] adj extremely impressive or exciting. ➤ **spectacularly** adv.

spectacular[2] n a spectacular display or show.

spectate v to be a spectator.

spectator n 1 somebody who attends a show or sports event. 2 an onlooker.

spectral adj 1 of or suggesting a spectre. 2 of or made by a spectrum.

spectre (NAmer **specter**) n 1 a visible ghost. 2 something that haunts the mind.

spectrum n (pl **spectra**) 1 the series of colours produced when a beam of white light is dispersed by a prism or in a rainbow. 2 the range of light in the order of wavelengths. 3 the entire range of wavelengths or frequencies of electromagnetic radiation or of any particular type of it. 4 an interrelated sequence or range.

speculate v 1 to form an opinion or theory without definite evidence. 2 to assume a business risk in the hope of gain. ➤ **speculation** n, **speculator** n.

speculative adj 1 involving speculation rather than firm evidence. 2 questioning or enquiring. ➤ **speculatively** adv.

speech n 1 the expression of thoughts in spoken words. 2 a public discourse or address. 3 a group of lines to be spoken by a character in a play.

speechify v (-ies, -ied) to make a speech in a pompous manner.

speechless adj unable to speak, from anger or revulsion.

speech therapy n therapy for people who have problems with speaking. ➤ **speech therapist** n.

speed[1] n 1 the act or state of moving swiftly. 2 rate at which something moves. 3 rate of performance or execution. 4 the sensitivity to light of a photographic film. 5 each of the gear ratios of a bicycle. 6 slang an amphetamine drug. ❋ **at speed** while moving fast.

speed[2] v (past tense and past part. **sped** or **speeded**) 1 to move or go quickly. 2 to travel at excessive or illegal speed. 3 archaic to meet with success or prosperity.

speedboat n a fast motorboat.

speed dating n a dating system in which people gather together to spend a few minutes with each of many potential partners before choosing one or more dates.

speedometer n an instrument for indicating a vehicle's speed.

speed up v to move or work more quickly.

speedway n 1 an oval racecourse for motorcycles. 2 the sport of racing motorcycles.

speedy adj (-ier, -iest) swift or quick. ➤ **speedily** adv, **speediness** n.

spell[1] n 1 a spoken word or form of words held to have magic power. 2 a state of enchantment. 3 a compelling influence or attraction.

spell[2] v (past tense and past part. **spelt** or **spelled**) 1 to name or write the letters of (a word) in order. 2 of letters: to form (a word). 3 to amount to or mean (something).

spell[3] n a short period or phase.

spellbind v (past tense and past part. **spellbound**) to hold the entire attention of. ➤ **spellbinding** adj.

spellchecker n a computer program that checks the spelling of words in a document.

spelling n 1 the forming of words from letters. 2 the sequence of letters that make up a word.

spell out v to explain clearly and in detail.

spend[1] v (past tense and past part. **spent**) 1 to use or pay out (money). 2 to wear out; to exhaust. 3 to cause or permit (time) to elapse. ❋ **spend a penny** Brit, informal, euphem to urinate. ➤ **spender** n.

spend[2] n informal an amount of money spent.

spendthrift n somebody who spends carelessly or wastefully.

sperm n (pl **sperms** or **sperm**) 1 the male fertilizing fluid. 2 a spermatozoon.

spermatozoon /ˌspuhmətəˈzohˌən/ n (pl **spermatozoa**) a male gamete, which fertilizes a female egg.

spermicide n a contraceptive that kills sperm. ➤ **spermicidal** adj.

sperm whale n a large toothed whale with a blunt head.

spew[1] v 1 to vomit. 2 to eject or be ejected in great quantity.

spew[2] n vomit.

sphagnum n a moss that grows in wet acid areas, e.g. bogs.

sphere n 1 a space or solid enclosed by a surface, all points of which are the same distance from the centre. 2 an area of knowledge or interest.

spherical adj having the form of a sphere. ➤ **spherically** adv.

sphincter n a muscular ring surrounding a bodily opening.

sphinx n (pl **sphinxes** or **sphinges**) an ancient Egyptian image in the form of a lion with a human head.

spice[1] n 1 a vegetable product, e.g. pepper, ginger, or nutmeg, used to season or flavour foods. 2 something that adds excitement or enjoyment.

spice[2] v 1 to season with spice. 2 (often + up) to add zest or relish to.

spick-and-span or **spic-and-span** adj spotlessly clean and tidy.

spicy adj (-ier, -iest) 1 having the strong flavour of spice. 2 strongly seasoned with spices. 3 somewhat indecent. ➤ **spicily** adv, **spiciness** n.

spider n a small invertebrate animal with eight legs, which makes webs for trapping its prey.

spiel n informal a glib line of talk designed to influence or persuade.

spiffing adj Brit, informal, dated extremely good; excellent.

spigot n 1 a small plug or tap to stop up a cask. 2 a projection on the end of a piece of piping that fits into the next piece.

spike[1] n 1 a thin pointed object or projection. 2 a metal projection set in the sole and heel of a running shoe to improve its grip. ➤ **spiky** adj.

spike[2] v 1 to pierce with a spike. 2 to add spirits or a drug secretly to (drink or food).

spike[3] n 1 a cluster of flowers growing directly from a single stem. 2 an ear of grain.

spill[1] v (past tense and past part. **spilt** or **spilled**) 1 to flow or cause to flow out of a container so as to be lost or wasted. 2 to cause (blood) to be shed. 3 to flow or empty out of something. 4 to spread beyond a limit; to overflow. 5 informal to divulge (information). * **spill the beans** informal to divulge information indiscreetly. ➤ **spillage** n.

spill[2] n 1 a quantity of liquid spilt. 2 a fall from a horse or vehicle.

spill[3] n a thin strip of paper or wood for lighting a fire.

spin[1] v (**spinning**, past tense and past part. **spun**) 1 to revolve rapidly; to whirl. 2 of wheels: to revolve rapidly without gripping. 3 of a ball: to revolve in the air and deviate from a straight line on bouncing. 4 to feel dizzy or faint. 5 to draw out and twist fibre into yarn or thread. 6 of a spider, silkworm, etc: to form (a web or silk) by sending out a sticky liquid in threads. 7 to dry (clothes) in a spin-drier. 8 to tell (a long involved tale). 9 informal to present (information, news, etc) in a way that creates a favourable impression.

spin[2] n 1 the act of spinning. 2 informal a particular interpretation or slant given to a piece of information. 3 informal a short excursion. * **in a spin** informal in a state of mental confusion.

spina bifida n a congenital defect in the formation of the spine, allowing part of it to be exposed.

spinach n a plant with large dark green leaves used as a vegetable.

spinal adj in the region of the backbone.

spinal column n the elongated structure of bone running from the head to the lower back and enclosing the spinal cord.

spinal cord n the cord of nervous tissue enclosed in the spinal column.

spindle n 1 a round stick with tapered ends used to form and twist the yarn in hand spinning. 2 a pin or axis round which something turns.

spindly adj (-ier, -iest) unnaturally tall or slender in appearance.

spin doctor n informal an official employed by a political party or individual to present information in the most favourable light.

spin-drier or **spin-dryer** n a machine that dries clothes by spinning them in a drum.

spindrift n sea spray.

spine n 1 the spinal column. 2 something forming a central axis or chief support. 3 the back of a book, holding the pages together. 4 a stiff pointed part of a plant or animal. ➤ **spiny** adj.

spine-chiller n a book, film, etc with a sinister terrifying theme.

spine-chilling adj exciting and terrifying.

spineless adj 1 having no spinal column. 2 lacking strength of character. 3 free from spines.

spinet n a small harpsichord.

spinnaker n a large triangular sail set forward of a yacht's mast and used when running before the wind.

spinney n (pl -eys) Brit a small wood with undergrowth.

spinning wheel n a machine for spinning yarn or thread by means of a spindle driven by a hand- or foot-operated wheel.

spin-off n 1 a by-product. 2 something which is a further development of some idea or product.

spin out v 1 to cause to last longer. 2 to extend or prolong.

spinster n an unmarried woman past the usual age for marriage. ➤ **spinsterhood** n.

spiral[1] adj winding round a centre or pole in a continuous curve ➤ **spirally** adv.

spiral[2] n 1 a spiral curve, object, or pattern. 2 a continuous increase or decrease in prices or incomes.

spiral[3] v (**spiralled, spiralling**, NAmer **spiraled, spiraling**) 1 to follow a spiral course. 2 to increase or decrease continuously or uncontrollably.

spire n a tall pointed structure on top of a church tower.

spirit[1] n 1 the non-physical conscious part of a person. 2 the soul. 3 a supernatural being. 4 (in pl) temper or state of mind. 5 liveliness, energy, or courage. 6 the prevailing character, attitude, or feeling in somebody or something. 7 the true meaning of something as distinct from the literal. 8 (also in pl) strong alcoholic drink, e.g. whisky or gin. 9 (also in pl) a readily vaporizing liquid obtained by distillation.

spirit[2] v (**spirited, spiriting**) (often + away) to carry off secretly or mysteriously.

spirited adj full of energy and determination. ➤ **spiritedly** adv.

spirit level n a device that uses the position of a bubble in a transparent tube of liquid to indicate whether a surface is level.

spiritual[1] adj **1** relating to the spirit as distinct from body. **2** relating to religious matters. **3** based on sympathy of thought or feeling. ➤ **spirituality** n, **spiritually** adv.

spiritual[2] n an emotional religious song of a kind developed among black Christians in the southern USA.

spiritualism n a belief that spirits of the dead can communicate with the living through a medium. ➤ **spiritualist** n.

spirogyra n a type of algae with cells containing spiral chlorophyll bands.

spit[1] v (**spitting**, *past tense and past part.* **spat** *or* **spit**) **1** to eject saliva, liquid, or food forcibly from the mouth. **2** to rain lightly. **3** to sputter. **4** (*often* + out) to utter (words) or express (feelings) vehemently. ✳ **spit it out** to say what is on one's mind.

spit[2] n **1** spittle or saliva. **2** the act of spitting.

spit[3] n **1** a slender pointed rod for holding and turning meat over a source of heat. **2** an elongated strip of sand or shingle extending into the sea.

spite[1] n petty ill will or malice. ✳ **in spite of** regardless of.

spite[2] v to annoy or hinder out of spite.

spiteful adj deliberately malicious. ➤ **spitefully** adv.

spitfire n a quick-tempered person.

spitting image n (**the spitting image**) the exact likeness.

spittle n saliva ejected from the mouth.

spittoon n a receptacle for spitting into.

spiv n Brit, informal a slick individual who lives by sharp practice or petty fraud. ➤ **spivvy** adj.

splash[1] v **1** to fall into or move through a liquid causing it to fly up and scatter in drops. **2** of a liquid: to be scattered in large quantities. **3** to make wet with scattered drops of liquid. **4** to display or print (something) in a conspicuous position. **5** chiefly Brit (usu + out) to spend money liberally.

splash[2] n **1** the action or sound of splashing. **2** a spot or daub from splashed liquid. **3** a vivid patch of colour. **4** a small amount of liquid added to a drink. **5** informal a conspicuous news item. ✳ **make a splash** to make a vivid impression. ➤ **splashy** adj.

splash down v of a spacecraft: to land in the sea. ➤ **splashdown** n.

splat n a splattering sound.

splatter[1] v to fall in or splash with heavy drops.

splatter[2] n a splash of liquid in heavy drops.

splay v to spread or open out.

spleen n **1** an organ concerned in the destruction of blood cells, storage of blood, and production of lymphocytes. **2** bad temper.

splendid adj **1** magnificent or sumptuous. **2** excellent. ➤ **splendidly** adv.

splendour (NAmer **splendor**) n **1** magnificent appearance or impression. **2** grandeur or pomp.

splenetic adj bad tempered or spiteful.

splice[1] v **1** to join (ropes) by interweaving the strands. **2** to join (lengths of film, magnetic tape, or timber) at their ends. ✳ **get spliced** Brit, informal **to get married**.

splice[2] n a joint made by splicing.

spliff n informal a marijuana cigarette.

splint n a support for an injured body part, e.g. a broken arm.

splinter[1] n a sharp thin piece of wood or glass, split or broken off lengthways.

splinter[2] v to split into splinters; to shatter.

splinter group n a small group that has broken away from the main part of an organization.

split[1] v (**splitting**, *past tense and past part.* **split**) **1** to divide or separate lengthways. **2** to separate (parts) by putting something between. **3** to break or burst apart. **4** to divide or share between people. **5** to divide (a political party) into opposing groups. **6** (*often* + up) to end a relationship or connection. ✳ **split hairs** to make trivial distinctions. ➤ **splitter** n.

split[2] n **1** a narrow break made by splitting. **2** the act of splitting. **3** a division into opposing groups. **4** (**the splits**) a jump or position with the legs extended at right angles to the trunk.

split infinitive n an infinitive with a word, usu an adverb, between *to* and the verb, as in *to fully agree*.

split-level adj of a room, house, etc: divided into two main levels.

split second n a very short moment. ➤ **split-second** adj.

splitting adj of a headache: intense and piercing.

splodge[1] n Brit, informal a large spot, smear, or blot.

splodge[2] v Brit, informal to mark with a large smear.

splosh[1] v informal to make a splashing sound.

splosh[2] n informal a splashing sound.

splurge[1] n informal **1** an extravagantly large amount of something. **2** an ostentatious display. **3** an extravagant spending spree.

splurge[2] v informal (*often* + on) to spend money extravagantly.

splutter[1] v **1** to make a series of noisy spitting sounds. **2** to speak hastily and confusedly.

splutter[2] n a spluttering sound.

spoil v (*past tense and past part.* **spoilt** *or* **spoiled**) **1** to damage or ruin. **2** to impair the enjoyment of. **3** to fill in (a voting paper) wrongly so as to render invalid. **4** to impair the character of (a child) by excessive lenience. **5** to treat indulgently. **6** to become unfit for use or consumption. ✳ **spoiling for a fight** very eager to fight.

spoiler n 1 a long strip on an aircraft wing that can be raised for reducing lift and increasing drag. 2 a strip across the front or rear of a car, for increasing stability at high speeds.

spoils pl n plunder taken in war or a robbery.

spoilsport n somebody who spoils the enjoyment of others.

spoke¹ v past tense of SPEAK.

spoke² n each of the radiating bars connecting the hub of a wheel with the rim.

spoken¹ adj speaking in a specified manner: soft-spoken.

spoken² v past part. of SPEAK.

spokesman or **spokeswoman** n (pl **spokesmen** or **spokeswomen**) a person who speaks on behalf of a group.

spokesperson n (pl **spokespersons** or **spokespeople**) a spokesman or spokeswoman.

sponge¹ n 1 a type of soft sea creature without a backbone, able to absorb water when wet. 2 a piece of sponge or similar material for cleaning. 3 a light type of cake or pudding. ▸ **spongy** adj.

sponge² v 1 to clean or wipe with a sponge. 2 informal to obtain money by exploiting people's natural generosity. ▸ **sponger** n.

sponge bag n Brit a small bag for holding toilet articles.

sponsor¹ n 1 a person or organization that pays towards the cost of a cultural or sporting event. 2 somebody who contributes to a charity by giving money for a participant's efforts in a fund-raising event. 3 somebody who introduces a bill in parliament. ▸ **sponsorship** n.

sponsor² v to be sponsor for.

spontaneous adj done from a natural feeling or sudden impulse. 2 unconstrained or uninhibited by nature. 3 developing without apparent external influence. ▸ **spontaneity** n, **spontaneously** adv.

spoof n informal 1 a humorous parody. 2 a hoax or deception.

spook¹ n 1 informal a ghost. 2 chiefly NAmer a spy.

spook² v to frighten or startle.

spooky adj (-ier, -iest) informal sinister and frightening. ▸ **spookily** adv.

spool¹ n a cylindrical device on which thread, wire, tape, etc is wound.

spool² v to wind onto a spool.

spoon¹ n an implement consisting of a small shallow bowl with a handle, used for eating or serving food. ▸ **spoonful** n (pl **spoonfuls**).

spoon² v to pick up or transfer with a spoon.

spoonbill n a wading bird with a long bill flattened at the tip.

spoonerism n a transposition of the initial sounds or letters of two or more words, e.g. in tons of soil for sons of toil.

spoon-feed v 1 to feed with a spoon. 2 to give help or information to (somebody) in a way that avoids the need for further thought.

sporadic adj occurring occasionally or in scattered instances. ▸ **sporadically** adv.

spore n a primitive reproductive body produced by plants, algae, etc.

sporran n a leather pouch worn in front of the kilt in traditional Highland dress.

sport¹ n 1 a competitive activity or game requiring physical skill and having a set of rules. 2 these activities collectively. 3 a person who is generous-minded and accepts defeat graciously.

sport² v 1 to wear (something distinctive). 2 literary to play about happily.

sporting adj 1 concerned with or fond of sport. 2 generous-minded. * **a sporting chance** a reasonable chance of success.

sportive adj literary cheerful and playful.

sports car n a small fast car.

sports jacket n a man's jacket for informal wear.

sportsman or **sportswoman** n (pl **sportsmen** or **sportswomen**) 1 a man or woman who engages in sports. 2 a fair and generous-minded person. ▸ **sportsmanship** n.

sporty adj (-ier, -iest) 1 fond of or skilled at sport. 2 of clothes: suitable for sporting activities or casual wear. 3 of a car: small and fast.

spot¹ n 1 a small round area different in colour or texture from the surrounding surface. 2 a dirty mark or stain. 3 a pimple or small blemish on the skin. 4 Brit, informal a small amount. 5 a place or area. * **in a spot/in a tight spot** informal in difficulties. **on the spot 1** immediately. 2 at the place of action.

spot² v (**spotted, spotting**) 1 to notice or detect. 2 to single out or identify. 3 to mark with spots. 4 Brit (with 'it' as subject) to fall lightly in scattered drops. ▸ **spotted** adj, **spotter** n, **spotty** adj.

spot check n a random check made to test quality, accuracy, etc.

spot-check v to submit to a spot check.

spotless adj 1 free from dirt or stains. 2 pure or unblemished. ▸ **spotlessly** adv.

spotlight¹ n 1 a lamp projecting a narrow intense beam of light focused on a person or place. 2 (**the spotlight**) full public attention.

spotlight² v (**spotlighting,** past tense and past part. **spotlighted** or **spotlit**) 1 to illuminate with a spotlight. 2 to direct attention towards.

spot-on adj Brit, informal absolutely correct or accurate.

spouse n a husband or wife.

spout¹ v 1 to eject (liquid, etc) or flow in a copious stream. 2 to express in a strident or pompous manner. 3 to declaim or recite.

spout² n 1 a projecting tube for pouring liquid from a kettle, pot, etc. 2 a downpipe carrying water from a roof gutter. **3** a forceful jet of liquid. ✳ **up the spout** *informal* ruined or useless.

sprain[1] *v* to wrench or twist (a joint) violently so as to stretch or tear the ligaments and cause swelling and bruising.

sprain[2] *n* **1** an instance of spraining. **2** a sprained joint.

sprang *v* past tense of SPRING[1].

sprat *n* a small sea fish of the herring family.

sprawl[1] *v* **1** to lie or sit with arms and legs spread out carelessly. **2** to spread over a landscape, etc.

sprawl[2] *n* **1** a sprawling position. **2** an irregular spreading mass or group.

spray[1] *v* **1** to discharge or apply (a fluid) as a spray. **2** to direct a spray of something onto (a surface) or throughout (a place). **3** of a male cat: to mark out its territory by urinating throughout (an area). ➤ **sprayer** *n*.

spray[2] *n* **1** fine drops of water blown or falling through the air. **2** a jet of vapour or finely divided liquid. **3** an aerosol or other device by which liquid is sent out in a spray. **4** a substance for spraying.

spray[3] *n* **1** a flowering branch or shoot of a plant. **2** a small bouquet of cut flowers.

spread[1] *v* (**spreading**, *past tense and past part.* **spread**) **1** to open or extend (something contracted or folded). **2** to distribute or be distributed over an area or period of time. **3** to cover (a surface) with an even layer of something. **4** to communicate to an increasing group. ➤ **spreader** *n*.

spread[2] *n* **1** the distribution or expansion of something. **2** a gap or span between two points. **3** a range of things. **4** the two facing pages forming an opening in a newspaper or magazine. **5** a food product designed to be spread. **6** *informal* a sumptuous meal.

spread-eagled *adj* stretched out with the arms and legs at an angle to the trunk.

spreadsheet *n* a computer program in which numerical data can be displayed in rows and columns, and rapid calculations made.

spree *n* a bout of unrestrained activity: *a spending spree*.

sprig *n* a small shoot or twig.

sprightly *adj* (**-ier, -iest**) usu of an elderly person: full of vitality and liveliness. ➤ **sprightliness** *n*.

spring[1] *v* (**sprang, sprung**) **1** to move suddenly with a jumping action. **2** to move by the release of a spring. **3** (*often* + up) of plants or buildings: to appear suddenly. **4** (*usu* + from) to appear suddenly or unexpectedly. **5** (*usu* + from) to originate or arise. **6** (+ on) to cause (something) to happen, be revealed, or be entrusted to somebody suddenly.

spring[2] *n* **1** the season of new growth between winter and summer. **2** a piece of bent or coiled metal that recovers its original shape when released after being compressed or stretched. **3** capacity for springing; resilience or bounce. **4** a jump or bound. **5** a source of water issuing from the ground.

springboard *n* **1** a flexible board on which a diver or gymnast springs to gain extra height. **2** something that provides an initial stimulus or impetus.

springbok *n* (*pl* **springboks** *or* **springbok**) a graceful southern African gazelle noted for its habit of springing suddenly into the air.

spring-clean *v* to give a thorough cleaning to (a house or furnishings). ➤ **spring-clean** *n*.

springer spaniel *n* a small spaniel of a breed once used chiefly for flushing small game.

spring-loaded *adj* operated by means of spring tension or compression.

spring onion *n chiefly Brit* an onion with a small mild-flavoured bulb and long green shoots that is chiefly eaten raw in salads.

springy *adj* (**-ier, -iest**) having an elastic or bouncy quality.

sprinkle[1] *v* **1** to scatter in fine drops or fine particles. **2** to scatter fine drops or particles over (a surface). **3** to dot here and there.

sprinkle[2] *n* = SPRINKLING.

sprinkler *n* **1** a nozzle installed in a ceiling as part of an automatic fire-extinguishing system. **2** an apparatus for watering a lawn by spraying.

sprinkling *n* a small quantity or number, *esp* scattered in drops or particles or distributed randomly.

sprint[1] *v* to run at top speed, *esp* over a short distance. ➤ **sprinter** *n*.

sprint[2] *n* **1** a running race of no more than 400m. **2** a short fast swimming or cycling race. **3** a burst of speed.

sprite *n* a fairy or elf, *esp* one associated with water.

spritzer *n* a drink of wine diluted with soda water or lemonade.

sprocket *n* a tooth or projection on the rim of a wheel, shaped so as to engage the links of a chain or the perforations on the edge of a film.

sprout[1] *v* **1** of a plant: to send out shoots or new growth. **2** to develop or grow (something).

sprout[2] *n* **1** a shoot, e.g. from a seed or root. **2** = BRUSSELS SPROUT.

spruce[1] *n* an evergreen coniferous tree with a conical head of dense foliage.

spruce[2] *adj* neat or smart in dress or appearance.

spruce[3] *v* (+ up) to make (oneself or another person) spruce.

sprung[1] *v* past part. of SPRING[1].

sprung[2] *adj* fitted with springs, or possessed of springiness.

spry *adj* (**sprier** *or* **spryer, spriest** *or* **spryest**) *esp* of an old person: vigorously active; nimble.

spud *n informal* a potato.

spume *n literary* froth or foam.

spun *v* past tense and past part. of SPIN[1].

spunk *n* **1** *informal* spirit; pluck. **2** *Brit, coarse slang* semen. ➤ **spunky** *adj*

spur[1] *n* **1** a pointed or wheel-shaped metal device on the heel of a rider's boot, used to urge the horse on. **2** a goad to action; an incentive. **3** a fruit-bearing side shoot. **4** a ridge that extends sideways from a mountain. **5** a short road or length of railway connecting with a major route. **6** ✳ **on the spur of the moment** suddenly; on impulse.

spur[2] *v* (**spurred, spurring**) **1** to urge (a horse) on with spurs. **2** (*often* + on) to encourage to make a greater effort.

spurious *adj* **1** false; fake; invented. **2** of argument or reasoning: apparently sound but containing flaws.

spurn *v* to reject with disdain.

spurt[1] or **spirt** *v* **1** to gush out in a jet. **2** to put on speed or increase effort.

spurt[2] or **spirt** *n* **1** a sudden forceful gush. **2** a sudden increase in effort or speed.

sputter[1] *v* to make, or to speak with, explosive popping sounds.

sputter[2] *n* the act or sound of sputtering.

sputum *n* (*pl* **sputa**) mucus and saliva that is coughed up.

spy[1] *v* (**-ies, -ied**) **1** to work for a government or other organization by secretly gathering data about enemies or rivals. **2** (+ on) to watch somebody secretly. **3** to catch sight of or spot.

spy[2] *n* (*pl* **-ies**) a person who keeps secret watch on somebody or something or collects information secretly.

spyglass *n* a small telescope.

spyhole *n Brit* = PEEPHOLE.

sq. *abbr* square.

squab *n* **1** a fledgling bird, *esp* a pigeon. **2** *Brit* a thick upholstery cushion for a chair, car seat, etc.

squabble[1] *v* to quarrel noisily, *esp* over trifles.

squabble[2] *n* a noisy quarrel.

squad *n* **1** a small group of military personnel assembled for a purpose. **2** a small group working as a team. **3** a group of players from whom a sports team is selected.

squaddy or **squaddie** *n* (*pl* **-ies**) *Brit, informal* a private in the armed forces.

squadron *n* **1** a unit of an air force consisting usu of between 10 and 18 aircraft. **2** a naval unit consisting of a number of warships on a particular operation.

squalid *adj* **1** filthy and degraded from neglect or poverty. **2** sordid; disreputable. ➤ **squalidly** *adv*.

squall[1] *v* of a baby: to cry noisily.

squall[2] *n* a noisy cry.

squall[3] *n* a sudden violent wind, often with rain or snow. ➤ **squally** *adj*.

squalor *n* the state of being squalid.

squander *v* to waste, dissipate, or misuse (e.g. money, time, or talents).

square[1] *n* **1** a plane figure with all four sides equal and four right angles. **2** an open usu four-sided space in a town. **3** a woman's head-scarf. **4** a quadrilateral space marked out on a board, used for playing games. **5** a T-shaped or L-shaped instrument used to draw or test right angles. **6** the product of a number multiplied by itself. **7** *informal, dated* a person who is excessively conventional or conservative. ✳ **back to/at square one** back where one started.

square[2] *adj* **1** having four equal sides and four right angles. **2** forming a right angle. **3** at right angles. **4** level or parallel. **5** of a shape or build suggesting strength and solidity. **6** denoting an area equal to that of a square whose sides are of the specified unit: *ten square feet*. **7** placed after a length measurement: denoting the area of a square expanse or object whose sides are of the specified measurement: *ten foot square*. **8** (*often* **all square**) even or equal, e.g. as regards a score or the settlement of accounts. **9** *informal, dated* excessively conservative; dully conventional. ✳ **square peg in a round hole** a person in an environment incompatible with their personality or abilities. ➤ **squarely** *adv*.

square[3] *v* **1** (*often* + off) to make square or rectangular. **2** (*often* + off) to mark (a surface) into squares or rectangles. **3** to multiply (a number) by itself. **4** (+ with) to be in, or bring into, agreement with. **5** to balance or settle (an account). **6** to even the score of (a contest).

square[4] *adv* **1** directly; precisely. **2** transversely across a cricket pitch or football field.

square dance *n* a dance for four couples who form a hollow square.

square deal *n* an honest and fair arrangement or transaction.

square leg *n* in cricket, a fielding position halfway to the boundary on the leg side, level with the batsman.

square meal *n* a nutritionally balanced and satisfying meal.

square up *v* **1** to settle a bill or debt. **2** (+ to) to face a challenge.

squash[1] *v* **1** to press or crush into a flat mass. **2** to squeeze or press into a space. **3** to suppress (e.g. a rebellion or rumour) forcefully. **4** to humiliate or silence, e.g. with a cutting remark. ➤ **squashy** *adj*.

squash[2] *n* **1** the situation where one is squashed, e.g. in a crowd. **2** an indoor game played by two people in a four-walled court with rackets and a small rubber ball that can be hit against any wall. **3** *Brit* a soft drink made by diluting sweetened and concentrated fruit juice.

squash[3] *n* (*pl* **squashes** or **squash**) a gourd whose flesh is cooked and eaten as a vegetable.

squat[1] *v* (**squatted, squatting**) **1** (*also* + down) to assume a position in which the knees are bent and the haunches rest on the heels. **2** to occupy property as a squatter.

squat[2] *n* **1** a squatting posture. **2** an empty building occupied by squatters. **3** the act of squatting in an uninhabited building.

squat[3] *adj* (**squatter, squattest**) short or low and broad.

squatter *n* a person who occupies otherwise empty property without rights of ownership or payment of rent.

squaw *n offensive* a Native North American woman or wife.

squawk[1] *v* **1** to utter a harsh abrupt scream. **2** *informal* to make a loud or vehement protest.

squawk[2] *n* an act of squawking.

squeak[1] *n* a short shrill cry or noise. ✳ **a narrow/near squeak** an escape barely managed. ➤ **squeaky** *adj.*

squeak[2] *v* **1** to make a squeak or utter in a squeak. **2** (+ through) to pass an examination or otherwise succeed, by the narrowest of margins.

squeaky-clean *adj informal* **1** absolutely clean. **2** morally unassailable; goody-goody.

squeal[1] *n* a shrill sharp cry or noise: *squeals of delight.*

squeal[2] *v* **1** to utter or make a squeal. **2** *informal* to turn informer. **3** *informal* to complain or protest.

squeamish *adj* **1** easily made to feel faint or nauseous. **2** easily shocked or offended.

squeegee *n* (*pl* **squeegees**) a tool with a rubber blade used for removing liquid from a surface, e.g. when cleaning a window.

squeeze[1] *v* **1** to compress by applying physical pressure to the sides. **2** to extract (liquid, etc) from something by pressure. **3** to force or cram into or through a restricted space. **4** (+ in/into) to fit (a person or task) into a tight schedule. **5** (+ out) to force (somebody) out of their job, area of activity, etc.

squeeze[2] *n* **1** an act of squeezing. **2** a quick hug or embrace. **3** a quantity squeezed out from something. **4** *informal* a condition of being crowded together. **5** financial pressure caused by restricting credit.

squeezy *adj* (**-ier, -iest**) of a plastic container: flexible, so as to dispense its contents when squeezed.

squelch[1] *v* **1** to make the sucking sound typical of somebody walking through mud. **2** *informal* to crush or suppress (opposition, etc).

squelch[2] *n* a squelching sound.

squib *n* a small firework that burns with a fizz.

squid *n* (*pl* **squids** *or* **squid**) a mollusc with eight arms, two long tentacles, and a long tapered body.

squiffy *or* **squiffed** *adj* (**-ier, -iest**) *chiefly Brit, informal* slightly drunk; tipsy.

squiggle *n* a short wavy twist or line, *esp* in handwriting or drawing. ➤ **squiggly** *adj.*

squint[1] *v* **1** to have a squint in the eye. **2** to look or peer with eyes partly closed.

squint[2] *n* **1** abnormal alignment of an eye, so that it turns permanently towards or away from the nose. **2** *informal* a quick glance.

squire[1] *n* **1** formerly, a young nobleman acting as a knight's attendant and training for knighthood. **2** the principal landowner of a district.

squire[2] *v* to escort (a woman).

squirm *v* **1** to twist about like a worm; to wriggle. **2** to feel acutely embarrassed or ashamed. ➤ **squirm** *n.*

squirrel[1] *n* a tree-dwelling rodent with a long bushy tail.

squirrel[2] *v* (**squirrelled, squirrelling,** *NAmer* **squirreled, squirreling**) (*usu* + away) to secrete somewhere or hoard for future use.

squirt[1] *v* **1** to issue, or squeeze out, in a jet from a narrow opening. **2** to direct a jet or stream of liquid at.

squirt[2] *n* **1** a small rapid stream of liquid. **2** *informal* a small, insignificant, or impudent person.

squish[1] *v* **1** to make a slight squelching or sucking sound. **2** *informal* to squash.

squish[2] *n* the sound of squishing.

Sr[1] *abbr* **1** senior. **2** Sister.

Sr[2] *abbr* the chemical symbol for strontium.

SS[1] *n* Adolf Hitler's bodyguard and special police force.

SS[2] *abbr* **1** saints. **2** steamship.

St *abbr* **1** Saint. **2** street.

stab[1] *n* **1** a thrust with a pointed weapon. **2** a sharp spasm of pain or emotion. ✳ **a stab in the back** an act of treachery. **have/make a stab at** *informal* to make an attempt at.

stab[2] *v* (**stabbed, stabbing**) **1** to pierce or wound with a pointed weapon. **2** to thrust or jab (a pointed object) somewhere. **3** to cause a sharp pain.

stability *n* the quality of being stable.

stabilize *or* **-ise** *v* to make or become stable. ➤ **stabilization** *n.*

stable[1] *n* **1** (*also in pl*) a building in which horses are kept. **2** (*also in pl*) an establishment where racehorses are kept and trained. **3** a group of people working as a team or under one person's management.

stable[2] *v* to put or keep (a horse) in a stable.

stable[3] *adj* **1** not likely to collapse, overturn, etc. **2** securely established so as to endure and be dependable. **3** not subject to change or fluctuation. **4** of a patient or their condition: not likely to deteriorate suddenly. **5** not subject to mental or emotional insecurity.

stablemate *n* another horse stabled with the one in question.

staccato *adj and adv* **1** of a piece of music: performed with each note produced in an abrupt, detached style. **2** of speech: with a jerky delivery.

stack[1] *n* **1** a pile, *esp* an orderly one. **2** a cone-shaped, rectangular, or cylindrical pile of hay or straw. **3** a number of aircraft circling an airport waiting their turn to land. **4** a chimney. **5** *informal* (*also in pl*) a large quantity or number.

stack[2] *v* **1** to pile (things) into a stack. **2** to fill with stacks of things. **3** to assign (an aircraft) to a particular altitude and position within a stack. **4** to shuffle (a pack of cards) in such a way as to enable one to cheat. ✳ **be stacked against/in favour of** to be highly likely to produce an unfavourable/favourable result for.

stadium *n* (*pl* **stadiums** *or* **stadia**) a sports ground surrounded by tiers of seats for specta-tors.

staff[1] *n* **1** the people who work for an institution, business, etc. **2** the teachers at a school or university. **3** a group of officers appointed to assist a commanding officer. **4** (*pl* **staves**) a long stick carried for support when walking or as a weapon. **5** a rod carried as a symbol of office or authority. **6** (*pl* **staves**) in music, the STAVE[1] 3.

staff[2] *v* to supply (an organization, etc) with a staff.

staff nurse *n Brit* a qualified hospital nurse ranking below a sister or charge nurse.

stag *n* an adult male deer.

stage[1] *n* **1** a raised platform. **2** the raised plat-form or other area in a theatre where actors perform. **3** (**the stage**) the acting profession. **4** a distinguishable period or step in the develop-ment of something. **5** a section of journey, race, or rally. **6** = STAGECOACH. ✳ **set the stage for** to provide the necessary conditions for the arrival, appearance, or occurrence of.

stage[2] *v* **1** to produce and perform (a theatrical work). **2** to organize (a public event).

stagecoach *n* formerly, a horse-drawn passen-ger and mail coach that ran a regular scheduled route.

stage fright *n* nervousness felt at appearing before an audience.

stagehand *n* a theatre worker who handles scenery, props, or lights.

stage-manage *v* **1** to be the stage manager of (a play, etc). **2** to arrange (an event, etc) so as to achieve a desired result. ➤ **stage manage-ment** *n*.

stage manager *n* a person who is in overall charge of the stage, cast, and technical staff during performances of a play.

stage whisper *n* a loud whisper by an actor, audible to the audience, but supposedly inau-dible to others on stage.

stagger[1] *v* **1** to move unsteadily or jerkily as if in danger of falling over. **2** to dumbfound or astonish. **3** to arrange (a set of things) so that

they are not in line, start at different times, or partially overlap.

stagger[2] *n* **1** a staggered arrangement. **2** a lurching movement.

staggering *adj* astonishing or overwhelming. ➤ **staggeringly** *adv*.

staging post *n* a regular stopping place for vehicles.

stagnant *adj* **1** of water: not flowing and usu overgrown or foul. **2** dull or inactive.

stagnate *v* to become or remain stagnant. ➤ **stagnation** *n*.

stag night *n* a party for men on the night before one of them is married.

stagy *or* **stagey** *adj* (**-ier, -iest**) artificially dra-matic; consciously theatrical.

staid *adj* unadventurous and usu old-fashioned in attitude.

stain[1] *v* **1** to mark, discolour, or soil. **2** *literary* to dishonour (a person or their character, reputa-tion, etc). **3** to colour (wood or a biological specimen) by using chemicals or dyes.

stain[2] *n* **1** a soiled or discoloured spot. **2** a moral taint or blemish. **3** a preparation, e.g. of dye or pigment, used in staining.

stained glass *n* glass coloured or stained, usu for use in leaded windows.

stainless *adj* **1** free from stain or stigma. **2** rust-resistant.

stainless steel *n* steel containing chromium and highly resistant to rusting and corrosion.

stair *n* **1** (*usu in pl*) a flight of steps for passing from one level to another. **2** any step of a stairway.

staircase *n* a flight of stairs with the supporting framework, casing, and balusters.

stairway *n* one or more flights of stairs, usu with intermediate landings.

stairwell *n* a vertical shaft in which stairs are located.

stake[1] *n* **1** a pointed wooden or iron post used for driving into the ground as a marker or support. **2** (**the stake**) a post to which a person was formerly bound for execution by burning.

stake[2] *v* **1** (*often + off/out*) to mark out (an area) with stakes. **2** to support (a plant) with a stake. ✳ **stake one's claim** to assert one's ownership of, or right to, something.

stake[3] *v* **1** to bet (a sum of money, one's reputa-tion, etc). **2** *chiefly NAmer* to back (a person or business concern) financially.

stake[4] *n* **1** something, *esp* a sum of money, that is staked. **2** an interest or share in an undertak-ing. **3** (*in pl*) what is to be won or lost in a contest or competitive situation. **4** (*in pl*) used after a noun to denote that an aspect of life is thought of as a competion between people: *not doing terribly well in the promotion stakes.* ✳ **at stake 1** to be won or lost. **2** at risk.

stake out *v informal* to conduct a surveillance of (a suspected area, person, etc). ➤ **stakeout** *n*.

stalactite *n* an icicle-like deposit of calcium carbonate hanging from the roof or sides of a cave.

stalagmite *n* a spike-like deposit of calcium carbonate growing upward from the floor of a cave.

stale *adj* **1** *esp* of food: no longer fresh; unpalatable or musty. **2** of news: no longer interesting. **3** lacking vigour or effectiveness through over-exertion or repetition. ➤ **staleness** *n*.

stalemate *n* **1** a position in chess representing a draw, where the king, although not in check, can move only into check. **2** a deadlock.

stalk¹ *v* **1** to pursue (a prey or quarry) stealthily. **2** to follow and watch (a person with whom one has become obsessed), to the point of persecution. **3** to walk in a stiff haughty fashion. ➤ **stalker** *n*.

stalk² *n* **1** the main stem of a plant. **2** the stem of a leaf or fruit.

stall¹ *n* **1** a compartment for a domestic animal in a stable or barn. **2** (*usu in pl*) a compartment in a mechanically operated device from which horses are simultaneously released to start a race. **3** any small compartment, e.g. one of a row of toilets. **4** a stand or counter at which articles are offered for sale, e.g. in a market. **5** *Brit* (*in pl*) the seats on the main floor of an auditorium, e.g. in a theatre. **6** a seat in the chancel of a church. **7** the cutting-out of a vehicle engine. **8** the condition of an aircraft when it loses lift, e.g. from moving forward too slowly.

stall² *v* **1** of a vehicle, engine, driver, aircraft, or pilot: to suffer a stall. **2** (*usu* **be stalled**) to be unable to progress. **3** to play for time; to delay. **4** to divert or delay (somebody), usu to give oneself more time.

stallion *n* an uncastrated male horse.

stalwart¹ *adj* **1** strong. **2** dependable; staunch.

stalwart² *n* a staunch supporter.

stamen *n* the organ of a flower that produces the male reproductive cell.

stamina *n* the capacity for sustained mental and physical effort.

stammer¹ *v* to speak or utter with involuntary stops and repetitions, *esp* of initial consonants.

stammer² *n* a tendency to stammer.

stamp¹ *v* **1** to bring down (one's foot) forcibly. **2** to walk with loud heavy steps. **3** to impress or imprint (words, etc) on something. **4** to leave (a permanent or indelible image) in someone's mind, etc. **5** of a quality, etc: to characterize (something). **6** to attach a postage stamp to (an envelope, etc).

stamp² *n* **1** a printed adhesive piece of paper used to indicate that postage has been paid. **2** an instrument for stamping a mark, etc on a surface. **3** the impression or mark made by stamping. **4** a characteristic quality. **5** the act or sound of stamping the foot.

stamp duty *n* a tax levied for legal recognition of certain documents.

stampede¹ *n* **1** a wild headlong rush of frightened animals. **2** a sudden mass movement of people.

stampede² *v* to run away or rush in panic, or to cause (people or animals) to do this.

stamping ground *n* one's favourite or habitual haunt.

stamp out *v* to eradicate or destroy.

stance *n* **1** a way of standing. **2** an intellectual or emotional attitude.

stanch *v NAmer* see STAUNCH¹.

stanchion *n* an upright bar, post, or support.

stand¹ *v* (*past tense and past part.* **stood**) **1** to support oneself on one's feet in an upright position. **2** to rise to this position. **3** to rest upright on the ground or other surface. **4** to occupy a position or location. **5** to remain stationary. **6** to have a particular attitude or opinion. **7** to remain valid. **8** (+ to) to be likely to receive or experience something. **9** to tolerate or like: *I can't stand her husband.* **10** to withstand. **11** to treat (somebody) to a meal or drink. **12** *Brit* to be a candidate in an election. ✳ **leave standing** to surpass spectacularly. **stand by 1** to wait in readiness. **2** to do nothing while something is happening. **3** to support or remain loyal to. **stand for 1** to represent. **2** to permit or tolerate. **stand on one's own feet/ two feet** to be self-reliant.

stand² *n* **1** a definite attitude taken towards something. **2** a determined effort to fight for or resist something. **3** (*also in pl*) a structure of tiered seats for spectators of a sport or spectacle. **4** a raised platform for a band, speaker, etc. **5** a small outdoor stall selling food, etc. **6** a frame or rack on or in which to place things. **7** (**the stand**) *NAmer* the witness-box.

standard¹ *n* **1** a level of quality or achievement. **2** a norm used for comparison. **3** (*in pl*) principles of acceptable behaviour. **4** a flag or banner.

standard² *adj* **1** regularly and widely used; accepted as a norm. **2** of language: used in the speech and writing of educated people and considered as the norm.

standard-bearer *n* **1** a person who carries a banner. **2** a conspicuous figure at the forefront of an organization, etc.

standardize *or* **-ise** *v* to make (things) conform to a standard. ➤ **standardization** *n*.

standard lamp *n* a lamp with a tall support that stands on the floor.

standard of living *n* a measure of the prosperity of an individual or community, shown *esp* by their level of consumption.

standby[1] n (pl **standbys**) **1** a person or thing held in reserve in case of necessity. **2** a state of readiness for duty or use.

standby[2] adj **1** held in reserve and ready for use or duty. **2** of tickets: unreserved and available for sale shortly before e.g. a performance.

stand down v Brit to relinquish an office or position.

stand in v to act as substitute for somebody.

standing[1] adj permanently existing, in force, or available.

standing[2] n **1** status, position, or reputation. **2** length of existence or duration.

standing joke n something that is a regular source of amusement or target of derision.

standing order n Brit **1** an order to a bank to pay a specified sum of money to another named account at specified times. **2** an instruction, e.g. to a supplier, in force until specifically changed.

standing ovation n a prolonged burst of applause during which the audience rise to their feet.

standoff n a state of deadlock between opponents.

standoffish adj derog reserved; aloof.

stand out v to be especially visible, noteworthy, or good. * **stand out for** to be stubborn in insisting on.

standpoint n **1** the position from which one views something. **2** one's point of view with regard to some issue.

standstill n a stationary state; a stop or impasse.

stand up v **1** to rise to a standing position. **2** to bear close scrutiny: *That argument won't stand up.* **3** informal to fail to keep an appointment with (somebody). * **stand up and be counted** to make one's views known. **stand up for** to defend against criticism. **stand up to 1** to confront or prepare to resist. **2** to withstand (wear, etc).

stank v past tense of STINK[1].

stanza n a number of lines forming a basic division of a poem.

staple[1] n **1** a small wire clip that can be driven through sheets of paper to secure them together. **2** a sharp-ended U-shaped metal loop, driven into a surface to secure something to it.

staple[2] v to fasten or attach with staples. > **stapler** n.

staple[3] n **1** the main element or constituent of something. **2** the main trading commodity or raw material of a region.

staple[4] adj **1** depended on as basic. **2** main.

star[1] n **1** a gaseous body that radiates energy and is visible as a point of light in the night sky. **2** a stylized figure with five or more points that represents a star. **3** a famous entertainer, performer, or sports personality. **4** the leading or

outstanding performer in a group. **5** informal a kind of generous person. > **stardom** n.

star[2] v (**starred, starring**) **1** of a film, play, etc: to feature (a certain star) in a leading role. **2** to play a leading role in a production. **3** to mark with a star or asterisk.

starboard n the right side of a ship or aircraft looking forward.

starch[1] n **1** a carbohydrate that is an important foodstuff, obtained chiefly from cereals and potatoes. **2** a powder or spray used to stiffen fabric.

starch[2] v to stiffen (clothes or fabric) with starch.

starchy adj (**-ier, -iest**) **1** of foods or other substances: containing a lot of starch. **2** of somebody's manner, etc: stiff and formal.

stare[1] v to look fixedly, often with wide-open eyes. * **stare somebody in the face** of a solution, etc: to be only too obvious.

stare[2] n a staring look or expression.

starfish n (pl **starfishes** or **starfish**) a sea creature with a body consisting of a central disc surrounded by five equally spaced arms.

stark adj **1** of a landscape, surroundings, etc: bleak or bare; desolate. **2** harshly clear or plain. **3** sheer; utter. > **starkly** adv.

starkers adj Brit, informal completely naked.

stark-naked adj completely naked.

starlet n a young film actress being coached for starring roles.

starling n a gregarious bird with glossy greenish black plumage.

starry adj (**-ier, -iest**) **1** of the sky: studded with stars. **2** informal relating to the stars of the entertainment world.

starry-eyed adj naively idealistic or over-optimistic.

starship n in science fiction, a large spaceship for interstellar journeys.

start[1] v **1** to come into operation or existence. **2** to begin functioning or moving, or to make (something) do this. **3** to begin (an activity or undertaking). **4** to cause (somebody) to do something. **5** to range from a specified amount: *Prices start from £300.* **6** to move suddenly or violently, esp as a result of shock or surprise. * **to start with** as the first thing to be considered.

start[2] n **1** the beginning of a movement, activity, journey, etc. **2** a starting place, e.g. for a race. **3** a lead conceded to a competitor at the start of a race. **4** a sudden involuntary bodily movement, e.g. from surprise or alarm. * **for a start** in the first place.

starter n **1** the person who gives the signal to start a race. **2** an automatic device that activates machinery, esp a vehicle engine. **3** chiefly Brit (also in pl) the first course of a meal. * **for starters** chiefly Brit, informal in the first place.

startle v to cause (somebody) to start in alarm, etc. ➤ **startled** adj, **startling** adj.

start off v to begin talking, operating, etc, or to cause (somebody or something) to do this.

start out v to begin a journey or undertaking.

start up v **1** to begin to operate, or cause (e.g. an engine) to begin to operate. **2** to begin a commercial undertaking. ➤ **start-up** n and adj.

starve v **1** to suffer severely or die from hunger. **2** to cause (a person or animal) to suffer from or to die of hunger. **3** informal to be ravenous. **4** (+ of) to deprive of. ➤ **starvation** n.

stash[1] v informal (often + away) to store in a secret place for future use.

stash[2] n informal a secret store of drugs, weapons, etc.

stasis n (pl **stases**) a state of static balance without activity or change; stagnation.

state[1] n **1** the condition or situation of somebody or something. **2** a politically organized community usu occupying a definite territory. **3** the operations or concerns of the central government of a country. **4** a constituent unit of a nation having a federal government. **5** (**the States**) the United States of America. **6** (**a state**) informal an upset, confused, or dirty condition. * **state of affairs** (also **state of things**) a situation. **state of emergency** a situation involving national danger or extreme disaster, during which the government assumes special powers. **state of play 1** Brit the current score in a cricket or football match. **2** Brit the current situation.

state[2] v to declare formally.

stately adj (**-ier, -iest**) imposing; dignified.

stately home n Brit a large country residence, usu of historical or architectural interest and open to the public.

statement n **1** a declaration or account of something given orally or in writing. **2** a summary of a financial account. **3** an account of events given to the police or in court.

state-of-the-art adj using the most advanced technology available.

statesman or **stateswoman** n (pl **statesmen** or **stateswomen**) an experienced and respected political leader.

static[1] adj characterized by a lack of movement, animation, or change. ➤ **statically** adv.

static[2] n **1** electrical disturbances causing unwanted signals in a radio or television system; atmospherics. **2** ≈ STATIC ELECTRICITY.

static electricity n an electrical charge built up, e.g. by friction, in a material from which it cannot be conducted away.

station[1] n **1** a regular or major stopping place for trains. **2** the place or position in which something or somebody stands or is placed. **3** standing; rank. **4** a place established to provide a public service. **5** an establishment equipped for radio or television transmission or reception. **6** a radio or television channel.

station[2] v to assign to a post or station.

stationary adj **1** having a fixed position; immobile. **2** neither progressing nor deteriorating.

Usage Note: Do not confuse this word with stationery.

stationer n a shopkeeper who deals in stationery.

stationery n paper, envelopes, and other materials used for writing, typing, etc.

Usage Note: Do not confuse this word with stationary.

stationmaster n an official in charge of a railway station.

station wagon n NAmer an estate car.

statistic n a single term or quantity from a collection of statistics.

statistical adj relating to or produced from statistics. ➤ **statistically** adv.

statistics pl n **1** a branch of mathematics dealing with the collection and analysis of masses of numerical data. **2** (treated as pl) a collection of numerical data relating to a subject. ➤ **statistician** n.

statuary n statues collectively.

statue n a likeness, e.g. of a person or animal, sculptured or modelled in a solid material.

statuesque adj tall, well-proportioned, and stately.

statuette n a small statue.

stature n **1** the natural height of a person when standing upright. **2** standing or reputation.

status n **1** the legal condition or standing of a person, territory, etc. **2** position in relation to others in a hierarchy or social structure. **3** prestige. **4** the state of affairs.

status quo n the existing state of affairs.

status symbol n a possession recognized as indicating high social status or wealth.

statute n **1** a law passed by a legislative body. **2** any of the permanent rules of an organization.

statutory adj **1** established, regulated, or imposed by statute. **2** informal standard; usual or expected. ➤ **statutorily** adv.

staunch[1] (NAmer **stanch**) v to stop the flow of (blood, etc).

staunch[2] adj steadfast in loyalty or principle. ➤ **staunchly** adv.

stave[1] n **1** an iron pole or wooden stick. **2** any of the narrow strips of wood placed edge to edge to form a barrel, bucket, etc. **3** a set of five horizontal spaced lines on which music is written.

stave[2] v (past tense and past part. **staved** or **stove**) (+ in) to crush or break (a hard casing, etc) inward.

stave off *v (past tense and past part.* **staved off)** to ward or fend off (a threatening danger), *esp* temporarily.

stay¹ *v* **1** to remain in a place and not move. **2** to remain in a particular state and not change. **3** to reside temporarily somewhere. **4** to delay or prevent (a judicial procedure, such as an execution). * **stay put** to stay where placed or left.

stay² *n* **1** a period of residing at a place. **2** the suspension of a judicial procedure.

stay³ *n* **1** *literary* somebody or something that serves as a prop or support. **2** *(in pl)* formerly, a corset stiffened with bones.

staying power *n informal* stamina.

stead *n* * **in somebody's or something's stead** in place of somebody or something else. **stand somebody in good stead** to be an advantage to somebody.

steadfast *adj* loyal or unwavering. ➤ **steadfastly** *adv.*

steady¹ *adj* (-**ier, -iest**) **1** firmly positioned or balanced; not shaking, rocking, etc. **2** showing, or continuing with, little variation or fluctuation. **3** not easily moved or upset. **4** constant and dependable; consistent; not erratic. ➤ **steadily** *adv,* **steadiness** *n.*

steady² *v* (-**ies, -ied**) to become or make steady.

steady³ *adv* * **go steady** *informal* to have a long-term relationship with a boyfriend or girlfriend. **steady on!** used to tell somebody to calm down.

steak *n* **1** a lean high-quality slice of meat, *esp* beef, suitable for grilling or frying. **2** poorer-quality beef suitable for braising or stewing. **3** a cross-sectional slice of a large fish.

steal¹ *v* (**stole, stolen**) **1** to take (something) without permission or illegally, with no intention of returning it. **2** to take (a look, etc) surreptitiously. **3** to come or go stealthily or unobtrusively. * **steal a march on** to gain an advantage over (somebody) by stealthy or underhand means. **steal the show** to make a bigger impression than other ostensibly more prominent participants.

steal² *n informal* a bargain.

stealth¹ *n* caution and surreptitiousness in movement or activity.

stealth² *adj* denoting *esp* aircraft designed to be able to avoid radar detection.

stealthy *adj* (-**ier, -iest**) characterized by stealth. ➤ **stealthily** *adv.*

steam¹ *n* **1** the vapour into which water is converted when boiled. **2** the mist formed when water vapour condenses. **3** energy or power generated by steam under pressure. * **let off/blow off steam** *informal* to release one's pent-up energy, emotional tension, etc. **under one's own steam** independently.

steam² *v* **1** to give off steam. **2** to move by means of steam power. **3** *informal* to move or

progress quickly. **4** (+ up) to become covered with steam. **5** to cook (food) in steam from boiling water. **6** to clean or press using steam. * **get steamed up** *informal* to get angry or agitated.

steamboat *n* a boat propelled by steam power.

steam engine *n* a stationary or locomotive engine driven by steam.

steamroll *v* = STEAMROLLER².

steamroller¹ *n* a machine equipped with wide heavy rollers for compacting newly laid road surfaces, etc.

steamroller² *v* (**steamrollered, steamrollering**) **1** to force acceptance of (a law, etc) by crushing opposition or curtailing discussion. **2** to force (somebody) into doing something.

steamy *adj* (-**ier, -iest**) **1** full of steam. **2** hot and humid. **3** *informal* portraying sexual activity.

steed *n archaic or literary* a horse.

steel¹ *n* **1** an alloy of iron with carbon, notable for its strength and hardness. **2** cold hardness or unyielding strength.

steel² *v* to nerve (oneself) to do something.

steel band *n* a band that plays instruments made from empty oil drums.

steel wool *n* steel fibres used for scouring and burnishing.

steelworks *pl n* a factory where steel is made.

steely *adj* (-**ier, -iest**) **1** resembling steel. **2** unyielding; relentless.

steep¹ *adj* **1** sloping sharply, or nearly vertical. **2** of a rise or fall in an amount, level, etc: substantial and rapid. **3** *informal* of a price: unreasonably high. **4** *informal* excessive. ➤ **steeply** *adv.*

steep² *v* **1** to soak or be soaked in a liquid. **2** (*usu* **be steeped in**) to be thoroughly imbued with.

steepen *v* to become or make steeper.

steeple *n* a church tower with a spire.

steeplechase *n* **1** a horse race over a racecourse with hedges and ditches for jumping. **2** a middle-distance running race over obstacles. ➤ **steeplechaser** *n,* **steeplechasing** *n.*

steeplejack *n* a person who climbs chimneys, towers, etc to paint or repair them.

steer¹ *v* **1** to guide or control the course of (a vehicle or ship). **2** to guide (somebody or something) in a certain direction. * **steer clear of** to keep well away from. ➤ **steering** *n.*

steer² *n* a bullock.

steerage *n* formerly, the section of a passenger ship for passengers paying the lowest fares.

steering wheel *n* a wheel that is turned by a driver or helmsman to steer a motor vehicle, ship, etc.

steersman *n* (*pl* **steersmen**) a helmsman.

stegosaurus /stegə'sawrəs/ *n* a large dinosaur with projecting bony plates along its back.

stellar *adj* relating to a star or stars.

stem n **1** the main stalk or trunk of a plant or shrub. **2** the slender stalk of a flower, leaf, or fruit. **3** the main unchanging part of a word. **4** a vertical stroke of a letter or musical note. **5** the tube of a tobacco pipe. **6** the slender support between the base and bowl of a wineglass. ✻ **from stem to stern** of a ship: from end to end.

stench n a stink.

stencil[1] n a sheet of e.g. paper or metal, perforated with a design or lettering through which ink or paint is forced onto the surface below.

stencil[2] v (**stencilled, stencilling,** NAmer **stenciled, stenciling**) **1** to produce (a design, etc) by means of a stencil. **2** to decorate (a surface) with a stencil.

stenography n the writing and transcription of shorthand. ➤ **stenographer** n, **stenographic** adj.

stentorian adj of a person's voice: extremely loud.

step[1] n **1** a movement made by raising one foot and bringing it down in front of the other in walking. **2** the space passed over in one step. **3** a short distance. **4** a flat supporting surface for the foot in ascending or descending. **5** (in pl) a stepladder. **6** a level or grade in a scale. **7** a stage in the progress of something. **8** an action, proceeding, or measure.

step[2] v (**stepped, stepping**) to move by raising one foot and bringing it down in front of the other, or in another position. ✻ **step aside 1** to stand clear of something. **2** to resign from a position. **step back** to distance oneself from a situation in order to assess it more objectively. **step forward** to volunteer one's services. **step on it/the gas** informal to drive or move faster; to hurry up. **step out of line** to fail to conform.

stepbrother n a son of one's stepparent by a former marriage.

stepchild n (pl **stepchildren**) a child of one's wife or husband by a former marriage.

stepdaughter n a daughter of one's wife or husband by a former marriage.

step down v to retire or resign.

stepfather n the husband of one's mother by a subsequent marriage.

step in v **1** to intervene. **2** to take somebody's place for a time.

stepladder n a hinged ladder with flat rungs and often a platform.

stepmother n the wife of one's father by a subsequent marriage.

stepparent n the husband or wife of one's parent by a subsequent marriage.

steppe n a vast grassy treeless plain, esp in southeastern Europe or Asia.

stepping stone n **1** a stone on which to step when crossing a stream. **2** something regarded as a means of progress or advancement.

stepsister n a daughter of one's stepparent by a former marriage.

stepson n a son of one's wife or husband by a former marriage.

step up v to increase the amount, speed, or intensity of.

stereo[1] n (pl **-os**) **1** stereophonic sound. **2** a stereophonic record-player, etc.

stereo[2] adj stereophonic.

stereophonic adj denoting a sound system using two different channels to give spatial effect.

stereotype[1] n a standardized simplistic image of a person or thing. ➤ **stereotypical** adj.

stereotype[2] v to represent (a person or thing) as a stereotype.

sterile adj **1** unable to produce young, seeds, or crops. **2** deficient in ideas or originality. **3** free from living organisms, esp micro-organisms. ➤ **sterility** n.

sterilize or **-ise** v to make sterile. ➤ **sterilization** n.

sterling[1] n British money.

sterling[2] adj **1** of a person's character or efforts: of genuine worth or quality. **2** of silver: at least 92.25% pure.

stern[1] adj **1** harsh, strict, or severe. **2** firm; uncompromising. ➤ **sternly** adv.

stern[2] n the rear end of a ship.

sternum n (pl **sternums** or **sterna**) the breastbone.

steroid n **1** a chemical compound of a class characterized by a ring of carbon atoms and including various hormones. **2** an anabolic steroid.

stertorous adj of breathing: characterized by a harsh snoring or gasping sound.

stethoscope n an instrument used to detect and study sounds produced in the body, esp by the heart and lungs.

Stetson n NAmer trademark a broad-brimmed high-crowned felt hat.

stevedore n a person employed to load and unload ships.

stew[1] n **1** a dish of meat, vegetables, or both, cooked in liquid in a closed pan. **2** informal an agitated state.

stew[2] v **1** to cook (meat, fruit, etc) in liquid in a closed vessel. **2** of tea: to become strong and bitter from prolonged brewing. **3** informal to be in a state of agitation. ✻ **stew in one's own juice** informal to suffer the consequences of one's own stupidity.

steward n **1** a person who attends to the needs of passengers on an airliner, ship, etc. **2** a person who supervises the provision of food and drink in a club, college, etc. **3** an official in charge of arrangements or crowd-control at a large public event. **4** a person employed to manage a large house or estate. ➤ **stewardship** n.

stewardess n a woman who attends to the needs of passengers on an airliner, ship, etc.

stick[1] n 1 a twig or slender branch from a tree or shrub. 2 a club or staff used as a weapon; a stave. 3 a walking stick. 4 an implement used for striking or propelling a ball or other object in a game. 5 something prepared in a long, slender, often cylindrical form. 6 the threat of punishment as a means of obtaining compliance. 7 informal critical disapproving comment. 8 (**the sticks**) informal, derog remote or backward rural areas.

stick[2] v (past tense and past part. **stuck**) 1 (often + into) of something sharp or pointed: to be fixed in something. 2 to thrust (a sharp or pointed object) into or through something. 3 informal to poke (something) somewhere. 4 informal to put somewhere, esp temporarily. 5 to attach (one thing) to another with adhesive. 6 (often + to) to adhere or become fixed or attached to a surface, etc. 7 to become fixed or unable to move. 8 chiefly Brit, informal to bear or stand (a person or thing). 9 to protrude or project. 10 (+ at) to persist at a task, etc. 11 (+ with) to persevere with something. 12 (+ to) not to deviate from something. ✳ **be stuck 1** to be unable to move. 2 to be unable to solve a problem, finish a task, etc. **be stuck for** to lack or need. **be stuck on** informal to be infatuated with. **be stuck with** informal to be unable to escape from. **get stuck in/into** informal to involve oneself wholeheartedly in a task, etc. **stick by** 1 to continue to support (somebody). 2 to honour (a promise, etc). **stick one's neck out** informal to take an initiative or risk that leaves one vulnerable. **stick together** to continue to support each other; to remain united.

stick around v informal to linger somewhere.

sticker n an adhesive label or notice.

stick insect n an insect with a long thin body resembling a stick.

stickleback n a small fish with spines on its back.

stickler n a person who insists on things being done exactly right.

stick out v 1 to jut out; to project. 2 to be prominent or conspicuous. ✳ **stick it out** informal to endure something to the end. **stick out for** to insist on or persist in demanding.

stick up v to stand upright or on end; to protrude. ✳ **stick up for** to defend against attack or criticism.

sticky adj (-**ier**, -**iest**) 1 adhesive. 2 viscous; gluey. 3 coated with a sticky substance. 4 of the weather: humid or muggy. 5 sweaty or clammy. 6 difficult; problematic. ✳ **come to a sticky end** informal to meet with ruin, disaster, a nasty death, etc.

stiff[1] adj 1 not easily bent. 2 of a handle, lock, etc: hard to operate or turn. 3 of the body or a part of it: not moving freely, or painful to move as a result e.g. of intensive exercise. 4 of a mixture: thick. 5 of social relations: not relaxed and friendly. 6 lacking in ease or grace. 7 of an alcoholic drink: strong. 8 of a punishment: harsh or severe. ✳ **a stiff upper lip** a stoical, dry-eyed self-control. ➤ **stiffly** adv, **stiffness** n.

stiff[2] n informal a corpse.

stiffen v to make or become stiff. ➤ **stiffener** n.

stifle v 1 to prevent (a person or animal) from breathing freely or suffocate (them). 2 to sup press (a yawn, a giggle, etc). 3 to curb or repress.

stifling adj uncomfortably hot and stuffy. ➤ **stiflingly** adv.

stigma n (pl **stigmas** or **stigmata**) 1 a connotation of disgrace associated with certain things. 2 (pl **stigmata**) (in pl) in Christianity, marks on a person resembling those left on Christ's body by the Crucifixion. 3 the part of a flower that receives the pollen.

stigmatize or -**ise** v (often + as) to describe or categorize in disapproving terms. ➤ **stigmatization** n.

stile n a step or set of steps for climbing over a fence or wall.

stiletto n (pl -**os** or -**oes**) 1 a slender rodlike dagger. 2 Brit an extremely narrow tapering high heel on a woman's shoe.

still[1] adj 1 not moving. 2 calm or tranquil. 3 of drinks: not fizzy. ➤ **stillness** n.

still[2] v to make calm or quiet.

still[3] adv 1 as before: Drink it while it's still hot. 2 in spite of that; nevertheless. 3 even; yet.

still[4] n 1 a still photograph, esp a single frame from a cinema film. 2 quiet; silence.

still[5] n an apparatus used in distillation, esp of spirits.

stillborn adj of a baby: dead at birth.

still life n (pl **still lifes**) a picture showing an arrangement of inanimate objects, e.g. fruit or flowers.

stilt n 1 either of two poles with a footrest, which enable the user to walk along above the ground. 2 any of a set of posts that support a building above ground or water level.

stilted adj of writing or speech: stiffly formal and unnatural.

Stilton n a strong variety of cheese, either white or with blue veins.

stimulant n something, e.g. a drug, that stimulates.

stimulate v 1 to cause (a physiological process) to take place, or increase the activity of (an organ). 2 to provoke increased activity or interest in (somebody). ➤ **stimulation** n.

stimulus n (pl **stimuli**) 1 something, e.g. an environmental change, that directly influences the activity of living organisms, e.g. by exciting a sensory organ. 2 an incentive or inducement.

sting[1] v (*past tense and past part.* **stung**) **1** *esp* of a plant or insect: to give an irritating or poisonous wound to. **2** of a part of the body: to smart. **3** to cause a pang of bitterness or pain in.

sting[2] n **1** a sharp organ in certain plants or insects that can wound by piercing and injecting a poisonous secretion. **2** a wound or pain caused by stinging. ✳ **a sting in the tail** a telling and unexpected climax to a story, etc.

stingray n a ray with a whiplike tail bearing a long poisonous spine.

stingy adj (**-ier, -iest**) *informal* mean or ungenerous.

stink[1] v (*past tense* **stank** *or* **stunk**, *past part.* **stunk**) **1** to give off a strong offensive smell. **2** *informal* to be highly suspect or very bad. ➣ **stinker** n.

stink[2] n **1** a strong offensive smell. **2** *informal* a row or scandal.

stinking[1] adj *informal* **1** severe and unpleasant. **2** having a strong offensive smell.

stinking[2] adv *informal* extremely: *stinking rich*.

stint[1] v **1** to restrict (somebody) to a small share. **2** (*often* + on) to be sparing or frugal.

stint[2] n one's quota or round of duty or work.

stipend n a fixed sum of money paid periodically as a salary or to meet expenses.

stipendiary adj receiving a stipend, as distinct from working voluntarily.

stipple v **1** to dapple, speckle, or fleck. **2** to texture or roughen (a painted or cemented surface).

stipulate v to specify as a condition of an agreement or offer. ➣ **stipulation** n.

stir[1] v (**stirred, stirring**) **1** to move (a liquid or semiliquid) around by repeated circular movement with a spoon, etc, usu in order to blend the ingredients. **2** to make a slight movement. **3** to wake and begin to move. **4** (*often* + up) to rouse (somebody) to activity. **5** *Brit, informal* to create trouble or ill-feeling between people by gossip, tale-bearing, etc. ➣ **stirrer** n.

stir[2] n **1** the act or an instance of stirring. **2** a sensation or commotion.

stir[3] n *informal* prison.

stir-fry v (**-ies, -ied**) to cook (small pieces of food) by stirring them together while frying them rapidly.

stirring adj rousing; inspiring. ➣ **stirringly** adv.

stirrup n either of a pair of D-shaped metal frames attached to a saddle in which a horse-rider's feet are placed.

stitch[1] n **1** a loop of thread or yarn left in material by a single in-and-out movement of the needle in sewing, embroidery, knitting, or crochet. **2** a method of stitching. **3** a sharp and sudden pain in the side brought on by running or exercise. ✳ **in stitches** laughing uncontrollably.

stitch[2] v to sew (fabric, a garment, etc).

stitch up v *informal* to incriminate maliciously.

stoa n (pl **stoas** or **stoae**) in classical Greek architecture, a portico, roofed colonnade, or colonnaded walk.

stoat n (pl **stoats** or **stoat**) a European weasel with a brown coat that turns white in winter in northern regions.

stock[1] n **1** a store or supply of raw materials or finished goods. **2** (*also in pl*) one's store or supply of anything. **3** farm animals. **4** the capital raised by a company through selling shares. **5** (*in pl*) the shares of a particular company or type of company. **6** the liquid in which meat, fish, or vegetables have been simmered. **7** the trunk or main stem of a plant. **8** a plant grown for its sweet-scented flowers. **9** a person's line of descent. **10** a breed or variety of a plant or animal. **11** (*in pl*) formerly, a wooden frame with holes in which an offender's feet could be locked as a public punishment. ✳ **in stock** in the shop or warehouse and available for delivery. **out of stock** sold out; having none available for delivery. **take stock** to review a situation.

stock[2] v **1** to supply (a place) with a stock of something. **2** to start or keep a stock of (something). ✳ **stock up** (*often* + on) to lay in a supply of something.

stock[3] adj *informal* commonly used; standard.

stockade n a line of stout posts set vertically to form an enclosure or a defensive barrier.

stockbroker n a broker who buys and sells securities. ➣ **stockbroking** n.

stock car n a strengthened assembly-line car used in races where drivers try to force each other off the track.

stock exchange n a stock market or the building housing it.

stocking n **1** a woman's closely fitting garment for the foot and leg. **2** *NAmer or archaic* a man's long sock. **3** (*also* **Christmas stocking**) an ornamental stocking hung up by children on Christmas Eve, to be filled with presents. ➣ **stockinged** adj.

stock-in-trade n **1** the equipment used in a trade or business. **2** the range of skills habitually used by an individual in an activity.

stockist n *Brit* a retailer who stocks goods of a particular kind.

stock market n a market where brokers buy and sell stocks and shares, or the transactions made there.

stockpile[1] n a reserve supply of something essential for use during a shortage.

stockpile[2] v to accumulate a stockpile of (an essential commodity, etc).

stock-still adv completely motionless.

stocktaking n the process of taking an inventory of goods or supplies held e.g. in a shop.

stocky adj (**-ier, -iest**) *esp* of a person: short and sturdy.

stodge n *chiefly Brit, informal* heavy filling starchy food, such as steamed pudding. ➤ **stodgy** *adj.*

stoic n a stoical person.

stoical *adj* bearing pain, hardship, and sorrow without complaining. ➤ **stoically** *adv.*

stoke v 1 to supply (a fire or furnace) with fuel. 2 to feed or encourage (an emotion). ➤ **stoker** n.

stole[1] v past tense of STEAL[1].

stole[2] n a large rectangular scarf or shawl worn by women across the shoulders.

stolen v past part. of STEAL[1].

stolid *adj* difficult to arouse emotionally or mentally. ➤ **stolidity** n, **stolidly** *adv.*

stomach[1] n 1 a saclike internal organ in which the first stages of digestion occur. 2 the part of the body that contains the stomach; the belly or abdomen. 3 appetite or inclination.

stomach[2] v 1 to find (food) palatable or digestible. 2 to bear (something irksome) without protest.

stomp v *informal* to walk or dance with a heavy step.

stone[1] n 1 the hard mineral matter of which rock is composed. 2 a piece of rock; a pebble. 3 a gem. 4 a piece of stone adapted to a particular function, e.g. a gravestone. 5 the hard seed in a peach, cherry, plum, etc. 6 (pl usu **stone**) *Brit* a unit of weight equal to 14 pounds (about 6.35 kilograms). * **a stone's throw** no very great distance. **leave no stone unturned** to make every possible effort to find or obtain something.

stone[2] v 1 to hurl stones at. 2 to remove the stones or seeds of (a fruit).

stone[3] *adv* completely: *stone deaf.*

Stone Age n (the Stone Age) the first known period of prehistoric human culture characterized by the use of stone tools.

stoned *adj informal* intoxicated by a drug, e.g. marijuana, or alcohol.

stonewall v 1 to be evasive or obstructive. 2 *chiefly Brit* to bat very defensively in cricket.

stony *adj* (-ier, -iest) 1 full of stones. 2 resembling stone. 3 cold or unresponsive. ➤ **stonily** *adv.*

stood v past tense and past part. of STAND[1].

stooge n 1 a person being used by somebody more powerful to do distasteful jobs. 2 the member of a comedy duo who is the butt of the other's jokes.

stool n 1 a seat usu without back or arms. 2 *esp* in medicine, a discharge of faecal matter. * **fall between two stools** to fail to fit into either of two categories or avail oneself of either of two possibilities.

stool pigeon n *chiefly NAmer* a police informer.

stoop[1] v 1 to bend the body forward and downward. 2 to lower oneself morally.

stoop[2] n a stooping position or posture.

stop[1] v (**stopped, stopping**) 1 to come or bring to an end. 2 to discontinue moving. 3 of a bus or train: to call at a place to take on or let off passengers. 4 to prevent from doing or continuing something. 5 to prevent from happening. 6 to cease or discontinue (an activity). 7 to block or plug (a leak, opening, etc). * **stop at nothing** to be unscrupulous in achieving one's ends. **stop dead** to come to a sudden halt.

stop[2] n 1 the act of stopping. 2 a place where a train or bus halts to let passengers on or off. 3 a device or mechanism that prevents movement. 4 a knob on an organ that brings a particular set of pipes into play. * **pull out all the stops** to do everything possible to achieve something. **put a stop to something** to prevent something from continuing.

stopcock n a valve for stopping or regulating flow, e.g. of fluid through a pipe.

stopgap n a temporary expedient; a makeshift.

stop off or **stop over** v to break one's journey somewhere, *esp* overnight.

stoppage n 1 an act of stopping. 2 a blockage. 3 a cessation of work by a group of employees as a form of industrial action. 4 *Brit* a deduction from pay for National Insurance, etc.

stopper[1] n a plug or bung.

stopper[2] v to close or secure with a stopper.

stop press n late news added to a newspaper after printing has begun.

stop up v 1 to block (a hole, passage, etc). 2 *Brit, informal* to delay going to bed until late.

stopwatch n a watch that can be started and stopped at will for exact timing of races, etc.

storage n 1 the act of storing. 2 space available for storing things.

storage heater n *Brit* an electric device that stores heat at night, when electricity is cheap, and radiates it during the daytime.

store[1] v 1 (*often* + up/away) to keep or accumulate as a reserve supply. 2 to place (property, furniture, etc) in a warehouse, etc for later use or disposal. 3 to enter (data) in a computer memory, on a diskette, etc, for future access.

store[2] n 1 a quantity of things kept for future use. 2 (*in pl*) in the armed forces, etc, a supply of food, equipment, ammunition, etc. 3 a collection or accumulation. 4 storage. 5 (*also* **department store**) a large shop selling a variety of goods. 6 *NAmer* a shop. * **in store** awaiting one in the future. **set store by something** to regard something as important and worthwhile.

storey (*NAmer* **story**) n (pl **-eys** or *NAmer* **-ies**) a horizontal division or level of a building.

stork n a large wading bird with a long stout bill and black and white plumage.

storm[1] n 1 a violent disturbance of the weather marked by high winds and usu by rain, thunder and lightning, etc. 2 a tumultuous outburst.

✻ **storm in a teacup** a disproportionate fuss about something relatively minor.

storm² v **1** to shout angrily; to rage. **2** to rush furiously. **3** of troops: to make a sudden violent attack on (a place) to capture it.

storm troops pl n = SHOCK TROOPS.

stormy adj (-ier, -iest) **1** wild, windy, or characterized by storms. **2** full of turmoil or fury.

story¹ n (pl -ies) **1** an account of real or imaginary events. **2** the plot of a literary or dramatic work. **3** a rumour. **4** a lie. **5** a news article or broadcast.

story² n (pl -ies) NAmer see STOREY.

stoup n a basin for holy water at the entrance of a church.

stout¹ adj **1** heavily built; fat. **2** strong and thick. **3** bold and brave. ➤ **stoutly** adv.

stout² n a dark sweet heavy-bodied beer.

stove¹ n **1** an enclosed appliance that burns fuel for heating. **2** a cooker.

stove² v a past tense and past part. of STAVE².

stow v to pack away in an orderly fashion in an enclosed space.

stowaway n a person who stows away, esp on a ship.

stow away v to hide on board esp a ship, as a means of travelling without payment or undetected.

straddle v **1** to stand, sit, or be astride. **2** to be on land on either side of.

strafe v to attack (ground troops, etc) with fire from low-flying aircraft.

straggle v **1** to lag behind or stray away from a body of people going somewhere together. **2** to grow or spread untidily. ➤ **straggler** n, **straggly** adj.

straight¹ adj **1** extending in one direction without bends or curves. **2** level, upright, or symmetrically positioned; not skew. **3** in a proper or tidy state. **4** honest or fair. **5** clear, simple, or logical. **6** candid; frank; not evasive. **7** of successes: following consecutively or uninterruptedly. **8** of an alcoholic drink: unmixed; neat. **9** informal conventional in appearance, habits, opinions, etc. **10** informal heterosexual. ✻ **keep a straight face** to refrain from laughing.

straight² adv **1** directly; in a straight line. **2** without delay or hesitation. ✻ **go straight** to leave one's life of crime and live honestly. **straight off/out** without hesitation.

straight³ n a straight part or piece of something, esp a racetrack.

straightaway or **straight away** adv immediately.

straighten v to make or become straight.

straightforward adj **1** truthful and direct. **2** presenting no hidden difficulties. ➤ **straightforwardly** adv.

straightjacket n see STRAITJACKET.

straightlaced adj see STRAITLACED.

strain¹ v **1** to exert (a part of one's body) to the maximum. **2** to wrench or sprain (a part of one's body) through over-exertion. **3** to make great or excessive demands on. **4** to pass (a liquid) through a sieve or filter.

strain² n **1** a pulling or stretching force exerted on something. **2** a great demand on one's strength, resources, etc. **3** mental or emotional stress. **4** an injury caused by excessive tension, effort, or use. **5** (also in pl) a tune or passage of music.

strain³ n **1** a breed or variety of an animal or plant. **2** an inherited but not dominant characteristic, quality, or disposition.

strained adj **1** done or produced with excessive effort; not spontaneous. **2** tense; uneasy. **3** showing the effects of strain.

strainer n a device, e.g. a sieve, to retain solid pieces while a liquid passes through.

strait n **1** (also in pl) a narrow channel connecting two large bodies of water. **2** (in pl) a situation of difficulty or distress.

straitened adj poverty-stricken or necessitating severe economies.

straitjacket or **straightjacket** n **1** an outer garment of strong material used to bind the arms of a violent prisoner or psychiatric patient. **2** something very restrictive or confining.

straitlaced or **straightlaced** adj excessively strict in manners or morals.

strand¹ v **1** to cause (a ship or whale) to run aground on a shore. **2** to leave (a person) in a strange place without the means to leave it.

strand² n literary a shore or beach.

strand³ n **1** any of the threads, strings, or wires twisted to make a cord, rope, etc. **2** any of the elements interwoven in a complex whole.

strange adj **1** not known, heard, seen, or visited before. **2** exciting wonder or surprise. ➤ **strangely** adv.

stranger n **1** a person with whom one is unacquainted. **2** a person unfamiliar in the place in question.

strangle v **1** to choke (a person or animal), esp to death, by compressing their throat. **2** to hinder the development of (something). ➤ **strangler** n.

stranglehold n **1** a grip round the neck that can lead to strangulation. **2** a total control or monopoly of something.

strangulation n the act of strangling.

strap¹ n **1** a strip of flexible material used for fastening, securing, holding together, or carrying. **2** (the strap) punishment by beating with a leather strap. ➤ **strapless** adj, **strappy** adj.

strap² v (strapped, strapping) to secure with or attach by a strap.

strapping adj of a person: big, strong, and sturdy.

stratagem n a scheme for deceiving and outwitting an opponent.

strategic adj **1** relating to the long-term pursuit of objectives. **2** relating to military effectiveness. **3** of weapons, missiles, etc: designed to attack the enemy homeland, rather than for use on the battlefield. ➤ **strategically** adv.

strategy n (pl -**ies**) **1** military planning on a broad scale for the conduct of a campaign or battle: compare TACTICS. **2** long-term planning in the pursuit of objectives. **3** a plan or method devised to achieve a long-term objective. ➤ **strategist** n.

stratify v (-**ies, -ied**) to form, deposit, or arrange (material, etc) in strata. ➤ **stratification** n.

stratosphere n **1** the layer of the earth's atmosphere above the troposphere at a height of 10–50 km. **2** informal the highest levels of something. ➤ **stratospheric** adj.

stratum n (pl **strata**) **1** a horizontal layer or series of layers of rock. **2** a socioeconomic level of society.

straw n **1** dry stalks of grain, used for bedding, thatching, fodder, etc. **2** a single stalk of grain. **3** a tube of paper, plastic, etc for sucking up a drink. **4** a pale yellow colour. ✷ **catch/clutch/grasp at straws** to turn in desperation to any means of saving the situation. **draw the short straw** to be the person chosen to do something unpleasant. **the last straw** the last of a series of misfortunes, which makes a situation unbearable.

strawberry n (pl -**ies**) a small sweet red fruit covered with seeds.

strawberry blonde n a reddish blonde hair colour.

straw poll n an unofficial test of opinion.

stray[1] v **1** to wander away from the main group, or from the proper place or route. **2** of an eye or hand: to move apparently casually in some direction.

stray[2] adj **1** of a domestic animal: having strayed; lost. **2** not in the proper place. **3** occurring at random or sporadically.

streak[1] n **1** a line or band of a different colour from the background. **2** an inherent quality, esp in somebody's character: a mean streak. **3** a series of successes, failures, etc.

streak[2] v **1** to make streaks on or in. **2** to move swiftly. **3** informal to run naked through a public place. ➤ **streaked** n, **streaking** n.

streaky adj (-**ier, -iest**) **1** marked with streaks. **2** of bacon: having lines of fat and lean.

stream[1] n **1** a body of running water, smaller and narrower than a river. **2** an unbroken flow, procession, or succession, e.g. of gas, traffic, or people. **3** Brit a group to which schoolchildren of the same age are assigned according to their general academic ability. ✷ **on/off stream** operational or available/not so.

stream[2] v **1** to flow in a stream, or in large quantities. **2** to trail or extend in a trail. **3** to run profusely with liquid. **4** Brit to divide (a school or an age group of pupils) into streams.

streamer n **1** a coiled strip of coloured paper for throwing at a party. **2** a pennant.

streamline v **1** to design (a vehicle, etc) so as to minimize resistance to motion, e.g. through air. **2** to make (an organization) simpler or more efficient.

street n a public road in a city, town, or village. ✷ **on the streets** earning one's living as a prostitute. **streets ahead/better** informal immeasurably better. **up/down one's street** suited to one's abilities or tastes.

streetcar n NAmer a tram.

streetwalker n a prostitute who solicits in the streets.

streetwise adj informal resourceful at surviving and prospering in modern urban conditions.

strength n **1** the physical power one has in one's body. **2** in a material object: ability to withstand pressure, prolonged use, etc. **3** the intensity of something. **4** the number of people who belong to or are needed for a particular type of group. **5** a good point. ✷ **go from strength to strength** to become ever more successful. **on the strength of** on the basis of (something).

strengthen v to make or become stronger.

strenuous adj **1** vigorous and wholehearted. **2** requiring effort or stamina. ➤ **strenuously** adv.

stress[1] n **1** pressure exerted on a physical object. **2** mental or emotional tension. **3** emphasis given to a syllable, word, etc. **4** relative importance attached to an idea, fact, etc.

stress[2] v **1** to emphasize (a point, etc). **2** to accent or emphasize (a word, syllable, etc). **3** (usu in passive, also + out) to subject to emotional or mental stress.

stressful adj causing mental or emotional tension.

stretch[1] v **1** to pull or extend (material) till it becomes taut. **2** of material, garments, etc: to have an elastic quality. **3** of materials, garments, etc: to become permanently enlarged. **4** to extend one's body or limbs to full length. **5** (+ out) to lie at full length. **6** to extend in space or time. **7** to provide an adequate challenge for (a person or their mind). **8** to strain (some resource, etc). ➤ **stretchy** adj.

stretch[2] n **1** an act of stretching. **2** elasticity. **3** an extent or area. **4** a period of time. **5** informal a period in prison. ✷ **not by any stretch of the imagination** not conceivably.

stretcher[1] n a light portable bed for carrying a sick, injured, or dead person, typically a sheet of canvas stretched between two poles.

stretcher[2] *v* to carry (an injured or sick person) on a stretcher.

strew *v* (*past part.* **strewn**) **1** to spread by scattering. **2** (+ with) to cover (a place) with something scattered.

striated *adj* marked with grooves, ridges, or streaks.

stricken[1] *adj* **1** horrified or distressed. **2** badly hurt or affected by illness, calamity, emotion, etc: *panic-stricken*.

stricken[2] *v NAmer* past part. of STRIKE[1].

strict *adj* **1** determined to enforce discipline and observance of rules. **2** rigorously conforming to rules or standards. **3** exact or precise. ➤ **strictly** *n*.

stricture *n* **1** a restraint or restriction. **2** a censure.

stride[1] *v* (**strode, stridden**) to walk with long steps.

stride[2] *n* **1** a long step. **2** a state of maximum competence or capability: *get into one's stride*. * **make strides** to make good progress. **take something in one's stride** to deal with something difficult or unpleasant calmly.

strident *adj* **1** loud and obtrusive. **2** expressing opinions, demands, etc loudly or urgently. ➤ **stridency** *n*, **stridently** *adv*.

strife *n* bitter conflict or dissension.

strike[1] *v* (*past tense* **struck**, *past part.* **struck** or *NAmer* **stricken**) **1** to hit with one's hand, a weapon, a bat, etc. **2** to collide with. **3** to carry out an attack. **4** to make a mental impact on. **5** to occur suddenly to. **6** to make and ratify (a bargain). **7** to indicate (the time) by sounding. **8** to create (a particular mood, atmosphere, etc): *The speech struck a gloomy note*. **9** to put (somebody) suddenly in a particular state: *The blow struck him unconscious*. **10** (*often* + out) to delete or cancel. **11** to cause (a match) to ignite. **12** to discover (something, *esp* minerals). **13** (+ off/out) to embark on a journey, *esp* in a particular direction. **14** to withdraw one's labour in protest against an employer.

strike[2] *n* **1** a stoppage of work by employees. **2** a discovery of a valuable mineral deposit. **3** a military attack, *esp* an air attack.

strike off *v* to forbid (*esp* a doctor) to continue in professional practice.

striker *n* **1** a football player whose main role is to score goals. **2** a worker on strike.

strike up *v* **1** to begin to sing or play. **2** to cause (e.g. a friendship or conversation) to begin.

striking *adj* attracting attention; unusual or impressive. ➤ **strikingly** *adv*.

string[1] *n* **1** a narrow cord used *esp* to tie or fasten things. **2** a length of gut, wire, etc used to produce notes in certain musical instruments, e.g. the violin and piano. **3** (*in pl*) the stringed instruments of an orchestra. **4** a group of objects threaded on a string. **5** a succession or sequence. **6** (*in pl*) conditions or obligations

attached to something: *a relationship with no strings attached*.

string[2] *v* (*past tense and past part.* **strung**) **1** to equip with strings. **2** to thread (things) on a string. **3** to tie, hang, or fasten with string. **4** (*often* + out) to extend, stretch, or prolong. ➤ **stringed** *adj*.

string along *v informal* to deceive or fool.

string bean *n* a bean with stringy fibres between the sides of the pods, e.g. a runner bean.

stringent *adj* rigorous or strict. ➤ **stringency** *n*, **stringently** *adv*.

string quartet *n* a group of four musicians playing stringed instruments, usu comprising two violins, a viola, and a cello.

stringy *adj* (-**ier**, -**iest**) resembling string; in long thin pieces or fibrous in texture.

strip[1] *v* (**stripped, stripping**) **1** to remove clothing, covering, or surface material from. **2** to remove one's clothes. **3** to remove (wallpaper, paint, etc) from a surface. **4** (+ of) to deprive of possessions, privileges, or rank. **5** to remove furniture, equipment, or accessories from (e.g. a house or ship). **6** (*often* + down) to dismantle (e.g. an engine).

strip[2] *n* the act of undressing, *esp* a striptease.

strip[3] *n* **1** a long narrow piece of material. **2** a long narrow area of land. **3** *Brit* the distinctive clothes worn by a sports team.

strip cartoon *n* a series of drawings forming a usu humorous narrative.

stripe[1] *n* a narrow band differing in colour or texture from adjacent parts. ➤ **stripey** *adj*, **stripy** *adj*.

stripe[2] *v* to mark stripes on. ➤ **striped** *adj*.

strip light *n* a long tubular fluorescent lamp.

stripling *n* *archaic or humorous* an adolescent boy.

stripper *n* **1** somebody who performs a striptease. **2** a tool or solvent for removing something, *esp* paint.

striptease *n* an entertainment in which a performer undresses gradually in an erotic manner.

strive *v* (*past tense* **strove** or **strived**, *past part.* **striven** or **strived**) **1** to try hard. **2** (+ against) to struggle against.

strobe *n* a bright intermittently flashing light, e.g. at a disco.

strode *v* past tense of STRIDE[1].

stroke[1] *v* to pass the hand over gently.

stroke[2] *n* an act of stroking.

stroke[3] *n* **1** an act of striking. **2** a striking of the ball in a game, *esp* one that constitutes the scoring unit in golf. **3** an unexpected occurrence: *a stroke of luck*. **4** a sudden disabling attack caused by rupture or obstruction of an artery of the brain. **5** a technique for propelling the body or a boat through water. **6** a repeated movement e.g. of a mechanical part such as a piston rod. **7** the sound of a striking clock. **8** a mark made by a single movement of a pen, brush, etc. **9** *Brit* a punctuation mark (/) used e.g. to separate alternatives. ✳ **at a stroke** by a single action. **off one's stroke** performing below one's usual standard.

stroll[1] *v* to walk in a leisurely manner.

stroll[2] *n* a leisurely walk.

strong *adj* **1** having or marked by great physical power or resistance. **2** having moral or intellectual power. **3** having great resources of wealth, talent, etc. **4** striking or superior of its kind. **5** effective or efficient, *esp* in a specified area. **6** forceful or cogent. **7** rich in some active agent, e.g. a flavour or extract; concentrated. **8** of a colour: intense. **9** full of passion or enthusiasm. **10** of a specified number: *an army ten thousand strong*. ✳ **(still) going strong** *informal* continuing to be active, effective, successful, etc. ➤ **strongly** *adv*.

strongarm *adj* using or involving undue force.

strongbox *n* a strongly made chest for money or valuables.

stronghold *n* **1** a fortified place. **2** a place dominated by a specified group.

strong room *n* a fireproof and burglarproof room in which money and valuables are stored.

strontium *n* a silver-white metallic element.

strop[1] *n* a leather band used for sharpening a razor.

strop[2] *n* *Brit, informal* an angry mood.

stroppy *adj* (**-ier, -iest**) *Brit, informal* quarrelsome or angrily uncooperative.

strove *v* past tense of STRIVE.

struck *v* past tense and past part. of STRIKE[1].

structural *adj* relating to or forming part of a structure. ➤ **structurally** *adv*.

structure[1] *n* **1** something constructed, e.g. a building. **2** the way in which something is constructed or organized.

structure[2] *v* to construct or organize in a particular way.

strudel *n* a dessert made from a thin sheet of dough rolled up with filling and baked.

struggle[1] *v* **1** to proceed with difficulty or great effort. **2** to make violent or strenuous efforts against opposition or confinement. **3** to make strenuous efforts to do something. ➤ **struggler** *n*.

struggle[2] *n* **1** a violent effort or exertion. **2** a determined attempt in adverse circumstances. **3** a difficult task.

strum *v* (**strummed, strumming**) to play (e.g. a guitar) by brushing the thumb, the fingertips, or a plectrum over the strings.

strumpet *n* *archaic or humorous* a prostitute or promiscuous woman.

strung *v* past tense and past part. of STRING[1].

strut[1] *v* (**strutted, strutting**) to walk with a proud or erect gait. ✳ **strut one's stuff** to show off one's skills or talents.

strut[2] *n* **1** a structural piece designed to support or strengthen a framework. **2** a strutting step or walk.

strychnine *n* a bitter poisonous chemical compound obtained from an Asian plant.

Stuart *adj* relating to the royal house that ruled Scotland from 1371 to 1603 and Britain from 1603 to 1649 and from 1660 to 1714.

stub[1] *n* **1** a small part of a chequebook page, ticket, etc left as a record of the contents of the part torn away. **2** a short remaining part of a pencil, cigarette, etc left after the larger part has been used up.

stub[2] *v* (**stubbed, stubbing**) **1** to strike (one's foot or toe) against a hard object or surface accidentally. **2** (+ out) to extinguish (e.g. a cigarette) by crushing the end.

stubble *n* **1** the stalky remnants of crops left in the soil after harvest. **2** a rough growth of short bristly hairs on a man's face. ➤ **stubbly** *adj*.

stubborn *adj* **1** determined, *esp* unreasonably determined, not to change or give way. **2** difficult to get rid of. ➤ **stubbornly** *adv*, **stubbornness** *n*.

stucco *n* (*pl* **-os** *or* **-oes**) a fine plaster used to coat or decorate ceilings and walls. ➤ **stuccoed** *adj*.

stuck *v* past tense and past part. of STICK[1].

stuck-up *adj* *informal* self-important or conceited.

stud[1] *n* **1** a solid button with a shank on the back inserted through an eyelet in a garment as a fastener or ornament. **2** a rivet or nail with a large head used for ornament or protection. **3** a small piece of jewellery for a pierced ear, etc. **4** a projecting piece, e.g. on a boot or tyre, to increase grip.

stud[2] *v* (**studded, studding**) **1** to decorate, cover, or protect with studs. **2** to set thickly with prominent objects.

stud[3] *n* **1** an animal, esp a stallion, or group of animals kept primarily for breeding. **2** a place, e.g. a farm, where such animals are kept. **3** *informal* a sexually active man.

student *n* **1** somebody who studies something, *esp* at a college or university. **2** a pupil at *esp* a secondary school.

studied *adj* carefully considered or prepared.

studio *n* (*pl* **-os**) **1** the workroom of a painter, sculptor, or photographer. **2** a place for the study of an art, e.g. dancing, singing, or acting. **3** a place where films are made. **4** a room equipped for the production of radio or television programmes.

studio flat *n* a small flat with one main room.

studious *adj* **1** pursuing studies seriously and with commitment. **2** deliberate and meticulous. ➤ **studiously** *adv*.

study[1] *n* (*pl* **-ies**) **1** the application of the mind to acquiring knowledge, *esp* by reading. **2** a careful examination or analysis of a subject. **3** a room devoted to study, writing, reading, etc. **4** a literary or artistic work intended as preliminary or experimental.

study[2] v (**-ies, -ied**) **1** to engage in study. **2** to engage in the study of (a subject). **3** to read, observe, or consider attentively or in detail.

stuff[1] n **1** materials, supplies, or equipment used in various activities. **2** personal property; possessions. **3** an unspecified material substance. **4** a group of miscellaneous objects. **5** subject matter or expertise. **6** the essence of a usu abstract thing.

stuff[2] v **1** to fill by packing things or stuffing inside. **2** to gorge (oneself) with food. **3** to fill out the skin of (an animal) for mounting. **4** to force or thrust into a confined space. **5** (usu + up) to block up (the nasal passages). **6** Brit, informal to defeat or thwart.

stuffing n **1** material used to stuff e.g. upholstered furniture, soft toys, etc. **2** a seasoned mixture of ingredients used to stuff meat, vegetables, etc.

stuffy adj (**-ier, -iest**) **1** badly ventilated; close. **2** of the nose: blocked or congested. **3** narrowly conventional in behaviour.

stultify v (**-ies, -ied**) to bore (somebody) by being tedious or repetitive. ➤ **stultifying** adj.

stumble[1] v **1** to trip in walking or running. **2** to walk unsteadily or clumsily. **3** to speak in a hesitant manner. **4** (+ upon/on/across) to find or discover unexpectedly or by chance.

stumble[2] n an act of stumbling.

stumbling block n an obstacle.

stump[1] n **1** the part of a tree remaining in the ground after the tree has been felled. **2** a remaining part. **3** in cricket, any of the three upright wooden rods that, with the bails, form the wicket. ✳ **on the stump** informal making a political speech as part of a campaign.

stump[2] v **1** informal to baffle or bewilder. **2** to walk heavily or noisily.

stumpy adj (**-ier, -iest**) short and thick; stubby.

stun v (**stunned, stunning**) **1** to make dazed or briefly unconscious, e.g. by a blow. **2** to overcome with astonishment or disbelief.

stung v past tense and past part. of STING[1].

stunk v past tense and past part. of STINK[1].

stunner n informal an unusually attractive or impressive person or thing.

stunning adj informal strikingly attractive or impressive. ➤ **stunningly** adv.

stunt[1] v to hinder the growth or development of.

stunt[2] n **1** a difficult feat displaying physical or acrobatic prowess. **2** something done purely as a way of attracting attention or publicity.

stuntman or **stuntwoman** n (pl **stuntmen** or **stuntwomen**) a man or woman employed as a substitute for an actor in scenes involving dangerous feats.

stupefy v (**-ies, -ied**) **1** to make groggy or insensible. **2** to astonish. ➤ **stupefaction** n.

stupendous adj marvellous. ➤ **stupendously** adv.

stupid adj **1** lacking common sense or intelligence. **2** dulled in feeling or perception. ➤ **stupidity** n, **stupidly** adv.

stupor n a stupefied condition.

sturdy adj (**-ier, -iest**) **1** strongly built or constructed. **2** showing determination or firmness of purpose. ➤ **sturdily** n.

sturgeon n a large edible fish whose roe is made into caviar.

stutter[1] v **1** to speak with involuntary hesitations, repetitions, or prolongations of sounds. **2** to make a series of abrupt sounds or movements. ➤ **stutterer** n.

stutter[2] n **1** the act of stuttering. **2** a speech disorder that produces stuttering.

sty[1] n (pl **-ies**) = PIGSTY.

sty[2] or **stye** n (pl **sties** or **styes**) an inflamed swelling at the edge of an eyelid.

Stygian adj literary extremely dark or gloomy.

style[1] n **1** a distinctive or characteristic manner of doing something. **2** a particular design or arrangement of something, e.g. hair. **3** a manner of expression in writing, painting, music, etc, characteristic of an individual, period, etc. **4** elegance or sophistication in dress, social behaviour, etc. **5** a prolongation of a plant ovary with a stigma at the top. ✳ **in style** with much elegance or extravagance.

style[2] v **1** to design or arrange in a particular style. **2** to designate by an identifying term.

styli n pl of STYLUS.

stylish adj **1** fashionably elegant. **2** characterized by elegance and skill. ➤ **stylishly** n.

stylist n **1** a hairdresser. **2** an artist, designer, etc who is an expert in matters of style.

stylistic adj relating to style. ➤ **stylistically** adv.

stylize or **-ise** v to represent or design with an artistically simplified, streamlined, etc shape rather than according to nature. ➤ **stylized** adj.

stylus n (pl **styli** or **styluses**) **1** a tiny piece of material, e.g. diamond, used in a gramophone to follow the groove on a record and transmit the sound. **2** a pointed instrument used in ancient times for writing on clay or waxed tablets.

stymie v (**stymies, stymied, stymying** or **stymieing**) to thwart.

styptic adj tending to contract tissues, esp to check bleeding.

suave adj **1** smoothly charming and polite. **2** esp of men: elegant and sophisticated. ➤ **suavely** n.

sub[1] n informal **1** a submarine. **2** a subscription. **3** a substitute, esp in a sport.

sub² v (**subbed, subbing**) *informal* to act as a substitute.

sub- *prefix* **1** under, beneath, or below: *submarine*. **2** lower or next below in rank. **3** a further or secondary instance of a specified action or process: *sublet*. **4** having an incomplete or partial resemblance to: *subhuman*.

subaltern n a commissioned officer in the British Army ranking below a captain.

subatomic *adj* **1** occurring within an atom. **2** smaller than an atom.

subconscious¹ *adj* existing in the mind but not admitted to consciousness. ➤ **subconsciously** *adv*.

subconscious² n (**the subconscious**) the part of the mind in which mental activity takes place below the threshold of consciousness.

subcontinent n a distinct, large subdivision of a continent.

subcontract v to engage a third party to perform all or part of (work included in an original contract). ➤ **subcontractor** n.

subculture n a sector of society whose members share a pattern of behaviour and values distinguishable from the mainstream culture.

subcutaneous *adj* situated or applied under the skin.

subdivide v to divide (a part of something already divided) into more and smaller parts. ➤ **subdivision** n.

subdue v (**subdues, subdued, subduing**) **1** to bring under control; to curb. **2** to conquer and bring (e.g. a people) into subjection.

subdued *adj* **1** lacking normal cheerfulness or liveliness; low-spirited. **2** reduced in force, intensity, or strength.

subedit v (**subedited, subediting**) *chiefly Brit* to edit (e.g. a newspaper article) in preparation for printing. ➤ **subeditor** n.

subhuman *adj* below the level expected of normal human beings.

subject¹ n **1** a branch of knowledge or learning, *esp* one taught or studied. **2** the person or thing that is being discussed, written about, studied, represented, etc. **3** in grammar, the word or phrase in a sentence or clause denoting the person or thing that performs the action of a verb. **4** somebody owing obedience or allegiance to a ruler.

subject² *adj* **1** (*often* + to) owing obedience or allegiance to. **2** (+ to) dependent or conditional on something. **3** (+ to) liable or exposed to something. **4** (+ to) prone to.

subject³ v **1** (+ to) to cause to undergo something. **2** (*often* + to) to bring (e.g. a people) under control or rule. ➤ **subjection** n.

subjective *adj* determined or affected by a particular individual's views and feelings. ➤ **subjectively** *adv*, **subjectivity** n.

sub judice /ˈjoohdisi/ *adv* currently being considered by a court and therefore not open to discussion.

subjugate v to bring under the control of another authority. ➤ **subjugation** n.

subjunctive¹ *adj* in grammar, denoting a verb mood that represents an act or state not as a fact but as a possibility or wish.

subjunctive² n a verb form expressing the subjunctive mood.

sublet v (**subletting**, *past tense and past part.* **sublet**) of a tenant: to lease or rent (all or part of a rented property).

sublimate v **1** in psychology, to divert the expression of (an instinctual impulse) into a socially or culturally acceptable form. **2** = SUBLIME². ➤ **sublimation** n.

sublime¹ *adj* **1** of the highest moral or spiritual worth; exalted. **2** astoundingly beautiful or grand. **3** outstanding or extreme. ➤ **sublimely** *adv*.

sublime² v in chemistry, to pass directly from the solid to the vapour state when heated, without liquefying.

subliminal *adj* existing or functioning below the level of conscious awareness. ➤ **subliminally** *adv*.

submachine gun n a portable rapid-firing gun.

submarine¹ n a vessel, *esp* a warship, designed for undersea operations. ➤ **submariner** n.

submarine² *adj* situated, occurring, or growing under the sea.

submerge v **1** to go or put under water. **2** to cover with water; to flood. **3** to cover or suppress completely.

submerse v *technical* to submerge. ➤ **submersion** n.

submersible¹ *adj* capable of going or operating under water.

submersible² n a vessel used for undersea exploration and construction work.

submicroscopic *adj* too small to be seen using an ordinary microscope.

submission n **1** the act of submitting. **2** something submitted for consideration, inspection, etc.

submissive *adj* willing or tending to submit to others. ➤ **submissively** *adv*.

submit v (**submitted, submitting**) **1** to yield to the authority or will of another. **2** (+ to) to allow oneself to be subjected to something. **3** (+ to) to subject to a process or practice. **4** to send (something) to another person or authority for consideration, examination, judgment, etc. **5** to put forward as an opinion; to suggest.

subordinate¹ *adj* **1** occupying a lower class, rank, or position. **2** of secondary importance.

subordinate² n a person of lower rank.

subordinate³ v (*often* + to) to treat as less important than. ➤ **subordination** n.

subplot *n* a subordinate plot in fiction or drama.

subpoena[1] *n* a writ commanding somebody to appear in court.

subpoena[2] *v* (**subpoenas, subpoenaed, subpoenaing**) to serve with a subpoena.

subscribe *v* 1 (+ to) to pay regularly in order to receive a periodical or service. 2 (+ to) to feel favourably disposed to something; to agree with it. 3 to give a written pledge to contribute (an amount of money). ➤ **subscriber** *n*.

subscript *adj* of a letter, number, etc: written or printed below another character.

subscription *n* 1 the act of subscribing to something. 2 a sum of money subscribed. 3 *Brit* membership fees paid regularly.

subsection *n* a subdivision of a section.

subsequent *adj* following in time or order; succeeding. ➤ **subsequently** *adv*.

subservient *adj* 1 obsequiously submissive. 2 subordinate. ➤ **subservience** *n*.

subside *v* 1 to become less forceful or intense. 2 to fall to a lower level or return to a normal level. 3 of ground: to cave in. 4 of a building: to sink into the ground.

subsidence *n* the slow sinking of an area of land.

subsidiary[1] *adj* 1 supplementary or auxiliary. 2 of secondary importance.

subsidiary[2] *n* (*pl* **-ies**) a company that is wholly controlled by another.

subsidize *or* **-ise** *v* 1 to provide with a subsidy. 2 to pay part of the cost of (a product or service), making it cheaper for those who buy or use it. ➤ **subsidization** *n*.

subsidy *n* (*pl* **-ies**) a grant or gift of money, e.g. by a government to assist an enterprise deemed advantageous to the public.

subsist *v* to have only the basic necessities of life.

subsistence *n* the minimum, e.g. of food and shelter, necessary to support life.

subsoil *n* the layer of weathered material that lies under the surface soil.

subsonic *adj* travelling at a speed less than that of sound in air.

substance *n* 1 a physical material. 2 the fundamental or essential part or meaning. 3 correspondence with reality. 4 material of real value or importance.

substandard *adj* of lesser quality than expected or prescribed.

substantial *adj* 1 significantly large. 2 ample to satisfy and nourish. 3 firmly constructed; solid. 4 relating to the essence of something.

substantially *adv* 1 for the most part; basically. 2 by a large amount; greatly.

substantiate *v* to establish (e.g. a statement or claim) by proof or evidence.

substantive *adj* having substance or significance. ➤ **substantively** *adv*.

substitute[1] *n* somebody or something that takes the place of another.

substitute[2] *v* (*usu* + for) to put (one thing) in the place of another. ➤ **substitution** *n*.

subsume *v* to include as a member of a group; to incorporate.

subterfuge *n* 1 deception or trickery used as a means of concealment or evasion. 2 a trick or ruse.

subterranean *adj* existing or occurring under the surface of the earth.

subtext *n* the underlying meaning or theme of a text.

subtitle[1] *n* 1 a printed text, e.g. a translation, that appears at the bottom of the screen during a film or television broadcast. 2 a secondary or explanatory title.

subtitle[2] *v* to provide a subtitle or subtitles for.

subtle *adj* 1 pleasantly or tastefully delicate; understated. 2 difficult to understand, analyse, or distinguish. 3 showing keen insight and perception. 4 cleverly contrived; ingenious. ➤ **subtlety** *n*, **subtly** *adv*.

subtotal *n* the sum of part of a series of figures.

subtract *v* to take (one number) away from another in calculating the difference between them. ➤ **subtraction** *n*.

suburb *n* an outlying part of a city or large town, *esp* a residential district.

suburbia *n* the suburbs of a city, or their inhabitants.

subversive[1] *adj* tending to undermine the established system, e.g. of government.

subversive[2] *n* a person engaged in subversive activities.

subvert *v* to overthrow or undermine the power of (e.g. a government or institution). ➤ **subversion** *n*.

subway *n* 1 *Brit* a passage under a street for pedestrians. 2 *NAmer* an underground railway.

succeed *v* 1 to achieve a desired object or end. 2 to attain wealth or fame. 3 (+ to) to inherit something, *esp* sovereignty, rank, or title. 4 to follow after another in order.

success *n* 1 the achievement of a desired object or end. 2 the attainment of wealth or fame. 3 somebody or something that succeeds.

successful *adj* 1 resulting in success. 2 having succeeded. 3 having gained wealth, fame, etc. ➤ **successfully** *adv*.

succession *n* 1 a number of people or things that follow each other in sequence. 2 the process of becoming entitled to a another person's property or title. ✳ **in succession** following one another without interruption.

successive *adj* following one after the other. ➤ **successively** *adv*.

successor *n* a person who succeeds another in a title, office, etc.

succinct *adj* clearly expressed in few words. ➤ **succinctly** *adv*.

succour[1] (*NAmer* **succor**) *n* assistance in time of difficulty.

succour[2] (*NAmer* **succor**) *v* to go to the aid of.

succulent[1] *adj* 1 of food: full of juice and flavour. 2 of a plant: having juicy fleshy tissues. ➤ **succulence** *n*.

succulent[2] *n* a succulent plant, e.g. a cactus.

succumb *v* 1 (+ to) to give in to something or somebody with superior strength or overpowering appeal. 2 to die from disease or injury.

such[1] *adj and adv* 1 of the kind, quality, or extent. 2 of that or the same sort: *There's no such place.* 3 of so extreme a degree or extraordinary a nature: *in such a hurry.* * **such as** 1 for example: *reptiles, such as lizards.* 2 the same kind as; like: *women such as my sister.*

such[2] *pron* (*pl* **such**) (*in pl*) similar people or things: *tin and glass and such.* * **as such** in himself, herself, itself, or themselves; intrinsically.

such and such *adj informal* not named or specified.

suchlike[1] *adj* of the kind mentioned; similar.

suchlike[2] *pron* (*pl* **suchlike**) a similar person or thing.

suck[1] *v* 1 to draw (e.g. liquid) into the mouth by creating a partial vacuum with the lips and tongue. 2 to draw liquid from (something) in this way. 3 to eat (e.g. a sweet) by means of sucking movements of the lips and tongue. 4 to draw in or up by suction. 5 (+ in/into) to draw (somebody) by irresistible force.

suck[2] *n* an act of sucking.

sucker *n* 1 a cup-shaped device, *esp* of rubber, that can cling to a surface by suction. 2 a mouth or other animal organ adapted for sucking or clinging to a surface. 3 a shoot from the roots or stem of a plant that can grow into an independent plant. 4 *informal* a gullible person. 5 *informal* a person irresistibly attracted by something specified.

suckle *v* 1 to give milk to (a baby or young animal) from the breast or udder. 2 of a baby or young animal: to take milk from the breast or udder.

suckling *n* an unweaned baby or young animal.

suck up *v informal* (*often* + to) to act in an obsequious manner.

sucralose *n* an artificial sweetener about 600 times sweeter than sugar.

sucrose *n* the form of sugar obtained from sugarcane and sugar beet and occurring in most plants.

suction *n* a force that draws something in or causes it to adhere, produced by a partial vacuum over part of its surface.

sudden *adj* 1 happening or coming unexpectedly. 2 marked by haste; abrupt. ➤ **suddenly** *adv*, **suddenness** *n*.

suds *pl n* the lather on soapy water.

sue *v* 1 to bring a legal action against (a person, institution, etc). 2 (*usu* + for) to make a formal request for.

suede *n* leather with a velvety surface produced by rubbing the flesh side.

suet *n* the hard fat round the kidneys and loins in cattle or sheep, used in cooking.

suffer *v* 1 (*often* + from) to be affected by or be subject to (an illness or condition). 2 to experience (something unpleasant). 3 to sustain loss or damage. 4 *archaic* to tolerate. ➤ **sufferer** *n*.

sufferance *n* tolerance implying a lack of objection rather than actual approval.

suffice *v* 1 to be enough. 2 to be enough for (somebody or something).

sufficiency *n* (*pl* **-ies**) 1 a sufficient amount. 2 adequacy.

sufficient *adj* enough; adequate. ➤ **sufficiently** *adv*.

suffix *n* a group of letters placed at the end of a word and affecting its meaning, e.g. *-ness* in *happiness*.

suffocate *v* to die or cause to die from being unable to breathe. ➤ **suffocation** *n*.

suffrage *n* the right to vote in political elections.

suffragette *n* a woman campaigning for the right to vote to be extended to women in Britain in the early 20th cent.

suffuse *v* to spread over or through.

Sufi *n* (*pl* **Sufis**) a Muslim mystic. ➤ **Sufism** *n*.

sugar[1] *n* 1 a sweet crystalline substance obtained from sugarcane or sugar beet. 2 a sweet water-soluble carbohydrate found in plant and animal tissue.

sugar[2] *v* to sprinkle, coat, or sweeten with sugar.

sugar beet *n* a variety of beet grown for the sugar in its roots.

sugarcane *n* a tall tropical grass with stout stems grown as a source of sugar.

sugar daddy *n informal* an elderly man who lavishes gifts and money on a young woman in return for sex or companionship.

suggest *v* 1 to put forward as a possibility or for consideration. 2 to call to mind by thought or association. 3 to express indirectly; to imply.

suggestible *adj* easily influenced by suggestion.

suggestion *n* 1 something, *esp* an idea or plan, suggested. 2 the impressing of an idea, attitude, etc on the mind of another person. 3 a slight indication; a trace.

suggestive *adj* 1 (*often* + of) tending to suggest; indicative or evocative. 2 risqué. ➤ **suggestively** *adv*.

suicide *n* 1 the act of killing oneself intentionally. 2 the ruining of one's own interests. 3 somebody who commits suicide. ➤ **suicidal** *adj*, **suicidally** *adv*.

suit¹ n **1** an outer costume of two or more matching articles of clothing, *esp* a jacket and trousers or a skirt. **2** a costume worn for a specified purpose. **3** all the playing cards in a pack bearing the same symbol, i.e. hearts, clubs, diamonds, or spades. **4** a lawsuit.

suit² v **1** to please or be convenient or good for. **2** to be becoming to or look right with. **3** to adapt (something) to a particular situation, circumstance, etc. * **suit oneself** to do as one likes. **suit somebody down to the ground** to suit somebody extremely well.

suitable adj appropriate for a particular person, situation, etc. ➤ **suitability** n, **suitably** adv.

suitcase n a rectangular case with a hinged lid and a handle, used for carrying clothes, etc when travelling.

suite n **1** a group of rooms occupied as a unit. **2** a set of matching furniture. **3** an instrumental musical form consisting of a series of pieces.

suitor n dated somebody who courts a woman with a view to marriage.

Sukkoth or **Succoth** n a Jewish harvest festival celebrated in September and October.

sulfur n NAmer see SULPHUR.

sulk¹ v to be moodily silent through resentment or disappointment.

sulk² n (usu in pl) a fit of sulking.

sulky adj (-ier, -iest) sulking or given to fits of sulking. ➤ **sulkily** adv.

sullen adj silently gloomy or resentful. ➤ **sullenly** adv.

sully v (-ies, -ied) to defile or tarnish.

sulphur (NAmer **sulfur**) n a non-metallic combustible chemical element that occurs naturally as yellow crystals.

sulphuric (NAmer **sulfuric**) adj containing sulphur.

sulphuric acid n a corrosive oily acid.

sulphurous (NAmer **sulfurous**) adj containing or derived from sulphur.

sultan n a sovereign of a Muslim state.

sultana n **1** a light brown seedless raisin. **2** a sultan's wife.

sultry adj (-ier, -iest) **1** oppressively hot and humid. **2** exciting strong sexual desire; sensual.

sum n **1** an amount of money. **2** the result of adding numbers. **3** a simple arithmetical problem involving addition, subtraction, multiplication, or division.

summarize or **-ise** v to reduce to a summary; to express concisely.

summary¹ n (pl -ies) a brief account covering the main points of something.

summary² adj **1** done quickly without delay or formality. **2** tried or triable in a magistrates' court. ➤ **summarily** adv.

summation n **1** the process of adding numbers. **2** the act of summing up. **3** a summary.

summer¹ n the season between spring and autumn. ➤ **summery** adj.

summer² v (+ in) to spend the summer in a particular place.

summerhouse n a small building in a garden designed to provide a shady place in summer.

summit n **1** the highest point of a hill or mountain. **2** the topmost level attainable. **3** a conference of heads of government.

summon v **1** to order to come. **2** to call people to attend (a meeting). **3** (often + up) to cause (a particular quality, e.g. courage) to show itself in oneself or others.

summons n (pl **summonses**) **1** a written notification ordering somebody to appear in court. **2** an order to come to a particular place, person, etc.

sumo n a Japanese form of wrestling.

sump n chiefly Brit a reservoir for lubricating oil underneath an internal-combustion engine.

sumptuous adj lavishly rich, costly, or luxurious. ➤ **sumptuously** adv.

sum total n the whole amount.

sum up v **1** to summarize. **2** to appraise concisely.

sun¹ n **1** (often **Sun**) the star round which the earth and other planets revolve. **2** a star. **3** the heat or light radiated from the sun.

sun² v (**sunned, sunning**) to expose (oneself) to the rays of the sun.

sunbathe v to lie or sit in the sun in order to get a suntan. ➤ **sunbather** n.

sunbeam n a ray of light from the sun.

sunbed n **1** a bed or reclining chair used for sunbathing. **2** a unit consisting of a couch and an array of sunlamps.

sunblock n a cream that protects exposed skin from the ultraviolet rays in sunlight.

sunburn n inflammation of the skin caused by overexposure to sunlight. ➤ **sunburnt** or **sunburned** adj.

sundae n a dish of ice cream served with a topping of fruit, nuts, syrup, etc.

Sunday n the day of the week following Saturday, the traditional day of worship for Christians.

Sunday school n a class of religious instruction for children, held on Sundays.

sunder v literary to break apart or in two.

sundial n an instrument that shows the time of day by the shadow cast by a pointer.

sundries pl n miscellaneous small articles or items.

sundry adj of various kinds; miscellaneous.

sunflower n a tall plant with large yellow-rayed flowers.

sung v past part. of SING.

sunglasses pl n tinted glasses worn to protect the eyes from the sun.

sunk v past part. of SINK¹.

sunken *adj* **1** submerged, *esp* lying at the bottom of the sea. **2** lying below the surrounding level.

sunlamp *n* an electric lamp that emits ultraviolet light, used *esp* for tanning the skin.

sunlight *n* light emitted by the sun; sunshine.

Sunni *n* (*pl* **Sunni** *or* **Sunnis**) **1** the major branch of Islam that acknowledges the first four caliphs as rightful successors of Muhammad. **2** a follower of Sunni.

sunny *adj* (**-ier, -iest**) **1** bright with sunshine. **2** cheerful, optimistic. **3** exposed to or warmed by the sun.

sunrise *n* the rising of the sun above the horizon or the time when this happens.

sunroof *n* an opening or removable panel in the roof of a car.

sunscreen *n* a substance or preparation that protects the skin from excessive ultraviolet radiation.

sunset *n* the descent of the sun below the horizon or the time when this happens.

sunshade *n* **1** a parasol. **2** an awning.

sunshine *n* the sun's light or direct rays.

sunspot *n* a transient dark marking on the visible surface of the sun caused by a relatively cooler area.

sunstroke *n* heatstroke caused by direct exposure to the sun.

suntan *n* a browning of the skin from exposure to the sun. ➤ **suntanned** *adj.*

sup[1] *v* (**supped, supping**) *chiefly dialect* to drink (liquid) in small mouthfuls.

sup[2] *n chiefly dialect* a sip.

sup[3] *v* (**supped, supping**) *dated* to eat one's evening meal.

super *adj informal* a general term of approval.

super- *prefix* **1** higher in quantity, quality, or degree than: *superhuman*. **2** extra: *supertax*. **3** to an excessive degree: *superabundant*. **4** surpassing others of its kind in size or power: *supertanker*. **5** placed above something: *superscript*.

superannuated *adj* **1** retired on a pension. **2** obsolete.

superannuation *n* the regular contribution made by employees to their pension scheme, deducted from wages or salary.

superb *adj* **1** of excellent quality. **2** grand or magnificent. ➤ **superbly** *adv.*

supercharger *n* a device supplying fuel and air to an internal-combustion engine at a pressure higher than normal for greater efficiency. ➤ **supercharged** *adj.*

supercilious *adj* coolly disdainful; haughty.

superficial *adj* **1** lying on or affecting only the surface. **2** apparent rather than real. **3** of a person: not capable of serious thought; shallow. **4** not careful, thorough, or deep. ➤ **superficiality** *n*, **superficially** *adv.*

superfluous *adj* exceeding what is necessary.

superglue *n* a very strong, quick-setting adhesive.

supergrass *n Brit, informal* a police informer who gives information about a large number of criminals.

superhero *n* (*pl* **-oes**) a character in a cartoon, film, etc with extraordinary powers that they use to fight crime, etc.

superhuman *adj* exceeding normal human power or capability.

superimpose *v* to place (one thing) over or above something else. ➤ **superimposition** *n.*

superintend *v* to be in charge of.

superintendent *n* **1** a person who supervises or manages something. **2** a British police officer ranking above a chief inspector.

superior[1] *adj* **1** of higher rank, quality, or importance. **2** excellent of its kind. **3** greater in quantity or number. **4** in printing, superscript. **5** conceited or supercilious. ➤ **superiority** *n.*

superior[2] *n* a person who is above another in rank or office.

superlative[1] *adj* **1** of the highest degree or quality. **2** in grammar, denoting the degree of comparison expressing an extreme or unsurpassed level, e.g. *smallest*.

superlative[2] *n* an exaggerated expression of praise.

superman *n* (*pl* **supermen**) *informal* a man of extraordinary power or achievements.

supermarket *n* a large self-service retail shop selling foods and household merchandise.

supermodel *n* a very successful fashion model who has become a celebrity.

supernatural[1] *adj* transcending the laws of nature, *esp* involving a god, spirit, devil, ghost, etc.

supernatural[2] *n* (**the supernatural**) supernatural forces or beings.

supernova *n* (*pl* **supernovae** *or* **supernovas**) a star that explodes, becoming immensely brighter for a few weeks or months.

supernumerary *adj* **1** exceeding the usual or stated number. **2** not listed among the regular members of a group.

superpower *n* any of a very few dominant nations in the world.

superscript *adj* of a letter, number, etc: written or printed above another character.

supersede *v* to take the place of (*esp* something inferior or outmoded).

Usage Note: Note the spelling with -sede not -cede or -ceed.

supersonic *adj* moving at a speed above the speed of sound in air.

superstar *n* an extremely popular or successful entertainer or sportsperson.

superstition *n* **1** irrational belief in the influence of the supernatural on human affairs. **2** a superstitious belief.

superstitious *adj* believing or suggesting, on no rational basis, that certain actions have supernatural repercussions and bring good or bad luck. ➤ **superstitiously** *adv.*

superstore *n* a very large supermarket, often on the outskirts of a town.

superstructure *n* **1** the structural part of a ship above the main deck. **2** the part of a structure built on top of a lower or more fundamental part.

supervene *v* to happen in a way that interrupts some plan or process.

supervise *v* to oversee (a task or workers). ➤ **supervision** *n*, **supervisor** *n*, **supervisory** *adj.*

supine *adj* **1** lying on the back. **2** weak and inactive.

supper *n* an evening meal or snack.

supplant *v* to oust or supersede.

supple *adj* able to perform bending or twisting movements with ease and grace. ➤ **suppleness** *n.*

supplement[1] *n* **1** something that completes or makes a useful addition. **2** a part issued to extend a book or periodical. **3** an extra charge payable for something.

supplement[2] *v* to add a supplement to. ➤ **supplemental** *adj.*

supplementary *adj* added as a supplement; additional.

suppliant[1] *adj* humbly imploring or entreating.

suppliant[2] *n* a person who supplicates.

supplicate *v* to ask humbly and earnestly for something. ➤ **supplicant** *n and adj,* **supplication** *n.*

supply[1] *v* (-ies, -ied) **1** to provide somebody with (something). **2** to provide for or satisfy (a need, etc). ➤ **supplier** *n.*

supply[2] *n* (pl -ies) **1** the quantity of a commodity needed or available. **2** (*usu in pl*) provisions or stores. **3** the act of supplying something. **4** a teacher who fills temporary vacancies in schools.

support[1] *v* **1** to serve as a foundation or prop for. **2** to help, e.g. by giving money. **3** to approve of, encourage, or defend. **4** to substantiate or corroborate. **5** to be an enthusiastic or loyal follower of (e.g. a football team). **6** to provide with a home and the means of subsistence. **7** to enable (e.g. life) to exist. ➤ **supporter** *n.*

support[2] *n* **1** the act of supporting. **2** something that holds something up or serves as a prop. **3** somebody who offers help and encouragement.

supportive *adj* providing help and encouragement.

suppose *v* **1** to believe or think probable, usu without proof. **2** to assume or presuppose.

✳ **be supposed to do something** to be expected or required to do something.

supposed *adj* believed or imagined to be such. ➤ **supposedly** *adv.*

supposition *n* something that is believed or thought likely, but is unproven.

suppository *n* (pl -ies) a cone or cylinder of medicated material intended to melt after insertion into the rectum or vagina.

suppress *v* **1** to put an end to by force. **2** to stop the publication or revelation of. **3** to restrain or inhibit (e.g. a feeling). ➤ **suppression** *n*, **suppressive** *adj.*

suppurate *v* to form or discharge pus. ➤ **suppuration** *n.*

supremacist *n* an advocate of group supremacy, e.g. of the superiority of one race over another.

supremacy *n* supreme authority, power, or position.

supreme *adj* **1** highest in rank or authority. **2** greatest, strongest, or most important. ➤ **supremely** *adv.*

Supreme Court *n* the highest judicial tribunal in a state.

supremo *n* (pl -os) *Brit, informal* a leader, or the person in charge of something.

surcharge *n* an additional charge, tax, or cost.

surd *n* in mathematics, a root, e.g. the square root of 2, that cannot be expressed exactly by dividing one integer by another.

sure[1] *adj* **1** marked by feelings of confident certainty. **2** (+ of) confident that something is true, will happen, etc. **3** certain; bound: *She is sure to win.* **4** true and reliable. ✳ **for sure** as a certainty. **to be sure** admittedly. ➤ **sureness** *n.*

sure[2] *adv chiefly NAmer, informal* certainly.

sure-fire *adj informal* certain to succeed.

surely *adv* **1** it is to be hoped or expected that. **2** without doubt; certainly.

surety *n* (pl -ies) **1** a person who assumes legal liability for the debt or failure in duty of somebody else. **2** a pledge given for the fulfilment of an undertaking; a guarantee.

surf[1] *n* the foam and swell of waves breaking on the shore.

surf[2] *v* **1** to stand or lie on a surfboard and ride on the waves towards the shore. **2** to browse through (the Internet or TV channels) randomly. ➤ **surfer** *n*, **surfing** *n.*

surface[1] *n* **1** the exterior or upper boundary or layer of something. **2** the uppermost level of a body of liquid. **3** the superficial aspect of something. ✳ **on the surface** to all outward appearances.

surface[2] *v* **1** to come or bring to the surface, *esp* of water. **2** to become apparent. **3** to give a surface to (e.g. a road).

surfboard *n* a long narrow buoyant board used in surfing.

surfeit *n* an excessive amount.

surge[1] *n* **1** a powerful rising or onrushing movement. **2** a sudden increase. **3** a sudden experience of an intense emotion.

surge[2] *v* **1** to move with a surge. **2** to increase suddenly.

surgeon *n* **1** a medical specialist who practises surgery. **2** a medical officer in the navy.

surgery *n* (*pl* **-ies**) **1** the branch of medicine that deals with disorders by cutting open the body to repair or remove damaged parts. **2** a surgical operation. **3** *Brit* a place where a doctor or dentist treats patients. **4** *Brit* a session at which a lawyer, MP, etc is available for consultation.

surgical *adj* **1** relating to or used in surgery. **2** providing support for a body part or correcting a deformity. **3** involving precision bombing. ➤ **surgically** *adv*.

surgical spirit *n* *Brit* a mixture consisting mainly of methylated spirits and used *esp* as a skin disinfectant.

surly *adj* (**-ier, -iest**) irritably sullen and bad-tempered.

surmise[1] *v* to imagine or infer on scanty evidence.

surmise[2] *n* a conjecture or guess.

surmount *v* **1** to overcome (a difficulty or obstacle). **2** to stand or lie on the top of.

surname *n* the name shared by members of a family.

surpass *v* to go beyond in quality, degree, or performance.

surplice *n* a loose white outer ecclesiastical vestment.

surplus[1] *n* **1** a surplus amount. **2** an excess of income over expenditure.

surplus[2] *adj* remaining over and above what is needed.

surprise[1] *n* **1** the feeling caused by an unexpected event; astonishment. **2** something unexpected or surprising. * **take somebody by surprise 1** to come upon somebody without warning. **2** to astonish somebody.

surprise[2] *v* **1** to fill with wonder or amazement. **2** to take unawares. **3** to attack or capture unexpectedly. ➤ **surprised** *adj*.

surreal *adj* having a strange dreamlike irrational quality.

surrealism *n* an artistic movement that used the incongruous images formed by the unconscious in its work. ➤ **surrealist** *n and adj*.

surrender[1] *v* **1** to admit defeat and submit to an opponent. **2** to hand over to the control or possession of somebody else. **3** *formal* to give up or hand in (e.g. a ticket). **4** (+ to) to allow (oneself) to be controlled by an emotion, influence, etc.

surrender[2] *n* the act of surrendering.

surreptitious *adj* done by stealth. ➤ **surreptitiously** *adv*.

surrogate *n* a substitute. ➤ **surrogacy** *n*.

surrogate mother *n* a woman who carries and bears a child for a couple who cannot have children.

surround[1] *v* **1** to encircle, or enclose on all sides. **2** to be associated with.

surround[2] *n* **1** a border or edging. **2** (*in pl*) surroundings.

surroundings *pl n* the area or circumstances by which one is surrounded.

surtax *n* a tax on an item charged in addition to an existing tax.

surtitle *n* a translation of the dialogue of an opera or play that is projected onto a screen above the stage.

surveillance *n* close watch kept over somebody, e.g. by a detective.

survey[1] *v* **1** to examine closely. **2** to contemplate as a whole. **3** to determine the form and features of (an area of land), prior to e.g. making a map of it. **4** *Brit* to examine and report on the condition of (a building, e.g. a house for sale). **5** to conduct a statistical survey on (a group of people). ➤ **surveyor** *n*.

survey[2] *n* **1** a statistical enquiry into the opinions or preferences of a group of people. **2** an act of surveying, e.g. an examination of a building to determine its condition. **3** a report drawn up by a surveyor.

survival *n* **1** the fact of continuing to live or exist. **2** something that survives, *esp* after others of its kind have disappeared.

survive *v* **1** to continue to exist or live. **2** to escape alive from (an accident or disaster). **3** to remain alive after the death of (somebody). ➤ **survivor** *n*.

susceptibility *n* (*pl* **-ies**) **1** the fact of being susceptible. **2** (*in pl*) feelings or sensibilities.

susceptible *adj* **1** open or vulnerable to some influence or agency. **2** easily moved or emotionally affected.

sushi *n* a Japanese dish of balls of cold boiled rice garnished with raw fish or other ingredients.

suspect[1] *v* **1** to imagine (something) to be true or probable. **2** to believe (somebody) to be guilty without conclusive proof. **3** to distrust (something).

suspect[2] *n* somebody who is suspected, e.g. of a crime.

suspect[3] *adj* likely to be false or dangerous.

suspend *v* **1** to hang (something), *esp* so that it is unsupported except at the top. **2** to cause to stop temporarily. **3** to defer (a prison sentence) on particular conditions. **4** to defer or delay (e.g. judgment) awaiting fuller information. **5** to debar temporarily from office, employment, or attendance at school.

suspended animation *n* temporary suspension of the vital body functions, e.g. in people nearly drowned.

suspender n **1** Brit a strap with a fastening device, attached to a belt or corset to hold up a woman's stocking. **2** NAmer (in pl) = BRACES.

suspense n a state of excited or anxious uncertainty as to a decision or outcome.

suspension n **1** the act of suspending, or the state of being suspended. **2** the system of devices, e.g. springs, supporting the upper part of a vehicle on the axles. **3** a state in which particles are mixed with but undissolved in a liquid.

suspension bridge n a type of bridge that has its roadway suspended from cables.

suspicion n **1** an unsubstantiated idea or feeling that something is the case, esp that somebody has done something wrong. **2** a feeling of mistrust. **3** a slight trace. ✳ **above suspicion** too honest or virtuous to be suspected of having done something wrong. **under suspicion** suspected of having done something wrong.

suspicious adj **1** tending to arouse suspicion. **2** inclined to suspect; distrustful. ➤ **suspiciously** adv.

suss v Brit, informal **1** (often + out) to uncover the truth about. **2** (often + out) to work out; to realize.

sustain v **1** to support the weight of. **2** to give support, sustenance, or relief to. **3** to cause to continue; to prolong. **4** to suffer or undergo. ➤ **sustained** adj.

sustainable adj **1** able to be sustained. **2** of energy, development, etc: not exhausting natural resources or damaging the environment. ➤ **sustainability** n.

sustenance n **1** food or provisions; nourishment. **2** the act of sustaining.

suture[1] n **1** a fibre used in the sewing together of parts of the living body. **2** a stitch made with a suture.

suture[2] v to close or secure with sutures.

suzerainty n control by one state of the foreign relations of another internally autonomous state.

svelte adj slender in an elegant and attractive way.

SW abbr **1** Southwest. **2** Southwestern.

swab[1] or **swob** n **1** a wad of absorbent material used for applying medication, cleaning wounds, taking specimens, etc. **2** a specimen taken with a swab.

swab[2] or **swob** v (**swabbed** or **swobbed**, **swabbing** or **swobbing**) **1** to clean (a wound) with a swab. **2** (often + down) to clean (a surface) by washing, esp with a mop.

swaddle v to swathe or envelop.

swaddling clothes pl n narrow strips of cloth formerly wrapped round a baby to restrict its movement.

swag n **1** an arrangement of fabric, plaster decorations, etc in a drooping curve. **2** informal goods acquired by unlawful means; loot.

swagger[1] v to walk with an air of overbearing self-confidence or self-satisfaction. ➤ **swaggering** adj.

swagger[2] n a self-confident or arrogant gait or manner.

swain n literary a male admirer or suitor.

swallow[1] n a small migrant bird with long wings and a forked tail.

swallow[2] v **1** to cause (food or drink) to pass from the mouth through the oesophagus into the stomach. **2** (often + up) to envelop or engulf. **3** to accept or believe without question.

swallow[3] n an act of swallowing.

swam v past tense of SWIM[1].

swamp[1] n an area of wet spongy land; a marsh. ➤ **swampy** adj.

swamp[2] v **1** to submerge. **2** to fill (a boat) with water until it sinks. **3** to overwhelm with too much of something.

swan[1] n a large long-necked mostly pure white aquatic bird. ➤ **swanlike** adj.

swan[2] v (**swanned, swanning**) Brit, informal to go around in a leisurely, aimless or ostentatious fashion.

swank[1] v informal to show off.

swank[2] n informal ostentation or boasting.

swanky adj (**-ier, -iest**) informal **1** fashionably smart and expensive. **2** inclined to show off.

swan song n a farewell appearance or performance, or a final work.

swap[1] or **swop** v (**swapped** or **swopped**, **swapping** or **swopping**) **1** to exchange (things), usu with another person. **2** to exchange or substitute.

swap[2] or **swop** n an act of exchanging things.

sward n a surface of short grass.

swarm[1] n **1** a large mass of flying insects. **2** a large number of honeybees, esp when emigrating from a hive with a queen bee to start a new colony elsewhere. **3** a group of people or things massing together.

swarm[2] v **1** to move or assemble in a crowd. **2** (+ with) to teem with something. **3** (+ up) to climb rapidly by gripping with the hands and feet.

swarthy adj (**-ier, -iest**) of a dark complexion.

swashbuckler n a swaggering adventurer or daredevil. ➤ **swashbuckling** adj.

swastika n **1** an ancient symbol in the shape of a cross with the ends of the arms bent at right angles. **2** this symbol used as the emblem of the German Nazi Party.

swat[1] v (**swatted, swatting**) to hit (an insect) with a sharp slapping blow. ➤ **swatter** n.

swat[2] n **1** a quick crushing blow. **2** a swatter.

swatch n a sample piece of fabric or other material.

swath n chiefly NAmer = SWATHE[1].

swathe[1] n **1** a row of cut grain or grass left by a scythe or mowing machine. **2** a long broad strip.

swathe² v **1** to wrap with a bandage or strip of material. **2** to envelop.

swathe³ n something that swathes or envelops.

sway¹ v **1** to move slowly and rhythmically back and forth or from side to side. **2** to change the opinions of others.

sway² n **1** a swaying movement. **2** controlling influence or power. ✴ **hold sway** to have influence or power.

swear v (**swore, sworn**) **1** to use profane or obscene language. **2** to utter or take (an oath) solemnly. **3** to promise emphatically or earnestly. ✴ **swear by** to place great confidence in. **swear to** to express certainty about.

swear in v to induct into office by administration of an oath.

swearword n a profane or obscene word.

sweat¹ n **1** fluid excreted through the pores from the glands under the skin, when one is hot, etc. **2** informal a state of anxiety or impatience. **3** informal hard work; drudgery. ✴ **no sweat** informal not a problem. ➤ **sweaty** adj.

sweat² v (past tense and past part. **sweated** or NAmer **sweat**) **1** to excrete sweat. **2** to emit moisture. **3** to work hard. **4** to feel tense or anxious. **5** to cook (vegetables) gently.

sweatband n a band of material worn round the head or wrist to absorb sweat.

sweater n a usu long-sleeved pullover.

sweatshirt n a loose collarless pullover of heavy cotton.

sweatshop n a place of work in which people are employed for long hours at low wages and under poor conditions.

Swede n a native or inhabitant of Sweden.

swede n a plant with a bulbous yellow-fleshed root used as a vegetable.

sweep¹ v (past tense and past part. **swept**) **1** to clean by brushing. **2** to remove with a single forceful action. **3** to move or carry along with irresistible force. **4** (+ away) to abolish or destroy completely. **5** to search (an area) systematically. ✴ **sweep somebody off their feet** to cause somebody to fall in love with one. **sweep something under the carpet** to conceal hoping that it will be ignored. **sweep the board** to win everything in a contest.

sweep² n **1** an act of sweeping. **2** (also **chimney sweep**) a person who cleans chimneys. **3** a curving course or line. **4** a broad extent. **5** scope. **6** informal a sweepstake. ➤ **sweeper** n.

sweeping adj **1** extending in a wide curve or over a wide area. **2** extensive; wide-ranging. **3** of a statement: marked by wholesale and indiscriminate inclusion.

sweepstake n (also in pl) a lottery or other form of gambling, e.g. on a horse race, in which the stakes form the prize or prizes.

sweet¹ adj **1** inducing a taste similar to that of sugar. **2** having a pleasant smell or taste. **3** of air or water: fresh and pure. **4** delightful or charm-

ing. **5** marked by gentle good humour or kindliness. **6** pleasing to the ear or eye. **7** satisfying. ✴ **sweet on somebody** informal, dated in love with somebody. ➤ **sweetly** adv, **sweetness** n.

sweet² n **1** Brit a small piece of confectionery prepared with sugar or chocolate. **2** Brit a dessert.

sweet-and-sour adj seasoned with a sauce containing sugar and vinegar or lemon juice.

sweetbread n the pancreas or thymus of a young animal used for food.

sweet corn n maize with kernels that contain a high percentage of sugar, used as a vegetable.

sweeten v **1** to make or become sweet. **2** to make less painful or trying.

sweetener n **1** a substance added to food or drink to sweeten it, esp one used instead of sugar. **2** chiefly Brit, informal a bribe.

sweetheart n a person that one loves.

sweetmeat n archaic a sweet or delicacy rich in sugar.

sweet pea n a climbing plant of the pea family with colourful fragrant flowers.

sweet potato n a plant with large sweet tubers used as a vegetable.

sweet talk n informal flattery.

sweet-talk v informal to persuade (somebody) to do something by flattering them.

sweet tooth n a fondness for sweet food.

swell¹ v (past tense **swelled**, past part. **swollen** or **swelled**) **1** to expand, esp to curve outwards or upwards. **2** to increase the number, volume, or intensity of.

swell² n **1** a rounded protuberance or bulge. **2** a gradual increase. **3** a surging or undulating movement of water.

swell³ adj NAmer, informal, dated excellent.

swelling n an abnormal bodily protuberance or enlargement.

swelter v to suffer from heat.

sweltering adj oppressively hot.

swept v past tense and past part. of SWEEP¹.

swerve¹ v to turn aside abruptly from a straight course.

swerve² n an instance of swerving.

swift¹ adj **1** moving or capable of moving at great speed. **2** occurring suddenly or lasting a very short time. ➤ **swiftly** adv, **swiftness** n.

swift² n a dark-coloured bird noted for its fast darting flight.

swig¹ n a quantity drunk in one swallow.

swig² v (**swigged, swigging**) to drink in long draughts.

swill¹ v **1** Brit (often + out) to wash, esp by flushing with water. **2** Brit, informal to drink or eat greedily.

swill² n food for pigs, composed of edible refuse mixed with water or milk.

swim¹ v (**swimming**, past tense **swam**, past part. **swum**) **1** to propel the body in water by bodily movements. **2** to be immersed in or flooded with a liquid. **3** to have a floating, whirling, or dizzy sensation. ➤ **swimmer** n.

swim² n a period of swimming.

swimming bath n Brit (also in pl) an indoor swimming pool.

swimming costume n Brit a close-fitting garment worn for swimming.

swimmingly adv informal very well; splendidly.

swimming pool n an artificial pool for people to swim in.

swimsuit n = SWIMMING COSTUME.

swindle¹ v to take money or property from by fraud or deceit. ➤ **swindler** n.

swindle² n an act of fraud or deceit.

swine n **1** (pl **swine**) formal a pig. **2** (pl **swine** or **swines**) informal a contemptible person. ➤ **swinish** adj.

swing¹ v (past tense and past part. **swung**) **1** to move freely to and fro when suspended. **2** to move in in a circle or arc. **3** to move into a new position by grasping a fixed support. **4** to throw (a punch) with a sweeping arm movement. **5** to fluctuate from one condition, position, or object of attention to another. **6** to influence decisively. **7** informal to succeed in doing or having (something).

swing² n **1** a suspended seat on which a person can swing to and fro. **2** a swinging movement. **3** a stroke or blow delivered with a sweeping movement. **4** a change in public opinion or political preference. **5** jazz played with a steady lively rhythm and simple harmony. ✴ **get into the swing of things** informal to accustom oneself to a situation or undertaking. **go with a swing** informal to be enjoyable and successful. **in full swing** at the height of activity. **swings and roundabouts** Brit, informal a situation in which a loss or disadvantage is balanced by a gain or advantage of another kind.

swingeing adj chiefly Brit severe or drastic.

swinging adj informal **1** lively and exciting. **2** sexually liberated.

swipe¹ v **1** informal to strike or hit out at with a sweeping motion. **2** informal to steal. **3** informal to pass (a card) through a machine that can read its magnetic stripe.

swipe² n informal **1** a strong sweeping blow. **2** an unexpected criticism.

swipe card n a plastic card containing a magnetic strip encoded with information that can be read when the card is passed through a special machine.

swirl¹ n **1** a whirling mass or motion. **2** a twisting shape or pattern. ➤ **swirly** adj.

swirl² v to move in eddies or whirls.

swish¹ n a hissing or brushing sound, or a movement causing it.

swish² v to move with a swish.

swish³ adj Brit, informal smart and fashionable.

Swiss n (pl **Swiss**) a native or inhabitant of Switzerland. ➤ **Swiss** adj.

Swiss roll n Brit a thin sheet of sponge cake spread with jam, cream, etc and rolled up.

switch¹ n **1** a device for making or breaking a connection in an electrical circuit. **2** a sudden shift or change. **3** a slender flexible twig or rod.

switch² v **1** to make a sudden change in. **2** to exchange (things).

switchback n Brit something, e.g. a road or rollercoaster, with alternating steep ascents and descents.

switchblade n chiefly NAmer a flick knife.

switchboard n a panel with switching devices that enable telephone calls to be directed manually to particular numbers.

switch off v **1** to turn off (e.g. a light or machine) by operating an electrical switch. **2** informal to lose interest.

switch on v to turn on (e.g. a light or machine) by operating an electrical switch.

swivel¹ n a device joining two parts so that one part can pivot freely.

swivel² v (**swivelled, swivelling,** NAmer **swiveled, swiveling**) to turn on a swivel; to turn rapidly and smoothly.

swiz or **swizz** n (pl **swizzes**) Brit, informal something that does not live up to one's hopes or expectations.

swob¹ n see SWAB¹.

swob² v see SWAB².

swollen v past part. of SWELL¹.

swoon¹ v to faint.

swoon² n a loss of consciousness.

swoop¹ v **1** esp of a bird: to descend steeply through the air, e.g. to seize prey. **2** to make a sudden attack or raid.

swoop² n an act of swooping. ✴ **at one fell swoop** see FELL⁴.

swop¹ v see SWAP¹.

swop² n see SWAP².

sword n a cutting or thrusting weapon with a long sharp-pointed and sharp-edged blade. ✴ **cross swords** to fight or argue.

swordfish n (pl **swordfishes** or **swordfish**) a large oceanic food fish with a sword-like beak.

swore v past tense of SWEAR.

sworn¹ v past part. of SWEAR.

sworn² adj **1** made under oath. **2** determined to remain as specified: *sworn enemies.*

swot¹ n Brit, informal a person who studies excessively.

swot² v (**swotted, swotting**) Brit, informal to study hard.

swum v past part. of SWIM¹.

swung v past tense and past part. of SWING¹.

sybarite n somebody who likes to indulge in sensual pleasures. ➤ **sybaritic** adj.

sycamore n **1** a Eurasian maple tree. **2** NAmer a plane tree.

sycophant *n* a self-seeking flatterer; a toady. ➤ **sycophancy** *n*, **sycophantic** *adj*.

syllable *n* a unit of spoken language that usu consists of one vowel sound with or without an accompanying consonant sound.

syllabus *n* (*pl* **syllabi** *or* **syllabuses**) a summary of a course of study or of examination requirements.

syllogism *n* a pattern of deductive reasoning consisting of two premises and a conclusion.

sylph *n* **1** a slender graceful woman or girl. **2** an imaginary being inhabiting the air. ➤ **sylph-like** *adj*.

sylvan *or* **silvan** *adj* **1** located in or characteristic of woods. **2** full of trees

symbiosis *n* (*pl* **symbioses**) the living together of two dissimilar organisms in intimate association, usu to the benefit of both. ➤ **symbiotic** *adj*.

symbol *n* **1** something or somebody that stands for or suggests something else by association or convention, *esp* a visible sign of something abstract. **2** a special sign used in writing or printing to represent something.

symbolic *adj* using or constituting a symbol or symbols. ➤ **symbolically** *adv*.

symbolism *n* the use of symbols to represent other things.

symbolize *or* **-ise** *v* **1** to serve as a symbol of. **2** to represent by means of symbols.

symmetrical *or* **symmetric** *adj* having the same proportions, shape, etc on both sides. ➤ **symmetrically** *adv*.

symmetry *n* (*pl* **-ies**) **1** the property of being symmetrical. **2** beauty of form arising from balanced proportions.

sympathetic *adj* **1** showing compassion and sensitivity to others' feelings. **2** favourably inclined. **3** congenial. ➤ **sympathetically** *adv*.

sympathize *or* **-ise** *v* **1** to share in distress or suffering. **2** to agree with somebody or something. ➤ **sympathizer** *n*.

sympathy *n* (*pl* **-ies**) **1** the act or capacity of sharing the feelings or interests of another. **2** inclination to think or feel alike. **3** (*also in pl*) a feeling of loyalty.

symphonic *adj* relating to, or having the form of, a symphony.

symphony *n* (*pl* **-ies**) an extended piece for orchestra, typically in four contrasting movements.

symposium *n* (*pl* **symposia** *or* **symposiums**) a formal meeting at which several specialists deliver short addresses on a topic.

symptom *n* **1** something giving indication of a disease or other physical disorder. **2** something that indicates the existence of *esp* something undesirable.

synagogue *n* the house of worship and communal centre of a Jewish congregation.

synapse *n* the point between two nerves across which a nervous impulse is transmitted. ➤ **synaptic** *adj*.

sync *or* **synch** *n informal* synchronization. ✳ **in/out of sync** in/not in harmony or agreement.

synchromesh *n* a system designed to synchronize the speeds of the different moving parts involved in a gear change.

synchronize *or* **-ise** *v* to cause to happen at the same time. ➤ **synchronization** *n*, **synchronizer** *n*.

synchronous *adj* happening or arising at precisely the same time. ➤ **synchronously** *adv*.

syncopate *v* to modify or affect (musical rhythm) by stressing a weak beat or omitting a strong beat. ➤ **syncopation** *n*.

syndicate[1] *n* a group of people or organizations who combine to carry out a particular transaction or to promote a common interest.

syndicate[2] *v* **1** to sell (e.g. a cartoon) to a syndicate for simultaneous publication in many newspapers or periodicals. **2** to manage by a syndicate. ➤ **syndication** *n*.

syndrome *n* a group of symptoms that occur together and characterize a particular medical disorder.

synergy *n* cooperation between two organizations or things that achieves more than both would achieve if they worked separately.

synod *n* **1** the governing assembly of an Anglican province, diocese, or deanery **2** a formal meeting to decide ecclesiastical matters.

synonym *n* any of two or more words in a language that are used with the same meaning.

synonymous *adj* **1** having the same meaning. **2** closely associated.

synopsis *n* (*pl* **synopses**) a condensed statement or outline.

syntax *n* the way in which words are put together to form phrases, clauses, or sentences.

synthesis *n* (*pl* **syntheses**) **1** the combination of separate or diverse elements into a coherent whole. **2** the artificial production of a substance by chemical reaction.

synthesize *or* **-ise** *v* **1** to produce by synthesis. **2** to combine (things) to form a whole. **3** to produce (sound) electronically.

synthesizer *n* an electronic keyboard musical instrument that produces a sound that can be altered, e.g. to mimic other instruments.

synthetic[1] *adj* **1** produced by chemical synthesis, *esp* as an imitation of something natural. **2** not genuine or sincere. ➤ **synthetically** *adv*.

synthetic[2] *n* a synthetic textile fibre.

syphilis *n* a serious sexually transmitted bacterial disease. ➤ **syphilitic** *adj and n*.

syphon[1] *n* see SIPHON[1].

syphon[2] *v* see SIPHON[2].

syrup (*NAmer* **sirup**) *n* **1** a thick sticky solution of sugar and water, often flavoured or mixed with medicinal substances. **2** the concentrated juice of a fruit or plant.

syrupy *adj* **1** like syrup. **2** cloyingly sweet or sentimental.

system *n* **1** a regularly interacting or interdependent group of items forming a unified whole. **2** a form of social, economic, or political organization. **3** an organized or established procedure or method. **4** order. **5** the body considered as a functional unit. **6** (**the system**) society or its rules regarded as stultifying or restrictive. ＊ **get something out of one's system** *informal* to stop thinking about something.

systematic *adj* methodical in procedure or plan; thorough. ➤ **systematically** *adv*.

systematize *or* -**ise** *v* to arrange according to a system.

systemic *adj* involving a system, e.g. affecting the body generally.

T¹ or **t** *n* (*pl* **T's** or **Ts** or **t's**) the twentieth letter of the English alphabet. ✳ **to a T** to perfection; exactly.

T² *abbr* the chemical symbol for tritium.

TA *abbr* Territorial Army.

Ta *abbr* the chemical symbol for tantalum.

ta *interj Brit, informal* thanks.

tab¹ *n* **1** a projecting flap, loop, or strip of material by which something can be held or lifted. **2** *chiefly NAmer* a bill, *esp* for a meal or drinks. ✳ **keep tabs on** *informal* to keep under close surveillance. **pick up the tab** *informal* to pay a bill, e.g. in a restaurant.

tab² *n* = TABULATOR.

tab³ *n informal* a tablet, *esp* one containing an illegal drug.

tabby *n* (*pl* **-ies**) a domestic cat with a brownish or grey coat striped with darker shades.

tabernacle *n* **1** (*often* **Tabernacle**) a tent sanctuary used by the Israelites during the Exodus. **2** the meeting place or church of Nonconformists or Mormons.

table¹ *n* **1** a piece of furniture consisting of a smooth flat slab of wood, etc fixed on legs or some other support. **2** a systematically arranged list of figures, information, etc. **3** (*also* **multiplication table**) a list of the results of multiplying a number by various other numbers. ✳ **on the table** *chiefly Brit* put forward for discussion. **turn the tables** to reverse the relative fortunes of two contending parties.

table² *v Brit* to place (a matter) on the agenda.

tableau *n* (*pl* **tableaux** or **tableaus**) a depiction of a scene by silent and motionless costumed participants.

tablecloth *n* a cloth that is spread over a dining table.

table d'hôte *n* (*pl* **tables d'hôte** or **table d'hôtes**) a meal consisting of a fixed number of courses with a limited choice, provided at a fixed price: compare À LA CARTE.

tablespoon *n* a large spoon used for serving.

tablet *n* **1** a small solid shaped mass or capsule of medicinal material. **2** a flat slab suitable for an inscription.

table tennis *n* a game, based on tennis, played with round wooden bats and a small hollow plastic ball on an indoor table.

tabloid *n* a newspaper having a relatively small page size and usu containing news stories written in a relatively simple style.

taboo¹ or **tabu** *adj* forbidden on grounds of morality, tradition, or social usage.

taboo² or **tabu** *n* (*pl* **taboos** or **tabus**) a prohibition imposed by social custom.

tabular *adj* of data or statistics: arranged in a table.

tabulate *v* to arrange (data) in tabular form. ➤ **tabulation** *n*.

tabulator *n* an attachment to a typewriter or a word-processing function used for arranging data in columns.

tachograph *n* a device for automatically recording the speed of a vehicle, *esp* a lorry.

tachometer *n* a device for indicating speed of rotation, e.g. of a vehicle engine.

tachycardia *n* relatively rapid heart rate, often indicative of disease.

tacit *adj* implied or understood but not actually expressed. ➤ **tacitly** *adv*.

taciturn *adj* not communicative or talkative. ➤ **taciturnity** *n*.

tack¹ *n* **1** a small nail with a broad flat head. **2** a long loose stitch used to hold layers of fabric together temporarily. **3** the direction of a sailing vessel with respect to the direction of the wind. **4** a change of course from one tack to another. **5** a course of action.

tack² *v* **1** to fasten or attach with tacks. **2** to sew together with tacks. **3** (*often* + on) to add as a supplement. **4** to change the course of (a sailing vessel) by turning the bow towards the wind. **5** to follow a zigzag course.

tack³ *n* equipment used in horse riding.

tack⁴ *n* cheap or worthless things or material.

tackle¹ *n* **1** a set of equipment used in a particular activity. **2** an assembly of ropes and pulleys arranged for hoisting and pulling. **3** an instance of tackling in sport.

tackle² *v* **1** to attempt to take the ball from (an opposing player) in hockey or football. **2** to set about dealing with (a problem, etc). **3** to speak to (somebody) about a difficult matter. ➤ **tackler** *n*.

tacky¹ *adj* (**-ier, -iest**) slightly sticky to the touch.

tacky² *adj* (**-ier, -iest**) *informal* in poor taste; vulgar.

tact *n* a keen sense of how to handle people or affairs so as to avoid giving offence.

tactful *adj* showing tact. ➤ **tactfully** *adv.*

tactic *n* a method for achieving an end.

tactical *adj* **1** carried out with only a limited or immediate end in view. **2** of voting: in favour of the candidate most likely to defeat the candidate one least wants to win rather than in favour of one's preferred candidate. **3** of nuclear weapons: of or designed for air attack in close support of ground forces. ➤ **tactically** *adv.*

tactics *pl n* **1** military planning concerned with the disposition and manoeuvres of forces in combat: compare STRATEGY. **2** the skill of employing available means to accomplish an end.

tactile *adj* **1** relating to the sense of touch. **2** of a person: in the habit of touching people in a friendly way.

tactless *adj* insensitive or likely to cause offence. ➤ **tactlessly** *adv.*

tad *n informal* a small amount. * **a tad** somewhat, rather.

tadpole *n* the larva of an amphibian, such as a frog or toad, that lives in water and has a rounded body, long tail, no legs, and external gills.

taffeta *n* a crisp lustrous fabric.

tag[1] *n* **1** a flap or loop on a garment by which to hang it up, or that carries information such as washing instructions. **2** an electronic monitoring device worn around the wrist or ankle by people convicted of a crime but not held in custody. **3** a trite quotation or saying. **4** an identifying word or phrase accompanying or replacing a name. **5** a rigid binding on an end of a shoelace.

tag[2] *v* (**tagged, tagging**) **1** to supply with an identifying marker, price label, etc. **2** to fit with an electronic tag. **3** (*often* + on) to attach as an addition. **4** (*usu* + along/on) to go with somebody.

tag[3] *n* a children's game in which one player chases the others.

tagliatelle *pl n* pasta in the form of narrow ribbons.

tail[1] *n* **1** a flexible extension of the rear end of the body of an animal or bird. **2** the rear part of an aircraft consisting of horizontal and vertical stabilizing and control surfaces. **3** the luminous trail behind a comet. **4** the lower or inferior part of something. **5** (*in pl*) = TAILCOAT. **6** (*in pl*) the reverse of a coin. **7** *informal* a person who follows or keeps watch on somebody. * **turn tail** *informal* to run away.

tail[2] *v* **1** *informal* to follow (somebody) for purposes of surveillance. **2** (*often* + back) to form a long queue. **3** (+ off/away) to diminish gradually in strength, volume, etc.

tailback *n* a long queue of stationary motor vehicles.

tailcoat *n* a man's formal evening coat with two long tapering skirts at the back.

tailgate *n* **1** a hinged board at the rear of a vehicle. **2** a door at the rear of a car, *esp* one that opens upwards.

tailor[1] *n* somebody whose occupation is making or altering clothes.

tailor[2] *v* **1** to make (a garment) for a particular customer. **2** (+ for/to) to adapt to suit a special need or purpose.

tailored *adj* cut so as to fit the figure well.

tailplane *n* the horizontal projection of an aircraft's tail.

tailspin *n* **1** a spiralling dive by an aircraft. **2** *informal* a state of chaos or panic.

tailwind *n* a wind blowing from behind a vehicle, aircraft, or ship.

taint[1] *v* **1** to spoil or contaminate. **2** to corrupt morally.

taint[2] *n* a slight trace of contamination or of something undesirable.

take[1] *v* (**took, taken**) **1** to reach for and hold. **2** to get into one's possession or control. **3** to remove. **4** to proceed to occupy. **5** to subtract (a number). **6** to choose. **7** to lead or carry to another place. **8** to use as a route or means of transport. **9** to bring to a particular state: *Her ability should take her far.* **10** to affect in a specified way: *The remark took us by surprise.* **11** to consume (food, drink, medicine, etc). **12** to adopt or advance (a particular view). **13** to be taught (a subject of study). **14** to hold or accommodate. **15** to need or call for. **16** to submit to or undergo. **17** to tolerate or endure. **18** to accept in payment. **19** to accept or make use of (a risk, opportunity, etc). **20** to regard in a particular way. * **take after** to resemble (an older relative) in appearance or character. **take against** *chiefly Brit* to come to dislike. **take apart 1** to dismantle. **2** *informal* to criticize or treat severely. **take it** to infer or assume. **take to 1** to form a liking for. **2** to begin to do (something). **what it takes** the qualities or resources needed.

take[2] *n* **1** the uninterrupted recording, filming, or televising of something. **2** proceeds or takings. **3** *chiefly NAmer, informal* interpretation or slant. * **on the take** *informal* taking bribes.

takeaway *n Brit* **1** a cooked meal eaten away from the premises from which it was bought. **2** a shop or restaurant that sells takeaways.

take away *v* **1** to remove. **2** to subtract. * **take away from** to detract from.

take back *v* **1** to retract (a statement). **2** to return (unsatisfactory goods) to the place where they were bought.

take down *v* **1** to remove or dismantle. **2** to write down on paper.

take-home pay *n* the part of gross salary or wages remaining after deductions, e.g. for income tax, insurance, etc.

tangent

take in v **1** to offer accommodation or shelter to. **2** *informal* to deceive or trick. **3** to make (a garment) smaller by alteration. **4** to include. **5** to understand.

takeoff n **1** a caricature or impersonation. **2** the launching of an aircraft or rocket.

take off v **1** to remove (clothing). **2** to deduct (an amount). **3** to mimic (somebody). **4** of an aircraft: to become airborne. **5** *informal* to leave abruptly. **6** *informal* to be quickly successful.

take on v **1** to agree to (a task or undertaking). **2** to engage (staff, etc). **3** to assume (an appearance or quality). **4** *informal* to become emotional or distraught.

takeout n *NAmer* = TAKEAWAY.

take out v **1** to extract or remove. **2** to obtain (authorization, insurance, etc). **3** to escort on a social occasion. ✻ **take it out of** to fatigue or exhaust. **take it out on** to vent one's anger or frustration on.

takeover n an act of taking over, *esp* of gaining control of a business company by buying a majority of the shares.

take over v to assume control or possession of.

take up v **1** to pick up or lift. **2** to become engaged or interested in (an activity). **3** to occupy or require (space or time). **4** to shorten (a garment). **5** to discuss or pursue (a matter) further. ✻ **take somebody up on 1** to accept (an offer) from somebody. **2** to venture to disagree about (something). **take up with** to begin to associate with.

takings pl n the amount of money earned by a business during a specified period.

talc n **1** = TALCUM POWDER. **2** a soft mineral with a greasy feel.

talcum powder n finely powdered talc, often perfumed, used for dusting the body.

tale n **1** a story. **2** a lie.

talent n **1** a special creative or artistic aptitude. **2** general ability or intelligence. **3** talented people. **4** *informal* people considered in terms of their sexual attractiveness. **5** an ancient unit of weight or money.

talented adj having a special natural aptitude or skill.

talisman n (pl **talismans**) an object believed to bring good fortune or produce magical effects.

talk[1] v **1** to convey information or communicate in speech. **2** (+ about/of) to make the subject of conversation. **3** (+ over/through) to discuss (something) at length. **4** to be able to speak. **5** to reveal secret or confidential information. **6** (+ into/out of) to persuade (somebody) by talking.

talk[2] n **1** a conversation. **2** (*also in pl*) a formal discussion or exchange of views. **3** an address or lecture. **4** rumour; gossip.

talkative adj given to talking a lot.

talk back v to answer impertinently.

talk down v (+ to) to speak in a condescending fashion to.

talking-to n (pl **talking-tos**) *informal* a reprimand or scolding.

talk round v to persuade or convince.

tall adj **1** of above average height. **2** of a specified height. **3** highly exaggerated; incredible: *a tall story*. ✻ **a tall order** an unreasonably difficult task or requirement.

tallow n the solid white rendered fat of cattle and sheep, used in soap and candles.

tall ship n a sailing ship with tall masts.

tally[1] n (pl **-ies**) **1** a record of items, amounts, or a score. **2** the current number of things achieved by somebody.

tally[2] v (**-ies, -ied**) **1** to correspond or match. **2** to make a count of.

tally-ho n (pl **-os**) a call given by a huntsman to the hounds on sighting a fox.

Talmud n the authoritative body of Jewish tradition.

talon n a curved claw, *esp* of a bird of prey.

tamarind n a pod-like fruit with sticky brown pulp.

tamarisk n a shrub with tiny narrow leaves and masses of minute flowers.

tambourine n a shallow one-headed drum with loose metallic discs at the sides, played by shaking or striking.

tame[1] adj **1** of an animal: not afraid of or dangerous to human beings. **2** of a person: docile and submissive. **3** lacking zest or interest. ➤ **tamely** adv.

tame[2] v to make tame.

tamp v (*often* + down) to pack (something) in or down by a succession of blows.

tamper v (+ with) to interfere or meddle without permission.

tampon n an absorbent plug put into the vagina to absorb menstrual bleeding.

tan[1] v (**tanned, tanning**) **1** to convert (animal skin) into leather. **2** to make or become light brown by exposure to the sun. ✻ **tan somebody's hide** *informal* to beat somebody severely.

tan[2] n **1** a brown colour given to the skin by exposure to sun. **2** a light yellowish brown.

tandem[1] n a bicycle having two seats one behind the other. ✻ **in tandem 1** in partnership or conjunction. **2** arranged one behind the other.

tandem[2] adv one behind the other.

tandoori n a North Indian method of cooking meat in a clay oven.

tang n **1** a sharp distinctive flavour or smell. **2** a projecting shank on a blade that connects with a handle.

tangent n **1** in mathematics, the ratio in a right-angled triangle between the sides opposite and adjacent to an acute angle. **2** a straight line touching a curve or surface at only one point. ✽ **fly/go off at a tangent** to change suddenly from one subject or course of action to another.

tangential adj **1** acting along or lying in a tangent. **2** incidental; barely relevant.

tangerine n a small loose-skinned citrus fruit with deep orange skin and pulp.

tangible adj **1** capable of being perceived by touch. **2** real; material. ➤ **tangibility** n, **tangibly** adv.

tangle¹ v **1** to intertwine in a disordered mass. **2** informal (often + with) to engage in conflict or argument. ➤ **tangled** adj.

tangle² n **1** a confused twisted mass. **2** a complicated state.

tango¹ n (pl **-os**) a Latin-American ballroom dance, characterized by long pauses and stylized body positions.

tango² v (**-oes, -oed**) to dance the tango.

tank n **1** a large receptacle for liquids or gas. **2** a container for fuel in a motor vehicle. **3** a clear-sided container in which to keep fish. **4** an enclosed heavily armoured combat vehicle that moves on caterpillar tracks.

tankard n a silver or pewter beer mug sometimes with a hinged lid.

tank engine n a steam locomotive that carries its own water and coal and does not have a tender.

tanker n a ship, aircraft, or road or rail vehicle designed to carry liquid in bulk.

tank top n a sleeveless pullover usu worn over a shirt or jumper.

tannin n a soluble astringent substance used in tanning and dyeing, and present in tea.

Tannoy n trademark a public address system that can broadcast throughout a large building.

tantalize or **-ise** v to tease by presenting something desirable that is just out of reach or promising something and then withholding it. ➤ **tantalizing** adj.

tantamount adj (+ to) equivalent in significance or effect to.

tantrum n (pl **tantrums**) a fit of childish temper.

Taoiseach n the prime minister of the Republic of Ireland.

tap¹ n **1** a device with a spout and valve attached to a pipe or container to control the flow of a liquid or gas. **2** a device that can be attached to a telephone to allow somebody to listen secretly to conversations. ✽ **on tap 1** of beer, etc: on draught. **2** readily available.

tap² v (**tapped, tapping**) **1** to pierce (a container, tree, etc) so as to let out or draw off a fluid. **2** to draw from (a source or supply). **3** to connect a listening device to (a telephone wire) in order to acquire secret information. **4** informal (usu + for) to ask for money or information from (somebody).

tap³ n **1** a light blow, or the sound it makes. **2** tap dancing.

tap⁴ v (**tapped, tapping**) **1** to strike lightly with a slight sound. **2** to give a light blow with (something).

tapas pl n light savoury Spanish snacks eaten with an alcoholic drink.

tap dancing n a style of dancing in which the steps are tapped out audibly by small pieces of metal fitted to the dancer's shoes.

tape¹ n **1** a narrow band of woven fabric. **2** the string stretched above the finishing line of a race. **3** adhesive tape, insulating tape, or masking tape. **4** = MAGNETIC TAPE. **5** a tape recording. **6** a cassette of audio tape or videotape.

tape² v **1** to fasten or bind with tape. **2** to record on magnetic tape. ✽ **have something taped** to be confident of one's ability to deal with something.

tape measure n a narrow strip of tape marked off in units for measuring.

taper v **1** to decrease gradually in thickness, diameter, or width towards one end. **2** (often + off) to diminish gradually. ➤ **tapering** adj.

tape recorder n a device for recording sounds on magnetic tape and reproducing them. ➤ **tape recording** n.

tapestry n (pl **-ies**) a piece of heavy fabric decorated with woven or embroidered designs.

tapeworm n a parasitic worm with a long, ribbon-like body that lives in the intestine of human beings.

tapioca n grains of cassava starch used esp in puddings.

tapir n (pl **tapirs** or **tapir**) a hoofed mammal with an elongated flexible snout.

tappet n a lever or projection moved by or moving some other piece, such as a cam.

tar¹ n **1** a dark viscous liquid obtained by distilling wood, coal, peat, etc. **2** a brown residue present in tobacco smoke.

tar² v (**tarred, tarring**) to cover or smear with tar. ✽ **tarred with the same brush** of two or more people: having the same faults.

tar³ n informal, dated a sailor.

taramasalata n a pinkish paste made from fish roe, olive oil, and seasoning, usu eaten as a starter.

tarantula n (pl **tarantulas** or **tarantulae**) **1** a large hairy spider of tropical and subtropical America. **2** a large southern European spider.

tardy adj (**-ier, -iest**) **1** delayed; late. **2** sluggish. ➤ **tardily** adv, **tardiness** n.

tare n the weight of an unloaded goods vehicle without its fuel.

target¹ n **1** an object to fire at in practice or competition, consisting of a series of concentric circles with a bull's-eye at the centre. **2** a person or object that is selected to be fired at, attacked, criticized, etc. **3** a goal or objective.

target² v (**targeted, targeting**) **1** to make

(somebody or something) a target. **2** (+ at/on) to aim (e.g. a missile) at.

tariff *n* **1** a duty imposed by a government on imported or exported goods. **2** the rates charged by a business, e.g. a hotel, or a list of these rates.

tarmac[1] *n* **1** a mixture of tar and aggregates used for surfacing roads. **2** a runway or other area surfaced with tarmac.

tarmac[2] *v* (**tarmacked, tarmacking**) to apply tarmac to (a road or path).

tarn *n* a small mountain lake.

tarnish[1] *v* **1** to dull the lustre of (something) by dirt, air, etc. **2** to bring discredit on.

tarnish[2] *n* a film of chemically altered material on the surface of a metal or mineral.

tarot *n* a set of 22 pictorial playing cards used for fortune-telling.

tarpaulin *n* a sheet of heavy waterproof tarred canvas.

tarragon *n* a herb with aromatic leaves.

tarry *v* (**-ies, -ied**) *archaic or literary* **1** to stay in or at a place. **2** to delay.

tarsus *n* (*pl* **tarsi**) the group of small bones in the ankle, heel, and upper part of the foot.

tart[1] *adj* **1** sharp or acid to the taste. **2** sarcastic or hurtful. ➤ **tartly** *adv*.

tart[2] *n* a pastry shell containing a sweet or savoury filling.

tart[3] *n informal* **1** a female prostitute. **2** a sexually promiscuous woman. ➤ **tarty** *adj*.

tartan *n* **1** a textile design of Scottish origin consisting of checks and stripes of varying colour, usu patterned to designate a particular clan. **2** a fabric with a tartan design.

tartar[1] *n informal* a formidable or irascible person.

tartar[2] *n* **1** a substance formed during fermentation that is deposited in wine casks as a reddish sediment. **2** an incrustation on the teeth consisting of calcium salts.

tartare sauce *n* mayonnaise with chopped pickles, olives, capers, and parsley, served *esp* with fish.

tart up *v* **1** to dress (oneself) up, put on make-up, etc. **2** to decorate or refurbish (a place) *esp* cheaply or gaudily.

task *n* an assigned piece of work; a duty. ＊ **take to task** to rebuke for a failure or mistake.

task force *n* **1** a temporary military grouping assembled to accomplish a particular objective. **2** a group of people that has been assigned a specific task.

taskmaster *or* **taskmistress** *n* a person who assigns tasks.

tassel *n* a bunch of cords or threads of even length fastened at one end, used as an ornament.

taste[1] *v* **1** to take a little (food, drink, etc) into the mouth to test its flavour. **2** to recognize (a substance, flavour, etc) by tasting. **3** (*often* + of)

to have a specified flavour. **4** to experience or undergo. ➤ **taster** *n*.

taste[2] *n* **1** the faculty of perceiving the flavours of substances through the taste buds and distinguishing them as sweet, bitter, sour, or salt. **2** the flavour of a substance as perceived by this sense. **3** an instance of tasting. **4** a small amount tasted. **5** an experience of something. **6** an individual preference. **7** discernment in aesthetic or social matters.

taste bud *n* any of the small organs on the surface of the tongue that transmit the sensation of taste.

tasteful *adj* conforming to good judgment or acceptable behaviour. ➤ **tastefully** *adv*.

tasteless *adj* **1** lacking flavour. **2** not conforming to good judgment or acceptable behaviour. ➤ **tastelessly** *adv*.

tasty *adj* (**-ier, -iest**) **1** having an appetizing flavour. **2** *informal* arousing interest. **3** *Brit, informal* sexually appealing.

tat *n Brit, informal* low-quality or tasteless goods.

tatter *n* an irregular torn shred of material. ＊ **in tatters 1** torn to pieces; ragged. **2** in a state of ruin or disarray.

tattered *adj* old and torn.

tattle[1] *v* to chatter or gossip.

tattle[2] *n* chatter; gossip.

tattoo[1] *n* (*pl* **-os**) an indelible mark or design on the skin made by tattooing.

tattoo[2] *v* (**tattooed, tattooing**) to mark (the body) by inserting pigments under the skin. ➤ **tattooist** *n*.

tattoo[3] *n* (*pl* **tattoos**) **1** an outdoor military display of marching, music, etc. **2** a rapid rhythmic beating or tapping.

tatty *adj* (**-ier, -iest**) *chiefly Brit, informal* shabby; dilapidated.

tau *n* the 19th letter of the Greek alphabet (T, τ).

taught *v* past tense and past part. of TEACH.

taunt[1] *v* to provoke or jeer at (somebody) in a mocking way.

taunt[2] *n* a sarcastic provocation or insult.

Taurus *n* the second sign of the zodiac (the Bull).

taut *adj* **1** stretched or pulled tight. **2** tense; stressed. ➤ **tauten** *v*, **tautly** *adv*.

tautology *n* (*pl* **-ies**) the needless repetition of an idea, statement, or word. ➤ **tautological** *adj*, **tautologous** *adj*.

tavern *n Brit, humorous or archaic* a pub or inn.

tawdry *adj* (**-ier, -iest**) **1** cheap and tastelessly ornate. **2** sordid or sleazy. ➤ **tawdriness** *n*.

tawny *adj* (**-ier, -iest**) of a warm sandy or brownish orange colour.

tax[1] *n* a charge imposed by a government on individuals, organizations, or property, *esp* to raise revenue.

tax[2] *v* **1** to levy a tax on (income, a person, etc). **2** to pay tax on (a vehicle). **3** to make strenuous demands on. **4** (+ with) to charge (somebody) with a fault, or blame them for it. ➢ **taxable** *adj*.

taxation *n* **1** the imposition of taxes. **2** revenue obtained from taxes.

tax-deductible *adj* legally permitted to be deducted from income or capital before tax is paid on it.

tax exile *n* a person who lives abroad in order to avoid paying high taxes in their home country.

tax haven *n* a country with a relatively low level of taxation.

taxi[1] *n* (*pl* **taxis**) a motor car that may be hired, together with its driver, to carry passengers.

taxi[2] *v* (**taxis** or **taxies**, **taxied**, **taxiing** or **taxying**) of an aircraft: to move at low speed along a runway before takeoff or after landing.

taxicab *n* = TAXI[1].

taxidermy *n* the art of preparing, stuffing, and mounting the skins of animals to give a lifelike appearance. ➢ **taxidermist** *n*.

taxing *adj* physically, mentally, or emotionally demanding.

taxi rank *n* a place where taxis park to wait for customers.

taxonomy *n* (*pl* **-ies**) **1** classification, *esp* of plants and animals according to their presumed natural relationships. **2** the scientific study of classification. ➢ **taxonomic** *adj*.

tax return *n* a form on which a person states their income and allowable deductions for tax assessment purposes.

tax year *n* the year that is taken as the basis for calculations of tax (in Britain generally from 6 April to 5 April).

TB *n* = TUBERCULOSIS.

Tb *abbr* the chemical symbol for terbium.

tbs or **tbsp** *abbr* (*pl* **tbs** or **tbsp** or **tbsps**) tablespoonful.

Tc *abbr* the chemical symbol for technetium.

Te *abbr* the chemical symbol for tellurium.

tea *n* **1** the leaves and leaf buds of an evergreen Asian shrub prepared and cured. **2** a drink prepared by steeping tea leaves in boiling water. **3** a drink made from the leaves, flowers, or fruit of various other plants. **4** refreshments, usu including tea with sandwiches, cakes, or biscuits, served in the late afternoon. **5** a late-afternoon or early-evening meal.

tea bag *n* a cloth or paper bag holding enough tea for an individual drink.

tea cake *n* a round sweet bun often containing currants, usu eaten toasted with butter.

teach *v* (*past tense and past part.* **taught**) **1** to cause (somebody or something) to know something or how to do something. **2** to impart the knowledge of (a subject, skill, etc). **3** to cause

(somebody) to understand something by experience. **4** to advocate. ➢ **teaching** *n*.

teacher *n* a person whose occupation is teaching, *esp* in a school.

tea cloth *n* = TEA TOWEL.

teacup *n* a small cup used for tea.

teak *n* the hard yellowish brown wood of a tall tree native to India and Southeast Asia.

teal *n* (*pl* **teals** or **teal**) a small freshwater duck.

team[1] *n* **1** a group of players forming one side in a sporting contest, game, etc. **2** a group of two or more people who work together. **3** two or more draught animals harnessed together.

team[2] *v* **1** (*often* + up) to come together as a team. **2** (+ with) to combine (e.g. an item of clothing) with another for a particular effect.

teammate *n* a fellow member of a team.

team spirit *n* willing and enthusiastic cooperation to achieve group objectives.

teamwork *n* mutual cooperation in a group enterprise.

teapot *n* a usu round pot with a lid, spout, and handle in which tea is brewed.

tear[1] *n* a drop of clear salty fluid secreted into the eye and often released as a result of grief or other emotion. ✳ **in tears** crying; weeping.

tear[2] *v* (**tore**, **torn**) **1** to rip or pull apart by force; to damage in this way. **2** to wound (e.g. a muscle or ligament) by tearing. **3** (*often* + from/ off) to remove by force. **4** (**be torn**) be unable to decide between two alternatives. **5** to move with great speed or haste. ✳ **tear a strip off** *informal* to rebuke (somebody) angrily. **tear into** to attack (somebody) physically or verbally without restraint.

tear[3] *n* a hole or rip made by tearing.

tearaway *n* Brit, *informal* an unruly and reckless young person.

tear down *v* to demolish.

teardrop *n* a single tear.

tearful *adj* **1** causing tears. **2** crying or inclined to cry. ➢ **tearfully** *adv*.

tear gas *n* a gas that causes the eyes to stream with tears and is used chiefly in dispersing crowds.

tearjerker *n* *informal* a very sad or sentimental play, film, etc.

tearoom *n* a restaurant where light refreshments are served.

tear up *v* to tear into pieces.

tease[1] *v* **1** to try, usu playfully, to irritate or embarrass (somebody) by making fun of them. **2** to arouse (somebody) sexually with no intention of permitting sexual fulfilment. **3** to disentangle and straighten (wool) by combing it.

tease[2] *n* *informal* somebody or something that teases.

teasel or **teazel** or **teazle** *n* a tall plant with flower heads that are covered with stiff hooked bracts.

tease out v to gain (information, the truth, etc) with difficulty, e.g. by working through a mass of data.

teaspoon n **1** a small spoon used for adding sugar, etc to hot drinks and stirring them. **2** = TEASPOONFUL.

teaspoonful n (pl **teaspoonfuls**) as much as a teaspoon will hold (about 5ml).

teat n **1** a nipple of the mammary gland of a female animal. **2** a rubber or plastic mouthpiece attached to the top of a baby's feeding bottle.

tea towel n a cloth for drying dishes after they have been washed.

technical adj **1** involving special and usu practical knowledge, esp of mechanical, industrial, or scientific subjects. **2** relating to or used in a particular subject: technical terms. **3** complicated or difficult to understand. **4** marked by a strict legal interpretation or rigid application of the rules. **5** relating to technique. ➤ **technically** adv.

technical college n a further education college that offers courses in practical subjects.

technicality n (pl **-ies**) **1** a detail meaningful only to a specialist. **2** a detail arising from a strict or literal interpretation of a rule or law.

technician n **1** a specialist in the technical details of a subject or occupation. **2** somebody employed to do practical work, e.g. in a laboratory.

Technicolor n trademark a process of colour photography in the cinema.

technique n **1** the manner in which an artist, performer, or athlete displays their skill. **2** a method of accomplishing a desired aim.

techno n a form of fast electronically produced modern dance music.

technology n (pl **-ies**) **1** the application of science for practical purposes esp in commerce and industry. **2** the study of applied scientific methods. ➤ **technological** adj, **technologically** n.

tectonic adj relating to the earth's crust.

teddy n (pl **-ies**) = TEDDY BEAR.

teddy bear n a stuffed toy bear.

Teddy boy n a male member of a British youth cult of the 1950s, characterized by supposedly Edwardian-style clothing, hair styled in swept-up quiffs, and enthusiasm for rock 'n' roll.

tedious adj dull, boring, and apparently interminable. ➤ **tediously** adv.

tedium n the state of being tedious.

tee[1] n a mark aimed at in various games, e.g. curling or quoits.

tee[2] n **1** the area from which a golf ball is struck at the beginning of play on a hole. **2** a peg used to raise a golf ball into position for striking at the beginning of play on a hole.

tee[3] v (often + up) to place (a golf ball) on a tee.

teem v **1** (+ with) to be filled with large numbers of moving and active beings. **2** Brit (also + down) to rain hard.

teen[1] adj informal = TEENAGE.

teen[2] n informal = TEENAGER.

teenage adj relating to or suitable for teenagers. ➤ **teenaged** adj.

teenager n a person who is aged between 13 and 19.

teens pl n the years 13 to 19 in a lifetime.

teeny or **teensy** adj (**-ier**, **-iest**) informal tiny.

tee off v to drive a golf ball from a tee.

teepee n see TEPEE.

tee shirt n see T-SHIRT.

teeter v to wobble or move unsteadily.

teeth n pl of TOOTH.

teethe v to cut one's milk teeth.

teetotal adj practising complete abstinence from alcoholic drinks. ➤ **teetotalism** n, **teetotaller** n.

telecommunications pl n the science and technology of communication at a distance, e.g. by telegraph, telephone, television, etc.

teleconferencing n the process of holding a meeting involving people in different places who are linked by telephone or video.

telegram n a message sent by telegraph and delivered as a written or typed note.

telegraph[1] n an apparatus or system for sending messages along a wire.

telegraph[2] v to send a message to (somebody) by telegraph.

telegraphic adj **1** of the telegraph. **2** concise; terse.

telekinesis n the supposed ability to move distant objects without physically touching them, esp just by concentrating the mind on them. ➤ **telekinetic** adj.

telepathy n communication that supposedly occurs directly from one mind to another without use of the known senses. ➤ **telepathic** adj.

telephone[1] n **1** a device for converting sounds into electrical impulses for transmission by wire or radio to a particular receiver. **2** the system of communications that uses telephones. ➤ **telephonic** adj.

telephone[2] v to speak to (somebody) by telephone.

telephone box n a booth containing a public telephone.

telephone directory n a book giving the telephone numbers of subscribers.

telephonist n Brit a telephone switchboard operator.

telephony n the use of telephones for communication, or the technology of telephones.

telephoto lens n a camera lens that produces a magnified image of a distant object.

teleprinter n a machine with a typewriter keyboard and printing device that transmits, and receives and prints, telegraphic signals.

telesales

telesales *pl n* sales or selling transacted by telephone.

telescope[1] *n* a usu tubular optical instrument for viewing distant objects in magnified form by means of a lens or a concave mirror. ➤ **telescopic** *adj.*

telescope[2] *v* **1** to slide one part within another like the cylindrical sections of a hand telescope. **2** to condense or shorten.

Teletext *n trademark* an information service provided by a television network.

telethon *n* a long television programme designed to raise money for charity.

televise *v* to broadcast (a programme, event, etc) by television.

television *n* **1** an electronic system for transmitting images together with sound as electrical signals along a wire or through space to a receiving device that then reproduces them. **2** a device with a screen and sound system for receiving and displaying television signals. **3** the television broadcasting industry. ➤ **televisual** *adj.*

teleworking *n* the practice of carrying on an occupation or business from home using a computer, modem, e-mail, etc to communicate with employers or clients. ➤ **teleworker** *n.*

telex[1] *n* **1** a communications service involving teleprinters connected by wire through automatic exchanges. **2** a message sent by telex. **3** a telex machine.

telex[2] *v* to send (a message) by telex.

tell *v (past tense and past part.* **told**) **1** to make known the incidents, characters, etc involved in (a story) to. **2** to give information to. **3** to order or instruct (somebody) to do something. **4** to distinguish. **5** *(often + on)* to have an effect: *The strain was beginning to tell.* ✳ **tell on** *informal* to inform on. **tell tales 1** to be untruthful. **2** to reveal secrets or spread gossip. **tell the time** to read the information on a clock or watch.

teller *n* **1** somebody who tells e.g. a story. **2** somebody appointed to count votes. **3** a member of a bank's staff who deals directly with customers' transactions.

telling *adj* producing a marked effect; significant. ➤ **tellingly** *adv.*

telling-off *n (pl* **tellings-off** *or* **telling-offs**) *informal* a harsh or severe reprimand.

tell off *v informal* to scold or reprimand.

telltale[1] *n* somebody who informs on somebody or their actions.

telltale[2] *adj* revealing, betraying, or indicating something.

telly *n (pl* **-ies**) *chiefly Brit, informal* = TELEVISION.

temerity *n* excessive boldness.

temp[1] *n informal* a person, e.g. an office worker, employed temporarily.

temp[2] *v informal* to work as a temp.

temper[1] *n* **1** an uncontrolled and often disproportionate rage. **2** proneness to displays of rage. **3** a characteristic cast of mind or state of feeling. **4** the degree of hardness or resilience given to steel by tempering. ✳ **keep one's temper** to keep one's anger under control. **lose one's temper** to show one's anger.

temper[2] *v* **1** to moderate (something harsh). **2** to bring (*esp* steel) to the right degree of hardness by reheating and cooling it.

tempera *n* a method of painting using pigment mixed with egg yolk and water.

temperament *n* a person's own particular mental and emotional character, *esp* with regard to its effect on behaviour.

temperamental *adj* **1** easily upset or irritated. **2** unpredictable in behaviour or operation. **3** arising from an individual's character or constitution. ➤ **temperamentally** *adv.*

temperance *n* abstinence from alcohol.

temperate *adj* **1** moderate in the indulgence of appetites or desires. **2** having a moderate climate. ➤ **temperately** *adv.*

temperature *n* **1** degree of hotness or coldness as measured on a scale, e.g. in degrees Celsius. **2** *informal* an abnormally high body heat, usu indicative of illness.

tempest *n* a violent storm.

tempestuous *adj* **1** characterized by passion, violence, and emotional turbulence. **2** characterized by storms and bad weather.

template *or* **templet** *n* **1** a pattern, mould, or stencil used as a guide when making, drawing, cutting out, or drilling something. **2** a thing that serves as a model.

temple[1] *n* a building dedicated to religious worship *esp* in non-Christian religions.

temple[2] *n* the flattened space on either side of the forehead.

tempo *n (pl* **tempi** *or* **tempos**) **1** the speed of a musical piece or passage. **2** the rate of motion or activity.

temporal *adj* **1** relating to time as opposed to eternity or space. **2** relating to lay or secular matters.

temporary *adj* lasting only for a limited time. ➤ **temporarily** *adv.*

temporize *or* **-ise** *v* to avoid making a decision or commitment.

tempt *v* **1** to make (somebody) feel strongly inclined to do something. **2** to attract or appeal to. **3** to try to persuade (somebody) to do something wicked, immoral, or unwise, by the promise of pleasure or gain. ✳ **tempt fate** to do or say something that suggests overconfidence and might bring disaster. ➤ **tempter** *n*, **tempting** *adj.*

temptation *n* **1** an urge to do, take, or enjoy something, *esp* something forbidden or unwise. **2** the state of being tempted. **3** something tempting.

temptress n a woman with very strong and obvious sex appeal.

ten n the number 10. ➤ **ten** adj.

tenable adj **1** capable of being defended or justified. **2** (usu + for) of a position, award, etc: to be held for a specified period.

tenacious adj **1** holding on very firmly. **2** unwilling to desist or to give up on something. ➤ **tenaciously** adv, **tenacity** n.

tenancy n (pl **-ies**) temporary occupancy of land, a house, etc under a lease or rental agreement.

tenant[1] n somebody who rents or leases a house or flat from a landlord.

tenant[2] v to live in (a property) as a tenant.

tench n (pl **tenches** or **tench**) a freshwater fish of the carp family with a greenish or blackish skin.

Ten Commandments pl n the commandments given by God to Moses, recorded in Exodus 20:1–17.

tend[1] v **1** to be likely or inclined to do something, or to have the habit of doing something. **2** to move in a specified direction.

tend[2] v **1** to be in charge and take care of. **2** to provide care and treatment for.

tendency n (pl **-ies**) **1** an inclination or predisposition to do something. **2** a general trend or movement.

tendentious adj presenting a biased view.

tender[1] adj **1** showing great gentleness and kindness. **2** showing love or affection. **3** of meat: easy to cut and chew. **4** sensitive or sore. **5** young and vulnerable. **6** demanding careful and sensitive handling. ✳ **tender mercies** unkind treatment. ➤ **tenderly** adv, **tenderness** n.

tender[2] n **1** a boat that carries supplies, passengers, etc to and from ships. **2** a vehicle attached to a steam locomotive for carrying a supply of fuel and water. **3** a road vehicle that carries tools, equipment, or personnel, e.g. for the fire service.

tender[3] v **1** to present formally for acceptance. **2** to offer (money) in payment. **3** (often + for) to present a bid in the hope of gaining a contract.

tender[4] n a formal offer or bid.

tendon n a cord or band of fibrous tissue that connects a muscle to a bone.

tendril n a slender coiling outgrowth that attaches a climbing plant to its support.

tenebrous adj literary dark; murky.

tenement n a large building divided up into separate dwellings.

tenet n a principle, belief, or doctrine.

tenner n Brit, informal a ten-pound note.

tennis n a game for two or four players that is played with rackets and a ball on a flat court divided by a low net.

tennis elbow n inflammation and pain of the elbow, usu resulting from overuse of the hand and forearm.

tenon n a projecting piece of wood specially shaped to fit into a matching slot.

tenor n **1** a male singer having a high voice but below the range of an alto. **2** the general meaning of something spoken or written.

tenpin bowling n an indoor bowling game using ten bottle-shaped pins and a large ball.

tense[1] adj **1** feeling or showing nervousness and anxiety. **2** marked by strain or suspense. **3** stretched tight; taut. ➤ **tensely** adv.

tense[2] v (often + up) to become or make tense.

tense[3] n a set of inflectional forms of a verb that express action taking place at a particular time.

tensile adj **1** able to be stretched or drawn out. **2** relating to tension.

tension n **1** the condition of being stretched tight. **2** the strain caused by two forces pulling in opposite directions. **3** mental or emotional unease; stress. **4** a feeling of nervous and excited anticipation or suspense. **5** a state of latent hostility between individuals or groups. **6** voltage or electrical potential.

tent n a collapsible shelter made of canvas or similar material supported by poles. ➤ **tented** adj.

tentacle n an elongated flexible animal part, usu around the mouth, used for feeling, grasping, etc.

tentative adj **1** not fully worked out or developed; provisional. **2** hesitant or uncertain. ➤ **tentatively** adv.

tenterhook n ✳ **on tenterhooks** in a state of suspense or nervous anticipation.

tenth adj and n **1** having the position in a sequence corresponding to the number ten. **2** one of ten equal parts of something.

tenuous adj **1** weak or flimsy. **2** not thick; fine. ➤ **tenuously** adv.

tenure n **1** the holding of a position or an office. **2** the conditions under which a property is held or occupied. **3** NAmer a secure employment status esp for teaching staff.

tenured adj NAmer providing secure employment status.

tepee or **teepee** n a Native American conical tent, usu made of skins.

tepid adj **1** moderately warm. **2** not enthusiastic.

tequila /tə'keelə/ n a strong Mexican alcoholic drink.

tercentenary n (pl **-ies**) a 300th anniversary.

term[1] n **1** a word or expression with a precise meaning. **2** (in pl) provisions relating to an agreement. **3** the time for which something lasts. **4** any of the usu three periods of instruction into which an academic year is divided. **5** the time at which a pregnancy of normal length ends. **6** a mathematical expression that forms part of a fraction, equation, ratio, etc. ✳ **be on good/bad terms with** to have a friendly/unfriendly relationship with (somebody). **come to terms** (+ with) to accept or resign oneself to something sad or unpleasant. ➤ **termly** *adj and adv.*

term² *v* to apply a particular term to.

termagant *n* an overbearing or nagging woman.

terminal¹ *adj* **1** forming an end, boundary, or terminus. **2** relating to or suffering from a disease that is certain to cause death. **3** *informal* extreme or irreversible. ➤ **terminally** *adv.*

terminal² *n* **1** the end of a transport route, with its associated buildings and facilities. **2** a building at an airport with facilities for arriving and departing passengers. **3** a point where a wire or cable can be connected to an electrical apparatus. **4** a device through which a user can communicate with a computer.

terminate *v* **1** to bring or come to an end. **2** to take action to end (a pregnancy) prematurely. **3** to reach a terminus. ➤ **terminator** *n.*

termination *n* the ending, *esp* of a pregnancy.

terminology *n* (*pl* -ies) the technical terms used in a particular subject. ➤ **terminological** *adj.*

terminus *n* (*pl* **termini** *or* **terminuses**) the end of a transport line or travel route.

termite *n* an insect with a pale-coloured soft body that lives in colonies and feeds on wood.

tern *n* a white seabird with a black cap and a forked tail.

ternary *adj* made up of three parts.

terpsichorean *adj literary or humorous* relating to dancing.

terrace¹ *n* **1** a level paved or planted area adjoining a building. **2** a horizontal ridge cut into a hillside and used for farming. **3** *chiefly Brit* a row of similar houses joined by common dividing walls. **4** *Brit* a series of shallow steps providing standing accommodation for spectators.

terrace² *v* to make (an area of ground) into a terrace or terraces.

terracotta *n* unglazed brownish red earthenware.

terra firma *n* dry land; solid ground.

terrain *n* an area of land, *esp* with respect to its physical features.

terrapin *n* a water reptile like a small tortoise.

terrestrial *adj* **1** relating to the planet earth or its inhabitants. **2** relating to land as distinct from air or water. **3** of organisms: living on or in land or soil. **4** of a television system: not transmitting programmes via a satellite.

terrible *adj* **1** *informal* of very poor quality. **2** *informal* highly unpleasant. **3** *informal* extreme or very great. **4** *informal* very unwell, upset, or guilty. **5** terrifying.

terribly *adv informal* **1** very. **2** very badly.

terrier *n* a usu small dog of various breeds, orig used to hunt out game from underground.

terrific *adj* **1** *informal* extraordinarily large or intense. **2** *informal* excellent or highly enjoyable. **3** arousing fear or awe. ➤ **terrifically** *adv.*

terrify *v* (-ies, -ied) to fill with terror. ➤ **terrifying** *adj.*

terrine *n* **1** an earthenware baking dish. **2** a food, *esp* pâté, cooked in a terrine.

territorial *adj* **1** relating to territory or land. **2** of an animal or bird: marking out and defending its own territory.

Territorial Army *n* in Britain, a voluntary force providing a trained army reserve for emergencies.

territory *n* (*pl* -ies) **1** a geographical area under the jurisdiction of a government. **2** an administrative subdivision of a country. **3** an assigned area; *esp* one in which an agent, sales representative, or distributor operates. **4** an area occupied and defended by an animal or group of animals.

terror *n* **1** a state of intense fear. **2** somebody or something that inspires fear. **3** acts of terrorism. **4** *informal* an annoying or appalling person.

terrorism *n* the systematic use of terror, violence, and intimidation for political ends. ➤ **terrorist** *adj and n.*

terrorize *or* **-ise** *v* to fill with terror or anxiety.

terry *n* (*pl* -ies) an absorbent fabric used *esp* for towels.

terse *adj* using few words. ➤ **tersely** *adv.*

tertiary *adj* **1** of third rank, importance, or value. **2** *Brit* relating to higher education.

tessellated *adj* paved or decorated with stones arranged in a pattern. ➤ **tessellation** *n.*

test¹ *n* **1** a means of assessing the quality, capabilities, reliability, etc of somebody or something. **2** a series of questions or exercises for measuring the knowledge, intelligence, ability, etc of an individual or group. **3** a real-life situation that subjects something or somebody to stress, difficulties, etc. **4** an *esp* chemical procedure, used to identify the presence of a substance. **5** = TEST MATCH.

test² *v* **1** to subject to a test. **2** to subject to severe strain. **3** (*usu* + for) to produce a specified result in a medical or chemical test: *She tested negative for HIV.* ➤ **tester** *n.*

testament *n* **1** (**Testament**) either of the two main divisions of the Bible. **2** a proof of or tribute to something. **3** a will. ➤ **testamentary** *adj.*

testate *adj* having made a valid will.

test card *n* a picture broadcast by a television transmitting station to facilitate the testing or adjustment of receivers.

test case *n* in law, a representative case whose outcome is likely to serve as a precedent.

testicle *n* either of the two oval sperm-producing organs of a male mammal, usu with its enclosing structures. ➤ **testicular** *adj*.

testify *v* (**-ies, -ied**) **1** to give evidence under oath as a witness in a court. **2** (*usu* + to) to serve as evidence or proof.

testimonial *n* **1** a letter of recommendation. **2** a public expression of appreciation or esteem.

testimony *n* (*pl* **-ies**) **1** a sworn statement or the evidence given by a witness in a court. **2** an outward sign; evidence.

test match *n* an international cricket or rugby match.

testosterone *n* a hormone that produces and maintains male secondary sex characteristics.

test tube *n* a thin glass tube closed at one end and used in chemistry, biology, etc.

test-tube baby *n* a baby conceived by fertilization of an ovum outside the mother's body.

testy *adj* (**-ier, -iest**) easily annoyed. ➤ **testily** *adv*.

tetanus *n* an infectious disease characterized by muscle spasms, esp in the jaw.

tetchy *adj* (**-ier, -iest**) irritably or peevishly sensitive. ➤ **tetchily** *adv*.

tête-à-tête[1] /ˌtet ah ˈtet, ˌtayt ah ˈtayt/ *adv and adj* in private; private and intimate.

tête-à-tête[2] *n* a private conversation between two people.

tether[1] *n* a rope, chain, etc by which an animal is fastened.

tether[2] *v* to fasten or restrain (an animal or person) by a tether.

tetrahedron *n* (*pl* **tetrahedrons** or **tetrahedra**) a polyhedron with four faces.

TETRA mast *n* a telecommunications mast erected as part of mobile phone communication system (Terrestrial Trunked Radio) being set up for use by the police.

Teutonic *adj* supposedly characteristic of the Germans.

text[1] *n* **1** printed or written words. **2** the main body of printed matter on a page or in a book, as opposed to illustrations, notes, etc. **3** a literary or other work selected for special study. **4** a passage of Scripture chosen *esp* for the subject of a sermon. **5** = TEXT MESSAGE. ➤ **textual** *adj*.

text[2] *v* to send a text message to. ➤ **texting** *n*.

textbook[1] *n* a book used in the study of a subject.

textbook[2] *adj* exemplary or typical.

textile *n* cloth, *esp* a woven or knitted cloth.

text message *n* a written message sent from one mobile phone to another. ➤ **text-messaging** *n*.

texture[1] *n* the visual or tactile surface characteristics of something, *esp* fabric. ➤ **textural** *adj*.

texture[2] *v* to give a particular texture to.

Th *abbr* the chemical symbol for thorium.

Thai /tie/ *n* (*pl* **Thai** or **Thais**) **1** a native or inhabitant of Thailand. **2** the national language of Thailand.

thalidomide *n* a sedative and hypnotic drug found to cause foetal malformation when used during pregnancy.

than *conj* **1** used to introduce the second element in a comparison: *She is older than I am.* **2** used to introduce an alternative or a contrast: *They would starve rather than beg.* **3** used after expressions such as *no sooner* to introduce what happened next.

thane *n* **1** an Anglo-Saxon nobleman holding lands in exchange for military service. **2** a Scottish feudal lord.

thank *v* **1** to express gratitude to. **2** (*usu* + for) to hold responsible; to blame. ✳ **thank you** used as a conventional and polite formula for expressing gratitude.

thankful *adj* **1** grateful. **2** expressing thanks. **3** pleased or glad. ➤ **thankfulness** *n*.

thankfully *adv* **1** in a thankful manner. **2** it is a relief that.

thankless *adj* **1** bringing neither profit nor appreciation. **2** not expressing or feeling gratitude.

thanks *pl n* **1** an expression of gratitude. **2** thank you. ✳ **thanks to 1** with the help of. **2** because of or owing to.

thanksgiving *n* **1** an expression of gratefulness, *esp* to God. **2** (**Thanksgiving**) a public holiday occurring in November in the USA and in October in Canada.

that[1] *pron* (*pl* **those**) **1** the thing or idea just mentioned. **2** a relatively distant person or thing introduced for observation or discussion. **3** (*in pl*) people. ✳ **and (all) that** *informal* and everything connected with it. **that is (to say)** in other words. **that's that** that concludes the matter.

that[2] *adj* (*pl* **those**) **1** denoting the person, thing, or idea specified, mentioned, or understood. **2** denoting the one farther away or less immediately under consideration.

that[3] *conj* used to introduce a noun clause or a subordinate clause expressing purpose, reason, or result.

that[4] *pron* used to introduce a restrictive relative clause identifying or characterizing a particular person, thing, or group: *The book that you want is on the table.*

that[5] *adv* **1** to the extent indicated or understood: *a nail about that long.* **2** very; extremely: *It's not that expensive.*

thatch[1] *n* plant material such as straw or reeds used as a roof covering.

thatch[2] *v* to roof (a building) with thatch. ➤ **thatcher** *n*.

thaw[1] *v* **1** to go or cause to go from a frozen to a liquid state. **2** (*often* + out) to become less numb or stiff from cold. **3** of the weather: to be warm enough to melt ice and snow. **4** to make or become less hostile or reserved.

thaw[2] *n* **1** a period of weather warm enough to thaw ice. **2** a lessening of hostility or aloofness.

the *definite article* **1** used before nouns when the object or person in question has been previously referred to or is obvious from the circumstances. **2** used to refer to somebody or something unique or universally recognized: *the pope*. **3** used before a singular noun to indicate generic use: *a history of the novel*.

theatre (*NAmer* **theater**) *n* **1** a building specially constructed for the presentation of dramatic performances. **2** dramatic literature or performances. **3** (**the theatre**) the world of actors, acting, and drama generally. **4** a place where significant events or actions take place. **5** (*also* **operating theatre**) *Brit* a room where surgical operations are carried out.

theatrical *adj* relating to the theatre or the presentation of plays. ➤ **theatricality** *n*, **theatrically** *adv*.

theatricals *or* **theatrics** *pl n* **1** the art of performing plays, or theatrical performances. **2** theatrical behaviour.

thee *pron archaic or dialect* used as the objective case: thou.

theft *n* the act or crime of stealing.

their *adj* **1** belonging to or associated with them. **2** belonging to or associated with an indefinite singular person.

Usage Note: Do not confuse this word with *there* or *they're*.

theirs *pron* the one or ones that belong to or are associated with them.

Usage Note: Note that there is no apostrophe in *theirs*.

them *pron* used as the objective case: they.

thematic *adj* **1** relating to or constituting a theme. **2** classified according to subject. ➤ **thematically** *adv*.

theme *n* **1** a subject or topic dealt with in a discursive or artistic work and usu forming a unifying thread running through it. **2** a unifying concept in the planning or design of something. **3** a group of notes or melody forming the basis of a musical composition.

theme music *n* a signature tune.

theme park *n* an amusement park based on a specific theme.

theme song *n* a recurring melody in a musical play or film that characterizes the production or one of its characters.

theme tune *n* a signature tune.

themself *pron* = THEMSELVES 2.

themselves *pron* **1** used reflexively or for emphasis to refer to the people, animals, or things that are the subject of the clause. **2** used reflexively to refer to an indefinite singular person that is the subject of the clause.

then *adv* **1** at that time. **2** soon after that; next. **3** besides or in addition. **4** in that case. ✷ **then and there** at once.

thence *adv* **1** from there. **2** *formal* consequently.

thenceforth *adv archaic or formal* from that time or point on.

theocracy *n* (*pl* **-ies**) government by priests. ➤ **theocratic** *adj*.

theodolite *n* a surveyor's instrument for measuring horizontal and vertical angles.

theologian *n* a specialist in theology.

theology *n* (*pl* **-ies**) **1** the study of God and the teachings of an organized religion. **2** a system of religious beliefs. ➤ **theological** *adj*, **theologist** *n*.

theorem *n* a proposition in mathematics or logic deducible from other more basic propositions.

theoretical *adj* **1** relating to or having the character of theory; abstract. **2** confined to theory, *esp* not involving practical experience. **3** hypothetical. ➤ **theoretically** *adv*.

theoretician *n* somebody who specializes in the theoretical aspects of a subject.

theorist *n* = THEORETICIAN.

theorize *or* **-ise** *v* to form a theory; to speculate.

theory *n* (*pl* **-ies**) **1** an idea or set of ideas put forward to explain why something happens. **2** the general or abstract principles of a subject. ✷ **in theory** on the basis of abstract principles or under ideal circumstances, but not necessarily in practice or reality.

therapeutic *adj* **1** relating to the treatment of disease or disorders. **2** having a beneficial effect on a person's health. ➤ **therapeutically** *adv*.

therapy *n* (*pl* **-ies**) treatment of physical or mental disorders, or a specific type of treatment. ➤ **therapist** *n*.

there *adv* **1** in, at, or to that place. **2** on that point or in that particular respect. **3** used to draw attention to something. ✷ **there is/are** used to introduce a sentence or clause stating that something exists or is true.

Usage Note: Do not confuse this word with *their* or *they're*.

thereabouts *adv* **1** near that place. **2** near that time, quantity, etc.

thereafter *adv formal* after that.

thereby *adv* by that means; as a result of which.

therefore *adv* because of that.

therein *adv formal* in that; *esp* in that respect.

thereof *adv formal* of that or it.

there's *contraction* **1** there is. **2** there has.

thereupon *adv formal* immediately after that.

therewith *adv* **1** *formal* with that or it. **2** *archaic* thereupon.

thermal[1] *adj* **1** relating to heat. **2** designed to prevent body heat from escaping. ➤ **thermally** *adv*.

thermal² *n* **1** a rising current of warm air. **2** (*in pl*) thermal underwear or clothing.

thermionic *adj* **1** relating to the emission of electrons from incandescent substances. **2** of e.g. a valve: using thermionic electrons as charge carriers.

thermodynamics *pl n* the branch ofphysics dealing with the relations between heat and other forms of energy. ➤ **thermodynamic** *adj.*

thermometer *n* an instrument that measures and indicates temperature, *esp* a glass tube containing a liquid, e.g. mercury, that rises and falls with changes of temperature.

thermonuclear *adj* relating to or making use of transformations occurring in atomic nuclei at very high temperatures.

Thermos *n trademark* a vacuum flask.

thermostat *n* an automatic device for regulating temperature. ➤ **thermostatic** *adj,* **thermostatically** *adv.*

thesaurus *n* (*pl* **thesauri** *or* **thesauruses**) a book listing words and their synonyms.

these *pron* pl of THIS¹.

thesis *n* (*pl* **theses**) **1** a proposition that a person offers to substantiate by argument. **2** a dissertation embodying the results of original research, *esp* one submitted for a doctorate.

thespian¹ *adj* relating to acting, drama, or the theatre.

thespian² *n formal or humorous* an actor.

theta *n* the eighth letter of the Greek alphabet (Θ, θ).

they *pron* **1** used to refer to a previously mentioned group of people or things. **2** used to refer to a single person of either sex previously mentioned. **3** people in general. **4** the authorities.

they'd *contraction* **1** they had. **2** they would.

they'll *contraction* **1** they will. **2** they shall.

they're *contraction* they are.

Usage Note: Do not confuse this word with *their* or *there.*

---

they've *contraction* they have.

thiamine or **thiamin** *n* vitamin B_1, found *esp* in cereals and beans.

thick¹ *adj* **1** having a relatively great distance between opposite surfaces. **2** of large diameter in relation to length. **3** containing closely-packed objects or material. **4** (+ with) covered with a thick layer of. **5** not flowing or pouring easily. **6** of fog, etc: not easy to see through; dense. **7** of speech: imperfectly articulated. **8** of an accent: marked. **9** *informal* stupid. **10** *informal* on close terms; intimate. ✳ **a bit thick** *Brit, informal* unreasonable or unfair. **be as thick as thieves** *informal* to be very friendly or intimate with each other. **give somebody/get a thick ear** *Brit, informal* to give somebody/receive a blow on the ear as punishment. **lay it on thick 1** to overstate or exaggerate something. **2** to flatter somebody excessively. **thick and fast** in very quick succession. ➤ **thickly** *adv.*

thick² *n* the most crowded or active part. ✳ **through thick and thin** in good times and bad times.

thicken *v* to make or become thick or thicker.

thicket *n* a dense growth of shrubbery or small trees.

thickhead *n informal* a stupid person. ➤ **thick-headed** *adj.*

thickness *n* **1** the distance through an object as opposed to its length or height. **2** a layer or ply.

thickset *adj* heavily built; burly.

thief *n* (*pl* **thieves**) somebody who steals. ➤ **thievery** *n,* **thievish** *adj.*

thieve *v* to be a thief.

thigh *n* the part of the leg that extends from the hip to the knee.

thimble *n* a metal or plastic cap worn to protect the finger and to push the needle in sewing.

thin¹ *adj* (**thinner, thinnest**) **1** having little depth between opposite surfaces. **2** of narrow diameter in relation to length. **3** without much flesh or fat on the body. **4** not dense or closely-packed. **5** more rarefied than normal. **6** few in number. **7** of a liquid: very diluted; lacking substance or strength. **8** flimsy or unconvincing. **9** of a voice or sound: somewhat feeble and lacking in resonance. **10** *informal* disappointingly poor or hard. ➤ **thinly** *adv,* **thinness** *n.*

thin² *v* (**thinned, thinning**) **1** to make or become thin or thinner. **2** (+ out) to reduce the thickness or density of.

thine *pron* (*pl* **thine**) *archaic* the one or ones that belong to or are associated with thee.

thing *n* **1** an inanimate object as distinguished from a living being. **2** an object or entity not able to be precisely named. **3** a matter, affair, or concern. **4** an event or circumstance. **5** (*in pl*) personal possessions, clothes, equipment, etc. **6** used with an adjective expressing pity, envy, etc: a person or animal: *Poor thing!* **7** (**the thing**) what is required or to be striven for. ✳ **one's (own) thing** *informal* something that one finds especially interesting or enjoyable.

think¹ *v* (*past tense and past part.* **thought**) **1** to produce or work on ideas in the mind. **2** to have a particular belief or opinion. **3** (+ of/about) to have in one's mind as the object of consideration or reflection. **4** (+ of) to remember or call to mind. **5** to expect or suspect. ✳ **think better of** to decide on reflection to abandon (a plan). **think nothing of 1** to be entirely unconcerned about. **2** to disregard. **think twice** to consider very carefully. ➤ **thinker** *n.*

think² *n informal* an act of thinking.

think over *v* to consider.

think tank *n* a group of people who evolve new ideas and offer expert advice.

thinner *n* a solvent used to thin e.g. paint or varnish.

third *adj and n* **1** having the position in a sequence corresponding to the number three.

2 one of three equal parts of something. **3** the third forward gear of a motor vehicle. **4** in Britain, a third-class honours degree. ➤ **thirdly** adv.

third degree n (**the third degree**) harsh interrogation or treatment to obtain information from a prisoner.

third-degree burn n a very serious burn characterized by destruction of the skin and the underlying tissues.

third party n somebody other than the people principally involved in an action.

third-party adj of insurance: covering loss or damage sustained by somebody other than the insured.

third person n in grammar, the term used to refer to a person or thing other than the speaker or the person addressed, represented by the pronouns he, she, it, or they.

third way n a political programme that is neither of the right nor left, but aimed at reaching a consensus in the centre.

Third World n the less industrialized nations of the world.

thirst[1] n **1** a desire or need to drink. **2** an ardent desire; a craving.

thirst[2] v **1** to feel thirsty. **2** (often + for/after) to crave eagerly.

thirsty adj (-ier, -iest) **1** feeling thirst. **2** causing thirst. **3** of a machine or engine: consuming large quantities of fuel. **4** having a strong desire. ➤ **thirstily** adv.

thirteen adj and n the number 13. ➤ **thirteenth** adj and n.

thirty adj and n (pl -ies) **1** the number 30. **2** (in pl) the numbers 30 to 39. ➤ **thirtieth** adj and n.

this[1] pron (pl **these**) **1** the thing or idea that has just been mentioned. **2** a nearby person or thing introduced for observation or discussion.

this[2] adj (pl **these**) denoting the person or thing that is nearer at hand or more immediately under consideration.

this[3] adv to the extent indicated or specified.

thistle n a prickly plant with dense heads of usu purple flowers.

thistledown n the fluffy hairs from the ripe flower head of a thistle.

thither adv formal to or towards that place.

tho' or **tho** adv or conj informal or literary though.

thong n **1** a narrow strip, esp of leather. **2** a skimpy bathing costume or piece of underwear resembling a G-string.

thorax n (pl **thoraxes** or **thoraces**) **1** the part of a mammal's body between the neck and the abdomen, or the cavity inside it. **2** the central section of the body of an insect, spider, etc carrying the legs and wings. ➤ **thoracic** adj.

thorn n **1** a short projecting plant part with a sharp point. **2** a woody plant, shrub, or tree

with branches covered with thorns. ✳ **a thorn in somebody's flesh/side** a cause of great irritation.

thorny adj (-ier, -iest) **1** covered in thorns. **2** full of difficulties or controversial points.

thorough adj **1** carried out with or showing great care and attention to detail. **2** complete; utter. ➤ **thoroughly** adv, **thoroughness** n.

thoroughbred[1] adj bred from the best members of the same breed, strain, etc over many generations.

thoroughbred[2] n a thoroughbred animal.

thoroughfare n a public way, e.g. a road, street, or path.

thoroughgoing adj **1** extremely thorough. **2** absolute or utter.

those pron and adj pl of THAT[1] and THAT[2].

thou pron archaic or dialect the one being addressed; you.

though[1] adv however.

though[2] conj **1** in spite of the fact that. **2** and yet; but.

thought[1] v past tense and past part. of THINK[1].

thought[2] n **1** the act or process of thinking. **2** serious consideration. **3** an idea, opinion, concept, or intention. **4** reasoning or conceptual power. **5** the views of a period, place, group, or individual. **6** (+ of) hope or expectation.

thoughtful adj **1** absorbed in thought. **2** showing careful reasoned thinking. **3** showing concern for others. ➤ **thoughtfully** adv.

thoughtless adj **1** rash. **2** lacking concern for others. ➤ **thoughtlessly** adv.

thousand n (pl **thousands** or **thousand**) **1** the number 1000. **2** (also in pl) an indefinitely large number. ➤ **thousandth** adj and n.

thrall n a state of complete absorption or enslavement.

thrash v **1** to beat soundly, esp with a stick or whip. **2** to defeat heavily or decisively. **3** (+ around/about) to move or toss about violently.

thread[1] n **1** a thin continuous strand formed by spinning and twisting together short textile fibres. **2** a projecting spiral ridge, e.g. on a bolt or pipe, by which parts can be screwed together. **3** a pervasive recurring element.

thread[2] v **1** to pass a thread through the eye of (a needle). **2** to pass something into or through. **3** to string (things) together on a thread. **4** to make one's way cautiously. ➤ **threader** n.

threadbare adj worn or shabby.

threat n **1** an indication of something unpleasant to come. **2** an expression of an intention to inflict punishment, injury, or damage. **3** something that is a source of danger or harm.

threaten v **1** to utter threats against. **2** to give ominous signs of. **3** to be a potential source of harm or danger to. ➤ **threatening** adj.

three n the number 3. ➤ **three** adj.

three-dimensional adj **1** having, or giving

the illusion of having, length, breadth, and height. **2** of a fictional character: lifelike.

threepence *n* the sum three old pence (1.25n) ➤ **threepenny** *adj*.

threesome *n* a group of three people or things.

threnody *n* (*pl -ies*) a song of lamentation, *esp* for the dead.

thresh *v* **1** to separate the grain from (harvested corn) by beating it with a machine or flail. **2** to move or toss about violently. ➤ **thresher** *n*.

threshold *n* **1** the plank, stone, etc that lies under a door. **2** a doorway. **3** the point or level at which something begins.

Usage Note: Note that there is only one *h* in the second half of the word.

---

threw *v* past tense of THROW[1].

thrice *adv archaic or literary* three times.

thrift *n* careful management, *esp* of money; frugality. ➤ **thrifty** *adj*.

thrill[1] *n* **1** a sudden feeling of pleasurable excitement. **2** something that causes such a feeling. **3** a sudden tremor of nervousness or emotion.

thrill[2] *v* **1** to cause to experience a thrill of excitement or emotion. **2** (+ at/to) to be pleasurably excited by.

thriller *n* a novel, film, or drama characterized by a high degree of suspense.

thrilling *adj* intensely exciting. ➤ **thrillingly** *adv*.

thrive *v* (*past tense* **throve** *or* **thrived**, *past part.* **thriven** *or* **thrived**) **1** to grow vigorously. **2** to prosper. **3** (+ on) to enjoy or be stimulated by something. ➤ **thriving** *adj*.

throat *n* **1** the passage through the neck to the stomach and lungs. **2** the front part of the neck. * **at each other's throats** quarrelling violently.

throaty *adj* (**-ier, -iest**) hoarse or guttural. ➤ **throatily** *adv*.

throb[1] *v* (**throbbed, throbbing**) **1** to pulsate with unusual force or rapidity. **2** of a pain: to come in rhythmic waves.

throb[2] *n* a beat or pulse.

throe *n* (*usu in pl*) a pang or spasm. * **in the throes of** undergoing the difficult process of.

thrombosis *n* (*pl* **thromboses**) the formation or presence of a blood clot within a blood vessel.

throne *n* **1** the ceremonial chair of a sovereign or bishop. **2** (**the throne**) sovereignty.

throng[1] *n* a large crowd.

throng[2] *v* to crowd into (a place).

throttle[1] *n* a valve for regulating the supply of a fluid, e.g. fuel, to an engine.

throttle[2] *v* **1** to strangle or choke. **2** (*usu* + back/down) to regulate, *esp* reduce the speed of (an engine).

through[1] (*NAmer* **thru**) *prep* **1** into at one side or point and out at the other. **2** (*usu* + all)

during the entire period of. **3** over the whole area of. **4** by means of. **5** because of.

through[2] (*NAmer* **thru**) *adv* **1** from one end or side to the other. **2** from beginning to end. **3** to the core; completely. **4** *chiefly Brit* connected by telephone. * **through and through** thoroughly; completely.

through[3] (*NAmer* **thru**) *adj* **1** allowing a continuous journey from point of origin to destination. **2** starting before and continuing beyond a particular place: *through traffic.* **3** having qualified for the next round of a competition. **4** finished.

throughout *adv and prep* **1** in or to every part. **2** from beginning to end.

throughput *n* the amount of material processed during an operation.

throve *v* past tense of THRIVE.

throw[1] (**threw, thrown**) **1** to send through the air by a forward motion of the hand and arm. **2** to cause to move violently into or against something. **3** to force (somebody) to fall to the ground. **4** of a horse: to unseat (its rider). **5** to put (somebody) in a specified position or condition, *esp* suddenly. **6** (+ on/off) to put (clothing) on or off hurriedly. **7** to direct (light, a look, etc) in a certain direction. **8** to move (a lever or switch). **9** to shape (a pot, etc) by hand on a potter's wheel. **10** to give (a party). **11** to have (a tantrum or fit). **12** *informal* to confuse or disconcert. * **be thrown back on** to have to rely on (something) when no other resources are available. **throw oneself into** to devote one's energy to (an activity). **throw one's weight about/around** *informal* to behave in a bullying or domineering manner.

throw[2] *n* **1** an act of throwing. **2** a light cover, e.g. for a bed. **3** *informal* a chance, try, turn, etc.

throwaway *adj* **1** designed to be discarded after use. **2** of a remark: made with deliberate casualness.

throw away *v* **1** to get rid of as worthless or unwanted. **2** to use in a foolish or wasteful manner. **3** to fail to take advantage of (an opportunity, etc).

throwback *n* an individual exhibiting the characteristics of earlier genetic type or phase.

throw in *v* **1** to add as a free item with other goods or services. **2** to introduce or interject (a remark, etc). * **throw in the sponge/towel** to abandon a struggle or contest.

throw-in *n* in football, a throw made from the touchline to put the ball back in play.

throw out *v* **1** to get rid of as worthless or unwanted. **2** to expel abruptly from a room or building. **3** to dismiss or reject (a plan, proposal, etc).

throw up *v informal* to vomit.

thrum[1] *v* (**thrummed, thrumming**) to make a monotonous hum.

thrum² *n* a thrumming sound.

thrush¹ *n* a light-brown bird with a spotted breast, noted for its singing ability.

thrush² *n* a whitish irritating fungal growth occurring *esp* in the mouth or vagina.

thrust¹ *v* (*past tense and past part.* **thrust**) **1** to push or drive with force. **2** (+ on/upon) to force or impose the acceptance of (something or somebody) on.

thrust² *n* **1** a push or lunge with a pointed weapon. **2** a concerted military attack. **3** the essential meaning. **4** the force exerted by a propeller, jet engine, etc to give forward motion.

thrusting *adj* aggressive or pushy.

thud *v* (**thudded, thudding**) to make a dull heavy sound. ➤ **thud** *n*.

thug *n* a violent person, *esp* a violent criminal. ➤ **thuggery** *n*, **thuggish** *adj*.

thumb¹ *n* the short thick digit of the hand that is separate from the other fingers. ✳ **under somebody's thumb** under somebody's control.

thumb² *v* **1** to leaf through (pages) with the thumb. **2** to request (a lift) in a passing vehicle by signalling with the thumb.

thumb index *n* a series of notches cut in the unbound edge of a book for ease of reference.

thumbnail *n* the nail of the thumb.

thumbnail sketch *n* a brief, concise description.

thumbscrew *n* an instrument of torture for squeezing the thumb.

thumbs-down *n informal* rejection or disapproval.

thumbs-up *n informal* approval.

thump¹ *v* **1** to thrash or beat. **2** to strike or knock with a thump. **3** of the heart: to beat rapidly. **4** to make a thumping sound.

thump² *n* a blow with something blunt or heavy, or the sound of this.

thumping *adj* **1** *Brit, informal* impressively large or excellent. **2** throbbing.

thunder¹ *n* **1** the low loud sound that follows a flash of lightning and is caused by sudden expansion of the air. **2** a loud reverberating noise. ➤ **thundery** *adj*.

thunder² *v* **1** to make thunder or a sound like thunder. **2** to roar or shout. **3** to move fast and noisily.

thunderbolt *n* a single discharge of lightning with the accompanying thunder.

thunderclap *n* a sudden loud sound of thunder.

thundercloud *n* a cloud charged with electricity and producing lightning and thunder.

thunderous *adj* **1** making a noise like thunder. **2** angry and threatening. ➤ **thunderously** *adv*.

thunderstorm *n* a storm accompanied by lightning and thunder.

thunderstruck *adj* extremely surprised; astonished.

Thursday *n* the day of the week following Wednesday.

thus *adv formal* **1** because of this preceding fact or premise; consequently. **2** in this way. **3** to this degree or extent.

thwack¹ *v* to whack.

thwack² *n* a sharp blow; a whack.

thwart *v* to prevent somebody from carrying out (a plan, etc).

thy *adj archaic or dialect* of thee or thyself.

thyme *n* a garden plant with small aromatic leaves used in cooking.

thymus *n* (*pl* **thymi**) a gland in the lower neck region that functions in the development of the body's immune system.

thyroid *n* (*also* **thyroid gland**) a large endocrine gland at the base of the neck that produces hormones that influence growth and development.

Ti *abbr* the chemical symbol for titanium.

tiara *n* a decorative jewelled band worn on the head by women.

tibia *n* (*pl* **tibiae** *or* **tibias**) the inner and usu larger of the two bones between the knee and ankle.

tic *n* a habitual spasmodic motion of particular muscles, *esp* of the face.

tick¹ *n* **1** a mark (✓) used to label something as correct, to check off an item on a list, etc. **2** a light audible tap or beat, or a series of such sounds. **3** *Brit, informal* a moment or second.

tick² *v* **1** to mark with a written tick. **2** (*often* + off) to label or count with ticks. **3** to make the sound of a tick. **4** (+ away/by) of seconds, minutes, etc: to pass, bringing the end of something closer.

tick³ *n* a bloodsucking arachnid that often transmits infectious diseases.

tick⁴ *n* ✳ **on tick** *informal* on credit.

ticker *n* **1** *informal* a watch. **2** *informal* the heart. **3** *NAmer* a telegraphic receiving instrument that automatically prints out information on paper tape.

ticker tape *n* the paper tape on which a ticker prints out its information.

ticket *n* **1** a printed card or piece of paper entitling its holder to certain services, *esp* showing that a fare or admission has been paid. **2** a tag or label. **3** an official notification issued to somebody who has violated a traffic regulation.

ticking *n* a strong linen or cotton fabric used to cover a mattress or pillow.

tickle¹ *v* **1** to touch (a person or a body part) lightly and repeatedly so as to cause uneasiness, laughter, or spasmodic movements. **2** to provoke to laughter. **3** to amuse or delight. ➤ **tickly** *adj*.

tickle² n **1** a tickling sensation. **2** the act of tickling.

ticklish adj **1** sensitive to tickling. **2** of a cough: causing irritation in the throat. **3** requiring delicate handling.

tick off v Brit, informal to scold or rebuke.

tick over v of an engine: to be turned on and running slowly with the transmission disengaged.

tidal adj of, caused by, or having tides. ➤ **tidally** adv.

tidal wave n **1** an unusually high sea wave. **2** an unexpected, intense, and often widespread reaction.

tidbit n NAmer see TITBIT.

tiddler n Brit, informal somebody or something small, esp a small fish.

tiddly adj (-ier, -iest) informal **1** chiefly Brit slightly drunk. **2** Brit very small.

tiddlywinks pl n a game in which the object is to flick small discs into a container.

tide n **1** the periodic rise and fall of the surface of the sea caused by the gravitational attraction of the sun and moon. **2** a general trend in events. **3** a powerful surge of feeling.

tidings pl n a piece of news.

tidy¹ adj (-ier, -iest) **1** neat and orderly in appearance or habits. **2** informal large or substantial: a tidy sum. ➤ **tidily** adv, **tidiness** n.

tidy² v (-ies, -ied) to put in order; to make neat or tidy.

tidy³ n (pl -ies) **1** an act of tidying. **2** a receptacle for odds and ends.

tie¹ v (ties, tied, tying) **1** to fasten or attach with cord, string, etc. **2** to form a knot or bow in. **3** to make a bond or connection between. **4** (often + down) to restrict the range of activity of. **5** to achieve an equal score in a game or contest.

tie² n **1** something that serves as a connecting link. **2** a narrow length of material designed to be worn round the neck and tied in a knot in the front. **3** Brit a match or game between two teams, players, etc. **4** a draw or dead heat in a contest.

tie break or **tie breaker** n a contest or game used to select a winner from among contestants with tied scores.

tied adj **1** Brit of a house: owned by an employer and reserved for occupancy by an employee. **2** of a public house: bound to sell only the products of the brewery that owns it.

tie-dye v to produce patterns in textiles by tying portions of the fabric or yarn so that they will not absorb dye.

tie in v **1** (usu + with) to bring into harmony with. **2** (usu + with) to correspond with.

tie-in n a related product issued to coincide with a film or television production.

tiepin n a decorative pin used to hold a tie in place.

tier n **1** any of several rows or levels of e.g. seating arranged one above and behind the other. **2** any of a series of levels, e.g. in an administration. ➤ **tiered** adj.

tie up v **1** to attach or fasten securely. **2** to bind a person's arms or legs to prevent them moving or escaping. **3** to conclude (a matter) satisfactorily. **4** to make unavailable for other activities or uses. **5** (+ with) to relate to something.

tiff n informal a petty quarrel.

tiger n a very large Asian cat with a tawny coat striped with black.

tight¹ adj **1** fixed very firmly in place. **2** stretched taut. **3** of clothing: fitting closely or too closely. **4** impermeable to e.g. liquid or gas. **5** of e.g. control: characterized by firmness and strictness. **6** set or packed close together. **7** of a space: difficult to move or manoeuvre in. **8** characterized by scarcity. **9** informal stingy or miserly. **10** informal intoxicated; drunk. ➤ **tightly** adv, **tightness** n.

tight² adv **1** firmly or securely. **2** very close together.

tighten v to make or become tight or tighter.

tightfisted adj informal reluctant to part with money.

tight-knit adj of a group of people: closely linked because of shared interests or affection.

tight-lipped adj **1** having the lips compressed, e.g. in determination. **2** reluctant to speak.

tightrope n a rope or wire stretched taut for acrobats to perform on.

tights pl n a skintight garment covering each leg and foot and reaching to the waist.

tigress n a female tiger.

tilde /'tildə/ n a mark (˜) placed over the letter n in Spanish or over vowels in Portuguese to indicate nasal pronunciation.

tile¹ n a thin slab of fired clay, stone, concrete, cork, etc used to surface roofs, floors, walls, etc.

tile² v **1** to cover (a surface) with tiles. **2** to arrange (windows) on a computer screen without overlapping. ➤ **tiler** n, **tiling** n.

till¹ prep and conj until.

till² n a cash register or drawer in which money is kept.

till³ v to work (land) by ploughing, sowing, and raising crops.

tiller n a lever used to turn the rudder of a boat.

tilt¹ v **1** to cause to slope or sit at an angle. **2** formerly, to point or thrust (a lance) in a joust.

tilt² n **1** the act of tilting. **2** a sloping position. **3** formerly, a joust. * **full tilt/at full tilt** with maximum speed.

tilth n the condition of tilled land.

timber n wood suitable for carpentry or woodwork.

timbre n the quality of tone distinctive of a particular singing voice or musical instrument.

time¹ n **1** the continuum of past, present, and future in which events succeed one another. **2**

the point or period when something occurs. **3** a moment, hour, day, or year as measured or indicated by a clock or calendar. **4** the period required or taken for an action. **5** an appointed, fixed, or customary moment for something to happen, begin, or end. **6** any of a series of recurring instances or repeated actions. **7** (*also in pl*) a historical period. **8** *informal* a term of imprisonment. **9** in music, a tempo. **10** a person's specified experience, *esp* on a particular occasion: *We had a good time.* ＊ **behind the times** old-fashioned. **for the time being** for the present. **have no time for** to be unable or reluctant to spend time on. **in no time** very soon; very quickly. **in time 1** sufficiently early. **2** eventually. **make time** to find enough time to do something. **on time** at the appointed time. **time off** time spent away from work or relaxing. **time out** a break or rest.

time² *v* **1** to measure the time, duration, or speed of. **2** to arrange the time of. **3** to regulate the moment or duration of, *esp* to achieve the desired effect.

time bomb *n* a bomb equipped with device that makes it explode at a predetermined time.

time capsule *n* a sealed capsule containing contemporary articles that is buried for people to dig up and open in future years.

time-honoured *adj* sanctioned by custom or tradition.

timekeeper *n* **1** somebody who records the time worked by employees, elapsed in a race, etc. **2** an employee considered with regard to their punctuality. ➤ **timekeeping** *n*.

timeless *adj* not affected by time; eternal.

timely *adj* occurring or done at an appropriate time.

timepiece *n* a clock, watch, etc.

timer *n* **1** a device that gives an indication when an interval of time has passed, or that starts or stops a device at predetermined times. **2** a stopwatch for timing races.

time scale *n* the amount of time allotted for the completion of something.

timeserver *n* **1** somebody who fits their behaviour and ideas to prevailing opinions or their superiors' views. **2** somebody who makes little effort at work because they are soon to retire or leave.

timeshare *n* **1** = TIME-SHARING. **2** a share in a property under a time-sharing scheme.

time-sharing *n* an arrangement whereby people buy a share of a lease on a holiday property, entitling them to spend a proportionate amount of time there each year.

time signature *n* a sign on a musical staff showing the number of beats in a bar.

timetable¹ *n* a schedule showing a planned order of events.

timetable² *v* to arrange or provide for in a timetable.

timid *adj* lacking in courage, boldness, or self-confidence. ➤ **timidity** *n*, **timidly** *adv*.

timorous *adj* timid or nervous.

timpani *or* **tympani** *pl n* a set of two or three kettledrums played by one performer in an orchestra. ➤ **timpanist** *n*.

tin¹ *n* **1** a silvery metallic element used for plating and in alloys. **2** *chiefly Brit* a hermetically sealed tinplate or aluminium container for preserving foods. **3** a container in which food is cooked.

tin² *v* (**tinned, tinning**) *chiefly Brit* to can (food). ➤ **tinned** *adj*.

tincture *n* **1** a solution of a substance in alcohol for medicinal use. **2** a slight addition; a trace.

tinder *n* a combustible substance used for kindling a fire.

tinderbox *n* formerly, a metal box for holding tinder and usu a flint and steel for striking a spark.

tine *n* a prong, e.g. of a fork.

tinfoil *n* a thin metal sheeting of tin, aluminium, or a tin alloy.

tinge¹ *v* (**tingeing** *or* **tinging**) **1** to colour with a slight shade. **2** to impart a slight smell, taste, or other quality to.

tinge² *n* a slight modifying quality, *esp* a trace of a colour.

tingle¹ *v* to feel a stinging, prickling, or thrilling sensation. ➤ **tingly** *adj*.

tingle² *n* a tingling sensation.

tinker¹ *n* **1** a travelling mender of pots and pans. **2** an act of tinkering.

tinker² *v* (+ with) to repair, adjust, or work with something in an unskilled or experimental manner.

tinkle¹ *v* to make or cause to make a short light ringing sound.

tinkle² *n* **1** a tinkling sound. **2** *Brit, informal* a telephone call.

tinnitus *n* a ringing or roaring sensation in the ears.

tinny *adj* (**-ier, -iest**) **1** having a thin metallic sound. **2** not solid or durable; shoddy.

tinplate *n* thin sheet iron or steel coated with tin.

tinpot *adj* *informal* paltry or inferior.

tinsel *n* strips of metal threaded on a string, used to produce a glittering effect, *esp* in Christmas decorations.

tint¹ *n* **1** a lighter or darker shade of a colour. **2** a hair dye.

tint² *v* **1** to apply a tint to. **2** to dye (the hair).

tintinnabulation *n* *formal* a ringing sound, *esp* made by bells.

tin whistle *n* = PENNY WHISTLE.

tiny *adj* (**-ier, -iest**) very small.

tip¹ *n* **1** the pointed end of something. **2** a small part serving as an end or cap of something.

✳ on the tip of one's tongue 1 about to be uttered. **2** not quite remembered.

tip² v **(tipped, tipping) 1** to supply with a tip. **2** to cover the tip of. ➤ **tipped** adj.

tip³ v **(tipped, tipping) 1** (often + over) to overturn or upset. **2** to tilt. **3** Brit to deposit (rubbish, etc) by tilting a container.

tip⁴ n **1** Brit a place for tipping something, e.g. rubbish. **2** informal a messy place.

tip⁵ n an extra sum of money given in appreciation of a service performed.

tip⁶ v **(tipped, tipping)** to give (somebody) a tip.

tip⁷ n **1** a piece of useful advice. **2** a piece of inside information which may bring financial gain, e.g. from betting or investment.

tip⁸ v **(tipped, tipping)** Brit to mention as a prospective winner, success, or profitable investment.

tip off v to give a tip-off to.

tip-off n informal a tip given usu as a warning.

tipple¹ v to drink alcohol, esp continuously in small amounts. ➤ **tippler** n.

tipple² n informal an alcoholic drink.

tipster n somebody who gives tips, esp as regards the likely winners of horseraces.

tipsy adj **(-ier, -iest)** slightly drunk. ➤ **tipsily** adv.

tiptoe¹ v to walk silently or stealthily with one's heels off the ground.

tiptoe² n ✳ **on tiptoe** or **tiptoes** balancing on the toes or on the balls of the feet.

tip-top adj excellent or first-rate.

tirade n a long vehement speech or denunciation.

tire¹ v **1** to become or make tired. **2** (+ of) to become bored with.

tire² n NAmer see TYRE.

tired adj **1** needing sleep or rest. **2** (+ of) bored or exasperated with. **3** trite; hackneyed. **4** lacking freshness. ➤ **tiredness** n.

tireless adj continuing without rest or loss of vigour. ➤ **tirelessly** adv.

tiresome adj wearisome; tedious. ➤ **tiresomely** adv.

'tis contraction it is.

tissue n **1** any of the structural materials of a plant or animal. **2** = TISSUE PAPER. **3** a paper handkerchief. **4** a web or network.

tissue paper n a thin gauzy paper.

tit¹ n a small tree-dwelling bird that lives on insects.

tit² n **1** coarse slang a woman's breast. **2** Brit, informal a stupid person.

titan n **1** (**Titan**) a giant god in Greek mythology. **2** somebody who is very strong, powerful, or notable for outstanding achievement.

titanic adj colossal or gigantic.

titanium n a grey metallic element that is light and strong and used mainly in alloys.

titbit (NAmer **tidbit**) n **1** a tasty piece of food. **2** an interesting piece of information.

titchy adj **(-ier, -iest)** Brit, informal small or short. ➤ **titch** n.

tit for tat n the act of retaliating by making the other person suffer an equivalent injury, loss etc.

tithe n a contribution of a tenth part of something, e.g. income, for the support of a religious establishment or other charitable work.

titillate v to excite pleasurably or sexually. ➤ **titillating** n.

titivate v informal to make smarter. ➤ **titivation** n.

title¹ n **1** the distinguishing name of e.g. a book, film, or musical composition. **2** a word indicating a person's job, status, etc. **3** a hereditary or acquired appellation given to a person or family as a mark of rank. **4** designation as champion. **5** legal ownership. **6** (usu in pl) written material introduced into a film or television programme to represent credits, dialogue, or fragments of narrative.

title² v **(usu in passive) 1** to provide a title for. **2** to designate or call by a title.

titled adj having an aristocratic title such as Lord or Lady.

title deed n the deed constituting evidence of ownership of property.

title music n music played while the titles are shown at the beginning or end of a film or television programme.

title role n the role in a film, play, etc whose name is used as the title of the work.

titration n a method of determining the amount of a substance in a solution by adding measured quantities of a reagent until a reaction occurs.

titter¹ v to giggle or snigger.

titter² n a giggle or snigger.

tittle n a very small part.

tittle-tattle¹ n gossip.

tittle-tattle² v to gossip.

titular adj **1** of or constituting a title. **2** in title only; nominal.

tizzy or **tizz** n **(pl tizzies** or **tizzes)** informal a highly excited and confused state of mind.

Tl abbr the chemical symbol for thallium.

Tm abbr the chemical symbol for thulium.

TNT n trinitrotoluene, a high explosive.

to¹ prep **1** used to indicate a terminal point or destination. **2** before the hour mentioned: five minutes to five. **3** used to indicate the the person or thing affected by an action. **4** used to indicate addition, connection, or possession. **5** used to indicate relationship or conformity. **6** used to introduce an infinitive form of a verb. **7** used to denote purpose: He did it to annoy them.

to² adv of a door or window: into contact, esp with the frame; shut. ✳ **to and fro** from one place to another; back and forth.

toad *n* a tailless leaping amphibian with a short squat body.

toadstool *n* a poisonous or inedible umbrella-shaped fungus.

toady[1] *n* (*pl* **-ies**) a sycophant.

toady[2] *v* (**-ies, -ied**) to be obsequious.

to-and-fro *v* (**toing-and-froing**) to move to and fro; to come and go.

toast[1] *n* **1** sliced bread browned on both sides by heat. **2** the act of drinking in honour of somebody or something. **3** a highly popular or admired person.

toast[2] *v* **1** to make (bread, etc) crisp, hot, and brown by heat. **2** to drink a toast to.

toaster *n* an electrical appliance for toasting bread.

tobacco *n* (*pl* **-os**) the leaves of an American plant, prepared for use in smoking or chewing or as snuff.

tobacconist *n* chiefly Brit a person who sells tobacco.

toboggan *n* a light sledge, used for gliding downhill over snow.

toccata /tə'kahtə/ *n* a musical composition, usu for a keyboard instrument, characterized by rapid runs and intended to show off the performer's technique.

tod ✳ **on one's tod** Brit, informal alone.

today[1] *adv* **1** on this day. **2** at the present time or age.

today[2] *n* **1** this day. **2** the present time or age.

toddle *v* **1** of a very young child: to walk unsteadily. **2** informal to take a stroll. ➤ **toddle** *n*.

toddler *n* a very young child who is just learning to walk.

toddy *n* (*pl* **-ies**) a hot drink of spirits mixed with water, sugar, and spices.

to-do *n* informal bustle or fuss.

toe[1] *n* **1** any of the digits of a human's or animal's foot. **2** the lower end or part. ✳ **on one's toes** alert; ready to act.

toe[2] *v* to touch, reach, or drive with the toe. ✳ **toe the line** to conform rigorously to a rule or standard.

toe cap *n* a piece of steel or leather attached to the toe of a shoe or boot.

toehold *n* a place of support for the toes, e.g. in climbing.

toenail *n* the nail of a toe.

toff *n* chiefly Brit, derog a rich or upper-class person.

toffee *n* a sweet with a texture ranging from chewy to brittle, made by boiling sugar and butter.

toffee-apple *n* a toffee-covered apple held on a stick.

toffee-nosed *adj* chiefly Brit, informal stuck-up.

tofu *n* a soft cheeselike food prepared from soya-bean milk.

tog[1] *v* (**togged, togging**) informal (+ up/out) to dress up.

tog[2] *n* Brit a unit used to measure the insulating properties of a quilt, a garment, etc.

toga *n* a loose outer garment worn in public by citizens of ancient Rome.

together[1] *adv* **1** in or into one place, mass, collection, or group. **2** in collaboration; as a group. **3** in or into contact. **4** in or into association, relationship, or harmony. **5** at one time; simultaneously. **6** to or with each other. ✳ **together with** as well as. ➤ **togetherness** *n*.

together[2] *adj* informal self-possessed and emotionally stable.

toggle *n* a crosspiece attached to a loop in a cord, chain, etc, to serve as a fastening.

togs *pl n* informal clothes.

toil[1] *n* tiring work.

toil[2] *v* **1** to work hard and long. **2** to proceed with laborious effort.

toilet *n* **1** a fixture for receiving and disposing of faeces and urine. **2** a room or compartment containing a toilet and sometimes a washbasin. **3** archaic or literary the act of dressing and grooming oneself.

toiletry *n* (*pl* **-ies**) (*usu in pl*) an article or preparation used in washing, grooming, etc.

toilet training *n* the process of training a young child to use the toilet. ➤ **toilet-train** *v*.

toilet water *n* a light perfume.

token[1] *n* **1** an outward sign or expression, e.g. of an emotion. **2** a souvenir or keepsake. **3** a coinlike disc for use in place of money, e.g. for a bus fare. **4** a voucher for a specified form of merchandise. ✳ **by the same token** furthermore and for the same reason.

token[2] *adj* done or given without enthusiasm merely for show or to fulfil an obligation.

told *v* past tense and past part. of TELL.

tolerable *adj* **1** capable of being borne or endured. **2** moderately good or agreeable. ➤ **tolerably** *adv*.

tolerance *n* **1** allowance or acceptance of beliefs or practices differing from one's own. **2** the physiological ability to endure the effects of a drug, virus, radiation, etc. **3** an allowable variation from a standard dimension.

tolerant *adj* **1** marked by forbearance or endurance. **2** exhibiting tolerance, e.g. to a drug or environmental condition. ➤ **tolerantly** *adv*.

tolerate *v* **1** to allow or accept (e.g. other people or their views) without prohibition, hindrance, or contradiction. **2** to endure the action of (a drug, etc) without grave or lasting injury. ➤ **toleration** *n*.

toll[1] *n* **1** a fee paid for some right or privilege, e.g. of passing over a highway or bridge. **2** an amount of loss or damage suffered, e.g. the number of casualties caused by an accident or disaster.

toll² *v* **1** to sound (a bell) by pulling the rope. **2** to announce by means of a tolled bell. **3** of a bell: to sound with slow measured strokes.

toll³ *n* the sound of a tolling bell.

tom *n* a tomcat.

tomahawk *n* a light axe used by Native Americans as a throwing or hand weapon.

tomato *n* (*pl* **-oes**) a rounded usu red pulpy fruit used as a vegetable, *esp* in salads.

tomb *n* a chamber or vault for the dead, built either above or below ground and usu serving as a memorial.

tombola *n Brit* a lottery in which the tickets that entitle people to prizes are drawn from a revolving drum.

tomboy *n* a girl who behaves in a manner thought of as typical of a boy. ➤ **tomboyish** *adj*.

tombstone *n* = GRAVESTONE.

tomcat *n* a male cat.

tome *n formal* a book, *esp* a large scholarly one.

tomfoolery *n* foolish behaviour.

tomography *n* a diagnostic technique using X-rays or ultrasound to produce an image of a cross-section of the body. ➤ **tomographic** *adj*.

tomorrow¹ *adv* on the day after today.

tomorrow² *n* **1** the day after today. **2** the future.

tomtit *n Brit* a blue tit or other bird of the tit family.

tom-tom *n* a long narrow drum beaten with the hands.

ton *n* **1** (*also* **long ton**) a unit of weight equal to 2240lb (about 1016kg). **2** (*also* **short ton**) *NAmer* a unit of weight equal to 2000lb (about 907kg). **3** a metric ton. **4** a unit approximately equal to the volume of one long ton of seawater, used in reckoning the displacement of ships, and equal to 0.99 cubic m (35 cubic ft). **5** *informal* (*also in pl*) a great quantity. **6** *chiefly Brit, informal* a score or speed of 100.

tonal *adj* **1** relating to tone. **2** of music: based on one of the traditional keys. ➤ **tonality** *n*, **tonally** *adv*.

tone¹ *n* **1** a vocal or musical sound. **2** an inflection of the voice expressive of a mood or emotion. **3** style or manner of verbal expression. **4** prevailing character, quality, or trend, e.g. of morals. **5** a musical interval comprising two semitones. **6** colour quality or value. **7** of muscles: normal tension or responsiveness to stimuli.

tone² *v* (*often* + up) to impart strength and firmness to (part of the body).

tone-deaf *adj* relatively insensitive to musical pitch.

tone down *v* to soften or reduce in colour, intensity, force, etc.

toner *n* **1** a cosmetic preparation applied to the skin to reduce oiliness. **2** powdered or liquid ink used in a photocopier, laser printer, etc.

tongs *pl n* a grasping device consisting of two pieces joined at one end by a pivot or hinged like scissors.

tongue¹ *n* **1** a fleshy muscular organ in the mouth used in tasting and swallowing food and as a speech organ. **2** manner or quality of utterance. **3** a language. **4** a long narrow strip of land projecting into a body of water. **5** the flap under the lacing or buckles on the front of a shoe. ✱ **hold one's tongue** to say nothing.

tongue² *v* (**tongues, tongued, tonguing**) to articulate (notes) on a wind instrument by interrupting the stream of air with the tongue.

tongue and groove *n* a joint in which a projection fits into a groove.

tongue-in-cheek *adj* characterized by irony or whimsical exaggeration.

tongue-tied *adj* unable to speak freely, e.g. because of shyness.

tongue twister *n* a word or phrase that is difficult to articulate.

tonic *n* **1** something that invigorates, refreshes, or stimulates, *esp* an invigorating medicine. **2** (*also* **tonic water**) carbonated, slightly bitter mineral water, often drunk with gin.

tonight¹ *adv* on this night or the night following today.

tonight² *n* this night or the night following today.

tonnage *n* **1** total weight in tons shipped, carried, or produced. **2** the size or carrying capacity of a ship in tons.

tonne *n* a metric unit of weight equal to 1000kg.

tonsil *n* either of a pair of small oval masses of tissue that lie one on each side of the throat.

tonsillectomy *n* (*pl* **-ies**) the surgical removal of the tonsils.

tonsillitis *n* inflammation of the tonsils.

tonsure *n* the shaved patch on a monk's or other cleric's head.

too *adv* **1** to a greater degree than is necessary, desirable, permissible, etc; excessively. **2** *informal* very. **3** also; in addition.

took *v* past tense of TAKE¹.

tool¹ *n* **1** an implement, e.g. a hammer or knife, used to carry out work of a mechanical nature. **2** something that is useful in performing an operation or necessary for one's work; an aid. **3** somebody who is used or manipulated by somebody else.

tool² *v* **1** to work, shape, or finish (something) with a tool, *esp* to letter or ornament (leather, etc) by means of hand tools. **2** (*often* + up) to equip (a plant or industry) with tools, machines, and instruments for production.

toot *v* to produce a short blast on a horn, etc. ➤ **toot** *n*.

tooth *n* (*pl* **teeth**) **1** any of the hard bony structures in the jaws used for biting and chewing food. **2** any of the regular projections on the rim of a cogwheel, a comb, or the blade of a saw, etc. ✳ **get one's teeth into something** *informal* to begin to make progress in tackling or understanding something. **in the teeth of** in direct opposition to. **tooth and nail** with every available means. ➤ **toothed** *adj*, **toothless** *adj*.

toothache *n* pain in a tooth.

toothbrush *n* a brush for cleaning the teeth.

toothcomb ✳ **with a fine toothcomb** *Brit* thoroughly.

toothpaste *n* a paste for cleaning the teeth.

toothpick *n* a pointed instrument for removing food particles lodged between the teeth.

toothsome *adj* **1** of food: delicious. **2** *informal* sexually attractive.

toothy *adj* (**-ier**, **-iest**) having prominent teeth.

tootle *v* **1** to toot gently or continuously. **2** *informal* to go along in a leisurely manner. ➤ **tootle** *n*.

top[1] *n* **1** the highest or uppermost point, level, or part of something. **2** a garment worn on the upper body. **3** a part serving as an upper piece, lid, or covering. **4** (**the top**) the highest position, e.g. in rank or achievement. **5** the highest degree or pitch. ✳ **off the top of one's head** without taking time to think about or research the matter; impromptu. **on top 1** resting on the highest point or surface of something. **2** in a dominant position. **on top of 1** placed on or above the highest part of. **2** in control of. **3** in sudden and unexpected proximity to. **4** in addition to. **on top of the world** in high spirits. **over the top** exaggerated; *esp* excessively dramatic.

top[2] *v* (**topped, topping**) **1** to be or become higher than. **2** to exceed, surpass, or be superior to. **3** to cover with a top or topping. **4** to rise to, reach, or be at the top of. **5** *informal* to kill.

top[3] *adj* **1** of or at the top. **2** foremost or leading. **3** of the highest quality, amount, or degree.

top[4] *n* a child's toy that has a tapering point on which it is made to spin.

topaz *n* a transparent or yellow gemstone.

topcoat *n* **1** a lightweight overcoat. **2** a final coat of paint.

top dog *n informal* a person in a position of superiority.

top-flight *adj* of the highest rank or quality.

top hat *n* a man's tall-crowned hat with a flat top and vertical sides.

top-heavy *adj* unstable or out of proportion because the top part is too heavy for the lower part.

topiary *n* (*pl* **-ies**) **1** the art of training and trimming trees or shrubs into ornamental shapes. **2** trees or shrubs cut in this way.

topic *n* a subject for discussion or consideration.

topical *adj* **1** concerned with events and matters of current interest. **2** relating to or arranged by topics. ➤ **topicality** *n*, **topically** *adv*.

topknot *n* an arrangement of hair on the top of the head.

topless *adj and adv* having the breasts exposed.

topography *n* **1** the configuration of a land surface, including its relief and the position of its natural and man-made features. **2** the practice of making detailed maps of a region. ➤ **topographic** *adj*, **topographical** *adj*.

topple *v* **1** to fall down or over, *esp* through being top-heavy. **2** to cause to topple.

topsoil *n* surface soil, *esp* the organic layer in which plants grow.

topspin *n* spin that causes a ball to rotate forwards in the direction of its travel.

topsy-turvy *adj and adv* **1** upside down. **2** in utter confusion or disorder.

top up *v* **1** to make up to the full quantity or capacity. **2** to increase (a sum of money). **3** to replenish (a drink).

top-up fees *pl n* additional fees to be charged by universities to bridge the gap between the basic tuition fees they receive and actual tuition costs.

tor *n* a mound, hill, or rocky peak.

torch[1] *n* **1** *Brit* a small portable electric lamp powered by batteries. **2** formerly, a stick of wood coated or wrapped with inflammable material and burned to give light.

torch[2] *v informal* to set fire to.

tore *v* past tense of TEAR[1].

toreador /'tori-ədaw/ *n* a bullfighter, *esp* one on horseback.

torment[1] *n* **1** extreme pain or anguish. **2** a source of torment.

torment[2] *v* **1** to cause severe usu persistent distress of body or mind to. **2** to tease unkindly. ➤ **tormentor** *n*.

torn *v* past part. of TEAR[1].

tornado *n* (*pl* **-oes** *or* **-os**) a violent or destructive whirlwind.

torpedo[1] *n* (*pl* **-oes**) a self-propelling cigar-shaped underwater explosive projectile used to attack ships.

torpedo[2] *v* (**torpedoes, torpedoed, torpedoing**) **1** to hit or destroy (e.g. a ship) by torpedo. **2** to destroy or nullify (e.g. a plan).

torpid *adj* inactive and lacking energy or vigour. ➤ **torpidity** *n*.

torpor *n* a state of sleepy inactivity or sluggishness.

torque *n* a force that produces rotation.

torrent *n* **1** a violent stream of water, lava, etc. **2** a violent outpouring.

torrential *adj* of rain: falling fast and in large quantities.

torrid *adj* **1** extremely hot and dry. **2** involving passionate sex. **3** very uncomfortable or unpleasant.

torsion *n* the process of twisting or the state of being twisted.

torso *n* (*pl* **torsos** *or* **torsi**) the human trunk.

tort *n* in law, a wrongful act for which a civil action for damages may be brought.

tortilla /taw'teeya/ *n* **1** in Mexican cooking, a thin maize pancake, usu eaten hot with a filling. **2** in Spanish cooking, a thick omelette containing potato.

tortoise *n* a reptile with a bony shell into which the head, limbs, and tail may be withdrawn.

tortoiseshell *n* **1** the mottled brown-and-yellow horny shell of some marine turtles used in making various ornamental articles. **2** a butterfly with striking orange, yellow, brown, and black coloration. **3** a cat of a breed with black, brown, and yellow markings.

tortuous *adj* **1** marked by repeated twists and turns. **2** circuitous or involved. ➤ **tortuously** *adv*.

torture¹ *n* **1** the infliction of intense physical or mental suffering as a means of punishment, coercion, or sadistic gratification. **2** anguish of body or mind. ➤ **torturous** *adj*.

torture² *v* to subject (a person or animal) to torture. ➤ **torturer** *n*.

Tory *n* (*pl* **-ies**) a supporter of the British Conservative Party.

toss¹ *v* **1** to throw with a quick, light, or careless motion. **2** to throw up in the air. **3** to move repeatedly to and fro or up and down. **4** to jerk (one's head, hair, mane, etc) backwards. **5** to move and turn (food) lightly in a liquid, flour, etc until well coated. **6** to flip (a coin) to decide an issue according to which face lands uppermost.

toss² *n* an act or instance of tossing. * **not give/care a toss** *Brit, informal* not to care at all.

toss off *v* **1** to produce or write quickly or easily. **2** *Brit, coarse slang* to masturbate.

toss-up *n* **1** the tossing of a coin. **2** *informal* an even chance or choice.

tot¹ *n* **1** a small child; a toddler. **2** a small amount of spirits.

tot² *v* (**totted, totting**) **1** *chiefly Brit* (*usu* + up) to add (figures or amounts) together. **2** *chiefly Brit* (+ up) to increase by additions.

total¹ *adj* **1** comprising or constituting a whole; entire. **2** complete or absolute. ➤ **totally** *adv*.

total² *n* the end product of adding two or more smaller amounts together.

total³ *v* (**totalled, totalling,** *NAmer* **totaled, totaling**) **1** to amount to (a figure). **2** to add (something) up. **3** *informal* to demolish completely.

totalitarian *adj* of a political regime: based on strict control over all aspects of the life and productive capacity of the nation. ➤ **totalitarianism** *n*.

totalizator *or* **totalisator** *n* **1** a machine for registering bets and calculating winnings in the tote betting system. **2** = TOTE².

tote¹ *v informal* to carry.

tote² *n* (**the tote**) *informal* a betting system, using a totalizator, in which winners are paid a proportion of the total amount staked, based on the size of their stake.

totem *n* a natural object or animal revered by and serving as the emblem of a family or clan. ➤ **totemic** *adj*.

totem pole *n* a pole carved and painted with totemic symbols erected by some Native American peoples.

totter¹ *v* **1** to tremble or rock as if about to fall. **2** to move unsteadily.

totter² *n* an unsteady gait.

toucan *n* a bird of tropical America with brilliant colouring and a very large beak.

touch¹ *v* **1** to bring the hand or other part of the body in contact with. **2** to grasp or move in any way or degree. **3** to meet or adjoin without overlapping or penetrating. **4** to harm. **5** to use, consume, or accept. **6** to concern or affect. **7** to move to sympathetic feeling. **8** *informal* to rival in ability or value. **9** (+ on/upon) to treat a topic in a brief or casual manner. * **touch wood** with luck.

touch² *n* **1** an act of touching. **2** the sense of feeling derived from physical contact *esp* with the hands. **3** a distinctive style or skill in dealing with something. **4** an effective and appropriate detail. **5** a small amount. **6** (a touch) a bit; a little. **7** in sport, the area outside the touchlines. * **in touch** having up-to-date information or contact. **out of touch** lacking up-to-date information or contact.

touch-and-go *adj* highly uncertain or precarious.

touch down *v* **1** in rugby, to score by placing (the ball) on the ground over an opponent's goal line. **2** of an aircraft or spacecraft: to reach the ground in landing. ➤ **touchdown** *n*.

touché /tooh'shay/ *interj* used to acknowledge a hit in fencing or the success of an argument or witty point.

touching *adj* capable of arousing tenderness or compassion. ➤ **touchingly** *adv*.

touchline *n* in rugby and football, either of the lines that bound the sides of the field of play.

touch off *v* to cause or ignite.

touchstone *n* a test or criterion for determining the genuineness of something.

touch-type *v* to type without looking at the keyboard.

touch up *v* **1** to improve or perfect by small alterations. **2** *Brit, informal* to make unwelcome physical or sexual contact with.

touchy *adj* (**-ier, -iest**) **1** ready to take offence on slight provocation. **2** calling for tact, care, or caution.

tough¹ *adj* **1** strong and flexible; hard-wearing. **2** of food: not easily chewed. **3** characterized by severity or uncompromising determination. **4** capable of enduring great hardship or exertion. **5** aggressive or threatening in behaviour. **6** extremely difficult or testing. **7** *informal* unfortunate or unpleasant. ➤ **toughness** *n*.

tough² *n informal* somebody who is aggressive and violent.

toughen *v* to become or make tough.

toupee *n* a wig or hairpiece worn to cover a bald spot.

tour¹ *n* **1** a journey, e.g. for business or pleasure, in which one visits several places. **2** a visit, e.g. to a historic site or factory, for pleasure or information. **3** a series of professional engagements involving travel.

tour² *v* to make a tour of.

tour de force /ˌtooə dəˈfaws/ *n* (*pl* **tours de force**) an extremely impressive feat, performance, piece of work, etc.

tourism *n* **1** the activity of visiting places, *esp* in foreign countries, for pleasure. **2** the organizing by commercial companies of travel, accommodation, etc for tourists.

tourist *n* **1** somebody who takes a holiday abroad. **2** a member of a sports team that is visiting another country. ➤ **touristy** *adj*.

tournament *n* **1** a series of games or contests for a championship. **2** a contest between two parties of mounted medieval knights armed with blunted lances or swords.

tourney *n* (*pl* **-eys**) a tournament in the Middle Ages.

tourniquet *n* a bandage or other device tied tightly around a limb to stop the blood flow.

tousle *v* to make (something, *esp* somebody's hair) untidy.

tout¹ *v* **1** to try to sell. **2** *Brit* to sell (tickets in great demand) at exploitative prices. **3** to praise or publicize extravagantly.

tout² *n* (*also* **ticket tout**) *Brit* somebody who offers tickets for an event at vastly inflated prices.

tow¹ *v* to draw or pull along behind.

tow² *n* the act of towing. ✳ **in tow 1** being towed. **2** in the position of a companion or follower.

towards *or* **toward** *prep* **1** moving or situated in the direction of. **2** along a course leading to. **3** in relation to. **4** turned in the direction of. **5** not long before. **6** for the partial financing of.

towel¹ *n* an absorbent cloth or piece of paper for wiping or drying.

towel² *v* (**towelled**, **towelling**, *NAmer* **toweled**, **toweling**) to rub or dry with a towel.

towelling (*NAmer* **toweling**) *n* absorbent fabric used for making towels.

tower¹ *n* **1** a tall and narrow building or structure, standing alone or attached to a larger structure. **2** a tall unit for storage.

tower² *v* to reach or rise to a great height.

tower block *n Brit* a tall multi-storey building, usu containing flats or offices.

towering *adj* **1** impressively high or great. **2** reaching a high point of intensity.

town *n* **1** a compactly settled area, *esp* one larger than a village but smaller than a city. **2** the business centre of a large town or city. **3** the townspeople. ✳ **go to town** to deal with or exploit something enthusiastically. **on the town** in pursuit of entertainment or amusement.

town crier *n* somebody employed to make public proclamations.

town hall *n* the chief administrative building of a town.

town planning *n* the arrangement of the various components of the urban environment for best results. ➤ **town planner** *n*.

townscape *n* the overall visual aspect of a town.

township *n* **1** *esp* formerly, an urban area inhabited by non-white citizens in South Africa. **2** in the USA and Canada, a subdivision of a county.

towpath *n* a path, e.g. along a canal, for use in towing boats.

toxic *adj* **1** = POISONOUS. **2** relating to or caused by a poison. ➤ **toxicity** *n*.

toxicology *n* a branch of biology that deals with poisons and their effects. ➤ **toxicologist** *n*.

toxin *n* an often extremely poisonous protein produced by a living organism, e.g. a bacterium.

toy¹ *n* **1** something for a child to play with. **2** something designed for amusement or diversion rather than practical use.

toy² *adj* **1** used as a toy. **2** denoting an animal of a breed of exceptionally small size.

toy³ *v* **1** (+ with) to touch or handle in an absent-minded or nonchalant way. **2** (+ with) to consider as a possibility but without committing oneself.

toy boy *n Brit, informal* a young man taken as lover by an older woman.

trace¹ *n* **1** a mark or line left by something that has passed. **2** a sign or evidence of some past thing. **3** a minute or barely detectable amount or indication. **4** the graphic record made by a recording instrument.

trace² *v* **1** to find by using signs, evidence, or remains. **2** to study in detail or step by step, *esp* working back towards the source or origin of something. **3** to follow the course or trail of. **4** to copy (e.g. a drawing) by following the lines or letters as seen through a semitransparent superimposed sheet. **5** to delineate or sketch. ➤ **traceable** *adj*.

trace element *n* a chemical element present in minute quantities.

tracer n **1** ammunition that is chemically treated to mark its trajectory by a trail of smoke or fire. **2** a substance used to trace the course of a chemical or biological process.

tracery n (pl -ies) **1** an ornamental pattern of stonework and spaces in architecture. **2** a decorative interlacing of lines.

trachea n (pl **tracheae** or **tracheas**) the tube by which air passes to and from the lungs.

tracheotomy n (pl -ies) the surgical operation of cutting into the trachea usu to relieve suffocation by inhaled matter.

track¹ n **1** a roughly made path or road. **2** detectable evidence, e.g. a line of footprints or a wheel rut, that something has passed. **3** a specially laid-out course, esp for racing. **4** the parallel rails of a railway. **5** a rail or length of railing along which something, esp a curtain, moves. **6** the course along which something, e.g. a missile, moves. **7** a single song or piece of music on a compact disc, record, or cassette. ✳ **keep/ lose track of** to remain aware/no longer be aware of the development or whereabouts of. **make tracks** informal to leave. **on the right/ wrong track** attempting to do something in way that is likely/unlikely to be successful.

track² v **1** to follow the tracks or traces of. **2** to observe or plot the course of (e.g. a spacecraft or missile) instrumentally. **3** to move a film or television camera towards, beside, or away from a subject while shooting a scene. ➤ **tracker** n.

track down v to search for until found.

track event n an athletic event that takes place on a track; a race.

track record n a record of the past achievements of an individual, organization, team, etc.

tracksuit n a warm loose-fitting suit worn esp by athletes when training.

tract¹ n a pamphlet on a religious subject.

tract² n **1** a region or area of land of indefinite extent. **2** a system of connected body parts or organs.

tractable adj **1** of a person or animal: easily taught or controlled. **2** of a problem: easy to deal with.

traction n **1** the act of pulling, or the force exerted in pulling. **2** in medicine, a pulling force exerted on part of the body to treat fractures, cure deformities, etc. **3** the adhesive friction of a moving body on a surface, e.g. a tyre on a road.

traction engine n a large steam- or diesel-powered vehicle used to pull heavy loads.

tractor n **1** a vehicle used for pulling farm machinery. **2** a truck with a short chassis and a driver's cab, used to haul a large trailer.

trad adj informal = TRADITIONAL.

trade¹ n **1** the business of buying and selling or bartering commodities. **2** the business or work

in which one engages regularly. **3** an occupation requiring manual or mechanical skill; a craft. **4** the people or firms engaged in a particular business or industry.

trade² v **1** to engage in the exchange, purchase, or sale of goods. **2** to exchange. **3** (+ on) to exploit or take advantage of. ➤ **trader** n.

trademark n **1** a legally registered name or distinctive symbol attached to goods produced by a particular firm. **2** a distinguishing feature firmly associated with somebody or something.

trade off v to sacrifice (something) for something else.

tradesman n (pl **tradesmen**) **1** a shopkeeper. **2** a worker in a skilled trade.

trade union (Brit also **trades union**) n an organization of workers formed for the purpose of advancing its members' interests. ➤ **trade unionism** n, **trade unionist** n.

tradition n **1** the handing down of information, beliefs, and customs from one generation to another. **2** a belief, custom, or practice inherited from previous generations.

traditional adj relating to or handed down by tradition. ➤ **traditionally** adv.

traditionalism n adherence to traditional methods, usu in preference to newer ones. ➤ **traditionalist** n and adj.

traduce v formal to defame.

traffic¹ n **1** the movement, e.g. of vehicles or pedestrians, through an area or along a route. **2** the vehicles, pedestrians, ships, or aircraft moving along a route. **3** the information or signals transmitted over a communications system. **4** the business of transporting passengers or freight. **5** trade, esp in illegal merchandise.

traffic² v (**trafficked, trafficking**) to trade in something illegal or disreputable. ➤ **trafficker** n.

traffic island n a paved or planted area in the middle of a road designed to guide the flow of traffic and provide refuge for pedestrians.

traffic jam n a line of vehicles that cannot move normally because of an obstruction.

traffic light n (usu in pl) an automatically operated signal with coloured lights for controlling traffic.

traffic warden n Brit an official who enforces parking regulations.

tragedian n **1** an actor who plays tragic roles. **2** a writer of tragedies.

tragedy n (pl -ies) **1** a disastrous or very sad event. **2** a serious drama in which the main characters meet an unhappy fate.

tragic adj **1** very sad, deplorable, or disastrous. **2** relating to literary tragedy. ➤ **tragically** adv.

tragicomedy n (pl -ies) a literary work in which tragic and comic elements are mixed. ➤ **tragicomic** adj.

trail¹ n **1** a trace or mark left by somebody or something that has passed. **2** a marked path through a forest or mountainous region. **3** a route followed or to be followed for a particular purpose. **4** something that follows or moves along as if being drawn behind something.

trail² v **1** to follow the trail of. **2** to draw (something) along behind one. **3** to hang down so as to sweep the ground. **4** (*usu* + along) to walk or proceed heavily or wearily. **5** to do poorly in relation to others. **6** (*usu* + off/away) to become quieter or weaker; to dwindle.

trailblazer n **1** somebody who finds a new route through wild country. **2** a pioneer; an innovator. ➤ **trailblazing** adj.

trailer n **1** a wheeled vehicle designed to be towed. **2** *NAmer* = CARAVAN. **3** the rear part of an articulated lorry. **4** a set of short excerpts from a film shown in advance for publicity purposes.

train¹ n **1** a connected line of railway carriages or wagons pulled by a locomotive. **2** a moving file of people, vehicles, or animals. **3** a connected series of ideas, actions, or events. **4** a part of a gown that trails behind the wearer.

train² v **1** to teach (a person or animal) to do something. **2** to undergo training. **3** to make oneself fit by exercise, e.g. in preparation for a race or contest. **4** to direct the growth of (a plant) by bending, pruning, and tying. **5** (*usu* + on) to aim (something) at an object. ➤ **training** n.

trainee n somebody who is being trained for a job.

trainer n **1** a person who trains people or animals. **2** *Brit* a sports shoe designed for running, jogging, etc.

trainspotter n *Brit* somebody whose hobby is to collect the numbers of railway locomotives. ➤ **trainspotting** n.

traipse¹ v to walk or trudge about, often to little purpose.

traipse² n a long or unpleasant walk.

trait n a distinguishing quality or characteristic.

traitor n **1** somebody who betrays another's trust. **2** somebody who commits treason. ➤ **traitorous** adj.

trajectory n (pl **-ies**) the curve that a moving object follows through space.

tram or **tramcar** n *chiefly Brit* a passenger vehicle running on rails and typically operating on urban streets.

tramline n **1** *Brit* a track on which trams run. **2** (*in pl*) either of the two pairs of sidelines on a tennis or badminton court marking the area used in doubles.

trammel¹ n **1** a net with three layers. **2** *literary* (*in pl*) something that impedes freedom of action.

trammel² v (**trammelled, trammelling**, *NAmer* **trammeled, trammeling**) to restrain or confine.

tramp¹ v **1** to walk or tread heavily. **2** to travel about on foot.

tramp² n **1** a homeless person who travels around and survives by taking occasional jobs or by begging. **2** a usu long and tiring walk. **3** the heavy rhythmic tread of feet. **4** *NAmer* a promiscuous woman.

trample v **1** to press down, crush, or injure by treading. **2** (*usu* + on/over) to treat ruthlessly or with contempt.

trampoline n a resilient sheet supported by springs in a frame, used for bouncing up and down on and performing gymnastic tricks in the air. ➤ **trampolining** n.

trance n **1** a state of semiconsciousness or unconsciousness with diminished sensitivity to external stimuli. **2** a state of altered consciousness or ecstasy in which religious or mystical visions may be experienced.

tranche n a portion.

tranquil adj calm, quiet, or peaceful. ➤ **tranquillity** n, **tranquilly** adv.

tranquillize or **-ise** (*NAmer* **tranquilize**) v to make calm, *esp* with drugs.

tranquillizer or **tranquilliser** (*NAmer* **tranquilizer**) n a drug used to tranquillize.

transact v to conduct (business).

transaction n **1** an instance of buying and selling or a business deal. **2** the act of conducting business.

transatlantic adj **1** crossing the Atlantic Ocean. **2** relating to people or places situated beyond the Atlantic Ocean.

transcend v **1** to go beyond the limits of. **2** to surpass.

transcendent adj **1** extraordinarily great, good, etc. **2** beyond the limits of ordinary experience. **3** of God: existing outside the material universe. ➤ **transcendence** n.

transcendental adj extending beyond ordinary experience, *esp* into the mystical realm. ➤ **transcendentally** adv.

transcontinental adj crossing a continent.

transcribe v **1** to make a written copy or version of. **2** to write (something) in a different medium; to transliterate. **3** to make a musical transcription of.

transcript n a written, printed, or typed copy *esp* of dictated or spoken material or shorthand notes.

transcription n **1** the act of transcribing. **2** a transcript. **3** an arrangement of a musical composition for some instrument or voice other than the original.

transept n either of the projecting arms of a cross-shaped church extending at right angles to the nave.

transfer¹ v (**transferred, transferring**) **1** to carry or take from one person, place, or situation to another. **2** to move to another location, job, etc. **3** to make over the possession or control of (e.g. property). **4** to change from one vehicle or transport system to another. ➤ **transferable** n.

transfer² n **1** an act of transferring. **2** Brit a graphic image transferred by contact from one surface to another. ➤ **transference** n.

transfiguration n **1** a change in form or appearance, esp to something more beautiful or exalted. **2** (**Transfiguration**) a festival of the Christian Church commemorating the transfiguration of Christ (Matthew 17:2 and Mark 9:2–3).

transfigure v to transform outwardly, esp to make more beautiful.

transfix v **1** to hold (a person or animal) motionless, esp with horror or shock. **2** to pierce through, e.g. with a pointed weapon.

transform v to change radically in structure, appearance, or character. ➤ **transformation** n.

transformer n a device that changes an electric current, usu from high voltage to low, or from alternating to direct.

transfusion n a medical procure to transfer a quantity of another person's blood into the body of a patient.

transgress v to do wrong, esp by violating a law, rule, command, etc. ➤ **transgression** n, **transgressor** n.

transient¹ adj **1** transitory. **2** staying or working in a place for only a short time. ➤ **transience** n, **transiently** adv.

transient² n a transient guest or worker.

transistor n **1** a semiconductor device that makes use of a small current to control a larger one. **2** (also **transistor radio**) a small portable radio using transistors in its circuits.

transit n **1** the act of passing through or over. **2** NAmer transportation.

transition n the process of passing from one state, stage, form, topic, etc to another. ➤ **transitional** adj.

transitive adj of a verb: having a direct object. ➤ **transitivity** n.

transitory adj of brief duration; not lasting.

translate v **1** to reproduce the meaning of (a word, text, etc) in another language. **2** to explain or interpret (something difficult to understand). **3** (usu + into) to convert or be converted into another medium.

translation n **1** the act of rendering from one language into another. **2** a version thus produced.

translator n somebody who translates from one language into another.

transliterate v to represent or spell (a letter or word) in the characters of another alphabet. ➤ **transliteration** n.

translucent adj allowing some light to pass through, but not enough for objects beyond to be seen clearly; semitransparent. ➤ **translucence** n.

transmission n **1** the act of transmitting. **2** something, e.g. a message or television programme, that is transmitted. **3** an assembly of parts by which power is transmitted from a motor vehicle engine to an axle.

transmit v (**transmitted, transmitting**) **1** to send or pass from one person or place to another. **2** to cause (e.g. force or energy) to be conveyed through a medium. **3** to send out (a signal) either by radio waves or over a wire.

transmitter n a device that sends out e.g. radio or television signals in the form of electromagnetic waves.

transmogrify v (**-ies, -ied**) to transform, often with grotesque or humorous effect. ➤ **transmogrification** n.

transmute v to change in form, substance, or characteristics. ➤ **transmutation** n.

transom n **1** the planking forming the stern of a square-ended boat. **2** a horizontal crossbar used to strengthen a structure.

transparency n (pl **-ies**) **1** the quality of being transparent. **2** a photographic slide.

transparent adj **1** transmitting light without appreciable scattering so that bodies lying beyond are entirely visible. **2** free from pretence or deceit. **3** easily detected or seen through. **4** readily understood. ➤ **transparently** adv.

transpire v **1** to become known. **2** to occur. **3** of plants: to give off water vapour from the surfaces of leaves. ➤ **transpiration** n.

transplant¹ v **1** to lift and reset (a plant) in another soil or place. **2** to remove (something) from one place and settle or introduce it elsewhere. **3** to transfer (an organ or tissue) from one part or individual to another. ➤ **transplantation** n.

transplant² n **1** the act of transplanting, esp a surgical operation to transplant an organ. **2** something transplanted.

transport¹ v **1** to transfer or convey from one place to another. **2** to delight or enrapture. **3** formerly, to send (a convict) to a penal colony overseas. ➤ **transportation** n, **transporter** n.

transport² n **1** the conveying of goods or people from one place to another. **2** a means of travelling or of conveying passengers or goods. **3** a ship or aircraft for carrying soldiers or military equipment. **4** an experience of strong and usu pleasurable emotion.

transpose v **1** to change the relative position of (two or more things). **2** to transfer from one place or period to another. **3** to write or perform (music) in a different key. ➤ **transposition** n.

transsexual or **transexual** n somebody physically of one sex with an urge to belong to or resemble the opposite sex.

transubstantiation n the miraculous change by which, according to Roman Catholic and Eastern Orthodox dogma, the bread and wine used at communion become the body and blood of Christ when consecrated.

transverse adj lying or set crosswise. ➤ **transversely** adv.

transvestite n somebody who adopts the dress of the opposite sex. ➤ **transvestism** n.

trap[1] n **1** a device for catching animals. **2** a plan or trick designed to catch a person unawares and put them at a disadvantage. **3** a situation from which it is difficult or impossible to escape. **4** a light carriage with springs, pulled by a horse or pony. **5** informal the mouth.

trap[2] v (**trapped, trapping**) **1** to catch in a trap. **2** to place in a position from which it is difficult to escape. **3** to stop or retain.

trapdoor n a lifting or sliding door covering an opening in a floor, ceiling, etc.

trapeze n an apparatus consisting of a short horizontal bar suspended by two parallel ropes, used esp by circus acrobats.

trapezium n (pl **trapeziums** or **trapezia**) Brit a quadrilateral that has only two sides parallel.

trapper n a person who traps wild animals.

trappings pl n **1** outward signs and accessories. **2** ornamental coverings and harness for a horse.

Trappist n a member of a monastic order noted for its vow of silence.

trash[1] n chiefly NAmer **1** junk or rubbish. **2** inferior or worthless literary or artistic work. **3** a worthless person or worthless people.

trash[2] v chiefly NAmer, informal to destroy or vandalize.

trash can n NAmer a dustbin.

trashy adj (**-ier, -iest**) of poor quality.

trauma n (pl **traumas**) **1** a disordered mental or behavioural state resulting from emotional stress or shock. **2** a deeply shocking or distressing experience. **3** in medicine, an injury, e.g. a wound. ➤ **traumatic** adj.

traumatize or **-ise** v to cause to suffer emotional trauma.

travail n literary (also in pl) painful or laborious effort.

travel[1] v (**travelled, travelling,** NAmer **traveled, traveling**) **1** to go on a journey or tour. **2** to journey along (a road) or through (an area). **3** to move or be transmitted from one place to another.

travel[2] n **1** the act of travelling. **2** (in pl) journeys, esp to distant or unfamiliar places.

travel agency n an agency that gives information on and arranges travel. ➤ **travel agent** n.

traveller (NAmer **traveler**) n **1** somebody who is on a journey or who travels frequently. **2** a gypsy, or a person who has an itinerant alternative lifestyle.

traveller's cheque (NAmer **traveler's check**) n a cheque purchased from a bank or travel agency that may be exchanged abroad for foreign currency.

travelogue (NAmer **travelog**) n a film, book, illustrated talk, etc on travel, usu to some exotic or remote place.

traverse v to travel or extend across, over, or through.

travesty n (pl **-ies**) a distorted or grossly inferior imitation.

trawl[1] v **1** to fish with a trawl. **2** to search through a large number of things.

trawl[2] n **1** a large conical fishing net dragged along the sea bottom. **2** an act of trawling.

trawler n a boat used in trawling.

tray n an open receptacle with a flat bottom and a low rim for holding or carrying articles.

treacherous adj **1** involving a betrayal of trust. **2** providing insecure footing or support. **3** marked by hidden dangers or hazards. ➤ **treacherously** adv, **treachery** n.

treacle n **1** chiefly Brit molasses. **2** golden syrup. ➤ **treacly** adj.

tread[1] v (past tense **trod**, past part. **trodden** or **trod**) **1** to walk or step. **2** to step or walk along, on, or over. **3** to press down with the feet; to trample. * **tread on somebody's toes/corns** to give offence to somebody, esp by encroaching on their rights. **tread water 1** to keep the body nearly upright in water by a treading motion of the feet. **2** to stay in the same position without making progress.

tread[2] n **1** the sound or manner of stepping or treading. **2** the upper horizontal part of a step. **3** the part of a tyre that makes contact with the road. **4** the part of a sole that touches the ground.

treadle n a lever pressed by the foot to drive e.g. a sewing machine.

treadmill n **1** a wide wheel with a horizontal axis turned by people or animals treading on steps inside it, formerly used to drive machinery or punish prisoners. **2** an exercise machine that has a continuous moving belt on which to run or walk. **3** a wearisome or monotonous routine.

treason n (also **high treason**) the offence of violating the duty of allegiance owed to one's sovereign or government. ➤ **treasonable** adj.

treasure[1] n **1** coins, jewels, and other valuable objects. **2** something of great worth or value. **3** informal somebody highly valued or prized.

treasure[2] v to treat as precious; to look after carefully, cherish, or prize.

treasure hunt *n* a game in which each player tries to be first to find an object that has been hidden.

treasurer *n* the person in charge of the finances of e.g. a society.

treasure trove *n* under English law until 1996, hidden valuables of unknown ownership that become the property of the Crown when found.

treasury *n* (*pl* **-ies**) **1** a depository where the collected funds or revenues of a state, organization, or individual are kept. **2** (*often* **Treasury**) the government department in charge of finance and the economy. **3** a collection of valuable or pleasing things.

treat[1] *v* **1** to behave towards or deal with in a certain way. **2** to care for or attend to medically or surgically. **3** to present and discuss (a subject). **4** to apply a process or substance to. **5** (+ to) to provide (somebody) with food, drink, or entertainment at one's own expense. **6** (+ to) to provide (oneself) with enjoyment or gratification. ➤ **treatable** *adj*.

treat[2] *n* something that gives great pleasure. ✳ **a treat** *Brit, informal* very well or successfully: *The speech went down a treat.*

treatise *n* a formal written report on a subject.

treatment *n* **1** behaviour towards somebody or something, or the way in which somebody or something is dealt with. **2** the medicine, therapy, surgery, etc involved in dealing with a patient, injury, or illness. **3** the discussion or presentation of a subject, theme, etc. **4** the use of a chemical substance to preserve, purify etc something.

treaty *n* (*pl* **-ies**) a formal agreement made by negotiation, *esp* between states.

treble[1] *adj* **1** having three parts. **2** being three times as great or as much. **3** relating to the range or part of a treble. **4** high-pitched or shrill.

treble[2] *n* **1** a boy singer with a high-pitched voice. **2** the higher portion of the audio frequency range.

treble[3] *v* to increase to three times as much or as many.

treble clef *n* in music, a clef placing the G above middle C on the second lowest line of the stave.

tree *n* **1** a woody plant with a single tall and erect main stem and, generally, few or no branches on its lower part. **2** a tree diagram. ✳ **be barking up the wrong tree** *informal* to be acting misguidedly.

tree diagram *n* a diagram in the form of branching lines.

tree house *n* a structure built in the branches of a tree for children to play in.

tree line *n* the upper limit of tree growth on a mountain.

treen *n* small domestic articles made of wood.

trefoil *n* **1** a wild plant with three-lobed leaves. **2** a stylized ornament, *esp* in architecture, in the form of a three-lobed leaf or flower.

trek[1] *n* a journey, *esp* a long or arduous one made on foot.

trek[2] *v* (**trekked, trekking**) to go on a trek. ➤ **trekker** *n*.

trellis *n* a frame of latticework used *esp* as a support for climbing plants.

tremble[1] *v* **1** to shake involuntarily, *esp* with fear or cold. **2** to quiver or vibrate. **3** to feel fear or apprehension.

tremble[2] *n* a fit or spell of involuntary shaking or quivering.

tremendous *adj* **1** very great in size, degree, amount, intensity, etc. **2** *informal* highly impressive, unusual, or exciting. ➤ **tremendously** *adv*.

tremolo *n* (*pl* **-os**) in music, a trembling effect produced by very rapid repetition of notes.

tremor *n* **1** an involuntary trembling or shaking, e.g. because of a nervous disorder. **2** a distinct small movement of the earth that precedes or follows an earthquake. **3** a sudden thrill of fear or excitement.

tremulous *adj* **1** shaking or quivering. **2** uncertain, timid, or fearful.

trench *n* **1** a long narrow excavation in the ground. **2** a deep ditch dug to provide cover for troops from enemy fire. **3** a long, narrow, and usu steep-sided depression in the ocean floor.

trenchant *adj* incisive and penetrating. ➤ **trenchancy** *n*.

trench coat *n* a double-breasted raincoat with a belt.

trencher *n* a wooden platter formerly used for serving food.

trend *n* **1** a general or prevailing direction or tendency, *esp* in the way things develop or change. **2** a current style, fashion, or taste.

trendsetter *n* somebody who popularizes a new fashion, idea, theory, etc. ➤ **trendsetting** *adj*.

trendy *adj* (**-ier, -iest**) *informal* very fashionable or up-to-date.

trepan[1] *n* formerly, a surgical instrument for removing circular pieces of tissue or bone, *esp* from the skull.

trepan[2] *v* (**trepanned, trepanning**) to remove a circular piece of bone using a trepan.

trepidation *n* a feeling of nervous agitation or fear.

trespass[1] *v* **1** to enter somebody's land or property unlawfully or without permission. **2** (+ on/upon) to make an unwarranted or uninvited intrusion on. **3** *archaic* (+ against) to commit an offence against. ➤ **trespasser** *n*.

trespass[2] *n* **1** to the act of trespassing on somebody's land or property. **2** *archaic* a sin.

tress *n* (*also in pl*) a long lock of hair.

trestle n a framework consisting typically of a horizontal bar held at each end by a pair of sloping legs, designed as a support *esp* for a table top.

triad n **1** a group of three related people or things. **2** (*often* **Triad**) a Chinese secret society engaged in organized crime.

trial[1] n **1** a formal examination of the evidence in a court case to determine an accused person's guilt or innocence. **2** a test or period of probation to ascertain whether something or somebody performs adequately or is suitable. **3** (*in pl*) a competition in which the individual skills of a person or an animal are tested. **4** a test of faith, patience, or stamina. ✳ **on trial 1** undergoing trial in a court of law. **2** undergoing testing.

trial[2] v (**trialled, trialling,** *NAmer* **trialed, trialing**) to test (something) in order to assess its quality, durability, performance, etc.

trial and error n a process of trying out a number of methods to find which achieves a desired result.

triangle n **1** a polygon with three angles and three sides. **2** a percussion instrument consisting of a steel rod bent into a triangle and sounded with a small metal rod. **3** a romantic or sexual relationship involving three people. ➤ **triangular** adj.

triangulation n the measurement of the angles and one side of a triangle to find an unknown position, distance, etc, *esp* in surveying.

triathlon n an athletic contest involving three events, typically long-distance running, swimming, and cycling. ➤ **triathlete** n.

tribalism n loyalty to one's tribe.

tribe n **1** in traditional societies, a group of people, families, or clans with usu a common culture, dialect, religion, and ancestry, led by a chief. **2** *informal* (*also in pl*) a large number of people or things. ➤ **tribal** adj.

tribesman or **tribeswoman** n (*pl* **tribesmen** or **tribeswomen**) a person who is a member of a tribe.

tribulation n a state or cause of great distress or suffering.

tribunal n **1** *Brit* a board appointed to decide disputes. **2** a court of justice.

tribune n an official of ancient Rome elected by the common people to protect their interests.

tributary n (*pl* **-ies**) a stream or river feeding a larger river or a lake.

tribute n **1** something, *esp* a gift or a formal statement, given or made as a demonstration of respect, gratitude, or affection. **2** evidence of the worth or effectiveness of something. **3** a payment formerly made by one ruler or nation to another more powerful one.

trice n ✳ **in a trice** very soon or immediately.

tricentenary n (*pl* **-ies**) = TERCENTENARY.

triceps n (*pl* **tricepses** or **triceps**) the large muscle along the back of the upper arm.

triceratops n a large plant-eating dinosaur with three horns.

trichology n the scientific study of hair and the scalp. ➤ **trichologist** n.

trick[1] n **1** a crafty action or plan intended to deceive, defraud, or outwit somebody. **2** a dexterous or ingenious feat designed to puzzle or amuse. **3** an illusion. **4** a mannerism. **5** a single round of a card game. ✳ **do the trick** *informal* to produce the desired result. **tricks of the trade** the techniques that are used by experts in a particular profession or craft. ➤ **trickery** n.

trick[2] v to deceive, defraud, cheat, or outwit.

trickle[1] v **1** to flow in drops or a thin slow stream. **2** to go gradually or one by one.

trickle[2] n a thin slow stream or movement.

trickster n a person who defrauds others by trickery.

tricksy adj (**-ier, -iest**) full of tricks; mischievous.

tricky adj (**-ier, -iest**) **1** of a task, problem etc: requiring great skill, care, or tact. **2** full of difficulties, hazards, or problems. **3** inclined to be sly or deceitful.

tricolour (*NAmer* **tricolor**) n a flag with three bands of different colours, *esp* the French national flag.

tricycle n a three-wheeled pedal-driven vehicle.

trident n a three-pronged spear.

tried v past tense and past part. of TRY[1].

triennial adj **1** lasting for three years. **2** occurring every three years.

trier n somebody who perseveres with something.

trifle[1] n **1** *Brit* a type of cold dessert made from sponge cake, fruit, jelly, custard, and whipped cream. **2** something of little value or importance. **3** an insignificant amount.

trifle[2] v (*often* + with) to behave frivolously, thoughtlessly, or disrespectfully towards.

trifling adj unimportant or frivolous.

trigger[1] n **1** a small lever that activates a mechanism, *esp* that makes a gun fire. **2** something that causes an event or reaction.

trigger[2] v **1** to activate (a mechanism). **2** (*often* + off) to initiate, bring about, or set off.

trigger-happy adj inclined to resort to violence or guns too quickly.

trigonometry n the branch of mathematics concerned with the relations between the sides and angles of triangles.

trilby n (*pl* **-ies**) *chiefly Brit* a soft felt hat with an indented crown.

trill[1] n **1** in music, a rapid alternation of a main note and one above it. **2** a high-pitched warbling sound.

trill[2] v to produce a warbling sound. ➤ **triller** n.

trillion n (pl **trillions** or **trillion**) **1** a million million (10^{12}). **2** Brit, dated a million million million (10^{18}). ➤ **trillionth** adj and n.

trilobite n an extinct sea creature with a three-lobed body.

trilogy n (pl **-ies**) a group of three closely related literary or cinematic works.

trim[1] v (**trimmed, trimming**) **1** to make neater, shorter, or smaller by cutting or clipping. **2** to reduce the size of (e.g. expenditure). **3** to decorate with ribbons, lace, ornaments, etc. **4** to adjust (a sail) to take advantage of the wind direction.

trim[2] n **1** an act of trimming. **2** material used for decoration or trimming. **3** the upholstery, interior, and decorative accessories of a motor vehicle. ✳ **in trim 1** fit and healthy. **2** well-maintained.

trim[3] adj (**trimmer, trimmest**) in good order; neat and smart.

trimaran n a yacht with three parallel hulls.

trimming n **1** (in pl) pieces cut off in trimming something. **2** a decoration added to clothing, upholstery, linen, etc. **3** informal (in pl) the traditional garnishes accompanying a dish or meal.

trinity n (pl **-ies**) **1** (**the Trinity**) according to Christian theology, the unity of Father, Son, and Holy Spirit as three persons in one Godhead. **2** a group of three people or things.

trinket n a small inexpensive ornament or piece of jewellery.

trio n (pl **-os**) **1** a group or set of three. **2** a group of three musicians or singers. **3** a musical composition for a trio.

trip[1] v (**tripped, tripping**) **1** (also + on/up/over) to catch the foot against something and stumble or fall. **2** (+ up) to make a mistake. **3** to dance, skip, or walk with light quick steps. **4** to cause (a device or mechanism) to start or stop operating. **5** informal to experience the effects of a psychedelic drug. ✳ **trip the light fantastic** to dance.

trip[2] n **1** a journey or outing. **2** the act of stumbling or falling. **3** informal a hallucinogenic experience induced by a psychedelic drug. **4** informal an obsessive, self-indulgent, or self-serving course of action. **5** a device that activates a mechanism.

tripartite adj **1** composed of three parts. **2** involving three parties.

tripe n **1** the stomach tissue of a cow or sheep used as food. **2** informal rubbish or nonsense.

triplane n an aircraft with three pairs of wings arranged one above the other.

triple[1] adj **1** consisting of three things or parts. **2** three times as much or as many.

triple[2] v to become or make three times as much or as many.

triple jump n an athletic field event in which a competitor takes a running start and then performs a hop, a step, and a jump in succession.

triplet n **1** one of three children or animals born at one birth. **2** a group of three musical notes performed in the time of two or four.

triplicate[1] adj existing in three identical parts or copies.

triplicate[2] v **1** to make three copies of. **2** to multiply by three.

tripod n a three-legged stand for supporting a camera, etc.

tripper n Brit, informal somebody who goes on a journey or outing for pleasure.

triptych n a picture or carving covering three panels.

trip wire n a concealed wire placed near the ground that is used to trip up an intruder or to activate an explosive or warning device.

trite adj of a remark, idea, etc: lacking originality; overused.

triumph[1] n **1** a notable success, victory, or achievement. **2** the feeling of happiness or satisfaction brought by success. **3** a highly successful or spectacular example of something. **4** in ancient Rome, a ceremonial procession for a victorious general. ➤ **triumphal** adj.

triumph[2] v **1** (often + over) to obtain victory. **2** to celebrate victory or success, esp boastfully.

triumphant adj **1** victorious. **2** jubilant. ➤ **triumphantly** adv.

triumvirate n a group of three rulers or powerful people.

trivet n a three-legged stand to support a cooking pot or kettle.

trivia pl n unimportant matters, details, or facts.

trivial adj of little worth or importance; insignificant. ➤ **triviality** n, **trivially** adv.

trivialize or **-ise** v to treat (something) as being unimportant or less important than it is. ➤ **trivialization** n.

trod v past tense and past part. of TREAD[1].

trodden v past part. of TREAD[1].

troglodyte n a person who lives in a cave.

troika n **1** a Russian vehicle pulled by three horses abreast. **2** a group of three people working as a team.

Trojan n a native or inhabitant of ancient Troy in Asia Minor. ✳ **work like a Trojan** to work very hard.

Trojan Horse n somebody or something that undermines an organization from within.

troll[1] n in Scandinavian folklore, an ugly dwarf or giant.

troll[2] v to fish with a hook and line drawn through the water behind a moving boat.

trolley n (pl **-eys**) Brit **1** a large basket or a small cart on wheels, used for carrying e.g. shopping or luggage. **2** a shelved stand on wheels used for conveying food or drinks. **3** a hospital stretcher on wheels used for transporting patients. * **off one's trolley** Brit, informal crazy or stupid.

trolleybus n an electrically propelled bus running on a road and drawing power from overhead wires.

trollop n a promiscuous woman.

trombone n a brass musical instrument with a movable slide to extend its length and thus vary the pitch. ➤ **trombonist** n.

troop[1] n **1** (in pl) soldiers or the army. **2** a subdivision of a cavalry or tank regiment. **3** an artillery unit smaller than a battery. **4** a group of similar people, animals, etc.

troop[2] v of a group of people: to move together.

trooper n **1** a private in a cavalry or tank regiment. **2** NAmer a state police officer.

trophy n (pl -ies) **1** a cup, medal, plate, etc awarded to a person or team as a symbol of victory in a contest. **2** a memento of a successful achievement.

tropic n **1** (**tropic of Cancer**) a line of latitude 23½° north of the equator. **2** (**tropic of Capricorn**) a line of latitude 23½° south of the equator. **3** (**the tropics**) the region between these two lines of latitude.

tropical adj **1** relating to the tropics. **2** of the weather or a climate: very hot and usu humid. ➤ **tropically** adv.

trot[1] v (**trotted, trotting**) **1** to progress or ride at a trot. **2** to run at a moderately fast pace.

trot[2] n **1** a moderately fast pace of a horse in which the legs move in diagonal pairs. **2** a period of trotting. * **on the trot** Brit, informal in succession.

troth n * **pledge/plight one's troth** to make a solemn promise to be faithful or loyal, esp in marriage.

trot out v informal to say or produce with tedious regularity.

trotter n the foot of a pig, used as food.

troubadour n a medieval poet musician.

trouble[1] n **1** difficulty, problems, or danger. **2** a cause or source of difficulty, etc. **3** a problem, snag, or drawback. **4** public unrest or demonstrations of dissatisfaction. **5** effort taken over something. * **ask for trouble** informal to do or say something that may lead to problems or punishment. **in trouble** liable to be punished or suffer something unpleasant.

trouble[2] v **1** to cause distress, anxiety, or inconvenience to. **2** (often + to) to make an effort or take the time to do or say something.

troubled adj **1** worried or anxious. **2** characterized by or experiencing trouble.

troublemaker n somebody who deliberately and habitually causes trouble.

troubleshoot v to identify the causes of faults, problems, or disputes and try to remedy them. ➤ **troubleshooter** n.

troublesome adj causing difficulty or problems.

trough n **1** a long shallow receptacle for the food or drinking water of domestic animals. **2** an intervening lower area, e.g. between waves or ridges. **3** in meteorology, an elongated area of low atmospheric pressure. **4** a notably low point, e.g. in a trade cycle or on a statistical graph.

trounce v to defeat decisively.

troupe n a touring group of actors or other performers.

trouper n **1** a veteran actor or entertainer. **2** a loyal or dependable person.

trousers pl n an outer garment extending from the waist to the ankles, with tube-like parts that cover each leg separately. * **wear the trousers** informal to be the dominant person in a relationship.

trousseau /'troohsoh/ n (pl **trousseaux** or **trousseaus**) the clothes, linen, and other items that a woman collects for her marriage.

trout n (pl **trouts** or **trout**) a fish related to the salmon, with distinctive spotted markings.

trove n a store of valuable things.

trowel n **1** a small hand tool with a flat blade used to apply, mix, and spread plaster, cement, etc. **2** a small hand tool with a scoop-shaped blade used for lifting small plants, turning earth, etc.

troy n a system of weights, used mainly for precious metals and gemstones, in which there are 12oz to the pound.

truant[1] n a pupil who stays away from school without good reason or permission. * **play truant** to truant. ➤ **truancy** n.

truant[2] v to stay away from school without good reason or permission.

truant[3] adj straying or wandering.

truce n an agreement between enemies to stop fighting, often for a set period of time.

truck[1] n **1** a lorry. **2** Brit a wagon for carrying goods by rail.

truck[2] n * **have no truck with** to refuse to have anything to do with.

truculent adj aggressively defiant, sullen, or antagonistic. ➤ **truculence** n, **truculently** adv.

trudge[1] v to walk with slow, weary, or laborious steps.

trudge[2] n a long tiring walk.

true adj (**truer, truest**) **1** in accordance with fact or reality. **2** genuine or real. **3** properly or strictly so called. **4** accurate. **5** correctly adjusted or aligned, esp upright or level. **6** steadfast, loyal, or trusted. **7** (usu + to) consistent with what is expected of. * **come true** to happen; to become real. **true to form/type** behaving as expected. **true to life 1** accurately reflecting what goes on in real life. **2** realistic or lifelike. ➤ **truly** adv.

truffle n **1** a fungus that grows underground and is considered a great delicacy. **2** a rich chocolate sweet.

trug n Brit a shallow wooden basket used for carrying fruit, flowers, and vegetables.

truism n a truth that is too obvious or unimportant to be mentioned.

trump[1] n **1** (in pl) in various card games, the suit of cards that has been chosen to have a higher value than the other three suits. **2** a card of the suit that is trumps. **3** (also **trump card**) something that can be used to gain an advantage. * **come/turn up trumps** chiefly Brit, informal to do what is needed or desirable, esp at the last moment.

trump[2] v **1** to play a trump on (a card of another suit). **2** to surpass by doing or saying something better.

trumpery adj **1** worthless or useless. **2** cheap or tawdry.

trumpet[1] n **1** the highest-pitched brass musical instrument, with a a flared bell and three valves. **2** the loud penetrating cry of an elephant. * **blow one's (own) trumpet** to boast about one's own abilities, achievements, etc.

trumpet[2] v (**trumpeted, trumpeting**) **1** to play a trumpet. **2** to make the characteristic sound of an elephant. **3** to proclaim (something) loudly or widely. ➤ **trumpeter** n.

truncate v to shorten by cutting off the top or end part. ➤ **truncation** n.

truncheon n chiefly Brit a short thick stick carried as a weapon by police officers.

trundle v to move slowly on wheels.

trunk n **1** the main stem of a tree. **2** a person's or animal's body apart from the head, limbs, and other appendages. **3** the long flexible muscular nose of an elephant. **4** a large rigid box with a hinged lid, used for storing or transporting personal articles. **5** NAmer the boot of a motor vehicle.

trunk call n Brit, dated a long-distance telephone call.

trunk road n a main road connecting major cities.

trunks pl n men's tight-fitting shorts worn swimming or boxing.

truss[1] n **1** a rigid framework supporting a roof or bridge. **2** a padded belt used as a support for a hernia.

truss[2] v **1** to tie up the wings or legs of (a chicken, turkey, etc) in preparation for cooking. **2** (often + up) to secure or bind tightly.

trust[1] n **1** confident belief in or reliance on the character, ability, honesty, truth etc of somebody or something. **2** responsibility for something or somebody. **3** an arrangement whereby money or other property is held by one person for the benefit of another. **4** something managed by trustees.

trust[2] v **1** to rely on or believe in the truthfulness, accuracy, ability, etc of. **2** to be confident about allowing (somebody) to do, have, or look after something. **3** (often + to/in) to place one's confidence in or rely on somebody or something. **4** (often + to) to place (somebody or something) in somebody's care or keeping. **5** to hope or assume: I trust you are well. ➤ **trusted** adj.

trustee n a person appointed to administer money or other property for a beneficiary.

trustful adj trusting. ➤ **trustfully** adv.

trust fund n property, money, shares, or other assets held in trust.

trusting adj showing great trust, often to the extent of risking being exploited or hurt. ➤ **trustingly** adv.

trustworthy adj known to be honest, truthful, and reliable. ➤ **trustworthiness** n.

trusty adj (**-ier, -iest**) archaic or humorous reliable; trustworthy.

truth n **1** the state or quality of being true. **2** (**the truth**) the facts regarding something. **3** something that is true or is believed to be true.

truthful adj **1** telling the truth. **2** of a portrait, sculpture, etc: realistic. ➤ **truthfully** n.

try[1] v (**-ies, -ied**) **1** to make an attempt (to do something). **2** (often + out) to test or operate (something) to see if it is working or effective. **3** to conduct the trial of (an accused person). **4** to make severe demands on. * **tried and tested** known to be reliable.

try[2] n (pl **-ies**) **1** an attempt. **2** an experimental trial. **3** in rugby, a score made by touching down the ball behind the opponent's goal line.

trying adj annoying, unpleasant, or tiring.

try on v to put on (a piece of clothing) to see if it is suitable.

tryst n literary a secret agreement for a romantic meeting.

tsar or **czar** or **tzar** /zah, tsah/ n an emperor of Russia before 1917. ➤ **tsarist** n and adj.

tsetse /'tetsi, 'tsetsi/ n a two-winged blood-sucking African fly that transmits sleeping sickness.

T-shirt or **tee-shirt** n a short-sleeved casual top.

T square n a T-shaped ruler for drawing right angles and parallel lines.

tsp abbr teaspoonful.

tsunami /tsoo'nahmi/ n (pl **tsunami** or **tsunamis**) a huge sea wave that is produced by an underwater earthquake or volcanic eruption.

tub n **1** a low wide lidless container used for holding water, growing plants, etc. **2** a small plastic or cardboard container for food. **3** informal an old or slow boat, esp one that is awkward to sail.

tuba n the largest and lowest-pitched of the brass musical instruments.

tubby adj (**-ier, -iest**) informal podgy or fat.

tuber n a short fleshy usu underground stem, e.g. of a potato, bearing buds that may develop into new plants.

tubercular adj relating to or affected with tuberculosis.

tuberculosis n a serious infectious disease characterized by fever and the formation of abnormal lumps in the lungs.

tub-thumping adj informal of a person, speech, etc: expressing opinions in an impassioned or overzealous way.

tubular adj **1** cylindrical and hollow, like a tube. **2** made of or fitted with tubes.

TUC abbr Brit Trades Union Congress.

tuck[1] v **1** to push or fold into a confined space or between two surfaces. **2** to push (something loose) into a more secure or tidy position. **3** (+ in/up) to settle (somebody or oneself) comfortably in bed with the bedclothes firmly in place. **4** (often + up) to draw or gather (esp one's legs) into a folded position. ✳ **tuck in/into** to start eating (food) with enjoyment.

tuck[2] n **1** a fold stitched into fabric or a garment. **2** Brit, dated, informal food eaten as a snack by schoolchildren.

tuck away v to store or hide in a place that is difficult to find.

tucker n Aus, NZ food.

Tudor adj relating to the royal house that ruled England from 1485 until 1603.

Tuesday n the day of the week following Monday.

tufa n a porous rock formed as a deposit by mineral springs.

tuffet n **1** a tuft or clump, esp of grass. **2** a low seat or footstool.

tuft n a small cluster of long hairs, feathers, grasses, etc attached together at the base. ➤ **tufted** adj, **tufty** adj.

tug[1] v (**tugged, tugging**) to pull hard or suddenly.

tug[2] n **1** a hard sudden pull or jerk. **2** (also **tugboat**) a small powerful boat used for towing larger boats and ships.

tuition n teaching or instruction.

tulip n a plant with a single richly coloured cup-shaped flower.

tulle n a sheer, often silk, net fabric used chiefly for veils and dresses.

tumble[1] v **1** to fall suddenly, helplessly, or awkwardly. **2** to roll over and over or to and fro. **3** to move hurriedly and confusedly. **4** of prices, etc: to decline suddenly and sharply. **5** informal (+ to) to realize, understand, or become aware of suddenly.

tumble[2] n **1** an unexpected fall or drop. **2** a confused heap or an untidy state.

tumbledown adj of a building, etc: in a state of disrepair.

tumble-dryer or **tumble-drier** n an electric machine that dries laundry by rotating it in hot air inside a metal drum. ➤ **tumble-dry** v.

tumbler n **1** a large drinking glass without a handle. **2** an acrobat. **3** a movable part of a lock that must be adjusted to a particular position before the lock can be opened.

tumbrel or **tumbril** n **1** an open-ended farm cart. **2** a cart of this kind used for carrying political prisoners to the guillotine during the French Revolution.

tumescent adj swollen or distended, or in the process of becoming so.

tumid adj esp of a body part or tissue: swollen.

tummy n (pl -**ies**) informal a person's stomach or the area around it.

tumour (NAmer **tumor**) n an abnormal growth of tissue that may be benign or malignant.

tumult n **1** a loud confused noise. **2** a state of violent mental or emotional agitation.

tumultuous adj **1** characterized by great enthusiasm, loud cheering, etc. **2** marked by turbulence or upheaval.

tumulus n (pl **tumuli**) an artificial mound over a grave.

tun n a large cask, esp for beer or wine.

tuna n (pl **tunas** or **tuna**) a large food fish of warm seas.

tundra n a vast treeless plain characteristic of arctic and subarctic regions, with a permanently frozen subsoil.

tune[1] n a succession of musical notes; a melody. ✳ **call the tune** see CALL[1]. **change one's tune** informal to adopt a noticeably different attitude or point of view. **in/out of tune 1** of a musician, singer, musical instrument, etc: having or not having the correct musical pitch. **2** of people: in or not in harmony or agreement. **to the tune of** informal to the amount of (a specified sum of money).

tune[2] v **1** to bring (a musical instrument) to a standard pitch. **2** (often + up) to adjust (the engine of a motor vehicle) for optimum performance. **3** (often + in) to adjust (a radio or television receiver) to respond to waves of a particular frequency. **4** (+ in to) to become aware of. ➤ **tuning** n.

tuneful adj having a pleasant tune. ➤ **tunefully** adv.

tuneless adj not pleasant to listen to. ➤ **tunelessly** adv.

tuner n **1** a person who tunes musical instruments, esp pianos. **2** the part of a stereo system that receives radio signals.

tungsten n a hard grey–white metallic element with a high melting point, used esp for the filaments in light bulbs.

tunic n **1** a simple loose sleeveless thigh-length or knee-length garment. **2** a close-fitting hip-length jacket worn as part of a uniform.

tuning fork n a two-pronged metal implement that gives a fixed tone when struck.

tunnel¹ *n* **1** an underground passage that allows people, vehicles, etc to pass under an obstruction such as a hill, river, or building. **2** a small underground passage excavated by a burrowing animal.

tunnel² *v* (**tunnelled, tunnelling,** *NAmer* **tunneled, tunneling**) to construct a tunnel.

tunnel vision *n* **1** an eye condition in which only objects straight ahead can be seen distinctly. **2** *informal* extreme narrowness of viewpoint.

tunny *n* (*pl* **tunnies** *or* **tunny**) a tuna.

tuppence *n Brit* see TWOPENCE. ➤ **tuppenny** *adj.*

turban *n* a headdress worn *esp* by Muslim and Sikh men, consisting of a long cloth woundeither round a cap or directly round the head. ➤ **turbaned** *adj,* **turbanned** *adj.*

turbid *adj* of a liquid: cloudy, thick, or opaque.

turbine *n* a power-generating machine with a wheel or rotor driven by the pressure of water, steam, exhaust gases, etc.

turbo *n* (*pl* **-os**) **1** a turbine. **2** a turbocharger.

turbocharger *n* a supercharger powered by a turbine driven by the exhaust gases from an internal-combustion engine. ➤ **turbocharged** *adj.*

turbofan *n* a jet engine with a turbine-driven fan to increase thrust.

turbojet *n* a jet engine with a turbine-powered compressor that supplies compressed air to the combustion chamber.

turboprop *n* a jet engine with a turbine-driven propeller.

turbot *n* (*pl* **turbots** *or* **turbot**) a large edible flatfish.

turbulence *n* **1** agitation, tumult, or disorderliness. **2** irregular atmospheric motion characterized by strong currents of rising and falling air.

turbulent *adj* **1** characterized by agitation or tumult; stormy. **2** *technical* denoting a disturbed flow in a gas or liquid. ➤ **turbulently** *adv.*

turd *n coarse slang* a piece of excrement.

tureen *n* a deep bowl for serving soup.

turf¹ *n* (*pl* **turfs** *or* **turves**) **1** grass and the soil that is bound to its roots, forming a thick mat. **2** a piece of this cut from the ground. **3** (**the turf**) the sport or business of horse racing. **4** *informal.* **5** an area regarded as the domain of a particular person or group.

turf² *v* to cover (an area) with turf.

turf out *v* **1** to force to leave. **2** to get rid of.

turgid *adj* **1** swollen or distended. **2** of language, etc: pompous or bombastic.

turkey *n* **1** a large domesticated game bird with a heavy rounded body and a bald head. **2** *chiefly NAmer, informal* a flop.

Turkish *n* the national language of the people of Turkey. ➤ **Turkish** *adj.*

Turkish bath *n* a therapeutic or relaxing treatment that involves sitting in hot steam followed by a rubdown, massage, and cold shower.

Turkish delight *n* a jellylike sweet, cut in cubes and dusted with icing sugar.

turmeric *n* **1** an Asian plant of the ginger family with a large rhizome. **2** a bright yellow aromatic powder obtained from this plant.

turmoil *n* an extremely confused or agitated state.

turn¹ *v* **1** to move round on an axis. **2** to move round so as to be facing in a different or the opposite direction. **3** to go round (*esp* a corner). **4** to make or become something: *The weather has turned cold.* **5** to sprain (an ankle). **6** to make or form using a lathe. **7** of milk: to become sour. * **turn against** to become hostile towards. **turn to** to have recourse to (somebody) for help or support.

turn² *n* **1** an act of turning. **2** a bend or curve in a path, road, river, etc. **3** a place where a road divides; a turning. **4** a point at the beginning or end of a century or other period. **5** an opportunity or obligation to do something: *It's your turn to drive.* **6** an attack of illness, faintness, dizziness, etc. **7** a short act or performance, e.g. in a variety show. **8** a short walk or drive taken for pleasure. * **by turns** alternately or successively. **do somebody a good turn** to do a favour for somebody. **in/out of turn** in/not in the correct order of succession. **take turns/ take it in turns** to do something alternately or successively. **to a turn** to the required degree.

turn away *v* **1** to reject or dismiss. **2** to start to leave or change direction.

turn back *v* **1** to return or go in the opposite direction. **2** to prevent from advancing.

turncoat *n* a person who switches support from one party or cause to an opposing one.

turn down *v* **1** to reduce the strength or intensity of (volume level, etc). **2** to decline to accept.

turn in *v* **1** to hand (somebody) over to the authorities. **2** *informal* to go to bed for the night.

turning *n* **1** a road, path, etc, that branches off another. **2** a road junction.

turnip *n* a large white edible root, used as a vegetable and livestock fodder.

turnkey *n* (*pl* **turnkeys**) *archaic* a jailer.

turn off *v* **1** to stop from working or flowing by operating a switch or tap. **2** to cause (somebody) to lose interest. **3** to leave one road and join another.

turn-off *n* **1** a turning. **2** *informal* somebody or something that a person finds repulsive or boring.

turn on v 1 to cause to start working or flowing by operating a switch or tap. 2 to attack (somebody) suddenly. 3 to make (somebody) interested or excited, *esp* sexually.

turn-on n *informal* somebody or something that a person finds attractive, exciting, or sexually stimulating.

turnout n the number of people attending or taking part in an event.

turn out v 1 to turn off (an electric light). 2 to empty (a room, pocket, etc). 3 to produce (work, etc). 4 to prove ultimately to be: *The play turned out to be a success.* 5 to make the effort to attend an event. 6 (**be turned out**) to be dressed.

turnover n 1 the amount of money taken by a business in a particular period. 2 the rate at which a business loses and replaces its staff. 3 the rate at which a shop sells and replaces stock. 4 an individual pie made by folding a circle of pastry in half to enclose a filling.

turn over v 1 to put or be put the other way up. 2 of an engine: to revolve at low speed. 3 to think about (a matter, problem, etc). 4 to search roughly through (a place). 5 to deliver to the proper authority.

turnpike n in the USA or formerly in Britain, a major road on which a toll is payable.

turn round v 1 to complete the handling or processing of (goods or work) in a specified time. 2 to reform (a failing concern) so that it becomes successful.

turnstile n a gate with pivoting arms that turns to admit one person at a time.

turntable n a circular rotating platform, esp one on which a gramophone record is placed while being played.

turn up v 1 to appear unexpectedly, *esp* after being lost. 2 to arrive or occur. 3 to find or discover. 4 to increase the strength or intensity of (volume level, etc).

turn-up n *Brit* 1 a hem on a pair of trousers that is folded up over itself on the outside. 2 *informal* an unexpected or surprising event or outcome.

turpentine n a liquid distilled from the resin of conifer trees, used *esp* as a solvent for paints and varnishes.

turpitude n *formal* baseness, depravity, or wickedness.

turps n *informal* turpentine.

turquoise n 1 a blue, bluish green, or greenish gemstone. 2 a light greenish blue colour.

turret n 1 a little tower, often at the corner of a larger building. 2 an armoured, *usu* revolving structure on warships, tanks, aircraft, etc in which guns are mounted. ➤ **turreted** adj.

turtle n a reptile with a bony or leathery shell, resembling a tortoise, but with limbs adapted for swimming. ✳ **turn turtle** *esp* of a boat: to capsize or overturn.

turtledove n a small wild dove with a distinctive soft cooing call.

turtleneck n 1 *Brit* a high close-fitting neck on a garment. 2 *NAmer* = POLO NECK.

turves n pl of TURF[1].

tusk n a very long tapering tooth, e.g. of an elephant, walrus, boar, etc, that is visible when the animal's mouth is closed.

tussle[1] v to struggle or fight roughly.

tussle[2] n a rough fight.

tussock n a compact tuft of grass, sedge, etc.

tutelage n *formal* 1 guardianship. 2 tuition.

tutelary adj *formal* acting as a guardian to somebody or something.

tutor[1] n 1 a person employed as a private teacher, *esp* one who teaches individuals or small groups. 2 *Brit* a university or college teacher who teaches a small group and often has responsibility for students' welfare.

tutor[2] v to act as a tutor to.

tutorial[1] n a session of tuition given by a university or college tutor.

tutorial[2] adj relating to a tutor or the work of a tutor.

tutu n a very short projecting stiff skirt worn by a ballerina.

tuxedo n (pl **-os** or **-oes**) *chiefly NAmer* a man's dinner jacket.

TV n television.

twaddle n *informal* trivial or nonsensical speech or writing; drivel.

twain n *archaic* two.

twang[1] n 1 a strong quick ringing sound like that of the string of a musical instrument being plucked. 2 a distinctive nasal quality in the speech of a person or region. ➤ **twangy** adj.

twang[2] v to make a twang.

tweak[1] v 1 to give a sudden slight jerk or twist to. 2 *informal* to make fine adjustments to.

tweak[2] n an act of tweaking.

twee adj (**tweer**, **tweest**) *Brit* excessively or affectedly sentimental, pretty, cute, or coy.

tweed n a rough woollen fabric, often brownish or greenish and flecked with other colours, used *esp* for suits and coats.

tweet[1] v to make the characteristic chirping sound of a small bird.

tweet[2] n a tweeting sound.

tweeter n a small loudspeaker that mainly reproduces higher frequencies.

tweezers pl n (also **pair of tweezers**) a small pincer-like device used for plucking out hairs and handling small objects.

twelfth adj and n 1 having the position in a sequence corresponding to the number twelve. 2 one of twelve equal parts of something.

twelve n the number 12. ➤ **twelve** adj.

twenty adj and n (pl **-ies**) 1 the number 20. 2 (in pl) the numbers 20 to 29. ➤ **twentieth** adj and n.

twerp or **twirp** n *informal* a stupid person.

twice adv **1** on two occasions. **2** in double the quantity or degree.

twiddle¹ v **1** (often + with) to fiddle with. **2** to rotate or twist lightly or idly. * **twiddle one's thumbs** to have nothing to do.

twiddle² n an act of twiddling. > **twiddly** adj.

twig¹ n a small woody shoot or branch of a tree or bush.

twig² v (**twigged, twigging**) Brit, informal to realize or understand something.

twilight n **1** the soft shadowy or glowing light between sunset and full darkness. **2** the period between sunset and full night. **3** a period of decline.

twill n a fabric with slightly raised parallel diagonal lines.

twin¹ n **1** either of two offspring born to the same mother at the same birth. **2** either of two people or things closely resembling each other.

twin² v (**twinned, twinning**) **1** (+ with) to link or pair (one thing) with another. **2** Brit (+ with) to associate (a town in one country) officially with a town in another.

twin³ adj denoting either of two children who are twins, or either of two objects that function as a pair.

twine¹ n strong string made from two or more strands twisted together.

twine² v (usu + round/around) to coil or twist around something.

twinge n **1** a sudden sharp stab of pain. **2** a moral or emotional pang.

twinkle¹ v **1** of a star, light, etc: to shine with a flickering or sparkling effect. **2** of a person's eyes: to have a bright sparkle, esp as a sign of amusement, mischief, etc.

twinkle² n a flickering or sparkling effect.

twinkling n * **in a twinkling (of an eye)** immediately or very quickly.

twin set n chiefly Brit a woman's jumper and cardigan designed to be worn together.

twirl¹ v to spin round rapidly.

twirl² n an act of twirling. > **twirly** adj.

twist¹ v **1** to cause to move with a rotating motion. **2** (often + round) to turn to face in a different direction. **3** to twine or coil. **4** to bend in a specified direction, esp out of true. **5** to follow a winding course. **6** to join (two or more things or parts) together by winding. **7** to wrench (a joint) painfully. **8** to distort the meaning of. **9** to dance the twist. * **twist somebody's arm** informal to persuade or force a person to do something.

twist² n **1** an act of twisting. **2** something with a spiral shape or made by twisting e.g. paper. **3** (**the twist**) a dance, popular in the 1960s, featuring exaggerated twisting movements of the hips and legs. **4** an unexpected turn or development. * **round the twist** Brit, informal completely mad.

twister n **1** Brit, informal a dishonest person; a cheat or swindler. **2** chiefly NAmer a tornado.

twit¹ n chiefly Brit, informal a silly or stupid person.

twit² v (**twitted, twitting**) informal to tease or ridicule, esp light-heartedly.

twitch¹ v to move with a sudden jerky motion.

twitch² n a twitching movement.

twitchy adj (**-ier, -iest**) informal nervous or anxious.

twitter¹ v **1** of a bird: to make a series of quick chirping sounds. **2** to talk quickly, esp in a nervous or giggling way.

twitter² n a twittering sound. * **all of/in a twitter** informal in a state of nervous agitation; quivering.

two n the number 2. * **put two and two together** to use the available evidence or information to draw a conclusion. > **two** adj.

two-dimensional adj **1** having two dimensions, esp length and breadth but no depth. **2** of a fictional character, etc: lacking depth; superficial.

two-faced adj insincere, double-dealing, or hypocritical.

twopence or **tuppence** /'tup(ə)ns/ n Brit the sum of two pence, esp before decimalization in 1971. > **twopenny** adj.

twosome n a group of two people or things.

two-time v informal **1** to be unfaithful to (a partner or lover) by having a relationship with somebody else. **2** to cheat or double-cross.

tycoon n a person in business or industry who has exceptional wealth and power.

tying v present part. of TIE¹.

tyke or **tike** n informal a cheeky or mischievous small child.

tympani n see TIMPANI.

tympanum n (pl **tympana** or **tympanums**) the eardrum.

type¹ n **1** a class or group of people, animals, or things that share similar characteristics. **2** a person or thing considered to be representative of a class or group. **3** informal a person who has a specified characteristic, nature, etc: He's the quiet type. **4** printed characters, words, etc, or the blocks used to print them.

type² v to write using a typewriter or computer. > **typing** n.

typecast v (past tense and past part. **typecast**) (usu **be typecast**) of an actor: to be repeatedly given the same kind of role.

typeface n in printing, a particular style of type.

typescript n a typed copy of a text.

typeset v (**typesetting,** past tense and past part. **typeset**) to arrange the printing type for (a text). > **typesetter** n.

typewriter n a machine with a keyboard for writing in characters resembling printed type.

typhoid *n* a serious infectious bacterial disease characterized by fever, spots, diarrhoea, headache, and intestinal inflammation.

typhoon *n* a violent tropical storm.

typhus *n* an infectious disease marked by high fever, delirium, intense headache, and a dark red rash.

typical *adj* **1** exhibiting the essential characteristics of a type. **2** characteristic of somebody or something. ➤ **typically** *adv*.

typify *v* (-ies, -ied) to be typical of.

typist *n* a person who uses a typewriter.

typo *n* (*pl* **typos**) *informal* a printing error.

typography *n* the style, arrangement, or appearance of printed matter. ➤ **typographer** *n*, **typographic** *adj*, **typographical** *adj*.

tyrannical *adj* characterized by oppressive, unjust, or arbitrary use of power. ➤ **tyrannically** *adv*.

tyrannize *or* -**ise** *v* to treat cruelly or oppressively.

tyrannosaurus *or* **tyrannosaurus rex** *n* a very large flesh-eating dinosaur that walked on its hind legs.

tyranny *n* (*pl* -**ies**) rule or government that is cruel or oppressive. ➤ **tyrannous** *adj*.

tyrant *n* **1** a cruel or oppressive ruler. **2** any person who exerts cruel or oppressive power.

tyre (*NAmer* **tire**) *n* a solid or inflated hollow rubber cushion fitted round a wheel.

tyro *or* **tiro** *n* (*pl* **tyros** *or* **tiros**) a beginner or novice.

tzar *n* see TSAR.

tzatziki *n* a Greek dip or side dish, made from yoghurt, cucumber, and garlic.

U¹ or **u** *n* (*pl* **U's** or **Us** or **u's**) the 21st letter of the English alphabet.

U² *abbr* the chemical symbol for uranium.

U³ *n* in Britain, a classification of cinema films suitable for all age groups.

ubiquitous *adj* existing or seeming to be everywhere. ➤ **ubiquitously** *adv*, **ubiquity** *n*.

U-boat *n* a German submarine, *esp* as used in World Wars I and II.

UCAS *abbr Brit* Universities and Colleges Admissions Service.

udder *n* a bag-like organ producing milk in female cattle.

UFO *n* (*pl* **UFO's** or **UFOs**) an unidentified flying object, *esp* one popularly believed to be of extraterrestrial origin.

ugly *adj* (**-ier, -iest**) **1** offensive or displeasing to see or hear. **2** ominous or threatening. ➤ **ugliness** *n*.

ugly duckling *n* somebody or something that appears unattractive or unpromising but turns out to be admirable or successful.

UK *abbr* United Kingdom.

ukulele *n* a small four-stringed guitar.

ulcer *n* an open sore on the skin or a mucous membrane. ➤ **ulcerated** *adj*, **ulceration** *n*, **ulcerous** *adj*.

ulna *n* (*pl* **ulnae** or **ulnas**) the bone of the human forearm on the side of the little finger.

ulterior *adj* of a motive: underlying but not expressed.

ultimate¹ *adj* **1** last in a progression or series. **2** eventual. **3** fundamental; basic. **4** best or greatest. ➤ **ultimately** *adv*.

ultimate² *n* (**the ultimate**) the most extreme or important of its kind.

ultimatum *n* (*pl* **ultimatums** or **ultimata**) a final demand before resorting to direct action or retaliation.

ultramarine *n* a vivid deep blue pigment or colour.

ultramicroscopic *adj* too small to be seen with an ordinary microscope.

ultrasonic *adj* of sound waves: having a frequency above the range of the human ear. ➤ **ultrasonically** *adv*.

ultraviolet *adj* of electromagnetic radiation: having a wavelength between the violet end of the visible spectrum and X-rays.

ululate *v* to howl or wail in grief. ➤ **ululation** *n*.

umber *n* a dark or yellowish brown colour.

umbilical *adj* relating to the navel or the umbilical cord.

umbilical cord *n* a ropelike tube that connects a foetus with the placenta.

umbilicus *n technical* the navel.

umbra *n* (*pl* **umbras** or **umbrae**) a region of total shadow in an eclipse.

umbrage *n* a feeling of pique or resentment.

umbrella *n* **1** a collapsible circular shade for protection against rain. **2** something that provides protection or cover. **3** (*used before a noun*) including a wide range of elements or factors.

umlaut *n* a mark (¨) placed over a vowel to show a change of sound.

umpire¹ *n* a referee in some sports.

umpire² *v* to act as umpire of.

umpteen *adj and n informal* very many. ➤ **umpteenth** *adj*.

UN *abbr* United Nations.

un- *prefix* **1** forming words denoting a lack or opposite: *unskilled*; *unrest*. **2** forming verbs denoting the reverse of an action: *undress*.

unabashed *adj* not embarrassed or ashamed.

unabated *adj* at full strength or force.

unable *adj* not able; incapable.

unacceptable *adj* **1** not satisfactory. **2** not permissible. ➤ **unacceptably** *adv*.

unaccountable *adj* **1** inexplicable. **2** not responsible. ➤ **unaccountably** *adv*.

unaccustomed *adj* **1** not usual or common. **2** (+ to) not used to.

unacquainted *adj* **1** (+ with) lacking experience of or familiarity with. **2** never having met.

unadulterated *adj* **1** not mixed with anything inferior. **2** complete; utter.

unaffected *adj* **1** not influenced by something. **2** free from affectation; genuine.

unaffordable *adj* too expensive for most people.

unaided *adj* done without help.

unalloyed *adj* **1** not mixed with another metal. **2** complete and perfect.

unalterable *adj* not capable of being altered; permanent. ➤ **unalterably** *adv*.

unambiguous *adj* not ambiguous; clear or precise. ➤ **unambiguously** *adv*.

unanimous adj 1 all of one mind. 2 having the agreement of all. ➤ **unanimity** n, **unanimously** adv.

unannounced adj 1 happening without warning. 2 not publicized.

unanswerable adj 1 having no answer. 2 irrefutable. ➤ **unanswerably** adv.

unappealing adj not appealing; unattractive.

unappetizing or **unappetising** adj not appetizing; unattractive.

unapproachable adj aloof or unfriendly.

unarmed adj having no weapons.

unashamed adj without shame or embarrassment. ➤ **unashamedly** adv.

unassailable adj 1 not open to question. 2 not able to be attacked or challenged.

unassisted adj acting or done without help.

unassuming adj modest.

unattached adj 1 not involved in a romantic or sexual relationship. 2 not joined or united.

unattended adj not cared for or looked after.

unauthorized or **unauthorised** adj not having official approval.

unavailable adj not capable of being obtained, contacted, etc. ➤ **unavailability** n.

unavailing adj futile; useless.

unavoidable adj not avoidable; inevitable. ➤ **unavoidably** adv.

unaware adj (often + of) not aware; ignorant or lacking knowledge.

unawares adv 1 without noticing or intending. 2 suddenly; unexpectedly.

unbalanced adj 1 mentally disordered or deranged. 2 biased or partial.

unbearable adj not endurable; intolerable. ➤ **unbearably** adv.

unbeatable adj not able to be defeated or surpassed.

unbecoming adj 1 not attractive or flattering. 2 improper.

unbeknown adj (+ to) without the knowledge of.

unbelievable adj 1 too improbable to believe. 2 extraordinary. ➤ **unbelievably** adv.

unbeliever n somebody with no religious belief.

unbend v (past tense and past part. **unbent**) 1 to return to a straight position. 2 to become more relaxed.

unbending adj aloof or unsociable.

unbiased or **unbiassed** adj free from prejudice; impartial.

unbidden adj 1 unasked or uninvited. 2 spontaneous.

unborn adj not yet born.

unbounded adj having no limits.

unbowed adj not defeated or subdued.

unbridgeable adj of a difference in opinions etc: extreme and unlikely to be resolved.

unbridled adj uncontrolled.

unbroken adj 1 not broken; intact. 2 not beaten or surpassed. 3 uninterrupted.

unburden v (**unburdened**, **unburdening**) 1 to free from a burden. 2 to relieve (oneself) of fears, worries, etc, by confiding in somebody else.

uncalled-for adj unnecessary and unwelcome.

uncanny adj (-ier, -iest) strange or mysterious. ➤ **uncannily** adv.

unceasing adj continuous or incessant. ➤ **unceasingly** adv.

unceremonious adj abrupt or rude. ➤ **unceremoniously** adv.

uncertain adj 1 not definitely known. 2 not confident or sure. 3 not reliable or trustworthy. ✳ **in no uncertain terms** forcefully and clearly. ➤ **uncertainly** adv, **uncertainty** n.

uncharitable adj harsh or unkind in treating others. ➤ **uncharitably** adv.

uncharted adj of an area of land or sea: not recorded or plotted on a map.

unchecked adj allowed to develop without restraint.

unchristian adj 1 contrary to the teachings of Christianity. 2 uncharitable.

unclassified adj 1 not placed in a class. 2 of information: not subject to a security restriction.

uncle n the brother of one's father or mother, or the husband of one's aunt.

unclean adj 1 dirty. 2 morally or spiritually impure.

Uncle Sam n the US nation, people, or government.

uncomfortable adj causing or feeling discomfort. ➤ **uncomfortably** adv.

uncommon adj 1 not normally encountered; unusual. 2 remarkable; exceptional. ➤ **uncommonly** adv.

uncommunicative adj not inclined to speak much; reserved.

uncomprehending adj not able to understand something. ➤ **uncomprehendingly** adv.

uncompromising adj not wanting to compromise; inflexible. ➤ **uncompromisingly** adv.

unconcern n a lack of interest; indifference. ➤ **unconcerned** adj.

unconditional adj not having any conditions attached. ➤ **unconditionally** adv.

unconfined adj 1 not confined or limited. 2 of an emotion: without restraint.

unconfirmed adj not confirmed as true.

uncongenial adj 1 not compatible or suitable. 2 disagreeable; unpleasant.

unconscionable adj 1 unscrupulous; unprincipled. 2 excessive; unreasonable. ➤ **unconscionably** adv.

unconscious¹ *adj* **1** not knowing or perceiving. **2** having lost consciousness. **3** not resulting from conscious thought or sensation. **4** not intentional or deliberate. ➤ **unconsciously** *adv*, **unconsciousness** *n*.

unconscious² *n* the part of the mind that one is not normally aware of but influences behaviour and feelings.

unconstitutional *adj* not in accordance with the constitution of a nation, organization, etc. ➤ **unconstitutionally** *adv*.

uncontrollable *adj* incapable of being controlled. ➤ **uncontrollably** *adv*.

unconventional *adj* not conforming with generally accepted behaviour or ideas. ➤ **unconventionally** *adv*.

unconvincing *adj* not convincing; implausible. ➤ **unconvincingly** *adv*.

uncooperative *adj* not willing to cooperate with others.

uncoordinated *adj* **1** lacking in bodily coordination. **2** badly organized.

uncouth *adj* uncultivated in speech or behaviour.

uncover *v* **1** to remove the cover from. **2** to reveal or discover.

uncritical *adj* not expressing criticism or using discrimination. ➤ **uncritically** *adv*.

unction *n* **1** the act of anointing as a rite of consecration. **2** exaggerated earnestness.

unctuous *adj* falsely sincere or courteous. ➤ **unctuously** *adv*.

uncut *adj* **1** not cut or cut off. **2** not abridged.

undaunted *adj* not discouraged by danger or difficulty.

undecided *adj* **1** not having decided. **2** without a result.

undemonstrative *adj* not showing one's feelings.

undeniable *adj* plainly true; incontestable. ➤ **undeniably** *adv*.

under¹ *adv* **1** in a position below or beneath something. **2** in a condition of subjection or unconsciousness.

under² *prep* **1** lower than. **2** vertically below but not touching. **3** covered or protected by. **4** subject to the authority or control of, or during the rule of. **5** inferior in rank to. **6** undergoing the action or effect of. **7** within the group or category of: *under this heading*. **8** less than.

under- *prefix* **1** situated below: *underground*. **2** lower in rank: *undersecretary*. **3** less than normal: *undernourished*.

underachieve *v* to achieve less than is expected. ➤ **underachievement** *n*.

under-age *adj* below the legal age.

underarm *adj and adv* made with the hand below shoulder level.

underbelly *n* (*pl* **-ies**) **1** the underside of an animal. **2** a vulnerable area.

undercarriage *n* the part of an aircraft's structure that supports it on the ground.

underclass *n* the lowest class of people, *esp* the very poor.

underclothes *pl n* underwear.

undercoat *n* a coat of paint applied as a base for another coat.

undercover *adj and adv* seeking information secretly.

undercurrent *n* a hidden or underlying feeling or tendency.

undercut *v* (**undercutting**, *past tense and past part*. **undercut**) to charge less than (a competitor).

underdeveloped *adj* of a region: lacking modern industries.

underdog *n* a competitor who is expected to lose in a struggle or contest.

underdone *adj* not fully cooked.

underdressed *adj* dressed less formally than is appropriate.

underestimate¹ *v* **1** to estimate as being less than the actual size, quantity, etc. **2** to regard (somebody) as less capable or powerful than they actually are. ➤ **underestimation** *n*.

underestimate² *n* an estimate that is too low.

underfoot *adv* **1** against the ground. **2** in the way.

undergarment *n* an item of underwear.

undergo *v* (**undergoes, underwent, undergone**) **1** to experience. **2** to be subjected to (something unpleasant).

undergraduate *n* a student at a college or university studying for a first degree.

underground¹ *adj and adv* **1** below the surface of the ground. **2** in hiding or in secret.

underground² *n* **1** a secret movement or group resisting a government or occupying enemy. **2** *Brit* an underground railway.

undergrowth *n* vegetation growing on the ground in a wood.

underhand *adj* done secretly or by deception.

underlay¹ *v* (*past tense and past part*. **underlaid**) to raise or support by laying something underneath.

underlay² *n* thick foam or felt laid under a carpet.

underlie *v* (**underlying, underlay, underlain**) **1** to lie or be situated under. **2** to be the basis or cause of.

underline *v* **1** to mark with a line underneath. **2** to emphasize.

underling *n* a subordinate or inferior.

undermine *v* **1** to weaken or destroy gradually. **2** to wear away the base or foundation of.

underneath¹ *prep and adv* **1** directly below. **2** so as to be hidden by. **3** on the lower side.

underneath² *n* the bottom part or surface.

underpants *pl n* an undergarment covering the hips, crotch, and upper thighs.

underpart *n* a part lying on the lower side.

underpass *n* a tunnel or road under another road or a railway.

underpin *v* (**underpinned, underpinning**) 1 to strengthen the foundation of (a structure). 2 to support or substantiate.

underplay *v* to represent as being less significant than is the case.

underprivileged *adj* lacking the normal social or economic conditions of a civilized society.

underrate *v* to undervalue or underestimate.

underscore *v* to underline.

undersea *adj* situated under the surface of the sea.

undersecretary *n* (*pl* -**ies**) 1 in Britain, a junior minister. 2 a civil servant subordinate to a principal secretary.

undersell *v* (*past tense and past part.* **undersold**) 1 to sell at a lower price than. 2 to make little of the merits of.

underside *n* the side or surface lying underneath.

undersigned *n* (**the undersigned**) the person or people whose names are signed at the end of a document.

undersized *adj* of less than normal size.

understaffed *adj* not having enough staff.

understand *v* (*past tense and past part.* **understood**) 1 to grasp the meaning of. 2 to have a thorough knowledge of or expertise in. 3 to assume or suppose. 4 to interpret in a particular way. 5 to supply mentally (something implied though not expressed). 6 to show sympathy or tolerance.

understandable *adj* 1 normal and reasonable. 2 capable of being understood. ➤ **understandably** *adv*.

understanding[1] *n* 1 a mental grasp or comprehension. 2 the power of comprehending. 3 a particular meaning or interpretation. 4 a friendly or harmonious relationship. 5 an informal mutual agreement. 6 tolerance or sympathy.

understanding[2] *adj* tolerant or sympathetic.

understate *v* to represent as being less significant than is the case. ➤ **understatement** *n*.

understudy[1] *v* (-**ies**, -**ied**) to study another actor's part in order to be able to take it over in an emergency.

understudy[2] *n* (*pl* -**ies**) an actor who learns another actor's part and takes it over if needed.

undertake *v* (**undertook, undertaken**) 1 to take on oneself as a task or responsibility. 2 to guarantee or promise to do something.

undertaker *n* somebody who prepares dead bodies for burial or cremation and organizes funerals.

undertaking *n* 1 an enterprise. 2 a pledge or guarantee. 3 the business of an undertaker.

undertone *n* 1 a low or subdued tone. 2 a quality or feeling underlying a statement or action.

undertow *n* an underwater current that flows in a different direction from the surface current.

underwater *adj and adv* situated or used below the surface of the water.

underwear *n* clothing worn under other clothing next to the skin.

underweight *adj* weighing less than the normal or suitable weight.

underwhelm *v humorous* to fail to impress.

underworld *n* 1 the world of organized crime. 2 in mythology, the place beneath the surface of the earth where the souls of the dead live.

underwrite *v* (**underwrote, underwritten**) 1 to assume liability for payment on (an insurance policy). 2 to guarantee financial support of. ➤ **underwriter** *n*.

undesirable[1] *adj* unwanted or objectionable. ➤ **undesirability** *n*, **undesirably** *adv*.

undesirable[2] *n* an undesirable or unpleasant person or thing.

undeterred *adj* not deterred by setbacks.

undies *pl n informal* items of underwear.

undisputed *adj* not questioned or challenged.

undistinguished *adj* lacking in distinction; not exceptional.

undivided *adj* 1 not split into separate parts. 2 complete; total.

undo *v* (**undid, undone**) 1 to open or loosen by releasing a fastening. 2 to reverse or cancel the effects of. 3 to destroy the standing or reputation of.

undoing *n* 1 ruin. 2 a cause of ruin or downfall.

undoubted *adj* not disputed; certain or genuine. ➤ **undoubtedly** *adv*.

undreamed *or* **undreamt** *adj* (*usu* + **of**) not unimagined or regarded as possible.

undress[1] *v* 1 to remove the clothes from (somebody). 2 to take off one's clothes.

undress[2] *n* a state of having little or no clothing on.

undue *adj* excessive or immoderate.

undulate *v* 1 to rise and fall in waves; to fluctuate. 2 to have a wavy form or appearance. ➤ **undulation** *n*.

unduly *adv* excessively.

undying *adj* eternal; perpetual.

unearned *adj* of income: not gained from employment.

unearth *v* 1 to dig up out of the ground. 2 to find or discover after searching.

unearthly *adj* 1 weird or mysterious. 2 *informal* unreasonable or preposterous: *at an unearthly hour*.

unease *n* a feeling of disquiet or awkwardness.

uneasy *adj* (-**ier**, -**iest**) 1 apprehensive or worried. 2 uncomfortable or awkward. 3 precarious or unstable. ➤ **uneasily** *adv*, **uneasiness** *n*.

unedifying adj unpleasant.

uneducated adj not well educated; ignorant.

unemployable adj not acceptable or fitted for any form of employment.

unemployed adj not having a paid job.

unemployment n 1 the state of being unemployed. 2 the number or percentage of unemployed people.

unending adj never ending; seeming to go on indefinitely. ➤ **unendingly** adv.

unenviable adj unpleasant or undesirable. ➤ **unenviably** adv.

unequal adj 1 not equal. 2 not fairly or evenly applied. 3 badly balanced or matched. 4 (+ to) not capable of taking on (a task). ➤ **unequally** adv.

unequalled (NAmer **unequaled**) adj better than all others.

unequivocal adj clear and unambiguous. ➤ **unequivocally** adv.

unerring adj faultless or unfailing. ➤ **unerringly** adv.

UNESCO abbr United Nations Educational, Scientific, and Cultural Organization.

uneven adj 1 not level or smooth. 2 irregular or inconsistent. 3 varying in quality. ➤ **unevenly** adv, **unevenness** n.

uneventful adj without anything important or interesting happening. ➤ **uneventfully** adv.

unexceptionable adj beyond reproach or criticism. ➤ **unexceptionably** adv.

unexceptional adj commonplace or ordinary. ➤ **unexceptionally** adv.

unexpected adj not expected or foreseen. ➤ **unexpectedly** adv.

unexpurgated adj not abridged or censored.

unfailing adj 1 able to be relied on; constant or sure. 2 continuous. ➤ **unfailingly** adv.

unfair adj not fair or just. ➤ **unfairly** adv, **unfairness** n.

unfaithful adj 1 not faithful; disloyal. 2 having sexual relations with a person other than one's spouse or partner. 3 inaccurate. ➤ **unfaithfully** adv.

unfasten v to loosen or untie.

unfathomable adj impossible to understand fully.

unfavourable (NAmer **unfavorable**) adj 1 expressing disapproval. 2 disadvantageous; adverse. ➤ **unfavourably** adv.

unfazed adj informal not disconcerted or daunted.

unfit adj 1 unsuitable or inappropriate. 2 in poor physical or mental condition. ➤ **unfitly** adv, **unfitness** n.

unflagging adj never flagging; tireless.

unflappable adj informal remaining calm and composed; imperturbable. ➤ **unflappably** adv.

unflinching adj not flinching or shrinking; steadfast. ➤ **unflinchingly** adv.

unfold v 1 to open and spread or straighten out (something folded). 2 to reveal or be revealed gradually.

unforeseen adj not predicted or expected. ➤ **unforeseeable** adj.

unforgettable adj memorable or exciting. ➤ **unforgettably** adv.

unforgivable adj too bad to be forgiven or excused. ➤ **unforgivably** adv.

unfortunate[1] adj 1 unsuccessful or unlucky. 2 resulting in misfortune. 3 unsuitable; inappropriate. ➤ **unfortunately** adv.

unfortunate[2] n an unlucky person.

unfounded adj lacking a sound basis; groundless.

unfrequented adj not often visited.

unfunny adj serious; not funny.

unfurl v to open out or unroll.

ungainly adj (-ier, -iest) clumsy or awkward. ➤ **ungainliness** n.

ungenerous adj not generous; mean or petty. ➤ **ungenerously** adv.

ungetatable adj informal inaccessible; unapproachable.

ungodly adj (-ier, -iest) 1 irreligious or impious. 2 wicked or immoral. 3 informal unreasonable or inconvenient. ➤ **ungodliness** n.

ungovernable adj not capable of being controlled or restrained.

ungracious adj 1 rude or impolite. 2 not pleasing; disagreeable. ➤ **ungraciously** adv.

ungrateful adj showing no gratitude. ➤ **ungratefully** adv.

unguarded adj 1 of a remark: hasty or careless. 2 without a guard or screen.

unguent n a soothing or healing ointment.

ungulate n a hoofed animal.

unhappy adj (-ier, -iest) 1 not happy; sad. 2 unfortunate; unlucky. 3 unsuitable. ➤ **unhappily** adv, **unhappiness** n.

unharmed adj not harmed.

unhealthy adj (-ier, -iest) 1 not in good health. 2 not conducive to good health. ➤ **unhealthily** adv.

unheard adj 1 not perceived by the ear. 2 disregarded.

unheard-of adj previously unknown.

unhelpful adj not helpful; uncooperative. ➤ **unhelpfully** adv.

unheralded adj not previously announced.

unhesitating adj prompt; without hesitation.

unhinged adj mentally unbalanced.

unholy adj (-ier, -iest) 1 wicked or immoral. 2 unnatural or harmful. 3 informal terrible; awful.

unhurried adj not hurried; leisurely. ➤ **unhurriedly** adv.

unhurt adj not hurt or harmed.

unhygienic adj not hygienic.

unicameral *adj* of a parliament: having a single legislative chamber.

UNICEF *abbr* United Nations Children's Fund.

unicorn *n* a mythical white horse with a horn on its forehead.

unicycle *n* a cycle with a single wheel. ➤ **unicyclist** *n*.

unidentified *adj* not known or identified.

unification *n* the process of unifying or the state of being unified.

uniform[1] *adj* not varying in character or appearance. ➤ **uniformity** *n*, **uniformly** *adv*.

uniform[2] *n* clothing of a distinctive design worn by members of a particular institution or group.

unify *v* (**-ies, -ied**) to make or become a unit or whole.

unilateral *adj* done or undertaken by only one person or group. ➤ **unilaterally** *adv*.

unimaginative *adj* 1 not given to creative thought. 2 not interesting or innovative. ➤ **unimaginatively** *adv*.

unimpeachable *adj* not to be doubted or blamed. ➤ **unimpeachably** *adv*.

unimportant *adj* having little or no importance. ➤ **unimportance** *n*.

uninhabited *adj* having no inhabitants.

uninhibited *adj* acting or speaking without regard for what others might think.

uninitiated *adj* lacking special knowledge or experience of something.

uninspiring *adj* not arousing interest or enthusiasm.

unintelligible *adj* impossible to understand. ➤ **unintelligibility** *n*, **unintelligibly** *adv*.

unintentional *adj* not done deliberately. ➤ **unintentionally** *adv*.

uninterested *adj* not interested or concerned.

Usage Note: Do not confuse *uninterested* with *disinterested*, which means 'impartial'.

uninterrupted *adj* 1 not interrupted; continuous. 2 not obstructed.

union *n* 1 the act of joining two or more things into one. 2 a unified condition. 3 a marriage. 4 a club or association. 5 an organization run by students. 6 a trade union. 7 (*also* **Union**) a political unit made up from previously independent units. 8 (**the Union**) the northern states during the American Civil War.

unionist *n* 1 a member or supporter of a trade union. 2 (**Unionist**) a member of a political party in Northern Ireland that favours union with Great Britain. ➤ **unionism** *n*.

unionize or **-ise** *v* to join or cause to join a trade union. ➤ **unionization** *n*.

Union Jack *n* the national flag of the United Kingdom.

unique *adj* 1 being the only one; sole. 2 without a like or equal. 3 (+ to) belonging to or occurring in only one person, place, etc. ➤ **uniquely** *adv*.

unisex *adj* suitable or designed for either sex.

unison *n* the performing of several parts in a musical passage in harmony at the same time.

unit *n* 1 a single thing, person, or group that can form part of a larger whole. 2 a part of an organization that has a specific function. 3 a distinct military force forming part of a larger force. 4 an apparatus or device serving one particular function. 5 a building or group of buildings having a specified purpose. 6 an agreed quantity used as a standard of measurement.

Unitarian *n* a member of a Christian denomination that rejects the doctrine of the Trinity and believes that God is a single being. ➤ **Unitarian** *n*.

unitary *adj* 1 of or relating to a unit or units. 2 undivided; whole. ➤ **unitarily** *adv*.

unite *v* 1 to join together to form a single unit. 2 to form, or cause to form, an alliance or association. ➤ **united** *adj*, **unitive** *adj*.

unit trust *n* a company that invests in a range of shares on behalf of investors who can buy units of shares.

unity *n* (*pl* **-ies**) 1 the state of being one or united. 2 agreement or concord. 3 a whole made up of related parts. 4 the number one.

universal *adj* 1 including or concerning all in the world or in a particular area or group. 2 present or occurring everywhere or under all conditions. 3 adjustable to meet any requirements. ➤ **universality** *n*, **universally** *adv*.

universe *n* 1 all things that exist. 2 a sphere of activity.

university *n* (*pl* **-ies**) an institution of higher education that undertakes academic research and teaches degree courses.

unjust *adj* not just or fair. ➤ **unjustly** *adv*.

unjustified *adj* not justified; unfair or inappropriate.

unkempt *adj* untidy or dishevelled.

unkind *adj* not kind or sympathetic. ➤ **unkindly** *adv*, **unkindness** *n*.

unknowable *adj* that cannot be known or understood.

unknowing *adj* not knowing; unaware. ➤ **unknowingly** *adv*.

unknown[1] *adj* 1 not known. 2 not famous or familiar.

unknown[2] *n* somebody or something that is little known.

unknown quantity *n* (*pl* **-ies**) an unpredictable or idiosyncratic person or thing.

Unknown Soldier *n* an unidentified soldier whose body is buried in a national memorial as a representative of all the armed forces who died in a war.

unladylike *adj* of a woman: not showing good manners.

unlawful *adj* against the law or the rules.
➤ **unlawfully** *adv.*

unleaded *adj esp* of petrol: not treated with lead or lead compounds.

unleash *v* to loose from restraint or control.

unleavened *adj* of bread: containing no yeast or other raising agent.

unless *conj* if not; except when.

unlicensed *adj* not having a licence to sell alcoholic drinks.

unlike¹ *prep* **1** different from. **2** not characteristic of. **3** in contrast to.

unlike² *adj* dissimilar; different.

unlikely *adj* (-**ier, -iest**) **1** not likely to exist or occur. **2** not expected or believable. ➤ **unlikelihood** *n.*

unlimited *adj* **1** lacking any controls or restrictions. **2** boundless; infinite.

unload *v* **1** to remove cargo from a vehicle, ship, or aircraft. **2** to get rid of (something unwanted).

unlock *v* to unfasten the lock of (a door or container).

unlooked-for *adj* not foreseen or expected.

unloose *v* to release from restraints.

unlovely *adj* disagreeable or unpleasant.

unlucky *adj* (-**ier, -iest**) experiencing or causing bad luck or misfortune. ➤ **unluckily** *adv.*

unmade *adj Brit* of a road: not having a finished surface.

unmanageable *adj* difficult or impossible to handle or control. ➤ **unmanageably** *adv.*

unmanly *adj* weak or cowardly.

unmanned *adj* not having or needing a human crew.

unmarried *adj* not married; single.

unmask *v* to reveal the true character or nature of.

unmatched *adj* not matched or equalled.

unmentionable *adj* not fit to be mentioned; unspeakable.

unmerciful *adj* showing no mercy. ➤ **unmercifully** *adv.*

unmindful *adj* (+ of) not conscious of or considering.

unmissable *adj* too easy or too good to miss.

unmistakable *or* **unmistakeable** *adj* not capable of being mistaken; clear or obvious. ➤ **unmistakably** *adv.*

unmitigated *adj* **1** not diminished in intensity. **2** complete; downright.

unmoved *adj* not affected by emotion.

unnatural *adj* **1** not in accordance with nature or what is normal. **2** artificial or contrived. ➤ **unnaturally** *adv.*

unnecessary *adj* not necessary. ➤ **unnecessarily** *adv.*

unnerve *v* to cause to feel discouraged or uncertain.

unnoticed *adj* not seen or noticed.

unobtainable *adj* impossible to obtain.

unobtrusive *adj* not easily seen or noticed. ➤ **unobtrusively** *adv.*

unoccupied *adj* **1** not lived in. **2** not busy.

unofficial *adj* not authorized or official. ➤ **unofficially** *adv.*

unopposed *adj* not challenged or opposed.

unorthodox *adj* not conventional in behaviour, beliefs, etc.

unpack *v* to remove the contents of (a bag, suitcase, package, etc).

unpaid *adj* **1** not yet paid. **2** not paying a wage or fee. **3** not receiving payment.

unpalatable *adj* **1** not pleasing to the taste. **2** unpleasant or disagreeable. ➤ **unpalatably** *adv.*

unparalleled *adj* having no equal; unique.

unpardonable *adj* that cannot be forgiven. ➤ **unpardonably** *adv.*

unperturbed *adj* not disturbed or concerned.

unpick *v* **1** to undo (sewing) by taking out stitches. **2** to analyse (an argument, theory, etc) in detail.

unpleasant *adj* not pleasant or agreeable. ➤ **unpleasantly** *adv,* **unpleasantness** *n.*

unplug *v* (**unplugged, unplugging**) **1** to disconnect (an electrical appliance) by removing its plug from the socket. **2** to remove an obstruction from.

unplumbed *adj* not known or explored.

unpopular *adj* not generally liked or approved of. ➤ **unpopularity** *n.*

unprecedented *adj* having no precedent; not previously done.

unpredictable *adj* not predictable; changeable or erratic. ➤ **unpredictability** *n,* **unpredictably** *adv.*

unprejudiced *adj* impartial; fair.

unpremeditated *adj* not planned or intended.

unprepared *adj* not ready or made ready.

unprepossessing *adj* not attractive or pleasing.

unpretentious *adj* not pretentious or ostentatious. ➤ **unpretentiously** *adv.*

unprincipled *adj* lacking moral principles.

unprintable *adj* too controversial or offensive to be printed.

unproductive *adj* not producing much or having much use.

unprofessional *adj* not conforming to the standards of a profession. ➤ **unprofessionally** *adv.*

unprofitable *adj* **1** not yielding profit. **2** useless; vain. ➤ **unprofitably** *adv.*

unpromising *adj* seeming unlikely to succeed or be worthwhile.

unpronounceable *adj* too difficult to pronounce.

unprovoked *adj* done or happening without provocation.

unqualified *adj* 1 not having the necessary qualifications. 2 complete; utter.

unquestionable *adj* not able to be doubted or challenged. ➤ **unquestionably** *adv*.

unquestioned *adj* not doubted or challenged.

unravel *v* (**unravelled, unravelling,** *NAmer* **unraveled, unraveling**) 1 to separate the threads of (something knitted, woven, or tangled), or to become separated. 2 to solve (a problem or mystery). 3 to begin to fail.

unreadable *adj* 1 not legible. 2 too difficult or tedious to read.

unready *adj* not ready or prepared.

unreal *adj* 1 lacking in reality or substance. 2 strange or illusory. ➤ **unreality** *n*.

unrealistic *adj* not in accordance with reality or practicality. ➤ **unrealistically** *adv*.

unreasonable *adj* 1 not based on or according with reason. 2 excessive or immoderate. ➤ **unreasonably** *adv*.

unrecognizable *or* **unrecognisable** *adj* not able to be recognized.

unrelenting *adj* 1 not weakening in determination or severity. 2 continuing to show vigour. ➤ **unrelentingly** *adv*.

unreliable *adj* not able to be relied on. ➤ **unreliability** *n*, **unreliably** *adv*.

unrelieved *adj* unchanging or uninterrupted.

unremitting *adj* constant; incessant; never lessening.

unrepeatable *adj* 1 incapable of being repeated. 2 too shocking or offensive to be repeated.

unrepentant *adj* showing no shame or regret for wrongdoing.

unrequited *adj* of love: not returned.

unreserved *adj* 1 unqualified; without any reservation. 2 frank and open in manner. 3 not booked or set aside. ➤ **unreservedly** *adv*.

unrest *n* agitation or turmoil, *esp* caused by rebellion or dissatisfaction.

unrivalled (*NAmer* **unrivaled**) *adj* unequalled; better than all others.

unroll *v* to open out; to uncoil or unwind.

unruffled *adj* 1 poised and serene in the face of difficulty. 2 smooth; calm.

unruly *adj* (**-ier, -iest**) difficult to control or manage. ➤ **unruliness** *n*.

unsafe *adj* 1 not safe; dangerous. 2 of a legal verdict: based on unreliable or inadequate evidence.

unsatisfactory *adj* not acceptable or adequate. ➤ **unsatisfactorily** *adv*.

unsaturated *adj* 1 able to form products by chemical addition, esp containing double or triple bonds between carbon atoms. 2 of a fat: containing a high proportion of fatty acids with double bonds and less likely to result in higher cholesterol levels.

unsavoury (*NAmer* **unsavory**) *adj* 1 disagree-

able or distasteful. 2 unpleasant to taste or smell.

unscathed *adj* entirely unharmed or uninjured.

unschooled *adj* untaught; untrained.

unscientific *adj* not in accordance with scientific principles. ➤ **unscientifically** *adv*.

unscrew *v* to unfasten or remove by twisting or by taking out screws.

unscrupulous *adj* without moral scruples; unprincipled. ➤ **unscrupulously** *adv*.

unseasonable *adj* 1 untimely. 2 not normal for the season of the year.

unseasonal *adj* not normal for the season of the year.

unseat *v* 1 to cause to fall from a seat or saddle. 2 to remove from a position of power.

unseeing *adj* not noticing anything.

unseemly *adj* not conforming to established standards of behaviour or taste.

unseen *adj* 1 not observed or perceived. 2 of a passage for translation: not previously seen by those for whom it is set.

unselfish *adj* not selfish; generous. ➤ **unselfishly** *adv*.

unserviceable *adj* not working or fit for use.

unsettle *v* to perturb or agitate.

unsettled *adj* 1 anxious or uneasy. 2 variable; changeable. 3 not resolved or worked out.

unshakable *or* **unshakeable** *adj* of a belief: incapable of being changed or set aside. ➤ **unshakably** *adv*.

unshaven *adj* not having shaved.

unsightly *adj* (**-ier, -iest**) not pleasing to the eye; ugly.

unskilled *adj* not having or needing a special skill.

unsociable *adj* not enjoying social activity. ➤ **unsociably** *adv*.

unsocial *adj* 1 unsociable. 2 of working hours: falling outside the normal working day. ➤ **unsocially** *adv*.

unsolicited *adj* not ordered or asked for.

unsophisticated *adj* 1 not socially or culturally sophisticated. 2 simple and straightforward.

unsound *adj* 1 not healthy or whole. 2 not firmly made or fixed. 3 not valid or true.

unsparing *adj* 1 hard or ruthless. 2 liberal; generous. ➤ **unsparingly** *adv*.

unspeakable *adj* too bad or shocking to be spoken. ➤ **unspeakably** *adv*.

unspoilt *adj* of a place: not spoilt by modern developments.

unstable *adj* 1 likely to fall; not firmly fixed. 2 unsteady or irregular. 3 given to changes of mood or an inability to control the emotions.

unsteady *adj* (**-ier, -iest**) 1 not firm or stable; likely to fall. 2 not uniform or even. ➤ **unsteadily** *adv*.

unstick *v* (*past tense and past part.* **unstuck**) to release from being stuck or fixed. ✴ **come unstuck** to go wrong.

unstinting adj done or given generously.

unsuccessful adj not successful. ➤ **unsuccessfully** adv.

unsuitable adj not suitable or appropriate. ➤ **unsuitability** n, **unsuitably** adv.

unsung adj not celebrated or praised.

unsure adj not certain or confident.

unsurpassed adj better than all others.

unsuspecting adj unaware of something dangerous or undesirable.

unsustainable adj not able to be maintained or supported.

unswerving adj not turning aside; constant.

unsympathetic adj not sympathetic or understanding.

unsystematic adj not systematic.

untangle v 1 to unravel or free from tangles. 2 to make less confusing.

untapped adj of a resource: not yet exploited.

untaught adj not educated; ignorant.

untenable adj of an argument, theory, etc: not able to be defended.

unthinkable adj impossible to contemplate; out of the question.

unthinking adj 1 without thinking; heedless. 2 inconsiderate. ➤ **unthinkingly** adv.

untidy adj (-ier, -iest) not neat; slovenly or disorderly. ➤ **untidily** adv, **untidiness** n.

untie v (**unties, untied, untying**) to undo or unfasten.

until prep and conj up to as late or as far as (a specified time or event).

untimely adj 1 occurring before the natural or proper time. 2 happening at an unsuitable time.

untitled adj not having a title.

unto prep archaic to (a place or person).

untold adj 1 too many to be listed. 2 not told or revealed.

untouchable¹ adj 1 not able to be touched. 2 unable to be criticized or equalled.

untouchable² n a member of the lowest and formerly segregated Hindu caste.

untouched adj 1 not touched or handled. 2 not influenced; unaffected.

untoward adj unexpected and unwelcome.

untrue adj 1 false. 2 not faithful; disloyal.

untrustworthy adj unable to be trusted.

unusable adj not fit for use.

unused adj 1 /un'yoohzd/ not used; fresh or new. 2 /un'yoohst/ (+ to) unaccustomed to.

unusual adj 1 uncommon; rare. 2 exceptional. ➤ **unusually** adv.

unutterable adj too bad or unpleasant to describe. ➤ **unutterably** adv.

unvarnished adj 1 not varnished. 2 of facts: plainly expressed.

unveil v 1 to remove a veil or covering from. 2 to make public (something new).

unwaged adj not in paid employment.

unwanted adj not wanted or needed.

unwarrantable adj not justifiable; inexcusable. ➤ **unwarrantably** adv.

unwarranted adj not justified.

unwary adj not alert or cautious. ➤ **unwarily** adv.

unwavering adj fixed; steadfast.

unwelcome adj not welcome or wanted.

unwell adj ill.

unwholesome adj 1 having a harmful effect on health. 2 unpleasant in appearance.

unwieldy adj (-ier, -iest) awkward in shape or size for moving or handling.

Usage Note: Note the spelling with -ie- and only one l.

---

unwilling adj not willing; reluctant. ➤ **unwillingly** adv, **unwillingness** n.

unwind v (past tense and past part. **unwound**) 1 to undo (something wound up). 2 to relax after effort or stress.

unwitting adj 1 not intended; inadvertent. 2 ignorant or unaware. ➤ **unwittingly** adv.

unwonted adj not usual or characteristic.

unworkable adj not practicable or feasible.

unworldly adj 1 naive or unsophisticated. 2 not interested in wealth or personal gain. 3 not of this world; spiritual. ➤ **unworldliness** n.

unworn adj not worn or damaged by use.

unworthy adj not worthy.

unwrap v (**unwrapped, unwrapping**) to remove the wrapping from.

unwritten adj of a law or rule: based on custom and precedent, and not codified.

unyielding adj 1 hard and inflexible. 2 stubborn or uncompromising.

unzip v (**unzipped, unzipping**) 1 to undo the zip of. 2 to decompress (a computer file).

up¹ adv 1 at or towards a relatively high level. 2 in or to a raised or upright position. 3 out of bed. 4 to the top; so as to be full. 5 in or into a relatively better condition. 6 above a normal or former level. 7 towards a higher number, degree, or rate. 8 in or into existence or prominence. ✳ **up against** 1 touching. 2 faced with; confronting. **up to 1** as far as; until. 2 equal to or good enough for. 3 being the responsibility or choice of.

up² adj 1 moving or directed upwards. 2 going on or taking place. 3 at an end. 4 of a road: being repaired.

up³ v (**upped, upping**) informal to increase or raise.

up⁴ prep 1 at or to a higher position on. 2 at the top of.

up-and-coming adj likely to succeed.

upbeat adj informal optimistic and cheerful.

upbraid v to scold or reproach.

upbringing n a particular way of educating and rearing a child.

upcoming adj about to happen; forthcoming.

upcountry adj and adv characteristic of an inland or outlying region.

update[1] *v* to bring up-to-date.

update[2] *n* **1** an act of updating. **2** something that has been updated.

upend *v* to cause to stand on end.

up-front[1] *adj* **1** paid or done in advance. **2** honest and candid.

up-front[2] *adv* in advance or at the beginning.

upgrade[1] *v* to improve the standard or performance of.

upgrade[2] *n* **1** the act or an instance of upgrading. **2** an upgraded version of something.

upheaval *n* a great disturbance or change.

uphill[1] *adv* upwards on a hill or incline.

uphill[2] *adj* **1** going up; ascending. **2** difficult or laborious: *an uphill task*.

uphold *v* (*past tense and past part.* **upheld**) **1** to give support to or maintain. **2** to support or defend against opposition or challenge.

upholster *v* to provide (e.g. a chair or sofa) with upholstery. ➤ **upholsterer** *n*.

upholstery *n* **1** the fabric, padding, and springs used to make a soft covering for furniture. **2** the art of upholstering furniture.

upkeep *n* the process or cost of maintaining something in good condition.

upland *n* (*also in pl*) an area of high land.

uplift[1] *v* **1** to raise or elevate. **2** to make (somebody) feel more hopeful or optimistic. ➤ **uplifting** *adj*.

uplift[2] *n* **1** the act or result of uplifting something. **2** support for the breasts provided by a bra, etc. **3** a quality or effect that produces hope or optimism.

up-market *adj* designed to appeal to more prosperous or sophisticated customers.

upon *prep formal* on or on top of.

upper[1] *adj* higher in physical position, rank, or order. ✳ **have/get the upper hand** to have or gain a position of control or advantage.

upper[2] *n* the parts of a shoe or boot above the sole. ✳ **on one's uppers** having no money.

upper[3] *n informal* a stimulant drug, *esp* an amphetamine.

upper case *n* capital letters, e.g. A, B, C rather than a, b, c. ➤ **upper-case** *adj*.

upper class *n* the class occupying the highest position in a society. ➤ **upper-class** *adj*.

uppercut *n* a swinging blow directed upwards with a bent arm.

upper house *n* in Britain, the House of Lords.

uppermost *adj and adv* in or into the highest or most prominent position.

uppity *adj informal* behaving in a superior or supercilious manner.

upright[1] *adj* **1** perpendicular; vertical. **2** having a greater height than width. **3** honest or honourable.

upright[2] *adv* in or into an upright position.

upright[3] *n* **1** a vertical support. **2** a piano with a vertical frame and strings.

uprising *n* a localized rebellion.

upriver *adv and adj* upstream.

uproar *n* **1** a noisy commotion or violent disturbance. **2** a noisy or violent protest.

uproarious *adj* **1** noisy and boisterous. **2** extremely funny. ➤ **uproariously** *adv*.

uproot *v* **1** to pull up by the roots. **2** to move (somebody) away from their home or country.

upscale *adj and adv chiefly NAmer* up-market.

upset[1] *v* (**upsetting**, *past tense and past part.* **upset**) **1** to make (somebody) unhappy, disappointed, or anxious. **2** to knock over or overturn. **3** to throw into disorder; to disrupt. **4** to make (somebody) slightly ill.

upset[2] *n* **1** an unexpected defeat or setback. **2** a slight illness. **3** an emotional disturbance.

upset[3] *adj* **1** unhappy, disappointed, or anxious. **2** physically disturbed or disordered.

upshot *n* the eventual result or outcome.

upside *n* the favourable aspect of something.

upside down *adv and adj* **1** with the upper and the lower parts reversed. **2** in disorder or confusion.

upsilon *n* the 20th letter of the Greek alphabet (Y, υ).

upstage[1] *adv and adj* at or towards the back of a theatre stage.

upstage[2] *v* to steal attention from (somebody else) by doing something better or more exciting.

upstairs *adv and adj* on or to a higher floor.

upstanding *adj* honest and respectable.

upstart *n* somebody who behaves arrogantly when given authority.

upstate *adv and adj* to or in the part of a US state away from city areas.

upstream *adv and adj* in the direction opposite to the flow of a stream or river.

upsurge *n* a rapid or sudden rise.

uptake *n* the act of accepting or starting to use something. ✳ **quick/slow on the uptake** *informal* quick or slow to understand.

uptight *adj informal* **1** tense or nervous. **2** angry or indignant.

up-to-date *adj* **1** knowing or including the latest information or developments. **2** abreast of the times; modern.

up-to-the-minute *adj* completely up-to-date.

upturn[1] *v* to turn up or upside down.

upturn[2] *n* a change towards better conditions.

upward *adj* moving or extending upwards; ascending.

upwards *adv* from a lower to a higher place or level.

upwind *adv and adj* in the direction from which the wind is blowing.

uranium *n* a radioactive metallic element used as fuel in nuclear reactors.

urban *adj* relating to or part of a city or town.

urbane *adj* **1** courteous and suave in manner. **2** elegant or sophisticated. ➤ **urbanity** *n*.

urchin *n* a poor and dishevelled young child.

Urdu *n* the language of Pakistan, Bangladesh, and parts of India.

ureter *n* a duct that carries urine from the kidney to the bladder.

urethra *n* (*pl* **urethras** or **urethrae**) the canal that carries urine from the bladder out of the body, and in the male also conveys semen. ➤ **urethral** *adj*.

urge[1] *v* **1** to encourage or try hard to persuade. **2** to advocate or demand.

urge[2] *n* a strong impulse or desire.

urgent *adj* **1** calling for immediate attention. **2** persistent or demanding. ➤ **urgency** *n*, **urgently** *adv*.

urinal *n* a fixture attached to a wall in a public toilet, for men to urinate into.

urinate *v* to pass urine out of the body. ➤ **urination** *n*.

urine *n* liquid waste material secreted by the kidney and stored in the bladder until passed out of the body. ➤ **urinary** *adj*.

URL *abbr* uniform resource locator: the address of a page on the World Wide Web.

urn *n* **1** a container for the ashes of a dead person. **2** a large closed container with a tap, for making and serving tea or coffee.

ursine *adj* of or resembling a bear.

US *abbr* United States.

us *pron* used as the objective case: we.

USA *abbr* United States of America.

usable or **useable** *adj* capable of being used. ➤ **usability** *n*.

usage *n* **1** established practice or procedure. **2** the action or manner of using something.

use[1] /yoohs/ *n* **1** the action or manner of using something. **2** the right or benefit of using something. **3** the ability or power to use a part of the body. **4** a purpose or end. **5** practical worth or application. ✳ **make use of** to use or take advantage of.

use[2] /yoohz/ *v* **1** to put into action or service. **2** to employ for a specified purpose. **3** to expend or consume. **4** to consume or take regularly. **5** to exploit (somebody) as a means to one's own ends. **6** to treat (somebody or something) in a specified manner.

used *adj* **1** /yoohzd/ secondhand. **2** /yoohst/ accustomed; habituated. ✳ **be used to** to be familiar with or accustomed to. **used to** expressing a habitual action or state in the past: *I used to play golf.*

useful *adj* having a practical worth or application. ➤ **usefully** *adv*, **usefulness** *n*.

useless *adj* **1** having no use or purpose. **2** *informal* lacking skill or aptitude. ➤ **uselessly** *adv*.

user *n* somebody who uses something.

user-friendly *adj* easy to operate or understand.

use up *v* to consume completely.

usher[1] *n* **1** somebody who shows people to their seats in a theatre, cinema, or church. **2** an official who performs routine tasks in a court of law.

usher[2] *v* **1** to guide or escort to a place. **2** (*usu* + in) to introduce.

usherette *n* a woman who shows people to their seats in a theatre or cinema.

USSR *abbr* formerly, Union of Soviet Socialist Republics.

usual *adj* commonly or ordinarily done or used. ➤ **usually** *adv*.

usurer *n* somebody who lends money at an exorbitant rate of interest. ➤ **usury** *n*.

usurp *v* to seize authority wrongfully from. ➤ **usurpation** *n*, **usurper** *n*.

utensil *n* a tool or container used in the household.

uterus *n* (*pl* **uteri**) the female organ that contains and nourishes the young before birth; the womb. ➤ **uterine** *adj*.

utilitarian *adj* practical and useful rather than attractive.

utilitarianism *n* the theory that what matters is the greatest happiness of the greatest number.

utility *n* (*pl* **-ies**) **1** fitness to be used for some purpose. **2** an organization performing a public service, e.g. providing gas, electricity, or water.

utility room *n* a room containing a washing machine and other domestic equipment.

utilize or **-ise** *v* to make practical use of. ➤ **utilization** *n*.

utmost[1] *adj* farthest, greatest, or most extreme.

utmost[2] *n* the highest point or degree.

utopia or **Utopia** *n* an imagined place or state of perfection.

utopian or **Utopian** *adj* impossibly ideal. ➤ **utopianism** *n*.

utter[1] *adj* absolute; total. ➤ **utterly** *adv*.

utter[2] *v* to emit as sound or language.

utterance *n* **1** a sound or statement made. **2** the act of speaking.

uttermost *adj* and *n* = UTMOST[1], UTMOST[2].

U-turn *n* **1** the forward turning of a vehicle to face the opposite direction. **2** a total reversal of policy.

uvula *n* (*pl* **uvulas** or **uvulae**) the fleshy lobe hanging from the back of the soft palate. ➤ **uvular** *adj*.

uxorious *adj* *formal* excessively fond of one's wife.

V¹ *or* **v** *n* (*pl* **V's** *or* **Vs** *or* **v's**) **1** the 22nd letter of the English alphabet. **2** the Roman numeral for five.

V² *abbr* volt.

V³ *abbr* the chemical symbol for vanadium.

v *abbr* versus.

vacancy *n* (*pl* **-ies**) **1** an unfilled job or position. **2** an unoccupied room in a hotel or guest house. **3** empty space.

vacant *adj* **1** of a job or position: awaiting an appointment. **2** of a room or building: not occupied or lived in. **3** of the face: showing no expression. ➤ **vacantly** *adv*.

vacate *v* **1** to give up the possession or occupancy of (a room or building). **2** to leave (a job or position). ➤ **vacatable** *adj*.

vacation¹ *n* **1** a period during which the activity of an institution, e.g. a university or law court, is suspended. **2** the act of vacating a place. **3** *NAmer* a holiday.

vacation² *v NAmer* to take a holiday.

vaccinate *v* to inject with a vaccine. ➤ **vaccination** *n*.

vaccine *n* a substance prepared from organisms that cause a disease, injected into the body to increase immunity.

vacillate *v* **1** to hesitate or waver about something. **2** to fluctuate. ➤ **vacillation** *n*.

vacuous *adj* **1** stupid; inane. **2** idle; aimless. ➤ **vacuity** *n*.

vacuum¹ *n* (*pl* **vacuums** *or* **vacua**) **1** a space containing no matter or from which air or other matter has been removed. **2** a state in which an important person or thing is missing and has not been replaced.

vacuum² *v informal* to clean using a vacuum cleaner.

vacuum cleaner *n* an electrical appliance for removing dust and dirt by means of suction.

vacuum flask *n Brit* a container with a vacuum between an inner and an outer wall used to keep liquids hot or cold.

vagabond *n* a wanderer or tramp.

vagary *n* (*pl* **-ies**) an erratic or unpredictable action, change, etc.

vagina *n* (*pl* **vaginas**) a canal in a female mammal that leads from the womb to an external opening. ➤ **vaginal** *adj*.

vagrant¹ *n* a person who has no home or means of support.

vagrant² *adj* living as a vagrant. ➤ **vagrancy** *n*.

vague *adj* **1** not precise in meaning or clearly expressed. **2** not thinking or expressing one's thoughts clearly or precisely. **3** not sharply outlined; hazy. ➤ **vaguely** *adv*, **vagueness** *n*.

vain *adj* **1** having or showing excessive pride in one's appearance or abilities. **2** of an attempt: unsuccessful or ineffectual. ✳ **in vain** without success or result. ➤ **vainly** *adv*.

vainglorious *adj literary* excessively proud or boastful.

valance *or* **valence** *n* **1** a piece of drapery hung as a border along the edge of a bed, canopy, or shelf. **2** a pelmet.

vale *n literary* a valley.

valediction *n formal* **1** an act of saying farewell. **2** a statement of farewell.

valedictory *adj formal* expressing a farewell.

valency (*NAmer* **valence**) *n* (*pl* **-ies**) the degree of combining power of an element as shown by the number of atomic weights of hydrogen with which the atomic weight of the element will combine or for which it can be substituted.

valentine *n* **1** a lover or sweetheart chosen on St Valentine's Day, 14 February. **2** a greeting card sent or given to such a person.

valerian *n* **1** a perennial plant, some types of which have medicinal properties. **2** a sedative drug made from the roots of valerian.

valet¹ *n* an employee who attends to day-to-day needs for a man, the guests at a hotel, etc.

valet² *v* (**valeted, valeting**) **1** to serve (somebody) as a valet. **2** to clean (a car) as a service.

valetudinarian *n formal* a weak or sickly person, *esp* a hypochondriac.

valiant *adj* showing valour or courage. ➤ **valiantly** *adv*.

valid *adj* **1** well-grounded or justifiable. **2** of an argument: logically sound. **3** having legal force or value. ➤ **validity** *n*.

validate *v* **1** to make legally valid. **2** to corroborate or authenticate. ➤ **validation** *n*.

valise *n* a small travelling bag or case.

Valium *n trademark* a tranquillizing drug used to treat anxiety.

valley *n* (*pl* **-eys**) a low-lying area between hills or mountains.

valour (*NAmer* **valor**) *n* personal bravery in the face of danger. ➤ **valorous** *adj*.

valuable adj **1** having high money value. **2** of great use or worth. ➤ **valuably** adv.

valuables pl n personal possessions having a high money value.

valuation n **1** the process of valuing property or valuables. **2** the estimated value of something.

value¹ n **1** the worth in money or commodities of something. **2** relative worth, usefulness, or importance. **3** (usu in pl) a moral principle or standard of behaviour. **4** a numerical quantity assigned or computed. **5** the magnitude of a physical quantity. **6** the relative duration of a musical note.

value² v (**values, valued, valuing**) **1** (often + at) to estimate the money worth of. **2** to rate in terms of usefulness or importance. **3** to consider or rate highly. ➤ **valuer** n.

value-added tax n a tax levied on goods and services based on the increase of value at each stage of their development.

valve n **1** a structure in the heart or a vein that restricts the flow of blood to one direction only. **2** a mechanical device for controlling the flow of liquid, gas, or loose material. **3** a device in a brass musical instrument for varying the tube length to change the note.

vamp¹ n informal a woman who uses her charm to seduce men. ➤ **vampish** adj.

vamp² v informal (+ up) to rework (something old) with new material or in a new way.

vampire n **1** a dead person believed to come from the grave at night and suck the blood of sleeping people. **2** (also **vampire bat**) a South American bat that feeds on blood. ➤ **vampirism** n.

van¹ n **1** a motor vehicle used for transporting goods. **2** Brit an enclosed railway goods wagon.

van² n the leading people in a group or movement.

vanadium n a grey chemical element used in alloys.

vandal n a person who deliberately destroys or damages property. ➤ **vandalism** n.

vandalize or **-ise** v to destroy or damage (property) deliberately.

vane n a thin flat or curved blade that is moved about an axis by wind or water.

vanguard n **1** the troops moving at the head of an army. **2** the leading people in an action or movement.

vanilla n a flavouring obtained from the pod of a tropical American climbing orchid.

vanish v **1** to pass quickly from sight; to disappear. **2** to cease to exist.

vanity n (pl **-ies**) **1** excessive pride in oneself; conceit. **2** the quality of being vain or futile.

vanity case n a women's small case for carrying toilet articles and cosmetics.

vanquish v literary to defeat or overcome.

vantage n a position giving a strategic advantage.

vantage point n a place or position that affords a clear view over an area.

vapid adj lacking liveliness or interest. ➤ **vapidity** n.

vaporize or **-ise** v to convert (liquid) into vapour. ➤ **vaporization** n, **vaporizer** n.

vapour (NAmer **vapor**) n **1** smoke, fog, etc suspended in the air. **2** a substance in the gaseous state that is liquid under normal conditions. ➤ **vaporous** adj.

variable¹ adj **1** able to vary or be varied. **2** of behaviour, etc: fickle or inconstant. ➤ **variability** n, **variably** adv.

variable² n **1** something that varies or that can be varied. **2** a quantity that may assume any of a set of values. **3** a symbol representing a variable quantity or entity. **4** a variable wind. **5** (in pl) a region where variable winds occur.

variance n **1** the fact or quality of being variable or variant. **2** the state of disagreeing or disputing. * **at variance with** not agreeing with.

variant n something that shows variation from a type or norm.

variation n **1** the act or extent of varying. **2** something showing variation. **3** a varied version of a musical idea.

varicose adj of a vein: abnormally swollen or dilated.

varied adj **1** having different forms or types. **2** having a variety of contents or parts.

variegated adj marked with patches of different colours. ➤ **variegation** n.

variety n (pl **-ies**) **1** the state of varying; diversity. **2** an assortment of differing things of the same general kind. **3** something differing from others of the same general kind. **4** a group of plants or animals ranking below a species. **5** theatrical entertainment consisting of songs, sketches, acrobatics, etc.

various adj **1** of differing kinds or forms. **2** more than one; several. ➤ **variously** adv.

varnish¹ n a liquid coating that forms a hard shiny surface when it dries.

varnish² v to apply varnish to.

vary v (**-ies, -ied**) **1** to show or undergo change. **2** (usu + from) to deviate. **3** to make a change in. **4** to ensure variety in.

vascular adj relating to the system of channels conducting blood, sap, etc in a plant or animal.

vas deferens /,vaz 'defərenz, ,vas/ n (pl **vasa deferentia**) the duct that carries sperm from the testis to the penis.

vase n an ornamental vessel used for holding flowers.

vasectomy n (pl **-ies**) surgical cutting out of a section of the vas deferens as a means of sterilization.

Vaseline n trademark a type of petroleum jelly.

vassal n in a feudal society, a man who vowed loyalty to a lord in return for protection and land.

vast adj very great in amount, degree, or intensity. ➤ **vastly** adv, **vastness** n.

VAT n Brit value-added tax.

Vatican n (**the Vatican**) the official residence of the pope in Rome.

vaudeville n a light theatrical entertainment combining pantomime, dancing, and song.

vault[1] n 1 an arched structure forming a ceiling or roof. 2 a cellar or room with an arched ceiling. 3 an underground room or store. 4 a strongroom or compartment for valuables. 5 a burial chamber beneath a church or in a cemetery. ➤ **vaulted** adj.

vault[2] v to leap over something using the hands or a pole. ➤ **vaulter** n.

vault[3] n the act of vaulting.

vaunt v to call attention to (one's achievements), proudly or boastfully. ➤ **vaunted** adj.

VC abbr Victoria Cross.

VCR abbr videocassette recorder.

VDU n a visual display unit.

veal n the meat of a calf.

vector n 1 a quantity, e.g. velocity or force, that has magnitude and direction. 2 an organism that transmits a disease-causing agent.

Veda /'veedə, 'vaydə/ n a collection of Hindu sacred writings.

veer v 1 to change direction. 2 of the wind: to shift in a clockwise direction.

vegan n a strict vegetarian who avoids products derived from animals.

vegetable n 1 a plant grown for food. 2 derog a person with impaired mental capability caused by brain damage.

vegetal adj formal relating to plants.

vegetarian n a person who does not eat meat. ➤ **vegetarianism** n.

vegetate v to lead a dull inactive existence.

vegetation n plant life.

vegetative adj 1 relating to nutrition and growth. 2 involving propagation by non-sexual processes. 3 relating to involuntary bodily functions. 4 inactive.

vehement adj intensely felt or expressed; impassioned. ➤ **vehemence** n, **vehemently** adv.

vehicle n 1 an object with wheels and an engine used to carry people or goods, e.g. a car, bus, or lorry. 2 a medium through which something is expressed or communicated. ➤ **vehicular** adj.

veil[1] n 1 a length of cloth worn by women as a covering for the head or face. 2 something that hides or obscures. 3 a disguise or pretext. 4 the outer covering of a nun's headdress. ✳ **draw a veil over** to avoid mentioning (something unwelcome).

veil[2] v to cover with a veil.

veiled adj 1 thinly disguised. 2 indistinct or muffled.

vein n 1 any of the tubes that carry blood towards the heart. 2 a blood vessel. 3 a streak of a different colour in wood, marble, cheese, etc. 4 any of the ribs forming the framework of a leaf. 5 any of the thickened ribs that stiffen the wings of an insect. 6 a deposit of ore, coal, etc in rock. 7 a distinctive element or quality. 8 a mood or frame of mind. ➤ **veined** adj.

Velcro n trademark a fastening device consisting of two strips of fabric that stick to each other.

veld or **veldt** /velt, felt/ n open grassland in southern Africa.

vellum n a fine parchment for writing on.

velociraptor n a ferocious dinosaur that walked on two legs.

velocity n (pl -ies) speed in a given direction.

velour or **velours** n (pl **velours**) a fabric with a pile or surface resembling velvet.

velvet n a fabric with a short soft pile. ➤ **velvety** adj.

velveteen n a fabric with a short pile like velvet.

venal adj open to bribery. ➤ **venality** n.

vend v to sell (goods) in a small way.

vendetta n a blood feud arising from the murder of a member of one family by a member of another.

vending machine n a coin-operated machine for selling small items.

vendor or **vender** n 1 a seller of small items. 2 in law, the seller of a property.

veneer n 1 a thin layer of wood, plastic, etc forming the surface of a cheaper material. 2 a superficially or deceptively attractive appearance. ➤ **veneered** adj.

venerable adj commanding respect through age, character, and achievements.

venerate v to respect or regard with honour. ➤ **veneration** n.

venereal disease n a disease contracted from sexual contact.

Venetian n a native or inhabitant of Venice. ➤ **Venetian** adj.

venetian blind n a window blind made of horizontal slats that can be adjusted to vary the amount of light admitted.

vengeance n punishment inflicted on somebody in retaliation for an injury received or offence felt. ✳ **with a vengeance** with great force or intensity.

vengeful adj wanting or seeking revenge. ➤ **vengefully** adv.

venial adj of a wrongdoing: minor and pardonable.

venison n the meat of a deer.

Venn diagram n a graph that uses circles to represent sets, the circles overlapping to show common elements.

venom n **1** poison secreted by the bites of snakes, scorpions, etc. **2** strong hatred or malevolence.

venomous adj **1** poisonous. **2** spiteful or malevolent. ➤ **venomously** adv.

venous adj relating to a vein or the veins.

vent[1] n an opening for the escape of a gas or liquid or for the relief of pressure. ✳ **give vent to** to express (feelings) forcefully.

vent[2] v **1** to release (gas, etc) through a vent. **2** to express (feelings) forcefully.

vent[3] n a slit in a garment.

ventilate v to cause air to circulate through (a room or building). ➤ **ventilation** n.

ventilator n **1** an apparatus or opening for circulating fresh air. **2** an apparatus for providing artificial respiration for a patient who cannot breathe normally.

ventral adj relating to the front, lower, or inner surface of something.

ventricle n a chamber of the heart that receives blood from a corresponding atrium and from which blood is pumped into the arteries.

ventriloquism n the technique of projecting the voice so that it seems to come from a source other than the speaker, used to make a dummy appear to speak, as entertainment. ➤ **ventriloquist** n.

venture[1] v **1** (often + out/forth) to proceed despite danger or difficulty. **2** to offer (a controversial opinion).

venture[2] n **1** an undertaking involving risk or danger. **2** money or property at risk in a speculative venture.

venturesome adj ready to take risks; daring.

venue n the place where a gathering or event takes place.

Venus flytrap or **Venus's-flytrap** n a plant with leaves that snap together to trap and digest insects.

veracious adj formal truthful; honest. ➤ **veracity** n.

veranda or **verandah** n a roofed open gallery or portico along the outside of a building.

verb n a word that expresses an action or state, e.g. run, give, be.

verbal adj **1** involving or expressed in words. **2** spoken rather than written. **3** of or formed from a verb. ➤ **verbally** adv.

verbalize or **-ise** v to express in words.

verbatim /vuh'baytim, və-/ adv and adj in the exact words used.

verbiage n use of an unnecessary number of words.

verbose adj using more words than necessary. ➤ **verbosity** n.

verdant adj green with growing plants.

verdict n **1** the decision of a jury about the guilt or innocence of an accused. **2** an opinion or judgment.

verdigris n a green or bluish deposit formed on copper, brass, or bronze surfaces.

verdure n growing green vegetation.

verge[1] n **1** something that forms a border or limit. **2** Brit a planted strip of land at the side of a road. **3** the brink or threshold of something.

verge[2] v ✳ **verge on** to resemble or come near to.

verger n a church official who acts as an usher and caretaker.

verify v (-ies, -ied) **1** to establish the truth, accuracy, or reality of. **2** to confirm or fulfil. ➤ **verifiable** adj, **verification** n.

verily adv archaic certainly; truly.

verisimilitude n formal the quality of appearing to be true.

veritable adj actual; not false or imaginary. ➤ **veritably** adv.

verity n (pl -ies) **1** the quality being true or real. **2** a true statement.

vermicelli /vuhmi'cheli/ pl n **1** pasta in the form of long thin threads. **2** tiny strands of sugar or chocolate used as a decoration on cakes.

vermilion or **vermillion** n a brilliant red colour or pigment.

vermin pl n **1** lice, rats, or other common harmful animals. **2** birds and mammals that prey on game. ➤ **verminous** adj.

vermouth n a dry or sweet wine flavoured with aromatic herbs.

vernacular n **1** the language spoken by the ordinary people of a region. **2** informal the mode of expression of a group or class.

vernal adj of or occurring in the spring.

verruca n (pl **verrucas**) a wart on the underside of the foot.

versatile adj able to turn to or be turned to a variety of activities or uses. ➤ **versatility** n.

verse n **1** writing having a fixed rhythm and metre. **2** a distinct short section of a poem, song, or hymn. **3** each of the short divisions of a chapter of the Bible.

versed adj (+ in) having knowledge of or skill in something.

versify v (-ies, -ied) to write verses, or turn (words) into verse. ➤ **versification** n.

version n **1** an account or description of something told from a particular point of view. **2** a form or variant of a type or original. **3** an adaptation or arrangement of a work of art or piece of music.

verso n (pl **-os**) a left-hand page.

versus prep **1** against. **2** in contrast to.

vertebra n (pl **vertebrae** or **vertebras**) each of the bony segments forming the spinal column. ➤ **vertebral** adj.

vertebrate n an animal that has a backbone, e.g. a mammal, bird, reptile, amphibian, or fish.

vertex n (pl **vertices** or **vertexes**) **1** the highest point. **2** in mathematics, the point where lines or curves meet or cross each other.

vertical[1] *adj* going up or down at right angles to a horizontal line or surface. ➤ **verticality** *n*, **vertically** *adv*.

vertical[2] *n* **1** verticality. **2** a vertical line or surface.

vertiginous *adj* very high or steep and likely to cause vertigo.

vertigo *n* a state of imbalance and dizziness caused by looking down from a high position.

verve *n* energy or vitality.

very[1] *adv* **1** to a high degree; exceedingly. **2** used for emphasis: *the very best*.

very[2] *adj* **1** actual; same: *the very man*. **2** mere: *the very thought of it*.

Vesak *n* a Buddhist festival held in May.

vespers *n* a service of evening worship.

vessel *n* **1** a large structure designed to travel on water; a ship or large boat. **2** a container for liquid, e.g. a jug, cup, or bowl. **3** a tube or canal in which fluid is carried in the body or in a plant.

vest[1] *n* **1** *Brit* a sleeveless undergarment for the upper body. **2** *NAmer* a waistcoat.

vest[2] *v* to give a legal right or title to.

vested interest *n* **1** a personal interest in the outcome of a situation or action, *esp* when bringing financial benefit. **2** an interest carrying a legal right.

vestibule *n* a lobby or chamber between the outer door and the interior of a building.

vestige *n* **1** a trace left by something that has disappeared. **2** a minute amount. ➤ **vestigial** *adj*.

vestment *n* a ceremonial garment worn by members of the clergy or of a church choir.

vestry *n* (*pl* **-ies**) a room in a church where the clergy put on vestments.

vet[1] *n* a veterinary surgeon.

vet[2] *v* (**vetted**, **vetting**) to subject (somebody) to thorough investigation or appraisal before giving them a job or responsibility.

vetch *n* a plant of the pea family, used for fodder and improving the soil.

veteran *n* **1** a person who has had long experience of an occupation or skill. **2** *NAmer* a former member of the armed forces.

veterinarian *n* *NAmer* a veterinary surgeon.

veterinary *adj* relating to the medical care of animals.

veterinary surgeon *n* a person who is qualified to treat diseases and injuries of animals.

veto[1] *n* (*pl* **-oes**) **1** the right to forbid or reject a decision or proposal. **2** the process of exercising this right.

veto[2] *v* (**vetoes**, **vetoed**, **vetoing**) to use a veto against (a decision or proposal).

vex *v* to cause annoyance or distress to. ➤ **vexation** *n*, **vexatious** *adj*.

vexed *adj* **1** annoyed or distressed. **2** of a question or issue: controversial and having no satisfactory solution.

VHF *abbr* very high frequency.

VHS *abbr* *trademark* video home system.

via *prep* **1** passing through or calling at (a place) on the way. **2** through the medium of; by means of.

viable *adj* **1** capable of working; practicable. **2** of a foetus: developed enough to be capable of living. **3** capable of growing or developing. ➤ **viability** *n*.

viaduct *n* a long bridge carrying a road or railway over a deep valley.

vial *n* = PHIAL.

viands *pl n* *archaic* food.

vibes *pl n* *informal* the emotional atmosphere of a place.

vibrant *adj* **1** oscillating or pulsating rapidly. **2** full of life and vigour. **3** of sound: strong and resonant. **4** of colour: vivid. ➤ **vibrancy** *n*, **vibrantly** *adv*.

vibraphone *n* an electric percussion instrument producing a vibrato.

vibrate *v* **1** to move to and fro rapidly. **2** of a sound: to resonate.

vibration *n* **1** the action of vibrating. **2** *informal* (*in pl*) the characteristic emotional atmosphere of a place.

vibrato /vi'brahtoh/ *n* an expressive musical effect produced by rapid slight variations in pitch.

vibrator *n* a vibrating electrical apparatus used in massage or for sexual stimulation.

vicar *n* in the Church of England, a member of the clergy in charge of a parish.

vicarage *n* a vicar's house.

vicarious *adj* **1** experienced through imaginative sharing of another's experience. **2** delegated. ➤ **vicariously** *adv*.

vice[1] *n* **1** immoral or corrupt behaviour. **2** criminal trade in prostitution and drugs. **3** a grave moral fault. **4** a habitual minor fault or shortcoming.

vice[2] (*NAmer* **vise**) *n* a tool with adjustable jaws that hold an object tightly to be worked on.

vice- *comb. form* next in rank to; deputy: *vice-president*.

viceroy *n* an official sent by a sovereign to govern a subject territory.

vice versa /ˌvies 'vuhsə, ˌviesi/ *adv* with the order changed or reversed; conversely.

vicinity *n* (*pl* **-ies**) a surrounding area or district.

vicious *adj* **1** cruel and violent. **2** fierce and dangerous. ➤ **viciously** *adv*, **viciousness** *n*.

vicious circle *n* a situation in which dealing with one difficulty creates a new difficulty that makes the original difficulty worse.

vicissitudes *pl n* unpredictable changes in human fortunes.

victim n **1** a person who is killed, injured, deceived, or mistreated. **2** a living animal or person offered as a sacrifice in a religious rite.

victimize or **-ise** v **1** to punish or mistreat selectively. **2** to make a victim of. ➤ **victimization** n.

victor n a person, country, etc that defeats an enemy or opponent.

Victorian adj relating to the reign of Queen Victoria (1837–1901).

victorious adj having won a victory or success. ➤ **victoriously** adv.

victory n (pl **-ies**) the act of overcoming an enemy or opponent.

victuals pl n archaic food.

video¹ n (pl **-os**) **1** pictures and sound recorded on a magnetic tape or disc. **2** a tape or cassette of recorded material. **3** a machine for recording and playing this material.

video² v (**videoes, videoed, videoing**) to make a video recording of.

videodisc n a disc on which digital information is stored.

video game n a computer game played on a VDU screen.

videophone n an electronic device for transmitting sound and pictures down a telephone line.

videorecorder n a machine for recording on and playing videotapes.

videotape¹ n **1** magnetic tape used for recording visual images. **2** a cassette of this magnetic tape.

videotape² v to record on videotape.

vie v (**vies, vied, vying**) to compete with others for something.

view¹ n **1** a scene or scenery seen from a particular position, e.g. a window. **2** the ability to see something; sight. **3** a picture or photograph of a place. **4** an attitude or opinion. ✳ **in view of** because of; considering. **with a view to** intending to.

view² v **1** to see or watch. **2** to regard in a specified way. **3** to inspect. **4** to consider.

viewer n **1** a person who watches television. **2** an optical device.

viewfinder n a device on a camera showing an image of what will appear in the photograph.

viewpoint n **1** a standpoint; a point of view. **2** a place from which something can be viewed.

vigil n a period of staying awake in the night, to keep watch or to pray.

vigilant adj alert to spot trouble or danger. ➤ **vigilance** n, **vigilantly** adv.

vigilante /vijiˈlanti/ n a member of a group of self-appointed guardians of law and order. ➤ **vigilantism** n.

vignette n **1** an engraving or photograph that shades off gradually into the surrounding background. **2** a short descriptive literary sketch. **3** a brief attractive incident or scene in a play or film.

vigorous adj **1** full of strength and energy. **2** done with vigour. ➤ **vigorously** adv.

vigour (NAmer **vigor**) n **1** active physical strength or force. **2** intensity of action or effect.

Viking n a Norse trader and warrior of the eighth to tenth cents.

vile adj **1** morally despicable or abhorrent. **2** unpleasant or repulsive. ➤ **vilely** adv.

vilify v (**-ies, -ied**) to speak slanderously or abusively about. ➤ **vilification** n.

villa n **1** Brit a detached or semidetached suburban house. **2** a holiday house abroad. **3** a large house of an ancient Roman.

village n a small group of streets and houses in the country. ➤ **villager** n.

villain n **1** a scoundrel or criminal. **2** a bad character in a story or play. ➤ **villainous** n.

villein n formerly, a peasant working for a feudal lord in exchange for land.

vim n informal energy and enthusiasm.

vinaigrette n a salad dressing of oil and vinegar flavoured with salt, pepper, mustard, and herbs.

vindicate v **1** to absolve from blame. **2** to provide justification for. ➤ **vindication** n.

vindictive adj **1** eager to seek revenge. **2** intended as revenge. ➤ **vindictively** adv, **vindictiveness** n.

vine n a climbing plant, esp one that bears grapes.

vinegar n a sour liquid obtained from wine, cider, etc and used as a seasoning or preservative. ➤ **vinegary** adj.

vineyard n a plantation of grapevines used in making wine.

vintage¹ n **1** a season's yield of grapes or wine from a vineyard. **2** a superior wine of a particular type, region, and year. **3** the act or time of harvesting grapes or making wine. **4** a period of origin or manufacture.

vintage² adj **1** denoting superior wine of a particular year. **2** of enduring value; classic.

vintner n a wine merchant.

vinyl n a strong tough plastic that is derived from ethylene.

viol n an early stringed instrument having six strings and frets.

viola¹ n a stringed instrument of the violin family, intermediate in size and range between the violin and cello.

viola² n a cultivated violet with flowers resembling pansies.

violate v **1** to fail to comply with (a rule or law). **2** to assault sexually. **3** to fail to respect (something sacred). ➤ **violation** n, **violator** n.

violence n **1** exertion of physical force so as to kill or injure or to cause harm to property. **2** intense or turbulent action or force. **3** vehement feeling or expression.

violent adj **1** using or marked by violence. **2** powerfully intense or furious. ➤ **violently** adv.

violet n **1** a plant with sweet-scented purple or blue flowers. **2** a bluish purple colour.

violin n a musical instrument having four strings, played with a bow and with one end held under the chin. ➤ **violinist** n.

violoncello /ˌvie-ələn'cheloh/ n (pl **-os**) formal = CELLO.

Usage Note: Note the spelling *violon-* not *violin-*.

VIP n a very important person.

viper n a poisonous snake of the adder family.

virago n (pl **-oes** or **-os**) a loud domineering woman.

viral adj relating to or caused by a virus or viruses.

virgin[1] n **1** a person who has not had sexual intercourse. **2** (**the Virgin**) the Virgin Mary. ➤ **virginal** adj, **virginity** n.

virgin[2] adj **1** not having had sexual intercourse. **2** not altered by human activity. **3** of olive oil: obtained from the first pressing of olives.

Virgo n in astrology, the sixth sign of the zodiac (the Virgin).

virile adj **1** having the nature or qualities typical of a man. **2** of a man: having a strong sexual appetite. ➤ **virility** n.

virtual adj **1** essentially or nearly as described though not definitely or actually such. **2** in computing, simulating reality or the appearance of reality. ➤ **virtuality** n, **virtually** adv.

virtual reality n a computer environment in which images are produced that have the appearance of reality and can be manipulated electronically as if they were real.

virtue n **1** thought and behaviour conforming to a high moral standard. **2** a good moral quality. **3** archaic chastity, esp in a woman. * **by virtue of** because of.

virtuoso /vuhtyooh'ohsoh, -zoh/ n (pl **virtuosos** or **virtuosi**) a person who excels in musical or artistic technique. ➤ **virtuosity** n.

virtuous adj **1** having virtue; morally good. **2** archaic chaste. ➤ **virtuously** adv.

virulent adj **1** of a disease: severe and developing rapidly. **2** full of malice; malignant. **3** objectionably harsh or strong. ➤ **virulence** n, **virulently** adv.

virus n **1** a parasitic micro-organism that can cause disease. **2** informal a disease caused by a virus. **3** a piece of computer code maliciously introduced into a system to destroy programs and data.

visa n an endorsement made on a passport allowing entry into or exit from a country.

visage n literary a face or countenance.

vis-à-vis /ˌvee zah 'vee/ prep in relation to.

viscera /'visərə/ pl n the heart, liver, intestines, and other internal organs.

visceral adj **1** relating to the viscera. **2** felt or known instinctively rather than by reasoning. **3** deeply or intensely felt. ➤ **viscerally** adv.

viscose n a solution made from cellulose and used in making rayon and other fabrics.

viscosity n (pl **-ies**) **1** the state or extent of being viscous. **2** the property of a liquid or gas that enables it to resist flowing.

viscount n a member of the British peerage ranking below an earl.

viscous adj **1** sticky or glutinous. **2** having high viscosity.

vise n NAmer see VICE[2].

visibility n **1** the state of being visible. **2** the clearness of the atmosphere as revealed by the greatest distance at which prominent objects can be identified visually with the naked eye. **3** this distance. **4** capability of affording an unobstructed view.

visible adj able to be seen or perceived. ➤ **visibly** adv.

vision n **1** the power of seeing. **2** something seen. **3** a beautiful person or sight. **4** imaginative thinking about the future. **5** the picture on a television screen, or its clarity. **6** something imagined or seen in a dream or trance.

visionary[1] adj **1** showing foresight or imagination. **2** able or likely to see visions. **3** of the nature of a vision.

visionary[2] n (pl **-ies**) a visionary person.

visit[1] v (**visited, visiting**) **1** to go to be with (a person) or stay at (a place) for a time. **2** to inflict (something unpleasant) on a person or place. ➤ **visitor** n.

visit[2] n an act of visiting.

visitation n **1** an official visit, e.g. for inspection. **2** an appearance by a supernatural being. **3** a punishment regarded as coming from God. **4** a severe trial or affliction.

visor or **vizor** n **1** a movable part of a helmet that covers the face. **2** a flat sunshade attached at the top of a vehicle windscreen.

vista n a pleasing view into the distance.

visual[1] adj relating to or produced by vision. ➤ **visually** adv.

visual[2] n a photograph, graph, chart, etc used for illustration or information.

visual display unit n Brit a device that displays computer data on a screen.

visualize or **-ise** v to form a mental image of. ➤ **visualization** n.

vital adj **1** of the utmost importance; essential. **2** necessary to maintaining life. **3** full of life and vigour. ➤ **vitally** adv.

vitality n physical or mental liveliness.

vitalize or **-ise** v to give vitality to; to animate.

vital statistics pl n informal the measurements of a woman's bust, waist, and hips.

vitamin n any of various organic substances naturally present in foods and essential for the maintenance of health and growth.

vitiate v **1** to make faulty or defective. **2** to invalidate.

viticulture n the process of cultivating grapevines.

vitreous adj consisting of or resembling glass.

vitreous humour n the colourless transparent jelly that fills the eyeball behind the lens.

vitrify v (-ies, -ied) to convert into glass or a glassy substance by heat and fusion.

vitriol n **1** virulent speech or feeling. **2** concentrated sulphuric acid. ➤ **vitriolic** adj.

vituperation n harsh or abusive language. ➤ **vituperative** adj.

viva[1] /'veevə/ interj an expression of goodwill.

viva[2] /'veevə/ or **viva voce** /,veevə 'vohchi/ n an oral examination for an academic degree.

vivacious adj pleasantly lively. ➤ **vivaciously** adv, **vivacity** n.

vivarium n (pl **vivaria**) an enclosure for keeping and observing plants or animals indoors.

vivid adj **1** of a light or colour: clear and bright. **2** producing strong feelings or mental pictures. ➤ **vividly** adv, **vividness** n.

vivify v (-ies, -ied) to give vitality or interest to.

viviparous adj of an animal: producing living young rather than eggs.

vivisection n the practice of operating on living animals for scientific investigation.

vixen n **1** a female fox. **2** a scolding ill-tempered woman.

viz. abbr (Latin) videlicet = namely; in other words.

vizor n see VISOR.

V neck n a V-shaped neckline on a piece of clothing.

vocabulary n (pl **-ies**) **1** the words used in a language or activity or by an individual or group. **2** a list of words with definitions or translations.

vocal[1] adj **1** relating to the voice or speech. **2** having or exercising the power of producing voice, speech, or sound. **3** expressing opinions frankly; outspoken. **4** of music: written for or including parts for the human voice. ➤ **vocally** adv.

vocal[2] n (usu in pl) a sung part in a piece of music.

vocal cords pl n each of a pair of membranes in the throat that vibrate to produce sound.

vocalist n a singer.

vocalize or **-ise** v to speak or utter (sounds or words).

vocation n **1** a strong inner feeling that one should follow a particular activity or course of action, esp a divine call to the religious life. **2** a person's work or career. ➤ **vocational** adj.

vocative adj of a grammatical case expressing a person or thing addressed.

vociferous adj loud and insistent. ➤ **vociferously** adv.

vodka n a clear alcoholic spirit made by distilling a mash of rye or wheat.

vogue n the prevailing fashion. ➤ **voguish** adj.

voice[1] n **1** sound, in the form of speech or song, produced by forcing air from the lungs through the larynx. **2** the ability to speak. **3** the power or ability to sing. **4** a melodic part in a piece of music. **5** the use of the voice in singing or acting. **6** the expressed wish or opinion. **7** in grammar, distinction between active and passive use of a verb to indicate the relation of the subject of the verb to the action. ➤ **voiceless** adj.

voice[2] v to express in words.

voice box n the larynx.

voice mail n a system for storing telephone messages in digitalized form.

voice-over n the voice of an unseen narrator in a film or television programme.

void[1] adj **1** having no legal force. **2** empty or unoccupied. **3** vain or useless. **4** (+ of) devoid of or lacking.

void[2] n an empty space.

void[3] v **1** to nullify or annul (a contract, transaction, etc). **2** to discharge or emit (urine, excrement, etc).

voile n a fine soft sheer fabric.

volatile adj **1** readily vaporized at a low temperature. **2** unstable or explosive. **3** characterized by rapid change. ➤ **volatility** n.

vol-au-vent /'vol oh vonh/ n a round case of puff pastry filled with meat or vegetables in a sauce.

volcanic adj **1** of or produced by a volcano. **2** explosively violent.

volcano n (pl **-oes** or **-os**) a hill or mountain with an outlet at the top from which molten rock and lava may erupt from the earth's crust.

vole n a small rodent with a blunt nose and short ears.

volition n the act or power of choosing or deciding for oneself.

volley[1] n (pl **-eys**) **1** a flight of arrows, bullets, or other missiles, or the simultaneous firing of these. **2** a rapid sequence of questions or criticisms. **3** in ball games, a return of the ball before it touches the ground.

volley[2] v (-eys, -eyed) to hit (a ball) before it touches the ground.

volleyball n a team game in which players volley a ball over a high net using their hands.

volt n the SI unit of electrical potential.

voltage n an electric force measured in volts.

volte-face /,volt 'fas/ n (pl **volte-face** or **volte-faces**) a sudden reversal of attitude or policy.

voluble adj talking readily and at length. ➤ **volubility** n, **volubly** adv.

volume n **1** a book, esp one forming part of a large work. **2** space occupied as measured in cubic units. **3** the amount of something occupying a space. **4** the degree of loudness of a sound.

voluminous *adj* **1** containing a large quantity; very large. **2** of clothing: having a lot of material. **3** writing much or at great length.

voluntary[1] *adj* **1** resulting from free choice or consent. **2** acting or done without payment. ➤ **voluntarily** *adv.*

voluntary[2] *n* (*pl* **-ies**) an organ piece played before or after a religious service.

volunteer[1] *n* **1** a person who undertakes a service by free choice. **2** a person who offers to enter military service.

volunteer[2] *v* **1** to offer freely to do something. **2** to express (a remark or opinion) spontaneously.

voluptuary *n* (*pl* **-ies**) a person who enjoys luxury and sensual pleasure.

voluptuous *adj* **1** involving luxury and sensual gratification. **2** shapely and sexually attractive. ➤ **voluptuously** *adv.*

vomit[1] *v* (**vomited, vomiting**) **1** to eject the contents of the stomach through the mouth. **2** to eject violently or abundantly.

vomit[2] *n* vomited matter.

voodoo *n* (*pl* **voodoos**) a set of beliefs and rituals practised chiefly in the Caribbean and involving trance-induced contact with spirits. ➤ **voodooism** *n.*

voracious *adj* **1** having a huge appetite; ravenous. **2** excessively eager; insatiable. ➤ **voraciously** *adv*, **voracity** *n.*

vortex *n* (*pl* **vortices** or **vortexes**) a mass of whirling water or air.

votary *n* (*pl* **-ies**) **1** a devoted admirer or follower. **2** a person who has taken religious vows.

vote[1] *n* **1** the formal process of making a choice between several candidates for office or courses of action. **2** (*usu* **the vote**) the right to take part in an election.

vote[2] *v* to cast one's vote in an election. ➤ **voter** *n.*

votive *adj* offered to a deity in fulfilment of a vow.

vouch *v* (+ for) to affirm that something is true or that somebody is genuine or trustworthy.

voucher *n* a ticket that can be exchanged for specific goods or services.

vouchsafe *v* **1** to grant in a gracious or condescending manner. **2** to condescend or deign (to do something).

vow[1] *n* a solemn promise or assertion.

vow[2] *v* to promise something solemnly.

vowel *n* **1** any of a class of speech sounds, e.g. /ee/ or /i/, characterized by lack of closure in the breath channel or lack of audible friction. **2** a letter or character representing such a sound.

voyage[1] *n* a long journey by sea or air.

voyage[2] *v* to make a voyage. ➤ **voyager** *n.*

voyeur /vwah'yuh/ *n* **1** a person who gets sexual gratification from watching other people's sexual activities. **2** a person who enjoys seeing other people's suffering or distress. ➤ **voyeurism** *n*, **voyeuristic** *adj.*

vs. *abbr* versus.

V sign *n* a contemptuous gesture made by raising the index and middle fingers outwards in a V.

vulcanize or **-ise** *v* to treat (rubber or similar material) chemically to give it elasticity or strength.

vulgar *adj* **1** lacking in cultivation or taste. **2** ostentatious in one's behaviour or lifestyle. **3** lewd or indecent. ➤ **vulgarity** *n*, **vulgarly** *adv.*

vulgar fraction *n Brit* a fraction expressed by numbers above and below a line.

vulgarize or **-ise** *v* to make vulgar or less refined.

vulnerable *adj* open to being attacked or harmed. ➤ **vulnerability** *n*, **vulnerably** *adv.*

vulpine *adj* of or resembling a fox.

vulture *n* **1** a large bird of prey that feeds on carrion. **2** a predatory person.

vulva *n* the external parts of the female genital organs.

vying *v* present part. of VIE.

W¹ or **w** *n* (*pl* **W's** *or* **Ws** *or* **w's**) the 23rd letter of the English alphabet.

W² *abbr* **1** watt(s). **2** West. **3** Western.

W³ *abbr* the chemical symbol for tungsten.

wacky or **whacky** *adj* (**-ier, -iest**) *informal* absurdly or amusingly eccentric or irrational.

wad¹ *n* **1** a mass or bundle of soft material used e.g. to stop an aperture or pad a garment. **2** a roll of paper, *esp* paper money.

wad² *v* (**wadded, wadding**) **1** to form (material) into a wad. **2** to stuff, pad, or line with some soft substance.

waddle¹ *v* to walk with short steps, swinging the body from side to side.

waddle² *n* an awkward clumsy swaying gait.

wade *v* **1** to walk through water or mud. **2** (+ through) to read something lengthy and tedious. **3** *informal* (+ in/into) to attack with determination or vigour.

wader *n* **1** (*usu in pl*) a high waterproof boot. **2** a long-legged bird, e.g. a sandpiper or snipe, that wades in water in search of food.

wafer *n* **1** a thin crisp biscuit. **2** a round thin piece of unleavened bread used in the Eucharist.

waffle¹ *n* a baked cake of batter that has a crisp dimpled surface.

waffle² *v* *chiefly Brit, informal* to talk or write inconsequentially and usu at length.

waffle³ *n* *chiefly Brit, informal* empty or pretentious words.

waft¹ *v* to be conveyed lightly *esp* through the air.

waft² *n* **1** a slight breeze; a puff. **2** something, e.g. a smell, that is wafted.

wag¹ *v* (**wagged, wagging**) to move to and fro rapidly.

wag² *n* *informal* a wit or joker. ► **waggish** *adj*.

wage¹ *n* (*often in pl*) a regular payment for *esp* manual work. ► **waged** *adj*.

wage² *v* to engage in or carry on (a war, conflict, etc).

wager¹ *n* a bet.

wager² *v* (*often* + on) to bet.

waggle¹ *v* to move repeatedly from side to side or up and down.

waggle² *n* the act of waggling.

wagon or **waggon** *n* **1** a usu four-wheeled vehicle for transporting bulky or heavy loads, usu drawn by animals. **2** *Brit* a railway goods vehicle. *** on the wagon** *informal* abstaining from alcoholic drink.

wagtail *n* a bird with a very long tail that it habitually jerks up and down.

waif *n* a stray helpless person or animal, *esp* a homeless child.

wail¹ *n* **1** a loud prolonged high-pitched cry expressing grief or pain. **2** a sound suggestive of wailing.

wail² *v* to utter a wail.

wain *n* *archaic* a wagon or cart.

wainscot *n* a usu panelled wooden lining of the lower part of an interior wall.

waist *n* **1** the part of the body between the chest and hips. **2** a narrow part resembling the human waist.

waistband *n* a band, e.g. on trousers or a skirt, fitting round the waist.

waistcoat *n* *Brit* a sleeveless upper garment that fastens down the centre front, often worn as part of a man's suit.

waistline *n* the body circumference at the waist.

wait¹ *v* **1** (*often* + for) to remain stationary or refrain from beginning an activity for a period until something happens. **2** (*often* + for) to pause for somebody to catch up. **3** to be delayed or postponed. **4** to act as a waiter. *** wait on/upon** to act as an attendant to.

wait² *n* the act or a period of waiting. *** in wait** in a hidden position, *esp* in readiness to attack.

waiter or **waitress** *n* somebody who serves diners, e.g. in a restaurant.

waive *v* to refrain from demanding or enforcing (e.g. a right).

waiver *n* **1** the relinquishing of a right. **2** a document giving proof of this.

wake¹ *v* (*past tense* **woke** *or NAmer* **waked**, *past part.* **woken** *or NAmer* **waked**) **1** (*often* + up) to stop sleeping, or to rouse (somebody) from sleep. **2** (+ up) to pay more attention to what is happening or what one is doing. **3** (+ up to) to become aware of.

wake² *n* **1** a watch held over the body of a dead person. **2** festivities after a funeral.

wake³ *n* the track left by a moving body, e.g. a ship, in a fluid, e.g. water. *** in the wake of** following and as a result of.

wakeful adj **1** not sleeping or able to sleep. **2** spent without sleep. **3** alert. ➤ **wakefulness** n.

waken v (often + up) = WAKE[1].

walk[1] v **1** to move along on foot, with at least one foot always in contact with the ground. **2** to pass on foot through, along, or over (e.g. a route). **3** to take (an animal) for a walk. **4** to accompany (somebody) on foot. ✳ **walk away/off with** informal **1** to win (a prize, trophy, etc). **walk it** informal to win easily. ➤ **walker** n.

walk[2] n **1** a journey or outing on foot. **2** a manner of walking. **3** a route or path for walking. **4** a relatively slow rate of motion or progress, as of a person or horse walking. ✳ **walk of life** a person's occupation or position in society.

walking stick n a stick used as an aid to walking.

Walkman n (pl **Walkmen** or **Walkmans**) trademark a small portable cassette or CD player with earphones.

walk-on n (also **walk-on part**) a small usu nonspeaking part in a play.

walkout n **1** a strike by workers. **2** the act of leaving a meeting or organization as an expression of protest.

walk out v **1** to go on strike. **2** to depart suddenly, often as an expression of protest. ✳ **walk out on** to abandon.

walkover n an easily won contest.

walkway n a passage, path, or platform for walking.

wall[1] n **1** an upright and solid structure of stone, brick, concrete, etc serving esp as the side of a room or building or to divide an area of land. **2** in anatomy, a lining or membrane enclosing a cavity or structure. **3** something that acts as a barrier or defence. ✳ **go to the wall** informal to go bankrupt or out of business. **off the wall** NAmer unconventional. **up the wall** into a state of exasperation or unreasoning fury.

wall[2] v **1** (usu + in) to protect or surround with a wall. **2** (+ off) to separate or shut out by a wall. **3** (+ up) to close (an opening) with a wall.

wallaby n (pl **wallabies** or **wallaby**) a small or medium-sized mammal closely related to the kangaroo.

wall bars pl n horizontal parallel bars that are attached to a wall and used for gymnastic exercises.

wallet n a flat folding holder for paper money and credit and similar cards.

walleye n an eye that turns outwards, showing more than a normal amount of white. ➤ **wall-eyed** adj.

wallflower n **1** a plant that bears clusters of sweet-scented flowers in early spring. **2** informal a woman who fails to get partners at a dance.

wallop[1] v (**walloped**, **walloping**) informal **1** to hit forcefully. **2** to beat (an opponent) by a wide margin.

wallop[2] n informal a powerful blow.

wallow v **1** to roll or lie around lazily or luxuriously. **2** (+ in) to indulge oneself immoderately. **3** of a ship: to struggle laboriously in or through rough water.

wallow[2] n **1** an act of wallowing. **2** a muddy or dusty area used by animals for wallowing.

wallpaper[1] n **1** decorative paper for the walls of a room. **2** in computing, a decorative background on a monitor.

wallpaper[2] v to apply wallpaper to (the walls of a room).

wally n (pl -**ies**) Brit, informal a silly or useless person.

walnut n an edible two-lobed nut with wrinkled surface.

walrus n (pl **walruses** or **walrus**) a large northern sea mammal, related to the seal, with ivory tusks.

waltz[1] n a ballroom dance in triple time.

waltz[2] v **1** to dance a waltz. **2** to move in a casually confident or overconfident manner.

waltzer n a revolving fairground ride that moves its cars up and down as it revolves.

wan adj (**wanner**, **wannest**) **1** suggestive of poor health; pallid. **2** lacking vitality; feeble. **3** of light: dim or faint. ➤ **wanly** adv.

wand n **1** a slender rod used by conjurers and magicians. **2** a slender staff carried as a sign of office.

wander[1] v **1** to go or travel without a fixed route or destination. **2** to deviate from a course, or from what one is supposed to be saying, thinking about, etc. ➤ **wanderer** n.

wander[2] n a walk or journey without a fixed route or destination.

wanderlust n eagerness to go travelling.

wane[1] v **1** of the moon: to diminish in apparent size or intensity. **2** to decrease or decline.

wane[2] n ✳ **on the wane** in a state of decline.

wangle v to bring about or get by devious means.

wank[1] v Brit, coarse slang to masturbate.

wank[2] n Brit, coarse slang an act of masturbating.

wanker n Brit, coarse slang a foolish or unpleasant person.

want[1] v **1** to have a wish or desire for. **2** to wish or demand the presence of (somebody). **3** to feel sexual desire for. **4** (**be wanted**) to be sought by the police. **5** chiefly Brit, informal to require: This room wants decorating. **6** (often + for) to lack; to be in need of.

want[2] n **1** lack. **2** grave and extreme poverty. **3** a need or desire.

wanting adj **1** not present or available. **2** not up to the required standard. **3** lacking or deficient in.

wanton *adj* **1** sexually promiscuous. **2** gratuitously brutal or violent. ➤ **wantonly** *adv.*

WAP *abbr* Wireless Application Protocol, the technology that allows mobile phone users to send e-mails and connect to the Internet.

wapiti *n* (*pl* **wapitis** *or* **wapiti**) a large North American deer.

war[1] *n* **1** a state or period of armed hostile conflict *esp* between states or nations. **2** a struggle between opposing forces or for a particular end.

war[2] *v* (**warred, warring**) to engage in warfare.

warble *v* to sing in a pure tone with many turns and variations.

warbler *n* any of a family of small insect-eating birds, many of which are noted singers.

war crime *n* a crime committed during or in connection with war.

war cry *n* a cry or slogan used to rally warriors in battle or people to a cause.

ward *n* **1** a room in a hospital for one or usu a number of patients. **2** a division of a city, town, or other area for electoral or administrative purposes. **3** somebody under the care or control of a legal guardian. **4** a projecting ridge of metal in a lock allowing only a key with a corresponding notch to operate.

war dance *n* a dance performed as preparation for battle or in celebration of victory.

warden *n* **1** an official charged with special supervisory duties or with the enforcement of specified laws or regulations. **2** *Brit* the title of the head of some colleges or schools. **3** *NAmer* a prison governor.

warder *n* *chiefly Brit* a prison guard.

wardrobe *n* **1** a large cupboard where clothes are kept. **2** a collection of clothes, e.g. belonging to one person. **3** a collection of stage costumes and accessories.

wardroom *n* a dining or common room in a warship for commissioned officers.

ware *n* **1** manufactured articles or products of art or craft: *tinware.* **2** (*in pl*) goods for sale. **3** a specified make of pottery or china.

warehouse *n* **1** a building or room for the storage of merchandise or commodities. **2** *chiefly Brit* a large retail outlet.

warfare *n* hostilities or war.

warhead *n* the section of a missile containing the explosive charge.

warhorse *n* **1** a powerful horse used in battle. **2** *informal* a veteran soldier or public figure.

warlike *adj* **1** military; useful in war. **2** threatening; hostile.

warlock *n* a man practising black magic.

warlord *n* a military leader, *esp* a regional commander operating outside government control.

warm[1] *adj* **1** having, experiencing, or giving out moderate heat. **2** serving to maintain or preserve heat. **3** enthusiastic or cordial. **4** affectionate and outgoing in temperament. **5** of a colour: in the range yellow through orange to red. **6** in children's games: near to a goal, object, or solution sought. ➤ **warmly** *adv.*

warm[2] *v* to make or become warm. ✳ **warm to/towards** to begin to like. ➤ **warmer** *n.*

warm[3] *n* (**the warm**) a warm place or state.

warm-blooded *adj* having a relatively high and constant body temperature more or less independent of the environment.

warmonger *n* somebody who attempts to stir up war.

warmth *n* the quality of being warm in temperature or in feeling.

warm up *v* **1** to do gentle exercises before more strenuous physical activity. **2** of an engine or machine: to come to the necessary temperature for efficient working. **3** to put (an audience) into a receptive mood, e.g. before a comedy show.

warn *v* **1** to give notice to beforehand, *esp* of danger. **2** to inform (somebody) of the likely adverse consequences for them of a course of action. **3** (+ off) to order to go or stay away.

warning *n* **1** notification or a sign of a possible threat or danger. **2** a statement cautioning somebody whose actions are likely to have adverse consequences. **3** advance notice.

warp[1] *v* **1** to twist or bend (*esp* something flat or straight) out of shape. **2** to distort, *esp* by making odd or abnormal.

warp[2] *n* **1** a twist or curve that has developed in something originally flat or straight. **2** a series of yarns extended lengthways in a loom and crossed by the weft.

warrant[1] *n* **1** a commission or document giving authority, e.g. a document authorizing a police officer to make an arrest, a search, etc. **2** a document authorizing somebody to receive money, goods, etc. **3** a ground or justification; proof.

warrant[2] *v* **1** to serve as adequate ground or reason for. **2** to guarantee. ➤ **warrantable** *adj.*

warrant officer *n* an officer in the armed forces holding a rank below commissioned officers but above non-commissioned officers.

warranty *n* (*pl* **-ies**) a usu written guarantee of the soundness of a product and of the maker's responsibility for repair or replacement.

warren *n* **1** a network of burrows where rabbits live and breed. **2** a crowded district usu with a maze of narrow passageways.

warrior *n* a person engaged or experienced in warfare.

warship *n* an armed ship for use in warfare.

wart *n* a lumpy projection on the skin. ✳ **warts and all** *informal* not disguising any blemishes. ➤ **warty** *adj.*

warthog *n* an African wild pig with two pairs of rough warty lumps on its face and tusks.

wary *adj* (**-ier, -iest**) cautious and watchful so as to detect and escape danger. ➤ **warily** *adv*, **wariness** *n*.

was *v* first person and third person sing. past tense of BE.

wash[1] *v* **1** to make clean by using water and soap or detergent. **2** of water: to flow along, dash against, or overflow. **3** to carry away or deposit (something) by the force of water in motion. **4** to cover lightly with an application of a thin liquid, e.g. whitewash or watercolour. **5** *informal* to be convincing: *The story didn't wash with me.* ✳ **wash one's dirty linen in public** *informal* to reveal one's private affairs openly. **wash one's hands of** to disclaim interest in or responsibility for. ➤ **washable** *adj*.

wash[2] *n* **1** an act of washing. **2** articles, *esp* clothes, that have been or are to be washed. **3** a thin liquid used for coating or painting a surface. **4** an antiseptic or soothing lotion. **5** a disturbance in water or the air produced by the movement of a boat or an aircraft.

wash bag *n Brit* a small waterproof bag for toiletries.

washbasin *n* a basin or sink for washing the hands and face.

washboard *n* a board with a corrugated rectangular metal surface set into a wooden frame, used for scrubbing clothes when washing.

washed-out *adj* **1** faded in colour. **2** listless or exhausted.

washed-up *adj informal* no longer successful or useful.

washer *n* **1** somebody or something that washes. **2** a thin flat ring often fitted round the shank of a bolt to protect a surface when the bolt is screwed into it.

washing *n* articles, *esp* clothes, that have been or are to be washed.

washing machine *n* a machine for washing clothes and household linen.

washing powder *n* powdered detergent for use in a washing machine.

washing-up *n Brit* dishes and utensils to be washed.

washout *n informal* a failure or fiasco.

wash out *v* (**be washed out**) **1** to be cancelled because of rain. **2** *informal* to be pale and exhausted.

washroom *n NAmer, euphem* a toilet.

washstand *n* formerly, a piece of furniture used to hold a basin, jug, etc needed for washing one's face and hands.

wash up *v Brit* to wash the dishes and utensils after a meal.

wasn't *contraction* was not.

wasp *n* a slender winged insect with black and yellow stripes and an extremely painful sting.

waspish *adj* irritable or spiteful. ➤ **waspishly** *adv*.

wasp waist *n* a very narrow waist. ➤ **wasp-waisted** *adj*.

wassail[1] *n archaic* revelry; carousing.

wassail[2] *v* **1** *archaic* to carouse. **2** *Brit, dialect or archaic* to sing carols from house to house at Christmas.

wastage *n* **1** the wasteful or avoidable loss of something. **2** an amount wasted. **3** reduction in workforce numbers usu caused by individuals leaving or retiring voluntarily.

waste[1] *n* **1** the act of wasting. **2** damaged, defective, or superfluous material. **3** a sparsely settled, barren, or devastated region; a desert. ✳ **go to waste** to be squandered or wasted. **lay waste to** to destroy (a place) completely.

waste[2] *v* **1** to spend or use carelessly or inefficiently. **2** to fail to use (e.g. an opportunity). **3** (*often* + away) to lose weight, strength, substance, or vitality. **4** (**be wasted on**) to fail to be understood or appreciated by.

waste[3] *adj* **1** discarded as refuse. **2** of land: not cultivated or used; not productive.

wasted *adj informal* drunk or affected by illegal drugs.

wasteful *adj* given to or marked by careless and inefficient use of resources. ➤ **wastefully** *adv*.

wasteland *n* an area of barren, uncultivated, or uninhabited land.

wastrel *n* somebody who spends or consumes wastefully.

watch[1] *v* **1** to look at attentively. **2** to take an interest in the progress of. **3** to keep under surveillance or protective guard. **4** to be careful or cautious about. **5** (+ for) to be attentive or vigilant. ✳ **watch one's step** to proceed with care; to act or talk warily. ➤ **watchable** *adj*, **watcher** *n*.

watch[2] *n* **1** a small timepiece worn on the wrist or carried in the pocket. **2** close observation; surveillance. **3** a period of time during which a part of a ship's company is on duty while another part rests. **4** a body of firefighters or police officers working a particular shift. ✳ **keep watch** to be on duty or on guard looking out for possible danger.

watchdog *n* **1** a dog kept to guard property. **2** a person or group that guards against inefficiency, undesirable practices, etc.

watchful *adj* carefully observant or attentive. ➤ **watchfully** *adv*, **watchfulness** *n*.

watchman *n* (*pl* **watchmen**) a guard whose job is to protect a building, *esp* at night.

watch out *v* to be careful or vigilant.

watchtower *n* a tower from which a lookout can keep watch.

watchword *n* a motto that embodies a guiding principle; a slogan.

water[1] *n* **1** the colourless odourless liquid that falls as rain and forms rivers, lakes, and seas. **2** (*in pl*) a stretch of sea under the control of a specified sovereignty. **3** a watery liquid, *esp*

urine. **4** (*usu in pl*) the amniotic fluid surrounding a foetus in the womb and discharged shortly before birth. ✳ **hold water** to stand up under criticism or analysis. **water under the bridge** past events that it is futile to try to alter.
▷ **waterless** *adj*, **watery** *adj*.

water² *v* **1** to moisten, sprinkle, or soak (e.g. plants or ground) with water. **2** to supply (e.g. a horse) with water to drink. **3** to be a source of water for (an area). **4** (*often* + down) to dilute. **5** (*often* + down) to make less forceful, controversial, etc. **6** to secrete tears or saliva.

water bed *n* a bed with a water-filled plastic or rubber mattress.

water boatman *n* an aquatic bug that swims on its back moving its long hind legs like oars.

water buffalo *n* an often domesticated Asian buffalo with large horns.

water cannon *n* a device for shooting out a jet of water with great force, e.g. to disperse a crowd.

water closet *n dated* a flush toilet.

watercolour (*NAmer* **watercolor**) *n* **1** a paint made from pigment mixed with water. **2** a picture painted with watercolours.

watercourse *n* a natural or artificial channel through which water flows.

watercress *n* a cress that grows in wet places.

waterfall *n* a vertical or steep descent of the water of a river or stream.

waterfowl *n* (*pl* **waterfowls** *or* **waterfowl**) a bird, *esp* a duck, that frequents water.

waterfront *n* a section of a town bordering on a body of water.

water hole *n* a natural hollow in which water collects, used by animals as a drinking place.

water ice *n* a frozen dessert of water, sugar, and flavouring.

watering can *n* a vessel with a handle and a long spout, used for watering plants.

watering hole *n* **1** a pool where animals come to drink. **2** *informal* a pub, hotel, etc used for convivial drinking.

water lily *n* an aquatic plant with floating leaves and usu showy colourful flowers.

waterline *n* the level on the hull of a vessel to which the water comes when it is afloat.

waterlogged *adj* filled or soaked with water.

watermark *n* a marking in paper visible when the paper is held up to the light.

water meadow *n* a meadow that is regularly flooded by a bordering river.

watermelon *n* a large melon with a hard green rind and sweet watery red pulp.

water mill *n* a mill whose machinery is moved by water.

water on the brain *n informal* hydrocephalus.

water polo *n* a game played in water by teams of swimmers who try to get an inflated ball into the opposing side's goal.

waterproof¹ *adj* impervious to water.

waterproof² *n Brit* a waterproof garment.

waterproof³ *v* to make waterproof.

watershed *n* **1** a dividing ridge separating streams, rivers etc that flow into different seas. **2** a crucial turning point. **3** *Brit* the time of day before which material considered unsuitable for children should not be shown on television.

water ski *n* a board used singly or in pairs for standing on while being towed over water at speed.

water-ski *v* (**water-skis**, **water-skied** *or* **water-ski'd**, **water-skiing**) to use water skis.
▷ **water-skier** *n*, **water-skiing** *n*.

waterspout *n* a funnel-shaped column of rotating wind and spray extending from the underside of a cloud to the surface of a sea, lake, etc.

water table *n* the level below which the ground is wholly saturated with water.

watertight *adj* **1** so closely sealed that water cannot pass through. **2** of an argument: impossible to disprove.

water tower *n* a tower supporting a raised water tank to provide the necessary steady pressure to distribute water.

waterway *n* a navigable route or body of water.

waterwheel *n* **1** a wheel made to rotate by direct action of water, and used *esp* to drive machinery. **2** a wheel for raising water.

waterworks *n* (*pl* **waterworks**) the reservoirs, buildings, and equipment used to supply water e.g. to a city.

watt *n* the SI unit of power, *esp* electrical power.

wattage *n* an amount of electrical power expressed in watts.

wattle *n* **1** a framework of poles interwoven with branches or reeds and used, *esp* formerly, in building. **2** a fleshy protuberance on the head or neck of a bird.

wattle and daub *n* wattle covered with clay, used, *esp* formerly, in building construction.

wave¹ *v* **1** to move the hand or something held in the hand to and fro in greeting, as a signal, etc. **2** to sway, flutter, or swing loosely to and fro. **3** to give a curving or undulating shape to (e.g. hair).

wave² *n* **1** a moving ridge on the surface of a body of water, e.g. the sea. **2** a shape or outline that has successive curves, e.g. in the hair. **3** a surge of sensation or emotion. **4** a sudden increase or wide occurrence of a phenomenon or activity. **5** an act of waving, *esp* as a signal or greeting. **6** in physics, a periodic disturbance or variation of a physical quantity by which energy is transferred progressively from point to point. ✳ **make waves 1** *informal* to cause trouble. **2** *informal* to create a considerable, usu good, impression.

wave band *n* a band of radio frequency waves.

wavelength n the distance from the peak of one electromagnetic wave to the peak of the next. ∗ **be on somebody's/the same wavelength** to have the same outlook, views, etc as somebody else.

wavelet n a little wave.

waver v 1 to vacillate between choices. 2 to sway unsteadily to and fro; to flicker. 3 to hesitate as if about to give way; to falter. ➤ **waverer** n.

wavy adj (-ier, -iest) having a wavelike form or outline.

wax [1] n 1 = BEESWAX. 2 a malleable substance that is similar to, but harder and less greasy than, a fat, used in making candles, polishes, etc. ➤ **waxen** adj, **waxy** adj.

wax [2] v 1 to treat or rub with wax. 2 to remove hair from (a part of the body) using melted wax.

wax [3] v 1 (of the moon): to have an increasing area of the illuminated surface visible. 2 to show the emotional quality specified, esp when speaking or writing: wax lyrical. 3 literary to increase.

waxwork n 1 an effigy in wax, usu of a person. 2 (in pl) an exhibition of wax effigies.

way [1] n 1 a method or manner of doing something. 2 a characteristic manner of behaving or happening. 3 a feature or respect. 4 a course leading in a direction or towards an objective. 5 a road or path. 6 an opening one can pass through: the way in. 7 space or room, esp for forward movement. 8 the length of a course; a distance. 9 a direction or side: a one-way street. 10 (in pl) used to denote a specified number of participants: They split the money four ways. 11 motion or speed of a ship or boat through the water. ∗ **by the way** incidentally. **by way of 1** via. 2 in the form of. **get/have one's own way** to get what one wants. **have a way with** to be good at dealing with (people, animals, etc). **in a way** to some extent. **in the way** obstructing movement. **no way** informal under no circumstances. **on the way 1** while moving along a course. 2 coming or approaching. **out of the way 1** secluded or remote. 2 done or completed. **under way** in progress; started.

way [2] adv informal considerably; far. ∗ **way back** long ago.

waybill n a document giving details of the nature, destination, etc of the goods carried on a vehicle.

wayfarer n literary a traveller, esp on foot.

waylay v (past tense and past part. **waylaid**) 1 to ambush and attack. 2 to accost and detain.

way-out adj informal out of the ordinary, esp in being daring or experimental.

wayside n the side of a road.

wayward adj unpredictable and difficult to control.

WC abbr Brit water closet.

we pron referring to the speaker and others associated with the speaker.

weak adj 1 deficient in physical strength and vigour. 2 not able to exert or sustain much weight, pressure, or strain. 3 not having or exerting authority or political power. 4 unable to withstand temptation or persuasion. 5 (often + in) lacking skill or proficiency. 6 deficient in strength or flavour; diluted. ➤ **weakly** adv.

weaken v to make or become weak.

weakling n a weak person or animal.

weakness n 1 the quality of being weak. 2 a fault or defect. 3 (+ for) a special desire or fondness. 4 something one is especially fond of.

weal or **wheal** n a raised mark on the surface of the body.

wealth n 1 abundance of money and valuable material possessions. 2 the state of being rich. 3 an abundant supply.

wealthy adj (-ier, -iest) having wealth; rich.

wean v 1 to accustom (a child or other young mammal) to take food other than the mother's milk. 2 (usu + off/from) to cause to abandon a usu unwholesome dependence on something. 3 (**be weaned on**) to have been acquainted with something from an early age.

weapon n 1 an instrument of attack or defence, esp in combat. 2 a means used to further one's cause in conflict. ➤ **weaponry** n.

wear [1] v (**wore**, **worn**) 1 to have (e.g. a garment) on the body as clothing or adornment. 2 to have or show (a specified expression) on the face. 3 to damage or diminish, or be damaged or diminished, by use. 4 to endure use: The carpet is wearing well. 5 (often + on) of time: to go by slowly or tediously. ∗ **wear the trousers** to have the controlling authority in a household. **wear thin** to become weakened or exhausted. ➤ **wearer** n.

wear [2] n 1 wearing or being worn. 2 clothing, usu of a specified kind or for a special occasion: swimwear. 3 minor damage or deterioration through use.

wear down v to overcome by persistence.

wearing adj causing fatigue; tiring.

wearisome adj causing weariness; tiresome.

wear off v to lose effectiveness gradually.

wear out v 1 to make or become useless by long or excessive wear. 2 to tire or exhaust.

weary [1] adj (-ier, -iest) 1 exhausted or tired. 2 expressing or causing weariness. 3 (+ of) no longer able to endure or enjoy. ➤ **wearily** adv, **weariness** n.

weary [2] v (-ies, -ied) 1 to make weary. 2 (+ of) to become fed up with.

weasel n (pl **weasels** or **weasel**) a small slender flesh-eating mammal with a mostly reddish brown coat.

weather [1] n the prevailing atmospheric conditions with regard to heat or cold, wetness or dryness, etc. ✳ **keep a weather eye on** to remain alert to. **make heavy weather of** *informal* to have unnecessary difficulty in doing or completing. **under the weather** *informal* mildly ill or depressed.

weather² *v* **1** to come safely through (e.g. a storm). **2** to undergo, or be resistant to, change caused by exposure to wind, rain, sun, etc.

weatherboard *n* **1** any of a series of overlapping horizontal boards forming a protective outdoor wall covering. **2** a sloping board fixed to the bottom of a door for excluding rain, snow, etc. ➤ **weatherboarding** *n*.

weathercock *n* a weather vane, *esp* one in the figure of a cockerel.

weatherman *or* **weatherwoman** *n* (*pl* **weathermen** *or* **weatherwomen**) a person, *esp* a meteorologist, who reports and forecasts the weather, usu on the radio or television.

weather vane *n* a revolving pointer attached to an elevated structure in order to show the direction of the wind.

weave¹ *v* (*past tense* **wove**, *past part.* **wove** or **woven**) **1** to form cloth by interlacing warp and weft threads. **2** to produce by elaborately combining elements into a coherent whole. **3** (*usu* + in/into) to introduce as an appropriate element.

weave² *n* a pattern or method for interlacing the threads of woven fabrics.

weave³ *v* to move in a zigzag course, *esp* to avoid obstacles.

web *n* **1** the netlike structure spun by most spiders as a trap for prey. **2** an intricate structure or network. **3** (**the Web**) the World Wide Web. **4** the tissue uniting the toes of a bird or animal that lives in water.

webbed *adj* having toes joined by a web.

webbing *n* a strong narrow tape used for straps, upholstery, or harnesses.

webcam /webkam/ *n* a camera, connected to a computer, that produces images for display on a web page.

web page *n* a hypertext document that can be accessed via the World Wide Web.

website *n* a group of related web pages giving information about a particular subject, company, institution, etc.

wed *v* (**wedding**, *past tense and past part.* **wedded** *or* **wed**) **1** to marry. **2** to unite (two things).

we'd *contraction* **1** we had. **2** we would. **3** we should.

wedded *adj* **1** of marriage; conjugal. **2** (+ to) committed to.

wedding *n* **1** a marriage ceremony, usu with its accompanying festivities. **2** a wedding anniversary or its celebration.

wedge¹ *n* **1** a piece of wood, metal, etc that tapers to a thin edge. **2** a shoe with a wedge-shaped sole. **3** an iron golf club with a broad face angled for maximum loft. ✳ **thin end of**

the wedge something apparently insignificant that is the forerunner of a more important development.

wedge² *v* **1** to secure with or as if with a wedge. **2** (+ in/into) to force into a narrow space.

wedlock *n* the state of being married; marriage.

Wednesday *n* the day of the week following Tuesday.

wee¹ *adj* (**weer**, **weest**) *chiefly Scot* very small.

wee² *n* *chiefly Brit, informal* urine or an act of passing urine.

wee³ *v* (**wees**, **weed**, **weeing**) *chiefly Brit, informal* to urinate.

weed¹ *n* **1** a wild plant that grows where it is not wanted. **2** *informal* a weak or unattractively thin person. **3** (**the weed**) *informal* tobacco. **4** *informal* cannabis.

weed² *v* **1** to remove weeds. **2** (+ out) to remove (harmful or undesirable people or things).

weedkiller *n* a substance used for killing weeds.

weedy *adj* (**-ier**, **-iest**) **1** covered with or consisting of weeds. **2** *informal* weak, thin, and ineffectual.

week¹ *n* **1** a period of seven consecutive days. **2** the working days, usu Monday to Friday, during each seven-day period.

week² *adv* *chiefly Brit* at a time that is seven days after a specified day: *Tuesday week.*

weekday *n* any day of the week except Saturday and Sunday.

weekend¹ *n* Saturday and Sunday.

weekend² *v informal* to spend the weekend.

weekly *adv and adj* **1** every week. **2** once a week. **3** by the week.

weeny *adj* (**-ier**, **-iest**) *informal* tiny.

weep¹ *v* (*past tense and past part.* **wept**) **1** to express grief or other emotion by shedding tears. **2** *esp* of a wound: to exude a liquid, pus, etc slowly.

weep² *n* a period of weeping.

weepy *adj* (**-ier**, **-iest**) **1** *informal* tearful. **2** sentimental.

weevil *n* a small beetle that is harmful to grain, fruit, and plants.

weft *n* the crosswise yarn that interlaces the warp in a fabric.

weigh *v* **1** to ascertain the heaviness of. **2** to have a specified weight. **3** (*often* + out) to measure (a definite quantity of something) on scales. **4** (*often* + up) to consider carefully in order to reach a conclusion. **5** (+ down) to be a burden to. **6** to be considered important; to count. **7** (*often* + on/upon) to be oppressive or a cause of worry to. ✳ **weigh anchor** to pull up an anchor preparatory to sailing.

weighbridge *n* a large scale used for weighing vehicles.

weigh in *v* **1** of a jockey, boxer, etc: to be weighed before or after a race or match. **2**

informal to make a contribution. ➤ **weigh-in** *n*.

weight¹ *n* **1** the amount that something or somebody weighs. **2** a system of units of weight or mass. **3** any of the units used in such a system. **4** a piece of metal of known weight for use in weighing articles. **5** something heavy. **6** a heavy object used to hold or press something down. **7** a heavy object lifted as an athletic exercise or contest. **8** a burden or pressure. **9** relative importance, authority, or influence. ➤ **weightless** *adj*.

weight² *v* **1** to make heavy or hold down with a weight. **2** to arrange in such a way as to create a bias.

weighting *n* **1** an allowance made to compensate for something that has a distorting effect. **2** *Brit* an additional sum paid on top of wages or salary, *esp* to offset the higher cost of living in a particular area.

weightlifting *n* a sport that involves competitors lifting progressively heavier weights. ➤ **weightlifter** *n*.

weighty *adj* (**-ier, -iest**) **1** having importance, influence, or consequence. **2** heavy.

weir *n* a low dam in a watercourse to control its flow.

weird *adj* **1** suggestive of or caused by the supernatural. **2** *informal* very strange or bizarre. ➤ **weirdly** *adv*, **weirdness** *n*.

weirdo *n* (*pl* **-os**) *informal* somebody who is very strange or eccentric.

welch *v* see WELSH.

welcome¹ *n* a greeting or reception on arrival or first appearance.

welcome² *adj* **1** received gladly into one's presence or companionship. **2** received gratefully, *esp* because fulfilling a need. **3** (+ to) willingly permitted to do or have something. ✳ **you're welcome** used as a reply to an expression of thanks.

welcome³ *v* **1** to greet (somebody) hospitably and with courtesy. **2** to receive or accept (something) with pleasure.

weld¹ *v* **1** to fuse (metallic parts) together by heating and/or hammering. **2** to unite closely or inseparably. ➤ **welder** *n*.

weld² *n* a welded joint.

welfare *n* **1** well-being. **2** aid in the form of money or necessities for those not able to provide for themselves.

welfare state *n* a social system in which the state assumes responsibility for the provision of pensions, benefits, health care, etc to its citizens.

well¹ *adv* (**better, best**) **1** in a good or proper manner. **2** with skill. **3** in a kind or friendly manner. **4** in a prosperous or affluent manner. **5** thoroughly or fully. **6** with good reason. **7** much or considerably. **8** in all likelihood; indeed. ✳ **as well 1** also; in addition. **2** with an

effect that is the same or preferable. **well out of** *informal* lucky to be free from or not involved in. **well up on** *informal* very knowledgeable about.

Usage Note: Adjectives such as *well-known, well-mannered*, etc should always be spelt with a hyphen when used before a noun: *a well-known story*. The hyphen is not usually necessary when the adjective is used after a verb: *As is probably well known to most of you…*

well² *adj* (**better, best**) **1** healthy, *esp* cured or recovered. **2** satisfactory or pleasing. **3** advisable or desirable. ➤ **wellness** *n*.

well³ *interj* **1** used to express surprise, indignation, or resignation. **2** used to indicate a pause in talking or to introduce a remark.

well⁴ *n* **1** a pit, shaft, or hole sunk in the earth to reach a supply of water or a natural deposit, e.g. oil or gas. **2** a space or hole made to contain liquid. **3** a source from which something springs. **4** an open space extending vertically through the floors of a structure, e.g. for stairs or a lift.

well⁵ *v* **1** (*often* + up) of liquid: to rise to the surface. **2** (*often* + up) of emotion: to arise within one.

we'll *contraction* **1** we will. **2** we shall.

well-advised *adj* acting with or showing wisdom; prudent.

well-appointed *adj* having good and complete facilities, furniture, etc.

well-behaved *adj* showing proper manners or conduct.

well-being *n* the state of being happy, healthy, or prosperous.

well-disposed *adj* having a favourable or sympathetic attitude.

well done *interj* used to express congratulations.

well-done *adj* of food, *esp* meat: cooked thoroughly.

well-heeled *adj informal* wealthy.

wellington *or* **wellington boot** *n Brit* a waterproof rubber boot usu reaching to the knee.

well-nigh *adv literary* almost or nearly.

well-off *adj* **1** prosperous or rich. **2** in a favourable situation. **3** (*usu* + for) well provided.

well-spoken *adj* speaking clearly, courteously, and usu with a refined accent.

well-to-do *adj* rich; prosperous.

well-wisher *n* somebody who feels or expresses goodwill towards a person, cause, etc.

welly *or* **wellie** *n Brit, informal* **1** = WELLINGTON. **2** power or effort.

Welsh *n* **1** (**the Welsh**) (*in pl*) the people of Wales. **2** the Celtic language spoken in Wales. ➤ **Welsh** *adj*.

welsh *or* **welch** *v* (*usu* + on) to evade an obligation, *esp* payment of a debt.

Welsh rarebit *n* a snack of melted cheese, mixed with seasonings, on toast.

welt *n* **1** a strip, usu of leather, fastening the sole of a shoe to the upper. **2** a weal.

welter *n* a chaotic mass or jumble.

welterweight *n* a weight in boxing and wrestling between lightweight and middleweight.

wench *n archaic or humorous* a young woman.

wend *v* to proceed on (one's way), often at a leisurely pace.

wendy house *n* (*often* **Wendy house**) *chiefly Brit* a toy house for children to play in.

went *v* past tense of GO¹.

wept *v* past tense and past part. of WEEP¹.

were *v* second person sing. past, plural past, and past subjunctive of BE.

we're *contraction* we are.

weren't *contraction* were not.

werewolf /ˈweǝwoolf, ˈwiǝwoolf/ *n* (*pl* **werewolves**) in folklore, a person who periodically transforms into a wolf.

west¹ *n* **1** the direction of sunset, 180° from east. **2** regions or countries lying to the west. **3** (*usu* **the West**) Europe and North America. ➤ **westbound** *adj and adv*.

west² *adj and adv* **1** at or towards the west. **2** of the wind: blowing from the west.

westerly *adj and adv* **1** in a western position or direction. **2** of a wind: blowing from the west.

western¹ *adj* **1** in or towards the west. **2** (*often* **Western**) of Europe or North America.

western² *n* a novel, film, etc dealing with cowboys, frontier life, etc in the western USA.

Westerner *n* a person from the western part of a country or from Europe or North America.

westernize *or* **-ise** *v* to cause to adopt the culture, economics, politics, etc of North America or Europe.

westward *adv and adj* towards the west; in a direction going west. ➤ **westwards** *adv*.

wet¹ *adj* (**wetter, wettest**) **1** covered or soaked with liquid, e.g. water. **2** of weather: rainy. **3** of paint, cement, etc: not yet dry or set. **4** *Brit, informal* of a person: feeble, ineffectual, or dull. ✳ **wet behind the ears** *informal* immature or inexperienced. ➤ **wetly** *adv*, **wetness** *n*.

wet² *n* **1** moisture or wetness. **2** (**the wet**) rainy weather. **3** *Brit, informal* a feeble, ineffectual, or dull person.

wet³ *v* (**wetting**, *past tense and past part.* **wet** *or* **wetted**) **1** to make wet. **2** to urinate in or on.

wet blanket *n informal* a person who spoils other people's fun, e.g. by a lack of enthusiasm.

wether *n* a castrated male sheep.

wet nurse *n* a woman who breastfeeds a child she did not give birth to.

wet suit *n* a close-fitting rubber suit that retains body heat so as to insulate its wearer in cold water.

we've *contraction* we have.

whack¹ *v informal* **1** to strike with a sharp or resounding blow. **2** to defeat. **3** to place or insert roughly, casually, or quickly.

whack² *n informal* **1** a sharp resounding blow. **2** *Brit* a portion or share. ✳ **top/full whack** *chiefly Brit* the maximum amount.

whacked *adj informal* exhausted.

whacking *adj Brit, informal* enormous.

whacky *adj* see WACKY.

whale *n* (*pl* **whales** *or* **whale**) a very large sea mammal with a tail modified as a paddle. ✳ **have a whale of a time** to have an exceptionally enjoyable time.

whalebone *n* a horny substance found in two rows of plates along the upper jaw of some whales.

whaler *n* a person or ship engaged in whaling.

whaling *n* the occupation of catching whales for oil, food, etc.

whammy *n* (*pl* **-ies**) *informal* something that has a bad effect.

wharf *n* (*pl* **wharves** *or* **wharfs**) a structure built along the shore of navigable water so that ships may load and unload.

what¹ *pron and adj* (*pl* **what**) **1** used to ask about the identity, nature, purpose, occupation, etc of something or somebody. **2** used to ask for repetition of something not properly heard or understood. **3** used to express surprise or excitement. **4** whatever. ✳ **what about** used to make suggestions. **what if** what will or would be the result if. **what of it** what does it matter. **what's his/her/its name** used to replace a forgotten name. **what's what** the true state of things.

what² *adv* in what respect?; how much?

whatever¹ *pron* **1** anything or everything that. **2** no matter what. **3** *informal* used for emphasis in place of the interrogative adverb *what*.

whatever² *adj* **1** no matter what. **2** of any kind at all.

whatnot *n informal* other usu related goods, objects, etc.

whatsoever *pron and adj* whatever.

wheat *n* a cereal grass whose grain yields a fine white flour.

wheatear *n* a small white-rumped bird related to the thrush.

wheat germ *n* the central part of the wheat kernel used *esp* as a source of vitamins.

wheatmeal *n* brown flour made from wheat with some bran and germ taken out.

wheedle *v* **1** to use soft words or flattery. **2** to influence, persuade, or entice by wheedling. ➤ **wheedler** *n*.

wheel¹ *n* **1** a solid circular disc, or a circular frame joined to a central hub by spokes, that is capable of turning on an axle. **2** (**the wheel**) the wheel that controls the steering of a ship or vehicle. **3** a curving or circular movement.

wheel² v **1** to move in a circle or curve. **2** to turn round to face in the opposite direction. **3** to push (a wheeled vehicle). **4** to convey or move in a wheeled vehicle. * **wheel and deal** to pursue one's own commercial interests, *esp* in a shrewd or unscrupulous manner.

wheelbarrow n a load-carrying device consisting of a shallow box supported at one end by a wheel and at the other by legs.

wheelbase n the distance between the front and rear axles of a vehicle.

wheelchair n a chair mounted on wheels for disabled people or invalids.

wheeler-dealer n a shrewd operator, *esp* in business or politics.

wheel out v *informal* to resort to with tedious regularity.

wheeze¹ v **1** to breathe with difficulty, usu with a whistling sound. **2** to make a sound like that of wheezing.

wheeze² n **1** a sound of wheezing. **2** *Brit, informal* a clever scheme. ➤ **wheezy** *adj*.

whelk n a large usu edible sea snail.

whelp¹ n **1** a young dog. **2** a disagreeable or impudent young man.

whelp² v to give birth to (e.g. a puppy).

when¹ *adv* **1** at what time? **2** at or during which time.

when² *conj* **1** at or during the time that. **2** as soon as. **3** whenever. **4** in the event that; if. **5** considering that. **6** although.

whence *adv and conj formal* **1** from which place, source, or cause. **2** to the place from which.

whenever¹ *or* **whensoever** *conj* **1** at every or whatever time. **2** in any circumstance.

whenever² *adv informal* used for emphasis in place of the interrogative adverb *when*.

where¹ *adv* **1** at, in, or to what place? **2** at, in, or to what situation, direction, or respect? **3** at, in, or to which.

where² *conj* **1** at, in, or to the place at which. **2** wherever. **3** in a case, situation, or respect in which. **4** whereas.

whereabouts¹ *adv and conj* in what vicinity.

whereabouts² *pl n* the place or general locality where a person or thing is.

whereas *conj* **1** while on the contrary. **2** in view of the fact that; since.

whereby *conj formal* by which means.

wherefore *adv formal* **1** why. **2** therefore.

wherein *adv formal* **1** in what respect. **2** in which.

whereof *conj, pron, and adv formal* of what, which, or whom.

whereupon *adv and conj* closely following which.

wherever¹ *adv* used for emphasis in place of the interrogative adverb *where*.

wherever² *or* **wheresoever** *conj* at, in, or to every or whatever place.

wherewithal n means or resources, *esp* money.

wherry n (*pl* **-ies**) a light rowing boat or barge.

whet v (**whetted, whetting**) **1** to sharpen (a blade). **2** to stimulate.

whether *conj* **1** used to indicate an indirect question involving alternatives. **2** used to indicate a choice between two alternatives. **3** used to indicate indifference between alternatives.

whetstone n a stone for sharpening an edge, e.g. of a chisel.

whey n the watery part of milk separated from the curd.

which¹ *adj* **1** used to ask for identification of one or ones out of a known or limited group. **2** whichever.

which² *pron* (*pl* **which**) **1** which thing, person, etc. **2** whichever. **3** used to introduce a nonrestrictive clause, *esp* in reference to an animal, thing, or idea.

whichever *pron and adj* (*pl* **whichever**) **1** any one or ones out of a group. **2** no matter which.

whiff¹ n **1** a slight or passing odour. **2** *Brit, informal* an unpleasant smell. **3** a quick puff or slight gust. **4** a slight trace.

whiff² v *Brit, informal* to smell unpleasant.

Whig n a member of a British political party of the 18th and early 19th centuries seeking to limit royal authority and increase parliamentary power.

while¹ n a period of time. * **a while** for some time. **worth one's while** worth the time and effort used.

while² *conj* **1** during the time that. **2** providing that; as long as. **3** when on the other hand; whereas. **4** although.

while away v to pass (time) in a leisurely and usu pleasant manner.

whilst *conj chiefly Brit* while.

whim n a sudden, capricious, or eccentric idea or impulse.

whimper v to make a low plaintive whining sound. ➤ **whimper** n.

whimsical *adj* **1** resulting from or suggesting whimsy. **2** full of whims; capricious. ➤ **whimsically** *adv*.

whimsy *or* **whimsey** n (*pl* **-ies** *or* **-eys**) **1** an amusingly or quaintly fanciful quality, *esp* in writing or art. **2** a whim or caprice.

whin n = GORSE.

whine¹ v **1** to utter a prolonged high-pitched cry, usu expressive of distress or pain, or make a sound resembling such a cry. **2** to complain querulously or peevishly.

whine² n a whining sound. ➤ **whiny** *adj*.

whinge¹ v (**whinges, whingeing, whinged**) *Brit, informal* to complain or moan. ➤ **whinger** n.

whinge² n *Brit, informal* a complaint.

whinny v (**-ies, -ied**) to utter a low gentle neigh or similar sound. ➤ **whinny** n.

whip¹ n **1** an instrument consisting of a flexible leather strip or cord attached to a handle, used for driving animals and for punishment. **2** somebody appointed by a political party to enforce party discipline and secure the attendance of party members for important votes. **3** Brit an instruction from a whip to be in attendance for voting. **4** a dessert made by whipping some of the ingredients. * **the whip hand** the advantage.

whip² v (**whipped, whipping**) **1** to strike (a person or animal) with a whip. **2** to beat (e.g. eggs or cream) into a froth. **3** to thrash about flexibly like a whiplash. **4** to take, pull, or move very quickly and forcefully. **5** Brit, informal to steal. ➤ **whipping** n.

whiplash n **1** the flexible part of a whip. **2** injury to the neck resulting from a sudden sharp movement, e.g. in a car collision.

whippersnapper n informal an insignificant but impudent person, esp a child.

whippet n a dog of a small slender short-haired breed related to the greyhound.

whipping boy n a person who is blamed or punished for the mistakes, incompetence, etc of others.

whippoorwill /wipəwil/ n a North American nightjar.

whip-round n Brit, informal a collection of money used usu for a benevolent purpose.

whip up v **1** to stir up or stimulate. **2** to produce in a hurry.

whirl¹ v **1** to turn abruptly or rapidly round on an axis. **2** of the head: to become giddy or dizzy.

whirl² n **1** a rapid rotating or circling movement. **2** a rapid succession of events, engagements, etc. **3** a confused or disturbed state. **4** informal a try.

whirligig n **1** a child's toy, e.g. a top, that whirls. **2** a merry-go-round.

whirlpool n **1** a circular eddy of rapidly moving water. **2** a bath equipped with a device to produce whirling currents of hot water.

whirlwind¹ n **1** a small rapidly rotating windstorm. **2** a confused rush; a whirl.

whirlwind² adj happening with great speed or suddenness: a whirlwind romance.

whirr¹ or **whir** v (**whirred, whirring**) to revolve or move with a continuous buzzing sound.

whirr² or **whir** n a whirring sound.

whisk¹ n **1** a small usu hand-held kitchen utensil used for beating food until frothy. **2** a small bunch of flexible strands, e.g. twigs or feathers, attached to a handle for use as a brush.

whisk² v **1** to mix or beat (e.g. egg whites) with a whisk. **2** to convey or remove briskly. **3** to flick.

whisker n **1** a long projecting hair or bristle growing near the mouth of an animal. **2** (in pl) the hair of a man's beard or moustache. **3** (a

whisker) informal a very small amount or narrow margin. ➤ **whiskery** adj.

whisky (NAmer and Irish **whiskey**) n (pl -ies) a spirit made by distilling barley or other grain.

whisper¹ v **1** to speak softly. **2** to make a hissing or rustling sound.

whisper² n **1** a very soft speaking voice or something spoken very softly. **2** a hissing or rustling sound. **3** a rumour. **4** a hint or trace.

whist n a card game scored by winning tricks.

whistle¹ n **1** a device with a slit through which air, steam, the breath, etc is forced to produce a loud high-pitched sound. **2** a shrill clear sound produced by forcing air through pursed lips or by a whistle. * **blow the whistle on** informal to report (a person acting wrongly or a wrong act) to an authority.

whistle² v **1** to make a shrill clear sound by blowing or drawing air through the puckered lips. **2** to make a whistling sound by rapid movement. **3** to blow a whistle.

whistle-blower n informal somebody who reveals or reports wrongdoing.

whistle-stop adj consisting of brief stops in several places.

Whit n Whitsuntide.

whit n * **not a whit** not in the smallest degree; not a bit.

white¹ adj **1** of the colour of new snow or milk. **2** very pale. **3** of wine: having a light yellow or amber colour. **4** Brit of coffee or tea: containing milk or cream. **5** of flour, sugar, etc: refined and white in colour. **6** relating to people having pale skin colour. **7** free from moral impurity. **8** of a wedding: in which the bride wears a white dress. * **bleed white** to deprive eventually of all money or resources. ➤ **whiteness** n.

white² n **1** a white colour or fabric. **2** the mass of albumin-containing material surrounding the yolk of an egg. **3** the white part of the ball of the eye. **4** a person belonging to a light-skinned people.

whitebait n the young of a herring or sprat eaten whole.

white-collar adj relating to non-manual employees, esp those who work in offices.

white elephant n a possession that is troublesome to maintain or no longer of value to its owner.

white feather n a symbol of cowardice.

white flag n a flag of plain white used to request a truce or as a token of surrender.

white goods pl n **1** major articles of household equipment, e.g. cookers and refrigerators. **2** household linen.

white-hot adj glowing white with heat.

white lie n a harmless or unimportant lie, e.g. told to avoid hurting somebody's feelings.

white magic n magic used for good purposes.

whiten v to become or make white. ➤ **whitener** n.

white noise *n* low-volume sound that has many continuous frequencies of equal intensity.

White Paper *n* a British government report containing information about or proposals on a particular issue.

white sauce *n* a sauce made with flour, butter, and milk or a chicken or fish stock.

white spirit *n* a flammable liquid distilled from petroleum and used as a solvent and thinner for paints.

whitewash[1] *n* **1** a liquid mixture, e.g. of lime and water, for whitening *esp* exterior walls. **2** a deliberate concealment of a mistake or fault.

whitewash[2] *v* **1** to apply whitewash to (e.g. a wall). **2** to gloss over or cover up (e.g. a mistake or fault).

whither *adv and conj formal or archaic* **1** to or towards what place? **2** to the place at, in, or to which. **3** what does the future hold for?

whiting *n* (*pl* **whiting**) a seafish related to the cod.

Whitsun *n* Whitsuntide.

Whit Sunday *n* a Christian feast commemorating the descent of the Holy Spirit at Pentecost, observed on the seventh Sunday after Easter.

Whitsuntide *n* the week beginning with Whit Sunday.

whittle *v* **1** to shape (wood) by cutting off chips from its surface. **2** (+ down/away) to reduce, remove, or destroy gradually.

whizz[1] *or* **whiz** *v* **1** to speed through the air with a buzzing, whirring, or hissing sound. **2** *informal* to move or go swiftly.

whizz[2] *or* **whiz** *n* **1** a whizzing sound. **2** (*also* **wiz**) *informal* somebody who is very clever or skilful.

whizz kid *or* **whiz kid** *n* a person who is unusually clever or successful, *esp* at an early age.

WHO *abbr* World Health Organization.

who *pron* (*pl* **who**) **1** what or which person? **2** used to introduce a restrictive or non-restrictive clause in reference to a person or people.

whoa /woh-ə, woh/ *interj* used as a command, e.g. to a horse, to stand still.

who'd *contraction* **1** who would. **2** who had.

whodunit *or* **whodunnit** *n* a play, film, or story dealing with the detection of crime or criminals.

whoever *or* **whosoever** *pron* **1** whatever person. **2** no matter who. **3** *informal* used for emphasis in place of the interrogative pronoun *who*.

whole[1] *adj* **1** each or all of; total or entire. **2** having all its proper constituents: *whole milk*. **3** unhurt or intact. ➤ **wholeness** *n*.

whole[2] *n* something that is complete in itself or that results from putting all the required component parts together. ✳ **as a whole** considered all together or in general. **on the whole 1** all things considered. **2** in most instances.

whole[3] *adv* in an undivided piece or state.

wholefood *n* (*also in pl*) food in a simple and natural form that has undergone minimal processing and refining.

wholehearted *adj* earnestly committed or devoted. ➤ **wholeheartedly** *adv.*

wholemeal *adj* of bread or flour: produced from ground entire wheat kernels.

wholesale[1] *n* the sale of commodities in large quantities usu for resale by a retailer.

wholesale[2] *adj and adv* **1** selling or sold by wholesale. **2** on a large scale, *esp* without discrimination.

wholesale[3] *v* to sell (commodities) by wholesale. ➤ **wholesaler** *n.*

wholesome *adj* promoting health of body or mind.

wholly *adv* **1** completely. **2** solely.

Usage Note: Note that the spelling is *wholly* and not *wholely*.

whom *pron* used in place of *who*, as the object of a verb or preposition.

whoop[1] /woohp/ *n* a loud yell of eagerness or jubilation.

whoop[2] *v* to utter or make a whoop. ✳ **whoop it up** *informal* to celebrate riotously.

whoopee[1] *interj informal* used to express exuberance.

whoopee[2] *n* ✳ **make whoopee 1** *informal* to celebrate noisily. **2** *informal* to have sexual intercourse.

whooper swan /'hoohpə/ *n* a European swan with a loud ringing call.

whooping cough /'hoohping/ *n* an infectious bacterial disease, *esp* of children, marked by a convulsive spasmodic cough followed by a crowing intake of breath.

whoops *interj* used to express dismay or apology, *esp* on being clumsy or making a silly mistake.

whoosh *or* **woosh** *v* to move quickly with a rushing sound. ➤ **whoosh** *n.*

whopper *n informal* **1** something unusually large or extreme of its kind. **2** a blatant lie.

whopping *adj informal* extremely big.

whore /haw/ *n* a prostitute or a promiscuous woman. ➤ **whorish** *adj.*

whorehouse *n informal* a brothel.

whorl /wuhl, wawl/ *n* **1** an arrangement of similar parts, e.g. leaves, in a circle round a stem. **2** something spiral in form or movement. **3** a single turn of a spiral.

who's *contraction* **1** who is. **2** who has.

Usage Note: Do not confuse this word with *whose*.

whose *adj and pron* of whom or which, *esp* as possessor or object of an action.

why[1] *adv* for what cause, reason, or purpose? ✳ **why not** used in making a suggestion.

why[2] *conj* **1** the cause, reason, or purpose for which. **2** on which grounds.

why[3] *interj* used to express mild surprise, approval, disapproval, or anger.

wick *n* a cord or strip of material through which a liquid, e.g. paraffin, oil, or melted wax, is drawn up for burning in a candle, lamp, etc. ✳ **get on somebody's wick** *Brit, informal* to annoy or irritate somebody.

wicked *adj* **1** morally bad; evil. **2** disposed to mischief. **3** very unpleasant, vicious, or dangerous. **4** *informal* extremely stylish or skilful; good. ➤ **wickedly** *adv*, **wickedness** *n*.

wicker *n* interlaced twigs, canes, or rods used to make baskets, furniture, etc. ➤ **wickerwork** *n*.

wicket *n* **1** in cricket, either of the two sets of stumps at which the ball is bowled. **2** a small gate or door.

wicketkeeper *n* in cricket, the fielder who is stationed behind the wicket.

wide[1] *adj* **1** having great horizontal extent; broad; vast. **2** having a specified width. **3** fully opened. **4** embracing much; comprehensive. **5** extending over a considerable range. **6** deviating from a target or from something specified. ➤ **widely** *adv*.

wide[2] *adv* **1** over a great horizontal distance or extent. **2** to the fullest extent. **3** so as to leave much space or distance between. **4** so as to miss by a considerable distance.

wide-awake *adj* **1** fully awake. **2** alert and watchful.

wide boy *n Brit, informal* a man who is involved in petty crime.

wide-eyed *adj* **1** amazed or astonished. **2** naive.

widen *v* to become or make wider.

widespread *adj* widely distributed or prevalent.

widgeon *n* see WIGEON.

widget *n informal* a small usu mechanical device whose name is unknown or irrelevant.

widow[1] *n* a woman whose husband has died and who has not remarried.

widow[2] *v* (**be widowed**) to become a widow or widower.

widower *n* a man whose wife has died and who has not remarried.

width *n* **1** the measurement taken at right angles to the length. **2** largeness of extent or scope.

widthways *adv* in the direction of the width; crosswise.

wield *v* **1** to handle (a tool or object) effectively. **2** to exert or exercise (power or influence).

Usage Note: Note the spelling with -ie-.

wife *n* (*pl* **wives**) a married woman, *esp* in relation to her husband. ➤ **wifely** *adj*.

wig *n* a manufactured covering of natural or synthetic hair for the head.

wigeon *or* **widgeon** *n* (*pl* **wigeons** *or* **wigeon**) a freshwater dabbling duck, the male of which has a chestnut head.

wiggle[1] *v* to move or cause to move from side to side or up and down with short jerky movements.

wiggle[2] *n* a wiggling movement. ➤ **wiggly** *adj*.

wigwam *n* a conical or dome-shaped framework of poles covered with bark, rush mats, or hides, used formerly by Native Americans as a dwelling.

wild[1] *adj* **1** living or growing in a natural state. **2** of land: not inhabited or cultivated. **3** uncontrolled or unruly. **4** *informal* (*usu* + about) passionately eager or enthusiastic. **5** *informal* very angry; infuriated. **6** not sensible or well-founded. ➤ **wildly** *adv*, **wildness** *n*.

wild[2] *n* **1** (**the wild**) a wild, free, or natural state. **2** (**the wilds**) remote country.

wild card *n* **1** a playing card able to represent any card designated by the holder. **2** an irregular or unpredictable person or thing. **3** in computing, a character that can be used, e.g. in searching, to represent any character or string of characters.

wildcat *n* (*pl* **wildcats** *or* **wildcat**) a cat living in the wild that resembles but is heavier than the domestic cat.

wildcat strike *n* a strike initiated suddenly by a group of workers without union approval.

wildebeest /'wildəbeest, 'vil-/ *n* (*pl* **wildebeests** *or* **wildebeest**) = GNU.

wilderness *n* **1** a region or area that is uncultivated and uninhabited by human beings. **2** the state of exclusion from office or power.

wildfire *n* ✳ **spread like wildfire** to spread very rapidly.

wildfowl *n* (*pl* **wildfowl**) a game bird, *esp* a waterfowl.

wild goose chase *n* a hopeless pursuit after something unattainable.

wildlife *n* the wild animals, birds, and insects of an area collectively.

wile *n* (*usu* in *pl*) a deceitful trick or stratagem.

wilful (*NAmer* **willful**) *adj* **1** deliberate. **2** obstinately and often perversely insisting on having one's own way. ➤ **wilfully** *adv*, **wilfulness** *n*.

will[1] *v* (third person sing. present tense **will**, past tense **would**) **1** used to express an action or state in the future. **2** used to express intention or determination. **3** used to express willingness or consent. **4** used to express a request or invitation. **5** used to express capability. **6** *formal, literary* to wish or desire.

will[2] *n* **1** a mental power by which one controls one's wishes, choices, intentions, etc or initiates action. **2** a desire, wish, or intention. **3** willpower; self-control. **4** a legal declaration of the manner in which somebody wishes to have their property disposed of after their death. ✻ **at will** as one wishes. **with the best will in the world** no matter how good one's intentions are.

will[3] *v* **1** (+ to) to bequeath (property) to somebody. **2** to decree or ordain. **3** to cause or attempt to cause by exercise of the will. ➤ **willer** *n*.

willies *pl n* (**the willies**) *informal* a feeling of nervousness or fear.

willing *adj* **1** consenting, ready, or eager to do something. **2** done or given without reluctance. ➤ **willingly** *adv*.

will-o'-the-wisp *n* **1** a phosphorescent light sometimes seen at night over marshy ground and often caused by the combustion of gas from decomposed organic matter. **2** an enticing but elusive goal.

willow *n* a tree with pliant branches bearing catkins of flowers with no petals.

willowy *adj* of a person: gracefully tall and slender.

willpower *n* self-control and resoluteness.

willy or **willie** *n* (*pl* **-ies**) *Brit, informal* a penis.

willy-nilly *adv* **1** whether one wants to or not. **2** in a haphazard or random manner.

wilt[1] *v* **1** of a plant: to lose freshness and become limp. **2** of a person: to grow weak, tired, or faint.

wilt[2] *n* a disease of plants marked by wilting.

wily *adj* (**-ier, -iest**) crafty.

wimp *n informal* a weak, ineffectual, or cowardly person. ➤ **wimpish** *adj*, **wimpy** *adj*.

wimple *n* a cloth covering worn over the head and round the neck and chin by women in the late medieval period and by some nuns.

win[1] *v* (**winning**, *past tense and past part.* **won**) **1** to gain the victory in a battle, contest, or dispute. **2** to gain (a prize) in a contest. **3** to get possession of. **4** (+ over/round) to gain the approval of or persuade somebody. ➤ **winnable** *adj*.

win[2] *n* a victory or success in a game or sporting contest.

wince *v* to shrink back or grimace involuntarily, e.g. in pain. ➤ **wince** *n*.

winceyette *n Brit* a lightweight cotton fabric with a nap.

winch[1] *n* a machine for hoisting or pulling by means of a rope or chain wound round a rotating drum.

winch[2] *v* to hoist or pull with a winch.

wind[1] *n* **1** a natural horizontal movement of air. **2** breath or the ability to breathe. **3** *Brit* gas generated in the stomach or the intestines. **4** musical wind instruments collectively. ✻ **get**

wind of to hear a rumour of. **in the wind** about to happen. **put the wind up somebody** *Brit, informal* to scare or frighten somebody. **take the wind out of somebody's sails 1** to frustrate somebody by anticipating or forestalling them. **2** to make somebody less confident or self-important. ➤ **windy** *adj*.

wind[2] *v* **1** to make short of breath. **2** *Brit* to help (a baby) to bring up wind after feeding.

wind[3] *v* (*past tense and past part.* **wound**) **1** to have a twisting or spiralling course. **2** to pass round an object or central core so as to encircle it, *esp* repeatedly. **3** to tighten the spring of (a clock, watch, etc), e.g. by turning a key, to make it operate. **4** to put into the specified state or position by winding: *Wind the video back to the beginning.* ➤ **winding** *adj*.

windbag *n informal* an excessively talkative person.

windbreak *n* something, e.g. a line of trees or a screen, that gives protection from the force of the wind.

windcheater *n chiefly Brit* a windproof coat or jacket, fitting closely at the neck, waist, and cuffs.

wind down *v* **1** *informal* to become gradually more relaxed. **2** of a clockwork mechanism: to become slower because of decreasing tension in the spring. **3** to bring to an end gradually.

windfall *n* **1** a fruit blown down by the wind. **2** an unexpected gain or advantage.

wind instrument *n* a musical instrument, e.g. a trumpet or clarinet, sounded by the player's breath.

windlass *n* a winch used on a ship, e.g. to raise the anchor.

windmill *n* **1** a mill operated by vanes that are turned by the wind. **2** a similar structure using wind power to generate electricity, pump water, etc.

window *n* **1** an opening in the wall of a building, side of a vehicle, etc to let in light and air, usu fitted with glass. **2** a transparent panel in an envelope. **3** in computing, a rectangular area on the screen within which a separate file can be displayed. **4** a brief time available for something.

window dressing *n* **1** the act of arranging a display of merchandise in a shop window. **2** the act of presenting or emphasizing the more attractive features of something in order to gain acceptance for it.

windowpane *n* a panel of glass forming part of a window.

window-shop *v* to look at the displays in shop windows without intending to buy anything. ➤ **window-shopper** *n*, **window-shopping** *n*.

windowsill *n* the shelf at the bottom of a window.

windpipe *n* = TRACHEA.

windscreen n Brit a transparent screen at the front of a motor vehicle.

windshield n NAmer = WINDSCREEN.

windsock n a cloth cone mounted on a pole, used to indicate the direction of the wind, esp at an airfield.

windsurfing n the sport of riding across water on a sailboard. ➤ **windsurfer** n.

windswept adj exposed to strong winds.

wind tunnel n a tunnel-like apparatus through which air is blown to test the aerodynamic properties of an object placed inside it.

wind up v 1 to bring to a conclusion. 2 to bring (a business) to an end by liquidation. 3 Brit, informal to deceive playfully; to tease. 4 informal to arrive in a place, situation, or condition at the end of a course of action.

windward adj and adv facing the direction from which the wind is blowing: compare LEE-WARD.

wine[1] n an alcoholic drink made from fermented grape juice.

wine[2] v ✳ **wine and dine** to entertain with good food and wine.

wine bar n an establishment serving wine and usu food for consumption on the premises.

wine cellar n 1 a room for storing wines. 2 a stock of wines.

winery n (pl **-ies**) a wine-making establishment.

wing[1] n 1 one of a pair of movable feathered or membranous appendages that enable a bird, bat, or insect to fly. 2 either of the horizontal structures projecting from the sides of an aircraft, which provide lift and stability. 3 a part of a building projecting from the main or central part. 4 a group or faction within an organized body, e.g. a political party. 5 (in pl) the area at the sides of a theatre stage out of sight of the audience. 6 the section near the sideline on the left or right of a playing field. 7 Brit a part of the body of a motor vehicle above the wheels. 8 a unit of the Royal Air Force larger than a squadron. ✳ **in the wings** in the background. **on the wing** of a bird: in flight. **under one's wing** under one's protection; in one's care. ➤ **winged** adj.

wing[2] v 1 to wound (a bird) in the wing. 2 to wound (somebody), e.g. with a bullet, without killing them. 3 to go with or as if with wings; to fly. ✳ **wing it** informal to perform or speak without rehearsal; to improvise.

winger n a player positioned on the wing in football, hockey, etc.

wing nut n a nut with projecting flanges so that it may be turned by finger and thumb.

wingspan n the distance between the tips of the two wings of a bird or aircraft.

wink[1] v 1 to shut one eye briefly as a signal or in teasing. 2 to gleam or flash intermittently.

wink[2] n 1 an act of winking. 2 a brief period, esp of sleep. ✳ **tip somebody the wink** informal to give somebody a useful piece of information, esp covertly.

winkle n an edible sea snail with a spiral shell.

winkle out v chiefly Brit 1 to extract from a snug or embedded position. 2 to extract (information) from somebody who is reluctant to give it.

winkle-picker n Brit, informal a shoe with a very pointed toe.

winning adj 1 endearing. 2 that wins or has won. 3 that results in victory. ➤ **winningly** adv.

winnings pl n money won, esp in gambling.

winnow v to remove waste matter from grain by exposure to a current of air.

wino n (pl **-os**) informal an alcoholic, esp one who drinks cheap wine.

win out v = WIN THROUGH.

winsome adj pleasing and engaging.

winter[1] n the season between autumn and spring.

winter[2] v to pass or survive the winter.

win through v to reach a desired or satisfactory end, esp after overcoming difficulties.

wintry adj (**-ier**, **-iest**) 1 of the weather: characteristic of winter; cold. 2 chilling or cheerless.

wipe[1] v 1 to clean or dry by rubbing lightly or quickly. 2 to remove by wiping. 3 to erase (e.g. data or a recording) completely. ✳ **wipe the floor with** informal to defeat decisively. ➤ **wiper** n.

wipe[2] n 1 an act of wiping. 2 a disposable moist cloth.

wipe out v informal 1 to destroy completely; to annihilate. 2 to obliterate or cancel.

wire[1] n 1 metal in the form of a flexible thread. 2 a line of wire, usu insulated, for conducting electrical current. 3 a telephone or telegraph wire or system. 4 informal, dated a telegram. 5 a microphone and transmitter concealed under somebody's clothes.

wire[2] v 1 to provide with wiring. 2 to connect or fasten with wire. 3 chiefly NAmer, informal, dated to send a message to (somebody) by telegraph.

wireless n chiefly Brit, dated a radio.

wiretapping n the act of tapping a telephone or telegraph wire, e.g. to monitor conversations to obtain information.

wiring n a system of wires carrying electric current in a device, building, etc.

wiry adj (**-ier**, **-iest**) 1 resembling wire. 2 lean and vigorous.

wisdom n 1 good sense; judgment. 2 accumulated learning, knowledge, and experience.

wisdom tooth n any of the four molar teeth at the back of the jaws in human beings that are the last to erupt.

wise[1] *adj* 1 characterized by deep understanding and sound judgment. 2 judicious or prudent. 3 *informal* (+ to) aware of. ➤ **wisely** *adv*.

wise[2] *n archaic* manner or way.

wisecrack[1] *n informal* a flippant remark or witticism.

wisecrack[2] *v informal* to make wisecracks.

wish[1] *v* 1 to feel or express a desire for; to want. 2 to express the hope that somebody will have or attain (something). ✳ **wish on** to hope that (somebody) will suffer (e.g. an unpleasant situation).

wish[2] *n* 1 an instance of wanting or hoping for something; a desire. 2 an object of desire. ✳ **best/good wishes** a conventional greeting or sentiment wishing people health, happiness, etc.

wishbone *n* a forked bone in front of the breastbone of a bird.

wishful *adj* 1 having a wish; desirous. 2 in accordance with wishes rather than reality: *wishful thinking*. ➤ **wishfully** *adv*.

wishy-washy *adj informal* 1 lacking in strength or intensity; watery. 2 lacking in character or determination; ineffectual.

wisp *n* a thin insubstantial strand, streak, or fragment. ➤ **wispy** *adj*.

wisteria or **wistaria** *n* a climbing plant with showy blue, white, purple, or rose flowers.

wistful *adj* 1 full of unfulfilled desire; yearning. 2 musingly sad. ➤ **wistfully** *adv*, **wistfulness** *n*.

wit *n* 1 (*also in pl*) reasoning power; intelligence. 2 (*also in pl*) sanity. 3 the ability to use words or ideas to create a humorous effect. 4 a person with this ability. ✳ **be at one's wits' end** to be so harassed or worried that one does not know what to do. **have/keep one's wits about one** to be alert. **live by one's wits** to make one's living by cleverness or cunning rather than honest work.

witch *n* a woman who is credited with supernatural powers or who practises magic for evil ends.

witchcraft *n* the use of sorcery or magic.

witch doctor *n* a professional sorcerer, *esp* in a tribal society, who is credited with healing and other powers.

witch hazel *n* a shrub whose bark and leaves are used to make a soothing astringent lotion.

witch-hunt *n* the searching out and harassment of those with unpopular or unorthodox views.

witching hour *n* (**the witching hour**) *humorous* midnight.

with *prep* 1 used to indicate accompaniment or association. 2 used to indicate reciprocal action or communication. 3 in the direction of. 4 in possession of; having or bearing. 5 in addition to. 6 by means of; using. 7 used to indicate manner of action. 8 in opposition to; against. 9 in relation to. 10 able to follow the reasoning of. 11 on the side of (a person or group); for. 12 employed by (a company, institution, etc).

withdraw *v* (**withdrew**, **withdrawn**) 1 to draw (something) back, away, or aside; to remove. 2 to remove (money) from a place of deposit, e.g. a bank account. 3 to retract (e.g. an offer or statement). 4 to leave a place, *esp* in retreat. 5 to retire from participation. 6 to become socially or emotionally detached.

withdrawal *n* 1 the act of withdrawing. 2 the discontinuance of use of a drug, often accompanied by unpleasant side effects.

withdrawn *adj* shy and unresponsive.

wither *v* 1 to become dry and shrivelled, e.g. from age or disease. 2 to lose vitality, force, or freshness. 3 to cause to wither.

withering *adj* scornful and humiliating. ➤ **witheringly** *adv*.

withers *pl n* the ridge between the shoulder bones of a horse.

withhold *v* (*past tense and past part.* **withheld**) 1 to refrain from granting or giving. 2 to check or restrain.

Usage Note: Note the spelling with -*hh*- in the middle.

within[1] *prep* 1 inside. 2 in the range of. 3 not further than a specified distance. 4 during or before the end of (a period of time).

within[2] *adv* 1 inside. 2 inside one's body or mind.

with it *adj informal* 1 up-to-date; fashionable. 2 mentally quick or alert.

without *prep* 1 used to indicate the absence or lack of something. 2 used to indicate that something does not happen.

withstand *v* (*past tense and past part.* **withstood**) 1 to be unharmed by. 2 to resist with determination.

witless *adj* foolish.

witness[1] *n* 1 a person who sees an event take place. 2 a person who gives evidence, *esp* in a court of law. 3 a person who watches another sign a document and adds their own signature as an indication of authenticity. 4 something that serves as evidence.

witness[2] *v* 1 to observe (an event) personally or directly. 2 to be the scene or time of (an event). 3 to act as legal witness of (e.g. the signing of a document). 4 (+ to) to testify to something.

witter *v Brit, informal* to talk in a long-winded fashion about inconsequential matters.

witticism *n* a witty remark.

witty *adj* (**-ier, -iest**) showing wit; cleverly humorous. ➤ **wittily** *adv*.

wives *n* pl of WIFE.

wizard *n* 1 a man with supernatural or magical powers. 2 a person who is very clever or skilful. 3 a computer program providing a step-by-step guide to a particular task. ➤ **wizardry** *n*.

wizened *adj* dry, shrunken, and wrinkled as a result of ageing.

woad *n* a plant formerly grown for the blue dye obtained from its leaves.

wobble *v* 1 to rock unsteadily from side to side. 2 of the voice: to tremble or quaver. ➤ **wobbly** *adj.*

woe *n* 1 *literary* great sorrow or suffering. 2 (*usu in pl*) a trouble or affliction. * **woe betide somebody** somebody will suffer or be punished if they do the specified thing.

woebegone *adj* looking very sorrowful.

woeful *adj* 1 feeling or expressing woe. 2 pitifully bad. ➤ **woefully** *adv.*

wok *n* a large bowl-shaped cooking utensil used *esp* for stir-frying in Chinese cookery.

woke *v* past tense of WAKE[1].

woken *v* past part. of WAKE[1].

wold *n* an upland area of open country.

wolf[1] *n* (*pl* **wolves** *or* **wolf**) a large predatory mammal of the dog family that hunts in packs. * **cry wolf** to raise a false alarm and risk the possibility that a future real need will not be taken seriously. **wolf in sheep's clothing** a person who hides hostile intentions behind a friendly manner. ➤ **wolfish** *adj.*

wolf[2] *v* (*often* + down) to eat (food) greedily.

wolfhound *n* a dog of a large breed formerly used in hunting wolves.

wolfram *n* = TUNGSTEN.

wolf whistle *n* a distinctive whistle sounded to express sexual admiration, *esp* by a man for a woman. ➤ **wolf-whistle** *v.*

wolverine /ˈwoolvəreen/ *n* a fierce flesh-eating mammal of northern forests that is related to the weasel and has blackish fur.

woman *n* (*pl* **women**) an adult human female.

womanize *or* **-ise** *v* of a man: to seek to have casual sexual relations with many women. ➤ **womanizer** *n*, **womanizing** *n* and *adj.*

womankind *n* women as a whole, *esp* as distinguished from men.

womb *n* the hollow organ in a woman's body in which a baby develops before birth.

wombat *n* a plant-eating Australian marsupial resembling a small bear.

won *v* past tense and past part. of WIN[1].

wonder[1] *n* 1 rapt attention, admiration, or astonishment at something unexpected, strange, beautiful, etc. 2 a cause of wonder. * **no wonder** it is no surprise. **work/do wonders** to have a positive effect.

wonder[2] *v* 1 to feel curiosity or doubt. 2 (*often* + at) to marvel.

wonderful *adj* unusually good; admirable or excellent. ➤ **wonderfully** *adv.*

wonderland *n* a place where strange or magical things happen.

wondrous *adj literary* wonderful.

wonky *adj* (**-ier, -iest**) *informal* 1 awry or crooked. 2 shaky or unsteady.

wont *n formal* customary practice: *as was his wont.*

won't *contraction* will not.

wonted *adj literary* customary or habitual.

woo *v* (**woos, wooed, wooing**) 1 to try to win the love of (somebody, *esp* a woman). 2 to try to win the support or favour of. ➤ **wooer** *n.*

wood *n* 1 a hard fibrous plant tissue that makes up the greater part of the stems and branches of trees or shrubs. 2 (*also in pl*) a dense growth of trees, usu smaller than a forest. 3 a golf club with a wooden head. 4 a wooden bowling ball. * **not see the wood for the trees** to fail to have overall understanding of a subject, situation, etc as a result of concentration on details. **out of the wood/woods** escaped from danger or difficulty. ➤ **woody** *adj.*

woodcut *n* a print taken from a wooden block with a design cut on it in relief.

woodcutter *n* a person who cuts down trees or chops wood.

wooded *adj* of land: covered with growing trees.

wooden *adj* 1 made of wood. 2 awkwardly stiff. ➤ **woodenly** *adv.*

woodland *n* (*also in pl*) land covered with trees.

woodlouse *n* (*pl* **woodlice**) a small ground-living animal with a grey segmented body.

woodpecker *n* a bird with a very hard bill used to drill holes in trees to find insects for food.

woodshed *n* a shed for storing firewood.

woodsman *n* (*pl* **woodsmen**) a man who lives in, frequents, or works in the woods.

woodturning *n* the art of producing wooden articles on a lathe. ➤ **woodturner** *n.*

woodwind *n* 1 any of a group of orchestral wind instruments including the clarinet, flute, oboe, and bassoon. 2 the woodwind section of an orchestra.

woodworm *n* the larva of a beetle that bores in dead wood.

woof[1] *n* the low gruff sound characteristic of a dog.

woof[2] *v* to utter a woof.

woof[3] /woohf/ *n* = WEFT.

woofer /ˈwoohfə/ *n* a loudspeaker that responds mainly to low frequencies.

wool *n* 1 the soft fibre forming the coat of sheep. 2 yarn made from wool by spinning. * **pull the wool over somebody's eyes** to blind somebody to the true situation; to hoodwink them.

woollen[1] (*NAmer* **woolen**) *adj* 1 made of wool. 2 relating to the manufacture or sale of woollen products.

woollen[2] (*NAmer* **woolen**) *n* (*in pl*) woollen garments.

woolly[1] (*NAmer* **wooly**) *adj* (**-ier, -iest**) 1 made of or resembling wool. 2 of an animal or plant: covered with wool or with soft hairs resembling wool. **3** marked by vagueness or confusion. ➤ **woolliness** *n.*

woolly² (*NAmer* **wooly**) *n* (*pl* **-ies**) *chiefly Brit* a woollen jumper or cardigan.

woozy *adj* (**-ier, -iest**) *informal* dizzy or slightly nauseous. ➤ **woozily** *adv.*

word¹ *n* **1** a meaningful unit of language that is usu set off by spaces on either side in writing or printing. **2** a short remark, statement, or conversation. **3** (*in pl*) the text of a vocal musical composition. **4** (*in pl*) an angry conversation. **5** (**the word**) an order, command, or verbal signal. **6** (**one's word**) a promise. **7** (**one's word**) what one says or claims about something. **8** news or information. ✻ **be as good as one's word** to keep a promise. **from the word go** from the beginning. **in other words** expressing the same thing in a different and usu more straightforward way. **in so many words** in exactly those terms. **take somebody at their word** to believe somebody literally. **take the words out of somebody's mouth** to say the very thing that somebody else was about to say.

word² *v* to express in particular words; to phrase.

word class *n* a group of grammatically similar words; a part of speech.

word-for-word *adj* in or following the exact words used.

wording *n* the words used in a text or to express something.

word of honour *n* a promise pledging one's honour.

word of mouth *n* oral communication.

word processor *n* a computer or program that enables text to be written, stored, and printed. ➤ **word processing** *n.*

wordy *adj* (**-ier, -iest**) using or containing too many words. ➤ **wordily** *n.*

wore *v* past tense of WEAR¹.

work¹ *n* **1** activity in which one exerts physical strength or mental faculties to do or produce something. **2** the activities that provide one's accustomed means of livelihood. **3** a specific task, duty, function, or assignment. **4** something produced in a specified way, by a specified person or thing, or from a specified material. **5** (*in pl*) a place where industrial activity is carried out; a factory. **6** (*in pl*) the working or moving parts of a mechanism. ✻ **have one's work cut out** to have a difficult task. **out of work** unemployed.

work² *v* (*past tense and past part.* **worked**) **1** to do work to achieve a result or earn one's living. **2** to cause (a person or animal) to do work. **3** of a machine: to operate or function. **4** of a person: to operate (e.g. a machine). **5** to produce a desired effect; to succeed. **6** to prepare or form into a desired state by kneading, hammering, etc. **7** to get into a specified condition by slow or imperceptible movements: *The knot worked*

loose. **8** to carry on an operation, e.g. farming or mining, in. **9** to bring about (an effect or result). **10** (+ on) to strive to influence or persuade somebody.

workable *adj* **1** capable of being worked. **2** of a plan: practicable or feasible.

workaday *adj* ordinary.

workbench *n* a bench on which *esp* mechanical or carpentry work is performed.

worked up *adj* emotionally aroused; angry or upset.

worker *n* **1** a person who works. **2** a member of the working class. **3** any of the usu sterile members of a colony of ants, bees, etc that perform most of the labour.

workforce *n* **1** the workers employed by a particular company or engaged in a specific activity. **2** the people potentially available for work.

workhouse *n* formerly in Britain, an institution maintained at public expense to house needy people.

working¹ *adj* **1** that functions or performs work. **2** engaged in paid work. **3** during which one works. **4** suitable for or used in work. **5** serving as a basis for further activity, discussion, etc.

working² *n* **1** (*usu in pl*) a mine, quarry, or similar excavation. **2** (*usu in pl*) the act or manner of functioning or operating.

working class *n* the class of people who work, *esp* manually, for wages. ➤ **working-class** *adj.*

working party *n Brit* a committee set up to investigate and report on a particular problem.

work load *n* the amount of work that somebody has to do.

workman *n* (*pl* **workmen**) **1** a manual worker. **2** a person considered with regard to their skill at their trade.

workmanlike *adj* skilful or competent.

workmanship *n* **1** the relative skill of a workman. **2** the quality or finish exhibited by a product.

workout *n* a period of usu vigorous physical exercise.

work out *v* **1** to solve (a question, problem, etc) by calculation or reasoning. **2** to elaborate (a plan, etc) in detail. **3** to prove effective or successful. **4** (*often* + at/to) to amount to (a total or calculated figure). **5** to engage in physical exercise.

work permit *n* a document authorizing a foreigner to do paid work in a country.

workshop *n* **1** a place in which manufacturing or repair work is carried out. **2** a brief intensive session of study, training, or discussion with an emphasis on active participation.

workstation *n* a self-contained unit, e.g. a VDU and keyboard, linked to a computer network in an office.

worktop *n Brit* a flat surface on a kitchen unit that is suitable for working on.

work-to-rule *n chiefly Brit* a form of industrial action designed to reduce output or efficiency by deliberately keeping very rigidly to rules and regulations.

work up *v* **1** (**get worked up**) to become agitated or angry. **2** (+ to) to approach something through a series of increasingly more intense or demanding preparatory steps.

world *n* **1** (**the world**) the earth with everybody and everything on it. **2** (**the world**) secular affairs as distinguished from religious or spiritual matters. **3** a distinctive class of people or their sphere of interest. **4** the personal environment of one's life or work. **5** an indefinite or very great number or amount. **6** a planet. ✳ **best of both worlds** the advantages of two alternatives, *esp* without their disadvantages. **bring/come into the world** to give birth to/be born. **out of this world** *informal* of extraordinary excellence. **think the world of** to have great love or admiration for.

worldly *adj* (**-ier, -iest**) **1** of this world and its pursuits rather than religion or spiritual affairs. **2** = WORLDLY-WISE.

worldly-wise *adj* possessing a shrewd understanding of human affairs; sophisticated.

world music *n* a type of popular music that incorporates elements of traditional music from various countries.

world power *n* a state powerful enough to affect the entire world by its actions.

world-shaking *adj* having tremendous importance.

world war *n* a war engaged in by most of the principal nations of the world.

world-weary *adj* bored with life and the material pleasures of the world.

worldwide *adj and adv* throughout or involving the entire world.

World Wide Web *n* a vast information system composed of interconnected sites and files to which individuals have access through the Internet.

worm[1] *n* **1** a relatively small elongated limbless invertebrate animal with a soft body, e.g. an earthworm. **2** (*in pl*) infestation with or disease caused by parasitic worms.

worm[2] *v* **1** to proceed by winding or wriggling. **2** to make (one's way) insidiously or deviously. **3** (+ out of) to extract (information) from somebody by artful or persistent questioning. **4** to rid (an animal) of parasitic worms.

wormcast *n* a small heap of earth or sand excreted by a worm on the surface.

wormwood *n* a plant that yields a bitter aromatic oil used to flavour absinthe and vermouth.

worn *v* past part. of WEAR[1].

worn-out *adj* **1** exhausted. **2** made useless by wear.

worried *adj* feeling or showing anxiety or concern. ➤ **worriedly** *adv*.

worrisome *adj chiefly NAmer* **1** causing distress or worry. **2** inclined to worry or fret.

worry[1] *v* (**-ies, -ied**) **1** to feel or cause to feel concern or anxiety, *esp* about unpleasant things that have happened or may happen. **2** to bother or disturb (somebody). **3** of a dog: to chase and harass (e.g. a sheep). **4** (+ at) of a dog: to bite, pick up, and shake (something) repeatedly. ➤ **worrier** *n*, **worrying** *adj*.

worry[2] *n* (*pl* -**ies**) **1** mental distress or agitation. **2** a cause of worry; a trouble or difficulty.

worse[1] *adj* **1** of a lower quality. **2** in poorer health. **3** more serious or severe. ✳ **the worse for** harmed by. **worse off** suffering worse circumstances, *esp* financially.

worse[2] *adv* **1** less well. **2** more seriously or severely.

worse[3] *n* something worse.

worsen *v* to make or become worse.

worship[1] *n* **1** praise, prayer, and thanksgiving offered to a divine being. **2** religious practices and rituals. **3** extravagant admiration or devotion. **4** (**Your/His/Her Worship**) *chiefly Brit* used as a title for various officials, e.g. mayors.

worship[2] *v* (**worshipped, worshipping,** *NAmer* **worshiped, worshiping**) **1** to offer prayer and praise to (a deity). **2** to regard with great or excessive admiration or devotion. ➤ **worshipper** *n*.

worshipful *adj* **1** rendering worship or veneration. **2** (**Worshipful**) *chiefly Brit* used as a title for various people or groups of rank or distinction.

worst[1] *adj* **1** of the lowest quality. **2** least appropriate or advisable. **3** most severe or serious.

worst[2] *adv* **1** least well. **2** most seriously or severely.

worst[3] *n* (*pl* **worst**) **1** the worst state or part. **2** (**the worst**) what is least desirable. ✳ **at worst/at the worst** under the worst circumstances. **do one's worst** to do the utmost harm of which one is capable. **if the worst comes to the worst** if the very worst thing happens.

worsted /'woostid/ *n* a high-quality fabric with no nap made from smooth compact yarn.

worth[1] *adj and prep* **1** equal in value to. **2** having money or property equal to (a sum). **3** deserving of. ✳ **for all one is worth** *informal* with all one's energy or enthusiasm. **worth it** worth the time or effort spent.

worth[2] *n* **1** value, *esp* financial value. **2** the equivalent of a specified amount or figure: *twenty pounds' worth of petrol*. **3** moral or personal merit.

worthless *adj* **1** valueless. **2** useless. **3** contemptible or despicable.

worthwhile *adj* worth the time or effort spent.
worthy[1] *adj* (**-ier, -iest**) **1** (+ of) good or important enough for; deserving. **2** deserving respect, support, etc, or deserving the position, title, etc attained. **3** commendable but dull. ➤ **worthily** *adv*, **worthiness** *n*.
worthy[2] *n* (*pl* **-ies**) *often humorous* a worthy or prominent person.
would *v aux* **1** the past tense of WILL[1]. **2** used to introduce a possibility or presumption. **3** used after a verb expressing a wish or request. **4** used to express a polite request or invitation. **5** used in reported speech to express an action or state in the future. **6** used to express a preference. **7** *literary* used to express a wish or desire.
would-be *adj* wishing or aspiring to be.
wouldn't *contraction* would not.
wound[1] *n* **1** an injury, e.g. from violence, accident, or surgery, that involves tearing, cutting, or breaking the skin. **2** a mental or emotional hurt.
wound[2] *v* to inflict a wound on. ➤ **wounded** *adj*, **wounding** *adj*.
wound[3] *v* past tense and past part. of WIND[1].
wove *v* past tense of WEAVE[1].
woven *v* past part. of WEAVE[1].
wow[1] *interj informal* used to express pleasure, admiration, or surprise.
wow[2] *n informal* a striking success.
wow[3] *v informal* to excite (e.g. an audience) to enthusiastic admiration or approval.
WPC *abbr Brit* Woman Police Constable.
wrack[1] *v* = RACK[2] (1).
wrack[2] *n* a brown seaweed, *esp* kelp.
wraith *n* an apparition of a living person seen shortly before or after death.
wrangle[1] *n* an angry or prolonged dispute or quarrel.
wrangle[2] *v* to quarrel angrily or at length.
wrap[1] *v* (**wrapped, wrapping**) **1** to cover, pack, or enfold in something flexible, e.g. paper or fabric. **2** to fold or wind (something flexible) round somebody or something.
wrap[2] *n* **1** a shawl. **2** material used for wrapping. ✱ **under wraps** secret.
wrapper *n* a covering for an article.
wrap up *v* **1** to dress in warm outer garments. **2** to complete or end. **3** (**be wrapped up in**) to be completely engrossed in.
wrasse *n* (*pl* **wrasses** or **wrasse**) a brilliantly coloured seafish with spiny fins, thick lips, and strong teeth.
wrath *n* strong vengeful anger. ➤ **wrathful** *adj*.
wreak *v* **1** to inflict (e.g. revenge). **2** to cause or create (havoc or destruction).
wreath *n* (*pl* **wreaths**) **1** flowers or leaves intertwined into a circular shape. **2** a curl, ring, or coil.
wreathe *v* **1** (**be wreathed in**) to be surrounded by a cloud, coils, etc of something. **2** to twist or move in coils.
wreck[1] *n* **1** a shipwreck. **2** destruction. **3** the broken remains of something, e.g. a building or vehicle, wrecked or ruined. **4** a person in very poor health or spirits.
wreck[2] *v* **1** (*usu* **be wrecked**) of a vessel: to sink, break up, or be destroyed. **2** to ruin or destroy by violent action or accident. **3** to bring disaster or ruin to (e.g. plans or a marriage).
wreckage *n* broken parts or material from a wrecked structure.
wren *n* a very small bird with a short erect tail.
wrench[1] *v* **1** to pull or twist violently. **2** to injure (a part of the body) by a violent twisting or straining. **3** to snatch forcibly.
wrench[2] *n* **1** a violent twisting or a sideways pull. **2** acute emotional distress caused by e.g. a parting. **3** a spanner, *esp* an adjustable spanner.
wrest *v* **1** to take by violent pulling or twisting. **2** to obtain with difficulty by force or determination.
wrestle[1] *v* **1** to take part in wrestling. **2** to engage in a violent or determined struggle. **3** to push, pull, or manhandle by force. ➤ **wrestler** *n*, **wrestling** *n*.
wrestle[2] *n* an act of wrestling, *esp* a wrestling bout.
wretch *n* **1** a profoundly unhappy or unfortunate person. **2** *informal* a despicable person.
wretched *adj* **1** deeply afflicted or unfortunate. **2** deplorably bad. **3** mean, squalid, or contemptible. ➤ **wretchedly** *adv*.
wriggle[1] *v* **1** to move to and fro with short writhing movements. **2** to move by twisting and turning. **3** (*usu* + out of) to extricate oneself by manoeuvring, equivocation, etc. ➤ **wriggler** *n*.
wriggle[2] *n* a wriggling movement. ➤ **wriggly** *adj*.
wring *v* (*past tense and past part.* **wrung**) **1** to twist or compress, *esp* so as to extract liquid. **2** (*often* + from/out of) to extort by coercion or with difficulty. **3** to twist (an animal's neck), *esp* so as to break it. **4** to twist (one's hands) together as a sign of anguish. **5** to shake (somebody's hand) vigorously in greeting.
wringer *n* = MANGLE[2].
wringing *adj* of clothes, etc: so wet that liquid is dripping out.
wrinkle[1] *n* a small ridge or crease formed in the skin, in fabric, etc.
wrinkle[2] *v* **1** to contract into wrinkles. **2** to become marked with wrinkles.
wrinkly[1] *adj* (**-ier, -iest**) having many wrinkles.
wrinkly[2] *n* (*pl* **-ies**) *Brit, derog* an elderly person.
wrist *n* the joint between the hand and the arm.
wristwatch *n* a watch attached to a strap and worn round the wrist.

writ *n* a formal document issued in the name of a court commanding or forbidding a specified act.

write *v* (**wrote, written**) **1** to form (legible words, symbols, etc) on a surface, *esp* with a pen, pencil, etc. **2** to be the author or composer of (a piece of writing, music, etc). **3** to compose and send (a letter). **4** to complete or fill in (e.g. a cheque) by writing.

write down *v* to record (information) in written form.

write off *v* **1** to deem to be irreparably lost or useless. **2** to cancel the record of (bad debt). **3** to damage (a motor vehicle) beyond repair.

write-off *n* something or somebody written off.

write up *v* **1** to write an account of. **2** to put into finished written form.

write-up *n* a written account or review.

writhe *v* to twist or squirm in pain or embarrassment.

writing *n* **1** the act or occupation of literary composition. **2** written letters or words, *esp* handwriting. **3** (*usu in pl*) a written composition. ✳ **the writing on the wall** an omen of impending disaster or ruin.

wrong[1] *adj* **1** not according to truth or facts; incorrect. **2** in error; mistaken. **3** wicked, immoral, unjust, or unfair. **4** not satisfactory, e.g. in condition. ✳ **get (hold of) the wrong end of the stick** to misunderstand. **on the wrong side of 1** out of favour with. **2** more than the specified age. ➤ **wrongly** *adv*.

wrong[2] *adv* **1** without accuracy; incorrectly. **2** without regard for what is right or proper. **3** out of proper working order.

wrong[3] *n* an injurious or unfair act. ✳ **in the wrong 1** mistaken or incorrect. **2** being or appearing to be guilty.

wrong[4] *v* to treat unjustly or unfairly.

wrongdoer *n* a person who behaves immorally or illegally. ➤ **wrongdoing** *n*.

wrong-foot *v* **1** *Brit* to make (an opponent) move in the wrong direction, e.g. in tennis or football. **2** to put at a disadvantage by a sudden change of approach.

wrongful *adj* wrong, unjust, or unlawful. ➤ **wrongfully** *n*.

wrongheaded *adj* perverse.

wrote *v* past tense of WRITE.

wrought *adj* **1** of metals: beaten into shape by tools. **2** formed by artistry or effort. **3** (+ up) deeply stirred.

wrought iron *n* a tough pure form of iron that is easily worked.

wrung *v* past tense and past part. of WRING.

wry *adj* (**wryer** *or* **wrier, wryest** *or* **wriest**) **1** ironically or grimly humorous. **2** bent or twisted, *esp* to one side. **3** contorted into an expression of distaste, disapproval, etc. ➤ **wryly** *adv*.

wunderkind /'voondəkint/ *n* (*pl* **wunderkinds** *or* **wunderkinder** /-kində/) a person who succeeds in a competitive field at an early age.

WWF *abbr* World Wide Fund for Nature.

WWI *abbr* World War I.

WWII *abbr* World War II.

WWW *abbr* World Wide Web.

wych elm *or* **witch elm** *n* a hardy elm that grows in northern Europe and Asia.

WYSIWYG /'wiziwig/ *adj* denoting a computer system in which all text and graphics displayed on screen can be reproduced in exactly the same form on printout (*what you see is what you get*).

wyvern *n* a mythical and heraldic animal represented as a two-legged winged creature resembling a dragon.

X or **x** n (pl **X's** or **Xs** or **x's**) **1** the 24th letter of the English alphabet. **2** the Roman numeral for ten. **3** somebody or something whose identity is unknown or withheld. **4** used as a symbol to mark something as incorrect. **5** used as a symbol for a kiss.

X certificate n formerly, a classification of a film as suitable for adults only.

X chromosome n a sex chromosome that is usu paired with another X chromosome in a female cell and with a Y chromosome in a male cell.

Xe abbr the chemical symbol for xenon.

xenon n a heavy colourless odourless gas.

xenophobia n intense fear or dislike of foreigners or strangers. ➤ **xenophobe** n, **xenophobic** adj.

Xerox n trademark a photocopier or photocopy.

Xmas n informal Christmas.

X-rated adj involving pornography, indecency, or extreme violence.

X-ray[1] n an electromagnetic radiation of very short wavelength that can penetrate various solids and act like light to expose photographic films or plates.

X-ray[2] v to examine, treat, or photograph using X-rays.

xylophone n a percussion instrument consisting of a series of wooden bars that are struck with two small hammers.

Y¹ or **y** *n* (*pl* **Y's** or **Ys** or **y's**) the 25th letter of the English alphabet.

Y² *abbr* the chemical symbol for yttrium.

yacht /yot/ *n* a relatively small sailing or powered vessel used for pleasure cruising or racing. ➤ **yachting** *n*.

yahoo *n* (*pl* **yahoos**) *informal* an uncouth or rowdy person.

yak¹ *n* (*pl* **yaks** or **yak**) a large long-haired wild or domesticated ox of Tibet.

yak² or **yack** *v* (**yakked** or **yacked, yakking** or **yacking**) *informal* to talk persistently; to chatter.

yam *n* an edible starchy tuberous root used as a vegetable.

yang *n* in Chinese philosophy, the masculine active principle in nature.

Yank *n informal, often derog* an American.

yank *v informal* to pull or extract with a quick vigorous movement. ➤ **yank** *n*.

Yankee *n* **1** *informal* an American. **2** *NAmer, informal* somebody from New England or the northern USA. **3** *NAmer, informal* a Federal soldier in the Civil War.

yap *v* (**yapped, yapping**) to bark in a high-pitched or snappish way. ➤ **yap** *n*, **yappy** *adj*.

yard¹ *n* **1** a unit of length equal to three feet (about 0.914m). **2** a unit of volume equal to one cubic yard (about 0.765m³). **3** a long spar tapered towards the ends to support and spread a sail.

yard² *n* **1** *chiefly Brit* a small usu walled and often paved area open to the sky and adjacent to a building. **2** an area with buildings and facilities set aside for a specified business or activity. **3** *NAmer* a garden of a house.

yardarm *n* either end of the yard of a square-rigged ship.

Yardie *n informal* a member of a West Indian criminal gang.

yardstick *n* a standard used for comparison.

yarmulke or **yarmulka** *n* a skullcap worn by Jewish males.

yarn *n* **1** thread prepared and used for weaving, knitting, and sewing. **2** *informal* a narrative of adventures, *esp* a tall tale.

yashmak *n* a veil worn over the face by Muslim women, so that only the eyes remain exposed.

yaw *v* of a ship, aircraft, or spacecraft: to deviate from a straight course, *esp* by side-to-side movement. ➤ **yaw** *n*.

yawn¹ *v* **1** to open the mouth wide and inhale, usu in fatigue or boredom. **2** to be menacingly wide, deep, and open.

yawn² *n* **1** a deep usu involuntary intake of breath through the wide open mouth. **2** *informal* a boring thing or person.

Yb *abbr* the chemical symbol for ytterbium.

Y chromosome *n* a sex chromosome that usu occurs paired with a dissimilar chromosome in the male sex and does not occur in the female sex.

yd *abbr* yard.

ye¹ *pron archaic* or *dialect* you.

ye² *definite article archaic* the.

yea /yay/ *adv archaic* yes.

yeah *adv informal* yes.

year *n* **1** the period of about 365¼ solar days required for one revolution of the earth round the sun. **2** a cycle of 365 or 366 days divided into twelve months beginning on 1 January and ending on 31 December. **3** a period of time equal to this but beginning at a different time. **4** a period of time during which something, e.g. a school, is in session. **5** the body of students who enter a school, university, etc in one academic year. **6** *informal* (*in pl*) a very long time. **7** (*in pl*) age.

yearling *n* an animal one year old or in its second year.

yearly *adj* done or occurring once every year; annual. ➤ **yearly** *adv*.

yearn *v* to long persistently or sadly. ➤ **yearning** *n* and *adj*.

yeast *n* **1** a minute fungus that is able to ferment sugars and other carbohydrates. **2** a commercial product containing yeast, used for the fermentation of alcohol or for raising bread.

yell¹ *v* to utter a sharp loud cry, scream, or shout.

yell² *n* a sharp loud scream or shout.

yellow¹ *adj* **1** of the colour of egg yolk or lemons. **2** *informal* cowardly. ➤ **yellowish** *adj*.

yellow² *n* a yellow colour. ➤ **yellowy** *adj*.

yellow³ *v* to make or become yellow.

yellow card *n* a yellow card held up by a football referee to indicate the taking of a player's name for committing an offence.

yellow fever *n* an often fatal infectious disease of warm regions, marked by fever, jaundice, and often bleeding.

yellowhammer *n* a common bunting, the male of which is largely yellow with a reddish brown back.

Yellow Pages *pl n trademark* a telephone directory that lists organizations and services alphabetically within sections classified according to the nature of their business.

yelp *v* to utter a quick shrill cry or bark. ➤ **yelp** *n*.

yen[1] *n (pl* **yen)** the basic monetary unit of Japan.

yen[2] *n informal* a strong desire or inclination.

yeoman *n (pl* **yeomen)** formerly, a small farmer who cultivated his own land.

Yeoman of the Guard *n* a member of a military corps who serve as ceremonial attendants of the sovereign and warders of the Tower of London.

yes[1] *interj* **1** used in answers expressing affirmation, agreement, or willingness. **2** used to indicate polite interest or attentiveness. **3** used to express great satisfaction or delight.

yes[2] *n (pl* **yeses** *or* **yesses)** an affirmative reply or vote.

yes-man *n (pl* **yes-men)** *informal* an obsequious supporter of superiors.

yesterday[1] *adv* on the day before today.

yesterday[2] *n* **1** the day before today. **2** time not long past.

yesteryear *n literary* **1** the years of the fairly recent past. **2** last year.

yet[1] *adv* **1** up to this or that time. **2** only having done so much or got so far. **3** as of now; still. **4** at some future time and despite present appearances. **5** in addition. **6** used to indicate a still greater degree; even. **7** nevertheless.

yet[2] *conj* but nevertheless.

yeti *n* = ABOMINABLE SNOWMAN.

yew *n* an evergreen coniferous tree with poisonous red fruits.

Y-fronts *pl n Brit, trademark* men's underpants in which the front seams take the form of an inverted Y.

Yiddish *n* a language closely related to German spoken by Jews chiefly in or from Eastern Europe. ➤ **Yiddish** *adj*.

yield[1] *v* **1** to bring forth as a natural product. **2** to produce as a result of expended effort. **3** to produce (money or its equivalent) as revenue. **4** *(often + up)* to give up possession of (e.g. a position of advantage or point of superiority). **5** *(often + to)* to give way to pressure or influence. **6** to give way under physical force. **7** to surrender or submit. ➤ **yielder** *n*, **yielding** *adj*.

yield[2] *n* something yielded, or the amount of it.

Usage Note: Note the spelling with -*ie*-.

yin *n* in Chinese philosophy, the feminine passive principle in nature.

YMCA *abbr* Young Men's Christian Association.

yob *n Brit, slang* a loutish young man. ➤ **yobbish** *adj*.

yobbo *n (pl* -**os** *or* -**oes)** *Brit, slang* = YOB.

yodel[1] *v* **(yodelled, yodelling,** *NAmer* **yodeled, yodeling)** to sing or call by suddenly changing from a natural voice to a falsetto and back. ➤ **yodeller** *n*.

yodel[2] *n* a yodelled song or call.

yoga *n* **1 (Yoga)** a Hindu philosophy teaching control of all activity of body, mind, and will so that the self may attain liberation. **2** a system of exercises for attaining bodily or mental control and well-being. ➤ **yogic** *adj*.

yoghourt *or* **yoghurt** *n* see YOGURT.

yogi *n (pl* **yogis)** somebody who practises or is a master of yoga.

yogurt *or* **yoghurt** *or* **yoghourt** *n* a slightly acid semisolid food made of milk fermented by bacteria.

yoke[1] *n* **1** a bar or frame by which two draught animals, e.g. oxen, are joined at the necks for working together. **2** two animals yoked together. **3** a frame fitted to somebody's shoulders to carry a divided load, e.g. two buckets or baskets. **4** a fitted or shaped piece at the top of a garment from which the rest hangs. **5** something that is felt to be oppressive or burdensome.

yoke[2] *v* **1** to put a yoke on (e.g. a pair of oxen). **2** to connect or couple (two things).

yokel *n* a naive or gullible country person.

yolk *n* the usu yellow round mass that forms the inner portion of an egg.

Yom Kippur /yom ki'pooə, 'kipə/ *n* a Jewish festival observed with fasting and prayer on the tenth day of the Jewish year.

yon *adj and adv literary or dialect* = YONDER.

yonder *adj and adv archaic or dialect* over there.

yonks *n Brit, informal* a long time; ages.

yore *n* ✻ **of yore** *literary* long ago.

you *pron (pl* **you)** **1** used as subject or object: the person or people being addressed. **2** a person; one.

you'd *contraction* **1** you had. **2** you would.

you'll *contraction* **1** you will. **2** you shall.

young[1] *adj* **(younger, youngest) 1** in the first or an early stage of life, growth, or development. **2** suitable for or characteristic of young people.

young[2] *pl n* **1** offspring, *esp* of an animal. **2 (the young)** young people.

youngster *n* a young person or creature.

your *adj* **1** belonging to or associated with the person or people being addressed. **2** belonging to or associated with people in general.

you're *contraction* you are.

yours *pron* (*pl* **yours**) the one or ones that belong to or are associated with you.

Usage Note: Note that there is no apostrophe in *yours*.

yourself *pron* (*pl* **yourselves**) **1** used reflexively or for emphasis to refer to the person or people being addressed. **2** = ONESELF.

youth *n* **1** the time of life when one is young, *esp* adolescence. **2** a young male adolescent. **3** young people. **4** the quality or state of being youthful.

youth club *n* a local organization providing leisure activities for young people.

youthful *adj* **1** relating to or characteristic of youth. **2** not yet mature or old; young. ➤ **youthfully** *adv*, **youthfulness** *n*.

youth hostel *n* a place providing inexpensive bed and breakfast accommodation, *esp* for young travellers or hikers. ➤ **youth-hosteller** *n*, **youth-hostelling** *n*.

you've *contraction* you have.

yowl *v* to utter a loud long wail of pain or distress. ➤ **yowl** *n*.

yo-yo[1] *n* (*pl* **yo-yos**) *trademark* a toy consisting of two joined discs that is made to fall and rise when held by a string attached and wound between the discs.

yo-yo[2] *v* (**yo-yoes** *or* **yo-yos, yo-yoed, yo-yoing**) to fluctuate.

yucca *n* a plant with long often rigid leaves and a large cluster of white flowers.

yuck *or* **yuk** *interj* *informal* used to express a sense of disgust and revulsion. ➤ **yucky** *adj*, **yukky** *adj*.

Yule *or* **Yuletide** *n* *archaic* Christmas.

yummy *adj* (**-ier, -iest**) *informal* delicious.

yuppie *or* **yuppy** *n* (*pl* **-ies**) *informal, derog* a young person in a professional job with a high income and a fashionable lifestyle.

YWCA *abbr* Young Women's Christian Association.

Z or **z** *n* (*pl* **Z's** or **Zs** or **z's**) the 26th letter of the English alphabet.

zany *adj* (**-ier, -iest**) fantastically or absurdly comical.

zap *v* (**zapped, zapping**) *informal* **1** to destroy or kill. **2** to move with speed or force. **3** to switch swiftly from channel to channel on a television set by means of a remote control. ➤ **zapper** *n*.

zeal *n* eagerness to accomplish something.

zealot *n* a zealous person; *esp* a fanatical partisan of a religious or political movement. ➤ **zealotry** *n*.

zealous *adj* filled with or characterized by zeal. ➤ **zealously** *adv*.

zebra *n* (*pl* **zebras** or **zebra**) a black and white striped fast-running African mammal related to the horse.

zebra crossing *n Brit* a road crossing marked by a series of broad white stripes to indicate that pedestrians have the right of way.

zebu *n* an Asian ox of a domesticated breed with a large fleshy hump over the shoulders.

zeitgeist /'tsietgiest/ *n* the general intellectual and moral character of an era.

Zen *n* a Japanese Buddhist sect that aims at enlightenment by direct intuition through meditation.

zenith *n* **1** the point of the celestial sphere that is directly opposite the nadir and vertically above the observer. **2** the highest point reached in the heavens by a celestial body. **3** the highest or most successful point.

zephyr *n literary* a gentle breeze, *esp* from the west.

zeppelin *n* (*also* **Zeppelin**) a large German airship of the early 20th cent.

zero[1] *n* (*pl* **-os** or **-oes**) **1** the arithmetical symbol 0; nought. **2** the point from which the graduation of a scale, e.g. of a thermometer, begins. **3** a temperature of 0° Celsius (32° Fahrenheit), the freezing point of water.

zero[2] *v* (**zeroes** or **zeros, zeroed, zeroing**) to return (a counter) to zero.

zero hour *n* the time at which an event, *esp* a military attack, is scheduled to begin.

zero in *v* **1** (+ on) to adjust one's aim so as to hit. **2** (+ on) to focus attention on.

zero tolerance *n* a policy of total strictness in law enforcement in which not even the most minor offences are overlooked.

zest *n* **1** enthusiastic enjoyment; gusto. **2** an exciting or stimulating quality. **3** the outer peel of a citrus fruit used as flavouring. ➤ **zestful** *adj*.

zeta *n* the sixth letter of the Greek alphabet (Z, ζ).

zigzag[1] *n* a line or course consisting of a series of alternate sharp turns in opposite directions.

zigzag[2] *adj and adv* forming or going in a zigzag.

zigzag[3] *v* (**zigzagged, zigzagging**) to proceed along a zigzag course.

zilch *n informal* zero.

zillion *n* (*pl* **zillions** or **zillion**) *informal* (*also in pl*) an indefinitely large number. ➤ **zillionth** *adj and n*.

Zimmer frame *n trademark* a tubular frame with four legs, designed to help people who have difficulty in walking.

zinc *n* a bluish white metallic element, used *esp* as a protective coating for iron and steel.

zing[1] *n informal* energy or vim.

zing[2] *v informal* to move briskly.

Zionism *n* a movement initially for setting up a Jewish homeland in Palestine, now for furthering the interests of the state of Israel. ➤ **Zionist** *adj and n*.

zip[1] *n* **1** *chiefly Brit* a fastener that joins two edges by means of two flexible rows of teeth brought together by a sliding clip. **2** *informal* energy or liveliness. **3** *NAmer, informal* nothing; zero.

zip[2] *v* (**zipped, zipping**) **1** (*often* + up) to close or open with a zip. **2** in computing, to compress (a file). **3** *informal* to move with speed and vigour.

zip code *n* (*also* **ZIP code**) a number used as a postcode in the USA.

zipper *n chiefly NAmer* a zip.

zippy *adj* (**-ier, -iest**) **1** *informal* lively or energetic. **2** fast; having good acceleration.

zircon *n* a brownish or semitransparent mineral used as a gem.

zirconium *n* a steel-grey metallic element that is corrosion-resistant.

zit *n chiefly NAmer, informal* a pimple on the skin, *esp* of the face.

zither *n* a musical instrument having usu 30 to 40 strings over a shallow horizontal soundboard and played with plectrum and fingers.

Zn *abbr* the chemical symbol for zinc.

zodiac *n* a band in the sky, through which the apparent paths of the sun, moon, and all the principal planets except Pluto pass and which is divided into twelve signs for astrological purposes. ➤ **zodiacal** *adj*.

zombie *n* 1 in voodooism, a human being who is believed to have died and been reanimated. 2 *informal* a person resembling the walking dead, *esp* a shambling automaton.

zone¹ *n* 1 an area distinct from adjoining parts. 2 any of the sections into which an area is divided e.g. for planning purposes. 3 (*also* **time zone**) an area where a common standard time applies. ➤ **zonal** *adj*.

zone² *v* to arrange in, mark off, or partition into zones.

zonk *v informal* to strike (somebody or something) hard.

zonked *adj* 1 *informal* completely exhausted. 2 *slang* (*often* + out) highly intoxicated by alcohol or drugs.

zoo *n* (*pl* **zoos**) a place where a collection of living animals is kept and usu exhibited to the public.

zoology *n* 1 the branch of biology that deals with animals and animal life. 2 the animals found in a particular area. ➤ **zoological** *adj*, **zoologist** *n*.

zoom¹ *v* 1 to move quickly. 2 to operate the zoom lens of a camera.

zoom² *n* 1 the action of zooming. 2 a zoom lens.

zoom lens *n* a camera lens allowing progressive change from long to short shot.

Zr *abbr* the chemical symbol for zirconium.

zucchini /zoo'keeni/ *n* (*pl* **zucchinis** *or* **zucchini**) *chiefly NAmer* a courgette.

zygote *n* a cell formed by the union of two gametes. ➤ **zygotic** *adj*.